Nineteenth-Century Literature Criticism

Guide to Thomson Gale Literary Criticism Series

For criticism on	Consult these Thomson Gale series
Authors now living or who died after December 31, 1999	*CONTEMPORARY LITERARY CRITICISM (CLC)*
Authors who died between 1900 and 1999	*TWENTIETH-CENTURY LITERARY CRITICISM (TCLC)*
Authors who died between 1800 and 1899	*NINETEENTH-CENTURY LITERATURE CRITICISM (NCLC)*
Authors who died between 1400 and 1799	*LITERATURE CRITICISM FROM 1400 TO 1800 (LC)* *SHAKESPEAREAN CRITICISM (SC)*
Authors who died before 1400	*CLASSICAL AND MEDIEVAL LITERATURE CRITICISM (CMLC)*
Authors of books for children and young adults	*CHILDREN'S LITERATURE REVIEW (CLR)*
Dramatists	*DRAMA CRITICISM (DC)*
Poets	*POETRY CRITICISM (PC)*
Short story writers	*SHORT STORY CRITICISM (SSC)*
Literary topics and movements	*HARLEM RENAISSANCE: A GALE CRITICAL COMPANION (HR)* *THE BEAT GENERATION: A GALE CRITICAL COMPANION (BG)* *FEMINISM IN LITERATURE: A GALE CRITICAL COMPANION (FL)* *GOTHIC LITERATURE: A GALE CRITICAL COMPANION (GL)*
Asian American writers of the last two hundred years	*ASIAN AMERICAN LITERATURE (AAL)*
Black writers of the past two hundred years	*BLACK LITERATURE CRITICISM (BLC)* *BLACK LITERATURE CRITICISM SUPPLEMENT (BLCS)*
Hispanic writers of the late nineteenth and twentieth centuries	*HISPANIC LITERATURE CRITICISM (HLC)* *HISPANIC LITERATURE CRITICISM SUPPLEMENT (HLCS)*
Native North American writers and orators of the eighteenth, nineteenth, and twentieth centuries	*NATIVE NORTH AMERICAN LITERATURE (NNAL)*
Major authors from the Renaissance to the present	*WORLD LITERATURE CRITICISM, 1500 TO THE PRESENT (WLC)* *WORLD LITERATURE CRITICISM SUPPLEMENT (WLCS)*

ISSN 0732-1864

Volume 174

Nineteenth-Century Literature Criticism

Criticism of the
Works of Novelists, Philosophers, and Other
Creative Writers Who Died between 1800
and 1899, from the First Published Critical
Appraisals to Current Evaluations

Jessica Bomarito
Russel Whitaker
Project Editors

THOMSON
GALE

Detroit • New York • San Francisco • New Haven, Conn. • Waterville, Maine • London

Nineteenth-Century Literature Criticism, Vol. 174

Project Editors
Jessica Bomarito and Russel Whitaker

Editorial
Kathy D. Darrow, Jeffrey W. Hunter, Jelena O. Krstović, Michelle Lee, Thomas J. Schoenberg, Noah Schusterbauer, Lawrence J. Trudeau

Data Capture
Frances Monroe, Gwen Tucker

Indexing Services
Laurie Andriot

Rights and Acquisitions
Margaret Abendroth, Emma Hull, Jackie Jones

Imaging and Multimedia
Dean Dauphinais, Robert Duncan, Leitha Etheridge-Sims, Lezlie Light, Michael Logusz, Dan Newell, Kelly A. Quin, Denay Wilding

Composition and Electronic Capture
Tracey L. Matthews

Manufacturing
Rhonda Dover

Associate Product Manager
Marc Cormier

LIBRARY OF CONGRESS CATALOG CARD NUMBER 84-643008

ISBN-13: 978-0-7876-8658-1
ISBN-10: 0-7876-8658-1
ISSN 0732-1864

Printed in the United States of America
10 9 8 7 6 5 4 3 2 1

Contents

Preface

Since its inception in 1981, *Nineteeth-Century Literature Criticism* (*NCLC*) has been a valuable resource for students and librarians seeking critical commentary on writers of this transitional period in world history. Designated an "Outstanding Reference Source" by the American Library Association with the publication of is first volume, *NCLC* has since been purchased by over 6,000 school, public, and university libraries. The series has covered more than 450 authors representing 33 nationalities and over 17,000 titles. No other reference source has surveyed the critical reaction to nineteenth-century authors and literature as thoroughly as *NCLC*.

Scope of the Series

NCLC is designed to introduce students and advanced readers to the authors of the nineteenth century and to the most significant interpretations of these authors' works. The great poets, novelists, short story writers, playwrights, and philosophers of this period are frequently studied in high school and college literature courses. By organizing and reprinting commentary written on these authors, *NCLC* helps students develop valuable insight into literary history, promotes a better understanding of the texts, and sparks ideas for papers and assignments. Each entry in *NCLC* presents a comprehensive survey of an author's career or an individual work of literature and provides the user with a multiplicity of interpretations and assessments. Such variety allows students to pursue their own interests; furthermore, it fosters an awareness that literature is dynamic and responsive to many different opinions.

Every fourth volume of *NCLC* is devoted to literary topics that cannot be covered under the author approach used in the rest of the series. Such topics include literary movements, prominent themes in nineteenth-century literature, literary reaction to political and historical events, significant eras in literary history, prominent literary anniversaries, and the literatures of cultures that are often overlooked by English-speaking readers.

NCLC continues the survey of criticism of world literature begun by Thomson Gale's *Contemporary Literary Criticism* (*CLC*) and *Twentieth-Century Literary Criticism* (*TCLC*).

Organization of the Book

An *NCLC* entry consists of the following elements:

- The **Author Heading** cites the name under which the author most commonly wrote, followed by birth and death dates. Also located here are any name variations under which an author wrote, including transliterated forms for authors whose native languages use nonroman alphabets. If the author wrote consistently under a pseudonym, the pseudonym will be listed in the author heading and the author's actual name given in parenthesis on the first line of the biographical and critical information. Uncertain birth or death dates are indicated by question marks. Single-work entries are preceded by a heading that consists of the most common form of the title in English translation (if applicable) and the original date of composition.

- The **Introduction** contains background information that introduces the reader to the author, work, or topic that is the subject of the entry.

- The list of **Principal Works** is ordered chronologically by date of first publication and lists the most important works by the author. The genre and publication date of each work is given. In the case of foreign authors whose works have been translated into English, the list will focus primarily on twentieth-century translations, selecting those works most commonly considered the best by critics. Unless otherwise indicated, dramas are dated by first performance, not first publication. Lists of **Representative Works** by different authors appear with topic entries.

- Reprinted **Criticism** is arranged chronologically in each entry to provide a useful perspective on changes in critical evaluation over time. The critic's name and the date of composition or publication of the critical work are given at the beginning of each piece of criticism. Unsigned criticism is preceded by the title of the source in which it appeared. All titles by the author featured in the text are printed in boldface type. Footnotes are reprinted at the end of each essay or excerpt. In the case of excerpted criticism, only those footnotes that pertain to the excerpted texts are included. Criticism in topic entries is arranged chronologically under a variety of subheadings to facilitate the study of different aspects of the topic.

- A complete **Bibliographical Citation** of the original essay or book precedes each piece of criticism.

- Critical essays are prefaced by brief **Annotations** explicating each piece.

- An annotated bibliography of **Further Reading** appears at the end of each entry and suggests resources for additional study. In some cases, significant essays for which the editors could not obtain reprint rights are included here. Boxed material following the further reading list provides references to other biographical and critical sources on the author in series published by Thomson Gale.

Indexes

Each volume of *NCLC* contains a **Cumulative Author Index** listing all authors who have appeared in a wide variety of reference sources published by Thomson Gale, including *NCLC*. A complete list of these sources is found facing the first page of the Author Index. The index also includes birth and death dates and cross references between pseudonyms and actual names.

A **Cumulative Nationality Index** lists all authors featured in *NCLC* by nationality, followed by the number of the *NCLC* volume in which their entry appears.

A **Cumulative Topic Index** lists the literary themes and topics treated in the series as well as in *Classical and Medieval Literature Criticism, Literature Criticism from 1400 to 1800, Twentieth-Century Literary Criticism,* and the *Contemporary Literary Criticism* Yearbook, which was discontinued in 1998.

An alphabetical **Title Index** accompanies each volume of *NCLC*, with the exception of the Topics volumes. Listings of titles by authors covered in the given volume are followed by the author's name and the corresponding page numbers where the titles are discussed. English translations of foreign titles and variations of titles are cross-referenced to the title under which a work was originally published. Titles of novels, dramas, nonfiction books, and poetry, short story, or essay collections are printed in italics, while individual poems, short stories, and essays are printed in roman type within quotation marks.

In response to numerous suggestions from librarians, Thomson Gale also produces an annual paperbound edition of the *NCLC* cumulative title index. This annual cumulation, which alphabetically lists all titles reviewed in the series, is available to all customers. Additional copies of this index are available upon request. Librarians and patrons will welcome this separate index; it saves shelf space, is easy to use, and is recyclable upon receipt of the next edition.

Citing *Nineteenth-Century Literature Criticism*

When citing criticism reprinted in the Literary Criticism Series, students should provide complete bibliographic information so that the cited essay can be located in the original print or electronic source. Students who quote directly from reprinted criticism may use any accepted bibliographic format, such as University of Chicago Press style or Modern Language Association style.

The examples below follow recommendations for preparing a bibliography set forth in *The Chicago Manual of Style,* 14th ed. (Chicago: The University of Chicago Press, 1993); the first example pertains to material drawn from periodicals, the second to material reprinted from books:

Franklin, J. Jeffrey. "The Victorian Discourse of Gambling: Speculations on *Middlemarch* and *The Duke's Children*." *ELH* 61, no. 4 (winter 1994): 899-921. Reprinted in *Nineteenth-Century Literature Criticism*. Vol. 168, edited by Jessica Bomarito and Russel Whitaker, 39-51. Detroit: Thomson Gale, 2006.

Frank, Joseph. "*The Gambler*: A Study in Ethnopsychology." In *Freedom and Responsibility in Russian Literature: Essays in Honor of Robert Louis Jackson,* edited by Elizabeth Cheresh Allen and Gary Saul Morson, 69-85. Evanston, Ill.: Northwestern University Press, 1995. Reprinted in *Nineteenth-Century Literature Criticism*. Vol. 168, edited by Jessica Bomarito and Russel Whitaker, 75-84. Detroit: Thomson Gale, 2006.

The examples below follow recommendations for preparing a works cited list set forth in the *MLA Handbook for Writers of Research Papers,* 6th ed. (New York: The Modern Language Association of America, 2003); the first example pertains to material drawn from periodicals, the second to material reprinted from books:

Franklin, J. Jeffrey. "The Victorian Discourse of Gambling: Speculations on *Middlemarch* and *The Duke's Children*." *ELH* 61.4 (Winter 1994): 899-921. Reprinted in *Nineteenth-Century Literature Criticism*. Eds. Jessica Bomarito and Russel Whitaker. Vol. 168. Detroit: Thomson Gale, 2006. 39-51.

Frank, Joseph. "*The Gambler*: A Study in Ethnopsychology." *Freedom and Responsibility in Russian Literature: Essays in Honor of Robert Louis Jackson.* Eds. Elizabeth Cheresh Allen and Gary Saul Morson. Evanston, Ill.: Northwestern University Press, 1995. 69-85. Reprinted in *Nineteenth-Century Literature Criticism*. Eds. Jessica Bomarito and Russel Whitaker. Vol. 168. Detroit: Thomson Gale, 2006. 75-84.

Suggestions are Welcome

Readers who wish to suggest new features, topics, or authors to appear in future volumes, or who have other suggestions or comments are cordially invited to call, write, or fax the Associate Product Manager:

Associate Product Manager, Literary Criticism Series
Thomson Gale
27500 Drake Road
Farmington Hills, MI 48331-3535
1-800-347-4253 (GALE)
Fax: 248-699-8054

Acknowledgments

The editors wish to thank the copyright holders of the criticism included in this volume and the permissions managers of many book and magazine publishing companies for assisting us in securing reproduction rights. Following is a list of the copyright holders who have granted us permission to reproduce material in this volume of *NCLC*. Every effort has been made to trace copyright, but if omissions have been made, please let us know.

COPYRIGHTED MATERIAL IN *NCLC*, VOLUME 174, WAS REPRODUCED FROM THE FOLLOWING PERIODICALS:

California Slavic Studies, v. 2, 1963 for "The Genesis of Leskov's Soborjane" by Thomas A. Eekman. Copyright © 1963 by Nicholas V. Riasanovsky and Gleb Struve. Reproduced by permission of the University of California Press and the authors.—*College Literature*, v. 29, winter, 2002. Copyright © 2002 by West Chester University. Reproduced by permission.—*Comparative Literature*, v. 46, winter, 1994 for "Hugo's Gilliatt and Leskov's Golovan: Two Folk-Epic Heroes" by Larry R Andrews. Copyright © 1994 by the University of Oregon. Reproduced by permission of the author.—*French Forum*, v. 3, January, 1978. Copyright © 1978 by French Foreign Publishers, Inc. All rights reserved. Reproduced by permission of the University of Nebraska Press.—*French Studies*, v. 52, April, 1998 for "Who Is the Narrator in *Indiana*?" by Peter Dayan. Copyright © 1998 The Society for French Studies. Reproduced by permission of the publisher and the author.—*George Sand Studies*, v. 11, spring, 1992. Copyright © 1992 *George Sand Studies*. Reproduced by permission.—*Germano-Slavica*, v. 6, 1988. Copyright © *1988 Germano-Slavica*. Reproduced by permission.—*Nineteenth-Century French Studies*, v. 19, winter, 1991; v. 31, spring-summer, 2003. Copyright © 1991, 2003 by *Nineteenth-Century French Studies*. Both reproduced by permission.—*Romance Languages Annual*, v. 8, 1996. Copyright © 1997 by Purdue Research Foundation. Reproduced by permission.—*Romance Notes*, v. 21, spring, 1981. Reproduced by permission.—*Slavic and East European Journal*, v. 12, winter, 1968; v. 44, spring, 2000. Copyright © 1968, 2000 by AATSEEL of the U.S., Inc. Both reproduced by permission.—*Southern Review*, v. 16, March, 1983 for "Feminism and Interpretation Theory: Sandpaper" by Anne Freadman. Copyright © 1983 by Anne Freadman. Reproduced by permission of the author.—*Studia Slavica*, v. 48, 2003. Copyright © Akadémiai Kiadó, Budapest, 2003. Reproduced by permission.—*Texas Quarterly*, v. 9, autumn, 1966. Copyright © 1966 by The University of Texas at Austin. Reproduced by permission.—*Tolstoy Studies Journal*, v. 10, 1998. Copyright © Tolstoy Studies Society. Reproduced by permission.—*University of South Florida Language Quarterly*, v. 20, spring-summer, 1982. Reproduced by permission.

COPYRIGHTED MATERIAL IN *NCLC*, VOLUME 174, WAS REPRODUCED FROM THE FOLLOWING BOOKS:

Burke, Tim. From "Ann Yearsley and the Distribution of Genius in Early Romantic Culture," in *Early Romantics: Perspectives in British Poetry from Pope to Wordsworth*. Edited by Thomas Woodman. Macmillan Press Ltd, 1998. Selection, editorial matter and introduction copyright © Thomas Woodman 1998. Chapter 12 copyright Macmillan Press Ltd 1998. Reproduced with permission of Palgrave Macmillan.—Christiansen, Hope. From "Masters and Slaves in *Le rouge et le noir* and *Indiana*," in *The Play of Terror in Nineteenth-Century France*. Edited by John T. Booker and Allan H. Pasco. University of Delaware Press, 1997. Copyright © 1997 by Associated University Presses, Inc. All rights reserved. Reproduced by permission.—Christmas, William J. From *The Lab'ring Muses: Work, Writing, and the Social Order in English Plebeian Poetry, 1730-1830*. University of Delaware Press, 2001. Copyright © 2001 by Associated University Presses, Inc. All rights reserved. Reproduced by permission.—Crecelius, Kathryn J. From *Family Romances: George Sand's Early Novels*. Indiana University Press, 1987. Copyright © 1987 by Kathryn J. Crecelius. All rights reserved. Reproduced by permission.—Daly, Pierrette. From "The Problem of Language in George Sand's *Indiana*," in *West Virginia George Sand Conference Papers*. Edited by Armand E. Singer, Mary W. Singer, Janice S. Spleth, and Dennis O'Brien. Department of Foreign Languages, West Virginia University, 1981. Reproduced by permission.—Daniels, Charlotte. From *Subverting the Family Romance: Women Writers, Kinship Structures, and the Early French Novel*. Bucknell University Press, 2000. Copyright © 2000 by Associated University Presses, Inc. All rights reserved. Reproduced by permission.—Dorn, Judith. From "The Royal Captives, a Fragment of Secret History: Ann Yearsley's 'Unnecessary Curiosity'," in *1650-1850: Ideas, Aesthetics, and Inquiries in the Early Modern Era*. Edited by Kevin L. Cope. AMS Press, 2000. Copyright © 2000 by AMS Press, Inc. All rights reserved. Reproduced by permission.—Edgerton, William B. From "Leskov and Gogol," in

Thomson Gale Literature Product Advisory Board

The members of the Thomson Gale Literature Product Advisory Board—reference librarians from public and academic library systems—represent a cross-section of our customer base and offer a variety of informed perspectives on both the presentation and content of our literature products. Advisory board members assess and define such quality issues as the relevance, currency, and usefulness of the author coverage, critical content, and literary topics included in our series; evaluate the layout, presentation, and general quality of our printed volumes; provide feedback on the criteria used for selecting authors and topics covered in our series; provide suggestions for potential enhancements to our series; identify any gaps in our coverage of authors or literary topics, recommending authors or topics for inclusion; analyze the appropriateness of our content and presentation for various user audiences, such as high school students, undergraduates, graduate students, librarians, and educators; and offer feedback on any proposed changes/enhancements to our series. We wish to thank the following advisors for their advice throughout the year.

Nikolai Leskov
1831-1895

(Full name Nikolai Semyonovich Leskov; also transliterated as Nikoli, Nikolay, Semenovich, Semionovich, Lyeskov; also wrote under the pseudonym M. Stebnickij; also transliterated as Stebnicki, Stebnitsky) Russian short story writer, novelist, essayist, and playwright.

The following entry provides an overview of Leskov's life and works. For additional information on his career, see *NCLC*, Volume 25.

INTRODUCTION

Regarded as one of the finest short story writers of nineteenth-century Russia, Leskov wrote tales depicting life among the various classes of Russian society, from uneducated peasants in remote rural areas to wealthy, sophisticated city dwellers and members of the Orthodox Church. Characterized by an adept use of colloquialism and regional dialect, witty and humorous wordplay, and a darkly comic worldview, Leskov's fiction has long been admired for what has been described as its quintessentially Russian quality. While Leskov is perhaps best remembered as the influential practitioner of the *skaz* genre, a colorful short story style that makes use of first-person accounts and anecdotal material within a larger narrative structure, he also wrote several lengthier works, which he described as "novelistic chronicles." Chief among these chronicles, *Soborjane* (1872; *The Cathedral Folk*) is considered a narrative masterpiece on the subject of the Russian Orthodox clergy. In this and many other examples of his fiction, Leskov has demonstrated his own deeply felt but unorthodox Christian spiritualism and his penetrating satirical capacity. Despite critical neglect during his lifetime, prompted in part by reaction to his frequently controversial positions on a number of major social, political, and religious issues, Leskov is acclaimed by modern scholars for his mastery of the *skaz* genre, for his skill and versatility as a storyteller, and for his vivid fictional portrayal of nineteenth-century Russian life.

BIOGRAPHICAL INFORMATION

Leskov was born to Semyon Dmitrievich Leskov, a minor bureaucratic official who had been trained for the priesthood, and his wife, Marya Alferieva, the daughter of a landowning family of the lesser nobility, at Gorokhovo in the Russian province of Orel. Leskov's childhood was troubled by family strife and financial difficulties, as were his school years at the Orel *gymnasium,* which he attended from 1841 to 1846. In 1847 he began a civil service career, first as a legal clerk and, following a move to Kiev in 1849, with the military bureaucracy. In Kiev Leskov met and married Olga Smirnova, the daughter of a merchant, with whom he had two children. The marriage was stressful and unhappy due to his wife's mental instability, and was dissolved when she was committed to an asylum in 1861. Prior to his divorce, Leskov served as an estate manager for a private corporation from 1857 to 1860, employment that entailed extensive travel, and thus he was exposed to a diverse range of Slavic dialects and folklore. In 1860 Leskov embarked on a journalistic career in St. Petersburg where, despite his desire to remain apolitical, he was soon caught up in an ongoing dissension between conservatives and the radical intelligentsia. After writing a controversial article misunderstood as an indictment of radicals, Leskov was labeled a conservative and consequently shunned by many of Russia's leading writers and thinkers. Leskov's bitterness toward his political opponents was expressed in his early novels *Nekuda* (1864; *No Way Out*), which portrayed liberal and radical leaders as fools and scoundrels, and *Na nožax* (1871; *At Daggers Dawn*), a narrative polemic against the ideological foibles of revolutionaries and nihilists. These novels aggravated the rift between Leskov and his opponents, and consequently his writings, including the many short stories he began to produce in the 1860s, were rejected by the leading progressive periodicals of the day. Undaunted, Leskov continued to write numerous stories, sketches, and loosely woven novels, or "chronicles," in the 1870s and 1880s, many of them subtly critical of religious and bureaucratic institutions. In 1874 Leskov received an appointment to the Ministry of Education, a position he held until 1883; his iconoclastic writings about the clergy then came under scrutiny and he was forced to resign his post. A short time later, a collection of his sketches, *Meloči arxierejskoj žizne* (1878), was banned by government censors as seditious. In his later years Leskov, who had scrupulously avoided any formal association with church organizations, came to advocate the biblically based doctrines of Protestantism over the liturgical traditions of the Orthodox Church. He recognized a spiritual ally in his contemporary Leo Tolstoy, with whom Leskov corresponded extensively regarding religion and moral issues prior to his death in 1895.

MAJOR WORKS

Scholarly attention to Leskov's writings has generally approached his works from one of two major perspectives: either concentrating on the stylistic innovation of his *skaz* stories, or considering his writings thematically by focusing on their spiritual content and evocation of the nineteenth-century Russian national character. The typical pattern of Leskov's *skaz* features a realistic frame story in which an ostensibly credible narrator (frequently a well-educated, urbane individual) sets the scene for a second but more involved first-person account, by a less reliable, often simple-minded character who relates a tale of bizarre (sometimes supernatural) events or describes an eccentric person. The central story is often told in humorous terms, with extensive use of regional dialects, colloquialisms, wordplay, and punning. Yet the light and entertaining tone typical of Leskov's *skaz* often masks a subversive commentary on corruption in the government or clergy. Leskov's earliest sketches feature his use of *skaz* narration, apparent in the 1862 story "Pogassee delo" ("A Case That Was Dropped"), a tale of bureaucratic corruption and peasant superstition. He further developed the technique in his later stories, the best known of which include "Očarovannyj strannik" ("The Enchanted Pilgrim"), concerning an itinerant monk who reveals to a group of fellow travelers stories of his tortured past and his struggles to expiate sin, and "Zapečatlennyj angel" ("The Sealed Angel"), which describes the "Old Believers," a sect of orthodox Christians whose revered icon, a depiction of an angel, is miraculously restored after government officials confiscate and mar it. Other frequently discussed and popular stories are "Belyi orel" ("The White Eagle"), in which Leskov offers a wryly subversive account of an honest man's inability to counter the pervasive bureaucratic corruption of the ruling powers, and "Levša" ("Lefty, Being the Tale of Cross-Eyed Lefty of Tula and the Steel Flea"), a humorous story that pits an untutored Russian craftsman against a team of English engineers. Leskov also made effective use of conventional narrative forms in some of his stories and sketches, including one of his most famous works, "Ledi Makbet Mtsenskogo uezda" ("The Lady Macbeth of the Mtsensk District"), which delves into the dark passions and ruthless actions of a young wife who murders three times in order to conceal her affair with a handsome servant.

In terms of theme, matters of religion and spirituality figure prominently throughout Leskov's literary oeuvre, although as his career progressed he often handled these issues ironically, as in "Na kraiu sveta" ("At the Edge of the World"), which follows a missionary priest to remote Siberia where he learns a fundamental principle of faith from his pagan guide. Leskov's fictional evocation of idiosyncratic characters, each with his own absurd but somehow saintly capacity, can be found in his early stories and sketches of the 1860s, including his "Ovtsebyk" ("The Musk-Ox") and "Kotin doilec i Platonida" ("Kotin the He-Cow and Platonida"), both centering on an unlikely hero who devotes his life to the care of others. Leskov confronted the issue of Church hypocrisy in "Vladychnyi sud" ("Episcopal Justice"), concerned with the subject of Jewish conversion and a father's efforts to exempt his son from military service. From the late 1870s Leskov became gradually more outspoken in his denunciation of the Orthodox Church and increasingly preoccupied with moral issues and the study of Christian doctrine, themes that he explored in a series of stories loosely based on the traditional tales of saints' lives collected in the Russian *Prolog*. In such works as "Odnodum" ("Singlethought") and the novella *Nesmertel'nyj Golovan* (1880; *Deathless Golovan*) Leskov depicted simple, virtuous men (known collectively as *pravedniki*) who demonstrate the strength and beauty of a righteous life. Among Leskov's longer, novelistic works, his well-known chronicle *The Cathedral Folk* is a compassionate examination of the lives of a group of rural Russian Orthodox priests, who, despite harsh surroundings and seemingly insurmountable difficulties, are faithful to their spiritual calling. Set in the fictional Stargorod (Old Town), the work offers what critics describe as an effective polyphonic narrative, in which the juxtaposed perspectives of its characters combine to render a complex portrait of conflict between orthodoxy and heretical belief among the peasantry in provincial Russia. Considered one of Leskov's most notable nonfictional pieces, *Evrei v Rossii* (1884; *The Jews in Russia*) is an eloquent plea for religious and cultural tolerance. Meanwhile, such stories as "Skazanie o Fedore khristianine i o druge ego Abrame zhidovine" ("The Tale of Fedor the Christian and his Friend Abraham the Jew") and "Zheleznaia volia" ("A Will of Iron") illustrate that Leskov was not above the use of folk prejudices and stereotypes for sardonic effect, especially in his later works.

CRITICAL RECEPTION

Although nineteenth-century Russian reviewers did not generally acclaim Leskov's literary accomplishments, such notable compatriots as Feodor Dostoevsky, who praised Leskov's ability to portray character types, and Leo Tolstoy, who admired his linguistic facility, applauded aspects of his work. By the beginning of the twentieth century Leskov's writings had declined into obscurity until they received the recognition of prominent Soviet critic Maxim Gorky, who offered high praise for his storytelling ability and the rich Russian flavor of his writing. Since this time a selection of Leskov's works have appeared in English, German, and French, despite certain difficulties in translating the Russian colloquialisms, puns, and allusive language typical of his style. In the contemporary period Leskov has been extolled as one of the earliest and most brilliant architects of the *skaz* genre. His mastery of character delineation and skilled manipulation of documentary and anecdotal material in these short works has traditionally elicited the majority of critical attention to the writer, whereas his longer chronicles have frequently been dismissed as artistically inferior—though recognition of the complex, nonlinear, decentralized, and polyphonic structure of these lengthier narratives has prompted a scholarly reassessment of this position. Contemporary English-language critics have also discussed Leskov's religious views and his stance on the political and social issues of his day. Additionally, his works have been favorably compared to stories by some of the finest European prose writers of his century, with Leskov usually numbered among the outstanding narrative stylists in the short fiction genre. Primarily, however, it is his perceptive portrayal of nineteenth-century Russian culture and customs that has elicited the greatest praise and interest of contemporary scholars, leading many to corroborate Gorky's description of him as "the truest Russian of all Russian writers" while delighting in Leskov's earnest and satirical evocations of the Russian national character.

PRINCIPAL WORKS

O raskol'nikakh goroda Rigi (prose) 1863

Tri rasskaza M. Stebnitskogo [as M. Stebnickij] (short stories) 1863

Nekuda [*No Way Out*] (novel) 1864

Oboidennye (novel) 1865

Ostrovitjane [*The Islanders*] (novel) 1866

Rastočitel' (play) 1867

Na nožax [*At Daggers Drawn*] (novel) 1871

Zagadochnyi chelovek. Epizod iz istorii komicheskogo vremeni na Rusi s pis'mom avtora k Ivanu Sergeevichu Turgenevu (prose) 1871

Soborjane. Stargorodskaia khronika v 5-ti ch. [*The Cathedral Folk*] (novel) 1872

Truženiki morja [adaptor and translator; from the novel *Les travailleurs de la mer*, by Victor Hugo] (prose) 1872

Zakhudalyj rod. Semeinaia khronika kniazei Protozanovykh. Iz zapisok kniazhny V. D. P. [*A Decrepit Clan*] (novel) 1874

Detskie gody (novel) 1875

Velikosvetskii raskol (Lord Redstok, ego uchenie i propoved'). Ocherk sovremennogo religioznogo dvizheniia v peterburgskom obshchestve [*Schism in High Society: Lord Radstock and His Followers*] (prose) 1877

Meloči arxierejskoj žizne (Kartinki s natury) (sketches) 1878; revised and enlarged, 1880

Nesmertel'nyj Golovan [*Deathless Golovan*] (novella) 1880

Evrei v Rossii [*The Jews in Russia: Some Notes on the Jewish Question*] (prose) 1884

Zametki neizvestnogo (short stories) 1884, 1917-18

Sobranie sočinenij. 10 vols. (short stories, novels, play, essays, and sketches) 1889-90

Nevinnyi Prudentsii. Skazanie (prose) 1892

Polnoe sobranie sočinenij. 36 vols. (short stories, novels, play, essays, letters, and sketches) 1902-03

The Sentry and Other Stories (short stories) 1922

The Musk-Ox and Other Tales (short stories) 1944

The Tales of Leskov (short stories) 1944

The Enchanted Pilgrim, and Other Stories (short stories) 1946

The Amazon, and Other Stories (short stories) 1949

Sobranie sočinenij. 11 vols. (short stories, novels, play, essays, letters, and sketches) 1956-58

The Enchanted Wanderer, and Other Stories (short stories) 1958

Nikolai Leskov: Selected Tales (short stories) 1961

Satirical Stories of Nikolai Leskov (short stories) 1968

Nikolai Leskov: Five Tales (short stories) 1984

N. S. Leskov o literature i iskusstve (essays) 1984

The Sealed Angel and Other Stories (short stories) 1984

Lady Macbeth of Mtsensk and Other Stories (short stories) 1988

Vale of Tears; and, On Quakeresses (short story and essay) 1991

On the Edge of the World (short stories) 1992

*Publication of this short story cycle began in 1884, in the journal *Gazeta A. Gattsuka*, but was halted by censorship and did not resume until 1917-18 when the last three stories appeared in the journal *Niva*.

CRITICISM

William B. Edgerton (essay date December 1953)

SOURCE: Edgerton, William B. "Leskov and Tolstoy: Two Literary Heretics." *American Slavic and East European Review* 12, no. 4 (December 1953): 524-34.

[*In the following essay, Edgerton discusses the major influences on Leskov's religious non-conformity, including the writings of Leo Tolstoy and Leskov's contact with English Protestantism.*]

We are not sectarians, but heretics. . . .

Leskov to Lidija Veselitskaja, about himself and
Tolstoy.[1]

Probably no other writer in pre-Revolutionary Russian literature ever suffered so much at the hands of politically-minded critics as Nikolaj Leskov. He once said that the role of the writer is to struggle against the prevailing current of his time,[2] and his own career illustrates both the application of that principle and its consequences. His independent attitude toward all intellectual fashions, whether nihilism in the 1860's or conservatism in the 1880's, led single-minded Russians of various political colors to suspect him of hypocrisy and duplicity. Doctrinaire Russian critics of the right and the left, accustomed to classifying all writers in such tidy categories as "religious reactionary" or "atheistic liberal," were even more bewildered by Leskov's own kind of non-conformity than by the Christian anarchism of his great associate Tolstoy. Tolstoy, after all, had the virtue of pushing his convictions to their logical extreme, in the best tradition of Russian maximalism; whereas Leskov, though he acknowledged himself to be a devoted follower of Tolstoy, refused to become doctrinaire even in his Tolstoyanism.

This failure on the part of Russian critics to understand the nature of Leskov's thinking, their inability to find a ready-made label to paste on his peculiar type of non-conformity, is probably responsible in large measure for the fact that his position in Russian literature is still undefined. Recent Soviet studies, though providing much valuable information, have been as unsuccessful in getting at the essence of Leskov's writings as studies before the Revolution. The fall of tsarism made it possible to publish a number of Leskov's works that had been suppressed by tsarist censors, including one of his greatest short novels;[3] but in general the change of regimes in Russia has simply meant the exchange of one set of limitations on the study of Leskov for another set just as narrow. The non-conformist religious outlook on life that colors virtually everything he ever wrote can be studied no more adequately within the framework of Soviet Marxism than it could within the framework of Pobedonoscev's Orthodoxy. If a satisfactory study of Leskov's thought is to be written in our day, it will probably have to be written abroad.

A chapter of crucial importance in the development of Leskov's thought is the story of his relations with Leo Tolstoy. From the time of their first meeting in 1887 until Leskov's death in 1895 he counted himself a follower of Tolstoy, but the nature of their relations was far more complex than that of mere teacher and pupil. After all, Leskov was only three years younger than Tolstoy himself, and when they first met in 1887 both men were in their late fifties.

The best way to describe Tolstoy's influence on Leskov might be to call him a sort of catalytic agent in Leskov's philosophy, crystallizing a set of convictions, a world outlook, that had been in the process of formation since Leskov's early childhood. Indeed, it is not going too far to say that Leskov had been groping toward the formulation of his own Tolstoyan philosophy long before Tolstoy himself worked it out. Both Tolstoy and Leskov confirm this fact. Leskov's biographer and close associate A. I. Faresov reports these words from his interview with Tolstoy in 1898: "Leskov was my follower, but not in a spirit of imitation. He had long before started out in the same direction I am traveling now. We met each other, and I am deeply moved by his agreement with all my views."[4] Faresov likewise quotes the following words from Leskov about Tolstoy: "They say I am imitating him. Not in the least! When Tolstoy was writing *Anna Karenina* [in other words, between 1873 and 1877], I was already close to that which I am now saying."[5] In a letter to Lidija Veselitskaja in 1893 Leskov offered this comment on a newspaper statement that he was a follower of Tolstoy:

> That is quite true. I have said and I do say that I long ago sought what he is seeking; but I did not find it, because *my light was poor.* On the other hand, when I saw that he had found the answer that *satisfied me,* I felt that I no longer needed my own insignificant light, *and I am following after him.* I seek nothing of my own, nor do I make a display of myself; but *I see everything in the light of his great torch.*[6]

D. S. Mirsky called Leskov "the most Russian of Russian writers and the one who had the deepest and widest knowledge of the Russian people as it actually is."[7] No one who has read very much of Leskov will be likely to question this. And yet, paradoxically enough, in the life of this most Russian of Russian writers there were certain strong English influences which have never been adequately studied and which may be largely responsible for the religious non-conformism that so profoundly influenced his literary career and finally led him to Tolstoy.

These English influences reached Leskov by way of an English family named Scott that lived in Moscow in the early nineteenth century. James Scott, Jr., and his four sons managed the great landed estates of the Naryškin and Petrovskij families; and one of the sons, Alexander, was married to a sister of Leskov's mother. Leskov himself stresses the close relations of his family to Protestantism through the Scotts and says that

> all of us children grew up with respect for the convictions and piety of our English relatives, whom our elders held up to us as models of the active Christian life, serving as examples for us in a great many ways. I think this reference alone should be enough to make clear to the reader how a little of the spirit of English religion made its way into our family.[8]

The Scott family in Moscow also served as a sort of informal placement bureau for English girls who came to Russia to work as governesses. Leskov tells us that these girls "were always very upright persons, sometimes highly educated and always strictly religious," and he adds that they were all either Methodists or Quakers.[9] Another of Leskov's aunts, a sister of his father, took one of these girls as a governess for her daughters; and in time she herself became a close friend and religious follower of her own governess. These two women, Leskov's Aunt Polly[10] and the English Quaker girl Hildegarde, served as the heroines of one of the best stories of Leskov's last years, **"Judol'"** (**"Vale of Tears"**), which describes their courageous and efficient relief work among the cholera-ridden peasants of Leskov's own Orël province in the great famine of 1840. The example of Christianity in action that nine-year-old Leskov saw in this young English girl made a profound and lifelong impression on him.

The aunt who married Alexander Scott was responsible for still further English connections in Leskov's family. When one of Leskov's cousins was left a widower with three small children, she advised him to go to Britain and bring back a Quaker wife to serve as their step-mother. He followed her advice, and his marriage to the Quaker girl he brought back from Scotland turned out so well that his brother went to Scotland and married her sister.[11]

Finally, when Leskov was twenty-six years old he quit a government position in Kiev to go to work for his English uncle in the newly-organized commercial and contracting firm of Scott and Wilkins. As a responsible agent of the company he spent the next three years traveling over European Russia almost from one end to the other. According to Leskov himself this rich first-hand experience among all types of people all over Russia provided him with enough material to last him a lifetime as a writer,[12] and he referred to his experiences with his English uncle in at least half a dozen stories.

To be sure, these English Protestant influences do not in themselves explain everything in Leskov's complex personality. Lack of space prevents any discussion here of such matters as his relation to Ukrainian and Polish culture, to the literature of the Orthodox Church, and to a number of prominent figures in the literature, philosophy, and religious thought of Western Europe and America. Nevertheless, the very use Leskov made of these other influences is in itself further evidence of the way in which his early English associations helped to shape his manner of thinking. These associations account for much of the intellectual independence that made his contemporaries misunderstand him and for many of the difficulties he had in working out his own philosophy of life.

All of us are the children, and the victims, of the society that has molded our thinking; and even our originality tends to express itself within the conventional patterns of thought and action that each society creates for its individualists. The rebel in nineteenth-century Russian society tended to express his rebellion through such traditional channels of non-conformism as hostility to the tsarist regime, defiance of the Orthodox Church (which he associated with all religion), and reverence for what he thought was science. In this the radical intellectual observed a standard of radical behavior that was probably as rigid in its own way as the conventions of the conservatism he opposed. Leskov's path of development, on the other hand, was difficult just because it was genuinely independent, and led in a direction that defied analysis in terms of the thought patterns that divided—and therefore united—the conventional radicals and conservatives of his time.

As late as 1871 Leskov referred to himself as a "humble and devoted son" of the Church and a "convinced Orthodox,"[13] but his devotion to Orthodoxy had always been far from uncritical. Even in his novel *The Cathedral Folk* (*Soborjane*), where he perhaps gave supreme proof of his independence by taking the much-scorned Russian clergy as his heroes, he pitted his courageous Archpriest Tuberozov against the intolerant, bureaucratic Church hierarchy in a way that makes the whole story a kind of speech by the loyal opposition.

Moreover, from the beginning of his literary career he had shown great interest in the various forms of Christianity that existed outside of the Orthodox Church. In the colorful multitude of characters that trouped through his stories we find innumerable Old Believers, who were the heroes of his short novel *Zapečatlennyj Angel* (*The Sealed Angel*), not a few Lutherans, and a sprinkling of Roman Catholics, Stundists, Moravians, Quakers, and fashionable followers of the evangelical English Lord Radstock. In all this assortment of unorthodox Christians, as well as in members of the State Church itself, Leskov was attracted, wherever he found them, by just those elements that Tolstoy was later to point out as the essence of the teachings of Jesus. Leskov, like Tolstoy, laid great emphasis on a proper understanding of the New Testament. Like Tolstoy, Leskov considered the heart of Christianity to be love of one's fellow man rather than membership in a particular church or the observance of a particular ritual. In fact, one of his best-known stories, **"At the End of the World"** (**"Na kraju sveta"**), contrasts the genuinely Christian spirit of an ill-smelling Siberian heathen with the spurious Christianity of certain ambitious missionaries to Siberia. Further, Leskov anticipated Tolstoy's belief that men who had been transformed individually by the teachings of Jesus could and should set about to transform society. In **"Nekreščennyj pop"** (**"The Unbaptized Priest"**) he tells with his characteristic humor the story of an Orthodox priest whose spiritual pedigree wasn't quite in order, but whose genuinely Christian life made a new place out of his parish.

In **"Odnodum"** (**"The One-Track Mind"**) he tells about an incorruptible Bible-reading policeman named Ryžov whose refusal to take bribes came close to upsetting the economic and political life of his whole town. Leskov makes it clear that this "Biblical socialist," as he calls him, has set himself free from all worldly ambitions, and therefore from all fear of worldly authorities; and the humorous, heroic account of his interview with the governor of the province has scarcely a parallel anywhere in Russian literature.

As early as 1865, in his novel *Obojdennye* (*Those Who Were Overlooked*), Leskov anticipates Tolstoyan nonviolence in his description of his hero's mother. He portrays her as a saintly Orthodox woman from whom nobody could steal because everyone was free to take what he needed from her without stealing. Her goodness and forgiveness not only shielded her from conflicts with her enemies but actually destroyed her enemies by turning them into friends. The very thought of human enmity or of violence and destruction filled her with spiritual anguish and led her to call on God's mercy for the evildoers, saying: "God is the judge of human wickedness, not man."[14]

The whole thorny question of Leskov's attitude toward Tolstoyan nonviolence (or, as Tolstoy himself called it, "nonresistance to evil") seems to have puzzled everybody who has ever written on the relations between the two men; and no one has yet explained it adequately.[15] The usual interpretation has been that Leskov strongly disagreed with Tolstoy's nonresistance and yet was attracted to him and the rest of his teachings in spite of this disagreement. Since what is generally called "nonresistance" lies at the heart of Tolstoy's whole philosophy, this interpretation seems to betray inconsistency either in the interpreters or in Leskov himself.

The one article by Leskov that might have clarified this whole matter has lain buried for nearly seventy years in the columns of an almost inaccessible newspaper, and seems to have been overlooked by every scholar who has ever written about him. It is **"O rožne. Uvet synam protivlenija"** (**"About Goads: An Exhortation to the Children of Resistance"**), which Leskov published in *Novoe Vremja* (No. 3838, pp. 2-3) on November 4, 1886. It is the last of seven different articles Leskov wrote about Tolstoy in that single year, and it is the most complete expression we have of his attitude toward Tolstoyan nonresistance.

At first glance, **"About Goads"** might appear to be an attack on the very arguments against Tolstoy's doctrine that Leskov himself had written five months before, in **"Zagrobnyj svidetel' za ženščin"** (**"A Witness From Beyond the Grave in Defense of Women"**),[16] which various scholars have pointed out as evidence of Leskov's opposition to nonresistance. The fact that the ear-

lier article was not published until the same month as **"About Goads"** would seem to support this theory, and the usual conception of Leskov does not make it hard to imagine him rushing into print with a *feuilleton* in *Novoe Vremja* to answer the arguments that he himself had abandoned since writing them in the previous June.

A close examination of the facts, however, makes it clear that the Leskov of November was not essentially different from the Leskov of June. In his earlier article he had made this significant statement about Tolstoy: "The Count's other theses, on nonresistance to evil, *are not understood* either by his supporters or by his opponents."[17] The little-known article **"About Goads"** is simply Leskov's effort to explain what Tolstoy did mean by "nonresistance" and to evaluate it justly.

Leskov begins by clearing away the unfortunate misconceptions to which the negative word "nonresistance" has given rise ever since Tolstoy first used it:

> . . . Tolstoy does advocate resisting evil, and he even offers a program for the conduct of this resistance with hope of giving good the upper hand over evil. . . . This program is outlined very clearly and well in his parable "The Godson" (Tolstoy's *Works,* Vol. 12, p. 499), which has attracted very little attention.

After a detailed analysis of this story, with references also to two others dealing with nonresistance, "Ivan the Fool" and "The Candle," Leskov reaches the following conclusion:

> In all truth, a fair-minded and sensible man would have to admit that Tolstoy allows resistance to evil only after a person has himself achieved 1) purity, 2) steadfastness, and 3) love, that is, great and "perfect love." As for what this "perfect love" is, Paul gives us a ready-made definition: "perfect love" is that which "seeks nothing for itself, is kind in all things, and casts out fear."

> Evil cannot prevail against the man who sets forth with this kind of love. But if he undertakes to "resist evil" without himself being *pure, steadfast,* and filled with unselfish *love,* then any kind of "resistance" by such a man will be vain and will do no good; on the contrary, it will only bring on redoubled bitterness and thus will occasion great harm.

Pointing out that this doctrine did not originate with Tolstoy, but was expressed long ago by Socrates, Marcus Aurelius, and Jesus Christ, Leskov says that it is also defended to a significant degree by contemporary humanists, and that even the everyday experience of ordinary, clear-thinking people is leading in the same direction. Then he asks:

> Why does Tolstoy's reasoning now appear all of a sudden so stupid, harmful, and insignificant? . . . Is it not because we feel, willy-nilly, that we are *not pure enough*

to purify others, not strong enough to strengthen others, and not sufficiently filled with love to frighten terror away instead of being frightened by it ourselves?

After devoting more than half of his article to an explanation and defense of Tolstoy's "nonresistance," Leskov then proceeds to make certain criticisms of it that throw light on his earlier polemics with Tolstoy in **"A Witness From Beyond the Grave."** His principal criticism is directed at Tolstoy's assertion that men have no right to resist evil in others until they themselves are free of evil. Leskov shares Tolstoy's great faith in the power of nonviolent means of resisting evil; and he realizes, like Tolstoy, that their effectiveness depends largely on the spiritual development of the person who attempts to use them. But Leskov disagrees with Tolstoy over the course of action to be followed by those who have not yet understood the power of nonviolence or who have not yet grown in spirit to the point where they can use it effectively. For these persons Leskov can find little in Tolstoy's teachings except "nonresistance to evil" in the literal meaning of the phrase, and this Leskov can never accept. Tolstoy, following the Russian revolutionary tradition in spite of himself, would divide history at the point where each man's spiritual revolution made him capable of overcoming evil with love. Tolstoy would concentrate on working for this inner revolution in each human soul, and leave the righting of everyday wrongs until after the revolution had taken place. Leskov, the sober realist, would set out toward the Kingdom of God from where men actually are. His view of the world was essentially organic and complex rather than mechanical and simple, and the notion that history—even one man's individual history—could be neatly divided into two parts was foreign to his conception of reality.

It is interesting to observe that in his views on nonviolent resistance to evil Leskov was much closer to the great Indian follower of Tolstoy, Mahatma Gandhi (who some would say far outstripped his teacher), than he was to Tolstoy himself. Gandhi, like Leskov, insisted to the end of his life that violent resistance to evil was better than passivity or cowardice, but he lived and died in the conviction that the world would eventually come to recognize the superior power of nonviolent resistance based on love.

Leskov's article **"On Goads"** makes it clear that his claim to be a follower of Tolstoy was based on a genuine understanding and acceptance of the essence of Tolstoy's teachings. Throughout the last eight years of his life he placed his literary talents beside those of Tolstoy at the service of the religious convictions that united them. A comparison of the way they illustrated their beliefs through art would in itself be a tempting subject for discussion, but space does not permit it here. I will limit myself now to venturing the no doubt controversial opinion that Leskov created a number of characters who are more convincing and attractive embodiments of the Tolstoyan religion of love than the characters of Tolstoy himself. With his at times dogmatic rationalism, his stern moralism, and his powerful satire, Tolstoy could attack the existing order of society with all the eloquence of an Old Testament prophet. Leskov at his best, however, was able to fulfill Tolstoy's own requirements for good art: he was able to "infect" the reader with feelings of unity with all mankind. Moreover, he did this in stories that were suffused with a warmth and humor that have no counterpart anywhere in Tolstoy. Space does not permit the discussion that ought to be given in support of this heretical opinion about these two gifted heretics. I will say only that in addition to the works already mentioned I have in mind such stories by Leskov as **"Pugalo"** (**"The Scarecrow"**), **"Figura," "Tomlenie Dukha"** (**"Anguish of Spirit"**), **"Skomorokh Pamfalon"** (**"Pamphalon the Clown"**), **"The Sentry"** (**"Čelovek na časakh"**), **"Pustopljasy,"** and **"The Beast"** (**"Zver'"**).

Toward the end of his life Leskov summed up his own difficult career in a letter that adds support to the evidence presented here about the influence of his English relatives. Writing to M. A. Protopopov, who had just published a study about him called "A Sick Talent,"[18] Leskov pointed out the fact that he had naturally been a child of his times.

> It was simply a matter of my having to free myself from the fetters that encumber a Russian child of the landowning class from his infancy. In writing about myself I would have called the article not "A Sick Talent," but "Difficult Growth." The tendencies of the landowning class, ecclesiastical piety, narrow nationalism and statism, glorification of the native land—I grew up in the midst of all that, and often it all seemed repulsive to me, but still—I could not see "where the truth lay." . . . Katkov had a great deal of influence on me, but it was while *Zakhudalyj rod* was being printed that he himself first said to Voskobojnikov: "We are mistaken; this man is not ours!" . . . He was right, but I did not know *whose* man I was. "A thorough reading of the Gospels" made it clear to me, and I at once returned to the free feelings and inclinations of my childhood.[19]

The turning point he mentions here took place in 1875, during his second visit to Western Europe. On July 29, 1875, he wrote from Marienbad, in Bohemia, to his old friend P. K. Sčebal'skij:

> In general I have become a "turncoat" and no longer burn incense to many of my old gods. Above all I have broken with clericalism, about which I have read to my heart's content in works that are forbidden in Russia. I have had an interview with young Naville[20] and—I was shaken in my beliefs. I believe more than ever in the great significance of the church, but nowhere do I see that spirit which becomes a society bearing the name of Christ. If the "reunion" for which our church prays

ever comes about, it will certainly not take place on the basis of agreement about "articles of faith," but rather in an entirely different manner. But I have been working at this so hard that it has tired me out. I will say only this: had I read all the many things I have now read on this subject and heard all that I have now heard, I would not have written **The Cathedral Folk** as I did write it, for that would have been distasteful to me. Instead, I am itching now to write about a Russian heretic—an intelligent, well-read, and free-thinking *spiritual Christian,* who has passed through all doubts for the sake of his search for Christian truth and has found it only within his own soul. I would call this story "Fornosov the Heretic," and I would publish it—but where would I publish it? Oh, these "political tendencies!"[21]

This remarkable letter makes it clear just what Leskov meant by the "free religious feelings and inclinations" to which he returned after reading the Gospels thoroughly. Whatever the influences were that made him itch to write "Fornosov the Heretic," they brought him close once again to the religion he had first seen as a child in Aunt Polly and the English governess Hildegarde; and they formed one more barrier to any sort of easy integration into the thought patterns of his Russian contemporaries. Years later, when Leo Tolstoy's powerful personality discovered this same kind of nonconformist Christianity, it is little wonder that Leskov found his own convictions confirmed and became his devoted follower.

Notes

1. Lidija Veselitskaja, "Pis'ma N. S. Leskova," *Literaturnaja Mysl'. Al'manakh* (Leningrad, 1925), III, 297.

2. A. I. Faresov, *Protiv tečenij. N. S. Leskov. Ego žizn', sočinenija, polemika i vospominanija o nem* (Petersburg, 1904), p. 398.

3. *Zajačij remiz.* English translation: *The March Hare,* in Nikolai s. Leskov, *The Amazon and Other Stories,* tr. by David Magarshack (London, 1949). (Works that have been published in English translation are cited hereafter with the English title preceding the Russian.)

4. Faresov, p. 71.

5. *Ibid.,* p. 307.

6. Veselitskaja, *op. cit.,* p. 272.

7. D. S. Mirsky, *A History of Russian Literature,* Francis J. Whitfield, ed. (New York, 1949), p. 320.

8. N. S. Leskov, "O 'kvakerejakh' (Post-scriptum k 'Judoli')," *Polnoe sobranie sočinenij* (3rd ed., Petersburg, 1903), XXXIII, 98. Hereafter cited as *Poln. sobr. soč.*

9. *Ibid.,* XXXIII, 99.

10. Aunt Polly's real existence has never been questioned in the literature about Leskov; but since this article went to press, the piecing together of numerous bits of biographical information from Leskov's works and letters makes it almost certain that she was actually a composite character, whom Leskov no doubt drew mainly from his mother's sisters Aleksandra Petrovna, the wife of Alexander Scott, and Natal'ja Petrovna, the wife of the wealthy eccentric, Mikhail Andreevič Strakhov, on whose estate Leskov spent much of his childhood.

11. *Ibid.,* XXXIII, 99-100.

12. A. N. Leskov, "Žizn' Nikolaja Leskova," in N. S. Leskov, *Izbrannye sočinenija* ("Ogiz," 1946), p. xxix.

13. Letter from Leskov to P. K. Ščebal'skij, June 8, 1871, *Šestidesjatye gody (sbornik)* (Moscow-Leningrad, 1940), p. 320.

14. *Poln. sobr. soč.,* VI, 27, 168.

15. Readers who are familiar with *Zakhudalyj rod (A Family in Decline), Poln. sobr. soč.,* XVII, may wonder why no mention is made here of this work, which was originally published in 1874—years before Tolstoy's conversion—and contains an important character, the schoolteacher Červev, who is a thoroughgoing Tolstoyan. Having originally been misled here myself, I offer this as striking evidence of the pitfalls awaiting the unwary in Leskov scholarship. If one compares the version in *Poln. sobr. soč.,* XVII, with the original version published in *Russkij Vestnik,* CXII-CXIII (July, August, October, 1874) and with the first edition in book form (Petersburg, 1875), it becomes clear that Leskov *inserted* most of the Tolstoyan element in the story years after its first publication—probably in 1889 when he prepared it for the first edition of his collected works, in which it formed a part of the ill-fated Volume VI that was burned by order of the censors soon after its publication.

16. *Istoričeskij Vestnik,* XXVI (November, 1886), 249-80. Leskov's letter of June 14, 1886, to S. N. Šubinskij, the editor of the *Istoričeskij Vestnik,* shows that he had finished the article by that date (Faresov, *op. cit.,* p. 178).

17. *Istoričeskij Vestnik,* XXVI, 276.

18. M. A. Protopopov, "Bol'noj talant," *Russkaja mysl',* XII, No. 12 (1891), 258-78.

19. December 23, 1891. Published in *Šestidesjatye gody,* p. 381.

20. The editor of *Šestidesjatye gody* (p. 352) identifies this name (spelled *Nevil'* in the published Russian text of the letter) as "a French theologian." Lesk-

ov's frequent references in the ensuing months to the writings of the Protestant Swiss philosopher Jules-Ernest Naville indicate rather that the person he met was a younger member of the scholarly Naville family of Geneva, probably Adrien, the professor of philosophy, or Edouard, the archaeologist.

21. *Šestidesjatye gody,* p. 330-31.

Thomas A. Eekman (essay date 1963)

SOURCE: Eekman, Thomas A. "The Genesis of Leskov's *Soborjane.*" In *California Slavic Studies.* Vol. 2, edited by Nicholas V. Riasanovsky and Gleb Struve, pp. 121-40. Berkeley: University of California Press, 1963.

[*In the following essay, Eekman details the lengthy composition and artistic development of Leskov's fictional chronicle* The Cathedral Folk, *while also summarizing critical reaction to the work and characterizing it as both Leskov's masterpiece and "the first great novel from the life of the Russian clergy."*]

In the past two decades the interest in Nikolay Semenovich Leskov has shown a steady increase, both on the part of the general public and among scholars. In the West there have been three recent studies about this writer,[1] whose life and work have so many intriguing facets, and present so many unsolved problems, that they certainly deserve study and comment.

Leskov is regarded as an extremely gifted storyteller who used a very rich and racy language, and as perhaps "the most inventive linguistic innovator" in Russian literature.[2] His role and his place in Russian letters, his beliefs and his views, have been a subject of controversy and various misunderstandings, and some of the latter have not yet been cleared up.

One of these misunderstandings centers in the often-told history of the novel *Soborjane* (*The Cathedral Folk*), which is generally considered to be one of the masterpieces, if not *the* masterpiece of Leskov. It is usually said that, by way of reaction to the violent attacks in the radical periodicals at the beginning of the 1860's, Leskov—who resented these attacks very strongly—vented his gall on the "nihilists" in his novel *Nekuda* (*No Way Out*), published in 1865, and then again, still more vehemently, in his next novel, *Na nožakh* (*At Daggers Drawn,* 1870-1871), after which he kept aloof from the political controversies of his day and, switching to the conservative press, devoted himself to depicting the life of the Russian clergy and discussing religious problems.[3] This new trend is said to have found its primary expression in *The Cathedral Folk* (published in Katkov's *Russkij Vestnik* in 1872),

as well as in his famous stories **"Zapečatlennyj angel"** (**"The Sealed Angel,"** 1872) and **"Očarovannyj strannik"** (**"The Enchanted Wanderer,"** 1873).

As we shall presently see, this view of the situation is not quite accurate, and in some respects is even quite wrong. It is nevertheless true that Leskov was the first Russian writer to offer to his public a broad picture of the life of the Russian Orthodox clergy. This entire class of Russian society had previously been almost completely neglected by Russian writers, despite the proverbial social-mindedness of Russian literature, which was said to be always concerned with problems of Russian society and to give a realistic and critical treatment of all social phenomena in contemporary Russia. There had been occasional figures of priests in Russian prose fiction before Leskov's time (for example, in Gogol's Ukrainian tales, though not in his *Dead Souls,* that broad canvas of Russian life, or in other works). After Leskov, we find clergymen depicted by Tolstoy (*Resurrection,* "And Light Shines in the Darkness," etc.), by Chekhov (in several short stories), and by a few other writers. But they remained exceptions even after Leskov. This is, of course, only in part to be explained by the demands imposed by the censorship. A more important reason was the social status of the priest, who remained throughout this period of classical Russian literature a humble, inconspicuous, or despised figure in Russian life, not worthy of the attention of its painters. "From my early days," Leskov wrote in a letter to Tolstoy, "I felt strongly drawn toward problems of faith, and I began to write about churchmen at a time when this was considered unbecoming and impossible."[4]

Thus it is Leskov's undeniable and lasting merit to have given a true and colorful picture of some representatives of this more or less hidden class of Russian society. But even though belonging to a hereditary caste, to a closed group, the Russian priest was at the same time, by virtue of his vocation, intimately bound up with the village community, or parish, and its daily life. The characters that Leskov introduces to us in his *Soborjane*—the archpriest Savely Tuberozov, the priest Zakharia Benefaktov, and the deacon Akhilla Desnitsyn—are not an isolated little group; they are closely connected with all the other strata of the population of the small fictitious town of Stargorod (that is, "Oldtown"), where the action of the novel takes place. These ties are particularly close with the so-called intelligentsia; we get acquainted with all the Stargorodian notables: the mayor, the judge, the police chief and his wife, the tax collector and the postmaster and their wives, the doctor, the teacher, army officers, and several landed proprietors from the surrounding countryside. As for other social groups, we meet only occasional merchants and the proletarian Danilka.

Above, I used the word "novel" to describe *Soborjane.* It should be noted, however, that Leskov himself preferred to call it "a chronicle." Apparently he felt that the novel form did not suit him too well. After 1872, the year of publication of **The Cathedral Folk,** he never again tried his hand at a novel (the same is true, by the way, of the drama, another genre at which he had tried his hand during the same period: in 1867 he wrote his play **Rastočitel'** (**The Wastrel**), but the moderate success that the play enjoyed did not stimulate him to any further playwriting). As for **Soborjane,** the success of this work with the Russian public was quite considerable. If he was to give up this genre, it must have been because by nature and by temperament, as well as by his abilities, he was better suited to creating relatively short works—stories with one central motif, with a certain purpose or tendency, or a sequence of such stories, loosely interconnected and often bordering on journalism. It is difficult to find a writer to whom the term "anecdotist" is so applicable as it is to Leskov.

His critics and biographers agreed with Leskov that he was not really a novelist, that his few novels were more or less failures, and that—to go back to **Soborjane**—his story of life in the town of Stargorod was rather a chronicle than a novel. When he began writing it he said: "It will be a chronicle, not a novel."[5]

Now, we may ask ourselves why this work should be denied the name of novel. A chronicle is a record of events that are not necessarily bound together by any inner cohesion but are arranged in the order of their occurrence—day by day, as in a diary, or year by year. In a novel this inner cohesion is imperative: it is a fictitious narrative, relating a connected series of events, or incidents, or scenes, and portraying the characters involved in them. In **The Cathedral Folk** there is, it is true, Tuberozov's diary, in which some past happenings, preceding the action in the novel, are recorded; and subsequently this record is carried on to the point at which that action begins and is even worked into that action. However, Tuberozov's "demi-cotton book," as Leskov calls his diary, encompasses only a relatively small part of the work. Moreover, the incorporation of a diary in a novel is quite a usual, widely practiced device, which need not disqualify the work as a novel. As far as the cohesion, the interrelation of incidents, and the plot are concerned, these are certainly to be found in **Soborjane**: we follow the fortunes of all the three characters involved in cathedral activities until their deaths. There is an unmistakable leading idea in the novel, which can be summed up as the fight waged by Tuberozov—a right-minded, honest, devout, and tenacious priest—against the rigid, inhuman, bureaucratic spirit of his superiors in the Church. In addition to this theme, which runs through the whole novel, there are also some side themes sustained throughout the book. We must thus conclude that Leskov was in fact wrong in describing his work as a mere "chronicle," and that it is a regular novel in the accepted sense of the word.

Having reached this conclusion we must, however, admit that this novel, this *sui-generis* artistic unity, is composed of various materials of divergent character. This does not mean that we do not enjoy **Soborjane** as a harmonious work of art. But, on closer observation, the different component parts are easy to discern. There is, of course, the main story of Savely Tuberozov and his two assistants, of their doings and adventures (it is especially in the case of Akhilla that we can speak of "adventures"), their fights and setbacks; and of how they were in the end taken away from Stargorod by death. In the second half of the novel (to be more exact, in the last two of the five parts into which it is divided), the action, centered around Savely and Akhilla, forms a whole and develops without interruptions, the only exception being the party held by the postmaster's wife in Part IV.

In Parts I-III, however, we find, to begin with, the flash backs provided through Tuberozov's "demi-cotton book"; these are related, of course, to the main line of action. Also connected with it is the parallel line of the teacher Varnava and his human bones. In Parts II and III there is a new, and important, parallel action—the arrival in Stargorod of the inspector Bornovolokov and his unscrupulous secretary Termosesov, who is a depraved would-be revolutionary (or ex-revolutionary). Finally, a break in the narrative is provided by the introduction of the dwarf Nikolay Afanasyevich and of the memories he brings up—memories of his life as a serf of the aged Lady Plodomasova, a neighboring landed proprietress (Part II, chaps. ii-v).

Let us look again at the view mentioned before, according to which Leskov first wrote his antinihilistic novels, but later, realizing the uselessness of continuing in this vein, turned to the portrayal of types from the clerical class and devoted to them his next major work, **The Cathedral Folk.** If we take a second look at the chronology of Leskov's writings during this period we shall see that the facts are somewhat at variance with this view.

The novel **No Way Out** was written for the most part in 1864; the last chapters were published early in 1865. In the next few months Leskov wrote several other works, this being an extremely fruitful period in his career. Among them were **"The Lady Macbeth of the Mtsensk District," "The Amazon"** (**"Voitel'nica"**), **Those Who Were Overlooked** (**Obojdennye**), and **The Islanders** (**Ostrovitjane**). Then, from January to July, 1866, Leskov worked at the first part of **The Cathedral Folk.** Fragments of it were published in the periodical **Otečestvennye Zapiski** in 1867 under the title **"Čajuščie dviženija vody"** (**"Those Waiting for the Moving of the Water"**). One section of these published chapters, dealing with the poor man Pizonsky and later omitted from the novel, was included in a volume of Leskov's stories published that same year (1867), and received the title **"Kotin doilec i Platonida"** (**"Kotin the Breadwinner and Platonida"**).

As a result of a disagreement with Kraevsky, the editor in chief of *Otečestvennye Zapiski,* the publication of Leskov's work in this well-known progressive periodical had to be discontinued: Leskov was annoyed by the fact that Kraevsky had made some arbitrary changes in his work and had even left out some passages. The next year eight chapters of the novel, this time bearing the title **"Božedomy"** (**"People of the House of God"**), appeared—with substantial changes in the text—in a rather obscure magazine, *Literaturnaja Biblioteka,* but once more the publication of Leskov's work was suspended. It is known that in June, 1868, Leskov negotiated with a certain Kashpirev, who was planning to launch a new monthly journal, *Zarja,* about the publication in it of **"Božedomy,"** but the launching of the journal met with difficulties, and thus for the third time Leskov had bad luck with his novel; the only result was an unpleasant lawsuit with Kashpirev.[6] In the March, 1869, issue of Katkov's *Russkij Vestnik* another work by Leskov began to be serialized; this was **"Starye gody v sele Plodomasove"** (**"Old Times in the Village of Plodomasovo"**), a work which, as we shall see below, was closely connected with *Soborjane,* and in part incorporated almost verbatim in it. Finally, in November, 1869, Leskov's novel *At Daggers Drawn* began to be serialized in the same *Russkij Vestnik.* In 1870-1871 **"Božedomy"** was an object of negotiations with S. A. Yuryev, editor of the Slavophile magazine *Russkaja Beseda,* but they led to nothing. Then, at last, as a result of a personal visit to Katkov in Moscow, Leskov succeeded in selling his **"Božedomy"** and securing a place for it in Katkov's periodical, in which the work appeared in 1872, this time under its final title of **"Soborjane."** That same year it came out in book form. The text had again been carefully revised, whole chapters having been suppressed and others changed.

This, in short, is the history of the publication of *The Cathedral Folk.* It makes quite clear that Leskov wrote this work not after but between his two notorious antinihilistic novels; that he wrote it, and partly published it, before he produced his most violent, pamphlet-like, tendentious work, *Na nožakh,* and right in the middle of his period of vigorous antinihilism or antileftism.

If we keep this in mind and turn once more to the text of the novel we shall find that the book contains passages of an antinihilistic, pamphlet-like nature that are at least as violent as those in his two professedly political novels. In chapter x of Part I, there is a discussion between the schoolteacher Varnava Prepotensky and a certain Daryanov; through Varnava's mouth Leskov voices, in a satirical way, his aversion to the nihilistic ideas of the 1860's: he mocks at the unwholesome interest in physics and at the longing for a revolution. Varnava expresses his conviction that "spies are necessary," for "you cannot do without spies when you introduce new teachings, because you must study society"; and he complains that the officials and the clergy in the town "retard things." "What do they retard?" asks Daryanov. "Well, don't you understand?" replies Varnava. "You mean the revolution?" "The teacher interrupted his work and nodded with a smile."[7]

But Varnava is an innocent boy when compared with Termosesov, the inspector's secretary. So far as we know, Termosesov is not modeled on any existing "nihilist," as were many characters in *No Way Out* and *At Daggers Drawn*; he is a product of Leskov's imagination, but he embodies all the characteristics which Leskov, in those days, regarded as typical of the Russian radicals, and above all, the insincerity of their radical views, to which they adhered only while it was fashionable to do so. Termosesov considers those views naïve, and if he ever did believe in them he has long since outgrown them; but he has preserved from his "nihilist" days a complete disregard of, and disdain for, all conceptions of morality. This is shown in his behavior towards his superior, Bornovolokov, towards his hostess Bizyukina, wife of the tax collector, and towards people in general; he even steals Bizyukina's diamonds.

It has been suggested that even though Leskov was writing a novel about the Russian clergy he could not refrain from injecting into his basically nonpolitical novel some antinihilistic characters and ideas. On examining the genesis of the work more closely, one sees, however, that some of the "radical" elements in *Soborjane*—among others the characters of Varnava and Bizyukina—appear in it right from the outset (viz., at the beginning of chapter iii of Part I). They contribute to the main line of action, or plot, of the novel throughout the greater part of it, and could not be left out. This is quite natural: to depict the fight which Tuberozov must wage against the negative elements in the town and the province, some light had to be shed on these elements, too; and so we meet the hidebound Old Believers, the intriguing Poles, the heartless Church dignitaries, the indifferent local intelligentsia, and—last but not least—the radicals, Leskov's pet aversion. Though in writing *At Daggers Drawn* a few years later Leskov was to give rein to this aversion, in *Soborjane,* fortunately, he kept himself under control and subordinated the "radical" elements to his main design. Being primarily a good storyteller, he was, I think, too much in love with his fascinating creation to let the story be marred by political bias.

As has been mentioned above, the antinihilistic element is one component of the novel but by no means the only one. There are two other elements to which I should like to draw attention: the "Pizonsky" and the "Plodomasovo" elements. As we know, the original title of Leskov's work was **"Those Waiting for the Moving of the Water,"** the subtitle being "Romaničeskaja khronika" ("A Novelistic Chronicle"). The title was derived from a passage in the Gospel According to St. John (5:2-9) describing a scene in which invalids are gathered around the pool of Bethesda—the blind, the lame, the paralyzed, all "waiting for the moving of the water" (John 5:3). For an angel comes down from time to time and stirs the water, whereupon the first invalid to enter the pool is cured (verse 4). There were people in Russia—such was apparently the idea behind Leskov's title—who were waiting impatiently for the moment when the dead waters of Russian life would be stirred and begin to move, and the disease with which the country was afflicted would be cured. As Leskov put it in a letter written in 1867: "I intend to bring to the fore some modern types and the present-day situations of people who await a lawful, peaceful, silent movement."[8] He did not mention the clergy, the cathedral folk, in his original title, and it is quite probable that when he originally conceived the plan of depicting some of those Russians who were waiting for the water to move he had in mind not only the archpriest Tuberozov, but also the *meščanin* Pizonsky, the serf and midget Nikolay Afanasyevich, and the *bojarynja* Plodomasova, as well as other positive characters of his novel.

That Pizonsky is such a positive character, for whom Leskov had destined a far more important role than came to be actually allotted to him, may be judged by the fact that about a third of the earliest version of the novel, the fragments of **"Those Waiting for the Moving of the Water"** published in *Otečestvennye Zapiski,* consisted of the detailed story of Kotin Pizonsky, who was portrayed as a simple, pure soul, a man who saves two little girls and affords shelter to the unhappy Platonida. In the volume of Leskov's stories published in the same year, the same story bore the title **"The People of Stargorod: Fragments from the Unfinished Novel** *Those Waiting for the Moving of the Water.* **I. Kotin the Breadwinner and Platonida."** So here Leskov was still regarding it as part of a broadly conceived work, giving a panorama of life in an old Russian town (Stargorod) and its environs.

But in the complete separate edition of the novel, in 1872, Leskov suppressed the whole of the original Pizonsky episode. Pizonsky himself, however, retained a place in **Soborjane**: albeit very modest, it was not without some importance, for he was the person who inspired Tuberozov as the latter watched him on the small island in the river, where he led his solitary life, recite an original sort of prayer. And Pizonsky again inspired the archpriest when he entered the cathedral in the course of Tuberozov's sermon: the priest held him up as an example, thus shocking the notables present and

involving himself in trouble. The later curtailment of Pizonsky's role was due to Leskov's wish, when revising the novel and preparing it for a definitive edition in 1872, to narrow its scope, to simplify its action. In its original conception it was probably too broad, too unwieldy, taxing too much the strength, the patience, and the temperament of the rather peppery author.

"Kotin the Breadwinner and Platonida" appeared in 1867, at an early stage in Leskov's work on *Soborjane,* when the last parts of the novel may have yet been unwritten. But the author already had the whole picture of his little town of Stargorod clearly in mind, as is evident from the fact that a number of characters from *The Cathedral Folk* are mentioned in the story. Father Tuberozov, the deacon Akhilla, the mayor, the postmaster and his wife—all of them, though only superficially painted, figure in **"Kotin the Breadwinner."** We may note in passing that one episode in this story of Kotin Pizonsky and Platonida—the one (chaps. xv-xix of **"Kotin"**) in which Platonida is threatened by her lecherous old father-in-law—reminds us very much of an episode in another of Leskov's stories, namely **"The Lady Macbeth of the Mtsensk District"** (see chaps. iv-viii). In action, in situation, in atmosphere, and in style, these two episodes are strikingly similar. In both, we are transported into the atmosphere of a sultry night, in which the element of passion is mingled with that of crime. In **"The Lady Macbeth"** the heroine dreams of a tomcat; in **"Kotin the Breadwinner"** a similar symbolic role is played by a night moth. Both stories were published in 1867, but **"The Lady Macbeth"** had been written as early as 1864, and therefore we must regard the episode in **"Kotin the Breadwinner"** as an echo—a somewhat muted echo—from the earlier story.

In the last chapter of **"Kotin the Breadwinner"** the heroine, Platonida, enters a nunnery: she has literally "wept her eyes out" (*ona vyplakala oči*) and has become blind; and in her eye sockets are set little icons. This motif—the hero entering a monastery at the end of his life or of his worldly adventures, a feature so common in Old-Russian literature—was one of Leskov's favorite endings (cf., for example, **"The Enchanted Wanderer"**); and the same details were used in the story **"Pavlin"** (**"The Peacock"**), in which the heroine, Lyuba, turns from the world and enters a small convent, and in due course gets "wept-out eyes," into the orbits of which "small, round mother-of-pearl icons" are set.[9] This is not the only point of similarity: the figure of Avenir in **"Kotin"** resembles that of Dodya in **"Pavlin."**

"Pavlin" dates from 1874. However, the last chapter of **"Kotin"** was written much later. It was added to the story when Leskov decided not to include it in *The Cathedral Folk.* Leskov published the story of Kotin, with this short concluding chapter, as late as 1890. So here again we see him using in **"Kotin the Breadwinner"** an element of another, earlier, story, in a shortened, less elaborate form.

There is a passage in the story where the author used the same words to characterize Kotin Pizonsky that he used to characterize Akhilla in *The Cathedral Folk,* of which it was originally intended to form a part. The progress of these two men in school is much the same, and both are expelled "on account of their great age and scant progress" (*za velikovozrastie i malouspešie*).[10] Such a detail proves that Leskov, when he was planning and writing his novel, in 1866-1867, had not yet wholly integrated the work, had not yet finished working at it and polishing it. We may point out here that such recurring motifs and details are rather frequent in Leskov's works.[11] Leskov was a born, indefatigable storyteller, who never shunned the repetition of a motif, a character, atmosphere, or a new word coinage.

"Kotin the Breadwinner" was a story of more or less the same character and with the same background as *The Cathedral Folk,* enacted in the same town of Stargorod and at the same time, and showing us some of the same characters. The other short story, or rather group of short stories, connected with *Soborjane*—the group centering about the Plodomasov family—has little in common with Stargorod or its inhabitants. This group, eventually entitled **"Old Times in the Village of Plodomasovo,"** consists of three fragments from the records of a typical Old-Russian boyar family, a family of landed gentry, and represents the rural and feudal element in the picture of Russian provincial life which Leskov had set out to depict in his chronicle. The first story, entitled **"The Boyar Nikita Yuryevich,"** takes place in the eighteenth century. Nikita Yuryevich abducts a young girl and forces a priest to marry them, but the girl shows her character by declaring that she has contracted the marriage of her own free will. She becomes the lady of the boyar house and changes the rude, belligerent Nikita Yuryevich into an obedient husband. This type of energetic, conscientious lady, representative of the Old-Russian nobility at its best, is one of the most convincing positive characters in Leskov's work, a type to which he returns again and again. It continues the gallery of positive female characters from the Russian noble class in nineteenth-century literature, of which Pushkin's Tatyana and Turgenev's heroines are such well-known examples.

Marfa Andrevna Plodomasova is also the main character in the next story (Leskov called them "sketches"), which bears her name. After the death of her husband she lives on as a woman known for her pure and irreproachable life, and therefore is called "the crystal widow." She demands the same blameless conduct of her son Aleksey Nikitich, an officer in a regiment of the guards, and when it turns out that a girl servant is ex-

pecting a child by the young Plodomasov she punishes him severely. At the same time she protects and helps the girl, and when a boy is born she succeeds in saving her son's honor by having the child entered in the church register as the son of a neighboring landowner by the name of Tuganov, whose own child dies at about the same time, soon after birth. So it is that the only scion of the Plodomasov family is registered as Parmen Semenovich Tuganov, and it is under this name that we encounter him again in *Soborjane*.

The third "sketch" of the series was called **"The Plodomasov Dwarfs."** Here at last we find ourselves in the town of Stargorod, where the local "intelligentsia" has gathered to celebrate the name day of the mayor's wife. Suddenly there appear two little figures, the midgets Nikolay Afanasyevich and his sister, former servants of the late Lady Plodomasova, and Nikolay tells the story of their life with Marfa Andrevna. It is generally known that Leskov, who cultivated the racy Russian vernacular in literature, often wrote his stories as first-person narratives, as though told by his characters, usually simple, uneducated people. No other writer in world literature used so often and so consistently the method of the *Rahmenerzählung*. Most of his short stories begin with the description of a company assembled, in which one of those present narrates some vivid tale, he himself being more often than not its main character. This device becomes rather monotonous, almost routine, in Leskov's works. The story of the Plodomasov dwarfs illustrates his use of this device both in his short stories and in his novels, for this third part of **"Old Times in the Village of Plodomasovo"** was, unlike the first two, taken over into *Soborjane*.

It is possible that the series **"Old Times in the Village of Plodomasovo"** was written by Leskov as early as 1867; in any case he had conceived the idea of writing it by that time. In the monthly *Literaturnaja Biblioteka* it was announced in 1867 that two works by Leskov would be published in it in the following year: not only **"Božedomy,"** but also a "sketch" entitled **"The bojarynja Plodomasova."** A few years later, Leskov wrote with reference to his three sketches: "I wanted to create a sort of trilogy, that is, to write about the grandmother, the *bojarynja* Plodomasova, about her daughter, Madame Tuganova, and her granddaughter."[12] When he included the three Plodomasovo sketches in a volume of short stories published in 1869, the third sketch was preceded by a note in which he remarked: "Here one should imagine a long gap in the Plodomasovo chronicle, for the three sketches which cover the later years of Plodomasova's old age, and the upbringing and life of the nobleman Tuganov, are for special reasons not included by the author in this volume."[13]

Here again a query arises. Leskov seems to have intended to write three further installments of his Plodomasovo chronicle. Did he actually write them and then, for reasons known only to himself, exclude them from his collection of short stories? Did they later disappear? It is one of the many as yet unsolved questions that I mentioned at the beginning. Mr. Plodomasov and Mr. Tuganov figure in *Soborjane,* but they appear there without any comment or description, out of the blue as it were, and the reader learns nothing about their descent, background, and so on, as if their life stories—the kind of thing upon which Leskov usually loved to dwell—had been left out of the book.

My reason for dealing at some length with these preliminary stages of Leskov's novel was to show that in 1866-1867 Leskov was planning to paint an elaborate and broad picture—broad both in its historical and in its social scope—of Russian life, situating the action of his novel in an imaginary provincial town and the adjacent countryside. The local clergy was to play its due role in this life, but not the dominant part eventually to be given to it in the final version of *Soborjane.* The 1868 edition bore the title **"Božedomy,"** which already indicated a narrowing of the scope, as is confirmed by a comparison between the original text and the 1868 edition. In the latter (*Literaturnaja Biblioteka,* January, 1868, p. 3) Leskov wrote, after describing the three cathedral people: "These three men constituted the spiritual aristocracy of Stargorod, the chronicle of which the author once intended to write, before he realized that the time for such a chronicle was not yet ripe."[14]

However, as we have seen, it was only reluctantly and gradually, and by no means completely and consistently, that Leskov abandoned his original, more ambitious plan. We may assume that among his reasons for doing so was his difficult financial plight in those years: rebuffed by the radical circles, he was not yet accepted by the conservatives (some conservatives—as, for example, Katkov—were never to accept him wholeheartedly). All prominent periodicals were closed to him; but Leskov lived by his pen, and in order to earn his livelihood he was forced to publish his writings in any paper that would accept them, and publish them as quickly as possible. He had no time now for lengthy, circumstantial, patiently elaborated works, although this does not mean that Leskov did not bestow enough attention and labor on his novel, for we shall see presently that he did. We have seen that the first parts of *The Cathedral Folk* were written in 1866-1867, but it is possible, though there is no proof of this, that the last chapters of the novel, with their more concentrated and quietly unfolding action, and their greater unity, came into being much later, perhaps only a short time before 1872, the year in which Leskov sold his work to Katkov and could at last be sure of its regular publication and of a decent income.[15]

To return for the last time to the Plodomasovo cycle: here, too, Leskov ran into trouble in his attempts to get his work accepted and published. The first two stories appeared in a second-rate weekly, *Syn Otečestva,* in rather short installments. The third was accepted by *Russkij Vestnik.* It was only in the volume of short stories published the same year (1869) that the three sketches were assembled. As we know, the third story was included in *The Cathedral Folk* as it appeared in 1872, also in *Russkij Vestnik;* this means that, within three years, the same story, the same text, was published twice in one and the same journal—a rather unusual occurrence.

But was it really the same text? In his note, added to the third Plodomasovo sketch, Leskov wrote: "This sketch was, in part, taken over into the chronicle *The Cathedral Folk.*" And the commentary to the Soviet edition of Leskov's *Collected Works* states: "'**The Plodomasovo Dwarfs**' was published again, with some alterations in the text, within the framework of *The Cathedral Folk.*"[16] Professor Setschkareff says, however, that the text of the sketch was "included almost verbatim in *The Cathedral Folk.*"[17] The exact relation between the two texts has apparently never been investigated. Comparison shows that while the two versions of the dwarfs' story are in their main lines identical, its details underwent various alterations and corrections. This is further proof of the fact, previously noted by other Leskov students, that he took great pains to polish his language and style, that he carefully and repeatedly emended his pieces and often rewrote them, sometimes as many as twelve times, paying close attention to various nice points. "I cannot stand slovenliness," Leskov once said; and he added: "I am ready to raise hell when I notice it in others."[18]

We see then that in the second version of the dwarfs' story Leskov introduced a number of minor changes; single words or lines, or even certain passages, usually of minor importance, were left out, or added, or modified. All this shows that he worked hard on his story, but does not disclose any clear-cut tendency. Sometimes he would change, for example, the endings of feminine nouns from *-oju* or *-eju* to *-oj* and *-ej,* or alter the punctuation or the division into paragraphs (in the second version, incorporated in *The Cathedral Folk,* there were far fewer paragraphs than in the first one; this, as well as the closer type of the second version by comparison with the first one as reproduced in the Soviet edition of *Collected Works,* accounts for the fact that the second version appears shorter than the first); occasionally, Leskov would also change the division into chapters: there were more chapters in the original version and they were shorter. For many of his minor alterations it is difficult to discover the motives.[19] At times they tend to simplify the text; at times, to embellish it. In general, we can see a tendency to emphasize, to intensify the original wording by the addition of such words as "even," "suddenly," and "terribly."

This tendency seems to be rather characteristic of Leskov. Leo Tolstoy was among those of Leskov's contemporaries who noticed and criticized Leskov's propensity to hyperbolical style and manner. Tolstoy spoke of the "exuberance" of his images, ideas, incidents, and descriptions. The same hyperbolism has been called the characteristic feature of Gogol, with whom Leskov had no doubt very much in common. Leskov loved Gogol and admired him for his "wordcraft" (*rečetvorčestvo*); and in several of the earlier as well as in some of the later works of Leskov there is unmistakable evidence of Gogol's influence.

It has often been pointed out that Leskov possessed and cultivated a special style, bringing it as close as possible to the racy vernacular and charging it with original, colorful figures—a quality for which he has been both praised and criticized. One of the contemporary critics, Menshikov, wrote about the *embarras de richesse* in Leskov's language, saying that it suffered from "supersaturation with Russian salt."[20] Less attention has been paid to this other feature, connected, to be sure, but not identical, with the first one: the "hyperbolism" in his use of language, the inclination to exuberance, to exaggeration, to overemphasis, to a certain "maximalism." This may be illustrated by one small example: Leskov would never write "We listened to his story"; with him it must be, "We *all* listened to his story." There are scores of examples of this laying of additional emphasis in Leskov's works.[21]

Once again we come back to **Soborjane,** the mosaic character of which (at least in its early parts) may now be understood to be the result of Leskov's wish to do several things at once. His primary intention was to give a broad and detailed picture of the people who were "waiting for a lawful movement," of contemporary "types," and of the situations in which they found themselves. They are represented by the noble-minded, poor Pizonsky, by the archpriest Tuberozov, and in part by the dwarf Nikolay Afanasyevich, the only man who helps Tuberozov to the very end. In addition, Leskov wanted to delve into the past, to portray some typical representatives of the old generation in the Russian countryside, making use, for this purpose, of his own reminiscences of life in Oryol Province, where he spent his boyhood. Among his early acquaintances was Natalya Sergeyevna Zinovyeva, a local landed proprietress, who seems to have possessed many of the characteristics with which Leskov endowed Lady Plodomasova. Like the latter, she was held in great esteem because of her intelligence and her noble and independent character.[22] And, like the aged Lady Plodomasova, she had a dwarf. Finally, there were the nihilists, who in those years caused Leskov much worry. In fact, it is possible to say that Leskov was handicapped in composing his novel by the fact that his imagination ran away with him, causing too many interesting, gripping stories to come crowding into his mind. He simply could not refrain from telling the vivid stories of the young widow Platonida, of the two dwarfs, of the malicious Termosesov, of the proletarian Danilka, and so on, although they had no organic connection with the main line of the narrative. In a letter he frankly admitted this shortcoming of his: "Whenever I conceive a plan, I trace an inordinately vast outline and wish to embrace entire worlds, and this is what harms me."[23]

Valentina Gebel says that "on none of his works did Leskov bestow so much attention and energy as upon his fictional chronicle **The Cathedral Folk**,"[24] and she speaks of Leskov's "truly Sisyphean labor" over his style.[25] Nevertheless, Leskov seems to have forgotten, at times, his overall view of the novel, and he was not able to rid it of certain inconsistencies, especially in the early parts. As has been noted, this may be accounted for by his strong *Lust zum Fabulieren,* by his temperament, and by the disturbing circumstances under which the work came into being. Examples of this curious heedlessness, despite all his care in rephrasing, and in simplifying the action, are to be found in the strange chronology of **The Cathedral Folk.** When we examine Tuberozov's diary we discover many chronological discrepancies: in this diary, as has been pointed out by the late Boris Tomashevsky, the year 1837 lasts about three years; and the little boy whom Pizonsky takes care of is said to have been born in 1836, but is still referred to as a little boy in 1861 and 1864.[26] But there are also other oddities. Tuberozov himself is said to be an aged man, well over sixty, but according to his dairy (which he terminated in 1864) he finished the ecclesiastical seminary and was appointed to Stargorod about 1832; he was still quite a young man at that time, and therefore should have been about fifty years old, rather than sixty or seventy, in 1864. Zakharia is presented as an old, feeble man, older in any case than Tuberozov; yet he has many children, one of whom is still an infant. Akhilla is said to be fifty years old; this hardly fits in with the picture we get of the deacon—his boyish behavior, his boisterous character, his energy and physical vigor—a picture of hardihood that is, moreover, maintained until the very end, as is illustrated by his fight with Danilka in the last chapters of the novel.

Still stranger are the anachronisms in the stories of the Plodomasovo characters. From the first story about the Plodomasovo village we learn that Marfa Andrevna was born in 1733. In **The Cathedral Folk** she dies in 1850, that is, at the age of one hundred and seventeen. Her son Aleksey Nikitich was born fifteen years after her marriage, that is, in 1763. But in **The Cathedral Folk** he appears as an active "marshal," or leader, of the district nobility, by no means old, although he should be one hundred and one years of age. As a matter of fact, in one point in the novel he is called "Nikita Alekseyevich," instead of "Aleksey Nikitich."[27] This would seem to indicate that the character in *The Cathedral Folk* is not the same Aleksey, son of *bojarynja* Plodomasova, but her grandson, which would certainly make more sense. It is obvious that Leskov did not pay much attention to these personalia.

As we remember from the Plodomasovo chronicle, Aleksey had a natural son, Parmen Semenovich Tuganov. This Tuganov appears also in *The Cathedral Folk.* He too is a marshal of the nobility, not of the district, however, but of the province (*gubernija*). Nowhere in the novel is there any mention of the fact that he is the son of Plodomasov. By the way, Leskov tells us in his sketch that Tuganov was born at a time when "the people raved about Pugachevism" (*narod bredil pugačevščinoj*). This would seem to refer to the years 1773-1775. But elsewhere there are many indications that he was born about 1783-1784—a discrepancy of some ten years. However, even had he been born at this later date he would have been eighty years old in 1864, the year in which the action of *The Cathedral Folk* takes place, whereas in fact there is no evidence that he is an old man; on the contrary, he is shown to us as a middle-aged gentleman (he refers to Father Tuberozov as "an old man").[28]

The same applies to the dwarf siblings. Nikolay Afanasyevich and his sister were bought by Marfa Andrevna in 1783 or 1784. At that time, it appears, they were already adults, but Nikolay Afanasyevich still plays an active part in 1864, as a dwarf of well over a hundred years of age. At one point, however, he states that he has "completed his eighth decade,"[29] and at the end Leskov refers to his being seventy years old not long before his demise.

There are also other discrepancies. One of the notables of the town, Porokhontsev, is described sometimes as *ispravnik* (a sort of district police chief) and sometimes as *gorodničij* (chief of the town), though these were two distinct functions in the Old-Russian administrative apparatus (in one place he is referred to as *uezdnyj načal'nik,* head of the district; in another as *gradonačal'nik,* head of the town).[30]

Of course, these inconsistencies or contradictions are not of major importance. They merely serve as illustrations of the chaotic way in which *Soborjane* was created: Leskov had many different ideas, and in his endeavor to remold and combine them he became entangled in discrepancies. Some of these ideas he soon developed in other works. The attack on the radicals and on the intriguing Poles, for example, came to fruition, even before *The Cathedral Folk* had appeared in print, in the novel *At Daggers Drawn.* The theme of the Old Believers, in a like manner, soon found its realization in the story **"The Sealed Angel,"** written in the year when *The Cathedral Folk* was published. And the

idea of writing a chronicle of provincial life was partly resumed when Leskov produced **"Smekh i gore"** (**"Laughter and Woe"**) in 1870 (a work in which some of the elements of *Soborjane* are present), *Detskie gody* (*Years of Boyhood*) in 1874, and especially *Zakhudalyj rod* (*A Family in Decline*) in 1873. The last-mentioned work is more of a chronicle than *The Cathedral Folk,* and has more unity. In it a true Russian noblewoman is portrayed; not unlike the old Lady Plodomasova, she also had Madame Zinovyeva for her prototype.

All this does not detract in the least from the artistic value of Leskov's novel, from the masterly way in which he puts his characters before us, especially Father Tuberozov and Deacon Akhilla, who both rightly became extremely popular with the Russian reading public.

Leskov's estimate of his own works did not remain constant. Once, in a letter in 1888, he wrote that he was more fond of *A Family in Decline* than of *The Cathedral Folk* and "The Sealed Angel": "It is more mature and written with greater care. . . . It is my favorite work," he wrote.[31] But on another occasion he said: "**'The People of God's House'** is perhaps my only work which will find its place in the history of our literature."[32] And elsewhere he repeated this opinion: "I enjoy myself fussing with them [that is, with *The Cathedral Folk*] (*ja sam rad s nimi vozit'sja*), and I know that it is perhaps my only work that will find a place in the history of literature."[33]

But there are also some critical pronouncements by Leskov—critical not of the artistic side of the novel, but of the ideological. They date from the last ten years of his life, when he had become a full-fledged follower of Tolstoy. Once he said: "*The Cathedral Folk* is excellently written. It is pure beauty! Art at its purest! However—can we develop along the lines of an idealized Byzantium?"[34] And elsewhere: "Anyway, I would not write it [that is, *Soborjane*] now, but I would gladly write 'The Memoirs of an Unfrocked Priest,' and maybe I shall still write it."[35] Finally, Leskov's biographer, Faresov, quotes him as saying, apropos of Goncharov's Oblomov:

> A figure of such dimensions I don't have. People say, however, that my Tuberozov and Akhilla seem to be alive. . . . I know one thing: in fifty years people will be reading Tolstoy, Turgenev and me. . . . *The Cathedral Folk* is my most elaborate work, but in fifty years it will no longer have any interest for the public, just as Pomyalovsky's *Bursa* does not interest them any more now—and yet is it [that is, *The Cathedral Folk*—T. E.] not a work of art? What is lacking in it is an author who is also a thinker and who can carry the reader on his shoulders across the filth of life, depicted in it, to a dry and clean shore. However, where my Tuberozov would carry his reader, and whether I would follow him, I don't know! . . . I really do not know what I

would do and say to Tuberozov, if he were to appear in person before me, with my ideas about Christianity and the state such as they are now. I created him, but I would meet him now as Taras Bulba met his sons when they came back from the Kiev College.[36]

We see thus that, toward the end of his life, Leskov felt an aloofness to his own hero; that the spirit in which **Soborjane** was conceived appeared to him as "idealized Byzantium"; that his own Tuberozov did not seem to him to be leading the reader to a worthy goal. Leskov himself had undergone a transformation in those twenty years. He had withdrawn from the official Orthodox Church, and his attitude toward it was now highly critical. These new convictions of Leskov's seemed to influence his attitude toward his earlier works. Is it true, however, that **Soborjane** is permeated with the "Byzantine" spirit? In other words, does Leskov advocate in this work an attitude of complete submission, of subordinating everything in the state, in society, and in the individual to the all-powerful Church, in accordance with the old Byzantine ideal? Was the novel inspired by reactionary motives? In my opinion, it was not. Leskov must have involuntarily succumbed, in the last years of his life, to the influence of a certain section of public opinion, as far as his earlier works were concerned. It was only natural that the radicals branded his novel about such a despised group as the clergy, with its anti-nihilistic tendency, as reactionary. On the other hand, Katkov did not trust Leskov either; he more or less forced him to introduce certain changes, especially toward the end of the final version, in the passage in which Tuberozov, just before he dies, forgives his enemies among the high Church dignitaries. In the original version the old archpriest remained adamant and immovable in his protesting attitude. But even after those changes had been made, the figure of Tuberozov remained a symbol of resistance to the official Church. It is greatly to Professor Edgerton's credit to have pointed out this fact. He writes:

> Even in the final version of the novel, archpriest Tuberozov's life represents a powerful indictment of the consistory system through which the government controlled the church, and of the relative intolerance and bureaucratic despotism fostered by the system at the expense of freedom of the spirit. But it seems clear that Leskov's original intention was to make the indictment even stronger.[37]

And elsewhere he says:

> The very fact that the heroes of his novel were members of the clergy was enough to confirm the radicals in their condemnation of Leskov as a reactionary. What they overlooked was the strong defense of religious freedom that ran through the novel from beginning to end, and the protest against all religious intolerance and all bureaucratic oppression of religion, whether coming from the government or from the higher clergy within the church itself.[38]

This attitude of protest was originally emphasized, as may be seen from one of the preserved manuscripts of **The Cathedral Folk,** in which the figure of archpriest Avvakum, the seventeenth-century fanatical leader of the Dissenters, or Old Believers, is introduced. In this version Avvakum figures as a forerunner of Father Savely Tuberozov and as an example to him. Leskov omitted this historical figure altogether in the final version.[39]

Having this in mind I can only partly agree with B. Drugov, who in his monograph on Leskov assumes that Leskov conceived the idea of writing **Soborjane** as an answer to the radicals, who were very critical of the Russian clergy.[40] And I disagree completely with the view advanced by Gromov and Eichenbaum, who, in their introduction to the eleven-volume Soviet edition of Leskov's **Collected Works,** maintain that "Leskov turned to the Russian provincial clergy under the obvious influence of Katkov's reactionary ideas."[41] No, Leskov was for some time under the influence of Katkov, but in **Soborjane** he clearly opposes Katkov's ideas.

Summing up my conclusions, I agree that **The Cathedral Folk** is "something unequaled amidst the rich narrative literature of the 1860's and 1870's; it is the first great novel from the life of the Russian clergy and as such is unsurpassed to this day."[42] But it is something more than just the depiction of a group of churchmen and their life; it has a broader scope and greater significance.

Notes

1. William B. Edgerton, "Nikolaj Leskov, the Intellectual Development of a Literary Nonconformist," MS, doctoral diss., Columbia Univ., 1954; Hugh McLean, "Studies in the Life and Art of Leskov," MS, doctoral diss., Harvard Univ., 1956; Vsevolod Setschkareff, *N. S. Leskov, sein Leben und sein Werk* (Wiesbaden: Harrassowitz, 1959).

2. McLean, *op. cit.,* p. 243.

3. Cf. A. L. Volynskij, *N. S. Leskov* (St. Petersburg, 1901), chap. v; R. I. Sementkovskij, Introduction to *Polnoe sobranie sočinenij N. S. Leskova,* Vol. I (St. Petersburg, 1902), pp. 33 and 47; A. Luther, *Geschichte der russischen Literatur* (Leipzig, 1924), p. 270; P. Kovalevsky, *N. S. Leskov* (Paris, 1925), chap. iv.

4. January 4, 1893; in N. S. Leskov, *Sobranie sočinenij v 11 tomakh* (Moscow, 1956-1958), Vol. XI, p. 519. Hereafter, when quoting Leskov, I refer to this eleven-volume Soviet edition of *Collected Works.*

5. Commentary to *Sobranie sočinenij,* Vol. IV, p. 519.

6. This affair is described by Leskov's son: Andrej Leskov, *Žizn' Nikolaja Leskova* (Moscow, 1954), p. 270. Cf., for the difficulties with "Božedomy," the whole chapter (Part IV, chap. ix).

7. *Sobranie sočinenij*, Vol. IV, p. 104.

8. Letter to the Russian Literary Fund (E. P. Kovalevsky), May 20, 1867, in *Sobranie sočinenij*, Vol. X, p. 264; cf. *ibid.*, Vol. IV, p. 519.

9. *Ibid.*, Vol. V, p. 277.

10. *Ibid.*, Vol. I, p. 226, and Vol. IV, p. 6.

11. To give but one of many examples: in "Smekh i gore" (*Sobranie sočinenij*, Vol. II, p. 497) Leskov tells about the hungry peasants who died from sudden overeating; two brothers, sitting opposite each other, toppled over and died; the autopsy showed that their mouths, throats, stomachs, and intestines were full of kasha. The same story is told in *Soborjane* (*Sobranie sočinenij*, Vol. IV, p. 305).

12. Valentina Gebel', *N. S. Leskov: v tvorčeskoj laboratorii* (Moscow, 1945), p. 130; *Sobranie sočinenij*, Vol. III, p. 599.

13. *Sobranie sočinenij*, Vol. III, p. 598.

14. *Ibid.*, Vol. IV, p. 522.

15. Minor mistakes are not altogether absent from the last parts: in the fifth (last) part, the dwarf Nikolay Afanasyevich repeatedly visits Tuberozov to induce him to humility; but Nikolay later falls ill, and it is Tuberozov now who visits him "in the large Plodomasov mansion"—the dwarf was, then, at home, in Plodomasovo (*Sobranie sočinenij*, Vol. IV, pp. 267-268). But when Nikolay Afanasyevich realized that all he had done was in vain he "got ready to go back to his town" (*ibid.*, p. 269). So he was *not* at home. (Was "his town" Stargorod, which was situated close to the village of Plodomasovo?)

16. *Sobranie sočinenij*, Vol. III, pp. 351, 598.

17. V. Setschkareff, *op. cit.* (in note 1, above), p. 74.

18. Quoted by V. Gebel', *op. cit.*, p. 117.

19. The name of Zakharia Benefaktov was given in the earlier version as Zakhary Benefisov, a name Leskov may have deemed too worldly, reminiscent as it is of the word *benefis*, "theatrical benefit."

20. Quoted by V. Gebel', *op. cit.*, p. 195.

21. For Leskov's language, see the chapter on this subject in V. Setschkareff, *op. cit.*

22. Cf., for example, Leskov's sketch "Dvorjanskij bunt v Dobrynskom prikhode," and *Sobranie sočinenij*, Vol. III, p. 600.

23. Letter of June 8, 1871, to P. K. Shchebalsky, in *Sobranie sočinenij*, Vol. X, p. 329. Also quoted by Leonid Grossman, *N. S. Leskov: žizn'—tvorčestvo—poètika* (Moscow, 1945), p. 264, but with a wrong date (May 26, 1871).

24. V. Gebel', *op. cit.*, p. 128.

25. *Ibid.*, p. 132.

26. B. Tomaševskij, *Pisatel' i kniga. Očerk tekstologii* (Leningrad, 1928), pp. 126, 127. Cf. also *Sobranie sočinenij*, Vol. IV, p. 521.

27. *Sobranie sočinenij*, Vol. IV, p. 131.

28. *Ibid.*, p. 193.

29. *Ibid.*, p. 132.

30. Cf. *ibid.*, Vol. IV, p. 63 (the *novyj gorodničij* is a *dobryj mužik*), p. 86 (here he is *ispravnik* and an *otstavnoj rotmistr*), pp. 88, 89; he is *not* the *gorodskoj golova* who is described as "a shortish, fat merchant," Vol. IV, p. 312.

31. To A. S. Suvorin, February 11, 1888, in *Sobranie sočinenij*, Vol. XI, p. 366. Also quoted by Andrej Leskov, *op. cit.* (in note 6, above), p. 309.

32. Quoted by L. Grossman, *op. cit.*, p. 103.

33. Letter of May 26, 1871, to P. K. Shchebalsky, in *Sobranie sočinenij*, Vol. X, p. 325.

34. Quoted by A. I. Faresov, *Protiv tečenij* (St. Petersburg, 1904), p. 90.

35. Letter to L. I. Veselitskaya, January 27, 1893, in *Sobranie sočinenij*, Vol. XI, p. 529; also quoted by Faresov, *op. cit.*, pp. 263-264.

36. Faresov, *op. cit.*, pp. 284-285.

37. Edgerton, *op. cit.* (in note 1, above,) p. 326.

38. *Ibid.*, p. 304.

39. Cf. Gebel', *op. cit.*, p. 134.

40. B. M. Drugov, *N. S. Leskov* (Moscow, 1957), p. 49.

41. P. Gromov and B. Ejkhenbaum, "N. S. Leskov (očerk tvorčestva)," in *Sobranie sočinenij*, Vol. I, p. xxxiv.

42. A. Luther, *op. cit.* (in note 3, above), p. 271.

Richard Bridgman (essay date autumn 1966)

SOURCE: Bridgman, Richard. "Leskov under the Bushel of Translation." *Texas Quarterly* 9, no. 3 (autumn 1966): 80-8.

[*In the following essay, Bridgman underscores the narrative brilliance of Leskov's stories, offering examples of the writer's evocative and finely realized characterizations in several pieces, including "The Musk-Ox" and "The Lady Macbeth of the Mtsensk District."*]

The Jacobean dramatists most often rise in the mind as one reads Leskov's stories. Like Ben Jonson, he possesses an uncanny range of technical knowledge about crafts and professions, which is complemented by a sharp ear for levels of speech. And like John Webster, Leskov encloses his people in a world clouded with savagery. Events close in upon men without warning, to torment and kill at their pleasure. The characters know this and, by doing their share of murdering, introduce themselves into the inexplicable scheme. This dangerous universe is ringed by terrors created in their own minds, for Leskov's people are unusually subject to hallucinations, visions, and marvels. This much is Websterian, the soup of poisoned paintings, amputated hands, and lycanthropic dukes. Leskov's characters respond to this surreal world as Webster's characters do to theirs. The same energy that animates it and projects delusions forth so invests the characters that they never snivel, never cower, but participate demonically in the world as is, and die dazzlingly. These are courageous, stoic characters, egoistic, demanding, dangerous. But they are not insensitive. This is a point worth making, since today we are not accustomed to the joining of power and sensitivity. They seem to us separate endowments. Leskov reminds us how far we have fallen from a conception of the full man.

Leskov's characters are flesh, bone, and often visible blood. One often thinks of them first as animals because of their brutal, candid activity, and Leskov encourages this metaphorically. But these are abundantly imaginative animals, whose minds teem with concretized images that leap out, blend with the feral scene, and surround them with a peculiar force and beauty. Moreover, these creatures are directly aware of powers controlling them, and worship them unabashedly. Their awe is not servile however, and rarely clots into inert theological forms. Vitality persists and forces religion to adapt to it—whereupon we come full circle, back to the animal energies animating, or put otherwise, making man.

Short of the radical step of learning the Russian language though, it sometimes seems that we shall never know how great a writer Nikolai Semenovich Leskov was. The universal plaint of his translators is that Leskov's style is a hurdle too high, and they have tripped, although capable of brilliant rhetorical turns. The trouble is that his style is essentially colloquial. Some intercultural significance may be made of the fact that Leskov was born in 1831, four years before our own colloquial master, Samuel Clemens. Leskov's translators go on to say that their failures are the more bitter since he is a writer of the first rank, and the most Russian of Russians. Gorki thought him a "magician of the word," and Tolstoi censured him for the winning fault of exuberance. "There were too many good things in his stories."

Painful as it is to be regaled with descriptions of a writer's narrative skill and verbal pyrotechnics and then be told they are hidden from view, still perhaps a strong enough light will burn the bushel. As a priest and his barbaric driver wait out a blizzard in a snow hollow roofed with reindeer skins, Leskov evokes a Siberian snore—"As if a large swarm of bees was humming and knocking gently on the sides of a dry, resonant beehive." The atmosphere of "human sweat, smoke, damp rottenness, dried fish, fish fat, and dirt" generates the following acerbly comic interchange, whose vivacity is a second heartening instance of Leskov's penetrating the barrier of intractable language.

> "Don't snore," I said.
>
> "Why, Bachka? Why shouldn't I snore?"
>
> "You snore horribly, you don't let me sleep."
>
> "You ought to snore too."
>
> "I don't know how to snore."
>
> "And I know how to, Bachka," and he instantly started droning at full speed.

Other metaphors shine forth. Reindeer skins resemble soapsuds. Gay laughter sounds "as if someone was tickling the water nymph of the lake." A Tarter resembles "a fresh and hardy vegetable." A Roman candle goes off "like a fiery bird with a burning tail." And a gypsy's grace is lauded: "I have seen actresses dance at a theatre, but pah, they were like an officer's horse on parade that fidgets for nothing, without any fantasy—there's no fire and no life about it. When this queen stepped out, she seemed to be sailing on a calm sea and yet you could hear her bones crack and her marrow run from bone to bone."

Few people know that Leskov is that exhilarating to read. Not much of his work is available, and what is is indifferently translated. But for the moment the first job is to get Leskov out in the open, to demonstrate that he is a splendid writer. Then we can quibble our way pleasantly toward fidelity.

The portrait of Leskov most frequently reproduced shows a doughty man, seated, arms firmly folded in front of him and supported on the arch of a cane. He is bearded and wears a kind of engineer's cap fixed squarely on his head. Leskov was the son of a civil servant. Like Pushkin and Tolstoi he had peasant nurses, but more important he early came into the aura of an Aunt Polly, whose Quaker beliefs sufficiently permeated him so that near the end of his life he approached sympathetically—but did not go ga-ga over—Tolstoi's radical Christianity. His uncle by marriage, an Englishman named Scott, managed some extensive estates near Kiev, and for ten years he employed his nephew as a business agent. Leskov's letters to Scott—so the story goes—were impressive enough for friends to encourage him to enter journalism.

Leskov's career now took a queer turn. Arriving at St. Petersburg as a committed journalist, he immediately reduced his market with an improvident article. St. Petersburg had been seriously burned in 1862 and the radicals were blamed for it. Leskov, by nature a partisan of objectivity, called for an official investigation to test the validity of these rumors to which, ironically, he seems not to have subscribed. The liberal press thinking they saw an act of betrayal at once denied Leskov publication in a sizable portion of the national press. Since he had intimately observed the condition of the serfs Leskov too desired reform, but he felt the liberals were too often fowl, squawking, pecking, hissing, and quacking in the barnyard while progress toward a genuinely humane and cultured Russia went a-begging in the wilderness. This position, consolidated by the personal attacks upon him, led him to write novels critical of the progressives, the titles of which suggest the Russian political climate: in 1864, *The Impasse* (sometimes translated as *No Way Out*), and in 1870, *At Daggers Drawn.* Being virtually ostracized did not shake Leskov artistically. His great stories are marked by stability, good humor, and under the circumstances, a notable lack of vindictiveness. He does not seem to have been obsessed by his persecution and won a wide reading public in spite of the boycott.

This same poise kept him in later life from falling into the excesses of Tolstoian piety. Although Leskov admired the glowing faith of Russian mystics, he readily satirized the clergy. **"On the Edge of the World"** (1876) concludes, "Gentlemen, reverence at least the holy modesty of the Orthodox Church, and understand that she has truly maintained the spirit of Christ, if she suffers all that God wills her to suffer. Truly, her humility is worthy of praise; and we must wonder at her vitality and bless God for it." Yet, before this reconciliation is reached, Leskov has led us through a bitterly hilarious account of a young priest on the Siberian frontier learning not to push conversion too strongly among the natives. If their genial pragmatism leads them to yield occasionally to the baptizing efforts of a vodka-peddling missionary, they still view Christ as a kind but essentially weak deity. The priest's driver, for example, admires Christ chiefly because he made a blind man see by spitting in his eyes, an appeal whose literalness naturally troubles the young, idealistic priest. Not long after, though, he awakens in his sledge with his eyelashes frozen shut. With no analogical fuss from Leskov, the driver spits in the priest's eyes and rubs them until they unfreeze.

Such ironic counterpoint is often perceptible in Leskov's work. In **"The Enchanted Wanderer"** (1874), the leading character is purchased at one point as a nurse for a little girl, who suffers from "the English illness," which according to normal nationalistic slurs would be venereal in origin but which here is apparently rickets. As a result, her legs are "round as wheels." Later the Wanderer is captured by Tartars, who slit the soles of his feet and pack chopped horsehairs into the wounds. The prickling forces the Wanderer to walk on his ankles until his legs too become "round as wheels." (The treatment enrages the Wanderer: "You damned Asiatics, what have you made of me? Better to have killed me outright, you vipers!" To which the Tartars reply soothingly, "Never mind, Ivan, never mind. Why make a fuss about nothing?")

Before the story of the young priest in Siberia ends, another savage has gobbled up the Holy Elements of the mass, drunk the consecrated oil, and stolen the ritualistic box in which they are carried. The acquisition of this sort of ruefully comic experience often makes Leskov's priests into sane men who know how to act with vigorous good sense. When the Wanderer turns lay brother, his religious fervor leads to fits of hallucination. Under the illusion that it is a suicide seeking his prayers—which he cannot in good conscience provide—he kills the convent cow. So the Father Prior locks him in a potato cellar. There he falls into incessant prophesying, whereupon the Father's next response is to transfer him to a building stripped of all furniture save the icon "Blessed Silence." When, after a winter in the exclusive company of a silent Christ, the Wanderer has not improved, the Father finally decides to send him "off somewhere to have a good run. Perhaps he has merely grown stale in one place."

This, the tolerant view, is the one most often taken by the ecclesiastical leaders in Leskov's world, but the stupid, the venal, and the petty appear too. In **"The March Hare"** (sometimes known as **"The Hare Park"** and published twenty-two years after Leskov's death in 1895) a priest learns during confession that a boy has stolen watermelons from his garden (Russian Missouri again) and hales the boy up and down the room by the hair. The boy's indignant father in turn berates the priest as a beast and usurer (he is), and as reparation wins from him a pound of foreign soap, a turkey cock and two turkey hens, a heifer, a young pig, and "a lovely piece of cloth that will make you a very excellent coat" (Russian Washington, D.C.).

Leskov's priesthood stands on the solid base of the simple lay believers. A caveat: these are spiritually simple men whose faith and vision have gradually clarified in the dark cellar of existence. Otherwise, they are demonstrably complex human beings, not in the slightest degree allegorical. The conclusion of the Wanderer's story can be misleading. "He had told us all his story with the unreserved frankness of his simple soul, and his prophecies are concealed in the hands of Him who has kept his decrees from the wise and has revealed them to babes and sucklings." The career of this babe and suckling leavens the simplistic sentiment. It begins when he tumbles a man under the wheels of a coach for which he rides postillion. The dead man comes to haunt the Wanderer, and the two confront one another forthrightly. "What do you want with me? Go away!" "You took my life without leaving me the time to repent my sins." "Things will happen."

This same matter-of-factness reappears when the Wanderer flogs a Tartar to death in an endurance match. In retrospect he comments, "His stubbornness and ambition caused him to depart stupidly from this world. You see, I am not to blame, it was his own fault." The Wanderer is no sadistic scoundrel. We are not appalled by his attitudes so much as we are slowly drawn to accept their inevitability in a pain-ridden and irrational world. Leskov's men are forceful, proud, and active and in a violent existence swirling with nightmarish visions they retain a stoic elan that is compellingly attractive. The Wanderer meets the abandoned mistress of a prince for whom he works. Wolf-eyed and big in stomach, she begs him to plunge a knife into her heart. "I shuddered all over and told her to pray. I couldn't kill her with the knife; I pushed her off the bank into the river." This Wanderer, the one whose way with a wild horse was to jump on his back, "seize him with my left hand by the ear and turn him aside with all my might, whilst I hit him with my right between the ears and ground my teeth most frightfully," *this* Wanderer earns the right to be simple, so fantastically and savagely complex is his enchanted world. His struggles in the weird web of life finally win him direct religious vision.

Leskov introduces us to another variety of spiritual response in **"The Musk Ox"** (1862). Vasilii Petrovich, the clumsy title figure whose arrival is presaged by "a series of heavy movements . . . behind the fence, following which [he] dropped into the little garden like a load of earth" is Leskov's most relentlessly pessimistic character. This tortured, earth-bound idealist plays out the misery of his life against an idyllic backdrop of forest monasteries, between which pilgrims travel slowly in country carts, the air fragrant with lilacs, golden carp and trout leaping in the thin vapours over the surface of wooded lakes, and "jackdaws pottering about in the greenery of the trees."

In the midst of this lyric serenity stands a gruff iconoclast and radical Christian. Accused of impractical idealism, the Musk Ox responds irritably, "What will you have me do? My heart cannot stand this civilization, this nobilization, this scoundrelization!" He suffers neither fools nor brutes easily, and as a consequence loses a tutor's job for assaulting a young aristocrat who had trapped and teased a maid on a ladder. And he is profoundly upset when he witnesses a governmental roundup of vagrant Jewish children for military service. "I can't follow all your la-di-das," he cries. "Your heads are full of stuff about the sheep being safe and the wolves being in good fettle too; only it can't be done. It never happens that way." His peculiar blend of spiritual pith and ferocious sympathy is caught in this small exchange: "Your mother is alive and well, I hope," asks the narrator. "Died in a poorhouse." "What, all alone?" "Well, who do people die with?"

The Musk Ox makes a series of unsuccessful withdrawals from society: to live among the Old Believers— "The truth is they are a lot of hair-splitters"; to a forest hermitage, from which he is soon expelled for holding free-thought seminars with pilgrims; and finally to a family of wealthy ex-serfs. Mooning and snarling at his hosts in the extremity of his spiritual malaise, he is sent to their lumber camp. There the Musk Ox makes his last retreat—to a stifling dark woodland nook where he hangs himself with his belt. The margins of his copy of Plato are filled with self-accusation: "A clown to the people, a curse unto thyself, a killer of ideas." Though Leskov's men are possessed with God in queer ways, and sometimes seem to win a salvation of sorts, they are quite as likely to end as disastrously as the Musk Ox, with his "bloodshot dilated eyes [staring] at the moon with the expression which is left in the eyes of a bull who has been struck several times on the head with a bludgeon, and then straightaway has had his throat slit."

Writing of peasants, Leskov never seems, like Turgeniev, to be a god descended temporarily among the commoners. He is sympathetic and shares their attitudes easily. He revels in odd details drawn from country life, so that here and there in his stories we learn that an "astronomer" is a horse that habitually jerks its head up; that the best way to assess the maturity of a pig is to pierce his back fat with an awl; and that if you put a burbot (not a turbot) in a wooden trough, tease it until its liver swells in rage, and then kill it, you are assured of a delicious soup. His eye for detail has a structural counterpart, for he customarily organizes his material in small units of narrative. His chapters are rarely more that three to five pages long, for he conceives his action in a series of discrete blocks linked by symbolic recurrence. He is fond of using a narrator; sometimes a brace of them with the first introducing the second who then tells the main story, even as the Conradian narrator introduces Marlow.

In **"The March Hare,"** for example, a narrator takes us to an asylum where one of its inmates, O., proceeds to describe how he became a rabid conservative. Although the tone is persistently ironic and the climax high farce, Leskov still generates sympathy for this poor devil of a subdistrict police officer, whose title alone must remind us of Orwell as a young sub-sub in Burma and

Melville's sub-sub librarian, and all the attendant ironies generated by debased bureaucratic titles.

O.'s route to obsession passes through the Church. Serving as a bishop's choirboy, he is instructed by a martinet who respects Facts and the kind of authority they breed. O. must memorize that the Virgin was born in the summer of 5486, and that seventy thousand saints were born in January, but only a hundred and thirty in June. Stuffed with such tripe, O. is sent home to become a police official. His distorted zeal sets him after those "underminers of foundations," the Socialists. He meticulously traps a governess into writing out and signing two apparently radical remarks ("The deceitfulness of riches chokes the Word"), which naturally turn out to be quotations from the New Testament. Tricked, cuckolded, and maddened to a frenzy by a real subversive in his employ, O. is sent off at last to the asylum where he spends his days knitting socks and his nights sitting on heron eggs in the swamps in order (so he believes) to hatch the fire bird. But as he remarks plaintively to the narrator: "The fire bird cannot be hatched out, if they all want to eat heron's eggs."

This badgered victim of an authoritarian education owns just one more of the many obsessions Leskov explores. If O. is shallow and mad, the Musk Ox introspective and self-destroying, and the Wanderer robust and peregrine, each displays a personality bent by the brilliant and mysteriously relentless pressures of life. As a rule, Leskov commiserates with those in the grip of savagery, but in at least one instance the savagery itself dominates his interest. In his major work, **"Lady Macbeth of Mtsensk"** (1865), we read a chilling story of the utmost emotional power and technical skill, totally lacking in pity. It moves from the classic opening of a bored merchant's wife thrown in the company of her handsome lackey, through a history of adultery, murder, and punishment—all without the faintest nod to guilt or remorse. Yet Leskov creates respect for the single-minded intensity of his characters, who, like trapped foxes, gnaw themselves free, indifferent to the mutilation they must inflict upon themselves.

The first of many low-keyed symbolic events in **"Lady Macbeth"** occurs when the husband is called away because a dam has burst and damaged his property. The central unifying gesture of the whole story is a symbolic cognate to this—the pressure of Katerina's breast, first felt when Sergei exuberantly squeezes her to him. Shortly he has made her his mistress, whereupon a large grey cat, strokable but—properly for an embodiment of passion—not seizable, lies between her breasts. After the lovers have murdered her father-in-law, this same cat assumes the dead man's face to comment, "I have come from the churchyard on purpose to see how you and Sergei Filipych are warming your husband's bed." Following this sardonic apparition, Katerina's husband

arrives to be dispatched with a blow from a candlestick, supplemented by strangulation. "For five quiet minutes" Katerina lies atop her husband's chest as her lover strangles him—listening to his heart slow, and stop.

This bizarre murder is a ghastly counterpart to their sexual passion, which is also consummated in eerie silence. When Sergei first takes Katerina, "a silence fell upon the room, which was broken only by the soft regular ticking of a watch." (It is her husband's.) They spend a passionate night later under an apple tree when "the air was still" and "It was difficult to breathe, and one felt an inclination to laziness, indulgence, and dark desires." A fresh murder takes place in an equally oppressive atmosphere, heightened by whispers, coughs, heavy breathing, hoarseness, candles being snuffed, shutters closed. Then Katerina "with one rapid movement covered the childish face of the victim with a large down pillow and threw herself on it with her firm elastic bosom."

Drunken passersby witness and interrupt the last moments of this murder with "deafening blows" upon the shutters. After this equivalent to the Shakespearian porter scene (which is omitted in Shostakovich's opera based upon this story), the lovers are sentenced to exile in Siberia. "When they handed her child to her [Katerina] only said: 'What do I want with him!' turned to the wall, and fell with her bosom on the hard pallet." During the long journey east, Sergei trifles with other female convicts. Once convinced of his infidelity, Katerina throws her chief rival overboard as the prisoners cross the Volga, then leaps into the water herself. Having this long sustained his remarkable metaphor of the breast's suffocating passion, Leskov concludes: "Katerina Lvovna rose from another wave almost to the waist above the water, and threw herself on Sonetka like a strong pike on a soft-finned minnow, and neither appeared again."

"Lady Macbeth"'s ending in a fish simile reminds us that Leskov's fiction swarms with imagery drawn from natural life. Human activity is characteristically punctuated by animal commentary—is, in fact, virtually absorbed in it. When Sergei and Katerina embrace under an apple tree, Leskov rises to a bravura paragraph, flavorsome, mixed, curious:

> A golden night! Stillness, light, aroma and beneficent vivifying warmth. On the other side of the garden, in the distance beyond the ravine, someone struck up a loud song; near the fence in a thicket of bird-cherries a nightingale poured forth its shrill song; in a cage on a high pole a sleepy quail jumped about; the fat horse breathed heavily behind the stable wall; and on the other side of the garden fence a pack of gay dogs ran noiselessly across the common and disappeared in the strange, formless, black shade of the old half-ruined salt warehouse.

Similarly, when the couple make love in a wretched corridor of a way station, a chorus of sounds surrounds them: a guard spitting idly at his boot tip, crickets chirping competitively, convicts snoring, a mouse gnawing a feather under the stove.

Leskov's grotesque juxtapositions of levels of natural life make the delusions his characters often suffer seem part and parcel of a weird whole. Sometimes the illusions are symbolic dreams like Katerina's cat of passion. Sometimes madness brings on the fantasies. One stage of O.'s progress out of hysterical delirium is marked by this vision: "Something dancing before my eyes, something very mysterious, some curiously tiny creatures, the size of pea-pods, just like the dwarfs children sometimes see in dreams, and these dwarfs seemed to be fighting with one another and waving steel spears about which flashed so brilliantly they almost blinded me."

At other times, Leskov's characters face bewildering physical illusions. At the very moment that a drunken priest lies down above a window under which there is a gateway, "a cartload of hay had driven into it, and he, in his fuzzled, sleepy state, imagined that it had driven into his inside." The priest refuses to budge until the cart is driven out again where he can see it. Such roughhouse fancy is matched by lyrical beauty. Caught in a snowstorm and abandoned by his driver, the young priest sees this:

> A gigantic winged figure floated towards me, clad from head to heels in a chiton of silver brocade, which sparkled all over; on its head it had a headdress that seemed to be seven feet high and glittered as if it were covered all over with diamonds, or, more precisely, as if it were a whole diamond mitre. . . . It was like a richly ornamented Indian idol, and to complete this resemblance with an idol and its fantastic appearance, from under the feet of my wonderful visitor sparks of silver dust spurted out on all sides, and he seemed to float upon them as on a light cloud.

Even though this particular vision turns out to be no more than the priest's frost-covered driver returning to rescue him, it is wonderful enough. The driver in his snow miter is no less a representative of salvation than a bishop in his golden one. Leskov's natural world repeatedly produces such scenes that reveal wonders truly beyond madness, and these constitute the last regality of Leskov's imagination. It leaps the boundaries of a perceived world to testify to the awesome splendor of man immersed in his own fantasies. Even as the lower animals envelop his characters' lives, so do these wonders that need not rise from madness or derangement:

> An ancient man came up to me, he mumbled incoherently; he was covered with wax and smelt of honey; yellow bees wriggled in his eyebrows.

What else shall we make of this forest creature than that he is Leskov's measure of life? And note: like the plain cup of water and honey-drenched cucumber that this old man provides as refreshment, Leskov's conceptions have a mysterious adequacy, even in English.

Thomas L. Aman (essay date winter 1968)

SOURCE: Aman, Thomas L. "Leskov's First Series of Sketches." *Slavic and East European Journal* 12, no. 4 (winter 1968): 424-34.

[*In the following essay, Aman concentrates on two of Leskov's early stories, "Razbojnik" and "V tarantase," probing the inventive narrative and anecdotal techniques Leskov developed in these travel sketches.*]

It is generally considered that Leskov is one of the masters of the short story in Russian literature. But this undisputed fact might be a closely guarded secret, for all the critical acclaim Leskov has received in English. Professor Edgerton has performed a titan's task in sorting through the maze of biographical material on the writer,[1] and Thomas Eekman has contributed to our overall understanding of Leskov's best known novel, *Soborjane*.[2] But Leskov's short stories have received very little attention indeed. Except for V. S. Pritchett's sparse comments,[3] it may almost be said that Hugh McLean has single-handedly contributed to whatever critical literature there is on Leskov's short works.[4]

The story of Leskov's extensive journeys over the wide expanse of Russia is well known. His keen powers of observation coupled with a lively imagination served him in good stead when he eventually determined to make his living by the pen. During his thirty-five years as a writer, Leskov created a prodigious body of literature encompassing an incredible variety of genres, topics, and characters. He was fairly brimming over with ideas, and his work at times gives the impression of having been written down helter-skelter, so much was he in a rush to get it to the printer's office in order to launch himself into a new project. This is, in most cases, an illusion, however, for what is in force is a technique both carefully contrived and controlled—a technique producing that apparent haphazardness which is the hallmark of Leskov's talent and which is so like life itself.

Occasionally Leskov's hand could not keep pace with Leskov's imagination. At times he planned entire series of stories in advance only to see these plans disappear as he got caught up by a different idea. His Lady Plodomasova, for example, was to be but the first character in a proposed trilogy.[5] In 1864 in a letter to Straxov Leskov mentions a projected series of eleven stories to follow **"The Lady Macbeth of Our District."**[6] Neither of these plans was ever realized. At other times he was more successful in bringing his projects to fruition, as witness his **"Rasskazy kstati"** and **"Rasskazy neizvestnogo."** But whether such projected series actually saw publication or remained mere plans, Leskov was attracted to the form.

Leskov's first effort of the pen, which is the first in a series of articles on the distilling industry in the Penza district, is dated 28 April 1860. Two years later, in March, Leskov published his first purely artistic work under the heading **"Pogašee delo."**[7] This was followed in a month by the sketch **"Razbojnik"**[8] and shortly thereafter by its continuation, **"V tarantase."**[9] The latter two stories were subsequently republished in the collection, *Tri rasskaza* (Peterburg, 1863).

Had Leskov's later works suffered the same fate that these first stories did, he would be utterly unknown to the Russian reading public today. Following the 1863 edition, **"V tarantase"** was never again published. **"Razbojnik"** had to wait 82 years from the time of its republication in 1863 before it again saw the light of day.[10] Then, as in the more recent edition of Leskov's *Collected Works* of 1956, it was presented without the follow-up sketch, **"V tarantase."** It is unfortunate that this should have happened, for the sketches form two parts of one comprehensive whole. It is also surprising, because **"V tarantase"** is, as A. Narkevič points out, at least as good a story as **"Razbojnik."**[11] One even gets the impression that the decision to publish one sketch without the other was purely arbitrary. Although the two stories are far from Leskov's best offerings, I do not believe that they should be so lightly dismissed as they are in Edgerton's statement: "neither of these two sketches is particularly good as a story."[12]

The two stories under discussion deal with a group of travellers on their way to the fair in Makar'eva. The time is fixed as "fair" time; no further definition is given except that it is hot and dry, therefore summer. The travellers' journey takes them through the Penza district, and the settings of the sketches are the open road and various wayhouses along the route. Leskov, the narrator and one of the travellers, is a non-participating observer.

The origin of the stories is unknown, but it is most probable that Leskov heard the anecdotes while journeying over the vast areas of Russia and then transformed them artistically into the state in which they appeared in 1862.[13] It is quite possible that Leskov originally planned a whole series of anecdotes which would have been narrated during the travellers' journey. In any case, the idea was one that certainly appealed to the author. The ancient mode of travel, with the attendant interesting conversations, must have attracted Leskov, for at the end of **"V tarantase"** he comments with a certain amount of nostalgia: "Perhaps, in time,

people won't travel in this fashion in Russia, and then, probably, such conversations will disappear and completely different ones will take place."

Almost twenty-five years later Leskov was to reiterate his remarks. In **"Žemčužnoe ožerel'e"** a group of friends sit around tea discussing literature and pondering over why inventiveness seems to have weakened in recent times.[14] Leskov, the narrator, recalls the deceased Pisemskij's ideas on the subject. There is a direct connection, he claims, between lack of inventiveness and the railroad system. With the railroads one can travel a great deal but travel is rapid and in no way offensive. Earlier one had to take his chances on all sorts of travelling conditions and many types of travelling companions. However, this served the keen observer with a wealth of impressions. And because it is a variety of impressions that activates the imagination, the railroads have proved harmful to literature.

The travellers, then, are riding in an old-fashioned springless Russian carriage. "There were five of us sitting there," Leskov informs us, and then proceeds to name them for the reader's future reference: "I, a merchant from Nižnij Lomov, a steward [*prikazčik*] from a certain Astraxan' commercial establishment, two young salesclerks attached to this same steward, and a trading peasant from the village Golovinščina."[15] The peasant rides on top of the *tarantas* with the coachman; the remaining five have assembled themselves in the carriage itself. "According to habit we all soon became acquainted with one another and were drawn together as only Russians are able to draw close while travelling. Our conversations did not cease for a minute. . . ." (1-2).

The convention is a timeworn and useful one; an author gathers together a group of people, one of these narrates a story he knows or has heard, and the others become his listeners. Such a gathering takes place occasionally in a cozy room before a fireplace, sometimes in a train station, or on board ship, in short, anywhere where two or more people congregate. The assumption is, of course, that in any group of people there will be at least one who has an interesting story to tell. With Leskov the story is usually interrupted at various junctures by the listeners' comments, interjections, and questions. These serve as a kind of punctuation marks in the story and remind the reader both of the listeners' continued presence and of the fact that the narrator of the events is not the author of the story. With Leskov the narrator is usually a participant in the action he relates.

In **"Razbojnik,"** the final statement quoted above not unexpectedly leads the reader to believe that a tale will be told during the journey itself. Actually, this is true; but the travelling tale is postponed till the second part of the story, **"V tarantase."**

Leskov's opening of **"Razbojnik"** is exceptionally felicitous. "We were driving toward Makar'eva, to the fair" (p. 1). A host of ideas must have been conjured up by this simple sentence for the contemporary Russian reader. Fair time, with all its attendant bustle and excitement, always offered a good subject or background for an interesting tale. In those days driving a long distance was at best a hazardous affair. If one did not have difficulty obtaining horses, perhaps the carriage would break down—not to mention the ever-present danger of being terrorized by assorted brigands and robbers. This last foreboding is strengthened by the title itself.

The sketch is divided into three parts: in the first Leskov briefly describes his travelling companions, the second comprises a series of conversations held in the tiny village where the travellers stop for the night, and the third part is dominated by the *skaz* tale of the young peasant from this village. The first two parts offer, as it were, a background and introduction to the third and most important segment. The narrator and his audience are presented to the reader and the scene is set. The entire party is sitting around the table with the exception of the narrator himself, a young local peasant, who remains standing before his audience. The listeners have already been somewhat prepared for the story; the conversation up to now has dealt with recent robberies in the neighborhood and their investigation by the local authorities. The travellers have repeatedly been warned not to drive on the same evening after dark, but rather to wait until dawn.

Fear on the part of the peasants, that same worry over one's skin which Leskov earlier noticed in **"Pogassee delo,"**[16] has conspired to help the robbers in their evil deeds. The peasants drive their passengers from one point to another and could very well shout out warnings when spying these robbers. But, as the peasant reasons, to whom would he yell out when returning along the same route, this time alone? By now the villain would have had time to round up his comrades and would be waiting to ambush the hapless coachman. Eventually the travellers reconsider and put off the continuation of their journey to the morrow.

"But did you ever see one?" The question concerning robbers is put to the young peasant (p. 7). The query serves the purpose of eliciting the subsequently related story in the form of an answer. The narrator begins: "'Bout six years ago, or probably even more, I got so scared that, good God!" Leskov inserts the remark, "We began to listen."

Not too far from where the travellers are resting is situated a village where a peasant wanted to sell his horse. The narrator, as it turned out, was in need of one. Early one morning, therefore, he slipped into his boot some forty rubles, a considerable sum in those days, and set off through the forest. Considering the possibility of being waylaid, he decided to cut a club with which to defend himself if the need should arise. Shortly thereafter he descried through the trees a soldier sitting by the pathway. Apprehensive, yet determined, the narrator continued on his way. When he drew level with the bedraggled soldier the latter suddenly asked him for a crust of bread. Receiving the reply that the peasant had none, the soldier then requested a *groš*. Wishing to help the poor man, yet fearful of showing all his wealth at once, the peasant again answered that he had none. With a cry that he would call his followers, the soldier then bent over and reached into his boot, as if to draw a knife. With no further thought, the narrator immediately took advantage of the opportunity thus afforded him, and gave the soldier a whack with all his strength. The man fell on the spot and "lay there, just like a frog" (p. 8).

A glance at the athletic build of the narrator is enough to assure the listeners that the soldier was either killed or very seriously hurt. The peasant, then, would kill out of fear for his own skin. In answer to the question, "But did you finish him off?" he says, "The Lord only knows. There's a sin on my soul if something happened. Only I didn't want to. . . ." (p. 9.) This, then, plus the fact that he confessed his crime to the priest, absolves him, as it were, from any more responsibility in the matter. The oldsters in the village merely caution him to be quiet about the affair, thus insuring immunity for the village from the authorities. As in the earlier **"Pogassee delo,"** silence before the law is shown as a primary instinct of the peasant and his community.

The peasant's narrative has produced a very strong impression on one of the listeners, however, the author himself. As the travellers clamber up into the hayloft for a night's rest, he falls into a fitful sleep in which a dream keeps haunting him. In this dream the narrator sees the wounded soldier crawling off toward the woods with "eyes bulging out, blue lips, tongue clenched between teeth, and blood welling from nose and eyes" (p. 10). From this point the imagination of the author carries him further and further: "There was also a small, cypress cross from Kiev, and in a bit of rag a pinch of his native earth. He'd surely carried that little piece of ground from afar, from his native land, where his old mother and father are awaiting their son on leave, and perhaps even a young wife is also waiting for him, or is she running after the Cossacks, or is she *already* at the midwife's. Keep waiting, friends, keep waiting." (p. 10.)

There are so many changes in tone and in emphasis in this final paragraph that it is difficult to keep track of them. The first part offers a description of the soldier which is ghastly. The greenish-hued face, blue lips, bloody eyes and nose, bulging eyes, and tongue clenched between teeth are all terms denoting physical corruption specifically utilized to induce terror in the face of death. The little knife with hand-made handle and the tiny cypress cross from Kiev are personal details, say something about the man himself, and evoke sympathy on the part of the reader. Death can be very impersonal, but personal detail increases the pain and fear many times.

The pinch of earth which the soldier has carried about with him for, perhaps, many years is an inserted bit of information which approaches the sentimental. The added touch that this is from his native land where his old parents are awaiting the soldier's return makes the sentimentality extreme, almost unbearable. Pathos is injected in this manner, but a pathos that is almost alien to the story in which it has been introduced. It is almost unfair that the parents have been included at this juncture, for we have already heard the peasant's story, feel sorry for the most probably innocent victim of his fear, and now it is as if the author were asking us to share the pain of the parents also. It is an irony of fate that we simultaneously know both of the soldier's death and of the old parents' expectancy.

It is at this point that Leskov puts in the master's touch. In a manner somewhat reminiscent of Gogol', Leskov succeeds in transforming a hypothetical idea into a living reality. "Perhaps," he writes, "even a young wife is also waiting for him. . . ." By the end of the sentence, however, it has already become ". . . or is she *already* at the midwife's." From the idea that a young woman is, perhaps, waiting for the soldier, comes the fully formed unfaithful wife who, it turned out, was unable to wait and succumbed to the charms of some passing Cossack. By this stroke, Leskov has managed to veil the tragic old parents in a mist and has once again forced the emphasis to return to the tragedy of the soldier, where it properly belongs. Perhaps even a certain relief is felt at realizing that the unhappy soldier will never be subjected to the pain of learning of his wife's infidelity.

If we bear in mind that **"Razbojnik"** is but Leskov's second artistic effort, then the dream sequence becomes even more significant for the sophistication of its representation. Leskov had attempted description of a dream in his earlier work, **"Pogassee delo."**[17] Here, however, the priest's dream appears, if not crude, at least somewhat obvious. The changing of tempo and progression of ideas in the dream with all their implications to the narrator of **"Razbojnik,"** on the other hand, are executed with the best combination of starkness of description and economy of means.

Less than two weeks after the publication of **"Razbojnik"** Leskov's **"V tarantase"** appeared. There can be no doubt that the sketch is a continuation of the

one preceding it. The same characters are present; they are still journeying to the fair in their huge, lumbering *tarantas*. The peasant who had told the story of his encounter with the poor soldier is now driving the company and even points out the spot where the confrontation had occurred. The time of the segment is the morning following the evening on which the travellers had prudently decided to postpone their trip.

If one were to judge literature by inventiveness alone (it is, after all, this inventiveness which Leskov has in mind when recalling Pisemskij's words above), then **"V tarantase"** would indeed claim a high place in belles-lettres. The setting of the story and the characters, in fact, even the technique involved, are ordinary enough. But the two anecdotes which constitute the major portion of the sketch are among the most original that Leskov ever described. And it is these anecdotes that are at the basis of both the story's literary purpose and its success.

In this sketch, as in **"Razbojnik"** before it, Leskov does not lead directly into the anecdote portion, but rather spends some time in preparation for it. The travellers have risen and seated themselves in the carriage where they continue to doze for a short while. Soon, however, they are fully awake, and the inevitable conversations begin. Much of this introductory section is monopolized by talk of drinking and by the merchant Gvozdikov's idle chatter. The company halts at a wayside inn, thus offering Leskov the opportunity to describe contemporary conditions in such an establishment. Travelling is enormously facilitated by the aid of a few drinks, for when the passengers resume their journey, the atmosphere becomes much gayer and a lively conversation ensues. As in so many of Leskov's tales a question provokes the central anecdote.

No doubt under the impression of the previous evening's tale about the suspected robber, the peasant riding on top queries, "Whyever would there be this stealing among our people?" The merchant has his predictable answer, "There's stealing among all people." It is Gvozdikov's remark which gives rise to the slight but amusing digression to follow. "But, no," he declares, "there's no stealing amongst the Germans." And, in fact, he adds that the Swedes do not have any robbers either—cheaters aplenty, but no robbers. Anfalov, the steward, with shrewd logic then inquires as to who makes Swedish locks. With sudden dawning, Gvozdikov reluctantly admits that there must be stealing amongst Swedes.

A short silence ensues, after which the peasant inquires about the English. The merchant assures all that the English are constantly employed in trading. Anfalov, or Yellow-eyes, as Gvozdikov calls him, seconds this, mentioning that they have "been destined" for this "from on high." In response to objections from the group, he relates the following story in a tongue that is, if archaic, extremely lively.

In olden times, he recounts, shortly after Christ's ascension, and when the ancient faith flowered throughout the land, a wanderer made his way about the world, preaching a godly life to the people. This wanderer at one time found himself in a country peopled by many nations and situated in the place where Rome now stands. His preaching eventually angered the cruel tsar of these people and the latter commanded that he leave his domain. When the preacher refused to depart, the evil tsar ordered his execution. The arrows shot at the holy man bounced off, however, and when the tsar's warriors returned to report, the various nationalities gathered round the preacher and discussed among themselves how best to free him. The English were the first to come up with a plan and, approaching the bound man, asked him, "Would you like us to go to the tsar and trade you away from him?" The holy man gave vent to his disappointment that his words had gone unheeded. The diverse peoples had failed to attain harmony among themselves. "You were not able to stand up for me as a community," the preacher answered them, "go, therefore, and trade your whole lives through." In similar fashion, he enjoins the French to "make war" and the Russians to "steal your whole lives through."

Thus, says Anfalov, were the different nationalities sent forth according to their calling. The tsar's warriors returned and drove a pike into the holy man's heart, but before the latter died he prophesied that from each drop of his blood would spring forth a man who would go about the people teaching love and harmony.

The tale produces a strong impression on the company, and for a time silence reigns. It is broken, however, by the merchant, who thoughtfully exclaims, "Something's not right." He admits the truth of the English trading all their lives but is skeptical about the remainder of what Anfalov has related. As proof he points to the French employed at a cast-iron works, asking, "What kind of war could be going on there?" The driver backs up the merchant by testifying to the proficiency of the French at stealing.

It is this same driver who now proceeds to tell an alternate version of why some people steal while others make war. Once, he claims, he was driving someone to the station from which this company had yesterday arrived. He had gone some five versts or so when he spied a man walking alongside the road. The peasant offered him a lift and after a short pause the pedestrian accepted and crawled into the wagon. The inevitable conversations immediately began. The wanderer let drop that he had been in Jerusalem and moved on to a dis-

cussion of why men were plagued by lechery, drunkenness, stealing, and other sins.

There was a holy man, he said, to whom God had entrusted the commandments written in His own hand on stone tablets. Everything was transcribed there as it should be: thou shalt not steal, thou shalt not kill, etc. This holy man carried the tablets down to his people from the heights of a great mountain. But, descending the mountain, the man froze in his tracks when he caught sight of his people. They had not had the patience to wait for him but had given themselves over to the devil. He was met by music, dancing, revelry, and all sorts of evil. So much did this upset the saint that he dropped the tablets which clattered down, breaking into pieces as they fell. The people, realizing their waywardness, scrambled to gather up the shattered pieces. But in no way could they put them back together again. The holy man continued his descent, surrounded by a heavenly light. So frightened became those holding the tablet fragments that they ran off in all directions, still clutching them in their hands. To those who remained, however, the saint brought a second set of commandments, and these lived out their lives in righteousness. But those who ran off were destined to lives of sin and hardship. The people carrying fragments which said "steal," "kill," etc., spent their days in stealing and killing. Those to whom fell the pieces on which was written "thou shalt not" became wanderers, outcasts without home or family.

Thus ends the coachman's tale of "why there would be stealing among our people." The merchant probably expresses the opinion of the majority when he states, "Now, that's more likely closer to the truth."

There is a remarkable unity in these two stories that could not have been achieved without careful planning. Each story is made up of two basic components, embellished with a certain amount of extraneous detail. In **"Razbojnik"** the various conversations about robberies in the village district make up the first component. These robberies are "real" events, of course, but somehow vague, impersonal, in a way, almost hypothetical. The second component in the story is the actual encounter with the soldier which the peasant relates. This is something which no longer merely forebodes; it touches the reader first because it *happened*, and secondly because it happened to someone with whom the reader has become acquainted.

The two basic elements in **"V tarantase"** are the two anecdotes themselves. Each of them has the purpose of explaining the events described the evening before. Here again, the first turns out to be the "hypothetical" case, for the explanation is rejected by the company as untrue. The second story is perfectly acceptable to all and thus becomes the established fact. The company continues its journey fully assured that it has discovered the logical reason for the happenings previously described as well as all other events of both the past and the future. Whether Leskov meant to produce such an impression by purposeful implication or whether such implication was inherent in his understanding of the peasant mentality, it seems to me that there is also present here the suggestion of the peasants' attitude of blind and utter subordination to the wiles of fate. In any case, it is significant that it is the same person, namely the young village peasant, who gives voice to the "real" segments in each of the two stories.

Quite apparent in these early stories of Leskov is the writer's essential objectivity. For example, nowhere does he make a definite pronouncement on whether the soldier in **"Razbojnik"** actually intended to rob the peasant. And the peasant's narrative holds just the right note of unconcern. After all, he felt justified in protecting himself and if he killed the soldier, well, he "hadn't wanted to." In **"V tarantase"** it is Leskov's intention to present, not his own, but the people's version of why men sin. His description of the travellers' rejection or acceptance of an explanation and their reasons for such is like a transcript of the participants' remarks. There is absolutely no intrusion by the author.

Present in these stories are the seeds of numerous themes, motifs, and characters which Leskov would later develop more fully. There is, for example, mention of a village priest in **"Razbojnik,"** a character for which Leskov would become well known in a few more years. Anfalov, it turns out, is an Old Believer, as is the wanderer who had told the peasant the story of the commandments. The Old Believers will, of course, become an object of extreme interest for Leskov and, eventually, the subject of one of his greatest stories. One may also discern in **"V tarantase"** the rudimentary idea of the *pravednik,* a character existing in almost all of Leskov's works.[18] Akin to the objectivity remarked above, there is a certain casualness, almost nonchalance, in the face of death in the story **"Razbojnik."** But this near callousness in describing death[19] will become tempered with humor as Leskov's literary development progresses. But it is noteworthy that he published very few works in which death of some sort does not figure. One other facet of Leskov's art which is slightly exhibited here is his fondness for animal imagery. When the peasant recalls how he struck down the soldier with his club, he remarks that "he lay there, just like a frog." Not only is the term one which would readily have occurred to the peasant's mind: it is also a most appropriate one for describing the felled soldier's utter helplessness.

Two other elements in the stories bear noticing for the light they shed on Leskov's future artistic development. His descriptions of the peasants' lives, traditions, and superstitions, of the village, the wayside inn, and the open road: all are but miniatures of what was to come later. These were facets of Russian society which Leskov knew well, and he never ceased to draw on his experiences when creating a new work.

Finally, a word about Leskov's language. It may be said without exaggeration that this is the only feature of Leskov's talent which has received anywhere near the recognition due it.[20] In the two stories under discussion many recognizable traits are already observable. Gvozdikov's verbal play in **"V tarantase"** is on a somewhat lower plane than that of Leskov's future characters, but gives an idea of things to come. The speech of the young peasant is full of dialect words and ungrammatical forms. The story told by Anfalov is monopolized by all sorts of archaic words drawn from the Old Church Slavic vocabulary. The important thing to note here is that from the very outset Leskov was attempting to individualize the speech patterns of each of his characters. He himself was occasionally wont to boast of his ability in this respect: "A writer's organization of voices consists in the ability to control the voice and language of his hero and not run off from alto to bass. In my work I tried to develop this ability and attained it, it seems, to the extent that my priests speak like priests, my nihilists like nihilists and my peasants like peasants."[21]

Notes

1. William B. Edgerton, *Nikolai Leskov: The Intellectual Development of a Literary Nonconformist* (dissertation, Columbia Univ., 1954).

2. Thomas Eekman, "The Genesis of Leskov's *Soborjane,*" *California Slavic Studies,* II (1963), 121-140.

3. V. S. Pritchett, "Leskov," *Oxford Slavonic Papers,* X (1962), 18-24.

4. See, e.g., Hugh McLean, "On the Style of a Leskovian *Skaz,*" *Harvard Slavic Studies,* II (1954), 297-322, and "The Priest and the Sorcerer: Leskov's First Short Story," to be published in a Chicago *Festschrift* dedicated to G. V. Bobrinskoy. Also worth mentioning here is A. Ansberg, "Frame Story and First Person Story in N. S. Leskov," *Scando-Slavica,* III (1957), 49-73.

5. Валентина Гебель, «Н. С. Лесков в творческой лаборатории» (М., 1945), 130.

6. Letter of 7 December 1864 to Straxov, Н. С. Лесков, «Собрание сочинений» (11 тт.; М., 1956-1958), X, 253.

7. М. Стебницкий, "Погасщее дело," «Век,» № 12 (25 март 1862).

8. М. Стебницкий, "Разбойник," «Северная пчела,» № 108 (23 апрель 1862).

9. М. Стебницкий, "В тарантасе," «Северная пчела,» № 119 (4 май 1862).

10. Н. С. Лесков, «Избранные сочинения,» ред. Б. Другов и А. Лесков (М., 1945), 3-7.

11. А. Наркевич, "Лесков и его комментаторы," «Вопросы литературы,» 1959, № 12, стр. 195.

12. Edgerton, 166.

13. Professor Edgerton has suggested to me the probability that the two anecdotes in the second of these stories represent undiscovered folklore elements and that these early sketches in general were influenced by as yet unidentified sources. No one, however, has had the opportunity thus far to fully explore these theories.

14. Н. С. Лесков, "Жемчужное ожерелье," «Собр. соч.,» VII, 432.

15. Н. С. Лесков, "Разбойник," «Собр. соч.,» I, 1. All further quotations in the text are taken from this edition.

16. М. Стебницкий, «Сборник мелких беллетристических произведений» (СПб., 1873), II, 110, reprinted here under the title "Zasuxa."

17. Ibid., 122.

18. This was mentioned by Edgerton, 166.

19. Cf., e.g., the description of Axilla's brother's death in *Soborjane* (*Sobr. soč.* [*Sobranie sočinenij*], IV, 70), and that of the old monk in "Očarovannyj strannik" (*Sobr. soč.*, IV, 398-399). This is, however, only apparent callousness. After all, as Leskov takes great pains to show, these are not his descriptions but rather those of his characters.

20. I list here but a few of the many articles dealing with Leskov's use of language: А. С. Орлов, "Язык Лескова: Материал к статье," «Язык русских писателей» (М.: АН СССР, 1948), 144-175; Н. С. Антошин, "О языке Н. С. Лескова," «Наукові записки» (Ужгородський Державний Унів.), XXXVII (1959), 70-97; Валентина Гебель, "О языке Н. С. Лескова," «Литературная учеба,» 1938, № 5, стр. 39-62.

21. А. И. Фаресов, «Против течений» (СПб., 1904), 273-274.

Hugh McLean (essay date 1974)

SOURCE: McLean, Hugh. "Iron, Dough, and a Kolyvan' Husband: Leskov Confronts the Germans." In *Mnemozina: Studia litteraria russica in honorem Vsevolod Setchkarev,* edited by Joachim T. Baer and Norman W. Ingham, pp. 267-80. Munich: Wilhelm Fink Verlag, 1974.

[*In the following essay, McLean surveys Leskov's sardonic and generally critical literary depictions of Germans and German contact with Russia.*]

One of the soul-stretching, but not necessarily pleasant aspects of foreign travel is the tourist's traditional pastime, culture-comparing. "U nas tak, a u vas ètak," as the formula goes in Russian: "You have it this way, but we have it that way." This game is likely to arouse strong, and conflicting, feelings in almost anyone, especially in people with little experience of foreign ways. One generally feels relatively helpless in a foreign country, linguistically lame, ignorant of the local ropes; and one's habits and desires cannot always be satisfied in accustomed ways. Everything is so much easier and more comfortable at home that to the weary traveller even the "smoke of the fatherland," as Griboedov put it (quoting Deržavin, who in turn was quoting the *Odyssey*), seems to smell better.

On the other hand, however, some of "their" ways inevitably strike us as better than "ours"—easier, more attractive, more opulent. Yet to acknowledge "their" superiority seems almost an act of self-treason—a depreciation of one's own nationality and thus of oneself. An emotional tug-of-war ensues, from which "we" normally emerge victorious: after all, the big emotional battalions, always eager to do battle in the name of self-defense (or self-congratulation), are solidly on "our" side. All the same, some residue of cultural relativism usually survives the war—an uneasy awareness that one's own national system of beliefs and social practices is only one of the many possible adjustments to the human condition.

For an educated Russian in the nineteenth century, however, the game was a bit harder to win. Most of the visible scoreboards kept showing "them" far in the lead. It was all too clear that in France, Germany, and England most people were better fed, better clothed, and better housed than they were in Russia; public services were more efficient; political institutions more responsive to the popular will; average levels of education and literacy higher; industrialization much further advanced; and so forth. The list of "their" superior scores was a long one. And on the Russian side there was nothing very concrete to offset them with. There were, to be sure, the extraordinary creative achievements of the Russian cultural elite during the preceding century or so, especially in literature; but still, even the totality of these achievements hardly matched the enormous cultural wealth accumulated in the West since the Renaissance. Lacking ponderable evidence of superiority, the Russian could only resort to intangibles: national character, the nation's "youth" (whatever that might mean), its pristine vigor—with, of course, the corollary that the West was "rotten," effete, and moribund. Cultural accumulation aside, "our" people, as people, were clearly better—nicer and more human. If they had accomplished less, there were plenty of historical and geographical excuses for that. And of course God loved them best, and their way of understanding and worshipping Him was superior to any other.

* * *

Nikolaj Leskov had been an *aficionado* of the game of culture-matching ever since his since his childhood. Although he was thirty-one when he made his first trip abroad (1862) and in general lacked the cosmopolitan experience of his more affluent and more aristocratic contemporaries, his aunt Aleksandra's marriage to an Englishman, semi-Russified though he was, had exposed Leskov very early to a revealing, and unsettling, juxtaposition of two cultures. If an admired and beloved uncle were one of "them," "our" ways could not seem, even to a child, so absolute, so divinely ordained.

This theme of the foreigner in Russia fascinated Leskov all his life, and he returned to it again and again. Whether the outcome were treated favorably or otherwise, the confrontation of two cultures provided both dramatic energy and a means of casting new light on Russian society and the Russian national character, which remained one of Leskov's most persistent cognitive concerns. Several times he resorted to direct literary incarnations of this uncle, Alexander Scott, who makes full-scale appearances at the beginning (**"Jazvitel'nyj" ["The Mocker,"** 1863]), middle (*Meloči archierejskoj žizni* [*Trifles from Episcopal Life,* 1878]), and end (**"Zagon" ["The Cattle-pen,"** 1893]) of Leskov's literary career; and he is referred to tangentially in many other works. His was a haunting presence, both personally and, as it were, nationally, symbolically.

In 1875 Leskov had made his second excursion to western Europe, spending much of his time at Marienbad recuperating from various ills of body and spirit.[1] Very likely this experience as the Russian abroad reactivated the obverse theme, the foreigner in Russia, setting him thinking once again about the character who, for Leskov, was its archetypal representative. Soon after his return to Russia Leskov decided to take up this theme once again. He therefore automatically opened his mental trunk to the drawer of memories from the "Scott" period of his life, the time (1857-60) when he had been an employee in "commercial service" for his uncle's agricultural management firm, Scott, Wilkins & Co. Perhaps because of his recent sojourn in Austria and Germany, he chose to focus this time not on Scott himself but on a former employee of his, a German engineer named Krüger. This Krüger, as an archetypal specimen of his nation, was to be given a treatment even more mocking than that administered to Scott in **"The Mocker."**[2]

Like most Russians, Leskov had always had rather ambivalent feelings about Germans. The Germans were not then, of course, the national enemy No. 1 they were

to become in the twentieth century. To be sure, there was in most Russians some residue of the age-old antagonism between Teuton and Slav; but the nineteenth-century Russians found much in the Germans to admire and envy. In the realm of the intellect, German philosophers, after all, provided the foundation stones for most of the "Russian" ideologies of the nineteenth (and twentieth!) centuries, from Romantic idealism (Schelling, Fichte, Hegel) through mid-century materialism (Feuerbach, Moleschott, Büchner) to "scientific" socialism (Marx, Engels) and "decadence" (Nietzsche). German music was obviously supreme; German literature, outstanding; and German science and scholarship, preeminent in a great many areas of learning. In the material sphere, German manufacturing was beginning to rival England's, with industrialization advancing by leaps and bounds. And under the sagacious rule of the "Iron Chancellor" the Prussian crown had at last succeeded not only in subjecting to its authority all the myriads of petty German principalities but had inflicted humiliating defeats on both Austria and France. Germany, which had entered the century politically divided and economically backward, had now "caught up with and overtaken" France and England as Russia still only aspired to do. Thus for many Russians Germany was the most immediate exemplar, the model for their own future.

On the other hand, sources of friction, either manifest or potential, were not hard to find. On the international scene, the major antagonist, for the time being, was not Germany, but Germanic Austria, Russia's chief rival for the spoils of the fast disintegrating Ottoman Empire. Russian imperialist ambitions in the Balkans were intensified and Russian emotions heightened against both Austria and Turkey by uplifting notions of pan-Slavic solidarity with Balkan Slavs and pan-Orthodox solidarity with Balkan non-Slavs. As long as Bismarck ruled, however, Germany itself remained neutral in this conflict and tried through the *Dreikaiserbund* to keep its Imperial partners on speaking and negotiating terms. But outside the government there was already alarming talk in Germany itself about *Lebensraum* and a *Drang nach Osten,* which augured ill for the future.

On the whole, however, the Russians' attitude toward Germans in Germany remained fairly positive during the latter 1870s, as feelings aroused by the Franco-Prussian War subsided. Toward Germans in Russia, however, antagonism was increasing. Here the chief villains were the Baltic (Livonian) barons. These relics of the ancient glories of the Teutonic Order and the Knights of the Cross had managed to retain their lands and their dominance over the indigenous Lettish and Estonian populations through several changes of national flag; and after the area's incorporation into Russia in the eighteenth century these German nobles came to play an increasingly important role at the St. Petersburg court and in the Russian administration generally. Some of them eventually became Russified in language and culture, with only their names serving as emblems of their Germanic origin; but those who retained their connection with their ancestral Baltic lands generally preserved their German speech and Lutheran religion.

These Baltic provinces, moreover, had never been fully incorporated into the Russian administrative and judicial systems, being allowed to retain their local law and customs; and the German language there had equal status with Russian in the courts. This anomaly of an enclave of German territory within the Russian Empire, with German officials presiding over its destinies, began to trouble the hearts of race-conscious Russian patriots as the nineteenth-century tide of ethnocentric nationalism tended more and more to engulf the older, "feudal" notion of multinational monarchical suzeranity. If political allegiance were based on ethnic and cultural identity, how could these Germans be trusted to serve the Tsar rather than the Kaiser? How could you be a Russian and a German at the same time?

The noted Slavophile Jurij Samarin had for years been conducting a campaign of journalistic indignation against German rule in the Baltic provinces, calling for the government to institute in that area something like the policy that was later, in the reigns of Alexander III and Nicholas II, actually adopted, bearing the ill-fated name "Russification." For the time being, however, Samarin's articles had to be published outside of Russia, and his patriotic propaganda even evoked punitive action against him from the Russian government whose national purity he sought to promote.[3]

Leskov himself visited the Baltic area many times, beginning with a subsidized excursion in 1863 to Riga to investigate the secret schools of the Old Believers. At that time the Baltic barons had received a not unfavorable assessment from Leskov. As Protestants and non-Russians, they could not understand, or sympathize with, the Russian government's persecution of the Old Believers, which was then Leskov's chief concern; thus he could use German tolerance as a means of shaming the Russian intolerance he deplored. The Baltic German officials, he reported, carried out "with disgust" the repressive orders of the Russian government.[4]

Leskov's sentimental idealization of the Petersburg Germans in **The Islanders** (**Ostrovitjane,** 1866) seems to mark the high water of his early pro-German sentiments. In the later 1860s, however, he began spending the summers at resorts in the Baltic area, and before long his feelings about Russian Germans took a decided turn for the worse. First, there was the "holy water and cigar affair." Although he claimed he was not, as the Germans charged, the first to publicize this incident in the Russian press, Leskov certainly did energetically

broadcast it later, and more than once. What happened was this. In 1866, in the Estonian town of Wesenberg (now Rakvere), the resident Russian officials and clergy decided to hold a public service of thanksgiving for the Emperor's survival of the assassination attempt of Karakozov. This Orthodox ceremony, held in the public square, involved the consecration of holy water. The local German burghers, not surprisingly, considered themselves spectators rather than participants in such a ceremony, whatever their feelings about the Emperor's survival; and they stood by their shops or in the square to watch the arcane Orthodox antics of their Russian compatriots—without, apparently, deeming it necessary to remove their hats or extinguish their cigars. During the ceremony some unseemly behatted and cigar-smoking German crowded up indecently close to the priest performing the service. A Russian major promptly had the German arrested for his insolence. This act aroused other Germans to come to his defense, and a mêlée ensued, in the course of which some Germans supposedly lit their cigars from the candles burning on the Orthodox altar. In the aftermath, the German officials of the Baltic region took no action against the arrested German and instead managed to get the major and the priest transferred out of their territory. This was obviously a story ideally designed to arouse righteous anti-German indignation in patriotic Russian breasts, and Leskov makes the most of it.[5]

Even closer to home was Leskov's own "wie Rauch" affair, which took place in 1869 or 1870. One evening in Reval Leskov and a Russian friend named Dobrov got into a tavern argument with three young Germans. Quoting Turgenev's novel with malicious satisfaction, one of the Germans proclaimed that *Smoke* offered the most basic of all insights into the destiny of Russia: Russia was a country where every undertaking "would dissolve like smoke" (*wie Rauch*). Cut to his patriotic quick, the good Dobrov rose to his country's defense with a cane, which he broke over the Germans' heads. According to his own account, Leskov remained disdainfully aloof from the physical combat, but he was nevertheless made a defendant in a suit for assault brought by his German antagonists. The suit dragged on for several years in the courts, with Leskov patriotically refusing to respond to German legal papers served on him in Petersburg, insisting that they be translated into Russian. The case went all the way to the Senate, where Leskov was apparently let off with a small fine—having already made a good deal of journalistic capital out of the affair.[6] Leskov's dislike of Baltic Germans, however, had become a permanent emotional resource, to be drawn on for such xenophobic caricatures as Count Funkendorf in **A Decrepit Clan** (**Zachudalyj rod,** 1874).

In 1875 Leskov seems to have returned from abroad with a renewed animus against Germans, into which his old resentments from his Baltic experiences were readily absorbed. He set about venting these feelings artistically in the story **"Iron Will,"** utilizing anecdotal material dating back to his days in Scott's employ.

Like **"The Mocker," "Iron Will"** was again to be based on the confrontation of two national archetypes, the "oral" Russian with the "anal" European, to invoke two indispensable Freudian categories; and in this case the German was to be shown as an even more extreme representative of "anality" than the Englishman exhibited in the earlier story. The outcome of such a confrontation, in a Russian story written for Russians, is not hard to predict: the national oriflamme (or favorite orifice) will be thoroughly vindicated. But Leskov is too good an artist—or perhaps too contrary a personality—to allow his story to become too obvious a display of national self-flattery. As in **"The Mocker," "Laughter and Grief," "The Cattle-Pen,"** and other works in which he deals with the "national character" theme, Leskov therefore carefully avoids the superficial satisfactions of chauvinism. His technique, already employed in both **"The Mocker"** and **"Laughter and Grief,"** is to spread his irony liberally over Russian and foreigner alike. If the foreigner comes to grief in Russia—and most of Leskov's foreigners do, at least initially—it is not because Russia is better and they are worse, but because their characters are not suited to Russian conditions. These conditions are in no way presented as "good," let alone better than those in the West; they are simply a reality to which the Westerner must adapt or perish.

Like so many of Leskov's stories, **"Iron Will"** begins as a discussion, in the course of which the main narrative will be brought in by way of illustration, "à propos." The author's spokesman in this discussion, Fëdor Afanas'evič Vočnëv, belongs to a character type of which Leskov was especially fond, reminding us a good deal of Bishop Nilus in **"At the Edge of the World"** and a little of Orest Vatažkov in **"Laughter and Grief"**: the wise oldster, reflective and rich in experience, benevolent and tolerant, yet acutely aware both of the imperfections of human nature and the frequent ironies of human fate. Vočnev knows that human affairs and human problems have a way of oozing out of the simplistic categories men concoct for classifying and the easy formulas they devise for solving them.

Like Nilus, Vočnev is a patriotic Russian; and he narrates a story which at first seems like the ultimate Russian put-down of the Germans. Vočnev-Leskov, however, not only manages to put the Germans to shame without making the expected corollary claim of Russian superiority; he even succeeds in making the very German ignominy a source of ironies directed against his own country. Vočnev is especially fond of "ironic boasts," if such an oxymoronic genre can be said to exist. The Russians are assured a great future, he announces, because a people that could produce such a scoundrel as Čičikov is invincible![7] With their thousand years of recorded history, he further insists, the Russian claim to some sort of national "youth" is an absurdity. And the antidote to German rationality, he wryly suggests, is simply Russian stupidity! As he quotes a famous Russian general, "What do we care if they [the Germans] make clever calculations? We'll do something so stupid to them that they won't even be able to open their mouths. . . ."[8] Likewise, the counterforce to Bismarck's iron is Russian "dough": "All right, so they're made of iron . . . and we are simply dough, soft, raw, unbaked dough. But you should remember that a mass of dough can't be cut with an axe, and you may even lose your axe in it." Or, as the Russian proverb which Leskov uses as the epigraph to his story puts it: Rust eats iron.

The narrative material of **"Iron Will,"** as usual with Leskov, consists of a series of anecdotes, connected, on the narrative plane, by the personality of the hero, and on the plane of abstraction, by the "idea" the whole story is supposed to demonstrate, namely, the futility and even danger of "iron will" as a basic human stance, especially in an environment of "dough-like" Russians. This idea is explicitly articulated at the beginning; but nevertheless, Leskov's narrative skill is so great that he avoids giving the impression that the illustrations have been concocted to justify the conclusion. Exaggerated and pointed up as they undoubtedly are, they have the ring of human authenticity.

The central character in **"Iron Will,"** its demonstration piece, is a German engineer named in the story Hugo Pectoralis (i.e., Krüger), imported into Russia by the narrator's English employers to service their milling machinery. This Pectoralis is the "anal" character incarnate, with its virtues and defects magnified to the point of caricature and shown off in bold relief against the background of Russian orality. He is first of all competent—a good engineer, conscientious, responsible, and technically resourceful; however deficient he may be in human relations, he deals most effectively with objects. He is thoroughly dependable, knows his job, and gets his work done on time. All these virtues are in sharp contrast to the characteristic vices of the Russian "oral" character—slapdash performance, unreliability about time and obligations, achievement in word rather than deed. Similarly, Pectoralis is a fanatic practitioner of that postponement of gratification which the here-and-now Russians apparently find so impossible. With money he is as thrifty as Benjamin Franklin; and in general he shows a stupendous capacity for stifling the urgings of his id. In fact, for Pectoralis life in the present is almost totally denied in the name of the power and glories he aspires to in the future. He lives in anticipation of that great day when he will proclaim his independence of his employers, establish his own business, marry, and commence the production of a new generation of solid, dutiful, responsible German accumulators.

Yet for all these impressive manifestations of the Protestant ethic, Pectoralis is in the end reduced to ignominy and his dream swallowed up in the sticky dough of Russian life. And it is precisely the virtue he most values in himself, his "iron will," his capacity for self-control, that in the end proves his undoing. Pectoralis's "iron will" is indissolubly bound up with two disastrous flaws of character which in the end prove literally fatal: a rigidity so extreme that it cannot make adjustment to, or even acknowledge the existence of some very impossible alternative of admitting his own fallibility. The great Pectoralis renders him unable to distinguish at all between real self-interest and fatuous face-saving.

Leskov—or rather Vočnev—relates with gusto a long series of episodes in the Russian education of Hugo Pectoralis (more correctly, his non-education, since he is incapable of learning from experience). Pectoralis is stoicism reduced to absurdity—a man who without a murmur could endure countless wasp stings or drink glass after glass of tea so strong it is practically pure tannic acid—these and many other self-injurious acts performed in order to avoid the impossible alternative of admitting his own fallibility. The great Pectoralis cannot make a mistake or require human aid.

In typically anal fashion, Pectoralis's dream of glory is carefully measured out with money. When his savings reach 3,000 thaler (a goal he has set himself before leaving for Russia), he sends for his German fiancée, and they are duly married, at least on paper. To the utter amazement of Pectoralis's weak-willed Russian associates, however, it later transpires that the German had set himself another, unspoken test of his gigantic will power: he will not consummate his marriage until his savings reach 10,000 thaler! Such inhuman (and pointless) abstinence proves too much for his good *Frau,* who first consoles herself with another German, a laborer, and finally departs in search of a husband with more blood and less iron.

Pectoralis, in short, is an inhuman and thoroughly unpleasant character, his meanness redeemed only by his absurdity. On the other hand, the two Russians who serve as his chief antagonists are anything but paragons; indeed, they seem to have been carefully screened by Leskov so as to exhibit only the vices and not the virtues of the Russian character. (It should be admitted, however, that these vices as Leskov represents them do seem less vicious, more human, more forgivable than Pectoralis's). The first is a horse trader named Dmitrij Erofeič—a notorious swindler, but a swindler who cheats people not in a dry, prosaic, "German" manner, purely for gain, but exhibitionistically, for the fun of it, "as an artist," "for glory." Without too much difficulty

this Dmitrij Erofeič manages to con Pectoralis into buying a blind horse, the animal's physical blindness appropriately symbolizing its new owner's spiritual anopsy. The face-saving Mr. Iron Will, when he discovers the fraud, makes no remonstrance or protest of any kind—he prefers to accept the loss rather than make a public admission of his folly; and this stoic silence so unnerves the rascally Russian, used to soul-satisfying scenes with his swindled victims screaming threats and imprecations at him, that he lives in terror of the dire plot he assumes the German must be hatching against him. To forestall it, he is eventually reduced to sending Pectoralis a good horse! But even now the German cannot admit his original mistake. He contemptuously rejects the new horse, remarking scornfully to Dmitrij Erofeič: "I'm ashamed of you. You haven't got any will power at all."

Will power or not, Dmitrij Erofeič is obviously a man of considerable intelligence and verve, however knavish the purposes to which they are put. These qualities, on the other hand, are quite lacking in the chief Russian antagonist of Pectoralis, Safronyč. Safronyč is the very epitome of all the "Russian" weaknesses. As the German's rival in the foundry business, Safronyč is hopelessly inferior—sloppy, incompetent, unreliable, and without the slightest ambition to improve. Where Pectoralis's life is a mountain of "cares," Safronyč by contrast is "careless," i.e. carefree, *bespečnyj*—a Russian word hard to translate fully, with all its overtones of lighthearted irresponsibility, frivolousness, and "oral" dependency. Predictably, this archetypal Russian failure is hopelessly addicted to the national oral vice, alcoholism.

In a fair fight between these two specimens of ethnic identity, we would naturally expect the hard-working, self-denying, persevering German to emerge victorious, however appealing the Russian may be in his childish insouciance. But this is art, not athletics; and of course the spice of Leskov's anecdote lies precisely in the frustration of this obvious expectation. In the end the German's rigidity proves even more self-destructive than the Russian's irresponsibility. Pectoralis is ordered by a court either to reopen the passage, which he had barred off, between Safronyč's house and the street (Safronyč's house and workshop can be reached only by a right-of-way across Pectoralis's land) or to compensate Safronyč for his lost business at the rate of fifteen rubles per day. At this point Pectoralis's touted iron will becomes a suicidal weapon. Confronted with the choice between backing down or saving face by making payments greater than he can possibly afford, Pectoralis stubbornly chooses the latter course. As he boasts in court, "I have an iron will, and everybody knows what I have once decided must remain as I have decided and cannot be changed. I will not open the gate." Grimly announcing that he will "eat pancakes at

Safronyč's funeral," Pectoralis duly squeezes out the daily contribution required of him. Financial ruin is preferable to compromise.

The ensuing situation is a perfect ironic illustration of the fatal flaws of both character types. For the oral Russian, Pectoralis's daily subsidy, unexpected and unearned, represents the realization of his most cherished infantile dreams. He can now revert to a state of total dependency, with no labor or productive output required of him at all, comfortably lie back and suck his bottle, as it were, in blissful idleness. That bottle, of course, is not filled with milk; and since Safronyč lacks any capacity for self-restraint, the quantity of alcohol he now ingests is prodigious—more than his body can tolerate for long. Thus the German's donation provides the means for the Russian's self-destruction; and at last Pectoralis, though by now financially ruined, is able to fulfill his vow to eat pancakes at Safronyč's funeral. German *Festigkeit* would thus seem to have gained a symbolic triumph, however hollow.

But Pectoralis's victory is not only Pyrrhic, but exceedingly short-lived. The victor is himself soon vanquished, not only financially, but physically, swallowed up, so to speak, in the maw of Russian orality. At Safronyč's funeral feast Pectoralis makes the disastrous mistake of engaging in a pancake-eating contest with a monumentally obese, gouty old priest, "who loves anything made from dough." Doggedly determined as ever, Hugo goes on desperately cramming down pancake after pancake until at last he slides under the table. It is discovered that he is dead. "And Father Flavian crossed himself, sighed, and whispering 'God with us,' reached for a new pile of hot pancakes."

As a story, **"Iron Will"** shows Leskov very near the top of his form. The anecdotal material is amusing in itself, and at the same time it effectively accomplishes its argumentative purpose. The various episodes are skillfully dove-tailed into one another; and the major one, the contest between Pectoralis and Safronyč, is beautifully "retarded" by various means, including a whole "anecdote within an anecdote" which shows us how superstitiously credulous lower-class Russians could be (the drunken Safronyč, sleeping off a binge in the attic of his house, is taken for a ghost, and an elaborate campaign of exorcism undertaken against him). The all-round irony, that characteristically Leskovian wryness and slyness of tone, effectively neutralizes the chauvinistic spirit inherent in the material itself, absolving Leskov of any charge of gross pandering to nationalist sentiments. In the moral balance the Russians fare little better than the German. Nor is there any of the sentimentality that mars so many of Leskov's efforts. The only charges that could validly be levelled against **"Iron Will"** are, first, that Leskov belabors his point excessively, harping endlessly on the phrase "iron will" and

on its absurd consequences; and second, that the limits of our credulity are pressed a little too hard by the exaggerations inherent in caricature. The demise of poor Pectoralis, for instance, from a belly overstuffed with doughy Russian *bliny* may strike us as more obedient to the laws of poetic justice and artistic timing than those of human physiology.

Nevertheless, **"Iron Will"** clearly ranks among Leskov's better stories.[9] The mystery about it, therefore, is why the author chose to exclude it from his ***Collected Works,*** published toward the end of his life, in which he found room for so many works of far inferior quality. Did he simply forget about it, or had he turned against it for some artistic or moral reason? Unfortunately, time seems to have obliterated the answer to this question.[10]

The subject of Germans and Russians, however, continued to occupy Leskov in later years, and ironic needling of Russian chauvinism remained one of his favorite gambits all his life. He returned to the Baltic German theme with two substantial articles published in the early 'eighties, **"Herod's Work"** and **"Russian Statesmen in the Ostsee Region."**[11] In these articles Leskov's basic strategy is similar to the one employed in many stories: through irony and ostensibly "naive" commentary to force the material to lead to conclusions quite different from the expected ones.

"Herod's Works," for instance, is an ironic deflation of the career as Livonian Governor-General of the recently deceased Prince Aleksandr Suvorov (1804-1882). Though a Russian through and through, grandson of the great general, this Suvorov, according to Leskov, outdid himself in favoring the interests of the German aristocracy over the Estonians and Letts; he was contemptuous of the Russian Orthodox clergy in Livonia and harshly oppressive toward the Russian Old Believers. **"Herod's Work"** is a vigorously acid piece of writing, an effective antidote to the saccharine obituaries that had filled the Russian press with eulogies of Suvorov's magnanimity. In a letter to his editor Leskov accurately advertised it as "a lively article, half-historical, half-polemical, with the admixture of several amusing and characteristic anecdotes."[12]

One of the balance wheels in Leskov's psychic mechanism, preventing him from veering off too violently in the direction of anti-German nationalism, was his long-standing spiritual affinity with German Protestantism. Whatever their faults as people (and these faults he ascribed more to the aristocrats than to common folk), the Germans, in Leskov's view, had come much closer than the Russians to making Christianity a meaningful moral force in their real daily lives in this world; and that, for Leskov, was where the value of religion should be measured. Where the Orthodox Russians were still engaged in primitive magical incantations designed to manipulate supernatural forces, the Lutheran Germans were reading the Gospel and trying to put its precepts into practice.

"Russian Statesmen in the Ostsee Region" continues from where **"Herod's Work"** left off. Leskov deftly makes use of an old letter by Samarin both to blacken still further the name of Suvorov and at the same time to polemicize with Samarin himself and the policy of Russification he advocated. With typical slyness Leskov poses as an ordinary Greek Orthodox Russian, but in his exposition he continually makes unfavorable comparisons between the ritualism and superstition of the Orthodox, including the Old Believers, and the sobriety and enlightenment of the Germans. In one of his anecdotes a simple and friendly old German, an amateur Gospel preacher, expatiates in bad but eloquent Russian to some Old Believers about the universal brotherhood of men in Jesus Christ. The Old Believers in their turn tell him that the Scriptures are all right in their place, but that he should read other, presumably more interesting holy books too. In the *Ray of the Spirit,* for instance, "it is written how a young widow used the abomination of women [menstrual blood?] to save herself from the demon of concupiscence." In such a comparison Leskov need hardly state where his (and presumably his readers') preference lies.

Later the same Russo-German theme and the same slyness of manner were combined again for more strictly literary ends in **"Kolyvan' Husband"** (1883).[13] As the title symbolizes, here the confrontation of Russian and German archetypes is at the same time represented as an aspect of the eternal battle of the sexes—which perhaps confuses the national issue somewhat. Kolyvan' is the medieval Russian name for the town called by Estonians (and present-day Russians) Tallinn, by Germans and other Europeans Reval, and by nineteenth-century Russians Revel'. The hero of the story, the ill-fated "husband," is a Russian of the Russians, Ivan Nikitič Sipačov, born deep in the heart of Kaluga province to parents of impeccable Russian ancestry. He even has a Slavophile Moscow uncle who is an authority on Slavic archeology and a friend of the Kireevskijs and the Aksakovs. As a Russian naval officer in Reval, however, Sipačov marries into the local German gentry. His wife is a woman of unimpeachable character and great beauty, and her mother and other female relations are also paragons of Protestant virtue; but each time a child is born to the Sipačovs, these wily German females manage in the father's absence to have it baptised a Lutheran. Thus instead of the long-awaited Nikita Ivanovič, heir to the Sipačov dynasty, there is a succession of anomalous Teutonic non-sons: Gottfried, Oswald, and Günther. Each time Sipačov rages and storms, threatening violence and murder and suicide; but after a while his oral outburst subsides, to be followed by an

aftermath of remorse and efforts to make amends. Meanwhile, the quietly persistent *Frauen* make no concessions whatever. "Yes, we are stubborn Germans," one of them says, "and we have the bad habit of pursuing a matter through to the end."

Fifteen years later, on a visit to Dresden, the narrator learns of the final ironies in the ultra-Russian career of Ivan Nikitič Sipačov. His wife Lina had died, on her deathbed bequeathing him to the tender mercies of her equally Germanic and even stronger-willed cousin, Aurora, whom he dutifully married. The marriage was illegal in Russia, however, and so at Aurora's insistence Sipačov had retired from the Navy (as a Rear Admiral) and moved to Dresden. There he had died, after begetting three daughters to match the three sons he had by Lina. He was buried in a German Protestant cemetery; and his six sons and daughters, despite their Slavic surname and their blood bonds with Kaluga, have lost all traces of Russianness and become devoted citizens of the Reich.

Pungent as its irony is, **"Kolyvan' Husband"** is much inferior to **"Iron Will"** both as a work of art and as a representation of national types. Its ambiguities are neutralizing rather than energizing. For one thing, the role of the narrator is unsatisfactory, both ideologically and technically. This narrator is represented as a person very similar to, if not identical with the author (he is a Russian writer spending the summer in Reval). Having no connection with the Sipačovs other than living in the same building, he is purely a spectator in the action. This lack of motivated connection causes considerable technical difficulties in the narration, requiring a good deal of highly implausible eavesdropping (involuntary, of course) on the part of the narrator. It also causes some confusion in characterization and consequently in ideology.

The narrator ostensibly holds himself aloof from Sipačov's strident nationalism (manifested entirely in words rather than deeds). He constantly expresses disapproval of Sipačov's outbursts of temper, and he is fully aware of the absurd discrepancy between Sipačov's ringing words and the actual balancesheet of his life. The louder Sipačov rants about asserting the Russian presence in Livonia, the more he is outmaneuvered by his German relatives. The narrator, though basically sympathetic, understands this, of course, and treats his compatriot with a good deal of irony. Correspondingly, the narrator repeatedly tells us how charming and beautiful and virtuous these German girls are and how noble and dignified their mother and their grandmother. But from the point of view of characterization there is a glaring discrepancy between these assertions and the narrator's actual account of the women's behavior. In their actions and even words, these lovely Teutonic maidens and matrons are shown as simply insufferable—self-righteous, arrogant, unforgiving, and deceitful. Thus the narrator's professed feelings seem utterly out of keeping with his narrative material, and this disharmony is not explained or utilized in any way. The result is a blurred impression, which perhaps results from a discrepancy between feelings and doctrine in the author himself.

Officially and doctrinally, Leskov opposed national exclusiveness and advocated general tolerance toward all nations and toward national minorities in particular; but on the emotional plane, Leskov basically disliked Germans. As a result, feelings and doctrine work at cross purposes in the story. In the characterizations of the German women, the attractiveness so insistently asserted by the narrator is never made believable, mainly because the author does not really believe in it himself. Nor is it really made comprehensible why Sipačov, even passive as he is, should twice allow himself to be maneuvered into marriages to such a pair of castrating prigs. Furthermore, the element of ironic amusement built into our attitude toward Sipačov has nothing to match it in our response to his women. There is nothing amusing about them, and no poetic justice in their grim and total conquest of their Russian male victim. Finally, our ideological response is equally confused. What was apparently intended as a plea for tolerance and a camouflaged attack on the then official policy of Russification of the Baltic area becomes in its emotional impact the exact opposite: we feel sympathy for the basically warmhearted, if ineffectual Sipačov and anger at the unyielding *Wille zur Macht* of the German females. The story has in fact been read by some Soviet commentators as an anti-German, nationalist tract.[14]

After **"Kolyvan' Husband,"** the "national character" theme was laid aside once again, but not abandoned. Leskov returned to it once more in **"The Cattle-Pen"** (1893), his boldest and most powerful statement on the subject, written, as it were, at the edge of the grave. In this final statement, however, the Russians are once again confronted not with Germans, but with Leskov's own archetypal foreigner, his English uncle.

Notes

1. For a discerning analysis of the significance of this trip, particularly as a turning point in Leskov's religious evolution, see William B. Edgerton, "Leskov's Trip Abroad in 1875," *Indiana Slavic Studies,* IV (The Hague, 1967), 88-99.

2. Krüger's name is found in an address book of Leskov's dating from the 1850s. See Andrej Leskov's note in N. S. Leskov, *Izbrannye sočinenija* (Moskva, 1945), p. 454.

3. Samarin's "Pis'ma iz Rigi" (1849) urged the Russian government to base its authority in Livonia on the Lettish and Estonian peasantry, not on the German barons. For this work Samarin was arrested and administratively banished to Simbirsk. Later he continued the campaign with *Okrainy Rossii* (Berlin, 1868-76), which again led to legal action against him, terminated only by his death in 1876. Samarin cannot, of course, be blamed for the repressions perpetrated in the name of Russification under Alexander III and Nicholas II, but nevertheless, his advocacy pointed in that direction.

4. "Iskanie škol staroobrjadcami," *Birževye vedomosti,* No. 37 (February 7, 1869); "Irodova rabota," *Istoričeskij vestnik,* No. 4 (April, 1882), p. 196.

5. Leskov tells the story in "Zakonnye vredy," *Russkij mir,* Nos. 313 and 320 (November 30 and December 11, 1872); in "Russkie dejateli v Ostzejskom krae," *Istoričeskij vestnik,* No. 12 (December, 1883), pp. 493-494; and again in "Podmen vinovnych," *Istoričeskij vestnik,* No. 2 (February, 1885), pp. 327-340.

6. The details of the case (from Leskov's point of view) are set forth in "Zakonnye vredy." Writing in 1872, Leskov says there that the incident had taken place three years before, i.e., in 1869, and that "for three years now people have been writing [legal documents] about it in German." Andrej Leskov, however, dates the affair in 1870, attributing the Germans' arrogance to their pleasure in their compatriots' victories in the Franco-Prussian War (Andrej Leskov, *Žizn' Nikolaja Leskova po ego ličnym, semejnym i nesemejnym zapisjam i pamjatjam* [Moscow, 1954], pp. 235-236). The truth could probably be ascertained from court records, but no one has taken the trouble to dig them out. Leskov also refers elusively to the case in *Smech i gore* (N. S. Leskov, *Sobranie sočinenij* [Moscow, 1956-58], III, 570). Hereafter references to this edition of Leskov's works will be by volume and page only.

7. A similar Gogolian insight is attributed to Artur Benni in *An Enigmatic Man*: "No noble principles can take hold among these Čičikovs and Nozdrëvs" (III, 368).

8. The general referred to is the famous Crimean War hero Stepan Aleksandrovič Chrulev (1807-70), a "character" noted for his unconventional style, and from whose lips Leskov perhaps heard the remark directly. Leskov was fond of it. He had used it before in *Smech i gore* (III, 544) and cited it again in "Kartiny prošlogo," *Novosti i birževaja gazeta* (May 12, 1883). See Andrej Leskov, *op. cit.,* p. 115.

9. In this assessment I venture to differ with my honored colleague Vsevolod Setchkarev, who believes

that the weaknesses of character Leskov chooses to exaggerate for his satirical purposes are not "typical," and the story itself therefore "unconvincing." See Vsevolod Setschkarev, *N. S. Leskov: Sein Leben und sein Werk* (Wiesbaden, 1959), p. 96.

10. "Železnaja volja" first appeared in *Krugozor,* Nos. 38-44 (1876). It was not reprinted in any of Leskov's collected works, including the commodious Marks edition of 1902-03. With an assist from Andrej Leskov, it was rescued from undeserved oblivion only in 1942, when it was reprinted in the Soviet magazine *Zvezda* (No. 3-4), obviously considered appropriate grist for the Soviet war propaganda mill. It has subsequently been reprinted many times. The only explanation I have seen for Leskov's exclusion of "Iron Will" from the *Collected Works* is that given by B. M. Drugov in this "Afterword" to the separate edition of 1946, namely "lack of space." But this is absurd: the story is only eighty pages long, and the edition was in twelve large volumes. See B. M. Drugov, "Posleslovie," in N. S. Leskov, *Železnaja volja* (Moskva-Leningrad, 1946), p. 198.

11. "Irodova rabota," *Istoričeskij vestnik,* No. 4 (April, 1882), pp. 185-207; and "Russkie dejateli v Ostzejskom krae," *Istoričeskij vestnik,* Nos. 11 and 12 (November and December, 1883), pp. 235-263 and 492-519.

12. Letter to S. N. Šubinskij of October 8, 1882 (XI, 262).

13. "Kolyvanskij muž (Iz Ostzejskich nabljudenij)," *Knižki nedeli,* No. 12 (December, 1888), pp. 1-77.

14. This is essentially the interpretation of Leonid Grossman, *N. S. Leskov* (Moskva, 1945), p. 187, and of Andrej Leskov, *op. cit.,* pp. 238-239. Both of these books, however, were written either during or immediately after the Second World War. Andrej Leskov is perfectly aware, however—and the fact is more fully emphasized in the excellent commentary to the story by A. I. Batjuto in VIII, 610-613—that the story, at least in its manifest content, is just as much a satire on latter-day pan-Russianism and in particular on Leskov's erstwhile mentor, Ivan Aksakov, who had died two years before.

Earl Sampson (essay date 1974)

SOURCE: Sampson, Earl. "The Madman and the Monk: Two Types of Narrative Construction in Leskov." In *Mnemozina: Studia litteraria russica in honorem Vsevolod Setchkarev,* edited by Joachim T. Baer and Norman W. Ingham, pp. 317-24. Munich: Wilhelm Fink Verlag, 1974.

[*In the following essay, Sampson illustrates Leskov's use of "centralized" (i.e. linear) and "decentralized"* *narrative construction in his fiction by comparing two short stories, "The Enchanted Wanderer" and his late "The March Hare."*]

One of the most characteristic aspects of Leskov's manner, alongside his highly developed *skaz* technique, is his extensive use of anecdote, "die Grundform seiner Kunst," in the words of Professor Setchkarev.[1] In virtually every one of his works anecdotes play an important, if not the leading role. His shortest stories are often no more than elaborated anecdotes; many a longer work consists largely of a series of anecdotes; his novels are full of them; he uses them to characterize personages, to maintain suspense, for comic relief, for satirical thrusts, and sometimes, apparently, simply out of love of story-telling.

This predilection for anecdote is one aspect of Leskov's overall technique, which, with its stress on detail and episode at the expense of overall composition and formal unity of the whole, has been characterized as mosaic-like.[2] This technique had its natural effect on Leskov's attitude toward and treatment of the various narrative genres. It is clear that such a technique is poorly adapted to the novel. Although Leskov did leave several novels and novel fragments, they are not considered among the better of his works, and he obviously felt constrained by the requirements of the genre.[3] On the other end of the scale, if we take the strict definition of the short story as a narrative form that treats a *single* incident and depends for its effect on a certain concentration of artistic means, then neither does this genre correspond well to Leskov's tendency to pile up incident. Still, he was more at ease here than with the novel. Some of his shorter works (e.g., **"Čelovek na časach," "Zver'"** and, to a lesser degree, **"Tupejnyj chodožnik"**) answer well to this definition: a single anecdote forms the core of the story; the depiction of detail is not indulged in to such an extent as to diffuse the impact, such secondary episodes as are introduced are not numerous or striking enough to distract attention from the central episode. On the other hand, a number of short works that in terms of length alone could be classified as short stories are so full of incident as to at least stretch the definition somewhat in terms of structure (e.g., **"Ledi Makbet Mcenskogo uezda," "Levša," "Štopal'ščik,"** *Nesmertel'nyj Golovan,* **"Belyj orel," "Zagon"**).

Many of Leskov's best and most characteristic works, then, fit into neither the classification of true novel nor true short story, and in fact are difficult to classify at all in terms of genre. As Gromov and Èjchenbaum remark, "Vešči Leskova často stavjat čitatelja v tupik pri popytke opredelit' ich žanrovuju prirodu."[4] To be sure, some may fairly be classified as short novels (*povest'*), e.g., **"Ovcebyk"**; and others belong to the forms where fictional genres border on nonfictional genres, namely the sketch (*očerk*), e.g., **"Razbojnik," "Produkt prirody,"** etc., and the chronicle, e.g., *Soborjane, Zachudalyi rod,* and especially *Zagadočnyj čelovek,* which carries the subtitle *Istinnoe sobytie,* and which is essentially a fictionalized biography of Arthur Benni. But many important works simply refuse to be forced into generic pigeonholes, and it is symptomatic of Leskov's freewheeling attitude towards genre that he invented a number of his own genre terms, such as "pejsaž i žanr" (**"Polunoščniki," "Zimnij den'"**), "kartinki s natury" (**"Meloči archierejskoj žizni," "Improvizatory"**), "rapsodija" (**"Judol'"**), and "byl" (**"Vladyčnyj sud"**).

Part of the difficulty in assigning so many of Leskov's works to an established genre lies in their unique construction. Leskov worked out his own compositional technique, which Setchkarev describes as follows: "Sowohl seine kleinen als seine großen Werke sind nach dem decentralisierenden Prinzip gebaut; er scheut die planvolle Organization des Ganzen, um im Detail um so genauer zu sein. Die Ereignisse werden nicht um ein kompositionelles Zentrum gruppiert, es wird kein Kreis geschlossen, sondern ein Band entwickelt, das beliebig aufgerollt werden könnte."[5]

This is an accurate description of the general tendencies that Leskov followed in the composition of his narratives. Of course, individual works manifest these tendencies in varying degrees, and while the majority of his stories (particularly the longer, *povest'*-length works) fits the description quite closely, there are some in which the tendencies are more weakly expressed, or in other words, which are noticeably more "centralized" in their structure, which come closer to a conventional plot structure (one of the implications of Setchkarev's formulation is the lack of a plot in the strict sense of the term). One of the best examples of the latter type of work is Leskov's last story, **"Zajačij remiz,"** while perhaps the best example of the "decentralizing principle" is **"Očarovannyj strannik."**

There are several reasons for choosing these two stories to exemplify the range of Leskov's compositional techniques. They are of comparable length (in the 1956-58 edition **"Zajačij remiz"** occupies 90 pages and **"Očarovannyj strannik,"** 128). In broadest outlines, their structures are quite similar. Both are *Rahmengeschichten,* introduced by the author in the first person, in which the hero relates the story of his life in a long narrative periodically interrupted by the listeners. This form of informal, oral first-person narration provides the possibility of that looseness of narrative line that Leskov knew so well how to exploit, with its chronological transpositions, digressions and inserted anecdotes (one indication of this broad similarity in narrative technique is the similarity of the subtitle of **"Zajačij remiz"**—"Nabljudenija, opyty i priključenija Onoprija Pereguda iz Peregudov"—to the title that **"Očarovannyj strannik"** carried in its first [serial] publication—

"Očarovannyj strannik, ego žizn', opyty, mnenija i priključenija.")[6] In both stories the narrative consists chiefly of a series of remarkable anecdotes. However, in **"Očarovannyj strannik"** this series of anecdotes is strictly linear—no one incident is more significant than the rest; there is no climax. It is truly a "Band, das beliebig aufgerollt werden könnte." **"Zajačij remiz"** is quite different; here the whole course of events leads and builds toward one climactic and central episode, the immediate cause of Peregud's madness: his discovery—too late—that his own coachman is the socialist he has been trying so hard to capture. Despite its abundance of anecdotes, the story is basically a single anecdote, expanded into a *povest'*. The central episode is the climax of Peregud's life, and all his foregoing life is related as preparation for this climax; the anecdotes that are told along the way are secondary to it.

Unlike **"Očarovannyj strannik,"** the story is brought to a final and definite end. This, by the way, would be true even without the epilogue telling of Peregud's death, for it is made clear enough in the final chapters that he is hopelessly but harmlessly mad, that nothing more is in store for him than to live out his life in the asylum in his peaceful pursuit of knitting stockings. (The epilogue, to be sure, somewhat contradicts this; but as Setchkarev points out, this last episode is not very well in accord with Peregud's character as developed in the rest of the story.[7])

From the very beginning it is made clear that events will be directed toward a decisive climax. In the first place, the very circumstance that the author met Peregud in the insane asylum indicates some extraordinary event in his life—extraordinary enough to unhinge his reason. The author's hints in the prologue are calculated to support this supposition: ". . . i potom 'sam že sebja žestočajše umen'čtožil'"; "Estestvenno, čto čeloveku s takim nastroeniem v konce koncov ne moglo byt' pokojno" (IX, 502). In his own narration Peregud continually alludes to what is to come, either immediately or eventually, it is not always clear which—probably a deliberate ambiguity. For example, at the end of Chapter viii: ". . . i ne proizošli by nastupajuščie neožidannye posledstvija." One of these allusions is repeated continually and becomes a sort of leitmotif: "mečty moi bezumny." The climax is further prepared by the incident of the theft of Peregud's horses: ". . . ja, toj samyj, ščo vsich konokradov izvodil,—vdrug sam sel peški!" (IX, 564). This is an anticipation of the results of his attempts to catch a socialist, as is another of the author's hints in the prologue: "A priroda ego byla takova, čto on ešče v detstve svoem begal sam za soboju vokrug bočki, nastojčivo starajas' sam sebja dognat' i vyperedit'" (IX, 502).

The effectiveness of such a story depends on a degree of discretion in the handling of episode. The separate incidents must be subordinated to the main line of development; the number of incidents and the breadth of their exposition must be limited enough so as not to draw too much attention away from the climax. Leskov followed these demands fairly closely in **"Zajačij remiz."** There are, to be sure, a number of anecdotes, some fairly extended, that have little or nothing to do with the development—for example, the description of Vekovečkin's detailed knowledge of religious "history," or the story of how he got his name (both in Chapter xi). Some of the incidents that actually play no role in the plot development are presented as if they did. For example, the incident of the burbot (*nalim*) has no real bearing on Peregud's fate, since the archpriest would have visited his father in any case, fish or no fish (as Chapters vii and viii make clear), and the same change in his situation (the move to town to sing in the church choir, and the half-baked "education" connected with it) would have taken place. Yet Peregud attributes all this precisely to the fish incident: ". . . sejčas budet vam skaz o moem vospitanii . . . kak ono sostojalos',—i glavnoe, sovsem neožidanno i zamet'te, sovsem s nepodchodjaščego povoda—iz-za nalima" (IX, 511); "A vot vy že sejčas uvidite, kak pri vsem ètom zatrudnenii obošlis' i čto ot togo v rassuždenii menja vyšlo" (IX, 517). But as the climax approaches, such digressions— both overt and "camouflaged"—gradually decrease in frequency and extent, and finally disappear altogether. As for the incidents that actually make up the plot line, Leskov is careful to make clear the connection of each with the foregoing and following, to make of them a cause-and-effect sequence leading to the climax. Thus, although the story could by no means be said to be tightly constructed, it does have a fair degree of plot organization, centered around the climactic incident, the core anecdote.

Hardly a trace of this sort of organization is seen in **"Očarovannyj strannik."** Constructed on the model of François Fénelon's *Les Aventures de Télémaque* (Leskov at first intended to entitle it "Černozemnyj Telemak"), this story presents a long series of adventures united only by the person of the hero, with no particular gradation among them, leading to no real climax.[8] Michajlovskij describes the composition as follows: "V smysle bogatstva fabuly èto, možet byt', samoe zamečatel'noe iz proizvedenij Leskova, no v nem že osobenno brosaetsja v glaza otsutstvie kakogo by to ni bylo centra, tak čto i fabuly v nem, sobstvenno govorja, net, a est' celyj rjad fabul, nanizannych kak busy na nitku, i každaja businka sama po sebe i možet byt' očen' udobno vynuta, zamenena drugoju, a možno i ešče skol'ko ugodno busin nanizat' na tu že nitku."[9]

At first sight, it appears as though there is a climax, or at least a clear-cut ending in store: the hero's eventual entry into the monastery. Thanks to the frame-introduction, we know that this has already taken place at the time of the narration, just as in **"Zajačij remiz"**

we know from the beginning that the hero will end up in the madhouse. As in **"Zajačij remiz"** there are occasional allusions in the course of the story to this eventual outcome. But unlike **"Zajačij remiz,"** there is no build-up: the narrator goes from incident to incident without apparently drawing any closer to a climax; the separate episodes do nothing to prepare it. In fact, the occasional references to it serve rather to push it into the background than to make it seem imminent: the narrative reaches a stage where it seems only probable that at this point our hero will finally bring an end to his wanderings and enter the monastery, for which he believes himself to be predestined, and a listener interrupts with a conjecture to this effect. But such turns out not to be the case, and it is emphasized that the wanderer still has many adventures to undergo before his fate is fulfilled. When he finally does enter the monastery, it happens quite unexpectedly and prosaically:

> . . . tak ja vzjal i pošel v monastyr'.
>
> —Ot ètogo tol'ko?
>
> —Da ved', čto že delat'-s?
>
> Det'sja bylo nekuda. A tut chorošo.
>
> (IV, 504)

And the "climax" turns out to be no climax at all, for he has still further misfortunes in the monastery, and his last words hint that his adventures are not yet over. Even his desire "to die for his people" (IV, 513) is not a reliable hint of an imminent end to his adventures, for when he entered the army he had hoped to die soon "za veru" (IV, 499), yet he fought for fifteen years in the Caucasus before being retired from the army, only to undergo still more vicissitudes.

All this is not to say that the story has no artistic unity. While it has little structural organization and its unity depends mainly on the figure of the hero, this figure is sufficiently powerful, individual and consistent to fulfill the task. Through all his manifold adventures he is invariably true to himself, to the unique laws of his own character. I cannot agree with the viewpoint of Gromov and Èjchenbaum that Fljagin lacks, in the beginning, any moral norms, that "v soznanii Ivana Fljagina net nikakoj opornoj točki, nikakoj niti, svjazujuščej otdel'nye projavlenija ego ličnosti," that his conduct is determined wholly by chance (I, xli-xlii). The incident that they use to support their argument, that of the child that Ivan is hired to "nurse," seems to me an excellent illustration of the contrary: it shows that two of the principles that guide Ivan's conduct are a strong sense of personal integrity and an equally strong sense of justice. The cause of the apparent inconsistency in his conduct in this case is the conflict between the two—between his sense of duty to his employer and his sympathy for the wife. The latter wins out when the woman's life is threatened.

We see Fljagin's life story through his own eyes, and bizarre as it may be, it becomes almost believable, certainly internally consistent, when reflected through the prism of this open, good-hearted, somewhat simple nature. For the most part, it is his own nature that leads him into his misfortunes and adventures. Quick-tempered and impulsive, supremely confident of his physical prowess and, within his limited sphere, of his talents, he often gets into situations that a better judgment would avoid. Equally, it is his own nature that enables him to survive it all. Alongside a purely physical strength and stamina of heroic proportions, he has an innate moral strength that enables him to act wholly according to his conscience—to volunteer himself for punishment when he feels himself in the wrong (and this happens often enough, for the strength of his emotions often carries him beyond the bounds of what is— again according to his quite personal and instinctive standards—right and honorable), and to defy any authority when convinced of his rightness. Fate plays little part in his adventures.

There is something of Il'ja Muromec in Ivan. Leskov calls him a *bogatyr'* several times and at the beginning compares him specifically to Il'ja: ". . . on byl v polnom smysle slova bogatyr', i pritom tipičeskij, prosto-dušnyj, dobryj russkij bogatyr', napominajuščij deduške Il'ju Muromca v prekrasnoj kartine Vereščagina i v poème grafa A. K. Tolstogo" (IV, 386-7). It is clear that he is intended, on one level, as a symbol of Russia (his name—Ivan Severjanovič—emphasizes this). But there is also something in him of the Greek hero, and while *Les Aventures de Télémaque* (and perhaps the *Odyssey* itself) served as one of the models for the composition of the story, the character of the hero is rather similar to that of Hercules. He is self-confident; frank; intellectually limited but good-hearted and capable of deep feeling; impulsive; incapable of harming anyone out of malice but guilty of more than one death; physically well-nigh invincible but subject to a life of suffering and misfortunes.

Typically for Leskov, the image of the hero is given through his speech as much as through his actions; his naive frankness and the vigor of his nature, as well as his social and educational level, are revealed in his manner of expression. Except for the opening frame, the concluding paragraph, and the short dialogues which arise between Ivan and his listeners, the entire story is in his own words. This gives the work a unity and individuality of style and tone. In this work Leskov avoids the excesses into which his love for *skaz* sometimes led him. *Skaz* here is confined mainly to the role of a device for characterizing and individualizing the hero and making him live; it does not become an end in itself, a self-conscious display of linguistic versatility.

The individuality of Ivan's speech is underlined by the several interruptions from his listeners for an explanation of a word or phrase that he has used in a special, personal sense, or simply invented (e.g., *vychody, pod-ščetinit', popal na fitu*). Other idiosyncrasies of his speech include a predilection for verbal interjections (*pljuch, brjak, šmyg, šlep, pryg, trach, chvat,* etc.; e.g., "I oba . . . rubachi snjali, i v odnich . . . portičsach ostalis', i pljuch odin protiv drugogo, seli na zemlju . . ."; IV, 421) and a habit, when reproducing a dialogue, of inserting the words "govorju," "mol," etc., in the most unexpected places, between words that are syntactically closely related: "Potomu, mol, čto ona mne . . . poverena" (IV, 411); "Nu, malo li, govorit, čto" (IV, 448); "Možet li, govorju, èto byt'?" (IV, 478); "Nu, i slava, mol, Bogu" (IV, 492); etc. In contrast to this individualized, yet socially typical manner of speech, the speech of Onoprij Peregud is stylized, satirically exaggerated. The leading characteristic of his manner of speech, besides the heavy Ukrainian element (used before by Leskov to the same comic effect; see **"Nekreščenyj pop"**) and the frequent repetition of certain tag-phrases (*požalujte, ej-Bogu*), is the overabundant use of superlatives in *-ejšij* and long compounds with superlative prefixes. Practically every page has such forms as *dobrejšich, samogo žestočajšego, vsenesomnennejšego, prevelikij, preveličajšij, samoj preudivitel'nejšej, samonežnejšej, nainesčastnejšij, prenaitjaželejšaja.* The unnatural frequency of these forms, and the linguistic absurdity of some of them, such as *popreblagorassmotritel'stvujuščegosja,* confirm that the artistic intent here is not the creation of a verisimilar, "living" character, as in **"Očarovannyj strannik,"** but rather the creation of a satirical grotesque. This of course is not to imply that the style of **"Zajačij remiz"** is cruder; on the contrary, the stylistic texture of **"Zajačij remiz"** is more complex than that of **"Očarovannyj strannik,"** and just as controlled. "Prošu menja ne osudit' za to, čto zdes' ego i moi slova budut peremešany vmeste," the author writes in Chapter i (IX, 503). These words ostensibly apply only to the first four chapters, which give some of the history of the Peregud family and the village of Peregudy; from that point on, supposedly, the author allows Peregud to tell his story in his own words. But the satirical intent of the story requires that the reader constantly be aware of the contrast between the hero's view of the events related and the author's, so that throughout the story, not so much the words, but the "voices" of author and hero are mixed together—that is, we detect the author's ironic tone underlying his hero's words (this "mixture of voices" is one of Leskov's favorite techniques; see for example **"Čelovek na časach," "Voitel'nica," "Polunoščniki"** and others). This subtle stylistic ambiguity is well sustained throughout most of the story, but unfortunately towards the end Leskov allows a false note to creep in; apparently afraid the reader might miss the moral, he makes the Marshall of Nobility and Julija Semenovna express it in a very stilted and unconvincing conversation (Ch. xxvii). I am not at all sure, by the way, that the *real* point of the story is expressed here; but discussion of that point would lead too far afield of the present topic, namely, into a discussion of what sort of a satire the story is.

The comparison of **"Očarovannyj strannik"** and **"Zajačij remiz"** shows that Leskov was capable of using successfully two quite different principles of composition, which one might call the linear and the circular, or using Setchkarev's terminology, the decentralizing and the centralizing. But it also shows that he was, after all, at his best and most at home in the former approach. **"Zajačij remiz"** is the "neater" of the two, the more tightly constructed and formally unified; but Leskov's tendencies for proliferation of anecdote constantly threaten to break down the unity. **"Očarovannyj strannik,"** on the other hand, has a unity of a different order, of the type referred to in Professor Setchkarev's statement: ". . . es gelang ihm in seinen besten Werken tatsächlich, eine künstlerische Einheit zu komponieren, die zu keinem der üblichen literarischen Begriffe passte."[10]

Notes

1. Vsevolod Setschkareff, *N. S. Leskov: Sein Leben und sein Werk* (Wiesbaden: Otto Harrassowitz, 1959), p. 157.

2. Leskov himself used the term at least once: "Ètot jazyk . . . daetsja ne legko, a očen' trudno, i odna ljubov' k delu možet pobudit' čeloveka vzjat'sja za takuju mozaičeskuju rabotu." (N. S. Leskov, *Sobranie sočinenij* [Moskva: Goslitizdat, 1956-58], XI, 348. All further references to this edition will be identified only by volume and page number.) Leskov was speaking of his language here, but the term can be applied equally well to his composition. See Setschkareff, *loc. cit.*

3. In a letter to Fedor Buslaev, Leskov wrote: ". . . forma èta [the memoir form—E. S.] mne kažetsja očen' udobnoju: ona živee, ili, lučše skazat', istovee risovki scenami, v gruppirovke kotorych i u takich bol'šich masterov, kak Val'ter Skott, byvaet vidna natjažka, ili to, čto ljudi prostye nazyvajut: 'slučaetsja točno, kak v romane'" (X, 452). And at the beginning of one of his first-person chronicles, *Detskie gody* (or *Bluždajuščie ogon'ki*; the work was published under both titles), the narrator, no doubt speaking for Leskov, states: "Ja ne stanu usekat' odnich i razduvat' značenie drugich sobytij: menja k ètomu ne vynuždaet iskusstvennaja i neestestvennaja forma romana, trebujuščaja zakruglenija fabuly i sosredotočenija vsego okolo glavnogo centra. V žizni tak ne byvaet." (V, 279).

4. P. Gromov and B. Èjchenbaum, "N. S. Leskov; Očerk tvorčestva" [in *Sobranie sočinenij*] (I, xlviii).

5. Setschkareff, p. 159.

6. The echo of Sterne in these titles is of course no accident. See Leonid Grossman, *N. S. Leskov: Žizn'—tvorčestvo—poètika* (Moskva, 1945), 262-263, regarding the influence of Sterne on Leskov.

7. Setschkareff, p. 156.

8. See Setschkareff, p. 89, and Grossman, pp. 164-165. While Fénelon's novel may have been the main structural model, Leskov's orientation in writing this story probably included the whole picaresque tradition. Leskov himself mentions two other famous representatives of this tradition in answering Ščebal'skij's criticisms of "Očarovannyj strannik": "Potom: počemu že lico samogo geroja dolžno nepremenno stuševyvat'sja? A Don-Kichot, a Telemak, a Čičikov?" (X, 360).

9. N. K. Michajlovskij, "Literatura i žizn'," *Russkoe bogatstvo,* 1897, No. 6, p. 104. Quoted in N. S. Leskov, *Sobranie sočinenij,* IV, 553.

10. Setschkareff, p. 159.

K. A. Lantz (essay date 1979)

SOURCE: Lantz, K. A. "Stories and Tales." In *Nikolay Leskov,* pp. 81-101. Boston: Twayne Publishers, 1979.

[*In the following essay, Lantz presents an overview of Leskov's short fiction, noting three examples of his best work in the genre—"The Sealed Angel," "The Enchanted Pilgrim," and "At the World's Edge"—and surveying additional tales that display Leskov's unorthodox understanding of Christianity and his satirical view of the Russian national character.*]

I THREE MASTERPIECES

Although Leskov did not abandon the novel in the 1870s, the emphasis in his work shifted to shorter genres which were more in harmony with his talents.

Two subjects close to his heart provided the stimulus for one of his finest stories, **"Zapechatlennyi angel"** (**"The Sealed Angel,"** 1873). He had been interested in the Old Believers since childhood, and his 1863 study of the question of separate schools for them proved that he had become something of an authority on their way of life. A series of newspaper and journal articles devoted to the Old Believers reveals that, although he admired their independence and tenacity in defending their faith and supported their right to preserve it, he did not in the least romanticize them. Their narrow faith based on the dead letter of their canonical literature led him to conclude that they could have little positive influence on Russian religious life. But he was fascinated by their anachronistic way of life, a living link with the past. In particular, the Old Believers' resistance to change had enabled them to preserve the traditional style of icon-painting free from later influences.

The art of icon-painting, and religious art in general, was another subject which had captured Leskov's attention from his youth. While in Orel he followed with interest the painting of the iconostasis in the Church of St. Nikita; the eleventh-century frescoes in the St. Sofia Cathedral were being restored during his stay in Kiev. Leskov read several contemporary studies of icon-painting and joined the author of one, Fedor Buslaev, in lamenting the loss of the genuine native tradition as Western influences entered Russian culture after the seventeenth century. At a time when icons were not highly regarded as works of art, Leskov wrote a number of articles showing a fine appreciation of their esthetic as well as religious qualities. A more immediate stimulus to the writing of the story came with his acquaintance with a master icon-painter, Nikita Racheyskov, who preserved the old tradition of painting. Racheyskov was especially noted for his miniatures, "which he executed with his enormous and seemingly crude hands in a manner as astonishly delicate and subtle as a Chinese."[1] Leskov spent a great deal of time with Racheyskov absorbing the techniques and the lore of iconography, and said that he wrote the **"Angel"** in Racheyskov's "hot and stuffy studio."

The angel of the title is a small icon depicting a guardian angel, highly revered by an itinerant band of Old Believer stonemasons. They carry their angel with them wherever they go and attribute their good fortune to its influence. The band comes to Kiev to work on the construction of the first suspension bridge across the Dnepr River, but they provoke the enmity of a local official who confiscates their "heretical" icons. Sealing wax is dripped on the angel's face and the icon marked with an official stamp. The Archbishop of Kiev, however, is enchanted with this exquisite work of art and places it on the altar of the cathedral. The Old Believers' attempts to retrieve their icon create the suspense in the story. Their plan is to find a suitable icon-painter who could make an identical copy of the angel and then to steal the original, leaving the copy in its place. The seeking out of the icon-painter Sevastyan and the purloining of the original, during which Luka, the group's leader, carries the icon across the Dnepr walking on the chains of the still incomplete bridge, are dramatic events skillfully narrated.

The narrative is set in a frame; it is told with sober dignity by one of the Old Believers, Mark Aleksandrov, in a language wonderfully combining archaisms, bookish terms, and earthy popular expressions. This gives the story a sense of veracity in spite of some of the improbabilities of the plot.[2]

Although the story was an immense success and, together with **Cathedral Folk,** won Leskov the attention and admiration of a whole new circle of readers, contemporary critics (notably Dostoevsky[3]) objected to its ending. When the copy of the icon is returned to the church, Luka is shocked to find that the seal which had been placed on it shortly before to make it perfectly identical with the original has miraculously vanished. This "miracle" has a quite prosaic explanation, but Luka interprets it as a sign that he must abandon his Old Belief. He confesses all to the archbishop, who graciously receives him and the members of his band into the official church. This ending is not as improbable as might appear: given the primitive nature of the Old Believer's faith, an apparent miracle together with the kindness shown by the archbishop could easily move them to abandon their faith. Neither is the ending totally unexpected, since the narrator, Mark, announces at the very beginning that he will tell of how he was led to the true path by an angel. Midway through the story, while seeking the icon-painter Sevastyan, Mark encounters the holy hermit Pamva, and is moved by the spiritual strength and goodness of this representative of the official church. "If there are but two such men in the church," he says, "then we [the Old Believers] are lost, for he is inspired by love." (4. 365). Pamva's example shakes Mark's faith, already weakened by the Old Believers he has met in Moscow, who appear totally mercenary and corrupt. All this, together with the kindness and tolerance of an English couple who aid the Old Believers, is enough to win him over.

But though the ending is logically and psychologically motivated, it is nonetheless esthetically unsatisfying. Had the Old Believers been portrayed as narrow-minded fanatics, their conversion to a religion of greater tolerance and love might have struck a truer note. But they appear as honest, industrious, upright men with a deep love and knowledge of iconography who simply want to be left in peace to continue their religious practices. They seem to have little need for conversion. Leskov later suggested that the ending had been forced on him by Katkov.[4] Considering the doubts about official Orthodoxy expressed in other works Leskov was writing at the time (**Cathedral Folk, "The Enchanted Pilgrim"**), as well as evidence within the story itself, it would appear that Leskov's original intention was to have his Old Believers arrive at a nondogmatic, humane form of Christianity, but not necessarily be slipped so neatly through the doors of the official church. His saintly hermit Pamva, for instance, although nominally Orthodox, has little "official" in his religion: his forest hut contains no icons at all nor any weighty tomes of sacred writings. When he learns of the Old Believers' quest to retrieve their angel, he says: "The angel lives in the hearts of men; he has been sealed by ignorance, but love will smash the seal" (4. 366). Leskov's point, suggested but not fully realized in the story, concerns the real function of icons, in which their religious significance is combined with their esthetic value. Mark is moved from a purely superstitious awe of the supposed wonder-working properties of the icon to a deep appreciation of its beauty, as his description of it in chapter 2 proves. For him it represents a higher ideal, a symbol of faith which gives meaning to life. Pamva suggests that this ideal in fact is "within the hearts of men." By the end of the story, Mark himself has come to this realization. The story thus affirms the highest and most serious purpose for art: to inspire people with the worthiest of ideals by unsealing the angel which lives within their hearts.

"Ocharovannyi strannik" ("The Enchanted Pilgrim") is another of Leskov's masterpieces too little appreciated by contemporary critics. In 1873 Katkov refused to publish it in *Russky vestnik,* regarding it as "raw material" rather than a finished work. Some years later the critic Nikolay Mikhaylovsky objected to its "lack of any center whatsoever" and compared its many incidents to a string of beads, each existing independently from the others. To be sure, the work contains enough incident to fill several conventional novels, but there is most definitely a center, and the incidents are arranged with great skill so that they do develop in a logical pattern. This may not be immediately evident, however, because of the technique of narration. The story is told by Ivan Flyagin, a man of immense vitality and spiritual depth but with limited powers of analysis. As a narrator he is not fully "reliable," in the sense that he simply relates his life's story as a jumble of highly colorful incidents, attributing things he cannot understand to the action of divine forces. Flyagin's lack of understanding of his own adventures often creates a fine irony, but a closer analysis of his story reveals that the "beads" which make up the plot are strung in a most artful and conscious manner.[5] Flyagin often takes literally what his listeners and readers must see symbolically if they are to make sense of his life's story. He is convinced, for instance, that the events of his own life happen not of their own accord but have been largely predetermined by his mother's vow that her son should enter a monastery. Until he does so, he believes, he will suffer but not die, although he will be at the point of death many times. Although this "enchantment" is a fine device for arousing and sustaining the reader's curiosity, it is misleading if taken literally. But his life can be seen symbolically in these terms as a quest for salvation and the events he relates form definite stages in his progress to this end.[6]

The frame which opens the story neatly introduces its main themes. A group of tourists sailing across Lake Ladoga find that the rugged Karelian landscape is so wild and desolate as to drive a man to despair and suicide. Flyagin is introduced and relates the story of an alcoholic Moscow priest whose position is so hopeless that he resolves to kill himself so as to compel his bishop to provide for his destitute family. But the priest is stopped from this when he thinks of the fate of his immortal soul. He then devotes himself, contrary to church law, to prayers for the souls of suicides. The priest's story—of self-sacrifice by *not* committing suicide because of concern for one's salvation—is a major theme of the work as a whole. The second part of the frame completes the introduction of the main themes. Flyagin announces that he is a *koneser,*[7] a man with exceptional talent for breaking wild horses. Flyagin admires the spirit of such animals but realizes that they must be tamed if they are to be of any use. His technique explains his success: "I'd grab his ear as hard as I could with my left hand and with all my strength I'd pull it to one side, and with my right fist I'd give him such a thump between the ears and grind my teeth at him in such a terrifying way that sometimes even his brains would start coming out of his nostrils along with the blood. Well of course after that he would be as gentle as a lamb" (4. 391). But Flyagin is careful not to dominate the beast so totally as to break its spirit. He describes one exceptionally wild stallion which he broke but which died shortly thereafter because "he couldn't get over his own character" (4. 393). Flyagin's own quest for salvation can be seen in much the same terms: his nature is as wild and ungovernable as the stallions he is so skilled at breaking. His life's adventures are analogous to the process by which he tames horses; his energies must be channeled to a positive purpose but his spirit left unbroken.

Flyagin's story, as V. S. Pritchett has written, is about "primitive energy,"[8] the basic life force which contains the potential for both goodness and destruction, the force which compels one to go on living even under the most desperate conditions. The unusual series of incidents which opens the story illustrates this primitive energy at work and reveals the contradictory aspects of Flyagin's character. He whips a monk asleep on a haycart whereupon the horses bolt and the monk is thrown off and killed. Flyagin does not explain his action, but the circumstances—the fine summer day, the lovely countryside—fill him with an exuberance which can find its outlet only in senseless violence. But Flyagin is equally capable of thoughtlessly risking his own life to save another's, as he proves when he is almost killed while saving the life of his master and family. His tenderness and unthinking cruelty are illustrated in the episodes describing his concern for his doves, followed by his torture of his mistress's cat. He can be affectionately devoted to the child he is given to nurse while maliciously provoking a duel with a haughty officer. The excruciating scene of his flogging match with the Tatar demonstrates his capacity both to inflict and to suffer pain.

The low point of his biography occurs when he is kept prisoner by the Tatars and literally brought to his knees. The Tatar captivity and the incidents which preceded it have been challenges which forced him to curb his exuberance as he himself has curbed the wildness of the horses he tamed. His sufferings to this point have been for his own transgressions, but after his escape he begins his progress to a new goal—suffering for the sins of others. His encounter with the "magnetizer" who cures him of his fondness for drink is a crucial one. For all its farcicality, this episode conceals a very serious point, as do many other comic scenes in the work. The magnetizer explains in literal terms what Flyagin does metaphorically in later life. The magnetizer continues to drink, he says, because it is his duty to do so: "It's a very difficult calling, my friend, and even quite impossible for many; but I have trained myself for it because I see that one must bear one's lot and I bear mine" (4. 459). He cannot drop the habit, he explains, because someone else might "pick it up": "And as for you, if you suffer from some sort of passion, you mustn't just drop it of your own account in case some other man might pick it up and suffer torments from it. But seek out a man who would take this weakness from you of his own free will" (4. 460). The magnetizer thus takes on Flyagin's drinking habit (an excessive burden, it seems, since he dies of drink shortly thereafter). The magnetizer episode also leads neatly to the next stage of his journey, the awakening of love. Flyagin must first be brought to an awareness of beauty, which to this point he has recognized only in horses. But his encounter with the gypsy girl Grusha reveals a new world to him. His attraction to her is at first only an enchantment with her art and a fascination with her physical beauty, but eventually through her he experiences for the first time love in the form of *agape* rather than *eros*. She can no longer bear to live after the Prince has begun to betray her and must either kill him or herself but can bring herself to do neither. She makes Flyagin swear that he will kill her since he will have the opportunity to repent and save his own soul. Thus, as the magnetizer advised, he takes on her sin and suffers for it. He continues his role when he takes the place of the only son of an elderly couple who is to be sent to the army and risks his life, hoping to expiate the sin of murdering Grusha. His role as scapegoat is played literally when he, dressed in goatskins, performs as the Devil in pre-Lenten carnivals and is beaten by the other actors. After all of these adventures his entry into the monastery (where significantly, he is given the name of Ishmael) comes almost as an anticlimax. His monastic life, although not without its farcical side, does develop his urge for self-sacrifice to its utmost. He learns more about his country and at the end of the story is about to leave the monastery to fulfill his urge to sacrifice his life for his people. As the magnetizer told him earlier, "We, the possessed, suffer so that it should be easier for the rest" (4. 460).

Implicit in all this is an undercurrent of criticism of a church which invests too much in the letter and too little in the spirit of Christianity. The story of the priest who prays for suicides suggests that Christian mercy, if it is to be genuine, must be extended to all. The Orthodox missionaries who refuse to help Flyagin because he is already "saved" by his baptism supply another such example. Flyagin himself, quite unconsciously, provides further evidence that the church's view of mercy is too narrow. He has been brought up in the conventional religion and has primitive faith based on ritual coupled with narrow-minded scorn for other faiths. He refuses to recognize the children of his Tatar wives, for instance, since they have not been baptized. Yet on occasions when he allows himself to be guided by love, he violates the acknowledged norms of the church in favor of genuine mercy. The best and most paradoxical example of this is his murder of Grusha, done out of genuine love and pity when he finds the only way he can save her is by killing her.

Ultimately, the "enchantment" of the pilgrim is the enchantment of life itself in which, as the monk in his dream prophesied, he would suffer much adversity, but not die until he had worked out his destiny and in so doing saved himself. The complex but very artful structure of the story beneath its apparent artlessness, the depth of Flyagin's character which exemplifies the Russian character as a whole, the marvelous language of the narrative, make this work one of the high points in Leskov's art.[9]

The search for a positive hero and the attempt to depict a basic, living form of Christianity are again the motives behind **"Na kraiu sveta" ("At the World's Edge,"** 1875). Leskov based this story on incidents from the life of Bishop Nil of Yaroslavl, who worked as a missionary in Siberia in the 1850s. The plot of the story, concerning a man who sets out to bring enlightenment to the heathen only to find that he is in greater need of it than they are, is not exactly novel, but Leskov's treatment of it produced another masterpiece. The aged bishop who narrates Leskov's story recalls his first assignment to a distant Siberian diocese and his zealous attempts to raise the level of the local clergy. Missionary work among the primitive Yakut nomads of his diocese seemed to be particularly lagging. The bishop seeks advice from Father Kiriak, a Siberian veteran, but Father Kiriak's advice is to limit the church's activities to basic education and provide a good example of behavior for the native population. He adamantly refuses to do any missionary work, claiming that the church's efforts to baptize the natives only harm them. The bishop decides that he must make a personal visit to the mission field and sets off on a long trek across the snows with Father Kiriak and two native guides. But they are caught in a fierce blizzard and the bishop and his guide are left without provisions. The bishop is not surprised when his pagan guide abandons him, and he resigns himself to death. But to his amazement, this same pagan risks his life to return with food and save his companion.

What Leskov does here once again is to contrast the cold religion of the church, intent on saving souls by reliance on the sacraments, with the living spirit of religion exemplified by the unnamed "heathen" guide. Leskov does this in a subtle and convincing manner, and produces a penetrating critique of established Christianity. The opening frame of the story already introduces his theme unobtrusively. The bishop narrator shows a group of visitors his collection of artistic portrayals of Christ, discussing each one in turn. He tells his listeners that the only artist who captured the true spirit of Christianity is the anonymous master who painted the icon which stands in his room. Although this image lacks the sophistication and refinement of later Western portrayals, in its unassuming simplicity and total sincerity it conveys the real essence of Christ's teachings. The story contains a certain mockery of the established church's efforts to make this essentially simple doctrine into something mysterious and complex. Father Kiriak, for example, explains to the bishop the impossibility of trying to convey to the natives such concepts as "martyr" and "baptist." "It is still more difficult to talk about the merits of the sacred blood of Christ," he says, "or about other mysteries of the faith, and it is quite pointless to construct some sort of theological system for them or even to mention the idea of virgin birth without a husband. Either they will understand nothing, which is the best that could happen, or else they will simply laugh in your face" (5. 468). The bishop persists in trying to explain the fundamentals of Orthodoxy to his guide and despairs at the latter's total lack of comprehension. He feels only scorn and pity for this poor "savage" who is, it seems, to be denied salvation. Better, thinks the bishop, that these hopeless people become extinct like the Aztecs. The guide refuses to be baptized: for not only will this earn him the enmity of rival religious groups, the Buddhists and the Shamans, but, he explains, those who are baptized can no longer be trusted. Baptism is like a license to commit crime since the baptized know that the priest will absolve them of any sins. The guide argues that the priest can only forgive those who have done some injury to him personally. The guide's only conception of Christianity is that Christ was a good and a merciful man. It is only

after the story's reversal that the bishop understands that his "savage" has a far better grasp of the essence of Christianity than does the bishop himself.

Leskov does not idealize his primitive; indeed he emerges as a very human and convincing figure. One of the best scenes in the story is the description of how the two wait out the blizzard huddled together under the snow, breathing on one another for warmth. The bishop is grateful for warmth, but would gladly sacrifice it because of the stench from his guide, compounded of "stinking reindeer hide, pungent human sweat, smoke, damp putrefaction, dried fish, fish oil, and dirt . . ." while his resounding snores "like the buzzing of a dense and powerful swarm of bees in a resonant, dry hive, softly beating against its walls" prevent him from sleeping (5. 491-93). These vivid touches help remove any aura of sentimentality which might surround this noble savage. Yet a series of symbols, subtly interwoven into a fabric of the story, makes it plain that the pagan guide embodies that very ideal of brotherly love toward which Christianity strives. The symbolism underlines his role, ironically enough, as the one who enlightens the would-be missionary. Among the few things the guide knows about Christ is that he once gave sight to a blind man by rubbing spittle on his eyes and that he miraculously fed the people with bread and fishes. After their first night in the blizzard, the bishop awakens in panic, unable to see because his eyelids have frozen shut. The guide restores his sight by spitting on his eyes and rubbing them. The cavity in the snow where the two wait out the blizzard seems like a grave to the bishop, and the stench from his guide worse than that of Lazarus after his four days in the tomb at Bethany. He has resigned himself to death and indeed, when his guide returns after four days, he scarcely knows whether he is alive or dead. The reappearance of the guide and the bishop's return to life seem to him truly miraculous; his hunger, fatigue, and the uncertain light of the short Siberian day play tricks with his vision. He sees a figure approaching which seems to "materialize" in the form of an angel. It is the guide, covered with frost, his hair piled high on his head and coated with ice (he left his hat as a pledge in the deserted *yurt* where he took food). "Toward me floated a gigantic winged figure enveloped from head to foot in a *chiton* of sparkling silver brocade; he wore an enormous headdress which appeared to be almost six feet high, a headdress which burned as if it were all encrusted with jewels, or as if it were a solid miter of jewels . . ." (5. 505-6). There seems little doubt that the "savage"—by restoring the bishop's sight, by wondrously providing him with food, and by giving him back his life—has worked miracles as genuine as any described in the Gospels.

The reversal in the story is all the more effective since the bishop is portrayed as a sensible and enlightened if perhaps overzealous man, but not as a bigoted fanatic.

He now understands that "Christ has revealed Himself to him [the guide] as much as is necessary . . ." (5. 510) and abandons his proselytizing. Amid the empty Siberian landscape, "at the world's edge," where nature is stripped to its very minimum, the bishop finds the essence of religion, a faith also stripped to its very minimum. This was the simplified form of Christianity which Leskov had arrived at after his trip abroad in 1875, a faith founded on brotherly love, with a system of ethics much broader than that of institutionalized Christianity (exemplified here by one who is formally a pagan). The beliefs expressed in the story anticipate those of Tolstoy.

II Unorthodox Views of Orthodoxy

Several other stories of the 1870s, although not of the caliber of the three discussed above, also explore highly unconventional attitudes to religion. **"Vladychnyi sud"** (**"Episcopal Justice,"** 1877) was written immediately after **"At the World's Edge"** and is linked directly to it. But its overall tone is startlingly different and appears to go counter to the humane and tolerant view of the earlier story. Leskov begins by explaining that, in spite of its popularity among readers, **"At the World's Edge"** was criticized by the clergy for its "tolerance of unbelief and even indifference toward Holy Baptism as a means of salvation" (6. 88).

To prove that his bishop's very liberal views were by no means unique among the clergy, he relates a story in the form of an incident from his own youth, when he had served in the Recruiting Section in Kiev in the 1850s. At that time the law allowed recruitment of Jewish boys into the army as early as the age of twelve. If, as was usually the case, no records of birth could be produced, the evidence of witnesses was sufficient to establish the boy's age. Such witnesses often made a profession of giving false testimony, thereby sending boys of seven or eight for military service. A Jewish bookbinder appears to Leskov one day in an agony of worry because his young son is about to be taken as a recruit. The father has, quite legally, paid for a replacement for his son, but only after selling all his possessions to do so. The replacement is about to cheat the father out of his due by requesting baptism into the Orthodox faith. This would free him from his obligation since the law allowed only a Jew to take the place of another Jew. Ultimately, it is Metropolitan Filaret of Kiev who solves the dilemma by deciding that the replacement is unworthy of baptism, thus ensuring that the boy will be spared.

Leskov provides a glowing tribute to Filaret, hailing his "infinite goodness" and supplying a number of anecdotes to show his human side. Yet the anecdotes do little more than make him appear a good-natured fool. Filaret's decision likewise seems scarcely more than el-

ementary human decency. But what is even more peculiar, even distasteful, is Leskov's own role in the story, specifically his attitude toward the grief-stricken father. Leskov admits he was deeply moved by the man's plight and conveys the father's utter desperation (he literally sweats blood). But he spares no opportunity to ridicule the Jew by painting him as some sort of subhuman creature, using the stereotyped devices of the crudest anti-Semitic propaganda of the day. In a farcical and unnecessary scene, he portrays the Jew fleeing in terror from a bulldog that he believes is a crocodile. When the Jew follows him home to implore him to help, Leskov allows him to spend the night curled up on the floor next to the dog. "I was satisfied with both the Jew and the dog," he remarks, "and left them to share their common pallet until morning . . ." (6. 116).

A solution occurred to him when he first learned of the Jew's plight—both father and son should themselves be baptized. But he does not suggest this to anyone, and indeed forgets the whole affair until by chance he is reminded of it on the following day and tells an acquaintance who intercedes with Metropolitan Filaret. Leskov's attempts to justify this lack of concern are revealing: he stresses that he was raised in a devout Orthodox family and from an early age was inculcated with the conventional attitudes of such a milieu. His reluctance to save the Jew through baptism stemmed from his respect for the sacrament and his unwillingness to see it improperly used. It would thus appear that he wishes to jolt his readers into greater awareness by showing in himself the unthinking anti-Semitism of the typical Russian of his day, whose concern for maintaining respect for the purely formal rites of the church overrides his feelings of elementary humanity. The passages describing the Jew as a very human, suffering father are presumably intended to shatter the blindly prejudiced, stereotyped view. But the technique simply does not work. Leskov's own motivations are never made clear, and his mockery of the Jew—even with the best intentions—remains distasteful.[10]

The story has other flaws as well. There is a good deal of irrelevant memoir material describing various people and events in Kiev in the 1850s which is intended to increase the tension by retarding the climax. But in such a story it serves only to distract from the very powerful central episode. An epilogue in which Leskov meets this same Jew some years later to find that he has now become a zealous convert to Orthodoxy is an unnecessary touch which also mars the story.

In **"Nekreshchenyi pop"** (**"The Unbaptized Priest,"** 1877) Leskov again uses baptism as a means to distinguish the spirit of religion from its purely formalistic side. In contrast to the preceding stories, he writes here in a comic mode. The story is set in a Ukrainian village, and portions of it are clearly modeled on Gogol's early stories, with their witches, devils, extramarital escapades, and extensive use of the Ukrainian language. But the good-humored tone and absorbing plot mask some very pointed criticism of the official church. Dukach, an independent and quarrelsome villager, is, after years of childlessness, at last blessed with a son. But his troublesome nature has earned him the enmity of his neighbors, and not one of them will consent to act as godparent for his son. He decides to hold the christening in a neighboring village and sends his none-too-clever nephew Agap along with the village pariah, Kerasivna, who is rumored to be a witch. The two are caught in a severe blizzard during which Dukach accidentally kills Agap. Dukach goes to prison and Kerasivna insists that the child has been properly christened Savva as his father wished. Savva is educated by a kindly man who has been strongly influenced by the Stundists[11] and eventually becomes the priest of his native parish. His good sense and charity win him the love of his parishioners. But on her deathbed Kerasivna confesses that the blizzard forced her to turn back before the christening could take place. The beloved Father Savva, she insists, is not even a Christian, much less a priest. This naturally causes great consternation among the villagers, who wonder if all their marriages, christenings, and confessions are invalid. But they are so devoted to their priest that they insist he remain, and their kindly and sensible bishop agrees.

A very deliberate contrast is drawn between Fr. Savva's activities and those of the quite legally baptized priest in the next parish. While his neighbor concerns himself with building a splendid stone church and acquiring a bell and wonder-working icon for it, Fr. Savva ensures that the orphans of his parish are fed and clothed and that a school is provided for the village. Savva's modest wooden church is full, even though the population of the surrounding area has largely gone over to the Stundists, while the neighboring priest ministers to the verger and the churchmouse. The formal rite of baptism again provides a point from which to launch an attack on a church whose stress on Byzantine ritual sometimes threatened to obscure the essence of Christianity.

The stories of the 1870s discussed above, then, are primarily concerned with demonstrating a system of Christian ethics which, in its simplicity and universality, already anticipates the ideas of Tolstoy, but which is not fully elaborated. The basis of this system is active love for one's fellow man; its ultimate manifestation is self-sacrifice. This system comes increasingly into conflict with the teachings of the established church. Leskov focuses on the sacraments of the church, through them pointing out the narrowness and dogmatism of official Christianity. Artistically, the best of these stories are related as *skaz,* relying on the individualized language of the distinctive narrator to give them life.

III The Russian Character

Many of Leskov's writings deal, in one way or another, with the Russian character,[12] but a group of stories from the late 1870s and early 1880s is specifically devoted to a skeptical examination of the strengths and weaknesses of his countrymen. One technique which Leskov uses to illuminate the Russian character is to focus on an encounter between a foreigner and the Russians. The foreigner does not necessarily provide any standard of behavior by which the Russians are measured; more often it is only his fresh point of view and different standards which make the idiosyncracies of the Russians stand out all the more clearly. Even in his very first newspaper articles at the beginning of the 1860s, Leskov drew comparisons between Russian and foreign practices. The adventures of his uncle Scott (much fictionalized, to be sure) enabled him to make many comments on Russian manners. The Germans are also contrasted with the Russians: the Biedermeyer cosiness of the Norks in *The Islanders* implicitly affirms the value of the family at a time when the institution was under attack from the radicals. Leskov's attitude toward Germans is generally favorable in this novel, and there is no doubt of his admiration for their energy and practicality (although the pompous Friedrich Schultz illustrates some of their less admirable qualities.)

In the 1870s Leskov was disturbed by the rise of German militarism (see the ending of **"The Enchanted Pilgrim"**), and some personal encounters with Germans in the Baltic left him with a strong distaste for their smugness and chauvinistic scorn for the Russians. The aftermath of the Franco-Prussian War and the rumblings of the Iron Chancellor make up part of the background to a fine satire, **"Zheleznaia volia"** (**"A Will of Iron,"** 1876).

The frame of the story portrays a group of Russians who express their fears that disorganized and undisciplined Russia would not fare well in a conflict with iron-willed Germany. Vochnev, an old man who has followed the discussion without comment, finally disagrees: "Iron they well may be, but we are dough, simple, soft, damp, unbaked dough—and you should remember that dough in a mass cannot be chopped up even with an ax. Indeed, you may well lose the ax" (6. 6). Vochnev then tells a story—loosely based on some of Leskov's own experiences when he worked for Scott and Wilkins—of an encounter between German iron and Russian dough. A German engineer, Hugo Pectoralis, arrives in a small Russian provincial town to supervise the installation of some agricultural machinery ordered from his firm in Germany. Pectoralis seems almost an accessory to the machinery he has come to install: precise, unyielding, utterly consistent. The quality he most admires in himself is his vaunted "will of iron": once he has set himself a goal he will never go back on his word no matter what the consequences. But his iron will proves to be his nemesis in Russia: after a long series of misadventures, in the course of which he is abandoned by his wife and his promising business is reduced to bankruptcy, he nonetheless keeps his promise to eat pancakes at the funeral of his archenemy, only to be outblinied by a gluttonous priest. The story is well constructed so that Pectoralis's reversals grow ever more serious until his final tragicomic demise.

Pectoralis is a caricature, of course, but a very successful one. One might expect that with such a ridiculous German at the center of the stage, the Russians in the story would appear as models of virtue. Indeed, a lesser author handling such a situation might easily have sunk into chauvinistic glorification of the Russian character. But the satire is double-edged, with both edges sufficiently honed so that the Russians are spared little more than Pectoralis. As Vochnev suggests at the beginning of the story, the chief advantage of the Russians in any conflict with the Germans is their stupidity, which would utterly confound the Teutonic mania for precision and thorough calculation: "I am not praising my countrymen," he slyly remarks, "nor am I censuring them: I am only saying that they will hold their own and, whether through intelligence or stupidity, they will manage to defend themselves" (6. 7). The Russian character emerges as a total, and scarcely favorable, contrast to the German, exemplified by Pectoralis: where he is industrious, they are lazy; he is firm, they are yielding; he is restrained and frugal while they spend lavishly; he is calculating, they are instinctively cunning. Yet Pectoralis's virtues are so exaggerated that he functions with coldly mechanical precision and predictability, whereas the Russians' vices at least make them warmly human.

Leskov was a master at relating with malicious glee the downfall of an innocent, often a foreigner, as he is inexorably swallowed up by Russian life. But he does portray the Russians here "without praise and without censure"; apart from Chekhov, no nineteenth-century writer regarded his countrymen with fewer illusions than Leskov.

"Besstydnik" ("A Man Without Shame," 1877) employs the same framing device as the previous story: in this case, a group of naval officers discusses life at sea as a means of developing character. One tells a story to illustrate the influence of environment on character which contains as dubious a compliment to the Russians as does **"A Will of Iron."** His story is set immediately after the Crimean War, when revelations of widespread corruption in the army's supply services outraged front-line veterans in particular. Once at an evening of cards the narrator began to abuse supply officers as parasites and thieves who filled their pockets while honest soldiers suffered and died at the front. His rage

does not subside when he discovers that a supply officer is sitting near him. The supply officer not only listens to the tirade with equanimity, but even takes some pride in providing further examples of how well he and his fellow officers profited from the war. Although unmoved by the attacks on his profession, he does take the narrator to task for insulting the Russian people as a whole: "We are all Russians," he insists, "and we all have been given as part of our rich nature the capacity to cope with any circumstances. . . . You were given the task of fighting and this you did the best way possible—you fought and died as heroes and your fame has spread all over Europe. But we are placed in a position where we could steal, and we, too, distinguished ourselves and stole enough to become renowned. But if, for example, we were ordered to change places and we went to the trenches and you to supply-points, then, we thieves would have fought and died and you would have . . . stolen" (6. 157-58). After twenty years of life experience, the narrator is forced to admit that the supply officer was right.

"Chertogon" ("Exorcising the Devil," 1879) is a brief story superbly illustrating some contradictory traits of the Russian character. It describes a "rite which can be seen only in Moscow" (6. 302): a wealthy merchant, driven by his demon of boredom and dissatisfaction with life, stages a tremendous orgy during which a restaurant dining room is utterly ravaged. The next day, after a bath and haircut, he prostrates himself on the floor of a church and prays with such intensity that his legs shudder spasmodically. At last he rises and announces that he has been forgiven: "Right from the very top of the church," he says, "I felt an open hand reach down from the cupola, grasp me by the hair, and set me right on my feet again" (6. 314). Although the merchant pays the 17,000 ruble bill in the restaurant with little hesitation, he delays his morning break for tea until joined by colleagues because the tavern gives groups of three a five kopek discount. Leskov manages, through careful selection of telling detail, to convey both the fury of the orgy and the fervor of the merchant's prayers. The point of view (the story is told by the merchant's naive young nephew, fresh from the provinces) adds to the effect. "Since then," the narrator concludes slyly, "I have come to know the national manner of falling so that one can rise again" (6. 314).

"Levsha" ("Lefty, The Tale of the Cross-Eyed Left Handed Craftsman of Tula and the Steel Flea") is another ambiguous tribute to the Russian character. Its original edition of 1881 was accompanied by a preface in which Leskov stated that he had recorded this "legend from the armory" from the works of an old craftsman of the Sestroretsk arms factory. The story had such an air of authenticity that one critic accused Leskov of simply acting as a stenographer. Only later did he reveal that, apart from the basic idea—summed up in a catch phrase "The English made a Steel flea but our Tula lads shod it and sent it back again"—the whole story was his own invention. More recent Soviet scholarship has confirmed this, but has also uncovered several possible historical prototypes of the craftsman and sources of some of the episodes.[13]

"Lefty" is one of Leskov's best known stories and, unfortunately, the one most likely to be fatally injured in translation.[14] The plot itself—the adventures of the Tula gunsmith who manages to outdo the English and preserve Russia's pride by putting shoes on the life-sized steel flea which the English have created to demonstrate the high standard of their craftsmanship—is outrageous enough, but the language in which all this is related is even more extravagant. Purely invented words (the marvelous *nimfozoria*), complex puns, mangled foreign words misused or wittily combined with Russian ones (*melkoskop* for "microscope," from *melkii*, "fine," "small"; *kleveton* for "feuilleton," from *kleveta*, "slander") make the story all but untranslatable. Leskov explained the motivation of such language elsewhere: "The language is dotted with capricious agglomerations of improperly used words from the most varied contexts. This arises, or course, from the overly assiduous attempts of the storytellers to hit upon the conversational tone of that social stratum from whence they take their characters. Deprived of the possibility of acquiring the real form of conversational language of these people, they attempt to achieve it through maximum vivacity in their retelling, putting as colorful and as fanciful speech as possible into the mouths of their characters so that it should be unlike the language of everyday" (7. 60-61). This explanation of course only partially accounts for Leskov's decision to use the language he did. He had an immense love of words in themselves, and the story can be seen as an attempt to uncover more of their full potential. But the language does give the story a sparkle and verve impossible to convey fully in translation. Leskov succeeds in doing with words what his legendary craftsman did in metal: he creates a unique and highly amusing curiosity, but one which also has a bite that the famous steel flea did not have.

There is no doubt of Leskov's admiration for the unacknowledged and often untutored craftsmen who delighted in pushing their skills to the limits of the seemingly impossible. He was enchanted, for example, with the skill of the Palekh icon-painters "who can portray distinctly, on an icon measuring three and one-half by four and one-half inches, 129 figures along with ornamentation, walls, mountains, the Garden of Paradise, graves and Hell, where angels beat and enchain 'Satan and all his angels.' And around the head of each of these 129 figures is an aureole of gold, within which is a title: 'St. Iliya,' 'St. Enokh,' 'St. Rakh, the Robber,' etc. These inscriptions are so minute that they are diffi-

cult to read and not everyone can do so with the naked eye."[15] The idea of the steel flea itself may be nothing more than a tall story, but the skill which shod it was real enough and Leskov pays it due tribute. The craftsman himself is not without his positive significance (indeed, Leskov included the story in his cycle of righteous men), and his gentle mockery of Lefty's naiveté and backwardness still leaves no doubt that the craftsman is quite sincerely concerned about the welfare of his country.

The saga of the steel flea is intended to deflate the Russians' pride in their capacity to surpass the West purely on the basis of instinct or innate ability, without painstaking and systematic work. The marvelous achievement of the Tula craftsmen obscures the fact that in shoeing the steel flea they have ruined its delicate mechanism, since the shoes are too heavy. As one of the Englishmen remarks when the Russians triumphantly return the newly shod curiosity: "You would be better off knowing at least the four ways of reckoning by 'rithmetic . . . Then you could figure out that each machine can only do things 'cording to its power. You are mightly clever with your hands, but you didn't count on the fact that such a little gadget as this *nimfozoria* here has been worked out even to the most exact precisity and it can't carry no horseshoes. On account of that this *nimforzoria* won't skip around any more and don't even dance the *dansé*" (7. 49-50). Leskov would not dispute with those who saw his Lefty as a symbol of the Russian people as a whole, adding that he had no wish either to flatter or to ridicule his countrymen. The thrust of his satire is against the backwardness of his country and the belief in the special talents inherent in the Russian character which was often used to excuse that backwardness.

Despite his talent and his love for his country, Lefty is a victim of his own nationality. His fondness for drink begins his downfall, and the system he collides with in his own country completes it. His treatment on return from England pointedly contrasts with that accorded to an Englishman with whom he had a drinking bout on the way back to Russia. The Englishman is taken to his embassy, where he is treated by a doctor and an apothecary, is given pills of gutta-percha and a drink of *heure-fixe,* and left to sleep it off in a comfortable bed. Lefty, on the other hand is dumped on the floor of the police station, grilled about his passport, and, after the police have relieved him of his money and his "tripeter" watch, is sent off to die in a paupers' hospital.

There is yet one more barb to Leskov's satire: simply because the English have done something absurd (making a mechanized steel flea), the Russians feel obliged to outdo them with something even more absurd (putting shoes on it). Thus Leskov manages simultaneously to ridicule what might be termed the

"Slavophile" view of Russia's destiny, with its obscurantist belief in the special talents of the Russians, as well as the "Westernizer" approach, with its uncritical assumption that everything coming from the West is good and should be adopted and improved upon in Russia. Even the language of the story, with its lexicon of undigested terms from several European languages, conveys this. The narrator's attempts to achieve a high tone in his speech are as laughable as are the frantic efforts of his countrymen to outdo the West.

Leskov at one time planned a series of tales similar to **"Lefty,"** but the series, entitled **"Historical Character in Fabulous Tales of Recent Composition,"** has only one other member, **"Leon, dvoretskii syn"** (**"Leon, the Steward's Son,"** 1881). Although it contains much clever word play, the story as a whole has less verve than **"Lefty"** and the display of verbal fireworks too often becomes simply an end in itself.

"Kolyvan'skii muzh" (**"A Kolyvan Husband,"** 1888) is another story in which a naive, weak-willed, but likable character is slowly drawn into a net of circumstances which renders him helpless. As in **"A Will of Iron,"** Leskov deals with the meeting of German iron and Russian dough, but this time the dough is thoroughly kneaded, formed, and baked into a neat *Brötchen*. Sipachev, a young naval officer, begins as the most Russian of Russians: he is born in Kaluga of an old family, and his father and uncle are ardent Slavophiles. In Reval (whose old Russian name was Kolyvan') he marries into a charming and cultured German family. His relatives are aghast, fearing he will lose his national identity, but they become reconciled to the marriage when he assures them that he will have a son, Nikita, to be raised as a good Orthodox and carry on the family name. But his German kin arrange for him to be away on duty whenever a child is due, and each time he returns he finds he has fathered a Gottfried, then an Oswald, and finally a Gunther, each baptized as a Lutheran. Sipachev himself ends as a good German and is buried in a Lutheran cemetery in Dresden.

Although the story has many pages which sparkle with wry humor, it lacks the fine irony of **"A Will of Iron."** Leskov's satirical impulses overflow to such an extent that the point of the story is not altogether clear. He no doubt had in mind the practice of baptizing Russian children in the Baltic area as Germans, a topic which had been noted in the press. There is little anti-German satire of any force: the Germans in the story are cultivated and not openly chauvinistic, but they are also so convinced of their own superiority that they cannot understand why anyone would not want to become a German. The Russian will to retain national identity is weak as well. "We are monkeys," warns Sipachev's uncle, "and we love to imitate" (8. 409). But Leskov

also assaults Russian chauvinism, especially that of the Slavophiles with their insistence on forced Russification of the Baltic provinces. He mocks their ideas and even their speech, which he reproduces as an archaic Russian heavily laden with Old Church Slavonicisms. Sipachev's own flabby will is another target. Thus the story's overall impact is reduced through diffusion.

This group of stories reveals Leskov's thorough knowledge of the Russian character and his healthily skeptical view of his countrymen. His tone of detached, wry amusement and his technique of simultaneously poking fun at the quirks of both the Russians and the foreigners give his works objectivity and universality. The choice of topic is also significant: the mood of society was growing increasingly chauvinistic in the later 1870s, and Leskov's attempts to deflate the excess pride of his countrymen once again set him against the current of his times.

Notes

1. "O khudozhnom muzhe Nikite i o sovospitannykh emu," *Novoe vremia*, No. 3389 (1886).

2. As Leonid Grossman points out (*N. S. Leskov*, pp. 170-71), "private" persecution of Old Believers was not likely, nor would the officer who confiscated the icon have tried to extort money from the group before witnesses.

3. See "Smiatennyi vid," *Dnevnik pisatelia, Sobranie sochinenii*, XI (Moscow-Leningrad, 1929), 55-57.

4. For a fuller discussion of the story and its ending see Hugh McLean, "Russia, the Love-Hate Pendulum and 'The Sealed Angel,'" *To Honor Roman Jakobson* (The Hague, 1967), pp. 1328-39.

5. To use E. M. Forster's terminology, Flyagin relates his adventures as a "story"; it is up to his readers to discern that they in fact do form a "plot." A detailed study of the plot is M. P. Cherednikova, "O siuzhetnykh motivirovkakh v povesti N. S. Leskova 'Ocharovannyi strannik,'" *Russkaia literatura*, 3 (1971), pp. 113-27.

6. Thus "pilgrim" is a better translation here for the Russian *strannik* than "wanderer" since it implies one who travels with a very definite purpose.

7. An untranslatable pun on *kon'* ("horse") and connoisseur.

8. "Leskov," *Oxford Slavonic Papers*, 10 (1962), p. 20.

9. This work contains echoes of Dostoevsky's Christianity with its emphasis on mercy and voluntary assumption of the sufferings of another. To be sure, Flyagin's sufferings are more physical than spiritual, yet they ultimately lead to his salvation. The

effect of his capricious will also has Dostoevskian overtones. The parallels seem more a result of an inherent affinity of outlook and reliance on a similar tradition in Orthodoxy than of conscious influence.

10. The degree to which the Leskov who narrates the story can be identified with the real Leskov cannot be definitely established, although his attitude toward the Jews was certainly equivocal. His background no doubt predisposed him to anti-Semitism, and his early journalism contains more than a few derogatory remarks about the Jews. In the 1880s, however, he published a series of newspaper articles explaining aspects of Judaism with much sympathy and understanding ("Religioznye obriady evreev," *Peterburgskaia gazeta,* Nos. 244, 245, 252, 254, 255 [1880]. Other articles on the Jews appeared here in 1881, 1884, and 1885). In 1883 a group of St. Petersburg Jews asked him to write a study of the Jewish situation in Russia for presentation to the "Palen Commission" examining laws pertaining to Jews. The study (*Evrei v Rossii: Neskol'ko zamechanii po evreiskomu voprosu* [St. Petersburg, 1884]) defended Jewish rights and called for an end to restrictions on settlement. He expressed his own contradictory attitude to [A. I.] Faresov: "I believe that it is best to live in brotherhood with all nationalities, and I express that opinion publicly. But I myself fear the Jews and avoid them. I am in favor of equal rights but I am not in favor of the Jews" (*Protiv techenii* [St. Petersburg, 1904], p. 300). Leskov's fictional treatment of Jews is examined in more detail by Hugh McLean, "Theodore the Christian looks at Abraham the Hebrew: Leskov and the Jews," *California Slavic Studies,* VII (Berkeley, 1973), 65-98.

11. A term used to describe various evangelical and pietist sects which spread in the Ukraine and Southern Russia in the nineteenth century. Their example of charity, practical Christianity, and reliance on individual reading of the Gospels won over many who were disillusioned with Orthodoxy.

12. See, for example, Hugh McLean's interpretation of "The Enchanted Pilgrim" in these terms in "Leskov and the Russian Superman," *Midway* (Spring, 1968), pp. 105-23.

13. See E. S. Litvin, "Fol'klornye istochniki 'Skaza o kosom Levshe i o stal'noi blokhe' N. S. Leskova," *Russkii fol'klor: materialy i issledovaniia,* I (Moscow-Leningrad, 1956), 125-34; B. Bukhshtab, "Ob istochnikakh 'Levshi' N. S. Leskova," *Russkaia literatura,* No. 1 (1964), pp. 49-64; V. Shklovskii, "Ob odnoi tsekhovoi legende," *Ogonek,* No. 19 (1947), p. 16.

14. The most successful English translation is William Edgerton's in *Satirical Stories of Nikolai Leskov* (New York, 1969), pp. 25-53.

15. "Blagorazumnyi razboinik (Ikonopisnaia fantaziia)," *Khudozhestvennyi zhurnal,* 5, No. 3 (March 1883), p. 197.

William B. Edgerton (essay date 1983)

SOURCE: Edgerton, William B. "Leskov and Gogol." In *American Contributions to the Ninth International Congress of Slavists: Kiev, September 1983.* Vol. 2, edited by Paul Debreczeny, pp. 135-47. Columbus, Ohio: Slavica Publishers, 1983.

[*In the following essay, Edgerton stresses the immense influence of Nikolai Gogol's writings on those of Leskov, tracing numerous structural and narrative parallels between Leskov's fictional works and Gogol's* The Inspector General *(1836) and* Dead Souls *(1842), while acknowledging Leskov's general superiority in delineating character.*]

In Leskov research the scholarly genre of "Great Writer and . . ." is represented by articles or chapters in books entitled "Leskov and Tolstoj," "Leskov and Dostoevskij," "Leskov and Gor'kij," "Leskov and Ševčenko," "Leskov and Herzen," even "Leskov and Skovoroda"; but to the best of my knowledge there is still no example in print of the title "Leskov and Gogol."

This is all the more paradoxical because no other writer had as much influence as Gogol on Leskov's literary formation. If it is still not clear to everyone just which Russian writer should get the credit for the famous statement that "we all came out of Gogol's *Overcoat,*"[1] there can be little doubt that much of Leskov's work came out of *Dead Souls* and *The Inspector General.* Boris Ejxenbaum said of Leskov: "Among all Russian writers he especially valued Gogol, though not at all as the originator of the 'Natural School,' but rather as a skillful storyteller, and incidentally with a Ukrainian flavor in his speech that Leskov greatly valued."[2] Leskov undoubtedly felt a certain kinship with Gogol precisely because Gogol was Ukrainian. Even before Leskov left his native Orel Province, he had become well acquainted with the exiled Ukrainian writer Opanas Markovyč, to whom he was indebted—in his own words—"for all my literary tendency and passion for literature."[3] When he moved to Kiev in 1849 at the age of eighteen, he took with him letters of introduction from Markovyč to Ukrainian friends. In the words of Ejxenbaum again, Leskov's "real spiritual homeland" was Kiev, "which at that time was not a Russian but a Polish-Ukrainian city." When he left Kiev in early 1861 and settled in Petersburg, "he entered Petersburg literature not only as a provincial but even as a foreigner."[4] One of the first persons he visited upon his arrival in Petersburg was his old friend the Ukrainian poet Taras Ševčenko; and in his obituary article on Ševčenko just a few weeks later, he felt so close to the Ukraine that he actually referred indirectly to himself as a Ukrainian![5]

Leskov's encounter with Gogol's works began at least by the early 1850s, long before he embarked on his literary career. By his own account he took part while living in Kiev in a benefit performance of Gogol's *Inspector General* sponsored by the all-powerful Princess Ekaterina Alekseevna Vasil'čikova, the wife of the Governor-General. Leskov and a lawyer named Jurov played the roles of Bobčinskij and Dobčinskij (VI, 116). Leskov's early articles and stories are peppered with references to Gogol. *The Inspector General* and *Dead Souls* helped to shape his perception of Russian reality; and such names as Skvoznik-Dmuxanovskij, Xlestakov, Čičikov, Nozdrev, and Sobakevič were a part of the vocabulary he used to organize his own thoughts and convey them to his readers. Indeed, many of Leskov's works cannot be fully understood apart from *The Inspector General* and *Dead Souls* as a kind of subtext. For example, in one of his earliest stories, **"Ovcebyk"** (**"The Musk-Ox"**), he says of the beautiful, highly intelligent, and equally virtuous wife of the businessman Sviridov: "But there were some desperate fellows who confessed their love to her and invited her 'to some shady stream' [под сень струй]." The last three words echo Xlestakov's proposal to the wife of the town governor in Act IV, Scene 13, of *The Inspector General*: "We shall flee to some shady stream [Мы удалимся под сень струй]" (I, 82), and create an ironic parallel between various landowners' attempts to seduce Nastas'ja Sviridova and Xlestakov's flirtation with the silly, simpering wife of Skvoznik-Dmuxanovskij. (Six years later, in a review of Tolstoy's *War and Peace,* Leskov was to use this same Gogolian phrase, "под сень струй," in reference to the account in Volume IV, Part 1, Chapters 4-5, of Nikolaj Rostov's reckless flirtation with the pretty young wife of a landowner in Voronež.)[6] A similar Gogolian subtext is found a few pages later in **"Ovcebyk"** when the protagonist says in a letter to the narrator: "I have resolved for myself the enigma, 'Russia, whither goest thou?,' and you need have no fear: I shall not leave here. There is nowhere for me to go" (I, 85). This quoted question from *Dead Souls* prepares the way for Ovcebyk's tragic answer at the end of the story: suicide by hanging.

A characteristic echo of Gogol's style is to be found in Chapter 8 of Leskov's early peasant novel *Žitie odnoj baby* (*The Life of a Peasant Martyress*). In this chapter the police chief comes upon the scene, followed by two men, "one of whom resembled an Englishman, and the other the letter *i*." From this point on to the end of the scene, Leskov consistently refers to the first man as

"the Englishman" and to the second as "the *i*," underlining the parallel to *The Inspector General* with the following words when the subject of medicine comes up:

> "That's your department," said the police chief, turning to the *i* and recalling Skvoznik-Dmuxanovskij in the scene with Gjubner.

> "Yah," answered the *i,* also recalling Gjubner in the scene with Skvoznik-Dmuxanovskij.

(I, 371-374)

In Book One, Chapter 30, of Leskov's first big novel, **Nekuda** (**No Way Out**), published in 1864, Gogol's *Inspector General* serves as the subtext for a scene in which a comical school inspector of Greek origin, speaking a barbarously Hellenized Russian, pays a visit to the school directed by Petr Lukič Glovackij. The parallel is made explicit to the reader when one character explains to another why old Petr Lukič is rushing about in such agitation:

> "State Councilor Saf'janos . . ."

> "What's that?"

> Pomada coughed, putting his hand over his mouth, and answered:

> "He's the Inspector General."

(II, 221)

As if to make sure that no reader will miss the parallel, Leskov goes on to describe old Petr Lukič's vain efforts to attach his sword properly to his ancient uniform; and then Liza, the friend of the school director's daughter, bursts out laughing and quotes her own version of Skvoznik-Dmuxanovskij's lines in Act I, Scene 4: "That confounded shopkeeper Abdulin! He doesn't see that the town governor has an old sword" (II, 222).

Similar echoes of Gogol's works, particularly *The Inspector General* and *Dead Souls,* can be found in Leskov's writing throughout his career. But Leskov's response to Gogol is not limited to such details as these. He himself recognized the structural parallels between *Dead Souls* and some of his own longer narratives. "I have frequently been compared to Gogol and Saltykov," he once wrote to A. S. Suvorin, "but I do not know whether I am worthy of that. Making the rounds of landowners in the manner of Čičikov has always interested me, and I tried it a little in **"Smex i gore"** [**"Laughter and Grief"**] and **"Očarovannyj strannik"** [**"The Enchanted Pilgrim"**]."[7] In reality, the parallels to these two works go far beyond mere structure. As Hugh McLean has pointed out in his excellent analyses of them, in both **"Laughter and Grief"** and **"The Enchanted Pilgrim"** Leskov portrays his native Russia as a country "where nothing can be accomplished by honest labor, and where there is no consistency in anything except in persecuting a man, if not by sharp torments, then by dull harassment" (X, 440).

In *Zagadočnyj čelovek* (*An Enigmatic Man*), published just a year before **"Laughter and Grief,"** Leskov recalls the reaction of his idealistic Polish-English friend Artur Benni when he read *Dead Souls* in prison just before his expulsion from Russia in 1865:

> Just imagine, only now, when I am about to be expelled from the country, do I see that I have never known Russia. I was told that one must study it first this way and then that, and the upshot of all those conversations was always pure nonsense. My misfortunes arose simply from the fact that I had never in my time read *Dead Souls*. If I had done that in London, or even in Moscow, then I would have been the first to consider it a matter of honor to prove that there can never take place in Russia the kind of revolution Herzen dreams of, . . . because no noble principles can ever take root among these Čičikovs and Nozdrevs.

> (III, 367)

Reflections of this pessimistic view of his native land can be traced throughout the rest of Leskov's life. In 1883 he wrote to his friend S. N. Šubinskij:

> I cannot forgive myself for never having learned the French language well enough to work in it like a native. I would not stay in Russia another moment and I would stay away forever. I am afraid it is possible to conceive a thorough-going hatred for her with all her nihilists and reactionaries. There is neither intelligence nor character nor any trace of dignity. What can ever become of this herd—this smug, self-satisfied herd?[8]

In December 1888 he wrote to his brother-in-law that he planned to spend the following summer in France. "I want to see life once more among people who are free," he wrote, "and not like us groveling slaves."[9]

A. I. Faresov, who saw a great deal of Leskov in the 1890s, quotes him as making the following despairing prediction about Russia:

> Am I to blame if reality is such that in fifty to a hundred years we shall have become so loathsome that we shall be faced with a European coalition? It is astonishing how Černyševskij could have failed to guess that on the very next day after the triumph of Raxmetov's ideas, the Russian people would pick out the most savage policeman to rule over them, and consequently that we could have gone forward under the government of the 1860s without turning the Raxmetovs loose against it.[10]

Among Leskov's most powerful literary transmutations of this pessimism are **"Laughter and Grief,"** already mentioned; **"Polunoščniki"** (**"Night Owls"**), with its attack on religious fanaticism and hypocrisy; **"Zagon"** (**"The Cattle-pen"**), with its bitter condemnation of

Russia's backwardness; **"Produkt prirody"** (**"A Product of Nature"**), which in McLean's words illustrates the truth that "any system of tyranny requires massive collaboration by the oppressed in their oppression";[11] **"Zimnij den'"** (**"A Winter Day"**), an unsparing picture of moral and political corruption in a Russian Sodom and Gomorrah; and **"Administrativnaja gracija"** (**"Administrative Grace"**), a deceptively merry account of political cynicism in high places. Along with these stories there is another one that occupies a special position in Leskov's work because of its relation to Gogol. In **"Otbornoe zerno"** (**"Choice Grain"**), artistically one of the most satisfying of the stories in this group, Leskov takes *Dead Souls* as his subtext and builds a satirical structure upon it that achieves epic proportions within the space of only twenty-five pages. As I have pointed out elsewhere in a detailed analysis of **"Choice Grain,"**[12] Leskov here presents an ironic defense of mutually beneficial Russian rascality, praising it under the name of "социабельность" ("sociable-ism")—which, as Leskov makes clear in the course of the story, is a Russian corruption of the imported foreign word "socialism."[13] This verbal corruption leads us back to what Artur Benni finally learned in a Russian prison when he read Gogol's *Dead Souls*: in the land of Čičikovs and Nozdrevs, Aleksandr Herzen's westernized socialism inevitably degenerates into социабельность.

Echoes from Gogol run throughout the story. In Chapter One, we are alerted to what is to come when the narrator happens to meet a landowner with whom he had gone to school in their boyhood. He tells us of their conversation: "I said I was just traveling, like Čičikov, for my own pleasure; and he jokingly prompted me with: 'Surveying the situation, no doubt'" (VII, 284). The Gogolian subtext provides further warning of rascality when the narrator says: "I can't tell you just why—whether . . . it was his genuine Nozdrëvism that repelled me; but anyhow I couldn't get rid of the feeling that once he had me in his home he would palm off a greyhound or a barrel-organ on me" (VII, 288). At the beginning of Chapter Two another Gogolian echo prepares us for the grain swindle:

> It goes without saying that the merchant to whom the choice grain had been sold was cheated unmercifully. All those Frenchmen who looked like Jews and all those Englishmen, as well as the *haute école* lady, were only what you might call the landowner's window-dressing, his agents, who played a part like that of the well-known Utešitel'nyj in Gogol's *Gamblers*.

> (VII, 293)

The climactic parallel to Gogol comes when the badly swindled merchant concocts a spectacular Russian "sociable-istic" scheme to recover his money without causing harm to any of his rascally compatriots. He goes back to the landowner who had cheated him and contracts to buy still more of his worthless wheat—enough to fill one whole barge. Then, after insuring the entire cargo with a German company for the highest possible amount, he bribes a peasant river-boat pilot to arrange for the barge to capsize at a convenient spot on the river, thus making it possible for him to collect his insurance money from the Germans.

The scene when the merchant goes back to the landowner to buy enough extra bags to fill the whole barge is a direct parallel to the bargaining scene between Čičikov and Sobakevič over dead souls in Gogol's novel.

> "How much more wheat do you want to buy from me?"
>
> "Why, I'll buy a lot more. . . . I need documentary evidence that I have loaded the whole barge with wheat. . . . How much will you charge for this extra purchase?"
>
> "I will charge no more than I would for dead souls."
>
> The merchant did not understand what this meant and hastily crossed himself.
>
> "What put that into your head? Their fate is to rot but ours is not. We are talking about the living. Tell me, how much will you charge for selling me something nonexistent?" . . .
>
> "Two rubles a bag."
>
> "Oh, come on, now! . . . No, now be a good Christian, let me have it for half a ruble."
>
> The landowner put on an expression of astonishment.
>
> "What do you mean? Half a ruble for a bag of *wheat*?"
>
> "After all, what kind of wheat is that!"
>
> "Now, we won't argue about whether it's one kind of wheat or another; the point is that you're trying to do me out of real money for it."
>
> (VII, 295)

Like Gogol, Leskov is a moralist; but the two writers are very different in the way they apply their moralism to literature. In *Dead Souls,* the protagonist Čičikov is portrayed as a thoroughgoing rascal; but as far as we can judge from the surviving fragments of Volume Two, Gogol intended to have Čičikov repent and reform by the end of the novel. In *The Inspector General* every single character is portrayed in a negative light, but Gogol brings them all to judgment in the final scene of the play with his announcement that the real Inspector General has arrived. In **"Choice Grain"** Leskov also presents only negative characters; but, unlike Gogol, instead of condemning them in the end, he ironically argues that the collective Russian rascality in this "sociableistic" utopia leads to unalloyed benefit for everybody—except the German insurance agents, of course, but they don't count since they are mere foreigners.

When Gogol moves on from portraying the human condition to prescribing his own cure for it, his own program for man's salvation, the Gogolian genius falters and his magic dissolves into nothingness. Kostanžoglo may be a model landowner and Murazov a thoroughly upright man, but Gogol's portrayal of them in the surviving fragments of Volume Two of *Dead Souls* is so uninspired, so deadly dull, that one is tempted to suspect that he revealed his artistic genius more effectively in destroying Volume Two than in creating it.

The final fragment of Volume Two, in which the Governor-General calls in all the officials of the town, from the town governor down to the lowliest titular councilor, including "all those who took bribes and those who did not, those who always acted against the dictates of their conscience, those who did it only now and then, and those who never indulged in it," is almost like a continuation of *The Inspector General* after the final curtain rang down. There is one great difference, however: *The Inspector General* is brilliant comedy, but the sermon against corruption and bribery that the Governor-General preaches to the assembled town officials is painfully artless and drearily earnest. Gogol was never able to portray convincing positive characters or to present a positive social program through his art.

Leskov, on the other hand, is unsurpassed in all Russian literature as a creator of believable positive heroes. Indeed, **"Odnodum"** (**"Singlethought,"** 1879), the first of his stories about *pravedniki,* or righteous men, lends itself to interpretation as Leskov's response to the challenge of Gogol's *Inspector General.* The central event in both plots is the same: the arrival in a provincial town of an allegedly high official on an inspection tour. The principal themes in Gogol's play are bribery, deception and self-deception, abuse of power, and love of ostentation. Everything in the play is false except the town officials' fear of the brash young government clerk whom they mistake for an Inspector General. In Leskov's story the inhabitants of the town of Soligalič are essentially the same as the characters in Gogol's play, but with one exception: Leskov's town is governed not by another Skvoznik-Dmuxanovskij but by a man who is devoted to honesty, truth, and justice, and who is singularly free of any love of ostentation or thirst for power. What strategies does Leskov use in order to make such a paragon of civic virtues believable? First of all, he places an unnamed fictive narrator between himself and his protagonist. This allows Leskov great flexibility: the narrator from his limited point of view can describe Aleksandr Ryžov's eccentric behavior with no obligation to explain it; and the narrator's expressions of surprise or bewilderment or indignation leave the readers free to judge for themselves the degree of irony concealed within his words, and hence the degree to which Ryžov's eccentricities are actually a judgment on the society around him.

A second strategy Leskov uses is to fit Ryžov into an archetype that is deeply rooted in Russian Orthodox culture: the *jurodivyj,* or "fool in Christ," who is familiar to readers and audiences all over the world through such well-known works as Tolstoj's early story "Childhood" and Musorgskij's opera *Boris Godunov.* This is not to say that Ryžov is a typical example of the archetype, or even that the archetype came down unchanged from medieval times to Leskov's nineteenth century. What can be said, however, is that the medieval Russian *jurodivye,* with their theatricality, their often shocking manner of speaking harsh truths in both words and actions to persons in power, prepared the way for a tolerance and even a sympathetic acceptance of the *čudak,* the eccentric, by the masses of ordinary Russian people which has not completely died out even to the present day.[14]

The rough-hewn, taciturn, and physically powerful Ryžov is what sociologists since David Riesman would call an inner-directed man, and the moral compass by which he keeps his life on course is the Bible. Even though he considers himself to be staunchly Orthodox, this emphasis on Bible-reading unconsciously brings him close to the spirit of western Protestantism. The only son of a widow who earned her living by baking and selling meat pies, Ryžov began supporting himself at the age of fourteen, carrying the mail on foot from Soligalič to the neighboring town of Čuxloma, with the Bible as his only companion. During those solitary journeys, reading his Bible as he walked, he became, in the words of Leskov's chronicler, "half a mystic and half an agitator in the Biblical spirit" (VI, 215); and at one favorite spot on his way, at the foot of an oak tree beside a lonely swamp, he would recite Isaiah's powerful verses into the empty air, shouting at the top of his voice such words as "Woe unto the mighty!" The perceptive reader can scarcely fail to recognize here a parallel to the Biblical story of John the Baptist, who spent his youth in the wilderness and then came forth preaching repentance to the "generation of vipers."[15] This parallel is confirmed in Leskov's statement about Ryžov's decision to quit his work as a mail carrier and find a new job in Soligalič: "Ryžov's development was completely finished, and the time was approaching for action in which he could apply the rules he had worked out for himself on his Biblical foundation" (VI, 215). Taking a job in Soligalič as the town policeman, he administers even-handed justice and protection to all the inhabitants; but eventually he gets into trouble because of his honesty. His absolute refusal to accept bribes threatens to undermine the system through which all the town officials supplement their income, from the lowliest clerk up to the town governor himself. As Leskov's narrator explains, with an allusion to a line in the first act of Gogol's *Inspector General,* "It was impossible to make ends meet without this 'squeezing,' and even the Voltaireans offered no objection to that" (VI, 217-218).

After the combined efforts of the town governor and the local archpriest fail to shake the stubborn policeman's refusal to accept any bribes, the archpriest thoroughly examines him at confession and reports to the governor that Ryžov is now beyond all hope: "He's filled his head with Bible-reading." In the ironic words of Leskov's chronicler, the archpriest and the governor

> felt sorry about it, and they became more charitable toward Ryžov. In our ancient Russian land every Orthodox knows that whoever has read the Bible all the way through and "even gotten to Christ" can no longer be held responsible for his actions; such people are like the well-known "fools in Christ" [*jurodivye*]—they will do queer things but they won't harm anybody, and no one is afraid of them.
>
> (VI, 222)

The principal action of the story gets under way with the appointment of a new provincial governor, Sergej Stepanovič Lanskoj, who begins by dismissing a great many corrupt officials, including the governor of Soligalič, and appoints Ryžov acting town governor in his place. The new appointment provides further evidence of Ryžov's immunity to the corrupting effect of power and his indifference to worldly honors and prestige. Having previously been neither willing nor financially able to buy a policeman's uniform on his salary, he now rules the town wearing the same old quilted jacket that he has worn ever since he carried the mail between Soligalič and Čuxloma. This lack of "uniformity" in their town governor does not disturb the inhabitants of Soligalič until they learn that the new provincial governor is soon to arrive on a tour of inspection. From this point on, the parallels between Leskov's story and Gogol's *Inspector General* become unmistakable. After devoting a whole chapter to describing the preparations that town officials customarily made for such a visit, painting the buildings, scrubbing the floors, patching the roads, clearing out some of the patients from the hospital (just as in Gogol's play), and having their uniforms cleaned, mended, and pressed, Leskov's narrator goes on to describe the dismay of the Soligalič officials over Ryžov's refusal to make any special preparations at all for the governor's visit:

> He did not tear down a single fence before the house of a single inhabitant [an allusion to the town governor's order in Gogol's play to tear down the old fence beside the cobbler's and make it look as if new streets were being laid out]; he repainted nothing with whitewash or ochre, and in general he undertook no measures either to spruce up the town or even to change his own absurd costume.
>
> (VI, 232)

In keeping with his sense of honesty, and in contrast to Skvoznik-Dmuxanovskij in Gogol's play, Ryžov refuses to create a "Potemkin village" out of Soligalič for the visit of the governor. "It won't do to make the people lose a lot of money on this," he says. "After all, is the governor coming to lay waste the land?" (VI, 232).

Since he insists on living within his ten-ruble monthly income, he cannot afford to buy a uniform himself, and he refuses to allow the townspeople to take up a collection and buy him one. "That's a gift," he explains, "and I won't take gifts." The only concession he finally makes is to allow the barrier at the town gates to be repainted in the national colors—black, white, and red—and to wear a uniform borrowed from the court assessor, who happens to be the same size as Ryžov. This concession prepares the way for the most ludicrous scene in the story, which illustrates another of Leskov's strategies in the portrayal of positive heroes—the blending of the virtuous and the comical. While waiting at the town gates for the first signal of the approach of the provincial governor, Ryžov absent-mindedly sits down to rest on the freshly painted log barrier, and when he rides off standing erect in the back of his open cart to meet the important personage, a general groan goes up as the townspeople see the Russian national colors brightly imprinted on the white pants of his borrowed uniform.

This farcical scene leads up to the final episodes of the story, which present a striking contrast to Xlestakov's interviews with Skvoznik-Dmuxanovskij and the other town officials in Gogol's comedy. Ryžov's reception of Governor Lanskoj, the Governor's reaction to Ryžov's eccentric behavior, and the opinions about Ryžov that the townspeople express in their interviews with Lanskoj—all this becomes intelligible and believable only when we view it against the background of traditional Russian culture and the place reserved in it for the *jurodivye*, the fools in Christ, and for eccentrics in general. When Governor Lanskoj, a typically Western-oriented, secular-minded Russian intellectual, begins his tour of Soligalič with the traditional visit to the cathedral, he shocks Ryžov's religious sensibilities by walking up to the altar erect, without making the sign of the cross or bowing in any direction. Ryžov strides up behind him, seizes the governor by the arm, and to the horror of the frightened townspeople says in a loud voice:

> "Sergej, thou slave of God! Come humbly, not haughtily, into the temple of the Lord, and present thyself as the greatest of sinners—like this!"

> With that he put his hand on the governor's back and gravely bent him over in a full bow, and let him go and stood at attention.

> (VI, 237)

This whole scene, and indeed the whole story, is filled with what the semanticists would call "directive statements." Needless to say, Leskov sought to make his tale

believable, but as a staunch opponent for art for art's sake he obviously wrote it not only to *reflect* Russian reality but also to influence its future development. Through his quixotic hero he implies that a courageous and incorruptible person, however humble his origins, can exert a powerful influence on the transformation of society. And through his portrayal of Governor Lanskoj's reaction to Ryžov's eccentricities, Leskov implies that even people in high places are not impervious to the moral influence of *pravedniki* who have the courage to "speak truth to power."

Leskov's chronicler tells us that after Ryžov's respectful reprimand in church, Lanskoj said not a word, but "crossed himself, turned around and bowed to all the people, and then quickly went out and left for the apartment that had been prepared for him."

Here, in another scene that parallels Gogol's play, the provincial governor receives the town officials one after another; but instead of duplicating Xlestakov in the collection of bribes, Lanskoj questions each official about the eccentric Ryžov. The whole scene is filled with typically Leskovian irony. For example, Lanskoj's remark to one official that Ryžov is insolent leads to the following exchange:

> "He's the humblest of men: if his superior sits on his neck, he will reason, 'This is what I must bear,' and he will bear it. Only, he's read the Bible a lot and that has unsettled him."

> "You are talking nonsense: the Bible is the book of God."

> "Yes, sir, that's right; only, it's not suitable for everybody to read: among the monks it arouses the passions, and among the laymen it disturbs the mind."

> "What twaddle!" Lanskoj answered, and went on with his questions:

> "And how is he about bribes—moderate?"

> "Oh, good heavens!" said the official. "He won't take any at all."

> The governor became even more skeptical.

> "That," he said, "I refuse to believe on any account."

> (VI, 237-238)

Lanskoj's comical interview with Ryžov himself is presented by Leskov's fictive chronicler as something beyond belief—but something that actually happened all the same. Ryžov's plain-spoken manner at first arouses Lanskoj's suspicions:

> "Do you have respect for the authorities?"

> "No."

> "Why not?"

"They are lazy, greedy, and hypocritical about the throne."

(VI, 240)

At another point Lanskoj asks: "So you are a connoisseur of the Bible, they say?" And Ryžov answers: "I read it as much as my time allows—and I also advise you to." (VI, 240)

Finally, Lanskoj almost loses patience and says:

"But you know, I could handle you in an entirely different way from the way I am handling you."

Ryžov looked at him in pity and answered:

"And what kind of evil can be done to somebody who knows how to support his family on ten rubles a month?"

"I could have you arrested."

"They eat better in jail."

(VI, 241)

In due time after Governor Lanskoj's visit, the chronicler tells us ironically, news came back to Soligalič "that was not only completely incredible but even impossible in a well-ordered system of government." The news was that on Lanskoj's recommendation Ryžov had been awarded the Cross of St. Vladimir, carrying with it hereditary nobility—the first Cross of St. Vladimir in all Russian history ever given to a policeman.

Thus ends Leskov's positive counterpart to Gogol's brilliant comedy. The bribe-taking and corruption, the love of power and ostentation, the deception and self-deception of Skvoznik-Dmuxanovskij and his henchmen ends with the chilling dawn of Judgment Day as the announcement is made that the real Inspector General has arrived; while in Leskov's story the quixotic, incorruptible, Bible-reading "fool in Christ" Ryžov insists on letting the provincial governor view the town as it really is, unwittingly lets himself be seen in a borrowed uniform with the Russian national colors on the seat of his pants, respectfully reprimands the governor for his conduct in church, and ends by receiving the cross of St. Vladimir. In **"Singlethought"** Leskov created the kind of positive "sermon in art" (to use the words of his contemporary, the critic M. O. Men'šikov)[16] that Gogol had tried in vain to create in the second volume of *Dead Souls* and in his *Selected Passages from Correspondence with Friends*. Like Gogol, Leskov too attacked the Russian plague of bribery and preached honesty, justice, integrity, and practical love of humanity; but thanks to his skillful use of such devices as an ironic fictive narrator, the Russian archetype of the fool in Christ, and the blending of the virtuous and the comic, Leskov succeeded where Gogol had failed.

"Choice Grain" and **"Singlethought"** are linked in various ways to one or both of Gogol's masterpieces, but they are also linked to each other. They are like two sides of the same coin—negative and affirmative treatments of the same set of moral and social problems. In **"Choice Grain"** Leskov's key word is "социабельность," his peculiarly Russian corruption of the imported term for socialism. In **"Singlethought"** his positive counterpart to "социабельность" appears in just one oblique reference, in the next to the last chapter, when his fictive chronicler refers in passing to Aleksandr Ryžov as a "Biblical socialist."

Notes

1. This question was settled some years ago by S. A. Rejser in his article "'Все мы вышли из гоголевской «Шинели»' (История одной легенды," Вопросы лимерамуры, 12, № 2 (1968), 184-187.

2. Б. Эйхенбаум, "'Чрезмерный писатель' (К 100-летию рождения Н. Лескова)," О прозе. Сборник смамей (Ленинград: Художественная литература, 1969), p. 336.

3. Letter of 23 July 1883 to S. N. Šubinskij; H. С. Лесков, Собрание сочинений в одиннадцами момах, XI (Москва: Художественная литература, 1958), 282. Subsequent volume and page references to this edition will be given in the text.

4. Эйхенбаум, p. 336.

5. In this article Leskov wrote that on the morning after Ševčenko's death "я с другим моим земляком и знакомым покойника, А. И. Н[ичипоренко], отправились в Академию." Since both Ševčenko and Ničiporenko were Ukrainians, this sentence as it stands can only mean that Leskov considered himself a Ukrainian too. In the absence of a manuscript or any other text of this article published in Leskov's lifetime, Soviet Russian and Ukrainian editors have hesitated between printing this sentence as it was first published in Русская речь in 1861 and printing it with the change of one little letter, the *и* in другим to an *о*, which with the addition of a comma after моим would "correct" Leskov's "mistaken" reference to himself as a Ukrainian: ". . . я с другом моим, земляком и знакомым покойника, А. И. Н[ичипоренко], отправились в Академию." For further discussion of this little textological problem see my article: Вильям Эджертон, "История одной буквы (Был ли Лесков украинцем?)," Новый журнал (Нью Йорк), кн. 89 (1967), pp. 82-86.

6. "Герои Отечественной войны по гр. Л. Н. Толстому," Биржевые ведомосми, № № 66, 68, 70, 75, 98, 99, 109 (1869); reprinted in Собрание сочинений, X, 130.

7. Letter of 22 April 1888 (XI, 385).

8. Letter of 17 August 1883 (XI, 283).

9. Letter of 15 December 1888 to N. P. Kroxin, quoted in Андрей Лесков, Жизнь Николая Лескова (Москва, Художественная литература, 1954), p. 463.

10. А. И. Фаресов, Промив мечений. Н. С. Лесков. Его жизнь, сочинения, полемика и воспоминания о нем (С.-Петербург, 1904), pp. 43-44.

11. Hugh McLean, *Nikolai Leskov: The Man and His Art* (Cambridge, Mass.: Harvard University Press, 1977), p. 449.

12. William B. Edgerton, "Leskov's Parody on Gogol': *Otbornoe zerno*," in *Lingua Viget: Commentationes Slavicae in Honorem V. Kiparsky* (Helsinki: Suomalaisen Kirjallisuuden Kirjapaino, 1964), pp. 38-43.

13. Soviet scholars have interpreted this word to mean nothing more than "гражданственность" 'civic spirit,' but there is evidence in the memoirs of P. D. Bororykin that the word was first used in the 1860s precisely as a disparaging corruption of "социализм." M. I. Kastorskij was censor of the Библиомека для чмения at the time when Boborykin edited it, and Kastorskij was constantly on the lookout for ideas of socialism and revolution. Once, Bororykin recalls, Kastorskij rejected an article with the explanation that he could not possibly allow it to be published: "Эта статья полна мизерабельности и социабельности." П. Д. Боборыкин, Воспоминания в двух момах (Москва, 1965), I. 342. Leskov undoubtedly heard about this while writing for Boborykin's journal in 1863-1864.

14. This is illustrated by the following passage (given here in English translation) from a personal letter written on 5 July 1969 by Academician D. S. Lixačev:

> Leskov's popularity was due especially to his eccentrics and righteous men [праведники и чудаки]. In Russia people have always loved eccentrics, and eccentrics have never been a rarity in our way of life. This is hard for a foreigner to understand, but this is what has led to the popularity of the юродивые. And I can give you some idea of how frequently these eccentrics and righteous men have appeared by citing an example . . . A Leskovian 'Odnodum' comes to see me at least once a month. He will drop in to reach a decision with me about some eternal question. He is more

than eighty years old. He is dressed in the shabbiest manner, even though he earns quite a lot. He gives away everything he receives. He is a graduate of Moscow University, but when you look at him, you would think he was an unskilled laborer. One of his eccentricities is his refusal to grant recognition to streetcars and busses. He goes everywhere on foot, and he eats mainly raw vegetables and black bread. He will come a good ten kilometers on foot in order to resolve some question or to ask what I think about this or that. He himself will often make fun of himself. Those around him love and revere him, and never get angry when he rebukes them for some misdeed they have committed. Oh, the fascination of this eccentric!

For a scholarly treatment of the *jurodivyj* in ancient Russian culture see Д. С. Лихачев, А. М. Панченко, «Смеховой мир» древней Руси (Ленинград: "Наука," 1976), particularly the chapters on "Древнерусское юродство," "Юродство как зрелице," and "Юродство как общественный протест," pp. 93-183.

15. Luke 2:2-14.

16. М. О Меньшиков, "Художественная проповедь (XI том сочинений Н. С. Лескова,)" Книжки недели, февраль 1894, pp. 160-183.

Thomas Eekman (essay date 1983)

SOURCE: Eekman, Thomas, "N. S. Leskov's *At Daggers Drawn* Reconsidered." In *Miscellanea Slavica: To Honour the Memory of Jan M. Meijer,* edited by B. J. Amsenga, A. H. van den Baar, F. Suasso, and M. D. de Wolff, pp. 195-221. Amsterdam: Rodopi, 1983.

[*In the following essay, Eekman imparts a preliminary study of Leskov's critically neglected and occasionally maligned novel* Na nožax, *considering the work's anti-nihilist theme, narrative structure, characterizations, and use of language.*]

The history of Leskov's three novels on topical social themes, **No Way Out** (**Nekuda**), **Cathedral Folk** (**Soborjane**) and **At Daggers Drawn** (**Na nožax**)[1], is rather confused and complex. They all originated in the period 1864-1871, and they all dealt with a problem which must have been very high in the author's mind: the existence in Russia (in Petersburg primarily, but also in Moscow, with some echoes in the province) of a group of quasi-idealistic, egoistic and immoral people who attempted to attain their selfish, materialistic goals while posing as idealists, socialists, "new men", "nihilists", or while boasting that they had been such idealists, but had become wiser, more mature and experienced since those days of youthful folly. Leskov must have met such people and been deeply disgusted by their unscrupulous behavior and their unclean way of thinking. Or perhaps his work was partly instigated by other prose and plays of the sixties in which a negative picture of the nihilists was presented. These works seemed to appeal to the large segment of the public that was afraid of revolutionary movements and opposed to trends that questioned the status quo or attempted to undermine the pillars of Russian society.

In an excellent book (which never drew much attention because it was published in the first year of World War II in an obscure place), *Iz literaturnoj polemiki 60-x godov* (Petrozavodsk: GIZ Karelo-finskoj SSR, 1941), V. Bazanov traces and discusses a great number of novels, shorter prose works, and plays written in a polemical, anti-nihilist vein that began to appear as early as 1855. In those times, when no real political life was possible in Russia, but when a growing number of people showed lively interest in the burning national and international issues, and when socio-political polemics took place in the guise of literary works, what was virtually a new genre of "political" or quasi-political prose came into being. Works like Turgenev's *Fathers and Sons,* Dostoevskij's *Possessed,* Leskov's **Cathedral Folk** or, to a certain extent, Tolstoj's *Contaminated Family,* which we look upon as literary works in their own right and evaluate for their intrinsic literary merits, themselves figured in the stream of polemical, pro- or, more often, anti-nihilistic writings.

We might see a parallel between the 1860's in Russia and the 1960's in Europe and the U.S. In the period of hippydom and student unrest a philosophical-political idealism and, here and there, a revolutionary zeal spread among young people, as had happened a century earlier in Russia. This mood later disintegrated and gave way to markedly pragmatic, practical, and self-centered attitudes, partly among those very idealists, now more sober and settled. As Hugh McLean put it: "Human societies, like human individuals, tire of excessive demands for altruism"[2].

This was what attracted Leskov's attention and raised his anger. However, he went much too far, describing these people as outright swindlers. Of his three so-called anti-nihilist novels, **At Daggers Drawn** met with the strongest disapproval of critics and public—both for its literary qualities, or rather lack thereof, and for its strong bias in its depiction of ex- or pseudo-nihilists as complete scoundrels. The work is by far the most voluminous Leskov ever wrote (830 pages); but it took him a relatively short time to finish it. He worked on it in 1870 and for part of 1871, during which time he also wrote **"Laughter and Grief"** (**"Smex i gore"**). It was published in *Russkij vestnik,* the Moscow monthly of a clear conservative, pro-government signature under the editorship of Mixail N. Katkov, in the issues 10-12 of 1870 and 1-8 of 1871; it then appeared as a book by the end of 1871. Dostoevskij's *The Possessed* (*Besy*) was printed in the same journal in the same period (1-11 of 1870, 11-12 of 1872) so that some readers confused the two works: their tone and, to a certain extent, their contents were similar[3].

The journalist D. Minaev wrote in his "Innocent Notes" (*Nevinnye zametki*) in the monthly *Delo* of November, 1871:

> People that got used to everything in the world also got gradually accustomed to the literary *quadrille* of the *Russkij vestnik*—a quadrille consisting of Messrs. Kljušnikov and Pisemskij, Dostoevskij and Leskov. The latter two novelists have been Katkovized [*okatkovilis'*] to such a degree that in their latest novels, *The Possessed* and **At Daggers Drawn,** they coalesced into one type of a sort of *homunculus* born in the famous ink stand of the editor of the *Moskovskie vedomosti*[4]. Both of these novelists, having thrown off the skin of their individuality, exasperated by the "new age and mores", and turned as green as the cover of the *Russkij vestnik* out of obscurantist spite, have provided themselves with a hunter's rattle to frighten the "red beast", i.e., the public, with various ghosts.[5]

Some similarities between Dostoevskij's and Leskov's works have been established[6]. A close analysis of **At Daggers Drawn** might well show more points of comparison—not just with *The Possessed,* but also with other works by Dostoevskij, specifically, *The Insulted and the Injured, The Idiot,* and *Crime and Punishment*—in themes, characters, atmosphere, and literary approaches and devices. That, however, is beyond the scope of this article.

Leskov himself had written off the theme as soon as he had finished his bulky product; he not only turned to different themes but, as is well known, broke with Katkov and, in the course of his later career, moved to the left, to a more liberal and critical view of the government. He wrote disapprovingly a few times about **At Daggers Drawn** and about his political novels in general:

> But when I forgot this inexorable requirement of artistic creation and portrayed only nihilist features, ignoring the whole human being, the result was one-sided denunciatory figures, marionettes, and not living types from the nihilist mold. These were pieces of patchwork, and very annoying and noticeable ones.[7]

But except for a number of disparaging remarks about **At Daggers Drawn** in his later works, articles, letters, or in conversations recorded by contemporaries, it seems that he tried to extinguish the memory of it[8] (although the novel was reprinted in 1875 and 1885 and included in his *Collected Works* published in 1889-1896). There was only one edition after Leskov's death, in five small volumes (XXIII-XXVII) of the *Polnoe sobranie sočinenij* (Petersburg, 1902-1903). The critics either remained silent or responded totally negatively. The exception was Dostoevskij, his comrade-in-arms from Katkov's magazine. On other occasions Dostoevskij was quite critical of Leskov as a writer, but in connection with *At Daggers Drawn* he wrote to his friend A. Majkov:

> Are you reading Leskov's novel in *Russkij vestnik*? A lot of idle talk, a lot of balderdash, as if it were taking place on the moon. The nihilists are distorted as if they were rogues. But on the other hand, certain types! How do you like *Vanskok*! [the nickname of a secondary character in the novel, an idealistic young woman]. In Gogol' there never was anything more typical and truer to life than she is. Believe me, I myself have seen and heard this *Vanskok,* I feel as if I have touched her! A remarkable personality! If nihilism of the early sixties dies out, this figure will remain as an eternal memento. She is the product of a genius! And what a master is he in portraying our little priests! What about that Father Evangel! . . . Strange is the fate of this Stebnickij [Leskov's pseudonym] in our literature. It would be worth analyzing such a phenomenon as Stebnickij critically and quite seriously.[9]

To this day Dostoevskij's advice has never been followed!

The negative comments were not prompted primarily, in this case, by indignation at the libelous nature of the book. In *No Way Out* many critics and readers, notably in Petersburg, recognized living persons, like the writer Slepcov, and situations, like the commune "Dom soglasija" in the third part. In *At Daggers Drawn* there are perhaps one or two recognizable persons[10], but even these were not generally recognized. One might expect Leskov to introduce the Petersburg fires of 1861, which indirectly caused his sudden rupture with the progressive groups and magazines, into one of his anti-nihilistic works, but he does not. Although there is a fire, caused by arson, in the Petersburg of *At Daggers Drawn,* it is not of the same type as the mysterious, widespread fires that in reality occurred in Petersburg and for which radical students were blamed.

One of the fiercest critics of the novel (and one of the few who paid any attention to it in pre-revolutionary Russia) was A. Volynskij, who, in his essay *N. S. Leskov* (Petersburg, 1898, reprinted, 1923), expressed both praise and criticism of the writer, though more of the latter than of the former. It was Volynskij's contention that, both in his journalistic work and his fiction, "whatever theme he elaborated on" Leskov would "express not one, but two opinions that could be reconciled only in a superficial way. His real feelings vanish in a mist of wordy reasonings. Nowhere does one find any firmness and logical harmony" (p. 32). The novella *The Islanders (Ostrovitjane)* had been, in Volynskij's eyes, "a mishmash of tearful romanticism and an entertaining, but very paltry comedy of the vaudeville type" (p. 194); *No Way Out* was full of "literary slander" (p. 209); and *At Daggers Drawn* was incredibly drawn-out and written without any talent—it lacked a clear construction and was rambling. "The novel is written in that vulgar style that authors of the boulevard type usually flaunt" (pp. 210-211). His negative comments are about four pages long; he complains of the stilted style, the "splendor of twopenny literature" with which the many characters were painted. "Leskov did not succeed in creating even one living personality. As a work of literature the novel does not exist. It is a two-volume work, the largest Leskov ever wrote, but at the same time it is a most trivial product," because "the idea, the style, the planning of the events, everything is rough-hewn, petty and not in a single respect worthy of Leskov's talent" (p. 213).

After this verdict, the novel was for a long time forgotten, eliminated, as it were, from Russian literature. Maksim Gor'kij held Leskov in high esteem; following Dostoevskij, he, too, praised the character of Vanskok, who was, according to him, "depicted with amazing art, totally alive"[11]. He considered it "Leskov's enormous merit that he apprehended these people so beautifully and depicted them so superbly"[12]. But otherwise Gor'kij ignored *At Daggers Drawn.* It should be added here that Vanskok plays only a very minor role in the novel, appearing in but four short chapters of part II.

Gor'kij's praise and the interest some critics of the formalist school bestowed on Leskov notwithstanding, he was considered a conservative, bourgeois, pro-clergy writer in the Soviet Union; his *oeuvre* and his name were more or less passed over in silence for several decades. The ban was lifted during and after World War II, when some articles and monographs began to appear. A nine-volume edition of his works came out in 1956-58 (the only Soviet *Sobranie sočinenij* so far), which did contain *No Way Out,* but not *At Daggers Drawn* (nor the novella *The Bypassed (Obojdennye)* and a few other, shorter works). The Soviet authors of studies on Leskov (B. Èjxenbaum, V. Vinogradov, V. Drugov, L. Grossman, V. Gebel', L. Čudnova, I. Stoljarova, N. Pleščunov, V. Troickij, M. Gorjačkina) either restricted themselves to a few lines on *At Daggers Drawn* or left it totally out of consideration, as if it had never existed. Only the work of Bazanov mentioned above contains six pages of (naturally, negative) comments. A few pages are devoted to it by Stoljarova in the two-volume *Istorija russkogo romana* of 1964.

A proscribed novel in the Soviet Union, it did not fare much better in the West. Unlike several other writings by Leskov, it never was the theme of any special study or article. In the books on Leskov published during the last quarter of a century in German (by V. Setschkareff, W. Girke, B. Zelinsky) or English (H. McLean, W. Edgerton, K. A. Lantz, J. Y. Muckle), precious little is said about *At Daggers Drawn.*

By now it is perhaps apparent that we are dealing with a failure of a novel, a lengthy, slanderous lampoon, an ill-constructed, pedestrian potboiler. Yet, if not the fact that Dostoevskij praised it, then at least the fact that Leskov is, after all, one of the masters of Russian prose of the second half of the nineteenth century may arouse our interest and make us desirous to see *what* exactly *made* the novel a failure and whether it has no redeeming features.

As was indicated above, Dostoevskij and Leskov, in spite of all their differences, had certain traits in common. Their socio-political views converged to a large extent, and as prose writers, they both had a bent for unexpected, thrilling developments that would keep the reader in suspense. Another common trait is their propensity for going to extremes. Nikolaj D. Mixajlovskij, in his extensive article on Leskov (*Russkoe bogatstvo,* no. 6, 1897), noted and documented this trait in Leskov's work; and the same has been said of Dostoevskij. Mixajlovskij called Leskov a "measureless" (*bezmernyj*) writer (in the sense of knowing no limits); he reproached him for his exaggerations that defied realism. On the one hand, he noted, Leskov strove to portray righteous people (*pravedniki*), totally positive, good and wise heroes; on the other, he seemed to enjoy depicting negative characters who were completely, unconditionally negative and evil. Mixajlovskij did not specifically discuss *At Daggers Drawn,* he probably never read it; but Leskov's characteristic trait, especially the apparent pleasure he took in presenting the reader with some absolutely wicked, monstrous characters, is very visible in this novel. Here one may see a resemblance to *The Possessed*[13] and possibly to other works by Dostoevskij[14]. It seems indisputable, though, that, even if the two writers have certain points in common, Dostoevskij's works have an incomparably greater literary significance and universal philosophical depth.

* * *

It is not and cannot be our intention to present in this paper an analysis of this novel of over eight hundred pages, nor to render its contents, which consist of a long series of events, actions, and discussions, interspersed with the author's comments. One feels, when reading *At Daggers Drawn,* that the contention is not quite tenable that Leskov was a poor novelist, that he was only good at writing short stories, sketches, anecdotes, some of his longer works being no more than concatenations of such anecdotal material (perhaps with the exception of *No Way Out* and *Cathedral Folk,*

though even they show marked constructional flaws). On the contrary, one might argue that the composition of the work is well thought out: there is a central plot, an uninterrupted development (or interrupted for compositional reasons), and a unity of characters and action, even though the structure is rather complex. The heroes all interrelate, meet each other at the necessary moments (without too many miraculous coincidences) and play their roles in moving the plot forward. There are occasional moments of suspense, and devices for keeping the reader interested. It is true that the villains are painted excessively black, but Leskov also attempts to portray two or three positive heroes. Most other characters show both positive and negative features. And after all, the crime element in the novel, by which some of his contemporary critics (and also some Soviet critics) were horrified, is very mild in comparison to the crime literature that developed in our century.

A typical example of Leskov's method of building suspense is the scene in which Vislenev, one of the main characters, decides in the night to open the pocket book of Gordanov (the most negative hero) with a knife:

> . . . but suddenly Vislenev shuddered, the knife vibrated and slipped out of his hand, as if it was snatched away by some foreign force, and fell down somewhere far away out of the window, in the thick grass; in the room, amidst the deepest silence of the night, a deafening noise broke forth, a roar, a crash, a hissing, whistling and rumble. . . .
>
> (XIII, 75)[15]

This turns out to be an old clock that has started to strike, frightening Vislenev, who was doing something illicit.

After all this has been said, it must be admitted that the criticism of the novel was not quite unfounded. The work is certainly too lengthy, full of long-winded conversations in a rather formal ceremonious literary language; its literary qualities, its characterizations, its ideas, contents and style are not strong enough to sustain the reader's interest. Leskov wrote it more or less in a hurry; the following quote would indicate that is was dictated:

> Only once I tried to dictate, and the results were terrible. I was ill and dictated the novel *At Daggers Drawn.* And that, in my opinion, is the sloppiest of all my inferior works.[16]

Elsewhere, somewhat contradicting this statement, he wrote:

> This whole novel is written in a hurry and printed right from my text on scraps of paper, often jotted down with a pencil in the printing office.[17]

More generally, he once qualified his anti-nihilistic works as "hasty, journalistic jobs"[18].

Yet the book has some features that arouse our attention because they remind us of other, better works by Leskov. First of all, the setting is partly in the capital, Petersburg, but for a much larger part in a provincial town and its surroundings; that is also the case in the other novels, *Cathedral Folk* (although the Petersburg part—Axilla's visit to the capital—occupies only one chapter in it) and *No Way Out* (here Moscow, as a third milieu, is the setting of the middle part), as well as in some shorter works. In all cases, the evil spirits of the work live and operate in, or emanate from, Petersburg (Termosesov in *Cathedral Folk,* Saf'janos, Belojarcev in *No Way Out,* Gordanov, Kišenskij in *At Daggers Drawn*), the positive characters are provincials (the clergy in *Cathedral Folk,* Rozanov, Ženni, Liza in *No Way Out,* Podozerov, Forov, Evangel in *At Daggers Drawn*). Of course, the province (the countryside or a small town: Stargorod in *Cathedral Folk,* the *uezdnyj gorod* in *No Way Out,* the *gubernskij gorod N.* in *At Daggers Drawn*) can at times breed perverse characters, too, like Prepotenskij in the first, to a certain extent Parxomenko in the second, Bodrostina in the third novel. And not all characters should be described strictly in terms of positive or negative: some are simply weak, susceptible to bad influences, like Vislenev in the third novel. However, there can be no doubt about Leskov's tendency to stress, on the one hand, the evil forces immanent in the big city, particularly the Russian imperial capital, where he spent a large part of his life and toward which he developed a sort of love-hate relationship, and, on the other hand, the noble forces that could be found in the province, the wide Russian land, repository of old Russian virtues and strength of character, from which he himself had emerged and which he tended to view in a positive light. Leskov did not idealize the province; sometimes his heroes complain of its terrible dullness. But it is the provincial nobility (or sometimes the clergy) from which he draws his most colorful characters. We remember the noble, strong-willed Lady Plodomasova from **"Old Years in Plodomasova" ("Starye gody v sele Plodomasove")**, who also figures in *Cathedral Folk,* and Varvara Proto-zanova in *A Decrepit Clan (Zaxudalyj rod).* In *At Daggers Drawn,* one of the heroines, Aleksandra Ivanovna Sintjanina, is portrayed in a similar way (part I, p. 21).

The devastating power of the "pseudo-liberals", the "nihilists", or, even worse, "nehilists" (ne-gilisty: gil' = rubbish; they reject all social and moral "rubbish") from the city over provincial simpletons is shown in what Gordanov does to Vislenev. Gordanov induces him to write an inflammatory article, and uses this manuscript as a pledge that puts Vislenev entirely in his power. It enables Gordanov to extort money from Vislenev, to force him to run into debt, and thereby to completely ruin Vislenev. He even forces Vislenev to marry against his will. All this without Vislenev even realizing that Gordanov is the villain who is behind it. Gordanov be-lieves that "in our society everything is forgiven and permitted to shameless impudence and to vice, covered up by hypocrisy" (XXV, 75). His intention to gain power over Vislenev and to marry Vislenev's sister Larisa, one of the principal female characters, constitutes one main plot line. (The other central story line is Glafira Bodrostina's wicked plan (with Gordanov as her accomplice) to dispose of her husband, the old General Bodrostin, in order to get hold of his fortune.)

Contrasted with Gordanov is the honest idealist, Podozerov. In a conversation with Sintjanina he declares: "I don't have any predilections and I am not a slave of any party: I respect and love all sincere and honest people in the world as long as they wish their fellow creatures happiness and believe in what they profess" (XXV, 93). And later on he exclaims: "Believe me, everything is moonshine except one thing: the good that one person can do for another" (XXV, 129).

Chapter 5 of part V describes Gordanov's rude advances to (the naturally disinclined) Larisa, and Podozerov's sudden intervention at exactly the right moment. This scene is dished up in the style of a standard romantic story, of a typical early nineteenth-century novel. The two adversaries insult one another, but a clash is prevented by another sudden and well-timed intervention: that of a secondary character, Vodop'janov (who figures in only a few chapters). In chapter 13 there is a scene in which Larisa is threatened during the night in her bedroom by the lascivious Gordanov—a sensual scene that Leskov repeated from his stories **"Kotin the He-Cow and Platonida" ("Kotin doilec i Platonida")** and **"The Lady Macbeth from the Mtsensk District" ("Ledi Makbet Mcenskogo uezda")**.

Continuing in the romantic manner, Leskov stages a duel between Gordanov and Podozerov. Here his endeavor to enhance the attractive, thrilling nature of the story prompts the use of a compositional device: first, the duel is announced, then a few chapters on different themes are inserted to heighten the suspense, the reader's impatient expectation. Subsequently, we are informed that Podozerov has been mercilessly killed. Two chapters later the course of events during the duel is, at last, described. Finally, we find out that Podozerov was not dead after all, but dangerously injured; he later gets the better of death. He then marries Larisa, although he feels no passionate love toward her (in spite of the fact that she is always presented as a physically most attractive person). This might indicate a desire on the part of the author to elevate his hero to a level of ideality that is superior to the sexes and sexual love—somewhat like Myškin in Dostoevskij's *Idiot*—although that would be contrary to Leskov's own very human and earthly inclinations.

Gordanov and the equally unscrupulous Kišenskij (a Jew) are mockingly labeled "our esteemed men-of-action" (*naši dostojnye dejateli*) by the author. And Bodrostina follows Katerina L'vovna from **"The Lady Macbeth from the Mtsensk District"** in her resolution to do in her old husband and to marry her beloved. She humiliates Vislenev (who is strongly attached to her) in every possible way. She is aware, however, of the qualities of the three men who surround her: Vislenev, she realizes, is a "*mizerija*"; another character, Ropšin, "even more repulsive" (*ešče gaže*); and Gordanov "a cold criminal and rascal, an insolent, self-confident, wicked, guileful traitor and her destroyer" (XXVII, 72). More and more, especially in the Petersburg part of the novel, the action revolves around Bodrostina's inheritance and thus the widely known motif of a struggle over a legacy becomes the central theme.

We may conceive of the negative characters as individuals who happen to indulge in immoral behavior, but we may also envisage them as typical representatives of a corrupt generation. Leskov himself hints at this by a remark of one of his characters: ". . . all people here in Petersburg are linked by a hatred of each other. All people here, my dear, are at daggers drawn" (XXVI, 93). A little later, Gordanov says to Bodrostina: "You and I have played at nihilism" (*nigilistničali*); but she interrupts him: "That is to say, *you* have played at nihilism." He: "Well, . . . whoever it was . . .", etc. (103). The whole idea of nihilism boils down, in their parlance, to acting dishonestly, without principles. There are many places in the book where the author vents his dislike of an amoral, unconscionable young generation (or at least a certain part of it). We should remember that 1871 was the year of the Nečaev trial, which revealed a horrifying criminal element among the revolutionaries. As K. A. Lantz put it:

> . . . the novel is not so much an attack on nihilism as a broad indictment of the cynical materialism of society as a whole[19] (i.e. in Leskov's Russia).

However, there exists a different conception of the term nihilism that is also represented in the book: nihilism in the sense of looking skeptically at surrounding reality, of reluctance to accept anything, any authority, at face value, of the desire to replace worn-out, fossilized values by new, higher and more meaningful ones. The bearer of this view is Major Forov, who is dubbed by his wife "the gray-haired nihilist". It is interesting that he professes to be an atheist and remains so until the end of his life. This honest and pure soul has as his closest friend a priest, Father Evangel, with whom he carries on lively conversations. Evangel represents the positive cleric; his moving relationship to his wife Painka, their love and mutual understanding are described in a way reminiscent of Father Tuberozov and his *protopopica* Natal'ja Nikolaevna in *Cathedral Folk*.

"Women—they are such a joy! They are our balm bearers [*mironosicy*]—without their tears this evil world would indurate!", he exclaims (XXV, 147). There are more instances in *At Daggers Drawn* where women are praised. This is one of the ways in which Leskov differs from his admired teacher Lev Tolstoj: he definitely had a more positive view of women[20]. And unlike many other Russian classical writers, he was able, his own unhappy family notwithstanding, to depict happy marriages: e.g., those of the Forovs and of Evangel and his wife in this case. They contrast with the strange, joyless, inauspicious marriage of Podozerov and Larisa.

The world of these morally pure and good people, to whom much attention (and much space) is given in the novel, is used by the author to offset the impure world of Gordanov, Bodrostina *e tutti quanti*. "No, there are no alliances anymore: they're all at daggers drawn!", is Forov's sad conclusion about that world (XXV, 166). It is interesting to note that Forov and Evangel are also true democrats, who even foment dissatisfaction among the peasants. This would indicate that *At Daggers Drawn* is not, as is claimed, a reactionary novel (the fire ceremonies and rebellion of the peasants (XVII, chapters 18, 29) are even described with some sympathy), although it is true that Leskov expresses his aversion for political twaddlers and his skepticism toward social progress (as he does in *No Way Out* through Rozanov). In the last lines of the novel Podozerov sighs: "It's all so amazing, Father Evangel. You were a rebel, I was a socialist—but who needed it?" To which Evangel answers: "I don't know." Podozerov: "And you will never find out." And Leskov ends the novel with his hero's prophetic words: "No, it's not easy to make out where we are moving while we're at daggers drawn . . . , it's all a prologue to something big that is most surely going to happen."

In a letter to A. S. Suvorin of March 20, 1871 (when he was still writing *At Daggers Drawn*) Leskov refutes a remark by his correspondent that the swindle

> 'came forth directly from nihilism', and that is not to be found in my novel and will not be in it. I believe and I am convinced, that *the swindle stuck* to nihilism, the same way it stuck, and is still stucking, to 'idealism, religion', and patriotism . . . An 'immediate continuation' of nihilism is Major Forov—a character who suffered the most by the concessions I had to make [to Katkov] . . . I don't take revenge on nihilism because scoundrels have slandered it . . .[21].

The introduction of Father Evangel gives Leskov the additional opportunity to introduce the speech and way of writing of a priest with his strong admixture of Church Slavic elements, of biblical terminology. This reminds us of Tuberozov, especially his *Demikotonnaja kniga*, in **Cathedral Folk**, of Fljagin's speech in **"The Enchanted Wanderer"** (**"Očarovannyj strannik"**) and many more clerical or monastic heroes in his works. In the epilogue Leskov renders a letter by Father Evangel, which gives him a chance to air seminary language for a few pages. He uses Church Slavic, church-related, biblical or old Russian words and expressions not only in the utterances of clerics or at solemn moments, but sometimes also with the purpose of adding a mocking or ironic twist to the conversation.[22]

As is well known, Leskov's specialty, his favorite form of narration, was the frame story (continuing an old tradition and particularly following Turgenev). *At Daggers Drawn* not only contains stories-within-the-story when the background of various characters is focused upon, but also a real frame story, "Rasskaz Vodop'janova" in vol. XXVI. This frame story is connected with the main story line, because the heroine of the story turns out to be Podozerov's mother.

The last volume of the novel in particular contains long, drawn-out conversations involving the principal characters. They are constantly meeting, and, having nothing else to do, discussing their problems of communication and their mutual affections and disaffections. The developments are much too slow and Leskov exemplifies the adage he liked to quote that all sorts of literature are good except the boring ones.[23] Suddenly, however, starting with chapter eight, there is action again and a thrilling, even sensational development, clearly reflected in the chapter titles: "It Happened in the Dark Night" (*Delo temnoj noči*), "Before the Last Blow" (*Pred poslednim udarom*), "Events Are Approaching" (*Sobytija bližatsja*), "Larisa's Secret" (*Larisina tajna*). In this section peasants play an active role for the first time, and Leskov is able to introduce that other jargon he was so familiar with (as we remember from **"The Life of a Peasant Martyress"** (**"Žitie odnoj baby"**) and other stories): Russian peasant speech, as well as his knowledge of peasant customs and superstitions.

The language Leskov uses in the rest of the novel, in all instances where no special group parlance is rendered, is interlarded with the unusual words, the rich vocabulary he was famous for: *babelina, Bož'ji ljudcy, mesjac jasnit, položajnik, šišimora, tak glagolemyj, sigat', temen', znat' vžive, bespereč', "Stalosja po skazannomu, kak po pisannomu"* (XXVIII, 49), etc.

Because of his colorful expressions and puns, it is believed by many that Leskov was an extraordinary stylist. Elsewhere I have argued[24] that he actually used a rather heavy style with many stiff, clumsy, often old-fashioned turns of phrase. His sentences are considerably longer than those of his contemporaries in Russian prose: Dostoevskij, Tolstoj, Turgenev, Saltykov-Ščedrin, Čexov; he uses more participles and especially more adjectives—modifiers that lengthen the sentence and make it heavier. His manner of writing occasionally has elements of officialese and is sometimes marred by unnecessary prolixity. Consider the following example from *At Daggers Drawn*:

> Položenie del našej istorii, dozvoljajuščee zaključit' ètu čast' romana rasskazannymi sobytijami, možet vzbudit' v kom-nibud' iz našix čitatelej želanie nemedlenno znat' neskol'ko bolee, čem skol'ko podnevol'noe položenie majora Forova dozvolilo emu otkryt' general'še Sintjaninoj.

(XXV, 71)

(Twice the noun *položenie*, twice the verb *dozvolit'*, a rather ponderous construction.)

This is a typically Leskovian sentence (with four participles):

> Kak panaceja ot vsex bed i neurjadic stavilas' "babuškina moral'", i k nej oborotili svoi nasuplennyje i nedovol'nye liki junye vnučki, s trepetom otrekšiesja ot užasnuvšego ix dviženija "bespovorotnyx" žric nedavno otošedšego ili tol'ko otxodjaščego kul'ta.

(XXV, 123)

The text abounds in stiff sentences like:

> Niva smerti zreet bystro . . . Ètot vsex udivivšij perevorot v čuvstvax doživavšej svoj vek Vislenevoj k molodoj general'še ne imel inyx ob''jasnenij, krome starušeč'ej prixoti. . . .

(XXIII, 20);

or:

> Prebyvanie Larisy u Bodrostinoj ne ostavalos' tajnoj ni dlja Kateriny Astaf'evny, ni dlja Sintjaninoj, kotorye, razumeetsja, i razojdjas' s Laroj, ne perestavali eju interesovat'sja. Obeix ètix ženščin novoe sbliženie Larisy s Glafiroj porazilo črezvyčajno neprijatno. S tex por, kak Bodrostina ukatila za granicu, ni ta ni drugaja iz nazvannyx nami dvux dam ne imeli o nej nikakix obstojatel'nyx svedenij. . . .

(XXVI, 149-50)

Leskov's literary language was shaped by his reading, which was both very extensive and very intensive, but he read mostly eighteenth and early nineteenth century prose. In *At Daggers Drawn* he mentions, next to his older contemporaries Dickens and Thackeray (*Vanity Fair*), the eighteenth century writers Lesage and Sterne and the early nineteenth century writer Paul de Kock; and he quotes from a comedy by the eighteenth century poet Nikolaj A. L'vov.

The circumstantial manner in which he wrote his novels and some of his shorter works, the (for his time) old-fashioned style and language can be traced back to these influences[25]. But they also explain the traditional ingredients out of which he builds up his story, the descriptions, developments and devices that are borrowed from classical fiction and drama. For example, every emotion or feeling is reflected in and immediately betrayed by the facial expression or gestures of a person; similarly, Leskov moves the story forward or explains what is going on by letting people overhear each other's conversations. This eavesdropping device is even somewhat overused in the novel (in part XXVII particularly): it happens too frequently and is introduced too naively.

Another habit that stems from the times of the early European novel is that of the author addressing the reader, talking to him and commenting on the heroes and the events. This was the practice of very many eighteenth and nineteenth century prose writers, and even today the habit has not completely disappeared. However, Leskov gave his author's comments more frequently than most of his contemporaries, except perhaps Turgenev. He follows Turgenev also in addressing the reader occasionally in the second person: *"Po dovol'no vysokomu krylečku vy vidite . . ."* (XXIII, 22) (cf. similar apostrophes in *Zapiski oxotnika*).

In the early novel tradition, such a work had to be concluded by an epilogue; and Leskov does provide us, of course, with a detailed, 26-page Epilogue (again, it was perhaps primarily Turgenev's example which he followed). This epilogue offers some elucidations and describes the further vicissitudes of the heroes. Many of them die; as Podozerov puts it: "The cemetery is expanding." And he, the central hero, remains alone. Such is the sad finale of Leskov's reviled and repudiated novel.

These remarks are short and of an introductory nature. It would be worthwhile to submit **At Daggers Drawn** to the same kind of careful methodological analysis as was applied by Bodo Zelinsky to **No Way Out, The Islanders, Years of Childhood** (**Will-o-the Wisps**), **Cathedral Folk** and **A Decrepit Clan**[26]. A closer investigation of the structure, the action, the narrative position, the temporal and spatial situations and the character depiction would yield results that would contribute to a better insight into and an appreciation of Leskov's novel; this is a task for further study.

Notes

1. The novella *The Bypassed* (*Obojdennye*) of 1865, "almost a novel", as Leskov called it, could be added to this series.

2. Hugh McLean, *Nikolai Leskov, The Man and His Art,* Cambridge (Mass.) and London: Harvard University Press, 1977, pp. 218-219.

3. Cf. the commentary by [P. N.] Tkačev in *Delo,* no. 11, 1871, p. 58: *"V suščnosti Besy i Na nožax est' odno celoe proizvedenie, xotja i napisannoe raznymi avtorami"* (quoted by E. Pul'xritudova, "Dostoevskij i Leskov k istorii tvorčeskix vzaimootnošenij", in *Dostoevskij i russkie pisateli,* Moscow, 1971, p. 96).

4. I.e., Katkov, who also edited this newspaper.

5. Quoted by V. Bazanov, *Iz literaturnoj polemiki 60-x godov,* Petrozavodsk: GIZ Karelo-finskoj SSR, 1941, pp. 49-50.

6. For the relationship between Dostoevskij and Leskov see the bibliography in K. A. Lantz, *Nikolay Leskov,* Boston: Twayne, 1979, p. 155; in particular: V. Vinogradov, "Dostoevskij i Leskov (70-e gody XIX veak)" in *Russkaja literatura,* no. 1, 1961, pp. 63-84, no. 2, pp. 65-97; K. P. Bogaevskaja, "N. S. Leskov o Dostoevskom (1880-e gody)", *Literaturnoe nasledstvo,* vol. 86: *Dostoevskij, novye materialy i issledovanija,* Moscow: Nauka, 1973, pp. 606-620; I. P. Vidučckaja, "Dostoevskij i Leskov", *Russkaja literatura,* no. 4, 1975, pp. 127-137; E. M. Pul'xritudova, see footnote 3.

7. Quoted by H. McLean, op. cit., p. 134, from *Russkie pisateli o literature,* ed. by S. Baluxatyj, vol. II, Leningrad, 1939, p. 303.

8. See McLean, op. cit., p. 217.

9. F. M. Dostoevskij, *Pis'ma,* vol. II, Moscow-Leningrad, 1930, pp. 320-321; quoted by Leonid Grossman, *N. S. Leskov, žizn'-tvorčestvo-poètika,* Moscow: GIXL, 1945, p. 142; by H. McLean, op. cit., p. 220; in *Istorija russkogo romana,* vol. II, Moscow: Nauka, 1964, p. 421, a.o.

10. L. Grossman, op. cit., p. 141, mentions that Leskov was blamed for taking the writer Vsevolod Krestovskij as the prototype for Vislenev.

11. In his Introduction to the edition of Leskov's *Izbrannye proizvedenija,* vol. I, Berlin, Petersburg, Moscow, 1923, p. 7.

12. M. Gor'kij, *Nesobrannye literaturno-kritičeskie stat'i,* ed. by S. M. Brejtburg, Moscow, 1941, pp. 87-88; quoted by L. Grossman, op. cit., p. 143.

13. Aleksej B. Ansberg in his study "Frame Story and First Person Story in N. S. Leskov", *Scandoslavica,* vol. III, Copenhagen, 1957, p. 63, thinks *At Daggers Drawn* was written under the influence of *The Possessed,* but Leskov's work appeared in the *Russkij vestnik* just before Dostoevskij's.

14. K. A. Lantz, op. cit., p. 63.

15. Henceforth we will cite quotations from Leskov referring to the *Polnoe sobranie sočinenij,* Petersburg: A. F. Marks, 1902-1903, vol. and page number.

16. From an interview he gave only a few weeks before his death: *Novosti i birževaja gazeta,* Feb. 19, 1895; quoted by H. McLean, op. cit., p. 217.

17. In a letter from 1871 quoted by L. Grossman, op. cit., p. 144, footnote.

18. Quoted by H. McLean, op. cit., p. 191.

19. K. A. Lantz, op. cit., p. 62.

20. Although in *No Way Out* most of the female characters are negative (except the two girls in the first part and a few young women in the third part), whereas the men are much more likable (especially in the first part). On Leskov's opinion about women cf. K. A. Lantz, op. cit., p. 158, footnote.

21. N. S. Leskov, *Sobranie sočinenij,* Moscow, 1956-1958, vol. X, p. 297.

22. For example, where Gordanov warns Kišenskij: ". . . *sovetuju že vam pročee vremja života vašego skončat' v mire i pokajanii*" (XXVI, 24).

23. See A. I. Faresov, *Protiv tečenij; N. S. Leskov, ego žizn', sočinenija, polemika i vospominanija,* SPb., 1904, p. 188 (in a letter from 1887).

24. Proceedings of the "Colloque Leskov", organized by the Institut des études slaves, Paris University, June, 1981.

25. L. Grossman, op. cit., pp. 164-165, points to some reminiscences from Fénelon's *Télémaque* in Leskov's *Očarovannyj strannik*. The original newspaper version bore the title "The Enchanted Pilgrim: His Life, Experiences, Opinions, and Adventures", which is, as H. McLean remarks (op. cit., p. 252), an echo of similar titles of 18th century novels like *Gil Blas, Tom Jones,* etc. The "opinions," however, McLean adds, "are clearly those of *Tristram Shandy,* a favorite of Leskov's." Grossman mentions that in Leskov's last notebook, from 1894, there was a quote from Fénelon's *Télémaque* (ibid.). K. A. Lantz (op. cit., p. 64) writes that Leskov's longer prose narratives are "closer in form to the eighteenth-century English novel of Fielding and Sterne than to its nineteenth century counterpart."

26. Bodo Zelinsky, *Roman und Romanchronik: Strukturuntersuchungen zur Erzählkunst Nikolaj Leskovs,* Köln-Wien: Böhlau, 1970.

F. K. Jakobsh (essay date 1988)

SOURCE: Jakobsh, F. K. "The Saints of Leskov and Böll." *Germano-Slavica* 6, no. 2 (1988): 91-102.

[*In the following essay, Jakobsh compares two modern literary interpretations of a medieval moral-didactic legend: Leskov's "Skomorokh Pamfalon" and Heinrich Böll's 1953 radio play* Mönch und Räuber.]

Literary works which are deemed to be in the moralistic and didactic tradition frequently postulate an imperative of goodness and then proceed to measure the actions of characters according to these peremptory standards. One thus encounters in numerous works from the Middle Ages to those of Bertolt Brecht saints and angels, gods and judges, all benefactors of man as well as paragons of wisdom and virtue. In such instances the author circumvents defining and justifying ethical categories by operating with figures who by definition are considered to be the personification of lofty moral standards. We might therefore question whether it is appropriate to consider these works as being moralistic; they ought, more accurately, to be characterized as didactic works, since their impact is directed entirely towards propagating generally recognized ethical standards. Moreover, in some instances the "holy man" functions merely as a device for the endorsement and propagation of the author's personal commitment to a cause.

Works in a less common literary tradition, which more appropriately are called moralistic, are those where the author or the characters grapple with the very nature of moral standards and at the end a personally endorsed set of values is presented. This kind of literary work presupposes not only an author with strong commitment to ethical values, but one in the progressive reform tradition of spiritual and religious concerns, who seeks to re-examine and re-define basic standards for application in his own time and place. In the following I shall examine a story which was initially conceived to deal with such concerns, and newer versions thereof, which have also been written for a similar purpose. The initial version of the story was written in the early Middle Ages, and more recently it has been adapted and re-told in French, Russian and German.

The story in question is Greek in origin, and is commonly dated from about the ninth century, although it probably is based on an older legend.[1] The earliest available version is contained in the *Synaxarion,* a liturgical breviary in the Orthodox Church for the moral and religious edification of the faithful. In the following centuries it circulated widely, appearing in numerous manuscripts with slight variations throughout the realm of the Greek Church. By the twelfth or thirteenth century it is available in Russian translation, within the *Prolog,* a compendium of stories arranged by feast days in the ecclesiastical calendar of the Russian Orthodox Church.[2] In accordance with the Byzantine cult of the saints, this story is the abbreviated life of a relatively unknown saint, part hagiography, part panegyric, part moral lesson, told in a child-like, artless form.

According to its simplest account the ancient story relates the following events: Theodulus the Stylite was a highly esteemed fourth-century prefect of Constantinople, when he resolved to devote himself to God by spending the remainder of his life on a pillar near Edessa. After forty years of this anchorite self-mortification, and attaining what religious people in his time considered the highest degree of holiness, he was prompted by divine revelation to seek a kindred holy man in Damascus. Theodulus finds the man, Cornelius, whom he considers far from saintly, since he is a mere entertainer for the nightly merriment of revelers in public houses. Only after extracting the story of Cornelius' life, which abounds in self-abnegating acts of charity, is Theodulus prepared to accept the entertainer as the saintly man of God and as his equal in Christian virtue. Having gained this insight from the encounter with Cornelius, Theodulus returns to his pillar to resume the asceticism of an anchorite holy man.

It is remarkable that the saintly monk at the end of the story is totally oblivious of the purpose of his encounter, and the pious author of this early version seems to have missed entirely the implications of his own material. Juxtaposing two totally different conceptions of holiness can only be for purposes of contrast, and since one of these was even recommended in revelation, there can be little doubt as to which of these is the more meritorious. The hidden meaning of the story therefore must be seen as a critical evaluation of certain monastic practices, as well as a reprimand to establishment conceptions of what constitutes the essence of Christian virtue. In its basic structure and purpose the story is not unlike other extended metaphors advocating Christian piety, such as the parable of the Good Samaritan.

While this parabolic story had received widespread circulation throughout the Eastern Church, and had survived in the *Prolog* into recent times, it was virtually unknown outside of church circles, especially in the West. Here it was revived for the first time by a nineteenth-century French journalist and author of philosophical essays, Ernest Hello, who included it in his *Physionomies de saints,* published in 1875.[3] Like many of the other "lives of saints" in this collection, the story of the two disparate holy men was presumably gleaned from Eastern Church sources.

On little more than three pages Hello sketches an episode from the life of Saint Paphnuce, an ancient holy man of the desert, who seeks his equal among saints, and in response is directed by voices to see "un musicien qui chante dans un village a quelque distance d'Heraclee."[4] When Paphnuce locates the man, he finds someone who does not correspond to his ideals of saintliness, a lowly tavern entertainer. Only after repeated prodding does the singer finally speak about himself, and he relates two acts of supreme charity. At this point the story breaks off, and the author of the story proceeds to expound on the lessons contained therein, which culminates in the observation: "Many live in hate, who believe they are in love; many believe they are in hate, who are in love."

It would do an injustice to Hello if one were to examine this story for its literary merit, since the author sought only to convey simple religious sentiments, just as the ancient legend did. He even reduced the scope of the original story, did not attempt to make it more contemporary or relevant for his readers, focusing only on one aspect and then expounding at length the moral to be drawn from that incident. But since the author presents it in such abbreviated form, the broader impact of the original material is entirely lost. We are not informed, for instance, what conclusion Paphnuce draws from this encounter, and what its implication might be for his perception of himself. And even the author's concluding homily, while clearly intending to convey that the secular singer is in the state of "love," leaves open whether Paphnuce is his equal or one of those others who only "believe they are in love." Hello has succeeded in reviving the fascinating story of the disparate saints for Western readers, but he failed entirely to recognize the implications of that legend, both in terms of its literary as well as its moral potential.

For a version that does greater justice to the material, attempting to bring the legend of the two saints "out of moth balls" for contemporary readers, we must turn to a version of the story published twelve years later, in 1887, by the Russian writer Nikolaj Leskov. Although Leskov had read extensively Western writings of a religious nature, there is no evidence that he encountered any of Ernest Hello's works. On the other hand, the Protestant tradition of Western Europe did influence him greatly,[5] as did Tolstoy's provocative spiritual ideals.[6] It seems obvious that his interest in this legendary subject was prompted by a certain spiritual affinity with the mildly iconoclastic religious figure of the unpretentious saint. For some time prior to writing this story he had been grappling with religious ideals. From the mid 1870s on his works revolve around righteous men (*pravedniki*), whose values are derived from individual conscience and personal faith. It is within this context that he publishes an updated rendition of the medieval legend under the title **"Skomorokh Pamfalon."**

In its formal features and detailed observations Leskov's story purports to be little more than a translation of the ancient *Prolog* tale, albeit of an "ancient unabridged" version rather than the common one available in nineteenth-century Russia. The language is frequently archaic, characters are medieval, dialogues rather stilted or tedious, and the plot is clumsy. But these are merely devices in the hands of a skilled author who uses them to imbue his story with an aura of authenticity, as are the numerous details he added to the original account. Apparently Leskov undertook extensive historical research relating to the legend prior to writing **"Skomorokh Pamfalon."**[7] Moreover, his account of the two saints has been expanded to many times the original length. As a result the updated version which Leskov published can be readily understood by contemporary readers, retains the characteristic attributes of an ancient tale, and clearly seeks to make a point on matters of a religious or moral nature.

In addition to the countless details embellishing the story, the most notable deviation from the *Prolog* version involves the two central characters. This is already indicated in the names he gives them. Theodulus the contemplative stylite is called Hermius in the Leskov story, while Cornelius the entertainer now has the unusual name of Pamfalon.

Pamfalon is not just any entertainer, but a "Skomorokh"—the designation is peculiarly Russian and untranslatable. Attempts at rendering the name in English have yielded terms such as mountebank, buffoon, juggler, clown, and singer.[8] The "Skomorokhi" were medieval minstrels and travelling performers who provided rustic entertainment for the peasantry and common folk. By placing Pamfalon in this fascinating Russian tradition Leskov has not only embued the story with authentic flavour, but revived specific historical associations. The significance of this designation becomes clear when one realizes that throughout their history the "Skomorokhi" were subjected to vicious suppression by the state church. And while the established religious authorities sought to discredit them as immoral vagabonds, they were greatly loved in outlying regions for their imaginative songs, narrations, and performing acts. Thus the mere name conjures up associations central to the very theme of the story.

Moreover, while in all previous accounts the story focused on the religious man, the title now raises Pamfalon to a position of preeminence. In the initial version Leskov had sought to make the hero even more sympathetic by calling the story **"The Tale of a God-pleasing Skomorokh."** This shift of emphasis brings about the peculiar constellation which has Pamfalon as the title figure of the story, while in every other respect Hermius undoubtedly is the main figure.

Hermius retains the main attributes of Theodulus except for the benign resignation at the end of the story. The reasons for this deviation are presented near the beginning, when Hermius repeatedly asks God to show him his equal among men. That question is posed out of a despair regarding this world, a concern that goodness has become extinct and the realm of blessed eternity will be rather deserted. At this point the monk is convinced of his own perfection and secure in the vain knowledge that he is the only good man left on earth. It is in response to this boastful attitude that God sends him to find Pamfalon. Upon returning to his desert perch, there is then no comfort for him in the realization that others are good—as was the case with the saint in the medieval legend. Instead, he is now greatly

troubled and acutely aware of his own imperfection, since he realizes that in terms of sanctity he is inferior to Pamfalon, and the years spent in self-mortification are of no credit whatsoever. When Hermius then finds that a flock of birds has nested on the pillar he formerly occupied, he says: "That is how it should be, . . . birds should live among the crags and men should serve men."[9] With this he abandons his ascetic life and spends the remaining years in prayer and useful activity among the people in the neighbourhood by herding their goats and teaching their children.

In terms of characterization, Pamfalon is a rather medieval "absolute" figure, forever unchanging in his natural goodness. By contrast Hermius is a modern character who develops as he learns from his experiences. He had earlier rejected the life of high society for the contemplative life in search of self-perfection as idealized by the Orthodox Church. But this brought him only distant admiration from people and an overbearing sense of righteousness. The encounter with the ever generous Pamfalon leads him to another re-evaluation, a spiritual awakening which prompts him to abandon asceticism in favour of humble service for his fellow man.

With this portrayal Leskov presents a concrete manifestation of his own spiritual ideals, the result of his life-long quest for "ideal Christianity."[10] The ideals of the Orthodox Church are rejected as a gross misconception of true Christianity, and in its stead he postulates a Protestant outlook along with Tolstoyan simplicity in the service of man. What has been called his "subversively anti-Orthodox moral"[11] permeates this entire story, to the point of oversimplifying the complex structure of the old legend. Not only does Hermius come to this realization, but Pamfalon is the personification thereof, and even God points towards it. The conflict of values as represented by two divergent saints has thereby been resolved in favour of the humble saint, and making Pamfalon the title-hero of the story amounts to a virtual overstatement of this moral. What nevertheless makes the story a "literary crown-jewel of all times and languages,"[12] as Johannes von Guenther called it, are the majestically archaic expressions, the sincerity of the pursuit of righteousness, and the subtle blending of ancient and modern elements, not only in form and content, but also in technique.

The most recent version of the disparate saints was written by Heinrich Böll in the 1953 radio drama *Mönch und Räuber* (it initially appeared under the title *Der Heilige und der Räuber*). Although the author is familiar with Russian literature and the Pamfalon story was available in German translation, he disclaimed any knowledge of the Leskov story at the time of writing the play.[13] There also is no evidence whatsoever of influence from that direction. On the other hand, Hello and his sketch of Paphnuce are quite familiar to Böll. It is peculiar that only in one edition of the play does he acknowledge this indebtedness, and then with the sub-title, *Hörspiel nach einer Legende von Hello.*[14] The familiarity with Hello most likely stems from the fact that both share a common philosophical outlook, they are frequently referred to as "Catholic writers" in the reform tradition. Carl Amery even speaks of Böll as a "Catholic revolutionary"[15] in the sense that he opposes recent social structures which threaten the traditional order of the human condition. This entire outlook has certainly been in the foreground of most commentaries on Böll's work, including the Nobel laudatio; however, it must be remembered that this play was written only in 1953, and therefore does not as yet possess many prominent features of his later oeuvre. It remains to be seen to what extent this work manifests the author's stated religious outlook.

From Hello Böll borrows the basic story of the two saints and a few key passages. Around this barren framework he constructs an elaborate radio play, involving twelve characters, numerous sub-plots, and sixteen chronological dialogue scenes. The authoritative 1953 production of the play (NWDR/SDR) has a duration of 65 minutes.

In the writings of Heinrich Böll this play represents a unique deviation, for the author who is otherwise renowned as one who only deals with contemporary German themes, here delves into a legendary subject. Yet the subject is not as remotely legendary as the other versions we have examined. The play is a parable only to the extent that the story makes no claim of its own representative reality, intending instead to typify moral and spiritual relations in the tradition of allegory. Beyond this, figures and events are quite realistic as well as contemporary. We might therefore call it a contemporary legend, since the setting is entirely within the scope of familiarity to the listening audience. But then the place setting removes events into a somewhat exotic realm, not specifically determined, but reminiscent of Eastern or South-Eastern Europe by the names of people and places, names such as Milutin, Baitha, Beguna, and Murdien.

In this remote mountainous region the monk Eugen, an old abbot in lugubrious isolation, is reminiscing about one of the most remarkable incidents in his life. In essence the entire play is Eugen's lengthy retrospective monologue about his life-long relationship to Mulz—otherwise called Milutin. The innocuous soliloquy is interjected with relatively short scenes, in which specific incidents come to life by means of acoustic blend and dialogue scenes involving the various characters. The first two and the last of these scenes involve the central characters.

In the early scenes the two are young boys, Eugen the son of a prosperous farmer, and Mulz the neglected son

of a robber. It is this family background which determines their entire future: Eugen attends school and church, which leads him directly into a monastery, while Mulz inevitably falls in with a gang of robbers and ends in jail. From this point on, however, their development is less predictable.

Eugen rises rapidly in his field, as abbot of his order he attains success as a leader, the respect of his peers, and a reputation as a saintly man of God. But upon reaching the apex of his career he feels isolated and dissatisfied, perhaps even uncertain about the value of his accomplishments in life. It is as a means of gaining certainty about himself in relation to others that he asks God at this point to show him his equal among men, and is told to find Milutin in the distant village of a neighbouring region.

What Hello had summarized as: "Il approche du village, il arrive; il demande le musicien," Böll develops into six scenes, as Eugen undertakes his troublesome search for the unknown saint. No one knows of such a holy man, and the church authorities along the way discourage and even mock his endeavour. When he finally locates him, a humble bar entertainer, it turns out to be his boyhood friend Mulz under his more formal name.

Eugen ascertains that Milutin/Mulz has led a capricious life, but in the past ten years he has been a beloved friend and helper to all the poor in the village. While a bar performer of entertaining ballads in his working hours, he offers all his time and money to aid the underprivileged around him. For this he is recognized as a saintly man by the working poor, but to the church authorities he as well as the people he associates with are the unworthy degenerates of an impoverished mining village. When Eugen becomes aware of the implications to be derived from what he has seen and heard, he is content and stealthily returns home. But there he renounces all his offices, and spends his remaining years in a distant monastic cell praying and meditating on the dictum (familiar from Hello, originally uttered by Angele de Foligno): Many live in hate, who believe they are in love; many believe they are in hate, who are in love.

The resolution Böll offers at the end of the play is somewhat problematic. As was the case in the Hello sketch, one inevitably associates the contrastive pair of Milutin-Eugen with those paradigmatic people who are said to be in "love" and in "hate." Both pairs draw attention to a fundamental contrast, and Milutin certainly is an illustration of those who think they are rejected while in fact they are loved by God. But can Eugen be said to be a representative of the other, as consistency would lead one to conclude? The story does not seem to allow such an equation, and Eugen does not determine in the end (as Hermius did in the Leskov story) that he was on the wrong track, for he does not abandon his monastic life, nor undertake any other drastic deviations from his pattern of life.

But neither does Eugen just resume his monastic life, as the monk in the *Prolog* had done. He is ill at ease in the former role, critical of his active life, seeking peace of mind. As a result of this he renounces all his offices upon returning to the abbey, and then becomes even more withdrawn. The summary of his final state of mind is reflected in his concluding words, which we might see as the wisdom of the old saint:

> Ich zog mich in eins unserer Klöster oben in die Baitha zurück, hörte den Wind wie in meiner Jugend dort heulen, sah die mageren Euter der Kühe, und ich verbringe den Rest meines Lebens in Gebet und in Betrachtung über den Satz: "Viele wohnen in Haß, welche glauben, in der Liebe zu wohnen, viele glauben in Haß zu wohnen, welche in der Liebe wohnen."

There is no remorse or resignation in this, nor any attempt to emulate Milutin, only the desire to meditate and contemplate the mystery of the affirmation from Foligno. Eugen in effect becomes a mystic in the end, not unlike the Buddhist monk or wise man who withdraws from society to ponder the nature of the universe. He has reached the state of enlightenment.

Since social activism as well as spiritual re-orientation have been excluded as lessons to be drawn from the encounter with Milutin, we are left with no obvious message to deduce at the end. Böll has only sensitized his audience to an issue, namely one that has to do with the nature of morality and spirituality. Instead of reducing the message to a single denominator, as Leskov had done, this story once again points in two directions, just as the early legend had. The one value certainly is social morality derived from private conscience, as exemplified by Milutin in his inconspicuous way. But the play also points to faith as a socially oriented phenomenon, as represented by the institutionalized church Eugen serves, as well as to the vast realm of personal spirituality to which he in the end dedicates himself. The former obviously is laudable, but not to the exclusion of the latter. In terms of Christian virtues, Milutin stands for love of fellow man, and Eugen for love of God, the two of them encompassing the grand commandment of Jesus. This is the spiritual insight Eugen has gained. So there is no need for conflict or choice between them, they are complimentary parts of one ideal.

One distinction between the Leskov version and that of Böll is already highlighted parenthetically in the titles. At the end of the story Leskov suspends the inherent dualism of the two saints, concentrating attention on the values represented by Pamfalon, to which the more traditional religiosity of Hermius and the church are mere digressions to be overcome. For Böll, on the other hand, the dualism of the ancient legend is retained in the title. We must conclude, however, that both the title and its implied dualism are highly problematic. First of all, the reference to Milutin as a robber is deceiving: while he may have been a member of such a gang at one time, he does not now nor ever did possess the characteristic attributes normally associated with this totally pejorative designation. Furthermore, the dualism of the play does not focus attention on conflicting values as represented by Eugen the monk and Milutin the robber. These two men have indeed been representatives of different worlds all their lives, but these differences are insignificant to the central theme the play dwells on. Instead of with Milutin the robber, Böll contrasts Eugen with Milutin the ex-robber, now singer and religious iconoclast, just as Hello and Leskov had done. The title and the dualism implied by it are therefore most inappropriate. It would appear that Böll has sought here to exaggerate unnecessarily the differences between the two figures.

Despite such minor flaws, Böll's *Mönch und Räuber* is a most remarkable play. Not that its structure and form are even remotely interesting, for this was an early work and his first attempt at writing an original radio play (if we may call it original). It is his subtle treatment of the legend, imbuing the ancient story with insight into contemporary spirituality, which makes it profound. And he has succeeded in dramatizing a most difficult subject. Quite obviously he must have been pleased with the result, because Böll was prompted by it success to write other radio plays with religious themes. As a matter of fact, it is quite remarkable that his obviously religious themes without exception are henceforth written in the form of radio plays.

We may now draw some conclusions from our discussion.

The medieval legend of the recognized saint and the private holy man was told simply to draw attention to the goodness of the latter, that he too was worthy of salvation. That message is so simple, that it is incompatible with the elaborate dualism determined by the structure of the plot. One can only conjecture that the medieval writer borrowed a rather involved story and reduced it to a simplistic moral. Hello re-told the story on that simple level, adding only an invocation to ponder the moral of the story. These versions we may simply call religious tracts for spiritual edification; they are relatively inconsequential except for their historical value and as raw material for more recent literary writers.

The two literary writers of recent times, Leskov and Böll, used the story of the legend merely as a plot-outline, around which each created an elaborately structured literary work, which in turn serves as a means for deeper reflection on the nature of the ultimate goodness.

The divergent direction of their moral reflection is quite fascinating. Of the two, Leskov draws the more consistent and radical conclusion. For him the comparison of the two figures allows only a choice between them, and he comes out strongly in favour of Pamfalon. He thereby makes a plea for a re-evaluation of religious values in the Protestant tradition, in that Hermius the monk not only abandons monasticism, but experiences something tantamount to a conversion which determines the direction of his life henceforth. Religious institutions no longer play an important role in this life, instead he emphasizes a spiritual life that is governed by his personal relationship with his God. Within this context the nature of goodness or the ultimate sanctity consists of being in communion with God and helping one's fellow man.

Böll aims for a conclusion which virtually is at variance with the old legend. The dualistic structure of the ancient parable, which Leskov had so effectively integrated for contrast, is here nothing more than a superficial and even largely distractive interpolation. Eugen and Milutin/Mulz are compared rather than contrasted, and found to be complementary. The reference to them as monk and robber is totally inappropriate, and the proverbial juxtaposing of the two groups at the end of the play does not correspond to the characterization of the figures. The two holy men are life-long friends, sharing common goals, and each accepting the other as his equal or more worthy of merit. The meeting between them only confirms them in their respective goodness and concludes in an all-embracing harmony. It therefore follows that the play does not yield any conclusions from contrast. But then, after the encounter between them, Böll adds a second conclusion, one which is totally unrelated to any comparison between the two. When Eugen, after returning to the monastery, relinquishes his various offices and religious functions, he makes a parenthetic statement about his life. This step remains totally unmotivated and unexplained. It relates to his life only insofar as he had previously been uneasy about his true worth, when he had sought to meet a kindred spirit. Now an older and wiser man, Eugen renounces all power and success, preferring instead that mystical tranquility which transcends all such discriminative involvements as social or religious activism, intellectualizing, or even partaking in social intercourse. In a strange way, we have come full circle, Eugen in the end is as remote as the ancient stylite monk.

It is obvious that neither Leskov nor Böll has sought to persuade his readers/listeners in a didactic manner. We might conclude that the nature of the content simply does not lend itself to such aims, since we are dealing with spiritual and thereby largely private matters. But these authors also manifest rather peculiar attitudes towards their public. Rather than act as teacher or propagandist, they function as poets, conveying their message by analogy, offering insight, seeking to evoke a highly personal response. In the Leskov story we can still detect a somewhat argumentative position, but in Böll's play even that has been entirely eradicated. Here we are left with the absolute moralistic position without didactic intent, seeking only to grope towards spiritual truth as it is meaningful to an individual in the context of his life and time. This attitude is not only moralistic, it is also in the best tradition of literature.

Notes

1. This may be concluded from the fact that the source in which it first appears also contains stories based on ancient Far Eastern and Near Eastern legends, such as those of the Buddha and of Oedipus.

2. For more detailed information on the *Prolog* see, Stephen S. Lottridge, "Nikolaj Leskov and the Russian *Prolog* as a Literary Source," *Russian Literature* 3 (1972), 16-39.

3. Hello is virtually unknown outside of Catholic circles. The said book is still available in a newer edition: Ernest Hello, *Physionomies de saints* (Paris: Perrin, 1921). The relevant part of the story of Saint Paphnuce is on pp. 79-82.

4. Ernest Hello, *Physionomies de saints* (Paris: Perrin, 1921), p. 79.

5. William B. Edgerton, "Leskov's Trip Abroad in 1875," *Indiana Slavic Studies* 4 (1967), 88-99.

6. William B. Edgerton, "Leskov and Tolstoy: Two Literary Heretics," *American Slavic and East European Review* 12 (1953), 524-34.

7. Vsevolod Setschkareff, *N. S. Leskov: Sein Leben und Werk* (Wiesbaden: Harrassowitz, 1959), p. 126.

8. It should be noted, that these terms have been used in secondary literature, with reference to the story or the figure, since the story has not appeared in English translation.

9. N. S. Leskov, *Sobranie sochinenii v odinnadtsati tomakh,* vol. 8 (Moscow, 1956-1958), p. 230.

10. E. Heier, in *Religious Schism in the Russian Aristocracy 1860-1900* (The Hague: Nijhoff, 1970), pp. 67-76, discusses Leskov as one who was preoccupied, especially in his later years, with the quest for "ideal Christianity."

11. Hugh McLean, *Nikolai Leskov: The Man and His Art* (London, Cambridge: Harvard, 1977), p. 566.

12. Johannes von Guenther, in the epilogue to his own translation of *Nikolai Lesskov, Der Gaukler Pamphalon* (Stuttgart: Reclam, 1953), p. 94.

13. Heinz Schwitzke, *Reclams Hörspielführer* (Stuttgart: Reclam, 1969), p. 89.

14. The edition in question is the official one, contained in the volume *Heinrich Böll Werke: Hörspiele, Theaterstücke, Drehbücher, Gedichte I* (Köln: Kiepenheuer & Witsch, 1978), p. 125.

15. Carl Amery, "Eine christliche Position," in *In Sachen Böll: Ansichten und Einsichten,* ed. Marcel Reich-Ranicki (Köln: Kiepenheuer & Witsch, 1968), p. 94.

Larry R. Andrews (essay date winter 1994)

SOURCE: Andrews, Larry R. "Hugo's Gilliatt and Leskov's Golovan: Two Folk-Epic Heroes." *Comparative Literature* 46, no. 1 (winter 1994): 65-83.

[*In the following essay, Andrews compares similar treatments of altruistic heroes in Leskov's* Deathless Golovan *and Victor Hugo's 1866 novel* Toilers of the Sea, *investigating the possible influence of Hugo on Leskov and key differences in their respective narratives.*]

Midway through his literary career Nikolaj Leskov set out to create a series of positive heroes for nineteenth-century Russia. Among his most impressive "righteous men" (*pravedniki*) is the "immortal" Golovan, protagonist of the 1880 novella *Nesmertel'nyj Golovan: iz rasskazov o trex pravednikax* (*Deathless Golovan: from Tales of Three Righteous Men*). At the end of the sixth chapter Leskov's narrator, a transparently autobiographical representation of Leskov himself, introduces an impromptu digression that enthusiastically compares Golovan to Victor Hugo's Gilliatt, protagonist of his 1866 novel *Les travailleurs de la mer*:

> When I avidly went through the pages of Victor Hugo's novel *Toilers of the Sea* and encountered Gilliatt with his severity toward himself and indulgence toward others (outlined with such genius), having attained the height of perfect selflessness, I was struck not only by the grandeur of this cast of mind and the power of his portrayal, but also by the identity [*toždestvom*] of the Guernsey hero with the living person I knew by the name of Golovan. One spirit lived in them, and their similar hearts both beat with a selfless impulse. Nor did they differ much in their fate: a sort of mystery grew thick about them their whole life just because they were too pure and clear, and there fell to the lot of one as well as the other not one bit of personal happiness.
>
> (*Sobr. Soč* [*Sobranie sočinenij*] 6:372; my translation here and subsequently)

This paragraph is striking because of its abrupt interruption of the story; it seems a spontaneous and happy recognition. Chapter 7 opens immediately thereafter

with a further juxtaposition of the two characters' unorthodox positions vis-à-vis organized religion. A comparative study of the two characters, starting from Leskov's own remarks and including not only their striking similarities but also their equally striking differences, suggests that the two are folk-epic heroes with a peculiar twist: they have certain personal quirks or eccentricities and they are situated inappropriately in a problematic and unheroic social environment, a world that no longer seems to produce or support heroes. The comparison also suggests that Leskov's conception of his character and its literary vehicle is the more original, if less powerful, of the two. Further, speculation about influence suggests that, much as Leskov apparently admired Hugo's work, his conception of Golovan and the literary form that embodies him was more probably rooted in his own reminiscences and native traditions.

In the text of the story Leskov's comparisons of the two characters are unusually direct; he makes few other literary allusions (e.g., a quotation from an old Russian tale and a mention that Golovan had memorized Pope's *Essay on Man*[1]). Leskov's comparison is also entirely positive—he mentions no differences between the two characters and speaks of them with unqualified praise. Leskov also speaks as if comparing indiscriminately a literary character (Hugo's) to someone in real life, supporting his claim to be writing a biographical sketch ("I want to try to put down on paper what I have known and heard about him [Golovan] so that in this way his memory, so worthy of notice, will endure in the world" (*Sobr. Soč* 6:352).

The context of the comparison with Gilliatt in Chapter 6 is Golovan's most legendary exploit in the eyes of the villagers, an exploit which epitomized Golovan's selflessness: during the plague he had cut off a piece of his own flesh and cast it into the river, supposedly as a propitiatory sacrifice to save the people. (We find out later that he had simply cut off a plague sore to save himself, though he had, in fact, tended plague victims at great risk.) The comparison with Gilliatt (cited earlier) crowns this story and heightens the image of heroism it conveys.

The context of the comparison in Chapter 7 is Golovan's "free-thinking"—his tolerant, deistic quasi-Protestantism that partly reflects Leskov's own beliefs at the time. And again the viewpoint is that of the common people, who are baffled by Golovan's friendship with the Jew Juška and the "crazy" freethinker, Anton the astronomer: "Golovan, like Gilliatt, appeared 'doubtful in faith'" (6:373). The quotation marks, the use of *sumnitelen* instead of *somnitelen,* and the verb "appeared" suggest the people's view, not that of the reliable author-narrator. Two pages later, to crown the peasants' doubts about Golovan's orthodoxy, Leskov mentions the uncertainty of his parish membership, an uncertainty created when Golovan's hut slid part way down a hill and apparently crossed the parish boundary. Here the comparison with Gilliatt is very precise; when questioned insistently about his parish affiliation (about which he seemed quite indifferent), Golovan would say:

> "I'm of the parish of the Almighty Creator"—but there was no such church in all Orel.
>
> Gilliatt, in reply to the question of where his parish was, just raised his finger and, pointing to the sky, said:
>
> "Up there," but the essence of both these replies was one and the same.

$$(6:375)^2$$

Golovan does, however, visit the priest for "confession" when he is dissatisfied with himself, and the priest affirms that "his conscience is whiter than snow" (6:375). The comparisons with Gilliatt help round out the end of the first half of the story, the general and anecdotal characterization of Golovan, before Leskov focuses on the religious pilgrimage to the unveiling of a new relic.

What essential similarities between the two heroes does Leskov emphasize in these passages? The most important is their altruism. Both men set high standards for themselves—Golovan's good deeds and sexual continence and Gilliatt's heroic conduct—but have compassion for others' weaknesses. Leskov cites many examples of Golovan's "perfect selflessness" (*soveršennogo samootverženija*): purchasing his family out of serfdom, succoring the plague victims, turning the other cheek to the insults of his rival Fotej, renouncing carnal love with Pavla, sharing "bread from his own hunk indiscriminately with everyone who asked" (6:373), and finally drowning in a cesspool while trying to save someone's life or property in a fire. Hugo's Gilliatt serves the community as a sailor, saves the lives of Landoys and of his eventual rival Caudray, rescues Lethierry's boat engine and money with heroic physical and mental labors, and then renounces his love for Déruchette, the prize his efforts have won, when he discovers that she loves another. He goes so far as to arrange Déruchette's quick marriage, provide a ring and the trousseau intended for his own bride, and then efface himself in suicide. The moral purity of both characters lends them "sublimity" or "grandeur" (*veličiem*)—an aesthetic appeal—as positive ethical and epic heroes. They are prototypes of the possibility of human greatness among the common people.

Precisely because both characters are "too pure and clear" compared to the society around them and are quiet, even taciturn men, their lives seem mysterious, even miraculous—their second point in common. The common people in both novels tend to exaggerate the heroes' virtues and distort their motives with superstitious assumptions. Thus in both cases the authors show not only the substance of a folk hero but also his accrued legend in the perceptions of others. Throughout his story Leskov often focuses more on these perceptions of Golovan than on Golovan himself, suggesting that he is equally interested in characterizing the mentality of the folk surrounding his hero. Hugo's early characterization of Gilliatt stresses the mystery of his foreign background, his isolation from the native Guernseyites, his taciturnity and dreaminess, and his reputation as an uncannily expert sailor. His practical knowledge of sailing, gardening, and the weather earns him the distrust of the Guernseyites, who regard him as a sorcerer, a *marcou*. When Gilliatt returns triumphant from the rescue, Lethierry suggests that the common people might with justice look on him as demonic for his incredible feat: "Mais comment as-tu fait? Tout le diantre était contre toi, le vent et la marée, la marée et le vent. C'est vrai que tu es sorcier. Ceux qui disent ça ne sont déjà pas si bêtes" (3: 201-02). Although, or perhaps because, the people in both stories find these heroes somewhat alien beings, they consult them for advice and willingly grant them mythical status as heroes.

Their third similarity is their inability to achieve "one bit of personal happiness," expressed in their unfulfilled loves. Golovan is forcibly separated from his youthful love, Pavla, when their master sends him to the army and marries her off to Fotej. Later he takes her into his household when she has been abandoned and left destitute by her husband. Although the villagers refer to her as "Golovan's sin" (*Golovanovym grexom*), he has maintained a chaste relationship with her because she is still married. Hugo's Gilliatt endures a tacit, four-year love for Déruchette and undertakes his grand rescue in order to win her as a bride. At the end, however, she has fallen in love with the clergyman Caudray, and he learns of this love in the most painful way at the most ironic moment. The loss of his love directly motivates his suicide.

Finally, although Leskov sees both characters as examples of Christian altruism, he points out that neither possesses conventional faith or adherence to an established church. Leskov was moving in this Tolstoyan direction perhaps sooner than Tolstoy himself. His righteous men can express their uprightness outside the bounds of organized religion, partly *because* they are independent of it. Golovan's ethical values transcend church attitudes about parish boundaries, the sectarians, and the sacraments. Gilliatt, too, in pointing to the sky as his parish, expresses both his Revolutionary background and Hugo's skepticism toward the church. Gilliatt transcends the narrow views of both Anglican and Catholic residents of the island. His parish is cosmic creation itself, and most of his drama occurs in the vast context of the sea, sky, and animal life. The portrayal of both Golovan and Gilliatt emphasizes less their doubts than their positive faith in life and in a power greater than themselves.

Besides these similarities to which Leskov explicitly calls attention, the two heroes share other qualities as well. Both are common workmen of the lower middle class—Golovan the dairyman and Gilliatt the fisherman and gardener—in a rural setting close to nature.[3] Both authors here and in other works (the left-handed gunsmith from Tula and Jean Valjean come to mind) show enormous respect for work and for practical know-how and good sense. Leskov emphasizes Golovan's practical skills in expanding his herd of cows and giving good advice to others about cures and dowsing. Hugo catalogs in expansive detail Gilliatt's knowledge of gardening, the weather, and the sea, his carpentry and smithing skills, and his amazing resourcefulness in saving the wrecked Durande. Furthermore, both men are physically healthy and strong, except for Golovan's game leg. Both act with heroic courage in a physical struggle with the elements—Golovan with the plague and the Orel fire and Gilliatt with the sea, the storm, and the giant octopus. Both demonstrate what Leskov describes as the sudden emergence of folk heroes in times of crisis:

> In such sorrowful times of general disaster the folk puts forth from its midst heroes of great spirit, fearless and selfless people. In ordinary times they are invisible and often stand out in no way from the crowd; but when a "pimple" [*pupyrušek*—a colorful colloquialism for a plague sore] has a go at people, the folk puts forth a chosen one, and he works wonders that make him a mythical, legendary, "deathless" figure.
>
> (6:364)

In addition to these folk-heroic qualities, both characters also possess similar personal quirks. Both men are extremely neat and tidy in their personal habits. Both combine with their skills and practical shrewdness a certain innocence and simplicity. Both seem abnormally shy around women and are, in fact, virgins. Both are viewed as odd and set apart from normal society, and their physical dwellings are set apart spatially and looked on as peculiar (Golovan's) or haunted (Gilliatt's).

The literary vehicles that dramatize the two heroes are also similar in some ways. Both stories are narrated at a historical distance from the events. Leskov constantly refers to "those days" of what must have been the 1830s and 1840s and tries to recapture what life was like in old Orel. Hugo writes of the Guernsey of 40 years earlier (1820s), contrasting it with present-day (1860s) conditions. This historical distance in both cases enhances the "legendary" quality of the heroes and may imply, especially in Hugo's case, that present times are no longer capable of producing such heroes. As a corol-

lary, both works also have local color as part of their design. Leskov's eye always wanders from his protagonist to the general customs and conditions of life, the *byt,* surrounding him. He pauses lovingly over minor characters and describes at length a religious festival whose connection to his hero primarily is a contrast. Hugo wrote a long prologue on the channel islands that he eventually decided to publish separately. And with his customary amplification, he frequently pauses in the novel itself to describe weather and sea conditions around Guernsey, the state of trade, local superstitions, local flora, and technical details of labor. Both works thus have a digressive narrative style, and in both, local color—important and interesting in its own right—also establishes a base in the people and their way of life for the emergence of a folk hero and the popular legends surrounding him.

In both works, too, the narrators strike an autobiographical stance, creating in **Golovan** what McLean calls an "ambiguous fictionality" (95). The narrator's point of departure in **Golovan** is an early childhood memory of Golovan's rescuing him from a mad dog. Leskov's home town of Orel furnishes the setting, his grandmother and uncle appear as characters who can tell him about Golovan, and the narrator refers directly to later events in Leskov's life as if it were his own. The author-narrator also freely offers opinions and generalizations on his material ("Great personal disaster is a bad teacher of charity," 6:364). Notably, Leskov does not use his *skaz* technique, with its colorful and unreliable narrator, here or in most of the *pravedniki* stories. Hugo also obviously speaks out of his experience and love of the island that gave him refuge during his years of political exile and to which he dedicated his novel. As narrator he refers to himself as a resident and to his earlier writings, and, in typical Hugolian fashion, never resists an opportunity to expatiate at large on a subject. Both narrators are also great lovers of language, including archaisms, colloquialisms, and trade jargon. This metadiscourse, this authorial presence dominating both works, is characterized abundantly by ironic distance. The educated narrators ultimately speak of uneducated commoners from the outside, with a mixture of admiration for their colorfulness, strength, and virtue and tongue-in-cheek irony regarding their superstitiousness and ignorance. Both authors find models of moral excellence in their folk heroes and models of stupidity and rascality (Leskov's Fotej) or hypocrisy and evil (Hugo's Clubin) in secondary characters. Both authors satirize institutionalized religion.

Less obviously, both works mix epic and novelistic genres in attempting to portray the possibility of heroism in an unheroic age. Marjorie Ferry, in her excellent dissertation applying narrative theory of Georg Lukàcs to Leskov's *pravedniki* tales, shows convincingly that **Deathless Golovan** and ten other tales experimentally combine the epic conception of a moral hero with a novelistic conception of a problematic, amoral world. The resulting hybrid "is designed to provide concrete evidence of the existence of a wholeness behind the chaos of Russian life" (Ferry 148; the tension between the two is explored further by Luigi Volta). His personal eccentricities make Golovan more of an individual than the traditional epic hero, though his positive qualities still make him rather static as a result of Leskov's quasi-hagiographic approach. At the same time Leskov redeems the work's didacticism from utopianism by showing that the protagonist's moral wholeness is "already active in the midst of a more novelistically interpreted society"; the protagonist realistically demonstrates a "successful existence in and occasional opposition to a seemingly meaningless world" (Ferry 148).[4] Gilliatt, too, represents an individuated folk hero who is contrasted, in his straightforward simplicity, with the problematic nineteenth-century world of criminality, class stratification, and disillusionment, as well as to such metaphysical problems as the ambiguity of destruction and creation in the forces of nature. In calling attention to the latter theme, Victor Brombert acknowledges that the novel has an epic intention and tone and that Gilliatt has the traits of the mythical hero engaged in a quest. But he further suggests that this "pattern of myth points to spiritual rather than strictly epic values," thus justifying the work's description as a "visionary novel" (150-52).

This account of the similarities of character and genre must, however, be heavily qualified. The same four qualities that Leskov singles out for resemblance of character also reveal significant differences. Although Leskov praises Gilliatt's "severity toward himself and indulgence toward others," altruism is not so clearly Gilliatt's key virtue as it is Golovan's. In addition to his service to others, Gilliatt is also competitive, as in the boat race. Above all, his main heroic feat, the rescue of the Durande, is motivated more by the desire to obtain Lethierry's niece as his wife than by the wish to help his neighbor. Golovan's parallel deeds, helping victims of the plague and the fire—communal, not personal, disasters—show no signs of self-interest. In Hugo the great deed dominates the plot, emphasizing Gilliatt's individual power, whereas in Leskov the great deeds receive the same emphasis as smaller, more down-to-earth examples of charity. We see in Golovan none of Gilliatt's defiant posture before the elements, and Golovan is presented more often in an active social role: for example, because of his honesty and fairness he is chosen to distribute food at communal tables and to record property sales. Gilliatt's selflessness and generosity are shown largely at the end, where his humble arrangement of the marriage (an arrangement which, incidentally, employs deceit) is so exaggerated a reversal that it stretches credulity and perhaps expresses the despair and resignation that leads to his death. Golovan's self-less behavior is constantly shown in more believable and practical acts of kindness throughout the work. Then, too, although both characters experience ironic reversals, Gilliatt's bitter sense of the futility of his herculean labors turns him against life—his self-effacement becomes self-erasure.[5] Golovan's sense of irony is constant, as seen in his "eyes, intelligent and good, but as if a bit mocking" (6:353), and it supports his amused tolerance of others and his positive attitude towards life. He is quite content to live in full awareness of the discrepancy between his apparently sinful relationship to Pavla and his real, chaste one. Golovan's ethical strength is intended to evoke an ur-Christian, eschatological standard of behavior; his simple advice to peasants seeking his help is to "pray and then act as you would if you were about to die" (6:358). Golovan's *caritas* is so clearly more exemplary than Gilliatt's general tolerance and ultimate resignation that one wonders if Leskov did not misread Hugo on this issue of altruism.

The mysterious and legendary quality of the two heroes also admits significant differences. Golovan is not the brooding dreamer Gilliatt is, and he keeps silent about his relationship with Pavla for the sake of her privacy, silent about cutting the plague sore from his leg out of a respect for folk belief: "Golovan . . . was so little burdened by the mystical cloud with which popular rumor surrounded him that he did not, it seems, make any effort at all to destroy anything that had taken shape around him. He knew that it would be in vain" (6:372). The people, too, seem more tolerant of his mysterious oddness than do the Guernseyites of Gilliatt's. His reputation as a savior of the people is positive, unlike Gilliatt's negative reputation as a sorcerer. Orel society is more open than Guernsey society to all kinds of sectarians and eccentrics; the Russian villagers give great freedom to Anton the astronomer by labeling him mad, and they worry little about Golovan's lack of religious affiliation.

More important are the differences in the two characters' supposed lack of "personal happiness." Both heroes, in fact, lead useful, stable, and generally contented lives. But Gilliatt undergoes a trial that crushes his hopes for love and his purpose for living. Golovan remains stable and optimistic; although he cannot marry Pavla and abstains from sex with her, he does live long and contentedly with her. An early description emphasizes his cheerfulness—the "calm and happy smile" perpetually on his lips and in his eyes (6:353). Leskov's comment about both heroes' not having found any happiness must therefore be qualified. Leskov himself provides the distinction at the end of his story. When the narrator remarks that Golovan and Pavla "deprived themselves of all their own happiness" on account of a good-for-nothing, his grandmother defines two kinds of happiness:

"But happiness is to be understood in this way: there is righteous happiness [*sčast'e pravednoe*] and there is sinful happiness [*sčast'e grešnoe*]. The righteous kind will never transgress against anyone, but the sinful kind will step over everything. And they [Golovan and Pavla] preferred the first to the second."

(6:397)

In renouncing Déruchette, whose uncle would force her to marry him, and in renouncing life, Gilliatt does not seem to earn the same degree of "righteous happiness." Leskov's simple comparison of the two heroes thus conceals a difference. Gilliatt's suicide over the loss of his love reveals the absence of any of Golovan's higher sources of sustaining happiness in life.

This difference is underlined by the differences in the two heroes' religious attitudes, in the broader sense. Although both transcend conventional religion and both show an intimate relationship with nature's life force, Golovan's reverence for the Creator and for creation is more consistent and his attunement to life more convincing. He is known for having unusually high-quality livestock and dairy products, for feeding people, and for divining water for wells. And as perceived by the folk mind, he fuses pagan and Christian values: his sacrifice of part of his leg to the river of life ends the plague, restores fertility, and "pays" for the community. His flexibility and resilience also reveal an Eastern patience with time and the elements. Gilliatt, in contrast, despite his gardening, fishing, life-saving, and extraordinary kinship with the sea and sky, becomes a brooding obsessive who must endure and outwit nature and kill its menacing monster for the sake of an unrequited love. On the one hand Hugo portrays Gilliatt as a dreamer immersed in the infinite mystery and power of the elements, and on the other he makes Gilliatt a "gladiator" striving to conquer these elements with his dauntless human will and ingenuity. Both traits belong to European romanticism—one thinks of Faust yearning to follow the sun in Part 1 yet building dikes to control the sea in Part 2. By introducing a conventional love motive into Gilliatt's character, Hugo unbalances him. It is then difficult to see his seasuicide as a positive return to transcendent nature. When Golovan loses his love when she is married off to another, he does not lose faith in life but becomes a good cook in the army, calmly buys his freedom, and frees and supports his relatives. When he is reunited with his love but remains frustratingly celibate, their relationship is integrated happily into a larger life of productivity and community. In terms of world-view, his consistent quality of acceptance, shown even in the smile the narrator remembers so clearly at the very moment Golovan snatched the mad dog and flung it into a cellar, is more convincing and interesting, if less emotionally powerful as fiction, than Gilliatt's mixed extremes of reverence, resistance, and resignation.

In addition to character differences, differences in style and genre also modify the similarities Leskov so emphasized in the two characters. Despite numerous stylistic parallels, Hugo's blend of the epic and the problematic (in Lukàcsian terms) in the relationship of the hero to his world is more dramatic and less unified than Leskov's. Gilliatt's sublime conquest of nature in the rescue resembles the traditional epic hero's feats of valor more than do any of Golovan's actions. In fact, however, the daily, practical "righteousness" of a person such as Golovan, as Leskov implies at the end of the story and in an 1881 article (**"O gerojax i pravednikax"**), is much more difficult to achieve than the traditional heroic deed (Muckle 51). Although Gilliatt seems more the epic hero, his personality is at the same time invaded more by the "problematic," through the love story and suicide, than is Golovan's. Because Golovan's heroism is embedded in daily life, the two modes—epic and novelistic—are more seamlessly interwoven.

Hugo's *Les travailleurs de la mer* is also a full-scale romantic novel with leisurely descriptions of a number of characters and a complicated, carefully structured plot. It draws on traditions of the gothic and exotic tale, the adventure novel, romantic love stories, and the fairy-tale quest (the rescuer of Lethierry's engine and "treasure" is promised marriage to his niece, the "princess"). It draws on all the resources of romantic style—protracted suspense, extravagant diction, high dramatic contrasts, clear moral conflicts, grotesque and exotic detail, coincidence, eavesdropping, emotional descriptions, clear internal characterization, and intense situational irony. Only secondarily is it a realistic novel about *travailleurs*. **Nesmertel'nyj Golovan,** in contrast, claims to be a biographical sketch, looks like a realistic, anecdotal *povest'*, and draws on traditions of moral fable, folk legend, and saints' lives. Its very linguistic texture, including the voice of the narrator, is permeated by oral folk traditions in a way Hugo's is not. Despite the work's far smaller size, its plot is less focused than Hugo's. The chronology is loose, the tone is casual and understated, and the lengthy treatment of the religious procession bears only indirectly on the protagonist. Some of Golovan's most interesting and heroic actions have already occurred when the story opens, and all information except the incident with the mad dog comes to the narrator at second hand. Leskov treats characters from the outside and refrains from artificially heightening the deeds of his hero. The surprise revelation of "Golovan's sin" at the end is but modestly climactic. Leskov introduces a Western love element only to submerge it and deprive it of traditional sentimental and romantic significance.[6] Despite the narrator's open admiration of Golovan, Leskov does a great deal to emphasize Golovan's realistic, concrete individuality by giving him eccentricities (his smile, his "gentlemanly" sash, his odd house, his single garment, his sisters' "spittle" yarn) and by avoiding romantic methods of portraying his hero.

Yet a hero Golovan is, emerging from the common background much as a folk hero or saint, and as basically unchanging and static as they are in their respective genres. He seems more static, despite the greater realism of Leskov's style, than Gilliatt, who is deeply affected by seeing his name in the snow in the opening incident and then conducts a near-silent courtship of Déruchette from a distance. If Golovan's consistency and quirky ordinariness are more convincing, Gilliatt's emotional intensity and sustained physical prowess are more gripping in the course of the plot. At the same time Leskov's treatment of an epic hero in an unheroic world is more original because he shuns the romantic clichés Hugo was still using in 1866 and because the contrast between his hero's heroic nature and the surrounding *byt* is less sharply drawn. Golovan is extraordinary in his very ordinariness; Gilliatt is extraordinary chiefly because of his one superhuman exploit.

This account of the differences between the two heroes and their literary frames suggests that Leskov's comments on Gilliatt in the story need not be taken as precise analysis or definitive appraisal. Leskov is acknowledging his admiration for Hugo, but he is also "doubling" his own character with another similar one and thus extending the number of *pravedniki* in this series of tales. At this time of transition in Leskov's life he was deliberately searching for examples of virtue to prove to himself (and to Pisemskij, with whom he debated the issue[7]) that the modern world was not doomed to moral disintegration. The literary example of a Gilliatt may have struck his imagination as a confirmation across national boundaries of the *pravedniki* he was discovering among the Russian people.

But did Hugo's character actually influence the composition of *Nesmertel'nyj Golovan* in a significant way? Leskov was a wide and voracious reader, copying passages from numerous Western authors into his notebooks (Gebel' 56) and referring to them in letters. But references to Hugo are sparse. Leskov seldom dealt with foreign writers in his journalistic articles, although in an 1869 article refuting complaints about the poverty of Russian literature, he does say that the French can boast only of Hugo (*O lit.* [*N. S. Leskov o literature i iskusstve*] 33). In an essay on Turgenev ("Čudesa i znamenija," 1878) he quotes in passing a wolf analogy from Hugo (*O lit.* 64), and in an 1891 letter advising the young artist Z. P. Axočinskaja to become better educated by studying great works of art, he says, "Make a first conquest over yourself: Read all of Puškin, then Shakespeare, and then Vict[or] Hugo" (*Sobr. soč.* 11: 481) In *Ostrovitjane* (*The Islanders,* 1866) the narrator reports that a priest told him that he had never seen "a condemned man in such state of mind as Victor Hugo

clumsily depicts in his *Dernier jour d'un condamné*" (title cited in French: *Sobr. soč.* 3:165-66) He alludes to Hugo in **"Skaz o tul'skom kosom Levše i o stal'noj bloxe"** in an insignificant reference to Quasimodo from *Notre Dame de Paris,* and one wonders if traces of Bishop Myriel from *Les Misérables* persist in the priest Tuberozov in **Soborjane** and in some of Leskov's good bishops, as they do somewhat in Dostoevskij's Zosima. But in general Leskov's creative thinking was not dominated by Western literature. He always asserted that experience of Russian life and knowledge of people were the most important things for a writer. He was not a typical aristocratic intellectual, thinking largely in terms of European literary tradition.

Most Russian, Soviet, and Western scholars are silent about Leskov's knowledge of Hugo (e.g., Drugov, Troitskij, Volynskij/Flekser, McLean, Edgerton, Macher) and have amply shown the plausible Russian literary and autobiographical sources for Leskov's *pravedniki*.[8] M. P. Alekseev emphasizes the great attention Hugo drew from translators and critics in the 1860s and 1870s but says nothing of Leskov (884-90). Vladimir Kostršica offhandedly mentions that **Deathless Golovan** "comments on . . . an episode from Victor Hugo's *Travailleurs de la mer*" (74), but he does not specify which episode; perhaps he is thinking simply of Leskov's explicit reference to Gilliatt's reply about his parish. Leonid Grossman quotes at length from Leskov's paragraph comparing the two heroes but does not explore the possible influence or compare the two characters in detail (199). Piero Cazzola mentions, without development, the comparison about parishes (745). Vladimir Semenov quotes and reaffirms Leskov's comparisons of Golovan with Gilliatt but without development or differentiation (129-30). Pierre Kovalewsky cites the possible influence of Hugo's novel but says that the subjects are so different that there could be no serious influence (210-11).

In the story itself, of course, Leskov as narrator says that he avidly read Hugo's novel. Did he read it in French? Andrej Leskov says that Leskov received very low scores in French in the gymnasium and that only his mother spoke French in the family (73-74). Leskov was apparently less comfortable in French than other major Russian writers were, and though he attended French theatre during his second sojourn in Paris in 1875, he visited primarily Russians.[9] He did not meet Hugo then, as, for example, Turgenev did in the 1870s. McLean speculates that "although he knew French literature reasonably well, he had probably read most of it in Russian translation. He could, however, and sometimes did, read French books" (28). He could have read *Les travailleurs de la mer* in Russian translation, either in its installments in *Otečestvennye zapiski* in 1866 (Nos. 6-8, 15-17) or in one of its book editions published in the same year. But he doubtless read the novel in French because in November 1872 he published a simplified version for young people of Hugo's novel, *Truženiki morja,* ostensibly his own translation, under his pseudonym M. Stebnickij.[10] Thus Leskov read *Les travailleurs de la mer* between 1866 and 1872, three to nine years before his second trip to France and eight to fourteen years before the composition of ***Nesmertel'nyj Golovan.*** (Semenov is thus a bit loose when he says that "At the time of composition of his ***Golovan*** Leskov became acquainted with V. Hugo's novel," 129.) The very fact that Leskov published a children's version of Hugo's novel, doubtless for its captivating adventure narrative and for its exemplary hero, supports the idea that the work had a great impact on him.

An examination of that translation produces two further revelations. The first is in Leskov's foreword (or, as he calls it, "In Place of a Foreword"), where he answers potential parental objections that the book is unsuitable for children. He argues:

> aside from an acquaintance with the customs of a little-known maritime population—an acquaintance that furnishes fresh and very interesting reading—the young reader can draw from it images of lofty spirit and worthy imitation of character, images whose outline is met far from often in children's novellas in that artistic form in which they appear in Victor Hugo.
>
> (M. Stebnickij, n.p.)

He is alluding here, of course, to the exemplary moral character of the protagonist Gilliatt, especially as captured imaginatively by Hugo in stirring scenes. This justification of the didactic suitability of his translation confirms Leskov's high opinion of Hugo's hero.

The second revelation comes out of the changes Leskov makes in rendering Hugo's original. Not unexpectedly, Leskov deletes many details and most of Hugo's expansive digressions on such topics as sorcerers, sailors' jargon, English aristocratic titles, French protestants, octopus lore, and the relations of the natural elements of wind and sea. These would tend to impede the plot movement for young readers. He also deletes passages that might be construed as objectionable on political, religious, or moral grounds (e.g., Norman jokes against royalty, a reference to the Tsar's repression of Poland, details about Lethierry's atheism, and descriptions of Déruchette's beauty and of naked girls bathing). But what is most relevant to this study is the way Leskov changes Hugo's ending. First, he completely veils Gilliatt's suicide by drowning in the cliff chair Gild-Holm-Ur. He deletes the details of Gilliatt's calculated progress to the rock and the painful, step-by-step rise of the tide until it covers his head, coinciding with the steady retreat of the boat bearing away the young lovers Déruchette and Caudray. He also eliminates the description of the complex expression on Gilliatt's face. The reader surely still gathers that Gilliatt is going to drown—the seat is mentioned by name and Gilliatt's rescue of Caudray from the seat earlier is still fresh. But the result of Leskov's change is that the suicide is minimized instead of being protractedly emphasized as in the original. Perhaps Leskov found such a scene too painful for his youthful readers, or he felt that this suicide ill-suited the noble character of Gilliatt. Leskov certainly sympathized with suicides, as in **"Očarovannyj strannik,"** but he preferred heroes attached to life, like his *pravedniki.* Surely, too, he had no desire to transmit without qualification what he considered the stale plot formula referred to earlier—"he fell in love and shot himself." If so, his changed ending is a critique or correction of Hugo, and Golovan could be considered a further response to Hugo's final treatment of his hero.

More important, besides deleting the description of Gilliatt's death, Leskov *inserts* several generalizations about Gilliatt's virtue that leave no doubt that Gilliatt evoked his highest admiration. These final didactic comments begin when he has Déruchette recognize Gilliatt on the rock (she does not recognize him in the original): "'Look, there's a person [*čelovek,* i.e., human being] there on the rock: it's he!' And it actually was *he,* it was Gilliatt, a *human being* in the full and great meaning of this word" (Stebnicki 440; Leskov's emphasis).[11] Here Leskov emphasizes Gilliatt's fulfillment of the highest conception of human potential.

After a brief literal translation of the boat's passing, Leskov concludes the novel with a fade-out that distances us as it generalizes about Gilliatt:

> Gilliatt remained on his spot as a model of sublime love, which stood higher than love for his own happiness.
>
> Let him thus remain on this rock and in the imagination of the reader as a model of noble energy [*obrazcom blagorodnoj ènergii*], goodness [*dobroty*], and submission to the holy will of Providence, which everyone who wishes to be a worthy human being should foster in himself.
>
> (440-41)

Leskov praises Gilliatt's self-sacrificing love—his altruism—just as he does eight years later in Golovan. He also singles out Gilliatt's tireless work ("noble energy") in the service of practical love and his essential kindness and goodness, again key qualities in Golovan himself. The final note, about Gilliatt's "submission" (*pokornosti*) to Providence, blurs Gilliatt's suicide, which in Hugo's work may be interpreted as either resignation or revolt and thus resembles only Golovan's resignation to his love's inaccessibility even in her proximity (an act of resignation not dramatized in the story). Leskov thus provides a generalized, didactic ending in place of Hugo's original concrete ending. It is a choice that reflects both Leskov's perception of his young audience and his enthusiasm for Gilliatt's moral qualities.

Still, it is a fair distance from noting Leskov's great admiration for Hugo's novel to ascribing significant influence to it in the conception and composition of ***Deathless Golovan***. Despite the similarities between the two heroes, the differences between them, along with what we know of Leskov's Russian sources, suggest that Leskov was directly and almost entirely influenced by native experience and tradition in creating his character Golovan. After all, Golovan was a historical person known to Leskov's family. Further, Leskov seemed to want to distance himself deliberately from Western genre traditions in fiction, as he had earlier in the *skaz* and the novel-chronicles. In ***Nesmertel'nyj Golovan*** he counters the romantic style, the obligatory love interest, the tight plotting, and the individualistic hero of Western novels such as Hugo's with an anomalous, hybrid Russian genre[12] and a hero intimately related to his community and intended didactically to represent a general moral ideal and a specific virtue in the Russian people. In concluding this comparison of the two heroes of these novels, we might very well find the differences between them more interesting and instructive than the resemblances with which Leskov was so taken.[13]

Notes

1. Although "having approved" of Pope's work, Golovan may have learned it partly because it was given to him by his patron, General Ermolov, and partly because he liked "lofty thoughts" in general; his memorization of it is presented as a bit eccentric—he knew Pope "not in the way people usually know an author, *by having read through his works*" (*Sobr. Soč.* 6: 375, Leskov's emphasis).

2. The original passage in Hugo comes in the scene in which Gilliatt has just rescued Caudray from the sea:

   "De quelle paroisse êtes-vous?"

   Gilliatt leva la main droite, montra le ciel, et dit:

   "De celle-ci."

   (Hugo 1: 204)

3. Hugh McLean (358-59) and Danilo Cavaion (47-48) both appropriately emphasize the petit-bourgeois economic independence and self-reliance of Leskov's *pravedniki*; Hugo's Gilliatt fits this description as well.

4. In a parallel fashion, O. E. Majorova also calls attention to two narrative levels in the story, the mythic and the social-psychological, as well as the mingling of two narrative points of view, those of the peasants and of the educated narrator (174).

5. Cf. Victor Brombert: "Gilliatt's ultimate sacrifice . . . cannot be attributed solely to selflessness and higher love . . . Gilliatt's withdrawal from life is not a simple matter of generosity; it is a refusal of the violence of passion, perceived as a threat and a fundamental evil . . . Gilliatt turns his back on the allurements of life" (159-60).

6. McLean alludes to Leskov's heavy guilt about sex in describing "puritan" desexualization as one of the three chief traits of the *pravedniki* (360). He finds Golovan's case especially remarkable because Leskov makes Golovan's relations with the women living with him the object of climactic interest, whereas the courage shown in the epidemic and fire seems more promising literary material for development (361). Walter Benjamin, however, finds the asexuality or bisexuality of Leskov's "maternal males" not something "privative" but the "pinnacle of creation" and "a bridge to a higher world" (97-98). If Leskov skirts the problematics of sex and Hugo touches on them (in Gilliatt's fantasies and subsequent pain), it is partly a question of genre, of Leskov's rejection of Western fictional treatments of love, about which he often complained. In his 1882 book review, "Žitie kak literaturnyj istočnik," for example, he scornfully characterizes some of Tolstoy's critics as "sorry that such a great artist is concerned with ascetics and not with ladies and cavaliers . . . It is incomprehensible and annoying to these people that it is possible to love something in another way than the endless variations on the theme: 'He fell in love and got married' or 'He fell in love and shot himself'" (*O Lit.* 39). See also A. I. Faresov's account of an interview with Leskov near the end of his life in which he said that the French, with their addiction to the trite love themes cited above, cannot hope to understand characters in Russian novels (241-43).

7. In his "Foreword" to the first edition of *Odnodum* Leskov tells amusingly how his talks with the "dying" Pisemskij were the genesis of his search for "righteous men" and the series of stories about them (*Sobr. soč.* 6: 641-43).

8. The key study here is Majorova's detailed comparison of *Golovan* with a number of saints' lives and the epic song of Egorij. See also A. A. Gorelov, *N. S. Leskov* (245-48), and A. A. Kretova. N. C. Mixajlova discusses Leskov's imitation of folk legend about the bogatyrs and finds that the juxtaposition of folkloristic and realistic elements works well (51). D. Straukaite and V. Gebel' (81) also point to folk sources. Andrej Leskov speaks of the influence of the *One Hundred Four Sacred Stories* (67)—mentioned in the story itself—and of several childhood incidents (43, 52-53).

McLean points to hagiographic models for the *pravedniki* (350) as well as personal models in Leskov's uncle Scott and in his early acquaintances Markovich, Benni, and the Kiev intellectuals (34, 54, 70). Leskov himself called attention to the saints' lives as rich sources for positive heroes in literature, including references to Tolstoy and Flaubert, in his 1882 "žitie kak literaturnyj istočnik" (*O lit.* 38-40).

9. Particularly two Russian Jesuits, as McLean (28) and William B. Edgerton (89) make clear. In fact, this trip may have influenced the development of his *pravedniki* because he was thoroughly rereading the gospels and was engaged in serious religious reconsiderations. This process would outweigh by far any influence of French literature at this time. Leonid Grossman also notes Leskov's weakness in French during his first stay in Paris in 1862-63, when he studied the Russian colony there (82, 92-93).

10. I am deeply indebted to Ljudmila Ivanovna Koval'čuk, head of the Information and Bibliography Group at Volgograd State University Library, for obtaining a microfilm of this rare book for me to use during my exchange visit in Volgograd.

11. Compare the original:

> "Vois donc. Il semblerait qu'il y a un homme dans le rocher."
>
> Cette apparition passa.
>
> Le *Cashmere* laissa la pointe . . .

(Hugo 3: 270)

12. Earl Sampson notes the difficulty of genre classification for *Nesmertel'nyj Golovan* and Leskov's other stories and cites a number of Leskov's own invented genre terms (317-18).

13. I am indebted to the Research Council of Kent State University for a summer research grant that made the completion of this article possible. I am also indebted to Prof. Hugh McLean for pointing out in private correspondence several of Leskov's references to Hugo.

Works Cited

Alekseev, M. P. "Viktor Gjugo i ego russkie znakomstva: vstreči; pis'ma; vospominanija." *Literaturnoe nasledstvo* 31-32. Moscow, 1937. 777-932.

Benjamin, Walter. "The Story-Teller: Reflections on the Works of Nicolai Leskov." Trans. Harry Zohn. *Chicago Review* 16 (1963): 80-101.

Brombert, Victor. *Victor Hugo and the Visionary Novel.* Cambridge, Mass.: Harvard University Press, 1984.

Cavaion, Danilo. "Per una tipologia dei 'Giusti' di Leskov." Cavaion and Cazzola 35-49.

Cavaion, Danilo and Piero Cazzola, eds. *Leskoviana.* Bologna: Editrice CLUEB, 1982.

Cazzola, Piero. "I 'Giusti' di Leskov." *Convivium* (Bologna) 36 (1968): 732-51.

Drugov, Boris. *N. S. Leskov: očerk tvorčestva.* Moscow: Xudožestvennaja literatura, 1961.

Edgerton, William B. "Leskov's Trip Abroad in 1875." *Indiana Slavic Studies* 4. Bloomington: Indiana University Press; The Hague: Mouton, 1967. 88-99.

———. *Nikolai Leskov: The Intellectual Development of a Literary Nonconformist.* Diss. Columbia University, 1954.

Faresov, A. I. *Protiv tečenij: N. S. Leskov. Ego žizn', sočinenija, polemika i vospominanija o nem.* St. Petersburg: M. Merkuševa, 1904.

Ferry, Marjorie Ann. *N. S. Leskov's Tales About the Three Righteous Men: A Study in the Positive Type.* Diss. Yale University, 1977.

Gebel', Valentina. *N. S. Leskov v tvorčeskoj laboratorii.* Moscow: Sovetskij pisatel', 1945.

Gorelov, A. A. *N. S. Leskov i narodnaja kul'tura.* Leningrad: Nauka, 1988.

———. "'Pravedniki' i 'pravedničeskij' cikl v tvorčeskoj èvoljucii N. S. Leskova." *Leskov i russkaja literatura.* Ed. K. N. Lomunov and V. Ju. Troickij. Moscow: Nauka, 1988. 39-61.

Grossman, Leonid. *N. S. Leskov: žizn'—tvorčestvo—poètika.* Moscow: Xudožestvennaja literatura, 1945.

Hugo, Victor. *Les travailleurs de la mer.* 5th ed. 3 vols. Paris: Librairie Internationale, 1866.

Kostršica, Vladimir. "O žanrovom svoeobrazii prozy N. S. Leskova." *Filologičeskie nauki* 2 (1974): 70-75.

Kovalewsky, Pierre. *N. S. Leskov: peintre méconnu de la vie nationale russe.* Paris: Presses universitaires de France, 1925.

Kretova, A. A. "Fol'klornye tradicii v povestjax N. S. Leskova 'Očarovannyj strannik' i 'Nesmertel'nyj Golovan.'" *Fol'klornye tradicii v russkoj i sovetskoj literature: Mežvuzovskij sbornik naučnyx trudov.* Ed. B. P. Kirdan et al. Moscow: Moskovskij gos. ped. inst. im. V. I. Lenina, 1987. 88-100.

Leskov, Andrej. *N. S. Leskov. Po ego ličnym, semejnym i nesemejnym zapisjam i pamjatijam.* Moscow: Xudožestvennaja literatura, 1954.

Leskov, N. S. *O literature i iskusstve.* Ed. I. V. Stoljarova. Leningrad: Leningrad University Press, 1984.

————. *Sobranie sočinenij v odinnadcati tomax.* Moscow: Xudožestvennaja literatura, 1956-58.

Lužanovskij, A. V. "Dokumental'nost' povestvovanija—žanrovyj priznak rasskazov N. S. Leskova." *Russkaja literatura* 4 (1980): 144-50.

Macher, Brigitte. *Nikolai Leskovs Verhältnis zur Orthodoxie.* Diss. Marburg University, 1952.

Majorova, O. E. "Rasskaz N. S. Leskova 'Nesmertel'nyj Golovan' i žitijnye tradicii." *Russkaja literatura* 3 (1987): 170-79.

McLean, Hugh. *Nikolai Leskov: The Man and His Art.* Cambridge, Mass.: Harvard University Press, 1977.

Mixajlova, N. G. "Tvorčestvo Leskova v svjazi s nekotorymi obrazami narodnogo èposa." *Vestnik moskovskogo universyteta: filologija* 3 (1966): 49-57.

Muckle, James Y. *Nikolai Leskov and the "Spirit of Protestantism."* Birmingham: Dept. of Russian Language and Literature, University of Birmingham, 1978.

Sampson, Earl. "The Madman and the Monk: Two Types of Narrative Construction in Leskov." *Mnemozina: Studia litteraria russica in honorem Vsevolod Setchkarev.* Ed. Joachim T. Baer and Norman W. Ingham. Munich: Wilhelm Fink, 1974. 317-24.

Semenov, Vladimir. *Nikolaj Leskov: vremja i knigi.* Moscow: Sovremennik, 1981.

Setschkareff, Vsevolod. *N. S. Leskov: Sein Leben und sein Werk.* Wiesbaden: Harrassowitz, 1959.

Stebnicki, M. [N. S. Leskov]. *Truženiki Morja. Roman Viktora Gjugo prisposoblennyj dlja detej.* St. Petersburg and Moscow: Izdanie knigoprodavca—tipografa M. O. Vol'fa, 1872.

Stoljarova, I. V. *V poiskax ideala (tvorčestvo N. S. Leskova).* Leningrad: Leningrad University Press, 1978.

Straukaite, D. "Antiklerikal'nye motivy v skazax N. S. Leskova i narodnaja satiričeskaja skazka." *Lietuvos TSR aukstyjy mokykly mokslo darbai, literatura* 6 (1963): 125-40.

Troickij, V. Ju. *Leskov-xudožnik.* Moscow: Nauka, 1974.

Volta, Luigi. "Aspetti tipologici e comparatistici della scrittura di N. S. Leskov." Cavaion and Cazzola 337-49.

Volynskij, A. L. [A. L. Flekser]. *N. S. Leskov: kritičeskij očerk.* 1898. St. Petersburg: Èpoxa, 1923.

Xaližev, V. and O. Majorova. "Leskovskaja koncepcija pravedničestva." *V mire Leskova: sbornik statej.* Ed. Viktor Bogdanov. Moscow: Sovetskij pisatel', 1983. 196-232.

Irmhild Christina Sperrle (essay date 1998)

SOURCE: Sperrle, Irmhild Christina. "Leskov, Tolstoy, and the Three Questions."[1] *Tolstoy Studies Journal* 10 (1998): 63-79.

[*In the following essay, Sperrle examines notable differences of opinion between Leskov and Tolstoy on the subjects of religion and morality, particularly as these divergences are demonstrated in Leskov's "The Hour of God's Will," which was based upon a theme suggested to Leskov by Tolstoy, and Tolstoy's 1903 story "The Three Questions," a response to "The Hour of God's Will."*]

Nikolai Leskov was drawn to religious questions all his life, a fascination which reveals itself in his fictional and journalistic work and made him a specialist on sectarian and orthodox issues. It is not surprising, then, that toward the end of his life he expressed great interest in and even allegiance to Tolstoyanism. More than other aspects of Leskov's life and art, his relationship to Tolstoy has received considerable scholarly attention.[2] Due to the scarcity of published primary material on Leskov as compared to the wealth of material on Tolstoy, however, most of these studies have looked at the relationship more from the Tolstoyan perspective, analyzing the writers' correspondence, as well as comments, letters, and memoirs of people close to Tolstoy. The picture of Leskov that emerges is of a devoted, although not uncritical, follower of Tolstoy during the last decade of his life.

The issue of Leskov's adherence to Tolstoyanism is complicated in several ways: first, by his clear turn toward didactic and moral fiction in his later years, which, though predating Tolstoy's religious writings, no doubt gained momentum from their relationship;[3] second, by his high regard for Tolstoy the person and writer, which somewhat overshadowed his feelings about Tolstoy's ethical beliefs; third, by the seeming enthusiasm with which he defended Tolstoy's views in public.[4] Although taken by themselves these points do not necessarily support such an idea, they have helped to create and reinforce the notion that Leskov and Tolstoy were *edinomyshlenniki*—"people of one mind."

The origin of the generally accepted view of Leskov's 'conversion' to Tolstoyanism in the 1880s may have been Leskov himself, since on many occasions he professed his devotion to Tolstoy and his ethical positions (albeit with some reservations). In 1887, roughly six months after the two writers met for the first time, Leskov wrote to Vladimir Chertkov, Tolstoy's secretary:

> About L. N[ikolaevi]ch everything is dear to me and everything is ineffably interesting. I am always in agreement with him, and there is nobody on earth who

might be dearer to me than he is. I am never troubled by what I cannot share with him: what is dear to me is the general, so to speak, governing disposition of his soul and the frightening penetration of his mind. Where he has weaknesses, there I see his human imperfection and I am astonished how rarely he makes mistakes; and then he does not make them in the main part, but in the practical applications, in that which is always deceptive and dependent on chance.

(*LIIT* [*Sobranie sochinenii v odinnadtsati tomakh*]
11: 356)

No doubt Leskov found inspiration in Tolstoy's moral strength. Considering his own somewhat eclipsed position in the literary world, he could only be flattered by Tolstoy's friendship[5] and the attention which 'the great writer' lavished on him. As one critic put it: "In his spiritual communion with L. N. Tolstoy, Leskov saw the greatest happiness that had occurred in his life" (Tunimanov 181).

When exploring the issue of Leskov's attraction to Tolstoyanism, it may be helpful to separate personal feelings from ethical beliefs. Up to his very death Leskov expressed his great respect and affection for Tolstoy, which, however, did not prevent him from rather vicious attacks on the Tolstoyans. "I love L. N. Tolstoy, but I don't like the 'Tolstoyans'," he confessed to Faresov (338).[6] As concerns Tolstoy's views, Leskov criticized the theory of nonresistance to evil, called Tolstoy's attacks on sex "an infringement on nature," passionately rejected his notion of women and education, disagreed with his positions on war and government, had his own ideas about the common people (*narod*), ignored the aesthetic principles of simplification (*oproshchenie*), and could not accept what Brigitte Macher called Tolstoy's *Kulturnihilismus* (103). These are hardly minor disagreements or mere "practical applications"!

There is much that unites the two writers. They both turned to the Gospel for religious guidance and urgently called for a moral renewal of society in the Christian spirit. The path each chose, however, seemed to have been very different. As Lovejoy suggests, it is often useful to distinguish between the motives that lead to the proclamation of a set of ideas and the ideas themselves, since "motives and reasons partly identical may contribute to the production of very diverse conclusions" (5). Examining the work of the two writers, as well as unpublished letters and other material by Leskov, will, I believe, give some new insights into the degree of their spiritual closeness. Notwithstanding Leskov's personal attraction to Tolstoy, I would suggest that Tolstoy only confirmed Leskov's own direction. Leskov's righteous people, furthermore—many of them created long before Tolstoy formulated his beliefs—do not embody the *specific Tolstoyan* understanding of Christian love, but merely demonstrate the *Christian*

ethic of love as expressed in the Gospels, and *lack* exactly what is usually called "Tolstoyan." A similar conclusion was reached by Luzhanovskii (1962-64) in his comparison of popular tales by the two writers. After first deploring the "belittling of Leskov's originality,"[7] he finds that an analysis of plots, characters, and literary technique in these stories shows that "in many issues—and it is important to stress, *in basic issues*—N. S. Leskov did not agree with L. N. Tolstoy, and, moreover, his aesthetic principles were diametrically opposed to those of Tolstoy"[8] (Luzhanovskii 1962-64: 241, 252; emphasis added).

Two stories—Leskov's **"The Hour of God's Will"** (**"Chas voli Bozhiei"**) and Tolstoy's *The Three Questions* (*Tri voprosa*)—are especially suited to explore the authors' spiritual closeness, since they share a common theme—a moral quandary and its solution—which, moreover, embodies essential principles of the Tolstoyan belief. Their close analyses will show that the two writers were not "people of one mind," and that the differences in their outlooks reflect not minor disagreements but two intrinsically opposed religious world views.

The theme was initially proposed to Leskov by Tolstoy in the late 1880s[9] and Leskov's version, **"The Hour of God's Will,"** appeared in 1890 in *Russian Review* (*Russkoe obozrenie*). Tolstoy was highly dissatisfied with Leskov's treatment of his subject. Eight years later he wrote in his diary: "Leskov used my theme, and badly. My marvelous thought was three questions: what time is the most important of all, what person and what action? The time is now, this very minute, the person is he with whom you are dealing, and the action is to save your soul, i.e. to do the work of love" (*PSS* [*Polnoe sobranie sochinenii v devianosta tomakh*] 53:198-199). In 1903 he decided to correct Leskov's 'mistake' and 'retaliated' with *his* version, the story called *The Three Questions*.

A comparison of the two stories should include but not be restricted to the all too obvious differences in the authors' literary styles. Except for a few stories by Leskov, imitatively 'written in the Tolstoyan manner,' the stylistic credo of the two could not be further apart. In this case we have Leskov's meandering twenty-seven-page story *vs.* Tolstoy's terse text of four pages. This imbalance usually becomes the focus in comparisons of the authors' literary works. As Lantz puts it: "Tolstoy's four page story achieves its power through the utter simplicity of its style, stripped of imagery and effects, and its total concentration on its moral point. Leskov's runs to twenty-seven pages and is written in a playful *skaz*-fashion with stylistic fireworks [. . .]; its moral point is all but lost amid hyperbole and farcical incident" (118).

In fact, Tolstoy's appraisals of Leskov's work in general persistently hark back to matters of style. He intensely disliked Leskov's manner of writing, and **"The Hour of God's Will"** would not be an exception.[10] After reading the story he wrote to Leskov:

> I began to read and [at first] I very much liked the tone and the unusual mastery of the language, but . . . then your particular shortcoming came to the fore, which, it would seem, could be so easily corrected and which in itself is a [positive] quality and not a shortcoming—an *exubérance* of images, colours, distinctive expressions which intoxicate and distract you. There is much that is unnecessary and disproportionate, but the *verve* and the tone are astonishing. The tale is still very good, but it is annoying that it could have been better were it not for an excess of talent.
>
> (*L6T* [*Sobranie sochinenii v shesti tomakh*] 3:342)[11]

Leskov, on the contrary, liked the story precisely for its linguistic qualities: "I somewhat like **"The Hour of God's Will"** for those difficulties with the language which I had to overcome" (to the literary critic Protopopov, April 30, 1894). He repeatedly admits his inability to write in the Tolstoyan manner, as for example in this letter to Chertkov: "I can't write as simply as Lev Nikolaevich. It is not part of my talent. [. . .] I've gotten used to the embellishment [*otdelka*] in my work and it is not possible for me to write more plainly" (*L11T* 11: 369).[12] If it is true that "nobody in this world is in a position to instill into his creative work a spirit that is different from the one that animates the creating person itself" (**"Zagrobnyi svidetel'"** 254), then the inability to write in a certain way would have to indicate the author's difference of spirit. As a close reading of the two selected stories will show, the writers' stylistic differences—Tolstoy's clarity *vs.* what Tolstoy called Leskov's "curliness" (*kucheriavost'*)—indeed correspond to different ways of thinking, and the values they cherish belong to two opposite world views—one which strives toward simplification and the other which treasures complication and plenitude.

Both writers opted for a fairy tale with a similar plot: A certain king (Leskov), or tsar (Tolstoy) desires to rule in an exemplary manner, and he comes to believe that the answers to the three questions will yield the ultimate guidelines for his kingdom. Thus, both stories illustrate their author's idea of how to implement a utopian kingdom.

The opening paragraphs already expose the rulers' personalities and indicate the different paths each author takes in resolving the task before him. Tolstoy does not waste any time with lengthy introductions. His ruler knows exactly the source of his problem and how to correct it. The story begins: "Once the tsar thought that if he always knew when to begin any affair, which people one should have contact with and which ones one should avoid, and most importantly, if he always knew which was the most important affair of all, he

would be successful in all things" (*PSS* 34: 134). He consulted his advisers but was unsatisfied since the responses he received were "all different." To find the "sure" answers he decided to call on a hermit (*PSS* 34: 135). In short, Tolstoy's ruler is self-sufficient and does not feel he owes anything to anybody. He rejects the advice of people around him because they propose different solutions, while obviously, in his understanding, the sign of the true answer is the one that all agree on.[13] In essence, it is *he* who thought up the questions and *he* who knows how and where to get the answers.

In Leskov's story the king does not have the slightest idea which questions are most crucial. In fact, he only reaches this point on page twelve of the story, when, after many failed attempts, he by chance overhears the three questions from three wise hermits. Page one reveals merely that the king, who is tellingly named *Dobrokhot*, the Well-Wisher, is wise and well-meaning, but in despair, because his affairs are not going as he would like:

> He loved to live according to the old manner, and ruled his kingdom with great piety, according to the traditions of his fathers and grandfathers, and all his efforts and worries were directed so that in his land truth would triumph over falsehood and all people in his kingdom would be happy, but all of this just never seemed to come out right. Dobrokhot would only have to begin to straighten out his affairs on one end, when—lo and behold!—they would come apart on the other. For a long time Dobrokhot tried all kinds of ways [. . .], wore himself out in his efforts up to the point of exhaustion, but to no avail whatsoever.
>
> (*L11T* 9:5)

Leskov's Dobrokhot is full of doubts. He knows only that things are not the way they ought to be, but has no idea of how to correct them. He needs help and accepts advice from people around him: First he follows his wife's suggestion to call a general assembly of his noblemen and advisors. These men, however, do not share the king's concern, but determine that everything is more or less satisfactory. When the king nevertheless insists that they discuss the issue, they first take a long nap, then quarrel, and finally come up with two possibilities for successful government: the conservative notion "do as your fathers did" and the liberal-progressive belief "value the future without troubling about the present." Neither solution satisfies the king, since neither provides any directive for the present. Next, the king is helped by his old nurse, a captive "from foreign lands," who urges him to find three old hermits. For this task he enlists the help of all roaming beggars, and thus, after all these efforts, he obtains the three questions from the three wise men. For the answers, however, the king needs to find a selfless maiden who can solve the riddle. He sends off his advisors who, once out of sight, squander the money for the task and return empty-handed. The king, then, under threat of punishment for noncompliance, sends off a public entertainer who returns with the final answers.

These fictional rulers strikingly reflect the personality of their respective creators. Tolstoy's tsar shows great confidence, refuses all advice, and chooses on his own where and to whom to go for the conclusive answers. The hero's unshakable belief in himself is found in the author as well. To Tolstoy, the author of *A Critique of Dogmatic Theology* (1881-2), *The Gospel in Brief* (1881-3), *What I Believe* (1884), *What Then Must We Do?* (1886), *The Kingdom of God is Within You* (1894), and other religious tracts, the truth is very clear and can be expressed in several concrete axioms. In an 1882 letter he writes: "[I]t seems to me now, that if Christ and His teaching had not existed, I would have uncovered this truth on my own. It seems so simple and clear to me; and I am convinced that it will seem the same to you" (*PSS* 63: 116). A bit further he repeats this thought: "Don't think that in Christ there would be anything unclear. Everything is as clear as day" (*PSS* 63:121). And it was up to Tolstoy to find this truth: "And how strange to say after 1800 years that I had to uncover this rule [of nonresistance to evil] as if it were something new" (*PSS* 63: 118).

In Leskov's case, the king's sentiments of doubt and his constant need for people whose knowledge or abilities might be of use are heard as well in the author. He writes to Tolstoy in 1891: "I know that I don't know anything and I never remain fixed in my position in anything, but I [always] discover something better and more useful" (*L11T* 11:496). The same self-questioning tone is heard again in an 1893 letter to Tolstoy:

> From my early years on I was attracted to questions of faith and began to write about religious people, when this was considered indecent and impossible [. . .], but I got mixed up all the time [. . .]. I approached *on my own* what I saw in you, but left to myself I was all the time afraid that this was a mistake, because, although in my consciousness there was the same light that I saw in you, in me everything was in chaos—troubled and unclear, and I didn't have confidence in myself.
>
> (*L11T* 11: 519)

To Leskov, who read the Gospels as eagerly as Tolstoy, the message was not that obvious. In a curious unpublished sketch, supposedly written shortly before his death, he mentions that his doubts about the Gospels' messages and his preoccupation with the meaning of Christ began in early childhood and remained with him all his life.[14] Moreover, in many letters to Tolstoy he singles out passages that have changed their meanings for him after repeated re-readings, or asks Tolstoy for advice on particular interpretations.

The amplitude of Tolstoy's diaries, letters, tracts, and articles provides much evidence that he, too, was plagued by doubts and kept rethinking his theory, and

passages can certainly be found in support of various slants in his world view. Yet, his basic beliefs, first formulated in the early 1880s, remained fairly consistent: for him the Christian religion of love was most fully embodied in the rule of nonviolence, and only total compliance with it would advance man in his struggle toward self-perfection. He wrote to Leskov in 1894: "I think that anybody who has read at the very least the Sermon on the Mount—I won't even speak of the whole Gospel—and who did not come to the conclusion that nonresistance to evil constitutes the basic condition of the Christian understanding of the world, such a person will not be convinced by any arguments" (*L6T* 3: 414).

Tolstoy's conviction that evil can be completely abolished by love is reflected in his story: The tsar reaches the hermit's hut and finds him digging in his garden. Repeated questions remain unanswered, and the tsar, feeling compassionate, helps the hermit in his work. When evening falls, and he once more requests an answer to his questions, they are interrupted by a severely wounded man who comes running towards them. The tsar attends to the sick man and stays the night. In the morning the stranger reveals himself as a former enemy who had planned to kill the ruler in revenge for previous punishment suffered. When the tsar was delayed from returning—due to his good deed—the man went to investigate, but was caught and nearly killed by the tsar's bodyguards. The tsar's aid effected a change of heart: "I wanted to kill you, but you saved my life. Now, if I remain alive and if you want this, I will serve you as your most faithful slave and will order my sons to do the same" (*PSS* 34: 137). The tsar, overjoyed at this reconciliation, forgives his enemy, returns his property, and offers other assistance. The story ends with a long speech by the hermit who tells the tsar that his actions are the answers to his quandary. His help first to the hermit and then to the wounded man saved his life and brought reconciliation. The hermit concludes:

> Therefore remember, the most important time is one: *now,* and it is most important because only then do we have power over ourselves; and the most important person is *that one with whom we are together now,* because nobody can know if he will ever have anything to do with another person again, and the most important deed—*to do a good deed* for him, because a person is sent into the world only for that reason alone.
>
> (*PSS* 34: 137)

Thus, at the story's end everything is tied up perfectly, everybody is happy and has profited: the hermit has finished his rows, the tsar has escaped regicide, is reconciled with his enemy, and has found his truth, and the enemy has turned into a faithful servant.

Leskov's story, on the other hand, ends rather curiously. His king had to go through an enormous amount of trouble and betrayal before he received the riddle's answers. However, when he wanted to rule according to this wisdom, he became afraid and thought:

> "what would happen if others in the neighbouring kingdoms didn't act the same way? After all, alone I wouldn't be able to rule in this manner amongst other temporal rulers." And he decided that he'd better sit the way he was sitting on his throne before, like all temporal rulers, and hold in one hand the sword and in the other the golden apple.
>
> (*L1IT* 9: 30)

He banishes the entertainer Razliuliai, who went through the ordeal of getting the answers from the wise maiden from the city and settles him in a pseudo-paradise where he could "eat honey with cucumbers to his heart's content." But he receives orders to avoid the marketplace, not to mingle with people and not to tell anybody about the young maiden and her prophesy. As his death approaches, the king has the whole story written down "without even the tiniest mistake."

> And Dobrokhot ordered that this scroll be rolled up in brocade and in damask and in fine gingham and be placed at the bottom of a small golden chest and be taken to the cellar of the tower behind seven locks and seven seals. May it lie there until the time for temporal rulers has passed.
>
> Precisely thus it was executed, and the scripture is still lying there behind the seals, and the affairs in the kingdom are as before, and everything goes so-so, not good not bad, the way it was at the time of the grandfathers and great-grandfathers. Obviously the hour of God's will has not yet arrived.
>
> (*L1IT* 9: 31)

Thus, the well-intentioned king refuses to obey these Tolstoyan principles, since he realizes that they do not provide protection from outside aggression. In a letter to Tolstoy, Leskov points out the necessity of ending the story in this manner: "[The story] got rather spoilt at the end 'because of fear,' but it wouldn't have come out otherwise" (*L6T* 3: 340).

Another passage in a letter to Tolstoy from 1891 shows how much Leskov was occupied with the interplay of Christian ethics and political power at that time, and how well thought out this ending was. He mentions a verse from Paul's Epistle to the Corinthians (I Cor XV, 24): "And then the end will come, *when* he will hand over the kingdom to God,—when he will eliminate any kind of rule, any kind of power and force" and sees it "as a *direct* indication that Christ *is concerning himself with the elimination of any kind of rule, of any kind of power and force,* and without this his task here is not finished. [. . .] This means, that while there exists 'a rule, power and force,' he can not 'hand over' the kingdom to God—the 'father'" (*L6T* 3: 362-63).[15] This passage and Leskov's interpretation probably did not

trouble Tolstoy, since he did not like St. Paul and, in fact, considered him a "false interpreter" of Christ's message (*PSS* 24: 809). Not recognizing the necessity of power structures and political institutions, Tolstoy thought that man could work toward the 'Kingdom of God on Earth' *while* those institutions were still in place by simply refusing to play a part in their existence. He firmly believed that 'this evil,' like any other, would eventually be "swallowed up" if people stopped using force to resist it (*PSS* 53:197). This technique—later called passive resistance—has been put to good use by Mahatma Gandhi who—as Edgerton expresses it— "some would say far outstripped his teacher" (Edgerton 532).

Leskov may have accepted the theory of nonviolence as an ideal, but was too practical-minded to believe in its universal usefulness. For him, this way of behaving is "very good, but not always" (**Leskov o literature** 137). In some cases, he even considered it harmful. In an article from 1886, **"On Goads: An Admonition to the Sons of Resistance" ("O rozhne")**, Leskov discussed several of Tolstoy's folk tales published that year, in which Tolstoy laid out his program of nonresistance. Leskov did not object to the theory's validity as such but elaborated on its shortcomings and considered Tolstoy's idealistic view of the effectiveness of nonresistance naive and unrealistic:

> In his depiction of the kingdom of Ivan-the-Fool[16] Count Tolstoy is not even faithful to the truth and realism that always distinguish him. The calm subjects of "Ivan the Fool" serve as successful illustrations for Tolstoy: they "resist" not at all, "but only cry." The soldiers who conquered them softened up as well: they "felt disgusted to abuse them, and there was no one to fight with." But such a thing does not happen in real war, which Count Tolstoy knows well. Everybody knows, for example, that defenseless people are beaten, too, and very often even more severe acts of violence are done to women. . . . How should one act when before one's eyes one's sister is raped, or one's wife or even one's mother? . . . Is it possible to look on, not to resist immediately, but go first and water one's charred pieces of wood? . . .[17]
>
> (**Leskov o literature** 137-38)

For Leskov, evil has to be resisted *before* one reaches the point of spiritual purity, and he even argues—calling on emotions understood "by all and everyone"— that, in certain situations, acts of violence are more human and important than the concern for self-perfection:

> I am speaking from *the side of the heart,* from the side of feelings, which is accessible and understandable by all and everyone. Judging from this side, I think that there are incidents when a person cannot remain human without having shown the quickest and strongest resistance to evil. And he has to show this resistance without cleansing himself and preparing himself, but exactly as *the person he is now,* with the exact same towel

that he has in his hand, with the unfirm block and the charred pieces of wood.[18]

(Leskov o literature 140)

Leskov's criticism of the theory of nonviolence by far predates Tolstoy's own formulation of his beliefs. In an article from 1870, for example, Leskov addresses issues that reappear in the fairy tale **"The Hour of God's Will,"** and one passage of this article even presents an 'alternative version' of the tale or its sequel, a 'what would have happened if?' situation[19] **("Russkie obshchestvennye zametki"** 1-2). There he depicts the collapse of an exemplary government whose ruler, "a certain 'well-meaning,' ideal prince Irinei," dogmatically adheres to the practice of nonresistance to evil. Leskov called this endeavour the product of an "endearing, but ridiculous and harmful disposition," and concludes that "many people are very much afraid of 'exemplary government' and share the opinion of Friedrich the Great, that 'philosophers are of no use at all as rulers'" **("Russkie obshchestvennye zametki"** 2). For Tolstoy, the axiom of nonresistance remained the cornerstone of his religious world view, and, considering Leskov's objections to this most integral portion of Tolstoy's ethics, it is hard to conceive how Leskov could have been a follower of Tolstoy *at any time.*

The moral of Tolstoy's tale *The Three Questions* is very clear. The king learns—and we are made to believe that he accepts—the rules given him for successful government. Accordingly, he must make the present the most important time. A fixation on the present corresponds to Tolstoy's reading of the Gospels, and to this precept he dedicates one of the twelve chapters of *The Gospel in Brief (PSS* 24: 885-893): "True life in the fulfillment of the will of the Father is not life in the past, nor in the future, but life in the present" *(PSS* 24: 887). This focus on the moment is not only part of the established truth in Tolstoy's tale; in a certain way it motivates its structure as well. The story depicts a particular incident without any extraneous material and there is a definite sense of "before" and "after": before the riddle was solved and after. However, we know very little about the past, the time of "before," of how and why the tsar arrived at precisely those questions, nor do we know anything about the future, how he applied the newly found wisdom. But thanks to the story's tight construction and the fact that all ends well and all have profited from the ordeal, one might be easily persuaded to accept its moral without questioning its feasibility. A philosophy that focuses on the moment, however, isolates a person's act from motives (past) and consequences (future). In our motives, we give credit to people or events that have inspired certain acts, and in looking at consequences we are forced to take responsibility for what we have done. In an essay posthumously titled *Towards a Philosophy of the Act,* Bakhtin (1993) develops a theory of action in which the act is not looked at by itself but becomes part of a never-ending chain of existence. The crucial aspect in this theory is answerability—*otvetstvennost'.*

A look at Tolstoy's story from this angle reveals some of the troubling parts in his teaching and shows how he controls the story to give a neat and succinct message. The reader—intrigued by the story's craftsmanship—easily overlooks inconsistencies in content. Since for Tolstoy earthly powers only create and perpetuate evil and, therefore, should be dispensed with altogether, it seems surprising that he chose a ruler in the first place to demonstrate his axiom of love. On the other hand, this ruler fits his role rather incompletely: he has appropriated only selected features of his position and rejected the more uncomfortable ones. Unlike many fairy-tale kings who send others on quests but themselves remain on the throne, Tolstoy's tsar departs for an unspecified amount of time—however long it will take to "find the truth." Moreover, his absence is not state-related, but prompted by a personal motive: He "wants to be successful in all things" *(PSS* 34: 134). This decision betrays irresponsibility, since his office entails the protection and care of his subjects, especially if he does not trust his advisers, which is made explicit in the otherwise very terse story. A negation of power structures poses the same problem as does the application of the theory of nonresistance, namely, the lack of protection of others and, incidentally, of oneself.

But in *The Three Questions* we also see that Tolstoy, an outspoken opponent of power, does not reject the *privileges* that come with a powerful position. His tsar, while leaving his kingdom unprotected, takes off surrounded by "guards carrying weapons (*oruzhenostsy*)," thanks to whom he remains alive and can accomplish his good deed. His good deed is thus the result of another's "bad deed," since obviously, when they wound the enemy, the guards are not acting out of love for the person they are with at the moment. Does that mean that the precept applies only to certain people and not to guards? Tolstoy's rigid application of his theory forces him to close his eyes to what happens outside—at the edge of the forest where the tsar's guards are positioned. Thus, while neglecting the tsar's responsibilities, Tolstoy makes extensive use of the ruler's privileges: his prerogative of personal inviolability and the right to punish and reward are the moving forces behind the story. They account for the rise and denouement of the evil force, and thus illustrate the moral's soundness. Tolstoy's tsar enjoys the advantages of his office without returning the gift by taking responsibility for his subjects, as well as for unpopular decisions.

The hermit's closing speech confirms the emphasis on personal advantage that makes the moral so palpable to the reader: The tsar's service to the old man saved him from being killed, his help to the wounded made possible the reconciliation with his enemy, and the reason for the good deed now is "because we do not know when we will die and whether we will ever have a chance of being with another person again," i.e., when we will have another opportunity to do good. Or as Tolstoy formulated it in the diary passage quoted above: The deed is "*to save your soul,* i.e. to do the work of love" (*PSS* 53: 199). An even greater stress on personal gain is expressed in a letter to Chertkov, in which Tolstoy mentions the theme for the first time: "And the most dear of all deeds is to do good to that person, because this is the only deed that is probably *of use to you* (*tebe na pol'zu*)" (*PSS* 86: 63; emphasis added). Most certainly, Tolstoy understood this "use" in terms of spiritual benefit. But in *Confession* and in other didactic stories (*Father Sergius,* among others), he condemned the mere thought of reward when doing good; the application of the language of commerce, of gain and loss, when talking about spiritual matters reveals pride and self-centredness.[20]

Leskov's king is less concerned with himself and thinks first of his duty as statesman. His motive for seeking the truth is not "that he should be successful in all things" but "that in his land truth would triumph over falsehood and all people in his kingdom would be happy." He rejects the "simple wisdom" meant to assure "that every person in his kingdom would be well in the present hour, in the here and now," since he feels he cannot afford to think only of the present but has to "glance into unreachable distances," where fear of the unknown lurks. In Leskov's story there is no neat division into "before" and "after" that characterizes a mind which concentrates only on the present. Nothing really has changed in the kingdom: affairs are as before, "not good not bad," and the king returns to rule with "the sword and the golden apple," that is, using the traditional methods of punishment and reward. The reader is not presented with a found truth, but let down. There is a feeling of anticlimax and confusion: all the energy spent on the quest, all the adventures and hardships encountered on the way have come to nothing, since the findings are hidden away "behind seven seals" and the person bringing this truth is isolated as if he were infected by a dangerous and contagious disease. He is banished from society and rewarded with a "golden cage."[21]

This is what happens to the entertainer Razliuliai, who, having done the good work, comes out worst of all. He is not only sent on the journey under threat of punishment to himself and even to his family (the latter to ensure his return), but is advised by the maiden to renounce his well-earned reward so he will be believed (*L11T* 9: 29). Leskov does not believe that good deeds are "of advantage" to the person doing them. As he shows in the righteous characters of his stories and as he writes to his sister, for him "honest people fare badly

(*chestnym khudo*)" (letter to Krokhina, March 4, 1892). He liked best and frequently quoted—often in a slightly distorted version—Saint Paul's definition of perfected love: "Love which seeketh nothing for itself,"[22] and saw man's task as an effort "to increase the sum of goodness in oneself and around oneself" (*Leskov o literature* 116).

This interpretation of the deed of love is evoked in **"The Hour of God's Will."** As was his habit with any source material, Leskov changed and reformulated the three answers given to him by Tolstoy. To the wise maiden, who delivers the key to the questions, the truth is also very obvious. On hearing the riddle she says to Razliuliai: "It is good that you didn't give me a hard task, one that would be beyond my simple understanding, but asked the task of God, the most simple and easy, the answer to which in an honest soul is as clear as the sun" (*L11T* 9: 28). She begs him to ask her the questions in order and he complies:

> —Tell me, dear maiden, which hour is the most important of all?
>
> —The *present one,*—answered the maiden.
>
> —And why?
>
> —Because each person only has power over the present hour.
>
> —True! And which person is the most important of all?
>
> —*The one with whom you are now.*
>
> —Why is that?
>
> —Because it now depends on you, from what you answer him, whether he will be happy or sad.
>
> —And which deed is the most precious of all?
>
> —*The good that you will manage to do in this hour to this person.* If all of you begin to live according to this, everything will go all right and be in harmony. And if you don't want to live in this manner, you won't set things straight.
>
> (*L11T* 9: 28-29)

This is a considerable shift from Tolstoy's self-centeredness. Here, there is no talk of any reward, no soul being saved, no settling of old scores. Leskov's reformulation focuses on responsibility: we are made accountable for the happiness or sadness of the person we are in contact with. And this act will not depend on or result in personal gain.

Of course, Tolstoy would not have rejected Leskov's definition. He, too, advocated active love but was quite tormented by his failure to depict such acts convincingly. The reason for this may be that he was too 'enamoured' of the figure of the hermit or elder, which appears frequently in his didactic stories. These characters come to know the truth—or what they believe is the true way of life—but live in isolation so that we never see how they would apply their new-found knowledge. As Luzhanovskii puts it: ". . . the story [*Two Elders*] is really constructed on the transmission of the hero's acts, his activities, but only up to his 'purification,' until he realized the meaning of life. Tolstoy breaks off the action in his popular tales at exactly that point" (Luzhanovskii 1962-64: 250). Another example would be Tolstoy's very effective story *Father Sergius*: The bulk of the story is about Sergius' withdrawal and asceticism, whereas the moral of 'going into the world and learning from simple peoples' is placed at the very end, and we are shown only in very broad terms how he fares in the world. Tolstoy was very aware of this dilemma. He wrote in his diary: "As concerns F[ather] S[ergius]. Alone he is good—with people he falls" (*PSS* 53: 204). Tolstoy's preoccupation with self-perfection, as well as his method for attaining it, prevent him from showing in his own work *how* this active love can be realized in actuality. Edgerton is not the only one who felt that "Leskov created a number of characters who are more convincing and attractive embodiments of the Tolstoyan religion of love than the characters of Tolstoy themselves" (532).

The most significant difference between Leskov's "righteous men" and Tolstoy's positive characters, however, seems to be that between selfless love as choice *vs.* selfless love as dedication. Leskov's characters live their not always blameless lives, but in decisive moments do the deed of love; they live like ordinary human beings but do saintly deeds, whereas in Tolstoy, positive characters tend to "live like saints"—dedicate themselves to others to the point of self-neglect. To this category belong the hermit-type who, since he has made a conscious choice, suffers from self-doubt and pride, as well as such characters as Pashen'ka in *Father Sergius,* Platon Karataev in *War and Peace,* or various dedicated serfs and servants, all of whom exemplify love as pure *agape.* Leskov admires this type in his *Prolog* tale **Innocent Prudentius** (**Nevinnyi Prudentsii,** 1891; *LIIT* 9: 50-116), but gives the last word to his character Prudentius who rejects this choice for its ruthless disregard for human nature. He says about selfless Melita: "Her spirit is too elevated and serious—it is too merciless in its conquest over the flesh. You [his wife] and I . . . we look [at life] more simply" (*LIIT* 9: 115). Leskov frequently voiced this argument against Tolstoy, namely, that he demands too much from simple human beings. Not everybody is capable of living a life of saintliness. Leskov's characters are more warm and loving than Tolstoy's because they show themselves to be human despite their often 'sinful' positions. They are able to compromise, and although they frequently suffer materially or physically for their loving deeds, they live at peace with their choices. Their attraction lies in the

fact that they include other people's concerns in their own ordinary life, instead of renouncing their life or having it belong to others.

Leskov's repeated and ardent show of support for Tolstoy's "main stream of thoughts" has created much confusion and prevented a fair evaluation of their relationship. What Leskov really saw and appreciated was Tolstoy's tireless effort to turn public attention away from materialistic ends and to advocate a return to Christian ethics. He himself had been recommending such a redirection long ago, as in this letter from 1875:

> "We are ruled"—as Panin told Catherine II—"by the grace of God and the stupidity of the people"; we need a "good enlightenment," that is, an enlightenment which is not hostile to the Christian ideal, instead of pursuing the political ideal according to the European model. As for all the rest: "God is with us," because if it were not for Him "who would deliver us from such ills?"
>
> (Chertkov 188)

Already in his early writings, Leskov had been working toward reversing what he considered the wrong social values that dominated Russian society, but his work was not getting sufficient attention. As he repeatedly stated, "his light was weak," and he greeted the arrival of "the strong light" that came from Tolstoy (Faresov 308).[23] Leskov saw in Tolstoy a figure who caught an important historical moment, as he stated in a 1890 letter: "Tolstoy does exactly what is ripe now: It is impossible to live without belief, but to believe in banalities is also impossible. To humanize the evangelical teaching is the most noble and a quite timely task" (*LIIT* 11: 456). Or as he wrote in one of his notebooks:

> In the interpretations and commentaries of L. N. T. "there are some things difficult to understand" (as Ap. Peter expressed it in regard to Ap. Paul[24]), but he elevated his contemporaries to a height which can't be attained by the banal view of life [*poshlost'*] that stops at the notions of "gain and loss"; and in all the people touched by him there will survive if not the conviction, then probably the recognition or the notion that "we don't live the way we ought to"—and this is the great service of Tolstoy.
>
> (*Zapisnaia knizhka* 3)

There is great evidence, however, that by the early 1890s, if not earlier, he was trying to distance himself from Tolstoy's views. He diplomatically avoids the issue of commenting on *particular* parts of Tolstoy's teaching and only in occasional letters shows his irritation with it, as for example in the yet unpublished letters to Men'shikov,[25] such as in this from 1893:

> [. . .] I cannot at all agree with the questions of celibacy and whatever else concerns the relationship of the sexes; and this troubles me very much. It seems to me without purpose and has a detrimental effect on the

great majority of people, the same effect as some kind of monstrous demand of a terrible price has on a poor buyer. . . . He is terrified, walks away and then never comes back and dissuades others from going there: "This is not for us." [. . .] We have to purify people's taste and not rip out the natural law of nature.

(Letter from June 29, 1893)

When Men'shikov reproached him that same year for not speaking up for Tolstoy, Leskov answers by sending him an article from ten years earlier, in which he defended Tolstoy and Dostoevsky against attacks by Konstantin Leont'ev (letter from November 12, 1893).[26] He writes that this article touched "a difficult and delicate question," and "that after that *as concerns himself*" he felt he was done with this problem (Leskov's stress). Considering that this article was written before the bulk of Tolstoy's religious writing appeared and only treats the story *What Men Live By*—whose source Leskov is quick to point out in Afanas'ev's collection of folk tales—the notion of Leskov as Tolstoy's follower and defender has to be examined more critically.[27] As he continues in his letter:

It is correct to say that I "coincided" with Tolstoy, and was not "drawn in" by him as B[ureni]n thinks. I didn't imitate him, but said the same thing *before him,* but only not effusively, not confidently, but timidly and with a bur. Feeling his enormous strength I threw away my little lantern and followed his strong light. I "coincided," but *am tired* continuing with that.

(Letter from November 12, 1893)

From the context of the letter, in which Leskov discusses people who could possibly support Tolstoy in public, it becomes clear that notwithstanding their temporary "coincidence" Leskov considers himself not one of them, that he is "tired of continuing" to defend Tolstoy. Despite his disagreements, he nevertheless observed great constraint in criticizing Tolstoy's teaching. As he said to Faresov: "There is no reason to trot his faults out into the street and trouble his old age. That is only 'making noise,' not seeking the truth" (214).

Besides the touchy question of Leskov's public support of Tolstoy, there is another issue that muddies the water and prevents us from seeing the relationship between the two writers more clearly: both writers use the same sources and see in the Gospel and its message of Christian love the model that mankind should follow. If we examine the concrete issues of how each writer defines good and evil and how they propose to cope with the latter, we can see a great divergence. Tolstoy tends to think in well-defined categories: in his writings right and wrong are always evident. He wants mankind to strive toward a definite end, the establishment of the Kingdom of God on Earth where evil has been overcome by love. Of course, he realizes that this is a utopia which can never be attained. He nevertheless be-

lieved that if everybody were to recognize and apply the teaching of nonresistance, and work to perfect himself, evil could be overcome. Tolstoy therefore strives toward a monolithic, static ideal—a humanity unified by love—and could be considered susceptible to what Lovejoy called the "monistic pathos," a state of mind which suggests that "one is oneself a part of the universal One" and which allows the imagination to escape "from the sense of being a limited, particular self" (13). Such a psychology, however, would have a static and 'nihilistic' quality which is seen in Tolstoy's interest in patience, 'non-action,'[28] and his rejection of all 'worldly structures,' political and cultural ones. Tolstoy's emphasis on the present time, which has been pointed out earlier, supports such a state of mind as well: when cut off from past and future, the present becomes immutable. Such a temporal orientation allows an enormous freedom, the freedom to create *ex nihilo,* since the mind is free from previous 'delusions.' Here we find echoes of Tolstoy's rejection of culture and of his theory of art.

The values cherished by Tolstoy include purity, perfection, non-contamination, simplicity, clarity, stillness, unity. He is part of the Platonic idealistic tradition which sees evil in the divergence from the norm, in mutability. For Tolstoy, evil does not really exist by itself but consists in the splitting up, the breaking off from an ideal, solid, monolithic structure. He writes in 1882: "One person cannot do anything evil. Evil is the separation of people" (*PSS* 63: 114). And as was shown in the example of the story *The Three Questions*, for Tolstoy evil can be overcome, swallowed up, eliminated. In his 1898 diary he writes:

Nonresistance to evil is not only important because man should act in this way for himself, for the attainment of perfect love, but also because only nonresistance stops evil, swallows it up into itself, neutralizes it, doesn't allow it to go further, the way it inevitably does, like the transfer of movement by way of bouncing balls, if this force doesn't exist, which eats it up. Active Christianity does not consist in doing, creating Christianity, but in the act of swallowing up evil.

(*PSS* 53: 197)

This view of evil colours Tolstoy's notion of love. If evil is disunity, love is the striving for ultimate unity. Perfect love, then, is a state that can only be reached in a metaphysical realm. Love of one's neighbour as a concrete notion Tolstoy considers an idea so "unclear and unrealizable that it remains only an empty phrase." He continues: "My opinion is that this principle is a metaphysical one, a very important one as such; but when this same principle is understood as a rule of life, as a law, then it is simply stupid. But unfortunately it is often understood that way" (*PSS* 63: 117).

Tolstoy nevertheless struggled with his notion of perfect love and tried to turn it into a theory of active love. He finally concluded that the most perfect love is that which continues even when it is rejected by the recipient. He wrote in his 1889 diary: "I thought: The sign of real, that is, self-renouncing love is, if a person whom I love and for whom I labour does not accept my efforts, despises them, and I nevertheless can't get angry at him and don't value my efforts. The opposite sign is faulty egoistic attachment" (*PSS* 50: 184). It may be ironic with respect to our comparison of the two writers that this entry immediately follows: "I read Leskov. False. Bad."

Leskov might say the same thing about Tolstoy, since he certainly would not agree with such a definition of love. In fact, he treated this theme in an article which was disguised as a 'defence' of Tolstoy, but ends up exposing the egoistic motives in a so-called Tolstoyan type of benefactor (**"Rasskazy kstati"** 2).

Tolstoy's notions of love and evil seem to be very much tied up with a sense of martyrdom. Evil is overcome by being 'swallowed up' by the good, that is, the better you are the more *you* have to work to absorb even more evil. *The Three Questions* illustrates this idea as well: The enemy's previous punishment and his murderous intention are wiped away by the good deed of the *tsar*, not by anything the enemy himself did. He confessed only *after* having been the recipient of the good deed. Furthermore, the troubling question remains: Why was the previous punishment not only reversed, but the enemy was rewarded *with more*? Does that mean that the punishment was not deserved in the first place?

Tolstoy clearly is working here with the model of Christ, the Saviour, who assumed sins on man's behalf.[29] But we have a long way to go to emulate Christ, which is why such a notion has to be accompanied by a theory of self-perfection. Leskov rejected this direction, which Tolstoy called the "regal way" ("*tsarstvennyi put'*") to attain perfect love, and found another Biblical image much closer to his heart: the image of the thief on the cross, whose previous evil deeds were wiped away by what *he* did. In **"On Goads"** he writes:

> According to the Gospel, the very best change in a living person can happen very quickly—"in the twinkling of an eye." A thief is hanging there, next to him a righteous person, and then another thief. And the thief was completely as he should be—a genuine thief. He didn't water any charred wood pieces, but then in his presence the other thief began to harass the meek one—and there immediately appeared all that is necessary:
>
> —Amen. From now on you will be with me. [. . .] The same happened with the fornicatress, as well as with Zaccheus and with the praying publican. In all cases a noble upsurge grabbing the heart, a holy movement of the soul, and not *a method* with charred wood. . . .
>
> (*Leskov o literature* 138-39)

Tolstoy did not like this notion, as his reaction to Leskov's legend **"Conscientious Daniel"** shows. D. P. Makovitskii, during one of his visits to Iasnaia Poliana in 1909, reports:

> Maria Nikolaevna had read **"Conscientious Daniel"** in Leskov's version, published in *The Intermediary* (*Posrednik*), and recounted it at breakfast. L. N. didn't approve of the end (I—Dushan Petrovich—don't remember the story itself. It was something to the effect that due to his deed, former evil done by him stopped being evil). L. N. didn't approve of this thought of Leskov. Maria Nikolaevna didn't agree, and couldn't really understand L. N.
>
> ("U Tolstogo" 52)

Leskov advocated exactly the opposite of what Tolstoy expressed in the diary passage quoted earlier: For Tolstoy "active Christianity does not consist in doing, creating Christianity, but in the act of swallowing up evil" (*PSS* 53: 197). For Leskov active Christianity was precisely "doing, creating Christianity," or, as he expressed it in **"The Hour of God's Will,"** the sign of the good deed is whether a person leaves happy or sad.

The two writers disagree furthermore not only on the notion of love but, more importantly, or resulting from it, on their idea of evil. Again, Leskov's concept of evil proves to be diametrically opposed to Tolstoy's. For Leskov, evil comes from closing one's mind to the surrounding world, from the conviction that the truth has been revealed to you alone. Throughout his whole writing career, he tirelessly attacked dogmatic thinking and showed the downfall of characters who preach and rely on what they think is an infallible truth. His targets include idealist socialists (**"The Musk-ox"**), nihilists and materialists (*No Way Out, At Daggers Drawn*), Slavophiles (**"The Kolyvan Husband"**), and proto-existentialists (**"Iron Will"**). It is not surprising, then, that toward the end of his life he would take on the Tolstoyans in **"A Winter's Day"** and in **"The Rabbit Carriage"** (**"Zaiachii remiz"**).[30] Unlike Tolstoy's, Leskov's righteous characters perform their deeds of love *unconsciously*. As Durylin characterized them: "[They are] Christians without Christ, righteous ones who do not know the name for their truth" (Durylin 74).

Leskov then is not prone to the 'monistic' cast of mind, but to what I would call the 'organic' pathos. He is attracted to unexpected but decisive moments, quick changes, distortions of norms, open-endedness, constant transformation, connectedness not in the metaphysical but in the actual realm, and to a certain "curliness" and "muddiness."

Of course, a mind that is always seeking, that is in constant doubt, that constantly rejects what it has found, would be very attracted to a mind that seems to have found a firm set of beliefs. Such was Leskov's attraction to Tolstoy. He had been "digging in the pile"[31] of Christian love all his life and was relieved that somebody "had found a solution," a "practical application" of Christianity which seemed very close to his heart. His intellectual restlessness shows itself as well in his boiling temperament, a quality which was remarked on by many people who knew him. And once he realized that he could never agree with Tolstoy, that his mind could never be directed toward a fixed solution, he rebelled against Tolstoy with all the force that he was capable of. He told Gurevich:

> He [Tolstoy] wants—and his son, and the Tolstoyans, and others as well—, *he* wants what is beyond human nature, what is impossible, impossible, because such is our essence. . . . I know myself . . . all my life I was a demon. I did such things, that . . . nobody knows this. And now—I am an old man, I am sick, and nevertheless, such feelings are boiling in me that I myself am not able to say what and why it is. I have dreams, terrible dreams which can't be expressed in words. And who knows what this is? And what for, why and where from? Can you call it sensuality? But after all I don't know myself what I need it for! I don't need anything, in my mind I don't want anything,—I am looking for peace of soul, but something is troubling and tormenting me. . . .
>
> (301)

Tolstoy was not spared the excesses of this passionate nature. Leskov attributed a lot of what he considered Tolstoy's misinterpretations to the latter's "withdrawal from the world," to the fact that he surrounded himself with people who fully and uncritically accepted his views. Dismayed that Tolstoy might be "spoilt once and for all" by having made up his mind and closed it to any objections, Leskov made it his mission to be that critical presence from afar whether Tolstoy liked it or not. A. M. Khir'iakov, an acquaintance of both writers, describes the relationship thus:

> It [was] not blind worship, but love with criticism, with a constant readiness for protest[. . .]. In Nikolai Semenovich this protest was expressed with special obstinacy.
>
> He loved Tolstoy very much and valued the correspondence of his own thought with that of this great writer. But when the great writer began to say something which was not acceptable to the mind and the heart of Leskov, then the protest would begin. Affectionate, but undoubtedly protesting letters were sent off to Iasnaia Poliana, and at home [. . .] his study would resound with denouncing and refuting tirades.
>
> —No, Modestych—he would say—it is not said for nothing, that it is not good for man to be alone. He sits there like a bear in his hole, in his Iasnaia Poliana, not seeing real people and losing an appropriate point of view. He should see people, follow up on everything that's going on in the world. . . . It would be good for him to go to Europe. Look at contemporary European life. Then he wouldn't have written *Non-Action* in this

manner. And who is around him? They are very nice people, these non-resisters, but can they really give him the necessary rebuff? He is breaking them, crushing them, and the result is a swamp, which is not offering him resistance, but sucking him in. But he needs rebuttal, he needs a fight. . . . Why am I worrying so much? Because what he says with such terrible force is so dear to me.

> (2-3)

In an attempt to prescribe the 'way to heaven,' Tolstoy had to ignore many elements that did not fit—sweep the dirt under the rug, or let others clean up the mess. "Sitting in his bear hole," he did not really appreciate the enormous task that Leskov had set for himself, the hard task of "cleaning up," tirelessly pointing out inconsistencies, wrong turns, false claims. As Leskov mentioned repeatedly, his task was to clean away "the dung that had accumulated outside the cathedral."[32]

Tolstoy did not see the relationship that way. From his point of view, Leskov was just one of his followers, although one with some unpredictable and troubling idiosyncrasies. As he remarked to Men'shikov several years after Leskov's death: "I was very struck at how completely Leskov attached himself to us in his later years, but I was always waiting unconsciously, that he would go ahead and present us with something really unexpected . . ." (249).

Notes

1. I would like to thank Donna Orwin and the two anonymous readers for their helpful and generous comments and suggestions. Research for this article was supported by two grants from the International Research and Exchanges Board, with funds provided by the US Department of State (Title VIII program) and the National Endowment for the Humanities. None of these organizations is responsible for the views expressed.

2. Apostolov, Azarova, Boiko, Edgerton, Filimonova, Gudzii, Kupriianovskii, Kurlanskaia 1985 and 1986, Luzhanovskii, 1962-64 and 1965, Sergeenko, Tunimanov, Viduetskaia.

3. See, for example, *Pravedniki,* his cycle of stories about righteous characters written in the mid-1870s through the 1880s, and his reworked *Prolog* legends.

4. Leskov followed Tolstoy's writing career with interest and, beginning with an early comprehensive review of *War and Peace* from 1869, he commented extensively on Tolstoy's work and mentioned Tolstoy or his teachings in more than thirty articles (not counting those on such Tolstoy-related subjects as vegetarianism, nonresistance to evil, marriage, education, or forgiveness of offences).

Significantly, his last published piece was "O pov-esti Tolstogo."

5. The two writers met for the first time on April 20, 1887. Their extant correspondence consists of 52 letters from Leskov to Tolstoy and 10 letters of Tolstoy from Leskov dating from April 1887 to October 1894. The majority of Tolstoy's letters unfortunately seems to have been lost due to the negligent handling of the Leskov archives after his death. Unlike other letters by Leskov, the majority of which are still unpublished to this day, his letters to Tolstoy—with the exception of one which was discovered later—received preferential treatment and appeared already in 1928 in the collection *Pis'ma Tolstogo i k Tolstomu*. The first complete publication of the correspondence is found in *L6T* 3: 334-415.

6. One of Leskov's most blatant attacks on the Tolstoyans is in *Zimnii den'* (*A Winter's Day*, 1894).

7. Leskov was aware of this trend to diminish his own contribution: "They say I am imitating him. Not in the least! When Tolstoy was writing *Anna Karenina* [between 1873 and 1877], I was already close to what I am saying now" (Faresov 307-08). Even Tolstoy admitted this fact in an interview in 1898: "Leskov was my follower, but not in a spirit of imitation. He had long before started out in the same direction I am travelling now. We met each other, and I am moved by his agreement with all my views" (Faresov 71).

8. Luzhanovskii's arguments were already brought up in 1897 by Sementkovskii, a largely forgotten Leskov critic.

9. Tolstoy mentioned the theme first in a letter to Chertkov from June 20, 1887. See Tolstoy's *PSS* 86: 2-63. A variant appeared in 1889 in the collection *Tsvetnik* which was the text supposedly used by Leskov (*PSS* 26: 245, 737).

10. Although Tolstoy's statements on Leskov are very inconsistent, depending on his interlocutor, as concerns Leskov's style they are almost invariably negative, as for example in a letter to Chertkov from January 23, 1887: "Leskov's article is excellent, except for the language in which one feels artificiality" (*PSS* 86: 18) or in a conversation after Leskov's death: "One should reexamine Leskov—there is much good in him. His style is heavy, with entanglements and long-windedness. This is why he has been totally forgotten. But in his thoughts is lots of good stuff" (Gusev 100). Apart from stylistic considerations Tolstoy was very fond of several of Leskov's pieces, in particularly his story *Pod prazdnik obideli* (*Offended Before Christmas*). He recorded, recited, and spoke

of it frequently. One must not forget, however, that even then he did not have *Leskov's* story in mind, but *his own* edited, cut, and renamed version. See Boiko.

11. The two italicized French words are the same in the original.

12. Apparently, the two writers discussed their stylistic differences. A visitor to Iasnaia Poliana reported a discussion from 1894 in which Tolstoy was asked whether he liked Leskov: "He answered that, in his opinion, certain places in Leskov were extraordinary (he began to recall the title of [some] pieces and scenes from them), but his basic shortcoming was an artificiality in his plots and in his language, and his particular little words (*slovechki*). He even 'dared to tell him that' when they met in person, but he [Leskov] answered that he was unable to write otherwise" (Lazurskii 23-24).

13. Tolstoy developed this idea in his article "Nedlanie" (1893), in which he rejects scientific truths—and with it all of science—exactly for that reason.

14. The sketch mentions two books from early childhood which made the most lasting impressions on him: *A Hundred and Four Holy Stories* with pictures, read at age five (Dostoevsky was intrigued by this book as well in his childhood), and *Readings from the Four Gospels* read at age ten. See Leskov's "Iz vsekh knig . . .".

15. Leskov's choice of title for his fairy tale, with its obvious reference to the Bible, and especially to the Second Coming, makes its link with this letter even clearer.

16. Leskov refers to *Ivan Durak*, one of the folk tales published in the 1886 Tolstoy volume.

17. The "charred pieces of wood" is a reference to the parable *The Goldchild* in the same volume. In this parable, the spiritual strength necessary to overcome external evil is gained by completing three preparatory steps symbolized by three objects: the step of 'cleansing oneself'—not using a dirty towel for cleaning; then, 'strengthening oneself in good work'—firmly attaching the wooden support necessary for moulding a rim; and 'warming with never-ending love'—making charred pieces of wood sprout again through patient watering.

18. The references are again to the parable *The Goldchild,* see note 17.

19. I am grateful to I. V. Stoliarova for pointing out this passage to me.

20. Konstantin Leont'ev called the idea of saving one's soul, the concern for personal salvation, "transcendental egoism." (Berdiaev 223).

21. The "banishment" of the entertainer which was added to the revised (published) version of the story shows that Leskov must have believed that the found wisdom did not only not work for rulers, but was something dangerous that had to be hidden away *in general*. He furthermore describes in great detail the isolation in which the wise maiden lives and her immense ignorance of all worldly matters. She does not even know the meaning of "king" (*L11T* 9: 27). In the earlier draft of the story which is much milder as concerns this point the king actually tries to apply the rules but could not manage and turns over the kingdom to his son, who in turn buries the found answers (*Skazka o korole*).

22. The quotation in question (1 Cor 13, 5) literally says "love seeketh not her own" (King James) or "love does not insist on its own way" (Revised Standard Version)—in Russian "*ne ishchet svoego*." Leskov often changed it into "love that seeketh nothing for itself" (*nichego ne ishchet dlia sebia*)." See, for example, *Leskov o literature* 136.

23. Hugh McLean has explored in great detail the 'rushlight (*ploshka*)' and 'torch (*fakel*)' trope which Leskov used when comparing himself to Tolstoy (529-530).

24. The quotation is from 2 Peter 3, 16.

25. The literary critic Mikhail Osipovich Men'shikov was personally acquainted with both Leskov and Tolstoy.

26. The article in question is *Graf L. N. Tolstoi i F. M. Dostoevskii kak eresiarkhi.*

27. Of course, Leskov did not stop "defending" Tolstoy after 1883 as he stated but wrote many more articles on Tolstoy-related issues. Many of them, however, follow the pattern of pointing out older sources of Tolstoy's thoughts and continuing roughly in this vein: "Why are you attacking Tolstoy for this. . . . This is not new, but can be found in such and such a book."

28. See his 1893 article *Nedelanie* (*PSS* 29: 173-201). As for more transcendent notions of non-action, in 1911, when he presented the essence of Taoism to the reader, he equated the Taoist abstinence from all corporal desires with the Christian notion of love as expressed in the first epistle of John (*PSS* 40: 351).

29. The previous titles of Tolstoy's parable *The Godchild*, mentioned above (see note 17), further support this view: *How the Godchild Redeemed the Sins of Others, The Godchild as the Man who Assumed the Sins of Others and How he Atoned for Them, How a Person Assumed the Sins of Others and How he Redeemed Them* (*PSS* 25: 725).

30. The usual translation of this title is *The March Hare* or *The Rabbit Warren*. I proposed this translation as an alternative in my PhD dissertation (Weinberg 174-181).

31. "*kopal tu kuchu*," see Faresov, 308.

32. See, for example, in a letter to Tolstoy, January 4, 1893 (*L6T* 3: 371).

Works Cited

Apostolov, N. N. "L. N. Tolstoy i N. S. Leskov." *Lev Tolstoy i ego sputniki.* Moscow: Komissiia po oznamenovaniiu stoletiia so dnia rozhdeniia L. N. Tolstogo, 1928. 218-225.

Azarova, N. I. "O narodnykh rasskazakh Tolstogo i Leskova." *Iasnopolianskii sbornik.* Tula: Priokskoe knizhnoe izdatel'stvo, 1974. 92-100.

Bakhtin, M. M. *Towards a Philosophy of the Act.* Trans. Vadim Liapunov. Austin, TX: University of Texas Press, 1993.

Berdiaev, Nikolai. *Konstantin Leont'ev: ocherk iz istorii russkoi religioznoi mysli.* Paris: YMCA Press, 1926.

Boiko, M. P. "N. S. Leskov: *Pod prazdnik obideli.*" *Tolstoi-redaktor: Publikatsiia redaktorskikh rabot L. N. Tolstogo.* Moscow: Kniga, 1965. 248-60.

Chertkov, L. "Pis'ma Nikolaia Leskova I. S. Gagarinu i I. M. Martynovu." *Simvol* 6 (1981): 185-188.

Durylin, S. N. "O religioznom tvorchestve N. S. Leskova." *Khristianskaia mysl'* 11 (1916): 73-86.

Edgerton, W. B. "Leskov and Tolstoy: Two Literary Heretics." *American Slavic and East European Review* 12, No. 4 (1953): 524-34.

Faresov, A. *Protiv techenii: N. S. Leskov: ego zhizn', sochineniia, polemika i vospominaniia o nem.* St. Petersburg, 1904.

Filimonova, N. Iu. "N. S. Leskov i L. N. Tolstoy." *Iazyk i stil': Tipologiia i poetika zhanra.* Volgograd: VPI im. A. S. Serafimovicha, 1976. 148-57.

Gudzii, N. K. "Tolstoy i Leskov." *Iskusstvo* 4, No. 1-2 (1928): 95-128.

Gurevich, L. Ia. "Iz vospominanii o N. S. Leskove (Popovodu ego smerti)." *Literatura i estetika: Kriticheskie opyty i etiudy.* Moscow, 1912. 295-302.

Gusev, N. N. *Dva goda s Tolstym.* Moscow, 1928.

Khir'iakov, A. M. "N. S. Leskov." *Rul'* [Berlin] No. 1296 (8 March 1925): 2-3.

Kupriianovskii, P. V. "L. N. Tolstoy i N. S. Leskov v zhurnale *Severnyi vestnik.*" *Uchenye zapiski Ivanovskogo P. I. im. Furmanova* 29 (1962): 101-50.

Kurlanskaia, G. B. "Leskov i Tolstoy." *Tvorchestvo N. S. Leskova: Mezhvuzovskii sbornik nauchnykh trudov.* Kursk: KGPI, 1986. 85-111.

———. "Tolstovskie motivy v *Zakhudalom rode* N. S. Leskova." *Problemy izucheniia kul'turnogo naslediia.* Moscow: Nauka, 1985. 273-79.

Lantz, K. A. *Nikolay Leskov.* Boston: Twayne, 1979.

Lazurskii, V. F. "Dnevnik." *L. N. Tolstoy v vospominaniiakh sovremennikov.* Vol. 2. Moscow, 1960. 5-42.

Leskov o literature i iskusstve. Leningrad, 1984.

Leskov, N. S. "Graf L. N. Tolstoy i F. M. Dostoevsky kak eresiarkhi: Religiia strakha i religiia liubvi." *Novosti* (April 1 and 3, 1883).

———. *Iz vsekh knig . . .* RGALI, *Fond* 275, *op.* 1, no. 101 [undated].

———. Letter to M. A. Protopopov from April 30, 1894. IRLI, *Fond* 391, no. 33.

———. Letter to M. O. Men'shikov from November 12, 1893. IRLI, *Fond* 22574 CLVIIIb. 61.

———. Letter to M. O. Men'shikov from June 20, 1893. IRLI, *Fond* 22574 CLVIIIb. 61.

———. Letter to Ol'ga Krokhina from March 4, 1892. IRLI, *Fond* 220, no. 42, sheet nr. 27.

———. "O povesti Tolstogo," *Peterburgskaia gazeta* (January 27 and 28, 1895).

———. "O rozhne: Uvet synam protivleniia," *Novoe vremia* (November 4, 1886). Rep. *N. S. Leskov o literature i iskusstve.* Leningrad, 1984. 128-41.

———. "Perepiska N. S. Leskova s L. N. Tolstym." *Sobranie sochinenii v shesti tomackh (L6T).* Vol. 3. Moscow: Ekran, 1993. 334-415.

———. "Rasskazy kstati: Nevynosimyi blagodetel' (Tolstovskii tip I prototip)." *Russkaia zhizn'* (December 20, 1893): 2.

———. "Russkie obshchestvennye zametki." *Birzhevye vedomosti* No. 15 (January 11, 1870): 1-2.

———. "Skazka o korole Dobrokhote i o prostovolosoj devke." Draft ms. RGALI, *Fond* 275, *op.* 1, no. 29.

———. *Sobranie sochinenii v odinnadtsati tomakh (L11T).* Moscow: Gosizdat, 1956-58.

———. *Sobranie sochinenii v shesti tomakh (L6T),* vol. III. Moscow: Ekran, 1993.

———. "Zagrobnyi svidetel' za zhenshchin," *Istoricheskii vestnik* (November 1886): 249-280.

———. *Zapisnaia knizhka* IRLI, *Fond* 612, no. 106.

Lovejoy, A. O. *The Great Chain of Being: A Study of the History of an Idea.* Cambridge, MA: Harvard University Press, 1961.

Luzhanovskii, A. V. "Narodnye rasskazy N. S. Leskova i L. N. Tolstogo." *Tolstovskii sbornik.* Tula: Tul'skii GPI im. L. N. Tolstogo, 1962-64. 241-54.

———. "Neopublikovannaia stat'ia N. S. Leskova o tolstovskom uchenii." *Russkaia literatura* 1 (1965): 162-67.

Macher, B. *Nikolai Leskovs Verhältnis zur Orthodoxie.* Diss. Marburg, 1952.

McLean, H. *Nikolai Leskov: The Man and His Art.* Cambridge, MA: Harvard University Press, 1977.

Men'shikov, M. O. "Iz zapisnykh knizhek." *Prometei* 12 (1980): 247-256.

Pis'ma Tolstogo i k Tolstomu. Ed. S. P. Shesterikov. Moscow-Leningrad, 1928.

Sementkovskii, R. I. "Nikolai Semenovich Leskov." N. S. Leskov, *Polnoe sobranie sochinenii.* Vol. 1. St. Petersburg, 1897. 5-66.

Sergeenko, P. A. "Leskov i Tolstoy." *Tolstoi i ego sovremenniki.* Moscow: Izdanie V. M. Sablina, 1911. 213-22.

Tolstoi, L. N. Letter to Chertkov from January 23, 1887 in: *PSS* 86: 18.

———. Letter to Chertkov from June 20, 1887 in: *PSS* 86: 62-63.

———. *Polnoe sobranie sochinenii v devianosta tomakh.* Moscow, 1928-58.

Tunimanov, V. A. "Leskov i L. Tolstoy." *Leskov i russkaia literatura.* Moscow: Nauka, 1988. 181-201.

"U Tolstogo—Iasnopolianskie zapiski." *Literaturnoe nasledstvo* 90, No. 4 (1979).

Viduetskaia, I. "Tolstoi i Leskov: Nravstvenno-filosofskie iskaniia (1880-1890-e gody)." *Tolstoy i literatura narodov SSSR.* Erevan: Izdatel'stvo Erevanskogo universiteta, 1978. 145-61.

Weinberg [Sperrle], I. Ch. *The Organic Worldview of Nikolaj Leskov.* PhD Dissertation, Columbia University, New York, 1996.

I. Christina Sperrle (essay date spring 2000)

SOURCE: Sperrle, I. Christina. "Narrative Structure in Nikolai Leskov's *Cathedral Folk*: The Polyphonic Chronicle." *Slavic and East European Journal* 44, no. 1 (spring 2000): 29-47.

[*In the following essay, Sperrle assesses Leskov's use of a multiperspective or polyphonic narrative mode in* The Cathedral Folk, *examining the Russian writer's efforts to depict a broad juxtaposition of many character viewpoints without attempting to synthesize them through a singular narrative consciousness.*]

The unusual form of Nikolai Leskov's *Cathedral Folk* (1872) has prompted many commentators on the work to raise the issue of genre. Most call it a novel, albeit a "flawed" one (Eekman 123-4; Zelinsky passim; McLean 174). The "flaws" include its uneven narrative structure, the mixture of heterogeneous materials and styles, factual discrepancies, an absence of psychological characterization, and the lack of a strong central plot. Such classification also inevitably invites a comparison with the genre's masters—Tolstoy and Dostoevsky—and results usually in a denigration of Leskov's work, which is thought to pale when placed next to the great nineteenth-century Russian novels.

Placing Leskov into the accepted nineteenth-century literary canon ignores the innovative features in his work that distinguish him from this tradition. Somewhat against the current, Marcadé credits Leskov with breaking the dominant structure of the nineteenth-century novel and creating a new type of genre "of which novelistic elements constitute only one part." He calls him a precursor of the experimental "cubist" narratives of the early twentieth century, such as those of Bely, Pilniak, Babel, or of such "chaotic compositions as those of Remizov" (364). Unfortunately, he does not develop this theme further. I will take his lead and especially borrow his term "cubist" (which he himself appropriated from Berdiaev) for this particular Leskovian narrative.

Cubism was foremost an experiment with form. The cubist painter of the beginning of the twentieth century rejected the traditional representational standards in an attempt to depict the "fourth dimension": "movement in depth, or time, or space-time, by the simultaneous presentation of multiple aspects of an object" (Canaday 458). This effort yielded a new concept of non-perspectival space. Instead of creating space by illusionistic devices (modeling and foreshortening), depth was achieved by overlapping different single views, and, later, by different layers of pasted material (collage) (Janson 527). When talking about *Cathedral Folk,* Leskov himself repeatedly raised the issue of form and insisted that it was not a novel, but—as its subtitle indicates—a chronicle (*khronika*). He was also well aware that this form was unusual and in his view represented "something new." Examining Leskov's chronicle as a cubist narrative, that is as a narrative that stresses *visual* multiperspectivity, will illuminate some of the more unconventional features in its narrative structure, as well as in the nature and role of the narrator.

Cathedral Folk is the final result of a vast epic work (conceived in 1866) in which Leskov intended to depict life in a typical Russian provincial town as reflected through characters from different social classes. The only completed part of this project centered on the clergy, and was published as *Cathedral Folk* in 1872. It focuses on the three men of the cloth who serve the town's principal cathedral: the archpriest Father Savely Tuberozov, the priest Zachary Benefaktov, and the deacon Akhilla.[1]

The work consists largely of trifling incidents, squabbles, and pleasant events that disrupt the humdrum existence of the inhabitants in Old Town (*Stargorod*). Instead of a main plot, there are several intersecting story lines, one of which describes Tuberozov's largely futile attempts to heighten his parishioners' moral awareness and to reform the rigid structures of the church apparatus. A second plot line deals with the arrival of nihilism as exhibited by the local schoolteacher, two Petersburg exrevolutionaries, and a few minor figures.

Commentators on *Cathedral Folk* have remarked that these two lines are not developed well enough, and that the two major issues—Tuberozov's run-ins with the ecclesiastic authorities and the threat of rationalistic views to Orthodox Russia—are somewhat trivialized. But these "shortcomings" are actually characteristic of the work's structure. In fact, the dynamic of *Cathedral Folk* rests not on plot development and suspense (i.e., on "perspective"), but on the sheer exuberance of anecdotal material (i.e., on the "collage" effect). This so-called "raw" material (episodes, anecdotes, notebooks, life stories)—which in itself is to a certain extent self-sufficient—is superimposed, recomposed and varied, and gradually accumulates different perspectives which interact with each other as in a cubist picture in order to form a final impression: a picture of the three clergymen who comprise the "Cathedral Folk." Thus, the formal devices mimic the ideational content of the work: a fictional rendering of the philosophical concept of *sobornost'*—variety in communion. Though these three members of the cloth represent a unity—expressed in the collective noun of the title *Soboriane*—Leskov shows how their common belief system, Orthodox Christianity, gets interpreted individually, and changes when confronted with life.

The three characters reveal their strengths and weaknesses precisely in trifles, in their personal reactions to challenges that threaten their traditional way of life. Surprisingly, considering their vocation, they do not engage in any discussions on the nature of faith or on what constitutes the right relationship with God. Even the intimate diary of Tuberozov, a person well-read in Church history, does not contain any sections treating abstract matters of faith. McLean is not alone when he expresses his dissatisfaction on this issue:

> Unfortunately, Leskov does not match either the cosmic sweep [of Dostoevsky and Tolstoy] or their emotional intensity. He shows us no Konstantin Lyovin or Ivan Karamazov wrestling agonizingly with the "ac-

cursed questions" of the existence of God and the moral order of the universe. Instead the whole theme is externalized and trivialized.

(McLean 200-201)

Leskov "zooms in" on the particular to draw conclusions about the general. As Old Town was to represent all of Russia, so in Leskov's view, trifles are true indicators of a person's real character. A few years after *Cathedral Folk,* he wrote: "As we know, a person is best understood in trifles" (6: 502).[2] In *Cathedral Folk* little is discussed. Yet precisely in the trifles that Leskov depicts and in the characters' reactions to these trifles, we are shown three different modes of spirituality and three different relationships with God. For Leskov, faith is not determined intellectually—by how one resolves for oneself the "accursed questions"—but by how one's beliefs stand up against the seemingly insignificant moral dilemmas encountered in daily life.

The concentration on trifles is a central part of Leskov's artistic intention. He, therefore, illustrates in exemplary manner Bakhtin's idea of the crucial importance of the everyday, the ordinary, of what Morson and Emerson call "prosaics" (Morson and Emerson 15). For Leskov, "trifles" are symbolic and conceal much larger issues. He writes in *Cathedral Folk*:

> Savely, Zachary and Akhilla were friends, but it would, of course, be greatly unjust to propose that they would not make efforts to vary their life with scenes of slight enmity and misunderstandings, [. . .] No, even here there was something of this sort, and the pages of Tuberozov's diary [. . .] will uncover many trifles which did not seem trifles at all for those who felt them, who fought with them and endured them.
>
> (4: 11)

Seen from this perspective, the work's designation as a chronicle makes sense. In a novel, events are deliberately selected and arranged around central characters, whereas in a chronicle events are recorded as they happen. The chronicler is an observer rather than a creator of events. A fictional chronicler will thus try to recreate this seeming objectivity and conceal his presence as much as possible by turning himself into something akin to a "secretary." Thus, the mechanism of fictionality, although no doubt operative, is less obvious in a fictional chronicle than in a novel.

Leskov repeatedly expressed his distaste for the novelistic genre. In a work from the mid-1870s, which was written in what was to become one of his favorite genres—namely the fictional memoir style—he comments on what he considers a new narrative technique:

> I will relate all of this not as it is told in novels; and this, it seems to me, can present a certain interest, and even, I may say, a novelty, and moreover, an edification.

> I will not cut short certain events and enlarge the significance of others, since I am not forced to do so by the artificial and unnatural form of the novel which demands the rounding off of the plot and the concentration of everything around one main center. Life does not happen that way. Human life takes its course, like a scroll that is unwinding from a spool, and in the notes I am offering here I will unfold it as simply as a ribbon.
>
> (5: 279)

For Leskov, the novel is "unnatural." It cannot represent life, since real life events are not shaped and concentrated around one center (one perspective) but happen in a chronological way: They "unfold."[3] Consequently, in Leskov's work there is often a sense that the narrator is not in control, and, moreover, that the author seems to be absent. Characters are overwhelmed by circumstances, and unlike Dostoevsky, who employs accidents and unexpected occurrences to advance the plot,[4] Leskov uses them to disrupt the story line, create endless digressions and place the hero in ever more new and seemingly unrelated situations.

Leskov's narrator, however, is not a mere recounter of facts and anecdotes. Nor is Leskov just a *bytopisatel'*—a depictor of bland daily life, as unsympathetic critics call him with stubborn insistence. His ideal is the *rasskaz-polu-byl'*—a mixture of truth and fiction—which Grossman called "an original and purely Leskovian genre" (255). Leskov rejected traditional literary genres and preferred his own improvisations, such as "rhapsody," "little pictures from nature," *"paysage et genre,"* "potpourri," "survey," *"revue,"* "story *à propos,"* and others. As Eikhenbaum remarked, for Leskov the word "genre" referred not to the literary term but to *genre* painting (348). This comment deserves closer examination. Genre paintings present scenes from life with an air of undeliberateness. The artist gives the impression that he has merely copied what happened to be before his eyes, that he merely depicted from life, so to speak. But in the final analysis he presents *his* arrangement of a typical scene. He takes what is considered typical material, characters, costumes and objects—everything that is needed to convey the flavor of a certain environment—and arranges them into a genre scene. The author of a genre painting is not an inventor, but first a meticulous observer and second a skillful arranger. The narrator of *Cathedral Folk* can best be characterized as first a genre painter and second a "cubist" painter, since in his final arrangement he superimposes multiple genre paintings in order to reveal a multiperspectival, synthetic, but unresolved image.

Leskov had determined the form of *Cathedral Folk* from the very outset, explaining to an editor that his work was not a "large fictional work" but a *"novelistic chronicle"* (emphasis his).[5] He also stressed the form's uncommonness, the fact that it presented "something new":

[It] will be a chronicle, and not a novel. That is how it was conceived, and in this manner it is growing according to the grace of God. This not a very customary thing in our society, but to make up for it we have an opportunity to learn something.

(10: 260)

Obviously, for Leskov, "chronicle" was not an empty label. Rather than convey content in the most advantageous manner possible, this new form—if it was accepted by the reader—would initiate some mysterious learning process. For Leskov, then, form, in addition to content, had become an instrument of enlightenment. He expressed the same attitude in the statement quoted earlier, in which he rejected the novel in favor of the fictional memoir style and suggested that this new form was not only "interesting" but presented "an edification" (*nazidanie*) (5: 279). To uncover this instructive element, these "new" genres, and the genre of the chronicle in particular, have to be examined more closely. For this analysis, I propose to interpret the term "chronicle" in its particular Russian context. Indeed, in describing to an editor the future ***Cathedral Folk*** as "a history of years bygone" (*istoriia let vremennykh*) (10: 281), Leskov clearly alluded to the early twelfth-century Kievan chronicle, *Povest' vremennykh let—A History of Bygone Years,* also called the Nestorian or Primary Chronicle. Moreover, in the first version of ***Cathedral Folk,*** when giving Old Town's prehistory, Leskov refers on the very first page to Nestor's chronicle, claiming that mention had been made of Old Town already on the "very early pages of both manuscripts" of this early Russian document. With this move and by quoting from an additional "trustworthy legend" (*dostovernoe skazanie*) which is "preserved" in Old Town, he clearly places his work into the chronicle tradition (Leskov 1867, no. 6:181).

A mosaic of heterogeneous material—historical as well as legendary facts, literary passages with dialogues, oral tales, excerpts from other chronicles and enlarged anecdotes—is the most distinctive feature of the Russian Primary chronicle. Moreover, the scope of the Old Russian Chronicle—the "documentation" of the history of Kievan Rus "from the very beginning" until its fragmentation in the twelfth century—exceeded the lifetime of a single compiler, and we have to assume several authors. But unlike the historian in a modern sense, the author or compiler of the Russian chronicle took great liberties in the handling of his material. In eleventh-century Rus there was no concept of "historical objectivity." Separate redactions of the chronicle have shown that the compiler not only collected material, that is, incorporated and copied older sources, but felt free to rewrite and shape this material to suit his regional point of view. The ancient chronicler then was a *reviser* of "factual material" who could embellish and exaggerate facts or omit them altogether.

These improvisational features—the compilers' liberal handling of source material[6] and the mosaic composition—are found in Leskov's chronicle as well and, perhaps not surprisingly, these are the very traits which were considered the "flaws of the novel." Like the Primary Chronicle, ***Cathedral Folk*** is an anthology of narrative structures: extended *skaz* sections, dramatic dialogues and an abundance of anecdotes alternate with the author's commentary and apostrophes to the reader. In addition, the large section of Tuberozov's diary, containing the protagonist's own stylistic idiosyncrasies and many factual inaccuracies, is like a chronicle within a chronicle inserted "verbatim" into the work.

The ancient chronicler could thus be called a genre painter as defined above. He pretends to show an objective, "historical" picture of reality, but it is a reality that he arranges according to his taste from collected material—a reality of *polu-byl'*. More than factual history, then, he was interested in presenting a genre, the flavor of a certain time, in telling the tale—the *povest'* of bygone years.

Leskov was guided by the same purpose in his chronicle, namely, to depict a microcosm of Russia at a certain historical period. Unlike the Old Russian chronicler, however, he did not concentrate on major events, but chose seemingly insignificant people and incidents. In a work from 1883 he expressed his interpretation of the historian's task:

I greatly appreciate and love this science [history] but I can serve only one aspect of it, the light and superficial aspect, the aspect of portraying certain unimportant people, who, however, by their very lives express to a certain extent the history of their time.

(7: 522)[7]

When calling his work "A History of Years Bygone," Leskov changed the customary word order of the title, thereby stressing the last word, the adjective *vremennykh*—"temporal." His title literally translates as "A History of Years in Temporal Terms." The ancient chronicler wanted to show God's design in history and tended to homogenize the various points of view of the miscellaneous material. Leskov is more modern: by juxtaposing diverging outlooks he emphasizes their temporal quality. The multiple, superimposed perspectives lack a unifying "authorial," that is "true" perspective, creating the unresolved "cubist" effect. For Leskov, any point of view is only temporary, one of many, and subject to change according to circumstances. He is suspicious of one "true" perspective, of "one truth," and in ***Cathedral Folk,*** as in his work in general, he demonstrates the pitfalls of trusting any exclusive vision.

Thus, Leskov rejects authorial omniscience and prefers narrators that have no ultimate authority, such as the highly individual voice of the *skaz*-narrator, or—as in the case of ***Cathedral Folk***—the chronicler, who merely compiles, presents, and rearranges other people's points of view. Both types of narrators allow Leskov to play games with perspectives and shake up our ways of perceiving. This may be the learning process he referred to earlier, a learning process intrinsic to the form of the work.

The depiction of Deacon Akhilla at the very beginning of ***Cathedral Folk*** may serve as an example of Leskov's "cubist" method. He explains his technique directly in the text: In order to "paint some kind of picture of the mighty Akhilla for the reader" he proposes to list all traits that are in currency about this character. Such a device, he feels, "would be somehow more satisfactory" for the task (4: 6). In other words, like a cubist painter he is presenting different perspectives of his subject, and like a chronicler, the "secretary to his time," he simply records and arranges other people's experiences. Even within this limited material the reader is shown how one attribute looks quite different through another person's eyes. Thus, to do justice to the pupil's "enormous size and his limited successes in class," the school inspector called Akhilla a "blockhead" (*dubina*). The rector, on hearing this evaluation, finds it quite inadequate and using now the literal meaning of this term—a wooden cudgel—explodes the metaphor:

> [M]arveling at his [Akhilla's] dimensions, his strength and his slow-wittedness he would say:

> "I think it would be insufficient to call you a cudgel since in my eyes you are at least a whole wagon full of fire wood."

> (4: 7)

Trying to surpass that depiction, the next person simply calls Akhilla "excessive," in fact "so excessive that it is difficult to know how to deal with him in a dignified manner." The author lists these attributes without comment and then reports a hilarious anecdote of how the bishop bestowed on Akhilla the title "the pierced one" (*uiazvlennyi*) (4: 7-9). Since Akhilla had a powerful voice, which was actually his main qualification for becoming a deacon, he was asked to sing the solo in the hymn "Pierced by Sorrows" during a festive service. During his moment of glory, as the author notes, "he should have been painted, since no pen can adequately depict him" (4: 8). That is, the author feels now that words are inadequate "to paint some kind of picture" of this character.[8] The outcome of this event demonstrates another facet of Akhilla's "excessiveness" which "cannot be dealt with in a dignified manner": he was so carried away that he could not stop improvising new melodies for the word "pierced" until he was forcefully dragged out of the church. After merely listing these "eye-witness" reports, the narrator completes "the picture of the mighty Akhilla" by adding some biographical details and by an external description.

Throughout the chronicle these attributes imparted to Akhilla reappear in numerous situations, are varied and enriched by new connotations, until at the end the initial values have been modified. There is a feeling that their "rough edges" had been "polished off." For example, Akhilla's physical strength was presented in the beginning as an overwhelming but admirable quality. In the image of the "blockhead" and the "wagon full of wood," his strength was coupled with his negative trait, an equally excessive stupidity. But by the end he is made to realize that his nemesis and source of weakness is not his slow wits, as expected, but what was admired before, namely, his strength. Whereas the attribute "the pierced one" had no intrinsic semantic value when it was accorded him, by the end, however, it reaches tragic proportions. It is reinvoked several times in the text, most prominently when Akhilla is in mortal agony over Tuberozov's death. At that point we witness the excessiveness of his pain, and he truly ends up as one who is "pierced by sorrows." In other words, the epithet "the pierced one," originally coined by the bishop in jest, has gained an unforeseen depth and has become a real character trait.[9] As happens frequently in Leskov, a trifle becomes symbolic. In this manner the author-chronicler freely uses information from previous sources—oral or written reports—for his own purposes and varies it as he sees fit: enlarging, reducing or using it in new contexts.

Many of the features of Leskov's chronicle that have been pointed out—mosaic construction, multiperspectivity, lack of author's omniscience, rejection of a unifying point of view, open-endedness (the chronicle as a scroll unfolding)—call to mind Bakhtin's reading of the polyphonic novel, and in particular Dostoevsky's chronicle-like novels. There is, however, a very crucial difference. Bakhtin (using examples from Dostoevsky) vehemently rejects what Leskov cultivates, namely secondhand knowledge. For Bakhtin secondhand definitions are part of a monologic design and fundamentally unethical (Morson and Emerson 265): "a *secondhand* truth, becomes a *lie* degrading and deadening him [the person being thus described]" (Bakhtin 59). The examples he chose, however, only demonstrate the secondhand characterization by one person of another person or by a collective group with a unified opinion ("us," "spies," "psychologists") (Bakhtin 60), but he does not seem to explore whether the same is true when secondhand descriptions of several different people—several distinct subjective visions—get superimposed, a technique Leskov employs with great mastery and liberty, as has been shown above. Instead, Bakhtin understood psychology in terms of inner speech (Morson and Emerson 173-230) and quoted as example one of Raskolnikov's so-called dialogized monologues in which he "inundates his own inner speech with [. . .] words of others, complicating them with his own accents or directly reaccenting them, entering into a passionate polemic with them" (Bakhtin 238). While considering this technique a crucial element of the polyphonic novel, Bakhtin, however, does not explain why a voice filtered through the hero's consciousness is not conveying a secondhand truth, since it is not really the other person's voice arguing with him, but the hero's, Raskolnikov's, version of what his mother, Marmeladov, Svidrigailov, etc., might answer to his objections.

In contrast to Dostoevsky, who concentrates on inner speech, for Leskov the world of the mind is very deceptive and can be far removed from reality, which may explain why he rejects authorial omniscience. One example that illustrates this philosophy is the bath scene in **Cathedral Folk** (4: 84-93), which has often been considered superfluous and totally unrelated to the "plot." This episode shows how the mind left to its own devices and refusing to check itself against reality creates a fantastic picture which has lost all ties to the outside world.

The scene is set in the deceptive and dim morning twilight. Three strange figures around whom "breathed the atmosphere of a northern saga" (4: 85) make their way down to the river. The first figure initially seems, "to superstitious minds," like the Old Town's house demon, but with a change of light it turns into some kind of a druid. The second figure, a woman, holds a large gleaming copper shield with a tuft of hair attached to it, a trophy which "seemed to have been just freshly taken from a skull together with the skin." The third figure, a black savage, seems to be carrying "instruments of torture" and "a bloody sack from which hung two human heads, pale, devoid of hair and which most probably breathed out the last bit of air during torture" (4: 85). From across the river towards the group something was moving "slowly and evenly," reminiscent of the avenging statue of the Commander from *Don Juan* (4: 86).

However, as soon as the sun rises in all its glory, "the mysterious saga disappears as if it had never existed," the group now represents three "human beings, although rather original ones," and the statue turns out to be Deacon Akhilla riding into the river on his horse. The three figures are Akhilla's bathing buddies getting ready for a swim, and the torture instruments turn out to be bathing paraphernalia: the shield is a large copper basin with a ragged sponge and a cloth mitten in it, the "black savage" is the prefect's coachman carrying a small bench, a little red rug, and a pair of ox-bladders which are blown up tight and fastened together. As the author concludes: "A picture of the most tranquil nature" (4: 87).

This little scene of visual deception is called "a *paysage and genre* of the simplicity of Old Town's life" (4: 89), a statement which could be considered metafictional. As

in his characterization of Akhilla, Leskov once more takes refuge in the visual arts. A true picture of "simple reality" is a combination of a *paysage*—an individual view of a landscape tied to its particular lighting and positioning, that is, a specific morning in deceptive twilight, etc.—with a *genre* scene, an habitual occurrence, that is, the daily bathing ritual. As he shows in the chronicle, the "simplicity" of life is complicated when insignificant, habitual actions acquire particular, individual interpretations. This scene also exemplifies Leskov's view of how real knowledge is gained. For Tolstoy, for example, real knowledge comes from experiencing, from being in the middle of the event, as is depicted in Pierre's contact with war in *War and Peace* or Levin's participation in mowing in *Anna Karenina*. For Leskov, real knowledge comes from being exposed to many views and drawing conclusions, which, however, must be open to redefinitions as new perspectives emerge. Knowledge is an open-ended, forward-moving process. Being too close to an event might be as problematic as being too far away; moreover, external circumstances, such as light, remoteness from the object—in the physical as well as figurative sense, as in prejudices and preconceived ideas—distort reality. The individual impression—the *paysage*—must be constantly checked against the general picture—the *genre*—and vice-versa to get closer to an understanding of the "simplicity of life."[10]

Thus, Leskov's choice of form reveals his epistemological position. The difference between the two modes of gaining real knowledge, of getting to the truth, can best be expressed in the two different meanings of experience: *Erlebnis* vs. *Erfahrung*. *Erlebnis* is the act of living physically through an event, of experiencing an event. This is the position that Tolstoy, for example, advocates. *Erfahrung,* on the other hand, is the result of a prolonged learning process, an accumulation of knowledge which is gained by constant exposure to the world, i.e. having experience. The second meaning is more extensive, since it includes not only one's personal experiences but also what one has learned about and from other people. Moreover, the two terms describe a different distance from the object. *Erlebnis* is the depiction of raw emotions, whereas *Erfahrung* is what Wordsworth called "emotion recollected in tranquillity," or what is meant in Russian by the term *sozertsanie*. For Leskov real knowledge is gained by being an "experienced (*erfahrener*) observer or listener."

This notion is inscribed into his work. He chooses an "experienced observer" in the figure of his chronicler, and moreover demands that the reader of his work become an "experienced observer." The "experienced listener-observer" must digest all pre-existing material "in tranquillity." Pre-existing material is anything that predates the present moment and includes what one has experienced oneself, that is, has seen previously (one's view of reality, one's perspective or *paysage*), as well as what one has heard or read about (source material, other people's experiences, the *genre*). This kind of observer has gained distance from what he describes; he reflects on and evaluates an event soberly after having received information on it from various sources. Since the mind, when tied to a momentary experience, can be deceived by unfortunate external circumstances—as is shown in the bath scene—it is important that people not reflect on their "feelings at the moment," but broaden out, look at their experiences after they have "cooled off," and compare them to other people's feelings ("create a collage").[11]

This feature distinguishes Leskov's chronicler from the type of chronicler we find in Dostoevsky, for example. In an article on this issue, Likhachev—using Dostoevsky's term—characterizes him as a chronicler of the present, of contemporaneity (*letopisatel' sovremennosti*), who like a journalist hurries to jot down the events, fearing that the facts may become distorted as time proceeds (Likhachev 91).[12] Dostoevsky's pictures are, therefore, not "cubist" since his chronicler does not work synthetically, soberly collecting and rearranging data, but, as Likhachev called them, "impressionistic" (93), in that his chronicler tries to reproduce an immediate (albeit polyphonic) "untainted" moment of the present.

Thus, the device of depicting a single event as seen by several people, which is found in Leskov as well as in Dostoevsky, is used by each writer differently and for very different ends. In Dostoevsky's *Brothers Karamazov,* for example, several characters describe the murder scene after the fact, but as if they are still experiencing it. Their perspective is that of participants, not experienced observers, their pictures are subjective impressions. Each of these observers has a "severely distorted" vision, since none of them sees the mysterious person in the garden but simply imagines somebody. We once more see proof of the mind's deceptiveness as concerns events of the present, its tendency to substitute for reality, which would fall into the category of Leskov's bath scene discussed above.[13] As in Dostoevsky in general, in this episode the imaginative world takes on enormous proportions and assumes a reality of its own which becomes part of the plot. Uncertainty—fantasy not tested by reality—builds suspense and moves the action forward, while the search for the puzzle's solution—"Who's done it?"—keeps the reader's attention focused.

Leskov's case is much more benign. Thus, in an early episode in *Cathedral Folk,* the Marshal of the Nobility presents to each of the three clergy members a staff, a gift which becomes a source of discord. The reader is first given the bare facts (4: 12), then Akhilla gives his interpretation (4: 12)—then we become witnesses of a dispute over it (4: 15-19), and later on, the event is shown through the eyes of Tuberozov who is reading—together with the reader—his version as he had described it earlier in his diary, thus in a twice-"digested" form (4: 80-81). By looking at one event from several angles we see how each view, as well as time to some extent, distorts the event, yet the separate versions do not change the event, as in the Dostoevsky example, in which the identity of the murderer changes. In Leskov the facts are clear, simple and known by all participants from the beginning. The reader is presented with several interpretations of one event, he becomes in a certain sense a "philologist." Moreover, Leskov's seemingly insignificant dispute takes on larger proportions, if we consider the symbolic meaning of a staff in the Biblical as well as literal sense.

In the Bible, the staff first suggests the Aaronic priesthood and is a metonymic emblem of priestly authority. In its broader application it is a metaphor of support and authority and symbolizes the body of rules that give its bearer steadfastness in his decisions. *Cathedral Folk* literally opens with this episode and its repercussion, and Leskov uses this "trifle" to reveal early on and with a light touch the spiritual weaknesses of the three recipients.[14] Thus the "distortion" inherent in any subjective vision, which in Dostoevsky leads to plot complications, in Leskov serves as a device of characterization. The priest Zachary remains largely unmoved by the disagreement that arises over the gift. His staff carried the inscription: "He gave him a rod into his hand."[15] He is a kind and gentle figure, but his form of Christianity—meekness personified—is firm and inflexible. Unlike the "restless Father Savely [Tuberozov]"—whose staff was symbolically inscribed "The rod of Aaron bloomed" (Num. 17: 8)—Zachary will never "make any waves" and disturb any existing order (4: 188). He is even afraid "to burden the earth with his weight," which, as it is, cannot be very significant since he looks "as if he were plaited out of straw" (4: 6). Tuberozov calls him "the humble Zachary who exists in a way as if he didn't exist at all" (4: 203). Such a man is too removed from the base concerns of life to be troubled by what he views as a mere "trifle."

Akhilla, the eternally irresponsible child, is found on the opposite side of the spectrum, since he is firmly engrossed in life and in the moment. He does not care about consequences and responsibilities, and the confusion over the gift is merely an opportunity to crack a clever joke which causes the others embarrassment and pain.[16] Therefore, Tuberozov deprives him of his staff with the justification that as a deacon he has no right to carry one in the first place. But apart from this legalistic reason, we are shown in what follows that Akhilla indeed does not "deserve a staff," since he has not yet found a firm authority that he can rely on. For Tuberozov he is "the daring Akhilla who lives like an elemental force, not knowing himself for what purpose he was put there" (4: 203). He is very endearing for his child-like qualities but badly needs guidance. He is a *bogatyr*—a kind of warrior for the faith—and displays all the virtues as well as the shortcomings of such a believer. He will serve his chosen master faithfully and absolutely. But the fact that in the beginning of the chronicle he wears spurs under his cassock (4: 67) indicates that he must overcome his primal, rebellious Cossack nature and turn his belief into more than a cloak, a superficial cover. Like an unbridled child, he is indiscriminately open to everything new—especially if it promises to be fun—since his intellectual capacities are not trained. This makes his understanding of the faith very literal and uncritical, and he is easily swayed to accept other masters, as is shown later on when, during a trip to Saint Petersburg, he momentarily "converts" to a nihilistic worldview, but equally easily renounces it again.

Tuberozov, the most conscious believer of the three, suffers most from the incident, since he is made to face his small-mindedness and pride. However, the affair with the three staffs is not explained or resolved. Symbolic repercussions echo throughout the chronicle, but as concerns the initial event, Leskov merely presents the different realities, forcing the reader to draw his own conclusions.

The exuberance of episodes and anecdotes in *Cathedral Folk,* therefore, gradually accumulates different perspectives on what one may call the chronicle's central theme: a juxtaposition of the different beliefs people hold and how these beliefs fare when confronted with life. Thus, each of the three clergymen cling to different spiritualities, yet all three profess Russian Orthodoxy. The juxtaposition between belief systems and their proponents illustrates once more Leskov's apprehension regarding matters of the mind: it is less important which faith one professes than how one adapts or interprets this faith to meet daily life. And once again, the mind is contrasted with reality, since although convinced in one's mind that one adheres to the "right" faith, one's actions may reveal the opposite. Leskov does not believe in theorizing but in acting. Thus his characters do not engage in intellectualizing belief systems, in discussions of the "accursed questions," but rather demonstrate how they apply the Gospels' ethics.

This philosophy pervades his poetics as well. In *Cathedral Folk* the author is not omniscient, and he does not penetrate his characters' minds or analyze their actions.[17] Instead, he is as human as his characters, a being with limited vision who merely compiles and records the actions of others. He thus allows his readers to judge what these actions reveal about their perpetrators. Leskov once expressed this view in an article:

> It was said long ago that "literature is life that is written down and a literary man is in his way the secretary

to his time." He is a recorder, not an inventor, and when he stops being a recorder and becomes an *inventor,* then any bond between him and society will disappear.

> (Gebel' 78 [emphasis his])

Leskov claims to be incapable of inventing; instead he looks towards the outside for inspiration. In an open letter to a friend and editor he wrote in 1884:

> The articles in your newspaper said that I for the most part *copied* my characters from life and that I related true events. Whoever the author of these articles was, he is *perfectly correct*. I have powers of observation and maybe a certain skill in analyzing feelings and motives, but I have *little imagination*. It is difficult and burdensome for me to make up anything, and therefore I always needed living people whose spiritual makeup can arouse my interest. They would take possession of me, and I would try to incarnate them in stories, which themselves I would also very often base on a real event. That is the way I have written almost everything . . .[18]

Of course, being one of the greatest storytellers of Russian literature, Leskov "added" a great deal to his so-called documentary material, and we should accept the above statement with a great deal of caution. What does seem significant in Leskov's work, however, is that he almost never enters the mind of his protagonists or records their thoughts. Other people's speech patterns can be imitated and recreated, since we can all hear them—thus the author can maintain his seeming stance of "objectivity," of being merely a secretary. Patterns of thoughts, on the other hand, will always remain pure "fiction," the author's invention, unless they are *his own* thoughts, since an individual can never experience how and in what pattern another person's thoughts proceed. The issue of depicting inner speech touches upon two philosophical issues: reality as perceived by others and reality as expressed. It is true that people experience their thoughts in words. But only "if the Logos becomes flesh," that is when these words are expressed, do they become real to *others*. As any creative person knows, there is a difference between words expressed vs. words experienced as thoughts. As Tiuchev put it: "A thought expressed is a lie." Inner dialogue thus has to be distinguished from external dialogue—be it fictionalized or real—since (as Bakhtin concedes) inner dialogue is a dialogue reflected through one consciousness, one point of view (48). Inner dialogue is carried on with an "imagined" partner, not with a real partner. And a person can really only know his own consciousness; those of others he has to conjecture. Fictional characters who think, reflect in essence the author's train of thought. Thus any fictional work that reproduces the inner life of characters can be polyphonic only up to a certain extent, since inner dialogue is filtered through one monologizing consciousness. Likhachev makes a similar observation regarding Dostoevsky's novels:

In the voices of these characters one often (much more often than in many other authors) hears the voice of Dostoevsky himself. Dostoevsky's worldview can be read in the words of Zosima, Vershilov, Ivan Karamazov, Stavrogin, Myshkin and others. Even if this is polyphony, it is the polyphony of a lyrical work—a polyphony that is subordinated to the expression of authorial feelings, ideas and thought-feelings. His novels are a lyrical chronicle.

(Likhachev 92)

Leskov tries to move away from this type of author and attempts, instead, to present other people's realities. He shies away from "inventing," and therefore, rejects what purports to be another person's thoughts, since they are not a "half-truth," but pure authorial invention. Consequently, his characters hardly ever think; they speak. They are characterized by how they are perceived by others. As Leskov explained in a conversation, he took great pains in recreating individual speech patterns, patterns which have objective reality, since they can be experienced:

> People tell me that it is fun to read my works. That is because all of us—my characters and myself—have our own voices. The voice is "pitched" in each of us correctly, or at least carefully. I am afraid of losing my way when I write: therefore my petty bourgeois speak in the manner of petty bourgeois and my lisping and burring aristocrats in their own fashion. And this is a talent that has to be formed in a writer. Yet developing it is not only a matter of talent but of tremendous labor. Man lives by words, and we must know at which moments of psychological life which of us will use which words.

(Faresov 274)

In this statement, Leskov applies the metaphor of the pitching of a voice to a writer's talent. A writer must be able to hear different voices and depict them as different voices, not homogenize them into his voice. A character in Leskov, then, is not defined by what he thinks, how he expresses himself to himself, but how he expresses himself to others, the world outside, in words and in deeds.

Thus, through his aesthetic principles, Leskov forces the reader to become an "experienced observer-listener." Leskov rejects the novel where the reader participates in the hero's tumultuous life and gets engrossed in experiencing events as they are being "concentrated around one center" by the author, thereby uncritically accepting the author's idea of how phenomena unfold in life. In Leskov's work we are presented with "scenes from life," his works are like collages where elements "represent" (are part of an image) and "present" (exist for their own sake). The reader is an observer in relation to the text, making his own conclusions as to the significance of these events, or the characters involved—gaining experience in interpreting character—

instead of having such conclusions served ready-made by the author, that is accepting one source of knowledge as the whole truth.

The nineteenth-century psychological representation of inner thoughts through authorial comments, internal monologues and stream of consciousness has conditioned readers to look for certain types of characterizations, and a hierarchy has been established, where an absence of this narrative mode devalues the work. The techniques associated with this mode somewhat correspond to modeling ("the rounding out of characters") and foreshortening ("close-up of a person's thoughts") in painting, devices that arrived with the Renaissance and its stress on a single perspective. In his study on multiple perspectives, Florenskii claimed that single perspective was a sign of a mentality that appeared with the arrival of individualism and the disintegration of the metaphysics of a generalized folk creation—when man put himself in the center and began to look at the world from his individual point of view only. He further sees the continuation of this development in Kantian philosophy. Florenskii contrasts this mode to icon painting with its "reverse perspective" and its multifocalization (*raznotsentrennost'*), and other painting traditions that lack single perspective (medieval, Chinese, Egyptian art).[19] In this system the drawing is constructed "as if the eye while changing its position were to look at several places in it" (46). Bakhtin taking his lead from Florenskii saw an attempt in Dostoevsky to move from single perspective, or a monologic design, towards the polyphonic novel and its multiperspectivity. The difference between Dostoevsky's multiperspectivity and Leskov's is that Dostoevsky's is speculative, a clash of ideas, which means, it is ultimately filtered through one consciousness. Leskov's multiple perspectives are visual, as Florenskii called them "*nagliadnye,*" a collection of "secondhand" descriptions. This narrative mode, which presents the characters' interaction with the external world, instead of their inner makeup, demands a talent of a different type, one that can come up with an abundance of varied situations, each of which revealing yet another character trait and adding yet another facet onto the cubist picture. Leskov's style has often been characterized as "excessive." But without the abundance of anecdotes the characters would not be developed. Throughout the chronicle, Leskov thus accumulates separate "genre scenes" which by the end are superimposed in the reader's mind and make up the cubist painting, with its aspect of multiperspectivity. It is the reader who must distill his own interpretation and pronounce the final or finalizing word.

Notes

1. The other sections planned were either never realized, exist only in fragments, or have turned into smaller separate pieces. Parts of an earlier version

of *Cathedral Folk* were published already in 1867 in *Otechestvennye zapiski* under the title *Waiting for the Movement of the Water* (*Chaiushchie dvizheniia vody*). For an account of the rocky publishing history and the antecedents of *Cathedral Folk* see Eekman; McLean 173-190.

2. All references to the 11 vol. Leskov edition (Leskov 1956-1958) will be in the text.

3. Leskov frequently mentions Sterne's novel *Tristram Shandy,* a book he had read early in life, and an argument could be made that his "dislike" of the novelistic genre might not include the "natural flow" of the Sternian type of novel—which Shklovskii called the "most typical novel of world literature" (204). Leskov's statements on Sterne, however, are not unambiguous. He uses him apologetically when justifying his own use of "digressions and ricochets" (see, for example, 11: 606), but as concerns the philosophy behind the Sternian construction, he either parodies its inherent fatalism (see 2: 325; Leskov 1996: 5), or criticizes its reluctance to establish values. Thus, in *Soboriane,* Tuberozov (who has read Sterne as well) laments that Russia is about to enter a phase of "Shandyism," a state of mind that has lost control and turns everything into an object of ridicule (4: 80). As will be shown later, Leskov's attempt to recreate the "unfolding" of events in life is quite different from depicting the "drifting along by the force of circumstances," an uncontrolled movement. Leskov's stance of "undeliberateness" is actually very deliberate, i.e. arranged.

4. One may think of the whole construction of *Crime and Punishment,* which almost exclusively rests on accidents, such as overhearing conversations, bumping into certain people, etc.

5. The early version of *Cathedral Folk* published in 1867 had the subheading *A Novelistic Chronicle* (Leskov 1867, no. 6: 181).

6. Leskov was notorious for his irreverent use of source material (Weinberg 97-110).

7. This statement explains Leskov's interest in and affinity with Sergei Solov'ev's view of history.

8. This would privilege painting over writing in the depiction of the truth, which may explain Leskov's "visual" approach to writing. See also a statement he made about a character in a (quasi-) autobiographical story: "I am afraid that I am quite unable to draw [*narisovat'*] his portrait precisely because I see him [before me] so well and clearly" (6: 353).

9. An additional subtext with further connotations and repercussions is provided by Akhilla's name, which is itself a cross between the Saint's name Akila (whose Saint's day is July 27) and the Greek hero's name Achilles (*Akhill* or *Akhilles* in Russian). Considering the Russian tradition of choosing a child's name according to the Saints' calendar—a ritual especially operative as concerns the clergy—the deacon's real name was most likely Akila (given the time of the chronicle, it would be inconceivable for him to be named after a pagan hero). His warrior-like appearance and superhuman strength quite naturally suggest the Greek hero's name and could easily provoke this distortion. Whether Leskov invented this name or had heard it somewhere, it is a successful illustration of the common Russian people's love of word puns and syncretic adaptations. In this context Akhilla's "vulnerability" (*uiazvlennyi* means literally "wounded") is especially telling, echoing Achilles' one vulnerable spot, his heel, which despite his legendary invulnerability becomes his nemesis. Incidentally, Leskov asserted that the model for his character was a deacon-*bogatyr'* of enormous size whom he knew personally (De-la-Bart 20).

10. An example from another work, in which Leskov demonstrates this theory, is the relationship between the sledge driver and the bishop in his later story "On the Edge of the World" ("Na kraiu sveta," 1875). To the bishop, the driver becomes a repulsive stinking savage when he is too close to him, a miraculous incarnation of a flying saint when seen from afar in the deceptive morning twilight, and at the end of the story, when he has reflected on all these varied "pictures," the bishop sees in him merely a decent human being.

11. In letters from his later life Leskov frequently uses the image of "cooling off." Thus, he writes to his sister: "[O]ne has to accept everything in the world with coolness [*s proxladoi*]" (Letter to Ol'ga Krokhina, sheet no. 3).

12. As concerns Dostoevsky's fear of distortion in connection with quotations (another form of source material) see Perlina. For Leskov, every version by definition (since it is individualized) is already a distortion. "Distortion" is therefore an unavoidable and even necessary part of the *polu-byl'* of reality.

13. It seems ironic that when discussing Leskov's bath scene in a review of *Cathedral Folk*, Dostoevsky called it "completely unnecessary" (Vinogradov 80).

14. When depicting this event the chronicler-narrator warns that this is one of the trifles that "turn out to be not a trifle at all for those who experience it" and that in fact "these staffs fell among the

priesthood of Old Town like the Biblical snakes, which the Egyptian sorcerers threw before the pharaoh" (4: 11,12). This reference to Exodus 7: 8-13, which uses the metaphor of the staffs to depict the victory of right over the wrong authority, thus provides the subtext of how to interpret this episode: each staff will turn into a "snake," i.e., the wrong authority, and consequently, reveal the flaws in each recipient's spirituality.

15. I have not been able to locate this seemingly Biblical quotation (*Dade v ruku ego posokh*).

16. Akhilla quickly "transposes" the Church Slavonic description of Zachary's rod: *Dade v ruku ego posokh* into its vulgar counterpart: *dana palka v lapu*, thereby effecting a semantic shift: instead of "receiving his staff" the priest "got spanked in the paw with a stick" (4: 18). Ironically, this joke becomes symbolic further on in the chronicle, when it becomes clear that Zachary's only recourse against heretical notions is force, namely, when he uses his priestly authority to demand that a youthful freethinker be spanked by his father (4: 73).

17. This is true for almost all of Leskov's work: his characters—with very rare exceptions—never think.

18. Letter to P. K. Shchebal'skii, the editor of *Varshavskii dnevnik* (*Shestidesiatie gody* 344). It is interesting to note that Gogol made a similar claim.

19. Florenskii, "Obratnaia perspektiva," 46, 50, and *passim*. Leskov illustrates a similar view in the frame narrative of his story "On the Edge of the World" ("Na kraiu sveta," 1875), when the bishop, comparing icons to Western depictions of Christ, rejects the latter because they are all individual interpretations; each is able to depict only a single aspect of Christ. Leskov collected icons, was very knowledgeable about icon painting, was personally acquainted with a master icon painter, and wrote extensively on this subject; his fictional or quasi-fictional treatments include "The Sealed Angel" ("Zapechatlennyi angel," 1873), the above-mentioned "On the Edge of the World," "Descent into Hell" ("Soshestvie vo ad," 1894), in addition to a great number of articles.

Works Cited

Canaday, John. *Mainstreams of Modern Art*. New York: Holt, Rinehart and Winston, 1959.

Bakhtin, Mikhail. *Problems of Dostoevsky's Poetics*. Caryl Emerson, ed. and tr. Minneapolis: U of Minnesota P, 1984.

De-La-Bart, F. Graf. "Literaturnyi kruzhok 90-kh godov (Iz vozpominanii o V. Solov'eve, N. S. Leskove i drugikh)." *Izvestiia obshchestva Slavianskoi kul'tury*, vol. 2, no. 1. Moscow: Tip. Riabushinskogo, 1912. 8-21.

Eekman, Thomas. "The Genesis of Leskov's *Soboriane*." *California Slavic Studies* 2 (1963): 121-140.

Eikhenbaum, Boris. "N. S. Leskov: K 50-letiiu so dnia smerti." In his *O proze*. Leningrad: Khudozhestvennaia. literatura, 1969. 327-345.

Faresov, Anatolii. *Protiv techenii: N. S. Leskov: ego zhizn', sochineniia, polemika i vospominaniia o nem*. St. Petersburg: Merkushev, 1904.

Florenskii, Pavel. "Obratnaia perspektiva." In his *U vodorazdelov mysli*. Moscow: "Pravda," 1990. 43-106.

Gebel', Valentina. *N. S. Leskov: V tvorcheskoi laboratorii*. Moscow: Sovetskii pisatel', 1945.

Grossman, Leonid. *N. S. Leskov: Zhizn'—tvorchestvo—poetika*. Moscow: Gosudarstvennoe izdatel'stvo khudozhestvennoi literatury, 1945.

Janson, H. W. *History of Art*. 9th ed. New York: Harry N. Abrams, 1973.

Leskov, Nikolai. "Chaiushchie dvizheniia vody." *Otechestvennye zapiski*, nos. 6, 7, 8 (March 15-April 15, 1867).

———. Letter to Ol'ga Krokhina, 13 April 1892. IRLI, Fond 220, no 43.

———. *Polnoe sobranie sochinenii v tridtsati tomakh*, vol 3. Moscow: "Terra," 1996.

———. *Sobranie sochinenii v odinnadtsati tomakh*. 11 vols. Moscow: Gosudarstvennoe izdatel'stvo khudozhestvennoi literatury, 1956-1958.

Likhachev, D. C., "'Letopisnoe vremia' u Dostoevskogo." In his *Literatura—real 'nost'—literatura*. Leningrad: Sovetskii pisatel', 1984.

Marcadé, Jean-Claude. "Les premières versions du *Clergé de la collégiale* de Leskov: *Ceux qui attendent le bouillonnement de l'eau* et *Les Habitants de la maison de Dieu*," *Revue des études slaves* 58.3 (1986): 347-364.

McLean, Hugh. *Nikolai Leskov: The Man and His Art*. Cambridge, MA: Harvard U P, 1977.

Morson, Gary Saul and Caryl Emerson. *Mikhail Bakhtin: Creation of a Prosaics*. Stanford, CA: Stanford U P, 1990.

Perlina, Nina. *Varieties of Poetic Utterance: Quotation in 'The Brothers Karamasov.'* Lanham, MD and London: U P of America, 1985.

Shestidesiatye gody: Sbornik (Materialy po istorii literatury i obshchestvennomu dvizheniiu). Moscow-Leningrad, 1940.

Shklovskii, Viktor. "Parodiinyi roman 'Tristram Shendi' Sterna." *O teorii prozy.* Moscow: "Federatsiia" 1929 (reprint Ann Arbor: Ardis, 1985). 177-204.

Vinogradov, V. V. "Dostoevskii i Leskov (70-e gody XIX veka)." *Russkaia literatura* 1 (1961): 63-84.

Weinberg [Sperrle], I. Christina. *The Organic Worldview of Nikolaj Leskov.* Ph.D. Dissertation, Columbia University, 1996.

Zelinsky, Bodo. *Roman und Romanchronik: Strukturuntersuchungen zur Erzählkunst Nikolaj Leskovs.* Cologne and Vienna: Böhlau Verlag, 1970.

Gabriella Safran (essay date 2000)

SOURCE: Safran, Gabriella. "Jew as Text, Jew as Reader: Nikolai Leskov." In *Rewriting the Jew: Assimilation Narratives in the Russian Empire,* pp. 108-46. Stanford, Calif.: Stanford University Press, 2000.

[*In the following excerpt, Safran explores Leskov's somewhat ambivalent representation of Jews in his short fiction, primarily concentrating on subjects of Jewish conversion to Christianity and Leskov's use of Jewish figures to implicitly critique Russian society and the Orthodox Church in his "Episcopal Justice" and "New Testament Jews."*]

If the state rewards converts to Christianity with money and privileges, should we attempt to distinguish a conversion based on conviction from a hypocritical one? When the government treats religious belief as a public service to be officially compensated, should any citizen imagine it instead as a personal relationship between an individual and God? While [Grigory] Bogrov's work spoke to a philosophical dilemma posed by the project of Jewish acculturation, and [Eliza] Orzeszkowa and her Russian translator considered political issues associated with it, two of Nikolai Leskov's stories reflect on some religious questions raised by the specter of Jewish conversion in the late-nineteenth-century Russian Empire. In his depictions of converts from Judaism, he touches on larger questions about the faith and the identity of the Russian Orthodox.

The many works that Leskov wrote about Jews reveal his fascination with the "Jewish question." From 1877 through 1886, he published six stories whose main characters were Jewish: **"Vladychnyi sud"** [**"Episcopal Justice"**] (1877), **"Rakushanskii melamed"** [**"The Melamed of Österreich"**] (1878), **"Zhidovskaia kuvyrkollegiia"** [**"Yid Somersault"**] (1882), **"Novozavetnye evrei"** [**"New Testament Jews"**] (1884), **"Ukha bez ryby"** [**"Fish Soup Without Fish"**] (1886), and **"Skazanie o Fedore-khristianine i o druge ego Abrame-zhidovine"** [**"The Tale of Fedor the Christian and His Friend Abraham the Jew"**] (1886).[1] During the 1880s, he produced a series of twenty articles on Jewish rituals, as well as several pieces on other topics related to Jews.[2] Finally, the St. Petersburg Jewish community commissioned him to write the book ***Evrei v Rossii*** [***Jews in Russia***] (1884), a refutation of certain accusations made against Jews, which was published anonymously and submitted to the Pahlen Commission, a body created to deliberate on the legal status of the empire's Jews.[3]

Those scholars who have addressed these texts are primarily interested in the question of Leskov's general attitude toward Jews. From Iulii Gessen and V. Vodovozov at the beginning of the twentieth century to William Edgerton and Hugh McLean near its end, critics observed that while the writer used ugly stereotypes to portray the Jewish characters in some of his earlier pieces, his later ones depicted Jews more positively, suggesting that he repented from or rethought his intolerance.[4] Indeed, especially in his later years, he seemed to have been self-conscious about his reflexive hostility to Jews, which he opposed to an ideal Christian morality. In a letter written in 1888, he first admitted that "I would rather order work from a German or a Russian than a Jew," then asserted that "a human being deserves our sympathy primarily because he is human."[5] His biographer A. I. Faresov quotes him on the difficulty of finding a single clear answer to the Jewish question: "I believe that one must live in a brotherly way with all nations, and I express that view, but personally, I am afraid of Jews, and I avoid them. I am for equality [*ravnopravnost'*], but [I am] not for Jews."[6]

For Leskov's biographers since Faresov, analysis of this Russian writer's feelings about Jews and the empire's other nationalities poses a fascinating psychological problem. In my study of depictions of the mutability of the acculturating Jew, I am most interested in Leskov's invocation of varying archetypes in his description of his own attitudes toward the Jews. If we accept the accuracy of Faresov's transcription, Leskov describes himself as "for equality," aligning himself with the liberals who believed that the future would and should contain a Russian state in which Jews could enjoy the same privileges as Christians, as well as Jews who would appreciate these rights. At the same time, Leskov admits that he is "not for Jews" and that, just like the ignorant soldiers who learn from Major Pleskunov's story in his own **"Melamed of Österreich,"** he is even afraid of them. In the vocabulary of his time, Leskov identifies alternately with the types of the sophisticated Judeophile and the primitive Judeophobe, that is, both the liberal, philosophizing Westernizer whose sympathy extends to everything human, and the conservative nationalist who refuses to patronize a Jewish business.

Leskov recognized his own inconsistency on this issue. In connection with his equivocations on the "Jewish question" and a few other matters, Faresov cites Leskov's musings on human inconsistency in general: "Varied people sometimes inhabit a single body. . . . It's not even always possible to sense what gorilla might be resurrected [*voskresnut'*] in each of us. That's why dissimilar children, Cain and Abel, can be born to a single family."[7] The debates about the status of the Jews, which focused on their loyalty to the Russian state and the Russian people, and the discussions of converts from Judaism, which centered on their loyalty to the Church, all forced Leskov to recognize the insubstantiality of some of his own loyalties. Even while he participated in the argument in his fictional and nonfictional texts, it would seem, Leskov acknowledged the logical flaw at the heart of the "Jewish question"—that is, the impossibility of reliably and permanently defining any person's allegiances.

Leskov identifies the irreconcilable human types in a single family or individual with Cain and Abel, the two sons of Adam and Eve whose story culminates in Cain's murder of his brother. The reference to Genesis in this context reveals the tendency that Leskov shared with many of his contemporaries to imagine the Jews of the Russian Empire in the framework of biblical archetypes. By using biblical terms, he signals that he sees Jews first of all as playing a role in Christian history. If the posited unreliability of the Jew compels the writer to admit his own inconsistency, then the problem of Jewish mutability inevitably forces him to confront questions about Christian faith and the Orthodox believer. After considering some of the ramifications of these questions for this writer, I will address Leskov's most complex "Jewish" story, **"Episcopal Justice,"** and the shorter **"New Testament Jews."** . . .

LESKOV, RUSSIAN JEWRY, AND THE CHRISTIAN QUESTION

Although Russian law had always made conversion to Christianity legally and economically advantageous, a perceived increase in Jewish baptisms in the late nineteenth century disturbed members of the Russian intelligentsia in various political camps and even some thinkers within the Orthodox Church.[8] On one end of the spectrum, some believed that baptized Jews were without exception hypocrites who posed a danger to Christianity, and that the Church should forbid their conversion rather than allow them to enjoy its benefits.[9] On the opposite end, others saw the phenomenon as a reason to change the law, to introduce equality and religious tolerance, rather than force people into religious hypocrisy.[10]

Doubt about Jewish conversions produced writings that worked to distinguish between "true" and "false" converts. Fictional and nonfictional images of these two

kinds of converts relied on mastertexts from the Gospels. The paradigmatic conversion narrative about the transformation of a Jew into a Christian begins when a light from heaven strikes Saul, who had persecuted the Christians, while he is on a journey to Damascus. Saul hears the voice of Jesus, loses consciousness, then, after baptism, comes to with a new faith and a mission to propagate it (Acts 9). His new name—Paul—signifies the completeness of his transformation. Similarly, Augustine, who had sinned, converts after hearing a voice that tells him to read the Bible, which brings "a peaceful light streaming into [his] heart."[11] The classic conversion tale recounts the path toward baptism, from crisis toward rebirth, featuring the sequence of guilt, retribution, redemption, and then blessedness, and the association with illumination and a journey or a road.[12] This conversion narrative coexists with a kind of double: the tale of a false or insincere conversion. Again, the New Testament furnishes the archetype: Judas Iscariot, one of Jesus' disciples, proves disloyal to him when he betrays him. This scene equates Judas with the Pharisee priests who bribe him, creating a story in which a Jew who has been baptized is revealed as no Christian but a Pharisee. In the lexicon of Leskov's era, in Russian and other European languages, "Pharisee" could mean "Jew," "religious hypocrite," or "hypocrite" more broadly defined.

The European tradition of writing on Jews and Jewish conversion tended to assign the biographies of all Jews—including assimilated and even baptized Jews—to one of these two categories. It defined Jews as either Pharisees—"blind" fools whose stories are frozen in the stasis of their eternal rejection and persecution of Jesus—or potential converts who can move forward to "see" the truth of Christianity.[13] In this system, Jews and Pharisees were associated with law instead of grace or mercy, and with formalistic approaches to texts and life. Unbaptized and unassimilated Jews could only be Pharisees, but those who reached out toward gentiles and gentile culture were liminal figures, who immediately brought up the question of categorization. They could fit the model of either Paul, the sincere convert, or Judas, the false convert and secret Pharisee.

The attraction of these opposing biblical stories as archetypes for Christian narratives about contemporary Jews stems from the tradition of figural reading; in Christian exegesis, the events in the Hebrew Bible portend those that appear in the Greek Bible. As Erich Auerbach explains, "*figura* is something real and historical which announces something else that is also real and historical."[14] That is, biblical events are seen as no less real for their placement in a symbolic system that defines them as leading toward a First and then a Second Coming. Postbiblical history, for the Christian exegete, always demands interpretation: "history, with all its concrete force, remains forever a figure, cloaked and needful of interpretation."[15] Thus just as Dostoevsky's characters in *The Idiot* read and reread Revelation, trying to fit their own experience into a biblical model of apocalypse and redemption, so their nonfictional late-nineteenth-century Russian counterparts wrote and rewrote the Jewish acculturation and conversion they witnessed, using the genres they had inherited from the Christian Bible.

In Russian journalistic polemics as in literature, the stories of Paul and Judas were clearly differentiated, the image of the sincere convert distinguished from that of the hypocrite who accepted Christianity for profit. Stories of "good" converts—whether cast as nonfiction, autobiography, or fiction—stress not the advantage that Russian laws gave to converts but instead the persecution of converts by the Jewish community (recalling the persecution of Jesus, as well as Paul).[16] Leskov wrote newspaper articles as well as fiction that worked with this model. For instance, in an 1885 piece he praised a group of Jews who espoused Christian beliefs without converting officially. The members of the "New Israel" "synagogue" in Kishinev believed in Jesus as the Messiah and rejected the Talmud. Leskov praised their movement: "this is a most important, free and sincere step toward spiritual rapprochement [*sblizhenie*]."[17] His enthusiasm reveals a catch-22 dilemma: by accepting the legal benefits of baptism, converts were in danger of appearing "false"; only those who somehow rejected the material advantages of conversion—like the "New Israel" congregation in Kishinev, whose members advertised their sympathy for Christianity, but did not convert—had the potential to be "true" Christians.

Even while some writers worked to imagine a "true" conversion, others described the "false" instance of it. In Aleksey Pisemsky's 1873 play *Baal,* the virtuous Russian characters are disgusted by a Jew who converts to Orthodoxy in order to marry a Russian woman, then happily accepts a fifty-ruble government payoff.[18] Mikhail Saltykov-Shchedrin, in a section of *Sovremennaia idilliia* [*A Contemporary Idyll*] published in 1883, refers to a Jew's plans to convert in order to obtain a residence permit for himself and his relatives as "blasphemous double-dealing" [*koshchunstvennyi gesheft*].[19] Leskov, too, in his newspaper articles, criticized both Jews who convert for the sake of material gain and the policy that encouraged them to do so. In an 1883 piece about government policy in the Baltics, he draws attention to a high-level administrator's distress at having to carry out a law according to which Jewish converts to Christianity received thirty rubles:

> The law did not please him [Governor-General Suvorov in Riga]. There's nothing wrong with that—that law didn't please a great many people, who much more broadly and truly than the prince understood the multifaceted danger that such an honorarium posed both to faith and to morals. This law, nicknamed the "Law

about the thirty pieces of silver," led to many of the very worst instances of "commerce in faith," and we can be sincerely happy that it has been eliminated.[20]

Suvorov's—and Leskov's—discomfort with this image is understandable. The law itself created a scenario that casted the Jewish convert as Judas, the person who received thirty pieces of silver in exchange for a betrayal of a worthy cause, making him by definition unlikely to be a good Christian, and it gave the role of the Pharisees to the tsarist government and its unwilling administrators. Leskov's commentary on the "law about the thirty pieces of silver" places him in unexpected company, evoking a fear similar to the one that Karl Marx articulated in the 1840s in his obscure essay "On the Jewish Question." In Marx's formulation, Jewish assimilation and emancipation occur in tandem with the growth of capitalism and the concomitant involvement of Christians in unethical transactions: "The Jew has emancipated himself in a Jewish manner. . . . money has become a world power and the Jew has become the practical spirit of the Christian people. The Jews have emancipated themselves in so far as the Christians have become Jews."[21] The liminality and the moral ambiguity of assimilating Jews for Marx and of Jewish converts for Leskov seem to taint the Christians who interact with them.

* * *

While many depictions of Jewish converts defined them either as "true" Christians or "false" Pharisees, cantonists who had converted to Russian Orthodoxy as children could not necessarily be assimilated into this binary system. By emblematizing the categoric dilemma posed by forced conversion, they could challenge the ancient archetypes. The decision to draft Jewish children was explicitly motivated by tsarist policy aimed at conversion of the Jews to Orthodoxy. One member of Nicholas's secret police even wrote a memorandum urging that the Jews be required to furnish only child recruits, since children were less likely than adults to refuse conversion.[22] Leskov's fictional narrator in **"Episcopal Justice"** confirms this when he observes that the government preferred child recruits, since "there was a conviction that small children adapted more quickly and could be more easily baptized [*legche krestilis'*]" (p. 90).[23] Indeed, to judge by the autobiographical accounts of surviving cantonists, army officials used force as well as persuasion to convince Jewish recruits to convert. Ultimately, half of the Jewish child recruits and significant numbers of adult soldiers were baptized.[24]

It is important to remember that regardless of this official preference for child recruits, the Jewish communities under Nicholas had the option of offering men ages eighteen to twenty-five. Nonetheless, a large percentage of the recruits whom communities turned in were boys, some even younger than twelve. Their decisions were influenced by several factors: first, Jewish boys eighteen and over were often already the heads of families, whose elimination would create a more severe economic impact on the community than would the drafting of young children; second, tsarist regulations permitted community officials to draft selectively rather than exacting the same number of boys from each family. Thus, the poor and unemployed and those who had no influence with community leadership or had offended it in some way were more likely than others to be drafted themselves or have their children given to the army. Not surprisingly, this policy exacerbated rifts within Jewish communities.[25]

Few non-Jewish Russian writers aside from Leskov took up the grim theme of cantonism. Aleksandr Herzen, while being sent on exile for political crimes, was shocked and "wanted to sob" when he ran across a detachment of child soldiers. For him, the fate of Jewish cantonists epitomized the "monstrous crimes . . . buried in the archives from the criminal, immoral reign of Nicholas."[26] By the 1870s, the story of the cantonists was no longer buried. Subscribers to *Otechestvennye zapiski* could read not only Bogrov's tear-soaked accounts of the cantonists' sufferings in the chapter "The Wanderings of Erukhim," near the end of *Notes of a Jew,* but also a story by the former cantonist Viktor Nikitin on the same topic, "Mnogostradal'nye" ["The Suffering Ones"], published in 1871.[27]

Like these writers who breached the topic of cantonism in the mainstream Russian press, Leskov was apparently inspired to write about it after witnessing it himself. He worked in Kiev on the "production of recruits" [*proizvodstvo nabora*] in the early 1850s, at a time when the government demanded ever increasing quotas of recruits from Jewish communities,[28] and his experience as a government official clearly conditioned his approach to the topic. Bogrov and Nikitin wrote of cantonism from the perspective of the child recruit or his Jewish friends; Leskov wrote from that of the administrator who processed recruits.

While Leskov's fiction, as we will see, deals ambiguously and figuratively with the responsibility of military administrators for the sufferings of child recruits, he addresses this topic explicitly in his journalism. In an article on the enforcement of Nicholas's decrees in the empire's Baltic borderlands, Leskov comes close to analyzing his own work in Kiev. He often wrote about a community in Riga of Old Believers, schismatics seen by the Orthodox Church as heretics.[29] In 1849, Riga General Governor Suvorov decided that Old Believer orphans should be enrolled into cantonist units. City policemen were required to pursue the defenseless boys, arrest them, and take them to another city, where, like the Jewish cantonists, they faced a probable forced conversion to Orthodoxy. The situation in Riga mirrored that in the Kiev story, because in both cities the officials who enforced the rules of recruitment and the cantonist boys represented different ethnic groups (most often the Riga policemen were not ethnic Russians, but from the Baltic German middle class).

Leskov's signal that he saw cantonism in Riga, as in Kiev, as a slaughter of the innocents is his frequent repetition in both contexts of a biblical citation about "lamentation in Ramah" ("Rachel weeping for her children . . . would not be comforted" [Matt. 2:18, quoted from Jer. 31:15]).[30] He appears intrigued by the officials who created this "lamentation" in Riga. In one article in 1869, Leskov cites a letter by Count Sologub, a local administrator who disagrees with the general governor. Sologub describes the behavior of the German policemen: "The more the local militia . . . feel an internal revulsion for their duties, the more severely they carry them out." In 1869, Leskov expresses the opinion that such repulsive duties provoke in the Germans an ever greater hatred for Russians. Thus, they carry out their duties more severely, hoping that the Old Believers will come to hate the tsarist authorities more strongly. In Leskov's retelling, the German policemen think, "So don't blame us, but your own kind—those who forced us into this chase, which is *repulsive* to us!"[31]

Nonetheless, Leskov does not limit himself to a single explanation of the phenomenon. Thirteen years later, in another article on Riga, he again cites that same sentence from Sologub's letter. This time he rejects the opinion that he himself had earlier proposed:

> Some people say that the Germans "had their own political motivations," that they wanted to show these settled people of the Russian breed [the Old Believers] that they are being crowded out and tormented not by Germans, but by Russians. Thus, as these people would have it, the Germans wanted to set them [the Old Believers] against the Russian government. But I think that is unlikely, empty speculation.

Leskov proffers a more subtle psychological analysis of the German militia's actions:

> A person who is compelled to do a repulsive thing tries to finish with it *as quickly as humanly possible*. It's the same as drowning cats. It's better to drown them right away and at such a depth that they can't climb out, than to torment them at length and to hear how they meow in the agonies of death.[32]

In the articles about the Riga Old Believers, Leskov offers two explanations for the militia's cruelty: either the German policemen hated the Russian Old Believers because they represented a different nationality, in which case their behavior reflects an ingrained racial or cultural hatred, or the Germans in fact sympathized with the Russians, and acted harshly because they did not want to prolong the agony of the child cantonists. The parallel between the German militia in Riga and Leskov's own employment in Kiev indicates that these answers might describe Leskov's ambivalence about his behavior as a military administrator. Given his experience when he came to Riga, he probably identified with the militia even while he doubted the wisdom and the theological justification for the capture and likely forced conversion of Old Believer children.

The situation of the Jewish cantonists Leskov encountered in Kiev may have troubled him because it produced a sort of cognitive dissonance. The New Testament, as well as the patristic literature that is so important in Eastern Orthodoxy, presents sincere Christians, in the model of Jesus, as the victims of sanctimonious Jews. Leskov, as he so often boasted, was far more literate in Church traditions than the average Russian writer of his time: he knew the Gospels and the Church Fathers well. The disjunction between the stereotype of the Christian victim in sacred literature and the reality of Jewish victims of what Leskov clearly saw as Christian religious hypocrisy could lie behind his fascination with Jews and Jewish converts to Christianity and his association of them with a reevaluation of Orthodox piety.

In questioning Orthodox practices, Leskov took part in a discussion that engrossed the intellectuals of his time: others too decried what they saw as hypocrisy and pharisaism in the state church and were attracted to what were identified as Protestant practices (Bible reading, lay preaching, spontaneous individual prayer, a pastoral focus for the work of priests, and a certain skepticism about ritual, miracles, and the Church hierarchy).[33] The most vocal critic of the Church was a friend of Leskov, Father Ioann Belliustin, whose scathing description of the inadequate education and ridiculous obligations of rural priests in his 1859 book (published abroad without his knowledge) provoked a scandal and loud cries for reform.[34] While the state did impose significant reforms on the Church and the priestly estate, it put up great resistance to "Protestant-style" innovations.[35] The state grouped the many Protestant movements among the peasantry under the title "Shtunda" and repressed them energetically. Meanwhile, the echoes of the debate are clearly audible in the Russian fiction of the period, from the Bible-reading prostitute in Dostoevsky's *Crime and Punishment* to Lydiia Ivanovna's patronage of foreign mystics in Tolstoy's *Anna Karenina*. In most of his writings, Leskov, rather like Belliustin himself, supported the criticism of Church practices (implicit in his 1870s work, but increasingly explicit later on) with examples drawn from his own provincial experience; at the same time, he emphasized his respect for certain aspects of Russian religious culture (icon painting, church architecture, etc.).

In 1877, though, Leskov published a book dealing with a more urban issue, a religious trend among the St. Petersburg aristocracy: an English Protestant, Baron Radstock, had decided to preach in Russia and attracted a host of followers.[36] In *Velikosvetskii raskol* [*Schism in High Society*], Leskov alternated between mocking Radstock and delicately pointing to the problems that might account for educated Russians preferring this exotic Protestant to their own Orthodox priests. As he would in the Jewish stories, Leskov took advantage of a seemingly peripheral topic to comment on the state of the Orthodox Church.

At the same time, in establishing a connection between Christian treatment of Jews and reform of Orthodox practices, Leskov took a stance similar to that of Vladimir Solov'ev, a contemporaneous religious philosopher whose critique of Orthodoxy owed nothing to Protestantism. In the 1884 essay "Evreistvo i khristianskii vopros" ["Jewry and the Christian Question"], Solov'ev explicitly defined negative attitudes toward Jews as a denial of the Christian doctrine laid out in the Bible: "If the commandment of the Gospels is feasible, if we can deal in a Christian way with everyone, not excluding even the Hebrews [*iudeev*], then we are completely to blame when we do not do this."[37] As Judith Kornblatt notes, the Jews constitute a key element of his Christian theology: "Solov'ev's interest in the Jews goes well beyond the 'Jewish question' and anti-Semitism. It in fact corresponded to his most central philosophical categories."[38] Critics have often used Leskov's writings on the Jews, like Solov'ev's, primarily as a litmus test measuring the writer's liberalism. Following Kornblatt's lead in her writings on Solov'ev, I want to set Leskov's depictions of Jews against the broader canvas of his understanding of the future of Russian Orthodoxy itself.

"EPISCOPAL JUSTICE"

The Jewish cantonist first appeared in Leskov's fiction in 1863, in the story **"Ovtsebyk"** [**"The Musk-Ox"**], where an encounter with a group of child recruits, some sick, provokes a crisis in the hero. Fourteen years later, in 1877, Leskov returned to the theme to address it at length. In **"Vladychnyi sud"** [**"Episcopal Justice"**], he weaves commentary on Judaism and Christianity into a characteristically complex plot. This story combines biblical and historical themes, describing an underage Jewish recruit like the ones whom Leskov might have processed when he worked in Kiev—and the narrator, like Leskov, works as an administrator at the recruitment office. The boy's father, a bookbinder, is a freethinker who has dipped into Christian works. To punish him for his heterodoxy, the Jewish community has selected his son as a recruit. In order to save his son, the bookbinder hires another Jew—paying him in advance—to take his place, but problems arise when this substitute recruit decides to convert to Russian Ortho-doxy before his army service begins, in order to make himself ineligible (since only a Jew could substitute for another Jew). The substitute recruit is clearly motivated by the urge to avoid army service, rather than by any true change in faith. The bookbinder, with the help of the narrator and a string of other people, eventually succeeds in convincing the metropolitan of Kiev to de-clare the substitute recruit "unworthy" of conversion, thus forcing him to enter the army as a Jew. In spite of this victory, we learn in the final chapters that the book-binder's son had been so abused by the soldiers who held him pending his recruitment that he died soon after his father had him freed. The narrator encounters the bookbinder many years later, long after the death of his son and his wife, and finds out that the bookbinder him-self has converted to Orthodoxy. In assigning responsi-bility for the bookbinder's problem, the narrator criti-cizes tsarist law and excoriates the Jewish community, but glosses over his own role and that of the other Rus-sian officials who processed the cantonists.

It is easy to situate this story in the tradition of Chris-tian writing about the Jew and to focus on the distinc-tion between the bookbinder, the real convert, whose story resembles Paul's, and the substitute recruit, the false convert, who evokes Judas. Within that context, the work becomes a lightly concealed attack on the hypocritical attitude toward the sacrament of baptism enforced under Nicholas I, which fails to distinguish between faith and profit.

Such a conclusion would follow a trail of clues that Leskov himself laid. He began **"Episcopal Justice"** with a digression about a story he had written two years before, **"Na kraiu sveta"** [**"On the Edge of the World"**] (1875). Critics have often analyzed Leskov's **"Episcopal Justice"** in the context of that better-known work, which also describes conversion to Christianity in Russia's borderlands.[39] Its hero, Father Kiriak, an Or-thodox missionary to the Far East, teaches the native peoples about Christianity but refuses to participate in a campaign to baptize masses of them as quickly as pos-sible. In **"Episcopal Justice,"** Leskov coyly notes that some had criticized that earlier story, accusing the priest of "indulgence of unbelief and even a careless attitude toward the salvation of souls through holy baptism" (p. 88). He then introduces his new story as proof that **"Na kraiu sveta"** was not the only incident of its type. This introduction makes it clear that Leskov saw both stories as revealing the hypocrisy of missionary efforts that promoted "baptism either from fear, or for material gain." Thus, the encounter with the baptized bookbinder at the end of **"Episcopal Justice"** mirrors the note at the end of **"On the Edge of the World"** that a "whole crowd" of pagans had converted to Christianity, repre-sented for them by the vision of Kiriak's God. Given the dichotomy of Paul and Judas, both works show that

voluntary baptism, inspired by the association of Chris-tianity with mercy and virtue, is better than forced, bribed, or bought conversion. Only voluntary converts, like Paul, can become "real" Christians.[40]

Ever-present references to the New Testament reinforce the connections between Leskov's Jewish converts and their biblical prototypes. The story begins with two bib-lical epigraphs, the first introducing the conflict be-tween true "Christian" mercy and a "pharisaical" or purely formal approach to law: "Judge not according to appearance, but judge righteous judgment" (John 7:24), Jesus' rebuke to the Pharisees who criticized his heal-ing on the Sabbath. The second epigraph prefigures the metropolitan's rejection of the substitute recruit: "For he shall have judgment without mercy, that has shown no mercy" (James 2:13).

Biblical citations describe both the torment of the book-binder's son and the Jews' responsibility for it. The re-cruitment of Jewish boys as cantonists, like the recruit-ment of Old Believer children in Riga, is compared to the Massacre of the Innocents in Bethlehem: "In all the Jewish towns and shtetls the 'lamentation in Ramah' was literally renewed: Rachel wept loudly for her chil-dren, and would not be comforted" (p. 90) (Matt. 2:18, from Jer. 31:15). The narrator uses strong language to emphasize the responsibility of Jews themselves for the situation: "Jewish entrappers [*sdatchiki*] tore the little Yids out of their mothers' embraces almost indiscrimi-nately" (p. 90). The "severity" of Russian law, he says, is only furthered by "the limitless cruelty of the Yids' injustice [*nepravda*] and trickery [*plutovstvo*]" (p. 90). Biblical epithets reinforce this negative depiction of Russian Jews: the narrator speaks of "stiff-necked Jews [*zhestokovyinoe evreistvo*]" (p. 96) (Acts 7:51; see Exod. 33:3, 34:9; Deut. 9:13) and anachronistically criticizes their "Pharisaic talmudism" (p. 96). (Few of the non-Jews who participated in the nineteenth-century debates surrounding the Jewish question in Russia seemed to realize that the Talmud was written several centuries after the events described in the Christian Bible, by which time the Pharisees no longer existed.)

The web of biblical subtext prefigures the eventual con-version of the unhappy bookbinder, who invokes Jesus: "Oh, Yeshua! Yeshua ha-Notsri ['Jesus the Nazarene' in Hebrew]! He [the substitute recruit, who is seeking baptism so as to avoid army service] wants to deceive you" (p. 100). The narrator then compares the book-binder to one of Jesus' patients, the possessed boy (p. 100) (Matt. 17:14-21; Mark 9:17-29; Luke 9:38-43), and imagines Jesus' sympathy for him: "isn't *He* com-ing to take up in His holy arm this unhappy sheep, per-haps by chance bleating out His name" (p. 113) (see Matt. 18:12-14). These references to Jesus' kindness and mercy make the bookbinder's sincere conversion seem inevitable.

The substitute recruit's false conversion is described in equally biblical terms. By converting in order to avoid the army, he would become the kind of Christian "due to whom 'the name of God is blasphemed among the Gentiles' [*imia bozhie khulitsia vo iazytsekh*]" (p. 138), the words Paul uses to accuse the Jews of disobeying religious laws: "For the name of God is blasphemed among the Gentiles through you, as it is written" (Rom. 2:24; see Isa. 52:5 and Ezek. 36:20). During the story's denouement, the metropolitan begins his refusal of baptism with another citation of Paul, heightening the contrast between sincere religious devotion and the actions of the substitute recruit. His words, "*Liuby nikoli ne oslabevaet*" (p. 141), are an archaic version of the first line of the verse, "Love never faileth, but whether there be prophecies, they shall be done away; whether there be tongues, they shall cease; whether there be knowledge, it shall vanish away" (1 Cor. 13:8).

After converting to Orthodoxy, the bookbinder offers one last reference to the New Testament. He asserts that although the Old Testament "about some things [*pro shcho*] is silent, like dumb Zachariah, and about others stutters [*gugnit*], like Moses . . . the evangelicum [*Evangelium*] is a simple, clear book" (p. 143). "Dumb Zachariah" is Zachariah, the father of John the Baptist, who didn't believe the angel who foretold the birth of his son and was punished for his doubt by temporary muteness (Luke 1:11-22). The bookbinder deems the Hebrew Bible an inadequate source of information and justifies his own conversion with reference to the text that inspired it, asserting that the Old Testament has been made irrelevant by the advent of Christianity and the New Testament.

The profusion of biblical citations reinforces the story's connection to the New Testament mastertext, identifying the substitute recruit with Judas and the bookbinder with Paul. The narrator makes this link between biblical and contemporary themes explicit: "Eighteen centuries have not altered this *ancient story*; but now I must return to my story" (p. 96).

IN SEARCH OF THE PHARISEES

However, Leskov's tale and the New Testament story are not perfectly parallel. Although **"Episcopal Justice"** contains easily identifiable counterparts for Paul and Judas, the search for characters who correspond to the New Testament's other leading players, the Pharisees, is more difficult. It first appears that the narrator, in the tradition of Christian Hebraics, associates the Pharisees simply with the contemporary Jewish community, assigning the Jewish leaders full responsibility for the plight of the freethinking bookbinder and his son:

> A man with a good conscience by nature had shifted his mental horizon slightly and, without betraying the faith of his fathers, tried to have his own opinion about

the spirit of the law, concealed by the letter . . . and the case against him was ready. He became a "dangerous freethinker"; pharisaical talmudism tries to destroy his kind, eliminate them, wipe them off the face of the earth. If he had . . . completely forgotten about Jehovah and never thought about His commandments, but never threatened the Pharisees' sanctimoniousness [*lzhepravednosti*], then it wouldn't matter. . . . But he demonstrated a kind of *breadth,* a kind of freedom of the spirit, and that's what these law-ridden [*podzakonnoe*] Yids cannot tolerate.

> (p. 96)

Given that he must have understood the rules concerning recruits, the narrator's assertions that Jews alone were to blame for the bookbinder's sad plight are intriguing. Of course, both the real Leskov and his narrator knew perfectly well that tsarist law encouraged the Jews to turn in underage boys as recruits. The paradoxicality of Leskov's description may in fact have been motivated by an attempt to provoke resistance in the reader. Dmitry Likhachev (after Viktor Shklovsky) calls this device in Leskov's work "false ethical evaluation."[41] Leskov's narrator offers an absurd opinion, what Likhachev calls a "provocative evaluation." The reader, of course, disagrees—but imagines that he or she is doing so against the will of the author. By 1877, several years after descriptions of the lives of the cantonists had been published in *Otechestvennye zapiski,* the readers of **"Episcopal Justice"** certainly could have understood the absurdity of the claim that the Jewish community was solely to blame for the excesses of the recruitment system.[42]

The force of the moral ambiguity surrounding the tsarist administrators draws the reader's attention to them and thus changes the center of the story's gravity, making it about them just as much as it is about the bookbinder and his redemption by the metropolitan. If the most important characters in the story are the bureaucrats, then the tale cannot fit as neatly as it seemed into the biblical genres inspired by Paul and Judas. However, the ever present references to the New Testament suggest that the life of Jesus must relate somehow to Leskov's tale. To follow Likhachev's logic, Leskov probably called those who abused the bookbinder and his son "Pharisees," then deliberately proposed inappropriate actors to fill their role, in order to urge the reader to seek out the real Pharisees. In this way he could lead the reader to read between the lines and discover his criticism of Nicholas's cantonism policy and those who carried it out.

We know that in Leskov's day, "Pharisees" meant hypocritical religious formalists. The definition best fits Aleksei Kirilovich Kliuchkarev, the narrator's boss, described at the beginning of the first chapter. Kliuchkarev is a "martinet" and "a bureaucrat from his head to his heels" (p. 89), a "severe and dry formalist"; he loves only his small dog and "precision in all things," but shows no mercy to human beings: "I never saw a time when a single muscle twitched in his dry, almost cruel face when he drove a civil servant with a large family from his job or sheared underage Jewish boys as cantonists" (p. 90).

"Pharisaical" epithets in this story apply not only to Kliuchkarev but also to other bureaucrats and to the system of cantonism in general. The division commanders who forcibly baptize child recruits are religious hypocrites, "in their own way carrying out Christian rites [*radevshii o khristianstve*] and, probably, understanding Christianity in their own way [*po-svoemu*]" (p. 91). In McLean's words, the sacrament of baptism is so "degraded" by their actions that the reader is led to question whether it "can . . . have any sacred content."[43] Baroness B., who helps and shelters the fleeing substitute recruit, has her own pharisaical trait, a "surface religiosity [*vneshnaia religioznost'*]" (p. 109). The narrator sees the law on cantonists itself as so unbendingly formal that it has no meaning: it allows for "no exceptions" (p. 128), regardless of circumstances. Such descriptions make it clear that the "truly pharisaical" business in the story and the real target of the author's criticism is not the Jews' wheeling and dealing, but rather the recruitment system itself. Thus, while Leskov at first seems to set his story within the traditions of Christian writings about Jews and to be prepared to focus on the distinction between Paul and Judas, "sincere" and "false" converts from Judaism, he steps over the boundaries of his genres by identifying not only Jews but also insincere Christians with the Pharisees.

THE JEW AS GOOD READER

"Episcopal Justice" is not only a critique of cantonism and the forced baptism to which it led. What makes the bookbinder's conversion real is his own confrontation with and comprehension of Christian doctrine, as represented by his solitary reading of the New Testament. By stressing this moment, Leskov approaches a criticism of Orthodox practices that goes beyond the call not to abuse the sacrament of baptism. Not only does he modify the biblical tradition so as to identify Christians as well as Jews with the Pharisees, but he also expands the framework of the conversion story to examine the sincerity of other Christians. While for centuries Christian theologians had distinguished between "true" and "false" Jewish converts, Leskov extends the comparison to differentiate between "true" Christians and pharisaical hypocrites. This difference emerges in their contrasting approach to text and in the sincere Christian's ability to read metaphorically.

The believer's metaphorical approach to text—specifically, to parable—is fundamental to the Evangelists' teachings. Jesus explains his allegorical style as a means

of distinguishing those who believe and understand from those who neither believe nor understand:

> And the disciples came, and said unto him, why speakest thou unto them in parables? He answered and said unto them, Because it is given unto you to know the mysteries of the kingdom of heaven, but to them it is not given. . . . Therefore speak I to them in parables, because they seeing, see not; and hearing, hear not, neither do they understand.
>
> (Matt. 13:10-11, 13)

Here the disciples are metaphorical listeners, who do not limit themselves to the letter of the story, but instead look for deeper meaning. Those who "seeing, see not, and hearing, hear not, neither do they understand" are pedantic listeners, who only see that which lies on the surface and can penetrate no deeper. Christian theologians such as Aquinas have expanded on the epistemological concerns expressed in Matthew to distinguish among the various levels—the literal, the metaphorical, the moral, and the anagogic—at which a reader might understand the Bible.

The allegorical nature of the Gospels emerges on two levels; not only does the primary hero, Jesus, speak in parables, but the Evangelists, like him, create a code, borrowing words, expressions, sentences, and literary devices from the Hebrew Bible, the text they know best. Their narrative style assumes a reader who knows that text equally well and who will be able to decipher a secret language that links ancient biblical predictions about the coming of a Messiah with events from the life of Jesus. The complex and paradoxical traditional attitudes of the Christian churches toward Judaism, the religion that gave rise to Christianity, and to the Jews themselves, arise against this literary background. The conversion of the Jews has, for most Christian denominations, seemed both more significant and more complicated than that of other non-Christians. As the "people of the Book," they can simultaneously represent the most appropriate objects of proselytism, the first and most logical potential converts, who know the Old Testament better than anyone and for that reason are better able than anyone to understand its hints about the future victory of Jesus; and, should they refuse conversion, they can appear to be Christianity's most stubborn enemies. In other words, given these stereotypes, Jews face a choice between two strictly defined roles: they can act either as the "best" readers of the Gospels, or the "worst," most adamant pedants.

These views of Jews as potential readers of the New Testament have a direct bearing on their roles in Leskov's stories. The Jewish father in **"Episcopal Justice"** is nothing if not a reader, one who works as a bookbinder, literally preserving and repairing books. Absurd and pathetic, but well-read, in his written appeal to the narrator he emphasizes that he has studied "the wisdom of God's word [*premudrost' bozhego slova*]" (p. 95). In the last scene, the bookbinder turns out to be not only a reader, but a "good"—that is, a metaphorical rather than a pedantic—reader. The narrator relays their conversation:

> "Who convinced you," I asked, "of the truth of Christianity?"
>
> "Well, that's clear in the Biblium [Bubel]: it's written there that the Messiah is supposed to come in the second Temple, and so that's what I saw, that he came. . . . What else can you seek [*shukat'*] or wait for, for he is already with us?"
>
> "But the Jews have all read that place, and they don't believe."
>
> "They don't believe because they've read too many talmuds and some other pointless [*pustogo*] things too, and came up with God alone knows what kinds of silly requirements, about what kind of Messiah he will be, and how he'll appear—who knows from where—and start to reign like a worldly power on earth, and they will begin to rule [*ponuvat*'; from Polish *panować*, "to reign"] the earth. . . . But that's all emptiness: he came in our form, a slave's form, and we need only hold to his teaching."

> (p. 143)

These statements recall Leskov's description of Baron Radstock's distribution of Bibles on the streets of St. Petersburg. According to the bookbinder, Bible reading is indeed the key to faith: in order to become a Christian one need only correctly read the New Testament and correctly interpret its references to the Old Testament, without insisting on the literal meaning of the descriptions of the coming of the Messiah. Saying disparagingly about other Jews that they have "come up with . . . silly requirements," the bookbinder agrees with the standard nineteenth-century Christian definition of Jews as those who rejected and continue to reject Christ; he criticizes their formalist approach to text. His own conversion, it is clear, results from his effort to be a good reader in spite of all resistance. By understanding biblical texts metaphorically rather than literally, he demonstrates that he is one of the Christian believers to whom "it is given . . . to know the mysteries of the kingdom of Heaven."

However, the bookbinder is not the only metaphorical reader in the story. The other characters, including the narrator, also confront a difficult "text" when they hear the bookbinder's tale. His very words pose an interpretive problem. Because Leskov is so well known for his ability to represent the accented or mannered speech of his characters, it is not surprising that his bookbinder's Russian is so peculiar, both in its phonetics and its vocabulary. Like many Russian writers at the time, Leskov conveyed a "Jewish accent" by making the bookbinder

confuse *s* and *sh* sounds: he says *vase* for *vasha* [your] and *gashpadin* for *gospodin* [mister]. As Leskov told his publisher, he did not know Yiddish.[44] Thus, with the exception of a few examples, such as *gval't* [help!] (p. 99) and *meshiginer* [crazy person] (p. 100), the non-Russian words the bookbinder uses come not from Yiddish but from Polish and Ukrainian, two languages that Leskov knew well. Actually, it is not improbable that a character such as the bookbinder would have used such words: Jews in the Pale of Settlement, living among Ukrainians and Poles, sometimes picked up their languages and used this knowledge to make themselves understandable among Russians.

The imbedded narrators in Leskov's stories often speak in idiolects that distance them from the reader, highlighting their ignorance, their foreignness, or their innocence and authenticity. In **"Episcopal Justice,"** the bookbinder's strange Russian creates a distance between himself and the narrator—a distance that the narrator traverses with some intellectual effort. When the narrator describes the process of his gradual comprehension of the bookbinder's problems, he begins with the bookbinder's letter, written in a combination of Russian, Polish, and Yiddish:

> It was impossible to understand what language it was in and even what alphabet. . . . Instead of rejecting the scrap of paper, given its incoherence [*neformennost'*], as "incorrectly submitted," I began to read it and "rebelled in my spirit—and then learned to read."[45] The absurdity [*nelepost'*] of the writing was nothing in comparison with that of the contents, but in that very absurdity desperation cried out yet more importunately.

> (pp. 94-95)

This attention to the difficult process of reading the bookbinder's strange prose reflects the story's central epistemological concern. Both the narrator, in reading the letter, and the bookbinder, in reading the Bible, like the original Christian disciples, overcome a pedantic need for complete and transparent clarity before they can locate a deeper and more complex meaning.

In a series of short chapters, the narrator recounts how, after he gets through the letter, his friend Drukart, then a higher official, and finally the archbishop of Kiev, slowly come to comprehend the bookbinder's tragedy. The bureaucrats who levy recruits cannot decide if they should mock the bookbinder or sympathize with him. Drukart, in contrast, grasps that although the substitute recruit's conversion would be in accordance with the policy of the Orthodox Church in Russia at the time, it would in fact be neither fair nor truly Christian. He demonstrates his ability to think allegorically by recognizing the bookbinder's cries about a "karkadyl" (presumably, a crocodile) as a description of his dog, and then referring to the bookbinder himself as a "karkadyl," saying, "Look what a vile thing they've done [*ish kakaia merzost' ustroena*] to this karkadyl" (p. 121).

The third audience of the story, Prince Illarion Illarionovich, can also see the position of the bookbinder metaphorically. His lack of pedantry is demonstrated in his sentences, themselves requiring interpretation: "Take that Yid too . . . in the sleigh . . . and go . . . with him . . . right away . . . to the metropolitan . . . (. . .) tell everything . . . and from me . . . bow to him . . . and say that I'm very sorry . . . and I can't do anything . . . since the law . . . Right-o . . . you understand" (p. 128). The prince hopes that the metropolitan will defy the law, but he does not say this directly. His evasive speech reveals his understanding of the complex situation.

The final and most influential person to hear the bookbinder's story is the metropolitan of Kiev, Filaret Amfiteatrov, to whom the narrator devotes seven of the story's fifty pages. Filaret's behavior in the story is often as surprising as that of the unpredictable Orthodox saints who were considered "fools for Christ" [*iurodivye*]. He has no respect for rank, and he insults practically all his suppliants, calling each of them "fool" and "stupid." He demonstrates his consistency by first calling the bookbinder these derogatory names (p. 140) and then saving his son by refusing baptism to the substitute recruit. The inanity of the metropolitan's answers testifies to his lack of formalism. He deals with aristocratic Russians and with poor Jews with the same absence of etiquette but, in the end, with mercy.

All of these characters demonstrate their ability to read a difficult situation metaphorically, and their struggles implicitly encourage the reader to adopt a similar interpretive strategy toward the story. The reader is in a privileged position, able not only to interpret the bookbinder's story, but also to evaluate all the characters' words and their reactions to the bookbinder and to one another. Thus, the reader can see **"Episcopal Justice"** not as a transparent text with a single meaning but as a complex, ambiguous "parable," whose deciphering might define a faith community, just as the interpretation of Jesus' stories unites Christians.

BLOODY SWEAT

One of the elements in the story that most urgently demands—and resists—interpretation is the Gothic image of the bookbinder's "bloody sweat." It is first mentioned in connection with the package of papers that the Jew brings out of his bosom, "soaked through with some kind of stinking brownish, somehow pus-like [*sukrovistoiu*] dampness—exceptionally nasty" (p. 102). Only after a few more pages, when the bookbinder tells his story to the bureaucrats, does the narrator elaborate on this "brownish" dampness:

All of us, with all our unfortunate experience of grief and suffering of this kind, were, it seemed, struck by the frightful horror of these frenzied torments, which produced in this poor fellow *bloody sweat.*

Yes, that . . . was nothing other than *bloody sweat,* which I saw with my own eyes on another human being only that one time in my life. . . .

To anyone who has never seen this *bloody sweat* . . . I would say that I saw it myself and that it is inexpressibly *horrifying.*

At least this dewy, cranberry-colored spot over the auricle still hovers before my eyes, and it seems to me that through it I see a gaping human heart, suffering from the most terrible torment—the torment of a father trying to save his child. . . . O, I will say it again: it was terrible! . . .

I involuntarily remembered the bloody sweat of the one whose righteous blood, through the fateful decision [*obrokom*] of their forefathers, was cast down onto the offspring of an outcast breed, and my own blood rushed into my heart and then quickly flooded back and sounded in my ears.

It was as though all my thoughts, all my feelings were swept away, underwent something both excruciating and sweet. It seemed that in front of me there stood not just a man, but some kind of bloody historical symbol.

(pp. 111-12; emphases in original)

This description is exaggerated, even surreal. This "bloody sweat" startled not only the story's characters but also Leskov's contemporaries. The critic from *Otechestvennye zapiski,* who in principle opposed Leskov and his political views, noted that he touchingly depicted the distress of the Jewish father.[46] Another reviewer pointed out the ghastliness of certain images: "wherever the author describes how recruitment used to happen here, horror wafts from the story."[47] Leskov's biographer Il'ia Shliapkin located precisely the image of "bloody sweat" as the center and the motivation of the story: "he [Leskov] was shocked by a frightened Jewish recruit, who emitted, out of fear, bloody sweat."[48] Following Shliapkin's lead, the author's son Andrei Leskov insisted on the authenticity of this image and on its importance for the writer. "He . . . tells with sincere feeling of the torments of the '*introligator*' ["bookbinder" in Polish], whose underage son was treacherously taken as a cantonist and who, praying for help and defense, became covered with 'bloody sweat.'"[49]

The image of bloody sweat may have so impressed the narrator and Leskov's critics not only because of its shock value but also because of its polyvalence. It evokes three scenes from the New Testament: first, the moment when Jesus refuses death, or "this cup," when "his sweat was, as it were, great drops of blood falling down to the ground" (Luke 22:44); second, the mixture of blood and water that dripped from Jesus' body after the Crucifixion, when "one of the soldiers, with a spear, pierced his side, and immediately came there out blood and water" (John 19:34); and, third, the Pharisees' assumption of guilt for the death of Jesus: "Pilate . . . took water, and washed his hands before the multitude, saying, I am innocent of the blood of this righteous person. See you to it. Then answered all the people, and said, His blood be on us, and on our children" (Matt. 27:24-25). Thus, the image can symbolize both the blood of Jesus, a suffering and innocent victim, and the guilt of the Pharisees in his death; it can be identified with both a perpetrator and a victim.

The strength of this vision of corporeal suffering challenges the millennia-old tradition of figural reading. Its resistance to formulaic interpretation may be what moved the critics, as well as the narrator and his co-workers. The bureaucrats' hearts have "become numb" due to their grim daily grind, since "even given the most obvious abuse of the weak, [we had] no time, means, or desire to judge, to lay down the law, or to stand up for him" (p. 92). Having seen so much horror, the officials who deal with the cantonists are no longer concerned with the justice of the rules that they are required to enforce. They probably seek comfort in a traditional Orthodox attitude toward the Jews as criminals, the inheritors of the Pharisees, who after their betrayal of Jesus merit any abuse. The bookbinder's bloody sweat can surprise and touch them because it calls Christian prototypes into question—within the context of canonical Christian text—by forcing them to see in the Jew a suffering human body with the "human heart" not of a criminal Pharisee, but of an innocent Jesus.

The image of bloody sweat functions in the story like a two-edged sword. On the one hand, it reinforces Christian stereotypes about Jews, defining the bookbinder as a Judas, a descendent of Pharisees, whom Christians are permitted to treat cruelly, and on the other hand, it shows that the bookbinder might be a victim rather than a criminal, in which case the Russian Christian administrators, including the narrator himself, become the Pharisees. The adjectives that describe the bloody sweat are yet more ambiguous: it is "horrible [*strashno*]" and it stinks, but also attracts the narrator, seeming in some way "both excruciating and sweet" (p. 112). Perhaps this sweetness reflects the deceptive, seductive simplicity of the story of a familiar literary type. If the bloody sweat symbolizes only Jewish guilt, then it is not criminal to recruit, baptize, or abuse the bookbinder's son, perhaps a "sweet" conclusion to the narrator. However, if the bloody sweat also symbolizes Jewish innocence, then its horror may lie in its incrimination of the narrator and his fellow functionaries as Pharisees.

The bloody sweat emblematizes the humanity of the bookbinder, which motivates Leskov's critique of Nicholas's cantonism. In conjunction with the many references to reading, it also exemplifies the kind of text that demands a metaphorical approach. This image spurs the story's characters to reconsider the ossified definitions regulating their Christianity. By situating this complex image of Jewish conversion at the center of his story, Leskov may have provoked his Christian readers to reexamine a number of concepts: their stereotypes about Jews, the way they were used to reading and interpreting the Bible so as to justify these stereotypes, and the narrative traditions within which they were used to telling stories not only about the Jews, but also about the Russian Orthodox.

"NEW TESTAMENT JEWS"

"Novozavetnye evrei" ["New Testament Jews"] (1884), in a sense, picks up where **"Episcopal Justice"** (1877) leaves off. The earlier story undermines archetypes of Jewish converts, portrays a Jew as an ideal reader of biblical text, and includes a lightly camouflaged criticism of Russian Orthodox practices surrounding baptism and a more deeply concealed criticism of Orthodox understandings of Jews. The later story, in showing the Jew Bazin, who, after reading the Bible, decides to convert to Protestantism rather than Orthodoxy, implicitly extends these criticisms. In fact, many Jews in the Russian Empire did, like Bazin, convert to Protestantism—the poet Osip Mandelstam being probably the best-known example. Bazin's tale, though, reveals less about the motivations of people like Mandelstam than it does about Leskov's unwillingness to identify the religion described in the New Testament exclusively with Russian Orthodoxy. As James Muckle meticulously documents, both Leskov's dissatisfaction with some aspects of Orthodoxy and his fascination with and attraction to some of the Protestant movements active in Russia, specifically to their emphasis on Bible reading rather than ritual, grew during the mid-1880s.[50] In **"New Testament Jews,"** as in **"Episcopal Justice,"** the figure of the Jew becomes a kind of lens facilitating a critical gaze on Russian society and Russian Orthodoxy. In reducing Bazin—even more than the bookbinder—to a penetrating readerly eye, Leskov participates in Solov'ev's project of testing Orthodoxy by investigating its relations with the Jews.

The 1884 story describes three Jews, all purportedly Leskov's acquaintances, "with Christian inclinations." The writer summarizes the lives of the first two heroes: An engraver in Kiev attended meetings of a group of Jews who were interested in Christianity, but he himself refused baptism, since he felt "ashamed to turn his back on [*brosat'*] his little Yids [*zhidkov*] while they had it badly and they themselves were stuck in the rubbish [*izdrianilis'*]" (p. 72).[51] A retired Jewish soldier, the second hero, reads the New Testament and lives according to its principles but does not agree with the proselytizing of an Irvingite lady.[52]

The biographies of the first two heroes preface the tale of the story's main hero, Bazin, a young rabbi, wise and learned, who one day happens to read the Gospels and immediately decides to convert to Christianity. The Jewish community persecutes him for his "betrayal" of Judaism, trying to turn him in as an army recruit or even to kill him, but he continues to believe in Jesus and even to convert other Jews to Christianity. Bazin carefully researches various branches of Christianity. He reads first the Orthodox catechism, then the Catholic one, but in neither does he find that which attracted him to Christianity when he read the New Testament. Finally he meets an English missionary, leaves for England, marries an Englishwoman, and himself becomes a Protestant missionary. Unlike the two other Jews described in the story, Bazin is an official convert.

Bazin's biography corresponds very neatly to the renditions of the tale of the Russian Jew as "true" Christian convert that appeared in evangelical literature.[53] The story seems to be based on a historical figure, a Jewish follower of Radstock, whom Leskov described in **Schism in High Society** as distinguished by a "phenomenal memory" and knowledge of the Bible.[54] However, Leskov's story seems to have owed something to his imagination. A contemporary reviewer in a Jewish newspaper notes that the picture printed along with Leskov's story above the caption "The Jew Bazin" actually showed not Bazin but Shapiro, a Jewish photographer from Petersburg, who had taken his own photo in the guise of a rabbi as a lark. . . .[55] Regardless of its accuracy, the story of Bazin shows that Leskov was intrigued by the story of a Jew reading the New Testament and then choosing Protestantism over Orthodoxy.

Like the bookbinder, the Jews in **"New Testament Jews"** not only read the Bible but are connected in other ways to images of written text. The first one, a carver of seals [rezchik pechatei] and an engraver, is involved with book production. And Bazin himself, like the Jewish Radstockite, resembles a book: "he knew the Old and New Testaments almost by heart in Russian, and he possessed a phenomenal memory; he was, one might say, a living concordance [zhivoiu 'Simfonieiu'], and had no need for printed references [pechatnykh svodkakh] or concordances ['Konkordantsakh']" (p. 81). The picture (of Shapiro) accompanying this story shows a Jew engaged in Bazin's favorite activity: reading a large tome. The link between these characters and text in general suggests that here, as in **"Episcopal Justice,"** Jews figure precisely as readers—ideally, readers of the Bible.

Like the bookbinder, Bazin, who is so strongly linked to books, can personify the ideal reader of the Bible and therefore the ideal Christian. Bazin's choice of Protestantism thus testifies to Leskov's lifelong conviction that Bible reading is fundamental to Christianity; he appears to be suggesting that both Jews and excessively formalistic Orthodox Christians could find inspiration in the New Testament for a new, less ritualistic religiosity. Leskov's fascination both with Jews who reject traditional Judaism (even while, like the "New Israel" congregation and the first two characters in **"New Testament Jews,"** they remain nominally Jewish) and with Russian Orthodox who are drawn to Protestant forms of Christianity is consistent with the utopian vision of a community united by the rejection of "empty," ritualistic religious traditions. This vision both draws on the imagery of the debate on church reform in the era and prefigures the Jewish-Christian friendship that Leskov would describe in 1886 in **"Skazanie o Fedore-khristianine i o druge ego Abrame-zhidovine"** [**"The Tale of Fedor the Christian and His Friend Abraham the Jew"**].

Notes

1. "Vladychnyi sud. Byl' (Iz nedavnikh vospominanii)," *Strannik,* vol. 1 (1877), nos. 1-2; "Rakushanskii melamed: Rasskaz na bivuake," *Russkii vestnik,* no. 3 (March 1878); "Zhidovskaia kuvyrkollegiia. Povest'. Ob odnom Kromchanine i o trekh zhidovinakh," *Gazeta A. Gattsuka,* no. 33 (14 August 1882), no. 34 (21 August 1882), no. 35 (28 August 1882), no. 36 (4 September 1882); "Rasskazy kstati: Novozavetnye evrei," *Nov',* vol. 1, no. 1 (November 1884); "Rasskazy kstati: Ukha bez ryby," *Nov',* vol. 8, no. 7 (February 1886); "Skazanie o Fedore-khristianine i o druge ego Abrame-zhidovine," *Russkaia mysl',* no. 12 (20 December 1886). In translating the titles, I follow Hugh McLean in *Nikolai Leskov* [(Cambridge: Harvard University Press, 1977)]. For a discussion of "Rakushanskii melamed," see Chapter 1.

2. These ethnographic articles are listed in the Bibliography.

3. *Evrei v Rossii* (St. Petersburg: 1884); reissued as *Evrei* [singular] *v Rossii,* with an introduction by Iulii Gessen (Petrograd, 1919). For an English translation, see Nikolai S. Leskov, *The Jews in Russia: Some Notes on the Jewish Question,* ed. and trans. Harold Klassel Schefski (Princeton, N.J.: Kingston Press, 1986). Although there is no proof that Leskov was paid to produce this book, it is unlikely that he wrote it for free.

4. See [V. Vodovozov], "Leskov, Nikolai Semenovich," in *Evreiskaia entsiklopediia* [(St. Petersburg: Brokgauz-Efron, n.d. (c. 1910), Facs. ed., Moscow: Terra, 1991)], vol. 10, pp. 415-18; [William B. Edgerton], "Leskov, Nikolay Semyonovich," in *Encyclopedia Judaica* (Jerusalem: Ketzer, 1971), vol. 11, pp. 45-46; Iulii Gessen's introduction to the postrevolutionary edition of *Evrei v Rossii*; Noé Gruss, "N. S. Leskov et les Juifs de Russie," *AMIF* (1974); Hugh McLean, "Theodore the Christian Looks at Abraham the Hebrew: Leskov

and the Jews," *California Slavic Studies* 7 (1973), and "Abraham the Hebrew," in *Nikolai Leskov*; Harold Klassel Schefski, introduction to Nikolai S. Leskov, *The Jews in Russia* [(Princeton, N.J.: Kingston Press, 1986)]; and A. A. Gorelov, *N. S. Leskov i narodnaia kul'tura* (Leningrad: Nauka, 1988), p. 167 n12.

5. N. S. Leskov, letter to K. A. Grehwe, 5 December 1888, *Sobranie sochinenii v 11 tomakh* (Moscow: Khud. lit., 1958), vol. 11, p. 404.

6. A. I. Faresov, *Protiv techenii* (St. Petersburg: M. Merkushev, 1904), p. 301.

7. Ibid., p. 293.

8. See the discussion of conversion from Judaism in the Introduction. Cf. the history of conversion to Orthodoxy in seventeenth- and eighteenth-century Russia in Michael Khodarkovsky, "'Not by Word Alone': Missionary Policies and Religious Conversion in Early Modern Russia," *Comparative Studies in Society and History: An International Quarterly,* vol. 38, no. 2 (April 1996).

9. This was the opinion of Prince Meshcherskii, the publisher of the journal *Grazhdanin.* See *Nedel'naia khronika Voskhoda,* 1 November 1887, p. 1099; cf. a series of articles in *Novorossiiskii telegraf*: "Po povodu perekhoda evreev v pravoslavie," no. 4184 (10 September 1888), "Po povodu perekhoda evreev v pravoslavie," no. 4200 (26 September 1888), "O perekhode evreev v pravoslavie," no. 4588 (7 November 1888). Many thanks to Ben Nathans for these articles!

10. "Iz obshchestvennoi khroniki," p. 869.

11. *The Confessions of St. Augustine,* trans. John K. Ryan (New York: Image Books, 1960), p. 202.

12. On the conversion tale, see Bakhtin, "Forms of Time and Chronotope in the Novel," [in *The Dialogic Imagination,* ed. Michael Holquist, trans. Michael Holquist and Caryl Emerson (Austin: University of Texas Press, 1981),] pp. 115, 116, 118, 120.

13. For discussion of the splitting of the image of the Jewish convert into the "real" and the "false," see [Sander L.] Gilman, *Jewish Self-Hatred* [(Baltimore: The Johns Hopkins University Press, 1986)], pp. 22-67.

14. Erich Auerbach, "Figura," in *Scenes from the Drama of European Literature* (Minneapolis: University of Minnesota Press, 1984), p. 29.

15. Ibid., p. 58.

16. For some typical stories of good converts, see Father Ioann Verzhekovskii, letter to the editor, *Kiev-lianin,* no. 124 (17 October 1867); an autobiographical account in Aleksandr Alekseev, *Obshchestvennaia zhizn' evreev, ikh nravy, obychai, i predrassudki, s prilozheniem biografii avtora* (Novgorod, 1868); and fictional depictions in Vl. Levinskii, *Perekreshchenets iz evreiskogo byta* (Moscow, 1870), and [Vsevolod Vladimirovich] Krestovskii, *Sobranie sochinenii* [(St. Petersburg: Obshchestvennaia pol'za, 1899)], vol 8. For more on Krestovskii, see Chapter 2.

17. [Anon.], "Novozavetnye evrei," *Peterburgskaia gazeta,* no. 4 (5 January 1885). This is not the story I discuss later, but a newspaper article with the same title. Inès Müller de Morogues, in *L'oeuvre journalistique et littéraire de N. S. Leskov: Bibliographie* (New York: Peter Lang, 1984), identifies the author as Leskov. On New Israel, see [I. Cherikover], "Novyi Izrail'," *Evreiskaia entsiklopediia,* vol. 11, pp. 769-71. On the leader of the movement, see Steven J. Zipperstein, "Heresy, Apostasy, and the Transformation of Joseph Rabinovich," in *Jewish Apostasy in the Modern World,* ed. Todd M. Endelman (New York: Holmes and Meier, 1987).

18. A. F. Pisemskii, *Polnoe sobranie sochinenii* (St. Petersburg: M. O. Vol'f, 1896), vol. 23.

19. M. E. Saltykov-Shchedrin, *Sobranie sochinenii* (Moscow: Khud. lit., 1973), vol. 15, pt. 1, p. 255.

20. N. S. Leskov, "Russkie deiateli v ostzeiskom krae," *Istoricheskii vestnik* (November 1883), p. 242.

21. Karl Marx, "*On the Jewish Question,* by Bruno Bauer," in *Selected Writings,* ed. David McLellan (Oxford: Oxford University Press, 1990), p. 59.

22. [Michael] Stanislawski, *Tsar Nicholas I and the Jews* [(Philadelphia: Jewish Publication Society, 1983)], p. 15; Shaul Ginzburg, *Historishe verk* [(New York: S. M. Ginzburg Testimonial Committee, 1937)], vol. 2, pp. 7-8.

23. Page numbers refer to N. S. Leskov, "Vladychnyi sud," *Sobranie sochinenii v 11 tomakh* (Moscow: Khud lit., 1957), vol. 6.

24. Stanislawski, p. 25; he cites N. Samter, *Judentaufen im 19ten Jahrhundert* (Berlin, 1906), p. 42.

25. Stanislawski, pp. 25-29.

26. Aleksandr I. Gertsen, *Byloe i dumy* (Moscow: Khud. lit., 1958), vol. 1, p. 209.

27. For a tremendously informative history of literary depictions of cantonists in Russian, Hebrew, and Yiddish, see Olga Litvak, *The Literary Response to Conscription* [(Ph.D. diss., Columbia University, 1999)].

28. Stanislawski, p. 184.

29. He wrote *O raskol'nikakh goroda Rigi, preimush-chestvenno v otnoshenii k shkolam* (1863); "S liud'mi drevlego blagochestiia," (1863) *Biblioteka dlia chteniia,* vol. 153, no. 11 (November 1863); "Iskanie shkol staroobriadtsami" (a series of feuilleton articles, 1869, in *Birzhevye vedomosti*); and many other articles in *Birzhevye vedomosti, Istoricheskii vestnik,* and other newspapers and journals, 1863-86.

30. *O raskol'nikakh goroda Rigi,* p. 33; "Iskanie shkol staroobriadtsami," 30 January 1869; "Irodova rabota," *Istoricheskii vestnik,* (April 1882), p. 191. In selecting this biblical verse to signify the mourning of the righteous oppressed, Leskov echoed one of his era's most popular books, in Russia as elsewhere: Harriet Beecher Stowe used the same line as the epigraph to vol. 1, chap. 12, of *Uncle Tom's Cabin.* In 1881, Dostoevskii would have Father Zosima quote the same line in *The Brothers Karamazov* (Dostoevskii, *Polnoe sobranie sochinenii,* vol. 14, p. 46).

31. "Iskanie shkol staroobriadtsami," 7 February 1869.

32. "Irodova rabota," p. 197.

33. See Gregory L. Freeze, *The Parish Clergy in Nineteenth-Century Russia: Crisis, Reform, Counter-Reform* (Princeton, N.J.: Princeton University Press, 1983).

34. I. S. Bellyustin, *Description of the Clergy in Rural Russia,* trans. Gregory L. Freeze (Ithaca, N.Y.: Cornell University Press, 1985).

35. Freeze, *The Parish Clergy,* p. 220.

36. Nikolai S. Leskov, *Velikosvetskii raskol* (St. Petersburg: V. Tushnova, 1877); N. S. Leskov, *Schism in High Society: Lord Radstock and His Followers,* trans. James Y. Muckle (Nottingham, England: Bramcote Press, 1995).

37. Vladimir Solov'ev, "Evreistvo i khristianskii vopros," in *Taina Izrailia: "Evreiskii vopros" v russkoi religioznoi mysli kontsa XIX-pervoi poloviny XX v.v.,* ed. V. F. Boikov. (St. Petersburg: Sofiia, 1993), p. 31.

38. Judith Deutsch Kornblatt, "Vladimir Solov'ev on Spiritual Nationhood, Russia, and the Jews," *Russian Review,* vol. 56, no. 2 (April 1997), p. 158.

39. See "Novye knigi," *Delo,* no. 9 (1879); "Bibliograficheskie izvestiia," *Pravoslavnyi sobednik* (April 1887); *Tserkovno-obshchestvennyi vestnik,* no. 54 (18 May 1877), p. 3; McLean, *Nikolai Leskov,* p. 311.

40. I would like to thank Inès Müller de Morogues for pointing out to me that one might make a similar observation about another story that Leskov wrote in 1877, "Nekreshchennyi pop" ["The Unbaptized Priest"].

41. Dmitrii S. Likhachev, *Literatura—real'nost'—literatura* (Leningrad: Sovetskii pisatel', 1984), p. 132.

42. This would be consistent with the reaction of the anonymous reviewer in *Otechestvennye zapiski,* no. 8 (August 1877), who rejects the substitute recruit as a representative of the morals of Jews in general: "In no place and at no time has it been possible to make judgments about the religiosity of a people based on the rabble of that people, for that matter the most base rabble" (p. 271).

43. McLean, *Nikolai Leskov,* p. 311.

44. N. S. Leskov, letter to A. S. Suvorin (Winter 1877-78), Rukopisnyi otdel Instituta russkoi literatury i iskusstva, St. Petersburg, f. 268, ed. khr. 131, l. 24.

45. Approximation of V. V. Kapnist epigram (Leskov, *Sobranie,* vol. 6, p. 632).

46. *Otechestvennye zapiski,* no. 8 (August 1877), p. 271.

47. *Nash vek,* no. 20 (March 1877), p. 3.

48. "K biografii N. S. Leskova (+21 fevralia 1895 g.)," *Russkaia starina* (December 1895), p. 206.

49. Andrei Leskov, *Zhizn' Nikolaia Leskova po ego lichnym, semeinym i nesemeinym zapisiam i pamiatiam, v dvukh tomakh* (Moscow: Khud. lit., 1984), vol. 1, p. 106; see also vol. 2, p. 27.

50. See James Y. Muckle, *Nikolai Leskov and the "Spirit of Protestantism"* (Birmingham, England: Birmingham Slavonic Monographs, no. 4 [1978]), pp. 113-25.

51. N. S. Leskov, "Rasskazy kstati: Novozavetnye evrei," *Nov'* (1 November 1884), pp. 71-84.

52. The movement begun by Edward Irving is known today as the Catholic Apostolic Church. Leskov referred to it in several stories; see Muckle, pp. 83-85.

53. Such a rendition appears in Russian in the biography of "James Adler," the son of a rabbi in the Pale of Settlement, who reads the New Testament, becomes a Protestant over the protests of his parents and community, leaves for England, becomes a missionary, and in that capacity returns to Russia in 1887. A. S. Ardov, *Evreievangelisty* (Moscow: N. L. Kazetskogo, 1914), p. 40. Also see the mentions of narratives of this sort in English literature in Michael Ragussis, *Figures of*

Conversion: "The Jewish Question" and English National Identity (Durham, N.C.: Duke University Press, 1995). He cites, for example, a work called *The Russo-Polish Jew: A Narrative of Conversion* (p. 45). For a discussion of the motivations of the Jews in the Russian Empire who became Protestants, see Endelman, "Jewish Converts in Nineteenth-Century Warsaw."

54. N. S. Leskov, *Schism in High Society,* p. 73.

55. *Nedel'naia khronika Voskhoda,* vol. 8, no. 45 (11 November 1884), p. 1284.

Bibliography

Leskov, Nikolai Semenovich. Articles on Jewish rituals, published in *Peterburgskaia gazeta*: "Religioznye obriady evreev." no. 244 (11 December 1880); "Religioznye obriady evreev," no. 245 (12 December 1880); "Religioznye obriady evreev: Shabash, ili prazdnik sedmits," no. 252 (20 December 1880); "Religioznye obriady evreev. Shabash, ili prazdnik sedmits," no. 254 (23 December 1880); "Religioznye obriady evreev: Novomesiachiia," no. 255 (24 December 1880); "Religioznye obriady evreev: Prigotovlenie opresnokov," no. 1 (1 January 1881); "Religioznye obriady evreev: Paskha," no. 8 (10 January 1881); "Religioznye obriady evreev: Mezhdu Paskhoiu i Piatidesiatnitseiu," no. 14 (17 January 1881); "Religioznye obriady evreev," no. 20 (24 January 1881); "Religioznye obriady evreev: Plach o razorenii Ierusalima," no. 26 (31 January 1881); "Religioznye obriady evreev: Prazdnik trub (ili Novogo Goda)," no. 38 (14 February 1881); "Obriady i sueveriia evreev: Den' ochishcheniia," no. 68 (21 March 1881).

———. [pseud. ***]. Articles on Jewish rituals, published in *Ezhenedel'noe novoe vremia*: "Evreiskaia nabozhnost' (Religioznye obriady i obychai u evreev)," no. 53 (3 January 1880); "Evreiskoe blagochestie v nachale dnia," no. 55 (17 January 1880); "Evreiskaia nabozhnost'. III," no. 57 (31 January 1880); "Evreiskaia nabozhnost': Vecher i noch' v evreiskom dome. IV," no. 59 (14 February 1880).

[———]. Articles on Jewish rituals, published in *Peterburgskaia gazeta*: "Kuchki (Zavtrashnii prazdnik u evreev)," no. 260 (21 September 1884); "Evreiskaia gratsiia (Verbnyi den' u evreev)," no. 265 (26 September 1884); "Radostnyi den' u evreev (Poslednii prazdnik oseni)," no. 268 (29 September 1884); "Religioznye illiuminatsii u evreev," no. 348 (18 December 1884).

[———]. "Evrei i khristianskaia krov'." *Peterburgskaia gazeta,* no. 20 (21 January 1892).

———. [pseud. N. L.]. "Evrei i obiazannosti khristian (Retsenziia)." *Istoricheskii vestnik,* no. 5 (May 1882).

[———]. "Evreiskie 'khedery' i 'melamedy.'" *Peterburgskaia gazeta,* no. 11 (12 January 1885).

———. "Irodova rabota." *Istoricheskii vestnik* (April 1882).

———. "Iskanie shkol staroobriadtsami." *Birzhevye vedomosti,* nos. 28, 30, 37, 43, 44, 48, 65, 71, 89, 102, 134 (1869).

[———]. "Kniga kagala (retsenziia)." *Novoe vremia,* no. 2186 (1 April 1882).

———. Letters to A. S. Suvorin. Rukopisnyi otdel Instituta russkoi literatury i iskusstva, St. Petersburg, f. 268.

[———]. "Novozavetnye evrei." *Peterburgskaia gazeta,* no. 4 (5 January 1885).

———. "Rakushanskii melamed: Rasskaz na bivuake." *Russkii vestnik,* no. 3 (March 1878).

———. "Rasskazy kstati: Novozavetnye evrei." *Nov',* vol. 1, no. 1 (November 1884).

———. "Rasskazy kstati: Ukha bez ryby." *Nov',* vol. 8, no. 7 (February 1886).

———. "Russkie deiateli v ostzeiskom krae." *Istoricheskii vestnik* (November 1883).

———. "Skazanie o Fedore-khristianine i o druge ego Abrame-zhidovine." *Russkaia mysl',* no. 12 (20 December 1886).

———. "S liud'mi drevlego blagochestiia." *Biblioteka dlia chteniia,* vol. 153, no. 11 (November 1863).

———. "U evreev." *Peterburgskaia gazeta,* no. 251 (12 September 1884).

[———]. "Vladychnyi sud. Byl' (Iz nedavnikh vospominanii)." *Strannik,* vol. 1, nos. 1-2 (1877).

———. "Zhidovskaia kuvyrkollegiia. Povest'. Ob odnom Kromchanine i o trekh zhidovinakh." *Gazeta A. Gattsuka,* no. 33 (14 August 1882), no. 34 (21 August 1882), no. 35 (28 August 1882), no. 36 (4 September 1882).

Faith Wigzell (essay date 2001)

SOURCE: Wigzell, Faith. "Nikolai Leskov, Gender and Russianness." In *Gender and Sexuality in Russian Civilisation,* edited by Peter I. Barta, pp. 105-20. London: Routledge, 2001.

[*In the following essay, Wigzell suggests that Leskov's fiction reflects established patriarchal cultural attitudes by typically gendering positive and heroic images of Russian character as male and negative archetypal Russian figures as female.*]

Gor'kii's dictum that Leskov was the most Russian of writers ("samobytneishii pisatel' russkii" (Gor'kii 1948-55, 24, 237)) has dominated subsequent critical assessment. While this essay conforms insofar as it discusses Leskovian characters who embody traditional Russian archetypes or ethnic stereotypes (national characterology), it takes as its focus the gender bias underlying Leskov's artistic recharacterisations. From lyrical appeals to his country (Rus'/rodina) to his colourful characters stylized à la russe, I shall argue that Leskov defeminizes and, more particularly, dematernalizes his symbols of traditional Russia. The aim is not to speculate on Leskov's biography, psychology or attitudes to women, but rather to uncover the writer's personal artistic slant on Russian national identity. I am, therefore, neither following the line pursued by Inès Muller de Morogues who examines female portraiture in terms of Leskov's response to the woman question, nor the psychologized approach of Hugh McLean (Muller de Morogues 1991; McLean 1977).

The works that lend themselves best to this type of discussion are those of the 1860s and 1870s where Leskov was responding to contemporary debate about Russian national identity and the Russian way forward. They are all set in the provinces, which was perceived by the Slavophile-inclined, here including Leskov, as the locus of real Russianness; **"The Life of a Peasant Martyress" ("Zhitie odnoi baby")**, 1863, **"The Enchanted Pilgrim"** (or "Wanderer") (**"Ocharovannyi strannik"**), 1873, together with three of the remaining parts of the unfinished chronicle of Russian provincial life, the novel *Cathedral Folk* (*Soboriane*), 1872, **"Kotin the He-Cow and Platonida" ("Kotin doilets i Platonida")**, 1867, and **"Olden Times in the Village of Plodomasovo" ("Starye gody v sele Plodomasove")**, 1869.[1] Some reference will also be made to the well-known story **"Lady Macbeth of Mtsensk" ("Ledi Makbet Mtsenskogo uezda")**, 1864.

For a writer to comment on the nature and future of Russia was not of course new. In particular, Leskov shares much with the Gogol' of *Dead Souls,* both in his (albeit more modest) apostrophes to Rus' and in the use of ethnic stereotypes as a basis for character portraits. By contrast with Gogol, however, Leskov's considerable knowledge of ordinary Russians, acquired in childhood and subsequently, as well as of their oral poetic heritage enabled him to broaden his sources for national characterology, thereby largely escaping the conventional negative connotations of ethnic stereotypes (the Russians as, for example, strong, ignorant and fond of drink) which dominate in *Dead Souls* (Møller 1997, 72)). It should have also permitted him to escape the negative gender stereotypes of women so often found in Gogol's work (women as gossipmongers, obsessed with trivia and so on), but here, as will be argued, Leskov ignored or reworked traditional images.[2] In any case, the debate about the qualities inherent in Russians which made them distinct and might determine their future had moved a long way since the early 1840s.

By the 1860s the question of how to bridge the cultural divide between the secularized culture of the élite and rural Russia's old pre-Petrine world view had become so pressing that few members of the intelligentsia, writers included, could ignore it (Hosking 1997, 263-85; 210-12). To solve the problem meant first defining Russia's essence and then advocating a path for the future. Not least was what to do with the majority of the population, the peasants. On the one hand they seemed irredeemably backward, on the other had preserved ancient customs and a rich national folklore, gems of which were being discovered and published in exactly this period: texts of the folk epic *byliny* with their heroic *bogatyri* (Rybnikov 1861-7) in particular, but Afanas'ev's folk tales and work on mythology (Afanas'ev 1855-7; 1865-9), P. V. Kireevskii's collection of songs (Kireevskii 1860-8) and Barsov's of folk-poetic laments (Barsov 1872) also spring to mind. Much of Leskov's work of this period was a response and artistic contribution to that debate, drawing on folk and religious material. Although he shared the Slavophile interest in the country's indigenous cultural roots, he felt his superior experience of rural Russia and its largely peasant population gave him a more balanced view than many. As Gor'kii remarked: "he loved Rus' in her entirety exactly as she was, with all the absurdities (*neleposti*) of her age-old way of life . . . but he loved it all without shutting his eyes to anything . . ." (Gor'kii, 24, 233). He was contemptuous of those whose ignorance of the "narod" led them to absurd idealisations (witness his ironical quotation from a Maikov poem at the end of **"The Life of a Peasant Martyress"** (1, 385; also 1, xxviii[3])), but equally disliked the semi-fictional ethnographic writings of populist writers with their exaggeratedly gloomy portrayals of peasant life (McLean 1977, 115-6). Leskov's use of folk images and national characterology allowed him to make ironic and sometimes bitter comment on contemporary Russia, while at the same time bringing forward what he saw as the positive heritage and potential of his country. However balanced his assessment of his country, Leskov's own gender bias nonetheless ensured a biassed selection and treatment of the images of Russianness.

His approach is evident even in his treatment of the varied terms for country that reflected the painful cultural divide: "Rus'" and "rodina" versus "Rossiia" and "otechestvo". Conceptually, "Rossiia" and "otechestvo" form a pair, connected to Russia as empire, with "otechestvo" implying concepts of noble duty or military and civil service in a cosmopolitan secular state. The two pairs of terms are gendered; obviously the term "otechestvo" is connected with the word for "father", but, over and above this, the concepts of state service and duty are essentially masculine ones, and so too is the Latinate term "Rossiia", despite its feminine gender (Gachev 1991, 150). The grammatical gender of the capital Petersburg (masculine), from where the tsar, the father of his people ruled (Dal' 1984, 1, 258), further assisted the view of the Russian autocracy and empire as male. Those interested in defining the essence of Russia, Leskov included, preferred the other pair, "Rus'" and "rodina", which are more than simply grammatically feminine. The word "rodina" is cognate with words like "roditel'" (parent) and "urozhai" (harvest). Through the associations with abundance, feeding and reproduction it is connected to the cult of Damp Mother Earth ("Mat' syra-zemlia"), the symbol of nurturing and care, enshrined in many traditional rituals and beliefs. In pre-Christian belief and the peasant world view the earth was seen as the womb of all civilisation, constantly renewing itself and providing succour to its children (Hubbs 1988, xiii-xvi; Barker 1986). "Your home ("rodimaia storona") is your mother—foreign parts are your mother-in-law" reads one of Dal''s proverbs (Dal' 1984, 255). Such concepts were also accepted by the intelligentsia: "I know why it is you weep, mother mine", declares Nekrasov in his poem ("Rodina"). "Rus'" like "rodina" is not simply feminine but, more specifically, possesses strong maternal overtones, often being popularly termed Mother Russia ("Matushka Rus'"). It had ceased to be a geographical term, denoting instead the qualities seen as essentially Russian, the language, tradition and religion located in a land seen as home ("rodina")—hence it was both the embodiment of Russianness and the epitome of the peasant world view. Key qualities were the supposedly female attributes of the submissive and humble, and, above all, of caring and nurturing (see Aizlewood 1996).[4]

In the work of the 1860s and 1870s under consideration here, Leskov not surprisingly ignores the terms "otechestvo"/"Rossiia", since his concern is the Russia of tradition and how to move the country into the modern world without destroying its essence. By contrast, the terms "Rus'"/"rodina" appear frequently, albeit often placed in the mouth of a narrator. Thus in the early story, **"The Life of a Peasant Martyress"**, the narrator, a local now resident in Petersburg, concludes a disquisition on the appalling rural habit of child beating, prevalent among the gentry as well as the peasants, as follows:

> O, my Rus', my native Rus' ("Rus' rodimaia"). How much longer will you dawdle in your dirt and squalor? Is it not time to wake, and take hold of yourself? Is it not time to unclench the fist, and turn to the mind? Revive, my own, much praisèd land! Enough of playing the fool, enough of wiping away the tears with fist and cudgel. . . .
>
> (1, 285)[5]

Although Leskov (here clearly perceptible behind the narrator) addresses Rus' in the familiar "ty", lyrically declaring his love for his country, he characterises Rus' as an uncaring mother, who responds to tears with brutality. Violence has overwhelmed caring maternal instincts.

Other instances of Leskov's use of the term "Rus'" reinforce the impression that he underplays the powerful maternal image of Rus'. A few years later, writing about the journey across Lake Ladoga in 1872, which is reflected in **"The Enchanted Pilgrim"**, Leskov expressed both admiration and despair about his "rodina" and its extraordinary people: "Whither are you going, whither are you sailing, oh holy motherland, on your rickety boat with its drunken sailors. How can you digest this combination of peas and cabbage, piety and drunkenness, spiritualist ravings and airy-fairy atheism, ignorance and conceit. . . . Oh be strong, my homeland! Be strong for you are crucial" (quoted in Gorelov 1988, 219). Here again Leskov affirms his love of Russia, but this time leaves out all reference to her feminine nature. The focus is instead on the country's incongruous contrasts and appalling problems, and rests partly on ethnic stereotypes (piety, drunkenness, ignorance, love of philosophizing) which are not gendered here. Though this invocation does not form part of **"The Enchanted Wanderer"** itself, the sense of Russia as a land of self-destructive contrasts (including piety versus drunkenness) underlies the story, in which positive features of Russianness are set against the negative in the person of the flawed hero. In this case the image of "Rus'"/"rodina" is not anti-maternal, but neither is it feminized. Only in the third example of an invocation to Russia, which comes in the novel ***Cathedral Folk*** is there any clear positive presentation of Rus' as feminine. On observing the kindness of the eccentric Pizonskii, who is bringing up an orphan on his own, the main character, Archpriest Savelii Tuberozov, exclaims: "Oh my soft-hearted Russia, how beauteous thou art!" (4, 36). It is no coincidence that this epitome of maternal qualities is a man, a point elaborated later. It may be concluded that, although Leskov is clearly deeply attached to his country as "Rus'"/"rodina", his view minimized the feminine aspects of the conventional concept. As will be seen, defeminizing or rather dematernalising is a feature of Leskov's literary Russianness as a whole.

It does not follow from the suggestion that "Rus'"/"rodina" is essentially feminine and "Rossiia"/"otechestvo" masculine that the former does not incorporate the masculine as well. Traditionally "Matushka Rus'" was seen as married to "Batiushka" (diminutive of father) tsar. Russians were seen as her children. While female positive images tended to replicate the supposed feminine qualities of Rus' (caring, long-suffering, passive and humble), male images were both contrasting and more varied, reflected in the religious and martial aspects of the old saying "Holy, Orthodox, heroic Rus', sacred Russian motherland" ("Rus' sviataia, pravoslavnaia, bogatyrskaia, mat' sviatorusskaia zemlia") (Dal' 1984, 1, 258; Platonov 1993, 6). Although no evidence exists to suggest that Leskov drew directly on the proverb in his depiction of his Russianized characters, this conception of "Rus'" with its tripartite division into maternal, religious and heroic qualities makes an excellent yardstick by which to evaluate Leskov's Russianness, and the respective roles played by male and female images in it.

The evaluation of Leskov's own selection of archetypes requires an understanding of the context of gender representation in Russian oral and literary tradition, the relevant aspects of which I shall, therefore, briefly outline. Surprisingly, the situation is more complex than might be assumed from the patriarchal structure of traditional Russian society. In folklore gender plays an important role, both in the "ownership" of a given genre and in the creation of typical images. Only the lament is performed solely by women, but in other genres women dominate. For example, the ballad, a narrative song focussing on family conflict, is frequently centred on female characters and women's problems (such as their powerlessness in the context of marriage in the patriarchal household). Though the sympathy between singer and subject matter is not overt, the ballad often expresses a female point of view and was generally sung by women (Balashov 1963, 14). It reflects national characterology in its emphasis on violence in the face of injustice, as well the figures of the victim heroine, the bold young man ("dobryi molodets") or the wicked mother-in-law. Apart from the ballad, a large body of lyric folk songs, mostly concerning love and marriage, are the property of women. More often than not they portray the sadness of a woman who is a victim of circumstances (married to a man she does not love, mourning a lost love and so on).

By contrast, the most obviously male genre in terms of subject matter and hero is the bylina. Perhaps not surprisingly, these epic songs (and the related genre of the historical song) were primarily sung by men. All the main heroes, the bogatyrs, are male, larger-than-life figures who defend Rus' by single-handedly overcoming hideous monsters, dragons or huge armies. Interestingly, whereas in the bylina and the folk historical song the ability to down buckets of "green wine" is a male attribute given positive value in the figure of the bogatyr, the ethnic stereotype of the Russians as prone to drink possesses negative connotations. Overall, the bylina heroes, in particular the best known, Il'ia Muromets, came to be regarded as the epitome of Russianness in its masculine variant, brave and active ("heroic Rus'").

Nonetheless, this "male" genre features not one, but two positive female figures. The first of these is the "polenitsa" (or "polianitsa"), a warrior maiden whose strength may rival or exceed that of the bogatyr with whom she fights (e.g. "Dobrynia and Nastas'ia"). It should, however, be noted that the "polenitsa" is always either tamed by marriage or killed by her husband for challenging his superiority (e.g. "Dunai"), and, further-

more, never fights to defend Rus'. The second is the hero's mother. In the bylina, just as in some folk historical songs, mothers play a significant role as caring figures who warn their sons not to take foolhardy action (e.g. "Dobrynia i zmei"), or pick up the pieces after their advice has been ignored, as in the bylina about Vasilii Buslaev and some variants of the song about the death of Mikhail Skopin-Shuiskii. But if the archetypal wise and caring mother has a raw deal in the bylina, fathers almost never appear.[6]

While positive mythologised images of women (even if often long-suffering and fatalistic) do exist in Russian folklore, they are rarities in Russian Orthodoxy. Just as Christianity is a male-dominated religion, though many of its most fervent ordinary supporters have always been women, hagiography, which mythologizes the deeds of saintly men and holds them up for emulation, is a genre composed by men, often monks, who mainly promoted misogynistic ideals. Female saints exist in Russia, as elsewhere, but they are few and far between and generally little venerated. The only female Christian figures to be universally venerated in Russia were those that incorporated age-old beliefs into their cult: Mary and St Paraskeva-Piatnitsa. In Russia more icons are devoted to Mary than to any other single figure, her cult emphasizing less her virginity than her role as the mother of God (Barker 1986, 87-123), most likely because of a confusion with the pre-Christian cult of Mother Earth.[7] Paraskeva-Piatnitsa similarly was linked with a pre-Christian female deity, Mokosh, who specifically protected women. The loving, giving mother is the supreme female image in Russian folk belief and folklore, just as the maternal facets of Rus' predominate. Overall the maternal figure is of major importance in traditional Russian culture (folk and written), certainly more so than the wise maiden of folk tales, or the unhappy victim of lyric song or ballad, trapped in a loveless marriage.

Outside hagiography women fare no better. The historical literature of early and Muscovite Rus' focusses on dominant figures who were overwhelmingly men. Only when women became widows, like Princess Ol'ga in the *Tale of Bygone Years* (*Povest' vremennykh let*), could they hold any real power. Not until the seventeenth century do literary portraits of strong women emerge in the descriptions of the lives of Uliian'ia Lazarevskaia, Boiarynia Morozova—supporter of the Old Belief—and Anastas'ia Markovna, the wife of the Archpriest Avvakum. Emphasizing the qualities of loyalty, steadfastness and infinite forbearance, these works present women as wives or mothers, to some extent, therefore, paralleling folk archetypes.

Female images of Russianness were thus available to Leskov. Despite this, the most distinctive of his epitomes of Russianness are male: the narrator hero of **"The

Enchanted Pilgrim", Ivan Sever'ianovich Fliagin, the priests Tuberozov, Zakhariia Benefaktov and deacon Akhilla Desnitsyn in *Cathedral Folk* as well as the lesser character of Konstantin Pizonskii (*Cathedral Folk* and **"Kotin the He-Cow and Platonida"**). By contrast, the positive female characters, especially those in the Stargorod cycle and in **"The Enchanted Pilgrim"**, are secondary, more passive or conventional. Tuberozov's wife, Natal'ia Nikolaevna, is a much less colourful character than her husband, while Platonida is neither as colourful nor as developed a character as Pizonskii, with whom she shares the story. In **"The Enchanted Pilgrim"**, the only striking and stylized female image is that of Grusha, who is not Russian but a gypsy (albeit a striking archetype of the passionate and tempestuous Romany). The sole dominant female character is Marfa Plodomasova (the old landowner from Tuberozov's diary and **"Olden Times in the Village of Plodomasovo"**). Only the early stories, **"The Life of a Peasant Martyress"** and **"Lady Macbeth of Mstensk"**, focus on heroines stylized à la russe. However, these characters and the nature of their Russianness must be understood in the context of Leskov's aims, which were less to create Russian archetypes than to make a polemical point.

The reasons for Leskov's choice of source material for Nast'ia Prokudina and Katerina Izmailova lie in his literary aims which at this very early stage of his writing career were more restricted than they became in the Stargorod cycle and **"The Enchanted Pilgrim"**. **"The Life of a Peasant Martyress"** was intended, like **"The Robber"** (1862), **"The Musk-Ox"** (1863) and **"The Mocker"** (1863), as a contribution to the peasant question. The story revolves around the tragic life and love of Nast'ia Prokudina, whose refusal to compromise her essential goodness and moral idealism (she has been forced into marriage to a near idiot as part of a business deal) leads to her destruction by the barbaric peasant environment in which she lives. Using his excellent first-hand knowledge, Leskov demonstrates the moral bankruptcy of the peasantry (McLean 1977, 115; Gorelov 1988, 146). The choice of a victim heroine with the archetypal Russian qualities of purity of soul and steadfastness was a natural one in the circumstances. To lend his character a typicality and enhance the tragedy of her fate, Leskov employed folk sources. The ending in which Nast'ia freezes to death in a forest inverts that of the well-known folk tale, "Jack Frost" ("Morozko"), about a victim heroine who, because of her goodness, escapes death in the forest in winter—real life, Leskov implies, is no fairy tale. Equally natural was the use of folk song as a means of lending a poetic colouring to Nast'ia's plight, and especially to the account of her love affair with an unhappily married man. Nast'ia is first drawn to Stepan because he sings superbly, just like Turgenev's "Singers" in *A Sportsman's Sketches*; she, too, possesses a remarkable voice, and the songs

they sing, both separately and together, are carefully chosen to reflect their feelings and situation. Nast'ia is stylized after the manner of the sad female figure of many folk songs, as a way of heightening the pathos of her fate and pointing out the contrast between her feelings and the brutal realism of her surroundings. In this way Leskov disputed the radicals' argument that serfdom was the cause of all peasant ills, suggesting instead that the peasants themselves were too often brutalized by life, causing harm to each other. The parallels render her a symbolic Russianized victim heroine in the service of a polemical argument, rather than an archetypal symbol of Russianness in general.

With Katerina Izmailova Leskov was responding not to political debate about peasant life but to a literary one about the relevance of Shakespearean archetypes in Russian settings (was tragedy possible in the Russia provinces?) as well as Leskov's own comment on the, as he saw it, overidealised merchant heroine of Ostrovskii's play, *The Thunderstorm* (*Groza*) (Guminskii 1983, 243-44; Wigzell 1989, 170-1). However, the desire to create his own versions of Russian archetypes as a function of a growing interest in the question "whither Russia" was already developing. In late 1864, just after completing **"Lady Macbeth"**, the writer declared his intention (subsequently unrealised) of making the story part of a cycle about typical Russian female characters (10, 253). The important word here is "typical". At this stage Leskov wanted to create recognisable provincial types, but not yet in characters who would embody the virtues (and failings) of Rus', thereby contributing to a general debate. Like Nast'ia, Katerina represents the victim heroine, but in the variant found in the folk ballad as opposed to magic tale or folk lyric. This heroine is driven by passion to the sort of action of which Nast'ia is incapable, murdering whoever stands between her and her lover, Sergei. The story contains numerous parallels both of plot and treatment with ballads (for details, see Wigzell 1989). As Lantz points out, the story supports the view of Leskov's alter ego in his novel *No Way Out* (1864) that the Russians possess a "direct and uncompromising nature . . . which would give their drama a unique flavour" (Lantz 1979, 44), a quality well expressed in the dramatic plot of the folk ballad. By underscoring the typicality of Katerina in this way, Leskov makes his point.

What becomes clear is that Leskov moved away from female characters as he began to focus on the problems of Russia. The victim heroine could not embody the positive values of old Russia, and in the Stargorod cycle features only once in the person of Platonida, who is given a much lighter Russian stylization than either Nast'ia or Katerina. Furthermore, when it came to depicting a happily married woman in Natal'ia Nikolaevna Tuberozova of *Cathedral Folk*, Leskov had no obvious folk source. Consequently Tuberozov's wife is paragon of wifely virtue according to conventional social norms, certainly also representing Leskov's own ideal spouse (caring, supportive, submissive, quiet, deferring to her husband's intellect and judgement), but Leskov also wanted to make her representative of the best in *traditional* Russian womanhood (Muller de Morogues 1991, 429-32). To this end he modelled Natal'ia Nikolaevna on the wife of Archpriest Avvakum, the most famous opponent of Church reform in the seventeenth century. Both are adjuncts to their husband, only once stepping forward to encourage him when his resolve falters (see Wigzell 1985, 332-4). Described by Deacon Akhilla as a "force", Natal'ia Nikolaevna is a softer, gentler person than her counterpart. Her "force" lies in her meekness and devotion to her husband. For his part, he derives moral and emotional strength from her presence by his side. Whereas there is some suggestion that Tuberozov might have done more to realise his potential and put his ideas into action, there is no such implied criticism of Natal'ia Nikolaevna. Like many, he clearly did not envisage women playing a more active role in the defence of Russianness and the development of his country.

When creating his trinity of clerical heroes in *Cathedral Folk,* Leskov, not surprisingly, shifted from women's to men's folklore. The bylina was an obvious choice, especially since public enthusiasm for it was at a height. Long believed defunct, it had been discovered flourishing in Olonets province. Interest culminated in Vereshchagin's famous portrait of Il'ia Muromets and in performances in Moscow in 1871 by singers brought from their villages (Gorelov 1988, 193). The second most important character in *Cathedral Folk,* the deacon Akhilla Desnitsyn, as well as the hero of **"The Enchanted Pilgrim"**, Fliagin, both draw on the male image of the epic hero. Termed bogatyrs partly because of their enormous size and strength (Leskov 1956-8, 4, 86, 298, 304, 386-7), both imbibe huge quantities of vodka, get involved in tests of physical strength (Akhilla in a fight with a German wrestler at a fair, Fliagin with a Tatar), and love their country (even though they do not serve it well). Both are also connected with horses; Fliagin becomes a "koneser", a connoisseur of horseflesh, Akhilla gallops the countryside like a Cossack (4, 67) and furnishes his spartan home in Cossack style (4, 10-11) (on Fliagin see Gorelov 1988, 197-204, Mikhailova 1966, Cherednikova 1971; on Akhilla, see Wigzell 1988a, 905-6)). Of course, despite their good qualities, neither has the sense of purpose of the epic bylina hero: Leskov's view of the past was a nostalgic one, but he realised that the epic qualities so admirable in the bogatyr were too often inappropriate or absurd in a latter-day hero. In evaluating aspects of his latter-day epic heroes' behaviour, he therefore drew on the ethnic stereotype of the Russians with its frequently negative connotations. Firstly, he shows how misplaced their strength often is, and, secondly, depicts their attachment

to vodka, especially binge drinking, as a failing. Nonetheless, their strength, spontaneity, basic decency and love of country make them both sympathetic figures in traditional epic vein and essential components of the nostalgic picture of old Russian life purveyed in *Cathedral Folk* on the one hand and the evocation of Rus' through the hero of **"The Enchanted Pilgrim"** on the other.

Important as the connection with the bylina is for one of Leskov's trinity of clerical heroes, it was not sufficient for the characterisation of the religious aspect of holy, Orthodox, heroic Rus'. Leskov chooses to present Father Savelii Tuberozov as a latter-day Avvakum, the conservative revolutionary who strove to reform Church life and then to protect Orthodoxy, as he conceived of it, from the attacks of the reforming Nikonites (Wigzell 1985, 321-5). Tuberozov's relative ineffectiveness in the modern world (as well as his occasional childishness) make him a more endearing but much weaker figure than the indomitable Avvakum. The counterpoint underlines Leskov's pessimism about the survival of old Russian virtues in a modern world, and rather suggests that, much as he admired the quintessentially Russian male qualities, he doubted how useful they were in the service of Russia.

Designed as a contrast to Tuberozov, the meek, kind Father Zakhariia Benefaktov of *Cathedral Folk* represents a different facet of Orthodox tradition. His humility and gentleness make him the embodiment of Russian kenoticism, like those Russian saints who espoused love and non-resistance to evil. One may observe that meekness and humility are close to the qualities displayed by Nast'ia Prokudina, but in this instance do not derive from folklore. There the suffering of women stems from their powerlessness in a given situation, these qualities thus forming a strategy for survival rather than a positive stance held up for emulation. One should note that the emphasis on the religious significance of humility and forbearance is to a great extent a nineteenth-century educated construct, just as the ideal of kenoticism has achieved its prominence only with Tolstoi, but its late provenance as part of a mythologised Russian tradition is of course just as valid in Leskov's artistic stylizations. The writer, as ever the pragmatist, could not admire uncritically, and he shows that Father Zakhariia's qualities are totally ineffectual in a Russia beset by atheism and alien Western influences; he is loved but not listened to.

If in *Cathedral Folk,* Leskov drew on the kenotic saint, the religious revolutionary and the heroic bogatyr' for this trinity of heroes, in **"The Enchanted Pilgrim"** he combined heroic and religious archetypes together in one character (male). Having largely given up hope that the reform of Russian life and moral leadership could come through the Orthodox Church, Leskov now focussed on a hero, epitomising the Russian "narod" with its moral strengths and failings, whose pilgrimage through life represents the people's own blundering path. With his propensity for violence and weakness for strong drink, Leskov seems to have found difficulty in finding appropriate models from lives of saints for his all too fallible hero, and hence restricted the hagiographical colouring to separate motifs and episodes, notably the dedication of the infant Pilgrim to God by his mother, his prophetic dreams, and his ultimate career as a monk, albeit of an unconventional kind. As a substitute Leskov turned to the late seventeenth-century literary work, depicting another fallible hero's journey through life, *The Tale of Misery-Ill Fortune* (*Povest' o Gore-Zlochastii*). In this lay morality tale, the foolish young man ("molodets"), ignoring his parents' advice, sets off on his own path in life. After constantly succumbing to the temptations afforded by strong drink, gambling, false friends and his own arrogance, he is hounded by the folk-poetic figure of Misery (Gore) and forced to take refuge in a monastery. Like the "molodets", Fliagin is prone to bouts of drinking and degradation followed by periods where he seems to be doing or making good. He, too, is finally forced to choose the monastery as the only way out (Wigzell 1997). Not least of the parallels is thematic; the "molodets" disobeys his parents and seventeenth-century behavioural precepts, while Fliagin, one of the children of Rus', not only ignores his real mother's dedication of him to God, but fails to pay sufficient respect to his motherland. In captivity among the Tatars Fliagin dreams longingly of the monastery domes in his own "baptised land", the beginning of inner change (4, 434). In the concluding pages of the story, the literally and metaphorically sobered Pilgrim hearkens to his mother's wishes, and places himself at the service of his Orthodox motherland (see Wigzell 1997, 760). Thus **"The Enchanted Pilgrim"** brings together the qualities of Russia, expressed in "holy, Orthodox, heroic Rus', sacred Russian motherland", although it should be noted that the maternal aspects of the saying are restricted to the end of the story, which leaves the reader with no real confidence that the hero can effectively defend his "rodina", doubts Leskov also shared.

Thus the active male Russianized heroes of the Stargorod cycle and **"The Enchanted Pilgrim"** are flawed by failings which reflect ethnic stereotypes of the Russians, but, thanks to their stylization through links with folk and religious literature, remain appealing figures. By contrast, the active Russianized heroine in these works is restricted to a single figure, that of Marfa Plodomasova. In general she represents a version of a historical image, the woman who gains power through widowhood. In early Russian literature this type is best represented by Uliian'ia Lazarevskaia, who dedicates herself to good works in the name of God after the death of her husband, while evidently continuing to

care for her children (her biography was composed by her son). Ever modest and self-abnegating, she uses power simply as a means of disposing of the family income in charitable activities. A more self-willed image is that of Boiarynia Morozova, who, against the wishes of her husband, dedicates herself to the cause of the Old Belief and so becomes a religious martyr. Neither provides a direct model for Marfa Plodomasova. Nor was the image of strong-minded widow relevant for the portrait of the younger Marfa, who, abducted at the age of fifteen by a dissolute neighbour and forced into marriage, refuses to repudiate her brutal husband when she has the chance because of her belief in the sanctity of marriage. Her decision to stand by him results in him reforming his ways. Although the principled Marfa is presented as a historical type, such as no longer exists (this part of the story is set in 1748), it seems likely that here Leskov drew on the contemporary literary archetype of the young heroine, who is morally stronger than the man she loves. He reverted to the historical image when depicting Marfa as a widow, autocratic but morally upright, courageous in the face of torture from bandits who invade her house. For the depiction of Marfa as a mother, on the other hand, he had the choice of numerous models, including that of Uliian'ia and the bylina mother, but Leskov presents her as severely lacking in caring and nurturing qualities. Her moral principles and the patriarchal precepts of the sixteenth-century guide to household management and good behaviour, the *Domostroi,* regulate her relations with her son. When she discovers that the twenty-year-old has made a serf girl pregnant, she orders a humiliating flogging. Although Marfa Plodomasova emerges as a pillar of virtue and a pious Christian, she is also a tyrant who has adopted the mores of male patriarchal society. As a mother she is the opposite of the loving, nurturing figure of folk and Orthodox tradition. That she was based on Leskov's grandmother and, more importantly, his mother (see McLean 1977, 15-23) goes some way to explaining the treatment of maternal images, not only in the person of Marfa but also elsewhere in these works.

While Natal'ia Nikolaevna is an ideal wife in Leskov's terms, she has no children. The decision not to make Tuberozov's wife a mother was certainly deliberate, since Tuberozov was to be seen as an ineffectual latter-day Avvakum who would leave no descendants of any kind. But it is clear that the playing-down of women as mothers goes further. Just as Leskov minimised the traditional maternal aspects of the concept of Rus', so the hugely important female maternal image finds practically no resonance in these stories. Katerina Izmailova's and Nast'ia Prokudina's efforts to become mothers end in tragedy with Katerina's rejection of her child and the death of Nast'ia's at two days old. Important male characters do not have mothers, while the Enchanted Pilgrim's mother dies when he was tiny, leaving no emotional or moral legacy other than her promise to dedicate him to God. By contrast, in the bylina the bogatyr has a mother (but no father), while the "molodets" of the *Tale of Misery-Ill Fortune* has both.

The only other mothers are all minor figures, none of whom is given a folk poetic colouring. In *Cathedral Folk* Zakharii Benefaktov's wife is mother to a whole tribe of children, but she is little more than a cipher, a reproach to Tuberozov's own childless wife. Leskov is so little concerned with her that he does not even bother to give her a name. In one of the episodes in **"The Enchanted Pilgrim"** Fliagin becomes nursemaid to a child whose mother has run off with an officer. He eventually allows the distressed mother to reclaim her child, but the episode is more important for its demonstration of Fliagin's essential humanity than of any point about the mother. What the episode does show is that Fliagin, the epitome of Russianness, carries within him the caring maternal impulse, though his child-care methods would make him the nanny from hell for a contemporary parent (he buries the child in sand up to her waist to keep her from running off).

Predictably, in the Stargorod cycle where the various facets of Russian tradition are largely kept separate, maternal benevolence is epitomised in one individual. The sole positive maternal image is a man, Konstantin (Kotin) Pizonskii. Brought up as a girl, Pizonskii is a ridiculous figure redeemed by his adoption of orphans (two girls in **"Kotin the He-Cow and Platonida"** and a boy in *Cathedral Folk*). His humility, acceptance of poverty and readiness to accept the scorn of others place him in direct line of descent from both the holy fool ("iurodivyi") and the "kaleki perekhozhie", the wandering beggar pilgrims of pre-Revolutionary Russia (who also appear in the bylina). Leskov underlines the resemblance in **"Kotin the He-Cow"** by calling him "nishchii, kaleka i urod" ("a beggar, cripple and freak") (1: 229), which in English translation lack the religious resonances of the Russian counterparts, where traditionally a connection is often, if not necessarily, made between physical deformity and true spirituality. Kotin is an odd and eccentric figure rather than a physical cripple. In his case the contrast is between his eccentricities in general and his inner moral values. As Kenneth Lantz noted, "the absurdity of Pizonsky's behaviour is one of his positive virtues" (Lantz 1979, 51). Although holy fools and "kaleki perekhozhie" could be men or women, Leskov's are male. The integration of a maternal image with theirs is not one found in folk or religious tradition. As already mentioned, Pizonskii's symbolic link with Rus' is made overt in the novel, indicating Leskov's admiration for traditional maternal values, but his unwillingness to embody them in a woman.

It may be concluded that for all Leskov's attachment to the Rus'/rodina pair of terms, his own personal psycho-logical make-up dictated adjustments to the conventional gendered perceptions of "Rus'"/"rodina" as a combination of the strongly maternal, and the male heroic (both secular and religious). Of the archetypal heroic and religious images used by the writer only the holy fool and the "kaleka perekhozhii" could be of either sex, but in Leskov they are male. The maternal image, so powerful and universal in folk belief and folklore as well as in the cult of Mother Earth and of the Mother of God is either neglected or inverted. At the same time, the maternal aspects of Mother Russia are played down, while actual female characters are either not seen in a maternal role or as mothers lack caring nurturing qualities. Indeed, the best "mothers" are men.

Overall, men furnish the great majority of positive embodiments of Russianness in the works examined. Whatever blemishes they possess or lapses they commit (such as a weakness for drink, ignorance or physical aggressiveness), their innate decency remains as a potential for good or for change. Furthermore, very often the particular stereotypical failings Leskov highlights are those which can have positive value in folklore (notably drinking, uncontrolled behaviour and even violence and ignorance). By contrast, few of these supposedly typical Russian failings are given to the women characters, to some extent because many ethnic stereotypes of Russians relate more to men than to women. Exceptions appear of two types, either those which render a character more negative than positive, such as Katerina Izmailova with her unbridled passions (but she is, after all, a type not an epitome of Russianness), or Marfa Plodomasova whose tyrannical behaviour is a means of presenting her as an inadequate mother. Similarly, as has been seen, for his positive female characters Leskov made limited use of models existing in oral tradition and early Russian literature. When it came to the depiction of Natal'ia Nikolaevna Tuberozova, a happily married woman, Leskov downplayed the strength and determination of her model, Archpriest Avakum's wife, to a point where Natal'ia Nikolaevna's "force" lies solely in her meekness and wifely devotion, for which he also drew on non-traditional cultural archetypes. Natal'ia Nikolaevna contributes neither to the heroic nor maternal dimension of Rus', and to the religious only passively. Marfa Plodomasova is an old woman and her principled attitudes are presented as anachronistic. In keeping with the patriarchal attitudes of his day, Leskov saw leadership largely in the hands of men. "Rus'" and "rodina" may be grammatically feminine, but for Leskov they seem to have been predominantly masculine.

Notes

1. I therefore exclude characters such as the hero of "The Musk-ox" ("Ovtsebyk"), 1863, or "The Battle-Axe" ("Voitel'nitsa"), 1866, because

Leskov makes little use of folk or traditional literary images in the creation of the main characters.

2. The situation with Gogol's female characters is similarly more complicated than it appears. The strongly negative tone of his portraits stem from the irreconcilable conflict between his own ideal of woman as the epitome of moral virtue and poetic inspiration, to which he had subscribed in his youthful essay "On Woman" (1831), and his own observations. Disillusion pushed him into the use of popular stereotypes.

3. References to Leskov's works are to the collected works, 1956-8, and are cited by volume and page number.

4. Writers and thinkers throughout the century, while seeing Russia as feminine, tended to emphasize the humble and submissive more than the maternal. Towards the end of the century, other female stereotypes, such as Blok's Russia as gypsy, began to play a role. There was a shift to the use of the term "Rossiia" by, for example, the philosopher Berdiaev, presumably because of the very specific connotations of "Rus'", though Berdiaev nonetheless chooses to refer to the Eternal Feminine as "bab'e", reflecting the peasant term for woman "baba" (Aizlewood 1996).

5. All translations are my own.

6. An obvious exception is "Il'ia Muromets i syn".

7. The Russian agrarian cycle was marked by festivals whose rites were intended to increase fertility and productivity of land, animals or people, sometimes overtly by reference to a mother figure or Mat' syra-zemlia.

List of Sources

Afanas'ev, A. N., 1855-63. *Narodnye russkie skazki* (Moscow: A. Semen).

———, 1865-9. *Poeticheskie vozzreniia slavian na prirodu* (Moscow: K. Soldatenkov).

Aizlewood, Robin, 1996. "Berdiaev and Chaadaev, Russia and feminine passivity", paper presented at the Conference on Gender and Sexuality in Russian Civilisation at the University of Surrey.

Balashov, D. M., 1963. *Russkie narodnye ballady* (Moscow-Leningrad: Sovetskii pisatel').

Barker, Adèle Marie, 1986. *The Mother Syndrome in the Russian Folk Imagination* (Columbus, Ohio: Slavica).

Barsov, E. V., 1872. *Prichitaniia severnogo kraia*, 2 pts (Moscow: Obshchestvo liubitelei rossiiskoi slovesnosti).

Cherednikova, M. P., 1971. "O siuzhetnykh motirovkakh v povesti N. S. Leskova 'Ocharovannyi strannik'", *Russkaia literatura,* 3, 113-27.

Dal', V. I., 1984. *Poslovitsy russkogo naroda,* 2 vols (Moscow: Khudozhestvennaia literatura).

Gachev, Georgii, 1991. *Russkaia duma: portrety russkikh myslitelei* (Moscow: Novosti).

Gorelov, A. A., 1988. *N. S. Leskov i narodnaia kul'tura* (Leningrad: Nauka).

Gor'kii, M., 1948-55. *Sobranie sochinenii,* 30 vols (Moscow: Khudozhestvennaia literatura).

Guminskii, V., 1983. "Organicheskoe vzaimodeistvie (Ot *Ledi Makbet* k *Soborianam*)", *V mire Leskova. Sbornik statei,* ed. V. Bogdanov (Moscow: Sovetskii pisatel').

Hosking, Geoffrey, 1997. *Russia. People and Empire 1552-1917* (London: Harper Collins).

Hubbs, Joanna, 1988. *Mother Russia: The Feminine Myth in Russian Culture* (Bloomington and Indianapolis: Indiana University Press).

Kireevskii, P. V., 1860-8. *Pesni, sobrannye P. V. Kireevskim* (Moscow: Obshchestvo liubitelei drevnei pis'mennosti).

Lantz, K. A., 1979. *Nikolay Leskov* (Boston: Twayne).

Leskov, N. S., 1956-8. *Sobranie sochinenii N. S. Leskova,* ed. P. Gromov and B. Eikhenbaum, 11 vols (Moscow: Khudozhestvennaia literatura).

McLean, Hugh, 1977. *Nikolai Leskov: The Man and His Art* (Cambridge, Mass./London: Harvard U. P.).

Mikhailova, N. G., 1966. "Tvorchestvo N. S. Leskova v sviazi s nekotorymi obrazami narodnogo eposa", *Vestnik Moskovskogo universiteta. Seriia Filologiia,* no. 3, 49-57.

Møller, Peter Ulf, 1997. "Counter images of Russianness: On the role of national characterology in Gogol's *Dead Souls*", *Celebrating Creativity: Essays in Honour of Jostein Børtnes,* ed. Knut Andreas Grimstad and Ingunn Lunde (Bergen: University of Bergen), 70-81.

Muller de Morogues, Inès, 1991. *"Le probleme feminin" et les portraits des femmes dans l'oeuvre de Nikolaj Leskov* (Slavica Helvetica 38) (Berne/Berlin/Frankfurt/New York/Paris: Peter Lang).

Platonov, O., 1993. "Russkaia tsivilizatsiia: dorogi tsivilizatsii", *Russkii vestnik,* 18-20 (101-03), 1-8.

Rybnikov, P. N., 1989-91. *Pesni, sobrannye P. N. Rybnikovym,* 3 vols, (Petrozavodsk: Karelia) reprinted from the 2nd edition ed. A. E. Gruzinskii Moscow, 1909-10.

Stoliarova, I. V., 1978. *V poiskakh ideala (Tvorchestvo N. S. Leskova)* (Leningrad: Izdatel'stvo Leningradskogo universiteta).

Wigzell, F., 1985. "The *staraya skazka* of Leskov's *Soboryane*: Archpriest Tuberozov and Avvakum", *Slavonic and East European Review*, 63, 321-35.

———, 1988a. "Leskov's *Soboryane*: a tale of good and evil in the Russian provinces", *Modern Language Review*, 83, 901-10.

———, 1989. "Folk stylization in *Ledi Makbet Mtsenskogo uezda*", *Slavonic and East European Review*, 67, 1989, 169-82.

———, 1997. "Bludnye synov'ia ili bluzhdaiushchie dushi: 'Povest' o Gore-Zlochastii' i 'Ocharovannyi strannik' Leskova", *Trudy otdela drevnerusskoi literatury*, 50, 754-62.

Oleg V. Nikitin (essay date 2003)

SOURCE: Nikitin, Oleg V. "Leskov's *Notes of the Unknown* (*Zametki neizvestnogo*): The Aesthetic Role of Language Stylization in Deconstructing the Characters and Circumstances of the Traditional Russian Culture of the 18th-19th Centuries." *Studia Slavica* 48, no. 4 (2003): 413-41.

[*In the following essay, Nikitin notes Leskov's appropriation of documentary material in his short story cycle* Zametki neizvestnogo, *then analyzes the writer's sophisticated use of language drawn from archaic and colloquial sources in order to create a rich and authentic literary style in his fiction.*]

A strange feeling took possession of me when I read Leskov for the first time. An astonishing world from the past opened before me. It was not dead, neither was it crowned with laurels, but it was lively and spontaneous, a bit ironic but cheerful, sometimes severely denouncing and at the same time most human. First of all it was the author's apt and vivid language that struck me as most interesting, where different semantic elements and archaisms lived together used with an original flavour and subtly charged with a new shade of meaning. It was also remarkable to see Leskov's ability to give a truthful representation of genuine Russian reality which at the time was more or less forbidden and was, indeed, skilfully avoided by his contemporaries. And besides, there was Leskov's all-forgiving identification with everything—nature, people, history. This comes from his philosophy and the depth of the suffering of his soul, a soul that was firmly loyal to the motherland and fully committed to serving her most resolutely. Leskov considered this service his mission.

During all his life Nikolaj Leskov would take steps which have never been treated adequately and for which he has been blamed and stigmatized again and again. It is a paradox but a fact now that Leskov's literary works were excluded from the school curriculum after the October Revolution. In higher educational establishments his activities and creative works were studied as selected passages (and so they are even today). For a long time his fiction (to say nothing about his religious and political writings or about his literary criticism) was unaccessible for the common reader. It was only his anticlerical stories, small domestic sketches and some novels which were discussed, but the critical response was limited due to the moralizing ethos of the time defined by the concept of socialist realism. The critics and advocates of socialist realism were too blind to see Leskov's superb craftsmanship and the disguised implications of his work. When the term socialist realism is used it should be remembered that Russian realism is a very capacious and complicated notion as compared to what it was stated to be in the Soviet theory of literature with its strictly confined boundaries and its submission to the exigencies of the revolutionary movement. There can hardly be any similar definition of realism, for instance, that would apply to the 19th and the 20th centuries. It can even be claimed that the 18th century in Russia was the age of progressive aesthetic and literary norms which are responsible for the kind of realism that appears in the masterpieces of Radiščev and Puškin, Žukovskij and Karamzin. The Russian cultural tradition appeared as a natural source of inspiration for writers. To the abyss of the coming *agitculture* they opposed the only value-man. The humanistic—and, in this sense, realistic—character of classical Russian literature consisted in a humane Weltanschauung which respected the dignity of man, and, in consequence, the principle of the independent, involuntary development of a human being. That was an ideology of добромолюбие (goodness) and wisdom which was eradicated later.

The fact that Leskov swam against the current of the time can be said to have determined the complexity of his vision as well as his creative attitude. On the whole, the entire inner world of his fiction is obviously permeated with an ideal or, better to say, disposition—духовносмь (spirituality). That is not only a reflection of a system of constant and firm moral values, of a commitment to a definite conception of art as a form of enlightenment but also of the quality of a soul, wistful and searching, tormented and plagued by contradictions. It is a prevalence of spiritual and intellectual interests over material being. It is the lot of few. Not to be crushed by gossip and threats, falsifications and mockery—such was the reward prepared for him. His adversaries never even pretended to forgive Leskov his spiritual truth and pure intentions, on the contrary, they tried to crush him by hook or by crook. Leskov, however, bore no grudge against them. His life and works are evidence of that.

The Russian dictionaries of the Soviet period define the notion духовносмь as 'obsolete' (!)—as though available but incompatible with the modern mentality and mode of life. Actually, it is not a slogan (that would not be typical of Leskov at all), духовносмь offers no promises of any kind, neither does it open up false perspectives. Духовносмь might be to some extent conservative, but it is not hostile to progress. It does not belong to any political party. On the contrary, it pleads for the protection of the best traditions and ideals of the past from inexpert or ruthless usage and interpretation by adherents of 'new' convictions. It should be remembered that the Latin *conservativus* means 'standing guard over smb., safe-guarding, protective'. 'Safe-guarding' has often boiled down to a complicity with inertness and stagnation. That is why Leskov was invariably shown to have been a writer of secondary importance, an effort to which the *Okhranka* (Secret Political Police in tsarist Russia) contributed, too. Leskov, however, was a guardian in the primary sense of the word—a guardian of the most important traditional values and ideals, i.e. the humanism and the spontaneity of the Russian character. That is why he resisted every attempt to level its originality, to blunt the intensity of the Russian spirit. In that we can see an actual necessity of our own time: the obligation to uphold the noble ideals of the ancient times, to adjust them to modern social processes and to look for ways in which they can be passed on to the future. That is where the great vitality of Leskov's power lies. His restitution has already come. Leskov for us is one of the modern authors occupying in the civil society of today.

The following note which Leskov jotted down in the album of G. P. Danilevsky seems to reflect his innermost pains; his words will help us to see him in a brighter, more appropriate light:

> In my literary time there was not a writer slandered more than I; nevertheless not in the least have I ever been sorry about that. I've always tried to accept the sufferings which have been falling to my lot through all the malice and libels for my good and have been very thankful for them: they've taught me to put up with them, and God help everybody in that.
>
> Nikolaj Leskov (Stebnitsky). 14th May, 1872. SPb.[1]

A lot has been said about the persuasiveness of Leskov's language, but the specific attributes of his style have never been properly defined, although the clarification of his reasons for the use of specific discourses might disclose much of the nature of his artistic world. It seems to be especially rewarding to try to detect the sources he drew upon while he elaborated his linguistic medium.

His essays and articles often touch upon questions of church life and as a matter of fact they frequently read as investigations of artistic problems. It was natural for the author to base them on documentary materials. For instance, '**Синодальные персоны. Период борьбы за преобладание (1820-1840 гг.)**' ['**Representatives of the Synod. The Period of Struggle for Predominance**'], '**Иродова рабома. Русские кармины в Осмзейском крае**' ['**Tyrant's Work. Russian Pictures in the East See Region**'], '**Церковные инмриганы. Исмsorические кармины**' ['**Church Intrigants. Historic Pictures**'], '**Поповская чехарда и приходская прихомь. Церковно-исмsorические нравы и кармины**' ['**Priest's Reshuffle and Parish Whims. Morals and Pictures from the History of the Church**'] and some other works written by Leskov and published in the journal *Istoričeskij vestnik* in the 1880s. Some of the aforementioned essays were later included by the author in the larger and prominent short stories and novels, others were organized into cycles like ***Zametki neizvestnogo***.

Leskov had testified to their authenticity: in the article '**Поповская чехарда . . .**' he says:

> I would like to offer the readers an interesting story (here and further on emphasized phrases are spaced by us—O. N.) I have borrowed from the original inquiry made in the Moscow department of the Holy Synod about priest Kirill about whom forty two persons from the parish of Spas in Nalivki "croaked".[2]

And in the introduction to the ***Notes of the Unknown*** the narrator describes an ancient manuscript which he has found introducing it to the readers in detail, besides declaring its authenticity. Then the author characterizes it substantially, and eventually he adds:

> Засим я предлагаю в подлиннике заметки неизвестного летописца в том порядке и под теми же самыми частными заглавиями, под какими они записаны в полууничтоженной рукописи.
>
> (Лесков 1973, IV: 257)

> (Hereafter I present the original notes of the unknown annalist in that order and with those and the same separate titles under which they appear in the half-destroyed manuscript.)

This is an interesting peculiarity of Leskov's not only in this instance but in general terms as well. In another article, '**Благословенный брак. Харакмерный пропуск в исмsorической лимерамуре раскола**' ['**Blessed Marriage. A Distinctive Omission in the Annals of the History of the Schism**'] the writer again refers to a rare manuscript book entitled О бракосочемании [*On Matrimony*], quotes the complete text and gives a minute description of it.[3]

One more important piece of information is offered by Leskov: as he begins his story the author points out to a familiar second-hand bookseller from the Sukharev tower from whom he claims he has bought a manuscript (Лесков 1973, IV: 257). It is known that since the middle of the 19th century Sukharev Square had been the venue of the famous book and art market. That was a centre of antiquities in Moscow (later on, at the time of Stalin, the tower was demolished). We may assume that Leskov the bibliographer knew that place and went there often enough to buy books.

Thus, fact and true-to-life fiction seem to merge. Those two references to reality are complemented by the writer in an inobtrusive, a most sophisticated way by a hint to an "artless presentation of events which in its own time seems to have interested an apparently very respectable, seriously disposed social circle" («безыскусственное изображение событий, интересовавших в свое время какой-то, по-видимому весьма достопочтенный, оригинальный и серьезно настроенный общественный кружок») (Лесков 1973, IV: 257).[4]

This circle was a mixed group of people including the secretary (from Искусный омвемчик), the assessor's wife with her small son Ignaty (Излишняя мамеринская нежносмь), "the spiritual student" («Чужеземные обычаи только с разумением применять можно»), etc. But the main characters of the cycle are, among others, a bishop, priests, a consistory man and the principal of the church seminary.

Leskov's acquaintances occasionally tried to exercise some pressure on him disapproving of his sharply critical views on the problems of church life. They wanted to soothe his anti-clerical leanings. Colonel Pashkov wrote to Leskov on the 22nd of September 1884:

> I find it unbearably regrettable to see that you, whose heart responded formerly to everything true and good, now sneer at . . . what was taught by the apostles. . . .
>
> (Другов 1957: 88)

The Slavophile I. S. Aksakov also approached Leskov with similar letters. But he had his own notions in this context: he fought for the moral purity of the custodians of religious traditions and despite the pressure of his friends or the censors' prohibition he never wavered in his position. (The cycle of short stories *Notes of the Unknown* was first published in *Gazeta A. Gattsuka* in 1884, № 2, 5, 9-14. Then publication was stopped by censorship, and it was only in 1917-1918 that the last three stories appeared in *The Niva*.) In Leskov's view people who are ordained should be inspired, i.e. inwardly ennobled and filled with elevated feelings and aspirations. These are people of Faith. Under the *klobuk* (headgear of Orthodox monk) and black robe with a smooth radiant cross Leskov saw not only a God's minister but first of all a man. Observing a deep abyss between the words of God's preachers and their deeds which hardly conformed to the established rules of morals the writer could not keep silent. It should be empha-

sized that the anti-clerical writings of Leskov should not be seen as an indication of a departure from God or Faith or religious feelings. They reflect no rejection on Leskov's part of God's commandments. They should be seen instead as true sketches of the life of the clergy, their domestic life and relationships. Some arguments of V. O. Klučevskij reflect the same view, e.g. his ironic question: "Do the clergy believe in God? They do not understand that question because they officiate God", or his statement: "In the West the Church has no God, in Russia God has no Church" (Ключевский 1990: 384).[5]

It has been established that it was scrupulous and protracted work in the archives that helped Leskov to realize the profound sense of the mentality of the past. That also considerably supplemented the knowledge derived from life. And, indeed, *Notes of the Unknown* contains much documentary information. Even some traits of the characters of this cycle were taken from the inquest deeds of the Synod. That is why what is presented in his narrative should be interpreted more than a fruit of Leskov's fantasy. It is the result of persistent research as well as the observation of the actual prototypes of his fiction. Leskov can actually be considered to have been a scholar, an explorer of the Russian antiquities and an investigator of the spirit of the past. Our suppositions are confirmed by looking through the files of the former Record Office of the Synod. A substantial part of them now is concentrated in the Russian State Record Office of Ancient Acts in Moscow. I was fortunate enough to be able to read some manuscripts kept in File № 1183 'Moscow Synodal Office' and analyze them.

In a manuscript entitled "The case of the shock which hieromonk of Novospassky Monastery, Arseny, had during divine service in Peter-and-Paul's Parish Church" there is the report of the following incident:

> . . . during the service of the hieromonk Arseny was overcome by a shock, he, however, had finished the liturgy; by the time he finished he had lost his tongue, the left arm and leg were paralyzed; soon after that a vomiting followed with eruption of holy donations at the altar; the ejected remained in a washbasin; after the exposure he had been taken to the church ward . . .[6].

At the end of this personal file a resolution was placed: a prohibition of divine service in churches of the Moscow eparchy. Later we shall see how Leskov used these sad and ironic facts in his domestic sketches.

From the other document under the heading 'About the presentation of a book for recording the evil deeds to the permanent inhabitants of the abolished George's Monastery' it is clear that a certain Grigory Nikolayev was lazy and negligent in performing his duty and showed no proper industry, and Zakhar Efimov abandoned himself to hard drinking and even violence. With reference to that, the applicant writes, your most humble servant asks the Office of the Holy Synod to give us a book for putting down in it every case of their improper conduct[7].

Here is another interesting and important document which helps us to find the sources of Leskov's prose. It testifies, in our opinion, to a curious accident, or as the writer might have said, to an extraordinary occurrence of a very unpleasant nature. Under the title 'About the expulsion of the novice Vasily Shiriayev from Voskresensky Monastery for improper conduct' it is told that "the lay brother Vasily Shiriayev was seen in a drunken state all during the Easter week . . .".[8]

Does not all that is cited above look like artistic discourse? Could not those picturesque passages connected with some actual events and facts be related to Leskov's *Notes of the Unknown*? At least we catch a likeness between them and the narrative. For instance, in his conduct and action "the regent of the bishop's choir", who was much of an Adonis («красик»—a dandy in Leskov's view.—O. N.)

> was so completely confused by the love stories of ladies who arrived for vespers, that . . . [he] wondered away from the choir or started winking at important females who were about to leave the church . . .
>
> (так в переплете любовных историй от приезжавших ко всенощной дам запутался, что . . . [он] с хор утекал или с направлявшимися к выходу женскими особами глазами перемигивался . . .)
>
> (Лесков 1973, IV: 287),

and Grigory Nikolayev who "was negligent and showed no proper industry in performing his duties". Who could know what was meant by such an impersonal definition? Only Leskov's creative imagination could see so clearly this cloaca maxima which was engraved on the worn and burnt pages of the invaluable manuscripts.

An old hierodeacon, who during the Lent was crazy about billiard, drank so truly that he became tipsy of empty wine-glasses (Лесков 1973, IV: 284-285), reminds the reader of the very cuctos morum who "all the Easter week was seen in a drunken state".

Lastly, Father Ioann from the story **'Как нехорошо осуждамь слабосми'** [**'It Is Wrong to Blame Foibles'**] being intoxicated permitted himself an "indecent thing": "having uttered an exclamation fell asleep, and did not wake up for a long time" («сделав возглас, заснул и не скоро пробудился») (Лесков 1973, IV: 259), and hieromonk Arseny who had a "shock" during divine service. In both of the examples veiled irony is implied.

After some possible parallels have been pointed out, a comparison of Leskov's style and approach to the description of every day events with some of the possible sources of his narrative style has been carried out. Our investigation suggests that the style of the business documents of national history, especially those of investigatory evidence connected with church life, is in a certain correlation with the text of Leskov's narrative. That interaction becomes particularly pronounced in the use of the words which have characteristic and determined meanings and may have served as formative models for him like буйсмво (tumult), разоблачение (unmasking), извем (false denunciation), справщик (corrector), дознание (inquiry), обыскная книга (a church book for registration of matrimonies), обыск (a note on marriage in a church book), консисморский приказный (consistorial bailiff). All these words had been used actively in the Old Russian legal system and in manuscripts in their primary meanings with different semantic and stylistic shades. For instance, the lexeme извѣть had nine ways of interpretation: 1. Pretext; excuse. 2. Cause. 3. Fraud, illegal actions. 4. Accusation; slander, calumny. 5. Proof, confirmation, evidence. 6. Denunciation. 7. Report, dispatch. 8. Advice. 9. Justification; apology, forgiveness (Словарь русск. яз. 1979: 116-118). Leskov accumulated them into a specific cover with a new meaning invented by him—'doubt'. On the one hand, it was a peculiar trait of his protagonist, the secretary of the consistory, who, after having been decorated with an order he had coveted, understood that

> after the departure of the foreign predicant (here preacher—O. N.) many of the simple folks who before in their lapsed life had never read the Gospel, appeared with the New Testament . . . Though,—the narrator proceeds,—in each of them were printed particulars as to the place and date of the publication, the secretary conceived an anxious doubt that those books were made at some printing-house in London, and the Russian imprint was put in by fraud, in order to reduce the incomes (?!—O. N.) of the orthodoxial department in Russia.
>
> (по отьезде иностран ного предиканта у многих простого звания людей, кои в прежде прошедшей жизни никогда Евангелия не читали, появилися в руках книжки Нового Завета . . . и хотя под кажою из оных было подпечатано обозначение выхода их из духовной типографии, но секретарь возымел беспокойное сомнение, что те книги произведены в типографии в Лондоне, а выход российский им обозначен обманно, собственно для подрыва доходов (?!—O. N.) православного ведомства в России.)
>
> (Лесков 1973, IV: 303-304)

On the other hand, the writer ridicules the pathological inclination of some protectors of orthodoxy who give in to the temptation of engaging in an absurd and feigned search of enemies of the national religion. Leskov's irony expressed in a veiled form takes another turn when the narrator gives a parody of the inquiry trial. It is held according to the secretary's извем. Being an expert in the Gospel he asks the chief справщик (corrector) from the gubernia printing-house, a German by birth, . . . to give him an explanation that would lead to conclusive evidence («призвал к себе из губернской типографии главного справщика, происхождением немца, . . . и предложил: не можете ли дать на сей преимет сведущего разъяснительного заключения») (Лесков 1973, IV: 304).

Because he had no doubt that an English publishing company, however hard they strived to falsify a legitimate Russian edition published with established blessings, would never be able to do so

> английское общество сколько бы ни стремилось всеми силами к тому обману, чтобы подделаться к законному русскому изданию, с установленного благословения изданному, никак того достичь не в состоянии.
>
> —А почему?
>
> —Потому, что там с такими грубыми несовершенствами верстки и тиснения и на столь дурной бумаге уже более двухсот лет не печатают
>
> (Лесков 1973, IV: 304)

(—And why? (asked the secretary—O. N.)

—Because there with page-reading and editing so imperfect, and on paper of such poor quality nothing has been printed in the last two hundred years.)

A fine and subtle hint of the title of this short story, **'Смесненная ограниченносмь англицкого искуссмва' ['The Constraining Limitation of English Art']**, gave Leskov the possibility to show the absurdity of the official Church and the pseudo-patriotism of the Russian zealots. It was his manner to invent affected titles, overloaded and intricate. The titles reveal the psychological attitude of Leskov to the specific tradition in question. He created his own system which distinguishes the notions 'book language' and 'local patois', 'living' and 'literary speech'. As a rule, the titles of his works are complicated and full of metaphors. This helped him to protect the original text from censorship covering the content behind the same neutral phrases which were hard to discern. In this episode the Old Russian word извѣть could have also been interpreted in a new sense because of the polysemanticism of its root: извѣть-вѣсть-вѣкъ-извѣчный, i.e. a primordial, old (difficult) problem. And in our view, the writer meant to make a step toward solving it by means of humour and irony, defending русскосмь (Russianness) and fighting against its mystificators.

The sarcasm with which he describes God's servants might suggest that Leskov's soul was entirely torn by the contradictions of reality. His characters are, to some extent, reflections of his own spiritual conflicts and awareness of social injustice. But his prose does not give the impression of despair concerning man's moral potential or lack of belief in the future. On the contrary, the writer was nourished on quite different stuff. Once he wrote to S. N. Shubinsky: "You should not at all be in time with 'the monde', but keep yourself to whatever is better than what it now approves of and encourages . . ." (Русские писатели 1955: 223). Leskov deeply felt the coming tragedy of nihilism. It was not only a trend in the environment of разночинец.[9] It was the beginning of a tyranny under which everyone would be left to the mercy of fate. That was an absolute negation and rejection of all human and social standards, principles, values established before. In this situation he was looking for bright ideals, and he found them in the rural provinces of Russia. Leskov listened to its spirit and movement with great attention. There he saw natural people and felt at ease. Leskov studied them through their customs and habits, through their language. Explaining the specific manner of the pronunciation and behaviour of people in the countryside Leskov retorted to the opponents of the 'artificiality' of his language:

> That very common, vulgar and artificial language in which many pages of my works are written is no invention of mine, it was collected while eavesdropping on the speech of a мужчк, of a half-wit, of a краснобай [phrase-monger—O. N.], of a юродивый [God's fool—O. N.] and of свямоши [hypocrites—O. N.]
>
> (Русские писатели 1955: 221)

When travelling about in the remotest places in Russia Leskov met uncommon characters having exceptional fates and strong tempers. Such is Ivan Severyanovich Flyagin the Очарованный смранник, depicted in a tale of the same name, who is a «типический, простодушный, добрый русский богатырь, напоминающий дедушку Илью Муромца» (Лесков 1973, III: 4-5) ('a typical, open-hearted, kind Russian богамырь [Hercules.—O. N.] reminding us of grandpa Ilya Muromets'). All Russia is compressed into his story. The Archpriest Savely Tuberozov (Соборяне), whose life is part of Russian hagiography, has gracelessly sunk into oblivion. In these characters Leskov saw the potential of a mighty spiritual force able to resist the general chaos of nihilism.[10] The writer visited a lot of monasteries where he could listen to unusual stories and read the messages of unusual, desperate souls from the past. Leskov found a way to reflect in a natural though elaborate form the innocent spontaneity of whatever he came across. For an example here is the entire text of a manuscript which deserved Leskov's attention:

> Честнѣйшій отець казначей Епифаній!
>
> Извѣстно вамь, что уже у нась на Крестно(м) островѣ открылся питѣйный домь, то во о(т)вращеніе противны(х) слѣдствій, по хр[и]с-

тіанской любви прош[у], а по должности моей и приказываю, сохраните пожал[у]йте какъ себя, такъ и др[у]ги(х) братій въ порядочно(м) воздержаніи, въ незазорно(м) поведеніи, і въ добродѣте(л)номъ состояніи, что б[у]деть Б[о]гу пріятно, о(т) ближни(х) заслужите себѣ почтеніе, а мнѣ во утѣшеніе и спокойствіе д[у]ха, ва(м) сіе пор[у]чено, и пор[у]чаю наблюда(т) сей порядокъ благосостоянія о чемь на вась надѣюсь и не с[у]мнюсь. Знаете, въ противно(м) случае какая мнѣ о(т)рада, я прин[у]жден, но б[у]д[у] соо(т)вѣтствова(т) моей должности. Извѣстны вы, что Б[о]жіею милостію, и монарши(м) благоволеніемъ доволнш пожалоованы, со временемъ поч[у]]ств[у]ете сами свою полз[у]. Сіе мое приказаніе, или паче усердіе, обявите и про(т)чей братіи. В про(т)чемь желая вамь всѣхъ благъ, пребываю

Вашь доброжелательный Архимандрить Макарій.
Маія 28 1780 года. Онѣга.[11]

That manner of speaking and style was very close to Leskov's as he pointed out himself:

My priests speak ecclesiastically, my nihilists—in a nihilistic way, my мужики—in a manly manner, the parvenus of them and the скоморохи [buffoons—O. N.]—freakishly, etc.

(Русские писатели 1955: 221)

Without any commentary the document will give an idea to the reader of the style and manners of the time so that he can compare it with the text of Leskov's *Notes of the Unknown.* The comparison will hopefully lead us to a new interpretation and a better understanding of the contents. The manuscript seems to be rich in the varieties of microstyles and syntactic constructions belonging to the church tradition, distributed in an appointed succession and with consistency which must have had an important meaning to Leskov. In the broad sense the writer drew upon the best traditions of classical Russian style so highly estimated in former times. Thus he could convey the inner world of his characters in a special language where "ornate sound of the words", he thought, was inadmissible. Here he followed the traditions of the literary language elaborated by M. V. Lomonosov and N. M. Karamzin, A. F. Vel'tman and the Russian Romantics, but he preserved, at the same time, his own individual voice, coherence of ideas and the linguistic character of his own vivid and clear style.

In this narrative Leskov, who was an outstanding experimenter, used striking Old Slavonic collocations and citations from the Holy Writ. That was an expressive recreation of the language used by the clergy, and it was a most ingenious device to achieve the ironic overtone of *Notes of the Unknown.* In the context of his own time we can call his style even avant-garde because specifically Russian elements are presented alongside with Slavonicisms like «. . . нимало сумняся . . .» (Лесков 1973, IV: 272) (not in the least

doubting), «. . . его же любяше» (Лесков 1973, IV: 277) (whom he had been loved by), «до умертвія . . .» (Лесков 1973, IV: 277) (up to death), «. . . въ превыспренние . . .» (Лесков 1973, IV: 279) (to the heavens), «нози» (Лесков 1973, IV: 280) (feet), «новоначатие» (Лесков 1973, IV: 259) (innovation), «мироносицы» (Лесков 1973, IV: 304) (here the meaning is not directly connected with myrrh, the referentiality of the word is altered and it means: female admirers of the chief of some sect), «войственники» (Лесков 1973, IV: 326) (put by the author instead of воины—soldiers), «борзяся» (Лесков 1973, IV: 330) (hastily), and others. And what is more, the writer borrows phrases from the Bible, which he uses in a slightly altered form to show the false learning of the ecclesiastics. The quotations in Leskov serve not for argument or evidence. They have the role of artistic analogies in relation to events and the characters' inner reality. Such a style gave the writer the possibility to disclose something of the secret deeds of God's servants. When explaining an episode which happened to Father Grigory, who was undecided as regards the difference between the Roman Catholic and the Protestant concepts of the sacrament of the holy penance (Лесков 1973, IV: 270), the narrator put his own thoughts into the Archbishop's words who "cleared up" the Father's problem in this way:

Они (взгляды—О. N.) весьма противуположны, но я их не осуждаю, а даже скажу: обои не худы. Но мы, как православные, должны своего не порицать и держаться—тем более, что у нас исповедь на всякий случай и особое применение в гражданском управлении имеет, которого нам лучше не касаться.

(Лесков 1973, IV: 270)[12]

(These [views—O. N.] are very contradictory but I don't condemn them and even say: neither of them is wrong. But we, as orthodoxials, should not dispute ours and should actually keep to it—especially because our creed has an application to every situation and a particular application in civil life, which should rather not be touched upon.)

The passage suggests that the author considers it an obligation for the priest to denounce political offence if he gets to know about it through a confession. It is not too much to say that Leskov, the avant-garde artist, applied Slavonicisms in a function not exploited before. It was not even their phonetic cover (the though decorative phonetic design of the word as a special stylistic method was originally adopted by the writer) he was interested in. Leskov used archaic expressions not for their lack of pleophony and abstruseness of meaning, for specific initial combinations or availability of compound sounds, etc. What mattered for him was the possibility to convey implicating intonations by means of Old Slavonic and express satirical laughter filled with the mixed feeling of sorrow and joy thanks to its spiritual rhythm.

We can find confusion of language units close in form in the prose of Pustozersk, i.e. in Жимие промопопа Аввакума and in his челобимные (petitions) to Tsar Alexey Mikhaylovich, and in 'literary' works (messages) by his coprisoners, инок (anchorite) Epiphany, priest Lazar', deacon Feodor. In these writings we can often see the Holy Scripture as interpreted by the authors correlated with what they want to say, which is similar to Leskov's way of giving parallels to the convulsions of modern life, as for example: «. . . свет его может просветиться пред человеки . . .» (Лесков 1973, IV: 309) (let his light so shine before men)—a free borrowing from the Gospel of Matthew, or «. . . что ми хощете дати?» (Лесков 1973, IV: 312) (what would you give me)—the question of Judas about the reward for his betrayal; or one more example: «. . . мня ся быти яко первым по фараоне . . .» (Лесков 1973, IV: 313) (I imagine myself to be as though the first after Pharaoh)—in Leskov's narrative it is said in honour of Father Pavel who considers himself to be the first after Pharaoh, and who, being very much displeased with refreshments prepared for him on a day of fast, finds an excellent remedy:

> a glass of undiluted punch rum with chemists' drops of English mint-*kholodianka* . . . , and, as a token of what it often compels, to alleviate pains. . . .

> (Лесков 1973, IV: 315)[13]

According to the biblical legend Joseph, who had been sold by his brothers into Egyptian slavery, became the first in Egypt after Pharaoh. A similar method of the interpretation of the Holy Writ was artistically used by Avvakum: he read contemporary events by the light of the holy rites. This elevates the occurrence described to the rank of a holy mystery (Пустозерская проза 1989: 33). In it his life-story and the end of the history of the world gets entangled:

> Ты, Господи, изведый мя из чрева матере моея, и от небытия и бытие мя устроил i аще меня задушат, причти мя с митрополитом Филиппом Московским. . . .

> (Пустозерская проза 1989: 45)

Epifany in Жимие says somewhat similarly:

> Господи Иисусе Христе, Сыне Божий! Помилуй мя, грешнаго, по благоиатп спаси мя, а не по долгу, ими ж веси судьбами.

> (Пустозерская проза 1989: 199)

Like in the case of Avvakum, where the change of the personal tone and the stylization of language lead to exposing the pathos of the preacher, Leskov uses archaic church elements in the oral colloquial speech of the characters in his *Notes* as well. In both works we see symbolic parallels corresponding to different parameters of view: жимие-narrative, saturation of the texts with church Slavonic terms, creative intuition to show events which happened during the life of each author, and eventually their religious moral stance is conveyed in the ancient book style in its primordial state. All that gives us the possibility to formulate the following conclusion: the permanent use of the literary aesthetic tradition and language heritage enables Leskov to create his own stylistic system. He was an avant-garde artist searching new ways of using words in their original and nonartificial hypostases. Just as Avvakum himself embodied a novel literary and language intention, Leskov tried to appropriate what he found there and accommodate it to the fresh conditions thereby developing his own standards. Our task is to understand this 'unintelligible' system of material linguistic integument and the means of its interior aesthetic organization.

When studying the problem, however, the danger of mixing up the two notions, style in its diachronic conception and the "normative" comprehension of it, might arise. The historic approach presupposes some system and we may easily be bogged down in multilingual and multicultural problems. Normative style is more or less a static category representing a whole complex of questions. It is a totality of indications characterizing an art or literary piece of a definite period and a tendency in attitude to the substantial idea and the artistic form. Here style has found its position on the basis of timelessness. We have a propensity for source study. It might appear an absolute necessity for anyone to develop analysis in such a key because Leskov compiled his work from original sources, and to elucidate his historic method has always born more substantial fruit than concentrating research exclusively on the text. It is also important to remember that "various styles of speech within limits of one and the same written language . . . can go back to different historic traditions" (Винокур 1959: 232).[14] For instance, it is known that in Russian literary speech of the beginning of the 19th century some Slavonicisms like млеко, брег, выя, вран, etc., which had their primordial Russian synonyms-duplicates, were in active use. In that particular period this trait characterized literary language on the whole in contrast to secular, epistolary or domestic language in its written form. Closer to the '30s the use of Old Slavonic was not any longer an attribute of the artistic mode of speech, it was rather a characteristic of the language of poetry as contra-distinguished from that of prose. Thus it would be an error to consider every language feature in Leskov's narrative as evidence for his use of the real language situation of his time. Here we should keep a linguistic distance and take into consideration essentially different conditions for the language in diverse spheres. That is why the writer's Slavonic world should be explained in the context of the literary aesthetic traditions of his time as well as of his own views expressed in letters, articles, etc. Seen in this way the abundance of Church Slavonic lexemes and syntactic constructions can be said to make no impression of a surcharge of the text as a result of primitive stylization. His comprehension of the notion of stylization is entirely different from some of the definitions we can find in modern dictionaries, e.g. "1. Stylization—imitation of outward [i.e. superficial—O. N.] forms, typical illustrations of a certain style. '. . .' 2. Literary work being as to the form an imitation of some style" (Лексические трудности 1994: 455). Stylization for him was not mere imitation, it was not even connected seriously to it (in this period of his creative activities). Leskov's inward requirement 'to stylize' comes out of his own artistic struggle against any unreasonable treatment of language ligatures on the one hand, and out of his speculations on artistic taste on the other. It is evident that Slavonicisms have a special part to play in the structure of his texts. Their emotional mood, musical pitch and grammatical harmony create a fascinating atmosphere of skilful puns and whimsical imagination. They are very carefully attributed to the oral characteristics of his protagonists and do not upset the balance of composition. Look at their inner phonation: епимимейка (Лесков 1973, IV: 269) (penance)—here used with the diminutive hypocoristic suffix instead of епимимья; примязание (Лесков 1973, IV: 257) (in the meaning of grabbing); дражае (Лесков 1973, IV: 284) (dearly, here in the sense 'having more importance'); снемлюмся (Лесков 1973, IV: 299) (are gathering); оспособлямь хозяев (Лесков 1973, IV: 298) (to help the hosts); . . . возгреваема духом благочесмивой ревносми . . . (Лесков 1973, IV: 299) (warming by the spirit of pious zeal)—describing the anger of a bishop; быв же через немалое время увещеваем . . . (Лесков 1973, IV: 309) (having been admonished during a long period of time); благочинный градских церквей . . . (Лесков 1973, IV: 305) (rural dean of the urban churches); . . . [быть] в напрасно посмыждающем конфузе (Лесков 1973, IV: 300) ([to be] in unfoundedly shameful embarrassment); . . . помещик . . . возмнил себя уже видящим небо омверсмо и смал проповедовамь . . . (Лесков 1973, IV: 298) (the landowner got too high an opinion of himself just seeing the Heaven open and began to preach); . . . омец же Иван . . . благословил его, а помом . . . лег паки (Лесков 1973, IV: 260) (Father Ivan blessed him, and then lay down again). Obviously, the use of archaic models of official business style filled with Slavonicisms and lexemes of religious meaning let us come to the conclusion that there is an appreciable connection between Leskov's language and some of the language features of the 17th century but Leskov's medium is more stylized. Leskov relied on a tradition which emerged in a later period, in the 1700s, when Old Slavonic words which used to have mostly ecclesiastic and cult semantics before were subjected to a redefinition of their language status, sometimes their field of dissemination was

narrowed down (or changed in a way) and they preserved their primary sense only in obsolete stylized church speech. Leskov was also right when he noticed the most peculiar feature of written business style in the 18th century: the collation of church speech with phraseological locutions with figurative meaning.[15] This made wordy modifiers metaphoric and inimitable in artistic beauty.

This statement is corroborated by our analysis of changes in Leskov's attitude to the literary language. He began with imitative genres, and the main form of stylization was 'mimicking of style' (of course, we have his fiction and not his essays or journalism in mind). That was not, however, simple imitation or assimilation to the concrete manner of writing but its intentional and spiritually realized reproduction. Moreover, Leskov came to literature with a definite view of Russian existence. In his first story, **'Овцебык'** (**'The Musk-ox'**) [1862], the principal traits of his artistic stance was already outlined: recollection, aptly combined with fantasy, was based on exposing the biography of a hero by short and impressive episodes (ЛЭС 1987: 216); short stories inserted into the main body of the text; a heightened sensitivity to folk speech and its richness in unexpected turns; trustworthy sketches of the clergy.[16]

'Жимие одной бабы' (**'The Life of a Woman'**) [1863] anticipates the characteristic components of his further literary activities—the subtitle «Из гостомельских воспоминаний» ('From the Gostomel reminiscences') suggests that Leskov's interest in giving a biographic turn to his narrative has deepened, and the folk *skaz* (tale) in his fiction obtains a dominant position for the first time.

In the second part of the '60s and '70s, Leskov's writing is notable for the broad range of expression. In this period the following language and style features of his literary works can be distinguished: a significant presence of elements of language naturalism, an active search for style-forming elements and modes of organizing the genre system, heightened sensibility to the minute description of the representatives of national types, and last but not least, a graphically pronounced social orientation of turns of speech (Соборяне, Запечамленный ангел, Очарованный смранник). Historic truth is subordinated to artistic truth in Leskov's literary works of this time just as in A. F. Vel'tman. The fantastic and real were the two principles forming the subject-matter of his fiction during the period. This perhaps indicated a shift from what is called conventional historicity, i.e. Leskov moved away from the important problems of modern life, which are screened by reveries and romantic dreams, to conscious historicism in which the tale as a source blends with a critical insight into the spiritual contradictions of the present.[17]

Later Leskov himself defined the method he used in the last period of his career. "I wrote in small chapters",—he said. L. P. Grossman (Гроссман 1945: 265) comments on Leskov's statement as follows:

> Leskov mastered this gift to cut up a story and enhance the interest of the reader by a skilful distribution of parts to perfection. He created his independent type of short story in sections: the general figure of his stories, which emerges in a series of quickly succeeding short chapters resumed nearly in every page, gives that lucid coherence to the whole which is assimilated by the reader with no strain or tiredness.

> (Гроссман 1945: 265)

Notes of the Unknown, indeed, consists of short but richly condensed chapters (all in all twenty two). Each of them has its own plot, each is certainly vivid, satiric and easily retained in memory. Every chapter has its own title, sometimes playful or ironic. Here are some of them: Искусный омвемвчик ['The clever respondent'], О вреде ом чмения свемских книг, бываемом для многих ['On the harm of reading secular books which affected a great many'], Излишняя мамеринская нежносмь ['Superfluous motherly tenderness'], Счасмливому осмроумию и непозволимельная вольносмь прощаемся ['The lucky wit is forgiven for inadmissible familiarity'], О безумии одного князя ['About the madness of a prince'], Османовление расмущего языка ['The stoppage of the growing tongue'], etc. It was one of Leskov's artistic habits to specify the title of the story by a subtitle either in brackets or without them, as for instance, **'О слабосми чувсмв и о напряженносми оных. (Двоякий приклад ом познаний и наблюдения)'** ['**Of the Weakness of Feelings and the Intensity of Theirs. (The Double Assiduity of Epistemology and Observation)'**] or **'О Пемухе и его демях. Геральдический казус'** ['**About Petukh and His Children. A Heraldic Casus'**]. A similar device to specify the main idea was applied by Leskov in his articles and essays, as we have already noticed. He thought that the title should be lively, sonorous, alluring and easy to memorize. Following this principle he created out-of-the-way, enigmatic and inviting titles.

The last story of the cycle is most remarkable in this respect. Let us first examine the title and its complex meaning—'A heraldic casus'. It emphasizes the mystery of the contents and creates a considerable metaphorical aura. This is the result of an unusual concept of the word, of its interior structure. In it the unit of the language appears not in the function of a conditional sign for expressing an idea but like an artistic image (Буслаев 1861: 1). We shall try to penetrate into the substance of this figurativeness. Thus, 'heraldic' can be traced back to the lexeme 'heraldry'. The 'Dictionary' of foreign words (Полный словарь 1894: 266) gives the following definition: it derives from Middle Latin

heraldus which can be traced back to herald. Heraldry is the science of insignia. The name comes from the fact that in the Middle Ages at the time of a tournament the armorial bearings of a new knight appeared, and the herald was supposed to explain the meaning of the arms depicted on the shield of the new contestant. But this interpretation does not contain the sense we are looking for, the very mysterious implication which Leskov managed to give the word. To reveal its concealed significance we shall follow the writer's mode of treating language: having 'turned' the word to one side we shall now turn it to the other. 'Herald' springs from Old German *hariwalt*—'steward of force'. It had three different meanings:

1. A public or town crier (in Russia—глашамай) in ancient times whose duty was to announce wars; 2. a person who proclaimed the names of knights in a tournament; 3. an official who announced important events to the public, e.g. coronations (Полный словарь 1894: 270). For the understanding of Leskov's intention the third meaning is of special interest. To get closer to it we have to remember that the word герольдия, which is obsolete today, was still widely used in the 19th century. This lexeme with some accurate definition would contain the main theme of the short story. Герольдия in Russia was a government institution which was responsible for the scrutiny of the rights of the nobles and for working out the insignia for various places and people. To confirm our hypothesis we shall address the short story **'About Petukh and His Children'**.

In it Leskov made use (with good effect) of events which were connected with the public marriage of an officer, son of a land-owning woman and a serf maid as well as the juridically illegitimate entry of their marriage. Showing the pictures of pre-reform Russia the writer touches lightly upon the very intricate and complicated theme of Russian cryptogamia (here the word is used in the meaning of clandestine marriage). Leskov's story seems true to us because he explains some details of the unusual case by references to one of the legal documents. In the second part ('A simple means') he inserts a footnote with some interesting information which proves that the story is true to historical fact. He mentions in a casual way the forty second paragraph of 'Instruction to Rural Deans', which was published in 1857, and quotes a few words from it:

> . . . in it the necessity is discussed to exercise "prudence in declaring couples husband and wife who were not married here"

> (где говорится об «осторожности в показывании супругами таких лиц, кои здесь не венчаны»),

and in witness of their marriage cannot produce evidence.

> Apparently,—infers the narrator,—there must have been some reason that made this warning necessary

(Очевидно, что предостережение это было чем-
нибудь вызвано).

(Лесков 1973, IV: 331)

As it becomes obvious by the passage quoted above, by
inobtrusive signs and remarks the author tries to bring
the reader closer to his true-to-life narrative style and
tries to convince him of the authenticity of his words.
As far as we can know on the ground of the written
evidence, Leskov was elaborating this problem at the
time of publishing the cycle and somewhat later in the
articles '**Благословенный брак . . .**'[18] and '**Брако-
разводное забвение. Причина разводов
брачных . . .**'[19] ['**The Divorce Unconsciousness. A
Motive of Divorce Proceedings . . .**']. In particular,
the writer cites a curious passage from a rare book
which has an indirect relationship to *The Notes of the
Unknown*. That is how Leskov describes an episode of
Russian cryptogamia [spacing out and sequence of
words made by the writer are presented here without
any changes—O. N.]: ". . . in the accomplishment of
marriage the church, i.e. 'the gathering of
believers' . . . , does not participate neither does any
'executor of *treb*' [occasional religious rites: christening, marriage, funeral, etc.—O. N.]. All the chanters
and benedictors only 'coattend', as witnesses, but 'the
performer [of rites—O. N.] is absent'[20]. This elliptical
device artistically confirms 'A heraldic casus' in which
Leskov, with grotesque metaphorical allusions, represents the fictive marriage (misalliance) of Petukh and
Pelageya describing the essence of the matter as a criminal farce. What is more surprising, the writer finds quite
a marvelous solution to settle the problem. It was really
'A Simple Means'—such is the title Leskov gave to the
final part of this short narrative. The consistory bailiff
comes to Luka's rescue who is so much in despair that
he has no idea of what to do, saying that

отчаяние есть смертный грех, а на святой Руси
нет невозможности.

(Лесков 1973, IV: 332)

(despair is a mortal sin, but in holy Russia nothing is
impossible.)

What is his 'remedy'? It is not a forgery or a criminal
act ("There is a mind not only in big heads but in small
ones" = «Ум-то не в одних больших головах, а и в
малых» Лесков 1973, IV: 333). So, Luka Aleksandrovich gets the book from the archives and finds the
name 'peasant Petukh' in it written in a different ink in
a scraped space. As soon as no one remembers who has
done it, an investigation is undertaken. During it all testify that Pelageya married Luka, and Petukh was simply
standing by. That proves to be a cogent argument, and
the true matrimony is confirmed. ". . . but the bailiff
did not do any forgery, he only added in the book the
very thing that he had wiped out in it. That was his

'simple means'" («а приказный никакой фальши не
сделал, а только подписал в книге то самое, что в
ней и вычистил. То было его "простое средство"»
Лесков 1973, IV: 333),—the narrator concludes finish-
ing the story. This final section differs from all the rest.
It manifests Leskov's greatness as an artist in the commanding humour, lenient irony and fully particularized
(as to characteristics and description) form. This part is
satiated with a special colouring supplied by the metaphorical devices and the amazing variety of verbalized
emotions. In it we find a most unusual combination of
circumstances skilfully brought together by Leskov and
joined with various style and language constructions:
the tradition of 18th-century business correspondence
acquires completely new shades of meaning, the lexis
of the inquiry deeds is put to very convincing use, vivid
Slavonicisms are combined with picturesque phraseological locutions. Even the very plot seems as if it was
borrowed from an ancient forensic manuscript with its
typical colophon, and the miscarriage of justice is
looked upon as a heraldic *casus.*

The second word of the subtitle has relatively richer semantic colouring. *Casus* means 'case'—this is the well-
known definition today. In the earlier period it also had
the meaning 'an awkward circumstance' or 'a remarkable case' (Полный словарь 1894: 438). Modern
sources add to the aforementioned definitions useful
and pertinent semantic explications, i.e. 1. Case, usually
difficult, intricate or uncommon, ridiculous; 2. *jur.* A
case, an accidental action, having external signs of
transgression but deprived of the element of a guilt
therefore non-punishable (СИС 1990: 211).

All these possible interpretations of 'heraldic case' are
important to take into account as they prompt us the
idea that the very word in Leskov's fiction appears in
the role of a literary image. It possesses not a single information ground but contains various groups of conditional indications and connotations which Leskov wants
to mobilize.

Somewhat later, in 1886, Leskov would reflect on the
problem of cases presenting highly convincing proofs
based on his own experience in the article
'**Геральдический муман. (Замемки о родовых
прозваниях).**' Alongside with some interesting facts he
gives in it an analysis of names and surnames which
seem foreign in origin, in term of their genealogy, however, they are primordially Russian[21]. At this point the
literary historian, E. P. Karnovich's Родовые проз-
вания и мимулы в России и слияние русских с ин-
оземцами (СПБ., 1886) [*Patrimonial Nicknames and
Titles in Russia and the Blending of the Russian with
the Foreign*] should be mentioned; Leskov appreciated
his knowledge of life and artistic gifts very highly.

Critics have pointed out the most characteristic pecu-
liarities of Leskov's fiction: his ability to create a lan-

guage which can convey the inner processes and the speech habits of his protagonists as well as the astonishing vividness of his description of domestic scenes. How is this manifested in the ***Notes of the Unknown,*** and what shades of textual meaning does his language display? We would like to return once more to the short story **'About Petukh and His Children'**. The narrator's speech is imperceptibly inserted into the dialogue so that what was said before could be explained:

> Petukh was a бесмяголбный (having no family) *muzhik* in the master's poultry-yard—dirty and half-witted, with a red nose, jabbering away in a squeaky voice, and was forty or so.
>
> (Был же Петух бестягольный мужик на господском птичьем дворе—нечистый и полоумный, с красным носом, и говор имел дроботливый с выкриком по-петушьему, а лет уже сорока и поболее.)
>
> (Лесков 1973, IV: 324)

Here the author employs specific words to create a true-to-life domestic atmosphere. The words have their own shades of meaning peculiar to the nature of the person implied, e.g. бесмягольный instead of бессемейный. In Old Russian мягло was used basically in two meanings: labour conscription or a family executing their duties at the time of serfdom. Interesting notes on it are given in the 'Dictionary' (Даль 1994: 900-901):

> . . . мягловой крестьянинь, который тянеть полное тягло, за двѣ души; . . . обычно крестьянинь; остается мяглымь отъ женитьбы своей до 60 лѣть, затѣмь либо онь идеть в полутяглые, и на четверть тягла, или смѣщается вовсе. . . . Тягло ср. мужь с женою или семья, вь крестьянствѣ, доколѣ мужикь, по лѣтамь своимь и по здоровью, числится тяглымь.

Leskov can very well be supposed to have known the numerous proverbs which were connected with this notion and which had wide currency in the social environment described by the writer in his cycle.

In the sentence quoted above Leskov uses дробомливый говор instead of more common words like quick, fast, pattering. And the sentence is immediately followed by the description of the conversation of the priest and his wife which is presented in another manner closer to *skaz*:

> Попадья ничего не внимала, а сказала такой сказ, что если поп ее заранее осведомит, когда бригадиршин сые сдедет в город, а Поленьку с мужиком свенчают, то она никакого мешанья не сделает, но если он от нее это скроет, то ее любопытство мучить станет, и тогда она за себя не поручится, что от нетерпения вред сделает.
>
> (Лесков 1973, IV: 324)[22]
>
> (The priest's wife didn't listen to him but said such a tale that if the priest informed her in advance when the brigadier's wife's son was going to go up to town, and

Polen'ka and the *muzhik* were going to be married, then she would not make any мешанья (trouble), but if he did that from her then she would be tormented by curiosity, and then she could not vouch for herself and might, out of impatience, do some harm.)

After this verbose skaz Leskov inserts a single statement: «поп уступил» (Лесков 1973, IV: 324) (the priest gave in). Nothing superfluous is added by the narrator. His syntactic phrases are efficiently constructed and thought out. This fluent passage gives the reader the impression that he can actually arrest the flow of the narrative and try to realize what is behind the narrator's words. That compositional device is called retardation. In connection with Leskov's *skaz* A. S. Orlov was the first to notice that particular narratological element. He claims that "the skaz of Leskov can be characterized by its excitement being supported by the curiosity of the listener to be able to hear how every person speaks in accordance with his typical nature" (Орлов 1948: 146). The priest uses a different language: there are no diffuse phrases, his voice sounds mild, and it is briefly interrupted by the narrator's elucidation:

> Ну, ладно,—говорит,—я тебе лучше все скажу, только уж ты знай, да никому здесь не сказывай.
>
> (Лесков 1973, IV: 324)
>
> (All right then,—he says,—I would better tell you everything, but remember you must not tell anyone here.)

Soon enough the speech of the officers is defined: it is shaped in the imperative mood without any additions and explanations; *skazovost'* here is not an expressive stylistic device to be applied. The traits of the people of this social stratum require another artistic method in another linguistic medium:

> —Сейчас нам отпереть! Ибо знаем, что в храме насильный брак совершается, и мы не допустим й сейчас двери вон выбьем. . . .
>
> (Лесков 1973, IV: 326)
>
> —(Open now [the door]! Because we know that in the church a forcible matrimony is happening, but we won't let it go on, we'll rather knock out the doors in no time. . . .)

Their speech is an expression of their intentions. This approach to representing character is most subtle. As we have already suggested, each estate in Leskov's fiction has its own unique language and style. By the means of speech constituting his characters Leskov creates a comic atmosphere. Manipulating elements of comedy, irony and satire the writer defines the characteristic features of the heroes' interior speech and inner world.[23] Though retardation is a stylistic device widely spread in longer literary pieces, there it has a different function; it appears, for instance, in lyrical digressions, in descriptions of nature or interiors, in insertion of external personages and separate short stories, etc., Leskov's mode of using it in the ***Notes of the Unknown*** differs, to some extent, from his usual treatment of the device. As we have mentioned, the author tried to slow down the speed and delay the events by using various ways of expressing the vocal characteristics of his protagonists. It is attained through a sharp change of textual key and alteration of the tone of narration. There is also one more detail which brings ***Notes*** close to folklore. It is the sequential construction of the narrative and the threefold reduplication of the typical episodes, which builds up tension. We find the latter used four times. Thirst is used in 'Излишняя мамеринская нежносмь' in this way: there is a mildly ironic and humorous depiction of Ignaty's fright which arises out of lying near бабка-голландка (Grandma Dutch) who keeps chuckling at him and making smacking noises with her lips up to the very morning (Лесков 1973, IV: 266). Here we see a two-way junction: the reinforcement of the inner tension of the hero (confirmed by him saying that he was looking forward to falling asleep with all his might) which takes place as if in a dream, and the skaz of two kinds when what happened in the past correlates to reality. We call this device an imaginary reduplication because the progress is infringed but the delay of the action is the result of the transmission of the thoughts and the voices of the characters through the sensibility of the narrator. In that particular episode skaz is one of the ways of showing reduplication where the situation of spontaneous improvisation conveys the disposition of the story-teller. We cannot fully affirm that this device is merely borrowed from national folklore. It is rather an element of sentimental prose which itself was affected by the oral folklore of the time. But the less it directly conforms to that dominant tradition or the literary norm the more original and interesting it is as to its form and metaphoricity. The problem is psychological rather than linguistic: it indicates what lies behind the narrator's apperception. Some parallel examples of retardation might be useful to analyze.

In the story **'Об иносмранном предиканме'** retardation appears in a different form: in the dialogue between Farther Georgy and владыка (member of the higher orders of the clergy). They discuss the question of the prohibition of preaching to the foreign предиканм (here 'preacher'). First of all the incident is described which arouses the interest in the reader as to why Georgy has refused to forbid the preacher to preach in the house of the предводимельша (the wife of a marshal of the nobility), Elena Ivanovna, who is called Elena Prekrasnaja for her 'delicate face' («за свое изящное лице») (Лесков 1973, IV: 299).

> Первая моя причина,—говорит,—та, что моего запрещения могут не послушаться, и я тогда буду через то только в напрасно постыждающем конфузе.
>
> (Лесков 1973, IV: 300)

(My first reason is,—he says,—that they might disobey my prohibition, in which case I put myself in a disreputable *konfuz'* in vain.)

That idea does not seem convincing enough to the bishop—«Это не что иное как гордость ума» (Лесков 1973, IV: 300) ('This is nothing else but the pride of the mind'). The second argument is as follows:

> . . . что предиканта того «развратителем» называть будет несправедливо, ибо он хотя и иностранец, но человек весьма хороших правил христианской жизни. . . .
>
> (Лесков 1973, IV: 300)

(. . . it would be unfair to call that *predicant* "a seducer" because though he is a foreigner, but a person of high Christian principles. . . .)

This reason does not seem to the bishop conclusive either who now begins to show his displeasure. To Georgy's third motive the bishop listens with testy impatience: ". . . it is not customary to the spirit of the orthodoxial belief to fear timidly any dissenting opinions, but on the contrary, it is characterized by laudable веромерпимсмво (toleration) and free expression and speech, just like the apostles advise": «Все слушать, а <u>хорошего</u> держаться» (Лесков 1973, IV: 300) (To listen to everything but hold to *the good*) [[underlined] by the author—O. N.]

The convincing argument for the bishop was that the governor himself was sitting behind the screen listening to the predicant.

> Услыхав это последнее,—продолжает повествователь,—владыка остановился и сказал:—Так для чего же вы мне об этом последнем с самого начала не сказали?
>
> (Лесков 1973, IV: 301)

(Having heard this,—the narrator continued,—the bishop stopped and asked:—Why didn't you tell me about this last thing at the very beginning?)

In this episode retardation comes after the second reduplication, and the dialogue serves the function of setting the story in motion. To some extent, the passage quoted above is connected with folklore motifs (the name of the lady ironically corresponds to a similar character of a well-known Russian tale). Leskov used the same device in the story **'About Petukh and His Children'**.

This brings us to an analysis of the syntactic system of the writer which is based (particularly in the last story) on N. G. Kurganov's Latinate syntax together with a sham (бутафория) of the beginning of the 19th century (Орлов 1948: 164-165). Actually, here we come across constructions which are not customary in Russian, i.e.

adverbial participles and verbs which change their positions and are placed by the author at the absolute end of the phrase, as for instance:

> The priest's wife his grief умишила (Лесков 1973, IV: 325) (calmed down); the Brigadier's wife took a deep breath and crossed herself, but that was because of a great confusion instead of a wedding ceremony, heaven knows what пемо бяху (had been sung), the deacon did not say . . . (Лесков 1973, IV: 330), or And you did not disgrace (пе опали) for that either me or anyone else through the rage of yours, but, by your usual mercy all of us покрыв (shielding), deliberated calmly and decorously . . . (Лесков 1973, IV: 329), etc.

The examples quoted above are not exceptional. If we examine them we understand the function of the transformations. Leskov seems to have intensified the real semantic and temporal sense of the endings of locutions by means of the utilization of verbal inversion. Thus, the full implication of the events is moved to the verbal forms which speeds up action and precipitates the evolution of the plot. It is in the verbs where the author perceives the substantial kernel of the passage. In conformity to the positional structure of the sentence Leskov uses the method of substitution. The writer's narrative style requires this in order to determine words and constructions which can freely occupy any syntactical position. This device amplifies the ways of the semantic expansion of the vocabulary because the shift of syntactical position does not always conform to valid aspects of syntax. We can see some elements of the method of transposition here as well where the transfer of words or collocations from one syntactic position to the other creates a different tone and defines the relations between the form of the word and its function in the sentence. As we can see, Leskov's method is experimental and uncommon. We have already touched upon this problem in the discussion of the gamut of the language colours in his prose.

Leskov's special interest in heraldry has already been pointed out. In *Notes of the Unknown* the names of the representatives of the clergy are selected very carefully. They can be read as labels which anticipate the roles these protagonists will play in the narrative. Some of them function as mirror reflections of certain tempers and moral characteristics. Of course, behind the form of the bearer of a proper name stands the narrator's ulterior device. Leskov liked one of the statements of Theocritus which he used as an epigraph at the beginning of the article **'Геральдический муман . . .'**: **'Everyone Gets His Name at a Blessed Hour'**[24]. Leskov himself followed this dictum in his creative writings. Thus, for instance Father Ioann (the name is a translation of the Hebrew 'God's grace') «прежде во всю жизнь свою не пил» (Лсков 1973, IV: 259) (he had not drunk all his life before); Father Pavel (from Latin *paulus*—

'small') «был роста высокого, осторожного понимания и в разговорах нередко шутлив» (Лесков 1973, IV: 261) (was of large stature, of keen comprehension, and in speech often enough jocular); Father Grigory (in Old Greek γρηγορω—'be awake, cheerful, vigilant') «в служенье хорош и весьма способен, но камоликовам, и то было в нем заимствованное . . .» (Лесков 1973, IV: 268) (in service is good and very capable, but камоликовам (is like a Catholic), and that was borrowed in him . . .); hieromonk Theodosy (the name is compound from the two Old Greek words: θεός—'God' and δόσις—'a gift', 'a donation', i.e. granted to God) «нарицаяся друг, но не верный, и втайне зложелатель . . .» (Лесков 1973, IV: 288) (called a friend, but not faithful, and secretly malevolent . . .); another Father Pavel, who imagined himself "to be as though the first after Pharaoh (мня ся быти яко первым по фараоне), endeavored to sit [in the дрожки] outstretched in a place for two . . ." (Лесков 1973, IV: 313); lastly, junior deacon (причемник) Porphiry (compare to Old Greek πορφύρεος—'purple, crimson; dark-red, violet; generally dark'; the name also has the root meaning 'purple clothes or a mantle') who was named 'the dull-born' (глупорожденный) and 'rough' (комовамый), was tall and of a very submissive disposition (нрав) (Лесков 1973, IV: 313).

It might be surprising to see that Leskov practically never mentions the surnames of his characters, especially if they belong to the church. Surnames were not used in clerical circles. Besides, it could have been rather a stiff and artificial device. Their real temper and deeds are of the greatest importance for Leskov who in hardly visible traits created picturesque satirical portraits of the local clergy.

Leskov's interest in the meaning of names and in their genealogy is obviously deeply rooted. In the 1870s he elaborated his own system of categorizing the surnames of the Russian priesthood. He established six categories: surnames which go back to the names of holidays (for instance, Rozhdestvensky), to the names of figures in antiquity like Platonov, or to words for virtues of character, etc. (Гроссман 1945: 272). Leskov's names are artistic images which have a life of their own and a complex aura of connotations. Somewhat later, in the 1900-1910s, the philosopher Father P. A. Florensky also expounded his view of names. He thought it was a grave mistake to "declare all the literary names,—*and the name as it is* [italicized by P. A. Florensky—O. N.],—arbitrary and accidental . . . Names are the main kernels of the very images . . ." (Флоренский 1993: 25). As well as Leskov, he considered names artistic images forming complex spiritual organisms and characterizing the persons who carry them. According to P. A. Florensky's concept, they possess various moods of their being (бымие): ecclesiastic, humiliated, diminutive (Флоренский 1993: 40, 94-96). The hypostasis of every name determines its significance and should be analyzed as part of the cultural process.[25] It may be interesting to compare the theological tradition with Leskov's own concept of names. His gift as a creative writer, his idealism and severe critical views helped him find an artistic form to convey his experiences as well as the findings of his research. In point of fact he formulated the very group of notions which later on were to become the basis of a modern branch of science—onomastics—the art of giving names (that is calque translation from the corresponding Old Greek word). Leskov's feelings and thoughts combined to find the concrete object of his writing—the representatives of the clergy. It was not only a coincidence but one of his stylistic devices permanently present in his literary works. This combination of satirical literary expressions and intellectual penetration to the depth of a problem seems to be the articulation of two features of his individuality: his intransigence as a social being confronting moral perversion and his profound intellect in search for truth. The very term 'onomastics' covers not only the art of giving names, but also scholarly proficiency in studying them. The latter now belongs to linguistics, Leskov, however, was the master of both approaches, and what is more, that ability of his appears in two forms: in scholarly conjectures and hypotheses which he managed to translate into the terms of the imaginative world of his art as a writer. Leskov's creative work, his world-view and his understanding of aesthetic problems merged all together in his fiction moulding his style and extending his penetration into national history and culture.

Leskov's work as a writer is most unique in the wide range of the questions he treats and the variety of ways he describes them. His narrative style is constituted of a great diversity of stylistic figures and dialects. The playful language abounds in parodistic elements given in a cover of archaic Slavonic expressions in combination with quotations from the Holy Writ which results in paronomastic effects. On the other hand, there are a lot of professional patterns and words of folk terminological lexis. Sometimes they are simply misrepresented in their meaning and structure. In another case, as though explaining the real sense of the word Leskov binds it in the consciousness of a speaker with a different lexeme. This device—attraction paronymique—is widely applied in **Notes of the Unknown.** It is used to express the difference in the cultural status of his characters (Орлов 1948: 167). Somewhere he changes the sense, and a wrong letter used by him, as if by mistake, has its own shade of meaning and colour indication. Thus, for instance, in the collocation посморонние вольнодомки (Лесков 1973, IV: 262) the letter o is substituted for u because those people were not 'free thinkers' (the correct root of the second word is дум), but people who stayed at home (на дому). In the sentence «Иеродиакон немолодых лет, но могумной

(of mighty flesh) плоти . . . имел страсть к биллиардной игре . . .» (Лесков 1973, IV: 284) the word могучий (might) is revised and changed into могумная which now absorbs the nuance of suggesting a self-indulgent, unrestrained character who never hesitates to take liberties. Father Preferants (whose nickname is associated with a card game preference) has a son богослов (theologian) who would better be called бог ослов (the God of donkeys) (Лесков 1973, IV: 291). In this example folk etymology is combined with the process of redistribution of the stem. As a result, quite an opposite meaning is suggested by the evocation of a curse commonly used in the 19th century in theological seminaries, an ironic nick-name for a foolish person, the same as 'ass' in English. After that statement the narrator defines the word by the following reference: «. . . [сын] по пороку беспамятства никак не мог научиться служению . . .» (Лесков 1973, IV: 291) ". . . [the son] because of a defect of unconsciousness could hardly be taught to preach . . .". This feature illustrates the significance of and the reason for the use of this rather uncommon idiomatic expression.

In the short story '**Удивимельный случай всеобщего недоумения**' ['**A Wonderful Case of General Perplexity**'] Leskov uses the word combination мадемуазель попадья (as a reference to a priest's wife) putting it in inverted commas. It is organized on the principle of placing together incompatible (because of their dissonant meanings) notions or of correlating words having contradictory meanings in a collocation. Similarly, for instance, to the French oxymoron *une sage folie* (a wise folly) (see: Марузо 1960: 186); or the Russian phrase: звонкая мишина (a ringing silence), etc.

This *alliance des mots* conveys a delicate sense of irony and humour, especially as those are words of different origins: *mademoiselle* (Fr.) + попадья (Rus.). When describing 'the spiritual inclination' to the unfrocked archimandrite the narrator says that

> в числе писем, оставшихся после смерти расстриги, было одно от женщины настоящего высокого звания русских фамилий, которая даже называть его прежнего сана не умела и заместо того, чтобы писать «архимандрит», выражалась: «парфемандрит», что ей было более склонно к французскому штилю.
>
> (Лесков 1973, IV: 310)

(in the number of letters remaining after the death of the unfrocked monk was one from a lady of one of the really high rank Russian families, who did not even know how to name his former order, and instead of "archimandrite" she wrote: "parfemandrite", which she found more familiar since it was closer to her French style.)

In the passage quoted above Leskov's neologism consists of the prefixoid парфе- which could be brought into correlation with the French adjective *parfait* (perfect, absolute). That is an instance based on an expression etymologically unclear for the national language environment. Here it is partly paraphrased just like револьвер at the turn of the 20th century when many borrowings were in active use. It was understood owing to its artificial rebuilding as ребродер²⁶.

Original puns are close in nature to folk etymology. They used to be organized as metaphoric idioms and constituted a phrase which had a double sense. Here are some characteristic examples of Leskov's individual thinking-in-words: неодолимая пассия (Лесков 1973, IV: 319) (irresistible passion), опымные резоны (Лесков 1973, IV: 320) (serious reasons); "And Polen'ka . . . became idleless, and having, as one can see, from her mother innate French кокемерия (coquetry) . . ." (Лесков 1973, IV: 320); "If he [Father Grigory—O. N.] на духу (with courage) for the better perspicuity exhorted in French, then this moved the audience so intensely that they гисмерически (hysterically) sobbed violently . . ." (Лесков 1973, IV: 320). The phrases quoted above can be interpreted in two ways: they provoke laughter because of a contradiction between their meaning and the actual situation of the characters, on the one hand, and because of the reference in them to the protagonists' civilized temper and bent for French manners and mentality, on the other. This idea has an interesting justification. The Russian каламбур (pun) has a concrete event for its origin, which, we may assume, was used by Leskov as a subtextual device.

It was known that in 18th-century French aristocratic memoirs the term *calambour* was explained in terms of the following genealogy: in a gathering of high society it was decided that everybody was to make up some verses for fun. There was a dull-witted abbot who had no idea about poetry. When his turn came, after some vain attempts, in a sweat at last he invented the following lines:

> *Pleurons tous dans ce jour*
> *A bois de calambour . . .*

This rot made the whole *monde* laugh to excess, and the *casus* was not forgotten for a very long time. Leskov may be supposed to have wanted to make use of the episode. We can say that puns (here on the preciosity of French style and manners) were very popular in Russia in the 18th-19th centuries.²⁷

We can also quote some specifically Russian puns and language pigments from Leskov's narrative, e.g. большая пресмрашка (Лесков 1973, IV: 331) (a great fear), примязание (Лесков 1973, IV: 257) (grubbing), сивуха (Лесков 1973, IV: 322) (in the context the horse is meant, but generally the word is associated with raw vodka), усилок (Лесков 1973, IV:

326) (strong man), в живоме (Лесков 1973, IV: 329) (during his life time), [deacon] положил . . . всему макое краеграненне (Лесков 1973, IV: 328) (began fabricating a story); «Священник . . . в разговоре голландский джин, отбивавший во вкусе своем мозжухой, даже критиковал . . .» (Лесков 1973, IV: 308) (During the conversation the priest . . . even criticized the Dutch gin which savoured of <u>мозжуха</u> . . . (here the [underlined] word is associated with juniper having the specific suffix -ух- (compare to крас-нуха—ten rouble banknote, etc.). These phrases have undoubtedly a vivid appeal to the senses. They all look unusual (as to their structure and meaning), they do not, however, break the rules of the genre. The analysis of similar instances would require an approach which is not exclusively linguistic.

We have tried to correlate the elements of Leskov's language with his peculiar stylistic system, with the facts of his biography and with the traditions of the history of literature. Looking for the sources of his fiction we have also tried to clarify the theoretic positions which could be useful for textological and source studies.

Thus, in the ***Notes of the Unknown*** different stylistic devices are combined. Creating picturesque portraits of the people of many professions and estates gives Leskov ample scope to charge his style and language with vivid features of various manners of speech and enunciation. Leskov's later style becomes a very complicated system, thoughtfully organized and elaborated to a nicety. His linguistic expressiveness, sophisticated use of words, his kind and keen irony, his ability to bring the narrator's speech closer to the tale tradition as well as the polysemanticism of the plot of each story based on original archive material lead to a conclusion of the following character: stylization in Leskov's later creative activities develops into an artistic principle which enables the writer to convey the complex vision he aspired to articulate.²⁸

Notes

1. GPB. F. 236, № 174, p. 56. Cited from: (Лесков 1991: 37). [Here as hereafter all translations into English are my own.—O. N.].

2. Историческій вѣстник 11 (1883) 2: 265. Though A. N. Leskov did not find a real manuscript with original *Notes* (see: Звезда 1935, 7: 226), I assume that linguistic and source studies will lead us to us some possible parallels.

3. Историческій вѣстник 20 (1885) 6: 506-509.

4. Ibid. p. 257. Later on Leskov said that he wanted to write 'Записки рассмриги' ['Notes of the unfrocked']; the hero of the story would be a young, sensitive and modest gentleman who becomes a priest in order to do what is possible

(we keep here the author's spacing out of the words—O. N.) *ad majorem Dei gloriam,* and discovers that there is nothing to do for God's glory. But this could hardly be published in our Fatherland,—inferred the writer. (See the epilogue by A. N. Leskov to one of the first publications of some stories from *Notes of the Unknown* in the journal Звезда 1935. 7: 226).

5. When writing this narrative Leskov's personal position was rather difficult. Besides the fact of having to stop publishing the *Notes,* there is one more detail. In that period E. M. Theoktistov (whom the writer called "a pig from Theatre Square") was the Head of the Central Department of State Seal. The Minister for Education D. A. Tolstoy who "disliked people who took their own stand", as Leskov said, was also ill disposed to him.

6. RGADA. F. 1183. L. 1, part 37, № 129, p. 1.

7. Ibid. № 134, p. 1.

8. Ibid. № 176, p. 6.

9. Разночинец—intellectual not belonging to the gentry in 19th-century Russia.

10. Нигилизм in its origin is borrowed from Latin *nihil*—'nothing'. N. O. Lossky gives a substantial analysis of the problem of Russian nihilism and its functions in literature. In his view the word "nihilism", not in an old theological but in the social sense, was used for the first time by N. I. Nadeždin in 1829. At that period it meant new tendencies in literature and philosophy. N. O. Lossky considered nihilism "the seamy side of the good qualities of the Russian people". See: Лосский 1991: 338-350.

11. RGADA. F. 1195. L. 4, № 445, p. 84 г. s. This manuscript is written in the traditional type of Russian handwriting of the 18th century—скоропись (tachygraphy). It is to some extent more developed as compared to the beginning of the century, and is closer to the modern manner of writing. It is characterized by a variety of letter scripts, an abundance of signs carried above the line and the absence of an elaborated system of punctuation. Figures representing the date of the composition of the document in the second part of the 1700s are not substituted for letters as a rule. In "()" we put letters written in the original above the line; in "<>"—the letters omitted but implied by the author, "[]" are used for the letters carried out under the title. Orthography and punctuation are given without any corrections in the original form.

12. Compare the statement by N. O. Lossky: "Reducing the Church to the stage of servitors of the state, the government converts ecclesiastics into social servants" (Лосский 1991: 248).

13. The very remedy was called by the spiritual males есмирмисменно вино from ес мир ми.

14. In his other article G. O. Vinokur posits an interesting thesis which can be usefully adapted to historical analysis. He claims that "in application to the tasks of the reproduction of an old *glossa* the means of language of the following four types can be distinguished: firstly, the means of generally historic and folk colouring; secondly, the means with bookish colouring imitating Church Slavonic speech; thirdly, the means of narrow chronological colouring; in the fourth place, the means in expressiveness of which the dialectally estranging momentum suppresses the historical momentum proper" (Винокур 1991: 424).

15. Compare also Leskov's following combinations to the business style of the 18th century: he uses the 18th century grammatical concord with prepositions thus ascribing to them the meaning they used to have then and brings them into correlation with one of their sensitive units to polysemantic Slavonicisms (we [underlined] them . . .): «. . . по принесении же белья эконом оное весьма смотрел в достоинстве проверял . . .» (Лесков 1973, IV: 278) (when the linen was brought the house-(exchequer-) keeper carefully looked through it and in virtue checked it up); «. . . [граф] в Петербург возвратясь, в мануфактур-совет, для испрошения медали . . .» (Лесков 1973, IV: 308) ([the count] came back to Petersburg, to the manufactory council, for asking a medal); «. . . случился к той поре на селе некий опытный брат, приезжий из недальней обители за нуждою монастырскою. . . . [он] сказал: "Брате, брате! Чего доспел еси?"» (Лесков 1973, IV: 311) (it came about at that time in the village that a certain experienced brother, a visitor from a cloister not far off, for monastery need. . . . [he] said: "Brother, brother! What have you made up?").

16. It can be mentioned here that one of Leskov's sisters, Natalija (1836-1920), was the nun Gennadija. See: Гроссман 1945: 26.

17. Compare, for instance, A. F. Vel'tman's 'Сердце и думка' ('Heart and Haze') to Leskov's 'Очарованный смранник' ('Encharmed Wanderer').

18. See: Историческій вѣстникъ 20 (1885) 499-515.

19. See: Историческій вѣстникъ 22 (1885) 509-524.

20. Cited from: Историческій вѣстникъ 20 (1885) 503.

21. See: Историческiй вѣстникъ 24 (1886) 598-613.

22. The usage of the rusificated French borrowing бригадирша is extremely significant. By probing into its genealogy the real contextual time can be revealed. The Russian бригадир springs from бригада (brigade) which has been known in Russia from the very outset of the 18th century. Since that time бригадир has been used as a military term. It was 'a brigade commander', an officer of the fifth class in the tsarist army of the 18th century, in between the colonel and the major-general, and in the navy it was the rank corresponding to the captain-commodore. Consequently, бригадирша (in the dictionaries it is defined as 'obsolete')—the wife of a brigadier—as a character's prototype could not exist beyond the first third of the 19th century. That is why we suppose that the real contextual time of this short story was the period between 1800 and the 1840s. See: Даль 1994: 313; Черных 1993: III; Макаров и Матвеева 1993: 47; ССРЛЯ 1991: 759. In the broad sense, Leskov gave a free rein to his imagination when describing pictures of pre-reform Russia. Apart from the aforementioned phenomenon, we think that there are some other striking illustrations of our conjecture, i.e. the problem of Russian *cryptogamia* described in this sketch, and the presence of tableaux vivants of the patriarchal mode of life in the Russian provinces in that period.

23. L. P. Grossman observed that "[Leskov] liked the inner world of his heroes by recreating their enunciation: one had a speech dull and unintelligible—his character is reserved and sullen; another spoke with such cunning word ligatures (извимия слов), that one is likely to get astounded by his speech,—but had a light and captivating temper" (Гроссман 1945: 270). See also the article О некоморых осoбенносмях языка «Замемок неизвесмного» (Азбукин 1963: 59-63).

24. Историческiй вѣстникъ 24 (1886) 598.

25. Compare the following definition made by bishop Antony (Florensov): "Name is an omen of the moral education of a person, of a Christian, a testimonial of his individuality and inclination to one or another kind of activity". See: Андроник (Трубачев) 1981: 76.

26. See the publication of 'Terminological Glossary on Linguistics (1935-1937)' from the Archives of the Academy of Sciences of the USSR (now RAN) in: Поливанов 1991: 392-393.

27. Some scholars have supposed that the term can be traced back to an anecdote about priest Kalember or about the German count Kalember whose command of French was poor. See: Поливанов 1991: 463; ЭСРЯ 1982: 24. P. Ja. Černych quotes a passage from "The Letters of the Russian Traveller" by N. M. Karamzin where the word "calanbur" was used, and considered that already from the beginning of the 19th century this expression was in use. In Russian dictionaries it is mentioned from 1804. See: Черных 1993: 370. As we know, anecdote is one of Leskov's vivid devices, which was artistically employed by him for language disguise.

28. I would like to thank Prof. Dr. V. Yu. Troitsky for his helpful comments while I was preparing this article and express special thanks to Prof. Dr. T. V. Androsova whose generous assistance and moral support I had ready at hand while working on it. I would also like to thank Mr. D. A. Dogadin for his technical recommendations and gestures of generosity during the time I was writing this article.

Literature

Азбукин В. Н. О некоторых особенностях языка «Заметок неизвестного»: Ученые записки Томского гос. ун-та. 1963. № 45. 59-63.

Андроник (Трубачев), иеродиакон. Епископ Антоний (Флоренсов)—духовник священника Павла Флоренского: Журнал Московской Патриархии. 1981. № 9. 71-77.

Буслаев Ф. И. Эпическая поэзия: Буслаев Ф. И. Исторические очерки русской народной словесности и искусства. 1. С.-Петербург 1861.

Даль В. И. Толковый словарь живого великорусского языка, 1-4. Москва 1994.

Другов Б. М. Н. С. Лесков. Очерк творчества. Москва 1957.

Винокур Г. О. Об изучении языка литературных произведений: Винокур Г. О. Избранные работы по русскому языку. Москва 1959.

Винокур Г. О. О языке художественной литературы. Москва 1991.

Гроссман Л. П. Н. С. Лесков. Жизнь—Творчество—Поэтика. Ленинград 1945.

Ключевский В. О. Собрание сочинений. В 9 т. IX. Материалы разных лет. Москва 1990.

Лексические трудности русского языка: Словарь-справочник. Москва 1994.

Лесков Н. С. Рукописное наследие. Каталог. Ленинград 1991.

Лесков Н. С. Собрание сочинений в шести томах. III, IV. Москва 1973.

Лосский Н. О. Характер русского народа: Лосский Н. О. Условия абсолютного добра. Москва 1991. 338-350.

Макаров В. И., Мамвеева Н. Р. От Ромула до наших дней: Словарь лексических трудностей художественной литературы. Москва 1993.

Марузо Ж. Словарь лингвистических терминов. Москва 1960.

ЛЭС = Литературный энциклопедический словарь. Москва 1987.

Орлов А. С. Язык Лескова. (Материалы к статье): Орлов А. С. Язык русских писателей. Москва-Ленинград 1948.

Поливанов Е. Д. Толковый терминологический словарь по лингвистике (1935-1937). В кн.: Поливанов Е. Д. Избранные труды по восточному и русскому языкознанию. Москва 1991. 318-506.

Полный словарь иностранных слов, вошедших в употребление в русском языке с означением их корней. Сост. Бурдон и Михельсон. С.-Петербург 1894.

Пустозерская проза: Сборник. Сост. М. Б. Плюханова. Москва 1989.

Русские писатели о литературном труде, 3. Ленинград 1955.

СИС = Словарь иностранных слов. Москва 1990.

ДРС = Словарь русского языка XI—XVII вв. Вып. 6. Москва 1979.

ССРЛЯ = Словарь современного русского литературного языка: В 20-и томах. Т. 1. Москва 1991.

Флоренский П. А. Имена: Малое собрание сочинений. Вып. 1 (Архив священника Павла Флоренского). Купина 1993.

Черных П. Я. Историко-этимологический словарь современного русского языка: В 2-х томах. Т. 1. Москва 1993.

ЭСРЯ = Этимологический словарь русского языка. Под ред. Н. М. Шанского, II/8. Москва 1982.

Abbreviations

Ed.: Edition

F.: Fund

GPB: Государственная публичная библиотека им. М. Е. Салтыкова-Щедрина (St. Petersburg). (now: Российская национальная библиотека).

L.: List (= опись)

RAN: Российская академия наук.

RGADA: Российский государственный архив древних актов.

R. s.: Reverse side

FURTHER READING

Biography

McLean, Hugh. *Nikolai Leskov: The Man and His Art.* Cambridge: Harvard University Press, 1977, 780 p.
    Detailed critical biography of Leskov.

Criticism

Alissandratos, Julia. "Leskov versus Flaubert as Connoisseur of a Medieval Narrative Pattern Closely Associated with Hagiography." In *American Contributions to the Tenth International Congress of Slavists: Sofia, September 1988,* edited by Jane Gary Harris, pp. 7-18. Columbus, Ohio: Slavica Publishers, 1988.
    Studies Leskov's employment of the Old Russian encomiastic narrative pattern (a story-telling structure generally employed in hagiography) in several of his short stories, then draws parallels between these and Gustave Flaubert's short story "La légende de Saint Julien l'Hospitalier."

Ansberg, Aleksej B. "Frame Story and First Person Story in N. S. Leskov." *Scando-Slavica* 3 (1957): 49-73.
    Describes Leskov's use of framing and first person narrative in his short stories.

Bowers, Catherine D. "Nikolaj Leskov's Reminiscences of Kiev: Examples of His Memoir Style." *Harvard Ukrainian Studies* 6, no. 4 (December 1982): 477-84.
    Considers the blending of fact and fiction in Leskov's memoir stories.

Chvany, Catherine V. "Stylistic Use of Affective Suffixes in Leskov." In *Mnemozina: Studia litteraria russica in honorem Vsevolod Setchkarev,* edited by Joachim T. Baer and Norman W. Ingham, pp. 64-77. Munich: Wilhelm Fink Verlag, 1974.
    Linguistic study of Leskov's writings, focusing on the use of diminutive grammatical forms in the stories "Grabež" and "Voitel'nica."

Edgerton, William B. "Leskov, Paškov, the Štundists, and a Newly Discovered Letter." In *Orbis Scriptus: Dmitrij Tschižewskij zum 70. Geburtstag,* edited by Dietrich Gerhardt, Wiktor Weintraub, and Hans-Jürgen zum Winkel, pp. 187-99. Munich: Wilhelm Fink Verlag, 1966.

Investigates Leskov's interest in two religious movements—the Štundists and the followers of Vasilij Aleksandrovič Paškov—and their potential influence on his writings.

Garnett, Edward. Introduction to *The Sentry and Other Stories,* by Nicolai Lyeskov, translated by A. E. Chamot, pp. vii-xiv. New York: Alfred A. Knopf, 1922.
    Considers the Russian critical reception of Leskov's fiction, particularly its denunciation by ideologues of the political Left and Right.

Ingham, Norman W. "The Case of the Unreliable Narrator: Leskov's 'White Eagle.'" In *Studies in Russian Literature in Honor of Vsevolod Setchkarev,* edited by Julian W. Connolly and Sonia I. Ketchian, pp. 153-65. Columbus, Ohio: Slavica Publishers, 1986.
    Describes Leskov's "The White Eagle" as "a cleverly disguised satirical story of political corruption and conspiracy" masquerading as a simple ghost tale, then evaluates Leskov's skilled use of unreliable and framed narrative in the work.

Lantz, K. A. "Leskov's 'At the Edge of the World': The Search for an Image of Christ." *Slavic and East European Journal* 25, no. 1 (spring 1981): 34-43.
    Finds that Leskov's short story "At the Edge of the World" reflects a radical decline in Leskov's support of the Russian Orthodox Church.

———. Introduction to *The Sealed Angel and Other Stories,* by Nikolay Leskov, edited and translated by K. A. Lantz, pp. vii-xiii. Knoxville: University of Tennessee Press, 1984.

Brief discussion of Leskov's life, influences, and his short stories. Characterizes Leskov as "one of Russia's great satirists."

Lottridge, Stephen S. "Nikolaj Leskov's Moral Vision in the *Prolog* Tales." *Slavic and East European Journal* 18, no. 3 (fall 1974): 252-58.
    Evaluates the Christian morality of Leskov's *Prolog* tales, a series of nine short stories based upon a popular collection of hagiographic writings and didactic narratives.

Norman, R. Introduction to *"The Musk-Ox" and Other Tales,* by Nikolai Leskov, translated by R. Norman, pp. vii-xiii. London: Routledge, 1944.
    Praises Leskov's inspired and enduring delineations of character in his short fiction.

Pritchett, V. S. "A Russian Outsider." 1947. Reprinted in *The Living Novel & Later Appreciations,* pp. 420-26. New York: Random House, 1964.
    Surveys Leskov's stories in English translation.

Sperrle, Irmhild Christina. *The Organic Worldview of Nikolai Leskov.* Evanston, Ill.: Northwestern University Press, 2002, 288 p.
    Full-length examination of Leskov's adherence to "organic" philosophy in his writings.

Wigzell, Faith. "Leskov's *Soboryane*: A Tale of Good and Evil in the Russian Provinces." *Modern Language Review* 83, no. 4 (October 1988): 901-10.
    Probes Leskov's portrayal of the Orthodox Church and Russian cultural traditions in his chronicle *The Cathedral Folk.*

Additional coverage of Leskov's life and career is contained in the following sources published by Thomson Gale: *Dictionary of Literary Biography,* **Vol. 238;** *Literature Resource Center*; *Nineteenth-Century Literature Criticism,* **Vol. 25; and** *Short Story Criticism,* **Vol. 34.**

Indiana

George Sand

(Born Amandine Aurore Lucile Dupin Dudevant)
French novelist, short story writer, and playwright.

The following entry presents criticism of Sand's novel Indiana *(1832). For coverage of Sand's complete career, see* NCLC, *Volumes 2, 42, and 57.*

INTRODUCTION

One of the most celebrated writers and controversial personalities of nineteenth-century France, Sand wrote prolifically in a variety of genres, producing more than eighty novels, three collections of short stories, a four-volume autobiography, numerous essays and dramas, and thousands of letters. She remains best known for her novels, which have been praised for their insightful studies of character, vivid evocations of nature, and masterful prose style. Sand began her literary career as a collaborative writer of fiction; *Indiana* was her first independently composed novel and is frequently considered one of her finest. Featuring a generic mixture of Romantic idealism and bourgeois realism, *Indiana* concerns itself with a young woman caught in a loveless marriage to a much older man. Seeking to find passion elsewhere, she falls in love with the charming and handsome Raymon de Ramière who, instead of fulfilling her emotional needs, deceives and betrays her, leaving her devastated before she recognizes the gentle, reliable, and protective love of her stalwart cousin Ralph. A major work of French Romantic fiction, *Indiana* is noted for its discerning critique of women's traditional role in marriage and is generally regarded as a significant precursor to Gustave Flaubert's 1857 masterpiece *Madame Bovary.*

PLOT AND MAJOR CHARACTERS

Indiana opens in the manor house of retired army officer Colonel Delmare at his Lagny estate in the Brie region of France, east of Paris. Residing with the aging colonel are his chaste nineteen-year-old wife, Indiana, and her English cousin, Sir Rodolphe (Ralph) Brown. Sand's narrator explains that Colonel Delmare claimed his bride from the Île Bourbon (modern Réunion Island in the Indian Ocean, off the coast of Africa), saving her at the age of sixteen from a brutal father and returning with her to France. A foreigner in Europe, with little understanding of the intricacies of French society, Indiana suffers from severe depression. Contracted into a passionless marriage, she endures the insensitivities of her husband who, though less cruel and violent than her father, is more concerned with bird hunting and the welfare of his small factory at Lagny than the affairs of his young wife. Only the caring, if sometimes detached, friendship of her phlegmatic cousin Ralph and her more intimate contact with Noun, her foster sister and attendant, provide Indiana with daily comfort. Like her mistress, Noun is a native of the colonies and referred to as a Creole, or foreigner of mixed descent. Sand's description of Noun also suggests that she is African—unlike the white-skinned Indiana whose parents were European—a fact that contemporary critics interested in the racial dynamics of the novel have found significant.

A quiet evening at Lagny is disturbed as Colonel Delmare and Ralph go in search of what they believe to be a thief on the manor grounds. Inside the house, Indiana and Noun hear a gunshot. Shortly thereafter the men return with a prowler wounded by Delmare's weapon. Only mildly injured, the alleged thief is revealed to be Monsieur Raymon de Ramière, a dashing young man of aristocratic lineage. As Indiana attends to his wounds, Raymon explains that he was indeed illegally on Delmare's property in order to spy on the Colonel's factory. The story, a lie that nonetheless satisfies Delmare, covers the truth of his presence: he is Noun's lover and sought to pay her a nocturnal visit. Having met the enchantingly beautiful Indiana, Raymon forgets his passion for Noun, which is supplanted by his immediate and overpowering desire for the Colonel's delicate young wife, in whom he likewise stirs feelings of love. As weeks pass, Raymon slowly plots his seduction of Indiana even as a distraught Noun endeavors to win him back. After luring Raymon into Indiana's bedchamber, Noun enjoys a night of passion with her former paramour. Their relationship is, nonetheless, at an end as Raymon's thoughts are fully concentrated on Indiana. In the same scene, he reveals his jealously of Ralph, noting a large portrait of him that hangs in Indiana's bedroom, diligently watching over her. In the days that follow Raymon remains dismissive of Noun.

She disappears, only to be discovered floating dead in the stream near Delmare's factory, having killed herself in the face of Raymon's betrayal.

Inconsolable after the loss of her dearest friend, Indiana falls deeper into depression. Ralph seeks to cheer her by taking her on a hunt with him, purchasing Raymon's horse for this purpose alone and then giving it to Indiana as a gift. Despite a momentary respite of happiness, Indiana's doubts magnify as her forbidden passion for the charming Raymon grows. Meanwhile, Ralph makes little effort to hide his dislike for Raymon as episodes of public flirtation between Indiana and the attractive young man about town escalate. After Colonel Delmare travels abroad in order to inquire into some distressing business matters with his Belgian partners in Antwerp, Raymon seizes the opportunity to seduce Indiana, but is interrupted by the unexpected return of her husband. As passions deepen between Indiana and Raymon, the financial ruin of Delmare's Belgian partners forces him to sell his property and manor at Lagny to Monsieur Hubert, an affluent industrialist. Subsequently, the Colonel decides to visit the Île Bourbon with his wife, taking her with him despite her protests. While they are away, Raymon, seeking to better his financial station, unexpectedly marries Laure de Nangy, the clever and highly capable adopted daughter of M. Hubert. Laure proves to be a cunning match for the scheming Raymon, and the two move into Lagny manor. When Indiana returns to her former home, she finds herself abruptly expelled by the new wife of the man she thought she loved. Forced to take refuge in a dreary hotel, Indiana expects to die there of despair until she is rescued by Ralph. After informing Indiana of her husband's death, Ralph professes his long hidden love for her. In a moment of impassioned madness, the two resolve to return to the Île Bourbon where they plan to commit suicide by plunging into Bernica gorge. Finding sanctuary in the secluded and remote colony after their journey, they recognize their deep, mutual affection for one another at Bernica, and instead decide to live out their lives in happiness far from the confines of conventional society.

MAJOR THEMES

Critics since Sand's time have recognized in *Indiana* a reflection of its author's rebellion against the bonds placed upon women in marriage. Freedom and self-determination in love and a rejection of socially proscribed gender roles are therefore generally seen as thematically central to the novel. Several scholars have also highlighted Sand's construction of a symbolic analogy between marriage and slavery in *Indiana,* and her representation of male-female relations as characterized by shifting moods of aggression, deceit, confrontation,

and submission. Indeed, the novel suggests the possibility that both love and marriage operate as oppressive and victimizing forces within a male-dominated society, and numerous scholars have highlighted the novel's juxtaposition of true (Indiana and Ralph) versus falsely perceived (Indiana and Raymon) love. Tensions between masculine and feminine principles are an additional focus of the novel, while commentators have also concentrated on the figure of Raymon de Ramière as integral to the work's critique of male duplicity. At first glance a sympathetic figure, Raymon later reveals himself to be a self-serving egoist who misuses the hierarchical structure of society to deceive, exploit, and seduce women. His capricious desires allow him to completely destroy Noun and to do nearly the same to Indiana prior to the intervention of Ralph. Additional thematic material in the novel includes its representation of dreaming, desire, wish fulfillment, and imaginative escapism, culminating in the retreat of Ralph and Indiana to a paradisiacal existence together in the French colonies. Lastly, the work demonstrates a political subtext from which its female characters are largely excluded. This occurs for the most part in the form of heated debates between Delmare, Raymon, and Ralph on the subject of post-revolutionary France, with each character respectively personifying the major political viewpoints of the period: Delmare embodying Napoleonic imperialism, Raymon the monarchism of the *ancien régime,* and Ralph the ideals of republicanism.

CRITICAL RECEPTION

Like Sand's novels that were to immediately follow it, including *Valentine* (1832), *Lélia* (1833), and *Jacques* (1834), *Indiana* was influenced by the Romantic narratives of Lord Byron and Jean-Jacques Rousseau in their depictions of passionate personal revolt against social conventions. Marked by Sand's critique of marriage and her incipient feminism, *Indiana* outraged some early British and American critics, but was extremely popular with the general reading public, prompting early reviewers to speculate as to the author's sex by identifying both "masculine" and "feminine" qualities in the novel's language and characterizations. In the contemporary period critics have preferred to argue the extent to which *Indiana* can be interpreted as a feminist novel, and many have studied Sand's manipulation of conventional gender categories through her transformations of Ralph and Raymon; the former emasculated then empowered, the latter suffering the opposite fate. The work has also been read as a critique of bourgeois domesticity and its circumscription of women within the household or private sphere. Concentrating further on character, modern scholarship has noted that Sand crafted the central personalities in *Indiana* from the stock figures of romance, with Raymon as a Don Juan type, the classic seducer, and Indiana as the weak feminine object of his irresistible passions. Sand, however, alters these clichés over the course of the novel, critics have asserted, by maintaining Indiana's control over her own sexuality and making Raymon subject to Laure de Nangy, a woman whose capacity for influence over others exceeds his own. In terms of the novel's genre, scholarly consensus has tended to view it as a combination of Romanticism and bourgeois realism, with commentators generally suggesting the prominence of the former in the work's thoroughgoing depiction of love-related themes, which overshadow any rendering of worldly practicalities. In this respect, *Indiana* has been said to owe a debt to the French Romance tradition stretching back to the courtly narratives of the Middle Ages. Its psychological portrayal of emotional relations between men and women, and weighty analysis of gender roles, however, attests to its realistic qualities. Still, the high romantic sentiment occasionally displayed in the novel—at, for instance, the moment in which Indiana and Ralph together decide to take their own lives at Bernica gorge—has been criticized as overwrought by modern standards. Likewise, the novel's somewhat awkward narrative construction has been assailed, particularly its anticlimactic conclusion, which appears to suggest a complete reversal of all that has proceeded it. Nevertheless, most contemporary critics have defended the overall aesthetic coherence of the novel, studying unifying elements within its narrative structure. The enigmatic qualities of the novel's masculine narrator has also led at least one commentator (Peter Dayan, 1998) to surmise that this unidentified figure may very well be Ralph, who through this interpretation becomes the central focus of both narrative point of view and character development in the novel. Another issue of interest to contemporary scholarship has been the novel's depiction of race. Centering on the figures of Indiana and Noun, both of whom are described as Creole (which can be taken to mean either an individual of mixed race or a European born in the French colonies), commentators have underscored Sand's analogous treatment of race and sexuality in the novel, elucidating her simultaneous critique of both gender and racial oppression. Finally, Sand's extensive use of natural imagery in *Indiana* has been interpreted as an abundant source of symbolic signification that both highlights the novel's central themes and prefigures the stylistic concerns of her later fiction.

PRINCIPAL WORKS

Rose et Blanche. 5 vols. [with Jules Sandeau] (novel) 1831

Indiana. 2 vols. (novel) 1832

Valentine. 2 vols. (novel) 1832

Lélia. 2 vols. (novel) 1833

Jacques (novel) 1834

André (novel) 1835

Leone Leoni (novel) 1835

Simon (novel) 1836

Lettres d'un voyageur [*Letters of a Traveller*] (prose) 1837

Mauprat (novel) 1837

L'Uscoque (novel) 1838

Spiridon (novel) 1839; revised, 1842

Gabriel (novel) 1840

*Les Sept Cordes de la lyre [*A Woman's Version of the Faust Legend: The Seven Strings of the Lyre*] (play) 1840

Le Compagnon du Tour de France. 2 vols. [*The Companion of the Tour of France*] (novel) 1841

Horace (novel) 1842

Consuelo (novel) 1843

La Comtesse de Rudolstadt (novel) 1844

Jeanne (novel) 1844

Le Meunier d'Angibault [*The Miller of Angibault*] (novel) 1845

Teverino (novel) 1845

Isidora (novel) 1846

La Mare au diable [*The Haunted Marsh*] (novel) 1846

Le Péché de Monsieur Antoine (novel) 1846

François le champi [*The Country Waif*] (novel) 1848

La petite Fadette. 2 vols. [*Little Fadette: A Domestic Story*] (novel) 1849

Le Château des désertes (novel) 1851

Les Maîtres sonneurs [*The Bagpipers*] (novel) 1853

Histoire de ma vie. 4 vols. [*My Life*] (autobiography) 1854-55

La Daniella (novel) 1857

Elle et lui [*She and He*] (novel) 1859

Le Marquis de Villemer [*The Marquis of Villemer*] (novel) 1861

Valvèdre (novel) 1861

Tamaris (novel) 1862

Mademoiselle de Quintinie (novel) 1863

Le Dernier Amour (novel) 1867

Mademoiselle Merquem (novel) 1868

Césarine Dietrich (novel) 1871

Nanon (novel) 1872

Contes d'une grandmère. 2 vols. (short stories) 1873-76

Ma soeur Jeanne [*My Sister Jeannie*] (novel) 1874

Flamarande (novel) 1875

Oeuvres autobiographiques. 2 vols. (autobiography and sketches) 1970

Correspondance. 26 vols. (letters) 1964-91

**This play was not produced on the stage; 1840 is the year of its publication.

CRITICISM

George Sand (essay date 1852)

SOURCE: Sand, George. Introduction to *Indiana,* translated by George Burnham Ives. 1900. Reprint, pp. ixx-xx. Chicago: Cassandra Editions, 1978.

[*In the following essay, originally written in 1852, twenty years after the first publication of* Indiana, *Sand responds to what she views as unfair attacks and false assessments made by the novel's critics.*]

I wrote *Indiana* during the autumn of 1831. It was my first novel; I wrote it without any fixed plan, having no theory of art or philosophy in my mind. I was at the age when one writes with one's instincts, and when reflection serves only to confirm our natural tendencies. Some people chose to see in the book a deliberate argument against marriage. I was not so ambitious, and I was surprised to the last degree at all the fine things that the critics found to say concerning my subversive purposes. Criticism is far too acute; that is what will cause its death. It never passes judgment ingenuously on what has been done ingenuously. It looks for noon at four o'clock, as the old women say, and must cause much suffering to artists who care more for its decrees than they ought to do.

Under all régimes and in all times there has been a race of critics, who, in contempt of their own talent, have fancied that it was their duty to ply the trade of denouncers, of purveyors to the prosecuting attorney's office; extraordinary functions for men of letters to assume with regard to their confrères! The rigorous measures of government against the press never satisfy these savage critics. They would have them directed not only against works but against persons as well, and, if their advice were followed, some of us would be forbidden to write anything whatsoever.

At the time that I wrote *Indiana,* the cry of Saint Simonism was raised on every pretext. Later they shouted all sorts of other things. Even now certain writers are forbidden to open their mouths, under pain of seeing the police agents of certain newspapers pounce upon their work and hale them before the police of the constituted powers. If a writer puts noble sentiments in the mouth of a mechanic, it is an attack on the bourgeoisie; if a girl who has gone astray is rehabilitated after expiating her sin, it is an attack on virtuous women; if an impostor assumes titles of nobility, it is an attack on the patrician caste; if a bully plays the swashbuckling soldier, it is an insult to the army; if a woman is maltreated by her husband, it is an argument in favor of promiscuous love. And so with everything. Kindly brethren, devout

and generous critics! What a pity that no one thinks of creating a petty court of literary inquisition in which you should be the torturers! Would you be satisfied to tear the books to pieces and burn them at a slow fire, and could you not, by your urgent representations, obtain permission to give a little taste of the rack to those writers who presume to have other gods than yours?

Thank God, I have forgotten the names of those who tried to discourage me at my first appearance, and who, being unable to say that my first attempt had fallen completely flat, tried to distort it into an incendiary proclamation against the repose of society. I did not expect so much honor, and I consider that I owe to those critics the thanks which the hare proffered the frogs, imagining from their alarm that he was entitled to deem himself a very thunderbolt of war.

James M. Vest (essay date January 1978)

SOURCE: Vest, James M. "Dreams and the Romance Tradition in George Sand's *Indiana*." *French Forum* 3, no. 1 (January 1978): 35-47.

[*In the following essay, Vest contends that far from simply being a work of literary realism, as Sand suggested in her early preface to the novel,* Indiana *is a "strange blend of realism and fantasy" concerned principally with dreams and wish fulfillment.*]

Dreams lie close to the heart of *Indiana.* More than sixty passages mention «rêve(r)» or «songe(r)» in the oneiric sense. Singly, many of these passages are crucial to plot or character development in the novel. Together, they contribute an element of thematic unity to the work. These references to nocturnal dreams and daydreaming may also help to resolve certain problems traditionally associated with the reading of this text, notably its «awkward» conclusion, its «loose» narrative structure and style, and its genre.

I

Indiana is essentially a book of wish fulfillment, in which most of the principal characters are endowed with a certain «faculté d'illusions» (p. 250)[1]. The Creole heroine is depicted as an «âme impressionnable,» a «femme rêveuse» who is sensitive to the «mystères» and «fantômes» of the night (p. 35). Raymon de Ramière is also portrayed as a dreamer (pp. 58-61), who would like to conquer her heart by insinuating himself into her dreams: «Quand tu rêvais d'un ami à l'île Bourbon, c'était de moi que tu rêvais» (p. 76). The stages of Raymon's amatory conquests over both Indiana and her servant Noun are noted in terms of sleeping and waking, sweet dreams and troubled sleep (pp. 68, 75, 87-89, 101, 135, 177, 183-84, 193, etc.). Indiana gradually becomes aware of the perfidy of her lover and attempts to tear herself away. Still, Raymon's appeal is strong, and she dreams of leaving her tyrannical husband for him (pp. 249-50, 272-73). She eventually escapes from the family retreat in the Indian Ocean and returns to France only to discover the extent of Raymon's duplicity: another woman has taken her place.

Of the «trois personnes rêveuses» mentioned in the novel's opening sentence, two come into their own as dreamers only in the final chapters. The night of his death, Indiana's churlish husband, Colonel Delmare, makes his sole helpful statement; and he makes it in his sleep. It is an ominous statement from the realm of his dreams: «Il rêvait en ce moment, et dit d'une voix faible et triste:—Prends garde à cet homme, il te perdra . . .» (p. 281). Finally, in the concluding chapters, the once lethargic Sir Ralph Brown emerges as the novel's true leading man. He becomes winningly gallant and persuasive precisely at the moment he is revealed to be a dreamer compatible with Indiana's own dream quest: «Le Ralph . . . qu'elle écoutait maintenant lui semblait un ami qu'elle avait vu jadis dans ses rêves» (p. 320; cf. pp. 325, 331, 333, 336). Since the colonel is now dead, Ralph and Indiana are free to pursue together their «rêves déliran[t]s» (p. 405).

Ranging from the commonplace to the profound, the recurrent oneiric references in *Indiana* help establish a visionary atmosphere where reverie and fantasy eventually become powerful enough to withstand society's persistent assaults. Nowhere is the dreamer's capacity for imaginative escape better illustrated than in the description of Indiana's reveries on île Bourbon. There, at sunset, on an isolated mountain overlooking the sea, she fantasizes to the point of ecstasy:

> La vue de la mer, tout en lui faisant mal, l'avait fascinée de son mirage magnétique. Il lui semblait qu'au delà de ces vagues et de ces brumes lointaines la magique apparition d'une autre terre allait se révéler à ses regards. Quelquefois les nuages de la côte prirent pour elle des formes singulières . . . d'autres fois c'étaient des flocons de nuées roses qui, dans leurs formes changeantes, présentaient tous les caprices d'architecture d'une ville immense. L'esprit de cette femme s'endormait dans les illusions du passé. . . . Un étrange vertige s'emparait alors de sa tête. Suspendue à une grande élévation au-dessus du sol de la côte, et voyant fuir sous ses yeux les gorges qui la séparaient de l'Océan, il lui semblait être lancée dans cet espace par un mouvement rapide, et cheminer dans l'air vers la ville prestigieuse de son imagination. Dans ce rêve, elle se cramponnait au rocher qui lui servait d'appui; et pour qui eût observé . . . elle eût offert tous les symptômes de la folie.

(pp. 249-50)

The forcefulness of her «magique apparition» lies in its evocation of a reality not physically present. It gradually creates images which transcend what is physically perceived and manages to validate the dreamer's aspirations. The waves, the clouds, and the mist all become visual correlatives for Indiana's longings. The effect of her act of imaginative transcendence is to transport her far beyond the lulling visions of casual daydreaming. There is a definite progression from reverie through a strange maelstrom of emotion and imagination to the very brink of madness. In this process, it is the emotional component, «le désir dans toute son intensité dévorante,» which effectively reifies illusion (p. 250).

Immediately after this moving portrait of psychic deliverance, the narrator indicates the importance of hopes and dreams but decries their futility when misdirected: «Elle vécut ainsi des semaines et des mois sous le ciel des tropiques, n'aimant, ne connaissant, ne caressant qu'une ombre, ne creusant qu'une chimère» (p. 250). Since the vicissitudes of the heroine's infatuation with this «chimère» form the principal subject of *Indiana,* we may wonder why an exotically beautiful person of her nature should waste herself on a scoundrel like Raymon. It may be because he, too, poses as a dreamer. His penchant for imagination and fantasy is evident, particularly in his dealings with women. His dreams figure prominently in his early social encounters with Madame Delmare (pp. 59, 60, 76-77) and in his affair with her servant Noun (pp. 85-90). But, unlike Indiana, Raymon adulterates, suppresses, and denies his dreams. The narrator finds him guilty of contaminating his legitimate dreams with «ses méditations politiques» and «ses rêves d'ambition et de philosophie» (p. 118; cf. pp. 124, 126, 134-35).

Sir Rodolphe Brown gradually replaces Raymon as chief object of Indiana's thoughts and desires as he presents himself as a dreamer and a suitable counterpart to Indiana. The emergence of Sir Ralph the dreamer becomes noticeable in the pages immediately following the description of Indiana's grand, misguided ecstasy, quoted above. Ralph now begins to resemble the great romantic heroes: at one with nature, he is a man haunted by sad memories, a melancholic dreamer, a wanderer battling society and «l'arbitraire de sa destinée» (p. 252). The final transformation into dreamer-hero is not completed, however, until he opens his heart to Indiana and recounts his life story in terms of his growth as a dreamer. Sir Ralph gains force and persuasiveness because he has learned to dare to dream. When he finally tells Indiana of his dreams and weeps with her by the waterfall of Bernica (pp. 333-35), she recognizes in him a being worthy of her trust and hope, worthy of sharing her ultimate dream. Together the two prepare to plunge into the torrent.

* * *

The final pages of *Indiana* deserve special attention. In these pages, the dreamers' dual achievement is revealed. With the recognition scene in Chapter 29, the pace and direction of the narrative change abruptly. Accepting each other as true dreamers, Indiana and Ralph come to realize that they have not only successfully rejected and eluded society's demands but have also, in a profound and disturbing way, discovered themselves. At last they are free to become partners in a final quest for fulfillment, in death. With the shock of recognition, the earlier dissonant tone of combat against repression or falsification of dreams gives way to a consummating *Liebestod* of dream coupling, as they embrace and prepare to die (p. 338).

The penultimate chapter's emotional crescendo is followed by the final chapter's sustained mood of integration and serenity. The cycle of conflict is completed in the last chapter, where the dreamers reappear, hale and hearty after their symbolic walk to the brink of destruction, and they seem at last to be socially acceptable. Society's initial ascendancy over instincts and emotions is finally reversed as the dreamers settle into a life of personal bliss and receive society's representative, the narrator.

Sand's narrator has traveled to île Bourbon «pour aller rêver dans les bois sauvages» (p. 339). He is an apprentice, eager to learn from the master dreamers. He immediately recognizes Sir Ralph as a figure from his own dreams and feels magnetically drawn to him (p. 345). Ralph offers two «explanations» for the couple's survival, one rational, the other purely fanciful: «Un médecin vous dirait peut-être qu'un vertige très supposable s'empara de ma tête et me trompa dans la direction du sentier. Pour moi . . . j'aime mieux croire que l'ange d'Abraham et de Tobie, ce bel ange blanc, aux yeux bleus et à la ceinture d'or, que vous avez vu souvent dans les rêves de votre enfance, descendit sur un rayon de la lune, et que, balancé dans la tremblante vapeur de la cataracte, il étendit ses ailes argentées sur ma douce compagne» (p. 349). Here the scientific logic of reason confronts the imaginative logic of fantasy. But imagination triumphs, and the narrator is prepared to accept the more fantastic explanation. Ralph persuasively replies to all of the narrator's objections—which are really those of society—and suggests that the couple's example might serve as a model for others who share their vision. *Indiana* concludes with Ralph's appeal to the narrator to ponder these mysteries as he goes forth into the world.

At least two major developments are suggested in *Indiana*'s conclusion. First the narrator is charged to take his newly-discovered revelations back into the world. Implicit in this commission is the idea that the narrator may perpetuate the couple's dream and that *Indiana* itself is one means of spreading the good news. A second development involves Indiana and Ralph, who are, in a sense, transfigured. In this chapter it appears that they are at last vindicated—certainly in the eyes of the narrator and possibly in the eyes of the world when it learns the dreamers' story. They have, in a sense, conquered death and society. Now, as their vision of truth becomes not just acceptable, but potentially universalized, their existence is shown to surpass that of mere mortals. They are portrayed as superior beings in their island paradise (pp. 340-42, 345-53). Somewhat like the dreamer in Victor Hugo's poem «Ce qu'on entend sur la montagne,» they can now oppose to civilization's strident, ephemeral noises the eternal truths revealed to those who sit receptively on a mountain by the sea.

Maligned as «factice, surajouté, irréel»[2], *Indiana*'s apparently inconclusive conclusion actually continues the dream imagery of the earlier chapters and fulfills the theme of dreams as an instrument of self-knowledge and transcendance. This chapter represents the culmination of the novel's central movement: a progression (in Northrop Frye's terms) from visualizing and questing after a better world to a reflective, idyllic view from above[3]. The concluding chapter expresses a spirit of freedom and integration, while allowing renewed and improved contact with the social order. Full of peace and light, it acclaims accomplishment and heralds happiness ever after.

In these respects, the ending of *Indiana* is typical of the finales of romance, that is, fairy tales and longer adventure romances like *Daphnis and Chloe* or medieval *romans courtois*. There are several reasons for interpreting *Indiana* in light of this generic tradition. Such an interpretation is useful in explaining not only the function of the conclusion but also the use of certain stylistic features of the work. However, it also raises the problems of assessment of *Indiana*'s «realism» and its relationship to the romance tradition[4].

II

Ample textual evidence contradicts the following statements made about *Indiana* by the author at the time of its first appearance: «[C'est] un récit fort simple où l'écrivain n'a presque rien créé»; «C'est de la vie ordinaire, c'est de la vraisemblance bourgeoise»[5]. A host of narrative features—including rampant exoticism, emotionalism, lack of chronological and naturalistic accuracy, and attention paid to an individual's malaise, aspirations and dreams—discourage us from ranking *Indiana* among the nineteenth century's great realistic novels. There is also evidence to suggest that George Sand did not, in actuality, believe her own proclamations of *Indiana*'s «vraisemblance.» Most notably, numerous explicit claims of veracity or verisimilitude, present throughout the earliest editions of the work, were repressed by the author and did not appear in editions posterior to 1833 (see variants, pp. 370, 371, 376, 379, 383, 394-95, 397)[6]. Perhaps we may credit Mme Sand's early pretentions to realism to what Henry James called her «peculiar power of self-defense, her constant need to justify, to glorify»[7].

In *Indiana* historical factuality and objectivity are repeatedly subverted by manifestations of that «faculté d'illusions» mentioned earlier. Although references to contemporary affairs play a part in the narrative, they are often glossed over or subordinated to more pressing emotional realities (e.g., pp. 55, 64-65, 113, 120, 259, 265)[8]. The objectivity of these allusions is often undercut by subcurrents of irony, bombast, «la rhétorique fleurie» (p. 158), and blatantly subjective judgments on the part of the narrator (especially pp. 66, 115-17, 132). A case in point, the most extensive passage of political discussion in *Indiana,* contains many sociologically verifiable details (pp. 155-61); but the immediacy of the political dispute is undermined by the use of the imperfect tense and generalizing expressions like «le soir,» and the value of the entire discussion is mocked by the narrator in a concluding sardonic apostrophe: «Heureux habitants des campagnes, s'il est encore des campagnes en France, fuyez, fuyez la politique, et lisez *Peau d'âne* en famille!» (p. 161). To Sand's narrator, fairy tales like *Peau d'âne* seem preferable to the mundane reality of corrupt politics and crass society.

Throughout *Indiana,* examples of the subordination of external reality to internal desires are readily apparent. In the intoxication of passion, Raymon sees an eighteenth-century country house as a «castel . . . qui avait une demitournure féodale,» and a serving girl becomes for him «une dame, une reine, une fée . . . une châtelaine du moyen âge» (p. 51). Indiana's appearance at the Parisian soirée where she meets Raymon on his own social territory is portrayed as a Cinderella-like «apparition» in a salon «que la lueur vive des bougies rendait féerique» (pp. 58-59). Events associated with the factory at Lagny are similarly veiled in fairy tale trappings. The factory at first serves as a convenient excuse for Raymon's appearance at Lagny; then the eerie, creaking sounds of its machinery guide Indiana ineluctably to Noun's floating body, and its spillway later recalls the haunting specter of the drowned girl (pp. 102, 126). We never learn what is manufactured there; nor do we need to, because its function is purely romanesque.

Thus both structurally and thematically, the central movement of *Indiana* is away from the confines of civilization toward a personal realization of individual freedom. This development is symbolized by the story's movement from the heavily ornate sitting room described in the opening pages, through the deceptively alluring salons and by-ways of Paris, toward the wild, open, «natural» setting of the conclusion. The text richly supports George Sand's prefatory claims that *Indiana* fundamentally reflects «la volonté aux prises avec la nécessité; . . . l'amour heurtant son front aveugle à

tous les obstacles de la civilisation» (p. 9). As Sainte-Beuve noted, the «langage naturel» and «encadrement familier» which constitute «la partie vraie, . . . observée du roman» give way to «invention presque pure» and «fantaisie»[9]. Like Sand's narrator, we may ask «Quel roseau mobile est-ce donc que la vérité, pour se plier ainsi à tous les souffles?» (p. 267), and we may conclude with Pierre Salomon that in *Indiana* «le réel finit toujours par se pénétrer d'éléments imaginaires» (edition cited, p. xvi). Like her heroine, George Sand imaginatively «construisait son ajoupa solitaire sous l'abri d'une forêt vierge, au bord d'un fleuve sans nom» (p. 273).

The sentence just quoted reflects pertinent stylistic and generic issues associated with *Indiana.* With its references to the *ajoupa* and the nameless river, this sentence evokes not only the conceptual category «exoticism» but also that vague atmospheric and stylistic ambiance that we associate with Sand's writing. Conceptually, we may link *Indiana*'s use of documented biotic exoticism to that found in the romances of antiquity. A reading of the romances of Longus, Chariton, Xenophon, Heliodorus, or Achilles Tatius will reveal similarities with *Indiana*'s strange blend of realism and fantasy. In these ancient romances, although the narrative emphasis is on sentimental, melodramatic adventures, the settings may be surprisingly recognizable. Descriptions of unusual flora and fauna contribute to the exotic appeal of these romances while, in a sense, adding to their credibility. The narrative function served by Achilles Tatius' accounts of crocodiles and hippos or Heliodorus' minutely described giraffe are quite comparable to those served by Sand's depiction of wildlife on île Bourbon. They help establish a fairy tale atmosphere of combined wonder and belief[10].

Without asserting that *Indiana* is totally or systematically a romance, we may note many other points of resemblance with the romance tradition, as represented by the sentimental Greek romances of the early Christian era and also by the chivalric romances of the Middle Ages. *Sir* Ralph is a knight engaged in an idealistic quest where persistent devotion to his beloved lady overcomes formidable obstacles. Although at first he appears phlegmatic, toward the end of *Indiana* his role is in many ways reminiscent of that of loyal and courteous love servants in *Amadas et Ydoine, Floire et Blancheflor, Yvain,* and other medieval romances. As in the older romances, the heroine is exquisitely attractive, a superior woman reduced to the position of a slave; the villains are self-serving, possessive ogres; the lovers are philosophical, lachrymose, and given to madness. Moreover, we find much travel, characters with symbolic or sound-alike names, a highly emotional recognition scene, and even shades of Ovidian love-sickness and enchantment. These are stock elements of antique and medieval romances. There is precedent for *Indi-*

ana's overt social protest in Achilles Tatius[11], and the detailed description of the sitting room at the beginning of Sand's novel may be related to the tradition of *Ekphraseis* (literary representation of a work of art or interior decoration) with which several older romances begin.

Still, no list of superficial similarities constitutes proof that *Indiana* is a romance. In fact, in addition to the resemblances, there are also several differences. Unlike many older romances, *Indiana* does not emphasize trial scenes and formal *débats,* mechanical and alchemical paraphernalia, or disguises; its pace seems (somewhat) less frantic, its characters less stereotypic. The character of Noun differs markedly from that of the ever-faithful servant or second in the romances of Achilles Tatius and Chrétien de Troyes. Indiana is less intrepid than the indefatigable heroines of Greek romances, less self-assertive than medieval heroines like Guinevere or Galeron. Yet insofar as her dalliance and self-deception are the chief obstacles to be overcome in the narrative, Sand's story resembles those in Chrétien's *Yvain* and *Erec et Enide,* where Laudine and Enide must finally be rewon by their knights-errant and restored to respectability.

Indiana is unmistakably romance-like in one essential respect: its central narrative concern for struggle, renewal, and reintegration. Whether this work is viewed as a «novel of initiation,» a «quest story,» a «prose melodrama,» or a «romantic *Bildungsroman,*» its dominant modal and structural aspects are those of romance. Typical of romance, Indiana and Ralph are two «beautiful» people who must work their ways through a series of exotic, mysterious, or archetypal perils. Significantly, their final test occurs at the cataract of île Bourbon. Like the heroes of many romances they pass through/over/by the dangerous waters and arrive, united and blissful, at their goal. This «incredible» capacity for survival and spiritual renewal may seem as ludicrous to ardent rationalists today as it did to the author of *Candide*; nevertheless, it is an essential feature of romance because it assures progress toward a sublime, ideal order. In this progression, *Indiana*'s finale assumes its true importance. In the penultimate chapter Ralph and Indiana are fully prepared to die. Their reemergence from the brink of destruction confirms their passage to an ideal plane: through a ritual of renewal they surpass life's trials and achieve their dreams. In the final chapter they converse with their adherent, the narrator, and, as in most older romances, we have reason to believe that the social order is to be renewed—for the better—as their personal reintegration is announced to the world. When Indiana and Ralph receive the narrator, they appear enthroned, in state as it were, like the noble lovers in the antique romances or the knights and their ladies returned to Camelot.

The fact that the lovers' domicile is more like the «ajoupa solitaire» than a princely palace is thoroughly in keeping with the tone and style of Sand's novel. Throughout *Indiana* the process of «natural,» instinctive, and imaginative wish fulfillment is conveyed in terms of a prose style which is itself meandering and, in many cases, oneiric. Full of «caprices tortueux et . . . enlacements sans fin» (p. 24), the lengthy passage cited earlier (pp. 249-50) effectively captures the spirit of Indiana's fanciful reverie in much the same way as the phrase about the «ajoupa» summarizes thematically and stylistically *Indiana*'s penchant for wish fulfillment and romance.

Considered in this light, the style of the novel seems thoroughly appropriate to the content, especially where dreaming is concerned. Early in the story, when the narrator describes Sir Ralph's state of mind as he futilely seeks assistance for Indiana, who has fainted, the account reads like the transcript of a labyrinthine nightmare: «Ralph, épouvanté, l'éloigna du feu, la déposa sur une chaise longue, et courut au hasard, appelant les domestiques, cherchant de l'eau, des sels, ne trouvant rien, brisant toutes les sonnettes, se perdant à travers le dédale des appartements obscurs, et se tordant les mains» (p. 36; cf. p. 305). Here Sir Ralph is introduced in a way that suggests not only his present sense of impotence but also his continuing dedication to Indiana and his well-concealed sensitivity. Later the description of Raymon's hallucinations while seducing Noun in Indiana's boudoir vividly evoke an atmosphere of hypnagogic fantasizing (pp. 85-86). Later still, in the depiction of Indiana's night walk along the Seine, the heroine's situation is rendered in terms which convey the distraught woman's insecurity and delusions (pp. 219-20). This passage vividly communicates the hallucinatory character of Indiana's experience and permits us to perceive her basic sense of instability in a labile world. That fluid movement which is associated with flowing water and time and life is essential to Indiana Delmare because it promises to take her elsewhere. It is thus a metaphorical correlative for her dreams of a better tomorrow.

The waters which flow through *Indiana* are closely linked with dreams as a source of psychological, thematic, and structural unity for the work. The ebbing tide of consciousness and the unstable flow of life are evoked metaphorically by repeated references to the allure of undulating water and to the psychic limpidity of dreams. The image of Noun's floating body returns to haunt Raymon's dreams and Indiana's suicidal reveries by the Seine. In île Bourbon, Indiana's dreams of escape are inspired by the sea. Her dreams are finally realized beside the waters of Bernica[12].

Sand's lovers would willingly sacrifice a princely palace for their «ajoupa solitaire . . . au bord d'un fleuve sans nom,» just as René would gladly swap all of Europe for the American wilds. Both stories concern «cette grande et terrible lutte de la nature contre la civilisation» (p. 272); their ideal is not one of happiness, but of self-fulfillment and freedom from society's constraints. Indiana's goals are vague: «un autre monde,» «une autre terre,» «un monde à part» (pp. 243, 249, 274). The dreams, reveries, visions, and longings which form *Indiana*'s structural core and animate its most memorable scenes evoke a fanciful world which is distinct from structured quotidian existence and is potentially superior to it. Freeing, sometimes savage, the imagination is associated with escaping from traditional views of social necessity. In *Indiana,* dreaming is seen as mysterious, compelling, and positive, even when it approaches madness.

To come full circle, we may note that the romance tradition is intimately associated with dreams and images of fluidity. Achilles Tatius' story of Cleitophon and Leucippe contains a dozen references to predictive dreams, which contribute directly to plot development. Dreams are also an integral part of Xenophon's *Ephesiaca,* Chariton's *Chaereas and Callirhoe,* and Heliodorus' *Aethiopica,* Bédier's «reconstituted» Tristan legend, and Malory's *Morte Darthur*[13]. Used in a context of mysterious revelation, predictive dreams enhance the subjective, essentially primitive character of these works. They thus contribute to a spirit of elemental conflict and eventual purification, as do the dreams in *Indiana.*

Even more striking than the dreams mentioned in these works is the oneiric quality of style, tone, and narrative development characteristic of them. Typically, romances are free-flowing and loosely associational, like dreams. The illogical, dreamlike transformations which characterize many romances are antithetical to the etiological organizational principles underlying many realistic novels. The latter are often concerned with the detailed representation of everyday life in terms of a logical, causal sequence of events. The romances of antiquity and the Middle Ages, on the contrary, are essentially vague in setting and tone, and their occasional realistic details are subordinated to the vagaries of emotion and coincidence[14]. Many of their incidents and encounters occur by chance. The *vague* manner in which these romance tales unfold is comparable to that of reverie or a dream (*rêve(r)* ← Lat. *vagus* 'vagabond') rather than to the logical structure of rational thought.

This «illogical,» dreamlike structure also characterizes *Indiana,* where transition by means of coincidence is common (pp. 78, 152-53, 168, 188, 194, 219-20, etc.). In a structure dominated by coincidence, time flow may be jumpy, nondirectional, and highly subjective. Thus, in *Indiana* chronological precision is occasionally neglected for romanesque effect (pp. 172, 238), and clock time is often subordinated to emotional time. Temporal reality frequently drifts into timeless reverie or appears condensed, attenuated, or disjunctive, as in a dream (pp. 58-61, 83, 85-89, 126, 175-77, etc.). Romance narratives develop according to a nonchronometric dynamic process, closer in nature to the raw emotionality of dreams than to waking notions of causality. The «never-never» land of romance is reminiscent of that described in Poe's «Dream-Land»: «a wild, weird clime that lieth sublime, / Out of SPACE—out of TIME.» When mundane awareness is temporarily suspended, the imagination is freed to confront the archetypal forces of the subconscious. The nonetiological, nonsequential aspect of *Indiana*'s style reflects the subjective and highly associational style and form of dreams.

III

If there is a single organizing principle or dynamic force in *Indiana,* it may well be «le désir dans toute son intensité dévorante.» This concept is reflected in the stylistic, thematic insistence on dreams, fluidity, and struggle toward a better existence. It is equally evident in the central narrative movement of *Indiana* away from the oppressive, conflicting demands of society toward personal integration and fulfillment in «un monde à part.» This basic movement may be equated with that of traditional romance, where disintegrative forces are combatted and, after many trials and much roaming, overcome. As in romance, an improved social order is implied at the end of *Indiana* through the reunion of the exemplary couple. In their meeting with society's representative, the dreamer-narrator, the transformation which has occurred on the personal level is also promised at the collective level. In the fundamental «lutte de la nature contre la civilisation» dreams are a vehicle for escape, wish fulfillment, and ultimate reintegration. As in older romances, the dreams in *Indiana* supplement, through their primitive emotional power and associational fluidity, the themes of struggle and reunification. If the dreams in *Indiana* tend to be compensatory, hallucinatory, or anagogic rather than predictive in nature, it may be because the author chose to emphasize the mysterious psychological power of «la faculté d'illusions.» Here dreams are perceived as an agent of transformation, a function of «le désir dans toute son intensité,» which offers hope for both personal integration and transcendance of «tous les obstacles de la civilisation.» In sum, George Sand used elements of the romance tradition for her own purposes and in her own way: eclectically, whimsically, in a manner befitting an admirer of Bernardin de Saint-Pierre and the early works of Balzac[15].

Many of the dreams and romance conventions employed in *Indiana* have strong emotional, hallucinatory, even psychotic reverberations, again associated with «le désir dans toute son intensité dévorante.» Throughout *Indiana* dreams are a manifestation of a strong desire for what one lacks. Their significant role in this fiction may reflect the author's personal concerns in the early 1830's, when she was breaking away from her husband, establishing herself in Paris, and creating the pen name George Sand. The insistent presence in the text of dream psychology, love of natural simplicity and spontaneity, and romance archetypes confirms her own judgments as to the central thrust of **Indiana**: it represents «*les passions* comprimées, ou . . . supprimées par *les lois*; c'est la volonté aux prises avec la nécessité» (p. 9)[16].

In this depiction of struggle, hope, and renewal, the delicate balance between actuality and imagination shifts gradually but pervasively toward the mysterious, the oneiric, the ideal. Dreams constitute an important link in this progression from the empirical toward the imaginary and the archetypal. The process is itself one of «illogical» impulse and chance association rather than one of «realistic» etiology. As the balance shifts toward romance, dreams become real and lead toward «un autre monde,» where the individual is freed to pursue an ideal of transcendency which is less evasive than visionary. Indiana's search for this «autre monde» involves her in a compelling search for an «autre moi»[17]. In this respect, **Indiana** is allied to Hugo's «rêveur sacré» and Olympio as well as to the dreamers in Nerval's *Aurélia* and «El Desdichado,» and looks ahead to the more sophisticated dream visions of Baudelaire, Rimbaud, Lautréamont, and Mallarmé. The dreams in **Indiana** not only provide relief from aggressive, confining social pressures; they also relate the dreamer to basic forces of the universe, thus leading to peace, harmony, and reintegration[18].

Notes

1. Parenthetical page references throughout this essay are to Pierre Salomon's critical edition of *Indiana* (Paris: Garnier Frères, 1962).

2. Béatrice Didier, «Ophélie dans les chaînes: Etude de quelques thèmes d'*Indiana*,» in Léon Cellier, ed., *Hommage à George Sand* (Paris: Presses Universitaires de France, 1969), p. 89. This statement is typical of many pejoratives raised against the formal «gaucherie» of the so-called «epilogue» (cf. Salomon, pp. v-vi, xlix). One of the reasons the conclusion seems to clash with the rest of *Indiana* is the extensive use of first person assertions by the narrator in this chapter; it should be noted, however, that many other passages employing the same narrational device occur throughout the text in the several printings of the 1832 edition (being deleted in the Gosselin edition of 1833 and thereafter), and that some lengthy passages of first person commentary still remain (e.g., pp. 202-03).

3. *Anatomy of Criticism* (New York: Atheneum, 1969), pp. 192, 200-02.

4. Among the sources which have informed the discussion of the nature of romance here and throughout this essay are: 1) Frye's *Anatomy of Criticism* and *The Secular Scripture: A Study of the Structure of Romance* (Cambridge, Mass.: Harvard Univ. Press, 1976); 2) essays included in Eleanor Terry Lincoln, ed., *Pastoral and Romance: Modern Essays in Criticism* (Englewood Cliffs: Prentice-Hall, 1969), especially F. O. Matthiessen's «The Crucial Definition of Romance,» and Richard Chase's «Novel vs. Romance»; 3) articles in Peter Haidu, ed., *Yale French Studies*, 51 (1974): *Approaches to Medieval Romance*, notably W. T. H. Jackson's «The Nature of Romance,» and Norris Lacy's «Spatial Form in Medieval Romance»; 4) Erich Auerbach, *Mimesis*, trans. Willard Trask (Princeton: Princeton Univ. Press, 1953); 5) Urban T. Holmes, *A History of Old French Literature from the Origins to 1300* (New York: Russell & Russell, 1962); 6) Ben Edward Perry, *The Ancient Romances* (Berkeley: Univ. of Calif. Press, 1967); and 7) the romances cited.

5. The first quotation is from the preface to the first edition of *Indiana* (p. 6; cf. pp. 9 and 10); the second is from a letter to Emile Regnault of 27 February 1832, when *Indiana* was in progress (Georges Lubin, ed., *George Sand: Correspondance, Tome II (1832-juin 1835)* [Paris: Garnier Frères, 1966], pp. 46-48). The principal early editions of *Indiana* are: (first) Roret et Dupuy, May 1832; Gosselin, 1833; Perrotin, 1842; and Hetzel, 1853.

6. Cf. also other textual changes in *Indiana* (notes 2 and 10). Additional circumstantial evidence includes the conventional nature of Sand's claims (e.g., «l'écrivain n'est qu'un miroir,» [p. 6], a *topos* common to Stendhal [*Le Rouge et le Noir*, II, 19], George Eliot [*Adam Bede*, XVII], *et al*); and especially Sand's assessment of «Le Réalisme» in 1857: «Quand les réalistes ont proclamé qu'il fallait peindre les choses telles qu'elles sont, ils n'ont rien prouvé pour ou contre la beauté et la bonté des choses de ce monde . . . car le monde vrai est sans relâche enveloppé de nuages et de rayons qui l'éclairent ou le ternissent avec une merveilleuse variété d'effets» (rpt. in *Questions d'art et de littérature* [Paris: Calmann-Lévy, 1878], p. 293).

7. *French Poets and Novelists* (London: Macmillan, 1919), p. 182; cf. pp. 155, 156, 183.

8. Mario Maurin refers to «la valeur symbolique de l'engagement politique» in this novel in «Un Modèle d'*Indiana*?», *French Review*, 50 (1976), 317-20; however, the political *arrière-plan* is not so cohesive a «symbolic» reflection of Indiana's personal struggle as Maurin appears to suggest.

9. In a review of *Indiana* published in *Le National,* 5 October 1832 (quoted by Salomon, p. xlviii); cf. similar comments by Musset, cited by Salomon, p. xlvii. Sainte-Beuve was incorrect in one respect: the fantastic tendencies of romance are not limited to the latter chapters of the book, as he suggests, but are already present and dominant in the first chapter (pp. 26-28). The tension between realism and romance in some other works by Sand is suggested by Kenneth Cornell in «George Sand: Emotion and Idea,» *Yale French Studies,* 13 (1954), 93-97.

10. Although numerous errors in her descriptions of topography, biota, and climate were brought to her attention and corrected for Hetzel's edition (1853), many inaccuracies remain (see Salomon's notes, pp. 248, 251, 254, 273, 276, 283, 318, 327, 340, 342); moreover, the function of these and other naturalistic references in *Indiana* is ultimately exotic and romanesque rather than concrete and realistic.

11. S. Gaselee, trans. (London: Heinemann, 1917): VI, 22; cf. VI, 12-13 and VIII, 5.

12. Some aspects of the aquatic imagery in *Indiana* are treated in Östen Södergård, *Essais sur la création littéraire de George Sand* (Uppsala: Almqvist & Wiksells, 1962), pp. 97-99; and in Didier, pp. 89-92.

13. Like *Indiana* all of these romances emphasize fluidity, and particularly the sea. There are romances which ignore dreams or scorn them as deceptive or debilitating, but these are often landlocked adventures, where Channel and Sea are not taken seriously: e.g., Chrétien's *Yvain,* where dreaming is related to falsehood or cowardice and openly derided (W. Foerster, ed., [Halle: Niemeyer, 1926], ll. 610-11, cf. ll. 171, 2503-07), and *Sir Gawain and the Green Knight,* where the bed and sleeping are explicitly linked with deception and Gawain's one opportunity for predictive dreaming is interrupted (J. R. R. Tolkien and E. V. Gordon, eds. [Oxford: Clarendon Press, 1925], III, 25, cf. III, 24).

14. These generalizations, which reflect a consensus of the writers mentioned in note 4, are based most directly on the formulations of Frye.

15. Although some debt to Bernardin's *Paul et Virginie* and *La Chaumière indienne* and perhaps to Balzac's *Le Rendez-vous* and *La Femme abandonnée* may be detected in *Indiana,* the question of contemporary influences is beyond the scope of this article (see Salomon, pp. iii, xi, xvi, *et passim*).

16. Although *Indiana* was the first novel to bear the nom de plume «G. Sand,» it was not Aurore

Dupin's first literary expression of interest in dreams; among her earlier works was the unfinished novel, *L'Histoire du rêveur,* which was printed in 1931 (Paris: Editions Montaigne).

17. Rimbaud's celebrated formula «*Je* est un autre» may be considered an example of the *Übertragung* effect, a universal component of oneiric self-projection, «un transfert intérieur [qui] nous change en un autre nous-mêmes» (Gaston Bachelard, *Poétique de la rêverie* [Paris: Presses Universitaires de France, 1960], p. 49. For other possible cross-currents with literary dreamers, see Albert Béguin, *L'Ame romantique et le rêve* (Paris: Corti, 1960), and Cellier, ed., *passim.*

18. This essay has profited from a Research and Creative Activities Grant made by Southwestern at Memphis and from the patient support of my wife Nancy. Portions of it were presented as a paper at the annual convention of the Modern Language Association of America, December 1975.

Tamara Álvarez-Detrell (lecture date 17 April 1980)

SOURCE: Álvarez-Detrell, Tamara. "*Indiana*: The Spanish Connection to George Sand." *University of South Florida Language Quarterly* 20, nos. 3-4 (spring-summer 1982): 15-17.

[*In the following essay, originally presented as a lecture on April 17, 1980, Álvarez-Detrell notes the extensive influence of Golden Age Spanish literature on the themes and characterizations of* Indiana, *particularly in its representation of social rebellion, individual self-worth, honor, and Don Juanism.*]

Most critics to date have exploited the autobiographical elements of George Sand's first novel, **Indiana.** Others have concentrated their efforts on the social aspect, analyzing the author's views on the situation of women, the abuses of marriage and contemporary laws.[1] The influence that Spain and Spanish literature may have exerted on the novelist has been all but neglected. It is the aim of this study to show the possible existence and nature of these cultural ties and to point out themes, ideas, or literary techniques present in **Indiana,** whose origin can be traced to Spanish tradition.

By taking a brief glance at the author's infancy, we shall be able to establish the source of these Iberian elements. In 1807 Aurore's father was sent to Spain as aide-de-champ to Murat; his wife and daughter soon followed. The stay in Madrid was brief, but the experience was intense—as Winmar points out: "the little girl stored in her impressionable mind the gloomy romance of a desolated nation"[2]. It can be logically assumed that during this three-month stay in a palace, the future George Sand was exposed to the language and many of the customs of the host country. Salomon believes that "Aurore devait garder le souvenir des montagnes d'Asturie et du luxueux palais de Goday, où Murat logeait avec son état-major."[3]

The attraction to this country enhanced by the travel experience to and from Madrid would last into her adult life and the fascination it held would be responsible for her future trips to Barcelona and Majorca.

It has been documented that Sand knew several foreign languages, but Spanish is never specifically mentioned.[4] Lacking formal training, however, does not exclude the possibility of becoming familiar with its rudiments, or even of possessing a basic conversational skill. Her contacts with the Spaniards began when she was three or four years old, and continued throughout her life; her circle of friends and intimates included several peninsular actresses and singers. That this exerted an influence on her works is evident when we consider not only *Indiana,* but *Consuelo* and the *Comtesse de Rudolstadt* as well.

The rôle of the Romantic movement in establishing a Spanish backdrop must not be overlooked. To the leaders of French Romanticism, Spain was the country of their choice, "the land of the hidalgos and of passionate women, of poetry, chivalry, romance and song. Victor Hugo made it the setting of his best-known tragedy . . . Spanish dances and Spanish costumes drew crowds in Paris . . . Spain was the dreamland of the poets, the Avalon of French Romanticism."[5] In 1830, George Sand was in Paris, two months after the première of *Hernani ou l'honneur castillan,* right in the midst of this dynamic literary movement. But even before she left for Paris, she had been surrounded by people who had contact with the literary and political worlds and who gathered at Nohant to read aloud, to discuss Hugo and the Romantics: "On faisait souvent des lectures à haute voix et on s'enthousiasmait surtout pour le chef du romantisme, Victor Hugo."[6]

Sand was influenced in her studies, her life and her work by writers who in turn owed some of their themes and ideas to the great volume of Spanish literature: Corneille, Molière, Hugo, Musset, Mérimée, Shakespeare, Byron and Hoffmann, among others. The French writers that were her contemporaries had produced works of Spanish inspiration prior to the realization of *Indiana.* Mérimée published the *Theatre de Clara Gazul* in 1825 and *La famille Carvajal* in 1828; Musset's *Contes d'Espagne et d'Italie* appeared in 1829. Hugo, in his 18-29 preface to *Cromwell,* adapts ideas from Lope de Vega's theatre, to include national themes, realistic customs, mixture of genres, moralizing, etc.; he is well acquainted with the works of Alarcón, Calderón,

Tirso and even Cervantes[7], as evidenced by *Notre Dame de Paris,* published in 1831 and inspired by one of the renowned Castilian's *Exemplary Novels* (*La Gitanilla*). Moreover, it is common knowledge that Sand had read Byron's *Don Juan* and Hoffmann's tale *Don Juan* in translation in the autumn of 1830.[8] Even if George Sand knew no Spanish, she could not have escaped the ever-present Spain in her literary studies and surroundings; one may observe the influence of its ideas and customs throughout her works.

Van Thieghem states that only Spanish writers up to the Golden Age affected the French Romantics: ". . . les sources d'inspiration fournies par l'Espagne seront les mêmes que celles auxquelles avaient puisé nos écrivains avant 1780 . . . les œuvres littéraires espagnoles utilisées sont des œuvres anciennes qui datent au plus du dix-septième siècle."[9] The eighteenth century is, after all, only a period of decadence for Castilian letters. The German critic Bouterwerk points out that the Romantics respected the main characteristics of the borrowed literature.[10] Some of these traits will be found in *Indiana*: love as an omnipresent force, the violent nature of human passions, a supreme sense of personal honor and individual worth, and a lyrical way of dealing with religious themes. One reason for the strong presence of Spanish elements in the Romantic is the fact that the essence of Spanish literature has a natural romantic side.[11]

It must be recalled that *Indiana* was the first novel published under the name "George Sand", the work that provided the writer with a literary identity, one that was to be hers alone. The importance of a literary identity mirrors the value of a human identity. The desire for being known as an individual, for being respected for one's worth is of paramount importance to the Spanish character and, as we shall see later, predominates in Sand's novels. In order to analyze this, as well as other Spanish aspects, we shall observe the affair between Noun and Raymon and the marriage of Indiana and Delmare.

The affair between Noun and Raymon is reminiscent of the relationship between Tisbea or Aminta and Don Juan in Tirso de Molina's *The Trickster of Seville* (*El Burlador de Sevilla*). Tisbea, a fisherwoman (Act I) and Aminta (Act III) are seduced by Don Juan Tenorio, a noble who misleads them into believing that he is promising matrimony, all the while knowing that he will never marry beneath his social class. The personal charm plus the fairy-tale situation of a poor woman being loved by and married to an aristocrat are tempting to the low-class women and they fall for his guiles. In parallel fashion, Raymon offers the maid-servant Noun the illusion of love and the temptation of marrying a young, handsome, rich nobleman. Sand points out to the reader that the chance of realizing those dreams is very slim:

Il vous est difficile, peut-être, de croire que M. Raymon de Ramière, jeune homme brilant d'esprit, de talents et de grandes qualités, accoutumé au succès de salon et aux aventures parfumées, eût conçu pour la femme de charge d'une petite maison industrielle de la Brie un attachement bien durable.[12]

He was clever enough to appreciate the advantage of his noble birth. He is attracted to Noun, in love with love, so to say, but does not love the person: "[il] était amoureux de la jeune créole aux grands yeux noirs . . . amoureux, et rien de plus" (p. 33). Like Don Juan, he is enticed by the spirit of adventure without considering the consequences of his behavior or the feelings of the woman:

Le jour où il triompha de ce cœur facile, il entra chez lui effrayé de sa victoire, et, se frappant le front, il se dit:—'Pourvu qu'elle ne m'aime pas'.

(p. 33)

Remorse being alien to his Don Juanesque being, he would swear his undying love and devotion as "il la préférait aux reines du monde" (p. 33), all words which Noun's simple mind was all too ready to believe.

Sand's portrayal of Raymon includes a brief period of self-analysis, a hypothetical episode where the young man explores the possibility of an unequal marriage: "il avait bien songé à l'élever jusqu'à légitimer leur union" (p. 34), but then rejects it as incompatible with social tradition:

cet héroïsme de vertu ressemble à Don Quichotte brisant sa lance contre l'aile d'un moulin; courage de fer qu'un coup de vent disperse, chevalerie d'un autre siècle, qui fait pitié à celui-ci.

(p. 35)

The futility of his ephemeral thoughts is again underlined by the disparity of birth; a high-born lady who sacrifices her reputation shows courage, but a maidservant risks nothing by her unorthodox behavior. Don Juan repeatedly declares that love creates equality, but the generous thought is forgotten with the realization of his amorous intentions. In a similar manner, when Raymon's interest in Noun cools, so does his belief in the equality of love.

Raymon's behavior prior to the Noun episode corresponds to the bachelor adventures of Tirso's trickster; like Don Juan, he is an exceptional being, eloquent and seductive, rather, seductive because of his eloquence: "ce n'était pas la passion qui le rendait éloquent, c'était l'éloquence qui le rendait passionné" (p. 41). Sand describes his methodology: "Il se sentait du goût pour une femme et devenait éloquent pour la séduire et amoureux d'elle en la séduisant" (p. 48). In the same fashion, Don Juan would fall in love with the idea of loving and would fall out of love as soon as he became the lover. His predecessor, though dishonest in love, was courageous and had to prove his valor with sword, usually after tarnishing the reputation of noblewomen. Raymon, likewise, "avait fait par amour ce qu'on appelle des folies . . . il avait compromis des femmes établies très haut; il avait trois duels éclatants" (p. 41). Raymon and Don Juan are fearless, above blame or ridicule; their daring makes them irresistible to the high-born women, tired of the respectable and boring average nobleman: "Dans le monde, un homme capable de folie en amour est un prodige assez rare, et que les femmes ne dédaignent pas" (p. 41).

Tragedy shadows the frivolous ways of the young aristocrats, for while enjoying life to the fullest, they forget something called honor. In Spanish the term used is 'pundonor' or point of honor, the motivating force behind many violent acts; 'pundonor' places a heavy burden on the individual, mainly the woman, but by extension affects the honor or reputation of husband, father and brothers. This is a fragile concept for it depends on the opinions of others and not on the actual guilt or innocence of the person concerned. It is a clean mirror that society places before every individual, but which can be easily tarnished by the breath of evil gossip. Once suspected of dishonorable behavior, whether rightly or wrongly so, one's family's name is soiled and must be cleansed by blood.

There is much speculation as to the real existence of the honor code in Spain; but there is no doubt as to the wealth of literary material that deals with the concept of 'pundonor'. The Golden Age playwrights, mainly Lope, Tirso and Calderón, dramatized the causes and consequences of the practice, usually pointing out the dangers of such a strict code.[13] It is partly because of the idea of honor, or its appearances, that Noun drowns herself in Sand's novel and that the Commander is killed in Tirso's play. Indirectly, Raymon and society kill Noun, the same way in which Gonzalo's honor concept causes the duel with Don Juan resulting in the former's death.

Of particular interest to our study is the insistence of Spanish writers on the individual worth of a person, regardless of class. In the sixteenth and seventeenth centuries several comedias dealt with that very theme, an intrinsic principle of the Spanish character. Repeatedly, one finds the low-born peasant or villager proud in spite of the lack of a title of nobility, for, after all, there is an interior side to the concept of honor, an idea akin to self-esteem. This ideal is the other reason why Noun drowns herself: she has lost her self-esteem as a result of her actions. Honor being much more valuable to the Spaniard than life, she drowns herself; her death restores her honor and that of her mistress.

In the *Mayor of Zalamea* (*El Alcalde de Zalamea*) by Calderón the main character states that "life and property belong to the King but honor is the patrimony of the soul and the soul belongs only to God" (Act I); he feels that it is his duty to provide food and shelter to King and soldiers, but he owes his reputation to no one. In Sand's novel, Indiana is aware of the chains which society has placed on a married woman, of the privileges given her husband as master of the household, but she will not relinquish the mastery of her will. The creole has stayed out all night and part of the morning; upon her return she faces an irate husband who demands answers. The passage is significant enough to be quoted at length:

> —Daignez-vous m'apprendre, madame, où vous avez passé la matinée et peut-être la nuit?

> * * *

> —Non, monsieur, mon intention n'est pas de vous le dire.

> —En vérité, vous espérez me le cacher?

> —J'y tiens fort peu. Si je refuse de vous répondre, c'est absolument pour la forme. Je veux vous convaincre que vous n'avez pas le droit de m'adresser cette question.

At this point Delmare becomes furious and alludes to the power and authority he possesses, because he has a beard. Indiana's calm answer parallels the mayor's in the Spanish play:

> —Je sais que je suis l'esclave et vous le seigneur. La loi de ce pays vous a fait mon maître. Vous pouver lier mon corps, garroter mes mains, gouverner mes actions. Vous avez le droit du plus fort, et la société vous le confirme; mais sur ma volonté, monsieur, vous ne pouvez rien; Dieu seul peut la courber et la réduire.

> (p. 168)

George Sand has indeed grasped the essence of the Spanish spirit. Indiana rebels against social laws, but even more important is the awareness of her own worth as an individual; thus she makes a statement of her will. She is taking the responsibility for her life, for her actions. The internal honor, her self-esteem has become more powerful than the exterior honor, the social mirror; the psychological awakening looks down upon society's disapproval of her behavior. She has left the house and has reflected; finally she has come back because she wants to: "je l'ai fait de mon plein gré. Mon cousin m'a accompagnée ici, et non pas ramenée" (p. 169). The choice of words is as powerful in 1832 as it was during the Spanish Golden Age.

That George Sand was influenced by Spanish literature is obvious; had it been her intention to hide this debt, she would not have made three of the characters of *Indiana* Spanish. The fact that critics have overlooked this trait may be due to a general attitude of neglect toward Spain or to the sometimes indirect nature of the contact, for often the ideas reach her through a Byron or a Molière. The instances of Iberian presence in *Indiana* are by no means limited to those mentioned in this study, nor are they limited to the novel in question. Given this rôle that Spain played in the French Romantic movement it would have been indeed strange had it spared our novelist. As Van Thieghem points out:

> L'imitation des œuvres espagnoles a donné à beaucoup d'ouvrages de l'époque romantique une occasion de peindre les passions dans toute leur intensité, de donner aux personnages une certaine armature morale que peu d'autres littératures pouvaient leur offrir, quelque chose de noble et d'austère, d'ardent et de sombre.[14]

Notes

1. For example:

   Wladimir Karénine, *George Sand: Sa vie et ses œuvres* (Paris: Librairie Plon, 1899-1926), I, 359-378, and II-IV, passim;

   Elme Marie Caro, *George Sand,* transl. by Gustave Masson (Port Washington, N.Y.: Kennikat Press, 1970);

   André Maurois, *Lelia ou la vie de George Sand* (Paris: Hachette, 1952), 166-8 and passim;

   Joseph Barry, *Infamous Woman: The Life of George Sand* (Garden City, N.Y.: Anchor Press, 1978), pp. 132-3, 152-9 and passim.

   Her first novels, *Indiana, Valentine* and *Lélia* in particular, are classified as autobiographical; they also deal with women and the abuses of marriage. Even her contemporaries, Musset, Sainte Beuve and others, chose to see autobiographical elements.

2. Frances Winmar, *George Sand and Her Times* (New York: Garden City Publishing Company, 1945), p. 50.

3. Pierre Salomon, *George Sand* (Paris: Hatier, 1953), p. 9.

4. For example, Karénine (*George Sand,* I, 181) mentions English and Italian, and in volume III, 100, quotes an elegy written in English by George Sand; cf. André Maurois, *Lélia,* pp. 41-42 and passim, and also Curtis Cate, *George Sand: A Biography* (Boston: Houghton Mifflin Co., 1975), pp. 40-44 and passim.

5. Winmar, *George Sand,* p. 87.

6. Karénine, *George Sand,* I, 313.

7. Philippe van Tieghem, *Les influences étrangères sur la littérature française* (Paris: Presses universitaires de France, 1967), pp. 210-12.

8. Renée Weingarten, *The Double Life of George Sand: Woman and Writer* (New York: Basic Books, 1978), p. 38.

9. van Tieghem, *op. cit.,* p. 205.

10. Bouterwek, *Histoire de la littérature espagnole,* cited in van Tieghem, *op. cit.,* p. 206.

11. Sismondi, *De la littérature du midi de l'europe,* cited in van Tieghem, *op. cit.,* p. 207.

12. George Sand, *Indiana,* notes by Jean Fuzier (Paris: Delmas, 1948), p. 38.

   All quotes from this work will be based on this edition and will be indicated by page number following the complete citation.

13. Other examples of Spanish works where the concept of pundonor plays a major part are *Fuenteovejuna* and *Peribañez* by Lope de Vega, *La venganza de tamar* by Tirso de Molina, and *El médico de su honra, El pintor de su deshonra, A Secreto agravio, Secreta venganza,* and others by Calderón de la Barca.

14. van Tieghem, *op. cit.,* p. 213.

Jeannee P. Sacken (essay date spring 1981)

SOURCE: Sacken, Jeannee P. "Nature Imagery as Narrative Structure in George Sand's *Indiana*." *Romance Notes* 21, no. 3 (spring 1981): 313-17.

[*In the following essay, Sacken suggests that Sand's use of natural imagery and geographic movement in* Indiana *underscores the novel's thematic shift from Indiana's repressive marriage to her regenerative relationship with Ralph.*]

At the end of **Indiana,** Sir Ralph and Indiana bid adieu to the narrator as he departs: "'Retournez au monde; si quelque jour il vous bannit, souvenez-vous de notre chaumière indienne.'"[1] This farewell recalls the geographical distance and the social differences between l'île Bourbon and Paris, the gorge of Bernica and the château of Lagny; moreover, it emphasizes the presence of nature imagery as a reinforcement of the thematic development. The incidents which occur on l'île Bourbon, as well as in Paris and at Lagny, convey the theme of physical and spiritual enslavement—a contrast to the Bernica described by Ralph: "'Tous nos jours se ressemblent; ils sont tous calmes et beaux; ils passent rapides et purs comme ceux de notre enfance. . . . La majeure portion de nos revenus est consacrée à racheter de pauvres noirs infirmes'" (p. 352). It is at Bernica that Ralph and Indiana discover the happiness, love, and freedom which had eluded them in Paris, at Lagny, and during their previous visits to l'île Bourbon.

Indiana, Ralph, and Delmare are first seen at Lagny where the surrounding environment is unnatural and dream-like. The interior of the house initially suggests the artificiality: the door to the main salon is "une porte surmontée d'Amours nus, peints à fresque, qui enchaînaient de fleurs des biches fort bien élevées et des sangliers de bonne volonté" (p. 24). The ceiling, painted to represent "un ciel parsemé de nuages et d'étoiles" (p. 28), again points to the falseness of the small, provincial château. When Laure de Nangy subsequently lives at Lagny, she describes the salon walls of which she has painted a pastiche:

> "Et cette jolie nature fausse et peignée . . . n'est-ce pas qu'il y avait dans tout cela de la poésie, des idées de mollesse et de bonheur, et le sentiment de toute une vie douce, inutile et inoffensive?"
>
> (p. 289)

These walls, with their evocation of the pastoral love enjoyed by Louis XV's nobles—itself merely a pretense—are witness to Indiana's and Raymon's love. For Indiana this spiritual love is the perfection of a long-desired ideal, while for Raymon it is only a means to impassion himself, a form of amusement as depicted by the figures on the walls.

Outside the house, the nature is equally artificial. The château's park encloses an orangery replete with rare and exotic plants—foreign to the region—to decorate this "jardin anglais" (p. 299). Despite its semblance of being natural, such a garden with its "arbres taillés" (p. 69) is just as artificial as "le jardin français." Indiana is described as "une belle fleur exotique" (p. 60)—a metaphor which strengthens her suggested affinity with nature; while free at Bernica during her youth, she fails to thrive once transplanted from her natural habitat.

Also in the park is a gazebo, which, when strewn with flowers, serves as the place for Noun and Raymon's frequent *rendez-vous*: ". . . dans le kiosque rempli de fleurs exotiques où elle venait l'enivrer des séductions de la jeunesse et de la passion, il oubliait volontiers tout ce qu'il devait se rappeler plus tard" (p. 51). During two of Raymon's visits to the garden, the description of the rainy or foggy weather suggests a certain unreality. When he meets Noun for the last time in Indiana's room: "La nuit était froide; un brouillard épais enveloppait les arbres du parc, et Raymon avait peine à distinguer leurs tiges noires dans la brume blanche, qui les revêtait de robes blanches" (p. 81). Subsequently traversing the garden for his tryst with Indiana, he encounters similar weather conditions: "Le hasard voulut que cette nuit-là fut blanche et opaque comme l'avaient été les nuits correspondantes du printemps. Raymon marcha avec incertitude parmi les arbres enveloppés de vapeurs" (p. 175). The foggy night acts as an opiate on Raymon, distorting his perception, as did the abundance of flowers and wine during his earlier *rendez-vous* with Noun. Although he is on his way to Indiana, his thoughts are of the dead Noun; and as he is overwhelmed by his conscience for his part in her suicide, the cry of a bird forces him to confuse the natural and supernatural, a cry "qui ressemble exactement au vagissement d'un enfant abandonné; et, quand il s'élance du creux des joncs, on dirait le dernier effort d'une personne qui se noie" (p. 176). Both nature and Raymon are seducers: Raymon, metaphorically described as a "vipère" (p. 334), seduces Noun and Indiana, and then is himself seduced by his hallucinations in the park and in Indiana's room with Noun.

The descriptions of the weather in Paris underscore the fate Indiana suffers at the hands of Raymon and in society. Her trips to Paris occur, symbolically, in winter. It is in Paris after a long winter that the dying Indiana meets and revives during three days of happiness with Raymon "quand la nature commençait à se réveiller" (p. 102). On a subsequent trip, she suffers Raymon's coldness throughout the entire winter until he abandons her on one of "les jours les plus froids de l'année" (p. 208).

While they are living at Lagny, and later in Paris and on l'île Bourbon, the image of the bird suggests Indiana's lack of freedom and her total subjugation to her husband. The initial description of M. Delmare as jealous and suspicious is amplified by his depiction as a *oiseau de proie*: "Il est certain que l'argus conjugal fatigua son œil de vautour sans surprendre un regard" (p. 26). A confrontation between Delmare and Indiana gives evidence of his potential cruelty and demonstrates that Indiana is a prisoner within her marriage:

> Il était tenté de l'étrangler, de la traîner par les cheveux, de la fouler aux pieds pour la forcer de crier merci, d'implorer sa grâce; mais elle était si jolie, si mignonne et si blanche, qu'il se prenait à avoir pitié d'elle comme un enfant s'attendrit à regarder l'oiseau qu'il voulait tuer.
>
> (p. 200)

Delmare's cruelty toward his wife is further underscored by the reader's realization that he does, in fact, shoot birds: "[il] s'exerce à tuer les hirondelles au vol" (p. 105). These images and events presage the outburst of Delmare's violence against Indiana: "Sans pouvoir articuler une parole, il la saisit par les cheveux, la renversa, et la frappa au front du talon de sa botte" (p. 269).[2]

On l'île Bourbon, nature is both a negative and positive force for the melancholy Indiana and the brooding Ralph. For both the sight of the sea is painful, reminding Indiana of the life her husband forced her to abandon, and Ralph of his unhappy life in France. Although

the house shared by the Delmares and Ralph is isolated in the mountains above the town, both Indiana and Ralph escape to a more profound solitude. Descending the gorges, Indiana finds solace in her thoughts of Paris and Raymon. Her ardent desire to return to France enables her to see the surrounding nature as the concretization of her memories: "Quelquefois les nuages de la côte prirent pour elle des formes singulières: tantôt elle vit une lame blanche s'élever sur les flots et décrire une ligne gigantesque qu'elle prit pour la façade du Louvre . . ." (p. 249). A retreat to the hidden gorges of Bernica allows Ralph to flee the unhappiness he associates with the sight of the sea just as he was able to seek refuge there when he was cast out of his family as a child. It was there that he helped raise Indiana, herself rejected by her father. A major portion of her limited education consisted in watching the different birds.

For the child Indiana, the observations of the birds' flight across the ocean were a form of amusement. Her adult vision of their flight has a modified significance however: "Le soir, elle suivait de l'œil le vol des oiseaux qui s'en allaient coucher à l'île Rodrigue. Cette île abandonnée lui promettait toutes les douceurs de l'isolement" (p. 273). The sight of the bird in flight has come to mean an escape from the emotional and social shackles imposed on her by her marriage to Delmare. Initially, her daydream allows her to picture herself in a small hut on l'île Rodrigue living freely and in complete isolation from society. Eventually, her plan is transformed into a flight from her husband to what is merely another form of enslavement—Raymon.

She hopes to accomplish what she believes to be a liberating flight, "'Au coucher de la lune . . . comme une pauvre pétrelle au fond de quelque récit bien sombre'" (p. 278). During her escape the canoe also is metamorphosed into a bird: "La pirogue bondit avec élasticité comme un plongeon sur les eaux" (pp. 284-85). The metaphor is repeated: "La goëlette *La Nahandove* les porta, rapide et légère comme un oiseau" (p. 314). It is this last trip back to l'île Bourbon, decided on by both Ralph and Indiana, that actually corresponds fully to the free flight of the bird. For Indiana, the victim of a social enslavement, and for Ralph, oppressed by an inability to express his emotions, the image of the bird in flight symbolizes their ideal of a liberated existence. While on the boat, Indiana regains her physical and mental health and Ralph's true personality begins to emerge from behind his imprisoning, expressionless exterior.

When they are once more in their childhood sanctuary of Bernica, Ralph is able to divulge his repressed love, confessing that he had previously looked to nature as a vicarious lover: "'Alors, j'étais ivre, j'étais fou; je demandais l'amour aux fleurs, aux oiseaux, à la voix du torrent'" (p. 325). Although nature seduces, it also reveals the truth, and allows Indiana to live "dans le cœur de Ralph tel qu'il était" (p. 337). With the discovery of their hidden, imprisoned selves, Ralph and Indiana are able to control their lives. This regeneration after social oppression is likened to the continuous renewal of nature after a storm:

> Les arbres, si frais et si beaux quinze jours auparavant, avaient été dépouillés entièrement de leurs feuilles, mais déjà ils se couvraient de gros bourgeons résineux. Les oiseaux et les insectes avaient repris possession de leur empire. . . . Tout revenait à la vie, au bonheur, à la santé.

> (p. 348)

Nature is ultimately an all-powered and divine force for Ralph and Indiana, and it is here that they are able to find God:

> "Pour nous l'univers est le temple où nous adorons Dieu. C'est au sein d'une nature grande et vierge qu'on retrouve le sentiment de sa puissance pure de toute profanation humaine."

> (p. 312)

Throughout *Indiana* there is a narrative progression from the psychological and marital enslavement and the social hypocrisy at Lagny, in Paris, and on l'île Bourbon to the self-discovery, freedom, and happiness at Bernica. Each thematic shift emerges through the characters' geographical movement, through the significance attached to the descriptions of nature within settings as it changes from the artificial imitations to its real, unadulterated state, and through the use of nature images. So we see that as the image of the bird in flight supersedes that of the birds destroyed by Delmare, the thematic meaning shifts also. Nature initially reflects the destructive cruelty of Delmare, Raymon, and society's treatment of Indiana. By the novel's end, for both Indiana and Ralph, nature is a beneficent, regenerative, and divine force.

Notes

1. George Sand, *Indiana* (Paris: Garnier Frères, 1962), p. 354. All future references will be to this edition and will be cited in the text.

2. Béatrice Didier, in her article, "Ophélie dans les chaînes," in *Hommage à George Sand,* ed. L. Cellier (Paris: Presses Universitaires de France, 1969), pp. 89-91, suggests that Delmare's cruelty towards Indiana's dog, Ophélie, symbolizes his cruelty towards his wife.

Pierrette Daly (essay date 1981)

SOURCE: Daly, Pierrette. "The Problem of Language in George Sand's *Indiana.*" In *West Virginia George Sand Conference Papers,* edited by Armand E. Singer, Mary W. Singer, Janice S. Spleth, and Dennis O'Brien, pp. 22-7. Morgantown: Department of Foreign Languages, West Virginia University, 1981.

[*In the following essay, Daly focuses on the male narrator in* Indiana *in order to elucidate the problem of masculine control over literary language illustrated in Sand's fiction.*]

> Rien n'est si facile et si commun que de se duper soi-même quand on ne manque pas d'esprit et quand on connaît bien toutes les finesses de la langue. C'est une reine prostituée qui descend et s'élève à tous les rôles, qui se déguise, se pare, se dissimule et s'efface; c'est une plaideuse qui a reponse à tout, qui a toujours tout prévu, et qui prend mille formes pour avoir raison.

> George Sand, *Indiana.*[1]

Literature is largely the collective production of men, and novels are chiefly creations of their imagination. It follows that literary figures and tropes are formulated from their point of view, and, correlatively, that the language of fiction itself is dominated by men. Today, many women writers express concern over the masculine structures of language and question the probability of ever transcribing a truly feminine experience within its elaborate system. Evidence of the inner conflict of women novelists struggling with the conventions of literature is present in the text, and it is often manifested by an awareness of the exclusion of the feminine in the male-dominated narrative system. One particular textual element which definitely presents a problem in French (as in some other languages) is that of the narrator who must identify with either the masculine or the feminine. Because there is no grammatical construction that is neuter, and because the masculine gender has been considered the so-called objective neutral, a novelist's narrator must be male in order to claim objectivity.

I propose to examine some of the ramifications of these problems in Sand's first novel, *Indiana.* My work will be divided into two aspects of the novel which permit sexual differentiation: the narrator and the characters. I have drawn together two male figures because of the similarity of their function. The relationship between Raymon and women in society corresponds to the one between the narrator and his female characters in the text. A critical exegesis of the text will demonstrate that the oppression expressed in *Indiana* is not, as the reductionist approach would have it, only a reflection of the author's own oppression in marriage, or of marriage in general as Sand herself says in her preface, but also a statement of the relation of a woman writer to the language of literature.

The convention which consists of writing through a masculine narrator is one that modern French women identify as the very first stylistic imperative to which they must conform, as the one which most alienates them, and which circumscribes the totality of their existence in literature. Marguerite Duras, for example, acknowledges that all writing starts with this imitation of the male. She captures the quintessence of the restriction: "La bonne à tout faire qui va danser se déguise en bourgeoise. La femme qui écrit se déguise en . . . , en homme. . . . Oui, ça commence toujours par cette singerie. C'est le premier travail à faire, ça."[2] Aurore Dupin, like all writers of her sex, narrates in the masculine, but she pursued the masquerade into other aspects of her life, adopting a masculine name for her *nom de plume* and transgressing societal sexual roles by wearing men's clothing: the first because of familial pressures not to publish under the Dudevant name, the second for economic reasons. Much has been written about the fact that she masqueraded in male attire in the Parisian world, but not much attention has been given to the male narrator in her writings. It is also subversively, by imitating his language, that she infiltrates the masculine structures and writes of women's experience through his voice. She officially gives birth to this male persona in *Indiana,* her first solo publication without the collaboration of Jules Sandeau.[3] In her mature life, she dropped this mask to speak in the feminine in her autobiography, and, in her later years, she also wrote through a grandmother's voice in *Contes d'une grand'mère.*[4]

Let me begin by attempting to verify the probability that the male voice in *Indiana* would falsify the expression of women's experience. In order to extricate his words from the other textual structures, I have compiled a list of interruptions identifying his voice as that of the dramatized narrator who intervenes to make commentaries.[5] They show that Sand's narrator uses a diversity of interruptions on the subject of women, ranging from confessions of ineptitude (inability to describe) to assertions of mastery over the subject. Among his many declarations of incompetence or lack of knowledge are found the ubiquitous "je ne sais quel," the repetitious "peut-être," and the qualifying adverb which reveals an opinion.[6] For example, in the erotic hunting scene, he says of Indiana: "Ses yeux et ses joues s'animèrent; le gonflement de ses narines trahit je ne sais quel sentiment de terreur ou de plaisir . . ." (p. 150). At the beginning, he also claims not to understand Indiana's feelings for men: "Mais peut-être la jeune et timide femme de M. Delmare n'avait-elle jamais encore examiné un homme avec les yeux . . ." (p. 26). Granted, these are well-worn narrative clichés, but they take on new meaning when examined from our perspective, that is, when we see that Sand's narrator distances himself from women repeatedly by using these terms in the context of feminine experiences and emotions.

One of these interventions of the narrator is his admitted difficulty in reproducing, in written form, the words of a woman. In a scene between Noun and Raymon, he interrupts the narration to declare himself unable to repeat her words: "Elle ne se servit peut-être pas des mêmes mots, mais elle dit les mêmes choses, bien mieux cent fois que je ne pourrais vous les redire." He then elaborates on her inimitable eloquence: "Où trouver le secret de cette éloquence qui se révèle tout à coup à un esprit ignorant et vierge dans la crise d'une passion vraie et d'une douleur profonde?" (p. 84). Noun's words are a blank in the written text.

On another occasion, the narrator also confesses to a certain inability to describe a woman's suffering, when he categorically refuses to report the moral pain inflicted on Indiana by the crew during the boat trip she undertakes after leaving her husband for Raymon: "Ce furent là de véritables tortures de cette infortunée durant le voyage, car, pour les fatigues, . . . je ne vous en parle pas" (p. 287). If this is a literary convention (the refusal to describe dates back in French literature to Chrétien de Troyes), it is still a refusal to describe, and the narrator chooses not to relate an experience. In this case, the feminist interrogation may well address itself to the lapsus in textual expression. Are a woman's words, her suffering, even her very existence, a blank in literature? She has indeed been endowed with a damning enigmatic quality which today's critics recognize.[7] There is no literary model for the woman writer in this context because novels are predominantly written by men, who, by design or inadvertence, have not given woman her full dimension. This stumbling-block is recognized by today's novelists. Duras, let us note, even makes the point that women's existence in her own novels is a suppression or a blank.[8]

Sand delegates to her male narrator the duty of educating women, ostensibly for their benefit. It is an obligation which he discharges through numerous interruptions showing mastery, either in sweeping generalizations, or through authoritative pronouncements such as "il est certain" or "sans doute." He uses these general statements to put women on their guard when they engage in a love relationship with a man. Let us note the sexual connotation of the word "puissant" in the following statement regarding men's rhetoric: "Le plus honnête des hommes est celui qui pense et qui agit le mieux, mais le plus puissant est celui qui sait le mieux écrire et parler" (p. 117). It is in fact later, when Indiana succumbs to Raymon's eloquent courting, that the narrator interrupts to say: "Honte à cette femme imbécile!" (p. 213), pointing an accusing finger at Indiana to teach women a lesson.

His interventions show that his voice is certainly not similar to the women's but to the men's. In fact, he resembles the principal male character, Raymon de la Ramière. Both men can be identified through their language as belonging to the dominant social class which imposes its views. Raymon's rhetoric echoes that of the masterly voice which interrupts the narrative.[9] Significantly, he is a pivotal character, one whose communications with women, whether oral or written, are the catalysts which cause the text to function. For instance, his last letter to Indiana elicits her suicide attempt, and his false speech is the reason for the death of her maid Noun.

He dominates the novel through his linguistic skill. In fact, the narrator warns of Raymon's powerful influence as if he were about to seduce the reader when he begins to court Indiana:

> Nous ne vous avons pas dit sur quoi était basée sa réputation d'esprit et de talent . . . ce Raymon, dont vous venez de suivre les faiblesses et de blâmer peut-être la légèreté, est un des hommes qui ont eu sur vos pensées le plus d'empire ou d'influence . . . vous avez été entraîné . . . par le charme irrésistible de son style, et les grâces de sa logique courtoise et mondaine.
>
> (p. 113)

Even though the hero may seem weak or fickle, his style is commanding. Here, the novelist reinforces the theme of the power of language by developing it on two registers, the advantage of Raymon's linguistic skill over the female characters, and the narrator's claims to a superior knowledge of rhetoric. The narrator *is* the one who points out the charm of Raymon's style: it is "irrésistible."

On the opposite side of the coin, when it is women's turn to be eloquent, their messages seem ineffectual. For example, when Noun writes to Raymon in one last attempt to express her feelings and entice him to return, she borrows her mistress' perfumed and satiny stationery, but, unlettered and unread, she is not aware that language has rules. Hence, the narrator addresses the reader with irony, calling her message a chambermaid's letter: "Mais l'orthographe! Savez-vous bien ce qu'une syllabe de plus ou de moins ôte ou donne d'énergie aux sentiments? Hélas! la pauvre fille à demi sauvage de l'île Bourbon ignorait même qu'il y eût des règles à la langue" (p. 53). A parallel can be drawn between the characters of Noun and her mistress, based on their relationship with Raymon and language. Indiana also totally fails to communicate with Raymon in her last letter. It does not reach its destination in time and he is already married to someone else when, following her own letter, she arrives from the island. Having left everything for him, she tries to commit suicide, as Noun had when she had also failed to appeal by letter. Both women are victims of Raymon's rhetorical skill as well as their own lack. In a paradoxical comment, the narrator satirizes Raymon's eloquence when he interrupts a love scene to remark: "il exprimait la passion avec art. . . . Seulement, ce n'était pas la passion qui le rendait éloquent, c'était l'éloquence qui le rendait pas-

sionné" (p. 62). Eloquence becomes an auto-erotic activity locking the hero into a closed world from which the addressee, in this case a woman, is excluded. It seems appropriate that both central female characters of the novel disappear. Noun's absence is doubly expressed: in nature, when, after acquiring Indiana's property, Raymon changes the course of the river to remove the bridge where she drowned, and in language, when everyone decides never to speak of her again. As for Indiana, she disappears from civilization at the end, and, when the narrator concludes the novel, he reports that he has searched for her on the island and has been told by the islanders that her existence is "une chose problématique" (p. 343).[10] Finally, in the last paragraph, she is neutralized, her voice blending with that of her faithful lover Ralph in one last greeting. It is the man's voice which ends the novel, Indiana's identity is fused into his, and her voice is stifled.

Through her hero, who has the finesse of the aristocrat, Sand warns women of the danger inherent in romances written by men who themselves know better than to take them seriously. Raymon warns Indiana that she is sentimental because she has learned life from novels: "Où avez-vous rêvé l'amour? dans quel roman à l'usage des femmes de chambre avez-vous étudié la société, je vous prie?" (p. 210). In her final letter to him, she admits that he is correct and that she has indeed mistaken life for novels: "j'avais appris la vie dans les romans à l'usage des femmes de chambre, dans ces riantes et puériles fictions où l'on intéresse le coeur au succès . . . d'impossibles félicités. C'est horriblement vrai, Raymon, ce que vous dites là! . . . vous avez raison" (p. 240). The novelist does show that men, in language and in literature, when they communicate with women, deceive them.

The theme of language, as it functions between Raymon and the women in the novel, is a reflection of the difficulties of the other fictional hero, the narrator, who was also created by the woman writer. Sand herself reveals an awareness of his fictional dimension when she writes about her first essays published under the title *Lettres d'un voyageur*: "Ce voyageur était une sorte de fiction, un personnage convenu, masculin comme mon pseudonyme, vieux quoique je fusse encore jeune; et dans la bouche de ce triste pèlerin, qui en somme était une sorte de héros de roman, je mettais des impressions et des réflexions . . ." (*OA* [*Oeuvres autobiographiques*], I, 7). This masculine persona is a convention which imposes its specific sexual features on the novel, thereby excluding what is characteristically feminine. In her attempt to be impartial or neutral, a woman writes through the masculine voice. But, it is only one subdivision of the polarization masculine/feminine. In this configuration, she opposes herself and speaks at times against women. Sand even goes so far as to say: "La femme est imbécile par nature" (p. 245).

The mask that the novelist is compelled to wear denies her sexual identity, and, from this false stand, she writes about women in a distorted, unfaithful, and sometimes disloyal, fashion. Outside the context of the masculine universality, women are the other, the alienated, or the nonexistent. The suppression of the voice of the woman writer is reflected in the novel by the disappearance of her two female characters.

The absence of women and the omniscience of men in the novel is the powerful metaphor that dominates the text. In the writings of the few women recognized in France, heroines also disappear. Corrine dies and the Princess of Clèves is hidden in a convent at the end. Sand's text questions its own power by alluding to the fact that novels are a tool for propaganda in the hands of the male dominant class, which, by lulling women into visions of idyllic life through sentimental portrayals of love, keeps them in an infantile state and contributes to the ignorance which enslaves them. It is also, as our analysis demonstrates, a statement of Sand's own relation to the language of literature. In the act of writing through the masculine voice, her identity as a woman is maintained at a distance. Her voice is suppressed and her feminine presence in the text is as problematic as her heroine's existence on the island. In Sand's works, it is the male voice which usually closes. This is particularly obvious in her major novel about the life of the artist, **Consuelo,** in which the singer-heroine loses her voice. In the end, it is Albert who speaks the last words of the novel.

Notes

1. P. Salomon ed. (Paris: Garnier Frères, 1962), p. 117. All references to this novel will hereafter be cited parenthetically in the text.

2. Marguerite Duras and Xavière Gauthier, *Les Parleuses* (Paris: Les Éditions de Minuit, 1974), p. 38. Duras adds: "les premières femmes qui ont écrit ont joué le rôle d'enfants terribles. . . . Elles ont fait les clowns pour amuser les hommes. . . . Colette a fait ça."

3. Granted, we find him in earlier writings such as "Voyage chez M. Blaise," but none of them has the breadth of a novel. In her early correspondence, we find a strange mixture of the alternation of masculine and feminine self-identification when she signs "Aurore" or "George." In her first literary attempts, she writes in a feminine voice; "Voyage en Auvergne" and "La Blonde Phoebe" are penned by a female narrator. The definite change to the masculine occurs in works which are destined for publication. All of the above are published in Sand's *Oeuvres autobiographiques* (Paris: Gallimard, 1971), hereafter cited parenthetically as *OA*.

4. *Contes d'une grand'mère* (Paris: Calmann-Lévy, s.d.).

5. Wayne C. Booth defines this concept in *The Rhetoric of Fiction* (Chicago: The U of Chicago P, 1961), pp. 151-52. I compiled a list of stylistic devices such as exhortations to the reader, claims of objectivity, refusals to describe, rhetorical questions, and exclamations.

6. My list of these, whether they treat of men or women, includes approximately twenty-five showing refusal, difficulty, or hesitation; but those showing mastery number over three dozen, many of which are included in the dissertation I am submitting this spring at Washington University in St. Louis, Missouri.

7. In an excellent analysis of a text by Balzac entitled "Adieu," Shoshana Felman in "Women and Madness: The Critical Phallacy," *Diacritics* 5 (Winter 1975): 2-10, shows that woman is *"the realistic invisible"* (p. 6), according to the critical concept of realism. Her madness, which is enigmatic and, therefore, beyond the realm of the explicable, situates her outside the objective norms of criticism. Felman concludes that, under the label of "madness," there is "nothing other than feminine difference" (p. 8). Nancy K. Miller, in "Emphasis Added: Plots and Plausibilities in Women's Fiction," *PMLA* 96 (1981): 36-48, observes that, in the relationship of women writers to literature, certain modalities of difference can be analyzed and that these have been dismissed as "implausible" by critics using the criteria of masculine "constructs" (p. 46).

8. "C'est des blancs" (op. cit., p. 12).

9. This study is based on the interruptions in *Indiana*. Sand's masculine narrator changes in her later novels. The narrative voice of *Consuelo,* as a case in point, is remarkably different from the one of this earlier novel. Sand also tries to escape from the ruling class by other means; she situates her women away from Paris in her rustic novels, for instance.

10. I believe that a case can be made for arguing that there are actually two male narrators telling Sand's story.

Nancy Rogers (essay date 1981)

SOURCE: Rogers, Nancy. "George Sand and Germaine de Staël: The Novel as Subversion." In *West Virginia George Sand Conference Papers,* edited by Armand E.

Singer, Mary W. Singer, Janice S. Spleth, and Dennis O'Brien, pp. 61-74. Morgantown: Department of Foreign Languages, West Virginia University, 1981.

[In the following essay, Rogers explores a thematic subversion of the patriarchal values of wealth, rank, title, and power in favor of "the more feminine qualities of love, peace, and tranquility" in Sand's Indiana *and Germaine de Staël's 1807 novel* Corinne.*]*

In an article in *Daedalus* Tony Tanner removes some of the layers of Rousseau's epistolary palimpsest, *Julie, ou la Nouvelle Héloïse* (1760), to arrive at some rather surprising conclusions concerning this pivotal novel.[1] Tanner outlines Julie's attempts to integrate extra-familial passion into her family life, the powerful love relationships between Julie and her father and Julie and her cousin Claire, and the ultimate failure of the heroine's experiment to combine all of her love relationships under her father's roof. This exciting and innovative study focuses on the disturbing elements in the Clarens household, the hidden but ominous signs of stress, of things amiss, in this bourgeois family. He calls Rousseau's novel "a book that not only bespeaks some kind of imminent crisis in the particular family structure on which Western society was based, but carries with it a sense of doom concerning the very emotions and institutions that the book strives to celebrate" (p. 23). Filial devotion and fear, paternal warmth, sexual desire, tranquil love between cousins, and Oedipal passion are, perhaps unintentionally on the part of Rousseau, shown as complex, contradictory, and shifting in this paradigm of the love novel. In addition, the ranks, names, and titles of the nobility, the Word of the father, and the *maison paternelle* itself are revealed as empty, meaningless, and subject to peril, pointing to the weakened figure of the father and to the fall of the bourgeois family in much of nineteenth-century fiction.

That Germaine de Staël and George Sand were greatly influenced by Rousseau is unquestionable. Staël's first literary effort was a critical study of Rousseau (*Lettres sur les écrits et le caractère de J. J. Rousseau*, 1788), which is the occasion of a plea for the literary edification of women,[2] and Sand's enthusiasm for her *maître à penser* is evident from the many tributes to his work in her *Histoire de ma vie* and throughout her correspondence. However, it is in the novels of these two women that Rousseau's influence is most noticeable, and it is especially interesting to study their examination of the institution of the *maison paternelle* in their fiction. In both *Delphine* (1802) and *Corinne, ou l'Italie* (1807) Germaine de Staël addresses herself to the question of woman's role in a patriarchal system. And of Sand's first eight novels, six relate directly to the issue of patriarchal heritage: *Indiana* (1832), *Valentine* (1832), *Jacques* (1834), *André* (1835), *Simon* (1836), and *Mauprat* (1837). All of these novels are concerned in some

fashion with the problems of rank, titles, inheritance, and propagation of family values. Both Sandian sons and daughters reject their heritage and turn elsewhere than to the house of the father to find harmony and happiness. In each case a new value system, usually based on the more feminine qualities of love, peace, and tranquility, is substituted for the patriarchal principles of wealth, power, and rank.

It is in Staël's last novel, *Corinne,* and Sand's first, *Indiana,* that this subject is most vitally and explicitly explored. Written during the proliferation of romantic novels, during a period which coincides with the rise to prominence of female authors, the age which Virginia Woolf hails as the "epic age" of women writers, these novels, both in conception and in ideology, offer many points of comparison. Each is a *Bildungsroman* of the quest of a woman for a fulfilling sexual union, and each records a relative degree of success or failure in this endeavor: the woman of genius is defeated in *Corinne,* as the heroine dies from that mysterious romantic malady which also struck Julie, Mme de Mortsauf, and Mme de Rênal; and the conclusion of *Indiana* places its heroine outside of society, united in a love-pact unsanctified by marriage, with her cousin Sir Ralph. Both of these novels are thus based on the search for love so common to fiction of the period. It is my contention, however, that beneath the thematic surface of the love novel, these two women authors explore the ramifications of the patriarchal system in a manner which, intentionally or subliminally, subverts that system.

I will first examine how the two authors treat such aspects of patriarchy as names, rank, titles, and various family structures and relationships. The role of the father will be closely studied as will the attempts by the two heroines to recreate a family unit outside the father's house. I will then turn to an aspect of novelistic organization which, in my opinion, points to the undermining of the patriarchal system.

In studying novels whose titles are proper names, especially when those names are female first names without a family or married name attached, the critic is naturally invited to examine the function of nomination in the work. Both Mme de Staël and George Sand use suggestive, colorful names for their female characters, following the lead of Chateaubriand and moving away from such classical names and titles as "la princesse de Clèves" and "Mme de Merteuil." The women characters in these two novels usually possess foreign, exotic names, such as Corinne, Noun, and Indiana, whereas the men retain such restrained, sober names as "le comte d'Erfeuil" and "Sir Ralph Brown." Thus, Staël and Sand express the new freedom and individuality of their heroines through names which by their connotative value establish the authors as apart from the realistic tradition explored by Constant and Stendhal. These are richly suggestive names, evoking far-off lands and unfamiliar values; such nominative practice represents a decided move away from contemporary life and problems. In each case the heroine is appropriately named. Corinne, the Italian poetess, recalls her famous predecessor in ancient Greece. Also, the exotic-sounding name, Indiana, reflects the leading character's Creole heritage (although Sand may actually have named her heroine for a friend in Bordeaux).

As the psychologists and anthropologists have demonstrated, naming is a phenomenon of social, cultural, and psychological significance. It can represent an attempt to transcend death on the part of the namer, an expression of ideology, and self-expression, and individuation, or self-creation, on the part of the one who accepts, assumes, or transforms his/her given name. The concept of "changing her name" is one that every woman who wishes to marry confronts in western society. She is also aware that in a patriarchal system, her name is never her own, but is merely a symbol of her link to a man, either her father or her husband. The name/marriage phenomenon is intimately related to the social structure of kinship and especially to the anthropological concept of the "gift-system" of patriarchy, in which men relinquish their sisters and daughters outside the immediate family.[3] Jacques Lacan has related the name of the father figure to the law: "C'est dans le *nom du père* qu'il nous faut reconnaître le support de la fonction symbolique qui, depuis l'orée des temps historiques, identifie sa personne à la figure de la loi."[4] The father's name is also related to the law in another sense in that a child who is refused his father's name is "illegitimate." At least in French, the father figure is thus related to both nomination (*le nom*) and to prohibition (*le non*), to use Foucault's terminology,[5] a redoutable combination for a daughter for whom a father is both a love object, to be worshipped or denied, and the image of ultimate masculine authority. It is of primary ideological importance that in these novels there is a conscious rejection by the heroine of her *nom de famille* as well as a diminishing of the worth of ranks and titles.

In *Corinne* the heroine is always referred to by her given name—no title or *nom de famille* is ever used by others when addressing her. She is presented as alone, independent, lacking the need for the conveniences of social status. "Son nom de famille était ignoré. Son premier ouvrage avait paru cinq ans auparavant, et portait seulement le nom de Corinne."[6] The importance of names and titles to the men of the novel is reiterated stylistically by the excessive repetition of titles; "Lord Nelvil," "le comte d'Erfeuil," and "le prince Castel-Forte" are almost always used to represent the male personages. As a point of contrast, the simple "Corinne" is striking, especially since the name alone is enough to evoke enthusiasm and adoration by the Roman people.

Yet Corinne's family name is of utmost importance to this novel in which name and nationality are closely linked. Early in the work Corinne asks her lover to promise something "au nom de votre père"; Oswald replies: "Ne prononcez pas ce nom; savez-vous s'il nous réunit ou s'il nous sépare!" (p. 207). This recognition of the importance of the patriarch's "*oui*" or "*non*," combined with Nelvil's sense of filial duty, causes Corinne to delay her confession, which consists of revealing her name and heritage. Oswald is aware that by marrying Corinne he will give her "le peu que je puis donner, un rang, un nom"; yet, he also fears that she will receive "la désapprobation de l'Angleterre" (p. 707). That Corinne will not be approved by a country, England, is a central issue in the novel, and Oswald's dead father is soon identified with that country whose value-system he championed. As a result of the prejudices of this northern *Weltanschauung,* the parental "*non*" has been pronounced against their marriage. Corinne, with her Italian traits of exuberance, enthusiasm, and passion, has been judged a poor match for a sober, duty-conscious, repressed Englishman. The disapproval of England for her Italian qualities has not derived from Oswald's father alone, but from Corinne's own family as well. For the heroine's family name is Edgermond, revelatory of the English past which she has rejected. Desperate because of her failure to animate a hostile and ungiving English society in her favor, the poetess has renounced her rights to the name "Miss Edgermond" and has obeyed the injunction of her stepmother: "vous devez à votre famille de changer de nom, et de vous faire passer pour morte" (p. 787). This is Corinne's dark secret: she has been cast out by her English father's new family and has turned to the sun and brilliance of Italy, leaving behind a society and a family which could not appreciate the Italian side of her identity. The crucial letter from Oswald's father, read after his death, serves to identify Corinne's half-sister Lucile with England ("la femme anglaise qui fera le bonheur de mon fils," p. 819) and Corinne with Italy ("l'Italie seule lui convient"). The dutiful son follows his father's directive and marries Lucile, once again demonstrating the rejection of Corinne (or Italy, as the title suggests) by the English nation. Thus, we see that Corinne's real name is not Edgermond after all, but "Italy." Her family name has been replaced by a national heritage, and her final poem, a eulogy to the glories of Italy, is her ultimate recognition of a bond stronger than that of a father.

In *Indiana* the question of nomination is of lesser importance than in *Corinne,* although it is closely linked to patriarchal tyranny. Indiana has loved neither her father nor her husband; both have been cold, powerful, and cruel. The narrator tells us that by changing her name from Carvajal to Delmare, Indiana "ne fit que changer de maître."[7] Thus, the husband's name is merely a transformation of that of the father; both represent tyranny and both imprison the heroine. Indiana's central purpose, as she struggles to define herself, is to battle the tyranny of the dominant male, whether as a daughter or as a wife; "résister mentalement à toute espèce de contrainte morale était devenu chez elle une seconde nature" (p. 69). For Indiana, her family name or married name is a symbol of limits upon her freedom; her dominant character trait in the novel is her rebelliousness, directed at the cruel constraints of both father and husband.

It is interesting to note a progression in the novel from an identification of the heroine with her married status to an emphasis on her as an independent being in the last section of the novel. Throughout the major part of the text, "madame Delmare" is used four or five times for every "Indiana," thus inescapably relating her to her marital status. Yet, at the end of the work, after "madame Delmare" has received her final rejection from the male world at the hands of her lover, Raymon de Ramière, a dramatic shift in nomination practice takes place. In the final two chapters and in the "Conclusion," the heroine is referred to as "Indiana" more than twice as often than as "madame Delmare." No legal change in name has taken place. In fact, Indiana and Ralph live in what is perceived as "un attachement criminel" by the inhabitants of the island. Isolated from an unjust society, the two have only each other; as Ralph says to their visitor, the young botanist from Paris: "Allez, jeune homme, poursuivez le cours de votre destinée; ayez des amis, un état, une réputation, une patrie. Moi, j'ai Indiana" (p. 353). And when their visitor leaves the island for the last time, he addresses them simply by their given names; gone are the titles which the world chooses to bestow. Indiana and Ralph have joined in a struggle against the hierarchical values of the "*colonel* Delmares" and the "Raymon *de* Ramières." The title "Sir Ralph Brown" has no validity in their world, and, in fact, like Paul and Virginie, the two work actively to rid their world of slavery and arrive at an equality of rank in which titles are worthless. Neither the title "madame Brown" nor "Lady Brown" will ever be Indiana's; her wholeness as a woman has no dependency upon society's approval. The two lovers have returned to the world of their childhood, where first names are all important. Their identities are intact as "Ralph" and "Indiana."

As we have seen, names and titles are symbols of the male world in both *Corinne* and **Indiana.** Neither heroine has accepted her father's name and each ends her life called only by her given name with no titles attached. Both Indiana and Corinne, in attempting to define themselves as women, have rejected the concepts of names and titles as well as the systems of value they imply.

It is evident from our examination of names and titles in these works that the figure of the father, and the family structure in general, are of central importance to the heroines. Each of these novels could be viewed from one perspective as a family novel, much in the same sense that *Julie, ou la Nouvelle Héloïse* can be approached. As Tanner describes in his article on Rousseau:

> It is almost as if, on the eve of what we roughly think of as the great period of the consolidation and domination of the bourgeois class and its growing belief in the myth of its own "perenniality" (Sartre's word), Rousseau wrote a book that had a manifest content of *l'amour* in all its more piercing, poignant, and plangent forms, and a latent content that said the bourgeois family would not work.
>
> (p. 23)

Although not ostensibly about the family, both *Corinne* and **Indiana** exhibit a decided attempt by the heroine to reconstruct a family life according to her own belief system and in contrast to that of her heritage. As with Julie, their attempts are doomed to failure. Yet, it is their struggle which is important, and that is the aspect of the novels upon which we will concentrate here.

Corinne is a woman who, as we have seen, has reached maturity bereft of a family name. Corinne does not often refer to her past family life; only in her confession (Livre XIV) does her bitterness at the early loss of her parents become clear. Except for an occasional reference to the pitiful lot of orphans, Corinne seems content with her status as the woman who incarnates "le culte du génie" (p. 668).

Yet, Corinne, that near-perfect woman of genius, exhibits a basic insecurity. When Lord Nelvil first sees her, he recognizes her need for "la protection d'un ami, protection dont jamais une femme, quelque supérieure qu'elle soit, ne peut se passer" (p. 663). And Corinne herself acknowledges this need when she says to Oswald: "c'est la femme qui révère profondément celui qu'elle a choisi pour son défenseur" (p. 800). This underlying insecurity most probably arises from her parentless state. Thus, in Corinne's life, it is the lack of the father figure ("le non du père," in Foucault's words) which is essential. Loss of her father has deprived her of the three essential elements of the patriarchal system: a family name and heritage, the protection and security of the *maison paternelle,* and an authority-figure for guidance and decision-making. She describes the effect of the death of her father in this way: "je perdis avec lui mon protecteur, mon ami, le seul qui m'entendit encore, dans ce désert peuplé" (p. 785).

However, the heroine's love for her father is not free of feelings of resentment and lack of comprehension. Her description of the reunion with her father after five years of education in Italy succinctly reveals these emotions: "il me sembla que sa figure avait pris un caractère plus grave" (p. 779). Thus, her beloved father has assumed some of the characteristics of England, those values which will ultimately destroy Corinne. Her feelings for her father, then, are a complicated mixture of love, need, and shame, the latter because of his new alliance with a northern value-system which rejects her most admirable qualities. The mediocrity of his new life dismays and betrays her, making her long for the land of her mother, Italy. It is hardly surprising, then, that she puts up little resistance when forced by her step-mother to give up her family.

Deprived of the sustenance of a traditional family existence, Corinne, like Julie in Rousseau's novel, undertakes the task of reconstructing a family system within which her worth can be recognized. Before her meeting with Oswald, she has formed an alliance with the symbolically-named Prince Castel-Forte, whose name and power seem to offer her the paternal strength, succor, and authority lost by the death of her father. This relationship is never fully explored by Staël, but we are left with the impression that he may harbor hopes of a more intimate rapport someday, whereas Corinne thinks of him only as a wise friend. The loss of her mother at the age of ten has left Corinne bereft of a successful female role-model during her adolescent and young adult years. Yet, the memory of her exuberant mother has served to reinforce her own belief in imagination, nature, and the exceptional (as opposed to "la médiocrité malveillante" [p. 787] which is England), and she has matured by rebelling against northern values. The lack of a mother and the heroine's relationships with women are too large a subject to be treated here, yet an absolutely essential one for a consideration of Corinne as a whole woman. We will limit ourselves to a discussion of the heroine's attempts to create a substitute family for herself through a series of complex, interconnected relationships with her half-sister Lucile, Oswald (Lucile's husband and Corinne's lost love), and her niece Juliette. At an earlier stage Corinne had made herself a surrogate mother for Lucile by undertaking the role of tutor to the young child. As we have seen, Oswald's father, whom Lucile calls her "second père," identifies Lucile with England and Corinne with Italy. A case could be made for the two sisters as contrasting halves of one entity; such a contention is actually made by Corinne on her deathbed, as she says to Lucile: "Il faut que vous soyez vous et moi à la fois" (p. 860). The interchangeability between the two is most evident in Corinne's role as surrogate mother of the child Juliette, who has her aunt's hair and eyes and whose name recalls Corinne's most famous stage role. The heroine's last act is to educate the child, instructing her in all the areas of her own talents, "comme un héritage qu'elle se plaisait à lui léguer de son vivant" (p. 859). Thus, Corinne has reconstructed a family for herself through her half-sister Lucile, Lucile's husband (and her own lover), and the product of the union of these two. The dissolution of her father's house has left Corinne destitute; through her psychological manipulations of those she cares for she has become eternally related to another patriarchal system, that of Oswald (although, as we shall see, this is not a simple, direct allegiance), who will attend her funeral "comme parent" (ibid.).

Indiana, likewise, has been abandoned by her "père bizarre et violent" (p. 68), who married her at sixteen to a man old enough to be her father and sent her into a foreign world, defenseless and without paternal protection. Married to Colonel Delmare, she has had to rely on her instincts—love, sex, self-preservation—for survival. In addition, she has been forced to recognize the deficiencies in her education, since she is "ignorante comme une vraie créole" (p. 164). Never having known her mother and desperate for an older, wiser person to guide her, the naive Indiana turns to the only sympathetic woman she knows, Mme de Ramière, the mother of her would-be lover. As the narrator tells us, "Indiana éprouvait le besoin de s'attacher à quelqu'un" (p. 128). This attempt to find a surrogate mother is naturally doomed to failure, since Mme de Ramière is much more sympathetic to her perfidious son than to his sweet and needy friend.

When this effort to find familial love fails, Indiana turns to the only stable relationship she has known, the one with her cousin Sir Ralph. (This is not to say, however, that their relationship has been a smooth one; some of the insights allowed by the narrator into Ralph's reactions to women are most interesting, although not of central importance here.) Ralph's feelings for Indiana are so all-encompassing that he sees her not only as sister and daughter but as lover as well. In other words, Ralph fills all the important masculine roles for his cousin. In their childhood, Ralph offered protection to Indiana from her despotic father. Indiana believes at first that she loves Ralph like a brother and Ralph, who has followed her from the île Bourbon to France, describes their attachment to Colonel Delmare in these terms: "Monsieur, lui dit-il, j'aime votre femme; c'est moi qui l'ai élevée; je la regarde comme ma soeur, et plus encore comme ma fille" (p. 147). This convoluted relationship can be extended from brother/sister and father/daughter to that of lovers only when the two return to the île Bourbon where Ralph can once again fill the roles "de tuteur et de père" (p. 306). The *béance* left by the father, the patriarchal husband, and the family has been filled; the *toit paternelle* has been replaced by the maternal qualities of nature and by the *toit éternel* of the peaceful skies over their retreat from the world of patriarchy. Thus, we see that Sand's solution to the problems posed by the male world for the superior woman is quite different from that of Staël, whose heroine is defeated; on the contrary, Indiana lives in a world in which her belief in freedom and love can flourish.

In order to conclude our discussion of these two novels, we will turn from theme to structure, or novelistic organization. In the critical exercise which Genette calls narratology, or the theory of the *récit,* it is evident that one of the most interesting and fruitful approaches is through an examination of how an author chooses to begin a narrative and at what point to conclude it.[8] The ideal beginning, or "narrative recipe," as derived from the epic, establishes a narrative model of clarity and order, providing such information as who, when, and where; it is this kind of beginning that one has come to expect from the early nineteenth-century novel. A comparison of opening and closing passages can also be helpful in defining the system of a text. Such an examination of the two novels in question reveals a perhaps unexpected novelistic process: one of erosion, in which a form of social power initially posited by the narrator is undermined in such a way that there is no longer a justification for the continuation of that power.

The opening lines of *Corinne* place the reader in the world of England, as symbolized by Lord Nelvil:

> Oswald, Lord Nelvil, pair d'Écosse, partit d'Édimbourg pour se rendre en Italie, pendant l'hiver de 1794 à 1795. Il avait une figure noble et belle, beaucoup d'esprit, un grand nom, une fortune indépendante; mais sa santé était altérée par un profond sentiment de peine, et les médecins, craignant que sa poitrine ne fût attaquée, lui avaient ordonné l'air du Midi. Il suivit leurs conseils, bien qu'il mît peu d'intérêt à la conservation de ses jours.
>
> (p. 653)

The initial sentence almost classically answers the who, when, and where of the "ideal" narrative and serves to introduce the text under the sign of the male: rank and social power ("Lord Nelvil, pair d'Écosse," "un grand nom"), activity (traveling as an act of movement and change—and so common for young men during the early part of the century), and wealth ("une fortune indépendante"). However, Oswald's social, physical, and monetary status are then subverted or lessened by his unhealthy state, combined with an indication of an unbalanced psychological condition. The cause of Oswald's sickness is his father's death, an event fed in Wertherian fashion by remorse for past actions and by his morbid imagination. The implication here is that Oswald wants to suffer ("il mît peu d'intérêt à la conservation de ses jours"), an implication made explicit by the generalizing statement terminating the first paragraph: "quand on souffre, on se persuade aisément qu'on est coupable." The opening passage thus proposes three antitheses: first, a comfortable social and financial position is undermined by self-induced bad health; second, longings for death are presented as an escape from an unhappy life, accompanied by indications of a subsequent death-in-life; and third, past indiscretions and guilt about them are placed in direct opposition to filial duty. The portrait of Oswald which emerges is that of a maladjusted, romantic, northern hero with a strong sense of *devoir.*

The last lines of *Corinne* are intimately related to the first, but they serve to undermine, through irony, Oswald's situation at the opening of the novel:

> Que devint Oswald! Il fut dans un tel égarement, qu'on craignit d'abord pour sa raison et sa vie. Il suivit à Rome la pompe funèbre de Corinne. Il s'enferma longtemps à Tivoli, sans vouloir que sa femme ni sa fille l'y accompagnassent. Enfin l'attachement et le devoir le ramenèrent auprès d'elles. Ils retournent ensemble en Angleterre. Lord Nelvil donna l'exemple de la vie domestique la plus régulière et la plus pure. Mais se pardonna-t-il sa conduite passée? le monde qui l'approuva le consola-t-il? se contenta-t-il d'un sort commun, après ce qu'il avait perdu? Je l'ignore; je ne veux, à cet égard, ni le blâmer, ni l'absoudre.
>
> (p. 863)

Oswald is in almost the same state as in the beginning of the novel, one of violent psychological alienation caused by a death (this time that of Corinne). Dislocation as an escape from grief is here a retreat to Tivoli, again alone, refusing the world of England, represented by his wife and daughter. But Oswald's sense of duty is now even stronger, taking him away from Italy and back to England. Romantic alienation and solitude, the conditions which allowed him to fall in love with Corinne/Italy during the course of the novel, have been replaced by attachment and duty, representing reaffirmation of patriarchal values. The romantic hero has settled for a bourgeois existence, and the possibilities for a life of spontaneity and genius have been rejected. The series of narrative questions with which the novel ends—all rhetorical since the reader knows that the answer to each must be a resounding "no"—is followed by the first-person narrative voice, rare in the work, which supposedly refuses to judge him, claiming ignorance. It is almost as if the "je" of the novel suddenly realizes how clearly this is an indictment of Oswald's behavior and decides to shun responsibility by a final lack of knowledge. But it is too late. Oswald is a condemned man, his English virtues and values eroded by his ultimate failure to love Corinne and, by extension, Italy. He, like Corinne's father, the other important patriarchal figure in the novel, has chosen to reject the very values which would have saved him from a "regular" (and mediocre) existence. The potential for destruction of his essence, posited by the opening lines, has been realized: duty, social position, wealth, family name, and England have brought him a death-like life.

The initial and final passages of ***Indiana*** also follow this pattern: a male character is the central focus in the opening scene, but his value system is undermined. The scene takes place in a patriarchal home, a small manor house, and the master of the house dominates the domestic tableau:

Par une soirée d'automne pluvieuse et fraîche, trois personnes rêveuses étaient gravement occupés, au fond d'un petit castel de la Brie, à regarder brûler les tisons d'un foyer et cheminer lentement l'aiguille de la pendule. Deux de ces hôtes silencieux semblaient s'abandonner sur eux; mais le troisième donnait des marques de rébellion ouverte: il s'agitait sur son siège, étouffait à demi haut quelques bâillements mélancoliques, et frappait la pincette sur les bûches pétillantes, avec l'intention marquée de lutter contre l'ennemi commun.

Ce personnage, beaucoup plus âgé que les deux autres, était le maître de la maison, le colonel Delmare, vieille bravoure en demi-solde, homme jadis beau, maintenant épais, au front chauve, à la moustache grise, à l'oeil terrible; excellent maître devant qui tout tremblait, femme, serviteurs, chevaux et chiens.

(pp. 23-24)

As is true in Staël's *Corinne,* Sand concentrates here on an active male. The tableau is interior, a passive, withdrawn world where time is suspended; timelessness is accentuated by the verb "cheminer" and by the consistent use of the imperfect tense. Yet, one of the three personages reacts against the monotony of timelessness, nervously moving about, yawning, and rebelling against "l'ennemi commun" (time). He makes the only pronounced gesture in the scene ("frappait la pincette"), while the other two silently abandon themselves to boredom and their dreams. This antithesis between the active and passive characters is reinforced by the vocabulary ("lutter"/"s'abandonner," "rebellion"/the idea of submission) and the opposition between the male principle—active, aggressive—and the female principle—passive, submissive—, which is thus established, even though we do not yet know if a female is present.

The second paragraph presents the masculine principle embodied in the rebellious member of the trio, Colonel Delmare. His powers, both of a patriarchal and professional nature, are stated ("maître de la maison," "colonel"), but are immediately undermined by the fact that he is a "vieille bravoure en demi-solde." Thus, his military title no longer has validity. Colonel Delmare is a man who must actively struggle against time, for his former glory is a thing of the past, as is his physical beauty. His balding head, thick body, and terrible look are intimidating to his inferiors (including his wife). Yet, the narrative decisively undermines his status, both by the ironic adjective "excellent" to describe his magisterial powers and by the description of his physical disintegration. The active male is thus the initial point of focus in *Indiana,* but narrative signals tell the reader that the associated system of values is subject to erosion and dissolution.

The closing passage of *Indiana,* like that of *Corinne* (although not focused so directly on the personage first presented), completes the process of erosion begun in the opening section:

Le lendemain, je quittai Ralph et Indiana; l'un m'embrassa, l'autre versa quelques larmes.

—Adieu, me dirent-ils, retournez au monde; si quelque jour il vous bannit, souvenez-vous de notre chaumière indienne.

(pp. 353-54)

Again, we are in a world of no precise time. The two passive members of the trio in the opening scene of the novel are again present and, once more, are set in opposition to another, the new "je" narrator in this case. They are part of a passive, motionless, interior existence, whereas he is actively involved in the process of leaving. He, like Colonel Delmare, has opted for the world of movement and time. They, instead, have chosen the solitary, inner existence predicted by their acceptance of the interiorization of the opening setting. Here, the relative grandeur of "un petit castel," symbol of patriarchy, is replaced by a humble "chaumière indienne" and the political world of France (which the two have shunned, progressively more actively, during the course of the novel) by the natural world of a remote island. The active-life struggle of Colonel Delmare is thus decisively rejected by Indiana and Ralph, who choose the peaceful, passive, isolated, timeless existence that only a romantic island can bring. Free from patriarchal values and laws, Indiana and Ralph live in harmony and love.

In both of these texts, we have seen that the openings are under the sign of the male; the heroine is either totally absent or mentioned only as a *personne.* The outer trappings of the male world are emphasized in both: titles; possessions such as land, family home, and money; and an active life. Each novel demonstrates either an explicit or implicit undermining of the world represented by these men, a patriarchal and hierarchical system in which daughters, wives, and mistresses have little power. The last few lines of each novel complete the erosion process through the reintroduction of the themes and antitheses of the opening lines, indicating a coherence of novelistic structure. This somewhat unusual, tidy structure, presenting the text as a continuous downgrading of the system posited by the opening pages, is perhaps the most dramatic proof that these are indeed subversive novels and that the male world is the target of that subversion.[9]

Whereas Rousseau's novel concentrates totally on the passional relationships of the daughter *within* the *maison paternelle*—Tanner shows, for example, that the most physical encounter in the text is between Julie and her father rather than her lover (p. 27)—those of Staël and Sand emphasize the extra-familial passions and the move by the daughter away from the father's house. Julie refuses all offers to leave the house of Clarens in any sense and becomes enslaved by both the "*nom*" and the "*non*" of her all-powerful father, acknowledging no other jurisdiction or authority than his, even though, as Tanner proves, the "Word of the father is even here in a very imperiled condition" (p. 35). This stance by Rousseau is wholly consistent with the antifeminism exhibited throughout his writings, especially in *Émile*. As Joseph Featherstone recently observed: "He was scarcely a women's liberationist—Emile's bride, Sophy, is a ghastly parody, anticipating what has been called the nineteenth century's cult of true womanhood. . . ."[10] Rousseau emphasizes obedience and submission in his discussion of education for a young girl and feels that a *fille savante* would be an aberration; the creative and intellectual aspirations of women were to be stunted in Rousseau's system. Corinne and Indiana, on the other hand, emphasize the problems of such uneducated women as Julie (trained only to embroider and to please a man), by concentrating on superior women and their struggle to be free. These novels differ from *Julie* in another extraordinary and significant fashion: neither Corinne nor Indiana has a child to further her father's line, thus avoiding the "destiny of biology" (in Simone de Beauvoir's term[11]) and the condition described by Adrienne Rich in her marvelous study of motherhood: "The woman's body is the terrain on which patriarchy is erected."[12] As Kate Millet has shown, the chief institution of patriarchy is the family, a structure which relies on the training of the young and on an inherited culture.[13]

Rather than staying in their father's house and propagating patriarchal values, Corinne and Indiana seek alternatives based on their own talents and beliefs. That Corinne fails and Indiana succeeds (with the help of a passive, peace-loving male) is less important than that they both try. Corinne is, evidently, a victim of patriarchy more completely than is Indiana, but, as we have seen, the system that destroys Corinne is so devastatingly undermined by the narrator that indications are that it cannot long survive. And the solution created by Indiana and her mate is set up in direct opposition to the male-dominated world they have left behind. The conclusions of both novels declare in a positive fashion the situation only indirectly confronted by Rousseau: that the father's house was in a state of disintegration.

That Staël and Sand used their novelistic skills to subvert the patriarchal system is perhaps a reflection of the position of women in their day. As Albistur and Armogathe state in their study of French feminism through history: "Les lendemains de la Révolution française sont les jours les plus sombres de l'histoire des femmes."[14] The institution of the Code civil, which determined the fate of women for a century, kept the female sex tied to her husband in every facet of her existence. The concept of woman as one of man's possessions (along with his children and servants) was also closely allied to the bourgeois notion of property.

Bourgeois ideals of the nineteenth century were notoriously anti-feminist, stressing the "bon ordre dans les familles" and the restoration of the authority of the father.

It is ironic, then, to find the romantic woman of literature so firmly placed upon a pedestal, the temptress/consoler to be worshiped from afar. Both Staël and Sand perceived the fallacy in the romantic myth of the woman as *muse/inspiratrice* in the style of Mme Récamier (although both were certainly placed in that category by the men around them and both profited from that position), while the mass of women were held in the most degraded position imaginable, unable to vote, be educated, obtain a divorce, dispose of their own property, have the right to a profession, or participate in any way in the political process. Woman was a victim of marital absolutism and was kept a minor for life. As Sheila Rowbotham has noted: "A domesticated romanticism produced a crop of egg-faced ringleted bonneted fragile girls. . . ."[15] Pampered and cared for, yet kept helpless, she became part of an oppressed cult. Thus, we see that the first half of the nineteenth century was a difficult time for women writers, who were often discredited both as women and as artists, since sentiment prevailed against the bluestocking. Overall, the romantic period was hardly favorable to feminist ideas; yet women kept writing and, as we have seen, were capable of examining and damaging the dominant system in their works.

The disintegration of the family is obviously not a subject indigenous to women writers. In fact, it becomes a major theme in the nineteenth-century novel, both in England and in France, and is seen in such varied works as Balzac's *Le Père Goriot* and *La Cousine Bette,* George Eliot's *Mill on the Floss* and *Daniel Deronda,* and Zola's entire *Rougon-Macquart* cycle, thus proving Tanner's contention that "the fall of the House of Clarens [is] a fall, to my mind, of inestimable importance for the subsequent history of European literature" (p. 44). Yet, it was the two most important women writers of nineteenth-century France who, quite soon after Rousseau, demonstrated more incisively and effectively than their *maître à penser* had in his novel, how the *toit paternel* might be replaced and the hegemony of patriarchy rejected. Expanding the concept of patriarchy to mean not just the rule of the father but the rule of men, as Kate Millet has shown, Staël and Sand attempted to combat the "sexual politics" of domination of their day. Feminist in their own politics they may not have been; feminist in their thinking they most decidedly were.

Notes

1. Tony Tanner, "Julie and 'La Maison paternelle': Another Look at Rousseau's *La Nouvelle Héloïse,*" *Daedalus* 105 (Winter 1976): 23-45; henceforth referred to in the text between parentheses.

2. For a thorough discussion of Staël's writings on Rousseau and feminism, see Madelyn Gutwirth's essay, "Madame de Staël, Rousseau, and the Woman Question," *PMLA* 86 (1971): 100-09.

3. See Marcel Mauss, "Essai sur le don," in *Sociologie et Anthropologie* (Paris: Presses Universitaires de France, 1966), pp. 145-279, and Claude Lévi-Strauss, chapter on "Endogamie et exogamie," *Les Structures élémentaires de la parenté* (Paris: Presses Universitaires de France), pp. 52-65.

4. Jacques Lacan, *Écrits I* (Paris: Éditions du Seuil, 1966), pp. 157-58.

5. Michel Foucault, "Le 'Non' du père," *Critique* 18 (March 1962), pp. 195-209.

6. Germaine de Staël, *Corinne, ou l'Italie* in *Oeuvres complètes,* I (Genève: Slatkine Reprints, 1967), 653. All subsequent citations will be taken from this edition.

7. George Sand, *Indiana* (Paris: Garnier, 1962), pp. 23-24. All subsequent citations will be taken from this edition.

8. This topic has been fully explored by Edward Said in *Beginnings: Intention and Method* (New York: Basic Books, 1975).

9. It may not be unusual to return to the beginning of a story, but I would judge it unusual to subvert, through language as well as through theme, the opening passage in the closing section.

10. "Rousseau and Modernity," *Daedalus* 107 (Summer 1978): 185.

11. Simone de Beauvoir, *Le Deuxième sexe* (Paris: Gallimard, 1949). See the chapter on "Les données de la biologie," in Part I ("Les Faits et les mythes"), I, 35-76.

12. Adrienne Rich, *Of Woman Born: Motherhood as Experience and Institution* (New York: Norton, 1976), p. 55.

13. Kate Millet, *Sexual Politics* (New York: Doubleday, 1970), pp. 82-84.

14. Maïté Albistur and Daniel Armogathe, *Histoire du féminisme français du moyen âge à nos jours* (Paris: Éditions des Femmes, 1977), p. 239.

15. Sheila Rowbotham, *Women, Resistance and Revolution* (New York: Pantheon Books, 1972), p. 38.

Carol V. Richards (essay date 1982)

SOURCE: Richards, Carol V. "Structural Motifs and the Limits of Feminism in *Indiana*." In *George Sand Papers: Conference Proceedings, 1978,* edited by Natalie Datlof et al., pp. 12-20. New York: AMS Press, 1982.

[*In the following essay, Richards analyzes a series of binary oppositions that form the thematic structure of* Indiana, *claiming that these dualities are mediated through several character triads (such as Indiana-Raymon-Ralph) in order to arrive at the novel's final theme of idealized love.*]

A close reading of George Sand's autobiography *Histoire de ma vie,* according to Germaine Brée, brings to light certain narrative patterns that are repeated in Sand's novels.[1] These narrative patterns exist in Sand's first novel *Indiana* (1832) with surprising clarity and lead us to a fresh understanding of the novel in which we see not the failure of love, as the editor of *Indiana* takes pains to show by using biographical data to interpret the text,[2] but the triumph of an ideal love which wins for the heroine the happiness she had missed in her loveless marriage. At the same time, the "Conclusion" of the novel, considered an afterthought of Sand's,[3] assumes an essential place in the economy of the work as a whole. Autobiography, not biography, serves to elucidate this piece of fiction.

Sand recounts in *Histoire de ma vie* that after her father's untimely death, she lived happily for a short time with her mother and grandmother. Brée shows that this threesome constituted a "happy triangle," the love of the two women, both mother figures, converging on the child. Later, however, in a series of permutations, the "two mothers" become successively "good" or "bad" depending on which one the young Aurore accepts as an influence on her life. Sand pictures herself as "the orphaned, wronged, incorruptible heroine: abandoned, slandered, betrayed, caught in Manichaean conflicts; wrested from her 'good' protectors, persecuted by 'bad' tyrants; deprived of her rightful position in society. But *always vindicated.*"[4] In addition to functioning as a "matrix of fabulation," the original emotional triangle is the source of the system of binary oppositions which informs Sand's world. My intent here is to show, by means of a close look at key passages, that, in the first place, the organizing matrix of the plot of *Indiana* is based on just such a series of binary oppositions encompassing: life, death; happiness, unhappiness; nature, civilization; the spiritual, the physical; "good," "bad"; secondly, that the conflict is played out by characters whose emotional relationships form the kind of triangles Brée found to be an integral part of Sand's autobiography, one character serving as mediator between two others whose essential characteristics are antithetical; thirdly, that on the outcome of the struggle depends the well-being of the heroine; and, finally, that Sand's views concerning her heroine's happiness are linked not only to her portrayal of marriage, but to what is the strongest dynamic principle of the action—a dialectic between sexual indulgence and sexual abstinence, a dialectic which betrays the limits of Sand's feminism at the same time as it defines her ideal of love and which is the central structuring motif of the novel.

In the opening chapter of the novel we meet the initial triangle composed of Indiana centered between two male figures, one actively malevolent and the other benign. The first is her much older husband Delmare, quick to anger and despotic; the second is the young and vigorous Ralph, noticeably calm and impassive. Sand wastes no time in condemning the institution of marriage and in particular the law which gives the master absolute rights over his property as over his wife. It is apparent that this law which chains the frail wife to the brutal husband causes such unhappiness that even death may follow, for the first words Indiana speaks are a plea to save a life.[5] She herself appears to be a near victim of this legal tyranny. The opening scene thus immediately raises two fundamental questions: the first concerns the fate of the heroine—who will provide her with an alternative to the injustice of her marriage? what will be the nature of the alternative?; the second concerns the identity of Ralph—why is he a third party to this unhappy marriage? and what explains his dispassionate stance?

The responses to these questions will not be fully given until the final two chapters of the novel (XXIX and XXX), when Ralph's secret is revealed and Indiana recognizes him as the man she should have loved. What sets into motion the static situation described in Chapter I, generating the bulk of the narrative material, is the arrival on the scene of Raymon, whose presence creates a second emotional triangle again centered on Indiana, at once the possible victim and the prize of the ensuing conflict. His entry into the action upsets the uneasy truce of Ralph-Indiana-Delmare by doubling the malevolent influence on the heroine's life. When Raymon first appears, it is as the nameless "thief" in the night of Chapter I. The purpose of his nocturnal entry onto the Delmare property—to visit his mistress Noun, Indiana's servant—is quickly comprehended by the two men of the household who keep this knowledge to themselves. Their discreet silence is responsible for the first instance of Indiana's misperception of Raymon. She does not realize then, or when they meet socially at a ball, that this young man of noble bearing is accustomed to many adventures in perfumed boudoirs, that he is often moved by his fiery passions (p. 49) rather than by reason or principle, that he is, in fact, seen by others as a Lovelace (p. 57). The "suspense" of the novel is generated by the fact that while the reader recognizes Raymon's charms to be those of a seducer, the heroine sees him as providing a secure haven of love to which to escape from the prison of her marriage. Within the larger frame of the mystery of Ralph's identity is placed, then, the narration of how Indiana is misled down the long perilous path toward a possible sexual union with Raymon. It is not until she has descended this path as far as she is able, until she has reached the depths of degradation and disillusionment, that the process of amelioration can begin. The knowledge of Raymon's true character allows for and precedes the awareness of Ralph's many virtues, and as Indiana gains this insight, the central conflict is resolved.

What begins as a tale of an unhappy marriage is quickly turned into the familiar narrative of the virgin defending her purity against the advances of a seducer.[6] This intrusion of a seduction scenario into a novel about marital injustice explains why Indiana's charms are those of a pure maiden. She is vulnerable on two counts: she is a Creole, having grown up on the Ile Bourbon (renamed La Réunion) in the Indian Ocean, and therefore naïve and socially inexperienced; and secondly, she had never known the happiness of affection: her bizarre and violent father had not loved her and when she married she had only exchanged one master for another (pp. 68-69). Like a princess in a tower, she had dreamt of deliverance, saving her heart for the hero who would deliver her (p. 69). Raymon's eloquent promises and platitudes of romantic love feed her dream of a liberator and she sees Raymon as she desires him to be (p. 71): "illusion," as Sand calls it, (Préface de 1832, p. 9) envelops the heroine. Henceforth, she imagines herself in a "tragic novel" playing the role of the "slave who was only waiting for a sign to break her chain" with the help of a savior who would battle her tyrant husband to the death (p. 71).

Raymon, however, is less interested in freeing Indiana than in pursuing his amorous adventures. In an unexpected twist to the pure maiden-seducer scenario, Raymon's verbal seduction of Indiana is given physical completion with her servant Noun. Yet, it is Indiana's image, as seen in her double Noun, that Raymon makes love to in the most intensely erotic episode of the novel (Chapters VII-VIII). While Raymon loved Indiana "with his whole soul," he "had loved Noun with his senses" (p. 80); during his carnal union with Noun, however, when he kissed her black hair he thought he was kissing Indiana's hair (p. 86) so that in a hallucinatory transport of all his senses, an erotic metamorphosis of Noun into Indiana is accomplished.

It is not Indiana, however, but Noun who suffers the immediate consequences of Raymon's outrage, for when the gullible servant learns that her lover of some time has also been courting her mistress, she drowns herself. And it is Indiana who discovers Noun's body floating on the surface of the water—an image of violent death, a reflection of her own possible future, a reverse image of the happiness so ardently desired.

This episode is doubly important: by setting up the narrative sequence of Noun's short existence in the novel as seduction-perfidy-death, the reader is alerted to the dangers Indiana will face if she continues to place her trust in the man who betrayed Noun. Secondly, in a triangle involving himself and the two women, Raymon mediates the fusion of purity and sexuality in his embrace of Noun; it is, however, only momentary. The synthesis of those antithetical opposites does not last. On the contrary, the polarity is reestablished after Noun's sacrificial death and Indiana's fate will continue to depend in large part on the conservation of her chastity.

Three elaborately constructed narrative sequences then bring Indiana within close range of Raymon's seductive powers. They each take place at night, in either Indiana's or Raymon's chambers, the place of greatest peril for a woman's virtue. With each episode, the pining princess Indiana becomes more actively audacious, and more foolhardy, as she herself pursues Raymon rather than waiting for him to come to her. In fact, Indiana becomes an actively seeking subject who copes with vicissitude and adventure, who courageously faces the hazards of a woman traveling alone, who risks all, comfort, security, reputation and social position to live out her romance to its most idealistic, and most illusory, conclusion. Not only does Raymon fail, of course, to match her own heroic efforts, but he also tires of Indiana's lofty concept of love and ends by making a loveless marriage of the sort to satisfy his ambitions. Although she has not been seduced, as was her double, Raymon's perfidy is so great and her despair so profound, that she barely escapes a fate analogous to Noun's: she is tempted, like Noun, by suicide as her romantic illusions are destroyed. Ralph, however, appears from nowhere to save her from this extreme consequence of her own recklessness. The seduction-perfidy-death sequence is thus averted for the heroine, in a kind of Manichaean struggle, Ralph watching over Indiana silently and secretly, then acting to rescue her. He embodies the "good" which counters the "bad" of Raymon. Furthermore, the Ralph-Indiana-Raymon triangle can be superimposed on the Ralph-Indiana-Delmare triangle in such a way as to equate Delmare and Raymon in the afflictions the heroine is made to suffer when under their power. Since Delmare is absent at the times when Indiana and Raymon draw near each other, Ralph combats the two forms of male evil—tyranny and seduction—in turn. Both of the malevolent male figures disappear from Indiana's life at nearly the same time (Chapter XXIX), Delmare's death preceding Raymon's marriage by only a few months.

In addition, it is the opposition between Ralph and Raymon/Delmare that the nature-civilization polarity is most sharply delineated. Delmare embodies the injustice of the Napoleonic Code, which made wives into chattel. Indiana has nothing but her own free will to redress the balance:

> I know that I am the slave and you are the lord. The law of this country has made you my master. You can tie up my body, bind my hands, rule over my actions.

> You have the rights of the strong and society concurs: but, over my will, sir, you can do nothing. . . .

> (p. 25)

Raymon is a product of the Restoration: scheming, self-serving, ambitious, frivolous, hypocritical; a man without a conscience, he represents a society where artifice is the rule of the game and "opinion" reigns. Ralph, however, is an outsider in the social hierarchy of France. Of English origins, much of his youth was spent on the tropical Ile Bourbon. He is frank where Raymon is merely eloquent; he is disinterested, self-sacrificing, generous, simple, socially inept, yet rich in self-knowledge and guided by a well-developed conscience and an unwavering devotion to Indiana. Indiana, too, is at odds with society by reason of her passion suppressed by the law; she represents, according to Sand, love itself up against all the obstacles of civilization (Préface de 1832, p. 9).

Ralph and Indiana are both linked to nature in its purest state. When, overwhelmed by their misfortunes, they decide on a double suicide, they choose the site of their childhood delights, an ennobling and purifying setting where reigns a pantheistic God (pp. 312-13). It is during the sea voyage back to the Ile Bourbon—to piety and purity—that Ralph wins the final victory over Raymon. Indiana's soul opens up to religious hope, her eyes discover the splendor of the sea and sky, and perceive, at last, Ralph's considerable merits (p. 315). Ralph in turn reveals his secret—a deep passion that he had resolutely suppressed in order to remain near his beloved and to serve her as friend, brother, and protector. Fortunately for this pure lover, Delmare was not a rival in love (p. 331) nor had he been able to aspire to becoming a father (p. 271), while Raymon did not, in fact, ever possess Indiana (p. 336).

The two narrative strands of Indiana's fate and Ralph's identity thus join as the hero turns out to be eminently qualified to provide Indiana with the ideal alternative to her loveless marriage: selfless, purified, love. There follows an apotheosis of "true" love defined as devotion founded on truth, nature and purity. Dressed in virginal white, her hair adorned with orange blossoms, Indiana accepts Ralph as her spouse in heaven and on earth. Their lips meet in an ethereal embrace which contains all the joys of this earthly life and the two leap to their death in the waters below (p. 338).

In a not totally unexpected reversal, the "Conclusion" of the novel presents the couple living in a state of harmony, peace and happiness in a secluded part of the far-away tropical island. Ralph's magnificent self-mastery has won him the prize, Indiana's need for love has been satisfied, and their trials have shown them to be equals in capacity for love as in suffering and misfortune. Their equality meets the ideal Indiana had at one time demanded of Raymon: "I must be loved totally, eternally and without reserve; you must be ready to sacrifice everything to me . . . everything, monsieur, because I shall place the same absolute devotion in my scale and wish it to balance" (p. 136). Although the conclusion seems anti-climactic and tacked on—especially since the focus of the narrative shifts to Ralph—it is nevertheless the logical outcome of a Manichaean struggle based on the preservation of purity; death is precluded when no illicit sex has occurred to be punished. Sand defines for the reader—and happy endings seem flat indeed—what is paradise on earth for the worthy. The conclusion proclaims the higher, more enduring happiness of the couple joined not by laws nor by desire, but by a "true" love, for "love can be a contract just as marriage is" (p. 52). It implies that such love is unattainable in civilized society, as is the union of the man and woman as equals. The virtues displayed by Ralph and Indiana are amply rewarded: generosity, devotion, sacrifice, and especially sexual continence, so as to sanctify the male-female union. Innocence and virtue triumph, to live happily ever after.

The novel thus suggests that the welfare of a woman such as Indiana is dependent upon the control of the fearsome power of sexuality and the ability to thwart its dangers. Indiana's own eroticism is clearly threatening: it is either displaced onto the double Noun, as if female sexuality is a "self" allowed expression only when detached from the heroine herself; or it is expressed in physical activity apart from the male, as in the two other frankly erotic episodes of the novel. The first of these is Indiana's ride on horseback, at which time we learn that hunting was the only passion that Indiana and Ralph had in common (suggesting their hidden and contained desire for each other, Chapter XIV, p. 150). The second takes place during Indiana's evening walks on the Ile Bourbon after her first frustrated attempt to join her fate to Raymon's and before her final disillusionment; alone on some mountain peak, she dreams of Paris, carried by her ardent aspiration towards "desire in all its devouring intensity" (p. 250). Both of these episodes are characterized by rapid, forward movement, intense excitement and unilateral physical pleasure. The many allusions to hair in the novel make it the erotic emblem *par excellence* and give it a thematic function: for example Indiana's hair is kissed voluptuously by Raymon and by Ralph (p. 149, p. 326); Noun's hair is allowed to hang seductively loose (p. 51); Indiana's hair falls out during the long illness preceding her final disillusionment signaling the end of her erotic attraction to Raymon (p. 298) and the exhaustion of her erotic energy. Thus desexualized and safe under Ralph's protective wing in the concluding pages, she fades into the background as he moves to center stage. Ralph alone speaks of their carnal union in veiled terms: "we have tasted happiness to the fullest" (p. 350). It is through him that physical love is purified and given transcen-

dent expression, and that a reconciliation between the chaste and the sexual is accomplished. Indiana's absence from the novel in the conclusion, leaving the reader to picture her happiness from Ralph's telling of it, betrays Sand's reluctance to allow her heroine full erotic expression, even with a hero as devoted and virtuous as Ralph. The sexuality of the heroine must somehow be transmuted, veiled or contained.

Freedom for the heroine is therefore not indulgence in unrestrained or illicit sexual activity. On the contrary, the dangers of such behavior are clearly demonstrated not only by the plot but by the seducer's character flaws and his link to French society. For Indiana, freedom is freedom to love as she sees fit, and to seek emotional contentment on her own terms. And that contentment is found through a mate equal to her in capacity to love, worthy of her exalted passion and so rich in virtue that her revolt against conjugal tyranny is fully vindicated. Indiana's dependence on Ralph to supply that vindication, as well as to save her from the consequences of her own folly, mark the limits to which Sand's feminist thought was developed in this, her first novel. Sand does not create a heroine who learns through experience, who develops a sense of self through which to achieve emotional independence, or who manages to stand on her own two feet so as to find some unconventional social niche for herself. In this respect, she appears a lesser woman than her creator, who had not only broken away from the confinement of marriage, but had begun what was to be a highly successful career with the very novel under discussion. And unlike Balzac and Stendhal, whose heroes grapple with social corruption, Sand in her novel condemns conjugal tyranny, the laws which uphold it and the hypocrisy which deceives the trusting heart, but her heroine does not learn how to survive in the so-called civilized world. While it can be said of both Indiana and her creator, although to different degrees, that of all the binary oppositions in Sand's world, the richest perhaps is that of her "social non-identification in a society where the feminine condition is socially defined,"[7] the social criticism implied by the heroine's rejection of the available roles of wife and mistress is circumscribed by the hero's major role in resolving the plot conflict. But more importantly, without saying how it can be done in society as she knows it, Sand declares in ***Indiana*** that women have the capacity as well as the right to be happy in love. We remember the boldness of Indiana seeking, however blindly, to take charge of her own destiny, and getting away with it. To love and to live—that is the vision Sand offers, the message that endures.

Notes

1. Germaine Brée, "George Sand: The Fictions of Autobiography," *Nineteenth-Century French Studies,* IV, no. 4 (Summer 1976), pp. 438-49.

2. George Sand, *Indiana,* ed. Pierre Salomon (Paris: Garnier, 1962), pp. xxx-xxxiii.

3. See Salomon, pp. v-vi.

4. Brée, p. 444.

5. Sand, *Indiana,* p. 29. All further references to this work appear in the text. Translations are mine.

6. For a concise summary of this tradition in 18th century fiction, of which *Indiana* is an undeniable descendent, see Nancy K. Miller, "The Exquisite Cadavers: Women in Eighteenth-Century Fiction," *Diacritics,* 5 (Winter 1975), pp. 37-43.

7. Brée, p. 446.

Anne Freadman (essay date March 1983)

SOURCE: Freadman, Anne. "Feminism and Interpretation Theory: Sandpaper." *Southern Review* 16, no. 1 (March 1983): 161-73.

[*In the following essay, Freadman presents a feminist-semiotic reading of* Indiana *that exposes the novel's rhetorical and generic manipulation of prior literary discourses, specifically those of Don Juan and the Muse.*]

It would be possible to interpret the project of my paper as resting on the assumption of the immanence of meanings; as if the structures of a text were inducible from the text taken in isolation; as if the text were significant in and of itself; as if George Sand's **Indiana**[1] could be made to disclose the secrets of women's writing, and to foreclose the formulation of important generalisations about that highly problematical object.

But a description such as that would be based on a set of assumptions about "formalism" grounded in the practices of North American New Criticism. I do not share these assumptions. So despite the possibility that I may be preaching to the converted, I beg leave to stipulate my use of the term. I take it, first of all, that formalism is the study of forms, insofar as form is the enabling condition of signification. On this view, form is not opposed to content.

Secondly, "form" is a theoretical object derived from the practices of formalism; it does not pre-exist those practices. Formalism must in general be characterised as the practice of differentiation. Since difference is the primary enabling condition of signification, it follows that formalism is not the principle of what has been called the "autonomous" text,[2] since "difference" supposes a field of pertinent comparison. It further follows, then, that formalism is not inductive. But it is the case that it takes as its domain of enquiry (and as its theoretical object) not the "individual text," but the text as individuated.

Thirdly, formalist theories of text are not necessarily, or properly, restricted to describing the linguistic forms deployed in any text. No theory of linguistic forms can of itself provide the foundation for a theory of textual forms. Theories of genre are formalist in precisely the sense in which I am using the term, that is, they are practices of differentiation which take as their criteria conventions or rule-governed strategies for the formation of texts.

My major methodological presupposition will be that any text is a rewriting of the field or fields of its own emergence, that to write, to read, or to speak is first of all to turn other texts into discursive material, displacing the enunciative position from which those materials have been propounded. I mean that "use" can always do something a little different from merely repeating "usage." In an attempt to do something towards specifying "women's writing," I shall suppose that it is in the business of transforming discursive material that, in its untransformed state, leaves a woman no place from which to speak, or nothing to say. The production of a speaking-position, with respect to discursive material that is both given and foreign, is what can be studied by a feminist formalism.

For the sake of convenience, I distinguish three kinds of discursive material, which I shall label "discourse," "genre" and "rhetoric." Discourse I take in a broad sense, as the sign as it has been used in a specifiable body of texts, and entailing the uses to which it has been put in those texts. Following Foucault,[3] if discourse consists of statements made in that body of texts which specify the objects of a knowledge and predicate of them in specifiable ways, then it follows that to read a sentence in terms of a discourse is at once to construe that sentence as a statement, and to count it (or not) as the same as another, as entailed in another, or as contradicting another of the same discourse. It is thus the determination of discursive value that determines the construals of logical inference. Such construals are conventional. It follows from this definition that discourse is a quasiformal entity, constraining interpretation. Since I hope I can take it for granted that no text is made only of statements, I suppose that the place of interpretation in the practices of reading is not determined by the theory of discourse as such. Genre I take as being in a limited way transdiscursive, a set of conventionalised practices for text-making.[4] The determination of genre is thus the determination of appropriate modes of reading. Rhetoric I take as techniques of persuasion, entailing the relationship of an "I" to a "you," and the invention of provisional relations of coherence between what must in principle be heterogeneous discourses; it thus manipulates the possible answers to the puzzle of what one proposition or set of propositions has to do with another. "You" is positioned in consonance of complementarity with "I" vis-à-vis these discourses. I suppose it is uncontentious that the rhetorical "I" and "you" together specify the enunciative position of the text, that they are both discursive constructs in principle distinct from empirical writers and readers, and that the enunciative position is a textual place from which the organisation of the discursive materials can proceed.

I shall accordingly read *Indiana* as a set of rhetorical and generic strategies that rewrite the material of two discourses. The first of these is the story of Don Juan. Now, you all remember Don Juan: he's the chap who confuses textuality with sexuality, the one for whom the seductive text is more than nine-tenths of the long something-or-other of the law. The discursive model for Don Juan's texts is the blandishments of the devil, while the generic model is something like the elegy, a form in which the dialogue structure is presupposed but rarely used. Were we to dramatise the elegy, the "you" of the text could respond only by resistance or collaboration: enthusiastic collaboration would either produce a lovestory on the model of the eighteenth-century rococo idyll, and thus put an end to the character of Don Juan as such, or Don Juan would reassert his role, cast the poor lady aside, and repeat himself. In the case of initial resistance, Don Juan would repeat himself until she stopped resisting, after which he would cast the poor lady aside, and repeat himself. My point is two-fold: on the one hand, whatever the lady says is predetermined by the form of the seductive text; as such, she has no control over discourse. She is left at the end of the story with only one text, the lament. But Don Juan is a bad listener, because he talks too much; and the lament is a powerless text. On the other hand, the narrative structure of the Don Juan story is anomalous amongst narrative structures in that it cannot end, and the generic problem for any narrativisation or dramatisation of it will be precisely that. Byron turns the tables on his hero, having him seduced by, instead of seducing, a formidable duchess, and leaving him at the end of his endless epic very tired indeed. Mozart and Molière both use the Commander. The point of this is that the theatre is precisely the medium to show the essential theatricality of the Don Juan role and the absolute lack of fit between the theatrical and the moral. Theatrical versions of Don Juan are generic paradoxes, and doubly satirical, since by the dramatisation of repetition, the repeated text becomes powerless, and the swagger of the Don is deflated; repetition itself works as judgement; but the explicitly judgemental gesture of the Commander is theatricalised, and as such emptied of moral content. Now let us suppose a novel written from the point of view of one of the Don's victims: the problem will be to retain the possibility of judgement-by-joke without undercutting the moral problematic, to individuate the victim from the list while retaining the list

as the essential statement about Don Juan, and to construct a speaking-position that will avoid the lament-and-reproach form.

The second discourse worked on by *Indiana,* and which in this case informs the narrative of the narration itself, is the myth of the Muse. The Muse is a thematics of form, and the Muse narrative is the story of the construction and the occupation of the speaking-position of a text. Just as in the Don Juan story, the two roles are always already distributed: the Muse is a female role, and the poet, on whom she bestows the gift of speech, is a male role. Nineteenth-century Muse narratives are invariably interpreted as erotic, where the encounter of Muse and poet is the enabling event for the production of speech. A convenient contrast is therefore to be made with the Don Juan story, since there text is instrumental to seduction, while in the Muse story, seduction is instrumental to text. But while the Don Juan story leaves a place for the speech of the victim, however unsatisfactory, the Muse story entirely eliminates the Muse as speaker. Not only is she silent, a "you" to the poet's invocation, but her role is over by the time the poem starts. There is only one speaking-position, and it has been usurped. Only the poet says "I." It is for this reason that the Muse narrative poses a serious problem for the woman writer.[5] What fiction is there available to speak the origin of women's texts, given that the Muse discourse makes the expression "woman writer" an oxymoron at best, and at worst, a contradiction? At periods when the Muse discourse is dominant, it is not possible merely to avoid it, while to reverse it would simply put the woman writer in the position of taking dictation from a pedagogical authority. The invention of an appropriate fiction, it seems to me, will always engage in some way with this account of the origins of speech which positions women as merely spoken.

The two major male characters of *Indiana,* Raymon and Ralph, and the stories of which they are protagonists, can be read in terms of these two discursive models. Raymon de Ramière is a Don Juan. In the course of the novel he has three love affairs, of which the central one is with Indiana herself, each of which in some way repeats the structures of the others. The first is with Noun, milk-sister, companion and maid of Indiana, and sometimes referred to as "la belle Indienne." These two women are treated in the novel as doubles, such that through the mediation of the mirror, Raymon sees each reflected in the other at the crucial moments of erotic encounter. The parallel is emphasised with various other details. The third lady in Raymon's life is Laure de Nangy, whom he meets when her adoptive father buys the property that had belonged to Indiana's husband. Paying his first courtesy call, he finds Laure seated at Indiana's place beside the fire. But there the parallel ends, since Laure is cleverer than Raymon and calls his bluff, calculating his submission to her designs rather than becoming the third in a string of replacement women victims, positioned as "the same" by the discourses of seduction.

Just as important for the interpretation of Raymon as a Don Juan is the series of descriptions of him as speaker of the seductive text. We are told that he "expressed his passion with art, and felt it with warmth. But it was not passion that made him eloquent, it was his eloquence that made him passionate" (p. 62). And again, "having so carefully thought out his plan of seduction, he had grown passionate, like an author warming to his subject, or a lawyer to his case; the emotion that he felt when he saw Indiana could be compared with that of an actor totally absorbed in his role . . ." (131). Raymon's eloquence is interpreted from the beginning as theatrical, and it is to its theatricality that the narrator attributes its power. Correspondingly, the women who fall victim to his power are not totally deprived of speech, but their speech is ineffectual. Noun writes Raymon a letter: "Poor girl!" exclaims the narrator, "it was the last straw. A chambermaid's letter! Although she had taken the satin writing paper and perfumed wax from Madame Delmare's writing desk, and she had formed the style in her heart . . . But the spelling! Do you know what a dreadful effect dropped syllables can have on sentiments?" (53). Indiana, too, writes letters, and more significantly, a journal: "This journal of her pains was addressed to Raymon, and although she had no intention of sending it to him, she conversed daily with him in it, telling him, sometimes with passion and sometimes with bitterness, of the evils of her life and the feelings she could not stifle" (268). Letters and diaries are of course "women's texts": both are private, since letters have single, personal interlocutors, and diaries are designed to be secret if not violated. But the place of letters and diaries is shown in the novel not to be a speaking-position, by the fact that they are effectively not read; and they are in no way the model for the narration. When the "you" of the seductive text starts talking, Don Juan's eloquence is already being addressed to another. The "I" who has no interlocutor is no "I" at all.

Ralph, by contrast with Raymon, doesn't like Noun much, and it never occurs to him to establish a parallel between her and Indiana. Equally by contrast with Raymon, he is inarticulate, given to heavy handed clichés and catastrophic frankness. Even his face is said to be insignificant, and he is compared unfavourably at the beginning of the text with the puffy face beaten into a metal fire-screen (25-26). Raymon finds him indistinguishable from his portrait, and speaks of his "mask of stone." But beneath all this, there is wisdom, passion, insight and love, and as his true character is revealed, his mask falls away, his "words take on the colour of his sentiments" (314); and just as his portrait hanging in Indiana's bedroom is covered with a triple layer of gauze, so it is said at the moment of his transformation that "the veil which hid such great virtues, such depth and strength of spirit, fell quite away, and the mind of this man rose to the level of his heart . . . words came to the aid of his thoughts, and this mediocrity who had never said anything but commonplaces in the whole of his life, became, at the end of it, eloquent and persuasive as Raymon had never been" (318). He is thus contrasted systematically with Raymon, who is said at the beginning to have a "happy face and a way with words" (49), but whose eloquence is gradually revealed to be a mask.

The transformation of Ralph has a narrative shape that resembles in a number of respects the Muse narrative. Firstly, it is a narrative of the transformation of silence into speech which not only reveals his true soul to Indiana, but crucially gives him the capacity to become the major narrative-relay of the text. That is, it is Ralph's account of the story which the narrator recounts. Furthermore, it is the sea voyage that takes Ralph and Indiana back to the Island which restores Indiana to health and Ralph to expressivity. Having planned a suicide pact, they are released from the pains of their former existences, and it is at this point that Indiana weeps on to the brow of Ralph, who is then and thereby freed to tell her of his love for her (320). Consummation occurs at the edge of a highly romantic version of the fountain of the Muses, a cataract, where their planned leap into the chasm becomes an unplanned orgasm, and they live, precisely, to tell the tale. Now this has every appearance of the classic Muse event, and its central function in the emergence of the narration will not have escaped you. We may remark on the fact that the major narrative-relay is a male character, as is the narrator, and that Indiana herself is sent out of the room at the moment of the transmission of the story from one to the other. How, we might ask, could George Sand have published in her first novel an account of the renunciation of the speaking-position? But to ask the question this way is to indulge in essentialism, and in particular, takes no account of the fact that Raymon and Ralph are opposed not merely as "characters" but as principles or modes of speech. "Men" may not be a category in this novel, and nor, indeed, may "women"; but "genre" certainly is. It is through the question of genre that the roles of the characters are specified. To ask the question of the "Muse interpretation" will not be to ask the question of Indiana's role *qua* woman, but to ask the question of her relationship with the taxonomy of genres whereby the conventions of this novel are described. Let me remind you that the Muse is conventionally not the Muse of a particular text so much as of the genre which governs that text.

The eloquence of Raymon is not merely the naked abuse of phallic speech. Raymon, we are told, was a man of "elegant manners, a studied life-style, and poetic loves"

(52). Meeting Noun in the forest at the dead of night, his fantasies are nurtured by "the poetry of the place" (51). Persuaded that Indiana's insistence on chastity is a proof of her coldness, he interprets her passionate letters and avowals of love as "an application of the exaggerated sentiments she had read about in books." Accordingly, he works on his own "passionate eloquence and dramatic improvisation, so as to keep up with his novelistic mistress, and he manage[s] to perpetuate the error. But for a calm and impartial audience, this love scene could only have been theatrical fiction disputing the stage with reality. The bombast of Raymon's sentiments and the poetry of his ideas, would have seemed a cruel and unfeeling parody of the emotions Indiana expressed with such simplicity" (196). You will no doubt have noticed the recurrence of the nineteenth-century version of the Aristotelian triad: the theatrical, the novelistic and the poetical are the predicates used to position Raymon's eloquence as false, in rather the same way as Byron says in *Don Juan* that his Muse is "the most sincere that ever dealt in fiction" (Canto 16, st. 2). Raymon's love-making is literary, yet it is Raymon who levels the accusation at Indiana, reproaching her with taking literally what she has read in books: "Where did you get your dreams of love? In what chamber-maids' novelette did you study society, I pray?" (210). She responds: "I was mad; I had, in your cynical language, learnt life from chamber-maids' novels, those carefree penny-fictions where the heart is inveigled by dreams of wild escapades and impossibly happy endings" (240). But if this is the definition of the novelistic, it is framed in this novel in such a way as not to be its model.

I take the theatrical to be the mode of insincerity, the poetical to be the mode of fantasy, and the novelistic to be that of illusion. Together they make up the literature of untruth, what the narrator calls "the art of words" as distinct from "the knowledge of things" (115). While of necessity partaking of the mode of prose narrative, this novel will be counterpointed to the novelistic as empiricism is to fiction. To observe, to watch, to listen and to understand are the predicates both of Ralph and of the narrator: "If somebody had observed closely Madame Delmare," we are told at the start of the text, "they would have seen in this trivial circumstance of her private life the painful secret of her entire existence" (29); and only four pages later, Indiana upbraids Ralph for knowing more, through his close observation of her, than she has ever permitted him to know. Ralph makes it his business, however, always to know what's going on. He is a sort of human watchdog to Indiana, whose first act in the novel is to light a candle and place it strategically so that Indiana's husband might notice her sickly state; his last is to tell the story. Observation, understanding, and illuminating the heroine so that others will understand is the role of the realist novelist; and when Ralph speaks, his text is not called a "novel," but a history, a narrative. Similarly, the narrator's preface claims that "the writer is but a mirror," that the "narrator recounts what he saw," that he is the "historian of Indiana," telling the story under the same construction as it was told to him (6-10). These claims, which are typically those of the realist novel, are specifically those of third-person narrative.

Just as the conventions of the literary are set against the realist novel as the false is to the true, so the other genres mentioned in the text are arranged in contrast. Political pamphlets, which are Raymon's forte and the main domain (apart from seduction) for the exercise of his eloquence, are by definition public, concerned with the manipulation of power rather than with truth. The opposite of these is Indiana's journal and her letters; the contrast lies in the opposition between the exclusively public text, which need only ever be performance, and the exclusively private text, which can only ever be truth, but which remains unheard. How to translate the public into the domain of the private is the rhetorical problem of Don Juan: the contrary problem—the translation of the intimate into public discourses, without either violating its secret or betraying its truth in the conventions of the literary—is the problem of the novelist of the personal. To solve it, to tell the story in such a way that the reader interprets it without relying on public opinion and the conventions of public morality, the novelist must construct an enunciative position that can speak from the domain of the personal. This is the problem solved by the figure of Ralph. But if it is at the same time to avoid the form of the lament and reproach, the first-person narrative that would have been Indiana's or Ralph's must be mediated. The narrative voice must be capable of gentle irony, the detachment of the sympathetic but lucid stranger, whose place is neither in the society characterised by public discourses, nor in the island refuge with its victims.

The people who tell stories in this story are above all good listeners, and it is only when a character is constituted explicitly as a good listener that another character can speak. This is the major model for the emergence of the narration. Its first occurrence is in the contrast between the two senior ladies of the novel, Madame de Carvajal, Indiana's aunt, and Madame de Ramière, Raymon's mother. On the morning of Indiana's escapade they discuss the matter: "the only thing that had struck Madame de Carvajal in Madame Delmare's disappearance was the scandal . . . Raymon's mother wept over Indiana's fate and sought to excuse her . . ." (228). Listening is not a simple, passive compassion; Madame de Ramière asks questions, and after this conversation with Madame de Carvajal goes off in search of news of Indiana (228). Similarly Ralph, the silent watcher, makes it his business to be in the right place at the right time, and his questions, though flat-footed, are always to the point. It is appropriate, then, that Madame de Ramière should discuss with Ralph the situation of Indiana, and that they should share their information to form a more or less complete story. Similarly, complementary narratives give us the necessary insight into Ralph's intimate life. Raymon's curiosity about him prompts Indiana into telling what she knows of his life story, but it is only when Ralph himself accedes to expressivity that the rest can be told, of course to Indiana herself. Indiana is thus positioned as listener by the fact that her version of Ralph's story is both true and compassionate, but incomplete. Now, Indiana in her role as listener is compared directly to the reader: "If the narrative of the inner life of Ralph has produced no effect on you, if you have not come to love this virtuous man, it is because I have been unskilled as the interpreter of his memories . . ." (337). If a reader is a listener like Indiana, whose job is to "come to love" Ralph as she does, then it must be because the reader is in possession already of enough of the facts of the matter for his own version of the story to be complemented but not contradicted by the revelation of a hitherto secret truth. These are the procedures of verisimilitude.

The presence of a good listener is signalled not so much by his or her response to a story as by his or her capacity to feel compassion before the story is told. Thus, Madame de Ramière weeps for Indiana *before* going off for news of her; the young narrator weeps *before* Ralph tells him the story; and Indiana's tears fall on to the brow of Ralph *before* he tells the story of his inner life. In each case, compassion is the sign of the listener, and it is the constitution of the "you" position that both constitutes the "I" and allows the succession of narrators to occupy it. The function of the prefaces is much the same, since they guide the reading towards compassion rather than condemnation, before the story begins.

The prefaces also function to define the genre and the mode of reading appropriate to it. The 1832 preface calls it a tale, and this word is used in several places in the novel in conjunction with descriptions of the characters as sculptural and motionless. In each case, however, the progression of the narrative will bring these fictional characters to life. The teller of tales has the job, claims the preface of 1832, of "amusing and not instructing" (8); and the 1842 preface, likewise, denies that the narrator is a pedagogue, claiming instead that he is "the true advocate of the abstract beings who represent our passions and our pains before the tribunal of force and the jury of public opinion. This is a task which has its gravity, beneath an appearance of frivolity . . ." (16-17). This is not incompatible, however, with the role of "teller of tales," since the later preface is written from the point of view of an author re-reading a book written and published ten years before. It is precisely the task of an understanding reading to seek the truth beneath appearances, just as it is the task of the teller of tales to give a form to truth. The realist novelist, and the realist reader, are defined by this dialectic.

Now, bringing a form to life is what Pygmalion does to Galatea, and we know from Ross Chambers' work on angels and automata that the Pygmalion myth is a variant of the myth of the Muse.[6] The transcendental Muse is claimed to be a source of the "I" position, and to bring from the realms of the unknown a Word which would remain inaccessible without her mediation. But the paradox is that the poet is "I" to the Muse's "you": her presence and her existence are contingent on his speech. Only when he has constituted her in her role can she play it, and she says what she is told. The Pygmalion myth makes this paradox explicit, but it is because of this that the roles can be reversed, where those of the transcendental Muse can not. To reverse the roles of the Pygmalion myth is to have a female Pygmalion breathe life into a male Galatea, and have him sing and dance at her bidding. When the walking portrait of Sir Ralph Brown receives the tears of Indiana on his brow, it is not she who is Muse, but he; in the role of Galatea, he speaks her story. His place as observer guarantees that in his role as eye to Indiana's "I" he controls the principal generic constraints of the novel, mediating the private to the tellable in order to produce the novel of the personal, and truth through the forms of fiction to produce the realist novel. The male Muse of verity is a stolid English empiricist.

The problem of speaking in this text is posed, then, in terms of who can tell the story; but the question of "who?" is in its turn raised in terms of "what genre?" Like Don Juan, Galatea is an actress; but unlike him, Ralph has only one part, asserting thereby the indissolubility of "form" and "content" in the conventions of genre, as in the myth of the Muse. Pygmalion, like all good authors, absconds from the text: it is Indiana's role to retire into privacy and silence at the end of the book, leaving Ralph to do the talking. She thus becomes the third person, that which must be told. She is the figure of truth, but for that very reason, she is not a figure of speech. We can see this as sundering the two traditional figures of Woman: her place in Philosophy, as Truth, and her place as Muse, in Poetry. But her occupation of the place of truth allied with her role as Pygmalion disturbs the picture somewhat, for Foucault has shown that these two roles together define the power of the speaking position.[7] Indiana as author and authority? Surely not. Yet it is her alliance with Ralph that allies truth with the genre of the realist novel, and provides the place of mediation for the personal to emerge into the public. And it is her role as Pygmalion that sets up the chain of narrative-relays. This alliance gives us a picture of the authorial position, as all good Muse stories should do. But the "author" is in the third person, spoken by a stranger who can say "I" only because he has no name and no face. Indiana is the very figure of the self-entailing ambiguity of "her story" that cannot be resolved into its disjuncts.

The man with the stone mask and the habit of resembling statues is not, then, a figure for the Commander in the Don Juan story, though he does have the last word over his Latin rival. The vengeance of the Muse is rather different in Raymon's case. He ends up married to a ruthlessly disdainful literary lady with the unmistakeably Muse name of Laure. She is busy, when we meet her, painting a copy of an eighteenth-century fresco. Her copy is exaggerated to bring out the mannered falsity of the rococo idyll, and she entitles it "Pastiche." But though she mocks it, with its "poetry" and its "ridiculous fictions" (289), it is no worse, she says, than the "sombre political elucubrations" of the present day. She thus marks the demise of Raymon's career not only as political pamphleteer but also as Don Juan. It is a sticky end indeed for the seducer, to be bound in holy matrimony with his own pastiche.

When Laure says of eighteenth-century art: "Is it not true that these sheep neither walk, nor sleep, nor graze like the sheep of today? nature is so pretty, so well-groomed . . ." (289), her description of the stylised depiction of nature must be set alongside the narrator's description of a part of the island where a volcanic disturbance has scattered rocks in the strangest patterns, suggesting half-formed sculptures and the outlines of architectural styles. Among this confusion, there is a "basalt obelisk, whose sides seem to have been chiselled and polished by an artist" (340). Laure's taste is neither for contemporary seriousness nor for eighteenth-century frivolity, and her double negative clears a space for the realist aesthetic of the narrator, for whom art is fashioned by the "chiselling and polishing" of the forms left by a natural disaster, a drama whose arena is the real world.

It is clear that the rhetoric whereby the realist novel is described is one that claims the transparency of discourse and the possibility of telling without interpreting and showing by reflection. But it is not clear to me that the use of this rhetoric in any text should be taken as an unproblematical statement of the case. Indiana's complicity with Raymon's eloquence is a function of her reading of novels, and in particular of her literal reading of them which presumes a perfect match with the world. She is thus the precise opposite of Laure, for pastiche is non-complicitous repetition, a denunciation of conventions. The rhetoric of realism is used in this novel as the opposite not simply of the illusory, but—crucially—of the use of the illusory in the discourses of seduction. It is the opposite not merely of a theory of representation, but of a discursive strategy. To be effective against the exercise of power, it must itself be an exercise in the play for power. It appears to derive its power from the claim to truth. But the narrative takes its distance. Ralph's portrait, the very model of realist art, is described in the following terms: "It was a painting of admirable skill, a true family portrait, a detailed

resemblance of infantile and careful perfection, a paragon of middle-class finickityness, a portrait that would make a nurse weep, the dogs bark, and a tailor swoon with pleasure" (92). The narrator is to the discourses of realism as Laure is to those of the illusory. After all, if seduction is a theory of reading to which we cannot subscribe, resemblance is a theory of writing that must on no account seduce.[8]

I wish to conclude with some remarks on the implications that work of the kind I have just done on *Indiana* might have for feminist reading-practices in general.

Let me take two specific examples of discursive difference from within the text. The first is the mirror, which functions for Raymon as that which frames the indistinguishability of one woman from another. For the narrator, however, the mirror is the metaphor for the novel which mediates private truths into public forms. This function is made all the more clear by the transformation of the mirror into the *face à face* at the door at the moment of the meeting of Ralph and the narrator (343). In the first case, the mirror is a metaphor for the discourses of seduction, in which no woman has an identity other than as woman; in the second case, like my mirror at home and no doubt yours, the mirror mediates the passage from the boudoir to the ball. In neither case is it the "same" mirror as Stendhal's, the metaphor for reflection theory, which is always already in the street.

The second example is *la lime,* which first appears in the narrator's prefatory remarks about the oppression of Indiana: "Indiana is will at odds with necessity, blind love striking its head against the obstacles of civilisation. But the serpent wears down and breaks its teeth in its attempt to bite into *la lime,* and the soul exhausts its strength in its fight against the positivities of life" (9).[9] Its second appearance is implicit: it is the means whereby the artist polishes the rocks thrown up by the volcano, thus turning them into the sculptures that stand as the first step of the Pygmalion story. In the first of these instances, *la lime* is the weapon of society, but it has changed hands in the second. The positivities of life are seduction, the law, and public opinion; these are discourses, whose power is the instrument of oppression. The fact that the metaphor changes hands—to be used *by* the writing instead of *against* the character—is the metaphor I have used for the enunciative position which disempowers the discursive materials on which it acts.

If reading and writing are practices that determine the way signs function under social conditions of some specificity, then they are indeed practices, and should be read as such. To read a nineteenth-century novel as if its discursive strategies were transparent, or enfeebled to the extent that it is taken to consist merely of words behaving like capricious nineteenth-century individualists, is to deny the readability of these strategies. However, to read those strategies is to commit oneself to the theory that textuality is a restriction on the so-called infinite possibilities of language. Discursive strategies are constraints on those possibilities, though in order to keep on working, they need to be reinvented, and their reinvention is of course their transformation. My claim about the mirrors is that they are different metaphors because they are constrained by different discursive formations; and that this difference is readable as a transformation by virtue of the postulate of the enunciative position of the text. I have further claimed that the Stendhalian mirror of the reflection theory of discourse is not a proper construal of either one of them. It is not entailed in the theory of textual constraints that only one construal of a text or of a sign is possible or true; but merely that certain construals are ruled out, and that we can say which ones these are. To rule out the possibility of certain construals—not by censorship but by textual strategy—is to insert one's speech at the point of the control of discourse. If, as Peirce is so often quoted as saying, the whole world is perfused with signs, then this is indeed what we must do. The alteration of meanings is a gesture of considerable political significance. It is incumbent upon me as semiotician to notice it.

It follows from this analysis that reading is a writing, certainly, and that writing is a reading, and my particular claim about the George Sand of *Indiana* is that she is a reader of the novelistic in precisely this sense, taking the position of Laure to Indiana, but also, of the narrator to Laure. While it is possible to compare the roles of Indiana and of Emma Bovary, it is also absolutely necessary to differentiate the procedures of the novels whose titles are their names. It is not good enough, after all, to assert that women were the reading public of the nineteenth-century novel, without taking the term "reading" in the strongest possible sense: Emma Bovary does not transform the genre of the novel: the authorial figure of *Indiana*/Indiana does.

To read textual constraints is thus to read the processes of difference. What is at stake is the possibility of specifying the objects of a feminist reading practice. A reading practice that works according to these principles will be reading the formation of texts from enunciative positions in an attempt to specify the "writing of women" as distinct from "women writers" and "feminine meanings," and "textual practices" as distinct from "expressivity" and "reflection." A formalist practice such as I have adumbrated, however, is necessarily a commitment to studying the particular, and is thus a challenge to two kinds of generalisation: women's writing cannot in this practice emerge as a unitary object, with certain essential properties; nor can it emerge as merely and necessarily derivative. Any history of women's writing will be a history of particular speaking positions as they tangle with particular and historically situated discursive materials. It will therefore be a history of specific transformations.

There is, however, a serious objection to limiting the sights of feminist criticism to "speaking-positions" rather than women writers, and that is that by so doing we seem to have tied our own hands. If the "woman writer" is not an a priori of feminist criticism, how (it may well be asked) could feminist criticism select a corpus of women's writing? My response is that we are not working in the void, any more than to speak is to transform silence. The woman writer is a given; but precisely, it is given in and by discourse. I can read that discourse, and rewrite it. George Sand is not as she is represented to be: prolix and repetitive when she is not just telling a good story, and when she is, a downright embarrassment to the modernist critic—and in either case, derivative to the point of abjection. In a reading such as I have done of *Indiana,* I have embarked on the rewriting of George Sand as a discursive object. The given of the history books is no more a biological source of meanings than the enunciative position I have sketched out today, though the discourses of biological authorship claim to locate a source of meanings, where mine does not.

It remains for me to define my own speaking-position. As semiotician, I claim that my reading is a reading "of" *Indiana,* but how can I read it without changing it? And as feminist, I claim that my reading changes the discourses within which George Sand has been read, but how can I so claim without claiming to know what they are? The paradox of my *Sandpaper* is that it partakes of the predicates both of the mirror and of *la lime*: it is a reflection upon, and an abrasion. This paradox cannot be solved by considering the work of reading as the production of a knowledge, defined by the epistemological dilemmas that run as a leitmotiv through current literary theory. But it is not the production of a knowledge; it is the plying of a craft, and as in any craft, its materials have their resistance. The material of the text we read does not simply evaporate by virtue of the assertion that we can only read it with language: diamond-cutting after all is done with diamonds. So you may think of "materials" as raw, or in the instrumental sense, as image or as mirror, as rock or rasp, as fresco or pastiche—as the telling or the tale, as the reading or the text. The difference, in this case, is immaterial, especially if you have the luck to be working with Sand.

Notes

1. George Sand, *Indiana,* ed. Pierre Salomon (Paris: Garnier, 1962). All references are to this edition; page numbers are given in the text; translations are my own.

2. See Walter Benn Michaels, "Against Formalism: The Autonomous Text in Legal and Literary Interpretation," *Poetics Today,* 1, Nos. 1-2 (1979), 23-34.

3. Michel Foucault, *L'Archéologie du savoir* (Paris: Gallimard, 1969).

4. See John Frow, "Discourse Genres," *Journal of Literary Semantics,* 9 (1980), 73-81.

5. See Anne Freadman, "Poeta (1st decl., n., fem.)," *Australian Journal of French Studies,* 16 (1979), 152-65.

6. Ross Chambers, *L'Ange et l'automate: variations sur le mythe de l'actrice de Nerval à Proust* (Paris: Lettres Modernes, 1971).

7. See Foucault, *La Volonté de savoir,* Vol. I of *Histoire de la sexualité* (Paris: Gallimard, 1976), and *Surveiller et punir* (Paris: Gallimard, 1975).

8. I am grateful to Ross Chambers for pointing out that the claim to truth, i.e. the claim *not* to seduce, is the ultimate seductive posture (see p. 70 above).

9. The allusion to the fable of La Fontaine, "Le serpent et la lime" (*Fables,* livre V, no. 16), constitutes in itself an ironic rewriting. The *moralité* of this fable interprets *le serpent* as *un esprit du dernier ordre* whose efforts to destroy *tant de beaux ouvrages* must necessarily be in vain:

> *Ceci s'adresse à vous, esprits du dernier ordre,*
> *Qui n'étant bons à rien cherchez sur tout à mordre;*
> > *Vous vous tourmentez vainement.*
> *Croyez-vous que vos dents impriment leurs outrages*
> > *Sur tant de beaux ouvrages?*
> *Ils sont pour vous d'airain, d'acier, de diamant.*

Kathryn J. Crecelius (essay date 1987)

SOURCE: Crecelius, Kathryn J. "*Indiana*: Heroic Romance and Bourgeois Realism." In *Family Romances: George Sand's Early Novels,* pp. 57-80. Bloomington: Indiana University Press, 1987.

[*In the following excerpt, Crecelius analyzes structure, theme, and characterization in* Indiana *by approaching the work as a synthesis of the heroic quest romance (featuring a heroine, rather than a hero) and the bourgeois, realist novel.*]

Sand intended *Indiana* as a serious portrait of everyday life, "bourgeois realism," as she called it (*C* [*Correspondance*] II, 46), without the frivolity, coarseness,

and diffuseness that characterized her and Sandeau's previous novel. While *Indiana* is a much more realistic work than *Rose et Blanche,* especially as concerns characterization and plot, it is best described as a romance, to use Northrop Frye's term.[1] More specifically, *Indiana* belongs to that mode which Fredric Jameson has called the "art romances of the Romantic period."[2] In her first long, independently written work, conceived and executed with an eye toward publication, Sand turned to one of the oldest literary genres, adapting and changing it for her own purposes.

Frye describes the quest romance as "the search of the libido or desiring self for a fulfillment that will deliver it from the anxieties of reality but will still contain that reality" (Frye, 193). He has identified in the romance six phases that "form a cyclical sequence in a romantic hero's life" (Frye, 198), as well as numerous characteristics particular to the genre, which all appear in *Indiana* with certain salient exceptions.

The most obvious difference between *Indiana* and Frye's examples concerns the reversals occasioned by the gender of the protagonist, who is a heroine rather than a hero, and who acquires at the end not a bride but a bridegroom. Nor is the reversal completely symmetrical, for Indiana does not rescue Ralph, as the hero does the lady, although he has the same psychological link to the oedipal father as the bride has to the mother. Indiana's quest is also far more spiritual than concrete and contains fewer physical adventures than the romances Frye describes, even though she does cross the ocean alone in a last, daring effort to be united with Raymon. This lack of external adventures has at least as much to do with Indiana's gender and women's circumscribed life as it does with the author's desire to relate a simple and natural story.

Indiana contains all the phases noted by Frye except the first, the birth of the hero(ine), which is not exceptional. Indiana's innocent youth (II) is described twice, by her and by Ralph, as an idyllic time spent in the pastoral setting of l'île Bourbon and characterized by the chaste love she and Ralph felt for each other. Her quest (III) involves the search for happiness and freedom and leads ultimately to self-knowledge, while her enemy is society and its laws, particularly those governing marriage, which allow women no voice in their own destiny. While Raymon at first appears to be the villain, especially in his more sadistic and diabolical moments, he is best seen as the catalyst that enables Indiana to understand the workings of French society and to appreciate the kind of alternative represented by Ralph.[3]

The fourth phase requires the "maintaining of the integrity of the innocent world against the assault of experience" (Frye, 201), and corresponds to Indiana's attempt to justify Raymon and his cowardly action in letting her leave France, rather than analyzing his behavior and recognizing that she and he have vastly divergent views of love and its consequences.

The fifth phase is complementary to the second in that it represents an idyllic, erotic world, but one where experience is comprehended rather than yet to come (Frye, 202). This phase encompasses Ralph and Indiana's voyage back to the île Bourbon, along with their moments at Bernica, where Ralph reveals his true self and Indiana understands the error of her choice of Raymon. This is also the point of epiphany, coming as it does at the top of a waterfall[4] and invoking a mysterious spiritual intervention that even the positivistic Ralph prefers to ascribe to an angel (*I* [*Indiana*], 349).[5] This moment of truth leads to the sixth and final phase, where Ralph and Indiana establish their own, separate household and withdraw as much as possible from the rest of society. The cycle renews itself, however, as Ralph recounts their story and describes their life to a young man whom they incite to follow their example, should society reject him. There is a potential sequel in this disciple's adventures in society that might lead to a similar, contemplative retreat; at the very least, Ralph and Indiana's experience is repeated in the young man's narration of the story.

By viewing *Indiana* as part of the romance tradition, we are able to demonstrate the unity of the novel as well as the necessity of the conclusion to the whole. The last chapter, which in the original edition was simply numbered 15, was later called "Conclusion. A Jules Néraud," and dedicated to the friend who had taught Sand so much about l'île Bourbon. Wladimir Karénine and Pierre Salomon both assert that this chapter was added after the novel had been completed, but before publication, either to avoid an unhappy ending or to lengthen the novel (*I,* v-vi). Neither suggestion is valid. George Sand would end her next two novels with the death of the protagonists, while *Rose et Blanche* did not have a happy ending, so she was not averse to tragic conclusions if necessary. As for the length of the novel, without this conclusion the two original volumes contain about the same number of pages (volume I fills 342 pages, volume II, 362, or 333 without chapter 15), so that the argument that the second volume was too short simply does not hold.

Rather than seeking external reasons for the ending of *Indiana,* we should examine the internal logic of the narrative. Seen from this perspective, the île Bourbon becomes the locus of the fulfillment of the desires that occasioned the story. Neither the real world, symbolized by France, particularly Paris, nor a fantasy world, l'île Bourbon is a French colony where French life is duplicated, but inexactly, so that the freedom to live differently than in French society exists. As is the case with its prototypes, *Indiana* ends in a rebirth that is also a reintegration, but on a different plane: at the end, Indiana is part of a couple, as at the beginning, only that couple is more genuine, being based on choice rather than coercion.[6]

This concluding chapter has a further structural function, for it provides the origin of the narrative and reveals the identity of the narrator. Throughout the novel, the narrator has been a mysterious figure. First-person interventions reveal him as well as his unknown narratee to be a man (*I,* 105), while his many tentative comments show that he is not omniscient but is occasionally underinformed as to all the circumstances of his tale. The conclusion allows us to understand the narrator's hesitancy, for he is merely repeating the story as he heard it from Ralph. This ending underlines the cyclical nature of the narrative as well, for it is only after the narrator has met Ralph and Indiana that he can tell their story, yet this meeting comes at the end, not at the beginning of the novel. Thus, *Indiana* ends where it properly should begin.

The discovery of the narrator's identity does not resolve all the ambiguities of the narrative, however. There are passages in the novel that seem clearly attributable to Sand herself, while others, especially those which express uncertainty about particular events, reveal the viewpoint of an outsider, the narrator. In Gérard Genette's terms, we can distinguish between "who sees?" (a female) and "who speaks?" (a male).[7] As noted in chapter 1, the use of a male narrator did not come easily to Aurore Dudevant. On some level, she felt from the first that narration was a male task, not a female one, or at least that a male narrator was more credible, while nonetheless continuing to assert her own voice. The alternation between "je" and "nous" in *Indiana,* as previously in *Rose et Blanche* and **"Jehan Cauvin,"** shows Sand's continued unwillingness to create an authoritative narrator who assumes complete responsibility for his narrative. However, there is a clear distinction between *La Marraine* or **"Histoire du rêveur"** and *Indiana,* in that the earlier works contain a male intradiegetic narrator and a female extradiegetic narrator who in some sense controls the text, whereas in *Indiana* the male narrator dominates. The female voice is still present, but it is harder to detect, for it has gone underground.

Although Sand systematically utilized a male narrator, she left gaps in all her texts where the female voice comes through—in perspective, in partial narration, as in *Lélia* and *Leone Leoni,* or in the inclusive "nous." The male narrator, like the male name, hides but imperfectly the female presence behind it. In revising her novel, as we know she did (*C* II, 46-48), Sand must have chosen to distance herself from the narrative, perhaps on account of its controversial content, perhaps because of earlier notions regarding male narrative authority, by interposing a separate narrator who, because of his gender and background, could not be assimilated to the author. This was accomplished by adding a final chapter, which served further to give more balance to the novel's plot. The "Conclusion" is therefore a positive and significant addition to the novel, and not the appendage it has been taken to be.

* * *

In addition to encompassing six phases, the romance is also characterized by a dialectical form (Frye, 187): the hero, symbol of light, combats the dark enemy, with all the other characters divided along similar lines. This binary opposition appears in **Indiana** on many different levels; it is found in the style, structure, and thematics of the novel.

The contrast between light and dark, white and black, is not seen in the characters, for the major ones all possess both good and bad traits, with only Mme de Carvajal and Delmare appearing predominantly negative and Mme de Ramière positive. Rather, the opposition is represented in a more sophisticated manner, both stylistically, in the black and white imagery that pervades the novel, and in the counterpoint that is set up between the enclosed, dark interiors of France and the open-air spaces of the île Bourbon. The structure of **Indiana** depends less on the four parts into which the novel is divided (Sand's primitive plan having been "four volumes about four characters" [*C* II, 47]) than on a series of interior scenes that are all variations on a theme. This structure has already been discerned in **Rose et Blanche.** and discussed in the preceding chapter. **Indiana** presents a more elaborate version of this method of composition.

The novel begins with a tightly composed scene painted in chiaroscuro, worthy of a Dutch miniaturist. Three immobile figures are seated in front of the hearth. A few pages later, a description of the fire, which crackles and dies, illuminating some objects while plunging others into shadow, gives an eerie, Gothic effect, particularly when Delmare is said to resemble a ghost as he paces back and forth. Clearly, something unpleasant is about to happen.

This claustrophobic atmosphere is repeated in the key scenes of the novel, which all take place in dark, confined spaces; even Indiana and Ralph's suicide attempt is set in the narrow gorges of the Bernica, during the night. Only the final discussion between Ralph and the narrator takes place in a fully light and open area, the garden. Significantly, the landscapes for which George Sand is famous and which had already appeared in **Rose et Blanche** are nearly absent from **Indiana,** as Sand herself admitted (*C* II, 48). The Brie countryside, Paris, Bordeaux, are barely evoked except for salient monuments (L'Institut, les Quinconces) and summary descriptions and appear more as names than as identifiable places. Only the interiors, where the action is played out, count. Although l'île Bourbon is carefully described, as befits the scene of a childhood paradise lost as well as an adult paradise regained, no important action takes place there until the very end of the novel.

The second crucial scene in **Indiana** is the one that inspired Musset's famous poem to Sand, which begins:

> Sand, quand tu l'écrivais, où donc l'avais-tu vue,
> Cette scène terrible où Noun, à demi nue,
> Sur le lit d'Indiana s'enivre avec Raimond?
> Qui donc te la dictait, cette page brûlante
> Où l'amour cherche en vain d'une main palpitante
> Le fantôme adoré de son illusion?
>
> (*I*, 87)

Sand, as you were writing the novel, how did you imagine this terrible scene where Noun, half nude, intoxicates herself in Indiana's bed with Raimond? Who dictated this burning page to you, where love seeks vainly with a trembling hand the adored ghost of its illusion?

The scene still makes a powerful impression on the reader today, charged as it is with eroticism, voyeurism, and energy.

After crossing the garden, a study in black and white, Raymon reaches Indiana's circular room, accompanied by Noun. Here, the same vacillating light as in the beginning creates strange shadows and blinds Raymon momentarily, while the mirrors seem to fill the room with ghosts, as Noun, dressed in Indiana's clothes, is reflected as both herself and her mistress. The light of the room contrasts with the dark of the night outside, while the virginal whiteness of Indiana's bed becomes the scene of debauchery. This episode is painful, for the reader sympathizes with Noun and her love of a man who, at the height of passion, is thinking of another woman. Like Musset, one feels impelled to ask how Sand imagined this scene, so disturbing in its depiction of a sexual act that is almost perverted.

This scene is repeated, and corrected, in Indiana and Ralph's suicide attempt at Bernica. It is dark when they begin their vigil, and only the white water is visible. The mist it gives off creates an atmosphere of mystery, and in the darkness, the ordinarily beautiful site becomes a frightening abyss. The moon rises, lighting the way, and after confessing his love for Indiana, Ralph picks her up in his arms "and carried her away [l'emporta] to hurl her with him into the torrent . . ." (*I*, 338; ellipses in original). The verb recalls that used in the earlier scene, when Raymon "entraîna sa créole échevelée" (carried off his disheveled Creole) (*I*, 86). The next day, in the more prosaic light, both men fall to their knees on the spot of their acts of passion, Ralph to thank God, and Raymon, in a rather unrealistic tirade, to beg Indiana's pardon for having profaned her bed and, by extension, her person.

The frankly sexual nature of both these scenes is reflected in the imagery Sand employs to describe their settings. In the first, Indiana's closed, circular room is reached by traversing dark corridors, described elsewhere as a "labyrinth" (*I*, 36). As Stirling Haig has perspicaciously noted, this room is a "veritable hermetically sealed Venusberg."[8] Its inaccessibility and secrecy are reminiscent of the invisibility of much of the female sexual anatomy. The female genitals are also discernible in the description of Indiana's bed, "this little bed half-hidden beneath the muslin curtains . . ." (*I*, 82), "narrow and virginal" (*I*, 83), which is appropriately adorned with a very male palm branch. The identity of the woman and the bed is made explicit in the narrator's comment that Raymon "shuddered with desire at the thought of the day when Indiana herself would open its delights to him" (*I*, 83). Raymon is never able to possess Indiana, who remains for him virginal and unavailable like her bed. His orgy with Noun, who had set out fruits "which coquettishly presented their rosy sides . . ." (*I*, 82), a metaphor for a woman ready for a sexual encounter, leads to tragedy precisely because she is the wrong woman in a forbidden place.

There is a different emphasis in the imagery of the gorges of Bernica. The most explicit description of the site comes fifty pages before the suicide scene. Here, the gorge is decidedly female, whereas the waterfall is a male image.

> C'est un lieu pittoresque, une sorte de vallée étroite et profonde, cachée entre deux murailles de rochers perpendiculaires, dont la surface est parsemée de bouquets d'arbustes saxatiles et de touffes de fougère.
>
> Un ruisseau coule dans la cannelure formée par la rencontre des deux pans. Au point où leur écartement cesse, il se précipite dans des profondeurs effrayantes, et forme, au lieu de sa chute, un petit bassin entouré de roseaux et couvert d'une fumée humide.
>
> (*I*, 251-52)

> It is a picturesque spot, a sort of deep and narrow valley, hidden between two perpendicular walls of rock, the surface of which is studded with clumps of saxatile shrubs and tufts of ferns.
>
> A stream flows in the narrow trough formed by the meeting of the two sides. At the point where they meet it plunges down into frightful depths, and, where it falls, forms a basin surrounded by reeds and covered with a damp mist.
>
> (*i* [*Indiana*, trans. George Burnham Ives], 231)

This setting represents sexual union, which for Ralph and Indiana is successful.[9]

The original scene between Noun and Raymon is replayed by Indiana and Raymon, with Noun's ghost haunting the room, not Indiana's. As Noun had worn her mistress's clothes, so does Indiana disguise herself as Noun to ascertain the truth about the servant's relations with Raymon. The action is prepared by the same white/dark imagery as earlier, with the trees hidden by fog and mist. Raymon is happy to leave the dark and eerie park, filled with memories of Noun's suicide, for the illumination of Indiana's room, but there he meets the by-now familiar vacillating light. The cruelty Raymon had shown toward Noun by using her to express his desire for Indiana in the previous scene is mirrored here as Indiana attempts to shock Raymon and force a confrontation between them. However, Raymon turns this scene to his advantage and tries deliberately to dominate and humiliate Indiana. Like its prototype, this encounter changes his love into hatred. Unfortunately for Raymon, this scene is interrupted by Delmare's arrival, as the first one was shattered by Indiana's entrance, and Raymon is not able to complete his seduction of Indiana.

This episode marks a turning point in the presentation of Raymon's character. From a daring young man-about-town, open to all romantic adventures, he becomes sadistic and egotistical, interested only in breaking Indiana's spirit and making her his slave. Like Laclos's Valmont, he carefully calculates his discourse and his letters so as to tell her what she wants to hear. He renews his attempt at seduction some pages later, when Indiana takes refuge in his room, expecting him to save her from having to accompany Delmare to l'île Bourbon. Unlike Indiana's room, Raymon's has no fire, and one imagines Indiana sitting in the cold and dark, awaiting Raymon's return. Their exchange is ended, as in the past scenes, by the arrival of daylight, which floods the apartment and brings with it Indiana's enlightenment. Raymon's rhetoric is similar to that which he had employed in the previous scene, while he uses the same physical insistence that stops just short of rape. In this case, though, it is Raymon himself who puts an end to the scene, saying to Indiana: "Come, madame, it is time for you to leave" (*I*, 214).

These final words are reproduced textually in the last scene in Indiana's room, when Laure de Nangy, now married to Raymon, says to Indiana, "Kindly leave" (*I*, 302). After having been sent away by Raymon from his room in Paris and accompanied out by his mother, she is definitively told to leave his room at Lagny by his wife. Indiana's home is no longer her own, and she has nowhere to go but a "lodging-house," which, curiously, is seen, like her room, as a refuge from an "inextricable labyrinth" (*I*, 305).[10] Yet the hotel room is not the white arena where virginal dreams are played out. On the contrary, "a dull, hazy light creeps regretfully over the smoky ceilings and soiled windows" (*I*, 304) of this anonymous room. Indiana's itinerary of lost illusions has shown her a somber, tarnished side of life that she had never imagined in her light, girlish room, where the travel books and etchings of Paul and Virginie's pastoral *amours* did not reveal the existence of grimy hotels and lovers such as Raymon.

Despite her despair, Indiana does not die in this dismal hotel room, as she so romantically imagines she will. She is rescued by Ralph and comes eventually to live happily with him in a traditional colonist's home, described earlier as "diaphanous" (*I*, 257) when compared with European houses. It is open and airy, without the dark, winding corridors and claustrophobic interiors she had known in France. The final scene of the novel corrects the opening one, where three people are seated silently in the dark: at the end, Indiana, Ralph, and the narrator converse in the outdoors.

The binary structure of the romance evident in the stylistic contrast between black and white imagery reappears on a thematic level in the opposition of ignorance and knowledge, which also represents a black and white dichotomy. Up until the end of the novel, Indiana is trapped in a conspiracy of silence and rhetoric: silence on the part of those who do not want her to know the painful truth about certain events, and rhetoric from those who tell her what they think she wants to hear. As the heroine of a woman author's romance, Indiana must undergo months of suffering and tests that consist not of slaying dragons but of understanding and combatting the society in which she lives as well as learning to know herself. This she does by listening to the language of men and evaluating the systems they represent. The male values expressed through language that Indiana must learn to recognize and reject pertain to love, politics, religion, and the military. Initially ignorant, she becomes enlightened, less in an intellectual sense than in a moral sense, and leaves sophistry behind for a world where she and Ralph mean what they say and say what they mean.

Love as defined in the novel is a verbal game whose rules both sides understand, although men created the rules first, and each side knows the possible moves open to it. Raymon is an expert at this game, for he is both a writer of political brochures and a persuasive speaker. His oratorical capabilities are shown in the novel not in a political forum, however, but rather in his love scenes with Noun and Indiana. Raymon is conscious of playing a role as he woos a woman; he elaborates speeches based on previous models of a lover's discourse. He tells women what they are conditioned to want to hear, and they respond accordingly. "[H]e knew that the promises of love did not involve honor, happily for society. Sometimes, too, the woman who had demanded these solemn oaths had broken them first" (*I*, 136). Indiana, however, is a stranger to French society

and does not even know that these games exist, much less how to play them. It is not insignificant that she is a Creole, descended from a Spanish father and brought up on an island far from her new home. Indiana is doubly an outsider in French society: she is a foreigner as well as a woman in a man's world.[11] Raymon is aware of this, and she is not.

> Et, quand il vit qu'elle ne se rendait pas, il céda à la nécessité et lui reprocha de ne pas l'aimer; lieu commun qu'il méprisait et qui le faisait sourire, presque honteux d'avoir affaire à une femme assez ingénue pour n'en pas sourire elle-même.
>
> Ce reproche alla au coeur d'Indiana plus vite que toutes les exclamations dont Raymon avait brodé son discours.
>
> (*I*, 186-87)

> And when he saw that she did not surrender, he yielded to necessity and reproached her with not loving him; a commonplace expedient which he despised and which made him smile, with a feeling of something like shame at having to do with a woman so innocent as not to smile at it herself.
>
> That reproach went to Indiana's heart more swiftly than all the exclamations with which Raymon had embellished his discourse.
>
> (*i*, 167)

Indiana is "[i]gnorant like a true Creole" (*I*, 164), not only of history and geography but also of the social realities of her time. Like Emma Bovary, for whom Indiana served as a model, she learned about love in books. "Where did you dream about love? in what novel intended for chambermaids did you study society, I beg you?" asks Raymon (*I*, 210). It is ironic that he should accuse Indiana of acting according to the prescriptions of novels, for his own language is precisely that of fiction and is a fiction she takes seriously. When one compares Raymon's rhetoric of love with Indiana's concept of love, derived from novels rather than experience, one finds many parallels.

Raymon's view of love is sadistic and of the "blame the victim" variety. Love remains on the periphery of his actions, separate from the rest of his life, as was the case with the men in *Rose et Blanche.* This is apparent first in his affair with Noun, which he sees as a lark, and later in his attitude toward Indiana's possible return from l'île Bourbon, which he intends to use as the occasion to take her as his mistress, not his wife.

Indiana accepts this sadistic concept of love. "She knew society so little that she made a tragic novel out of life . . ." (*I*, 71). When she receives Raymon's letter, she reacts mechanically to his call.

> Tel était son enthousiasme, qu'elle craignait de faire trop peu pour lui. . . . Elle eût donné sa vie sans croire que ce fût assez payer un sourire de Raymon. . . .
>
> (*I*, 275)

. . . L'Amour, c'est la vertu de la femme; c'est pour lui qu'elle se fait une gloire de ses fautes, c'est de lui qu'elle reçoit l'héroïsme de braver ses remords. Plus le crime lui coûte à commettre, plus elle aura mérité de celui qu'elle aime. C'est le fanatisme qui met le poignard aux mains du religieux.

(*I*, 281)

So great was her enthusiasm that she feared that she was doing too little for him. . . . She would have given her life, with the idea that it was too small a price to pay for a smile from Raymon. . . .

(*i*, 254-55)

. . . Love is woman's virtue; it is for love that she glories in her sins, it is from love that she acquires the heroism to defy her remorse. The more dearly it costs her to commit the crime, the more she will have deserved at the hands of the man she loves. It is like the fanaticism that places the dagger in the hand of the religious enthusiast.

(*i*, 260)

Pierre Salomon, in a note to his edition, attributes these sentiments to Sand herself and calls them "a way of hiding an unpleasant reality under an honorable mask . . ." (*I*, 281). However, Sand is not so much justifying Indiana's conduct (or her own, for that matter) as explaining its source. Love, for Indiana, means sacrifice of self and others for the beloved. It is this sort of love that is found in novels and preached by Raymond. Just as he held her responsible for his unhappiness and frustration, so does she accept this responsibility.

[E]lle n'agissait point en vue d'elle-même, mais de Raymon; . . . elle n'allait point à lui pour chercher du bonheur, mais pour lui en porter, et . . . dût-elle être maudite dans l'éternité, elle en serait assez dédommagée si elle embellissait la vie de son amant.

(*I*, 281)

[S]he was no longer acting in her own interests but in Raymon's; . . . she was going to him, not in search of happiness, but to make him happy, and . . . even though she were to be accursed for all eternity, she would be sufficiently recompensed if she embellished her lover's life.

(*i*, 260-61)

In her study of women's moral development, Carol Gilligan concludes that women are taught to be self-sacrificing and to place the needs of others ahead of their own. Indiana's thoughts are not an expression of bad faith, as Salomon implies, but rather represent a typical female viewpoint, one that Sand both depicts and exposes as deleterious to woman's existence.[12]

Raymon and Indiana's sadomasochistic relationship might actually have succeeded, had their reunion not been interrupted by his wife, who arrives before Raymon can hide Indiana, as he had earlier planned to do.

For once, Raymon the orator is speechless. "But Raymon answered nothing; his admirable presence of mind had abandoned him" (*I*, 301). Shocked by Indiana's return, he speaks only eleven words in three pages. His verbal spell over Indiana is broken, and her *amour romanesque* will soon fade, to be replaced by another, more genuine love.

If Raymon is reduced to silence, Ralph becomes more eloquent as he and Indiana return to their childhood home with the intention of committing suicide. "His words were marked by his feelings, and for the first time, Indiana knew his true character" (*I*, 315). As she learns to know Ralph, Raymon disappears from her heart. His words, too, have a powerful effect on Indiana, as they await death by the waterfall, but far from being the artificial rhetoric of Raymon, Ralph's discourse is the exact reflection of his thought. There is a correspondence between the signifier and the signified in his speech that is lacking in Raymon's. Ralph speaks as the moon rises, and his vocabulary repeatedly uses words of light: "brille," "feu," "lumière" (*I*, 318). It is a moment of truth, of honesty, when everything hidden is brought into the open. The authenticity of Ralph's love, the revelation of his character, show Indiana that she has been mistaken in both her appraisal of Ralph and her choice of Raymon. Ralph's love is genuine while Raymon's was just talk. Ironically, had Ralph revealed his real feelings earlier, Indiana would never have fallen for Raymon's lines. Yet the narrative structure of *Indiana* requires the characters' ignorance for the novel to continue: if Indiana had truly understood Ralph, if she had been apprised of the real cause of Noun's suicide, if Raymon had told her and Delmare of Ralph's love, there would have been no novel.

The end of the novel, with its insistence on transparency and candor and the image of the veil that is finally lifted, has a Rousseauistic ring. Raymon is shown to be a false love object, a mere "héros de roman," while Ralph, unremarkable as he is, is Indiana's true companion. When the narrator meets Ralph and Indiana, he remarks significantly: "Neither of them was particularly brilliant" (*I*, 346). Their words express their feelings and are the more powerful for their simplicity. Sand gives Indiana a chance that is denied to Emma Bovary, that for happiness outside of the novelistic world she had created for herself and men like Raymon had fostered. Like Rousseau before her and Flaubert after, however, she repeats the paradox of criticizing novels within a novel; she uses fiction to show a "realistic" alternative to fiction based not on rhetoric, ignorance, and illusion, but on truth and understanding.

In addition to love, politics is another one of the men's verbal games that are illustrated in the novel. Political discussions as well as the recounting of specific political events of the era occupy a large place in this novel and serve to situate it in the precise time frame of October 1827-January 1832. This places the novel astride the major political crisis of the romantic age, the revolution of 1830. Indiana is noticeably absent from the heated discussions between Delmare, Raymon, and Ralph, each of whom represents a different political perspective. It is not surprising that she does not join in these debates, for all three systems supported by the men exclude women from political participation. Her lack of partisanship, attributed by the men to her ignorance, has a deeper meaning, for she develops her own political ideas, formulated outside of the received ideas that the men had assimilated as part of their education. Her condition as outsider, unfettered by previous socialization, again allows her to see more clearly the positions defended by the men. Her questions are "naïves," her spirit "neuve et ingénue" (*I*, 164), only in relation to male society's expectations and conventions.

Through these discussions, Indiana learns that political systems are less the expression of indisputable truths than the codification of existing power structures. They consist merely of the "interests of civilization constituted into principles . . ." (*I*, 164). Indiana's political ideals, on the other hand, depend on "the straightforward ideas and simple laws of common sense and humanity . . ." (*I*, 164), and derive from a Rousseauistic opposition between civilization and nature, although she is more optimistic about humanity's inherent goodness. These views contrast sharply with both Delmare's Napoleonic dreams and Raymon's monarchistic opinions, which are twice designated by the narrator as "utopies" (*I*, 158, 165) and are therefore not in conformity with political reality. Significantly, Ralph's republican ideal, which, with certain important modifications, is at the base of Indiana's opinions, is not ridiculed as impractical or unrealistic.

Delmare and Raymon become fast friends, despite their political differences. In fact, by the end of the novel, Raymon feels more loyal to Delmare than to Indiana. "He was too much Delmare's friend, he owed too much consideration to the confidence this man had in him to steal his wife; he had to content himself with seducing her" (*I*, 212). This expression of male solidarity would be funny if it were not made at the expense of Indiana, who has no idea that men can be more faithful to the principles of male bonding than to the women they love. Raymon's concept of marriage is quite similar to Delmare's despite his superior education and manners. He assures Indiana that, had she been married to him, ". . . you would have blessed your chain" (*I*, 75). The word *chaîne* appears several times as the metaphor for her marriage to Delmare, along with the word *esclavage* (slavery), and it is therefore significant that it recurs in Raymon's discourse. Ralph and Indiana, on the other hand, once they have left French society behind, use their money to free the slaves of Bourbon. Furthermore, they are not married according to civil or religious law but simply live together, unfettered by socially defined ties.

Religion is another area in which Raymon and Indiana have opposite views. Hers are expressed in a letter to Raymon.

> [J]e ne sers pas le même Dieu, mais je le sers mieux, et plus purement. Le vôtre, c'est le dieu des hommes, c'est le roi, le fondateur et l'appui de votre race; le mien, c'est le Dieu de l'univers, le créateur, le soutien et l'espoir de toutes les créatures. . . . Vous vous croyez les maîtres du monde; je crois que vous n'en êtes que les tyrans.
>
> (*I*, 242)

> [I] do not serve the same God, but I serve Him more loyally and with a purer heart. Yours is the god of men, the king, the founder and the upholder of your race; mine is the God of the universe, the creator, the preserver and the hope of all creatures. . . . You deem yourselves the masters of the world; I deem you only its tyrants.
>
> (*i*, 224)

This letter contains the clearest formulation of the dichotomy between male and female values in the novel and links male institutions all together in one mutually supportive system: religion is used to justify government and society, to create and perpetuate oppression. Indiana is fully aware that her life is ordained not by God but by men. She follows her husband because to refuse him would mean being rejected by all other men, as Raymon has already proven, and would leave her without any means of survival.

Indiana only arrives at her concept of religion during the course of the novel, as can be seen in her explanation of her two suicide attempts. At first she rejects suicide because it is forbidden by God, and she justifies her walk into the Seine by the fact that she was unaware of her actions. Her second attempt is deliberate, for she is by then convinced by bitter experience that the usual image of an intolerant God propagated by society is not the only one. "Unhappiness, in entering my life, gradually taught me another religion than that taught by men" (*I*, 311). In religion, as in love and politics, Indiana learns to reject men's views for her own. It is important to note, however, that *Indiana* does not condemn men, but male institutions and those men who seek to perpetuate them. Both Delmare and Raymon are shown to be products of their society and, by implication, eventually changeable.

Indiana is not only a romantic heroine but the heroine of a romance as well. Sand set her novel in the France of her time but structured it in an ageless fashion, updating the form to suit her needs. She utilized five of the six phases of the romance and reproduced its ordinarily repetitive structure (the hero undertakes several quests, meets with several obstacles, etc.) by organizing the novel around one key scene that is reprised and modified until a successful outcome is obtained. Furthermore, Sand integrated the oppositions central to the romance into the thematics and the imagery of the novel, thereby retaining a key element of the form without being forced to present the one-dimensional characters usually found in the genre. The plot of the novel remains the same as that of the romance, for Indiana learns to recognize and conjure the evils of male social and religious conventions, ultimately emerging victorious from her struggle.

In a provocative article, Leslie Rabine asserts that Sand reproduced in **Indiana** the nineteenth-century ideology of the passive and chaste woman. That is not the case. Although Rabine is partly correct in stating that Indiana's "independence is contained in her dependence on a man . . . ," Indiana still achieves a major spiritual victory over society, one that is transmitted by the novel and is reproducible by the reader.[13] Laws, attitudes, and social customs have changed dramatically in the last 150 years, so it is easy for us to forget just how radical **Indiana** really was. Feminists today study male discourse and analyze patriarchal institutions, as Sand did, and they draw the same conclusions. Sand was not the first to criticize women's condition in society through her fiction. Graffigny's *Lettres d'une Péruvienne* (1747) did so overtly, particularly attacking women's insufficient education, while novels by all women did so covertly. Sand goes further than her predecessors both in demonstrating that religious, social, and political systems combine to oppress women and in locating their power in language. She posited a difference between men's and women's language in **"La Fille d'Albano,"** and in **Indiana** she proves it.

It is instructive in this context to compare **Indiana** with Hugo's *Notre-Dame de Paris,* published the previous year. Esmeralda is also victimized by the church, the law, and love, represented by Claude Frollo, Jacques Charmolue, and Phoebus de Châteaupers. She goes to the scaffold without ever realizing that she has become a sacrifice, a scapegoat.[14] Critics of the time, almost all of whom were male, reacted positively for the most part to Sand's castigation of society, although it is doubtful they understood just how subversive her program was. Charles Rabou, who wrote: "Let us make the author of **Indiana** give up her professorship in Social Economics and reduce her to being merely a powerful painter of passions," was one who did recognize the extent of Sand's rebellion and wanted it suppressed.[15] Women did heed her message, not only in France but in Europe and America, and hailed her as their champion.

The fact that Rabine can criticize Sand for not going far enough shows how great a distance women have traveled since 1832.

* * *

Sand used a traditional narrative genre to depict contemporary mores and problems. More important, **Indiana** proposes solutions to the insufficiencies of the society Sand criticizes, thereby fulfilling the didactic function of the romance and its related forms, the folktale and the myth. One of these solutions has already been described as representing the sixth or *penseroso* phase of the romance, that of contemplation and retirement, where the intimate desires that occasioned the story are realized within an idealized version of the real world, in this case l'île Bourbon. Sand also presents a more pragmatic solution to the social ills she diagnoses, one that is applicable to the France of her time. This solution becomes evident when we consider the evolution of the triangular configurations formed by the lovers in the novel, as in **Rose et Blanche.**[16]

At the beginning of **Indiana,** there are three people seated in the salon at Lagny—Indiana, Delmare, and Ralph. Indiana and Delmare are married, although in name only, and Ralph is Indiana's cousin and childhood companion, who is now the friend of the couple. Soon we are introduced to Noun, Indiana's *soeur de lait* and servant, and Raymon; these two are having a secret affair. This initial configuration gives way to a brief, transitional triangle consisting of the two women and Raymon. His attempts to romance them both quickly fail, and Noun's suicide removes her forever from an infernal game she was unprepared to play.

Raymon and Noun's love scene, commented on above, is the moment when the Indiana-Noun-Raymon triangle gives way to the central triangle of the novel, that of Indiana, Ralph, and Raymon. After the revelries of the previous night have passed, and daylight brings Raymon to his senses, he notices a covered portrait of Ralph in Indiana's room, and is incensed that this man is, figuratively at least, allowed to see Indiana every hour of every day, in all her most intimate moments. He later learns that Ralph has literal access to her room as well. The thought of Ralph's privileges incites Raymon's jealousy and deepens his desire for Indiana. This becomes clear in the hunt scene that soon follows. Raymon sees Ralph kiss Indiana on the lips, although presumably in a purely fraternal spirit, and he later becomes envious that Ralph has the pleasure of buying a horse for Indiana. Moreover, this episode reveals to Raymon that Ralph's feelings for Indiana go beyond friendship. He witnesses Ralph's attempt at suicide when Indiana has been reported killed, and recognizes the depth of Ralph's love for her. The *désir triangulaire* described by René Girard, in which a man's desire for a woman depends on another man's love for her, determines Raymon's courtship of Indiana, for it is Ralph that Raymon concentrates on in his seduction, not Indiana herself.[17]

First, Raymon wants to replace Ralph in Indiana's room and in her affections, and to claim her even more completely than Ralph, for Raymon knows that Indiana's relationship with her cousin is merely platonic. Second, he wants to prove his own superiority to Ralph himself, by eluding his vigilance on the way to Indiana's room. Finally, he tries to show Indiana that his politics are superior to Ralph's, less because he is convinced of the divine right of monarchy than because he is humiliated that dull Ralph's opinions should carry more weight than his brilliant arguments. In his desire to best Ralph, of course, his feelings for Indiana get somewhat lost, and even she herself senses that his political orations are not really aimed at her. "In those moments, it seemed to Indiana that Raymon was not paying attention to her at all . . ." (*I*, 166).

By contrast, Ralph's jealousy functions very differently. In his hatred of Raymon, he never loses sight of Indiana, her needs and desires. Rather than trying to crush his enemy, he is courteous and generous toward him, so that Indiana will not be hurt. Unlike Raymon, who demands that Indiana relinquish everything for him, Ralph explicitly tells her: ". . . [I] don't want such a sacrifice, I will never accept it. Why should my life be more precious than yours?" (*I*, 311). Ralph's jealousy does not obscure his love, and he does not participate in the same way as Raymon in this triangle.

The passage from this central triangle to the final configuration is made via two ephemeral triangles: that of Indiana, Delmare, and Raymon, where Indiana is torn between love and duty, and the Raymon, Indiana, and Laure de Nangy triangle, which parallels the earlier Raymon, Indiana, Noun relationship and is even more short-lived.

The end of the novel mirrors the beginning, but in a more stable and acceptable way. Indiana and Delmare's paternalistic, chaste marriage has become M. Hubert and Laure's father-daughter relationship, with Raymon occupying the third place in the triangle as Laure's husband. This arrangement provides a more normative family picture and replaces a marriage that was ill-assorted on several levels with one that is a partnership of equals. In addition, the illicit, morganatic relationship between Raymon and Noun is replaced by Ralph and Indiana's unsanctified marriage. Moral as well as social equals, they find the love and spiritual contentment that elude Laure and Raymon.

Just as the debonair Raymon is the contrary of the stiff, quiet Ralph, Laure de Nangy is the opposite of Indiana. Worldly, sensible, able to identify and protect her inter-

ests, Laure has no illusions as to what the future holds for an heiress like herself. "[S]he had too much good sense, too much knowledge of contemporary society, to have dreamed of love when two millions were at stake" (*I*, 293). Although Laure is a minor character, the contrast between her and Indiana is made explicit in two key scenes, one at the beginning and another toward the end of the novel, where each woman is shown against the same background, the eighteenth-century decor of the salon at Lagny. Indiana is overwhelmed by this setting, seated as she is under the mantel of a "huge white marble fireplace inlaid with gilt copper."[18] She is compared to a "flower born yesterday and forced to bloom in a Gothic vase," where "gothic" means old or outdated (*I*, 25). The description of the decoration of the room reinforces her passivity, for the sculptures are "tortuous" and far too complicated for the eye to follow with any success. Laure, however, is able to understand this room well enough to do a pastiche of it. She controls her surroundings, changing them at will, while Indiana is dominated by them.

> C'était une chose charmante que cette copie, une fine moquerie tout empreinte du caractère railleur et poli de l'artiste. Elle s'était plu à outrer la prétentieuse gentillesse de ces vieilles fresques; elle avait saisi l'esprit faux et chatoyant du siècle de Louis XV sur ces figurines guindées.
>
> (*I*, 288)

> The copy was a fascinating thing, a delicate satire infused with the bantering yet refined nature of the artist. She had amused herself by exaggerating the pretentious sweetness of the old frescoes; she had grasped the false and shifting character of the age of Louis XV on those stilted figures.
>
> (*i*, 266)

In her study of *Indiana*, Clotilde Montaigne calls Laure a "cold and dominating woman" and compares her to Balzac's Foedora.[19] Yet although Laure is totally unlike Indiana, I would argue that she is not meant to be a negative character, any more than Raymon is. She is simply an appropriate partner for Raymon. Both are products of their society. They are equal in rank, intelligence, and experience of the world. Laure's legal inferiority with respect to her husband is counterbalanced by her superior "cleverness" (*I*, 293). The final image of her is one of strength, whereas Indiana cowers on her knees before Raymon and Laure. In this scene Laure speaks, while Raymon is silent, and she identifies herself as the owner of the property: "You are in my house, madame" (*I*, 302).

Both final pairings are better socially and emotionally than those at the outset of the novel, but neither is perfect. Ralph and Indiana live outside of society on an island paradise that is an escapist's dream. While they try to change that society by purchasing slaves, their efforts are limited by their financial resources and do not attack the roots themselves of law and convention. In addition, Ralph and Indiana's relationship borders on the incestuous. Ralph not only is Indiana's cousin but during her youth served as her father, while during her marriage he acted as a protective older brother. His confession to Indiana before their suicide attempt repeatedly uses different words of kinship: "I made you my sister, my daughter, my companion, my pupil, my world" (*I,* 322); "My kisses were those of a father . . ." (*I,* 324); "I swore . . . to never forget my role as your brother . . ." (*I,* 331); and, finally, "It is now I who am your brother, husband, lover forever more" (*I,* 336).

This overdetermined union is in accord with the romance tradition, though, for the bride won by the hero after his quest has a "psychological connection with the mother in an Oedipus fantasy . . ." (Frye, 193). Here, as throughout the novel, the roles have been reversed, and Ralph represents the father. Indiana has gone from marriage to an overt father figure, an older man, to union with a covert father figure. L'île Bourbon, then, represents a double return to the past for Ralph and Indiana. They go back not only to the physical setting of their childhood but to its emotional climate as well, repeating the close relationship that they had had in their youth while adding to it a sexual component. This is indeed the realization of a girl's oedipal fantasy.[20]

Indiana shows a further development of *Rose et Blanche* in that two women are involved with a man who turns out to be the wrong man, but the situation is righted in the end as Indiana discovers that Ralph is her ideal partner. The scene between Raymon and Noun, where Raymon imagines he is making love to Indiana, touches a raw nerve because of its oedipal content: the women are more than rivals in love, they are mother-daughter figures loved by the same man. That is why the scene disturbed Musset and continues to carry a strong erotic charge.

Raymon is a necessary transitional figure on two levels: he is the catalyst both in the romance plot, enabling Indiana to identify concepts inimical to her happiness, and in her relationship with Ralph. As the initial triangular situation was set up, Indiana never would have recognized Ralph's qualities, nor would Ralph ever have indulged in a relationship with Noun. In order for Indiana to turn from Delmare to Ralph, she has to pass through Raymon. This arrangement can be seen as a flaw in the novel, for Ralph's true personality and the depth of his love are kept hidden from Indiana until the end. His characterization relates to the problem of point of view and narration, for Ralph is essentially presented as Indiana saw him and not in an objective way, which gives rise to certain inconsistencies. Sand compressed her scenario further in subsequent novels, eliminating this intermediate figure and refining her presentation.

On the other hand, Laure and Raymon remain within the confines of society and conform to its rules. Theirs is not a love match but a marriage of convenience. Yet inasmuch as the solution of the île Bourbon is the stuff of romance and wish fulfillment, so is Lagny the site of contemporary social realism. Laure and Raymon are the ideal couple of 1830, and their marriage is of the kind often portrayed by Balzac, for it represents the union of bourgeois fortune and noble blood. Unlike Balzac, however, Sand is not interested in the source of these recent fortunes, but rather in their use.

George Sand's awareness of the economic realities of her time appeared discreetly in *Rose et Blanche,* where money and its ability to buy almost anything informs the plot in a significant way. Horace buys Lazare a boat as a recompense for having saved his life; later, after his rape of Denise, Horace pays her a pension and places her in a convent. He also resolves to pay for Rose's education in order to protect her from being forced to supplement her income through prostitution. Money, or lack of it, prevents Laorens from marrying Blanche, while the power money bestows helps Mlle Cazalès to bring pressure on Blanche and coerce her to marry Horace. As already indicated, the alliance of the nobility with the wealthy bourgeoisie is touched upon comically, as the girls in the convent stoically envisage the possibility of marriage with the heir to an industrial fortune as the only alternative to remaining single. In *Indiana,* economics forms an integral part of the plot as well. Sand describes in detail the financial situation of the characters and, like Jane Austen, gives specific figures.[21] This orientation is not surprising from a woman who was raised to run an important estate and who, as we have seen, was an astute businesswoman, both where Nohant and her book contracts were concerned.[22] Ralph has "fifty thousand francs in private income" (*I,* 108), while Laure de Nangy possesses "two millions" in capital (*I,* 293). Delmare is described as the "proprietor of a comfortable manor with its dependencies, and, what is more, a manufacturer fortunate in his speculations . . ." (*I,* 24).

In fact, Delmare's factory provides the underpinning of the plot. When caught climbing the wall of Delmare's property, Raymon does not admit that he is Noun's lover but rather explains that he came to spy on Delmare's manufacturing techniques. This excuse gains him entry to the factory, and his visit enables him to see Indiana again while kindling his relationship with Delmare. Delmare's commercial enterprise is soon threatened, however, due to the bankruptcy of a Belgian firm, and he must leave for Antwerp to ascertain the damage to his fortune. His absence from Lagny allows Raymon access to Indiana, while his unexpected return prevents Indiana's seduction. Indiana and Delmare are ruined by the Belgian failure and must sell Lagny to pay their creditors. The property is bought by M. Hubert, a wealthy industrialist who had adopted Laure after the death of her father, the former owner of the château Hubert had bought to invest his money. She therefore combines aristocratic blood with a bourgeois upbringing and a commercial fortune, making her an especially attractive partner. This background suits Raymon perfectly, for he seeks a wife of both rank and assets.

> Il appartenait à une haute et rigide famille qui ne souffrirait point de mésalliance, et pourtant la fortune ne résidait plus avec sécurité que chez les plébéiens. Selon toute apparence, cette classe allait s'élever sur les débris de l'autre, et, pour se maintenir à la surface du mouvement, il fallait être le gendre d'un industriel ou d'un agioteur.
>
> (*I,* 263)

> He belonged to a family of high rank and unbending pride which would brook no mésalliance, and yet wealth could no longer be considered secure except in plebeian hands. According to all appearance that class was destined to rise over the ruins of the other, and in order to maintain oneself on the surface of the movement one must be the son-in-law of a manufacturer or a stockbroker.
>
> (*i,* 243)

Raymon resolves to marry Laure in order to acquire this fortune, and she accepts him. This marriage precipitates the end of the novel, as Indiana at last acknowledges Raymon's true character and subsequently learns to understand Ralph.

The end of *Indiana,* then, posits two distinct options: one can either try to accept the new bourgeois society or withdraw completely from it. The latter solution is more valorized emotionally, although it is also recognized as the less feasible, while the more realistic solution is shown to be the way of the future.

> [I]l faut trop d'énergie pour rompre avec le monde, trop de douleurs pour acquérir cette énergie. . . . Allez, jeune homme, poursuivez le cours de votre destinée; ayez des amis, un état, une réputation, une patrie. . . . Ne rompez point les chaînes qui vous lient à la société. . . .
>
> (*I,* 353)

> [T]oo much energy is required to break with society, and too much suffering to acquire that energy. . . . Go, young man, follow the course of your destiny; have friends, a profession, a reputation, a fatherland. . . . Do not break the chains that bind you to society. . . .
>
> (*i,* 327)

This dual conclusion is typical of the art romance, as Jameson has defined it: "Romance as a form thus expresses a transitional moment, yet one of a very special type: its contemporaries must feel their society torn between past and future in such a way that the alternatives are grasped as hostile but somehow unrelated worlds" (Jameson, 158).

George Sand, like others of her contemporaries, particularly Stendhal and Hugo, is using this form as a symbolic attempt "to come to terms with the triumph of the bourgeoisie and the new and unglamorous social forms developing out of the market system" (Jameson, 158), with the important difference that she welcomes rather than fears these changes. Charles Rabou was absolutely right in comparing Sand to a professor of Social Economics.

Sand is at a crucial point in the development of her social thought. On the one hand, she promotes the new order of intermarriage between classes even before it becomes fashionable to do so.[23] On the other hand, she is far from suggesting the radical class modifications portrayed in some of her later works. The resolution of the novel's romantic entanglements produces not only emotional stability but traditional class conformity as well. Both members of each couple are of equal social rank, whereas the initial couples represented less socially acceptable alliances.[24] Despite the reestablishment of more normative unions, there is a clear *embourgeoisement* in the lifestyle of both couples and a willing acceptance of the end of *ancien régime* social practices. Sand is above all pragmatic, here as in most of her novels, in her economic vision; she knew that total abolition of class distinctions was utopian and unrealistic, whereas her proposed marriages were not, as the nineteenth century was to prove.

The requirements of the art romance narrowly correspond to those of Sand's family romance, and she has brilliantly cast her own, special scenario in an original literary form. She has made the quest romance accessible to a heroine, while giving it a purely psychological and social dimension and eliminating the physical adventures. Sand created the kind of novel Hugo envisioned, a contemporary amalgam of idealism and realism: "After the picturesque, but prosaic, novel of Walter Scott, there will be another novel left to create, more beautiful and more complete, in our opinion. It is the novel that is both drama and epic poem, picturesque but poetic, real, but ideal, true, but great, which will combine Walter Scott with Homer."[25] The review of *Indiana* that appeared in the *Journal des Débats* on July 21, 1832, uses similar language in describing the novel as "pages both ideal and true that only a woman could have written. Let us all thank her for having dared to do so."[26] The synthesis forged in *Indiana* was an impressive achievement both for Sand and for the nineteenth-century novel.

Notes

1. Northrop Frye, *Anatomy of Criticism: Four Essays* (1957; rpt. Princeton: Princeton University

Press, 1973), pp. 186-206. Further references are in the text as Frye.

2. Fredric Jameson, "Magical Narratives: Romance as Genre," *New Literary History* VII, i (Autumn 1975): 158. Further references are in the text as Jameson.

3. The notion of Raymon as catalyst is derived from Jameson's view of Heathcliff as mediator rather than villain. See Jameson, p. 149.

4. The site of Ralph and Indiana's suicide attempt is doubly significant, for it combines a mountaintop and a waterfall. James M. Vest has thoroughly analyzed water imagery, so important to the romance, in *Indiana*. See "Fluid Nomenclature, Imagery, and Themes in George Sand's *Indiana*," *South Atlantic Review* 46, 2 (May 1981): 43-54. For a discussion of mountaintops and ceremonial ladders that link earth to sky in traditional symbolic systems, see Mircea Eliade, *Images et symboles: Essais sur le symbolisme magico-religieux,* 2d ed. (Paris: Gallimard, 1952).

5. Angels as the symbols of providence or luck appear twice in the text before this scene. Raymon describes Indiana as his "bon ange" (*I,* 77), for caring for him when he is brought wounded into the salon at Lagny; an angel is said to save Indiana herself from succumbing to Raymon's rhetoric when she seeks refuge in his room (*I,* 214). As Jameson has pointed out (p. 144), the magical elements of the romance have been secularized in the art romance; in *Indiana,* angelic intervention has become a metaphor for protection or, better, self-preservation.

6. "The initiatic work is the drama of a rebirth; the initiatic work illustrates the principle 'dying to be reborn.' The higher level which the hero reaches is in fact that which he had left before his fall; the rebirth is thus a reintegration into society." Léon Cellier, "Le Roman initiatique en France au temps du Romantisme," in *Parcours initiatiques* (Grenoble: Presses Universitaires de Grenoble, 1977), p. 123.

7. Gérard Genette, "Discours du récit," in *Figures III* (Paris: Seuil, 1972), p. 203.

8. Stirling Haig, "La Chambre circulaire d'*Indiana*," *Neophilologus* LXII, 4 (Oct. 1978): 507.

9. See Ellen Moers, *Literary Women* (Garden City, N.Y.: Anchor Books, 1977), pp. 369-401, for a discussion of female sexual imagery.

10. Frye remarks that "the hero travels perilously through a dark labyrinthine underworld . . ." (p. 190). Here, that underworld has become the heroine's own home.

11. See Hans Mayer, *Outsiders,* trans. Denis M. Sweet (Cambridge, Mass.: MIT Press, 1982), for an enlightening study of the outsider in literature.

12. Carol Gilligan, *In a Different Voice: Psychological Theory and Women's Development* (Cambridge, Mass., and London: Harvard University Press, 1982).

13. Leslie Rabine, "George Sand and the Myth of Femininity," *Women and Literature* 4, ii (1976): 14.

14. The comparison between the two novels is not arbitrary but is occasioned by Sand's own parallel in a letter of July 1832 where she recounts a scene in which Jules Janin, after having praised *Indiana* as the best novel of manners of the period, is visited by an angry Hugo, hurt that his novel was passed over. This exuberant letter, one of Sand's funniest, is, I think, not to be taken literally, particularly since no such review by Janin has been found. An anonymous article in the *Journal des Débats,* for which Janin was theater critic, appeared two weeks later (July 21) and used somewhat similar language, but there is no indication that Janin wrote it; he did write a major article on Sand much later, in 1836. Even if the anecdote is false, as I suspect, it is nonetheless important to note that Sand again chooses to compare herself favorably to Hugo, as she had in "Jehan Cauvin." See *C* II, 119-20.

15. Quoted in Annarose Poli, "George Sand devant la critique," in Simone Vierne, ed., *George Sand: Colloque de Cerisy* (Paris: CDU-Sedes, 1983), p. 96.

16. Carol V. Richards's article "Structural Motifs and the Limits of Feminism in *Indiana*," in *The George Sand Papers: Conference Proceedings 1978,* Hofstra University Center for Cultural and Intercultural Studies 2 (New York: AMS Press, 1982), pp. 12-20 came to my attention after this chapter was written. She covers some of the same ground, but from a different viewpoint and with different conclusions.

17. See René Girard, *Mensonge romantique et vérité romanesque* (Paris: Grasset, 1961). Sand was aware of the importance of this triangular mechanism, for she assigns it a role in the structure of woman's desire as well: "Women's hearts are so made that they begin to see a man in a young boy as soon as they see him esteemed and caressed by other women." *La Petite Fadette* (Paris: Garnier, 1958), p. 164.

18. Mme de Fonbreuse is "seated under the mantelpiece of a huge gothic fireplace" in *La Marraine,* p. 327.

19. Quoted by Salomon in *Indiana*, p. 293.

20. Mireille Bossis, in her article "Les Relations de parenté chez George Sand," *Cahiers de L'Association Internationale des Etudes Françaises* 28 (mai 1976): 297-314, underscores Ralph's paternal role throughout the novel and his father-daughter relationship with Indiana, which is fully assumed by both at the end. She describes him as a "unique and all-powerful character who removes the incest taboo . . ." (p. 309). I think she underestimates the sexual nature of the bond, apparent in the passage she quotes from the novel, and I find her final mother/child image applicable, in part, only to the dynamics of Ralph's earlier relationship to his mother, as she shows.

21. Ellen Moers points out that Austen is always very specific about the sums of money involved in her novels. See *Literary Women*, p. 102.

22. Sand's private notebooks contain much information, dating from her teens, on her financial affairs: money spent, profits received or anticipated from Nohant, and so forth.

23. According to Jean-Hervé Donnard, "Balzac carefully documented a social phenomenon that was to occur more and more frequently . . ." (p. 148). "On the other hand, during Napoleon's reign, society was so mixed that there weren't too many social obstacles to the marriage of a young nobleman and the daughter of a shopkeeper. Under Louis XVIII, such a marriage would have been scandalous; in any event, it would not have taken place so easily" (p. 251). See *Balzac: Les Réalités économiques et sociales dans La Comédie humaine* (Paris: Armand Colin, 1961).

24. Leslie Rabine is partly correct in her assessment that "George Sand did not settle accounts with the existing ideology . . ." ("Myth of Femininity," p. 13), in the sense that traditional class distinctions are maintained and the social order is not radically changed, as it would be if a noblewoman were to marry a peasant. However, her linking of Sand's class values to Noun seems to me to be wrong on several counts. Not only is there a long literary tradition of the nobleman marrying the poor woman, but this option is explicitly raised and thoroughly examined by the narrator (*I*, 52-53) and discarded not on account of class differences but rather because Raymon no longer loves Noun. Furthermore, this kind of union does appear in *Valentine*. As I have shown, Noun is eliminated from the novel for other reasons.

25. Victor Hugo, "Sur Walter Scott: A propos de *Quentin Durward*," in *Oeuvres complètes* (Paris: Le Club Français du Livre, 1967), vol. 5, p. 131.

26. *Journal des Débats*, July 21, 1832, p. 3.

Abbreviations

C: *Correspondance*, ed. Georges Lubin (Paris: Garnier), Vol. I, 2d ed., 1964; Vol. II, 1966; Vol. III, 1967; Vol. IV, 1968; Vol. VI, 1969.

I: *Indiana*, ed. Pierre Salomon (Paris: Garnier, 1962).

i: *Indiana*, trans. George Burnham Ives (1900; rpt. Chicago: Cassandra Editions, 1978).

Sandra Beyer and Frederick Kluck (essay date winter 1991)

SOURCE: Beyer, Sandra, and Frederick Kluck. "George Sand and Gertrudis Gómez de Avellaneda." *Nineteenth-Century French Studies* 19, no. 2 (winter 1991): 203-09.

[*In the following essay, Beyer and Kluck trace numerous parallels of theme and character between Sand's* Indiana *and Gertrudis Gómez de Avellaneda's 1841 novel* Sab, *suggesting the strong influence of the former writer on the latter.*]

That George Sand's works were of great importance in the English, Russian and American literary worlds is extremely well documented. Paul Blount asserts in his *George Sand and the Victorian World*, "It is not an exaggeration to say that a cult of George Sand existed in Victorian England and that among its participants were some of the most important figures in the literary world."[1] Among those, he cites Matthew Arnold, George Eliot, Jane Carlyle, Elizabeth Barrett Browning and Charlotte Brontë. Patrick Waddington, in his *Turgenev and George Sand: An Improbable Entente*, says, "The moral and political impact of George Sand upon the writers of post-decembrist Russia was phenomenal."[2] Turgenev himself said, "George Sand understood us as well as if she had been born a Russian—but then, she understood everything; she was an absolutely exceptional person, like no one else on earth" (*Turgenev* [*Turgenev and George Sand*], 105).

In America, the impact of Sand's works on Walt Whitman was monumental. Joseph Barry, in his *Infamous Woman: The Life of George Sand*, states that Whitman's reading of *Consuelo*, ". . . changed his life, his language, his life-style."[3] He quotes Esther Shephard's remark that, ". . . what had turned the irascible newspaper editor, angry and sometimes vituperative . . . into the . . . serene and happy and all-embracing expounder of love . . ." (*IW* [*Infamous Woman*], 285), was the epilogue of *The Countess of Rudolstadt*. The

American feminist writer, Margaret Fuller, after visiting George Sand in Paris, stated, "I never liked a woman better" (*IW*, 295).

In addition to England, America, and Russia, Sand's life, works and ideals had an important impact on the Hispanic world. If this impact was less dramatic there than elsewhere, it is perhaps because, in contrast especially to England and America, the Hispanic world was much less open, less free in the circulation of ideas, especially when expressed by one whose life and writings were considered scandalous, blasphemous even. Despite such barriers, Sand was read by the most important Spanish and Latin-American romantic writers, such as Larra, Espronceda, Hartzenbusch, Valera, and Gertrudis Gómez de Avellaneda, who admired her works along with those of her contemporaries, Chateaubriand, Lamartine and Hugo.[4]

Of these Hispanic writers, it was Avellaneda, also known as la Tula, who both acknowledged and best demonstrated George Sand's influence in her work. Avellaneda's importance in Hispanic literature is stated by two contemporary critics, Diez-Echarri and Roca Franquesa, who call her, ". . . la figura mas destacada de todo el romanticismo en Hispanoamérica . . . [que] no ha tenido rival en la literatura del Nuevo Continente" (". . . the most outstanding figure in all of Spanish American Romanticism who has had no equal in the literature of the New Continent").[5] According to these two critics, ". . . la Avellaneda se nos revela como la más grande escritora de nuestra lengua desde el Siglo de Oro" ("Avellanedo proves herself to be the greatest writer in our language since the Golden Age" (*HLEH* [*Historia de la literatura española e hispanoamericana*], 947).

Born into Cuba's aristocracy in Puerto Príncipe, in 1814, Avellaneda later renounced her claim to the world of privilege. "Mi familia pertenece a la clase que llaman noble, pero yo no pertenezco a ninguna clase. Trato lo mismo al duque que al cómico. No reconozco otra aristocracia que la del talento" ("My family belongs to the class that is called noble, but I belong to no class. I treat dukes no differently than I do wandering minstrels. I recognize no aristocracy other than that of talent").[6] This statement of class attitudes will sound a familiar chord in the Sand scholar.

At age 18, Avellaneda voraciously read history, magazines and novels, particularly those of the French authors in vogue. In addition to reading Chateaubriand and Hugo's *Notre Dame de Paris*, ". . . she discovered the early works of the woman some asserted Tula herself took as a model, Aurore Dupin, known to the world as George Sand."[7]

In 1836, when Avellaneda was 22, the family moved to Spain. After spending a short period of time in La Coruña, she went to Seville, where her late father's family lived. At this time she was reading French authors, including George Sand, the English Romantics, and the Spanish Romantics, the Duque de Rivas, and Zorrilla. She sent poems to the newspaper, *La Aureola*, thus beginning her career in Spain.

In 1840, la Tula and her brother moved to Madrid to participate in the lively literary life of that city. There she became an important contributor to the Spanish romantic movement and led a life of independence that recalls Sand's. Like Sand, she was, ". . . a woman writer in a sexist culture and period,"[8] who earned her livelihood from her literary output. Like George Sand, whom Avellaneda greatly admired, she ". . . became a celebrity, the female possessor of a 'literary life,' and a successful professional woman" (Miller, 178). In plots, themes, characters and statements, her work, like George Sand's, was feminist. While she was primarily a poet, she wrote plays and novels as well, and it is in her novels that George Sand's influence is the most notable.

Critics have long recognized the influence of Chateaubriand's *René*, Goethe's *Werther* and Rousseau's *La Nouvelle Héloïse* on Avellaneda's first and most important novel, *Sab*, published in 1841. The suffering of René is reflected in that of Sab, the hero of Avellaneda's novel; comparisons between Goethe's Charlotte and Carlota, the heroine of *Sab*, have been drawn; and the questions of social injustice touched upon by Avellaneda in her work have been considered as having their source in Rousseau's great epistolary novel.[9] However true such comparisons may appear, it seems that critics have overlooked a much more fertile source of inspiration for Avellaneda's novel: Sand's **Indiana**, first published in 1831. Indeed, parallels between the themes, characters and situations in the two novels abound. This is not surprising, given first, George Sand's importance in Avellaneda's Parnassus, and second, the views expressed by the two women with regards to such burning social questions as slavery and the place of women in male-dominated societies.

Both **Indiana** and *Sab* are novels of unrequited love. Indiana, the heroine of Sand's novel, is married to a cruel older man. She falls in love with Raymon de Ramière, who, although he professes to love Indiana, finally tires of her passion for him and marries a wealthy woman. Indiana returns to the Ile Bourbon, where she enters into a suicide pact with her cousin, Sir Ralph, whom she had always believed to be cold and unfeeling. Before their attempted suicide, however, he reveals the depth of his love for her. The suicide attempt fails, and years later, they are discovered living happily in isolation from society and its conventions.

In Avellaneda's novel, Sab is a mulatto slave on the plantation of Don Carlos de B. . . . He is hopelessly in love with Carlota, his master's daughter. Carlota, however, loves Don Enrique Otway, the proud son of a British merchant living in Cuba. Carlota's constant companion is her poor orphaned cousin Teresa, who is secretly in love with Don Enrique. Sab realizes that Don Enrique's interest in Carlota is motivated by greed, but because Carlota loves the Englishman, the slave finds a way of bringing them together, and then dies. The marriage, however, is an unhappy one, as Carlota eventually learns the truth about Don Enrique. Thereafter, she seeks solace from Teresa, who has become a nun. In the conclusion of the novel, Teresa gives Carlota a letter Sab wrote years earlier in which he confesses his eternal devotion to Carlota. Teresa dies, and Carlota has no choice but to continue her life with her merchant husband.

In *Sab* as well as in **Indiana,** women are presented as victims. Both Carlota and Indiana are victims of a society where marriage is a business arrangement excluding love and the aspirations of women. To underscore the innocence and emotional purity of the women-victims in contrast to their male exploiters, Sand and Avellaneda have made their heroines outsiders to European civilization (both are creoles).[10] The men who use them are Europeans, representatives of a corrupt, jaded, money-hungry society. Carlota and Indiana, because of their innocence and idealism, are easily duped by Don Enrique and Raymon, whose declarations of love are false. Don Enrique declares his love for Carlota in order to marry into a rich family. Raymon's love for Indiana, although at first appearing to be genuine, cannot sustain itself. He is terrified by the intensity of her passion for him, deserting her for wealth and social position. Not until the end of both novels do the heroines realize that there exists a man who truly loves them. These two men, Ralph and Sab, although from markedly different social backgrounds, have, in their emotional histories and devotion, much in common. They are both *âmes supérieures,* who have been conditioned by emotionally sterile childhoods to hide their true feelings. As a result, both appear to the other characters as cold and reserved. Both are presented in the dual and seemingly conflicting roles of father to and adorer of the heroine. Sab speaks of his care for Carlota when she was an infant: "Yo he mecido la cuna de Carlota, sobre mis rodillas aprendió a pronunciar 'te amo.'" ("It was I who rocked Carlota's cradle. It was on my lap that she learned to say, 'I love you'").[11] Ralph's revelation or his feelings for Indiana at the end of that novel include a description of his protective, father-like behavior towards her: ". . . je vous ouvrais mes bras avec une joie pure; vos caresses rafraîchissaient mon front; j'étais heureux, j'étais père."[12]

Interestingly, both authors clearly demonstrate that while Sab and Ralph are father figures, they are clearly aware of the woman in the child. Paradoxically, potentially incestuous relationships are presented as developing into the purest of loves. Because society has made any other relationship between the sexes so cynical (Raymon) or mercantilistic (the two husbands), a man must pass through the protective, joyful love of a father for his daughter if he is later to be able to recognize her individuality and her rights. Without the earlier father-daughter relationship, the man is quite literally unable to *see* the woman as anything more than a potential sexual conquest and/or an article in a business contract.

The secondary women characters in both of the novels are very similar, and serve to accentuate women's plight in society. Noun and Teresa are denied the support systems that family connections and money can provide. Noun, because she is a servant, and Teresa, because she is a poor relation, have absolutely no hope of achieving their goals. Their only role in life is to dream another, more apparently fortunate, woman's life. Noun and Teresa are totally loyal to Indiana and Carlota. Even though the loves experienced by the heroines are tawdry and bring nothing but heartbreak, they do constitute life for a woman of the time. Noun commits suicide and Teresa goes to a convent: both acts of death are dictated by a society that offers no alternative to women on the fringe.

In addition to the presentation of women as victims and in addition to the presence of similar types of secondary characters in both novels, the element of place is of great significance. **Indiana** takes place mainly in France, which Sand offers as a center of corruption; *Sab* takes place in Cuba, and the Cuban cities inhabited and developed by Europeans mirror the corruption found in any European city. The Ile Bourbon of Indiana's origins produces innocent, good people in harmony with nature and the universe. The plantation in *Sab* isolates the inhabitants in their rustic simplicity and goodness. In each novel, there is to be found an ultimate refuge from the world and its corruption. In the case of **Indiana,** it is the Bernica Gorge. This is the *lieu privilégié* where Indiana and Ralph were happy in their roles of father and child; the place where they came to die, and eventually found life. Its equivalent in *Sab* is the garden cultivated by Sab for Carlota's pleasure. The special nature of this garden is emphasized by Avellaneda in her novel. She states that, "no había en Puerto Príncipe en la época de nuestra história, grande afficción a los jardines" ("at the time of our story, there was not much interest in gardens in Puerto Principe" [*Sab,* 85]). Neither a *jardin à l'anglaise* nor a *jardin à la française,* Carlota's garden shows no European influence whatsoever. It is, instead, a perfect expression of Sab's devotion to his adored Carlota, as it contains all of the flowers dear to her. It is important to note that the only characters who enter the garden are Sab and Carlota. In both novels, the special character of the *lieu privilégié* is underscored by the fact that, after the heroines are tempted by the European dream of happiness as represented in one case by Raymon and in the other by Don Enrique, and after their illusions are shattered, they return to the Eden of their childhood, the only place on earth where happiness may possibly be attained.

In the case of **Indiana,** happiness *is* found, but only after Ralph and Indiana have cut themselves off totally from the world. Although they do not commit suicide, they do, in a sense, die to the world, breaking all ties with society and entrusting themselves entirely to Nature. *Sab* ends with the death of the mulatto slave and Carlota's forced return to the world. Indeed, Avellaneda speculates that she must have had to leave Cuba forever, accompanying her husband to "la populosa Londres" ("crowded London" [*Sab,* 231]), a city that symbolizes all that is foreign to the passionate, innocent creole and to her native isle.

Although Sand and Avellaneda give what appear to be totally different endings to their novels, the conclusions to be drawn from these endings are the same. They both emphasize the repressive nature of a European male-dominated society that holds all women and all other races in bondage. The slavery issue treated in *Sab* is, in fact, central to both novels, as women are portrayed in both as slaves to a system that pardons them nothing. Sab, in his assessment of his life of suffering, sees clearly that his lot, however, miserable, is perhaps better than Carlota's. "Oh! ¡las mujeres¡ ¡Pobres y ciegas víctimas! Como los esclavos, ellas arrastran pacientemente su cadena y bajan la cabeza bajo el yugo de las leyes humanas. sin otro guía que su corazón ignorante y crédulo, eligen un dueño para toda la vida. El esclavo, al menos, puede cambiar de amo, puede esperar que, juntando oro, comprará algun día su libertad, pero la mujer, cuando levanta sus manos enflaquecidas y su frente ultrajada para pedir libertad, oye al monstruo de voz sepulcral que le grita: 'en la tumba'" ("Oh, women! Poor, blind victims! Like slaves they patiently drag their chains and lower their heads under the yoke of man-made laws. With no guide other than their innocent, credulous hearts, they choose a master for life. The slave, at least, can change masters. He can hope that, by saving money, he may one day buy his way to freedom. But when a woman raises up her wraithlike arms and lifts up her outraged face to beg for freedom, she hears Death proclaiming, 'only in the tomb'" (*Sab,* 227). Indiana, in a passionate outburst, echoes Sab's plaint, while asserting her refusal to accept such slavery passively: "Je sais que je suis l'esclave et vous le seigneur. La loi de ce pays vous a fait mon maître. Vous pouvez lier mon corps, garrotter mes mains, gouverner mes actions. Vous avez le droit du plus fort, et la société vous le confirme; mais sur ma volonté, Monsieur, vous ne pouvez rien, Dieu seul peut la courber et la réduire. Cherchez donc une loi, un cachot, un instrument de supplice qui vous donne prise sur elle: C'est comme vous vouliez manier l'air et saisir le vide" (**Indiana,** 203-204). Despite such an affirmation of her independence, however, Indiana gains her freedom only when she flees "la loi de ce pays" and when the "maître" dies. The idyllic ending of **Indiana** is, in fact, as tragic as the *dénouement* of *Sab*. Indiana is condemned to live as an outsider if she is to find happiness, while Carlota is a prisoner of the social order. Neither can be both free and in society. Until such freedom exists for women, there is no real freedom for them anywhere.

Notes

1. Athens: The University of Georgia Press, 1979, 7.

2. Totowa, New Jersey: Barnes and Noble Books, [1981,] 17. Henceforth cited in the text as *Turgenev.*

3. Garden City, N.Y.: Anchor Books, 1979, 285. Henceforth cited in the text as *IW.*

4. For a discussion of the influence of the French Romantics on Hispanic writers despite the closed nature of Hispanic society, see Ricardo Navas-Ruíz, *El Romanticismo español, historia y crítica* (Salamanca: Anaya, 1970) 58-60.

5. Emiliano Díez-Echarri and José Maria Roca Franquesa, *Historia de la literatura española e hispanoamericana* (Madrid: Aguilar, 1966) 893. Henceforth cited in the text as *HLEH.* Translations are ours.

6. Quoted in Florinda Alzaga, *Las Ansias de infinito en la Avellaneda* (Miami: Ediciones Universal, 1979) 19.

7. Hugh A. Harter, *Gertrudis Gómez de Avellaneda* (Boston: Twayne Publishers, 1981) 22.

8. Beth K. Miller, "Avellaneda, Nineteenth-Century Feminist," *Revista/Review Interamericana,* 4:2 (Summer 1974): 177. Henceforth cited in the text as "Miller."

9. Alberto J. Carlos, "*René, Werther* y *La Nouvelle Héloise* en la Primera Novela de la Avellaneda," *Revista Iberoamericana,* 31 (1965): 223-39.

10. Our use of "creole" is in accord with the definition given in the *Grand Dictionnaire Encyclopédique Larousse* (Paris: Larousse, 1982) 3: 2760: "se dit d'une personne dont les ascendants sont originaires d'Europe et qui est née dans les anciennes colonies européennes (Antilles, Réunion, etc.)."

11. Gertrudis Gómez de Avellaneda, *Sab* (Salamanca: Ediciones Anaya, 1970) 151. Henceforth cited in the text as *Sab.*

12. George Sand, *Indiana* (Paris: Michel Lévy Frères, 1857) 293. Henceforth cited in the text as *Indiana.*

Doris Y. Kadish (essay date spring 1992)

SOURCE: Kadish, Doris Y. "Representing Race in *Indiana*." *George Sand Studies* 11, nos. 1-2 (spring 1992): 22-30.

[*In the following essay, Kadish claims that in its representation of Creole characters (including both Indiana and Noun),* Indiana *exhibits a mixture of socially resistant and conformist attitudes toward race that distinguish the novel as one of the most "enlightened" fictional texts on the subject produced during the nineteenth century.*]

This paper looks beneath the surface of the ostensibly all white society depicted in George Sand's *Indiana* in an attempt to discover the author's conflicted attitudes, and ours as readers and critics as well, toward race and the problems of slavery and racial oppression in general. Those attitudes are examined here as indications of this novel's "ideology," not in the traditional, prescriptive connotation of some reprehensible bias or false consciousness, but in the more recent, descriptive sense which serves to characterize the kinds of unarticulated or "preconscious" attitudes that we all hold, which are inextricably related to some general historical and political context or other. Looking at the revealing treatment or in many cases the equally revealing "nontreatment" of two main topics affecting the representation of race—color and sexuality—, I shall argue that in *Indiana,* Sand both conformed to and resisted her society's values concerning race. On the negative, conformist side, Sand will be seen to resemble other white middle or upper-class members of French society of her time in being driven to contain the potential threat to society by racial "others," for example by seeming at an explicit level to make all of her major characters white and by disapproving of intermarriage. On the positive, resisting side, however, resistance will also be found in the novel's strong, albeit implicit, identification with and appeal on behalf of persons of color and the disempowerment in society generally. While in the remarks that follow I shall want to acknowledge the ideological limitations that mark Sand's writings, as we all of course similarly suffer from blind spots and ideological limitations, I shall want to place special emphasis on resistance, which to my mind is more interesting than conformity and marks *Indiana* as an enlightened representation of race.

Beginning the consideration of the topic of color outside the text, the very use of the word "créole" in French is curious and problematic. Traditionally, as a noun, the word means a "personne de pure race blanche, née aux colonies." At the same time, however, definitions of the word as an adjective introduce a multiracial meaning that definitions of the unqualified noun exclude. As Léon-François Hoffman explains about the historical use of the adjectival form, "L'adjectif 'créole' qualifie d'ailleurs, quelle que soit leur pigmentation, les natifs de l'île Bourbon aussi bien que ceux de la Guadeloupe ou de Saint-Domingue" (52-53). Since the adjective form sometimes indicates mixed or black race while other times it means a white person from the colonies, there is conflict not just between the noun and adjective but in the different uses of the adjective, which allow for ambiguity. Today, some dictionaries record the distinction between noun and adjective (e.g. Littré) while others adopt the monoracial, nominal definition exclusively (e.g. Larousse).

The conflict apparent in the very meaning of the word "créole"—the conflict between explicitly denying and implicitly acknowledging differences of race as fundamental to the identity of the inhabitants of the French colonies—is not, I think, merely a linguistic curiosity, but reflects a fundamental conflict about French thinking about their colonies. That conflict is also apparent in Sand's novel with respect to the two feminine characters both described as "créole." The treatment of these two characters duplicates textually the problematic denial of difference of race that also occurred historically, socially, and linguistically. On the conformist side, the novel tends to shy away from openly acknowledging differences in color. Indiana, the wife of the prototypical colonialist, Colonel Delmare, is described as a "créole" in what would seem to be the sense of a white colonial ("Le blanc mat de son collier, celui de sa robe de crêpe et de ses épaules nues, se confondaient à quelque distance," 80), although there are few places in the novel where her race is explicitly identified. Far more problematic is the use of the same nominal form "créole" for Indiana's servant Noun ("M. de Ramière était amoureux de la jeune créole aux yeux noirs," 73) especially in the absence of any direct evidence that she is white, and in the presence of considerable hints in the text that she is in fact black or of mixed race. For example, her hair is referred to as being "d'un noir nègre," (192); and her arms as "frais et bruns," (104). And toward the end of the novel, Indiana's cousin and eventual soul mate Ralph Brown refers in passing to Noun as "créole dans l'acceptation la plus étendue" (321), but without spelling out this more extended sense of the term.

Aside from the curious use of "créole" coupled with a sprinkling of hints about color, however, race hardly ever plays an explicit role in *Indiana*: that it affects the main characters personally is rarely made clear, despite the fact that the novel is set in the French colonies at a historical moment when racial tensions and slavery were urgent and unresolved social issues, and despite the fact that Noun is a servant. And yet I have found that most readers, both French and American, when asked their impression of Noun's color, will respond that she is not white; and curiously, she appears as a person of mixed race in the illustration in the Garnier edition of the novel, although there is no acknowledgment in the introduction to this edition that race is an issue in either the illustration or the novel.

The conformist refusal in **Indiana** to acknowledge directly differences of color reveals an unwillingness in Sand's society, if not in ours still today, to recognize the actual conditions in which persons of color live. Instead, there is a tendency to pretend that they and whatever problems are associated with them simply do not exist. Thus Noun's and Indiana's tragic love stories often seem to be merely the tales of any two French women and not specifically two women from the colonies, where issues of race are to the forefront. Because the word "créole" in French, as noted earlier, has both monoracial and multiracial meanings, the text can function conservatively to avoid the issue of color by seeming to rely only on the monoracial meaning. For example, when there is talk of the class disparity in Noun's love affair with the aristocratic Raymon de la Ramière, but no mention of the issue of race, the text and the strict nominal sense of "créole" tempt one into thinking of her as white.

Sand's conformist indirectness in representing race lives on among her critics, who typically follow Sand's lead in failing to raise openly the issue of Noun's color. For example, Kathryn Crecelius provides a fascinating indepth study of black and white imagery in **Indiana** (63-70) but astoundingly without ever acknowledging the possible relevance of that imagery for the issue of race. And in another important and interesting study, Leslie Rabine dwells on Noun as a lower-class woman but without looking as carefully at the issue of race as she does at that of class. Rabine states, for example, that "Sand makes the pure and desirable woman a white bourgeoise while the sensual and unattractive woman is a lower class Creole" (13). What is surprising about this statement is the claim that Noun is unattractive, since Sand stresses her beauty consistently in the novel. It is also surprising to find "white bourgeoise" contrasted with "lower class Creole" since in Sand's novel "créole" is applied to both Indiana and Noun and thus, at the level of explicit usage, clearly does not stand in opposition to white. Given the ambiguity surrounding the word "créole," Rabine may thereby be introducing the issue of race into her analysis; but, following Sand's lead, she does so only indirectly, failing to unpack the meanings of the word and the ideological implications of its usage, not only Sand's usage, but her own, a usage which, as I have indicated above, may not be free of racist overtones, assuming that Rabine did intend indirectly to raise the question of race. In Rabine's analysis, the issue of class overshadows the issue of race. Thus Noun, a character that Sand portrays as a respectable servant from the colonies, is treated by Rabine as a lower-class prostitute:

the use of Noun in the novel demonstrates how the prostitution of lower class women was necessary to preserve the chastity of bourgeoise women. . . . Finally, in the novel, the lower class woman must be sacrificed to maintain the innocence of the bourgeoise woman and the stability of the social order.

(14)

By failing to come to grips adequately with the issue of race in **Indiana,** Rabine's interpretation is in some ways even more conformist than Sand's novel, which as we shall now see also displays a highly significant resisting thrust.

That there exists a resisting side of **Indiana,** and thus that conformity goes hand in hand with resistance in Sand's novel, is apparent in the various intrusions of black and mixed race in the novel, intrusions that reveal a willingness to recognize racial difference, even if such often merely implicit recognition does not seem to go very far by today's standards. Resistance can be discovered in the very fact that Indiana and other apparently white inhabitants of the colonies often seem indirectly imbued with the attributes of mixed race that can occur in the adjectival form of "créole." Consider for example the very fact of setting the novel in the West Indies and giving its ostensibly pure white heroine a name connoting the non-white race of Indians. The novel thereby resists conformity to the rigid standards of the times whereby whites were set off from persons of other races in an absolutely separate and superior category. Indiana, in her very essence, bridges a gap that racists and anti-abolitionists wished to preserve as absolute and unbridgeable. Consider also that Indiana reveals at one point that the woman who nursed her was black ("il me vit venir à lui dans les bras de la négresse qui m'avait nourrie," 157). Not only does this revelation suggest that Indiana's "soeur de lait," her servant Noun, may have been the daughter of the wet-nurse and thus black or of mixed race, but it also stresses that Indiana was nurtured with the non-white, racially "other" milk of her wet-nurse and thus is herself partially non-white, too. I might point out that the suggestion that milk was connected with racial purity is not without historical precedent. We learn, for example, that Portuguese Franciscans opposed admission of non-European born inhabitants of the colonies into their order, alleging that "even if born of pure white parents [they] have been sucked by Indian ayahs in their infancy and thus had their blood contaminated for life" (Anderson 60). The term "soeur de lait," used on a number of occasions in **Indiana,** thus carries racial connotations that heighten Indiana's association with persons of color.

The resisting side of **Indiana** is also apparent in the many passages in the novel in which Indiana herself voices resistance to the analogous oppression imposed on women and slaves, passages that make the point that blacks, whites, and persons of color do indeed share the common identity that definitions of the adjective "créole" acknowledge. The following passage is representative:

> en voyant le continuel tableau des maux de la servitude, en supportant les ennuis de l'isolement et de la dépendance, elle avait acquis une patience extérieure à toute épreuve, une indulgence et une bonté adorables avec ses inférieures, mais aussi une volonté de fer, une force de résistance incalculable contre tout ce qui tendait à l'opprimer. . . . Elle n'aima pas son mari, par la seule raison peut-être qu'on lui faisait un devoir de l'aimer, et que résister mentalement à toute espèce de contrainte morale était devenu chez elle une seconde nature, un principe de conduite, une loi de conscience. . . . Élevée au désert, négligée de son père, vivant au milieu des esclaves, pour qui elle n'avait d'autre secours, d'autre consolation que sa compassion et ses larmes, elle s'était habituée à dire: "Un jour viendra où tout sera changé dans ma vie, où je ferai du bien aux autres. . . .
>
> (89)

On occasion Indiana even serves as a spokesperson for ideas of resistance by slaves themselves to their oppressors, ideas that have a clear abolitionist ring:

> Dieu ne veut pas qu'on opprime et qu'on écrase les créatures de ses mains. S'il daignait descendre jusqu'à intervenir dans nos chétifs intérêts, il briserait le fort et relèverait le faible; il passerait sa grande main sur nos têtes inégales et les nivellerait comme les eaux de la mer; il dirait à l'esclave; "Jette ta chaîne, et fuis sur les monts où j'ai mis pour toi des eaux, des fleurs et du soleil."
>
> (249-250)

In this passage and elsewhere in the novel, Indiana, referring to herself metaphorically as a slave although she is white, grounds her plea for resistance in the multiracial meaning of the word "créole" noted above. Indiana's implicit non-whiteness is proudly proclaimed here in her use of the first-person plural "nos" in speaking together with black slaves of "nos chétifs intérêts" and "nos têtes inégales."

Commenting on Sand's metaphorical use of the notion of slavery, Nancy Rogers rightly concludes that "Indiana joins the other rebellious runaway slaves so often depicted in the literature of the times. . . . Indiana is branded as blatantly as any runaway slave recaptured by his master" (31). There is thus an important sense in which one could say that by choosing to live in the colonies and to live apart from its white colonialist inhabitants, both Indiana and Ralph can be seen as joining the ranks of a non-white community at the end of the novel and thus symbolically becoming honorary full members of the black slave community. The novel closes, revealingly, with Indiana and Ralph devoting their efforts to helping black slaves—if not to escape

slavery altogether at least to bear its burden with less suffering in sickness or old age: "La majeure portion de nos revenus est consacrée à racheter de pauvres Noirs infirmes. C'est la principale cause du mal que les colons disent de nous. Que ne sommes nous assez riches pour délivrer tous ceux qui vivent dans l'esclavage!" (342).

I might add that it is not surprising to find Ralph coupled with the racially impure Indiana and often treated like her. A native of the colonies, he too is a "créole," with all of the ambiguity that surrounds that word for Indiana and Noun. As Isabelle Naginski's analysis of *Indiana* makes it possible to see, he is also an androgynous double of the feminine writer, "a working model for the author's double-gendered voice" (65). And like Indiana, although he is white, his identity and hopes for the future are as rooted in the dream of the abolition of slavery and oppression as if he were black: "Ralph allait donc toujours soutenant son rêve de république d'où il voulait exclure tous les abus, tous les préjugés, toutes les injustices; projet fondé tout entier sur l'espoir d'une nouvelle race d'hommes" (167). It is thus possible to see in the couple, Indiana and Ralph, about which I shall have more to say later, a locus of combined masculine and feminine, white and non-white, resistance against the oppression and racism that for Sand characterizes the colonies generally and the colonialist Colonel Delmare specifically.

The treatment of sexuality in *Indiana* provides another occasion to observe both conformity and resistance in Sand's representation of race. Conformism is apparent in the deprecation or denial of non-white sexuality. Deprecation often occurs through the dichotomy established, typically from Raymon's point of view, between Indiana and Noun as (at least at the implicit level) a woman of color. In that dichotomy, Noun is physically disparaged more often than Indiana because an emphasis, typical in Western culture, is placed on her physicality as a person of color. The following description of the two women is representative: "Noun, grande, forte, brillante de santé, vive, alerte, et pleine de sang créole ardent et passionné, effaçait de beaucoup, par sa beauté resplendissante, la beauté pâle et frêle de madame Delmare . . ." (60). To Indiana is granted the delicacy and light color of the white colonial woman. To her servant is reserved the animal-like strength and the lustiness implying sexual availability typically associated by colonialists with black women slaves. Elsewhere that same sensuality reappears, as when Raymon is making love to Noun and thinking about the sexual opposition between her and her mistress:

> C'était Indiana qu'il voyait dans le nuage du punch que la main de Noun venait d'allumer; c'était elle qui l'appelait et qui lui souriait derrière ces blancs rideaux de mousseline; ce fut elle encore qu'il rêva sur cette

couche modeste et sans tâche, lorsque, succombant
sous l'amour et le vin il y entraîna sa créole échevelée.

(105)

Raymon blames the physicality of his "créole éche-velée" for his own abandon and debauchery ("succombant sous l'amour et le vin"); he interprets her seductiveness as solicitation ("le nuage du punch que la main de Noun venait d'allumer," "c'était elle qui l'appelait"). He further denigrates her, speaking of "l'ardeur insensée qui consume les flancs de cette créole lascive" (106).

Another of Sand's conformist practices consists, paradoxically, in the opposite of dichotomizing the two women. This practice consists, instead, in lumping the two women together and treating them both as inferior, along with all those who live in the colonies. The sexualization and diminution of women of color thus extends to all "créoles," again playing on the multiracial sense of that term. In the following passage, for example, Raymon subjects Indiana to the same sexualization as her servant:

en reconduisant madame de Carvajal et madame Delmare à leur voiture, il réussit à porter la petite main d'Indiana à ses lèvres. Jamais baiser d'homme furtif et dévorant n'avait effleuré les doigts de cette femme, quoiqu'elle fût née sous un climat de feu et qu'elle eût dix-neuf ans; dix-neuf ans de l'Ile de Bourbon, qui équivalent à vingtcinq ans de notre pays.

(84)

Although Indiana's sexual purity is overtly proclaimed in this passage, its covert message is her inherent propensity to the same excessive passion, the same "lasciviousness," as Noun. The novel similarly emphasizes that both women have the same luxurious, erotic dark hair: "S'il baisait ses cheveux noirs, il croyait baiser les cheveux noirs d'Indiana" (104).

Conformism is similarly directed at men born in the colonies, who, because they belong to a multiracial society, are implicitly disparaged sexually and relegated, like women, to the inferior category of the European male's sexual "other." A notable example is Indiana's soul mate Ralph. Throughout the novel, Ralph is symbolically emasculated and feminized through analogy with women, slaves, and members of oppressed groups; we read for example that "Ralph n'avait connu de la vie que ses maux et ses dégoûts" (166). No less than Noun and Indiana, he is a powerless and thus symbolically impotent victim of the masculine oppression of the colonialist system, which is consistently associated with slavery. Thus Ralph states: "Mon père . . . était prêt à me maudire si j'essayais d'échapper à son joug. Je courbai la tête; mais ce que je souffris, vous-même, qui fûtes aussi bien malheureuse, ne sauriez l'apprécier" (323). Unlike powerful masculine Europeans such as Indiana's husband Delmare and her lover Raymon,

Ralph is denigrated through his portrayal here in a symbolically feminine and slavelike guise as weak, submissive, silent, all-suffering, impotent, and asexual. Indeed, James M. Vest rightly captures the reader's overall impression of Ralph when Vest designates him as phallically "oarless," in contrast with the oarsmen ("rameurs") who kill Indiana's defenseless female dog Ophelia and with Raymon de *Ram*-ière (53). Denying the sexuality of male slaves, including the actual practice of castration, were facts of colonial life with which the literary desexualization of Ralph is consistent (Jordan 154).

The existence of conformist sexual and racial standards in *Indiana* is further evident in this novel's implicitly negative message about mixed marriage and children of mixed race, a message that the novel never openly acknowledges but that is revealing of its conflicted ideological attitudes toward race. When Noun, the servant, becomes pregnant by Raymon, the European aristocrat, the death of the mother before bearing the child precludes any possibility of racial mixture. One might conclude, although the novel itself refrains from openly addressing the issue of mixed marriage, that mixing races would be too radical a solution to the problems of slavery and oppression that *Indiana* explores. And indeed Sand states in the preface to the 1842 edition that her goal in that novel was to find moderate solutions to social problems: "Je cherchais . . . le moyen de concilier le bonheur et la dignité des individus opprimés par cette même société, sans modifier la société elle-même" (44). Michèle Hirsch observes along similar, conformist lines that the political revolt depicted in the novel at the moment of Indiana's arrival in Bordeaux in 1830 seems to be dismissed as illegitimate in *Indiana* (125).

It is crucial to stress again, however, that conformity goes hand in hand with resistance in the treatment of sexuality and race in *Indiana,* pace interpretations such as Crecelius's—"classes are left in place in the marriages and bourgeois values dominate," (80)—that only acknowledge the conformist meaning. Resistance in *Indiana* consists of granting women and men, to whites and non-whites alike, the right to enjoy a combined emotional and physical sexuality that transcends an exclusively carnal or reproductive bond. For women and slaves who have been relegated to the inferior roles of mere sexual object or procreative resource, such a more humane and expansive definition of sexuality constitutes a significant form of resistance against forces in society that refuse to recognize racial and sexual differences.

An interesting contrast that points up the resisting side of Sand's treatment of sexuality and race is suggested in Gayatri Spivack's analysis of Charlotte Brontë's *Jane Eyre,* a novel that was also written by a nineteenth-century woman but later, at what Spivack identifies as an imperialist phase of history, in which bearing children and saving souls were the chief roles assigned to middle-class English women. Spivack emphasizes the sharp opposition that Brontë draws between Jane and Rochester's first wife, the white Jamaican Bertha Mason; and Spivack argues that in order for Jane to replace Bertha as the lawful wife and mother, Bertha must be subjected to the kind of egregious animalization and sexualization that was often applied to women of color from the colonies. For Spivack, Brontë's treatment of Bertha serves "as an allegory of the general epistemic violence of imperialism, the construction of a self-immolating colonial subject for the glorification of the social mission of the colonizer." It is an allegory, Spivack claims, in which the woman from the colonies is "sacrificed as an insane animal for her sister's consolidation" (270).

The sharp difference between *Jane Eyre,* at least upon Spivack's reading, and **Indiana** is striking and reaches to the heart of Sand's resistance to conformist notions of sexuality and race. Although sometimes presented as more sexual than Indiana, Noun is subjected to little of the violent denigration that Bertha Mason receives. Nor are Noun and Indiana radically separated in their fate as either sexual partners or mothers, as Bertha and Jane are. On the contrary, Sand's novel repeatedly emphasizes the shared sexual experiences of the mistress and her servant and thus implicitly of women of all races. Indeed, the ambiguity surrounding the word "créole" in Sand's novel, with its admittedly negative function of sidestepping issues of race, also functions positively to emphasize the commonality of the two women. Both Noun's sexuality and her eventual childlessness are also Indiana's. Nurtured on the same milk; both destined to play subservient roles as women; treated similarly as slaves; mistreated by the same unfeeling lover; cut off from power, language, successful marriage, and enduring progeny: Noun and Indiana serve less as models of the oppressed and the oppressor than as joint illustrations of slave women's sexual oppression. In their shared oppression, they are offered to the reader for sympathy and understanding. Most importantly, unlike *Jane Eyre,* **Indiana** allows readers to recognize the racial implications of feminine sexuality. Sand's novel thus provides an implicitly contestatory, resisting representation of sexual practices in colonial society.

Resistance, at least as much as conformity, thus marks Sand's treatment of feminine sexuality and race in **Indiana.** It is perhaps not surprising, then, that at the end of the novel, Indiana and Ralph live together in what appears to be a spiritually if not a legally sanctioned union. True, on the conformist side, Ralph's feminization implicitly calls into question his ability to play a standard masculine, paternal role in society, just as Indiana's symbolic non-whiteness raises the specter of intermarriage. More importantly, however, on the resisting side,

the refusal to assign to Indiana the traditional roles of wife and mother constitutes an attempt to recast traditional notions of sexuality and love in new forms. That refusal needs to be interpreted as a resistance to the idea of relegating Indiana to the kind of biologically and socially reproductive role as mother and model of national values to which Spivack claims that Jane Eyre conforms. Naomi Schor perceptively discerns in **Indiana** "a yearning to be delivered both from the base desire for carnal possession characteristic of male sexuality and the injustices of a manmade system of laws that enables the enslavement of both women and blacks"; and thus she sees in Sand's refusal to assign a reproductive role to Indiana a refusal to "legitimate a social order inimical to the disenfranchised, among them women" (73).

Along with Rogers and Naginski, Schor correctly reads **Indiana** as an emancipatory text of resistance, as against Crecelius, Hirsch, and Rabine, who, to my mind, over-emphasize its conformist side. Common to those readings that privilege resistance is a feminist perspective that sees beyond the sexual compromises that Sand's characters inevitably make. Those readings acknowledge Sand's protest against injustice in **Indiana** and her willingness to fight that injustice through the limited means that she found available to the disempowered in the society of her time. Clearly Sand could not totally transcend or stand outside the ideology of her times with respect to race. Clearly, too, her positive representation of race in **Indiana** today appears to be largely indirect and symbolic. In short, conformity is an inescapable ingredient in that novel as in her writings generally. At the same time, it needs to be remembered that in a work such as **Indiana,** Sand does endorse many of the most liberal and enlightened views that were available to people of the nineteenth century, an endorsement that we today as critics need as much to applaud as to critique.

Works Cited

Anderson, Benedict. *Imagined Communities: Reflections on the Origin and Spread of Nationalism.* London: Verso, 1983.

Crecelius, Kathryn. *Family Romances: George Sand's Early Novels.* Bloomington, Indiana: Indiana University Press, 1987.

Grand Larousse de la langue française, II. Paris: Gallimard, 1968.

Hirsch, Michèle. "Questions à Indiana." *Revue des sciences humaines* 42.165 (1977): 117-129.

Hoffman, Léon-François. *Le Nègre romantique: personnage littéraire et obsession collective.* Paris: Payot, 1973.

Jordan, Winthrop D. *White over Black: American Attitudes Toward the Negro, 1550-1812.* New York: W. W. Norton, 1968.

Littré, Emile. *Dictionnaire de la langue française,* II. Paris: Gallimard, 1968.

Naginski, Isabelle. *George Sand, Writing for Her Life.* New Brunswick, New Jersey: Rutgers University Press, 1991.

Rabine, Leslie. "George Sand and the Myth of Femininity." *Women and Literature* 4 (1976): 2-17.

Rogers, Nancy. "Slavery as Metaphor in the Writings of George Sand." *French Review* 53.1 (1979): 29-35.

Sand, George. *Indiana.* Paris: Gallimard, 1984.

Schor, Naomi. "Idealism in the Novel: Recanonizing Sand." *Yale French Studies* 75 (1988): 56-73.

Spivack, Gayatri Chakravorty. "Three Women's Texts and a Critique of Imperialism." *"Race," Writing, and Difference.* Ed. Henry Louis Gates, Jr. Chicago: University of Chicago Press, 1985: 262-280.

Vest, James M. "Fluid Nomenclature, Imagery, and Themes in George Sand's *Indiana.*" *South Atlantic Review* 46.2 (1981): 43-54.

Sandy Petrey (essay date 1993)

SOURCE: Petrey, Sandy. "George and Georgina Sand: Realist Gender in *Indiana.*" In *Textuality and Sexuality: Reading Theories and Practices,* edited by Judith Still and Michael Worton, pp. 133-47. Manchester, England: Manchester University Press, 1993.

[*In the following essay, Petrey maintains that the realism of* Indiana *lies in its status as a realist study in gender that focuses on socially constructed identities and roles.*]

George Sand, Honoré de Balzac, Stendhal: when Sand's novel *Indiana* appeared in 1832, readers hailed it as a superb contribution to the new fictional form developed by *The Wild Ass's Skin* and *Scarlet and Black.* The assimilation of Sand to Stendhal is especially striking, for it came during a period when *Scarlet and Black* was far from a stock literary reference. Bernard Weinberg's classic study of critical reactions to French realism defines the period 1831-8 as 'seven years of an almost absolute silence' concerning Stendhal.[1] It's therefore all the more noteworthy that a large percentage of those who reviewed *Indiana* were impelled to break the silence to tell their readers what Sand's work was like.

For one reviewer, *Indiana*'s characters are 'drawn with that vigour of observation you admire in *Scarlet and Black*'.[2] For another, Sand represents the world in the 'raw and bold tones of Beyle'.[3] Even when the reviewer got the spelling wrong, he had enough confidence in generic identity to set Sand's work among those novels in the process of establishing 'the school of Sthendal [sic]'.[4] *Scarlet and Black* stands commandingly at the origin of French social realism by virtue of its comprehensive integration of contemporary society into the novel form. Two years after *Scarlet and Black,* **Indiana** assumed a prominent place beside it as the prototype of fiction in which literary creation and historical insight are reciprocally invigorating.

In the years since 1832, two currents of literary scholarship with little else in common have collaborated in distancing Sand's work from the foundational realist texts with which it was first equated. The masculinist operations of traditional criticism put Balzac and Stendhal far above their female colleague, and the revisionist impulse of feminist criticism has tended to maintain the opposition while refusing the hierarchy. Different though their attitudes toward Sand's achievement have been, critics have generally agreed that it's not Balzac and Stendhal's. The most striking aspect of Sand's first reception, however, is that invocation of realist authors proceeded from an unexceptionable understanding of realist achievement. The reasons **Indiana** and *Scarlet and Black* were originally put together are the same as those subsequently invoked to set them apart.

Realism's most consequential innovation—its foundational vision of the world—was awareness that the socio-historical conditions in which human existence unfolds have determinant impact on its course. Characters and age constitute a single whole to effect precisely the integration of individual and collective that furnished the leitmotif of Sand's reviewers. **Indiana**'s representation of the human heart, mind and soul was seen as credible because this novel historicises inner states as thoroughly as conventional fictions historicise outer appearance. '**Indiana** is the story of modern passion'.[5] 'The particular merit of **Indiana** [. . .] resides above all in a profoundly true sentiment of the sufferings and moral turpitudes of our epoch'.[6] '**Indiana** is our story, the story of the human heart as it is now' (Boussuge). 'On opening this book, we saw ourselves introduced into a world that was true, living, *ours* [. . .] we found customs and characters as they exist around us'.[7] To the eternal and universal paradigms of psychological delineation consecrated by classical humanism, realist fiction opposes the time-bound model of a selfhood formed by the forces that also define an era. That lesson was schematised again and again in the discussion provoked by **Indiana.**

Besides their impressive proclivity for the language that would identify realism as a whole, reviews of **Indiana** were also characterised by speculation on the author's sex. Much of this sexual commentary simply recycles inherited ideas on male and female writing: 'this is a novel written with all the strength of a man's grip and all the grace of a woman's pen'.[8] But the experience of reading *Indiana* stimulated some critics to open a consequential inquiry into the cultural practices that produce (rather than express) masculine and feminine sensibilities. Like hearts, thought, passion and suffering, for some of *Indiana*'s first readers gender too figured among the components of human existence that vary with time, place and customs. To the list of prophetic tropes organising early reactions to *Indiana* must be added a complex of issues with intense contemporary resonance, those addressing the interrelationship of gender and genre.

That George Sand and Aurore Dudevant were the same person was anything but a closely guarded secret in the small world of Paris literary circles in 1832, and reviewers with interesting things to say about the sexual identity of the authorial voice knew or suspected that the actual author was a woman who had taken a man's name. As Sainte-Beuve put it, this transsexual gesture was by itself enough to destabilise the narrating voice and integrate the author and his/her gender into the fictional universe: 'The author of *Indiana,* we are assured, is a woman [. . .] as far as we're concerned, everything in this harrowing production justifies the suspicion that has been circulating and creates a reading that is doubly novelistic, through the interest of the story in itself and through some mysterious and living identity, invincibly imagined behind the story by the reader' (pp. 473-4). For Sainte-Beuve, the author is as much caught up as characters in the socialised representation configuring the fictional world of *Indiana.* Cross-naming brought the person named into the novel, where his and/or her 'mysterious and living identity' underpins the contemporary reality enclosing Indiana and her supporting cast. Because a woman had written herself as a man by taking a masculine name and mastering a masculine style, the fictions of gender were brought into dynamic interaction with those of love.

While Sainte-Beuve located the novel of the author in the novel proper, Gustave Planche went farther. He took the combination of a name and a writing that both reverse gender expectations as demanding their own narrative, and he amenably provided it. Planche's protagonist is Georgina Sand, a name he derived from 'translating' the 'mysterious anonymity' on *Indiana*'s title page (p. 701). Georgina's biography can be effortlessly inferred from her compositional techniques:

> This must be a woman with an acute sensibility, but one who early on acquired personal direction of her actions. Such premature freedom gave her mind a somewhat virile character. Beside an idea that could come only from eiderdown, from under the laces of a bonnet, next to an emotion that springs from a heart impris-

oned by a corset, there are others indicating a daring horseman, riding crop in hand, tearing across fields in the early morning, pulling in great gulps of air, leaping ditches at the risk of his horse's neck.

(p. 701)[9]

Why does Georgina sound like George? She led the life George would have had if he existed. If sex is given and gender constructed, Planche's George and Georgina Sand exemplify gender alone. They/she/he write the way they do not because their bodies so dictate but because society has marked their bodies with corsets and bonnets or the chance not to sit side-saddle.

While Planche sees George and Georgina as the product of androgynous socialisation, he believes Georgina ultimately had to betray herself. By definition, androgynous socialisation can't be completely masculine, and the author of *Indiana* doesn't display some of the traits male instruction necessarily conveys. 'A man, on the contrary, introduces his mind and the artifice of his thought into expression of his every feeling. He schemes, he organises each outpouring of emotion. Often he even prefers effects to truth in a tête-à-tête; all the more reason to do so in a book' (pp. 701-2). When they confront a choice between truth and effect, men are trained to choose effect, and the author of *Indiana* takes truth instead.

Planche gives two instances of unseemly and unmasculine candour: delineation of Raymon de Ramière, the man with whom Indiana falls in love, and the narrator's misogynistic remarks on women's lack of intelligence. 'A man would never have agreed to paint Raymon's selfishness so pitilessly, or to pronounce this brutal aphorism: Woman is imbecilic by nature' (p. 700). However imbecilic he considers women, however selfish he considers other men, a man doesn't say so in books.

Sainte-Beuve, who also found Raymon too real a man to have been invented by one, crowns his reasons why a woman must have written *Indiana* like this: 'above all the character of Raymon, this disappointing character brought to light and exposed in detail with all his miserable selfishness in a way no man, not even a Raymon, would ever have been able to see or dared to say' (p. 473). The author of *Indiana* got Raymon exactly right, and that's something no man could have possibly done.

Which features of Raymon's textual presence are incompatible with character delineation as men practise it? The question is crucial, for it asks what 'truth' about themselves men are so unwilling to reveal that only a woman would put it into words. I believe the answer is that Sand represents Raymon's manhood as a social performance rather than a natural fact and thus challenges every claim that men's social position merely recognises their natural capabilities. In the terms of the essentialist/constructionist debate on identity, *Indiana* sets itself squarely on the constructionist side. It depicts—and enacts—male and female *being* as the consequence of culturally circumscribed patterns of masculine and feminine *behaviour,* a compelling repudiation of received ideas that goes far towards explaining early reader response. Reviewers' consistent attention to both the author's sexual identity and the setting's historical specificity was the appropriate response to a text that takes social production of men and women as its dominant concern. The narrator and characters of *Indiana* collaborate in a sustained demonstration that gender is no less a social phenomenon than the class distinctions so prominent in the works of Sand's realist colleagues.

The opposite of realist gender is naturally—physiologically, corporeally—determined sex, and *Indiana* takes pains to show that what looks like natural sexuality is in fact a social role. Raymon de Ramière, the character Planche and Sainte-Beuve saw as revealing the limits on a woman's ability to write like a man, is a perfect example. Raymon is a hugely successful lover, the sort of man whose standard depiction exalts manhood. In Sand's representation, however, Raymon's amatory prowess derives not from his manhood but from his discourse. He talks his desire into existence and in so doing separates desire from its supposed origin in male hormones. The sequence isn't lust followed by seductive language but seductive language followed by lust. 'He expressed passion with art, and he felt it with warmth. Only it was not passion that made him eloquent, it was eloquence that made him passionate' (p. 62).[10] Like that of sex, the essentialist vision of sexuality posits the control of behaviour by anatomy. In the realist vision of *Indiana,* Raymon's behaviour is cause rather than effect. He comes to feel with intensity what he articulates with skill, fabricating successive selfhoods that are simultaneously solid and factitious. What he is derives from how he acts.

As readers have long recognised, Raymon acts like an exemplary avatar of Don Juan. To my knowledge, however, no one has ever thought that Don Juan must be the creation of a woman because no man could ever depict a fellow male in so unflattering a light. On the contrary: Don Juanism is more like a secret ambition than a secret shame in masculinist ruminations on the subject. By no stretch of the imagination is a male character who seduces and abandons women a figure that 'a man would never have agreed to paint'. Too many men have painted such characters with too much success for any reviewer, much less one with the credentials of Planche and Sainte-Beuve, to argue that a man actually wouldn't do any such thing.

What sets Raymon apart from other Don Juans is that his treatment of women doesn't derive from his character but institutes it, which is why the rules of manly writing decreed that he be left undepicted. The eternal masculine mythologised in figures like Don Juan becomes a silly bit of nonsense as *Indiana* severs what counts as masculine from everything that could conceivably be considered eternal. 'Since his first literary creation, the definitive expression and determination of Don Juan has been precise: *a man without a name,* which is to say a sex and not an individual'.[11] By giving her Don Juan a local habitation and a name that are responsible for everything he does, Sand was equally precise: Raymon embodies a gender and not a sex. He becomes a Don Juan not through surging testosterone but through interactive dynamics.

Yet the desire produced by those dynamics is powerful and substantial, for Sand's vision of realist gender pays close attention to the fact that what society imposes on its members becomes their lived reality. When men and women come together in *Indiana,* the sparks still fly. The novel's specificity is ascribing the heat to ideology rather than physiology. Characters' mutual attraction is a social fabrication, their indulgence of it a social rite; the novel consequently makes its only representation of the sexual act its most powerful figuration of gendered desire.

When Noun senses that she's losing Raymon, she makes a final effort to keep him by dressing herself in Indiana's clothes before bringing her lover into Indiana's bedroom. Raymon's response is satisfactorily erotic. What turns him on, however, isn't the body he takes but the setting in which it's presented, a setting filled with the signs of a socio-economic status far superior to Noun's. Physically with the maid, emotionally taking the mistress, Raymon sees Indiana in her mirrors, feels her in her clothes, senses her in her curtains, caresses her on her bed: 'Noun took all these transports for herself, when Raymon saw of her nothing except Indiana's dress' (p. 86).

Like Indiana, Noun is a paragon of female beauty, but her anatomical perfection is erotically non-functional. Her beauty is in fact inimical to her lover's desire: every time Indiana's possessions convince Raymon he's with the woman he wants, one of Noun's body parts pushes itself forward and reminds him he's not.

> It was but a momentary error: Indiana would have been more hidden . . . her modest breast would not have been revealed through the triple gauze of her bodice; she might perhaps have adorned her hair with natural camellias, but it would not have lain on her head in such exciting disorder; she could have enclosed her feet in satin slippers, but her chaste dress would not have thus revealed the mysteries of her darling leg.

> (p. 83)

However Don Juan might react to them, women's breasts, legs and hair turn Raymon off. He's excited not by female flesh but by feminine clothes, pictures, crystal and lace. Anatomy is not destiny. Ideology is, and the ideology of gender activating Raymon's desire leaves anatomical attributes out.

For Don Juan, any female body reflects every other. For Raymon, the desired reflection comes not from female bodies but from feminine signifiers. When he wants 'a purer reflection of Indiana' (p. 83), he looks away from the body before him and to the musical instruments and embroidery behind it, ignoring the physical identity that sets Noun and Indiana together for the social identity that sets them apart. The substitution culminates, famously, when sex with the maid produces a hallucinatory vision of sex with the mistress. 'The two panels of mirrors sending Noun's image back and forth between them an infinite number of times seemed to be filled with a thousand shadows. In the depths of this double reverberation, he made out a slimmer form, and it seemed to him that, in the last misty, vague shadow of Noun reflected there, he saw the slender and elegant body of Madame Delmare' (p. 86). Clothes ordinarily manifest social position in ways a naked body does not. In *Indiana,* however, nakedness too is socially defined. Even when engaged in the most undeniably physiological component of gendered relations, Raymon demonstrates that physiology can never inform a serious understanding of either their causes or their effects.

Although Noun has 'a beauty of the first order,' (p. 52), she isn't desirable to Raymon because her beauty doesn't matter unless it's combined with first-order status. 'The wife of a peer of the realm who would so immolate herself would be a precious conquest; but a chambermaid!' (p. 52). Social standing and gendered desirability are both collective fabrications that interact to generate libido as well as protocol. Physically, Noun and Indiana are alike. Socially, they are a world apart, and Raymon's hallucinatory vision of the socially validated mistress while he engages in physical love with her maid is a striking feature of *Indiana*'s realist view of men and women together. *Every* component of gendered interaction is socially marked.

Indiana replaces Noun in Raymon's mirror because France's social organisation defines her as more desirable. Since social organisation is fluid rather than fixed, sexual desirability vacillates as well, which means that the woman adored can always become a woman scorned if she loses the status responsible for her appeal. Indiana can herself be replaced, as she is when the novel repeats substitution of one woman for another in its title character's bedroom. Raymon is again the figure for whom the substitution occurs, but Indiana becomes the woman expelled instead of the woman invoked when she returns from the Ile Bourbon to find Raymon married to Laure de Nangy. The political revolution that occurred between Indiana's miraculous appearance and ignominious expulsion from the same space figures a

different sort of social change: like forms of government, gendered relations vary with historical conditions.

Noun vanishes despite a physical beauty and a loving heart the narrator exalts unreservedly, Indiana despite qualities with analogous certification. As if to show that what actually gets to men has little to do with women's physical or emotional attributes, the prologue to Indiana's rejection by Raymon is her total surrender to him of her body, mind and heart.

> 'Won't you recognise me,' she exclaimed; 'it's me, it's your Indiana, it's your slave [. . .] Dispose of me, of my blood, of my life; I'm yours, body and soul; I came three thousand leagues to belong to you, to tell you so; take me, I'm your property, you're my master.' [. . .] She attached herself to him with the terror of a child who does not want to be left alone one instant and dragged herself on her knees to follow him.
>
> (pp. 300-2)

The abjection is spectacular, the offer of sexual slavery verbally explicit and gesturally confirmed. Raymon can't respond because—unlike Don Juan—he's not a sexual but a social being.

The same site, Indiana's bedroom, encloses two of the novel's most dramatic sexual encounters, and the outcome of both is a lesson on how much more than sex is involved in each. On a first level, the display could be understood as a simple instance of the dominance of property over human relations in realist fiction. Who gets the man? The woman who owns the bedroom. Nothing else counts—not beauty, not sacrifice, not intensity of desire, not magnitude of devotion. The absent Indiana is present in the space she possesses, the present Indiana might as well be absent from the space Laure has bought. Sand's novel incorporates classic tropes of standard bedroom plots, but it refuses to let them determine what happens in bed.

Although Sand appropriates the economic vision that a certain Marxist tradition has ascribed to Balzac's works, economics alone is far from exhausting the realist configuration of Laure de Nangy's mastery over the man other women beg to master them. Laure rules not just because she's rich but because she's noble as well, a combination with special importance in making *Indiana* what its readers saw as the 'infallible history' (Pyat, p. 194) of their age. Laure, the only descendant of an imposing aristocratic family, is also the only heir to an imposing bourgeois fortune. She thus enjoys superior status in both the elite groups recognized under the early July Monarchy, when aristocratic and financial notables were coming to rule side by side. In the high realist tradition, Laure's person manifests the global configuration of her age.

The importance in *Indiana* of the July Revolution's social and political transformation of France is largely responsible for contemporary readers' penchant for describing the novel in the language used for masterpieces of realism. Laure's special status in relation to July Monarchy elites foregrounds the reciprocal impact of genre and gender establishing the specificity of *Indiana* within the realist corpus, for the power granted Laure by historical changes effects nothing less than the obliteration of male hegemony. In describing Raymon's relations with Noun and Indiana, Sand socialises (and thus demystifies) masculine authority but leaves the man in the controlling role. In Raymon's relation with Laure, demystification completes itself by making the male the submissive rather than the dominant partner. Society may well restrict gendered contact to exercises of dominance and submission, Sand seems to be saying, but nothing requires either sex always to occupy the same position. Because the world validates hierarchies other than those of gender, a woman like Laure need not be a 'woman' when she's with her man. Her contact with Raymon is the studied, systematic reversal of Noun and Indiana's because her position in the France of the early 1830s precludes her assumption of anything vaguely like their gender roles.

Which of course means that Raymon's gender role must be cast aside as well. In the fable of Don Juan's sexual drive, every woman is a point on a line that never ends. In the realist narrative of gendered identity that is *Indiana,* the woman who stands above Raymon in collective perception orders that the line be cut, and she is obeyed. When Don Juan is between two women, he takes the new and leaves the old behind. When Raymon, 'his eyes sparkling' and 'a terrible smile playing on his lips' (pp. 301-2), has Indiana at his feet, Laure pronounces his desire null and void. The pronouncement's impact is the ultimate demonstration that gender roles and sexual physiology are independent variables. Laure 'was the woman who was to subjugate Raymon, for she was as far above him in skill as he was above Indiana' (p. 293). Much more than his sexual exploitation *of* women, it's Raymon's exploitation *by* one that makes him the kind of man no other man would have 'agreed to paint'.

On finding Indiana in despair, Laure's reaction—anything but sisterly—is a 'bitter, cold and contemptuous smile' (p. 302). Female solidarity would affirm the fundamentalist, anatomical vision of female identity repudiated by Laure, who can no more sympathise with the woman at Raymon's feet than she could put herself there. She therefore withdraws, 'triumphing in secret over the position of inferiority and dependence in which this incident had placed her husband in relation to herself' (p. 303). The tableau created when Indiana is at Raymon's feet and Raymon under Laure's thumb encapsulates substitution of gender for sex in Sand's first novel. The roles to be assumed in sexual contact are set by society, but no extra-social feature like bodily attributes can determine who will play them. Two charac-

ters—Indiana and Raymon, a woman and a man—take the feminine 'position of inferiority and dependence'. Two characters—a man and a woman, Raymon and Laure—take the masculine role of 'subjugating' their partners. The message all characters convey is that formulated when Noun's perfect beauty disappears during her socially imperfect love affair: the body counts only in so far as society decrees that it shall.

Accordingly, it's after Raymon's standing in society has been compromised by his political miscalculations that his body stops making him a man. His phallic superiority turns out to be not genital but political. Among the principal defenders of 'a royal house that was degrading itself and bearing him with it as it fell' (p. 260), Raymon experienced France's expulsion of that house during the July Revolution as a catastrophic end. His marriage to Laure was an effort to align himself with those for whom the events of July were an exhilarating beginning. Revolutionary transformations of governmental and gendered hierarchies coincide because both depend absolutely on a societal acquiescence that can always be withdrawn. Neither kings nor men actually rule by divine right.

There's another way *Indiana* employs the standard tropes of realist history to represent gendered existence: its depiction of the human consequences of France's marriage laws, which placed women in a permanently inferior position to their men. In one of the novel's most quoted passages, Indiana makes an eloquent protest against the French marital system, defending all women's right to disobey their husbands by forcing hers to consider the contrast between legal bondage and spiritual freedom. 'I know that I am the slave and you are the lord; the law of this country has made you my master [. . .] You have the right of the strongest, and society confirms it for you; but over my will, sir, you have no rights' (p. 225). Marital relations are in *Indiana* as pointed and precise a historical reference as dynastic successions, and the title character repeatedly defines revolution in the home as no less important than revolution in the palace.

Yet France's legal codification of unjust marital relations is far from the most significant component of realist gender in Sand's first novel, which understands perfectly that women's emancipation as traditionally understood would be only a part of the solution to their gendered submission. The end of juridical subservience to Delmare would do nothing about moral subjection to Raymon, as the text emphasises by repeating the key terms of Indiana's protest against being one man's wife in her abject plea to become another man's lover. The same woman who indignantly announces to Delmare that the law makes him the master and her the slave piteously cries out to Raymon that she has come three thousand leagues to say that she is his slave, he her master. Gender is an internal mystification as well as an external constraint, and the parallel between Indiana's pleas for freedom and for slavery pointedly define her womanhood as something she enacts as well as endures. Sand's men and women are a pulsating agglomeration of internalised ideologemes. Indiana makes herself Raymon's *woman* as surely—as ignominiously—as the laws make her Delmare's wife.

Indiana's enthusiastic performance of feminine submission has been hard for some of Sand's feminist readers to take. Conventional concepts of femininity seem to structure character delineation throughout this novel, in which women sometimes conform to time-dishonoured roles with at least as much commitment as men. My argument is that anything less would betray the fundamental principle of realist gender, an internalised reality as well as an ideological mystification. Indiana can't just say no to feminine emotions because her experience of them has been a constant feature of the processes establishing her selfhood. The revolution marking the contrast between Laure and Indiana also expresses the magnitude of the social cataclysm necessary for a meaningful change in gender roles. Laure can assume masculinity because great upheavals have defined her as a person in whom feminine traits are ludicrously incongruous. The upheavals in Indiana's life have the opposite effect, that of exaggerating her 'position of inferiority and dependence'.

Although Indiana's femininity meshes smoothly with Sand's representation of realist gender, the characters whom reviewers saw as betraying the author's actual identity were both male: Raymon and the narrator. In Planche's comments on the latter, the telltale clue was open contempt for the sex defined as 'imbecilic by nature' in the opening clause of a classically misogynistic authorial comment on the action being described. 'Woman is imbecilic by nature; it seems that, in order to counterbalance the eminent superiority over us given her by her delicate perception, heaven expressly set in her heart a blind vanity, an idiotic credulousness' (p. 245). What distinguishes this from innumerable similar distinctions between men's intellect and women's sensitivity? Why does this particular definition of women's delicate perception and dull brain stand so far apart from those written by hosts of men that its writer couldn't possibly be a man?

The answer is a variant on the reason why Raymon is radically unlike all the other Don Juans in Western literature: the narrator's masculinity too is performative instead of natural, and the more male it sounds the more it problematises maleness. Identical to the intensity of Raymon's sexual drives, George's patriarchal judgements of women are a discursive fabrication deconstructed by the very fact of their expression. What Sainte-Beuve called the narrator's 'mysterious and liv-

ing identity, invincibly imagined behind the story', is an androgynous being whose self-classification as naturally intelligent rather than perceptive refutes the idea that either men or women are by nature anything whatever. It's because the author identified on the original title page as G. Sand writes so much like George that Georgina's message comes through. The more sexualised the narrative voice, the more forcefully it reveals that all human voices are in fact gendered. Like Indiana's feminine subservience, like Raymon's masculine impetuousness, the phallic resonance of the narrator's voice configures gender by its very success in validating sex. Sand's narrator wrote his manhood as a blend of substance and artifice. Whereas the ideology men absorb from the cradle up has no difficulty with either sexual substance or gendered artifice in isolation, it provides no way to think the blend.

And that blend is central to ***Indiana,*** in which Raymon is both a raging bull and a henpecked wimp, in which George writes like a woman-hating pig and Georgina's mysterious, living identity undoes all he says. The *effects* of gendered existence are here overpoweringly conventional, their *cause* radically problematised. Raymon isn't just a man, he's a Don Juan; Indiana isn't just a woman, she's a groveling masochist; the narrator doesn't just recount, he does so in the Voice of the Father to cry out 'Shame on this imbecilic woman!' (p. 213) whenever female masochism warrants it. But because Don Juan and George are also the opposite of the male horrors they present themselves as being, the text dissociates all gendered features from sexual physiology. What they are comes not from anatomical attributes but from received ideas.

One of the novel's most forceful dissociations of gender from genitals occurs when Sir Ralph tells Indiana that he was placed with the 'eunuchs' (p. 332) because her behaviour towards him had nothing in common with standard male-female interaction. Eunuchs here come from communal rather than surgical operations. Prevented from performing masculinity by his determination to conceal what he feels for Indiana, Ralph can't be a man despite possessing manhood's consecrated attributes. His assimilation of himself to a eunuch immediately precedes his complaint that Indiana acted as if he lacked 'a soul and senses' (p. 332). He doesn't come right out and say what else eunuchs don't have, but his recognition that *everything* constituting maleness disappears unless masculinity is continuously performed remains striking.

Ralph's confession of his castrated feeling, however, comes at a point in the novel where the feeling has left him because masculine and feminine gender roles are reattaching themselves to male and female bodies. Ralph and Indiana are about to leave France for a tropical island where they will live happily ever after, about to enter a world where soul and senses reacquire their conventional association with anatomical distinctions. Sand's conclusion refuses the realist setting of its first four parts for an exotic elsewhere, so insulated from collective dynamics that Ralph and Indiana prosper in a slave economy while having no contact with slaves except to buy and set free 'poor enfeebled blacks' (p. 352). The novel's last words, spoken by Ralph and Indiana in unison, contrast their home to *le monde,* the term France and its realists consecrated to signal that society *was* the world for those within it. Where there is no *monde* there is no realism, and the happy couple's valedictory address perfectly caps the idyllic story they at last come to live.

The characters' removal from the realist universe coincides with the end of their performance of realist gender. Whereas Indiana continues to play the submissive woman, it now seems *natural* for her to do so because her man is so worthy of her respect. Raymon was only a gendered creature, 'true in his acting' (p. 213); Ralph is a sexual creature 'true in his passion' (p. 337). As a consequence, Indiana's assumption of conventional feminine submissiveness comes to appear as intelligent as it was formerly 'imbecilic'. At the conclusion of *Indiana,* the Couple reappears, purged of historically contingent behaviour, resplendent with forever unchanging devotion. Like Raymon, Indiana enacts the Couple Plot with three different partners. But whereas Raymon ends up with the ultimate figure for existence as socially defined—Laure de Nangy—Indiana's final partner categorically repudiates social definition of whatever kind. Ralph and Indiana are 'returned to truth, to nature' (p. 337) and thus removed from society and history. Conventional masculinity and femininity retain their textual force, but the text organises itself so that they seem to be not conventional but innate. In one of her last novelistic appearances, Indiana—smiling sweetly and silently—removes herself while one man, Ralph, tells her story to another, the narrator. The phallic order is preserved.

Except that, once more, the phallic order is eerily unnatural because one of the men performing it is also a woman. Ralph's progress from the state of a eunuch to triumphant testicularity is chronicled by a figure who undoes all his story's essentialist messages, George/Georgina Sand. Ralph and the narrator's exchange of Indiana's story, a classic instance of male bonding, also disassembles maleness by severing it from foundationalist thought. George Sand joins Sir Ralph in an offensively paternalistic exchange of stories culminating in the frequently misogynistic novel coming to a close; Georgina Sand remains a living identity that detaches paternalism and misogyny from any conceivable ground. Identical to the intensity of Indiana's desire for Raymon, the narrator's complacent masculinity is, despite appearances, a dramatically feminist proclamation.

Although it finally abandons realist history, **Indiana** never stops exploring realist gender.

The significance of George Sand's performative masculinity increases in the works that followed **Indiana,** almost all of which perpetuate the refusal of realist techniques that marks **Indiana**'s conclusion. The demarcation of realism from idyll in Sand's first novel holds good well beyond it, for her subsequent works establish an ever-greater distance from the realist project. Naomi Schor's validation of what she calls Sand's idealism attends to the refusal of French society effected when Indiana and **Indiana** leave France behind for an 'epilogue which so spectacularly exceeds the bounds of bourgeois realism'.[12] Schor's emphasis is appropriate, for **Indiana**'s abandonment of history was the beginning of Sand's lifelong commitment to developing an alternative to the realist style with which she began her career.

Yet throughout that career Sand's narrative voice clearly and insistently declared its masculinity. Proper and common nouns, adjectives, pronouns—every gendered mark of the French language represented George Sand as a man until he and his creator died. The principal product of realist gender in **Indiana,** the narrative presence of George Sand, remains a central constituent of the works that subsequently called realism to task. The radical destabilisation of the ideology of sex accomplished by **Indiana** continues throughout the writing career of that novel's most celebrated character, whose realist gender never ceases to repeat that sexual identity is constructed rather than inherited.

Notes

1. Bernard Weinberg, *French Realism: The Critical Reaction,* New York, 1937, p. 12.

2. Félix Pyat, review of *Indiana, L'Artiste,* 27 May 1832, p. 195. All further references to this review are given in the text. All translations are my own.

3. Gustave Planche, 'Georges Sand', *Revue des Deux Mondes,* 30 November 1832, pp. 687-702 (p. 701). All further references to this review are given in the text.

4. H. Boussuge, review of *Indiana, Cabinet de lecture,* 24 June 1832, p. 13. All further references to this review are given in the text.

5. H. de Latouche, Review of *Indiana, Le Figaro,* 31 May 1832, no page numbers.

6. Anonymous, review of *Indiana, Le Temps,* 14 June 1832, no page numbers.

7. Charles-Augustin de Sainte-Beuve, review of *Indiana* reprinted in his *Portraits contemporains,* Paris, 1870, I, pp. 470-81 (p. 471). All further references to this review are given in the text.

8. Edouard d'Anglemont, review of *Indiana, La France littéraire,* IV, 1832, pp. 454-7 (p. 457).

9. Since Planche knew Sand quite well and may even have helped her write the preface to *Indiana,* his claim to have intuited her life from her writing is spurious. The important point, however, isn't whether he was actually deriving gender from style but the steps he saw as enabling someone to do so.

10. George Sand, *Indiana,* Paris, 1962. All page references are given in the text.

11. Gregorio Marañon, *Don Juan et le donjuanisme,* trans. Marie-Berthe Lacombe, Paris, 1958, p. 24.

12. Naomi Schor, 'Idealism in the Novel: Recanonising Sand', *Yale French Studies,* LV, 1988, pp. 56-73 (p. 71).

Pratima Prasad (essay date 1996)

SOURCE: Prasad, Pratima. "(De)Masking the 'Other' Woman in George Sand's *Indiana.*" *Romance Languages Annual* 8 (1996): 104-09.

[*In the following essay, Prasad studies Sand's representation of femininity through her pairing of Indiana and Noun as a Romantic doubling of the Self and the Other.*]

The emergence and profusion of doubles in the European literary imagery marks the heyday of Romanticism. It finds its roots perhaps in the Romantics' assumption that character is mutable and not fixed, or in their pathology of alienation, which made them express the distinction between Self and Other in terms of a self-division. There have been many studies of this recurring motif in literature, grounded in psychoanalysis, theology, as well as in literary and cultural history. I would instance Otto Rank's pioneering study, which, drawing mostly on folk legend and anthropological evidence, traces the motif of the double to narcissistic self-love and the wish for a defense against death.[1] An example of a more contemporary interpretation of the double can be found in Paul Coates's work, who juxtaposes the emergence of the double with the expansion of colonialism: the double is a sign of the unrepressed vitality of the Other, which the Self continually strives to cocoon in projections (2). Most studies on the double identify the works of E. T. A. Hoffmann, Jean Paul Richter, Alfred de Musset, and later in the century, Dostoëvsky and Maupassant, as the most creative and effective manipulations of the motif. The characteristic Romantic double, coined as *Doppelgänger* by Jean Paul Richter, takes different forms, sometimes emerging as a shadow or a reflection of the hero that seems to have a life of its own (Hoffmann's *Lost Reflection,* 1820, and

Musset's *Nuit de Décembre,* 1835), or a figure with a strong and uncanny physical resemblance to the hero (Jean Paul's *Siebenkäs,* 1796, and Hoffmann's *The Devil's Elixirs,* 1815).

George Sand, whose fictional works are replete with doubles, does not receive mention in any of these critical analyses. In fact, gendered doubling, or the splitting of the ego for the feminine subject has not been adequately problematized. In this study, I examine Sand's innovative rewriting of the *topos* of the double in one of her early works, ***Indiana*** (1832). I will argue that ***Indiana,*** by mapping both race and class difference on the female double, makes a claim for a revitalized, hybrid feminine subject, one that goes beyond the existing paradigms of nineteenth-century French fiction. In addition, I hope to account for the centrality of the masquerade in Sand's working through of the dual feminine subject. In Sand's text, doubling is both produced by, and expressed through the motif of the masquerade.

When Sand's heroines, Indiana and her chamber maid Noun, first make their appearance in the text, they are neither mirror images nor two parts of the same soul, but two clearly demarcated antithetical subjectivities. They differ both in physical and in emotional stature:

> Noun était la sœur de lait de madame Delmare; ces deux jeunes personnes, élevées ensemble, s'aimaient tendrement. Noun, grande, forte, brillante de santé, vive, alerte, et pleine de sang créole ardent et passionné, effaçait de beaucoup, par sa beauté resplendissante, la beauté pâle et frêle de madame Delmare.
>
> (60)[2]

Moreover, Indiana and Noun are separated racially, socially, and sexually: Indiana is the daughter of a white colonizer, now married to the bourgeois industrialist Delmare; Noun, her chamber-maid, is a black Creole from the island of Bourbon. This social polarization is transposed onto the sexual axis as well: Indiana is a sensually deprived, chaste bourgeois woman while Noun is a sexually active lower-class woman. References to Indiana's sexuality, when there are any at all, underscore not just her chastity, but speak of her as though she were a virginal child-woman: "Le sourire des anges reposait toujours sur ses lèvres roses comme celles d'une petite fille qui n'a connu encore que les baisers de sa mère" (173). Caught up in a sterile marriage with a man who is more a violent father figure than a partner, and to whom she is bound by the rules of bourgeois marital fidelity, Indiana is divorced from her own desire. Noun, on the other hand, imposes herself as subject of her own desire with her lover Raymon.

On a first level of reading, the sexual and the social poles are presented as irreconcilable for the two female protagonists. Not surprisingly, ***Indiana*** has been read as a distressing account of Sand's traditionalist representation of women. Leslie Rabine, in a particularly trenchant essay ("George Sand and the Myth of Femininity"), states that Sand inscribes her first novel within the dominating masculine ideology of the nineteenth century according to which Noun's, or the lower class woman's prostitution was necessary to maintain the chastity of the upper class woman and the stability of the social order. While Rabine's reading remains compelling, I would argue that if the representation of femininity in **Indiana** is marked by the paradigm of male-authored texts, it does not mimetically reproduce that model. First, Rabine's discussion is centered on class and fails to take into account the racial differences between the two heroines. The implications of race and origins (which I discuss later) are crucial to the reading of the female double in **Indiana.** Second, Sand's borrowings from another male-centered dualist literary model, the Romantic double, offers a different perspective on the Indiana-Noun pair.

As John Herdman's study of the Romantic double has shown, Jean Paul defined the *Doppelgänger* as a second self that is dependent on, but not dominated by the self (Herdman 13-14). Now, it must be remembered that beyond Indiana's white, bourgeois identity lies another self, reflected in her beginnings outside the metropole. Bought up in the colonies in the absence of her biological mother, she is nursed by a Creole woman who happens to be Noun's mother. In fact, Indiana's experience in the text is likened to that of the slaves with whom she spent most of her childhood ("vivant au milieu des esclaves," 89; "cette femme esclave," 90). Having grown up with a violent father and been married off to an equally violent husband, she moves from one despotic master to another. Subordinate to those around her, she is in many ways just another Noun: "En épousant Delmare, [Indiana] ne fit que changer de maître, en venant habiter le Lagny, que changer de prison" (88). Men of society perceive her as an exotic "rose de Bengale" (80), a term that is associated on another occasion with the identity of Noun. Most importantly, Indiana and Noun are both Creoles, according to the varying definitions of the word (a Creole being a person of either European or African descent, born and naturalized in the West Indies, Mauritius, Bourbon Island, etc.). What at first seems like a pure and simple opposition between the two women is compounded by a likeness that comes from their shared creolization, their common experience. Noun is the alter-ego who embodies Indiana's ex-centric, marginal origins and her experience of subordination. Hence, strains of the Romantic *Doppelgänger* are not absent from the Indiana/Noun pair.

We can now nuance Sand's position with respect to two contemporary literary paradigms, the dual Romantic subject and the dual woman. On the one hand, as we have already said, while appropriating the paradigm of

the Romantic double, she distances her characters from Hoffmann's or Musset's doubles. Noun is a character in her own right and not just a projection of Indiana's self-division or psychic disintegration. On the other hand, the polarization of the two women at two ends of the social and sexual axes is undermined by the solidarity and likeness that binds them together.

This process of splitting and assimilation of the two female subjects pervades the entire text and is recapitulated in two key masquerade episodes. Feminine disguise alternately opposes and merges the identities of the two female protagonists. The masquerade scene in **Indiana** functions as a focal point, an exclusive space in the text wherein Sand's characteristic female double is represented in metaphorical terms. I will start by briefly contextualizing these two episodes. Of the two masquerade scenes, the first one occurs quite early, in the first section of the four-part novel. The novel's first section contains some of the ingredients of an emerging love triangle whose agents are Indiana the heroine, her friend and chamber maid Noun, and Raymon, a savvy Don Juan of sorts belonging to the nobility. When the novel opens, Raymon has already successfully wooed and seduced Noun. Raymon and Noun keep their relationship a secret, mostly because of the large gap between their respective social classes. As early as in the opening chapters of the novel, Raymon is already weary of Noun. His attentions have now turned to her mistress, the unhappy Indiana. It is at this narrative juncture, when both maid and mistress are still unaware of Raymon's real intentions, that our first scene takes place. The Delmares being absent for a few days, Noun has set up with Raymon a nightly *rendezvous* in Indiana's bedroom. Having taken over her mistress's private domain, Noun then goes on to appropriate her garments and accessories, which, combined with some other decorative effects, provide a perfect setting for a ceremony of seduction:

> A force de penser aux séductions que le luxe devait exercer sur son amant, Noun s'avisa d'un moyen pour lui plaire davantage. Elle se para des atours de sa maîtresse, alluma un grand feu dans la chambre que madame Delmare occupait au Lagny, para la cheminée des plus belles fleurs qu'elle put trouver dans la serre chaude, prépara une collation de fruits et de vins fins.

> (99)

In an unusual twist to what would have been another clandestine meeting between Noun and her paramour, the phantom of Indiana insinuates itself into the scene. Raymon, described by the narrator as particularly susceptible to illusion, and provoked by the sight of Noun in Indiana's clothes, starts to interchange the identities of the two women: "Raymon fut saisi d'un étrange frisson en songeant que cette femme enveloppée d'un manteau, qui l'avait conduit jusqu'là, était peut-être Indiana

elle-même" (101). The confusion of identities in Raymon's mind is deepened as the night goes by. Noun's
disguise, coupled with the inebriating strength of the
wine, produce a hallucinatory effect on Raymon, and he
finally succumbs to his illusions. He spends the entire
night with Noun, imagining that he is in Indiana's arms.
Sand describes in fine detail the disturbing effect of Indiana's attire on Noun's body and of the power of clothing to masquerade identity in a passage that is one of
the most shining examples of her prose.

> Si elle [Noun] n'eût pas été ivre comme lui, elle eût
> compris qu'au plus fort de son délire Raymon songeait
> à une autre. Elle l'eût vu baiser l'écharpe et les rubans
> qu'avait portés Indiana, respirer les essences qui le lui
> rappelaient, froisser dans ses mains ardentes l'étoffe
> qui avait protégé son sein; mais Noun prenait tous ces
> transports pour elle-même, lorsque Raymon ne voyait
> d'elle que la robe d'Indiana. . . . C'était Indiana qu'il
> voyait dans le nuage du punch que la main de Noun
> venait d'allumer; c'était elle qui l'appelait et qui lui
> souriait derrière ces blancs rideaux de mousseline; ce
> fut elle encore qu'il rêva sur cette couche modeste et
> sans tache, lorsque, succombant sous l'amour et le vin,
> il y entraîna sa créole échevelée.

(104-05)

The aftermath of this scene proves to be fatal: Noun
commits suicide after discovering Raymon's love for
her mistress Indiana. Much later in the text, beginning
to suspect the real reason behind Noun's death, Indiana
prepares to unearth the truth in a most disingenuous
manner. In this second episode for our consideration, it
is the mistress who "dresses up" as her maid. Although
Indiana does not carry her disguise to completion like
Noun, she engages in a similar play on appearances that
befuddles Raymon's perception.

> Indiana lui tournait le dos, elle était enveloppée d'une
> pelisse doublée de fourrure. Par un étrange hasard,
> c'était la même que Noun avait prise à l'heure du
> dernier rendez-vous pour aller à sa rencontre dans le
> parc. . . . Madame Delmare ne se doutait point de
> l'effet qu'elle produisait sur Raymon. Elle avait entouré
> sa tête d'un foulard des Indes, noué négligemment à la
> manière des créoles; c'était la coiffure ordinaire de
> Noun. Raymon, vaincu par la peur, faillit tomber à la
> renverse, en croyant voir ses idées superstitieuses se
> réaliser.

(190-91)

As if to exacerbate this effect, Indiana supplements the
unusual head-gear by displaying a lock of the dead
Noun's hair in her hands, thereby giving Raymon the
impression that she has cut off a lock of her own hair.
When Raymon discovers that it is actually the dead
Noun's hair, he experiences, as Maryline Lukacher puts
it, "an uncanny return of the repressed," and faints (77).

In this text, Sand gives the masquerade a distinctive
form within the private sphere in a creative use of the
apparatus of feminine clothing. Ballroom dresses, madras overalls, and colourful scarves serve as a disguise-
kit for Sand's female protagonists, who manipulate vestimentary codes to transcend the boundaries between
appearance and reality. As is evident, these two scenes
put forth a number of parallels, structural as well as
thematic. They both take place in Indiana's bedroom,
which is a privileged locus in the novel, in part due to
the symbolic significance of its circularity.[3] Moreover,
both scenes occupy strategic locations in the text itself:
the first episode dramatically concludes the first section
of the novel, while the second episode inaugurates the
third section. The same three characters are involved,
and in both cases it is the masculine subject of desire
who is duped by the artifice of feminine clothing. Both
scenes involve seduction, although in the second case
the sexual act is not carried through. In short, these two
narrative moments reveal Sand's predilection for the
masquerade as *topos*. As though propelled by some
kind of diegetic compulsion, she returns to the same
scene twice in order to milk its creative potentialities.
For our purposes, however, the most characteristic feature of these two narrative episodes is the doubling of
the female protagonists and their subsequent assimilation or fusion *via* the masquerade, a diegetic paradigm
that any reader of Sand's later texts would clearly recognize as a distinctive Sandian mark.

Of the two masquerade scenes in **Indiana,** the episode
in which Noun seduces Raymon has been much commented upon. Musset was among the first persons to be
entranced by Sand's literary imagination in this scene,
and went as far as to write a poetic interpretation of it.
He read the episode as Raymon's aspiration towards a
higher love, in which Noun and Indiana occupy allegorical positions of the Real and the Ideal respectively.[4]
Musset recognizes the thematic of the double in the
scene, but evokes it in terms of a splitting of the *object*
of desire. Among more recent interpretations of this
episode, Sandy Petrey, in a fascinating essay, contends
that Raymon's desire for Noun is "gendered": it is not
just Noun's beauty, but the socially-coded attributes
with which she surrounds herself (the clothes, the crystal, the lace, etc.) that arouse his desire. Leslie Rabine
recognizes the two extreme positions (angel/whore) assigned to woman, but deciphers the episode through the
double prism of Raymon's desire and the male narrator's comments. Critics in general have been more interested in the presence of the male desiring figure, and
have pondered on Raymon's motivations and comport-
ment. It is time now to look at how the feminine *subject* conceives of her "doubleness" and of her identity
in general. Noun is far from passive and her libidinal
economy equally governs the unfolding of the scene.
More specifically, in the act of wearing her mistress's
clothes, she sends out certain sartorial messages that
deserve a closer look. Moreover, since John Carl Flügel's psychological work in 1930, theorists have postu-
lated the will to "dress up" in human beings as an act

propelled by diverse and sometimes contradictory motivations. The Lacanian psychoanalyst Eugénie Lemoine-Luccioni goes so far as to say that clothes not only express desire but also reveal the manner in which the wearer conceives of his/her subject position.

I propose, first, to move the focus away from the center of the episode towards the passages that frame it. The passage that immediately precedes Raymon's entry, when Noun is alone in Indiana's room, is a rare moment in the text. If Noun hardly speaks at all in the novel, here the reader penetrates her consciousness, or, to use Genette's terms, witnesses a moment of "internal focalization" with Noun (206). By examining some of her interior monologues, Noun's dual appropriation of her mistress's clothes and private space become clearer. Dressed in Indiana's clothes, Noun looks at herself:

> [Elle] apprêta en un mot toutes les recherches du boudoir auxquelles elle n'avait jamais songé; et, quand elle se regarda dans un grand panneau de glace, elle se rendit justice en se trouvant plus jolie que les fleurs dont elle avait cherché à s'embellir.
>
> —Il m'a souvent répété, se disait-elle, que je n'avais pas besoin de parure pour être belle, et qu'aucune femme de la cour, dans tout l'éclat de ses diamants, ne valait un de mes sourires. Pourtant ces femmes qu'il dédaignait l'occupent maintenant. . . . Peut-être que cette nuit je ressaisirai tout l'amour que je lui avais inspiré.

(99-100)

Beyond the most palpable motive of rekindling Raymon's waning interest in her, Noun expresses here the Rousseauist paradigm of the "natural" woman imposed on her by her paramour. She seems to realize that in his praise of her natural beauty, Raymon confirms her in her naturalness and thereby in her exclusion from the social order. More importantly, presented as she is in self-absorbed contemplation in front of a mirror, Noun is emphasizing her own alienation. Specular identification with oneself can be profoundly alienating for the subject, as the self sees and relates to itself as other, doubled and projected on the specular image. In this passage, Sand incorporates the motif of the-woman-before-the-mirror within the larger scheme of Noun's social alienation. As Noun gazes into the mirror, she sees not just a split image of herself, but a figure draped in a muslin dress, satin shoes, and ribbons, all of which are sartorial emblems of another social class. And significantly, her thoughts dwell upon her difference from that other class of women, the "women of the court." By imitating Indiana, her closest known prototype of those upper-class women, Noun reveals the inner anxiety of her alienation and symbolically enacts a private vision of otherness, and the desire to transcend the determinations of her identity. But, paradoxically, in the moment of self-recognition in the mirror, she encounters her alterity, the actual fact of her difference.

Noun's self-contemplation is cut short when Raymon makes an irruption into this private fantasy. In fact, Noun gazes at herself in anticipation, as she prepares to be contemplated by Raymon. Through Noun's self-display in dress and adornment, Sand puts forth the notion that self-recognition, as theorists of clothing tell us, is dependent on the gaze of the other. Kaja Silvermann and Lemoine-Luccioni, who ground their arguments in Lacanian psychoanalysis, both underline that the gaze of the Other is central in the constitution of an individual's subject position ("C'est l'Autre qui détient l'être du sujet," Lemoine-Luccioni 78). The visual mediation of the mother during the mirror-stage of a child's development demonstrates that subjectivity, at the most profound level, is determined by the gaze that is outside. They point out further that clothing draws the body and makes it visible to the outside gaze, and is therefore another necessary condition for subjectivity. Travestied in her mistress's clothing, then, what exactly does Noun wish for Raymon to identify? To accurately answer the question, it is necessary to examine Noun's disguise in juxtaposition with her appropriation of Indiana's private bedroom, which she also transforms considerably.

In this central scene, Noun rearranges the configuration of the space of their encounter. The very site of this episode, we realize, is governed by her will: it is she who shifts the place of her nightly tryst with Raymon from an outside kiosk (their regular meeting place) to the interior of Indiana's bedroom, a decision that will later take Raymon by surprise. Noun's manipulation of the spatial configuration puts forth a certain conscious or unconscious desire on her part for her so far illicit relationship with Raymon to be sanctioned. That which is exterior to legitimacy (clandestine meetings in the woods) is symbolically imported by her into an interior space, Indiana's bedroom. This becomes all the more meaningful since in Noun's context, legitimacy is a doubly charged notion. At this point in the text, Noun has discovered that she is pregnant with Raymon's illegitimate child. If Noun's identity as the Creole maid of a bourgeois family is characterized by an alienation from the social structure, that estrangement is now total.

More importantly, Noun "disguises" Indiana's private space, much like the sartorial transformation over her own body. Just as she manipulates the signs of her identity through costume, she alters the setting in which she has chosen to introduce Raymon. The circular bedroom, as described by the narrator, carries with it all the signs of chastity that constitute Indiana's sexual identity. From the bed ("ce lit blanc et pudique comme celui d'une vierge," 101) to the engravings on the walls ("ces gravures que représentaient les pastorales amours de Paul et Virginie," 101), every part of Indiana's private living space carries the label of her sexuality. When

Noun takes over this space, it is transfigured: the austere whiteness is replaced with a celebration of the senses:

> Noun avait effeuillé des roses du Bengale sur le parquet, le divan était semé de violettes, une douce chaleur pénétrait tous les pores, et les cristaux étincelaient sur la table parmi les fruits, qui présentaient coquettement leurs flancs vermeils, mêlés à la mousse des corbeilles.
>
> (100-01)

In Noun's hands, the virginal setting is transformed into an erotic tableau. She plants the distinctive mark of her own identity, that of the sensual woman, on to her mistress's private space. Not only does she encroach upon Indiana's territory, but she also metamorphoses the visual semiotics to make it truly her own.

Noun's manipulation of vestimentary signs and the transformation of Indiana's room are doubly transgressive and, seen together, throw light upon her motives. On a space that is marked by Indiana, she engraves symbols that point to her specificity, her sexual identity. Similarly, if there is some loss of her own specificity in her mistress's clothing and adornment, her identity is not obliterated behind this artifice. She borrows the white dress of the virgin, only to recast it in the framework of a ceremony of seduction. As Raymon regretfully remarks, she wears white camelias in her hair, as Indiana would have, but unlike her mistress, she lets the flowers play with her hair sensuously ("dans [un] désordre excitant," 101). In donning Indiana's dress and adornment, Noun does not, in any manner, extinguish her sexuality to "become" another Indiana. If, as we have already stated, self-recognition is dependent on the apprehension of the outside gaze, Noun's gesture is a symbolic one. By masquerading in her mistress's clothes, Noun makes a demand for *recognition* in the dual sense of the word. First, her recourse to disguise is much less an attempt to disappear by taking on Indiana's identity than a means of escaping the fixedness of her identity and exploring the ambiguity created by costume. Behind the costume of the virginal upper-class woman, she calls on Raymon to recognize her, the real Noun. Second, her act is a claim for recognition in the sense of legitimation, or sanctioning of her status.

However, Noun's attempt is a failed one. The danger for Noun lies, paradoxically, in Raymon's gaze itself, which fails to acknowledge her call for recognition. Moreover, Noun's private fantasy is not compatible with Raymon's. Unable to negotiate the ambiguity created by Noun's disguise, Raymon's gaze seeks to relocate her identity on well-defined binary poles of sexuality. As revealed by his regretful laments after the orgiastic night, he addresses Indiana as one would invoke a divinity ("l'asile de ta pudeur sacrée," 105; "l'ange qui gardait ton chevet," 106), whereas Noun is

associated with carnal lubricity ("les flancs de cette créole lascive," 106). The process of repressing Noun occurs through her disguise itself. Her white dress is read metonymically, to represent a part of Indiana's identity, namely her sexuality ("sa chaste robe," 101). This in turn gives rise to a chain of metonymies and fetishistic associations for Raymon. Looking at Noun in the mirror, his gaze wanders towards a "purer" reflection of Indiana on her virginal bed ("le lit étroit et virginal," 102). Every attribute that surrounds Noun becomes a metonym for Indiana's untouched body and sexuality: "cette couche modeste, sans tache," "ceinture pudique" (105), "le lin virginal de ta couche" (106). In this scene of high fetishism, Noun, the sensual woman, disappears behind the figure of the ethereal, chaste image conjured by Raymon's imagination. Noun's suicide is an expression of that suppression. She becomes a prisoner and a victim of her own game.

After Noun's death, the menace of suicide, particularly of drowning, follows Indiana throughout the text, and links her destiny to that of her double. Traditionally, as Otto Rank has pointed out, the double is the emissary of death for the Self. The appearance of the double, especially in folkloric tales, is a sign that foretells the imminent death of the hero.[5] In Indiana's case, encounters with near-death are many, the most prominent one being the failed suicide pact with her cousin Sir Ralph. However, the novel's concluding section in the island of Bourbon is ultimately life-affirming: Indiana and Ralph have triumphed over the death instinct to lead a new, utopian existence in the colonies, outside the bounds of the French bourgeois universe. What is more, the text also suggests a certain sexual liberation for the heroine, as she shares her life with her partner outside the realm of marriage. Indiana's textual trajectory, then, I would argue, is a return to the "Indian" space, that is, to merit or live out her name (Indiana, *l'indienne,* the Indian woman, or Noun), to reaffirm that part of her subjectivity that Raymon refused to recognize, or suppressed. But she has to do so without literally becoming another Noun, i.e., without dying.

In this perspective, the second scene in Indiana's bedroom, when Indiana wears Noun's head-dress, is crucial. This second episode is in many ways a "correction" of the first, as though Indiana were avenging Noun's death. Firstly, Raymon is being put to test. Indiana's preparation for the encounter is both deliberate and premeditated as a test: "Elle risqua tout son sort sur une épreuve délicate et singulière contre laquelle Raymon ne pouvait être en garde" (190). Secondly, if Raymon smothered both Noun's body and her sexuality in the earlier scene, here Indiana corporally reinscribes the repressed woman within the economy of desire. Thirdly, while the fetish was an agent of repression for Raymon, here the lock of hair, fetish *par excellence,* and disguise are instruments of resuscitation; they revive both Noun's silenced body and Raymon's memory. Indiana's creole head-dress and Noun's hair are interlocked to fabricate before Raymon's eyes a dual and indeterminate female object of desire. Raymon is brutally confronted with the ambiguity of feminine identity that he earlier refused to acknowledge.[6]

The function of the masquerade is thus to delimit Indiana's identity as double and to reintegrate that which Noun represents in Indiana, indeed to mask difference. But Indiana's doubleness is already contained in her name. The name "Indiana" incorporates in its morphological structure both *Diane* (Diana) and *Indienne* (Indian), and each recounts a different story about her. We have already discussed our heroine's identity as *l'Indienne* or the "outsider." Her likeliness with the mythological Diana is also a striking one. Diana, Apollo's twin sister, is most commonly known for her passion for hunting and her sexual abstinence. The chaste Indiana also has an immense passion for hunting, as Raymon discovers to his surprise. When hunting wild boar, she displays a vigor, resolution, and physical courage that mark her as an illustrious descendant of Diana. Indiana's textual destiny, then, is to live out the dual narrative that is inscribed in both *Diane* and *Indienne,* narratives that are sometimes incompatible and contradictory. Through the scene of the masquerade, Sand makes an attempt to fuse the split antithetical subjectivity of her heroine, an attempt that seeks to recuperate the alienated double, and the alienated name. It is an effort to reconcile the two extreme images of woman, and to recuperate the "virtuous" and the "degraded" woman as one.

Sand's own words help shed light on the representation of women in her first novel. When the novel was still in its germinal stage, she described her heroine Indiana (then called Noémie) in a letter to Emile Regnault dated June 1831. For Sand, a series of antitheses qualify at best Noémie's subjectivity. She is both strong and weak, timid and audacious, capable of carrying the weight of the sky and yet tired by the weight of air, disdainful of the vanities of her century, yet seduced by the man who embodies all of them. These antitheses, however, do not constitute a contradiction for the author. She even goes on to state that "woman" in general can be characterized in a similar manner:

> Voilà je crois la femme en général, un incroyable mélange de faiblesse et d'énergie, de grandeur et de petitesse, un être de deux natures opposées, tantôt sublime, tantôt misérable, habile à tromper, facile à l'être.
>
> (*Correspondance* 2:46)

For all its essentialist pathos, what is interesting in this theorization of feminine subjectivity is the notion of *mélange* or amalgam. Sand lays down a set of received binary oppositions about female nature, only to make the claim that feminine subjectivity is a mixture of tendencies that gravitate towards both ends. The novel *Indiana* follows a similar pattern. Sand first borrows from conventional binaries of feminine subjectivity and subsequently transcends them through a process of hybridization: opposing narrative destinies are fused and contained in the subject Indiana. The scene of the masquerade emerges as the textual space where Sand theorizes her stance on identity. Through the masquerade, with its power to blur distinctions between Self and Other and to merge antithetical subjectivities, Sand formulates the model of a creolized, hybrid subject as an alternative representation of femininity in nineteenth-century French fiction.

Notes

1. See Rank, especially chapter 2: "Examples of the Double in Literature."

2. *Indiana* (Paris: Gallimard, 1984). All subsequent references are to this edition.

3. Indiana's circular room has been described as a privileged space in the novel, indeed the textual analogue of the island of Bourbon, where part of the novel is set. See especially Haig.

4. Musset's poem is reproduced by Pierre Salomon in the 1962 Garnier Frères edition, 87-88n.

5. See Rank, Chapters 4 and 5.

6. It should be noted that it is at the cost of Raymon's desire that Indiana's identity is reclaimed. When faced with the reality of this double female subjectivity, Raymon faints, and wakes up to discover that he no longer loves Indiana. Through this metaphoric death, Sand seems to suggest that Raymon can conceive of female subjectivity only in binary terms. In the scheme of masculine desire, the desired woman occupies only fantasy positions.

Works Cited

Coates, Paul. *The Double and the Other: Identity as Ideology in Post-Romantic Fiction.* London: Macmillan P, 1988.

Flügel, John Carl. *The Psychology of Clothes.* New York: The International Psychoanalytical Library Hogarth P, 1930.

Genette, Gérard. *Figures III.* Paris: Seuil, 1966.

Haig, Stirling. "La chambre circulaire d'Indiana." *Neophilologus* 62 (1978): 505-12.

Herdman, John. *The Double in Nineteenth Century Fiction.* London: Macmillan P, 1990.

Lemoine-Luccioni, Eugénie. *La Robe.* Paris: Seuil, 1983.

Lukacher, Maryline. *Maternal Fictions: Stendhal, Sand, Rachilde and Bataille.* Durham: Duke UP, 1994.

Musset, Alfred de. *Poésies complètes.* Paris: Gallimard, 1957.

Petrey, Sandy. "George and Georgina Sand: Realist Gender in *Indiana.*" *Textuality and Sexuality: Reading Theories and Practices.* Ed. Judith Still and Michael Worton. Manchester, England: Manchester UP, 1993. 133-47.

Rabine, Leslie. "George Sand and the Myth of Femininity." *Women and Literature* 4:2 (1976): 2-17.

Rank, Otto. *The Double: A Psychoanalytical Study.* Trans. Harry Tucker Jr. Chapel Hill: U of North Carolina P, 1971.

Sand, George. *Correspondance.* Paris: Garnier, 1964.

———. *Indiana.* Paris: Garnier Frères, 1962.

———. *Indiana.* Paris: Garnier Flammarion, 1984.

Silvermann, Kaja. "Fragments of a Fashionable Discourse." *Studies in Entertainment: Critical Approaches to Mass Culture.* Ed. Tania Modleski. Bloomington: Indiana UP, 1986. 139-52.

Hope Christiansen (essay date 1997)

SOURCE: Christiansen, Hope. "Masters and Slaves in *Le rouge et le noir* and *Indiana.*" In *The Play of Terror in Nineteenth-Century France,* edited by John T. Booker and Allan H. Pasco, pp. 197-208. Newark: University of Delaware Press, 1997.

[*In the following essay, Christiansen highlights an affinity between* Indiana *and Stendhal's 1830 novel* Le rouge et le noir *in both works' evocation of master/slave dynamics associated with emotional relations between men and women.*]

Contemporary by date, but not often considered together, Stendhal's *Le rouge et le noir* and George Sand's *Indiana* might on the surface seem to have relatively little in common, yet they share at least one intriguing feature: a pervasive play of master/slave imagery.[1] One might even say that the tension between these two extreme modes of behavior drives the plot in key parts of each novel. Both Julien and Indiana test the master/slave dynamic in their relationships with members of the opposite sex, but ultimately, it is only when they abandon it that they achieve happiness and, at the narrative level, that their stories come to an end.[2]

It is important to acknowledge at the outset that the subject of master/slave relationships is very complex. In *Le rouge et le noir* it is intertwined with questions of social hierarchy; Julien's behavior with Mme de Rênal and with Mathilde de La Mole is often described by a master/*servant* vocabulary. In *Indiana,* on the other hand, the master/*slave* dynamic is inseparable from gender issues: it exists precisely because women have so little power—and men have so much—under the Napoleonic code. While these broader contexts are of interest in their own right, the focus here will be limited to master/slave imagery as it figures in love relationships, primarily those between Julien and Mathilde and between Indiana and Raymon.

In order to appreciate the complexity of the master/slave dynamic in *Le rouge et le noir,* one might consider a scene from Part I where Julien's interaction with Mme de Rênal not only prefigures the relationship with Mathilde, but also announces his *prise de conscience* at the end of the novel. The scene in question takes place several months after Julien's arrival in the Rênal household, where Mme de Rênal enjoys literal power, or "mastery" over Julien; Julien's goal—in large part *because* of that power—quickly becomes that of "mastering," or subjugating, her, as if she were the enemy in a military campaign. This struggle is further complicated by the fact the two have gradually come to love each other. In this passage (which precedes the celebrated seduction scene), Julien, in the presence of the subprefect, touches Mme de Rênal's foot, causing her to drop her scissors and to warn, "—Be careful, I order you" (Stendhal 1964, 107). He instantly takes offense at Mme de Rênal's choice of terms: "she could say to me *I order you,* if it were something relating to the children's education, but in responding to my love, she assumes equality. One cannot love without *equality*" (107). Julien's statement at this early stage is but a preview of the lesson offered ultimately by both *Le rouge et le noir* and *Indiana*—that there is no place for real love as long as the relationship is based on a disparity of power, whether it be real or figurative.

If this basic dynamic were not complicated enough, given the intermingling of master/slave and master/servant vocabulary, there is also a tendency on the part of Julien and Mme de Rênal to play *both* roles (a pattern of behavior which will resurface later in the novel in the relationship between Julien and Mathilde). Shortly after Julien and Mme de Rênal make love for the first time, for example, it is the latter who instructs the hero ("That education in love, given by an extremely ignorant woman, was a pleasure" [118]). She wields a power—albeit a loving one—over him that closely resembles, as the narrator affirms, her authority over her children (119). "A moment later," however, "she admired him as her master" (120). Julien, too, tests both roles; later, in the final pages of Part I, while hiding in the Rênal house just before his departure for Paris, he sees Mme de Rênal at once as a "truly superior woman" (236), because of her child-like gaiety and her expertise in orchestrating visits to his room, and as a woman whose heart has become his "kingdom": "ah! there is a heart in which it is glorious to reign" (236). Elena Russo views Julien's adoption of this sort of slave-like posture as a rather painful, but ultimately productive, means of self-motivation: "that feeling of inferiority makes him experience 'horrible torments,' but it is also the principal motive that pushes him beyond himself and gives him the desire to take hold of the place of the master."[3]

Assuming that Russo's interpretation of Julien's behavior is valid, one could say that his interaction in Part II of *Le rouge et le noir* with the aristocratic Mathilde only intensifies that process of self-realization through the master/slave dynamic. It becomes obvious very quickly that many of the same patterns of behavior manifested in the Julien-Mme de Rênal relationship will also figure in that between Julien and Mathilde. In describing one of their early encounters at a ball, for example, the narrator again uses a mix of master/slave and master/servant vocabulary which reveals the two distinct, yet inseparable, types of relationships featured in the novel: "[Julien] did not deign to raise his eyes to Mathilde. She, with her beautiful eyes, opened extraordinarily wide and fixed upon him, appeared to be his slave. Finally, as the silence continued, he looked at her as a valet looks at his master, to receive his orders" (Stendhal 300-301). The narrator's choice of terms is revealing: while Julien is, literally, the "valet" for the La Mole family, and Mathilde, consequently, the literal "maître," she already imagines for herself the more figurative role of "esclave." Moreover, the use of the expression "to appear" suggests Mathilde's tendency to play a role rather than be herself; she may never truly *be* Julien's slave, but she can *appear* to be.

What this brief passage shows is that the play of master/slave is just that for both Julien and Mathilde, a *game,* albeit with real, serious consequences, in which both attempt to reverse their respective roles. Mathilde will increasingly "play the slave" because it corresponds to a romanesque ideal that introduces a sense of meaning into her otherwise boring life, in which she is, paradoxically, "enslaved." Julien, in turn, not only has much to gain in a real sense by "mastering" the aloof, aristocratic Mathilde, but he, too, models his behavior throughout the novel (and particularly in the context of love relationships) on a self-imposed sense of duty.

Once established, this basic pattern of behavior is recycled, with increasing intensity, over and over again. Recognizing that Julien might help realize her fantasy of imitating the story of her glorious ancestor, Boniface de La Mole, Mathilde initially assumes the role of master, in order to verify that Julien is "worthy" of her. In the seduction scene, for example, she tells him first how to use a ladder to reach her room, then how to ease it to the ground by rope; she gleefully informs him, once he obeys her commands, that he will, later, be obligated to

use a more direct means of transit—the door. Ironically, his willingness to "lower" himself by following her orders has the effect of elevating him, in her eyes and in his own, to her level, as Mathilde herself expresses: "Ah! how this man is worthy of all my love!" (Stendhal 345). It is paradoxical that once Julien proves his worth, she almost immediately regrets having surrendered the dominant role; she is furious, "shocked by [his] air of triumph. So he is my master, she said to herself" (347). Yet on the very next day she revels in his "masterly" gestures, such as when he impulsively brandishes a sword, as if ready to kill her: "Mademoiselle de La Mole, delighted, could think only of the happiness of having been on the verge of being killed. She went so far as to say to herself: he is worthy of being my master, since he was about to kill me" (353). The constant oscillation in her reactions, from scorn to submission, is matched by corresponding behavior on the part of Julien, who shifts from anguish, even "crazy ideas" (354), to aggression, treating Mathilde as "the enemy" (423) or even "a demon" (424).

Ultimately the very playing out of the master/slave dynamic becomes the relationship's only reason for being. As René Girard suggests, neither Julien nor Mathilde desires the other directly, but rather through the image of what the other should be:

> Like two dancers obeying the baton of an invisible conductor, the two partners observe a perfect symmetry: the mechanism of their desire is identical . . . In double mediation each one stakes his freedom against the other's. The struggle ends when one of the partners admits his desire and humbles his pride. Henceforth no reversal is possible, for the *slave's* admitted desire destroys that of the *master* and ensures his genuine indifference. This indifference in turn makes the slave desperate and increases his desire. The two sentiments are identical since they are copied from each other; they exert their force in the same direction and secure the stability of the structure.

> (Girard 1965, 109-10)

The word *stability* is critical, for it captures the essence of the Julien-Mathilde relationship: as long as they are driven to play out the master/slave dynamic, there can be no resolution, no equality—indeed, no true self-realization—just a constant, increasingly intense, rotation of roles.

One scene in particular illustrates just how perverse the dynamic can become. During the reconciliation phase of a typical cycle of behavior, Mathilde dramatically begs to be punished: "—Punish me for my atrocious pride . . . you are my master, I am your slave, I must beg your forgiveness on my knees for having tried to rebel. . . . Yes, you are my master . . . reign forever over me, punish your slave severely when she tries to rebel" (363). She then cuts off one side of her hair, offering the following explanation: "—I want to remember . . . that I am your servant: if a dreadful pride ever comes to lead me astray, show me this hair and say: it is no longer a question of love, it is not a matter of the emotion that your soul may feel at this moment, you have sworn to obey, obey on your honor" (363). Shortly thereafter, just after Julien has descended the ladder, he feels something fall on his hands; Mathilde has dropped her shorn hair, declaring: "There is what your servant sends you . . . it is the sign of an eternal obedience. I renounce the exercise of my reason, be my master" (364). That the relationship is based on artificial behavior is revealed by Mathilde's need to *remind* herself of her role as slave. More important, she substitutes for "slave" the term "servante"—which corresponds to Julien's actual role of "valet" mentioned earlier—a role which is literally impossible for the aristocratic Mathilde, but which indicates her desperate need to push to a new extreme her enactment of submission. Here she tries to *be* his *servante,* whereas earlier she only *appeared* to be his *esclave.*

While Julien may for a time derive pleasure from the *role* of master, he will eventually come to realize that it does not represent true happiness. It is only in prison, condemned to die after shooting Mme de Rênal, that he is able to recognize the duplicity of his power struggle with Mathilde and the potential for a simple and honest relationship with Mme de Rênal. Master/slave vocabulary virtually disappears in the final pages of the novel, as Julien and Mme de Rênal discover a peaceful state of equilibrium: "For Julien, except in the moments usurped by Mathilde's presence, he was living on love and almost without thinking about the future. Through a strange effect of that passion, when it is extreme and without the slightest dissimulation, Mme de Rênal almost shared his carefree attitude and his gentle gaiety" (496-97). Julien's conclusion that "man has two beings in him"[4] suggests his new awareness of the difference between the "inauthentic" self caught in the cycle of master/slave behavior, and the "authentic" one who finds love and happiness precisely because he ultimately considers Mme de Rênal his equal.[5]

A strikingly similar sense of duality quickly comes to the fore in Sand's novel as well, once again in the context of the master/slave dynamic. *Indiana,* still much less widely read than *Le rouge et le noir,* may be memorable above all for its complicated plot which includes nocturnal, mist-shrouded rendez-vous, dangerous ocean crossings, and a plan for a suicidal plunge into a waterfall. It tells the basic story of a woman who, trapped in a loveless marriage, first becomes involved in a troubled relationship with Raymon de Ramière, and then finds a fulfilling bond based on equality with her cousin Ralph. From the very start it is clear that "masters" have shaped the heroine's life—Indiana's husband, Delmare, "an excellent master before whom everything trembled, wife,

servants, horses, and dogs" (Sand 49), only takes over where her domineering father left off. Yet Indiana also possesses "two beings in [her]," to use Julien's phrase: in addition to the submissive one, there is another, which manifests itself as "an iron will, an incalculable force of resistance against everything that tended to oppress her" (Sand 88). She possesses, in short, an inner strength that belies—and is in fact a consequence of— her subservient position. Just as Julien's early comment "One cannot love without equality" effectively expresses, as it turns out, what he is to discover through his relationship with Mathilde, this emphasis on Indiana's strength forecasts the ultimate resolution of the master/slave dynamic in Sand's novel.

The ambiguity inherent in Indiana's nature shows itself from the very beginning of her relationship with Raymon. While she initially seems to play the role of slave, and Raymon that of her liberator, the reader soon realizes that neither role is as stable as it first appeared. The narrator's pointed suggestion, "Had she not been born to love, this slave woman who was waiting only for a sign to break her chain, for a word to follow him?" (Sand 90), suggests that Indiana, once freed from Delmare, might enjoy a more equal relationship with Raymon. However, from the moment Raymon recognizes that Indiana loves him, his role shifts to that of subjugator: "He did not need to see the joy that was shining through her tears to understand that he was the master and that he could dare" (93). His desire to control the relationship is further illustrated when, in the same dramatic scene, Raymon makes an impassioned speech in which he explains how his love would differ from that of Delmare, how he is prepared to position himself, as he says to Indiana, "at your feet, keeping you as a jealous master, serving you as a slave . . ." (95). Even if he casts both roles in a positive light (the jealous master protects, and the slave serves willingly), he exercises his authority by effectively denying Indiana a role at all, designating himself both master *and* slave.

Yet in spite (or perhaps because) of Raymon's appropriation of the more dominant role, Indiana herself shows signs of "masterly" behavior, articulating that very strength of character revealed through the narrator's voice in the early passage. In an important conversation between the two after the death of Noun (Indiana's companion who, unbeknownst to the heroine, was also involved with Raymon) Indiana outlines what Raymon must do if he is to be her lover: "You must love me without sharing, without change of heart, without reserve; you must be ready to sacrifice everything to me, fortune, reputation, duty, business, principles, family; everything sir, because I will put the same devotion on to the scales and I want them to be equal" (148). Indiana clearly envisions, even this early, an equal distribution of power, one similar to that shared by Julien and Mme de Rênal at the end of *Le rouge et le noir*, but which proved impossible between the hero and Mathilde.

Further evidence of Indiana's authority and independence is revealed shortly thereafter when she participates in the hunt, a striking scene which foreshadows later developments in the master/slave dynamic with Raymon. Indiana's strength in this passage actually frightens and revolts Raymon, who obviously cannot conceive of her in a "masculine," or "masterly," role. As the narrator explains, "Men, and lovers especially, have the naive self-conceit of wanting to protect the weakness rather than admiring the courage of women" (162).

This passage establishes a cycle of behavior which turns out to be very similar to that seen in *Le rouge et le noir* between Julien and Mathilde: once Raymon recovers from the initial shock of discovering Indiana's aggressive side, his desire to "master" her grows in direct proportion to her displays of strength and lucidity. Evidence of this can be found in what may very well be the most dramatic scene of the novel, when Indiana, after finally agreeing to receive Raymon in her room, decides to "test" him in order to resolve her suspicions about his relationship with Noun. Indiana offers him a mass of hair which he assumes is her own, until he realizes that it was cut from Noun's head after her suicide. This represents a turning point for Raymon: after hearing Indiana speak of equal roles, witnessing first her physical strength and then her calculating behavior, he decides that he no longer loves her. For him, interaction with Indiana now becomes an outright war: "Then he swore, in his bitterness, that he would triumph over her; he no longer swore it out of pride, but out of vengeance. It was no longer for him a question of winning a pleasure, but of punishing an affront; not of possessing a woman, but of subduing her. He swore that he would be her master, even if for only one day, and that he would then abandon her to have the pleasure of seeing her at his feet" (200). Raymon can only be satisfied with a relationship that leaves Indiana conquered, punished, possessed, "reduced."

His plan to seize definitively the role of master by "playing the slave" recalls the dynamic between Julien and Mathilde in *Le rouge et le noir*. Immediately after deciding to "conquer" Indiana, Raymon declares himself once again "worthy" of her and begs her forgiveness, pledging, in terms that bring to mind those of Mathilde, to be her slave: ". . . command, Indiana! I am your slave, you know it well . . . I will be submissive! . . ." (201). While Raymon pretends to be something he is not, Indiana remains honest; when she does escape from Delmare, planning to hide in Raymon's apartment until her husband leaves for l'île Bourbon,

she calmly tells Raymon: "Today, I come to get the reward for my faith; the time has come: tell me, do you accept my sacrifices?" (216), as if to remind him once again that he, too, will have to make sacrifices. Renowned for his eloquence, Raymon comes to rely on inflated rhetoric in his efforts to reassert his mastery, lauding Indiana's superiority, her divine, otherworldly nature, while simultaneously depicting himself as a mere mortal, enslaved by his natural instincts: "You were too perfect to play in this world the same role as we, vulgar creatures, subject to human passions, slaves of our coarse makeup" (240). It is, of course, the height of irony that Raymon speaks the truth about his own nature while being utterly hypocritical.

The growing tension apparent in the master/slave dynamic between Indiana and Raymon also characterizes the relationship between the heroine and her husband, as is revealed by a decisive confrontation just after Indiana's aborted suicide attempt. Indiana, now back with Delmare, defends her view of the two roles of master and slave; acknowledging her legal servitude to her husband, she nevertheless affirms her moral independence: "—I know that I am the slave and you the lord. The law of this country has made you my master. You can tie up my body, bind my hands, control my actions. You have the right of the strongest, and society confirms it; but you can do nothing about my will, sir, God alone can bend it and reduce it. So find a law, a prison cell, an instrument of torture, which will give you a hold over me! It is as if you wanted to handle air and seize the void" (232). When Delmare attempts to silence her, she replies: "You can impose silence on me, but not prevent me from thinking" (232); and then, when the quarrel reaches a peak of intensity, "I have spent a few hours free from your domination; I went to breathe the air of freedom to show you that you are not morally my master and that I depend only on myself on earth" (233). Thus Indiana not only confirms the dual nature of slavery, but also shows, ironically, what Raymon's behavior has already revealed, that "outward" servitude has nothing to do with "inward" freedom.

Indiana's speech serves effectively as a declaration of her independence and self-liberation from Delmare. After orchestrating her escape and surviving a treacherous sea voyage from l'île Bourbon back to France, she arrives at the house which Raymon now shares with a wife, Laure. Surprising him and falling at his feet, Indiana declares: "It is I, it is your Indiana, it is your slave, whom you called back from exile and who have come three thousand leagues to love you and to serve you; it is the companion of your choice who has left everything, risked everything, braved everything, to bring you this instant of joy! . . . I come to bring you happiness, to be all that you want, your companion, your servant, or your mistress. . . . I have come three thousand leagues to belong to you, to tell you that; take me, I am your possession, you are my master" (296-97). Unlike Raymon, who used strikingly similar terms to *act* the part of slave, Indiana resolves to *be* the slave. Instead of indicating weakness, Indiana's words and behavior in fact represent her determined pursuit of the dream of a life based on equality with Raymon, and as such are cast in a positive light. Indiana may be terribly mistaken about Raymon's nature, but she shows courage and sincerity in trying to turn the posture of slave into something meaningful. One need only remember that whatever her sacrifices, she expected an equal number from him.[6]

The lesson that true happiness lies beyond the master/slave polarity is illustrated by the contrasting fates of Indiana and Raymon. Indiana will go on, in the novel's rather unrealistic conclusion, to find a fulfilling relationship with her cousin in a peaceful, idyllic setting.[7] This relationship, unlike that with Raymon, is founded on equality, an equality that is expressed by the couple's commitment of the rest of their lives to freeing slaves.[8] Raymon, in contrast, seems destined to continue acting out the struggle for power. He has apparently met his match in the woman he marries, Laure de Nangy, who intends to play with Raymon the way he did with Indiana, as the narrator explains: "Less generous than madame Delmare, but more clever, cold, and flattering, vain and calculating, she was the woman who was to subjugate Raymon; because she was as superior to him in skill as he himself had been to Indiana . . . she derived a malicious pleasure in using that liberty which still belonged to her, and in making her authority felt for some time over the man who aspired to take it away from her . . . for her, life was a stoic calculation . . ." (289-90).

It is ironic that Laure, whose attitude calls to mind that of Mathilde, should see *liberté* as a product of subjugating Raymon, for if the "lesson" learned by Julien and Indiana is taken to be true, then such "freedom" must undoubtedly be just an illusion. *Subjuguer,* the verb attributed to Laure here and elsewhere to Raymon, is also used repeatedly by Stendhal to describe Julien's attitude toward women until he finally abandons the role-playing, having realized that fulfillment comes only by "improvising" and treating the other as an equal.[9]

Given the dénouements of both novels, it is clear that a resolution of the tension between master and slave is difficult to achieve in the "real" world; after all, Julien finds happiness with Mme de Rênal only under a death sentence; Indiana with Ralph only after nearly committing suicide, then living an isolated existence on an island. But in the final analysis, both Stendhal's *Le rouge et le noir* and Sand's **Indiana,** two novels which seem on the surface to have so little in common, offer, within an intricate play of master/slave imagery, the same important message—that it is perhaps not the degree or

the duration of the freedom which matters most, but rather, that freedom is tasted at all, and under what conditions. Julien and Indiana, in a word, become "masters" of their destinies by refusing to become "slaves" to the ultimately unfulfilling struggle for power and authority which so permeates the worlds in which they live.

Notes

1. Similarities between *Le rouge et le noir* (1830) and *Indiana* (1832) were noted as soon as the latter was published. David Powell, discussing the public's reaction to *Indiana,* states that some readers made favorable comparisons of Sand's novel to *Le rouge et le noir* and Hugo's *Notre-Dame de Paris* (Powell 29); Curtis Cate shows that Sand did indeed meet Stendhal, in Venice (Cate 280), and explains that Henri Boussuge, a noted critic of the period, compared Raymon de Ramière to Stendhal's Julien Sorel, adding that *Indiana* displayed an "immense superiority of style" over *Le rouge et le noir* (Cate 203); Joseph Barry also refers to a critic who found *Indiana* "unjust" and "bitter," but who praised Sand's talent, "placing 'his' [it was assumed that the work, published under the pen name J. Sand, had been written by a man] novel alongside Stendhal's recent *Le rouge et le noir*" (Barry 133). Marie-Jeanne Pécile, in her article on Sand's literary encounters, mentions Balzac, Hugo, and other important figures, but not Stendhal, except to say that "In her time, [Sand] was more famous than Stendhal and Flaubert and she was considered the equal of Balzac and Victor Hugo" (Pécile 52) and that Sand did not like Stendhal's "coarseness" (Pécile 61). In her preface to *Indiana,* Béatrice Didier suggests George Sand's familiarity with *Le rouge et le noir:* "One senses that she was nourished by Balzac. One can also think that she remembers Stendhal and that she knows *Le rouge et le noir* well. For her, as for Stendhal, the novelist is a mirror" (Didier 15-16). Nancy E. Rogers, in her article on stylistic similarities between Sand and Balzac, mentions in passing that the Sandian narrator's observations and personal commentary are in the manner of Stendhal, but lack his irony (Rogers 134); Marie-Jacques Hoog discusses parallels in character and theme; and Kristina Wingard shows that "There is in [Sand] . . . a narrative voice as characteristic as in Stendhal, although entirely different" (Hoog 392-93). Finally, after explaining that the publication of *Indiana* sparked renewed interest in *Le rouge et le noir* because of the striking parallels that critics perceived between the two novels, Sandy Petrey posits that since 1832, both traditional and feminist criticism have effectively disconnected *Indiana* from the realist texts with which it was initially equated (Petrey 133). "The

reasons *Indiana* and *Scarlet and Black* were originally put together," he continues, "are the same as those subsequently invoked to set them apart" (Petrey 134).

2. Other critics have noted the presence of master/slave imagery, especially in *Indiana*. See for example, Rogers 1979; Massardier-Kenney, who sees the "circular room" as a trap, and discusses "the enslaving effect of interior places" (Massardier-Kenney 68); Haig, who considers the addition of slavery to the scene in the "circular room" "not as a veneer of concern or a contrived dénouement, but rather as an integral part of George Sand's sorrowful vision of love, irrespective of her feminist program" (Haig 1987, 37); and James M. Vest, who explores similarities between *Indiana* and romance tradition: "As in the older romances, the heroine is exquisitely attractive, a superior woman reduced to the position of slave" (Vest 41). More generally, one might also relate the master/slave dynamic in the novels (particularly in *Le rouge et le noir*) to the Hegelian master/servant dialectic, as René Girard has done (Girard 110).

3. Russo 8. Russo links the struggle against authority to what might be called a literal building of character: "it is in struggling against all forms of power that the character establishes himself as such, that he is able to shape himself into a character . . . it is in protecting oneself against an arbitrary will that one discovers oneself as 'other,' a different and unique being" (Russo 1).

4. Stendhal 1964, 479. Victor Brombert has written at length about Stendhal's tendency to "experience everything in terms of opposites" (Brombert 1968, 77) and explains such polarities as "all part of a mechanism of action and reaction in which notions of offensive and defensive are essential movements of a psychological duel. These tensions . . . activate at every point a sense of projection into the as yet unlived moment" (Brombert 84).

5. Russo highlights this significant moment, affirming that in *Le rouge et le noir*, "the relationship between equals is very rare, occurring at privileged moments" (Russo 8).

6. Highlighting the ambiguity of Indiana's attitude, Petrey states: "The end of juridical subservience to Delmare would do nothing about moral subjection to Raymon, as the text emphasises by repeating the key terms of Indiana's protest against being one man's wife in her abject plea to become another man's lover . . . Gender is an internal mystification as well as an external constraint, and the parallel between Indiana's pleas for freedom and for slavery pointedly define her womanhood

as something she enacts as well as endures" (Petrey 143). Béatrice Didier's interpretation of Indiana's behavior here, on the other hand, is far more negative; she believes that the heroine is actually more enslaved by Raymon than by her husband: "The lover . . . is even more disappointing than the husband, to the extent that the heroine expected more from him. And society is such that when she is without a husband and without a lover, really alone, woman is reduced to nothing . . . The portrait that [Sand] gives of Indiana is, all in all, rather severe. She denounces her as eager to exchange one enslavement for another, ready, once liberated from her husband, to submit to all the humiliations on the part of her lover, incapable of living her freedom . . ." (Didier 1984, 26). Didier goes so far as to suggest, furthermore, that Indiana often derives pleasure from being mastered, and that "it is not difficult to find in the text a whole interplay of sadomasochistic images" (Didier 1984, 27).

7. Vest also emphasizes the positive turn of the plot for Indiana, stating that "both structurally and thematically, the central movement of *Indiana* is away from the confines of civilization toward a personal realization of individual freedom" (Vest 40).

8. Schwartz argues, in contrast, that "Indiana has an equal mature relationship with no one—she is Delmare's slave, Raymon's toy (or prey), and Ralph's 'child'" (Schwartz 72-73).

9. For an interesting discussion of the role of Laure in the novel, see Petrey 140-42. He cites the following passage where Laure revels in her feelings of superiority, "secretly triumphing from the inferior and dependent position in which this incident had just placed her husband in relation to her" (Sand 298), and concludes: "The tableau created when Indiana is at Raymon's feet and Raymon under Laure's thumb encapsulates substitution of gender for sex in Sand's first novel . . . Two characters—Indiana and Raymon, a woman and a man—take the feminine 'position of inferiority and dependence.' Two characters—a man and a woman, Raymon and Laure—take the masculine role of 'subjugating' their partners" (142).

Works Cited

Barry, Joseph. *The Infamous Woman: The Life of George Sand.* Garden City, NY: Anchor Press, 1978.

Brombert, Victor. *Stendhal: Fiction and the Themes of Freedom.* New York: Random House, 1968.

Cate, Curtis. *George Sand.* Boston: Houghton Mifflin, 1975.

Didier, Béatrice. "Ophélie dans les chaînes: Etude de quelques thèmes d'*Indiana*." *Hommage à George Sand.* Edited by L. Cellier. Paris: Presses Universitaires de France, 1969.

———. Préface. *Indiana*. Paris: Folio, 1984.

Girard, René. *Deceit, Desire and the Novel: Self and Other in Literary Structure.* Translated by Yvonne Freccero. Baltimore: Johns Hopkins University Press, 1965.

Haig, Stirling. "The Circular Room of George Sand's *Indiana*." *The Madame Bovary Blues: The Pursuit of Illusion in Nineteenth-Century French Fiction.* Baton Rouge: Louisiana State University Press, 1987.

Hoog, Marie-Jacques. "George Sand Reader of Stendhal ou *Le défi sandien*." *George Sand: Collected Essays.* Edited by Janis Glasgow. Troy, NY: Whitson, 1985.

Massardier-Kenney, Françoise. "*Indiana*: Lieux et personnages féminins." *Nineteenth-Century French Studies* 19 (1990): 65-72.

Pécile, Marie-Jeanne. "George Sand's Literary Encounters." *The George Sand Papers: Conference Proceedings, 1976.* New York: AMS, 1976.

Petrey, Sandy. "George and Georgina Sand: Realist Gender in *Indiana*." *Textuality and Sexuality: Reading Theories and Practices.* Edited by Judith Still and Michael Worton. Manchester: Manchester University Press, 1993.

Powell, David. *George Sand.* Boston: Twayne, 1990.

Rogers, Nancy E. "George Sand and Honoré de Balzac: Stylistic Similarities." *The George Sand Papers: Conference Proceedings, 1978.* New York: AMS, 1978.

———. "Slavery as Metaphor in the Writings of George Sand." *French Review* 53 (1979): 29-35.

Russo, Elena. "*Le rouge et le noir*: Jeux de l'autorité." *Nineteenth-Century French Studies* 16 (1987-1988): 1-14.

Sand, George. *Indiana.* Paris: Gallimard/Folio, 1984.

Schwartz, Lucy M. "Persuasion and Resistance: Human Relations in George Sand's Novels, *Indiana* and *Lélia*." *The George Sand Papers: Conference Proceedings, 1978.* New York: AMS, 1978.

Stendhal. *Le rouge et le noir.* Paris: Garnier-Flammarion, 1964.

Vest, James M. "Dreams and the Romance Tradition in George Sand's *Indiana*." *French Forum* 3 (1978): 35-47.

Peter Dayan (essay date April 1998)

SOURCE: Dayan, Peter. "Who Is the Narrator in *Indiana*?" *French Studies* 52, no. 2 (April 1998): 152-61.

[*In the following essay, Dayan takes Ralph to be the "hidden narrator" of* Indiana, *arguing that Ralph's point of view and gradual personal development (rather than Indiana's) shape the narrative structure of the novel.*]

George Sand's first novel **Indiana** has been one of the set texts on our second-year literature course for several years now. It is, on the whole, popular with the students. They like it partly because, unlike the work of the uncontroversially canonized (such as Baudelaire or Flaubert), it provides topics for debate on which the students feel they can take sides, for or against. One such topic has been dividing readers and critics since the novel was first published: the question of the literary desirability of the conclusion. At the end of the fourth part of the novel, we are promised the perfect Romantic lovers' suicide: Ralph takes Indiana in his arms, 'et l'emporta pour la précipiter avec lui dans le torrent . . .'. But, in the conclusion which follows, we find they have decided to live happily ever after instead. This has always been felt by some to be a bold rupture with the realist tradition, and by others to be a let-down, an abdication both of verisimilitude and of Romantic nobility for reasons of unworthy sentimentality. The 'points de suspension' at the end of the above quotation, however, do not merely signal the suspension of the realist mode, replaced in the conclusion by the idealist (according to the contrast between realism and idealism so well established by Naomi Schor).[1] The conclusion also differs from the rest of the novel in having an intradiegetic first person narrator, whereas the rest of the novel seems to have an extradiegetic omniscient narrator in the Balzacian mould.

In the conclusion, the point of view is strictly, in accordance with the traditional rules governing such narration, that of the narrator. We can only see what he can see. To him, Ralph and Indiana are enigmas, and he clearly knows virtually nothing about them other than through public rumour until Ralph himself tells him their story. The question of point of view in the rest of the novel is more complex and problematic. It is certainly impossible to believe that the apparently omniscient narrator is simply coterminous with George Sand.[2] Particularly, even if one could discount the question of gender (he is masculine), he appears to have paternalist ideas concerning the character of women and their proper place in society which are obviously opposed to those of Sand herself. He consistently presents women as intellectually weak and necessarily dependent on men. He never even considers the possibility that a woman could lead the kind of independent life that Sand herself had just embarked on at the time she wrote the book. This possibility emerges in many of the novels Sand wrote in the following decade—**André, Jacques, Lélia, Consuelo,** for example; but I think it would be uncontroversial to say that, in **Indiana,** women are unable to imagine a fulfilling life that does not rely on a man as partner, support, or father-figure, or at the very least as interface with the public sphere. Indeed, the very structure of the narrative depends on the assumption that Indiana needs a man to make her happy. We are told near the beginning that this is the case, and that she is dying for want of a lover. Raymon saves her—then betrays her; and final salvation comes through Ralph. *Indiana* tells the story of a woman who achieves happiness not through independence and self-realization, but by finding the right man. The assumption that she needs a man is never questioned.

In many of Sand's later novels, there is a fascinating contradiction between the point of view of the narrator and the apparent signification of the events that he describes. One can often analyse this as the product of the friction between the paternalist, realist narrative stance that Sand used to structure her novels, and a more complex human and especially feminine reality that disturbs that structure, often without perturbing the narrator himself. It is fairly easy, in such cases, to tease out a distinction between the author (responsible for the subversive features) and the narrator (responsible for the discourse that attempts, happily and necessarily without success, to suppress the meaning of those subversive features). However, in *Indiana* there is no such contradiction. The events correspond to and support the discourse. In other words, *Indiana,* considered on its own, has an ideological coherence that many other Sand novels lack, because there is little internally obvious difference between the narrator and the implied author. If one read the novel without knowing any of Sand's other work (and since it was her first novel, that is how it was originally read), one would have little reason to suspect that its author's opinions were in many ways diametrically opposed to those of its narrator; that opposition becomes plain only when one compares the ideas expressed in the novel to those put forward elsewhere by Sand, especially in her letters, articles, and autobiographical writings. Within *Indiana,* the morals suggested by the events and characters seem, on the whole, to support the views of the narrator (save, as we shall see, in one exceptional passage). One might ask who this narrator is, and why Sand appears to have delegated to him such wide-ranging control over the world view presented in her work. I would like to propose a simple answer to these questions, which also aims to elucidate the relationship between the extradiegetic narrator of the first four parts and the intradiegetic narrator of the conclusion.

Frequently—for example, in *Mauprat, Le Dernier Amour, Les Maîtres Sonneurs*—Sand begins her novel with a first-person frame narrator who introduces to us one of the novel's main protagonists, and tells us how that protagonist told him his story; then the frame narrator recounts for us that story, which constitutes the body of the novel. (Thus the first-person frame narrator appears intradiegetic in the frame, but extradiegetic in the main story.) Normally, the story is recounted orally to the frame narrator, and he claims to reproduce with the minimum of editorial intervention the words of the teller; so, in the main part of the text, 'je' refers not to the frame narrator, but to the story-telling protagonist who is being quoted more or less verbatim. This is what happens, for example, in *Mauprat,* or in *Le Dernier Amour.* However, it is not unknown for the frame narrator to retell the story in the third person, basing it entirely on the information given to him by the protagonist, but not claiming to reproduce exactly the protagonist's words. This is how *La Mare au diable* is presented. In the second chapter of that novel, the narrator (who refers to himself as 'l'auteur') describes how Germain has told him his story; he then states his intention to write this story down for the benefit of his literate readers. Germain, being an illiterate peasant, 'n'en saura rien et ne s'en inquiétera guère'. But the narrator will enjoy retelling it. In the retelling, he, the frame narrator, remains in the first person; and Germain, who originally told it, is in the third person.

It is possible to read *Indiana* in the same way, as a story told to the narrator by Ralph, although in the retelling, Ralph, like Germain, remains in the third person. In the conclusion, the intradiegetic narrator goes to visit Ralph and Indiana at their remote home on the île Bourbon. He describes his main motivation as a desire to learn about Ralph and his history. Just before he leaves, disappointed at having learnt little, he stings Ralph with a tactless remark concerning the islanders' low opinion of him. Ralph is at first angry, particularly because Indiana, who knows nothing of this low opinion, has overheard the remark; but then he consents to tell all, once Indiana is safely out of the way.

> Quand la nuit fut venue, elle se retira dans sa chambre, et sir Ralph, me faisant asseoir à côté de lui sur un banc dans le jardin, me raconta son histoire jusqu'à l'endroit où nous l'avons laissée dans le précédent chapitre.[3]

The words 'précédent chapitre', here, can only refer to the end of the novel's fourth part. Who, then, is 'nous'? It seems to me only logical to suppose that it includes 'vous' (the addressee, whom one could see as either the reader, or J. Néraud, to whom the conclusion is dedicated, and who is addressed in the second person) and 'je', the narrator; in which case we must assume that 'je' and 'vous' reached the end of the 'précédent chapitre' together. This clearly implies that the narrator of the conclusion is the same person as the narrator of the rest of the novel; and that the story in the novel's first four parts is the one which Ralph told to him on that night in Bourbon. The formal difference between *La Mare au diable* and *Indiana* would then be simply this: in the former, we are told at the beginning that the narrator had the story from Germain; in the latter, it is only at the end, in the conclusion, that we discover the relationship between Ralph and the narrator.

But even this discovery, as Kathryn Crecelius says, 'does not resolve all the ambiguities of the narrative'.[4] For in many ways, the attitudes and the narrative strategies of the authoritative and extradiegetic narrator of the first four parts seem incompatible with those of the hesitant and intradiegetic narrator of the conclusion. It is these incompatibilities which lead Robert Godwin-Jones simply to propose that the narrator of the conclusion should not be seen as the same person as the narrator of the first four parts.[5] In this, he articulates the gut feeling of the average reader: in my experience, everyone, on a first reading, tends to assume that there are indeed two different narrators, and no one sees any need to conflate them. Nonetheless, as I have shown, and as most critics recognize, the text does explicitly invite us to operate just such a conflation. So are there two narrators in **Indiana,** or one? This question ceases to be problematic if one understands the sudden change in the narrative approach which distinguishes the conclusion from the rest of the novel as a consequence of the fact that in the first four parts, the narrator is giving us Ralph's version and interpretation of events, from Ralph's point of view, though in the third person; whereas in the conclusion, he is speaking in his own voice.

My intention, in this essay, then, is to see what happens when one reads the first four parts of **Indiana** resolutely and consistently as the transposed narration of Ralph, as Ralph's story ('son histoire', as the narrator calls it), a story both about Ralph and told by Ralph, rather than about Indiana and told from the point of view of the narrator. I do not think that a rigorous attempt at such a reading has been made before; and it has wide-reaching implications. The first is that Ralph's ideology must be assumed to pervade the narrative. And that ideology is certainly not a neutral or uncontroversial one. Ralph is a man of strong views, deeply idealistic, with a much firmer grasp on principle than on reality. We need not, therefore, look in the novel either for an 'objective' view, or for George Sand's (or Indiana's) view; it is an exercise, sustained with peculiar virtuosity, in reconstructing the world from the point of view of a certain masculine idealism.

Ralph's opinion concerning the difference between the sexes is clear and almost uncontested in the novel. Women, to him, are less rational, less intelligent than men; they are more generally prone to enthusiasm, to fanaticism, and to deceiving and being deceived. This, of course, corresponds to the traditional Romantic equation of femininity with the heart, and masculinity with the head. In the case of Indiana herself, Ralph has done his best to turn it into a self-fulfilling prophecy. It was he who brought her up, who was her teacher, guide and mentor; and he gave her the education he thought appropriate to her sex. He taught her to love nature and beauty, but not to reason. (It is perhaps worth remem-

bering that George Sand was also educated by a male tutor—Deschartres; but he gave her a man's education, very different from Indiana's.)

> Ignorante comme une vraie créole, madame Delmare [. . .] avait été élevée par sir Ralph, qui avait une médiocre opinion de l'intelligence et du raisonnement chez les femmes, et qui s'était borné à lui donner quelques connaissances positives et d'un usage immédiat. Elle savait donc à peine l'histoire abrégée du monde, et toute dissertation sérieuse l'accablait d'ennui.[6]

Except, that is, when it is the man she loves who is talking; then 'la poésie de son langage' appeals to her. It is not reason which convinces a woman; it is love. This unfortunately means that a woman can be convinced to do irrational and indeed dishonourable things in the name of love, as the fanatic does in the name of religion.

> L'amour, c'est la vertu de la femme; c'est pour lui qu'elle se fait une gloire de ses fautes, c'est de lui qu'elle reçoit l'héroïsme de braver ses remords. [. . .] C'est le fanatisme qui met le poignard aux mains du religieux.[7]

Thus it is, the narrator tells us, the imbecility of woman, her inability to understand the full context of her actions and her willingness to dupe and be duped, that explains the apparent heroism and strength of character of Indiana. She does not, as a man would, think through and face up to the often terrifying social and ideological implications of what she does; that would indeed require exceptional force. But a woman is as untroubled by prescience as by notions of categorical imperatives or collective responsibility. She is able to base her whole world view on 'un jour de délire', to see the world not as it is, but as her fantasies would wish it to be; so that in behaving in accordance with those fantasies, she can commit extraordinary acts without extraordinary courage or intellectual merit. (In the following quotation, 'nous' obviously refers to men, as opposed to women, and supposes, therefore, that both the narrator and his primary addressee are men.)

> La femme est imbécile par nature; il semble que, pour contrebalancer l'éminente supériorité que ses délicates perceptions lui donnent sur nous, le ciel ait mis à dessein dans son cœur une vanité aveugle, une idiote crédulité. [. . .] Voilà ce que je vous répondrais si vous me disiez qu'Indiana est un caractère d'exception [. . .]. Je vous demanderais où vous avez trouvé une femme qui ne fût pas aussi facile à tromper que facile à l'être; qui ne sût pas renfermer dix ans au fond de son cœur le secret d'une espérance risquée si légèrement un jour de délire.[8]

These are the terms in which Indiana is always presented by the narrator. From the very beginning, we are told that she has a dream—that one day a saviour, a 'libérateur', a 'messie', will appear and spirit her away from her dull life. "'Un jour viendra . . . un homme viendra . . .'".[9] When she believes Raymon is that man, she is happy; when she loses faith in him, she lives only for death, until she acquires a new faith in Ralph as true saviour. Only once, I think, does this elementary analysis of Indiana's character fail to account for her words or deeds.

When critics wish to present Indiana as a genuinely progressive feminine character (rather than as the projection of a sexist male imagination or as a simple rebel against oppression), the passage they turn to is the letter which she sends to Raymon from the île Bourbon.[10] In that letter, she describes a quite astonishingly daring and ferociously anti-Catholic and anti-royalist system of beliefs, based on the principle that might must never be confused with right, and that the right to flee is the most fundamental of all. This is revolutionary stuff, and it is doubtless as incompatible with Ralph's republicanism as with Raymon's royalism (it foreshadows, in its assertion of the rights of the individual against the rule of the collectivity, Sand's later anti-Jacobinism). Surely it shows that Indiana is by no means a stranger to philosophical, religious and political speculation. Furthermore, she is also well aware of the gap between her ideals and reality. She has no illusions concerning the likely realization of her dreams, she analyses lucidly the circumstances in which she was able to believe that Raymon would sacrifice all for her, and she is clearly capable of seeing through and refuting his arguments in self-justification. This contrasts strangely with the way she had been presented to us, as a 'faible femme' buffeted by circumstance, and at the mercy of Raymon's flattery.

If one takes it that the narrator's point of view is Ralph's, the exceptional status of this letter becomes explicable. It is used by Sand as a device to give Indiana, just once in the novel, a chance to speak for herself, and to allow us to judge to what extent her future partner does her justice. The narrator's reaction (which, I repeat, I take as synonymous with Ralph's) is indeed revealing. He sees in the letter nothing more than another manifestation of her feeble-mindedness. The words that follow it are: 'L'infortunée se vantait'; and the following paragraph is the one beginning 'La femme est imbécile par nature', which I have quoted and discussed above. In fact, he ignores the content of four-fifths of the letter. He does not comment at all on its ideological or intellectual implications. To him, its sense is this: Indiana is trying to persuade Raymon that she is now in a state of 'douleur profonde et calme', and has ceased to long for him. It is on that interpretation of the letter that he bases his affirmation that she 'se vantait', and is easily deceived; after all, with hindsight, he knows that she will soon succumb to Raymon's wiles again. But is that really what she says in the letter?

Surely not. She speaks neither of 'profondeur' nor of 'calme'; she says only: 'ma douleur est digne de l'amour que j'eus pour vous' . . . which, given the violently paradoxical nature of that love as she has just described it, certainly does not suggest a stable resignation. In fact, I would suggest that she is well aware of the weakness of her position. She knows full well what no man in the novel will admit: that as a woman, she would be able to realize herself fully only if she could escape from them all—for all of them see woman as subject to their law. But she also knows that escape is impossible. She cannot obey the laws of God; she must submit to the law of man. That submission will be a derogation; but she can have no life without it.

> En me soumettant, c'est au pouvoir des hommes que je cède. Si j'écoutais la voix que Dieu a mise au fond de mon cœur, et ce noble instinct d'une nature forte et hardie, qui peut-être est la vraie conscience, je fuirais au désert, je saurais me passer d'aide, de protection et d'amour; j'irais vivre pour moi seule au fond de nos belles montagnes [. . .]. Mais, hélas! l'homme ne peut se passer de son semblable, et Ralph lui-même ne peut pas vivre seul.[11]

The narrator ignores this deep and eternally frustrated longing for independence, and continues to present Indiana as a 'faible femme' in need of a strong man. Certainly, Indiana is unable to do what Sand herself did (and many of her female protagonists, such as Thérèse, in *Elle et Lui*; Geneviève, in *André*; Consuelo and Jeanne, in the novels named after them): she cannot work for a living, and thereby acquire a social status of her own. But the reason for that is surely simple. One cannot work if one has no education and no skills. Indiana has none because of the way she was brought up—by Ralph. Ralph has thus made her dependent; at the end of the novel, he plainly means to keep her dependent; and in the story as he tells it, all evidence that she might not want to be dependent has been erased—except in the letter to Raymon, which, we may assume, is quoted verbatim, and has thus not been filtered through Ralph's eyes. The narrator is clearly aware that the letter's content needs to be belittled; he does not, however, see any need to take account of its real message.

Indiana's character, then, is presented by the narrator as constant, coherent, and fairly simple. Her circumstances change dramatically in the course of the novel, but her personality does not; the portrait of her that we receive in the first part remains valid. One could say the same of Delmare, of Raymon, indeed of all the characters in the book with one exception: Ralph; and this seems to me one of the clearest indications of the special relationship between Ralph and the narrator. Ralph remains an enigma almost until the end of the fourth part. He is an enigma to the reader, in that his behaviour is clearly not fully explained. But he also seems, strangely, to be an enigma to the narrator, challenging the latter's omniscience. Indeed, it is possible to put together quite an impressive catalogue of instances in which Ralph's behaviour seems to be either ignored or flatly contradicted by the narratorial commentary, whereas explanations are always forthcoming where the other characters are concerned. I shall take just two examples. Right at the beginning of the book, in the opening scene, we are given first a long portrait of Delmare, which subsequent events confirm; then an equally prophetic portrait of Indiana; and then a portrait of Ralph of which practically every detail turns out to be a red herring. He appears physically handsome, 'dans toute la force et dans toute la fleur de la jeunesse', elegant, self-satisfied, 'vermeil et blond', 'dormeur et bien mangeant'; but 'fade' and 'monotone', passionless and cold as his English origins would stereotypically suggest. In fact, we learn later that he has led a complex and tormented life, is emotionally old before his time, indeed 'flétri', exists in a permanent state of internal turmoil and self-contradiction, cares nothing for public opinion, and is, without exception, the most obsessively passionate character in the book, as well as the one with the greatest capacity to vary his appearance and social role. One is tempted to say that the portrait is designed to deceive. But the most extreme example of deception occurs halfway through the book, when Indiana is telling Raymon about Ralph's life, and how he approached her husband to ask for permission to come and live with them.

> 'Monsieur, lui dit-il, j'aime votre femme; c'est moi qui l'ai élevée; je la regarde comme ma sœur, et plus encore comme ma fille. C'est la seule parente qui me reste et la seule affection que j'aie. Trouvez bon que je me fixe auprès de vous et que nous passions tous trois notre vie ensemble. [. . .] Quand je vous aurai donné ma parole que je n'eus jamais d'amour pour elle et que je n'en aurai jamais, vous pourrez me voir avec aussi peu d'inquiétude que si j'étais réellement votre beau-frère. N'est-il pas vrai, monsieur?' [12]

This is quite simply a lie, as we discover at the end of the novel. He had always loved her. But the curious fact is not that a character should lie; after all, Raymon lies often enough. It is that, throughout, the narrator presents Ralph as a paragon of probity; and yet this lie is allowed to pass without comment. Obviously, the narrator simply does not want to tell us the truth either about Ralph's emotions, or about his character, which, given his ability first to tell and then to sustain this lie, must be much more complex than is ever suggested. Why not? There is one obvious answer: to maintain suspense and tension in the book. We slowly discover, one step ahead of Indiana all the way, that Ralph is not what he seems, and that despite appearances he is destined to be her soul-mate, for 'c'était lui qu'il aurait fallu aimer'. [13] But if one accepts my suggestion that the narrator is merely a front for Ralph, another reason, more essential, emerges.

However honest Ralph may be in other ways, he is in most circumstances constitutionally incapable of telling the truth about himself. Particularly, he can never engage in meaningful dialogue. In all the conversations he has, he turns out to have been playing a role which betrays his true nature. That nature can only emerge in narrative monologue. Furthermore, that monologue cannot be internal; Ralph needs a sympathetic and admiring ear. His first such monologue comes at the end of part IV, when he tells his story to Indiana. His second is the tale he tells to the narrator in the conclusion, and which, I have been suggesting, serves as the basis for the whole novel. Why should Ralph thus refuse both dialogue and self-analysis in the abstract? Naturally, it is partly because his circumstances make it impossible for him to tell the truth without causing scandal. But a broader consideration of the refusal of dialogue and of self-analysis in Sand's work suggests a more organic explanation. There is a whole class of characters in her novels who are apparently unable or unwilling to discuss their thoughts and feelings with others. These characters are necessarily, in one sense, not central; they cannot have the main speaking part in the book, for they speak little. However, they exert a certain fascination on those around them. They often inspire passionate attachments, sometimes temporary, sometimes permanent; above all, they have a curious ability to appear somehow more authentic, more real, than those who readily express themselves. They tend thus to become the centre of gravity of the work. I have in mind, for example, Marie in *La Mare au diable,* or la petite Fadette; Edmée, in *Mauprat*; Félicie, in *Le Dernier Amour*; Jeanne, in *Jeanne*; Boisguilbault, in *Le Péché de Monsieur Antoine.* There is a parallel to be drawn, though I have not the space to do it here, between their mutism, and that which Sand so frequently attributes to herself, not least in *Histoire de ma vie.* Mutism, loss of voice, frequently equates with loss or lack of social power, as Isabelle Hoog Naginski shows. [14] But it also signifies hidden depths; and it is an unquestioned tenet of Romantic fiction that a character with hidden depths is more interesting than a character who is clearly explained. Ralph, in *Indiana,* alone has these depths; his is the only character that one cannot appreciate without not only re-reading, but also careful reconstruction. In that sense, reading *Indiana* means discovering Ralph. The other characters appear simple, because that is how Ralph sees them. He does not, however, see himself as simple. Like most people, he is able to pigeon-hole others, but he can only conceive of himself through narrative, through the story of how he became what he is; static portraits always seem betrayals to the sitter. It is, then, because Ralph is the hidden narrator that he appears qualitatively different from the other characters. *Indiana* is indeed Ralph's story—not only the tale he tells, but also the narrative that constitutes him. And that is the reason for what one might call the inversion of the frame in the novel. Why is it only at the end that we discover who told the story? And why is Ralph in the third person, not the first? Because the novel traces his acquisition of a voice. At the beginning, he has none; he is unable even to think thoughts worthy of expression. It is only when he becomes able to live (or die) according to his ideals that he acquires the capacity to establish his personality in language, by speaking himself through narrative. Central to those ideals, as to that narrative, is a certain status relative to woman: Ralph needs a 'femme faible' to love and protect, he needs to save a woman from the world. Indiana gives him the opportunity to do so. It is her submission to him that gives him a history and therefore a voice; before that, he had been divorced from his own first person.

Notes

1. In *George Sand and Idealism* (New York, Columbia University Press, 1993). Kristina Wingård Vareille analyses similarly the 'rupture franche avec le code "réaliste" que constitue la fin'; see her *Socialité, sexualité et les impasses de l'histoire: L'évolution de la thématique sandienne d''Indiana' à 'Mauprat'* (Uppsala, Acta Universitatis Upsaliensis, 1987), p. 61.

2. As many critics have pointed out; see, for example, Robert Godwin-Jones, *Romantic Vision: The Novels of George Sand* (Birmingham, AL, Summa Publications, 1995), p. 15.

3. George Sand, *Indiana* ed. Béatrice Didier, Folio (Paris, Gallimard, 1984), p. 339. All references will be to this edition.

4. In *Family Romances* (Bloomington, Indiana University Press, 1987), p. 62.

5. See R. Godwin-Jones, op. cit., p. 303, n. 15. I am grateful to Nigel Harkness for bringing the critical debate on this matter to my attention.

6. *Indiana*, p. 174.

7. Ibid., p. 279.

8. Ibid., pp. 251-52.

9. Ibid., p. 89.

10. See, for example, R. Godwin-Jones, op. cit., p. 24; I. Hoog Naginski, *George Sand: Writing for her Life* (New Brunswick, Rutgers University Press, 1991), p. 73; K. Wingård Vareille, op. cit., pp. 54-55; K. Crecelius, op. cit., p. 72.

11. *Indiana*, p. 250.

12. Ibid., p. 159.

13. Ibid., p. 330.

14. Op. cit., pp. 218-20. Although Naginski does not go so far as to see Ralph as the source of the narrative perspective, her analysis of the novel as a narrative of the acquisition of speech does lead her to view Ralph as in many ways its emblematic character, 'la grande figure du livre' (p. 76).

Françoise Massardier-Kenney (essay date 2000)

SOURCE: Massardier-Kenney, Françoise. "Victimization in *Indiana* and *Jacques*." In *Gender in the Fiction of George Sand*, pp. 15-52. Amsterdam: Rodopi, 2000.

[*In the following excerpt, Massardier-Kenney explores Sand's manipulation of gender roles in* Indiana *in order to focus on the novel's themes of victimization and the oppression of women.*]

George Sand's life-long investigation of the meaning of "woman" and her questioning of the hierarchical binary oppositions between men and women is evident in her first novel, the famous *Indiana* (1832) and the lesser known fine epistolary novel *Jacques* (1834). In these two works, Sand began to lay bare the cultural mechanisms responsible for gender inequalities and began a pattern of using ambiguous protagonists in order to bring attention to the incoherence of established gender positions. Sand's first novel (1832) attracted considerable attention when it was first published and is one of the few among her works to be systematically discussed by contemporary critics. In 1832, critics focused on its realism and compared it to the work of Stendhal, while recent critics have perceived it as Sand's attempt to find a literary voice separate from realism (i.e., something called "idealism"). As Sandy Petrey has demonstrated in his analysis of the critical reception of 1832, *Indiana*'s appeal at the time was a "realist" appeal whereby the novel shows that life is formed by forces that very with time and place, and it is also the reason for its appeal now: gender is one of the "components of human existence that vary with time, place and customs" (134); and gender is interrelated with genre.[1]

However, beyond the continuity of its appeal, *Indiana* continues to give rise to opposite interpretations of what Sand's novel says about gender matters and what character is used to represent Sand's position. In *Writing for Her Life*, Isabelle Naginski has argued that the novel registers Sand's new found literary voice, which is embodied by the character of Ralph[2]; whereas Maryline Lukacher reads *Indiana* as the impossible attempt to choose between two mother figures: Sand's aristocratic grandmother and her plebeian mother and sees a parallel, not between Sand and Ralph, but between Sand and Raymon[3]. Some critics see the end of the novel where Ralph and Indiana escape to the idyllic setting of Bernica, as a flaw in a realist text[4] while others attempt to justify the ending as befitting an idealist and/or a feminist text. For instance, in his justification of the end, Nigel Harkness rereads *Indiana* as proposing an essentialist view and the end as claiming a feminist silence[5], while Petrey demonstrates that the novel is based on a constructivist notion of gender. Last, some, like Leslie Rabine, argue that Sand represents woman as passive and chaste (i.e., as reproducing a conservative nineteenth-century ideology) while others, like Kathryn Crecelius, point out that Sand shows how "religious, social, and political systems combine to oppress women" (73)[6]. Kristina Wingard Vareille also stresses the importance of Sand's critique of marriage and of the condition of women in *Indiana* but also points out that this critique is not limited to women since Sand shows that men almost as much as women are victimized by traditional marriage.[7]

These varied and sometimes contradictory interpretations stem from the novel's own contradictions and from a number of narrative shifts that prevent critical attempts to interpret it as a coherent narrative because precisely the novel's theme is the incoherence of gender positions. In *Indiana* Sand is analyzing and bringing to the surface mechanisms of victimization based on gender, race, and class and is questioning the stability of gender boundaries that buttress power inequalities through a systematic undermining of narrative authority and consistency. Although the final episode of the plot is usually the place where the disruption of the "idealist" is perceived, Sand has undermined the coherence of her own narrative well before the end through the manipulation of the omniscient narrator and through contradictory presentations of characters.

Although interpretations of *Indiana* vary greatly, there seems to be a critical consensus about the fact that the final episode of *Indiana* is an idealist happy ending. Whether critics approve of it or criticize it for its switch in mode, they consider what happens after the scene where Ralph and Indiana leap to their death a positive outcome: the protagonists don't die and live together happily ever after. However, their lives on a secluded plantation where they employ old or weak former slaves that they have freed may seem an "idealist" or "happy" solution only if readers identify with the patriarchal omniscient narrator. For this final episode obliterates the character of Indiana who becomes passive and silent[8]. The narrative is made by the male narrator for a male friend as recounted by Ralph the male protagonist who thus becomes the hero of the novel.

Indiana's transformation from a rebellious and articulate victim[9] into a sweet and languid character [according to the narrator, her eyes have a "douceur incomparable/unique sweetness" (337) and her manners have "quelque chose de lent et de triste qui est naturel aux créoles/something slow and sad that comes naturally to creole women" (337)] starts with the suicide scene where Ralph not only takes over discourse and recounts his long hidden passion for her but also directs all their actions ["il prit sa fiancée dans ses bras et l'emporta pour la précipiter avec lui dans le torrent/he took his fiancée in his arms and led her away to hurl her with him in the torrent" (330)]. The following "idyllic" episode repeats this pattern whereby Ralph controls discourse and action. When the narrator alludes to gossip concerning them among the colonists, Ralph silences him, and once Indiana is out of earshot, he accepts to tell his story "je vous dirai mon histoire, mais pas devant Indiana. Il est des blessures qu'il ne faut pas réveiller/I shall tell you my story, but not in front of Indiana. There are wounds that should not be reopened." (338) [note that he refers to it as *his* story, not hers], repeating a pattern of silence and withdrawal of information justified by the mistaken goal of protecting weak women. All of a sudden, Indiana's story has become Ralph's story and the novel ends with a dramatic shift away from the mechanisms of victimization of women to the emergence of the male Romantic hero.

While Ralph's own victimization and opposition to patriarchal structures may explain some critics' acceptance of his Romantic positioning as representing the voice of the author, his participation in those very patriarchal power structures and his final effective silencing of Indiana should warn the readers that identifying the author's position may be more difficult than the surface narrative would lead us to expect.

Ralph's surprising and seductive transformation into a passionate, articulate opponent of the debased values of Restoration society, and his endorsement by the omniscient narrator trap the readers into glossing over Indiana's erasure and, more importantly, into ignoring Sand's careful construction of Ralph as a character who participates in the victimization of women even though he is himself the victim of patriarchal law and even though, as Doris Kadish has noticed, he has been "symbolically emasculated and feminized through analogy with women, slaves, and members of oppressed groups" (27).

Sand's association of Ralph with some feminized traits, however, must be seen as part of her attempt to show that the unequal status of the two "sexes" is not based on any natural division but is a complex set of gender positions occupied by men and women who have different amounts of control over their lives. To see that Ralph is silent and submissive (i.e., positioned as a woman) does not mean that he represents the voice of the author. An examination of Ralph's history and personality reveals both his victimization and the extent of his participation in the structures that disenfranchise most women. Thus Sand's construction of Ralph is paradoxical.

Sand uses the omniscient narrator to present Ralph in a deceiving and ultimately inconsistent way. As Crecelius has noted, the presentation of Ralph gives rise to "certain inconsistencies" (77) because he is presented from the point of view of Indiana rather than in an objective way, as Sand's use of an omniscient narrator would lead the readers to expect. I would argue that the entire presentation of Ralph is suspect. The details describing Ralph given at the beginning of the novel consistently undermine the portrait made later. The Ralph of the beginning of the novel is characterized by the omniscient narrator as a well fed, dull character, an "homme dormeur et bien mangeant" (51). His features are "régulièrement fades/regularly dull" (51), his portrait in Indiana's room is insignificant and "only the original is more insignificant than the portrait" (108); still according to the narrator Indiana's and Ralph's personalities are totally incompatible (51). Moreover, Ralph is presented as a friend of Delmare, Indiana's tyrannical husband. Ralph also despises women as the narrator's description of his innermost thoughts indicate. When Ralph expresses his distrust of rhetoric as opposed to ideas (in the idealist belief, one assumes, that ideas can be evaluated separately from the language in which they are articulated), he blames women especially for paying more attention to form than to content, and for being highly susceptible to flattery. Indiana's reaction to his remarks "vous avez un profond dédain pour les femmes/you have a great disdain for women" (58) correctly interprets his comments as expressing his belief in the inferiority of women.

When Noun, Indiana's servant becomes agitated upon hearing that Delmare is out with a gun and risks wounding her secret lover Raymon de Ramière, and when Indiana also shows concern, the narrator makes us privy to Ralph's thoughts "Ces deux femmes sont folles, pensa Sir Ralph. D'ailleurs ajouta-t-il en lui-même, toutes les femmes le sont/these two women are crazy, thought Sir Ralph. Anyway, he thought on to himself, all women are" (61). He adds later "Quelles misérables terreurs de femmes/what miserable women terrors" (62). This is the same Ralph who at the end of the novel is presented as Indiana's ideal lover and interpreted as Sand's voice.

Furthermore, the theme of women's ignorance and specifically of Indiana's ignorance is linked throughout the novel to Ralph's conception of women as intellectually deficient. When, near the end of the novel, Ralph finally tells Indiana of his passion for her and recounts his role in her life: "Je fis de vous ma soeur, ma fille, ma compagne, mon élève, ma société/I made you my sister, my daughter, my companion, my student, my community" (316), the reader may be seduced by his passionate language (his "rhetoric") and forget that it is Ralph's upbringing that has made Indiana into an ignorant person whose subsequent intellectual weakness

confirms his patriarchal belief about women's innate inferiority. As the omniscient narrator had reminded the reader, Indiana had been brought up by Ralph "qui avait une médiocre opinion de l'intelligence et du raisonnement chez les femmes. . . . Elle savait donc à peine l'histoire agrégée du monde et toute discussion sérieuse l'accablait d'ennui/who had a poor opinion of women's intelligence and capacity for reasoning. . . . Thus she hardly knew any world history and any serious discussion bored her to tears" (174). This reminder by the narrator about Ralph's responsibility in Indiana's lack of intellectual maturity not only contradicts the same narrator's later endorsement of Ralph but is part of the novel's insistence on the role of men's prejudice in propagating women's ignorance and then blaming them for it. Sand ties the question of women's ignorance to the mechanisms of victimization through which knowledge is withheld from disenfranchised groups, be they women, servants or slaves. Because of her class, Indiana has at least learned to read and write as her letters to Raymon indicate. However, such is not the case for her servant and friend Noun; she makes a number of spelling errors in her letter to the same Raymon, who, upon receiving her letter, decides to leave her as such lack of control of French grammar clearly marks Noun's social inferiority and reminds him of the impossibility of continuing his affair with her.

The withholding of knowledge and of information because of the male characters' belief in the inability of women to understand the information is not the sole prerogative of Ralph; it characterizes all the male characters who have some power but it indicates that Ralph participates in the reproduction of patriarchal structures that are inimical to women. Besides his denial of education to Indiana, who is his sole love and anchor, Ralph also withholds from her crucial information about Noun and Raymon. In agreement with Delmare, Ralph keeps silent about the fact that Indiana's friend and maid is having a secret affair with Raymon, and thus further isolates Noun and allows Indiana to fall prey to Raymon's schemes. Similarly, at the end of the novel, he prevents the narrator from repeating what he has heard in order to protect Indiana as if she were a child. Ralph's role in denying women access to knowledge is incompatible with interpreting him as an ideal androgynous character. On the contrary it suggests that weak and silent characters may participate in their own victimization, as we shall see with Indiana' and Noun's attitudes toward their lover.

Even the facts of Ralph's early life as recounted by Indiana suggest Ralph's acquiescence and implication in the victimization of women. Significantly, it is Indiana who tells Ralph's story, in contrast to the end of the novel where Ralph is in control of the narrative. Indiana recounts to Raymon Ralph's first unhappy years during which he is rejected by his parents who prefer his less shy and more demonstrative older brother. Ralph is so depressed by his life that he is on the verge of committing suicide by drowning in the ocean[10] when he sees his young cousin Indiana (then five years old) who runs to him and hugs him. He decides to live for her and to take care of her (158). Ralph is thus saved from despair by the love of a child. As an adolescent he takes care of the orphaned Indiana, but after his own brother's death, he is forced to marry his brother's fiancee for unspecified family reasons (the reader assumes it is a financial arrangement between the two families). Ralph leaves for England with his wife who loved his brother and abhors him; has a son, and returns to the island of Bourbon after the death of his wife and son. Raymon, to whom Indiana is recounting this story, astutely wonders why Ralph didn't marry Indiana and she invokes her lack of wealth as a reason. The narrative of Ralph's life emphasizes the necessity of having a child-like woman for the melancholy hero to survive, but also Ralph's own victimization. The novel represents the patriarchal pattern of victimization which includes women, slaves, and men who don't occupy a position of power. Ralph is the second son, rejected by his parents and forced to marry for social and financial reasons while Indiana is also ignored by her relatives and married off to a much older man. In both cases families have broken down and have lost their protective vocation. Family structure is presented as the occasion to consolidate power positions. The pervasive corruption of the traditional family in which fathers no longer protect and mothers no longer nurture indicate Sand's conviction that the oppression of the weak—children, women, men, slaves—is endemic to the Restoration society she represents and that, by the logic of their own participation in such family structures, her characters can turn oppressors too.

By agreeing to marry his dead brother's betrothed, even though he knows of her love for his brother, Ralph puts himself in the position of a Delmare. Moreover, since Ralph had a son with this woman, whereas the question of Delmare's actually consummating his marriage with Indiana is left ambiguous, the reader must assume that Ralph forced himself on his wife to produce an heir or at least that he consumed his union knowing of her repulsion. Ralph's consent to marry is explained by his unwillingness to be disowned by his father (by which one assumes he will be disinherited since he has already been rejected emotionally by his parents).

Thus his allegiance to patriarchal values and his participation in oppressive practices, and his long lasting contempt for women must not be forgotten even in the context of his being later presented as the prototypical melancholy and isolated Romantic hero of the "idyllic" end of the novel. Ironically, Ralph is the character who had claimed the superiority of actions and ideas over words, but who is absolved because of his final control

of the narrative. The complexity of Ralph's role, the mix of victim and victimizer allows Sand to show the difficulty of escaping oppression as long as human beings accept binary systems of opposition whereby one category is posed as inferior to the other (women to men, slaves to masters). By luring the reader into accepting Ralph as the "idealist" solution to Indiana's fate, by carefully constructing him as the Romantic figure who finally comes to speech, Sand problematizes any notion of liberation that is not accompanied by a radical rethinking of gender and social categories. Ralph loves and saves Indiana but his adherence to paternalistic views of women condemns him to play the role of a traditional husband, one surely more palatable than the old, tyrannical Delmare, but still one which spells the end of Indiana's psychological and moral autonomy.[11]

This interiorization of patriarchal values by characters who articulate their opposition to the political or social aspects of these structures is shared by women characters as well, an idea to which Sand will return on several occasions and even more pointedly in later novels and which explains in part her reluctance to accept the category "women" as a rallying point because this very notion of woman often stands, as she demonstrates, for definitions of women articulated by and for the benefit of patriarchal subjects.

Women characters in **Indiana** follow Ralph's pattern of rebellion against the patriarchy while internalizing its norm or simply accepting and reproducing these structures if their position on the power scale allows it. Sand uses a range of women to show their implication in these oppressive practices: from a wealthy aristocrat (Laure de Nangy) to a servant who is possibly a former slave (Noun).

At one end of the power spectrum, Laure de Nangy who marries Raymon because he has the right pedigree and she can control him, occupies the position of "male" power. As Petrey has noticed, "the power granted Laure by historical changes affects nothing less than the obliteration of male hegemony" (141), but it is not so much male hegemony that is obliterated as the demonstration that gender performance has replaced notions of natural biological sexual differences to found inequalities. Laure de Nangy performs as a male. The obliteration of the power of the individual male leaves the structure intact. The character of Laure occupies a "masculine" position and thus further demonstrates the constructedness of notions of masculinity and femininity. Her social and economic position (an orphan from an old noble family who has been adopted by a rich industrialist), gives her the power to assess the desirability of potential male partners and to decide whom she will marry. Even before she becomes a major character, Sand introduces her as one of the spectators and commentators at the ball where Raymon recognizes Indiana and starts flirting with her. While Indiana innocently falls for Raymon's attentions, Laura watches him and invites gossip and information about him in a scene that inverts gender roles by placing her as the subject gazing. Laura's biological sexual identity is compensated by her social position; her gender role is that of male domination in contrast to Indiana's lower position and victimization, and later adoption of female submission. By providing these opposite examples of feminine performance, a tactic she will use as well in the novels discussed in subsequent chapters, Sand suggests that masculinity and femininity are positions that are linked to social and economic power more than to "nature" and that they could be negotiated. Sand shows that these gender inequalities are enforced through external pressures and through internal mechanisms (when individuals internalize imposed definitions and come to consider them natural, i.e., women can't think, women are weak, women are natural mothers, etc.).

Whereas Laure de Nangy's mental attitude is one of extreme power, Indiana's and Noun's reflect their inferior status and their ultimate acceptance of their inferiority. The orphan Indiana, daughter of an impoverished noble family, was given to a much older man (she is sixteen and he is sixty), ex-soldier turned business man whose money endeared him to her relatives, whereas Noun is a servant who follows Indiana wherever she moves. Although we are given no details (we don't know whether Noun's mother was a slave or free, or even whether Noun is black), her position as a domestic is clear and provides a more pronounced version of Indiana's own situation of servitude.

What is less evident is the importance of servitude in shaping these characters' own attitudes. Indiana may denounce the inequity of the laws that allow her husband's domination but when she leaves Bourbon to join Raymon, she can only speak in terms of abjection and servitude "c'est ton esclave que tu as rappelée de l'exil/ here is your slave that you called back from exile" (296), and "Je viens pour te donner du bonheur, pour être ce que tu voudras, ta compagne, ta servante ou ta maîtresse/I come to give you some happiness, to be what you want, your companion, your servant or your mistress" (296), "je suis ton bien, tu es mon maître/ I am your thing, you are my master" (297). Indiana's discourse, which is steeped in the vocabulary of slavery and which is a part of a pattern where relationships between men and women are described with a vocabulary of enslavement and subjection, reveals Sand's understanding of the mechanisms of subjection: the long-lasting subjection and state of ignorance in which women have been forced to live have resulted in their acceptance and internalization of the hierarchical structures that created their bondage; as a result, even when these structures of coercion are removed (i.e., when Indiana escapes from her husband), the women characters

retain a mental frame that conceptualizes "love" as bondage or as a relation of inequality.

When Noun attempts to regain Raymon's favors after she finds out that she is pregnant, she rejects his offers of financial support and uses the same metaphors that Indiana would later use. She even proposes to Raymon to work as his servant (as she is already his mistress, it is the only position that she can envision). She tells him "Je ne suis pas exigeante; je n'ambitionne point ce qu'une autre à ma place aurait peut-être eu l'art d'obtenir. Mais permettez-moi d'être votre servante/I am not demanding; I don't hope for what another woman in my place would have been artful enough to obtain. But allow me to be your servant." (110). So while Noun feels insulted by Raymon's offer of money (an offer which clearly means the end of their relationship), she is ready to surrender her whole being in order to be next to him. Isabelle Naginski has remarked that Noun is almost without speech (64) but actually it is the force of her eloquence that convinces Raymon not to break up as he intended. The narrator's comment on her appeal "Noun parla longtemps ainsi. Elle ne se servit peut-être pas des mêmes mots, mais elle dit les mêmes choses, bien mieux, cent fois que je ne pourrais les redire/Noun spoke thus for a long time. She perhaps did not use exactly the same words, but she said the same things, much better, a hundred times better than I could repeat them" (102). Noun may use the language of female subjection as Naginski and others have argued, but it is an extremely articulate language that describes accurately that state of mental bondage that characterizes women who don't benefit from a social position that can counterbalance gender positions. Indiana's and Noun's statements both articulate their acceptance that what they are is defined by what the male other wants. Indiana's "Je serai ce que tu voudras/I will be what you want" (296) echoes Noun's "Je me hais puisque je ne vous plais plus/I hate myself since I no longer please you" (102). The grammatical slip of the "what" instead of a "who" indicates the extent of Indiana's vision of herself as an object rather than as a subject, even in a situation which is the result of her will and of remarkable determination and courage.

In *Indiana,* love is thus presented as another locus for women's oppression. Not surprisingly Laure de Nangy, the only powerful woman in the novel, rejects the idea of "love" because she knows that, paradoxically, her wealth will make it impossible for her to disentangle genuine affection from ambition or greed. The ignorant and powerless Indiana and Noun who embrace romantic notions of love are destroyed by their acceptance of love as a relation that disempowers them. Whether this love includes a sexual relation or not, it is a negative experience[12]. The sexual relation just increases the chance that the woman will be victimized more quickly, as happens with Noun or with the other women that Raymon has discredited. Sexuality, like romantic love and marriage, has no positive ideological function in *Indiana*. The new order proposed at the end of the novel is very problematic as the previous analysis of its implication has shown. Although Kristina Wingard argues that Sand discretely suggests that Ralph and Indiana consummate their union[13] and that Indiana can finally accept her sexuality without danger or suffering, the final episode is curiously ambiguous about their status as a couple. This ambiguity reflects Sand's own ambiguity about the limits of the figure of Ralph as a solution. Her heroes are cut off from the external social structures of the world but they have interiorized gender roles. Thus the question of sexuality is erased[14]. Criticism of Sand for representing Indiana as a chaste *bourgeoise* fails to notice that Sand presents all the scenarios possible for a woman: marriage with sex (Laure de Nangy), love and sex (Noun), love without sex (Indiana), and that none of these scenarios can be fulfilling because of the power structure[15].

Sand's commitment to providing her readers with a constructivist conception of gender is such that the novel presents an unusual number of women who either are not mothers (thus whose lives as women contradicts traditional conceptions of "femininity" that rely on maternity as its linchpin or who as mothers or mother figures function as agents of reproduction of the social order). Sand's deconstruction of stable gender categories includes a reexamination of the roles of mothers in the reproduction of patriarchy and femininity.

First of all maternity and the ability to procreate among women of child bearing age is associated with death. Ralph's wife and his young son are dead by the beginning of the novel and, of course, Noun commits suicide while pregnant because her lover Raymon no longer wishes to carry on their affair. The other protagonists who are young women and who survive—Indiana and Laure de Nangy—are both childless and their own mothers are dead, an interesting coincidence if one recalls Sand's discussion of gender differences in which she mentions maternity as the only difference separating the sexes.[16]

The older women who are actual mothers (for instance, Raymon's mother) or who are mother substitutes (Mme de Carvajal, Indiana's aunt) are both aristocrats who are presented as opportunistic survivors of political and social upheavals or as educating their male offsprings to be victimizers. Mme de Carvajal, who has ignored her niece, starts to show her much affection when she realizes that Delmare has become a successful businessman ("Madame de Carvajal aux yeux de qui la fortune était la première recommandation, témoigna beaucoup d'affection à sa nièce et lui promit le reste de son héritage/Madame de Carvajal who considered wealth of

foremost importance, showed her niece much affection and promised her the rest of her inheritance") (86). The details of her life provided by the narrator draw the portrait of an opportunist for whom fortune and appearances are foremost: a widowed Spanish aristocrat who was an admirer of Napoleon, she has made a fortune speculating on the stock market and, according to the narrator "A force d'esprit, d'intrigues et de dévotion elle avait obtenu, en outre, les faveurs de la cour/ Through her wit, schemes, and devotion she had moreover obtained the favors of the court" (85). Mme de Carvajal uses her pretty niece Indiana to attract young fashionable men to her salon. She sees no objection to her niece's involvement with Raymon but is ready to disown her when gossip about their alleged affair threatens to break out and sully her reputation as a pious older woman. Sand's biting portrait of Mme de Carvajal as a crafty maneuverer who adopts the current ideologies (religiousness and the monarchy) and who gains power and money shows how little room there is to nurture and protect younger women like Indiana. These characters represent such disparate human types (one powerful, savvy, and independent; the other powerless, naive, and ignorant) that the fact that they are both women becomes irrelevant and cannot lead to any allegiance based on their sex.

In fact, Sand's presentation of women protagonists who belong to an older generation suggests that what these older women nurture is the reproduction of the very patriarchal structures that allow younger women without power to be bartered and exploited. An analysis of the presentation of Raymon's mother also shows the care with which Sand constructed her not as the positive character which most critics have seen, but as a very ambiguous, misguided, not to say negative, figure[17]. Sand's portrait of Raymon's mother as a good mother is ironic since that characteristic is always invoked in the context of his mistreatment of women. When the narrator describes Raymon's desertion of the pregnant Noun, he links his action to a class prejudice "Pour lui, une grisette n'était pas une femme/for him a *grisette* was not a woman" (75), which the narrator exonerates by commenting "Tout cela n'était pas la faute de Raymon; on [read his mother since his father has been long dead] l'avait élevé pour le monde/All this was not Raymon's fault; he had been brought up for fashionable society" (75). His mother is held responsible for his considering lower class women subhuman and not warranting the treatment reserved to "women," that is women of one's class who can provide social and financial alliances.

Thus in *Indiana,* as in the works examined in the other chapters, being a woman has a host of different meanings depending on the class to which an individual woman belongs. The higher the class, the more power she has and the less she shares with other women. The disparity of interests between younger poorer women and older aristocratic women is emphasized by Raymon's reactions to Noun after he attempts to break off with her. The omniscient narrator explains Raymon's eagerness to get rid of Noun by invoking his mother "Il en coûtait à Raymon de tromper une si bonne mère/It was difficult for Raymon to deceive such a good mother" (76).

Raymon's mother is thus directly linked to his treatment of Noun. The narrator follows with an ironically positive portrait of Raymon's mother as a woman with intellectual and moral qualities who has given him "ces excellents principes qui le ramenaient toujours au bien/those excellent principles that always brought him back to good" (78). Since the reader was just told how Raymon avoids responsibility [that would be the "bien" to which he returns] by invoking the need to spare his mother, the principles that his mother has taught him are reduced to simple narcissism[18]. Sand thus uses the omniscient narrator to say one thing but to mean another. The positive portrait of Raymon's mother seems to be used to excuse the behavior of the son but actually serves to implicate his mother in his corruption.

The ambiguity of the role of Raymon's mother is further developed through the narrator's comments alluding to the vicissitudes of her life. She is a woman who went through "des époques si différentes que leur esprit a pris toute la souplesse de leur destinée/such different times that their mind has adopted the suppleness of their destiny" (78). While the narrator presents this information positively, it parallels his other comments about Mme de Carvajal's ability to adapt to different moral codes, an ability, as we have seen, which is a sign of corruption. After Noun's suicide, the narrator explains that Raymon feels remorse and thinks of blowing his brains out but "un sentiment louable l'arrêta. Que deviendrait-sa mère . . . sa mère âgée, débile/a worthy feeling stopped him. What would become of his mother, so old and weak?" (127). Again his mother is the excuse for his failure to act.

The role of Raymon's mother as the explanation and justification for his narcissistic behavior is linked not only to Noun's fate but also to Indiana's. After Noun's suicide, Indiana refuses to see Raymon, but her husband imposes Raymon's visit on her because he has been charmed by Raymon's mother (122). Raymon in turn uses his mother to come visit Indiana who is seduced by her charm "qu'un esprit supérieur joint à une âme noble et généreuse, sait répandre dans ses moindres relations/that a superior mind linked to a noble and generous soul can infuse in all her relationships" (140). Indiana's "fascination de coeur" with Madame de Ramière is linked to her not having known her own mother (141).

The complexity of Raymon's mother's role is further demonstrated in the episode in which Indiana compromises herself by coming to see him late at night and he attempts to make her leave by asking his mother to help. Mme de Ramière acts very generously toward Indiana but as the narrator's analysis makes clear, she has created Raymon's selfishness and self-indulgence: "Le caractère de ce fils impétueux et froid, raisonneur et passionné était une conséquense de son inépuisable amour et de sa tendresse généreuse pour lui . . . mais elle l'avait habitué à profiter de tous les sacrifices qu'elle consentait à lui faire. . . . A force de générosité, elle n'avait réussi qu'à former un coeur égoïste/The character of this impetuous and cold, reasoning and passionate son was a consequence of her unending love and her generous affection . . . but she had accustomed him to profit from all the sacrifices she was willing to make for him. . . . By dint of generosity, she had only succeeded in shaping a selfish heart" (223). This analysis presents Raymon's narcissism, not as a natural "male" trait, but as the product of his mother's indulgence, that is as the product of specific cultural practices that reproduce hierarchies. Loving a son means encouraging narcissistic behavior and victimizing women. Ironically, mothers, as Sand presents them in *Indiana,* are the social agents through which gender inequalities are passed on to the next generation.

Sand's early description of the cultural mechanisms at work in the construction of gender inequalities and her reliance on highly ambiguous protagonists to suggest the complexity of oppressive practices was to find another expression two years later in *Jacques,* an epistolary novel written during her stay in Venice and published in 1834. The novel received universal negative criticisms from journalists and fellow writers because they found the story offensive: a man (Jacques) marries a younger woman without a dowry (Fernande) and attempts to have an "enlightened" marriage based on mutual respect rather than on duty. Consequently, when Fernande falls in love with a young man by the name of Octave, Jacques decides to disappear in what appears to be a mountain climbing accident in order to let her live her life. Sand's criticism of the indissolubility of marriage and her decision to sacrifice the hero in order to save the happiness of the adulterous wife ran counter to tradition[19] and offended sensibilities in so far as the husband is no Delmare figure. Jacques is presented as a superior man, an articulate and gifted former soldier mined by the *mal du siècle,* a much improved version of Ralph.

More recently, critics have identified Jacques with Sand's own position and tied Sand's pessimism to the specific circumstances in which she wrote the novel (i.e., the painful break-up with Musset in Venice). More importantly, however, the concerns exhibited in *Indiana* resurface, and the type of the Romantic hero presented as a solution to women's victimization in **Indiana** is finally rejected. Furthermore, Sand's exploration of the constructedness of gender roles becomes more daring and her analysis of the difficulty of changing roles becomes more pointed. Also, contrary to what she did in **Indiana,** Sand creates women characters whose sexuality is not evaded, but explored in ways that reveal the anxiety it fosters. Last her representation of a variety of women characters shows even more clearly than in **Indiana** how problematic the notion of woman is.

Notes

1. See Sandy Petrey, "George and Georgina: Realist Gender in *Indiana.*" Pp. 133-47 in *Textuality and Sexuality: Reading Theories and Practices.* Eds. Judith Still and Michael Worton. Manchester: Manchester University Press, 1993.

2. She states "the story of Ralph recapitulates the writer's progress from initial uncertainty and hesitation to ultimate assurance and eloquence" (56).

3. Lukacher specifically argues that Raymon figures Sand herself "before the impasse of the double feminine identification" (77). Maryline Lukacher, *Maternal Fictions.* Durham: Duke University Press, 1994.

4. This seems to be the view of the French editors of *Indiana.* See for instance the introduction of Pierre Salomon, ed. *Indiana.* Paris: Garnier, 1962; and Béatrice Didier, ed. *Indiana.* Paris: Gallimard (Folio): 1984.

5. See Nigel Harkness, "Writing under the Sign of Difference: The Conclusion of *Indiana.*" *Forum for Modern Language Studies* 33.2 (1997): 115-128.

6. See Kathryn Crecelius, *Family Romances.* Bloomington: Indiana University Press, 1987. Like Harkness, Crecelius also believes that Sand posits a difference between men's and women's language (73).

7. Vareille focuses on the character of Delmare to show that, for Sand, the victims of marriage are men as well as women since they are also frozen in a social role over which they have no control. See Kristina Wingard Vareille, *Socialité, sexualité et les impasses de l'histoire: l'évolution de la thematique sandienne d'Indiana (1832) à Mauprat (1837),* 32-34.

8. I have showed elsewhere that Sand has constructed Indiana as a very strong character both morally and physically. See Françoise Massardier-Kenney, "*Indiana*: Lieux et personnages féminins." *Nineteenth-Century French Studies* (1990): 65-71. Vareille has also showed that while Indiana is pre-

sented as a "faible femme" who faints, cries, is emotional, she is also very strong morally: she attends to wounded men, she stands up to her husband, etc. As she will do later in *Jeanne,* Sand redefines traditional notions of physical and moral strength. It should be noted as well that the very characteristics that mark her as a "femme faible" (crying, fainting, etc) are also typical of the male characters: all three male characters cry at one point or another. Raymon faints when the body of Noun is discovered and Ralph almost swoons when he thinks Indiana died from a horse accident.

9. Although Indiana is clearly presented as the victim of patriarchal institutions and although the narrative is controlled by a male voice, it is her voice whether in direct discourse or through letters that is the most present. Even the prolix Raymon is not given more space in letters or actual speech than is Indiana.

10. While a number of critics have noted the link that Sand establishes between water and women, I maintain that they miss a number of occurrences when water is associated with men as well. Noun does commit suicide in the river and, after wandering in Paris, Indiana almost drowns in the Seine, but there are as many incidents linked to water that are associated by male characters: for instance, Ralph's early suicide thoughts, Raymon's near fall in the very river where Noun drowned, and of course, Ralph's later planned leap in the waterfalls of the Bernica. As I have showed in "*Indiana*: Lieux et personnages féminins," Ophelia is not a figure for women; it is the name of Indiana's dog and it is the dog that dies from drowning, not Indiana. When Indiana escapes her husband to sail back to France, the dog follows the boat and is killed by coarse sailors. It should not surprise us that Sand refrain from associating women with water, since it would be an essentialist gesture.

11. Sand's contradictory portrait of Ralph as a positive Romantic figure who opposes conservative social and political practices but whose own gender ideology is ultimately patriarchal will find a development in *Jacques* (1834), where she will explore the very possibility of the contradictions expressed by the Ralph figure.

12. Vareille notes the negativeness of sexuality for women: "for women, sexuality can only be a trap, a threat, an aggressive and destructive domination exerted by the male" (43), but she does not extend her remarks to romantic love in general which is also a domination exerted by the male in that it destroys the female's subjectivity.

13. Her evidence is mostly based on the fact that the word "virginal" is no longer used in the utopic episode (footnote 61, p. 63) and that Indiana dresses as a bride in the suicide scene.

14. Of course, Sand's decision to leave the couple childless is a further detail that marks the absence of sexuality from their relation.

15. In any case, chastity is by no means reserved for women: since Ralph's wife died, he has remained single and sexless.

16. See the Introduction for a detailed discussion of maternity as an irreducible gender difference.

17. For example Maryline Lukacher interprets Raymon's mother as a figure representing Sand's grandmother because her last words to Raymon are the same as those Sand's grandmother actually said to her on her death bed (77). Similarly Vareille, who is usually a very astute reader, fails to notice Sand's irony in depicting Madame de Ramière.

18. The theme of male narcissism and the role of mothers in fostering such narcissism will be developed and amplified in later novels, most notably in *Lucrezia Floriani* (1846).

19. See Bill Overton's *Novel of Adultery,* for a discussion of that tradition where women are punished for their sins.

Bibliography

Crecelius, Kathryn. *Family Romances.* Bloomington: Indiana University Press, 1987.

Didier, Béatrice, ed. *Indiana.* Paris: Gallimard (Folio): 1984.

Harkness, Nigel. "Writing Under the Sign of Difference: The Conclusion of *Indiana.*" *Forum for Modern Language Studies* 33.2 (1997): 115-128.

Kadish, Doris Y. *Politicizing Gender: Narrative Strategies in the Aftermath of the French Revolution.* New Brunswick: Rutgers University Press, 1991.

Lukacher, Maryline. *Maternal Fictions.* Durham: Duke University Press, 1994.

Massardier-Kenney, Françoise. "Indiana: Lieux et personnages féminins." *Nineteenth-Century French Studies* 19:1 (1990): 65-71.

Naginski, Isabelle Hoog. *Writing for Her Life.* New Brunswick: Rutgers University Press, 1991.

Overton, Bill. *The Novel of Female Adultery: Love and Gender in Continental European Fiction 1830-1900.* New York: St. Martin's Press, 1996.

Petrey, Sandy. "George and Georgina: Realist Gender in *Indiana.*" *Textuality and Sexuality: Reading Theories and Practices.* Ed. Judith Still and Michael Worton. Manchester: Manchester University Press, 1993. 133-47.

Rabine, Leslie. "George Sand and the Myth of Femininity." *Women & Literature* 4.2 (1976): 2-17.

Salomon, Pierre, ed. *Indiana.* Paris: Garnier, 1962.

Sand, George. *Indiana.* 1832. Ed. Béatrice Didier. Paris: Gallimard, 1984.

Vareille, Kristina Wingard. *Socialité, sexualité et les impasses de l'histoire: l'évolution de la thèmatique sandienne d'Indiana à Mauprat.* Uppsala: Acta Universtatis Upsaliensis, 1987.

Charlotte Daniels (essay date 2000)

SOURCE: Daniels, Charlotte. "After the Revolution(s): George Sand's *Indiana.*" In *Subverting the Family Romance: Women Writers, Kinship Structures, and the Early French Novel,* pp. 103-42. Lewisburg, Penn.: Bucknell University Press, 2000.

[*In the following excerpt, Daniels interprets* Indiana *as a critique of bourgeois domesticity and the gendered construction of public and private spheres that it entails. The critic likewise probes the novel through a series of cultural and literary intertexts that elucidate its relationship to nineteenth-century gender ideology.*]

CROSS-VOICING IN *INDIANA*

> L'auteur d'***Indiana,*** cet écrivain hermaphrodite. . . .
>
> —Unsigned review of *Heures du soir, livre des femmes, Figaro,* May 20, 1833

George Sand, like the most colorful revolutionary women of fifty years earlier, favored trousers and boots over dresses and feminine shoes.[1] She writes in ***Histoire de ma vie*** (1855) that her preference for male attire, and in particular for boots, stemmed from the freedom they afforded her to walk easily in the streets of Paris, an activity that provided the young woman with a heady sense of her independence:

> Je ne peux pas dire quel plaisir me firent mes bottes: j'aurais volontiers dormi avec. . . . Avec ces petits talons ferrés, j'étais solide sur le trottoir. Je voltigeais d'un bout de Paris à l'autre. Il me semblait que j'aurais fait le tour du monde.[2]

Sand's decision to wear male attire is intriguing on a number of levels. Her male costume, in which, she tells us, she resembled "un petit étudiant de première année," enabled her to pass from the private into the public sphere defined as accessible to one gender only.

Likewise, in the literary world, the adoption of a male persona allowed Sand forays into the public sphere of the market that, given the literary establishment's general hostility toward women, would otherwise have been impossible.[3] It was only by using the name of her friend and sometime collaborator Jules Sandeau, that Sand was able to write and have her articles published in *Le Figaro, La Revue de Paris,* and *La Mode.* Sand had also published two novels in collaboration with Sandeau before changing their joint pseudonym "J. Sand" to "G. Sand" and devoting herself to establishing an independent career.[4]

Indiana was an immediate bestseller. The novel went through three editions within four months and received warm praise from the critical establishment. A critic in *La France Littéraire,* for example, wrote that *Indiana* was "digne d'être distingué parmi les meilleurs romans de notre époque." Another critic commented that "Monsieur" Sand had "un talent d'observation et d'analyse morale très distingué."[5] For several months after the publication of *Indiana,* critics generally assumed that its male authorial voice corresponded to a male author. It was not long, however, before the question of the author's real gender became a matter of great speculation. Even after they knew that Sand was in fact a woman, some critics fueled the guessing game by presenting their readers with an almost flirtatious game of peek-a-boo with the real authorial body. Sand capitalized on her ambiguous gender identity, privately female, publicly male, to create for herself a highly marketable literary persona.[6]

Sand successively wrote three different prefaces to *Indiana* for the 1832, 1842, and 1852 editions of her novel. The first was written at the behest of her editor, who, concerned with the public's response to certain sensitive points in the novel such as female sexuality and adultery, requested a little "padding." This padding takes three forms. First, Sand disassociates herself completely as a woman from the authorial voice of the preface. Sand creates a *préfacier* who is not only male, but who is referred to exclusively with distancing third-person forms ("il," "l'historien," or "le narrateur"), as though he were simply another character in the work. The "je" in this preface is masked.

Secondly, we find in the preface a disassociation of the male authorial voice from any notion that the novel it precedes deals with issues of specific concern to women. Sand's narrator makes a single reference to her female protagonist of the novel and then only to present *Indiana* as an abstract symbol of (unbodied) repressed emotion:

> Indiana, si vous voulez absolument expliquer tout dans ce livre, c'est un type; c'est la femme, l'être faible chargé de représenter les *passions* comprimées, ou si

> vous l'aimez mieux, supprimées par les lois; c'est la volonté aux prises avec la nécessité; c'est l'amour heurtant son front aveugle à tous les obstacles de la civilisation.[7]

Sand's narrator hereby associates Indiana with what has become a trope in romantic fiction. Rather than specifically female sentiment, she symbolizes "human" passions unrecognized by the increasingly rigid structures of bourgeois bureaucracy. This notion of an ungendered, or rather, double-gendered humanity is underlined by Sand's oscillation between male and female grammatical genders in the above passage. "La femme" is "l'être faible" (masculine), *"la* volonté," "l'amour" (masculine). This lack of gender specificity and tendency toward abstraction is true as well of Sand's references to other characters in the novel. The *préfacier* refers, for example, to "des plaintes arrachées à ses personnages par le malaise social dont ils sont atteints," and to "quelques cris de souffrance et de colère épars dans le drame d'une vie humaine." Sand's play with gender markers leads to a vagueness that refuses clear divisions between masculine and feminine. The reader would certainly not guess from this preface that the novel that follows treats the woes and passions of an unhappily married woman.

Finally, this authorial persona distances himself from the subject matter that follows by claiming a passive role vis-à-vis his subject:

> Si quelques pages de ce livre encouraient le grave reproche de tendance vers des croyances nouvelles, si des juges rigides trouvaient leur allure imprudente et dangereuse, il faudrait répondre à la critique qu'elle fait beaucoup trop d'honneur à une oeuvre sans importance.

(37)

He is simply "une machine qui . . . décalque, et qui n'a rien à se faire pardonner si ses empreintes sont exactes, si son reflet est fidèle." Sand's refuge behind the notion that literature is the reflection of society, a classic ruse during this period for male as well as female writers, serves as an extra distancing measure from issues of specifically female concern.

When Sand wrote her second preface in 1842, her prefatory strategy changed. By this time, the reading public was well aware she was a woman. The fact that she continued to use her male literary persona long after it had outgrown the function of disguise suggests a new relationship to cross-voicing. Sand intersperses third-person references to her "narrateur" with an occasional "je," which suggests a more direct link between author and reader. While adjectival endings still signal a masculine(ized) identity, this "je" identifies himself with female categories (even though they may be gendered male):

J'ai cédé à un instinct puissant de plainte et de re-
proche que Dieu avait mis en moi, Dieu qui ne fait rien
d'inutile, pas même les plus chétifs êtres, et qui intervi-
ent dans les plus petites causes aussi bien que les
grandes.

(46)

Given gender stereotypes prevalent in the literary world
of the nineteenth century, "les plus chétifs êtres" and
"les plus petites causes" may be assumed to refer to
women and their concerns. It is among this feminine
group that the male authorial voice places him/herself.
Moreover, that the "chétifs êtres" and "les petites
causes" referred to above signal women and their concerns becomes explicit as the narrator continues:

Mais quoi! celle que je défendais est-elle donc si petite? C'est celle de la moitié du genre humain, c'est
celle du genre humain tout entier; car le malheur de la
femme entraîne celui de l'homme, comme celui de
l'esclave entraîne celui du maître.

(46)

Sand's authorial voice, which in the first preface tended
to disassociate itself from women, here becomes feminized (despite the fact that it continues to be grammatically male), and it allies itself far more directly with the
importance of women as subject matter in *Indiana.*
Rather than refer to women as abstract symbols of human suffering as had been the case in the first preface,
the narrator here speaks of women as a specific segment of society. While woman's cause is associated
here with the suffering of a generalized humanity, she is
no longer the symbol of that suffering. Rather her suffering is painted as one part of a larger system. The
narrator reinforces and renders specific "his" alliance
with women when "he" makes reference to a deep concern about "l'injustice et de la barbarie des lois qui
régissent encore l'existence de la femme dans le mariage, dans la famille, et dans la société" (46-47). Sand's
cross-voicing has gone from disguise to what Naomi
Schor has aptly called "bitextuality," a kind of writing
that plays with language and its role in the construction
of gender. Sand implicitly suggests that gender, the
great dividing line of the nineteenth century, is finally a
set of external signs subject to manipulation. She, as a
woman who controls masculine forms of language,
maintains an outside perspective within officially recognized modes of discourse. As a cross-voiced writer, she
can be man and woman at the same time.

In Sand's short third preface, written after her literary
career had become well established, she maintains the
use of a masculine "je" ("Je fus étonné au dernier point
. . ."), but her tone has shifted far from the conciliatory
tones of the first preface. She takes on the "race de critiques . . . qui [portent] non seulement sur les oeuvres,
mais encore sur les personnes" (35), and insists on the
right to create storylines that defy reigning bourgeois
standards of morality.

Let us move backward from Sand's prefaces—for all of
them were written after the novel itself—to the text of
Indiana. Many of the issues raised in the prefaces play
an important role in the novel itself. I now consider the
ways in which cross-voicing within the novel allows for
an exploration of the complex interrelations between
public and private worlds in the post-revolutionary period, and in particular, the place of women within this
structure.

To be sure, in *Indiana,* none of the cast of Sand's characters cross-dresses or takes on cross-gendered names
to gain access to worlds from which access would otherwise be denied. On the contrary, Sand's characters
seem to follow Chaumette's implicit prescription to the
revolutionary women before him, to whom he "taught"
the desires of nature ("She has said to man: 'Be a man:
hunting, farming, political concerns, toils of every kind,
that is your appanage.' She has said to woman: 'Be a
woman. The tender cares owing to infancy, the details
of the household, the sweet anxieties of maternity, these
are your labors.'") The men in Sand's novel have positions in the larger world; the women are confined to the
private sphere where they obey, serve tea, and have nervous spells. Sand's characters—a father-figure husband,
a willowy wife, a sexy chambermaid, a rake, and a restrained handsome Englishman—are stock characters
by this point in the trajectory of the novel genre. But
while Sand's characters are in some ways quite conventional, we will see that they are also put into question.
Sand writes her novel within and against a tradition of
"romans à l'usage des femmes de chambre," sentimental, gothic, and fantastic novels whose drama depends
on the relationships between manly men and womanly
women. One of the ways this is achieved is through the
use Sand makes of her male narrator.

Sand's novel opens with a domestic scene. We are introduced to the Delmare family on a dark and rainy
night as they sit in a circle around the hearth. What
might be a romantic view into the domestic interior of
the "familles très unies" that dominated the nineteenth-
century French imagination is, in Sand's novel, something else entirely.[8] The characters present, Monsieur
Delmare, his young wife Indiana, and her cousin Ralph,
are all manifestly bored and miserable, "gravement occupés . . . à regarder brûler les tisons du foyer et cheminer lentement l'aiguille de la pendule" (49). The
painting-like stillness of the family scene is broken by
M. Delmare, who rises and begins to pace back and
forth through the shadows all the while glaring at his
young wife (Indiana) and her cousin (Ralph). From the
beginning, M. Delmare is treated pitilessly by the narrator. M. Delmare, who, in many respects, holds a position equivalent to that of the venerated M. de Wolmar
in *La Nouvelle Héloïse* [(1760)], is presented as pathetic and ridiculous, a caricature of the respectable
head of the bourgeois family:

Il quitta enfin sa chaise, évidemment impatienté de ne savoir comment rompre le silence, et se prit à marcher pesamment dans toute la longeur du salon, sans perdre un instant la roideur convenable à tous les mouvements d'un ancien militaire, s'appuyant sur les reins et se tournant tout d'une pièce, avec ce contentement perpétuel de soi-même qui caractérise l'homme de parade et l'officier modèle. . . . Il était l'époux d'une jeune et jolie femme, le propriétaire d'un commode manoir avec ses dépendances, et, de plus, un industriel heureux dans ses spéculations.

(50)

Delmare is defined by his private life ("l'époux d'une jeune et jolie femme, le propriétaire d'un commode manoir") and his public life ("un homme heureux dans ses spéculations").[9] While, as Habermas has shown, the eighteenth-century novel played an essential role in the emergence of such a subjectivity, it did so in a somewhat indirect way. Rather than portraying the family as a unit within a larger system, it instilled the illusion of a private life independent of the outer world, a "natural" world independent of the artificial world of commerce and politics. In fact, the whole system was dependent on people living their lives in this "natural" way. Sand, especially in the early portion of her novel, instead *emphasizes* the link between the private family and a larger ideological system, and thereby undermines its seeming naturalness. Rather than hide it, she underlines the ways in which public structures support private individuals, and vice versa. Already in the opening pages, the narrator uses his/her masculine gender status to gaze upon both the private and the public worlds with a distinctly female critical eye.

We saw above that the Napoleonic code translated the division between public and private spheres into legislative rules by allotting men increased power in the household while decreasing women's in both the home and in political and economic matters. Delmare's notion of honor depends on just such Napoleonic notions: "Toute sa conscience, c'était la loi; toute sa morale, c'était son droit" (134). His bourgeois insistence on individual economic rights according to abstract laws is coupled with an insistence of his right to a private life in which no outsiders have the right to interfere:

Pourvu qu'il respecte religieusement la vie et la bourse de ses concitoyens, on lui demande pas compte d'autre chose. Il peut battre sa femme, maltraiter ses gens, ruiner ses enfants, cela ne regarde personne. . . . Telle était la morale de M. Delmare. Il n'avait jamais étudié d'autre contrat social que celui-ci: Chacun chez soi.

(132)

Sand shows a remarkable awareness of the interrelation between public and private. Delmare needs a sense of being a private person, "chez soi," to function as an individual in the world of the bourgeois market "où il respecte la vie et la bourse de ses concitoyens." Here this link between the two worlds is made explicit and criticized.

Delmare lived his glory days during Napoleon's empire. He is physically strong, with a tendency toward violence, "il avait de larges épaules, un vigoureux poignet" (132). In the first chapter of Sand's novel he threatens to kill both a dog and shortly thereafter an intruder on his property, the latter of whom he does, in fact, shoot in the hand. He is a hunter, and on two separate occasions he physically abuses his wife; on others he imagines hurting her. This presentation of the bourgeois as a brutish character was not unusual in novels of the first half of the nineteenth century. In *The Battle of the Bourgeois,* Clark shows that, on the contrary, "from whatever angle he might be viewed, the bourgeois appeared as the enemy."[10] But such an explicit presentation of the link between public and private spheres and an exploration of the resulting abuse *was* unusual. Even before it was generally known that Sand was a woman, she was chastised for her introduction into the narrative of this unorthodox kind of socioeconomic commentary. Charles Rabou wrote in *Le Nouvelliste,* "Faisons descendre l'auteur d'*Indiana* de sa chaire d'économie sociale et réduisons-le à n'être qu'un puissant peintre de passions."[11] When this critic insists that the novel should be a forum of passions to the exclusion of "l'économie sociale," no matter what his declared political position, he is defending a particular (bourgeois) ideology that depends on an unquestioned division between public and private spheres.

In *Indiana* the male authorial voice is undermined in a subtle way by Sand's use of cross-voicing. All the male characters in *Indiana* have deprecatory thoughts or make derogatory comments about women. Delmare says, "Ah comme la ruse est innée chez cesêtreslà" (69). Ralph, Indiana's cousin, thinks "Ces deux femmes sont folles. . . . D'ailleurs . . . toutes les femmes le sont" (61), and Raymon complains about "un amour de femme" (221). Despite the narrator's harsh criticism of Delmare (and, as we will see, Raymon as well), "he" himself occasionally slips into the kind of language one hears in the mouths of *Indiana*'s male characters. Cross-voicing allows Sand to explore territory unavailable to a female narrator; like cross-dressing, it can also function as a parody of the assumed gender, in this case the male gender. When the narrator exclaims, "La femme est imbécile par nature" (251), "he" is parodying male assumptions about women. By undermining his own voice, he undermines the power of a more generalized male authorial voice.[12]

The narrator's voice functions parodically because it makes more blatant the kinds of assumptions about women more generally present in fiction. But the narrator does more than simply parody the male authorial voice. He also subtly introduces ideas that counter the views of this authorial voice. In the continuation to his comment regarding the imbecility of women, we find the following words:

Il semble que, pour contrebalancer l'éminente supérior-
ité que ses délicates perceptions lui donnent sur nous,
le ciel ait mis à dessein dans son coeur une vanité
aveugle, une idiote crédulité.

(251)

The narrator includes himself in the general category of
men ("nous") in a shared assumption that women are
stupid, proud, and gullible. But he also slips in a comment on the superiority of women in terms of their
abilities in the matter of "délicates perceptions." This
quality, recognized to be essential for any writer of fiction, is, significantly, attributed to women. Sand thereby
introduces a subtle association between women and
writing novels.

Sand's cross-voiced narrator alternates between identification with male models—sometimes serious, sometimes parodic, and a female position critical of these
models. The reader is invited to read doubly, on the one
hand, in terms of dominant models—male authorial
voice, conventionally gendered characters—and, on the
other hand, in terms of that which is neglected by those
models—female perspectives, a critique of conventional
gender roles.

OLD PLOTS

The male narrator's focus on public life allows for a
consideration of a series of plots depicting the relationships between men and women, within the broadest
possible variety of settings. In *Indiana* we find two of
what had become classic plots of sentimental fiction:
the marriage plot and the passion plot ending with the
death of the heroine. Both of these are treated critically
in Sand's novel, before she moves on to a consideration
of new plots in which new female subjectivities are
imagined. The first of the "classic" female plots we will
consider is Indiana's (post-)marriage plot. Sand begins
her novel where most novels of the period end. Marriage, the goal in so many eighteenth- and nineteenth-
century novels, is the baseline condition in *Indiana.* Indeed, Indiana and Delmare have been married and
submerged in the bourgeois domestic family for three
years by the time the novel opens. They live within a
well-defined domesticity clearly demarcated by the high
walls surrounding the "parc" of the Delmare property.[13]
We learn little concerning the details of the Delmare
(pre)marriage plot other than that the ceremony occurred on the île Bourbon and that shortly thereafter
Delmare decided for economic reasons to move to
France with his young wife. In Sand's novel, the details
leading up to this bourgeois marriage plot are less important than the state of marriage itself. *La Nouvelle
Héloïse,* the prototypical bourgeois plot of the later
eighteenth century, likewise focuses on life after, rather
than before, marriage. In Rousseau's work, the stability
of the family plot depends on a precarious resolution of

contradictions involved in shifting from one kinship
system (aristocratic, alliance-based) to another
("classless," dependent on the creation of a new domestic unit). Sand too presents an "after marriage plot" but,
in rewriting Rousseau, she dispenses with his sentimen-
talization of the domestic interior.

In accordance with the Napoleonic code, Indiana is entirely dependent, both legally and economically, on her
husband.[14] Sand presents us with a heroine who manifests, in an exaggerated, almost parodic form, the degraded status of women in "la famille très unie" of the
nineteenth century. Within her marriage, Indiana be-
haves like the unpaid laborer that, according to French
law, she is:

Parfois [Delmare] donnait chez lui un ordre mal
exprimé, ou bien il dictait sans réflexion des ordres
nuisibles à ses propres intérêts. Madame Delmare les
faisait exécuter sans examen, sans appel, avec
l'indifférence du cheval qui traîne la charrue dans un
sens ou dans l'autre.

(208)

Indiana's exaggerated respect for the legal and economic stipulations of marriage is coupled with a refusal
to make any concessions to the notion of bourgeois in-
traconjugal affection demanded by the myth of the
privatized family: "Elle n'aima pas son mari, par la
seule raison peut-être qu'on lui faisait un devoir de
l'aimer" (88-89). The bourgeois family in the eighteenth century had depended on the notion of conjugal
love as a means of defining a new family unit against
the preexisting family tradition of the old regime.

By the time Sand was writing, the bourgeois family had
become the dominant, albeit not uncontested, model.
While it still depended *symbolically* on the notion of
conjugal affection, it in fact depended increasingly less
on love and increasingly more on financial concerns; a
beautiful wife was still desirable, but as a prize rather
than as a companion. Delmare thinks of his wife as "un
trésor fragile et précieux" (50). Through her overblown
acceptance of her slavish role, Indiana fights back
against the family in a passively aggressive way: "Indiana était roide et hautaine dans sa soumission. . . . Sa
résignation, c'était la dignité d'un roi qui accepte des
fers et un cachot, plutôt que d'abdiquer sa couronne et
de se dépouiller d'un vain titre" (207). Indiana's submission is critical, disdainful, and provocative.

Indiana's strict adherence to her legally defined duties
brings out a parallel exaggeration of Delmare's hus-
bandly characteristics as they are defined by the law.
He resents Indiana's refusal to behave like a "real" wife
in accordance with the myth of the loving family. His
position of power becomes ridiculous without the crutch
of his wife's reverence and love: "Si son amour-propre

eût souffert de n'être pas le maître absolu, il souffrait bien davantage de l'être d'une façon odieuse ou ridicule" (208). When, in response to Delmare's irritation, Indiana points out that "elle n'avait fait qu'obéir strictement à ses arrêts" (208), Delmare responds in a manner that makes visible the violence usually latent in the nuclear family: "Il était tenté de l'étrangler, de la traîner par les cheveux, de la fouler aux pieds pour la forcer de crier merci" (209).

Indiana insists on her ability to resist absorption into the mask she wears. In a manner reminiscent of Laclos's Madame de Merteuil in *Liaisons dangereuses* (1782), Indiana makes a great effort to preserve another subjectivity beneath the mask of wifehood:

> Résister mentalement à toute espèce de contrainte morale était devenu chez elle une seconde nature, un principe de conduite, une loi de conscience.
>
> (89)

Unlike Merteuil, however, Indiana is a virgin, and she does not seek out the sexual pleasures that Merteuil's mask afforded her. When we are introduced to Indiana she is not in good health. In the opening scene, her condition stops her husband's abusive words short:

> Il remarqua l'air de souffrance et d'abattement qui, ce soir-là, était répandu sur toute sa personne, son attitude fatiguée, ses longs cheveux bruns pendants sur ses joues amaigries, et une teinte violacée sous ses yeux ternis et échauffés.
>
> (55)

Indiana is feverish, her blood flows irregularly, and she is subject to fainting spells and nervous spasms that last for hours. In fact, she is described through all of her time with Delmare as hovering in a space between life and death:

> Un mal inconnu dévorait sa jeunesse. Elle était sans force et sans sommeil. Les médecins lui cherchaient en vain une désorganisation apparente, il n'en existait pas; toutes ses facultés appauvrissaient également, tous ses organes se lésaient avec lenteur; son coeur brûlait à petit feu, ses yeux s'éteignaient, son sang ne circulait plus que par crise et par fièvre; encore quelque temps, et la pauvre captive allait mourir.
>
> (89)[15]

Freud tells us that hysterical symptoms are hieroglyphs needing to be decoded. If we accept this, what might be the hidden meaning of Indiana's body language? We might interpret Indiana's symptoms as an exaggerated, corporeal inscription of social power relations in which women's bodies are treated as the object of a complicated set of social/sexual disciplines.[16] We might read them too as a refusal of the libidinal economy that prescribes fulfillment for women within the role of wife and mother. We are told:

> La nuit avait pour cette femme rêveuse et triste un langage tout de mystères et de fantômes qu'elle seule savait comprendre et *traduire*.
>
> (my emphasis, 59)

In *La Jeune Née*, Catherine Clément and Hélène Cixous debate whether the hysteric should or should not be celebrated/romanticized as a resisting heroine. The debate could be continued at length with respect to Indiana and her role in the family. I would like to have it both ways. I see Indiana's symptoms as the translation of a repressed "langage de mystères et de fantômes," that is, a language that refuses the definitions of "enlightened" men and laws, a language of protest against the role allotted women in the family and in literature; it is also a language eventually retranslatable into something less self-destructive and more communicable than bodily suffering. Sand's novel provides the beginnings of such a retranslation. I will return to this in the next section but, before doing so, we will consider the second "classic" female plot included in Sand's multiply plotted novel: the passion plot ending in the death of a heroine.

Within the first few pages of *Indiana,* we are introduced to the rake of the novel, Raymon de Ramière, an aristocratic neighbor who penetrates the Delmare bourgeois interior. Our introduction to Raymon takes place in the Delmare living room, where he has been brought after being shot in the hand while scrambling across the wall surrounding the Delmare property. Indiana tends to his wounded hand while Raymon, in a feigned state of semi-consciousness, takes in the scene. We learn, though Indiana does not, that before Raymon's dramatic entrance into Indiana's life, the better part of another seduction plot has been played out. By the time he enters Sand's novel, Raymon has already met, been enchanted by, and seduced Indiana's extremely sensual childhood companion (*soeur de lait*) and chambermaid, Noun. This plot comes to a traditional ending in the body of the text when Noun discovers that Raymon has betrayed her by falling in love with her mistress, Indiana. In despair, she drowns herself in the river flowing through the Delmare property.

The death of the heroine, especially the sexualized heroine, was certainly not anomalous in the nineteenth century. In fact, this cathartic resolution served a social function:

> Qui trouvera-t-on autour du lit de l'agonisante? . . . Tous ceux qui ont fait cortège à sa vie. . . . Mais il semble que toute malveillance, toute nocivité les ait abandonnés par miracle; en eux, le "public" se fait soudain faste et pieusement attentif, le monde des hommes rend enfin hommage à l'être exceptionnel qu'il n'a pas pu conserver. L'agonie est l'heure de toutes les réconciliations, de tous les ralliements.[17]

Fauchery points out that the death of the heroine is usually conservative, a ritualistic way of confronting social contradictions and resolving them novelistically through pathos rather than ideological change.

Noun's tragic plot might easily fill an entire "roman à l'usage des femmes de chambres," planting in the hearts of readers like Noun the longing for a love that would transcend class differences and sweep them into blissful security with a man their social superior. But Noun, who is sensual, dark, and exotic, drowns herself in an "appropriate" manner so that her lover may continue to live a peaceful and socially acceptable existence in the future.[18] Noun's death is rendered unromantic and unacceptable by the very starkness of its presentation:

> Un cri déchirant attira en ce lieu les ouvriers de la fabrique; madame Delmare était évanouie sur la rive, et le cadavre de Noun flottait sur l'eau, devant elle.
>
> (119)[19]

We are not grateful for a good cathartic cry here. Moreover, the death-of-the-heroine ending is only the beginning of Sand's novel. Indeed, Noun's story is condensed into the first of the four books that make up *Indiana.* In the second book we are told that the causes of Noun's death were silenced in the Delmare household to shelter Indiana from the true story and thereby to avoid further aggravating her symptoms: "Il y eut une convention tacite de ne jamais en parler devant Indiana, et bientôt même on n'en parla pas du tout" (125). While Ralph and Delmare may stop discussing Noun, Sand's novel does not. *Indiana,* its plot constantly looping back on itself in a series of echoes and dissections, constitutes, finally, the undoing of both the marriage plot (in which the heroine suffers the woes of hysteria) and the passion plot (in which the heroine ends up dead).

New Plots

It seems at first glance that Indiana's story simply replays Noun's relationship with Raymon, that she steps in to replace the gap left in Raymon's life by Noun's absence. But the plots of the two women are entangled in complicated ways well before Noun drowns herself. Indeed, it is Raymon's involvement with Indiana that motivates Noun's decision to end her life. For Raymon, the two women, both Créole, represent two extremes of womanhood: on the one hand, Noun, the hypersexualized, lower-class woman, and, on the other, Indiana, the desexualized, angelic, upper-class woman. The doubling of Raymon's plot, once with the sexualized "sister," once with her angelic "sister," allows for some ingenious play with literary views of women.

While it is Noun's frank sensuality that attracts Raymon when he first sees her at a social event, he soon grows tired of this woman who has surrendered sexually to him: "Pour lui une grisette n'était pas une femme" (75). It is not long before he is able to desire

her only by imagining her as something she is not: "Noun, en déshabillé blanc, parée de ses longs cheveux noirs, était une dame, une reine, une fée; lorsqu'il la voyait sortir de ce castel de briques rouges" (74). It is precisely these qualities that lead to his passionate attraction to Indiana. She seems really to be all the things that he has had to project onto Noun. She is wealthy, delicate, and, above all, she is fairylike. At the ball where she meets Raymon for the second time, Indiana is actually described as a vision straight out of "les contes fantastiques [qui] étaient à cette époque à toute la fraîcheur de leur succès":

> Le blanc mat de son collier, celui de sa robe de crêpe et de ses épaules nues, se confondaient à quelque distance, et la chaleur des appartements avait à peine réussi à élever sur ses joues une nuance délicate comme celle d'une rose de Bengale éclose sur la neige. C'était une créature toute petite, toute mignonne, toute déliée; une beauté de salon que la lueur vive des bougies rendait féerique et qu'un rayon de soleil eût ternie. En dansant, elle était légère sans vivacité, sans plaisir.
>
> (80)

At the ball, Raymon and this rosebud are considered a perfect romantic pair, especially in the view of one "femme *artiste,*" who whispers to her neighbor:

> N'est-ce pas qu'auprès de cette jeune personne si pâle et si menue, le ton *solide* de l'un fait admirablement ressortir le ton *fin* de l'autre?
>
> (81)

Sand's readers, familiar with Noun's story, know to read this romanesque couple more skeptically than does the woman at the ball. The narrator, by way of the same sort of ironic distance we have already considered in his presentation of Delmare, has made certain that we view Raymon as a less-than-admirable man: we know (although Indiana does not) that Raymon has already seduced and is in the process of abandoning Noun by the time he sweeps Indiana off her feet at the ball. The narrator has already described for us how Raymon "honorably" decides to break off his relationship with Noun:

> Oui, sur mon honneur! il avait songé [au mariage]; mais l'amour, qui légitime tout, s'affaiblissait maintenant; il s'en allait avec les dangers de l'aventure et le piquant du mystère. Plus d'hymen possible; et faites attention; Raymon raisonnait fort bien et tout à fait dans l'intérêt de sa maîtresse.
>
> (75)

Such passages recounted by the narrator in Noun's story invite us to read Indiana's story with a good deal of critical distance.

Raymon "reads" his mistresses in terms traditionally provided in literature, i.e., the fallen woman or the madonna. For him, Noun represents the sexualized heroine, while Indiana represents the virginal heroine. Sand's novel shows the ways in which these terms are hurtful to women. This becomes even more clear in perhaps the most frequently cited passage in *Indiana,* a bedroom scene in which Raymon melds the two relationships into one. As he continues his "courtship" of Indiana, Noun's pregnancy becomes more apparent and her terror more pressing. To spend time in the Delmare household, Raymon has had to juggle his relationship with Indiana along with that of Noun in such a way that neither woman is aware of his relationship with the other. He finally resolves to send Noun away with money so that he can be free of her. Noun greets Raymon at the arranged time and place, but she is unexpectedly dressed in Indiana's clothes. She leads Raymon into Indiana's virginal chambers. In the presence of Noun draped in Indiana's white lace, his resolve fades. Despite the fact that Noun's disguise is only partially successful—she is "belle comme une femme et pas comme une fée"—he gives in to her seductions and makes passionate love to her on Indiana's narrow white bed:

> Elle l'entourait de ses bras frais et bruns, elle le couvrait de ses longs cheveux; ses grands yeux noirs lui jetaient une langueur brûlante, et cette ardeur du sang, cette volupté tout orientale qui sait triompher de tous les efforts de la volonté, de toutes les délicatesses de la pensée. Raymon oublia tout, et ses résolutions, et son nouvel amour, et le lieu où il était. Il rendit à Noun ses caresses délirantes.
>
> (104)

There is something profoundly egalitarian in the shared eroticism of this scene. But in Raymon's imagination, this experience of submission to women's sexuality is frighteningly dangerous. He can only conceptualize Noun's forthright sexuality in terms of what he sees as Indiana's angelic lack of sexuality. Coming back to his "senses" and addressing his thoughts to Indiana, Raymon bemoans his encounter with Noun and casts it and her in a demonic light:

> Quels songes impurs, quelles pensées âcres et dévorantes ne viendront pas à ton cerveau pour le dessécher? Ton sommeil, pur comme celui d'un enfant, quelle divinité chaste voudra le protéger maintenant? N'ai-je pas ouvert au démon de la luxure l'entrée de ton alcôve? . . . L'ardeur insensée qui consume les flancs de cette créole lascive ne viendra-t-elle pas . . . s'attacher aux tiens pour les ronger?
>
> (106)

Raymon's tendency to pit the two women against each other results in an inability to see either of them. Earlier he had been unwilling to read the letter that Noun sent him ("C'était peut-être un chef-d'oeuvre de passion naïve et gracieuse; Virginie n'en écrivit peut-être pas une plus charmante à Paul lorsqu'elle eut quitté sa pat-

rie. . . . Mais M. de Ramière se hâta de la jeter au feu" [77]). Likewise, Raymon's expressed regrets show a profound *mis*reading of Indiana's situation. We know that what he assumes to be Indiana's tranquil innocence, "[son] sommeil pur comme celui d'un enfant", is a far cry from the actual sleepless and pain-filled nights she experiences regularly, nights that contribute to the "feminine" frailty Raymon finds so tantalizing.

In Raymon's imagination, the two women shift into and out of the whore/madonna roles. On occasion, Indiana becomes the sexualized heroine, and Noun the submissive angel. This is the case when Raymon witnesses Indiana's remarkable behavior on horseback:

> Il ne se doutait pas que, dans cette femme si frêle et en apparence si timide, résidât un courage plus que masculin. . . . Raymon fut effrayé de la voir courir ainsi, se livrant sans peur à la fougue de ce cheval qu'elle connaissait à peine, le lancer hardiment dans le taillis, éviter avec une adresse étonnante les branches dont la vigueur élastique fouettait son visage, franchir les fossés sans hésitation, se hasarder avec confiance dans les terrains glaiseux et mouvants, ne s'inquiétant pas de briser ses membres fluets, mais jalouse d'arriver la première sur la piste fumante du sanglier. Tant de résolution l'effraya et faillit le dégoûter de madame Delmare. Les hommes, et les amants surtout, ont la fatuité innocente de vouloir protéger la faiblesse plutôt que d'admirer le courage chez les femmes. L'avouerai-je? Raymon se sentit épouvanté de tout ce qu'un esprit si intrépide promettait de hardiesse et de ténacité en amour.
>
> (162)[20]

Indiana's impressive maneuvering on horseback attests to her capacity for sensual experience *other* than bodily pain. In Raymon's imagination, these momentary signs of life shift Indiana into what had previously been Noun's role. Confronted with Indiana expressing vitality and pleasure, he compares her in negative terms to the now-dead Noun, whom he has transformed in his imagination into a timid creature: "Ce n'était plus le coeur résigné de la pauvre Noun, qui aimait mieux se noyer que de lutter contre son malheur" (162). For Raymon, which role the woman occupies ultimately seems less important than that she occupy one or the other.

As was the case with Delmare, Raymon's behavior in his personal life is inseparable from his behavior in public life. He is a glib journalist with an ability to convince his listener/reader of almost any position on any issue. While he claims his views are based on principles, these shift incessantly according to the needs of particular individuals within a particular power structure, in this case the constitutional monarchy:[21]

> Dispensé par sa fortune d'écrire pour de l'argent, Raymon écrivait par goût et (disait-il) par devoir. Cette rare faculté qu'il possédait, de réfuter par le talent la vérité positive, en avait fait un homme précieux au ministère.
>
> (130)

Indeed, Raymon in his public and private lives is a storyteller, a teller of fictions. And yet, again and again, Raymon accuses the women in his life of behaving as if *they* were characters in a novel when they make demands on him or show surprise at his behavior. In these moments, he implies that novels are simply women's foolishness rather than an integral part of the world *he* inhabits.

Shortly into Indiana's (unconsummated) love affair with Raymon, Delmare suddenly loses his wealth and announces to his wife that they must return to île Bourbon. On the eve of their planned departure, Indiana breaks out of her house (where her husband has literally locked her in) and goes to the Ramière residence. She waits for Raymon in his chambers, thereby losing all claim to public respectability. Raymon has already foreseen "qu'un instant viendrait le mettre aux prises avec cet amour de femme, qu'il faudrait défendre sa liberté contre les exigences d'une passion romanesque" (234). When he arrives home after a long and festive night to find Indiana waiting for him, he cries out: "Dans quel roman à l'usage des femmes de chambre avez-vous rêvé l'amour, je vous prie?" (221).

But the romanesque project to live together outside the law that Raymon attributes to Indiana's imagination and to novels is actually a project that Raymon and Indiana conceived together on the evening of their second meeting. Sand's prose blends the perspectives of the two participants on the evening of the ball. The narrator moves from reporting the thoughts of one character in the *style indirect libre* to reporting those of the other with no clearly defined transition between the two:

> Elle ne pensa pas non plus que cet homme pouvait être menteur ou frivole. Elle le vit comme elle le désirait, comme elle l'avait rêvé, et Raymon eût pu la tromper, s'il n'eût pas été sincère. Mais comment n'eût-il pas été auprès d'une femme si belle et si aimante? Quelle autre s'était jamais montrée à lui avec autant de candeur et d'innocence? Chez qui avait-il trouvé à placer un avenir si riant et si sûr? N'était-elle pas née pour l'aimer, cette femme esclave qui n'attendait qu'un signe pour briser sa chaîne, qu'un mot pour le suivre? Le ciel, sans doute, l'avait formée pour Raymon, cette triste enfant de l'île Bourbon, que personne n'avait aimée, et qui sans lui devait mourir.

(90)

The first portion of the passage describes Indiana's perspective ("Elle ne pensa pas . . . rêvé"), and the second Raymon's perspective ("Raymon eût pu la tromper . . . si sûr"). Finally the third passage once again presents Indiana's perspective ("N'était-elle pas née pour l'aimer . . . mourir")—for how could Raymon, meeting her unexpectedly at this ball after only the encounter in which she had nursed his wound, know that she was from the île Bourbon and that she had never been loved?

Thanks to the omniscience of the narrator, we find in this remarkable passage an agreement between the two on the terms of a still-unspoken project.[22] *Both* characters imagine devoting themselves to each other in a joyously secure future.

In fact, it is clear that Raymon takes the more active role in initiating the romance plots into which he encourages both Noun and Indiana to enter. To cite but one example, Raymon sneaks into the Delmare residence following the evening of the ball and falls at Indiana's feet with the following rush of words:

> Ce ne sont pas des circonstances vulgaires qui nous ont réunis, vois-tu; ce n'est ni le hasard ni le caprice, c'est la fatalité, c'est la mort, qui m'ont ouvert les portes de cette vie nouvelle. . . . Reste là, Indiana, reste contre mon coeur, c'est là ton refuge et ton abri. Aime-moi, et je serai invulnérable.

(96)

He continues to participate in and to encourage the co-authorship of this romance plot even when he has given up any relationship between the fiction and the events of his life: "Il se retrancha dans l'opinion où il était que [Indiana] appliquait maintenant à sa situation l'exagération des sentiments qu'elle avait puisée dans les livres. Il s'évertua à l'éloquence passionnée, à l'improvisation dramatique, afin de se maintenir au niveau de sa romanesque maîtresse, et il réussit à prolonger son erreur" (205). When Indiana enters into his story without making distinctions between what happens in books and what happens in life, enters his story with her heart and her soul, Raymon accuses *her* of being *romanesque*. Indiana and Noun, as his trusting "readers," are left dead or abandoned when he fails to make good on his *romanesque* promises. Raymon presents the women's stories in the same manner as he writes his articles, to assure himself immediate gratification without true concern for the fates of his readers.[23] In this way, Sand's novel points out how dangerous it is for women to take at face value the ubiquitous love plots of sentimental fiction, be they passion plots or bourgeois marriage plots.

After Raymon's refusal to take her under his wing, Indiana, stunned and desperate, comes close to repeating Noun's passion/death plot by drowning herself in the Seine. Indiana's plunge is cut short, however, by Ralph and his dog Ophélia, who come upon Indiana ankle deep in the river. After rubbing her numbed feet, Ralph accompanies her home. This felicitous twist in the traditional passion plot—Indiana survives—opens the way for the presentation of a new plot. In fact, the protagonist emerges from her disastrous experience with Raymon to assume a stronger position than she had held before she met him. Indiana is able to articulate her resistance to her husband more forcefully and directly than earlier, when her only communication had taken the form of hysterical symptoms. When her husband's violence takes concrete rather than abstract form, Indiana finds her tongue:

> Je sais que je suis l'esclave et vous le seigneur. La loi de ce pays vous a fait mon maître. Vous pouvez lier mon corps, garrotter mes mains, gouverner mes actions. Vous avez le droit du plus fort, et la société vous le confirme; mais sur ma volonté, monsieur, vous ne pouvez rien, Dieu seul peut la courber et la réduire.
>
> (232)

When Delmare refers to Indiana's words as "des phrases de roman," he is not referring to the same sentences that defined the plots we have thus far considered. Here they refer to sentences that subvert dominant plots. Just what these plots composed of such "phrases de roman" might consist in, is articulated in a long letter Indiana writes to Raymon after she has returned to île Bourbon with her husband. She is responding to a letter from Raymon in which the clichés of what I have been referring to as the "old plots" stand out. Raymon writes:

> Je vous l'ai dit souvent Indiana, vous n'êtes pas une femme, et, quand j'y songe dans le calme de mes pensées, vous êtes un ange. Je vous adore dans mon coeur comme une divinité. . . . Pourquoi, pur esprit, avais-tu pris la forme tentatrice d'une femme? Pourquoi, ange de lumière, avais-tu revêtu les séductions de l'enfer? Souvent j'ai cru tenir le bonheur dans mas bras, et tu n'étais que la vertu.
>
> (240)

After this reduction of Indiana once again into a bipolar being, at once angel and demon, he congratulates himself, and her too, for not giving in to the temptations of the flesh: "Dieu nous récompensera d'un tel effort; car Dieu est bon. Il nous réunira dans une vie plus heureuse" (242).

Raymon's words, which have always assured him success in both public and private affairs, are here refused by Indiana. Indiana begins her response to Raymon with an apology for disturbing him and a claim that she is writing to ease his mind. She urges him to forget her, and assures him she is well: "Soyez heureux, soyez insouciant; oubliez-moi; je vis encore, et peut-être vivrai-je longtemps . . ." (245). But from this passive, forgiving posture, she moves quickly to less docile tones, particularly in her response to Raymon's earlier charge that she has imagined her life in terms typical of "des romans à l'usage des femmes de chambre." Rather than denying the charge, Indiana embraces it and defines the ladies' novel as a potential means of resistance to the social limitations placed on women like herself. She turns Raymon's accusation that she is overly *romanesque* back on him by suggesting that it is he who is not *romanesque* enough:

> C'est que, selon votre expression cynique, j'avais appris la vie dans les romans à l'usage des femmes de chambre, dans ces riantes et puériles fictions où l'on intéresse le coeur au succès de folles entreprises et d'impossibles félicités . . . j'ai puisé dans l'exaltation de mes sentiments la force de me placer dans une situation d'invraisemblance et de roman, et que vous, homme de coeur, vous n'ayez pas trouvé dans votre volonté celle de m'y suivre.
>
> (247)

Indiana associates novels here with sentiment and implausibility.

In "Vraisemblance et motivation," Gérard Genette describes the relationship of plausibility to ideology:

> C'est-à-dire un corps de maximes et de préjugés qui constitue tout à la fois une vision du monde et un système de valeurs. . . . Ce qui subsiste, et qui définit le vraisemblable, c'est le principe formel de respect de la norme, c'est-à-dire l'existence d'un rapport d'implication entre la conduite particulière attribuée à un tel personnage, et telle maxime générale implicite et reçue.[24]

Indiana's refusal to behave "plausibly" represents then a refusal to adhere to certain maxims governing feminine behavior within a particular political structure. Indiana undermines this particular world view by showing how it rests on a specific conception of God, the guarantor of truth and of legitimacy within it:

> Ne m'exhortez pas à penser à Dieu; . . . Pour moi, j'ai plus de foi que vous; je ne sers pas le même Dieu, mais je le sers mieux, et plus purement. Le vôtre, c'est le dieu des hommes, c'est le roi, le fondateur et l'appui de votre race; le mien, c'est le Dieu de l'univers, le créateur, le soutien et l'espoir de toutes les créatures. . . . Vous vous croyez les maîtres du monde; je crois que vous n'en êtes que les tyrans. . . . Toute votre morale, tous vos principes, ce sont les intérêts de votre société que vous avez érigés en lois et que vous prétendez faire émaner de Dieu.
>
> (248-249)[25]

Indiana, the survivor of both the marriage plot and the passion plot, here defends her right to imagine and inhabit an entirely different social structure from the one in which Delmare and Raymon wield such power. Her hysterical symptoms have found a way into the language of dominant culture, a way into the words of novels, at least for a short while.

ALL IN THE (SAINT-SIMONIAN) FAMILY

> Mes soeurs, ma mère! vous serez obéies, vous serez aimées par delà tous les siècles! Car le règne de Dieu commence et le règne de Dieu n'aura pas de fin, et là où toute puissance, tout amour sont enlevés à la force brutale, vous avez des droits à la gloire aussi bien qu'à l'amour.
>
> —Anonymous exhortation to Saint-Simonian "family" gathering, circa 1830

Sand, in the preface to the 1852 version of *Indiana,* writes: "Du temps que je fis *Indiana,* on criait au saint-simonisme à propos de tout" (36). Her evocation of the Saint-Simonians, even in the form of an implicit denial of their influence, points to the importance of utopian socialist ideas during the period in which she began writing. "On criait au saint-simonisme à propos de tout" because the Saint-Simonians were in fact a significant presence in the social and intellectual landscape of the early 1830s.[26] The Saint-Simonians began to give public lectures in the late 1820s, and by 1832 their meetings were drawing significant public attendance.[27] Despite her disclaimers, Sand does refer to the Saint-Simonians in her correspondence in the early 1830s, sometimes quite favorably.[28] We have no way of knowing whether Sand was sincere in her denials of Saint-Simonian influence, although in 1852 she certainly had reason to distance herself from a movement whose ideals were given up after the 1848 revolution. What concerns me here is not Sand's sincerity or lack thereof, but rather the ways in which utopian socialist ideas, borrowed consciously or unconsciously, function in *Indiana.*

The Saint-Simonians were not a literary movement, but rather a social and religious movement. The "père" Enfantin who headed the movement from the late 1820s through the early 1830s, "rejected radical individualism in favor of a harmonious association of differentiated classes and . . . sexes."[29] In accordance with this vision, Enfantin imagined a family that extended beyond the boundaries of the nuclear family to include members linked by cooperation and mutual support—what the utopian socialists termed "association"—rather than by blood.

We find a rendition of this anti-individualistic notion of family in *Indiana.* Let us return for a moment to the opening scene in the Delmare salon. The only sign of tenderness and vitality is presented in animal rather than human form. Ralph's dog, the bright-eyed, furry Ophélia, "heureuse et caressante" (51), enters the room and, after being reprimanded by her master, approaches Indiana. The dog's presence provides an outlet for Delmare's pent-up frustrations. As M. Delmare pulls out his hunting whip and approaches the cowering dog, Indiana holds on to the dog protectively and begs her husband to show pity: "De grâce monsieur, ne la tuez-pas!" (54). In the argument that ensues—to which the narrator ironically refers as a "conversation conjugale"—, we learn that Indiana has good reason to expect the worst: Delmare has already killed Indiana's beloved spaniel. Some moments later, a servant announces that he suspects an intruder on the Delmare premises, probably a coal thief. Delmare claims that "[il] le tuera comme un chien" (56). In response to his wife's protests he adds disdainfully: "Si vous connaissiez la loi, madame, vous sauriez qu'elle m'y autorise."

Sand immediately sets up a coalition of sorts among Indiana, Ophélia, and the intruder, who is assumed to be a poor wretch (but who in fact turns out to be Raymon de Ramière) all united in the face of Delmare's violence and the law that legitimizes his behavior. Over the course of the novel, the number of members of this "family" expands through a system of echoes and analogies. Noun is related to Indiana through their shared childhood as well as their exploitation at the hands of Raymon. Noun's death by drowning is echoed by Indiana's near-drowning in the Seine and by Ophélia's eventual death as well.[30] In Sand's novel, the bonds between these beings unrelated by blood undermine the validity of the Delmare "family" by showing its destructiveness to all involved. They set up an ideal that transcends the nest version of the family to move toward a broader conception of fraternity (and sorority)—which challenges notions of bourgeois individualism rooted in the nuclear family.

One of the last engravings in the illustrated version of Bernardin de Saint-Pierre's enormously successful *Paul et Virginie* [(1788)]—a work that plays an important role in *Indiana*—depicts the virginal heroine Virginie rising angelically, her finger pointing toward the distant glow of heaven. The Saint-Simonians conceived of heaven as something quite different from this apotheosis of domestic bliss. Saint-Simon wrote in 1824: "L'âge d'or n'est pas dans le passé, il est dans l'avenir."[31] According to Saint-Simonian doctrine, the new familial economy of "association," less private and less selfish than its bourgeois counterpart, would be realized in a future paradise on earth. Saint-Simonian thought brought heaven down to earth in a utopian vision of the future. Adherents believed that this golden age of egalitarianism and cooperation would be overseen by a benevolent and socially concerned God.

This idea of a providential history is frequently evoked in *Indiana.* We see it in the narrator's repeated references to the instability of historical processes in passages such as the following: "Je vous parle d'un temps bien loin de nous, aujourd'hui que l'on ne compte plus par siècles, ni même par règnes, mais par ministères" (128). Several times, Ralph refers to this condition of instability as a precursor to a stable and more just social organization. In reference to Raymon, for example, we read:

> C'étaient des hommes d'un grand talent, en effet, que ceux qui retenaient encore la société près de crouler dans l'abîme, et qui, suspendus eux-mêmes entre deux écueils, luttaient avec calme et aisance contre la rude vérité qui allait les engloutir.
>
> (130-131)

The utopian socialist aspect of this future "rude vérité" becomes even more explicit in Indiana's letter to Raymon from île Bourbon in which she discusses her very utopian socialist notion of God, "le Dieu de toutes les créatures":

> Vous pensez que Dieu vous protège et vous autorise à usurper l'empire de la terre; moi, je pense qu'il le souffre pour un peu de temps, et qu'un jour viendra où, comme des grains de sable, son souffle vous dispersera.

(249)

Significantly, it is during the time on île Bourbon when Indiana is, so to speak, between couple plots—that is, when she is thinking less about Raymon in France ("elle s'habituait à penser moins à Raymon" [274]) and has not yet been introduced into Ralph's plot—that Indiana is the most forward-looking in her vision and independent in her actions. Ophélia, her beloved dog, is still alive, and Ralph figures as a comforting presence, but he keeps his distance. Indiana is free to explore the island and to dream. In her letter to Raymon from île Bourbon, Indiana has already described her dreams:

> Voilà mes rêves; ils sont tous d'une autre vie, d'un autre monde où la loi du brutal n'aura point passé sur la tête du pacifique, où du moins la résistance et la fuite ne seront pas des crimes, où l'homme pourra échapper à l'homme, comme la gazelle échappe à la panthère, sans que la chaîne des lois soit tendue autour de lui.

(250)

Sand's descriptions of her reveries during her solitary forays in the wilderness suggest a link between her social vision as described above and a new sexual economy:

> Suspendue à une grande élévation au-dessus du sol de la côte, et voyant fuir sous ses yeux les gorges qui la séparaient de l'Océan, il lui semblait être lancée dans cet espace par un mouvement rapide. . . . Dans ce rêve, elle se cramponnait au rocher qui lui servait d'appui; et pour qui eût observé alors ses yeux avides, son sein haletant d'impatience et l'effrayante expression de joie répandue sur ses traits, elle eût offert tous les symptômes de la folie. . . . Chez elle tout se rapportait . . . à une ardente aspiration vers un point qui n'était ni le souvenir, ni l'espoir, ni le regret, mais le désir dans toute son intensité dévorante.

(254)

The combination of a new social vision with this frankly erotic evocation of female extramarital desire contributes to making this "inbetween plot" the richest and most subversive of all Sand's subplots. The narrator refers to Indiana's reveries as "[des] projets romanesques et [des] projets extravagants" (273), pointing toward a new novel that might truly subvert the family romance. But Sand is writing in 1832, and she has to make a living. The Ralph-and-Indiana romance is waiting in the wings.

AFTER THE FALL (AT BERNICA): INDIANA AND SIR RALPH'S "NATURAL MARRIAGE"

> Les femmes n'ont encore rien à dire, ce me semble. Que ferontelles par la révolte? Quand le monde mâle sera converti, la femme le sera sans qu'on ait besoin de s'en occuper.
>
> George Sand, *Correspondance*

Thus far, I have given little attention to Indiana's cousin and faithful friend, Ralph. He is a constant if restrained presence throughout Sand's novel, his life story (also Indiana's life story) recounted in short passages between what I have referred to as the marriage plot and the passion plot. In these passages we learn that Ralph, like Indiana, was rejected as a child from the house of his father, and that he and Indiana, along with Noun, spent all their days together exploring île Bourbon's plethora of hills and valleys. This seemingly blissful state of affairs continued until Ralph, called upon to marry his brother's widow, moved to England. He is ten years older than Indiana, seven years older than Noun. By the time he returned to the island—after the death of his wife—Indiana was married to Delmare, and the couple was preparing to leave for France. Ralph, unable to bear his solitude on île Bourbon, bought himself a piece of land near Lagny, the Delmare property, and introduced himself into the Delmare household with the following proposition to Indiana's husband:

> Monsieur, j'aime votre femme; c'est moi qui l'ai élevée; je la regarde comme ma soeur, et plus encore comme ma fille. . . . Quand je vous aurai donné ma parole que je n'eus jamais d'amour pour elle et que je n'en aurai jamais, vous pourrez me voir avec aussi peu d'inquiétude que si j'étais réellement votre beau-frère. N'est-il pas vrai monsieur?

(159)

At that time, Delmare, convinced that Ralph posed no danger to his marriage, honorably accepted the offer. Indiana, equally convinced, considered Ralph to be a passionless and egotistical presence in the household. He has been living at Lagny for several years when we are introduced to the Delmare family in the opening pages of Sand's novel.

Throughout the novel, Ralph's position in the social structure is presented as different from that of the other male characters. Both Delmare and Raymon hold well-defined roles in the public sphere. Delmare represents a bourgeois who has made, and then lost, his fortune according to the competitive laws of the market. Raymon represents a class of opportunistic aristocrats who use their influence and connections (in Raymon's case through his pen) to balance themselves on the edge of precarious reigning political systems in such a way that their own comforts are consistently assured. The presentation of both Delmare and Raymon makes clear that their public lives are inseparable from their private lives. As we have seen, Sand seems to undermine the notion, prevalent even among the most critical romantics, that personal life takes place in some private psychological realm outside society. Sand provides no comparable role for Ralph in public life. He is associated with a political view, but it is not one linked to a series of routine daily activities, as are the political views of Delmare and Raymon. In the political arguments that become ever more frequent among the men in the Delmare household once Raymon has entered the picture, Ralph consistently supports what is nominally a republican point of view:

> Ralph allait donc toujours soutenant son rêve de république d'où il voulait exclure tous les abus, tous les préjugés, toutes les injustices, projet fondé tout entier sur l'espoir d'une nouvelle race d'hommes.
>
> (167)

Ralph's "rêve de république" and his "nouvelle race d'hommes" seem to be consistent with Indiana's dream of "une autre vie, un autre monde où la loi brutale n'aura point passé sur la tête du pacifique" (250). Ralph's position recalls the forward-looking vision prevalent among utopian socialists and especially among the Saint-Simonians as much as it does a past revolutionary ideal. This vision, however, is complicated by its association with the works of Bernardin de Saint-Pierre, and in particular with his *Paul et Virginie.*

Paul et Virginie is a topos throughout Sand's novel. The first reference to the work is in Noun's passion plot with Raymon. Noun's letters—which never have much of an effect on Raymon—are compared by the narrator to those that Virginie might have written: "Virginie n'en écrivait peut-être pas une plus charmante à Paul lorsqu'elle eut quitté sa patrie . . . mais M. de Ramière se hâta de la jeter au feu, dans la crainte de rougir de lui-même" (77). We find a second reference to Bernardin's work in Sand's descriptions of Indiana's bedroom, its walls adorned with lithographs depicting scenes from the lives of Paul and Virginie:[32]

> Le goût exquis et la simplicité chaste qui présidaient à l'ameublement; ces livres d'amour et de voyages, épars sur les planches d'acajou; ce métier chargé d'un travail si joli et si frais, oeuvre de patience et de mélancolie; cette harpe dont les cordes semblaient encore vibrer des chants d'attente et de tristesse; ces gravures qui représentaient les pastorales amours de Paul et de Virginie, les cimes de l'île Bourbon et les rivages bleus de Saint-Paul; . . . tout révélait madame Delmare.
>
> (101)

Sand's interweaving of themes from Bernardin's well-known novel into *Indiana* is certainly more than simple pastoral decoration. The juxtaposition of Paul and the Créole Virginie's "pastorales amours" with Raymon's seduction of the Créole Noun in the Créole Indiana's bed invites comment. We might read the lithographs as the myth of romantic (familial) love in contrast to the much less palatable reality of romantic love represented in Raymon's passion plots first with Noun and then with Indiana. These plots might serve as critiques then of the *Paul et Virginie* plot. But this reading would lead us far astray in the consideration of Sand's novel as a whole. Despite the critiques we have thus far considered, *Indiana* is not readily classified as an antiromantic novel. On the contrary, in the final love story between Ralph and Indiana, Sand exalts romantic love, and Bernardin's vision plays an important role in this exaltation.

To come to some understanding of Sand's return to Bernardin, it is helpful to take a brief detour through *Paul et Virginie.* Bernardin published his novel in 1788, on the very eve of the French Revolution. The novel went through thirty editions between 1789 and 1799, more than any other novel during the same period and, as was the case with *La Nouvelle Héloïse,* resulted in hundreds of fan letters to the author.[33] Bernardin, like Rousseau, preached a "return" to nature and virtue. In the preface to *Paul et Virginie,* he states: "Notre bonheur consiste à vivre suivant la nature et la vertu."[34] His novel tells the story of two children who grow up in a feminized paradise far removed from the world of France and of kings, where they taste the delights of intrafamilial love and sensuality. Blissfully ignorant of political or economic events, they live with their single mothers (one is a widow, the other was callously abandoned by a nobleman), each day reveling in nature and mutual tenderness:

> Ils croyaient que le monde finissait où finissait leur île, et ils n'imaginaient rien d'aimable où ils n'étaient pas. Leur affection mutuelle et celle de leurs mères occupaient toute l'activité de leurs âmes.[35]

In case of any doubt that what is being portrayed is a new ideal of the family, Bernardin points it out explicitly in his repeated references to this small group of individuals as "les familles heureuses" or "ces familles si unies." Additionally, we find a strikingly explicit lesson on the naturalness of the small loving family in the following exclamation addressed to Paul by Virginie:

> O mon frère! les rayons du soleil au matin, au haut de ces rochers, me donnent moins de joie que ta présence. J'aime bien ma mère, j'aime bien la tienne; mais, quand elles t'appellent mon fils, je les aime encore davantage. Les caresses qu'elles te font me sont plus sensibles que celles que j'en reçois. Tu me demandes pourquoi tu m'aimes; mais tout ce qui a été élevé ensemble s'aime. Vois nos oiseaux: élevés dans les mêmes nids, ils s'aiment comme nous; ils sont toujours ensemble comme nous.[36]

Amidst the economic and political changes underway in France, Bernardin proposed what *seemed* to his readers an escape from the turmoil. In fact, far from being an escape, his vision was intimately linked to events in France. He, like Rousseau, presents a naturalized, private, affectionate family from which emerge the self-conscious individuals demanded by capitalism.[37] *Paul et Virginie* celebrates privacy and domesticity in a utopian world where the public sphere is so remote as to be nonexistent. While this may seem incompatible with the *embourgeoisement* of society, where the two spheres are interdependent, and where the public sphere justifies its existence by producing material abundance, I would argue that in fact it is not. One of the qualities of the new intimate sphere was that it *seemed* entirely independent from outside forces. Goulemot makes this point:

> Je suis Paul ou je suis Virginie; ce que le livre raconte, c'est mon histoire; ce qu'éprouvent les héros, ce sont mes sentiments, mes aspirations, mes émotions. Le livre agit comme un révélateur et la lecture comme une reconnaissance de soi et un déchiffrement. Ce que je ressentais en moi et n'arrivais pas à exprimer, cette intimité profonde, ce caché spécifique, voilà qu'un livre lu par hasard, assis sur un banc, à l'ombre d'un arbre, me permet soudain de le comprendre et d'en avoir une conscience claire.[38]

The "je" thus interpellated is precisely the one demanded by the public sphere. Focusing on women in the home, Bernardin's presentation of an isolated feminine utopia is entirely in keeping with the imagination of the private sphere, which, with its complementary opposite of the public sphere, was defined as a whole against the structure of absolute monarchy.

While Bernardin focuses on the private realm, discussions of the social and political complement to his familial vision occasionally creep in. He opposes one social structure, symbolized by the loving "family," against another in the following passage, which transcribes the words of Paul's mother, Madame de La Tour, to her companion, Marguerite (who is also Virginie's mother): "J'ai goûté plus de consolation et de félicité avec vous, sous ces pauvres cabanes, que jamais les richesses de ma famille ne m'en ont fait même espérer dans ma patrie" (66)[39]. Here Madame de La Tour (note the aristocratic particle) expresses to her bourgeois friend how happy she is to be part of a loving family and how relieved to be free of her previous aristocratic existence. The monarchy, historically the protector of the aristocracy, is also presented in negative terms as a system in which it is impossible for most individual subjects to achieve well-being: "Le roi est un soleil que les grands et les corps environment comme des nuages; il est presque impossible qu'un de ses rayons tombe sur vous."[40]

Just as Paul and Virginie are feeling their first pubescent sexual pangs within the family, Virginie is called upon to leave for France to stay with a rich aunt who has promised to make the young girl her protégée. Ber-

nardin's France, represented by Virginie's great aunt, is overly invested in old-regime values, including some semblance of education for women and arranged marriages. This France scorns Virginie's bourgeois aspirations of becoming a good housewife. Virginie writes to her mother from France:

> Ma grand'tante fut bien surprise à mon arrivée, lorsque, m'ayant questionnée sur mes talents, je lui dis que je ne savais ni lire ni écrire. Elle me demanda qu'est-ce que j'avais donc appris depuis que j'étais au monde; et, quand je lui eus répondu que c'était à avoir soin d'un ménage et faire votre volonté, elle me répondit que j'avais reçu l'éducation d'une servante. Elle me mit, dès le lendemain, en pension dans une grande abbaye auprès de Paris, où j'ai de si faibles dispositions pour toutes les sciences, que je ne profiterai pas beaucoup avec ces messieurs.
>
> (87)

Bernardin's heroine, almost certainly modeled on Rousseau's Sophie, is willfully inept at any kind of learning not linked to her role in the domestic realm. She has no ambition to participate in any activities other than those preparing her for her place within the confines of the bourgeois family. Her domestic (and sexual) purity, untarnished by public matters, is elevated to mythical heights by the conclusion to Bernardin's novel. When Virginie refuses the marriage her great aunt arranges for her in the traditional mode of the old regime, Virginie is sent back to her family across seas made turbulent by winter storms. Any sympathies the reader might have had with this aunt's position are hereby extinguished. Bernardin makes it clear that the timing of Virginie's return to her "family" was calculated to assure the highest degree of danger. His novel in hardly veiled terms puts the blame for Virginie's eventual death squarely in this aristocratic woman's hands, underlining Rousseau's theory that aristocratic (public) women were a menace to society. The boat that carries Virginie homeward sinks in sight of the shoreline from which Paul, helpless, watches his beloved Virginie drown. She might have been saved but, unwilling to undress for the swim across the waters, she is doomed. Virginie's elaborate funeral is attended by all the islanders, and the reader is invited to interiorize her image as the essence of true womanhood.

Bernardin's novel continued to be read well into the nineteenth century. In fact, the work was read more widely during the Restoration than before.[41] Some of this can be explained by advances in printing technology, but certainly other reasons prolonged the novel's success. Arguably, Bernardin's presentation of familial issues reaffirmed readers' views of themselves as privatized individuals within the politically tumultuous postrevolutionary society; that is, it served as a conservative rather than disruptive force. His myth of a natural private life provided psychic stability within a culture rocked by the broad array of post-revolutionary, post-empire political positions.

Let us return to ***Indiana.*** After Ralph has saved Indiana from the boarding house where she lies destitute and dying after Raymon's second rejection, the two return to île Bourbon where they plan to commit suicide together.[42] On a moonlit night the two "promeneurs solitaires" make their way through fragrant foliage to Bernica, a steep-walled valley in which they spent many days together as children. There have already been hints regarding Ralph's true feelings for Indiana: certain glances, his near-suicide when he fears that Indiana may have died, the fact that he kisses her on the lips, and so forth. But it is only in the final pages of the fourth (and last) book, as Ralph and Indiana prepare for the leap into the shared deliverance of suicide *à deux,* that Ralph finally makes explicit his story. Ralph, whose verbal clumsiness has been contrasted throughout the novel with Raymon's verbal facility, is at last able to speak. Through his tale, imbued with passion finally set free, we learn that he suffered as much as did Indiana from what he calls the "simulacrum légal" (323) of the Delmare marriage.[43] Ralph's story, the true marriage plot as opposed to this simulacrum, is laden with references to *Paul et Virginie.*[44] Above the cataracts crashing into the abyss below, he tells Indiana:

> Quand je vous lisais l'histoire de Paul et Virginie vous ne la compreniez qu'à demi. Vous pleuriez, cependant; vous aviez vu l'histoire d'un frère et d'une soeur là où j'avais frissonné de sympathie en apercevant les angoisses de deux amants. . . . Moi, je relisais seul les entretiens de Paul et de son amie, les impétueux soupçons de l'un, les secrètes souffrances de l'autre. Oh! que je les comprenais bien, ces premières inquiétudes de l'adolescence, qui cherche dans son coeur l'explication des mystères de la vie, et qui s'empare avec enthousiasme du premier objet d'amour qui s'offre à lui.
>
> (318)

Ralph's description of falling in love with Indiana, "le premier objet d'amour qui s'offre à lui," echoes Virginie's "tout ce qui a été élevé ensemble s'aime." Again and again Ralph, a cousin by marriage to Indiana, emphasizes a more immediate familial relationship with his beloved:

> Je fis de vous ma soeur, ma fille, ma compagne, mon élève, ma société. . . . Vous n'étiez que mon enfant, ou tout au plus ma petite soeur; mais j'étais amoureux de vos quinze ans quand, livré seul à l'ardeur des miens, je dévorais l'avenir d'un oeil avide.
>
> (316-317)

Like Paul and Virginie, the two lovers in this "natural" marriage are presented as symbolically linked by blood, their desire incestuous.

Thus far, my reading of ***Indiana*** has suggested that Sand was highly *critical* of bourgeois domesticity and the position in which it placed women, that she dero-

manticizes the domestic interior by showing its complicity with oppressive economic and political positions. She also imagines an alternative realm in her incorporation of utopian socialist notions of progress toward a less competitive, more egalitarian society. If, as I have suggested, Bernardin's novel constitutes an extended hymn to bourgeois domesticity, what are we to make of Sand's weaving its themes through her novel, and in particular through descriptions of the relationship between Indiana and Ralph? How are we to resolve Sand's critique of the private domestic sphere with her celebration of Bernardin? These questions point to fundamental ambiguities in Sand's relationship to the myth and the reality of gendered public and private spheres. Up until this point, Sand's novel constitutes a scathing critique of both the nuclear family and the free-market economy based on individual competitiveness. In the final pages of her novel, however, she looks nostalgically toward the vision of domestic bliss that Bernardin provides. After opening the possibility of new conceptions of public and private lives, Sand in the final marriage scene and the following conclusion presents what has become a conservative vision.

Indeed, the marriage ceremony between Indiana and Ralph is entirely compatible with bourgeois notions of romantic love. Indiana is dressed in white at Ralph's request: "Si j'ai mérité d'être sauvé, j'ai mérité de te posséder. C'est dans ces idées que je t'ai priée de revêtir cet habit blanc; c'est la robe de noces" (329). (Significantly, the custom of bridal whites was inaugurated in the mid-eighteenth century while the bourgeois family was emerging.) Any suggestion of the adulterous nature of Indiana's relationship with Ralph is doubly offset; first by the fact that her legal husband is dead, secondly by the fact that Indiana is still a virgin when she "marries" Ralph at the "altar" above the waterfall. Moreover, Ralph, who himself has fathered a child with another woman, puts great stock in Indiana's purity: "J'eusse souffert de voir un autre homme vous donner une parcelle de bien-être, un instant de satisfaction, c'eût été un vol que l'on m'eût fait" (327).

As in Françoise de Graffigny's *Lettres d'une Péruvienne* [(1747)] and Isabelle de Charrière's *Lettres écrites de Lausanne* [(1785)], we are invited to read beyond the ending. In Sand's brief conclusion, we learn that the planned suicide turns out instead to be a rebirth, the marriage a baptismal rite. In a sense, we are provided with a second, miniature "after-marriage plot." The narrator, now a flesh-and-blood participant in the events recounted, comes across Ralph and Indiana on a remote part of the island. The couple live alone together in a rustic cabin enjoying the same sort of timeless bliss depicted in the early portions of *Paul et Virginie.* The Saint-Simonian elements of their respective visions play no role in this after-plot. Indeed, both Noun and Ophélia, the other members of the Saint-Simonian family, are dead. Ralph and Indiana's isolation from the rest of the islanders is emphasized; the family folds back in on itself in a way that precludes Indiana moving out of the confines of domesticity. We are told: "Quant à madame Delmare, sa retraite avait été si absolue, que son existence était encore une chose problématique pour beaucoup d'habitants" (334). So much for Saint-Simonian notions of fraternity! Indiana speaks only to encourage her husband to do so and thereby, with a touch of coquetterie worthy of a Sophie, to invite the visitor to admire Ralph's great wisdom:

> Elle est avide d'apprendre ce que les préoccupations de sa vie l'ont empêché de savoir; et puis peut-être y eut-il un peu de coquetterie de sa part à questionner sir Ralph, afin de faire briller devant moi les immenses connaissances de son ami.

(337)

While Indiana is presented as learning more than she was able to in her other plots, and presumably more than her counterparts Sophie and Virginie, this fact is softened by the narrator's suggestion that her questions may well be more for Ralph's sake than for her own. Indiana, in other words, is bound up in an old role.

The narrator tells Ralph:

> Quelques moralistes blâment votre solitude; ils prétendent que tout homme appartient à la société, qui le réclame. On ajoute que vous donnez aux hommes un exemple dangereux à suivre.

(343)

This myth, presented as dangerous or subversive, in fact fully coincides with prevailing notions of privacy and individualism. Against the often robust critique found in the rest of the novel, we find posited a conservative rendition of the privatized "natural" family.[45]

I am not trying to prove here that Sand is somehow finally an antifeminist, that her work, because of its occasional nostalgia for a reromanticized version of the privatized family and the bourgeois elements of its conclusion, is *ultimately* complicitous with the romantic visions of domesticity that limited the emotional and intellectual horizons of a century of women.[46] For reasons we considered in the introduction to this chapter, one would imagine that Sand would be particularly sensitive to the hazards involved in transgressing certain conventions while writing her first independent work, particularly in the area of gender politics. Sand is the only nineteenth-century woman writer who has become canonized, and certainly this is linked to her concessions to certain romantic tropes, including the exaltation of the private sphere.

In her analysis of Sand's **"Lettres à Marcie,"** Naomi Schor suggests that Sand is ultimately unable to imagine a life not defined by gendered public and private spheres:

> Ce qui est non pas l'impensé mais l'impensable pour Sand c'est le franchissement par la femme (comme par l'homme) de la barre qui sépare les deux sphères. Pour Sand la séparation des sphères est sacrée, inscrite dans la nature, et doit être maintenue, car l'ordre social en dépend.

(31)

My reading of the conclusion to *Indiana* supports Schor's view. Sand does indeed take the married romantic couple as a basic building block, confined within a household from which only the man may venture freely. I hope to have shown, however, that Sand's relationship to the division between public and private spheres is more complicated than Schor suggests. Sand's final glowing presentation of Indiana and Ralph's marriage hardly supplants completely the criticism of the institution we find in the rest of the novel. One critic's comment that *Indiana* constituted "un long cri contre le mariage" would seem to support this view.

If we move our focus away from Ralph and Indiana and toward the narrator in the volcanic landscape beyond the cabin, we discover a questioning of the public/private divide even in the conclusion to Sand's novel. I began my study of Sand with a consideration of her cross-voicing as a rhetorical strategy for transcending the barrier between public and private realms. The narrator in Sand's conclusion is both cross-voiced and cross-dressed (since he is now voice *and* body). "He" directs his words to Jules Neyraud, a naturalist whose work Sand draws on in her descriptions of île Bourbon: "Le sol avait conservé l'empreinte de vos pas" (331). Now the narrator's boots (presumably) like the ones Sand herself liked to wear are leaving their own impressions in the landscape. He is free to explore and record the private life of Indiana and Ralph but will return to the public world of France. Ralph tells him: "Allez jeune homme, poursuivez le cours de votre destinée; ayez des amis, un état, une réputation" (343).

Before arriving at Ralph and Indiana's cabin, the narrator comes across an intriguing phenomenon amidst the lavishly described tropical flora:

> Ces pierres volcaniques offrent souvent le même phénomène. Jadis leur substance, amollie par l'action du feu, reçut, tiède et malléable encore, l'empreinte des coquillages et des lianes qui s'y collèrent. De ces rencontres fortuites sont résultés des jeux bizarres, des impressions hiéroglyphiques, des caractères mystérieux, qui semblent jetés là comme le *seing* d'un être surnaturel, écrit en lettres cabalistiques.

(332-333)

The narrator stands transfixed in front of the incomprehensible language transcribed in the volcanic rock:

> Je restai longtemps dominé par la puérile prétention de chercher un sens à ces chiffres inconnus. Ces inutiles recherches me firent tomber dans une méditation profonde pendant laquelle j'oubliai le temps qui fuyait.

We might see in these hieroglyphs, as in Indiana's earlier hysterical symptoms, a female language that, in the nineteenth century, could be included in the narrative, only by moments, or in coded form.[47]

Notes

1. To my knowledge, Sand never makes mention of revolutionary women and the role they played in the events of 1789-1793. If she did know about them, it is highly unlikely she would have made any effort to associate herself with them. The cross-dressers and women involved in any way in the Revolution, had, by the nineteenth century, become symbols of the dangers associated with the disruption of the "natural" order. Cross-dressing was so threatening that it had already been reason for arrest before the Revolution under the terms of fraud. For an examination of cross-dressing in the eighteenth century, see Lynn Friedli, "'Passing Women': A Study of Gender Boundaries in the Eighteenth Century," in *Sexual Underworlds of the Enlightenment*, eds. G. S. Rousseau and Roy Porter (Chapel Hill: University of North Carolina Press, 1988), 234-60.

2. George Sand, *Histoire de ma vie* (Paris: Stock, 1945), 281.

3. That Sand was aware of this hostility to women is manifest in a letter written to her friend Charles Duvernet. She stresses the fact that, without the cover of a male name, she would have little hope of publishing in *La Revue,* given the editor's misogyny: "Il est bon que je vous dise que M. Véron, le rédacteur en chef de *La Revue* [*de Paris*] déteste les femmes et n'en veut pas entendre parler" (*Correspondance,* ed. Georges Lubin [Paris: Garnier frères, 1964], vol. 1, 784).

4. In fact, the spines of many late-nineteenth-century editions of Sand's works bear the name Dudevant rather than Sand. The fact that even the editors (and presumably admirers) of Sand's work felt impelled to associate this woman writer with her "real" name, that is, the name of her father or husband, rather than the name that she chose to identify herself by, bears witness to the tenacity of the need to categorize women according to "the name of the father" from which Sand was trying to escape. For a discussion of women writers and the complicated question of names, see Marie Maclean, *Name of the Mother* (London, New York: Routledge), 7-9; and DeJean *Tender Geographies,* 1-16.

5. Cited in Annarosa Poli, "George Sand devant la critique, 1831-1833," in *George Sand,* ed. Simone Vierne (Paris: Editions SEDES, 1983), 95, 96.

6. Ezdinli, *George Sand's Literary Transvestism,* iii.

7. George Sand, *Indiana* (Paris: Gallimard, 1984), 40. All subsequent references to *Indiana* and its prefaces will be to this edition, and page numbers will be cited parenthetically in the text.

8. The scene is then quite unlike the novels Georges May and Henri Coulet point to as typical of the genre at the end of the eighteenth century, novels that openly support bourgeois family values of which Marmontel's *Contes moraux* (1761, 1789-1792) are a striking example. In Sand's first preface she comments: "Si vous voulez absolument qu'un roman finisse comme un conte de Marmontel, vous me reprocherez peut-être les dernières pages" (39). She claims to write self-consciously against these late-eighteenth-century plots.

9. Delmare, entirely a creation of his position within the greater world, talks to Indiana "sur un ton moitié père, moitié mari." In the Freudian paradigm a woman falls in love with a man reminiscent of her father. This is an organizing principle of bourgeois plots on which Freud based his theory of the Oedipus complex. In a sense Indiana fits into this world (as did Julie in *La Nouvelle Héloïse*). She does marry someone reminiscent of her father. But in Sand's novel this father is hardly a revered figure. He is described as "un père bizarre et violent" (88) who neglected his daughter. We are told that when Indiana married she simply changed masters and prisons: "En épousant Delmare elle ne fit que changer de maître, en venant habiter Lagny que changer de prison et de solitude."

10. Clark, *Battle of the Bourgeois,* 170-71.

11. Poli, "George Sand devant la critique," 96.

12. This decision to use a male-gendered narrating voice has been seen by many recent critics as profoundly antifeminist in its impulse. One calls Sand's choice to use a male authorial voice "anathema to the feminist spirit" (Nancy Rogers, "George Sand and Germaine de Staël: The Novel as Subversion," in *West Virginia George Sand Conference Papers,* eds. Armand E. Singer et al. [Morgantown: West Virginia University, Dept. of Foreign Languages, 1981], 94). Another writes, "The mask that the novelist is compelled to wear denies her sexual identity, and, from this false stand, she writes about women in a distorted, unfaithful, and sometimes disloyal, fashion" (Pierrette Daly, "The Problem of Language in George Sand's *Indiana*," in *West Virginia George Sand Conference Papers,* eds. Armand E. Singer et al. [Morgantown: West Virginia University, Dept. of Foreign Languages, 1981], 26). And another: "To the most deeply rooted part of her self, Sand was as ruthless as any male model of exte-

rior domination she had encountered" (Erdmute Wenzel-White, "George Sand: She Who Is Man and Woman Together," in *West Virginia George Sand Conference Papers,* eds. Armand E. Singer et al. [Morgantown: West Virginia University, Depart. of Foreign Languages], 1981, 103). I would argue that the readings of these critics do not sufficiently account for the limitations placed on women writers during the early nineteenth century, nor the ways in which women like Sand were actually able to exploit the *form* of the constraints (male authorial voice, distance from female point of view, disclaimers, and so forth) to undermine the male domination of the profession and to present feminist alternatives.

13. In his *Dictionnaire* (1863-1872), Littré writes: "Private life should be lived behind walls. No one is allowed to peer into a private home or to reveal what goes on inside." Cited in Perrot, *Histoire de la vie privée,* vol. 4, 341.

14. This is true even though the money that fronted Delmare's manufacturing business came from Indiana's aunt, Mme de Carvajal.

15. Of these hysterical symptoms, René Doumic writes in 1909: "La femme incompromise . . . elle est pâle, elle est frêle, elle est sujette à s'évanouir. A la page 99, j'ai compté le troisième évanouissement; je n'ai pas compté plus loin. Ne croyez pas que ce soit l'effet d'une mauvaise santé! Mais c'est la mode" (*George Sand: Dix Conferences sur sa vie et son oeuvre,* [Paris: Perrin, 1909], 93).

16. In Charrière's *Lettres* we saw an exploration of the discipline of the marriageable female body, implicit in the bourgeois marriage plot. In Sand's novel we find an exploration of the constraints imposed on the female body in the bourgeois *post-marriage* plot.

17. Fauchery, *La Destinée féminine dans le roman européen du dix-huitième siècle,* 799.

18. Raymon at one point actually makes this explicit when he cries: "Elle s'est tuée, afin de me laisser l'avenir. Elle a sacrifié sa vie à mon repos" (184). But because Raymon's reaction is so blatantly self-interested, the event loses its poignancy.

19. A link between Noun's death in a plot concerning what the narrator calls "de bourgeois amours" and a larger economic system is suggested by the fact that she dies in the river whose water makes Delmare's manufacturing firm function; she is surrounded, moreover, by workers of the factory.

20. We find in this scene another instance of the narrator using cross-voicing. Interspersed with his

critique of Raymon's view of women, he actually takes Raymon's point of view of Indiana and borrows his voice: "Le principal charme des créoles, selon moi, c'est que l'excessive délicatesse de leurs traits et de leurs proportions leur laisse longtemps la gentillesse de l'enfance" (153). The male narrator adopts Raymon's perspective in this passage. He does so after systematically showing his reader that Raymon is, in fact, a despicable character. His words echo Raymon's hackneyed ideas about Créole women, but they do so with an ironic distance not present when Raymon's thoughts are transcribed directly. Again, the words in the narrator's mouth seem to almost parody Raymon's (and romantic literature's) obsession with virginal girl-children.

21. Though he always rationalizes his political views with a social justification—"Raymon soutenait sa doctrine de monarchie héréditaire, aimant mieux, disait-il, supporter les abus, les préjugés, toutes les injustices, que de voir relever les échafauds et couler le sang innocent" (167)—he supports the monarchy out of self-interest rather than abstract conviction.

22. We have seen that Sand's narrator moves in and out of omniscience. Sometimes, as is the case here, he knows everything. Other times he is more tentative: "Le gonflement de ses narines trahit je ne sais quel sentiment de terreur ou de plaisir" (161). This shifting allows Sand a certain ironic distance vis-à-vis her narrator.

23. "Comment eût-on pu persuader à ces jeunes appuis de la monarchie constitutionnelle que la constitution était déjà vieille, qu'elle pesait sur le corps social et le fatiguait, lorsqu'ils la trouvaient légère pour eux-mêmes et n'en recueillaient que les avantages? Qui croit à la misère qu'il ne connaît pas?" (130). Raymon's relationship with Indiana suggests the injustice of the constitution vis-à-vis "le corps social," as well as the injustice of relationships between men and women within such a system. Raymon is a grand exploiter of both the social body in his work, and of specific women's bodies in his private life. The love story doubled by a political allegory plays out dramatically the relationship between injustice at the level of public and private spheres.

24. Gérard Genette, *Figures II* (Paris: Seuil, 1969), 73-75.

25. Rousseau's *Emile* was condemned for its similarly iconoclastic views of God, particularly in the "Profession de foi" portion. For women, however, Rousseau felt that religion, regardless of whether it were true, was necessary to keep women firmly entrenched in their "natural" roles: "Quand cette

religion seroit fausse, la docilité qui soumet la mère et la fille à l'ordre de la nature efface auprès de Dieu le péché de l'erreur. Hors d'état d'être juges elles mêmes, elles doivent recevoir la décision des pères et des maris comme celle de l'Eglise" (*Emile*, 721).

26. "En 1832, la France subit les transformations de la révolution industrielle, connaît la misère urbaine, on est en plein saint-simonisme" (Frank Bowman, "La Nouvelle en 1832: la société, la misère, la mort et les mots," *Cahiers de l'association internationale des études françaises* 27 [1975]: 198).

27. "During this time, the Saint-Simonians were particularly active in Paris and Lyons, where they presented lectures several times a week to audiences that commonly numbered in the hundreds" (Claire Goldberg Moses, *French Feminism in the Nineteenth Century* [Albany: State University of New York, 1984], 45).

28. "De vives sympathies me lient de coeur et d'intention aux saint-simoniens; mais je n'ai pas encore trouvé une solution aux doutes de tout genre qui remplissent mon esprit et je ne pourrais en accepter aucune que je n'eusse bien examinée. . . . Comme je ne puis me défendre de l'intérêt et de la sympathie, je ne crains pas de déclarer que j'aime le saint-simonisme parce que l'avenir qu'il offre aux hommes est admirable de vigueur et de charité." Cited in Jehan d'Ivray, *L'Aventure saint-simonienne et les femmes* (Paris: Félix Alcan, 1930), 11.

29. Moses, *French Feminism in the Nineteenth Century*, 47.

30. Sailors brutally attack the dog as she swims after Indiana, who is clandestinely being rowed to the boat that will carry her to Raymon in France.

31. Cited in Ivray, *L'Aventure saint-simonienne*, 1.

32. Bernardin de Saint-Pierre was known as Bernardin during his lifetime.

33. Hunt, *Family Romance of the French Revolution*, 31.

34. Bernardin de Saint-Pierre, *Paul et Virginie* (Paris: Editions Gallimard, 1979), 1.

35. Ibid., 16.

36. Ibid., 58.

37. Rousseau instituted the modern father figure in *La Nouvelle Héloïse*. That the father figure in *Paul et Virginie* is left out in no way changes the novel's complicity with a bourgeois social structure. Lynn Hunt suggests that the absence of the father figure

in novels published during the revolutionary period played an important role in mitigating anxieties related to the removal of the king father-figure from his sacred place of power in the old regime. We might also note that, while no actual fathers are present, there is, much as in Rousseau's *Emile*, a tutor figure. This "vieillard" dispenses Rousseauian words of wisdom to his charge at intervals throughout the novel.

38. Goulemot, "Tensions et contradictions de l'intime dans la pratique des Lumières", 19.

39. Bernardin de Saint-Pierre, *Paul et Virginie*, 66.

40. Ibid., 102.

41. Jean-Marie Goulemot, "L'Histoire littéraire en question: l'exemple de Paul et Virginie," in *Etudes sur Paul et Virginie et l'oeuvre de Saint-Pierre*, ed. Jean-Michel Racault (Paris: Didier-Erudition, 1986), 203.

42. Before Ralph's story and after the exchange of letters between Indiana and Raymon, Sand's novel loops back into the Raymon-Indiana plot. Raymon, moved by Indiana's words, writes her a letter asking her to return to him. At great peril she does. Her trip takes months, and by the time she arrives in France, Raymon has forgotten all about his letter to her. In fact, confronted with "une société prête à se dissoudre," he is taken with a sudden urge for bourgeois comforts: "Raymon en tira cette conclusion, qu'il fallait à l'homme, en état de société, deux sortes de bonheur, celui de la vie publique et celui de la vie privée, les triomphes du monde et les douceurs de la famille" (262). He marries the daughter of the rich bourgeois who bought Lagny from M. Delmare, and the newly-weds are living there by the time Indiana arrives. Indiana enters her old bedroom and falls at the knees of Raymon, who had been reading. He is stupefied. Then, sensing an opportunity to ravish Indiana at last, moves to shut the door. Not quickly enough, however, for his wife enters and bids him to arrange Indiana's immediate departure. The coach leaves her at the pension where Ralph finds her.

43. This reference to Rousseau is interesting. Sand doubles Rousseau's "promeneur solitaire" to include a woman in this foray into a natural paradise. As we will see, however, this nominal inclusion of woman does not change the entirely Rousseauian presentation of the Ralph-Indiana marriage plot. Indiana's earlier solitary vagaries through the wilderness during her "promenades solitaires" (254) are far more suggestive of a truly new social vision.

44. In case we are not sufficiently moved by Ralph's story, or convinced this is the true marriage plot

as opposed to the "simulacrum légal" of the Delmare marriage, the narrator, addressing us directly, prods us into appreciation:

> Si le récit de la vie intérieure de Ralph n'a produit aucun effet sur vous, si vous n'en êtes pas venu à aimer cet homme vertueux, c'est que j'ai été l'inhabile interprète de ses souvenirs, c'est que je n'ai pas pu exercer non plus sur vous la puissance d'un homme profondément vrai dans sa passion.
>
> (329)

45. The couple's new life bears resemblance to the characters of another Bernardin novel, *La Chaumière indienne* [(1791)], the title of which actually makes up the final words of Sand's novel: "Souvenez-vous de notre chaumière indienne" (344). Sand has already waxed nostalgic about the privatized family earlier:

> Raymon apporta dans leur solitude toutes les subtilités de langage, toutes les petitesses de la civilisation. . . . C'est une grande imprudence d'introduire la politique comme passetemps dans l'intérieur des familles. Si il en existe encore aujourd'hui de paisibles et d'heureuses, je leur conseille de ne s'abonner à aucun journal, de ne pas lire le plus petit article de budget, de se retrancher au fond de leurs terres comme dans un oasis, et de tracer une ligne infranchissable entre elles et le reste de la société; car, si elles laissent le bruit de nos contestations arriver jusqu'à elles, c'en est fait de leur union et de leur repos.
>
> (170-71)

The irony here is that, by the time we read this passage, we have already seen what a disaster the Delmare family was before Raymon's arrival. The narrator seems to blame the disintegration on the "subtilités de langage" that Raymon introduces into the household, but we know there were serious problems in the Delmare family from the moment the novel opens.

46. Carol Richards argues just this: "Indiana's dependence on Ralph to supply her [vindication against conjugal tyranny], as well as to save her from the consequences of her own folly, mark the limits to which Sand's feminist thought was developed in this, her first novel" ("Structural Motifs and Limits of Feminism in Indiana," in *George Sand Papers,* ed. Natalie Datlof [New York: AMS Press, 1978], 19).

47. For another reading of Sand's ending and her use of the exotic landscape, see Nancy K. Miller, "Arachnologies: The Woman, the Text, and the Critic," in *Poetics of Gender,* ed. Nancy K. Miller (New York: Columbia University Press, 1986).

Works Cited

Bowman, Frank Paul. "La Nouvelle en 1832: la société, la misère, la mort et les mots." *Cahiers de l'association internationale des études françaises* 27 (1975): 189-208.

Charrière, Isabelle de. *Oeuvres complètes.* Eds. Jean-Daniel Candaux et al. Amsterdam: G. A. van Oorschot, 1979-1984.

Cixous, Hélène, and Catherine Clément. *La Jeune Née.* Paris: Unions générale d'éditions, 1975.

Clark, Priscilla. *Battle of the Bourgeois: The Novel in France, 1789-1848.* Paris: Librairie Marcel Didier, 1973.

Daly, Pierrette. "The Problem of Language in George Sand's *Indiana.*" In *West Virginia George Sand Conference Papers.* Eds. Armand E. Singer et al. Morgantown: West Virginia University, Department of Foreign Languages, 1981, 22-27.

DeJean, Joan. *Tender Geographies: Women and the Origins of the Novel in France.* New York: Columbia University Press, 1991.

Doumic, René. *George Sand: Dix Conferences sur sa vie et son oeuvre.* Paris: Perrin, 1909.

Ezdinli, Leyla. *George Sand's Literary Transvestism: Pre-texts and Contexts.* Ph.D. dissertation. Princeton University, 1987.

Fauchery, Pierre. *La Destinée féminine dans le roman européen du dix-huitième siècle 1713-1807, Essai de gynécomythie romanesque.* Paris: Armand Colin, 1972.

Friedli, Lynn. "'Passing Women': A Study of Gender Boundaries in the Eighteenth Century." In *Sexual Underworlds of the Enlightenment.* Eds. G. S. Rousseau and Roy Porter. Chapel Hill: University of North Carolina Press, 1988, 234-60.

Genette, Gérard. *Figures II.* Paris: Seuil, 1969.

Goulemot, Jean-Marie. "L'Histoire littéraire en question: l'exemple de Paul et Virginie." In *Etudes sur Paul et Virginie et l'oeuvre de Saint-Pierre.* Ed. Jean-Michel Racault. Paris: Didier-Erudition, 1986, 201-214.

————. "Tensions et contradictions de l'intime dans la pratique des Lumières", *Littérales* 17 (1995): 13-21.

Graffigny, Françoise de. *Lettres d'une Péruvienne et autres romans d'amour par lettres.* Eds. Bernard Bray and Isabelle Landy-Houillon. Paris: Flammarion, 1983.

Habermas, Jürgen. *Structural Transformation of the Public Sphere: An Inquiry into a Category of Bourgeois*

Society. Trans. Thomas Burger. Boston: Massachusetts Institute of Technology Press, 1989 (orig. *Strukturwandel der Öffentlichkeit: Untersuchungen zu einer Kategorie de bürgerlichen Gesellschaft.* Neuwied and Berlin: Hermann Luchterhand, 1962. Fr. trans. *L'Espace public: archéologie de la publicité comme dimension constitutive de la société bourgeoise.* Trans. Marc B. de Launay. Paris: Payot, 1978).

Hunt, Lynn. *The Family Romance of the French Revolution.* Berkeley: University of California Press, 1992.

Ivry, Jehan de. *L'Aventure saint-simonienne et les femmes.* Paris: Librairie Félix Alcan, 1930.

Maclean, Marie. *The Name of the Mother.* London and New York: Routledge, 1994.

Miller, Nancy K. "Arachnologies: The Woman, the Text, and the Critic." In *Poetics of Gender.* Ed. Nancy K. Miller. New York: Columbia University Press, 1986, 270-95.

Moses, Claire Goldberg. *French Feminism in the Nineteenth Century.* Albany: State University of New York Press, 1984.

Perrot, Michelle. *A History of Private Life: From the Fires of Revolution to the Great War.* Ed. Trans. Arthur Goldhammer. Vol. 4. Cambridge: Harvard University Press, 1990.

Poli, Annarosa. "George Sand devant la critique, 1831-1833." In *George Sand.* Ed. Simone Vierne. Paris: Editions SEDES, 1983, 95-100.

Richards, Carol V. "Structural Motifs and Limits of Feminism in *Indiana.*" In *George Sand Papers.* Eds. Natalie Datlof et al. New York: AMS Press, 1978, 12-20.

Rogers, Nancy. "George Sand and Germaine de Staël: The Novel as Subversion." In *West Virginia George Sand Conference Papers.* Eds. Armand E. Singer et al. Morgantown: West Virginia University, Department of Foreign Languages, 1981, 61-73.

Rousseau, Jean-Jacques. *Emile. Oeuvres complètes.* Eds. Bernard Gagnebin and Marcel Raymond. Vol. 4. Paris: Gallimard, 1969.

Saint-Pierre, Bernardin de. *Paul et Virginie.* Paris: Gallimard, 1979.

Sand, George. *Histoire de ma vie.* Paris: Editions Stock, 1945.

———. *Correspondance.* Ed. Georges Lubin. Vol. 1. Paris: Garnier frères, 1964.

———. *Indiana.* Paris: Gallimard, 1984.

Schor, Naomi. "Le Féminisme et George Sand: Lettres à Marcie." *Revue des sciences humaines* 226 (1992): 21-35.

Wenzel-White, Erdmute. "George Sand: She Who Is Man and Woman Together." In *West Virginia George Sand Conference Papers.* Eds. Armand E. Singer et al. Morgantown: West Virginia University, Department of Foreign Languages, 1981, 85-95.

Deborah Jenson (essay date 2001)

SOURCE: Jenson, Deborah. "Analogy: Slavery to Duplicity in Sand's *Indiana.*" In *Trauma and Its Representations: The Social Life of Mimesis in Post-Revolutionary France,* pp. 183-209. Baltimore: Johns Hopkins University Press, 2001.

[*In the following essay, Jenson problematizes Sand's use of analogy, particularly her overarching analogy between marriage and slavery, in* Indiana.]

The Colonial Social Life of Mimesis

In recent years, Homi Bhabha, Michael Taussig, Chris Bongie, and others have made the case that (what I would call) the *colonial* social life of mimesis is a drama of mimicry. The English literary figure of the "Mimic Man" stages the desire for "a reformed, recognizable Other, *as a subject of difference that is almost the same, but not quite.*"[1] Bhabha traces the line of descent of the mimic man through Kipling, Orwell, Naipaul, and Benedict Anderson. The mimic man is for Bhabha a feature of the post-Enlightenment English colonialism in which the civilizing mission typically yields texts rich in irony, repetition, and mimicry.

Taussig, examining naturalist and ethnographic texts of Euramerican encounter, focuses on a different dimension of mimicry, not the "native" mimic of colonial manners but the "mimicry by the colonizer of the savagery imputed to the colonized."[2] In this "colonial mirror of production," colonizers who have already diagnosed the inhabitants of the New World as possessing only rudimentary linguistic and cognitive skills (best suited to mimicry rather than language and thought) go on to "mimic" what they perceive as "savage violence." Taussig says, "The imaginative range essential to the execution of colonial violence in the Putumayo at the turn of the century was an imagining drawn from that which the civilized imputed to the Indians, to their cannibalism especially, and then mimicked" (65).

These two categories of colonial mimicry may have broad applicability, but they are drawn from specific historical contexts. The mimic man in English literature is a fiction of the subaltern in the late-nineteenth- and early-to-mid-twentieth-century imperial bureaucracy and Christian missions. The colonial mirror of production is the rationalization of a type of refractive "savagery" proper to frontiers into even the late twentieth century, when the extraordinary apparatus of Empire may have fragmented, yet localized conflicts between Indians and "poor peasant colonists" (63) persist. Colonial mimicry, in other words, is not just one game of charades, played by the same rules everywhere.

How does mimicry play out in the post-Revolutionary French social life of mimesis? In *Islands and Exiles,* Bongie, who reads mimicry in Victor Hugo's *Bug-Jargal,* theorizes that the post-Enlightenment "forked tongue" of the discourse of colonialism is particularly self-conscious in the French post-Revolutionary context. He argues that Hugo "globalizes" the "already well-established critique of colonial populations or primitive peoples as prone to imitation,"[3] extrapolating from the critique of imitation in colonial populations to the critique of representation itself. Bongie ties this extension of the paradigm of colonial mimicry to the lingering idealism of the French Revolution: "This postrevolutionary awareness of a contaminatory mimesis that cuts across supposedly fixed (e.g., racial) boundaries is the monstrous double of the Enlightenment belief in a commonly shared human nature into which we can all be educated and thus be (in Bernardin's phrase) 'reunited' despite all our differences" (245). This hypothesis that the French Revolution left the legacy of a more than usually "contaminatory" colonial mimesis is central to my reading in this chapter of Creole identity in George Sand's ***Indiana.*** I argue, consistently with Bongie's remarks, that the trope of colonial mimicry, hybridized with the post-Revolutionary trauma of likeness, spawns a colonial mimesis that pervades the spectrum of subject-object relations and makes French Romantic colonial texts more than usually duplicitous and self-contestatory. But instead of focusing on the paradigm of mimicry, I define my field rhetorically, as the Romantic interrogation of the mimetic politics linking analogy and slavery.

RHETORICAL POLITICS

Rhetoric has played such a primary role in late-twentieth-century theorizations of colonialism and race, from Henry Louis Gates through Toni Morrison and Bhabha, that one might wonder whether rhetoric provides a kind of linguistic parallel for mimicry itself. The key to this parallelism lies in the capacity of both rhetoric and mimicry to overdetermine *or* undermine essentialist identities.

Mimicry has a paradoxically anti-essentialist potential, in that, according to Bhabha, in the chapter "Of Mimicry and Man," in *The Location of Culture,* it is "constructed around an *ambivalence*; in order to be effective, mimicry must continually produce its slippage, its excess, its difference" (86). Mimicry thus destabilizes the notion of mimesis as the representation of reality or nature, casting mimesis as the performance of the clown

or the mime. Similarly, rhetoric can be used to transform any nonironic formulation of identity by means of exaggeration or cliché or countersymbolism; any essentialism of colonial or racial identity is subject to the operations of rhetoric.

Bhabha defines the desire of colonial mimicry along one particular rhetorical axis: the "*metonymy of presence*" (89). Metonymy contrasts with metaphor, where, as Barbara Johnson explains, "the substitution is based on resemblance or analogy"; in metonymy, the substitution is based "on a relation or association other than that of similarity (cause and effect, container and contained, proper name and qualities or works associated with it, place and event or institution, instrument and user, etc.)."[4] For Bhabha, mimicry as the metonymy of presence relies on the contiguity of plural and contradictory beliefs about such things as "the difference between being English and being Anglicized" and "the identity between stereotypes which, through repetition, also become different" (89-90). These contiguous associations have an accidental rather than a meaningful quality; Bhabha says that mimicry as the metonymy of presence is "an erratic, eccentric" strategy of colonial discursive authority.

But of course the traditional colonial discourse of mimicry ostensibly serves the purposes of domination, and rhetoric is also frequently associated with the creation of illusions of essentialist identity. James Snead, in *Figures of Division,* takes a startling approach when he subordinates racism itself to the purposes of rhetorical domination, as if the desire for rhetorical domination came first and racism then lent itself particularly well to the rhetorical project: "Racism might be considered a normative recipe for domination created by speakers using rhetorical tactics."[5] Toni Morrison, in *Playing in the Dark: Whiteness and the Literary Imagination,* likewise argues that the deployment of race as a figure is more threateningly politically consequential than "race" as biology: "Race has become metaphorical—a way of referring to and disguising forces, events, classes, and expressions of social decay and economic division far more threatening to the body politic than biological 'race' ever was."[6]

Both mimicry and rhetoric, in other words, represent the paradox that the mimetic construction of reality can easily be turned to the *construction of essentialism.* Artifice is required for the representation of authenticity. Critics and writers have long been fascinated with the politics of the capacity of rhetoric to design thought, to create a linguistic infrastructure of philosophical implication and affiliation. As a case in point, Bhabha's association of colonial mimicry with the politics of metonymy is hardly an isolated contemporary use of the paradigm of metonymy to configure an important problem of social reality. Johnson, in "Metaphor, Metonymy, and Voice in *Their Eyes Were Watching God*," problematizes the anomalous importance of metaphor and metonymy in the poststructuralist worldview: "How did it happen that such an arcane rhetorical opposition was able to acquire the brief but powerful privilege of dividing and naming the whole of human reality, from Mommy and Daddy or Symptom and Desire all the way to God and Country or Beautiful Lie and Sober Lucidity?" (155).

While rhetoric always has the privilege to "divide and name" the whole of human reality, different elements of rhetoric may be especially privileged in different eras and contexts. With regard to the mimetic treatment of colonialism in the racially conscious era of French social Romanticism, in the late 1820s, 1830s, and 1840s, Johnson's question could be phrased differently: How did it happen that *analogy* acquired the privilege of comparing and naming the problem of *slavery*? I broach this question through Charles Fourier's bizarre but influential paradigm of the politics of analogy.

THE ROMANTIC POLITICS OF ANALOGY AND THE RHETORIC OF SLAVERY

Analogy is conventionally defined as the rhetorical construction of correspondence between otherwise dissimilar things. But in Fourier's fantastical 1829 vision of *Le Nouveau Monde industriel* (*New Industrial World*), analogy also has didactic, metamorphic, political, and material powers. Consider the example of the humble beet, which offers itself for consumption under Fourier's system as a "vegetal hieroglyphic." Its vermilion juices make it a *"fruit de sang"* or "blood fruit," a status that evokes in turn "the image of slaves forced to the simple unity of action by torture."[7] Not only does the juice of the beet offer analogy to the expression of blood from slaves' tortured bodies, in other words, but the exploitation of that juice/blood in the making of beet sugar is analogous to the corruption of collective work ("l'unité simple d'action") by force. "The knotted leaf of the beet depicts the violent work of slaves and workers," he asserts. Sugar from the beet is therefore "a caricature of true sugar, just as the material unity of action in our colonial slave labor camps is a caricature of the passionate unity of harmonian works." In relation to the calorific "work" (analogous to the body at work in harmonian society) of the sugarcane, which yields a more concentrated sweetener, the beet's sugary violence is a *contre-sucre* or "countersugar"—superficially nutritive but fundamentally inferior to noncoercive and unbloodied unities of action.

The example of the beet illustrates Fourier's surreal use of analogy to transform simple things into intertexts, serving as a vast natural resource to be tapped for effective exegesis of the previously inscrutable "*great book of nature*" (366). As the poetico-industrial foundation of

the new economy of "Harmony," the inauguration of "this new *true, useful, and beautiful* science" (358) would lead even naturalists to condemn their existing epistemological systems. "Everyone," claims Fourier, "will rally to the analogy that marries two classifications." The inhabitants of the globe would exist in a flurry of impatience to learn analogies because of their "hidden properties" (357).

The prominence of slavery analogies in Fourier's formulation of the economy of the harmonian industrial world has its own complex rhetorical "unity of action." For Fourier, analogies have a homeopathic role as the "natural antidotes" to the maladies of civilization. "The logic of analogy . . . unveils all hypocrisy; it tears off civilized masks and proves that our alleged virtues are actually vices in the order of nature: Bernardin de St.-Pierre rightly named them '*frivolous and theatrical virtues*'" (366). Analogy in this sense serves as an extreme example of the Romantic trend toward what Théophile Gautier criticized as "useful art."

Fourier's vision of analogy as the foot soldier of the "harmony" at the center of Romantic social philosophy illustrates, if parodically, the stakes of "the social life of mimesis." Rhetoric, a foundational ingredient of verbal representation, was attributed revolutionary power in everything from patriarchal love relations to colonial subject relations in the utopian deliriums of France in the 1830s.

Analogy is the comparative structure at the foundation of metaphor; it unites two different terms by likeness in such a way that their relative difference or likeness is more defining than the qualities of either term by itself. Quintillian's famous example is "Peter is as strong as a lion." Analogy, like metaphor, is organized, as Roman Jakobson notes, by "various degrees of similarity,"[8] whereas metonymy operates on the axis of contiguity. Metaphor involves "selection and substitution"; metonymy involves "combination and contexture" (109). Unlike metaphor and metonymy, metaphor and analogy cannot be defined through opposition. The distinction between metaphor and analogy derives largely from the fact that in metaphor, the comparative basis of analogy is finessed, condensed; metaphor is a kind of abridged or elliptical form of reasoning by analogy. Quintillian defines metaphor as "a comparison without a comparative tool. Instead of saying 'Peter is as strong as a lion,' one says, 'Peter is a lion.'"[9]

Jakobson established that "Romanticism is closely linked with metaphor, whereas the usually intimate ties of Realism with metonymy usually go unnoticed" (114). Not *all* of Romanticism can be affiliated with metaphor, however. Metaphor is a dominant epistemology in Romantic lyricism, for instance in the early work of Lamartine or Musset, and in the prose genres most closely related to metaphoric lyricism, notably the *genre intime* (intimate writings). But as Romanticism in France became *social,* Quintillian's "comparative tool" became essential to literary construction. The social consciousness of Romanticism could not derive its examples and identifications from the space of solipsistic consciousness; it relied, instead, on comparisons *between* rich and poor, male and female, and master and slave.

Jakobson considered poetic language to be privileged over everyday speech in the exercise of linguistic freedom: "In the combination of linguistic units, there is an ascending scale of freedom. In the combination of distinctive features into phonemes, the freedom of the individual speaker is zero: the code has already established all the possibilities which may be utilized in the given language. Freedom to combine phonemes into words is circumscribed; it is limited to the marginal situation of word coinage. In forming sentences with words, the speaker is less constrained" (98). The activities of selection or substitution, combination and contexture, allow the speaker to play with the elements of the "code" and thereby achieve a limited degree of linguistic autonomy.

But analogy, which by this description would be a strong manifestation of linguistic freedom, is nevertheless characterized by the "chaining" of one term to another. In comparative formulas, one term cannot get free of the other, even though one may dominate the other. Such dramas of freedom, comparativity, and dominance are common to the analogical literature of social Romanticism. Analogy is, after all, the construction of a sort of paradoxical double subject. If Peter is as strong as a lion, the lion is presumably as strong as Peter. But even if the lion takes Peter's place as grammatical subject, the lion only exists in the phrase to describe Peter.

Fourier's choice of the beet and slavery to illustrate the powers of analogy resonates with this drama. The *politics* of slavery are in a sense metaphorical of the *politics* of analogy. Slavery compels analogy. The negative transformation of human existence into a walking exchange value signifies that the yoke of comparison, the insertion of the slave into a system or at least a pairing of values, is necessary to the constitution of slavery as a value. In Marxist terms, slavery is to analogy as the commodity is to exchange; both the slave and the commodity depend on their harnessing to other, dissimilar, terms, such as *freedom,* for their entry into a system of value. Or in Hegelian terms, the master consciousness depends on the consciousness of the slave.

However, even if slavery depends on another term, such as *freedom,* for its freedom from the negation of total abstraction, this animation of value through comparison is not in itself identificatory. The identity conferred

upon slavery through analogy is also the subordination of identity to comparison. Slavery, in this sense, may *compel* analogy, but analogy also *contains* slavery; analogy yokes slavery to another term.

Discussions of Fourier's analogical thought often return to such problems of rhetorical politics. Michael Spencer writes in "A(na)logie de Fourier" ("Fourier's A(na)logy") that "Fourier, enemy of hierarchies, democratizes metaphor."[10] In Fourier's philosophy, "everything is linked to everything else and everything is explained by analogy," especially the relationships between "the social movement and other movements." Analogy in Fourier's work is a metaphor for "association," "association being founded on the properties of the passions" (31). Analogy is the rationale for social linkage, in which hierarchy dissolves in intimacy.

This "democratization" has to do with the equality Fourier ascribes to both terms in any given analogical identification. Spencer notes that "the pitfall of traditional metaphoric practice is the subordination of the *comparant* (the comparing term) to the *comparé* (the compared term). In the case of the metaphor 'this man is a lion,' the lion is 'used' by the man, the seme 'courage' is extracted from the comparison, and the animal, who has no further utility, is rejected from the comparison." Spencer argues that Fourier's analogies avoid the sacrifice of one term to the constitution of value in the other, even if it is an avoidance based on chaos, on a-logic, and on the arbitrary proliferation of analogical significance: "This never happens with Fourier, first of all because the dissemblance between the *comparant* and the *comparé* is such that it guarantees their independence and prevents this type of exploitation; and secondly because, even as independent 'agents,' they participate in the creation of *other* analogies. The subordination of one term to the other is impossible" (42).

Fourier's use of "root" analogies like the "slave" beet are meant to function as "natural antidotes" to colonial slavery by making it accessible to consciousness, giving it a new cognitive circulation. "Let us perform the drama of the beet," proposes Fourier. "This plant will explain to us one of the methods to follow in the search for analogies, the rule of the contact of extremes" (355). The notions of *race* and *racine* or "root" may not be etymologically linked, yet the implied parallel between the philological, the political, and the organic in the example of the beet suggest that something in language and its relation to the mute world, the world devoid of linguistic representation, is responsible for generating a mutually exegetic field.

Fourier's democratization of metaphor through analogical thought can only go so far, however, as he gives each analogy a scientific stability. Analogy, for Fourier, is a form of *knowledge.* The beet is enslaved to its colonial identification,[11] and in a sense, slavery is overshadowed by the beet. Once the beet has become the slave hieroglyphic, the historical association of sugarcane with the blood of slaves in the colonies can never become "emblematic." Even in the chaotic profusion of images, there is tyranny and tradition in many of Fourier's analogies: "The rose depicts the modest virgin; the carnation depicts the girl harried by the need for love" (354).

Fourier's cult of analogical knowledge is also profoundly challenged by the modern psychological finding that in scientific experiments, "subjects can solve randomly generated analogies."[12] Michael Johnson and Tracy Henley "had subjects solve incomplete randomly generated analogies of the form 'Horse is to girl as sun is to——'" (56). The subjects generally were able to "generate valid analogy solutions." The researchers were left with the "unresolved antinomy in which the demonstrated fact of 'almost infinite flexibility' clashes with the need for some form of structural stability." Randomness is a "freedom" Fourier did not want to grant to analogy.

Although Fourier had noticed the ability of people to solve analogies, he contextualized this ability in terms of the discovery of knowledge essential to the new harmonian industrial society. He was convinced that analogy could actually produce wealth—for anyone, slave or freeman, one might add, endowed with the power of analogical thought. Since the book of established analogies would be a bestseller into perpetuity, "*devoured*" (377) at each printing, men and women would have only to contribute a single analogy, written up in say forty lines, to the definitive gloss on the rhetoric of the world, in order to earn "500,000 francs" (357). Analogy would therefore supply an abundant epistemological and financial capital, and a prolific creator of analogies would live very well indeed.

THE RHETORICAL POLITICS OF "CREOLE" IDENTITY

George Sand was powerfully drawn in the late 1820s and 1830s to the Fourierist and Saint-Simonian visions, above all for their articulations of women's rights and the legitimacy of free love. She was also chronically concerned as a single mother with issues of revenue per page; perhaps she had the model of the analogical "slave" beet in mind when she made the seductions of slavery *by* analogy—slavery as an analogy for marriage—a recurrent characteristic and theme of her first novel, **Indiana.** Published in 1832, **Indiana** tells the story of the life, loves, and protests of an upper-class Creole woman, Indiana, in relation to a social hierarchy in which she was simultaneously the dominated (husband/wife, seducer/fallen woman) and the dominator (mistress/servant or slave).

The term "créole" is a particularly obscure signifier in nineteenth-century France. Christopher Miller describes its complicated history: "A 'Creole' in its original meaning was 'a person born or naturalized in the country [usually the West Indies or other tropical dependency] but of European (usually French or Spanish) or of African Negro race: *the name having no connotation of color,* and in its reference to origin being distinguished on the one hand from being born in Europe or Africa and on the other hand from being aboriginal' (*OED*; emphasis mine). The word thus speaks of a double differentiation or exile and opens the question of race while distinctly providing no answer to it."[13] It is supposed to derive its meaning metonymically, which is to say, following Jakobson's classifications, along the axis of contiguity: to be Creole ostensibly signifies nothing more than association with a *place*—being born in the colonies, notably the *Antilles,* the West or East Indies. In fact, the term *Creole* initially designated specifically persons of white European descent. But because these places were under colonial rule, and because they relied on slaves as tools in their economy of agriculture and trade, *race* comes to elbow *place* in the semantic axis of contiguity. Because of this secondary metonymical association of place with slavery, the axis of contiguity yields to the axis of the condensation of meaning, and point of origin—place—becomes metaphorically colored—colored as race.

This slippage between the identification of master and slave, which seems historically anomalous, nevertheless parallels the rhetorical politics of "white" and "black" neighborhoods as analyzed by Johnson in "Metaphor, Metonymy, and Race": "The tendency of contiguity to become overlaid by similarity, and vice versa, may be summed up in the proverb 'Birds of a feather flock together'—'qui se ressemble s'assemble.' One has only to think of the applicability of this proverb to the composition of neighborhoods in America to realize that the question of the separability of similarity from contiguity may have considerable political implications" (157). As Miller says in his analysis of work by Baudelaire, "The surprise . . . is that there is no question of a real racial distinction to be made between white Frenchmen and white Creoles, yet every sign points in that direction" (94). These signs include the "'physical personality' of the Creole," including "'fragility,' the shape of the forehead, the quality of the gaze" (95), "'velvet eyes'" (94), and a "'black and yet luminous'" (100) quality, apparently in reference to hair or eyes, or both.

Such descriptions of the non-biologically based observation of mixed-race attributes in the white Creole in nineteenth-century French literature may be rooted above all in the *racialization of the mimetic faculty.* Miller notes the importance of Baudelaire's description of "a natural faculty of imitation, which they share with

Negroes." The truism of the imitative primitivism of the "savage," when extended to the white of non-European birth, suggests either that *imitativeness is environmentally derived* or that "racial" *imitativeness has a mimetic contagion that extends to others in the same environment* and transcends race. In either case, the inhabitants of the colonial dependencies are irresistibly imitative; they live under the mimetic spell of a mimetic land.

The condensation of similarity at work in this notion of Creole mimeticism means that the comparative axis of analogy is necessarily destabilized in analogies involving *créolité*. Analogy, conventionally defined as the rhetorical construction of correspondence between otherwise dissimilar things, is problematized by *créolité* because one cannot tell exactly *what créolité is* dissimilar *to*. If *créolité* in nineteenth-century France is effectively the metaphoricization of race, it should be an analogy buster, since analogy relies on a stable nonmimetic relation between the terms in question.

Ironically (or perhaps it is not so surprising given that the Creole in nineteenth-century literature seems to figure the fascination with figuration), George Sand uses *créolité* as the backdrop for obsessive fictions of analogical identity in ***Indiana.***

The plot of ***Indiana*** makes central use of the slippage inherent in the term "créole." On the one hand, the two major female characters seem virtually to divide up between themselves the disjunctive extremes of the clichés of Creole identity, along the axes of Indiana's unhealthy psychological susceptibility (encoded as white) and Noun's sexual red-bloodedness (encoded as mixed race). Indiana is described as "une créole nerveuse et maladive"[14] (a nervous Creole in poor health),[15] while her servant, Noun, is characterized as "overflowing with the full-blooded ardour and passion of a Creole" (25).

Nevertheless, as the text progresses, even the man who is intimately involved with them both will not always be able to tell them apart, putting their racial difference into question. Naomi Schor notes, "No more than it can be ascertained whether Indiana is a virgin or not, can one assert that Noun is black or white." And yet, she says, most readers "assume that she is black."[16] Of course, by the terms of Christopher Miller's analysis of the Creole, it should also be clear that Indiana's whiteness may be mimetic of blackness, adding to the confusion.

Doris Kadish points out that "toward the end of the novel, Indiana's cousin and eventual soul mate Ralph Brown refers in passing to Noun as 'créole dans l'acception la plus étendue,' but without spelling out this more extended sense of the term."[17] Sand deepens the ambiguity of racial difference within the category of the Creole by referring to Noun as the "soeur de lait" (60) or "milk sister" of Indiana. Although this expression is often translated as "foster sister" (25), it also suggests that Indiana and Noun were nursed by the same woman, who, as Kadish notes, *is* identified as black in the novel. Noun, says Kadish, "may have been the daughter of the wet-nurse and thus black or of mixed race . . . Indiana was nurtured with the non-white, racially 'other' milk of her wet nurse and is thus partially non-white, too . . . the suggestion that milk was connected with racial purity is not without historical precedent" (24). The category of the "milk sister" could also explain the text's ambiguity concerning Noun's legal status as servant or slave. Moreau de Saint-Méry in his 1797 *Description* of the French part of Haiti described the prevalence of wet nursing of Creole children by slaves. He conflates "blood" and "milk" in his description of the wet nurse's sacrifice and notes that wet nurses were commonly freed in payment for their services: "Creole women are reduced to soliciting from a slave the sacrifice of her blood to conserve the being to whom they were only able to give life. But their children are fed under their very eyes; the Creoles have to win their children's caresses away from the nurse who is almost always emancipated as the price of this good deed."[18]

In the same measure that the *difference* between Indiana and Noun is both proposed and deconstructed in the text, the *likeness* between them is both highlighted and problematized through an endlessly reiterated analogy between marriage and slavery. Just as both women are "Creole" in ***Indiana,*** even though one is white and one is probably not, both women are "slaves," even though one is the daughter of a slave-owning family and the other had probably been either a slave herself or the daughter of former slaves.

"LE SANDISME" AND RHETORICAL BONDAGE

Because she is married, Indiana sees herself as "this enslaved woman who was only waiting for a sign in order to break her chain" (52). The oppressiveness of marriage makes marital resistance "sweet and legitimate to the oppressed slave." She complains that she cannot "patiently endure the yoke which is crushing me," the yoke of a marriage in which "I am his servant; he asks nothing more of me" (159). Indiana's husband, Monsieur Delmare, is, as Schor writes, the "instantiation of an idea, the Law, which reduces women to the status of objects of exchange, to the abjection of virtual slaves" (xiii).

In this Sand, as an "emancipated muse of love," echoed not only the Fourierist cult of analogy in general but also the specific Saint-Simonian analogy between both free love and free labor and marriage and slavery. As Claire Moses and Leslie Rabine note, the feminist exploitation of the ideas of the comte de Saint-Simon, as interpreted by Enfantin, had by the late 1820s "begun to emphasize the more romantic elements of his work and especially his ideas for a 'new religion' based on love. Woman and the sociosexual relationship between the sexes then emerged as the movement's chief concern."[19] For a time, Sand gained notoriety as a kind of informal spokesperson for this socialist utopia.

The early-twentieth-century critic Marcel Bouteron summarized, for the entertainment of his readers, the scandal of Sand's fictionalization of social utopian theories: "Enfantin's completely wild theories on love and marriage, passing via the pen of George Sand, sowed great disorder in feminine souls. . . . Saint-Simon wanted to reform society, the human race; he wanted to deliver women, the proletariat, the oppressed, and to inaugurate on this lowly earth the reign of happiness through communal work and love."[20]

Bouteron called the wide-ranging influence of Sand's association of "l'amour libre" with the cause of freedom from marital slavery "le Sandisme." The expression dates to an article by Balzac in the *Muse du département* in which Balzac criticized his friend Sand for propagating legions of a feminine type he labels "'le bas-bleu du coeur'" (cited in Bouteron, 178). Sandism was a "sentimental leprosy" in which women make their marital complaints into a "claim to genius." So widespread was the critique of *le Sandisme* in the nineteenth century that Sand's husband, Casimir Dudevant, on whom the figure of Monsieur Delmare is partly based, felt justified in asking Napoleon III for the cross of the legion of honor on the basis of his endurance of "'conjugal woes of historical dimensions'" (179).

The 1830s were in fact an era of remarkable feminism. Feminist journals, including the *Journal des femmes, L'Opinion des femmes, La Mère de famille, Le Conseiller des femmes, La Gazette des femmes, Le Globe, La Femme libre, La Phalange,* and the *Phalanstère* theorized that a new politics of love was necessary to the revolutionary transformation of the social order. George Sand, along with writers and politicians such as Jeanne Deroin, Flora Tristan, and Pauline Roland,[21] was an important theorist of the meaning of domestic politics for the questions that had previously been defined only in terms of the "public" sphere. Many women were inspired by the insistence of utopian theorists that economic ills and social injustices could not be remedied until a fundamental corruption of gender relationships had been redressed. Fourier's community of the Phalange was intended to undo the perfidious effects of patriarchal hierarchy on society by instituting free love. Enfantin, the primary disseminator of the ideology of Saint-Simon, wrote in 1829, "The Saint-Simonian era will be announced BY THE COMPLETE ENFRANCHISEMENT OF WOMEN."[22]

Within this climate of utopian upheaval, an 1832 debate in the Saint-Simonian *Journal des femmes,* whose contributors included not only Sand but also many of the other leading *femmes de lettres* of the day, demonstrated the new analogical currency of the terms *slavery* and *liberty* with regard to marriage. Suzanne Voilquin, in a letter to the editor, rages against a previous article that she views as having been "dictated by the genius of the feudal centuries, . . . [telling us] in the 19th-century, after two great revolutions, 'Women, let us keep our slavery as it is.'" If the writer of that article had been "from the proletarian ranks, like my sisters and me, she would know this slavery that weighs on woman!"[23]

Voilquin illustrates the literal applicability of the term *slavery* to marriage in an anecdote from her own social experience. "The husband of one of my friends, outraged to hear talk of liberty, of the emancipation of women, formally declared to his wife that he regarded her as '*his* thing, *his* property, and that he would *punish* in her all women who might wish to escape from a too oppressive yoke'" (215). Another writer, Marie Reine, also invokes the backlash against the ideological prominence of the notion of marital slavery: "We are told that we have not demonstrated sufficiently clearly *how it is that we are slaves.*"[24]

The Mimetic Trauma of Slavery

In *Indiana,* this theme of marriage as a form of slavery by analogy recurs with such numbing force that it produces a political mutation: the term *slavery* virtually sacrifices its meaning to the term *marriage.* The referential mutability or subordination of slavery through the vehicle of the marriage analogy is troublingly exemplified in Indiana's use of first-person plural personal and possessive pronouns when she describes the suffering of her own slaves on the Île Bourbon:

> Living in the midst of slaves, for whom she had no other aid, no other consolation than her compassion and her tears, she had become accustomed to saying, "A day will come when everything will be changed in my life, when I will do good for others; a day when someone will love me; . . . while waiting, *let us* suffer, *let us* keep our silence; let us save *our* love for whoever will deliver *me*."
>
> (89, from French text; my translation and italics)

> [Vivant au milieu des esclaves, pour qui elle n'avait d'autre secours, d'autre consolation que sa compassion et ses larmes, elle s'était habituée à dire: "Un jour viendra où tout sera changé dans ma vie, où je ferai du bien aux autres; un jour où l'on m'aimera, . . . en attendant, *souffrons*; *taisons-nous*; et gardons *notre* amour pour récompense à qui *me* délivrera."]

Indiana's helpless empathy for her father's slaves involves the substitution of her own emotional agency for theirs. The slaves operate as a kind of Greek chorus for her own dramas of emotional liberation. Indiana exhibits the Romantic "pathology" of mimetic trauma, in which the sufferings of the social "other" become the paradoxical stuff of narcissism. In this part of the text, slaves are referred to in effect to "perform" Indiana's own sense of oppression and suffering. It is an unequal mimetic analogy, however, a potentially traumatic form of mimesis for the fictional slave who might be unable to accept the mistress's marital woes as a proxy for his or her own experiences.

Indiana's very name suggests an identity more "Indian" than that of the residents of the Île Bourbon themselves; Noun refers to herself once as "la pauvre Indienne" (99), but the white Creole's name appropriates Indianness. By contrast, the name Noun suggests the proper name in the abstract, the English *noun* that is the French *nom*, homophonous with the negative *non, no*. Throughout the novel, Indiana creates a communal identification through introjection and projection of slave characteristics, but she incidentally renders race unreadable. The married white woman becomes a sort of *master slave.*

Appropriation of the term *slavery* to describe other, less drastic, forms of oppression had been popularized during the Revolution. Srinivas Aravamudan, in *Tropicopolitans: Colonialism and Agency, 1688-1804,* notes that Jean-Paul Marat's best-seller *Les Chaînes de l'esclavage (The Chains of Slavery)* "uses the word *esclavage* to discuss metropolitan politics—while being completely oblivious to the colonial referent of the word."[25] French deputies used the term *esclaves* to describe the status of the French until colonial issues arose, at which point the term was sporadically replaced by the euphemism "unfree persons."

The politics of slavery in Sand's use of the term are crossed with the trope of being a "slave to love." It is intuitive that any analogy in which slavery is a term would have two negative poles, as in "marriage is like slavery," but Sand alternatively uses slavery as an analogy for Indiana's *willing* subjugation to desire in love: "It's me, it's your Indiana; it's your slave, whom you recalled from exile . . . to love and serve you" (231). The interchangeability of the positive and negative connotations of slavery ("you would have loved me too and would have blessed your chains" [56]) in regard to love is emphasized in the ironic reversibility of master and slave subject positions in Raymon's amorous paradoxes: "On awakening, Indiana, you would have found me at your feet, guarding you like a jealous master, serving you as a slave" (56).

Through these constructions and deconstructions of likeness, of the psychology of mimesis, the novel problematizes the effect of empathic resemblance on difference. The erasure of race through the marriage/slavery and love/slavery analogies is dramatized with many twists and turns in the novel through the obscurities of the resemblance and identification between Indiana and Noun. The development of this *doppelgänger* structure symbolizes both the violence and the altruism of analogy in social and literary relations with the cultural other.

Both women, Indiana and Noun, love the same man, Raymon, who embodies racial, gender, and class prejudices and whose speech veils the violence of prejudice with linguistic seductions. He seems to savor the drama of Indiana's language of marital abolitionism, and he certainly knows how to talk the talk: "Indiana! Men and their iron laws have disposed of you" (57). But in considering the two women's attraction to him, he ruminates to himself on the greater deliciousness of an upper-class wife's self-immolation in love: "The wife of a peer of France who sacrificed herself in that way would be a prized conquest; but a lady's maid! What is heroism in the one becomes impudence in the other" (38).

The novel reminds us again and again not to trust Raymon's ability to use Indiana's sincere speech for his own selfish purposes: "She had fits of anxiety and terror, thinking that perhaps all these grand, noble sentiments, so well expressed, were only a pompous display of words, the ironic fluency of a lawyer" (126). Raymon's speech is attributed more mastery over the Creole, white or not white, than over the European woman who is in a less mimetic rapport to slavery: "Women of France, you do not know what [being] a Creole is like. No doubt you would have been convinced less easily, for you are not the one who is being deceived and betrayed!" (103).

In contrast to Raymon, when Indiana discourses on her "slave" status to her husband, saying, "I know I'm the slave and you're the lord. The law of the land has made you my master. You can tie up my body, bind my hands, control my actions" (176), he responds, interestingly enough, "Be quiet. . . . Your novelistic language annoys us" (177). The fact that Raymon, who represents only a duplicitous affective and sensual investment in the cultural other, is occasionally moved by the slave/wife analogy, while Indiana's unpleasant husband identifies it as the stuff of literary cliché, signals the depth of the novel's ambivalence toward the politics of its own identifications.

The novel's problematization of the slavery/marriage analogy is developed through the doubling of Indiana and Noun in relation to Raymon. Noun, who is pregnant with Raymon's illegitimate child, is unaware of Raymon's growing interest in her mistress, just as Indiana is unaware that Raymon has seduced Noun. This love triangle plot becomes a triangulation of *mirroring* among the three characters. The mimetic trauma of the marriage/slavery analogy is developed as a trauma of specularity.

THE COLONIAL MIRROR STAGE

Noun, in this humiliating innocence of her real competition, dresses up virtually *as* Indiana one night: "Noun thought of a way of making herself more attractive to him. She decked herself out in her mistress's finery" (60). She leads her lover to Indiana's room for their tryst and Raymon, at the sight of her there in Indiana's mirror, is momentarily unable to distinguish between mistress and servant: "The cloaked woman . . . was perhaps Indiana herself. This absurd idea seemed to be confirmed when he saw a white, bejeweled figure appear in the mirror in front of him, the ghost of a woman, who, entering a ballroom, casts aside her cloak to reveal herself, radiant and half-naked in the brilliant lights" (62).

The suggestion here that Noun's nakedness is "white" may be paradoxical, particularly given that once Raymon has recovered from his confusion, Noun is no longer described as white but as an exotic, and therefore dark, creature: "She put her young, brown arms around him, she covered him with her long hair, her large black eyes looked at him with the burning languor, the ardent temperament, and the oriental sensuality which can overcome all efforts of the will" (64). Yet perhaps Noun is white in her radiance after all, since after Raymon has succumbed, against his best intentions, to Noun's dark charms, his confusion is renewed and amplified, made into a prism of conflicting identifications.

> The two mirrored panels reflected Noun's image endlessly from one to the other and seemed peopled by a thousand phantoms. In the depths of this double reflection he espied a more slender form, and in the last dim, blurred shadow, which was Noun's reflection in it, he thought he could see the slender, willowy form of Madame Delmare.
>
> (64)

> [Les deux panneaux de glace qui se renvoyaient l'un à l'autre l'image de Noun jusqu'à l'infini semblaient se peupler de mille fantômes. Il épiait dans la profondeur de cette double réverbération une forme plus déliée, et il lui semblait saisir, dans la dernière ombre vaporeuse et confuse que Noun y reflétait, la taille fine et souple de Madame Delmare. . . .]

Or conversely, perhaps Indiana's often-reiterated paleness is not entirely an effect of whiteness, since Raymon, who no longer sees in Noun anything more than the charm of Indiana's clothing—"all that Raymon saw of her was Indiana's dress"—goes on to confuse Noun's dark traits with those of Indiana: "When he kissed her black hair, he believed he was kissing Indiana's black hair" (64).

If Indiana and Noun are in fact of different racial backgrounds, as the novel suggests, this cross-racial prism presents an interesting twist on the Lacanian mirror stage, which, in Frantz Fanon's *Black Skin, White Masks* becomes a colonial mirror stage. Fanon, unlike Lacan, is intrigued by the problem of psychology ("internalization") conceptualized on the level of skin ("epidermalization").[26] Homi Bhabha's reading of Fanon's colonial mirror stage insists that epidermalization should not function as a "fixed phenomenological point" but rather as "the necessary negation of a primordial identity" that "enables the 'cultural' to be signified as a linguistic, symbolic, historic reality."[27] Henry Louis Gates notes that Bhabha "wants Fanon to mean Lacan rather than, say, Jean-Paul Sartre," meaning that he is more interested in finding a poststructuralist critique of identity in Fanon than an existential colonial alienation. In Sand's ***Indiana,*** the colonial prism raises questions of psychological "epidermalization"; however, any Manichean distinctions are blurred not only by Creole ambiguities but also by the refraction of gender and class in the love triangle. We do not know how Noun sees herself or how Indiana sees herself; we only know how Raymon sees and desires the one when he thinks he is seeing the other.

Noun's resemblance to her mistress and Indiana's resemblance to her servant is also a device that serves as the double of the marriage/slavery analogy. In the eyes of the man who is attracted to both women, Noun's race becomes literally undecipherable in the text. What *is* decipherable is that Indiana's "slavery" as a married upper-class woman is far more potent in its seductions than Noun's more literal servitude. Incredibly, the text informs us that Noun would have been more appealing than her mistress had Indiana not had, "to make her more beautiful, her slavery and her suffering" (103, my translation).

Lacking *figurative* slavery to redeem her literal servitude and make her appealing to Raymon, Noun, in an Ophelia-like scene, drowns herself. The poignancy of the Shakespearean quotation is rendered much more bitter by the fact that Indiana's *dog* is actually named Ophelia. The binding of tragic heroine to dog is yet another marker of Sand's resistance to her own analogies. The dog Ophelia, the dogness of the abandoned woman, the creature quality of the feminine, is hard to kill: much later in the text Indiana, fleeing her husband's abuse, watches sailors crush the dog's skull as she tries to swim after her mistress. Noun drowns like Shakespeare's Ophelia; the dog Ophelia drowns like Sand's Noun.

After the self-immolation of her unprivileged double, Indiana, in an accusing reversal of Noun's attempt to seduce through resemblance to her mistress, puts her own seductiveness to the test by imitating her dead servant to Raymon. It is a scene that underscores her status as both a Creole and the double of Noun: "She risked her whole fate on a strange, subtle test that Raymon could not be on his guard against" (138). She cuts off Noun's black hair and puts it on the floor in front of her as though she had just cut her own hair, and she dresses in the same mantle that Noun had worn to a meeting with Raymon just before drowning herself, the meeting at which Raymon had earlier confused Noun with her mistress. When Raymon first perceives Indiana in this guise, he flashes back to his earlier confusion, which is now transformed into the inverse confusion—he now believes that Indiana is the drowned Noun: "I don't know if you remember that Raymon had had then, for a moment, the improbable idea that the woman wrapped up and concealed in the cloak was Madame Delmare. Now, . . . he drew back involuntarily. He stayed at the door, fixing his frightened gaze on the motionless figure and trembling like a coward in case, when it turned around, it would reveal the livid features of a drowned woman" (139).

The relation of Raymon's "horrified gaze" to the myth of the Medusa's head is underscored by what happens next, but this is a Medusa of cross-racial likeness as well as phallic castration: Indiana "had tied a scarf of Indian silk loosely round her head in the Creole manner. It was Noun's usual head-covering" (139). Because of the scarf, it is plausible to Ramon that Indiana has cut off her own hair. He picks up the fallen hair and "he experienced, too, an indefinable nervous shudder when he felt it was cold and heavy, as if it had already been cut a long time" (140). Death is added to the brew of sex and race in the "castrated" locks: "And then he examined it closely and sought in vain for the blue sheen which made it look like a crow's blue-tinged wing. This hair was completely black, like Indian hair, heavy and lifeless." While Indiana watches him, Raymon becomes aware of the deception, crying, "It's not yours!" and tears the scarf off her head to confirm that her hair is intact. Indiana continues to show him the cut locks and demands, "Don't you recognize that hair, then? Have you never admired it, never caressed it?" (140). Raymon faints dead away onto the floor. When he awakens, a contrite Indiana is kneeling beside him, begging his forgiveness. But having passed through this not-so-fun hall of mirrors, the text informs us, "Raymon no longer loved her" (141).

As a woman humiliated in love through the drama of her morbid resemblance to a rejected rival, Indiana's recuperative identification with slaves suddenly reverses and becomes "une effrayante parité" (200), an appalling parity: "In such a future I can see only a frightening equality with Noun" (147), she writes to Raymon.

It is ironic that it is in the shift from marital to adulterous relationships that the politics of slavery by analogy shift from the emancipatory to the exploitative. Marriage as a legal construct privileging patriarchy is critiqued in the analogy with slavery, but Indiana's own tyranny emerges in the context of illicit love.

The referential mutability of slavery in *Indiana* through the operations of analogy—*who* is really the slave? is the slave the master or the slave? does the slave love slavery? and is the slave black or white?—casts doubt on the "harmonious" Fourierist capacity of analogy to transform discrete things into relations. The omnipresent vocabulary of "chains" in *Indiana* not only liberally links the problem of slavery to the problems of love and marriage; it also performs what is arguably the violence of harnessing difference to likeness. As Schor notes, the reader's typical assumption that there is a racial difference between Indiana and Noun is subtly informed by the obviousness of class difference between the two: "They are reading a series of cues in the novel that would lead them to read blatant indications of class difference as signs of a repressed racial difference" (xvii). But the omnipresent signs of class difference are masked by Indiana's rhetoric of analogical bondage.

Critics of *Indiana* have seen ethical conundrums in the novel's depiction of race but not in the novel's analogical identifications of marriage with slavery. Kadish divides Sand's attitude toward race in the novel into a "negative, conformist side," which consists of "seeming at an explicit level to make all of her major characters white," and a "positive, resisting side," which consists of "the novel's strong, albeit implicit, identification with and appeal on behalf of persons of color" (22). But this dichotomy of negative conformism that erases difference and positive resistance in the identification of difference begs a question: Can't identification be a form of *resisting* resistance? Can't it be "negative" resistance of threatening tensions, in the psychoanalytic sense? Rather than "positive" resistance in the World War II sense?

Which raises another question: What is signified by the pervasive critical identification with Indiana rather than Noun? Or at least, by the critical identification with Indiana's analogies? For critics have consistently reproduced her analogies. Kadish states, "Nancy Rogers rightly concludes that 'Indiana joins the other rebellious runaway slaves so often depicted in the literature of the times. . . . Indiana is branded as blatantly as any runaway slave recaptured by his master'" (25). Kadish's use of the term "rightly" to qualify Rogers' extension and exaggeration of Indiana's analogy to the slave is questionable given that Indiana's "branding" is the wound of an abused wife—she is marked on the forehead by the heel of her husband's boot—but it is not a permanent proprietary trademark legally identifying another person as a possession. "Rebellious runaway slaves," by contrast, are branded in a "blatantly" literal and permanent sense. Indiana, unlike the branded slave, immediately receives help from a ship captain who is dismayed that a man would hurt a pretty woman. And isn't it pertinent that Indiana feels *free* to discourse to her husband, to his face, on his analogical relation to the "slave master"?

Implicit critical identifications with Indiana reflect an elision similar to what bell hooks, in her introduction to *Ain't I a Woman?*, diagnoses as a rhetorical politics of borrowing and exclusion in white feminist analogies between "women" and "blacks."

> Like many people in our racist society, white feminists could feel perfectly comfortable writing books or articles on the "woman question" in which they drew analogies between "women" and "blacks." Since analogies derive their power, their appeal, and their very reason for being from the sense of two disparate phenomena having been brought closer together, for white women to acknowledge the overlap between the terms "blacks" and "women" (that is the existence of black women) would render this analogy unnecessary. By continuously making this analogy, they unwittingly suggest that to them the term "woman" is synonymous with "white woman" and the term "blacks" synonymous with "black men."[28]

"Women are like black women," in other words, would make no more sense than "Black women are like women"; to make an analogy between ostensibly *like* terms in order to *create equality* between those terms is tautological, paradoxical. One would see the likeness between both groups of women without the recourse to analogy if one were not seeing skin color and on that basis excluding some races from the category "woman." By contrast, the idea that "women are like blacks" derives its meaning from the notion that white women and black men are two similarly marginalized but different groups. In Sand's pervasive analogy between "black slaves" and "white married women," there is no space for black women slaves or black married women to participate in the identification.

Sand's ***Indiana*** is, paradoxically, not just a drama of slavery by analogy but also a drama of slavery *to* analogy. None of the problematic uses of analogy in ***Indiana*** are separable from Sand's thematization of the possibility that slave chains can be reduced to symbols of *analogical* "bondage." Not only the Creole heroine but the narrator(s) of the text are tremendously anxious about being the dupes of language: "Nothing is so easy or so common as self-deception when one does not lack intelligence and is familiar with all the subtleties of language. It is like a queen turned into a prostitute who, demeaning and raising herself, plays all parts, who disguises herself and decks herself in finery, dissembles and conceals herself; it is like a litigant who has an answer to everything, who has always foreseen everything, and has a thousand ways of being right" (85). One can hypothesize that Sand, like the Saint-Simonians

in the *Journal des femmes,* wanted her use of the slavery analogy to be emancipatory but had a premonition of the same anxieties that would haunt the fields of feminism and African American studies in the wake of identity politics: the anxieties of authenticity, of a realism of identity, of "firsthand" phenomenological experience.

Indiana is concerned with the problem of "firsthand" altruism and the second- and third-hand removes of language: "Who believes in poverty when he has no experience of it?" (85). Indiana believes—falsely—that she knows the misery of slavery firsthand, just as Raymon is repeatedly seduced by his own admittedly insincere language of love. But if one refrains from any politics that are not firsthand, politics become a form of slavery to the self. The case of the wife is, after all, not irrelevant for the case of the slave; many slaves were wives. Why study culture if one cannot look beyond the domain of the proper—beyond what is proper to oneself, to the proper name, to the "noun," to the "no" to the other?

Sand goes to acrobatic lengths to illustrate the impossibility of a non-mystificatory language. She does this especially through the trope of mystificatory trauma: trauma that is threatened but not sustained, or trauma that was sustained but is denied, or physical trauma transposed into a discourse of figurative trauma. This begins in the opening pages of the book when Indiana and her husband terrorize each other in what becomes a predictable pattern in the book. His behavior suggests an impending violence that will not in fact be realized, even though there are some precedents to expect it. Indiana then reproaches him by begging him not to carry out an action far more violent than the one that was threatened.

She begs his mercy when he threatens to hit the dog, Ophelia, saying with "indefinable fear," "Don't kill her" (19). Shortly after this scene, the colonel does "shoot" an unknown intruder, and the intruder collapses, but the colonel protests that the gun was loaded only with salt and that the intruder has collapsed from fright. Indiana responds, "But this blood, Monsieur, . . . was it fear that made it flow?" (27). But she later excuses her husband's violence to his victim, Raymon, with a transposition of the vocabulary of mortal blame into a vocabulary of flirtatious exchange: "You would pardon him for unintentionally wounding you, for his heart certainly bled more than your wound" (45). Raymon forgives him "with all my heart" because of her "hands which poured balm on my wounds." As he says this, he presses her hand gently and "all the young woman's blood surged gently back to her heart." Raymon is less affected because "he had the ease of manner that comes from some experience in affairs of the heart." Yet, "his heart did not belie his tongue" (46). And on it goes, a long riff on the troubling mimetic divide between rhetoric and the real. Sand seems to point to the terror of the fact that, in the space of representation, we cannot dependably distinguish between blood and emotion, heart and body, one person's body and the next person's body. The blood of language may flow, but can it ever express the other's social wounds?

The only character whose authentic altruism is tried and tested in the novel is Ralph, but his altruism is shackled by his quasi-autistic inability to put thoughts and feelings into words: "I don't know the subtleties of your language" (22), he says in the beginning of the novel when distressed by his inability to comfort Indiana. At the end of the novel we learn, in his sudden accession to linguistic self-revelation, that in his childhood "it was decided that no one would love me because I couldn't express my affection to anyone" (248). His characterization is both extremely awkward and a literary tour de force: the expression of altruistic empathy without recourse to rhetoric and its ethical deceptions.

Is the slippage of referentiality in language a source of Fourieresque wealth—the ability to walk in another man's shoes, to be a talk-traveler of different psyches and spaces? Is it freedom, or is it the betrayal of the slave? In analogy, the bondage of two nouns by the "comparative tool," does the analogist become a slave to the politics of mirroring? Schor argues that "*Indiana* is centrally concerned with the lure of narcissism, the impossibility of escaping the prison of self-reflection characteristic of the romantic ego and replacing it with a mimesis that strives to accommodate the other's otherness, but which more often than not is simply a more perfect model of the primary mirror of narcissism" (xviii). That mirror of otherness/narcissism is figured in *Indiana* as analogy, and it is a particularly powerful model because of the exaggerated mimeticism associated with *créolité*.

COLONIAL MIMICRY AND GENDER PERFORMANCE

In Sand's marriage/slavery analogy, the subject is female. But what it means to be female is plotted on the axis of race. The essential ambiguity of Creole "race" correspondingly undermines any essential gender identity, for all Indiana's almost parodically "feminine" weakness and wiles.

Judith Butler theorizes that the gendered body is a performative construct, constituted by "acts, gestures, enactments" including "words" and "desire." The rule of the performativity of essentialist gender identities is best illustrated by its most theatrical exceptions, such as drag. "*In imitating gender, drag implicitly reveals the imitative structure of gender itself.*"[29] Gender parody does not imply the presence of an original; "Indeed, the parody is *of* the very notion of an original" (138). Drag and other forms of gender "parody" can be seen as forms of *mimicry* that parody the relationship of mimesis to the real.

As such, the paradigm of gender performance has obvious parallels with the paradigm of colonial mimicry. But the *significance* of those parallels is less obvious. Is colonial mimicry the equivalent of racial "drag"? Is race a performance the way that gender is a performance? What is the difference between the mimetic underpinnings of race and gender?

What Bongie calls "endemic" or "contaminatory" mimesis in the specifically French Romantic treatment of colonialism is used in *Indiana* to dramatize not only the instability of racial identity but also the emotional attachment to a nonimitative identity. Indiana wants to experience interpersonal mimesis in analogical terms, meaning that she will create likeness where dissimilarity reigns; she will break free of marital inequity and free slaves. But despite the fact that she valorizes likeness above all else in her political vision of the world, she fears parity with Noun in her relationship with Raymon. And despite her commitment to the politics of analogy, she fears the ability of language to produce seductive mimetic slippage and confusion. In the French colonial social life of mimesis, both race and gender are performative, and the question of what gender *is,* is performed through mimicry of race. Yet Indiana, prototypical Romantic heroine and speaker of "novelistic language," courts the fiction of originality—if only by analogy.

Notes

1. Homi K. Bhabha, *The Location of Culture* (New York: Routledge, 1994), 86.

2. Michael Taussig, *Mimesis and Alterity: A Particular History of the Senses* (New York: Routledge, 1993), 66.

3. Chris Bongie, *Islands and Exiles: The Creole Identities of Post/Colonial Literature* (Stanford, Calif.: Stanford University Press, 1998), 244.

4. Barbara Johnson, *A World of Difference* (Baltimore: Johns Hopkins University Press, 1987), 155.

5. James A. Snead, *Figures of Division: William Faulkner's Major Novels* (New York: Methuen, 1986), x.

6. Toni Morrison, *Playing in the Dark: Whiteness and the Literary Imagination* (Cambridge: Harvard University Press, 1992), 63.

7. Charles Fourier, *Le Nouveau monde industriel* (Brussels: La Librairie Belge-Française, 1840), 356.

8. Roman Jakobson, *Language in Literature* (Cambridge: Harvard University Press, 1987), 99.

9. "C'est d'ailleurs sur cet aspect-là que Quintilien fonde sa définition de la métaphore: une comparaison sans outil comparant. Au lieu de dire que 'Pierre est fort comme un lion,' on dit 'Pierre est un lion.'" Michèle Aquien, *Dictionnaire de poétique* (Paris: Libraire Générale Française, 1993), 177.

10. Michael Spencer, "A(na)logie de Fourier," *Romantisme* 11.34 (1981): 42.

11. I mean here that *within* the terms of Fourier's "scientific" methodology the beet would logically be constrained to one analogical identification, but in fact, Fourier changed the terms of his analogies frequently. In *Analogie et cosmogonie,* the beet family represents robust republican familial happiness: "Les grosses raves républicaines ou espèces grossières et épaisses nous représentent le bonheur qu'on goûte sous le chaume" (The fat republican beets or the thick and vulgar species represent the happiness one tastes under the thatched roof of the cottage). On an illustrative chart, the "betterave rouge" is associated with "amitié" and the "betterave sucrée" is associated with "famille." *Oeuvres complètes de Charles Fourier (Manuscrits publiés par la Phalange)* (Paris: Éditions Anthropos, 1968), 12:88-89.

12. Michael G. Johnson and Tracy B. Henley, "Finding Meaning in Random Analogies," *Metaphor and Symbolic Activities* 7.2 (1992): 55.

13. Christopher L. Miller, *Blank Darkness: Africanist Discourse in French* (Chicago: University of Chicago Press, 1985), 93.

14. George Sand, *Indiana* (Paris: Gallimard, 1984), 58. Quotations from *Indiana* in French are from this edition.

15. George Sand, *Indiana,* trans. Sylvia Raphael (Oxford: Oxford University Press, 1994), 24. Quotations from *Indiana* in English are from this edition, unless otherwise noted.

16. Naomi Schor, introduction to *Indiana,* trans. Sylvia Raphael (Oxford: Oxford University Press, 1994), xvii.

17. Doris Kadish, "Representing Race in *Indiana,*" *George Sand Studies* 11.1-2 (1992): 23.

18. Moreau de Saint-Méry, *Description Topographique, physique, civile, politique et historique de la partie française de l'isle Saint-Domingue* (Philadelphia: Published by the author, 1797), 21.

19. Claire Goldberg Moses and Leslie Wahl Rabine, *Feminism, Socialism, and French Romanticism* (Bloomington: Indiana University Press, 1993), 6. In the essay "'Difference' in Historical Perspective" in that volume, Moses argues that socialists from this period held that "the French Revolution's espousal of universal rights had actually masked a policy of entrenched inequality" (27) and that Romanticism therefore valorized difference over equality. Though this is a very valuable account of the Romantic socialist relationship to history of the Revolution, it seems to me that the evidence presented by Moses highlights ongoing tensions between liberty, with its potential to be read as "difference," and likeness, rather than signifying a decisive Romantic affiliation with difference.

20. Marcel Bouteron, *Muses Romantiques* (Paris: Le Goupy, 1926), 143-44.

21. See Édouard Dolléans, *Féminisme et mouvement ouvrier: George Sand* (Paris: Éditions Ouvrières, 1951).

22. Père Enfantin, letter to Charles Duveyrier, August 1829, in *L'École Saint-Simonienne et la femme,* ed. Maria Teresa Bulciolu (Pisa: Golliardica, 1980), 54.

23. Suzanne Voilquin, in ibid., 215.

24. Marie Reine, in ibid., 227.

25. Srinivas Aravamudan, *Tropicopolitans: Colonialism and Agency, 1688-1804* (Durham, N.C.: Duke University Press, 1999), 306.

26. Frantz Fanon, *Black Skin, White Masks,* trans. Charles Lam Markmann (New York: Grove Weidenfeld, 1967), 11.

27. Homi Bhabha, "Remembering Fanon: Self, Psyche, and the Colonial Condition," cited in Henry Louis Gates, Jr., "Critical Fanonism," *Critical Inquiry* 17 (spring 1991): 461.

28. bell hooks, introduction to *Ain't I a Woman?* (Boston: South End Press, 1981), 8.

29. Judith Butler, *Gender Trouble: Feminism and the Subversion of Identity* (New York: Routledge, 1990), 137.

H. Adlai Murdoch (essay date winter 2002)

SOURCE: Murdoch, H. Adlai. "Ghosts in the Mirror: Colonialism and Creole Indeterminacy in Brontë and Sand." *College Literature* 29, no. 1 (winter 2002): 1-31.

[*In the following essay, Murdoch approaches the tropes of alterity, identity, and social oppression depicted in Sand's* Indiana *and Emily Brontë's 1847 novel* Jane Eyre *by examining the destabilizing presence of Creole figures in these works.*]

I

The colonial encounter raises myriad possibilities for reinscribing the terms of subjectivity in the post-colonial condition. Issues of alienation, difference and desire framed the imperial will to conquest, at the pinnacle of the colonial project in the mid-nineteenth century. Despite their differences, both France and Britain as European colonial powers came to represent the Creole as the unnamable third term, the impossible indeterminacy excluded by the colonial binary's *neither/nor* dyad. Because discursive form provided the key to authority and control over a myriad of people and places, literary tropes helped construct, elaborate, and reinforce a hierarchical, race-based discourse of inequality. This essay, then, compares the tropological subversion in unwonted reflections of the Creole in two nineteenth-century texts: Charlotte Brontë's *Jane Eyre* and George Sand's **Indiana.** Both texts seek to contain the complexities of the Creole by negating these disturbing, dangerously indeterminate figures whose subjectivity is paradoxically both unacknowledged and restrained, reflecting a colonial dyad that signifies metropolitan notions of lack and excess. For both *Jane Eyre* and **Indiana**—despite their disparate political and sociocultural contexts—are defined by a climactic subjective moment in which their female metropolitan protagonists are forced to give way to an instability signified by a Creole counterpart reflected in the mirror. When this Creole figure confronts the gendered metropolitan subject in the mirror of the colonial imagination, the resultant reversal and discursives undermine those presumptions of subjectivity and knowability that undergird the colonial site. Both scenes, then, inscribe critical contexts that allow us to question colonial binaries through their links to identity, alterity, and knowledge.

Held in thrall to the comprehensive discourse of domination and desire in the colonial text, contemporary figures of racial division tended to subsume the "exotic" differences produced by the encounter with the Other, allowing metropolitan authors to ignore colonialism's nascent ambiguities and to appropriate a variety of figures of blackness as repressed elements of the social whole, constructing simulacra of identity that reveal to the reader the dependent framework of metropolitan subjectivity, and provoking the interwoven Creole complexities to increasingly critical strategies of substitution. Principles and patterns of literary re-presentation, then, help shape the imaginary alienation that marks colonial identity, as Homi Bhabha remarks, "The visibility of the racial/colonial Other is at once a *point* of identity . . . and at the same time a *problem*. . . . [T]he recognition and disavowal of 'difference' is always disturbed by the question of its re-presentation or construction" (1994, 81; emphasis in the original). As literary discourse re-presented the authoritarian violence of the colonial encounter through figures of cultural subjection

and exclusion, transposing its hierarchies of self and Other into conventions of class and gender, metropolitan subjectivity was forced to confront the binary relation between metropolitan lack and Creole excess in the alterities of the Creole's erupting, unavowed, supplementary pluralities.

The psychological interaction between the subject and its mirror reflection also informs the principles underlying this reading. To sum up, in Lacanian terms, the mirror stage acts as a site of misrecognition and alienation, a moment of crisis that also doubles as the source of secondary identifications. But while these Creole figures do not necessarily act as the metropolitan subject's ideal reflection, they do allow her to be defined through an external image, in a process which, as Kaja Silverman points out, "is to be defined through self-alienation." More important for this subject and her colonial context, perhaps, are the binary patterns of ambivalence that emerge from such structures; as Silverman continues, "it entertains a profoundly ambivalent relationship to that reflection . . . unable to mediate between or escape from the binary oppositions which structure all of its perceptions" (1983, 158). It is precisely this alienated binary thinking, I contend, that grounded not only contemporary colonial discourse, but also the forms of metropolitan subjectivity through which the pluralisms of the Creole were ultimately dismantled and disavowed.

The destabilizing function of Creole figures in canonical metropolitan texts suggests that the conventions circumscribing nineteenth-century French and English articulations of identity excluded the complexities and contradictions implied by the term "Creole" itself. A product of the colonial encounter, the term "Creole" has been variously used to describe, or define, both of the oppositional categories that mark the schismatic vision of society imposed by colonial ideology. In fact, the 1989 edition of the *OED* defines the word "Creole" as a substantive whose primary context occurs "In the West Indies and other parts of America, Mauritius, etc.: *orig.* A person born and naturalized in the country, but of European (usually Spanish or French) or of African Negro race: the name having no connotation of colour, and in its reference to origin being distinguished on the one hand from born in Europe (or Africa), and on the other hand from aboriginal."[1] In this way, a Creole subject can be white, black, or the product of both ethnic groups; indeed, s/he may be either metropolitan or African, or, for that matter, colonizer or colonized, figuring an ambiguity that both mediates and ruptures the dominant strategies of containment and difference inscribed as the traditional corollary of the colonial encounter. This undefinability and strategic slippage of the Creole expose colonialism's false opposition of cultural traits and mine the unstable ground of social and cultural self-invention. By strategically locating these ambivalent articulations of the Creole, these authors find their oppositional constructions of metropolitan subjectivity unsettled and undermined by the uncanny contingencies of its multipartite mosaic.

These discourses of metropolitan colonialism, then, create a pervasive tropological instability that underlies the inscription of the Creole in gendered inflections of the colonial scene. At the same time that Jane and Indiana are made to confront the conflation of their reflections with the unheralded instantiation of their Creole counterparts, these reflections reverse and disperse themselves into a ghostly apparition, whose now insistent insubstantiality itself reflects the ambivalent desire and subjective misrecognition that lay at the heart of writing about colonialism and race. Indeed, by constraining such misapprehensions of the Creole subject, contemporary discourse marked the culmination of an obsession with colonialist textuality and its attendant assumptions of binary difference, giving rise to the racial and cultural misprision that define what Deirdre David calls "Jane's complex position in writing the nation, and . . . the often contradictory nature of Victorian writing about class, gender, and race" (1995, 81). This indeterminacy was reflected in a literary discourse marked by Africanist texts and subjects which sought to appropriate the themes and tropes of colonialism to distinctly metropolitan ends. Such formulations tend to reinforce the argument that the refusal to acknowledge the simultaneous subjection of both colonizer and colonized to a colonial discourse is ultimately repressed in the colonial process. This double gesture of implicit expression and repression has been remarked by Edward Said: "the empire functions for much of the European nineteenth century as a codified, if only marginally visible, presence in fiction . . . taken for granted but scarcely ever more than named . . ." (1993, 63). Thus the very vocabulary of colonial racism, the constitutive presence of the colonial experience in France and England, was ineluctably present even in texts that were ostensibly not about colonialism at all. By constructing the metropolitan subject as the unacknowledged other of the colonized, and by inscribing the metropolitan subject as all that the colonized was not, nineteenth-century French and British fiction that sought to transpose gendered for racial subjection confronted a destabilization and dislocation of its essential assumptions, a subversion of its binaries enacted by the polysemous patterns of the Creole.

The contemporary British novel had long been rife with colonial contexts and associations. Indeed, Britain, to all intents and purposes, led the continent in this regard, as Said points out: "Nearly everywhere in nineteenth- and early twentieth-century British and French culture we find allusions to the facts of empire, but perhaps nowhere with more regularity and frequency than in the British novel" (1993, 62). The link between home and

away was indissoluble to the extent that issues of identity, property, and social progress in the metropole were largely predicated upon successful management and regulation overseas. As Said again reminds us, "the values associated with such higher things as ordination, law, and propriety must be grounded firmly in actual rule over and possession of territory. . . . What assures the domestic tranquility and harmony of one is the productivity and regulated discipline of the other" (1993, 87). Thus the myriad colonialist tropes of Brontë's *Jane Eyre* (1847) provide telling examples of various metropolitan figures drawn on contemporary colonial practice, engendering a plausible pretext for the advancement of the novel's English setting that results in the ineluctable imbrication of both colonizer and colonized. As Margaret Cezair-Thompson puts it in her reading of *Jane Eyre,* "As a colonialist text it plays an important role in the postcolonial literary tradition, bequeathing a legacy of marginality that the postcolonial writer and critic must come to terms with in the decolonization and reconstruction of national literatures" (n.d., 3). Indeed, most of the novel's major characters, including Rochester, his imprisoned wife Bertha, and even Jane herself are associated with colonialism and slavery. Rochester, while British by birth, lived in Jamaica, acquired a Jamaican wife during his sojourn, and made a fortune by trading in goods whose production was based on slave labor. The subliminal threat signified by these subtexts of colonialism and slavery extends to the complex framework of Rochester's secret marriage. As Said suggests, "Bertha Mason, Rochester's deranged wife in *Jane Eyre,* is a West Indian, and also a threatening presence, confined to an attic room" (1993, 62). It is of critical importance that Bertha, Rochester's mad, violent spouse, is a Caribbean Creole, and as we shall see, the necessary indeterminacy of her inscribed identity destabilizes the re-presentational subjectivity of Jane herself.

This inscription of Antoinette (Bertha) Mason as a Caribbean Creole is elaborated and interrogated in Jean Rhys' intertextual *Wide Sargasso Sea* (1966). Purporting to be the untold story of Bertha Mason's life prior to her marginal appearance in *Jane Eyre,* this "prequel" to Brontë's text deliberately destabilizes received, supposedly singular notions of "colonizer," "colonized," and "Creole" as they were used in nineteenth-century British prose. By revealing and underlining the doubleness and instability in contemporary conceptions of social relations and "racial" categories, Rhys undermines key notions of knowing and perception, principally, in Judith Raiskin's words, "by insisting on the fluidity of the categories and of the power relations inscribed in them" (1996, 102). Concentrating on the shifting trope of Bertha's Caribbean Creole heritage, Raiskin shows that the term creole itself, and particularly its contemporary shifts in meaning from "white, native West Indian" to "'colored' native of mixed racial origin" (97), allowed Rhys to mine its critical implications of instability, undoing the binary opposition of self and Other upon which the Victorian novelistic tradition was largely based, as well as its concurrent notions of definitive social and cultural division.

By deliberately underlining and subverting the doubled, dissonant trope of Creole identity, Rhys undermines our notions of the oppositional relation between self and Other; the very discursive act of bringing this text into being undoes the presumed instability of the "mad Creole," as Raiskin explains, by "claiming a subjectivity for a character denied a stable position in any cultural or social space. Antoinette's 'various' social positions shift with every change in her name and put her in-between the symbolic orders of English culture and black Caribbean culture" (1996, 109). By pointing out the impossibility for this subject of belonging completely to either of the dominant social and "racial" categories, Rhys interrogates the key issues of colonialism, race, and otherness that "are so normalized in Brontë's text that they barely create a ripple in the story of Jane Eyre's 'progress' (1996, 114)." But it is by projecting a complex cast onto this fluid framework, generating "nativist" Creole subjects inscribed through the conflict between the desire to belong and the recognition of exclusion, that the metropolitan counterpart attains a discernible, if transitory capacity for degrading Creole subjects.

In this way, Brontë's characterization of Bertha Mason as a foil constructing a social identity for Jane Eyre and, by extension, the nineteenth-century female metropolitan subject, offer mediating racial and cultural terms and structure Bertha's cultural marginalization. As the *OED* definition indicates, the contemporary understanding of the Creole was at best ambiguous, the very absence of a specific connotation of color suggesting plural possibilities of double differentiation and opening vistas of discursive possibility and of cultural and identitarian ambivalence. The discourse of *Jane Eyre* does little to dispel this lack of clarity, since terms like "dark" or "blackened," although appearing within the text itself, were not exclusively applied to Blacks or Asians. Of greater import, however, are the implications of Bertha's definition as a Creole, for it is here, I contend, that the text constructs key ambiguities of race and culture upon which her own *métissage,* as well as the framework of Jane's metropolitan subjectivity, are ultimately drawn.

Critics have long disagreed over whether Bertha Mason is white or black. Gayatri Spivak, for example, characterizes Bertha as a "white Jamaican Creole," a "native subject" who, by virtue of her Creole status, remains excluded from the claims to individuality that metropolitan subjectivity bestows upon Jane (1986, 266-67). In this case, however, in a key point that Spivak's op-

position of Antoinette to her black servant, Christophine, appears to elide, the fact that Creole whites were themselves also natives does not necessarily imply the exclusion imposed on slaves and their descendants, as the structure of plantation societies tended to privilege whiteness, whether indigenous or imported. Gilbert and Gubar have also described Bertha Mason as Creole subject as "Jane's truest and darkest double: she is . . . the ferocious secret self Jane has been trying to repress . . ." (1979, 360). But while the ground of Bertha's presumptive whiteness remains unclear in Spivak's text, the terms of Gilbert and Gubar's definition lean more toward the psychological than the racial; Gilbert and Gubar do not use "darkness" in racial terms. They avoid the text's thorough articulation of racial tropes. Indeed, their construction of Bertha as Jane's "darkest double" almost constitutes a study in itself, a discursively constructed cultural evasion: with figures of race undergirding the tenor of the text, Bertha's racial positionality—as well as any critical refusal to acknowledge its significance—becomes crucial to her subjective structure. This fatally flawed discursive displacement of Bertha's ethnic and cultural lineage simply gets the Creole scenes wrong, as Cezair-Thompson claims, and "perpetuates the very silence it denounces by its own disregard and/or distortion of colonial history" (n.d., 3). These opposing (mis)readings of Bertha's textual inscription, of the key question of whether she is determined, both racially and psychologically, by this "darkness" or if she is indeed a white Creole, draw on specifically racialized typologies which will overdetermine the largely binary re-presentations of subjectivity in the novel, which are themselves based on the elaboration of fixed markers of racial and cultural difference.

On the other hand, Susan Meyer's recent study of the interpolation of race in Victorian women's fiction sees the figure of race as critical to the narrative structure of *Jane Eyre,* since she reads the text's tropes and figures as signs that "all insistently and conventionally mark Bertha as black . . . the ambiguously dark blood Bertha has inherited from her maternal line becomes fully evident" (1996, 69). However, as I shall argue, such a reading of the text overstates the case for racially typing Bertha as black, and indeed the ambivalence connoted by this "ambiguously dark blood," the result of Bertha's racially Creolized genealogy, determines the novel's appropriation of colonial signs into metropolitan contexts, producing its strikingly dissonant elaboration of cultural identity.

While her Creoleness is indeed inscribed in the text, Bertha's Creole lineage paradoxically remains both clear and unclear. While this Creoleness is an integral part of Richard Mason's attestation to the marriage between Rochester and Bertha in Spanish Town, Jamaica, whether or not she is both racially and culturally Creole remains at issue; she is given in the text as the daughter "of Jonas Mason, merchant, and of Antoinetta his wife, a Creole" (Brontë 1847, 366). While the *place* of Antoinetta's inscription is unquestioned, her *race* remains an unanswered question; in Jamaica's contemporary population structure, consisting of a relatively small white planter class, an overwhelmingly large black slave class, and a growing category of free colored people, she could be white, black, or any of several shades in between. When Rochester himself confirms her Creole parentage some pages later, it is more to inscribe tropes of madness and debauchery as the product of her West Indian heritage than to stipulate her racial makeup: "She came of a mad family:—idiots and maniacs through three generations! Her mother, the Creole, was both a mad woman and a drunkard!" (369). This racial indeterminacy leaves Bertha Mason's social and cultural identity an open question, and permeates the novel's textual vocabulary, producing a latent discursive instability that ultimately governs Jane's confrontation with her counterpart when Bertha finally appears in Jane's mirror.

For Jane, self-representation takes place from the outset under the sign of slavery and oppression, but as the narrative progresses, the discourse is increasingly at odds with itself in its terms for those "other" civilizations whose social practices Jane uses to construct comparative patterns of oppression and tyranny. Indeed, in addition to the African slaves who serve as her primary metaphor, Jane manages to draw parallels of marginalization with Indians, Turks, Persians, and native American Indians and to establish several unflattering associations between the British and Roman empires. But by conflating this succession of so-called "dark races" into an apparently unified trope of subaltern suffering, the discourse misapprehends the identitarian strictures governing racial and cultural difference. When the text does not distinguish between these disparate paradigms of imperial culture, it ultimately reinscribes and reinforces the very divisions and dualities whose binary logic it seeks to bridge through the undifferentiated individualism of metropolitan identity. When she is attacked by John Reed, the loathsome son of her benefactors, for example, Jane compares him to "a slavedriver," a dictator "like the Roman emperors," and claims for herself the status of his victim, since "like any *other* rebel slave,* I felt resolved, in my desperation, to go all lengths" (Brontë 1847, 8; my emphasis). This double comparison between slavery and subjection to Roman rule inscribes Jane as gendered metropolitan subject squarely between two discontinuous frames of reference, where the only commonality between contemporary slavery and ancient Rome is the slave culture that supposedly binds them together. When, at Lowood, Mr. Brocklehurst punishes her by making her stand on a stool, she couches her response to fellow pupil Helen Burns' silent gesture of support in parallel terms: "It was as if a martyr, a hero, had passed a *slave or victim,*

and imparted strength in the transit" (73; my emphasis). By playing upon the contemporary awareness of social injustice that helped bring about the recent abolition of slavery, Brontë assimilates Jane's subordinate social status to one of oppression and human bondage, but at the cost of appropriating the colonial signifier and attempting to disconnect it from its cultural signified. For as a freeborn metropolitan white woman, Jane's social condition cannot realistically be assimilated to that of either slave or victim; this outrageous, if not offensive comparison has the unwarranted effect of either debasing Jane as subject or alleviating the brutality of slavery, implying in any event an equality between various types of victimage. This orientalization of subaltern subjects inscribes an ambiguity that prepares the textual framework for the binary patterns and tropes that insistently ignore the Creole.

The contradictory traces of this disjunctive representation of slavery and oppression continue to surface in the narrative; the shower of gifts rained upon her during her engagement to Mr. Rochester, for example, elicits a similar comparison: "I thought his smile was such as a sultan might . . . bestow on a slave his gold and gems had enriched," and she suggests in return that he seek out "the bazaars of Stamboul without delay; and lay out in extensive slave-purchases some of that spare cash you seem at a loss to spend satisfactorily here" (Brontë 1847, 277-78). However, the orientalization of the narrative, in its references to "sultan" and "Stamboul," shifts the frame of reference from Africa to the Orient and enacts a series of contradictions in which the subtleties of cultural diversity illuminate Brontë's ambiguity on the question of difference. By using slavery to conflate the worlds of Africa and the Orient, in conjunction with the orientalist stereotype implicit in a phrase like "bazaars of Stamboul," Brontë's text insists on joining fixed definitions of difference, such that opposing cultures, similar only in their alterity, appear to become interminably interchangeable with each other, a discursive phenomenon that Edward Said has tellingly described: "it is enough for us here to note how strongly the general character ascribed to things Oriental could withstand both the rhetorical and the existential force of obvious exceptions. . . . The unisons are made within general categories, not between categories and what they contain" (1978, 101-02). This substitution reduces even the suggested consanguinity of colonial cultures to an unrecognizably amorphous abstraction in which difference from the one—a difference that the Creole complexities of race, gender and culture render insistently double—is translated into marginalization. Through this rhetorical sleight of hand, Brontë rehearses the very discursive gesture through which colonial discourse imposed an "Otherness" upon the colonial subject that dislocated it from any specific figural or cultural foundation.

This, then, is an overview of the discursive and cultural contradictions that culminate in the climactic moment of Jane's apprehension of Bertha's reflection in her mirror. So far, we have sought to show that since the Creole framework that undergirds the inscription of Bertha Mason—the pivot of the novel's plot—is critically and profoundly ambivalent, this unacknowledged ambivalence shapes the descriptive discourse of the novel, and particularly the multiple metaphors of oppression that figure Jane, such that they themselves are also fatally paradoxical. Such a development suggests that the key metropolitan context of the novel, which derives its distinction from the network of Caribbean slavery and cultural difference to which it stands in singular opposition, is irreparably divided. It thus displays a pattern of split sensibilities that are repeatedly undermined by the substitutive supplementarity of the Creole figure. With the discourse of metropolitan subjectivity articulated as the other of this unacknowledged Creole ambivalence, it must itself also undergo irregularity and dislocation. Thus it is that finally, at the key moment of Jane's replacement by Bertha's reflected image, a subtle combination of ambiguity and insubstantiality invades Jane's recounting of it:

> —Fearful and ghastly to me—oh, sir, I never saw a face like it! It was a discoloured face—it was a savage face. I wish I could forget the roll of the red eyes and the fearful blackened inflation of the lineaments!
>
> —Ghosts are usually pale, Jane.
>
> —This, sir, was purple: the lips were swelled and dark; the brows furrowed; the black eye-brows wildly raised over the bloodshot eyes.
>
> (Brontë 1847, 358)

The myriad forms ascribed to Bertha's color and mien in this passage constitute the place and space of difference; it is here that she will be identified and named. As such then, the passage merits an especially close reading.

At the outset, Jane describes the face whose reflection she has seen in terms of its character, attempting to ascribe attributes of some stripe to the unsettling phenomenon she has just witnessed. Thus she describes the face as "fearful," "ghastly," generalized adjectives that convey the shocking effect of this apparition upon her rather than representing the distinctiveness of what she has seen. So far, then, the face is simply disturbing; none of its features yet sets it apart from a generic, racially undifferentiated visage. The first precise indications of difference then follow; the face becomes "discoloured" and "savage," the latter appellation simply placing it into the broad, undifferentiated category of the Western world's supposedly uncivilized other. But an effect of discoloration suggests something out of kilter, a sign, perhaps, of disease or infection, a temporary aberration or affliction rather than an unalterable inscription of racial identity. The combined effect of these characterizations places increasing significance upon Bertha's distance from the delineation of metropolitan subjectivity, joined by a growing inability to locate her cultural connections.

As this face acquires more detail, we are given the "roll of the red eyes" and the "fearful blackened inflation" of its features. While, for Meyer, these reddened eyes suggest a drunkenness that Brontë associated with Africans since her childhood (1996, 69), their rolling, unfocused gaze can also suggest madness or delirium, the precise attribute of her maternal lineage as attested to by Rochester himself. Despite its "inflation," or swollen character, however, this last characterization cannot be conflated into unmistakably Negroid features. Further, the face is notably "*blackened*," not "black," suggesting a change effected from the *outside* rather than an intrinsic racial or ethnic distemper. In other words, the inscription of Bertha Mason remains insistently, inscrutably interstitial; she is neither a fully-fledged metropolitan subject nor its sociocultural other, the captious African counterpart to the oppressed middle-class Englishwomen that Jane represents. Her domain lies between both worlds, an overdetermined sign whose ambiguous frame of reference returns to destabilize the metropolitan figure who beholds her own subjective displacement in the mirror's double reflection.

Rochester himself, no doubt in a spirit of appeasement, proposes the possibility that Jane might have seen a ghost. But even in these terms, the insubstantiality of the figure he suggests is simply the other side of a colonial discourse's regressive recourse to substitution; the indefinable essence undergirding Bertha's appearance mediates her metamorphosis into Rochester's suggested specter of otherness. Unlocalizable and fragmented, projected onto and reflected by Jane's mirror, this ghostly presence draws on Bertha's Creoleness to enact Jane's subjective splitting. Bertha's "discoloured" mien, projected alongside the bewildered horror of Jane's pale features, generates through this double disjuncture the play of displacement that destabilizes a metropolitan subjectivity constituted as the opposite of its disempowered "darker races." The ghost in the mirror is thus instantiated as the return of an unacknowledged, discontinuous Creole iteration that colonialism cannot contain; in the supplementarity of its figures it incessantly undermines metropolitan assumptions of coherence, hierarchy, and difference.

Ultimately, despite Jane's asseverations, it goes without saying that a countenance coded as "purple," even one whose "lips were swelled and dark," the "black eyebrows raised over the bloodshot eyes," can by no means act as a marker of racial or cultural origin; indeed it suggests rather a face whose distorted but indeterminate hue may be the result of lighting, perceptual misapprehension, madness, or disease; and while Bertha's "swelled and dark" lips may conceivably fall somewhere between the bounds of physiognomy and phantasmagoria, neither the "black eyebrows" nor the "bloodshot eyes" differentiate her sufficiently, even as a Creole, from any Caucasian counterpart to warrant her incontestable inscription as a black subject. Thus Susan Meyer's claim that "the Jamaican Bertha-become-black is the fiction's incarnation of the desire for revenge on the part of colonized peoples" (1996, 69) not only misreads the signifiers of race and color in the novel by neglecting to take into account the fact that with Bertha never actually textually *defined* as black, the term "Jamaican Creole" covered an almost infinite range of ethnic *métissage*. Further, it also reveals itself to be caught up in the same transpositions of colonial oppression onto a metropolitan framework that informs Brontë's discourse. Bertha's incontrovertible indeterminacy, then, remains, and indeed becomes the primary marker of her racial and discursive identity in the text; and it is precisely this undecidable inscription, this *neither/nor* by which the intrinsic supplementarity of the figure is engaged and extended, that ultimately undermines both Jane's metropolitan subjectivity and the converse contours of Caribbean difference.

What is critical in these characterizations is the way in which their tropes now specifically denote neither the conventions of the metropole nor those of its stereotypical other. As the multivalent figure of the Creole displaces the capacity of the dependent metropolitan subject to apprehend its singular reflection, it generates a doubled misrecognition that forecloses the capacity of this subject to recognize either itself or its supposed counterpart. Susan Meyer suggests that "Brontë makes class and gender oppression the overt significance of racial otherness, displacing the historical reasons why colonized races would suggest oppression . . . to nineteenth-century British readers" (1996, 64). But this globalizing claim of oppression may not be as significant as it at first appears because, conversely, Brontë's text in fact may be said to conjure colonial figures of partial presence. Brontë's strategy appropriates the colonial signifier by detaching it from its characteristic signified, a specific moment of metropolitan social oppression through representation that approximates to the racial and political framework of slavery, but this discursive gesture is itself simultaneously undermined and undone by the pervasive, plural disjunctions of the Creole, dooming to failure this representation of Jane as paradigmatic "slave or victim." Jane's "others" are revealed as ultimately, intrinsically disparate, with Jane's prepossessing subjectivity displaced by the Creole indistinctness of her dark, silent double.

Bertha's silence, while apparently threatening, takes on its own discursive significance. For Bertha's reticence is part of a larger symbolic pattern; indeed, the rare black women present in Victorian texts remain stubbornly silent, as Cezair-Thompson suggests: "To configure Bertha as black is to disregard the very real absence and silence of black women in Victorian colonialist texts, and to confer on them a power which they simply did not have" (n.d., 22). In a critical analogy that codes the terms of this discourse as ultimately self-defeating, the unacknowledged racism undergirding Brontë's discourse may also be read as an ahistorical figure of transcendent authoritarianism. In Benedict Anderson's terms, for example, such discursive patterns represent an iterative moment that "dreams of eternal contaminations . . . outside history. . . . The dreams of racism . . . justify not so much foreign wars as domestic repression and domination" (1983, 136). This very repeatability of racist tropes initiates the instability of Brontë's subject and its corollary of indeterminate repression; a discursive position of specific historical bent underlines racism's peculiar inscription in Brontë's text while the multiple character of the Creole reinforces the subjection of the novel's characters and context to the disjunctive double vision of the colonial encounter. By exposing the instability of these paradigmatic figures, cultural signifiers drawn on the paradoxes of the colonial moment, a Creolized reading reflects and recuperates the slippery slope of colonial subjectivity on which such figures are implicitly constructed. For in reducing the colonial subject to an essentially exchangeable value, Brontë allows an infinite substitution of stereotypes, racial formulas, and cultural variables to invade the discourse. Subsequently, through a logic of opposition that the Creole figure now demonstrates to be fundamentally flawed, she tries to reduce the difference of colonial subordination and the dependent alterity of its metropolitan component to a continuation of racialized thought.

Thus Brontë's discursive task is grounded in an ineluctable opposition; on the one hand, in representing Jane Eyre through signifiers of slavery and oppression, she sought to underscore the plight of the modern female subject by substituting a recognizable contemporary for the devalorized figure of the native. Through this metropolitan appropriation of a spectrum of subaltern groups, erasing the terms and specificities of cultural and historical difference, the unstable inscription of these racialized colonial figures ultimately surpassed the unified signifying space onto which the narrator sought to map it. For given the signifier's further destabilization by an uncanny Creole ambivalence in the enigmatic, mysterious figure of Bertha Mason, the discourse could not sustain the complex displacement needed to bridge the shift from colonialist oppression through the plural dislocations of the Creole to engender an assumption of metropolitan mastery. At this juncture, we may read the relation between metropolitan subject and colonial Other as an inverse inscription of Homi Bhabha's formulation of colonial mimicry, as that which "must continually produce its slippage, its excess, its difference." As Bhabha suggests, these figures are ultimately undergirded by a "metonymy of colonial desire . . . that, through the repetition of *partial presence,* which is the basis of mimicry, articulates those disturbances of cultural, racial, and historical difference that menace the narcissistic demand of colonial authority" (1984, 126; 129, emphasis in the text). Here, since both colonizer and colonized are made subject to the articulative ambivalences of the Creole, both categories undergo an unqualified disruption, rendered fragmentary and incomplete by a metropolitan imposture whose insistence on a binary *either/or* subverts its claims to authorial ascendancy.

Brontë's colonialist discourse reflects a larger contemporary English concern with the implications of race and culture for the elaboration of national identity, since this identity itself was articulated as a function of racial difference. Ashcroft, Griffiths, and Tiffin argue the centrality of this point: "The self-identity of the colonizing subject, indeed the identity of imperial culture, is inextricable from the alterity of colonized others . . ." (1998, 12). The instantiation of Creole indeterminacy disguises and dislocates the colonist's assumption of the specular alterity of the other, its tertiary patterns setting the discourse upon an ambivalent axis of instability. A continued textual insistence upon displacement and misrecognition ultimately posits the possibility of constitutive identity for the metropolitan subject and simultaneously dissolves it through the unacceptable monstrosity of the hybrid. This intrinsic textual dissonance is racially produced, as Robert Young argues, when an "antagonistic structure acts out the tensions of a conflictual culture which defines itself through racial ideologies" (1995, 19). The contradictory space opened up by this play of opposition and difference illuminates the logical inconsistencies which propel colonial discourse. In the interstices of this subjective ambiguity, in Gayatri Spivak's words, "the white Creole . . . is caught between the English imperialist and the black native"; for identitarian assumptions such as these are ultimately grounded in the same dualities that subvert Brontë's colonialist discourse, and they force us to confront the unacknowledged complexities of colonial otherness (1986, 269). Through a Creoleness that is intrinsically neither black nor white, but more than the sum of both, Bertha's interstitial identity inverts and distends this intrinsically indeterminate signifier of colonial alterity, its subsequent rupture reversing and reframing the chimeric authoritarianism of a fatally flawed model of metropolitan mastery, a continuously contested cultural identity which, as Young puts it, "has often been constructed as a heterogeneous, conflictual composite of contrary elements, an identity which is not identical with itself" (1995, 3). In this way, the discursive contingencies that both secure and subvert

Brontë's work reaffirm the very disjunctions of identity and desire on whose precipitate logic she founds the implausible inhibitions of her protagonist.

II

French metropolitan discourse produced strikingly similar collisions between contemporary notions of colonial and metropolitan identity, and these provide context for the contradictions undergirding the two primary female protagonists of George Sand's first fictional work, *Indiana* (1832). French colonialist writing in general during this period, ranging from Bernardin de Saint-Pierre's *Paul et Virginie* (1788),[2] through Chateaubriand's *Atala-René* (1801-02) and Claire de Duras's *Ourika* (1823), reveals an almost obsessive fascination with the supposed otherness of the colonial site and with the peoples that were its inhabitants, whether they were transplanted metropolitans, Africans, Native Americans, or Creole Blacks. Paradoxically, while this French colonialist discourse was based on the perception of racial and cultural difference as the cardinal criterion of metropolitan identity, it also proclaimed universal subjectivity for all, at least when these diverse subjects gathered beneath the protective and instructive umbrella of French culture. In France's *mission civilisatrice,* the other, while acting as the locus of the metropole's prohibitions and inhibitions, could yet find in French supremacist culture a transcendent perfection to which it could aspire and from which it could hope for acceptance.

In these terms, the plot of *Indiana,* ostensibly a cautionary tale of a young woman's quest for romantic consummation, is marked both by its inscription of an "exotic" locale and by a complex cultural duality that draws on these assumptions of binary opposition to link Indiana, the privileged young heiress, to Noun, her Creole servant. Indeed, the physical and psychological parallels between these two in the opening section of the novel extend to patterns of naming; both Noun and Indiana fall somewhere outside the lexicon of "typical" names ascribed to French novelistic characters. But while Indiana appears most directly derived from Native American sources, consciously or unconsciously echoing the stereotyped elaboration of exoticism accomplished by Chateaubriand's earlier use of the "Meschacébé" and the "Muscogulges" in *Atala-René,* the name Noun is of an altogether different order. Drawn both lexically and etymologically on an alternative exotic axis, Indiana's other is framed by patterns of Arab writing and religion. Her name itself is a verbal transcription of the Arabic letter "Noûn," that introduces the Sûrat 4, An-Nisâ, a critical chapter of the Koran entitled "The Women."[3] This is but one of a number of Sûrats in the Qur'an that begin with separate letters, not forming any words, but always included in the recitation. *Inter alia,* punishments and perspectives for adulteresses are described here, with an initial punishment of confinement (4:15) later abrogated by the Sûrat An-Nur (24:2), which ordains lashing for unmarried and stoning to death for married adulteresses. While other verses address such subjects as man's superiority over woman and women's necessary obedience (24:34), proscriptions on marriage (24:22-24), and the partitioning of an inheritance (24:11), such an astonishing cultural parallel between the name and its signifier begs the question here of the Creole woman of color's textual assimilation to paradigms of transgression, lechery and lasciviousness. But it is the adulterous context itself, as it fleshes out Noun as cultural subject, that provides the critical framework that overdetermines these protagonists. Through this opposition between discourses deemed "exotic" by the metropole, issues of orientalized difference frame these subjects, establishing an implicit hierarchy that inscribes the one in a "natural," island simplicity and the other, to all intents and purposes, in sin and culpability. By discursively linking Noun to contexts of transgression *avant la lettre,* the text leaves no doubt that she is doomed, a racialized counterpart to Indiana inscribed as a literally "dark double" whose Creole background renders her actions both the converse and the repressed underside of Indiana's desire. And again, the articulation of the intrigue draws upon codes at work within a colonial discourse whose primary desire is grounded by the role of difference in a metropolitan identity's construction of subjectivity.

The desire that determines Indiana as subject and drives the actions of Noun, the colonized counterpart, enacts a complex dialectical relationship grounded, in a paradoxical sense, by the binaries of the colonial encounter. For if desire marks, at bottom, a desire for recognition, and mediates between the colonial subject and his/her object of desire, then it is the textual repression of this authoritarian colonial structure that allows the apparently platonic relationship between these two women to proceed. This discursive displacement allows Indiana's repressed, unlicensed desire to resurface through the desire of the culpable, colonized Other, as Noun's desire for Indiana's fiancé, Raymon, translates a desire for recognition by the colonizer's discourse.

The resonances of this complex colonialist narrative trace these antinomies of the colonial experience while weaving its identitarian and ideological components into a simulacrum of cultural coherence. As the text eventually inverts this series of colonial oppositions, it draws on the integral role played by assumptions of difference in the elaboration of colonial hierarchies, allowing us to link questions of difference and desire to the underlying notions of opposition and substitution through which a colonial discourse maintains its play of authority and codes its congruences. Revealing colonial authority as a fatally flawed discourse of domination and desire between self and Other suggests that while producing patterns of alienation and repression in its attempt to demarcate the cultures and contexts of the colonial site, it also reflects the presence of its own prohibitions and the extent of its own anxiety. As Homi Bhabha has pointed out, "In the doubly inscribed space of colonial representation where the presence of authority . . . is also a question of its repetition and displacement . . . domination is achieved through a process of disavowal that denies the *différance* of colonialist power . . . in order to preserve the authority of its identity . . ." (1986: 172). In other words, by enacting its script through a doubled frame of reference this discourse exposes its intrinsic fallibility; ambiguities of inscription arise when these persistent patterns of colonial repression, the contradictions and oppositions that remain unacknowledged nonetheless constitute the colonial framework.

These discursive inconsistencies and incongruities plague the protagonists and principles of *Indiana.* Trapped by a passionless marriage of convenience to a retired military officer several times her age, plagued by a succession of psychosomatic illnesses, Indiana is a typical example of unsatisfied nineteenth-century female desire complicated by constraints of class. Her bourgeois world of early nineteenth-century France, enervated by the subordination of women under the *Code Napoleon* and the subjugation of blacks beneath the persistent practice of slavery—not to be abandoned in French territories until 1848—embodied a patriarchal society imbued with the power and the means to articulate its authority in both its metropolitan and its colonial sites. In mapping the oppression marking contemporary gender-power relations, Sand aimed primarily at unmasking conventions of feminine repression; placing her not only within the bounds of what Nancy Miller terms "female plot . . . both what the culture has always already inscribed for woman and its reinscription in the linear time of fiction" (1988, 208), but also inscribing her within a system of colonial authority where deconstructing its assumptions of difference would reveal the insufficiencies of metropolitan subjectivity.

It is through this gender-based marginalization—one in which, as Naomi Schor points out, Sand's novels "focus on the institution of marriage as the keystone in the system of exchange of women between men that organizes patriarchal societies"—that the author seeks to inscribe the heroine's difference by subverting the order of masculine social domination (1989, 657). However, if colonialism can be inscribed as the *ne plus ultra* of patriarchal acts, *Indiana*'s characterizations reveal a paradoxical attempt to undermine this domination by providing the protagonist with a counterpart whose actions engage an unsanctioned subjective desire that challenges the society's traditional confines of class, race, and gender. Despite—or indeed because of—constructing her identity as an avatar of the Creole—a category whose ambivalence and inherent slippages have already been elaborated—Indiana's colonial origins ultimately subordinate her to the same patterns of unacknowledged racial and cultural ambiguity that subtend the image of her counterpart. She is a cultural dyad both colonial and metropolitan, a doubled subject whose attempt to suborn a social system based on hierarchies of difference paradoxically reveals a system of subjective exchange produced and propagated by colonial discourse.

The trio of Indiana, her Creole servant and foster-sister, Noun, and the egotistical seducer Raymon de la Ramière also form an interesting variation on the model of triangular desire elaborated by René Girard. If, as Girard contends, "Triangular desire is the desire which transfigures its object," then not only is Raymon's desire for Indiana mediated by Noun and her critical metamorphosis, but also by Indiana's desire through Noun to appropriate the space of difference signified by the shifting, ambivalent alterity of the Creole (1965, 17). Raised together on the Ile Bourbon, as the French island of Réunion was then known[4] Indiana and Noun are marked both by similarity and by difference:

> Noun was Madame Delmare's foster-sister; the two young women had been brought up together and loved each other dearly. Noun was *tall and strong,* glowing with health, active, alert, overflowing with *ardent, passionate creole blood*; and she far outshone with her resplendent beauty *the frail and pallid charms* of Madame Delmare; but the tenderness of their hearts and the strength of their attachment killed every feeling of *feminine rivalry.*
>
> (Ives 1978, 15; emphasis mine)
>
> [Noun était la soeur de lait de madame Delmare; ces deux jeunes personnes, élévées ensemble, s'aimaient tendrement. Noun, grande, forte, brillante de santé, vive, alerte, et pleine de sang créole ardent et passionné, effaçait de beaucoup, par sa beauté resplendissante, la beauté pâle et frêle de madame Delmare; mais la bonté de leur coeur et la force de leur attachement étouffaient entre elles tout sentiment de rivalité feminine.]
>
> (Sand 1832, 36-37)

As foster-sisters, Noun and Indiana are at the same time joined and separated, both self and other, the same yet different; both are referred to quite interchangeably in the text as *la créole.* Yet Noun is given pride of place in this articulation of binaries, and is defined as the arbiter of desire to which Indiana aspires. Indeed, it is her "Creole blood," necessarily, since stereotypically, "passionate" and functioning as a "racial" signifier that separates Noun's mixed-race ethnicity from Indiana's inscription as a displaced metropolitan subject; in this symbolic hierarchy, it is the exoticization of Noun's Creoleness that signifies "health" and "passion" while Indiana's excessively pale and delicate whiteness denotes "frail and pallid charms." This description of the passivity of the metropolitan feminine identity is mark-

edly at odds with the apparent vigor and vitality of Noun's disposition, creating a situation in which the subjective counterpart appears to enjoy a paradoxical primacy. Yet despite this stereotypical exoticism, the text will soon seek to reverse the hierarchy of this representation; the implicit valorization of an indeterminate, colonial Creole doubleness that appears to have escaped the confines of contemporary characterization will be revised by the moral degeneracy—itself also stereotypical—that propels Noun's secret subversion of her mistress's desire.

There is a clear dichotomy between Indiana, the product of a colonial upbringing on the Ile Bourbon, and her "others," those whose inferior social position and racial coloration limit their inclusion. She is thus marked both by her difference from metropolitan "norms," and by her difference from the slavery that supports and makes possible her privileged existence and by the intolerance for repression with which it imbues her:

> But, by dint of watching the constant tableau of the evils of slavery . . . she had acquired . . . an adorable kindliness toward her inferiors, but also an iron will and an incalculable power of resistance to everything that tended to oppress her.
>
> (Ives 1978, 46)
>
> [Mais, en voyant le continuel tableau des maux de la servitude . . . elle avait acquis . . . une indulgence et une bonté adorables avec ses inférieurs, mais aussi une volonté de fer, une force de résistance incalculable contre tout ce qui tendait à l'opprimer.]
>
> (Sand 1832, 68)

This spirit of resistance and revolt, which draws on slavery's oppression to articulate a subjective strategy that functions in contradistinction to it, has already been seen in *Jane Eyre,* and traditionally frames initiatives of identity for the colonized subject; here it has been appropriated to elaborate a differential metropolitan subjectivity. Indiana's identity is thus defined both through and in relation to the experience of the colonial other, rendering her the arbiter of an alterity already inscribed in the colonial discourse that determines the social and political realities of the Ile Bourbon, and establishing a context for the transpositions that are to follow.

Noun soon becomes an unwitting site of sociocultural slippage, a pluralized, polyvalent signifier whose contradictory vitality and otherness mediate the narrator's doubled vision of this unacceptable colonial hierarchy, since her Creoleness is made the contentious converse of the difference from the metropolitan which Indiana already embodies. And since the narrative persistently and, at times, confusingly, refers to both women as "la jeune créole," it exacerbates the critical doubleness and slippage that simultaneously join and separate them. This insistent discursive mirroring of subject and counterpart figures the pervasive ambiguity that ultimately presides over the entire text. More immediately, however, Raymon appears to be in pursuit of immediate gratification where Noun is concerned, for, we are told, he "was in love with the young Creole with the great black eyes . . . but he was in love and nothing more" (Ives 1978, 28). ["Monsieur de Ramière était amoureux de la jeune créole aux grands yeux noirs . . . mais amoureux et rien de plus" (Sand 1832, 73).] As he scales the walls of the Delmare estate to pursue another secret rendezvous with Noun, he is discovered, and immediately falls under the sway of her mistress' charms. Indiana initially forces Raymon into the traditional labyrinths of amorous circumlocution and deferral, seeking more to compensate for her husband's withdrawal from her than to take the relationship to a point of consummation. At the same time, Noun is inscribed for Raymon under the sign of the very cultural doubleness that will ultimately undo their relationship,

> Noun, in white *déshabilé,* with her long black hair for ornament, was a lady, a queen, a fairy. . . . But when Noun . . . came to him . . . with her white apron and neckerchief coquettishly arranged according to the fashion of her country, she was nothing more than a maid and a maid in the service of a pretty woman.
>
> (Ives 1978, 30)

> [Noun, en *déshabillé* blanc, parée de ses longs cheveux noirs, était une dame, une reine, une fée. . . . Mais, lorsque . . . Noun vint le trouver avec son tablier blanc et son madras arrangé coquettement à la manière de son pays, elle ne fut plus qu'une femme de chambre et la femme de chambre d'une jolie femme.]
>
> (Sand 1832, 74)

Through the opposition between purity and alterity traced from the whiteness of her "déshabillé" to the "tablier" and "madras"—this last a bit of traditional garb, a multicolored, checkered headscarf long associated with Creole societies and an incontrovertible sign of tropical "exoticism" and otherness, the knowledgeable note on the particulars of its knotting a sign of the penetration of Creole culture into the metropolitan consciousness—Noun functions as a sign of cultural slippage, written as a complex conundrum whose doubleness mediates the unavowed excess of the colonial Creole.

With Raymon's interest transferred to Indiana, Noun then realizes she is pregnant. Raymon, however, now under Indiana's spell, ceases all contact with Noun; indeed, he appears to have made the transition from physical to emotional attachment, "He had loved Noun with his senses; he loved Madame Delmare with all his heart" (Ives 1978, 57). ["Il avait aimé Noun avec les sens; il aimait madame Delmare de toute son âme" (Sand 1832, 99).] This shift in his affections forces her to write to him in desperation seeking a change of heart.

In a prefigurative episode, she makes use of Indiana's writing paper and wax, in an attempt at appropriation that only reveals her embarrassing lack of education and expression,

> Yet she had taken satin-finished paper and perfumed wax from Madame Delmare's desk, and her style from her heart. But the spelling! . . . Alas! the poor half-civilized girl from Ile Bourbon did not know even that there were rules for the use of language.
>
> (Ives 1978, 32-33)

> [Elle avait pourtant pris le papier satiné et la cire odorante dans l'écritoire de madame Delmare, le style dans son coeur . . . Mais l'orthographe! . . . Hélas! la pauvre fille à demi sauvage de l'île Bourbon ignorait même qu'il y eût des règles à la langue.]
>
> (Sand 1832, 76-77)

As the narrative commentary marks the shift from the allure of "the young Creole" to "the poor half-civilized girl" whose displacement and disease are summarily exposed, it signals the impending reversal of subjective hierarchies, as Noun's Creole mutability must ultimately be controlled and foreclosed by the discourse of the metropole.

Noun finds herself forced, in what is perhaps the most critical encounter in the narrative, to adopt a ruse of identitarian deception and role reversal on the occasion of one of Raymon's visits to Indiana to reestablish communication, in the hope of getting him to stand by her. It is at this point that the subjective dyad of Noun and Indiana comes together in a simulacrum of subjective similarity: taking advantage of Indiana's absence,

> Noun thought of a scheme for making herself more agreeable to him. She arrayed herself in her mistress's clothes, lighted a great fire in the room that Madame Delmare occupied at Lagny. . . .
>
> (Ives 1978, 58)

> [Noun s'avisa d'un moyen pour lui plaire davantage. Elle se para des atours de sa maîtresse, alluma un grand feu dans la chambre que madame Delmare occupait au Lagny. . . .]
>
> (Sand 1832, 99)

Already marked by the traces of a tendency toward transgression from which Indiana has carefully been excluded, Noun seeks an appropriation of her mistress's identity as the route to replacing desire, closing the door of difference by adopting the physical and the spatial trappings which still separate her subjective structure, socially as well as racially, from Indiana's station.

When Raymon approaches this figure of seduction, mistaking her vague outlines for Indiana's across the body of Creole difference and subjective doubleness that he already desires, he is already a victim of a critical misrecognition: Noun's shadowy figure soon indicates to him that she will join him momentarily. As he then enters Indiana's room, Raymon is at first taken in by the metonymical fragments of culture and class which he associates with Indiana as metropolitan subject:

> the engravings representing . . . the *peaks of Ile Bourbon* and the blue shores of Saint-Paul; and, above all, the little bed half-hidden behind its muslin curtains, as *white* and as *modest* as a *maiden's* bed. . . .
>
> (Ives 1978, 59; emphasis mine)

> [les gravures qui représentaient . . . les cimes de l'île Bourbon et les rivages bleus de Saint-Paul; mais surtout ce petit lit à demi caché sous les rideaux de mousseline, ce lit blanc et pudique comme celui d'une vierge. . . .]
>
> (Sand 1832, 101)

This mediatory moment ambiguously represents the absent Indiana; her physicality is assumed by the impassioned Raymon even as her cultural alterity is figured both by the colonial engravings of the island, signifying a geopolitical space to which she simultaneously does and does not belong, and by the suggested transgression of the metropolitan virtue and chastity embodied in this moment of illicit promise, construed by the whiteness of the maiden's bed. It is at this moment of identitarian exchange, in which Raymon assumes Indiana to be present as a metonymical abstraction of the decor that surrounds her, that the narrative most clearly marks the differential inscription of both women in colonialism's system of discursive exchange; Raymon sees the double figure of Noun/Indiana but, blinded by his desire, misconstrues the former and registers only a fleeting impression of the latter: Noun's Creolized, polysemic presence is elided by the very cultural trappings and furnishings that figure the absent Indiana she seeks to displace, and whose presence, in their turn, suggestively remembers the difference and duality of her absent mistress and foster-sister. The complexities of opposition and exchange that lie tacitly in this double moment of misapprehension and erasure mark the point at which subject and counterpart are most completely overdetermined by the logical limitations and multiple displacements inscribed in this representative scheme based on the binaries of racial division.

The subversion of this hierarchical framework, in which the privileging of Indiana as subject is cemented by reversing and erasing the image of the degenerate, ambiguous Creole counterpart parallels Raymon's growing awareness of the paradoxes and contradictions confronting him. Seeing what he wants to see, it is ultimately sexuality, and its repression and prohibition that form the core of this paradigm of doubleness and difference:

> he saw, *in the mirror opposite*, a *white* figure, the *phantom* of a woman . . . appear[ing] radiant and half-nude, in the dazzling light. But it was only a momen-

tary error—Indiana would have concealed her charms more carefully . . . her chaste gown would not have betrayed thus *shamelessly* the mysteries of her shapely legs . . . Noun . . . was graceful but *lacked nobility of bearing*. . . .
>
> (Ives 1978, 60; emphasis mine)

> [il vit apparaître dans la glace en face de lui une forme blanche et parée, le fantôme d'une femme . . . se montrer radieuse et demi-nue aux lumières étincelantes. Mais ce ne fut que l'erreur d'un instant: Indiana eut été plus cachée . . . sa chaste robe n'eût pas ainsi trahi les mystères de sa jambe mignonne . . . Noun . . . avait de la grâce, mais de la grâce sans noblesse. . . .]
>
> (Sand 1832, 101-2)

Forced to confront this chimera, Raymon realizes that he faces only a simulacrum of grace and nobility that ultimately betrays itself. His eventual recognition of Noun's appropriation of Indiana's subject position reveals the phantom's inscription in partial presence, a mirror reversal that announces not only the subject's ultimate destabilization by the polysemic possibilities of Creoleness, but the inevitable elision of these Creole complexities by a discursive construct of metropolitan mastery that will not tolerate such strategies of independence from a supposedly subordinate other. With the erasure of Noun as object of desire, the textual transgression ascribed to the counterpart undergoes a double displacement that punishes her while valorizing Indiana, redeeming her from being simply a pale reflection of Noun's vitality. For Raymon, functioning now as catalyst in this *schéma* of subjectivity, the phantom figure that he ultimately perceives in the mirror, unrecognized at first glance, is now in fact revealed to be an unseemly apparition, a discursively constructed dyad that is the projection both of his displaced desire for Indiana and of the discursive threat of male submission to the notoriously promiscuous Creole female. Indeed, both Raymon's image and Indiana's double are now progressively erased from the mirror's frame, paradoxically revealing the morally degenerate Noun not only as the only reflected subject but also the only one facing an imminent, discursively necessary erasure. Standing alone as the locus of this deformed desire in this double moment of recognition—in which Noun functions both as herself and as "Not Indiana," an impostor aspiring to metropolitan purity—her dual inscription in both absence and presence marks the climactic moment of a colonial identity-crisis. Here the polyvalent pluralism of the doubled Creole counterpart, having threatened to usurp Indiana's subjective space—one already made ambivalent by being constructed as the opposite of the metropolitan "norm"—is rejected and reinscribed as the defrocked, devalued pretender to the supposed superiority of metropolitan civilization and culture.

As Noun's body signifies and shapes the dualities underlying the carnal mysteries she so shamelessly reveals, her actions—and indeed her very identity—are betrayed by that "nobility of bearing" that she so patently lacks, so that the absent but threatened subject of metropolitan mastery is ultimately reinscribed through the double gesture that undergirds Raymon's act of recognition. Indeed, it is he who subsequently suggests that they leave Indiana's "sanctuary": "Let us leave this room; we are not in our proper place here, and I must have some respect for Madame Delmare, even in her absence" (Ives 1978, 63). ["Sortons de cette chambre, nous n'y sommes pas à notre place; et je dois respecter Madame Delmare, même en son absence" (Sand 1832, 102).] However, the mirror's reflection, and the repression it signifies, insistently return, generating through this repetition an infinite, itinerant multiplicity that joins desire to misrecognition and effectively makes colonial Creoleness a functional framework that mediates recognition of the doubled metropolitan subject:

> The two glass panels which repeated Noun's image *ad infinitum* seemed to be peopled by a thousand phantoms. He gazed into the depths of that multiple reflection, looking for a slenderer figure there, and it seemed to him that he could distinguish, *in the last hazy and confused shadow of Noun's image the graceful and willowy form of Madame Delmare.*
>
> (Ives 1978, 63; emphasis mine)

> [Les deux panneaux de glace qui se renvoyaient l'un à l'autre l'image de Noun à l'infini semblaient se peupler de mille fantômes. Il épiait dans la profondeur de cette double réverbération une forme plus déliée, et il lui semblait saisir, dans la dernière ombre vaporeuse et confuse que Noun y reflétait, la taille fine et souple de madame Delmare.]
>
> (Sand 1832, 104)

At this juncture of doubling and paradox desire in fact drives misrecognition, the incessant fragmentation of the otherness of Noun's reflected image allowing Indiana's trace to be inscribed in between its ambiguous axes. But here as well there appears a critical misapprehension of the axes of alterity. The desire to which both subjects succumb is marked by an inadvertent shift in Noun's cultural inscription, such that she is suddenly made generically oriental rather than "Réunionnaise," "her great black eyes . . . betrayed that ardor of the blood, that purely oriental lust which is capable of triumphing over all the efforts of the will" (Ives 1978, 63). ["ses grands yeux noirs lui jetaient . . . cette ardeur du sang, cette volupté toute orientale qui sait triompher de tous les efforts de la volonté" (Sand 1832, 104).] In an uncanny echo of the orientalist misprision we have already witnessed in *Jane Eyre*, Sand's attempts to cleave her Creole subject to negative stereotypes of irresistible sensuality result in a locational ambiguity and contradictions in characterization, so that this discursive doubling ultimately illuminates the extent to which such misapprehensions were a pervasive part of the contemporary consciousness.

Ultimately, this Creole figure and the slippages it represents are made to recede into the background, as an imagined Indiana supplants Noun as the object of a desire approaching its climax,

> It was Indiana whom he saw in the fumes of the punch which Noun's hand had lighted; it was she who smiled upon him and beckoned him from behind those white muslin curtains; and it was she of whom he dreamed upon that chaste and spotless bed, when, yielding to the influence of love and wine, he led thither his dishevelled creole.
>
> (Ives 1978, 63-64)

> [C'était Indiana qu'il voyait dans le nuage du punch que la main de Noun venait d'allumer; c'était elle qui l'appelait et qui lui souriait derrière ces blancs rideaux de mousseline; ce fut elle encore qu'il rêva sur cette couche modeste et sans tache, lorsque, succombant sous l'amour et le vin, il y entraîna sa créole échevelée.]
>
> (Sand 1832, 105)

But this is a coupling permissible only because it is inscribed in misrecognition; given the negative nuances that oppose colony to metropole and, concomitantly, desire to discipline through the "créole échevelée" and the "couche modeste et sans tache" that she despoils, the textual dismantling of the discursive and sexual threat that Noun's unbounded creoleness embodies is all but assured.

In the end, as this colonialist discourse dictates she must be, Noun is undone by her multilayered difference, her polyvalent pluralism threatening to dismantle the dependent subjectivity of an Indiana paradoxically both metropolitan and colonial. Raymon's metropolitan desire that we see framed in the mirror must ultimately be displaced, for it marks Noun's critical displacement of the singularities of metropolitan culture. Her pluralism forces the threatened metropole to turn her "shamelessness" and "lack of nobility" into markers of Creole transgression that make her subjective slippage the critical factor insistently separating her from her metropolitan counterpart. By exposing and undoing colonialism's binary logic here, then, Noun's Creole figure threatens the pristine presumptions of superiority and inviolability undergirding metropolitan identity, and suffers the ultimate discursive punishment—textual erasure—for this act of transgression. With Noun-as-Creole-subject necessarily reduced to a phantom figure, this resurgence of an indefinable, polysemic "ghostly apparition" in the mirror of French metropolitan mastery echoes the intolerable supplementarity of the Creole subject already inscribed in British metropolitan discourse, and marks the transformative return of the metropolitan repressed.

As the initial terms of partial presence—originally definitive of Indiana—are reversed and applied instead to Noun, this displacement resuscitates and resituates Indiana, arresting the anxiety of her absence by drawing from the mirror's frame a signifier of gendered metropolitan subjectivity written through the fundamental doubleness of colonial discourse. Although critically absent from the mirror in this instance, Indiana's submissive but resurgent subjectivity reveals the peripatetic place of Creole alterity in a colonial discourse of self-definition forced to rescue metropolitan identity from the arbitrary, ambiguous patterns of a Creolized Other whose alterity lies outside its binary frame. Her precipitate return forecloses this romantic idyll and jolts Raymon into recognizing the extent of his social transgression. By sketching subjectivity through a doubled Creoleness whose oscillations between metropole and the Ile Bourbon are the mark of a pervasive textual ambiguity, this metropolitan discourse of desire sought to evade and erase its conflictual sense of substitution and contradiction. Later in the novel, in an episode encompassing both parallels and reversals, the phantom figure of Noun will resurface to displace Indiana even further; in a scene bordering on necrophilia, Indiana will greet Raymon at their first romantic rendezvous seated in the shadows, attired not only in the coat worn by Noun to her last meeting with Raymon, but also in Noun's habitual madras headscarf beneath which she has covered her own hair with the dead Noun's salvaged locks. Raymon, in the dark, is at first fearful of having seen a ghost, but finally decodes this deliberate dissimulation—one in which the uncertainties and slippages that are the corollary of the Creole return within a framework of death and disease to allow this critically doubled subject to foreclose the love triangle's consummation. This scene of repetition salvages the sanctity of the marriage contract even as it initiates new directions for the plot, as Raymon's amorous desire is replaced by the desire for revenge.

If we read the figure of Noun as well as the literal erasure her character ultimately undergoes—unsurprisingly, she subsequently drowns herself from an irrecoverable sense of shame—as signifying an unacknowledged avatar of colonial ambivalence, generating a critical hybridity that makes her counterpart, Indiana, a sort of metonymic catalyst of constantly shifting identity—*almost the same but not quite,* in Homi Bhabha's phrase—she plays an uncannily crucial role in the text, embodying the paradox beneath colonialism's repressed fear of the similarity of the Other. This sort of colonialist inscription seeks to efface the protean hybridity that threatens to destabilize both the discourse and the supposedly fixed hierarchies separating the desiring colonial subject from the counterpart as desired object. But, as Homi Bhabha points out, "Both colonizer and colonized are in a process of miscognition where each point of identification is always a partial and double repetition of the *otherness* of the self" (1994, 97; emphasis in the original). By making Noun's Creole excess the *bouc émissaire* of Indiana's colonial in-

sufficiency, the text reveals the anxieties and inconsistencies that drive alterity in a colonial context. Such implosions of apparent parallels and opposites is an inalterable symptom of colonial discourse, in that while its inscriptions tend to allow a series of binary substitutions, safeguarding this logic will not permit the articulation of an independent, amorphous alterity.

In both of these examples, there is strong evidence of the captious conventions that tended to govern both the discursive articulation of female subjectivity and the representation of the stereotyped colonial subject in nineteenth-century France and Britain. In general terms, contemporary narrative practice sought to capitalize on society's vision of the oppressed female classes by comparing their plight with the subjected races and peoples that were increasingly in the forefront of the metropolitan imagination. This explains the emphasis laid by Brontë and Sand upon tropes of slavery and social difference; the relationship to empire in which these authors participated encouraged a certain complicitousness with imperialist ideology, if only in the attempt to reverse their own hierarchies of subordination. As Jenny Sharpe has noted, "English women's bid for gender power passes through a colonial hierarchy of race . . . the story of European woman cannot be told in the absence of reading for the signs of colonial exploitation" (1993, 12). Indeed, such exploitation favored those female figures whose presence unknowingly threatened to negate female metropolitan subjectivity, since these discourses aimed at constructing functional models of feminine agency from the fields of gender- and race-based oppression. In other words, in the attempt to rehabilitate the condition of both these subjected groups, the discourse constructed for itself an undifferentiated symbolic space, displacing but ultimately reinscribing the very racial hierarchies it was seeking to overturn.

This scenario of a participatory misrecognition is complicated even further, however, by the entry of the complex figure of the colonial Creole. On one level, Noun's eventual suicide accomplishes the textual erasure of the excessive, destabilizing threat her existence as polysemic Creole subject signifies. But it is the paradox undergirding this culture of representation, based as it is on a subtle substitution of discrete colonial subjects, that explains a vision of self and Other grounded in metropolitan values of subjection and exclusion that are themselves based on racial and social division. It is in those moments when the apparent authority of the colonial text is inadvertently undermined by the ambivalence of its anxieties, then, when the colonial framework diverges from the terms and teleologies of its metropolitan presuppositions, that its narratives reveal alternative articulations that its binary economy of exchange simultaneously seeks to stifle.

III

The transformative tenor of the racial and cultural *métissage* figured by Bertha Mason's and Noun's inscriptions in the mirror of the metropolitan imagination is an important one; while it does not suggest an absolute equality of perception or practice between the colonialist discourses of France and Britain, it does nonetheless articulate a cultural and discursive phenomenon whose roots lie in a hierarchical context of subjective repression, colonial desire and cultural difference. The feared figure of the Creole has long been linked to negative patterns of sterility, miscegenation and racial impurity. The patriarchal system of domination through which a European minority imposed its will upon the majority of inhabitants of the colonial site produced, *inter alia,* a praxis of racial difference as the primary means of maintaining the superiority of the colonizing powers. Yet at the same time, the physical proximity of these groups militated against maintaining the racial essentialism that lay at the heart of the colonizing process. Indeed, the intrinsically interdependent nature of the colonial encounter would tend to encourage precisely the sort of ethnic and cultural exchanges that would ultimately establish the modernity of *métissage* as a primary aspect of postcolonial culture. For in the end, all the actors in the colonial drama are touched by the double scene of cultural intervocality: the hallmark of global postcoloniality, from Antigua to Zimbabwe, is the fact of its having been spawned by the inhuman institution of slavery and nurtured by the paradoxical pluralisms of its cultural intersections. In other words, societies engaged in colonialist praxis would necessarily, if unconsciously, adopt a double discourse of revision and foreclosure, reflecting an interstitial inscription driven by the principles of both colonizer and colonized.

Over the long term, this double discourse of the colonial would be displaced by the transformative terrain of cultural *métissage,* by emergent, Creolized patterns of identitarian self-definition whose potential would eventually be realized in a postcolonial future rather than in a colonial past. In subverting the dominant notions of ethnic and cultural separation, *métissage* draws initially on these essentialist notions of discursive division and subjective singularity in order to deliberately dissolve the false ground of their fundamental hierarchies. The principle of anxiety articulated through the colonial network of hierarchical oppositions is thus made to confront the resurgence of its repressed Other; the unnameable sterile monster of the infertile hybrid is the unallowed, disavowed, strategic threat, the third term which is less than either one but simultaneously more than the sum of both. This discursive and historical conjunction of both lack and excess, then, marks the advent of difference through what was once the stereotypical, unplaceable *métis*. As a Creolized culture of difference supplants this imbrication of colonizer and colonized, it elaborates a functional alternative to the unitary colonial myths of absence and otherness.

This polysemous pluralism is intrinsic to the figures of the Creole, and allows it to counter the presumed primacy of metropolitan colonial subjectivity. As colonial discourse seeks to extend its presumptions of mastery, the substitutive ground of colonial otherness through which it functions essays a strictly limited binary system of exchange between metropolitan self and colonial Other. But given colonialism's simultaneous generation of Creole constructs that perpetually (re)produce their own difference, and whose incessant slippages eventually reduce the colonial binary to a paradigm of partial presence, these figures ultimately foreclose the very metropolitan identity the unfathomable Creole Other is meant to validate.

These works mark the emergence of a momentous nineteenth-century discursive act, a system of colonial signification based on a binary presumption of difference and a regressive interchangeability of signifiers and signifieds. By seeking to articulate the colonial subject as that which the colonized was not, colonialism's impossible inscription of the polysemous Creole sign revealed the inherent instability of this discourse, the gaps and contradictions of its own unacknowledged authoritarian fictions. But it is in accepting these fictions as both monolithic and monologic that we as readers signify our own corruption by the subjective metropolitan perspectives we have inherited. Even articulations of a postcolonial identity inscribed in alterity and elaborated and engaged from the margin can ultimately produce a differential discourse that still is shaped by those pressing patterns of homogeneity that persist even in the wake of domination's dispersal. As Henry Louis Gates contends: "The threat to the margin comes not from assimilation or dissolution . . . but . . . from the center's attempts to preserve . . . alterity, which result in the homogenization of the other as, simply, other" (1992, 298). Escaping the horns of this discursive dilemma, one that projects otherness as a simulacrum of the same, lies in dismantling its hierarchies of signification, in revealing strategic aporia where these moments of textual slippage permit the exposure of the intrinsic inconsistencies within colonialist ideologies of domination and difference, and in mapping new discursive designations of an affiliative, interstitial heterogeneity. The threatened erasure of these signal ghosts that repeatedly recur in the mirrors of metropolitan alterity can be contested through the strategic displacement of the margin, and by appropriating the multiple, disjunctive modernities of creolization and *métissage*.

Notes

1. *The Oxford English Dictionary,* IV. 7.

2. In an interesting geographical coincidence given the setting of *Indiana,* this work is itself set in the

Ile de France, the contemporary name for the island of Mauritius until it became a British possession in 1810.

3. See *An Interpretation of the Meanings of The Noble Qur'an in the English Language* (122-63). The letter Noûn also begins Sûrat 68, "The Pen." While the significance of these letters in Islamic culture is a matter of debate, and remains decipherable only through mystical illumination, this Sûrat includes a parable—of crucial importance given the contextualization of Sand's character—on the letter of the law, the wages of sin and the price of transgression and forgiveness. Further, in his *Dictionnaire des symboles musulmans,* Malek Chebel points out that the letter "Noûn/ *Nun*"—which he refers to as a "lettre talismanique"—is placed precisely at the center of the Arabic alphabet, splitting the alphabet in two (258), rendering it a fulcrum of difference whose resonances of latent doubleness locate Sand's character even more precisely within a framework of discursive and cultural duality. In poetic terms, the Arabic letter Noûn can be read as even further inscribed in ambivalence, thus framing its fictional homonym in additional layers of difference and paradox. By virtue of the duality of its form as written sign, it also engages what the poet Jean Sénac has called the "Signe des Deux Terres," extrapolating from this intrinsic ambiguity the simultaneity of secrecy and femininity as well as the possibility of latent linkages between superficially contradictory cultural sites. See Jean Sénac (1968), particularly the poem "Le Maître du Noûn." See also Christiane Chaulet-Achour's reading of the ambiguity of this sign and its value for the female discursive subject (1998), particularly the prefatory notes, which refer to "*Noûn /lettre de l'autre alphabet/Noûn/ sourcil et sein/ secret du féminin.*" While I have been unable to pin down any concrete references to an interest in or exposure to Islamic culture on Sand's part, it would appear that the myriad discursive resonances associated with this nomenclature make its choice more than coincidental. I would like to thank Jane Kuntz and Samira El Atia of the University of Illinois French Department for their invaluable help with these references.

4. See the entry "Réunion," in *Dictionnaire général de la francophonie.* The island bore the name of the Ile Bourbon between 1642 and 1793, and again from 1810 to 1848; it was known as Réunion Island during the Revolution and has been so known since 1848. In explaining Indiana's origins, Sand's text points out that, at the end of the Napoleonic period, "Indiana's father had taken refuge in the French colonies [*"le père d'Indiana s'était réfugié aux colonies françaises*" (42/85).] But while Cre-

ole stereotypes and misconceptions are culled in order to consistently inscribe Indiana in non-metropolitan difference, conveying orientalisms that conjoin heat and lasciviousness, such as "she was born in a fiery climate and [had] nineteen years of Ile Bourbon, which are equivalent to twenty-five in our country" [*"elle fût née sous un climat de feu et qu'elle eût dix-neuf ans de l'île Bourbon, qui équivalent à vingt-cinq ans de notre pays*" (41/84)], or the further fact that she was "Ignorant as a genuine creole" [*"Ignorante comme une vraie créole"* (141/174)] the Ile Bourbon is never discursively or geographically placed in any other part of the globe. Assertions such as the one made by Naomi Schor, then, in an article also cited elsewhere in this essay, that Indiana "is . . . a beautiful young woman from the West Indies" (657), are incontrovertibly incorrect.

Works Cited

Anderson, Benedict. 1983. *Imagined Communities: Reflections on the Origin and Spread of Nationalism.* London: Verso.

Ashcroft, Bill, Gareth Griffiths, and Helen Tiffin. 1998. *Key Concepts in Post-Colonial Studies.* New York: Routledge.

Bhabha, Homi. 1994. *The Location of Culture.* New York: Routledge.

———. 1986. "Signs Taken for Wonders: Questions of Ambivalence and Authority under a Tree Outside Delhi, May 1817." In *"Race," Writing, and Difference,* ed. Henry Louis Gates, Jr. Chicago: University of Chicago Press.

———. 1984. "Of Mimicry and Man: The Ambivalence of Colonial Discourse." *October,* 28 [(spring, 1984)]: 125-33.

Brontë, Charlotte. 1969. *Jane Eyre.* 1847. Reprint. Oxford: Clarendon Press.

Cezair-Thompson, Margaret. n.d. "The White Woman in the Attic: Charlotte Brontë, Jean Rhys, and the Colonialist Legacy of *Jane Eyre.*" Unpublished paper.

Chaulet-Achour, Christiane. 1998. *Noûn—Algériennes dans l'écriture.* Biarritz: Atlantica.

Chebel, Malek. 1995. *Dictionnaire des symboles musulmans* Paris: Albin Michel.

David, Deirdre. 1995. *Rule Britannia: Women, Empire, and Victorian Writing.* Ithaca: Cornell University Press.

Gates, Henry Louis, Jr. 1992. "Ethnic and Minority Studies." In *Introduction to Scholarship in Modern Languages and Literatures,* ed. Joseph Gibaldi. New York: MLA.

Gilbert, Sandra M., and Susan Gubar. 1979. *The Mad-woman in the Attic.* New Haven: Yale University Press.

Girard, René. 1965. *Deceit, Desire, and the Novel: Self and Other in Literary Structure.* Trans. Yvonne Frec-cero. Baltimore: Johns Hopkins University Press.

An Interpretation of the Meanings of The Noble Qur'an in the English Language. 1993. Trans. Dr. Muhammad Taqî-ud-Dîn Al Hilâlî and Dr. Muhammad Muhsin Khân. Riyadh, Saudi Arabia: n.p.

Luthi, J-J., A Viatte, and G. Zananini, eds. 1986. *Dictionnaire général de la francophonie.* Paris: Letouzey and Ané.

Meyer, Susan. 1996. *Imperialism at Home: Race and Victorian Women's Fiction.* Ithaca: Cornell University Press.

Miller, Nancy. 1988. *Subject to Change: Reading Feminist Writing.* New York: Columbia University Press.

Oxford English Dictionary. 2nd ed. 1989. Oxford: Clarendon Press.

Raiskin, Judith L. 1996. *Snow on the Canefields: Women's Writing and Creole Subjectivity.* Minneapolis: University of Minnesota Press.

Said, Edward. 1993. *Culture and Imperialism.* New York: Vintage.

———. 1978. *Orientalism.* New York: Vintage.

Sand, George. 1984. *Indiana.* Trans. George Burnham Ives. 1832. Reprint. Chicago: Academy Chicago Publishers.

Sénac, Jean. 1968. *Avant-corps, précédé de Poèmes iliaques et suivi de Diwân du Noûn.* Paris: Gallimard.

Schor, Naomi. 1989. "The Scandal of Realism." In *A New History of French Literature,* ed. Denis Hollier, Cambridge: Harvard University Press.

Sharpe, Jenny. 1993. *Allegories of Empire: The Figure of Woman in the Colonial Text.* Minneapolis: University of Minnesota Press.

Silverman, Kaja. 1983. *The Subject of Semiotics.* New York: Oxford University Press.

Spivak, Gayatri Chakravorty. 1986. "Three Women's Texts and a Critique of Imperialism." In *"Race," Writing, and Difference,* ed. Henry Louis Gates, Jr., Chicago: University of Chicago Press.

Young, Robert. 1995. *Colonial Desire: Hybridity in Theory, Culture, and Race.* New York: Routledge.

John T. Booker (essay date spring-summer 2003)

SOURCE: Booker, John T. "*Indiana* and *Madame Bovary*: Intertextual Echoes." *Nineteenth-Century French Studies* 31, nos. 3-4 (spring-summer 2003): 226-36.

[*In the following essay, Booker observes textual similarities in the seduction scenes of* Indiana *and Gustave Flaubert's 1857 novel* Madame Bovary, *while acknowledging differences in the two authors' handling of narrative outcome in each situation.*]

In his book, *Rereading,* Matei Calinescu uses the felicitous term "haunting" to evoke an experience that is no doubt familiar to most readers: "there are texts that haunt other texts," he observes, "in the sense that they appear in them as expected or unexpected visitors and even, one might say, as phantoms or specters, if such notions could be freed of their sinister connotations" (xi). Richly metaphorical, Calinescu's phrasing alludes, not to something that exists in either work by itself, but to a perception that occurs when the two come together in the mind of a reader.[1] The relative dates of the texts are of little import, Calinescu adds: it is the one that an individual knows first or best that will seem effectively to "haunt" the other. Roland Barthes, in one of his provocative musings, voiced a similar notion when he confessed that, for him, "l'œuvre de référence" (59) was invariably that of Proust, to the extent that, while perusing something by Stendhal or Flaubert, for example, he might have the unexpected impression of suddenly "finding" Proust (58-59). George Sand's **Indiana** (1832) and Flaubert's *Madame Bovary* (1857) offer an intriguing illustration of such a "*souvenir circulaire*" (Barthes 59) or "circular haunting" (Calinescu xi). Whether one discovers them in the order of their publication or comes to the earlier novel only after the much more famous one, striking textual echoes in key sequences may very well bring the two together in the reader's mind.

The sequences in question both lead toward scenes of seduction, although the actual outcomes are quite different. Emma Bovary is in fact seduced by Rodolphe Boulanger, at a time when she is especially vulnerable. The end of a platonic relationship with Léon leaves her all the more sensitive to what she sees as the dreary, sterile nature of her everyday life. Rodolphe, "de tempérament brutal et d'intelligence perspicace" (1:167), immediately sizes up the situation: "Pauvre petite femme! Ça baille après l'amour, comme une carpe après l'eau sur une table de cuisine" (1:167). Sure that he can have Emma, his only concern is for what one might call, in today's military parlance, an "exit strategy": "mais comment s'en débarrasser ensuite?" (1:167). The crude, dehumanizing tone of this monologue establishes a frame of reference against which the reader can subsequently appreciate (and judge) the finely crafted language that Rodolphe brings to bear on Emma during the *comices agricoles.* When he reappears after a strategic absence of six weeks, he does not have to wait much longer: once Emma has been able to procure the proper riding costume—an *amazone*[2]—the two set off on horseback for the forest where she will succumb to his advances.

In **Indiana,** the sequence of events unfolds at Paris (chs. 5-6), in the apartments of Madame de Carvajal, the heroine's aunt. Married to the brutish Colonel Delmare, Indiana has been introduced at a ball to an attractive young nobleman, Raymon de Ramière.[3] The two meet again a few nights later in Madame de Carvajal's *salon*, where in spite of the stultifying atmosphere Raymon manages to convey his feelings to Indiana, who promptly falls under the spell of his charm. Raised by a "père bizarre et violent" (68), Indiana has grown up starved for affection, clinging to a dream: "Un jour viendra où tout sera changé dans ma vie [. . .], où l'on m'aimera, où je donnerai tout mon cœur à celui qui me donnera le sien; en attendant, souffrons; taisons-nous, et gardons notre amour pour récompense à qui me délivrera" (69). Later passages will confirm what this one already suggests, that Indiana, like Emma Bovary, has what Raymon comes to call, derisively, a "tête romanesque" (217). A short time in the presence of M. de Ramière is enough to make Indiana believe she has met the man of her dreams: "Elle le vit comme elle le désirait," explains the narrator, "comme elle l'avait rêvé" (71). Fearing instinctively for Raymon's safety, should Delmare become suspicious, Indiana feigns illness the following evening rather than attend another ball. When Raymon sees Mme de Carvajal arrive alone, he surmises that her niece is avoiding him, promptly leaves to find her, and surprises Indiana, weeping alone in her aunt's apartments, where he addresses her boldly by first name:

> —Indiana, lui dit-il, vous pleurez . . . Pourquoi pleurez-vous? . . . Je veux le savoir.
>
> Elle tressaillit de s'entendre appeler par son nom; mais il y eut encore du bonheur dans la surprise que lui causa cette audace.
>
> (74)

Reading that passage, anyone familiar with *Madame Bovary* is likely to think at once of Rodolphe's carefully considered use of Emma's name, a tactic he tries out when he reappears after the *comices*:

> —Emma . . .
>
> —Monsieur! fit-elle en s'écartant un peu.
>
> —Ah! vous voyez bien, répliqua-t-il d'une voix mélancolique, que j'avais raison de vouloir ne pas revenir; car ce nom, ce nom qui remplit mon âme et qui m'est échappé, vous me l'interdisez! Madame Bovary! . . . Eh! tout le monde vous appelle comme cela! . . . Ce n'est pas votre nom, d'ailleurs; c'est le nom d'un autre!
>
> (1:188)

However base his intentions, Rodolphe's insight is excellent and his analysis to the point; he has a keen sense of how a woman such as Emma Bovary—or Indiana, one might add—whose existence has always been defined by her relationship first to father, then to husband, will react when she hears a man use her "own" name, and thereby appear to recognize her true identity.[4] His studied reply articulates what Emma herself presumably

feels, and while this first initiative does not yield immediate results from Rodolphe's point of view, it helps set the stage for a very different issue at a later moment.

If the approach of Raymon and Rodolphe seems similar, the two are nonetheless quite different by temperament. Rodolphe, going about the task of seduction in a deliberate manner, owes his eventual success in large measure to the self-control he exercises over his actions and especially his language. Raymon can be just as calculating on occasion, but he is fundamentally much more impulsive. As the Sandian narrator remarks early in the novel: "C'était un homme à principes quand il raisonnait avec lui-même; mais de fougueuses passions l'entraînaient souvent hors de ses systèmes" (49). While Rodolphe never loses sight of the fact that he is using cliched language for a specific end (witness his cool, circumspect attitude when it comes time to draft a *lettre de rupture*), Raymon tends to get swept away by his own rhetoric: "ce n'était pas la passion qui le rendait éloquent," the narrator reveals at another point, "c'était l'éloquence qui le rendait passionné" (62).

That such is the case becomes apparent when Raymon addresses Indiana at length after surprising her. Brushing aside her protestations of respect and love for Delmare, he claims to be able to "read" her unhappy situation—"je sais tous les secrets de votre destinée" (75)—and begins to evoke what might have been, had they only met earlier. As he fills out that hypothetical scenario, Raymon's phrasing grows increasingly incantatory. By the time he envisions himself watching over the young woman as she sleeps, waiting for her to awaken, he seems to draw from his own words the same sort of emotional charge that he will momentarily elicit from Indiana:

> J'aurais baisé sans bruit les tresses de vos cheveux, j'aurais compté avec vol-upté les palpitations de votre sein, et, à votre réveil, Indiana, vous m'eussiez trouvé là, à vos pieds, vous gardant en maître jaloux, vous servant en esclave, épiant votre premier sourire, m'emparant de votre première pensée, de votre premier regard, de votre premier baiser . . .
>
> —Assez, assez! dit Indiana tout éperdue, toute palpitante; vous me faites mal.
>
> (76)

The phrasing of Indiana's interjection here recalls a moment during the outing on horseback in *Madame Bovary,* when Rodolphe advances on Emma with clenched teeth and a fixed, purposeful stare. Her frightened reaction—"Oh! vous me faites peur! vous me faites mal! Partons" (1:192)—has an immediate effect, although it only makes her eventual surrender all the more certain; seeing that an aggressive approach will not work, Rodolphe quickly reverts to his proven strategy of playing on Emma's romanesque sensibilities. Indiana's use of the same phrase, on the other hand, is less a response to menacing behavior than a release of pent-up emotion; as delighted as she must be to hear such language for the first time, she feels duty-bound, given her situation, to reject the sort of impossible fantasy that Raymon is conjuring up: "ne me montrez pas le ciel sur la terre," she laments, "à moi qui suis marquée pour mourir" (76).

Far from silencing Raymon, Indiana's fatalistic remarks serve only to fan the flames of his rhetorical ardor, and a second long speech sounds like a rehearsal of material on which Rodolphe draws, much more cynically, during the *comices*. Abandoning the past conditional, Raymon assures Indiana that he will not allow her to die, that his life is henceforth tied to hers, for she is the woman he has always dreamed of finding: "De tout temps, tu m'étais destinée, ton âme était fiancée à la mienne, Indiana!" (76). In light of Indiana's life-long dream noted earlier, one can easily imagine her reaction to this rhapsodic phrasing. The laws of men may have given her to another, Raymon continues, but she remains the companion God has chosen for him: "Vois-tu, Indiana, tu m'appartiens, tu es la moitié de mon âme, qui cherchait depuis longtemps à rejoindre l'autre" (76). However incongruous the circumstances of their first meeting (in the opening scene, Raymon, shot while scaling the walls of Delmare's property, was carried wounded to Indiana's feet) it was no coincidence, he insists, that brought them together: "ce n'est ni le hasard ni le caprice, c'est la fatalité" (77).

For the reader of *Madame Bovary,* this sort of language in general—and that last phrase in particular—will bring to mind the campaign of seduction waged during the *comices agricoles* at Yonville. Rodolphe, too, portrays himself as one of those "âmes sans cesse tourmentées" (1:178), searching for happiness, which it is destined to find one day in the form of a fellow soul, similarly disposed; when that rendez-vous at long last occurs, "On ne s'explique pas, on se devine. On s'est entrevu dans ses rêves" (1:178). In counterpoint to the public speaker's praise of those who lead a modest existence, content to "do their duty," Rodolphe appeals to a higher sense of "duty" to appreciate all that is great and beautiful in life, which can come, he affirms, only from the passions: "Ne sontelles pas la seule belle chose qu'il y ait sur la terre, la source de l'héroïsme, de l'enthousiasme, de la poésie, de la musique, des arts, de tout enfin!" (1:179). As the official below drones on, Rodolphe edges closer to Emma and condemns "cette conjuration du monde" (1:180) that would prevent "deux pauvres âmes" (1:181) from finding one another: "Oh! n'importe, tôt ou tard, dans six mois, dix ans, elles se réuniront, s'aimeront, parce que la fatalité l'exige et qu'elles sont nées l'une pour l'autre" (1:181).[5]

In each case, this invocation of "fate" has a dramatic impact on the heroine, although the tangible results are less immediate in *Madame Bovary.* Rodolphe's mesmerizing performance during a public ceremony can serve only as a prelude, laying the groundwork for a conquest that will come some two months later, once he has worked out a scenario in which he can be alone with Emma. Raymon, by contrast, enjoys a much more private setting and forges ahead to make the most of the occasion. Having claimed that destiny, working ironically through the violence of Indiana's husband, has brought the two of them together, he assures her that nothing can henceforth separate them, at which point Indiana finally finds her voice once more:

> —Lui, peut nous désunir! interrompit vivement madame Delmare, qui, s'aban-donnant aux transports de son amant, l'écoutait avec délices. Hélas! hélas! vous ne le connaissez pas; c'est un homme qui ne pratique pas le pardon, un homme qu'on ne trompe pas. Raymon, il vous tuera! . . .
>
> Elle se cacha dans son sein en pleurant.
>
> (77)

This is a pivotal moment, as Indiana effectively surrenders to Raymon. Beyond her body language, the fact that she now addresses him by his first name (after he has used hers ten times in the course of his two extended speeches) signals an acceptance of intimacy on her part. That no physical seduction actually occurs is an early indication that the "laws" which govern this fictional world are more melodramatic in nature than realist. When Raymon, taking advantage of Indiana's emotional turmoil, presses his lips to hers, she faints, and he rings for the servants.[6] As it turns out, this is but the first in a series of close calls for Sand's heroine, who is periodically delivered from perilous circumstances at the last moment (most often, subsequently, by her ever-vigilant protector, Sir Ralph.)[7]

If we hold in mind this passage from **Indiana,** and turn to the scene of seduction in *Madame Bovary,* we find striking similarities. When Emma agrees to go horseback riding with Rodolphe, leaving behind her unsatisfying existence in Yonville, she places herself at his mercy. As he searches for the right approach (even resorting momentarily to a show of force, as we have seen), Rodolphe draws liberally once again upon his stock of cliches: "Est-ce que nos destinées maintenant ne sont pas communes?" (1:192), he intimates at one point, in a phrase worthy of Raymon. Emma is for him, he assures her, "comme une madone sur un piédestal" (1:193) whom he needs in order to live: "Soyez mon amie, ma sœur, mon ange!" (1:193). In the end, however, it is not rhetorical flourish, but Rodolphe's use of her name (for only the second time in this case) which serves to overcome a final measure of resistance:

> —J'ai tort, j'ai tort, disait-elle. Je suis folle de vous entendre.

—Pourquoi? . . . Emma! Emma!

—Oh! Rodolphe! . . . fit lentement la jeune femme en se penchant sur son épaule.

Le drap de sa robe s'accrochait au velours de l'habit. Elle renversa son cou blanc, qui se gonflait d'un soupir, et, défaillante, tout en pleurs, avec un long frémissement et se cachant la figure, elle s'abandonna.

(1:193)

Differences in context notwithstanding, these two passages share a remarkable number of textual features. To be sure, it is hardly surprising to find certain touches—the shedding of tears, the gesture of the woman burying her face against the man's shoulder or chest—in what must have already been, by the time *Indiana* was published, something of a stereotypical scene of seduction. Even the presence of the same verbs—*se cacher, s'abandonner*—might seem natural enough under the circumstances, although it is notable that the second of these two expressions becomes an important recurring motif in each novel. But when one takes into account as well the decisive play of names, all of this together can seem more than just coincidence.

Given these similarities, one naturally wonders if the author of *Madame Bovary* might have drawn inspiration directly from *Indiana,* although there is no hard evidence to make such a case. As a young man, Flaubert was an avid reader of Romantic literature (Bruneau 17-38), but in his early correspondence he mentions the work of Sand only sporadically. In a letter of October 1838, he urges Ernest Chevalier to read *L'Uscoque* (12:347); several months later (March 1839), he confides to the same friend: "Tu me dis que tu as de l'admiration pour George Sand; je la partage bien et avec la même réticence. J'ai lu peu de choses aussi belles que *Jacques*" (12:354). Up to the time of *Madame Bovary*, those are the only references to novels by Sand, and if the tenor of the remarks seems positive enough, the narrator of his first *Education sentimentale* (1845) alludes disparagingly to the "écoliers de quatrième" and the "couturières qui lisent George Sand" and who, by virtue of that fact, are not to be considered "gens d'esprit" (8:73). In late 1852, already at work now on *Madame Bovary*, Flaubert urges Louise Colet in characteristically coarse terms to avoid, in her own writing, the example of Sand: "Dans George Sand, on sent les fleurs blanches; cela suinte, et l'idée coule entre les mots comme entre des cuisses sans muscles" (13:250). A few years later, finally, in a letter to Louis Bouilhet (May 1855), he conveys his reactions to *Histoire de ma vie,* which he is then reading: "Tous les jours je lis du George Sand et je m'indigne régulièrement pendant un bon quart d'heure" (13:499). Beyond the correspondence, neither the Pommier-Leleu "reconstruction" of *Madame Bovary* nor Yvan Leclerc's recent edition of the *Plans et scénarios* reveals any indication of interest on Flaubert's part in the work of Sand, let alone an awareness of *Indiana.*

In fact, from what we know today, it would seem to be the publication of *Madame Bovary* that eventually brings a copy of *Indiana* into Flaubert's possession. Until installments of his novel began to run in the *Revue de Paris* in late 1856, George Sand, herself a well-known figure—the "most celebrated novelist" of the July Monarchy, claims Margaret Cohen (122)—would have had no reason to have heard of Flaubert. When the latter sends her a copy of his published novel the following spring, he inscribes it, with appropriate modesty, "A Madame Sand, hommage d'un inconnu" (Jacobs 50). It is only some years later that a regular correspondence, and gradually a warm and genuine friendship, develops between the two.[8] Following a cordial visit to Croisset in 1866, Sand sends Flaubert a complete edition of her works, presumably including *Indiana* (Tricotel 52).

Absent any proof of direct influence, one might be inclined to see in textual echoes such as those highlighted above just one more illustration of Flaubert's often noted penchant for recycling, to ironic effect, Romantic cliches and topoi. After all, to the extent that Emma Bovary "désire à travers les héroïnes romantiques" (14), as René Girard argued, the young woman we see at this early stage of Sand's novel would appear to be a fitting model for Flaubert's heroine. Having drawn from books a notion of what life should be like, and with her dream of an ideal man still unsullied by reality, Indiana falls as easily for Raymon's rhetoric as Emma does for that of Rodolphe. Not surprisingly, critics have suggested on occasion that Indiana is indeed a literary precursor of Emma Bovary. Henri Peyre, for example, once asserted in passing that "*Indiana* had in several respects anticipated *Madame Bovary.* Sand's novels, one remembers, were among the readings that had led Emma astray into romantic dreams" (xi). For Naomi Schor, Emma is Indiana's "most illustrious descendant" (53), a phrase repeated by Sand's most recent biographer, Belinda Jack (195). Béatrice Didier, alluding to Indiana's «bovarysme» avant l'heure (*George Sand* 66), explains: "Indiana annonce Emma Bovary; elle a la beauté de ces héroïnes qui souffrent du contraste entre l'infini du rêve et la pauvreté de leur existence de femmes esclaves, confinées dans l'univers étroit de la vie quotidienne" (*George Sand* 70-71).[9]

And yet, in certain ways, Indiana does *not* make a likely model for Emma. If both start out with a "conception romanesque de l'existence" (Salomon 143n), Sand's protagonist, unlike Flaubert's, comes in due course to recognize and accept that fact. In a letter to Raymon, Indiana admits he was right to accuse her of having "appris la vie dans les romans à l'usage des femmes de chambre, dans ces riantes et puériles fictions où l'on intéresse le cœur au succès de folles entreprises et d'impossibles félicités" (240). Indiana's phrasing here evokes the kind of fiction that Emma also finds so seductive; it is as if both women have read the same body of literature. But whereas Indiana learns from disillusioning experience and eventually faces up to the reality of her situation, Emma persists in believing that she should be able to live her life like a novel and becomes increasingly bitter when she is unable to do so.

What is more, the behavior of the two protagonists is quite different in one fundamental respect. It is clearly a mimetic impulse that leads Emma to embrace adultery, but had **Indiana** been one of those unnamed works of Sand (and Balzac) to which she turned in her boredom at Tostes, she would hardly have found in it the sort of "assouvissements imaginaires pour ses convoitises personnelles" (1:99) to which the narrator alludes. For while Indiana runs the risk of being seduced by Raymon, and effectively offers herself to him more than once, in the end she never does actually belong to that "légion lyrique de [. . .] femmes adultères" (1:195) who figured in Emma's youthful reading and whose number she is delighted to join after the outing on horseback with Rodolphe. Sand herself, in her **"Lettre à M. Nisard,"** pointed out that in **Indiana** "il n'y a pas d'adultère commis" (1:936), and Nathalie Buchet Rogers puts the matter very well: "Indiana représente la passion adultère séparée de tout désir physique et de toute jouissance corporelle" (136).[10] By her actual behavior, in short, Indiana is simply not the kind of heroine Emma Bovary longs to emulate.

In the final analysis, then, the coincidence of textual features in these two novels seems to defy logical explanation. The heroines, alike in some respects, are nonetheless quite dissimilar in others and the respective scenes of seduction lead to very different outcomes. Occurring as they do in key scenes, the echoes are prominent enough to make one wonder if Flaubert might indeed have come across **Indiana** at some point and been struck, if only unconsciously, by certain details which then resurfaced in his own novel. We will never know for sure, of course, and as Didier cautions more generally, "les «sourciers» doivent toujours faire preuve de prudence, car, chez les écrivains dignes de ce nom, et dans le creuset de la création littéraire, les influences fusionnent, se métamorphosent" (*George Sand* 45). In a very real sense, moreover, the search for sources is less productive than the sort of musing that inevitably occurs when two works come together this way in the experience of reading. Whichever one may appear at a given moment to "haunt" the other, to recall Calinescu's phrasing, the reader is sure to see *both* in a new, better perspective.

Notes

1. Christiansen, in her comparative reading of *Eugénie Grandet* and *Un cœur simple,* also draws on Calinescu's model. For a similar conception of the reader's experience, framed within a discussion of literary allusion, see Pasco 12-14.

2. Indiana, during the hunting episode in the second part of Sand's novel, wears an *amazone* (141) and in fact acts the part of the mythical female warrior—much to Raymon's discomfort (150-51); in a typical touch of Flaubertian irony, Emma, although "properly" dressed in her own eyes, ends up giving herself to Rodolphe during their outing on horseback.

3. Maurin highlights interesting parallels between this ball scene and an analogous moment in *La Princesse de Clèves* when the heroine and Nemours first see each other.

4. Just how sensitive Emma is to this use of her first name will be confirmed the day after the eventual seduction, when she entreats Rodolphe to "l'appeler encore par son nom" (1:195). For a lucid study of names in *Madame Bovary,* see Hemmings, whose analysis would apply as well to the situation of Indiana.

5. In his insightful reading of the *comices* scene, Haig focuses on the double seduction taking place and "the *efficacy* of worn rhetoric: Emma is no less responsive to Romantic clichés than is the crowd to the councillor's platitudes" (71).

6. While Raymon, in certain respects, may seem to be a descendant of the libertine hero, he differs from Valmont, for example, who is more than willing to take full advantage of the unconscious Présidente de Tourvel (*Les Liaisons dangereuses,* Letter cxxv).

7. In the context of a study of intertextual echoes between these two novels, it is interesting to note that Sir Ralph is also identified on several occasions as M. *Rodolphe* Brown. In spite of the similarity of names, Sand's character and Flaubert's Rodolphe Boulanger obviously play quite different roles.

8. For treatments of the correspondence and friendship between Flaubert and Sand, see Didier, *George Sand* (571-99); Jacobs; Reid; Schor (185-211); Tricotel.

9. For other passing comparisons of either the two novels or the two heroines, see Crecelius 68, 70; Didier, "*Indiana,*" 14-15; Freadman 172; Harkness 123. The only study I have found that actually compares some aspect of the two novels is a brief article by Massardier-Kenney, who sees in Sand's descriptive practice certain general similarities to that of Flaubert.

10. The preceding discussion points up more generally the rather loose sense in which we tend to

talk about Flaubert's recycling of Romantic cliches—a critical cliche in its own right—and the value of recent attempts, such as those by Cohen and Rogers, to distinguish more clearly between different kinds of novels written during the first half of the nineteenth century.

Works Cited

Barthes, Roland. *Le Plaisir du texte*. Paris: Seuil, 1973.

Bruneau, Jean. *Les Débuts littéraires de Gustave Flaubert, 1831-1845*. Paris: Colin, 1962.

Calinescu, Matei. *Rereading*. New Haven: Yale UP, 1993.

Christiansen, Hope. "Two Simple Hearts: Balzac's Eugénie and Flaubert's Félicité." *Romance Quarterly* 42 (1995): 195-202.

Cohen, Margaret. *The Sentimental Education of the Novel*. Princeton: Princeton UP, 1999.

Crecelius, Kathryn J. "*Indiana*: Heroic Romance and Bourgeois Realism." *Family Romances: George Sand's Early Novels*. Bloomington: Indiana UP, 1987. 57-80.

Didier, Béatrice. *George Sand écrivain*: "*Un grand fleuve d'Amérique*." Paris: PUF, 1998.

———. "*Indiana*, ou la naissance d'un écrivain." Préface. *Indiana*. Paris: Gallimard (Folio), 1984. 7-32.

Flaubert, Gustave. *Œuvres complètes de Gustave Flaubert*. 16 vols. Paris: Club de l'Honnête Homme, 1971-75.

Freadman, Anne. "Sandpaper." *Southern Review: Literary and Interdisciplinary Essays* 16 (1983): 161-73.

Girard, René. *Mensonge romantique et vérité romanesque*. Paris: Grasset, 1961.

Haig, Stirling. "*Madame Bovary*." *Flaubert and the Gift of Speech: Dialogue and Discourse in Four "Modern" Novels*. London: Cambridge UP, 1986. 53-106.

Harkness, Nigel. "Writing under the Sign of Difference: The Conclusion of *Indiana*." *Forum for Modern Language Studies* 33 (1997): 115-28.

Hemmings, F. W. J. "Emma and the 'Maw of Wifedom.'" *L'Esprit Créateur* 10 (1970): 13-23.

Jack, Belinda. *George Sand: A Woman's Life Writ Large*. NY: Knopf, 2000.

Jacobs, Alphonse, éd. *Gustave Flaubert-George Sand: Correspondance*. Paris: Flammarion, 1981.

Leclerc, Yvan. *Plans et scénarios de Madame Bovary: Gustave Flaubert*. Paris: CNRS Editions/Zulma, 1995.

Massardier-Kenney, Françoise. "*Indiana*: A Textual Analysis of Facial Description." *International Fiction Review* 15 (1988): 117-22.

Maurin, Mario. "Un Modèle d'*Indiana*?" *French Review* 50 (1976): 317-20.

Pasco, Allan H. *Allusion: A Literary Graft*. Toronto: U of Toronto P, 1994.

Peyre, Henri. "Keynote Address: George Sand, Our Contemporary." *The World of George Sand*. Ed. Natalie Datlof, Jeanne Fuchs, David A. Powell. NY: Greenwood P, 1991. xi-xix.

Pommier, Jean, et Gabrielle Leleu, éds. *Gustave Flaubert*: Madame Bovary. *Nouvelle Version précédée des scénarios inédits*. Paris: Corti, 1949.

Reid, Martine. "Flaubert et Sand en correspondance." *Poétique* 85 (1991): 53-68.

Rogers, Nathalie Buchet. *Fictions du scandale: Corps féminin et réalisme romanesque au dix-neuvième siècle*. Purdue UP, 1998.

Sand, George. *Indiana*. Ed. Pierre Salomon. Paris: Garnier, 1983.

———. "Lettre à M. Nisard." *Lettres d'un voyageur. Œuvres autobiographiques*. 2 vols. Ed. Georges Lubin. Paris: Gallimard/Pléiade, 1971. 936-43.

Schor, Naomi. *George Sand and Idealism*. New York: Columbia UP, 1993.

Tricotel, Claude. *Comme deux troubadours: histoire de l'amitié Flaubert-Sand*. Paris: SEDES, 1978.

FURTHER READING

Criticism

Harkness, Nigel. "Writing under the Sign of Difference: The Conclusion of *Indiana*." *Forum for Modern Language Studies* 33, no. 2 (April 1997): 115-28.

　　Analyzes *Indiana*'s often critically maligned conclusion, finding it to be a refusal of patriarchal ideology.

Little, Roger. "The First Novels of Hugo and George Sand: A Link?" *French Studies Bulletin*, no. 86 (spring 2003): 7-8.

　　Suggests a possible affinity between the opening of *Indiana* and that of Victor Hugo's novel *Bug-Jurgal*.

Massardier-Kenney, Françoise. "*Indiana*: A Textual Analysis of Facial Description." *International Fiction Review* 15, no. 2 (summer 1988): 117-22.

　　Studies Sand's narrative depiction of characters' faces in *Indiana*, finding that her descriptions influenced those of Gustave Flaubert's *Madame Bovary*.

Naginski, Isabelle Hoog. "*Indiana* or the Creation of a Literary Voice." In *George Sand: Writing for Her Life,* pp. 53-76. New Brunswick, N.J.: Rutgers University Press, 1991.

Considers *Indiana*'s thematic concern with the triumph of authentic discourse and the transfiguring power of spoken and written communication.

Sandars, Mary F. "*Indiana* and *Valentine.*" In *George Sand,* pp. 95-107. London: Robert Holden & Co. Ltd, 1927.

Praises *Indiana* as a significant work of social critique aimed at the inequities of nineteenth-century marriage, while highlighting the stylistic merits of the work and acknowledging that certain aspects of the novel's romantic sentiment appear dated in the early twentieth century.

Schor, Naomi. "Idealism in the Novel: Recanonizing Sand." *Yale French Studies,* no. 75 (1988): 56-73.

Calls for the recanonization of Sand and considers why her literary reputation suffered its decline; also assesses whether *Indiana* should be considered an idealist novel.

Schwartz, Lucy M. "Persuasion and Resistance: Human Relations in George Sand's Novels, *Indiana* and *Lélia.*" In *George Sand Papers: Conference Proceedings, 1978,* edited by Natalie Datlof et al., pp. 70-6. New York: AMS Press, 1982.

Evaluates dialogue between male and female characters in *Indiana* and *Lélia.*

Thackeray, William Makepeace. "Madame Sand and the New Apocalypse." In *The Paris Sketch Book.* Vol. 2, pp. 102-51. London: John Macrone, 1840.

Impressionistic essay that lauds Sand's *Indiana* as "most exquisite prose."

Thornton, Hermann H. Introduction to *Indiana,* by George Sand, pp. ix-xxvii. New York: Charles Scribner's Sons, 1935.

Brief bio-critical study noting the stylistic and Romantic qualities of *Indiana.*

Vest, James M. "Fluid Nomenclature, Imagery, and Themes in George Sand's *Indiana.*" *South Atlantic Review* 46, no. 2 (May 1981): 43-54.

Considers the significance of the sea and other watery imagery in *Indiana.*

Ward, Margaret E., and Karen Storz. "Fanny Lewald and George Sand: *Eine Lebensfrage* and *Indiana.*" In *The World of George Sand,* edited by Natalie Datlof, Jeanne Fuchs, and David A. Powell, pp. 263-70. New York: Greenwood Press, 1991.

Compares the portrayal of marriage in *Indiana* with that in Fanny Lewald's novel *Eine Lebensfrage.*

Additional coverage of Sand's life and career is contained in the following sources published by Thomson Gale: *Dictionary of Literary Biography,* **Vols. 119, 192;** *DISCovering Authors*; *DISCovering Authors 3.0*; *DISCovering Authors: British Edition*; *DISCovering Authors: Canadian Edition*; *DISCovering Authors Modules: Most-studied Authors* **and** *Novelists*; *European Writers,* **Vol. 6;** *Feminism in Literature: A Gale Critical Companion,* **Ed. 1:3;** *Feminist Writers*; *Guide to French Literature, 1789 to the Present*; *Nineteenth-Century Literature Criticism,* **Vols. 2, 42, 57;** *Reference Guide to World Literature,* **Eds. 2, 3;** *Twayne's World Authors*; **and** *World Literature Criticism.*

Ann Yearsley
1753-1806

(Born Ann Cromartie) English poet, novelist, and playwright.

INTRODUCTION

Known to her contemporaries as "The Milkwoman of Bristol," Yearsley was a highly recognizable working-class poet of late eighteenth-century England. Her short-lived career coincided with a period of public interest in the so-called primitive poets—unschooled writers of alleged natural genius. Though her works have suffered relative obscurity since before her death, contemporary scholars consider Yearsley one of the outstanding plebeian female poets of the period whose writings are widely thought to merit renewed historical and literary scrutiny. With the financial assistance of her early patron Hannah More, Yearsley published her first collection of lyric verse *Poems, on Several Occasions* in 1785. Yearsley followed this successful volume with two additional full-length poetic collections, as well as several examples of minor and occasional verse, most of which were originally printed in pamphlet form. Her works in other genres include a Gothic romance inspired by the novels of Ann Radcliffe and Horace Walpole, and a historical play concerned with the early days of the French Revolution.

BIOGRAPHICAL INFORMATION

Born into poverty in the village of Clifton Hill, near Bristol, Yearsley received no formal education as a child, relying instead upon the instruction of her brother William, who reputedly taught her to write, and thereafter pursuing her own project of reading and self study. She married John Yearsley in 1774, a man of very limited capacity as a family breadwinner. Yearsley's principal occupation at this time was that of a milkwoman, but the meager wages she earned selling milk door to door proved hardly enough to keep herself and her family from a life of destitution and potential starvation. By the early months of 1784, Yearsley, her husband, their six children, and Yearsley's mother were evicted from their cottage and forced to find shelter in a stable. When shortly thereafter a certain Mr. Vaughan discovered them there, Yearsley's mother had already died of exposure. Several months later the details of Yearsley's plight came to the attention of Christian philanthropist and poet Hannah More. Learning that Yearsley was herself an unlettered poet, More and her associate Elizabeth Montagu would become her literary patrons by the summer of 1784. Providing Yearsley with financial support, the women called upon a circle of friends and subscribers, seeing to it that Yearsley's work could be published and circulated among them. The appearance of the working-class poet's first collection *Poems, on Several Occasions* in 1785 was a public success, with readers delighted by the unlearned Yearsley's poignant lyrics. Rather than granting the profits made from the sale of the volume directly to Yearsley (and thus making them available to her dissolute husband), More placed the money into a trust and named herself as its executor. When Yearsley subsequently asserted her right to the funds, More reacted with indignation, refusing the request. The two women quarreled publicly over the dispute for years. Meanwhile, Yearsley continued to write and publish, relying on the silent financial patronage of the Earl of Bristol, Frederick Hervey, and the Bishop of Derry for her second volume *Poems, on Various Subjects* (1787). In a harrowing episode in 1789, Yearsley's three young sons were severely flogged when caught playing in the field of the affluent Levi Eames. This offense moved her to litigation and prompted her to publish the small poetic volume *Stanzas of Woe* (1790), which bears the subtitle *Addressed from the Heart on a Bed of Illness, to Levi Eames, Esq., Late Mayor of the City of Bristol.* An invective against Eames's abuse of authority in assigning the children corporal punishment for the minor infraction of trespassing, *Stanzas of Woe* demonstrates Yearsley's return to the elegiac mode of her early verse, in which she confronted the worldly sorrows that had followed her throughout her life. Near the end of her career Yearsley tried her hand at prose composition, producing a Gothic romance entitled *The Royal Captives* (1795-96), designed to appeal to the popular demand for such fiction at the time. As interest in Yearsley's writings dissipated by the late 1790s, she sought other means of enhancing her income, devoting her time to the operation of a circulating library outside Bristol that unfortunately produced only meager profits. Once again impoverished, Yearsley died in 1806, having written no further works of literature after *The Rural Lyre,* a poetry collection published in 1796.

MAJOR WORKS

An elegiac evocation of the poet's life in her native village, "Clifton Hill"—from Yearsley's debut verse collection *Poems, on Several Occasions*—is said to be representative of her finest early verse. Referring to herself via the persona of Lactilla the milkmaid, Yearsley reflects on her lack of education in the poem, musing upon the source of her burgeoning poetic impulse. Another major theme in Yearsley's early verse, from the point of view of modern criticism, concerns the oppressive powers of patriarchal culture and hierarchical class structure, which combined to silence feminine and working-class poetic voices such as her own. Thus, in many of her early pieces, such as "On Mrs. Montagu" and "Night. To Stella" (the latter name a pseudonym for Hannah More), Yearsley simultaneously praised her patrons while subtly lamenting the limitations they had placed upon her. Yearsley demonstrated her considerable literary-critical capacity in the poem "To the Honourable H_____e W_____e, On Reading *The Castle of Otranto*. December, 1784." Written in response to noted author Horace Walpole's Gothic novel, Yearsley's poem employs Walpole's figure of Bianca (a castle servant and minor character in *The Castle of Otranto*) as its first-person narrative persona, engaging from her feminine point of view the gendered limitations of the grotesque fictional world in which she exists. The appearance of Yearsley's second collection *Poems, on Various Subjects* occurred at the zenith of her public clash with former patron More. The volume includes several pieces in which the poet sought to defend herself as a professional writer, including "To Those Who Accuse the Author of Ingratitude" and a poem "Addressed to Ignorance, Occasioned by a Gentleman's Desiring the Author Never Assume Knowledge of the Ancients." Yearsley also responded to the intellectual condescension in the collection's "On Being Presented with a Silver Pen." Increasingly radicalized in the later years of her short career, Yearsley turned to subjects of political and topical interest in several pieces of occasional verse. First published in pamphlet form in 1788, Yearsley's *A Poem on the Inhumanity of the Slave-Trade* is the most notable example of these; it features a long narrative tale in verse centered on the figure of Luco, an African slave exploited by hypocritical, nominally Christian, slavers. Yearsley's literary apprehension of the unfolding French Revolution was recorded in her drama *Earl Goodwin*, performed in 1789, which voices her admiration for the French peasantry newly freed from their aristocratic oppressors and the sympathetic figures of the upper-class who supported them. As the utopian ideals of the revolution began to dissipate in the bloodshed of royal execution, Yearsley visited the subject again in a series of occasional poems published in 1793: *Reflections on the Death of Louis XVI*, her *Sequel to Reflections on the Death of Louis XVI*, and *An Elegy on Marie Antoinette, of Austria, Ci-devant Queen Of France: With a Poem on the Last Interview between the King of Poland and Loraski*. Yearsley's only novel, *The Royal Captives*, is generally characterized as a Gothic romance crafted in the tradition of Ann Radcliffe. Set in eighteenth-century France, the work makes use of the popular legend that King Louis XIV had a twin brother imprisoned behind an iron mask in the Bastille, and of a framing device that describes the fictional text as the memoir of a certain Henry Capet, the son of Louis's supposed twin. Returning to verse in her last work, *The Rural Lyre*, Yearsley expressed her doubts on a variety of subjects, from the visionary aspects of utopian politics and social transformation to the efficacy of religion. Included in the volume is her final retreat from the literary world and its petty squabbles into a natural state of pure poetry with the farewell poem, "The Indifferent Shepherdess to Colin."

CRITICAL RECEPTION

The debut of Yearsley's verse in the late eighteenth century coincided with the vogue of so-called primitive poetry in England and a highpoint of curiosity in the discovery of natural poetic genius untouched by the shaping forces of conventional education and culture. In a letter of 1787 Anna Seward described Yearsley as a "muse-born wonder," reflecting the widespread notion that untrained poets of miraculous talent could be found among the laboring classes. In her 1791 review of Yearsley's *Stanzas of Woe*, Mary Wollstonecraft heavily criticized this romantic idea, suggesting that primitive poets in general, and Yearsley in particular, had been considerably overrated. Wollstonecraft decried the movement to find a modern Homer or Hesiod whose uneducated genius could produce verse that equaled or surpassed in quality that of trained, professional poets. She additionally lamented what she viewed as the labored artificiality of Yearsley's writing in the volume, and its failure to demonstrate any intensification of the early poetic potential featured in Yearsley's *Poems, on Several Occasions*. Well received by its initial readers, this earlier volume had been heavily endorsed by Hannah More, who promoted its spontaneous and natural lyric qualities. The sober analysis of Yearsley's writings, however, devoid of the sentimentality that More and others had used to frame them, contributed to a rapid decline in interest and the relatively swift end to Yearsley's literary career.

This generally negative critical estimation of Yearsley endured throughout much of the twentieth century until a new generation of scholars began to focus on not only the stylistic qualities of Yearsley's writings, but also their historical, social, and gender contexts. In addition to studying her works with regard to eighteenth-century discourse on the subject of genius, contemporary scholars have also frequently discussed the extent to which primitive poets such as Yearsley were excluded from and defined by mainstream literary culture. Mary Waldron, Yearsley's contemporary biographer and the leader of a critical reassessment of her writings, has also questioned the traditional classification of Yearsley as a rustic poet. Noting the general absence of bucolic themes or the veneration of rural splendor in any of her writings, Waldron has echoed an aspect of analytical evaluation first made by Mary Wollstonecraft two centuries before her, while generally viewing Yearsley's work in a much more positive manner than Wollstonecraft. Critics have additionally recognized a pre-Romantic quality in Yearsley's verse, observing its personal and self-analytical orientation. Much of her work has also been seen as hinting at elements of nineteenth-century feminism, although in a rather rudimentary form. Contemporary commentary has additionally probed the relationship between Yearsley and her patron Hannah More, investigating the class dynamics of More's financial control over Yearsley's literary labor. Led by Waldron, many modern critics continue to urge that Yearsley has been largely misunderstood and unappreciated as a writer. By the early twenty-first century her works had remained available only in the rare book collections of select libraries, and are, according to Waldron, poised for a complete critical reevaluation as the expressive product of a unique, independent poetic voice in the late eighteenth century.

PRINCIPAL WORKS

Poems, on Several Occasions (poetry) 1785

Poems, on Various Subjects (poetry) 1787

A Poem on the Inhumanity of the Slave-Trade (poetry) 1788

Earl Goodwin (play) 1789

Stanzas of Woe, Addressed from the Heart on a Bed of Illness, to Levi Eames, Esq., Late Mayor of the City of Bristol (poetry) 1790

The Dispute: Letter to the Public. From the Milkwoman (letter) 1791

An Elegy on Marie Antoinette, of Austria, Ci-devant Queen Of France: With a Poem on the Last Interview between the King of Poland and Loraski (poetry) 1793

Reflections on the Death of Louis XVI (poetry) 1793

Sequel to Reflections on the Death of Louis XVI (poetry) 1793

The Royal Captives: A Fragment of Secret History. Copied from an Old Manuscript. 4 vols. (novel) 1795-96

The Rural Lyre: A Volume of Poems (poetry) 1796

CRITICISM

Hannah More (letter date 20 October 1784)

SOURCE: More, Hannah. "A Prefatory Letter to Mrs. Montagu. By a Friend." In *Poems, on Several Occasions*. 3rd ed., by Ann Yearsley, pp. iii-xiii. London: T. Cadell, 1785.

[*In the following letter, dated October 20, 1784 and affixed as a preface to Yearsley's debut poetic collection, More, the poet's first literary patron, describes her "discovery" of an unlearned working-class versifier of extraordinary talent in Yearsley.*]

Bristol, October 20, 1784

Dear Madam,

There is nothing more inconvenient than a high reputation, as it subjects the possessor to continual applications, which those of a contrary character entirely escape. The delight which you are known to feel in protecting real genius, and in cherishing depressed virtue, exposes you to the present intrusion, from which a cold heart, and an illiberal spirit, would have effectually secured you.

On my return from Sandleford, a copy of verses was shewn me, said to be written by a poor illiterate woman in this neighbourhood, who sells milk from door to door. The story did not engage my faith, but the verses excited my attention; for, though incorrect, they breathed the genuine spirit of Poetry, and were rendered still more interesting, by a certain natural and strong expression of misery, which seemed to fill the heart and mind of the Author. On making diligent enquiry into her history and character, I found that she had been born and bred in her present humble station, and had never received the least education, except that her brother had taught her to write. Her mother, who was also a milk-woman, appears to have had sense and piety, and to have given an early tincture of religion to this poor woman's mind. She is about eight-and-twenty, was married very young, to a man who is said to be honest and sober, but of a turn of mind very different from her own. Repeated losses, and a numerous family, for they had six children in seven years, reduced them very low, and the rigours of the last severe winter sunk them to the extremity of distress. For your sake, dear Madam, and for my own, I wish I could entirely pass over this part of her story; but some of her most affecting verses would be unintelligible without it. Her aged mother, her six little infants, and herself (expecting every hour to lie in), were actually on the point of perishing, and had given up every hope of human assistance, when the Gentleman, so gratefully mentioned in her

Poem to STELLA ["**Night. To Stella**"], providentially heard of their distress, which I am afraid she had too carefully concealed, and hastened to their relief. The poor woman and her children were preserved; but— (imagine, dear Madam, a scene which will not bear a detail) for the unhappy mother, all assistance came too late; she had the joy to see it arrive, but it was a joy she was no longer able to bear, and it was more fatal to her than famine had been. You will find our Poetess frequently alluding to this terrible circumstance, which has left a settled impression of sorrow on her mind.

When I went to see her, I observed a perfect simplicity in her manners, without the least affectation or pretension of any kind: she neither attempted to raise my compassion by her distress, nor my admiration by her parts. But, on a more familiar acquaintance, I have had reason to be surprised at the justness of her taste, the faculty I least expected to find in her. In truth, her remarks on the books she has read are so accurate, and so consonant to the opinions of the best critics, that, from that very circumstance, they would appear trite and common-place, in any one who had been in habits of society; for, without having ever conversed with any body above her own level, she seems to possess the general principles of sound taste and just thinking.

I was curious to know what poetry she had read. With the *Night Thoughts,* and *Paradise Lost,* I found her well acquainted; but she was astonished to learn that Young and Milton had written any thing else. Of Pope, she had only seen the *Eloisa*; and Dryden, Spenser, Thomson, and Prior, were quite unknown to her, even by name. She has read a few of Shakespeare's Plays, and speaks of a translation of the *Georgics,* which she has somewhere seen, with the warmest poetic rapture.

But though it has been denied to her to drink at the *pure well-head* of Pagan Poesy, yet, from the true fountain of divine Inspiration, her mind seems to have been wonderfully nourished and enriched. The study of the sacred Scriptures has enlarged her imagination, and ennobled her language, to a degree only credible to those, who, receiving them as the voice of everlasting Truth, are at the pains to appreciate the various and exquisite beauties of composition which they exhibit. For there is, as I have heard you remark, in the Prophets, in Job, and in the Psalms, a character of thought, and a style of expression, between Eloquence and Poetry, by which a great mind, disposed to either, may be so elevated and warmed, as, with little other assistance, to become a Poet or an Orator.

By the next post, I will send you some of her wild wood-notes. You will find her, like all unlettered Poets, abounding in imagery, metaphor, and personification; her faults, in this respect, being rather those of superfluity than of want. If her epithets are now and then bold

and vehement, they are striking and original; and I should be sorry to see the wild vigour of her rustic muse polished into elegance, or laboured into correctness. Her ear is perfect; there is sometimes great felicity in the structure of her blank verse, and she often varies the pause with a happiness which looks like skill. She abounds in false concords, and inaccuracies of various kinds; the grossest of which have been corrected. You will find her often diffuse from redundancy, and oftener obscure from brevity; but you will seldom find in her those inexpiable poetic sins, the false thought, the puerile conceit, the distorted image, and the incongruous metaphor, the common resources of bad Poets, and the not uncommon blemishes of good ones.

If this commendation be thought exaggerated, qualify it, dear Madam, with the reflection that it belongs to one who writes under every complicated disadvantage; who is destitute of all the elegancies of literature, the accommodations of leisure, and, I will not barely say the conveniencies, but the necessaries of life: to one who does not know a single rule of Grammar, and who has never even *seen* a Dictionary.

> Chill Penury repress'd her noble rage,
> And froze the genial current of her soul.

Though I have a high reverence for art, study, and institution, and for all the mighty names and master spirits who have given laws to Taste, yet I am not sorry, now and then, to convince the supercilious Critic, whose mass of knowledge is not warmed by a single particle of native fire, that genius is antecedent to rules, and independent on criticism; for who, but his own divine and incomprehensible genius, pointed out to Shakespeare, while he was holding horses at the play-house door, every varied position of the human mind, every shade of discrimination in the human character? all the distinct affections, and all the complicated feelings of the heart of man? who taught him to give to the dead letter of narrative the living spirit of action; to combine the most philosophic turn of thinking with the warmest energies of Passion, and to embellish both with all the graces of Imagination, and all the enthusiasm of Poetry? to make every description a picture, and every sentiment an axiom? to know how every being which *did* exist, would speak and act in every supposed circumstance of situation; and how every being, which did *not* exist but in imagination, *must* speak and act, if ever he were to be called into real existence.

But to return to the subject of my Letter: When I expressed to her my surprise at two or three classical allusions in one of her Poems, and inquired how she came by them, she said she had taken them from little ordinary prints which hung in a shop-window. This hint may, perhaps, help to account for the manner in which a late untutored, and unhappy, but very sublime genius of this town [Chatterton], caught some of those ideas which diffuse through his writings a certain air of learning, the reality of which he did not possess. A great mind at once seizes and appropriates to itself whatever is new and striking; and I am persuaded that a truly poetic spirit has often the art of appearing to be deeply informed on subjects of which he only knows the general principle; by skilfully seizing the master feature, he is thought artfully to reject the detail, with which, in fact, he is unacquainted; and obtains that credit for his knowledge which is better due to his judgment.

I have the satisfaction to tell you, dear Madam, that our poor Enthusiast is active and industrious in no common degree. The Muses have not cheated her into an opinion that the retailing a few fine maxims of virtue, may exempt her from the most exact probity in her conduct. I have had some unequivocal proofs that her morality has not evaporated in sentiment, but is, I verily believe, fixed in a settled principle. Without this, with all her ingenuity, as she would not have obtained my friendship, so I should not have had the courage to solicit for her your protection.

I already anticipate your generous concurrence in a little project I have in view for her relief. It is not intended to place her in such a state of independence as might seduce her to devote her time to the idleness of Poetry. I hope she is convinced that the making of verses is not the great business of human life; and that, as a wife and a mother, she has duties to fill, the smallest of which is of more value than the finest verses she can write: but as it has pleased God to give her these talents, may they not be made an instrument to mend her situation, if we publish a small volume of her Poems by subscription? The liberality of my friends leaves me no room to doubt of success.—Pressing as her distresses are, if I did not think her heart was rightly turned, I should be afraid of proposing such a measure, lest it should unsettle the sobriety of her mind, and, by exciting her vanity, indispose her for the laborious employments of her humble condition; but it would be cruel to imagine that we cannot mend her fortune without impairing her virtue.

For my own part, I do not feel myself actuated by the idle vanity of a *discoverer*; for I confess, that the ambition of bringing to light a genius buried in obscurity, operates much less powerfully on my mind, than the wish to rescue a meritorious woman from misery, for it is not fame, but bread, which I am anxious to secure to her.

I should ask your pardon for this dull and tedious Letter, if I were not assured that you are always ready to sacrifice your most elegant pursuits to the humblest claims of humanity; and that the sweetness of renown has not lessened your sensibility for the pleasures of be-

nevolence, nor destroyed your relish for that most touching and irresistible eloquence, *the blessing of him who was ready to perish.*

> I am,
> > Dear MADAM,
> > > Your much obliged,
> > > And very faithful
> > > > Humble servant,
> > > > > HANNAH MORE.

William Upton (poem date 1788)

SOURCE: Upton, William. "Verses Occasioned by the Perusal of the Poems of Ann Yearsley, the Milkwoman of Clifton, near Bristol." In *Poems on Several Occasions*, pp. 102-03. London: John Strahan, 1788.

[*In the following poem, Upton lauds the natural poetic genius of Yearsley.*]

> O thou, whose pow'r surpass the bounds of praise,
> > Omniscient Being, heav'n's eternal King!
> Who can'st, from void and impotent nothing, raise
> > The meanest worm—thy mightiest deeds to sing.
>
> Unlearn'd, untaught, in Education's page,
> > The humble rustic pin'd awhile unknown;
> 'Till thou, Infinite, didst her cause engage,
> > And form'd ideas—to magnify thy own.
>
> Fashion'd each thought with supernat'ral sense,
> > And "Fancy bade" with heav'nly ardour glow;
> Then deign to accept th' grateful recompence,
> > The hymn of praise—'tis all she can bestow.
>
> Illumin'd Yearsley, whose prolific mind
> > Teems with Imagination's noblest flights;
> Around thy head be bloomless laurels twin'd,
> > Serene thy days, and joyous be thy nights.
>
> Long may sweet Inspiration fire thy breast,
> > And future lays illustrious Virtue tend;
> Lays that in lofty flowing numbers dress'd,
> > Have prov'd thee Nature's universal friend.
>
> What tho' no pedigree thy name enrol,
> > Bristol shall long its rural minstrel hail;
> While Fame records her to each distant pole,
> > The admir'd poetress of *Clifton Dale*.

Mary Wollstonecraft (review date April 1791)

SOURCE: Wollstonecraft, Mary. Review of *Stanzas of Woe*, by Ann Yearsley. *Analytical Review* 9, no. 4 (April 1791): 447-48.

[*In the following review, Wollstonecraft derides* Stanzas of Woe, *suggesting that in this collection Yearsley demonstrates bitterness, confusion, and lack of poetic acumen.*]

It has been the fate of several poets, whom *good-luck* has pushed forward, to see their blooming honours fade, and to find by painful experience, that premature fame, though sweet to the taste, becomes bitter in digestion. We scruple not to rank Mrs. Y. among the number; for the praise which she has received has been, in our opinion, much warmer than she ever merited. But the pleasure of exalting a wonder, till puffed up by the breath of popular applause, it grows most wonderful, intoxicates the public of the day, and the ephemeral buzz is mistaken for the awful sanction which time gives to the general voice. Mrs. Y. certainly has abilities; but instead of 'native wood-notes wild,' stale allusions obscure her poems, in which, however, we discover an independent mind and feeling heart.

The present Stanzas [*Stanzas of Woe*] are the effusions of indignant anger, on account of a recent, and forming a judgment from her statement, a cruel insult, which had a serious effect on her health. We shall select three stanzas, in which she alludes to the death of her child, who was hurried into the world to die by the inhuman treatment that inspired her complains.

> Go to the cheated tygress of the plains,
>   Robb'd of her young she'd scare thy coward soul;
> Maternal agony high in her veins!
>   What pow'r of thine would her fierce wrath controul?
>
> Insolent tyrant! humble as we are,
>   Our minds are rich with honest truth as thine;
> Bring on thy sons, their value we'll compare,
>   Then—lay thy infant in the grave with mine.
>
> Ah, heed me not! but clasp it to thy heart
>   Till thy thought ache with rapture o'er thy child,
> Dwell on its beauties; stranger to the smart
>   Of her, whom thou hast of this bliss beguil'd.

A second poem is addressed to William Cromartie Yearsley, on his becoming a pupil to Mr. ***. We now expected to have heard the simple effusions of maternal fondness; but the trite illustrations from classical lore, which we have already noticed, met our view in every page; and the sense is rendered still more intricate by that confusion of thought, which shews struggling energy not sufficiently strong to cultivate itself, and give a form to a chaotic mass.

The following "Advertisement" is prefixed to these poems.

> At the time of hay-harvest, 1789, many village children playing in Mr. Eames's field, the author's sons (the eldest twelve, the youngest nine years of age) were singled out by that gentleman's footman, and horse-whipped in a most cruel manner, the youngest in the field, the other in the author's house where he fled for shelter: no person being in the house, the child embraced the man, endeavouring to soften him by en-

treaty and to elude his blows; all was in vain; till the boy's cries being heard, the fellow was forced from him with all that raging reluctance to which barbarous spirits are subservient: the child's skin wore a savage livery, yet the author, advising with her friends, agreed to forget this deep injury. Her second son expostulating with the footman in a childish manner, was way-laid from behind a wall several nights after, and beat till he could not stand, by the same servant, and at Mr. Eames's door. These repeated insults made it a duty in Mrs. Yearsley to summon the servant of Mr. Eames: she did so, and the offender was defended by a petty-sogging attorney who is a dependent on the magistrate. Mrs. Yearsley demanded of this sagacious counsellor, if he would countenance murder? He replied, "Had *I* been there, I would have given it them so EFFECTUALLY, that they *never* should have come there again." The author's attorney, justly supposing her purse not to be *quite* so heavy as Mr. Eames's, advised her to drop the prosecution.

June 1790, Mrs. Yearsley was sitting near her own door, when a man rushed furiously down Mr. Eames's field (which is nearly adjoining) swearing he would dash out the brains of two children that ran from him. The children were strangers, and escaped: his fury immediately turned upon the author; he treated her in a vulgar opprobrious manner. On her enquiring, and being informed that he was servant to Mr. Eames, she withdrew; but being in a state that claims gentler treatment, the shock was too violent: her life was preserved, her infant expired the same night.

Rayner Unwin (essay date 1954)

SOURCE: Unwin, Rayner. "Day Trips to Parnassus." In *The Rural Muse: Studies in the Peasant Poetry of England,* pp. 68-86. London: George Allen and Unwin Ltd, 1954.

[*In the following excerpt, Unwin characterizes Yearsley as a mediocre poet whose limited literary talent and failure to come to terms with her patron Hannah More led to her failure as a professional writer.*]

"The mediocres," wrote Southey, "have long been a numerous and an increasing race, and they must necessarily multiply with the progress of civilization." The second half of the eighteenth century produced more than enough uneducated poets to justify such a remark. Sometimes mediocrity was inherent in the man, as in the case of Henry Jones, who was brought from Ireland by the Earl of Chesterfield, quarrelled with his patron, failed to fulfil himself as a poet, and later had the misfortune to be run over when drunk. Sometimes a man, gifted in other spheres, unwisely strayed into verse. William Huntington, the tenth—and illegitimate—son of the wife of a Kentish labourer, had no aptitude for poetry, though he was undeniably gifted as a preacher of Methodism. Unfortunately he occasionally wrote doggerel that contrasts sadly with his virile and pungent prose. One of the most well-thought-of verse-writers of her day, the pathos of whose life-story overcame the indifference of her verse, was Ann Yearsley, a milkwoman of Bristol.

Lactilla (for so Ann Yearsley called herself) knew better than almost any poet the bitterness of poverty and starvation. She sold milk from door to door, mothered a rapidly-increasing family, but failed to prosper. When a Mr. Vaughan discovered her gift for poetry, she, her six children and her mother were dying from want; indeed the latter it proved impossible to save. These circumstances came to the ears of Hannah More, who immediately adopted Lactilla's cause as her own. She wrote to her numerous friends, Horace Walpole and Mrs. Montagu amongst them, lobbying on behalf of the unfortunate but talented milkwoman. "It is not intended," she assured them, "to place her in such a state of independence as might seduce her to devote her time to the idleness of Poetry." Ann was to be a wife and a mother first and foremost; but the most pressing reason for collecting subscriptions was to gain for her the wherewithal to live. "It is not fame, but bread, which I am anxious to secure to her."

Ann Yearsley was twenty-eight when Hannah More adopted her. She had had no formal education, beyond being taught to write by her brother. She knew nothing of grammar, and although she read intensely, her range was small. The melancholy of *Night Thoughts* and an inflated grandeur, imitated from *Paradise Lost,* show the two greatest influences on her writing. Of Dryden, Thomson, Spenser or Prior she had not even heard. A small volume of translations from the *Georgics* she greatly admired, and her knowledge of classical myth was gleaned from the pictures in print-shop windows.

In the first enthusiasm for her protégée Hannah More declared, as Spence did of Duck, that she had a natural critical faculty. "Without having ever conversed with any body above her own level, she seems to possess the general principles of sound taste and just thinking." The desire to find the natural poet, critically instinctive, and perfect in judgment, has already been commented on; Hannah More, a woman of unbounded enthusiasm, was certain that she had discovered such a "natural" milkmaid. Even Walpole, replying to Miss More in 1784, had few reservations. "Were I not persuaded by the samples you have sent me, Madam, that this woman has talents, I should not advise her encouraging her propensity, lest it should divert her from the care of her family, and, after the novelty is over, leave her worse than she was."

The indefatigable Hannah More secured a good subscription list, and Lactilla's poems were published in 1785. Society was charmed by the unacrimonious melancholy that they expressed, and the lurid, heavily-powerful use of descriptive words.

> The too gaudy Sun
> Shines not for me,

she complains in the opening poem, **"Night,"**

> no bed of Nature yields
> Her varied sweets; no music wakes the grove;
> No vallies blow, no waving grain uprears
> Its tender stalk to cheer my coming hour;
> But horrid Silence broods upon my soul,
> With wing deep-drench'd in Misery's torpid dews.

"I should be sorry to see the wild vigour of her rustic muse polished into elegance," Hannah More wrote to Mrs. Montagu. This was a new approach to a proletarian poet. Half a century after Duck had been dieted with a belated neo-classical education, Ann Yearsley was to be allowed to use her perfect ear and instinctive judgment as she pleased. Unfortunately such freedom came to the wrong person, and too late. The culture that she received would seem to have influenced her little, and grammatical correctness was the extent of her adult learning.

In her verses Lactilla expresses due humility and a desire to perfect her craft through the good offices of her new-found friends. In particular she asked them to

> Teach me to paint the tremors of the soul
> In Sorrow's deepest tints.

In the dedication of a subsequent volume she claimed that her works were "the effusions of NATURE only," but she freely admitted that nature needed to be perfected by the art of hands more skilled than her own. Thus she abandoned the freedom of expression that Hannah More had wished her to retain, and willingly disciplined herself as a novitiate to the established poetic order. Her orthodoxy can be seen in the lines she addressed **"To Mrs. V-N."**

> Bright sentiment, if unimprov'd, must die,
> And great ideas, unassisted, fall;
> On Learning's wing we pierce th'empyreal sky;
> But Nature's untaught efforts are but small.

Typical of Ann Yearsley's early poems is **"Clifton Hall,"** which presents something of a discursive seasonal commentary on the countryside around Bristol with which she was familiar. Autobiographical material is sparse, except when, in the depths of winter,

> half sunk in snow,
> LACTILLA, shivering, tends her fav'rite cow.

But melancholy thoughts are never far distant. The sight of Clifton Church, where her mother lay buried, leads, as might be expected, to a lengthy and lugubrious meditation. Even the joyful advent of spring is accompanied by a seasonal warning to the village girls.

Ye blooming maids, beware,
Nor the lone thicket with a lover dare.
No high romantic rules of honour bind
The timid virgin of the rural kind;
No conquest of the passions e'er was taught,
No meed e'er given them for the vanquish'd thought.

"Clifton Hall" is a more sustained poem than Ann Yearsley commonly wrote, but like all her verses it contains many of the faults, and few of the virtues, of an uneducated poet's writings. Personification is common, imagery and metaphor florid and laboured. Her style was puffed out rather than elevated, and more affected than natural. Southey was puzzled by the slight results from so promising a potential when he summed up her work. "With extraordinary talents, strong feelings, and an ardent mind, she never produced a poem which found its way into any popular collection."

The sale of the first volume of her poems produced £350, which sum Miss More and Mrs. Montagu put in trust for Ann and administered on her behalf. It was not an entirely satisfactory arrangement. Patronage puts its recipient under an obvious debt of gratitude, but Lactilla's money was her own; and despite the obligation she felt towards Hannah More she considered herself entitled to some voice in the administration of the trust. Inevitably there was a quarrel, which reflected little credit on Hannah More. To be so much as questioned put that lady on her dignity, and made discussion impossible. "Are you *mad*, Mrs. Yearsley? or have you drank a glass too much?" she exclaimed when she was asked for a copy of the deed of trust. Further interviews produced no accord. Hannah referred to Lactilla as a savage, and accused her of a miscellany of failings, such as gambling, drunkenness, and extravagance. Ann defended herself fairly effectively, but they were never reconciled.

Without the business ability and influence of Hannah More, Ann Yearsley never prospered. Her books continued to sell for a few years, but interest waned, just as it had with her predecessors, and as Walpole had predicted it might with her. For a while she ran a circulating library near Bristol, grew penurious again, and died, probably insane, in 1806.

Apart from being (if we except Mary Collier) the only woman proletarian poet, there is little that can be satisfactorily said either in praise or in blame of Ann Yearsley. Her station in life was one of the least conducive to the production of verse that it is possible to imagine, and we can only judge her achievements sympathetically in the manner that Johnson judged a woman preaching. Her early reading in *Paradise Lost* had an unfortunate effect upon her style, for Miltonic verse, as Keats realized, "cannot be written but in the vein of art"—and artlessness was essential to a writer with so meagre an intellectual equipment as Lactilla.

The wide dissemination of Milton's poems even amongst the lower classes of society, and the influence they had amongst poets who were not initially prejudiced in their favour, is one of the most interesting and constant factors conditioning the growth of the uneducated poet movement in England. Ann Yearsley seems to have received other influences too late for them to be very apparent. She never developed as a poetess, and perhaps her lack of response to cultural opportunities helped to turn Hannah More against her. But poetry could never be an all-absorbing occupation for her. She was not responsible just to herself, but to her family; and they surely must have echoed Crabbe's cry,

Can poets soothe you, when you pine for bread?

Tim Burke (essay date 1998)

SOURCE: Burke, Tim. "Ann Yearsley and the Distribution of Genius in Early Romantic Culture." In *Early Romantics: Perspectives in British Poetry from Pope to Wordsworth*, edited by Thomas Woodman, pp. 215-30. Houndmills, England: Macmillan Press Ltd, 1998.

[*In the following essay, Burke studies Yearsley's poetry with respect to the eighteenth-century conceptualization of genius, while focusing on the discourse of class and gender suppression contained in Yearsley's early verse.*]

Oft as I trod my native wilds alone,
Strong gusts of thought would rise, but rise to die;
The portals of the swelling soul, ne'er op'd
By liberal converse, rude ideas strove
Awhile for vent, but found it not, and died.
Thus rust the Mind's best powers. Yon starry orbs,
Majestic ocean, flowery vales, gay groves,
Eye-wasting lawns, and Heaven-attempting hills,
Which bound th'horizon, and which curb the view;
All those, with beauteous imagery awaked
My ravished soul to ecstasy untaught,
To all the transport the rapt sense can bear;
But all expir'd, for want of powers to speak;
All perish'd in the mind as soon as born,
Eras'd more quick than cyphers on the shore,
O'er which the cruel waves, unheedful, roll.

(Ann Yearsley, '**On Mrs. Montagu**' (1785), ll. 51-66)[1]

'**On Mrs. Montagu**' appears in Yearsley's debut volume of poetry, published in 1785. The poem invokes some familiar early romantic conventions in its detailing of solitary melancholy and sensory breakdown. We can readily recognize the poem's thwarted lyric expression and the speaker's sense that the poetic voice is muted and mutilated by the painful blockage of the sublime. The concession of defeat—'expir'd' and 'eras'd'—is not simply an aesthetic matter: this speaker has not so much a silent voice as a voice silenced. Such muting is frequently the social and literary experience of the labouring-class poet, and especially the woman labourer poet, in the second half of the eighteenth century. Yearsley, a milkwoman by trade, frequently writes of her sense of being silenced by patriarchal culture and the mores of a hierarchical class society, while subtly interrogating the social and textual impropriety of a labouring-class woman giving vent to her voice. Like Susannah Harrison and Ann Candler, Yearsley deploys the only available discourse which can, albeit temporarily, legislate speech: the quasi-religious sublime, whose paradox is the need to articulate one's silencing by a higher and potentially destructive force. Donna Landry, in an extended materialist reading of Yearsley, suggests that the poet's 'want of powers to speak' can be made good by 'a combination of recognition, encouragement, material support, and access to publication.'[2] I would suggest that Yearsley's undoubted desire for an authentic voice cannot be so easily granted. For one, the terms on which working female poets are granted publication often depend, as their patrons and prefacers insist, upon their immediate return to more conventionally feminine roles—as 'wife and mother', to quote Yearsley's first patron—which tend to restrict opportunities for public voices.[3] Second, the notion of 'genius', an attempt to explain the source of the rare creative abilities of uneducated labourers, offers strong theoretical arguments to exclude women from intellectual creativity.

Yearsley's contemporary readers could hardly have failed to notice the speaker of **'On Mrs. Montagu'** wrestling with this discourse of genius. The metaphors of conception and birth and the pitching of 'rude ideas' and 'ecstasy untaught' against 'liberal converse' indicate the poet's theoretical awareness of the class and gender implications of genius, a term whose highly specialized sense in the eighteenth century has become diluted in our own. Christine Battersby has argued that whether creativity is thought to be an inspiration from heaven or an innate characteristic, whether a Rousseauvian excess of passion or a Kantian perfection of reason, theories of genius have ensured that 'whatever faculty is most highly prized is the one that women are seen to lack'.[4] In the middle of the eighteenth century, influential theoretical texts offer greatly differing accounts of the source of creativity, ranging from the divine to the natural, from the educational to the accidents of social class, but certainly agreeing on one thing: that genius is a male preserve, a masculine and masculinizing faculty.[5] This perhaps is why **'On Mrs. Montagu'** has to wrestle quite so vigorously with its sense of muted blockage. I will return to this and other poems by Ann Yearsley in the second half of this essay, after the politics of genius have been more thoroughly scrutinized.

IDEAS AND IDEOLOGIES OF GENIUS

From Stephen Duck and Mary Collier in the 1730s, through Mary Leapor, James Woodhouse, Yearsley,

Robert Burns, Janet Little, Ann Candler and Robert Bloomfield and others to John Clare in the 1820s, the so-called 'peasant poets' enjoyed a long vogue. In early romantic culture, the uneducated labouring-class poet is a cultural curiosity, bearing some resemblance to Rousseau's 'noble savage' and the 'child prodigy' exemplified by Chatterton. Their achievements, against all the odds of class privilege and educational deprivation, readily prompt the charitable sensibilities of patrons and admirers in the period. Astonishment and admiration, and no little resentment, surrounded these poets; however, a rational explanation of the untaught worker's unlikely talents and capacities proved rather more difficult. Patrons and more disinterested theorists alike resort to the rubric of genius to account for such achievements. At some point in their career, each of the poets mentioned above is described, whether by a prefatory essayist, a reviewer or a patron, as a type of what became known as the 'natural' or 'unlettered' genius.

The popularity of such works within fashionable circles in this period signals in part a complicated nostalgia for a less organized, more organic society perceived to have been lost. The rural labourer, certainly, is thought to enjoy a close proximity to nature in his or her material engagement with it in the act of labour; thus, certain proletarian sensibilities had remained untainted by the ongoing commercialization of the nation, in which the bourgeois civic subject flourished at the price of alienation from the organic community. Long before Wordsworth's interest in recuperating the 'real language of men', the labourer poet was thought able to enjoy and spontaneously represent an intimate acquaintance with the salubrious and restorative powers of the natural world. One explanation of the unlettered genius is that the genius, in tune with nature, appears to offer a window onto a lost world.

In this essay, I want to go beyond the nostalgic associations prompted by the figure of the genius in later eighteenth-century patrons and readers to look more closely at the class and gender politics which construct and condition this theoretical discourse. Before this is possible, however, some explanation of the difficulty of such a study is necessary. That the discourse of genius is not readily associated with the political is a result of the romantic legacy that persists in some of our own critical practices at the end of the twentieth century. For the romantics, genius is a strictly aesthetic affair, and for them the aesthetic is ideally and profoundly separated from the social. The clichéd romantic genius is the solitary visionary, the child of nature, a uniquely gifted (and invariably male) individual who scorns the accountable material world in order to reveal the imaginative excesses to which he is partial. However, the tendency of specific historical and economic conditions to continually seep back into the realm of the aesthetic is a touchstone of recent historicist and materialist criticism.[6] Even Wordsworth's host of golden daffodils cannot escape the tainted association with 'wealth'. It will be necessary therefore to distinguish 'romantic' and what I will call the 'early romantic' ideas of genius. In the latter, genius is a term more knowingly and openly saturated with the politics of gender, class and nation.

English romantic writers certainly tend to be hostile to the rationale of political economy, but recent studies have argued that romanticism owes it a number of debts. The romantic notion of genius, for instance, has origins in Adam Smith's *The Wealth of Nations* (1776), in which the genius is dismissed as the unproductive scholar, critic or poet who contributes nothing tangible to the economy of truck, barter and exchange. It is Smith who erects the barrier between imaginative or intellectual genius and the concerns of economy and politics; the romantics, belatedly, attempt to sustain it. Smith's intervention marks a crucial ideological shift, for before 1776 theorists of genius had been concerned with how aesthetic and intellectual labour overlaps with other more tangible forms of productive activity as joint contributions to a broadly conceived national wealth. As Zynep Tenger and Paul Trolander have argued, the romantic idea of genius emerges amid the ruins of this earlier, highly politicized discourse:

> The marginalization of the [earlier] discourse of genius was intimately linked to the success of the emerging discourse of political economy. In the 1760s and 1770s, both discourses sought to define and structure social and economic relations and therefore were tacitly in competition with one another. But by the early nineteenth century, political economy had made great headway as a model of social relations and an agent of economic and civil progress. The romantics appropriated the discourse of genius when it was no longer considered relevant to social and economic policy.[7]

In the third quarter of the eighteenth century, what I am calling the early romantic discourse of genius was concerned with much more than aesthetic categories or literary facility. Genius as an embodied quality was openly acknowledged as a national asset, much prized and not to be wasted or frittered, and the individual of genius had a duty to cultivate and rationalize naturally or divinely endowed talent in order to optimize its productivity. As Tenger and Trolander suggest:

> Mid- to late-eighteenth-century writers on genius frequently argued that the productive forces of society were, or ought to be, organised according to the distribution of natural or acquired intellectual powers. Genius, or intellectual prowess, created and ordered the mental and mechanical practices that structured society and provided for its needs and wants. Discussions of literary and artistic originality were located within the framework of these more central assumptions.

(p. 170)

The classical *genius loci,* the spirit guarding a specific person or place, cannot be fully relocated into the inner space of the creative individual sensibility until a civil society and its political economy comprises productive and self-determining individual agents.

Locating a critical site outside the romantic ideology of genius requires critics to reconstruct it as a more politicized discourse than previously thought. A range of productive modes, from the production of new commodity objects to the creation of fixed class identities, from scientific innovation to biological reproduction, are at the heart of early romantic genius theory's concerns. If maximizing the output of original inventions was thought to be crucial to the nation's economic well-being in the 1750s, then so was the optimization of population, and there are significant links between the new interest in the origins of genius and the supply of bodies. It was widely thought—incorrectly as it happens—that the population was shrinking at the moment when the national economy needed more bodies than ever to sustain its expansion. Through the 1750s and 1760s especially, and continuing in the 1770s and beyond, economists were engaged in a debate on whether the population numbers of Britain are falling or rising. The discourse of population theory provoked passionate arguments from both positions, not least because Britain's fledgling economic power was thought to be at risk. The consensus held that numbers were falling, with potentially disastrous consequences in an era of burgeoning capital when productive capacity depended on maximizing a labour force.

In such a historical moment, biological reproduction is highly prized. The burdens placed upon women's bodies can be imagined from contemporary representations. The spinster figure is increasingly subjected to disparagement in contemporary conduct manuals for daughters, which continue to stress the importance of marital fidelity. It is not difficult to fathom the ideological import of the numerous prints and engravings—versions of Jean Baptiste Greuze's 'The Beloved Mother' (*c.* 1765) were among the most popular—depicting exhausted but dutiful women, surrounded by sometimes a dozen children, under the approving but unassisting gaze of the husband. One might also expect woman to be cast as the model of creative energy and reproductive potential in aesthetic theories at a time of (imaginary) population crisis, but genius theory in these decades sets out to privilege explicitly masculine forms of intellectual reproduction.

In the heyday of early romantic genius theory, questions of population and reproduction certainly appear to be on the minds of its leading exponents. In his *Essay on Genius,* Alexander Gerard urges his 'penetrative' genius to combine 'fertility' with the power of 'regularity'; the man of genius in William Duff's *Essay on Original Genius* possesses an imagination which 'creates and peoples worlds of its own' (Gerard, p. 54; Duff, p. 282).

It should be no surprise that creativity is phrased in metaphors of fertility, pregnancy and biological birth. It is difficult to conceive—even this term is instructive—of other figures that could effectively supplant them. Indeed, the etymological sources of genius lie in signals of nature's randomness and familial tradition, reflecting the term's Latin origins in *gignere* (to produce or to beget) and *genialis* (relating to birth or marriage). Standing alongside the discourse of population at a moment of reproductive crisis, however, the use of these figures in eighteenth-century genius theory becomes more than figurative, escaping their metaphorical status to have material effects in the cultural field. Before 'test-tube' technology in our own century, and the Frankensteinian imagination in the last, eighteenth-century men sought to appropriate the previously 'sacred' powers of reproduction in the discourse of genius. In the discourse of genius and the discourses which overlap and satellite around it, woman is central to, and yet erased from, the very process of generation. The feminine finds itself, in various degrees, the marginalized denominator of theories of creativity:

> A man of mere judgement is essentially different from a man of genius. The former can employ his reason only on subjects that are provided by others; but the latter can provide subjects for himself.
>
> (Gerard, p. 38)

Gerard here stresses a central contention of his thesis, that the genius's powers of imaginative association leave him dependent on no other economic or sexual or aesthetic unit for his self-perpetuation and reproduction. The man of genius able to 'provide subjects for himself' is not only self-authenticating, but self-perpetuating as well. It is notable that in *Conjectures On Original Composition,* Edward Young uses similar terms to refute the increasingly popular claim that Pope's poetry had demonstrated true genius and originality. As an imitator of the genius of others rather than a genius *per se,* 'Pope's noble muse may boast her illustrious descent . . . yet is an *Original* author more nobly born'. And while 'mule-like imitators shall die without issue', Young's more distinguished genius is, like Duff's, able to proceed 'of himself . . . his own progenitor' (Young, p. 30). Gerard displays similar disdain for the 'imitator', and the 'man' whose 'weakness of association' leaves him incapable even of imitation is almost beyond contempt: 'Every production of a man who labours under this debility of mind, bears evident marks of barrenness, a quality less apposite to true genius than any other' (Gerard, p. 42).

The genius is thus a remarkable model of masculinity, one who can enter the world and repopulate it independently of woman. His is therefore a more than merely 'noble' birth. In genius theory's 'virgin father' myth, the genius has a quasi-divine origin, and masculinity is the state closest to divinity. Young locates this divinity

within the self. His two dictums for the 'true Original' are 'I. *Know thyself*; 2ndly, *Reverence thyself*' (Young, p. 24). Impregnated by nature, the genius discovers the grounds on which he may legitimately revere his own impregnable and quasi-divine identity. Genius theory's uninterrupted male procreation stands as a figure for a quest towards abstraction, whose social effect was to redirect and relegate women's productivity to the material domain of senses and body.

More than any of the other theorists, it is Gerard's proposed 'union' of female fertility and male regulation which betrays most comprehensively the anxiety of the male who has embellished his masculinity with feminine characteristics. The crisis occurs when Gerard comes to stress the importance of materializing one's creative fecundity, by bringing the internalized objects ('conceptions') into the world:

> [Genius] must possess the power of employing a proper vehicle, congruous to the nature of that art, for conveying the conceptions of his imagination to the senses and souls of other men. It is this that puts it in the power of genius to show itself: without this its finest conceptions would perish, like an infant in the womb; without this, the brightest imagination would be like a vigorous mind confined in a lame or paralytic body.
>
> (Gerard, p. 419)

This man speaking to men is a precursor of the ideal Poet set out in Wordsworth's 'Preface' to the *Lyrical Ballads.* In Gerard, however, the process by which the artefact or the commodity is materialized is problematically gendered female, and involves a necessary intervention of female reproduction into the closed circuit of male communication.

Gerard's exceptional, 'penetrative' mind cannot simply be dismissed as phallic. Following the logic of the passage cited above, it also functions as a (metaphoric) female womb. The female power of creativity, which must so urgently be harnessed in Gerard's theory, functions as a sort of Platonic *chora,* as an incubus or cradle of masculine Form, enabling it/him to become 'fully formed' and speak to 'other men'. As Battersby suggests:

> Before the eighteenth century there had been a direct link between the word 'genius' and male fertility; now 'genius' was presented as both an expression of, and a threat to, maleness. Genius was seen to feminise the male body and mind. But genius was also a male preserve, in that only the highest and best males could withstand it.
>
> (p. 124)

Genius is thus delineated in terms of male procreativity, and woman (or more specifically the womb) becomes a site of necessary engagement but danger for the male genius. It could be objected, perhaps, that the feminization of aesthetic principles and artistic practices was familiar enough in the rhetoric of eighteenth-century aesthetic theory. The image of 'pregnant fancy', for instance, was a common figure, and was even applied to Yearsley's work by *The Monthly Review,* but given the recurrent discourse of penetration, fertility and frigidity that had gone before it, the womb, like so many other terms in genius theory, here exceeds its metaphoric function. Syntagmatically, the womb is a 'lame or paralytic' body. Masculine 'vigour' risks still-birth in the 'debilitating' process of incubation and materialization that Gerard casts here as a feminine creative principle in service of the male. The womb, as site of the formation and materialization of 'real' offspring and a metaphor for the process of transmitting ideal genius in material artefacts, is fraught with the prospect of failure and debility. The passage to genius, or rather to the display of genius, necessitates a fraught encounter with the unassimilable Other (the body, or the female which stands as a synecdoche for it), and the rapid colonization of that other in the guise of 'union'. The effect of this encounter is a systematic theoretical exclusion of women from displaying or even comprehending the sort of creativity characterized as genius.

'WANT OF POWERS TO SPEAK': YEARSLEY'S REDISTRIBUTION OF VOICE

Theories of creative genius thus perpetuate the cultural silencing of the female voice. Although Yearsley was by all accounts a woman thoroughly prepared to speak out against perceived injustice to herself, a number of early poems dramatize the difficulty of vocalizing and materializing imaginative labour in public. The poem that opened this essay uses recognizably Gerardian terms to express its failure of expression:

> Strong gusts of thought would rise, but rise to die;
> The portals of the swelling soul, ne'er op'd
> By liberal converse, rude ideas strove
> Awhile for vent, but found it not, and died.
>
> . . . all expir'd, for want of powers to speak;
> All perish'd in the mind as soon as born,
> Eras'd more quick than cyphers on the shore,
> O'er which the cruel waves, unheedful, roll.

('On Mrs. Montagu', ll. 51-4, 63-6)

Yearsley's vacant yet swelling 'portals' function here rather as the 'womb' that so terrifies Gerard's *Essay,* suffocating raw ideas which strive for birth and air but 'expir[e]' for want of powers to speak'. 'Rude ideas' cannot—or possibly must not—be materialized. The woman who speaks is like a poem carved in sand on a beach: destined to be submerged and drowned out by the din of an overwhelmingly muscular poetics of genius, or saturated with those discourses to the point at which a distinctive and de*cypher*able feminist poetics is overwritten and made invisible by the 'cruel' and 'unheedful' waves of a dominant and dominating culture. Genius embodied as a woman 'expires' not so much for 'want' of 'powers to speak' as the lack of an audience to listen, or, more accurately, want of an aesthetic in which she can be heard on her own terms. The solitary poet, painfully undergoing the blockage of the sublime and unable quite to escape the 'eye wasting' world by which it is prompted, ultimately opts out of the challenge to create her own terms for expression. The speaker relies instead on the example of Elizabeth Montagu, an early patron, described here as a 'bright Moralist':

> Such timid rapture as young EDWIN seized,
> When his lone footsteps on the Sage obtrude,
> Whose noble precept charm'd his wondering ear.
> Such rapture filled LACTILLA's vacant soul,
> When the bright Moralist, in softness dressed,
> Opes all the glories of the mental world,
> Deigns to direct the infant thought, to prune
> The budding sentiment, uprear the stalk
> Of feeble fancy, bid idea live,
> Woo the abstracted spirit from its cares,
> And gently guide her to the scenes of peace.

('On Mrs. Montagu', ll. 67-77)

In this and other poems, Yearsley retreats into an inner world of deathly peace, but leaves intact the terms in which woman is disqualified from Gerard's material expression. Organic and cultural metaphors, of budding and pruning, might well equally 'bid idea live', but they reconcile the body to its regulated productivity, natural and artificial. The comparison to 'young Edwin', the solitary but eventually inspired hero of James Beattie's popular poem *The Minstrel* (1771-4) is not exact, for Yearsley quickly learns that 'all the glories of the mental world' do not equip her to deal better with the 'cares' of the world, only to opt out of them 'in peace'. This poem of 'timid rapture' forces its own, for us unsatisfactory, closure as the potential female genius dies intestate, to be reborn in the image of bluestocking morality and gentility.

In other poems, however, Yearsley's speakers try to construct an alternative site, beyond the 'liberal converse' of the polite and what is described as the 'vulgar' din generated by the community of workers. Foreseeing a way out of the quasi-religious sublime and the culturally enforced silence of labourers who aspire to more than vulgarity, the poet chooses (like other working women poets in the period) to actively embrace silence. This is, of course, a risky strategy, all too easily co-opted into the dominant culture's expectations. However, in one of her best poems, printed last in the debut volume, Yearsley's speaker looks down from the hill on a 'noisy' party of homecome sailors, whose 'clumsy music' brings only 'rough delight', and her response is self-muting yet emphatic:

Yours be the vulgar dissonance, while I
Cross the low stream, and stretch the ardent eye
O'er Nature's wilds; 'tis peace, 'tis joy serene,
The thought as pure as calm the vernal scene.

('Clifton Hill', ll. 192-5)

Just as here Yearsley dramatizes her movement out of a 'low' culture towards the polite and pure silence enjoyed at the raised summit of Clifton Hill, so in the opening poem of her debut volume, **'Night. To Stella'**, the speaker charts her movement out of ignorance into the enlightenment that Hannah More—often apostrophed as 'Stella'—initially represents. The poet opts to remain silent in the face of Stella's 'song sublime', remembering again that for a labouring-class writer voice betrays ignorance and brutality, and that before discovery she was herself just another savage:

Thus desperately I reason'd, madly talk'd—
Thus horrid as I was, of rugged growth,
More savage than the nightly-prowling wolf;
She feels what Nature taught; I, wilder far,
Oppos'd her dictates—but my panting soul
Now shivers in the agony of change . . .

('Night. To Stella', ll. 189-94)

Though bemoaning the fact that the world is 'unheedful' and will not listen, this is a poem which powerfully suggests the profound agony of change that Yearsley has experienced in terms of both lived and textual practice, from the brink of starvation to successful publication, from an earthy and authentic voice to a muted and stringently edited text.

If these poetic voices resemble Ann Yearsley's own, we should not be overly surprised by her unwillingness to use her poetry as a site for the construction of a resistant labouring-class identity. Yearsley's class origins are complex and a matter of some dispute.[8] The details remain sketchy, but it seems that during a period of economic hardship, the Yearsley family refused to apply to the parish for relief, holing themselves up in a disused barn in what appears to be a suicide pact. Virtually starved herself and her mother already dead from hunger, the poet and her husband and children are rescued when she is overheard reciting her work by a local gentlemen, who engineers a meeting between the poet and Hannah More, a member of the bluestocking circle around Montagu. Both More and Montagu are fascinated by the capacity of creativity to flourish in such desperate conditions and, in a grand performance of charitable sensibility, More arranges Yearsley's (highly successful) publication by subscription. Despite her enthusiasm for Yearsley's 'native genius', More's preface to the volume warns Yearsley that by speaking of her desire to escape and exceed her previous 'savagery', she risks being the victim of 'seduction' by wealth, fame and originality, the phallocentred trappings of masculinized genius. Of her 'little project' to help Yearsley, More says that:

It is not intended to place her in such a state of independence as might seduce her to devote her time to the idleness of Poetry. I hope she is convinced, that the making of verses is not the great business of human life; and that as a wife and a mother, she has duties to fill, the smallest of which is of more value than the finest verses she can write: . . . it would be cruel to imagine that we cannot mend her fortune without impairing her virtue.

(More, pp. xv-xvi)

More is interested less in natural genius than the naturalization of existing social relations. Yearsley's potential rise to subjective 'independence' is framed here in an eroticized discourse of 'seduction'. To be a self-made woman is to win one's subjectivity by resigning the twin virtues of maternity and femininity. Like the genius theorists, More constructs a hierarchy of moral, economic and aesthetic value in which abstract maternal virtue triumphs over female artistic-creative practice. Yearsley's creativity is seen as a form of 'idleness', an inferior species of the true labour of motherhood. Yet, thanks to More's triumph of marketing, the poet is herself created, an object of creativity. Once she was Ann Yearsley, now she is 'Lactilla', a saleable and perfectly packaged commodity: not *a* but *the* 'Poetical Milkwoman'. Yearsley becomes, in a sense, Hannah More's 'monster', a starving, homeless broken fragment until she is 'mended'—More's own phrase—by 'one' who claims to be 'not motivated by idle vanity'. Yearsley's poetic identity is therefore doubly displaced, first by the cultural saturation of ideas about genius, motherhood and charitable sensibility, and then by the impossible injunctions placed upon her at a local level by More.

Yearsley's poetry is not, of course, the chance or divinely inspired work of some naive noble savage, and nor does she accept the rustic *nom de plume* 'Lactilla' without turning it to irony. It is in colonizing and revising the politics of silence, however, that Yearsley most effectively creates a poetics of subtle and effectively understated resistance to the masculine creative cycle set out by Gerard and reiterated by Hannah More. (Perhaps inevitably, in 1786 Yearsley and More quarrelled irreparably, ostensibly over monies. A very public feud developed, forcing the poet to seek new patrons and publishers.) In conclusion, two citations, the first here from a poem in Yearsley's second collection, serve to illustrate the depth of Yearsley's despair with what she calls 'alphabets (misused)' and the power of her resistance to them:

Florus, canst thou define that innate spark
Which blazes but for glory? Canst thou paint
The trembling rapture in its infant dawn,
Ere young Ideas spring; to local Thought
Arrange the busy phantoms of the mind,
And drag the distant timid shadows forth,
Which, still retiring, glide unform'd away,

Nor, rush into expression? No; the pen,
Tho' dipp'd in awful Wisdom's deepest tint,
Can *never* paint the wild extatic mood.

('To Mr. ****, An Unlettered Poet, On Genius Unimprov'd', ll. 1-10)[9]

The title is indicative of Yearsley's sharp distinction between genius and genius materialized. Finally, at the end of Yearsley's eleven-year career as a published writer, the experience of sublime 'blockage' that forced the contrived termination of the poem to Montagu becomes a precondition for achieving higher, idealized planes of conception in which she might at once preserve her silent interiority and 'bid idea live' without the risk of creative stillbirth:

                       . . . feeble sounds
Give not my soul's rich meaning; or my thought
Rises too boldly o'er the human line
Of alphabets (misused). Why should I wish
For words to form a picture of the world
Too rare? O world! What hast thou in thy sounds
So dear as silent memory when she leads
The shade of the departed? Ask despair
What renovation is, when friendship bends
To kiss her tears away; but ask her eyes;
The pleasing anguish dwells not on her tongue.

('Remonstrance in the Platonic Shade, Flourishing on an Height', ll. 49-59)[10]

Notes

1. Ann Yearsley, *Poems, on Several Occasions* (1785; London, 4th edn, 1786). 'On Mrs. Montagu', and the other poems discussed in this essay, frequently appear in modern anthologies of eighteenth-century poetry. See, for instance, the Yearsley selections in Moira Ferguson (ed.), *First Feminists: British Women Writers 1578-1799* (Bloomington, IN and Old Westbury, NY: Indiana University Press and The Feminist Press, 1985); Roger Lonsdale (ed.), *Eighteenth-Century Women Poets* (Oxford: Oxford University Press, 1989).

2. Donna Landry, *The Muses of Resistance: Labouring-Class Women's Poetry in Britain, 1739-1796* (Cambridge: Cambridge University Press, 1990), p. 127.

3. Hannah More, 'A Prefatory Letter to Mrs. Elizabeth Montagu', in Yearsley (1786), p. xv.

4. Christine Battersby, *Gender and Genius: Towards a Feminist Aesthetics* (London: The Women's Press, 1989), p. 113.

5. The key theoretical texts of early romantic genius include William Sharpe, *A Dissertation Upon Genius* (1755; rpt New York: Scholar's Press, 1973); Edward Young, *Conjectures On Original Composition. In A Letter to the Author of Sir Charles Grandison* (1759; rpt Manchester: Manchester University Press, 1918); William Duff, *An Essay on Original Genius* (1767; rpt Gainesville, FL: Scholar's Press, 1964); and Alexander Gerard, *An Essay on Genius* (Edinburgh and London, Cadell, 1774).

6. The permeability of the romantic aesthetic to the political which it would exclude is most fully detailed in Kurt Heinzelman, *The Economics of the Imagination* (Amherst: University of Massachusetts Press, 1980) and Alan Liu, *Wordsworth: The Sense of History* (Stanford, CA: Stanford University Press, 1989).

7. Zynep Tenger and Paul Trolander, 'Genius versus Capital: Eighteenth-Century Theories of Genius and Adam Smith's *Wealth of Nations*', *Modern Language Quarterly*, 55 (1994), 171.

8. The disagreement about Yearsley's social status revolves around her possible ownership of commercial property and her entrepreneurial status as sole owner of a dairy business. Moira Ferguson, in 'Resistance and Power in the Life and Writings of Ann Yearsley', *The Eighteenth Century: Theory and Interpretation,* 27 (1986), 247-68, reads Yearsley's work as unproblematically within a tradition of labouring-class poetry stretching at least as far back as Duck and Collier in the 1730s. Mary Waldron, in *Lactilla, Milkwoman of Bristol: The Life and Writings of Ann Yearsley, 1753-1806* (Athens, GA and London: University of Georgia Press, 1996), sees Yearsley's ability to not only write, but manage her property and financial accounts, as a mark of social differentiation. Landry, however, argues that Yearsley's writing enacts only an *imaginary* 'emancipation from social exigency, to take upon herself the illusory freedoms of the bourgeois subject while remaining critical of historical developments from which her class and gender cause her increasingly to dissent' (p. 125). Other critics have attempted to deconstruct Yearsley's rhetorical silences. See Lucinda Cole and Richard Swartz, 'Why Should I Wish for Words? Literacy, Articulation, and the Borders of Literary Culture', in M. A. Favret and N. J. Watson (eds), *At the Limits of Romanticism: Essays in Cultural, Feminist, and Materialist Criticism* (Bloomington: Indiana University Press, 1994), pp. 143-69.

9. Yearsley, *Poems on Various Subjects* (London, 1787).

10. 'Remonstrance' first appears in Yearsley's last published work, *The Rural Lyre* (London, 1796). Since 1787, Yearsley had also produced a number of short political poems, most notably *A Poem on the Inhumanity of the Slave Trade* (London, 1788), plus a novel, *The Royal Captives* (London, 1795), and a performed stage play, *Earl Goodwin* (London, 1791).

Madeleine Kahn (essay date 1998)

SOURCE: Kahn, Madeleine. "'A By-stander Often Sees More of the Game Than Those That Play': Ann Years-ley Reads *The Castle of Otranto*." In *Making History: Textuality and the Forms of Eighteenth-Century Culture*, edited by Greg Clingham, pp. 59-74. Lewisburg, Penn.: Bucknell University Press, 1998.

[*In the following essay, Khan explicates the poem "To the Honourable H_____e W_____e, On Reading* The Castle of Otranto. December, 1784," *arguing that Yearsley's perceptions therein highlight the hidden dynamics of gender and class in Walpole's Gothic novel.*]

When Horace Walpole heard that the bluestocking Hannah More had given his novella *The Castle of Otranto* to her protégé, Ann Yearsley, to read, he chastised his friend for thinking an uneducated milkwoman such as Yearsley would be able to read his Gothic tale in the spirit in which he wrote it:

> What! if I should . . . take the liberty of reproving you for putting into this poor woman's hands such a frantic thing as the *Castle of Otranto*? It was fit for nothing but the age in which it was written, an age [which did not care] whether its amusements were conformable to truth and the models of good sense; . . . but you will have made a hurly-burly in this poor woman's head which it cannot develop and digest. . . . her imagination is already too gloomy, and should be enlivened.[1]

Walpole clearly expects Yearsley to be an impressionable and therefore unsophisticated reader. He imagines that she will take the Gothic fancies of *Otranto* too literally and so be terrified and confused by them. In at least one respect he turned out to be correct: as Yearsley's poem on the topic, **"To the Honourable H_____e W_____e, on Reading *The Castle of Otranto*. December, 1784,"**[2] tells us, she was quite an impressionable reader and, at least for the purposes of her poem, she professed to be terrified by some of the supernatural events in the novella:

> Thy jawless skeleton of Joppa's wood
> Stares in my face, and frights my mental eye;
>
> (ll. 69-70)

> I shudder, see the taper sinks in night,
> He rises, and his fleshless form reveals.
>
> (ll. 75-76)

Here Yearsley's speaker shares the terror of one of Walpole's characters; the world of *Otranto* is real to her. These lines seem to offer support for Walpole's idea that Yearsley is too unsophisticated and too gloomy by nature to be an appropriate reader for *Otranto*. The editor of Walpole's letters, W. S. Lewis, quotes them as proof that Walpole was correct, but I believe Lewis has

mistaken one small part of the poem for the burden of the whole. Yearsley's response to *Otranto* is not limited to this fearful credulity, nor is her relationship to Walpole simply that of an unlettered reader to a skilled author. But in one way Lewis is quite right to cite these lines as typical, for they are a good example of the way Yearsley's poem renders her reading experience so immediate. She writes in the present tense; she relives the terror and misery of each of the characters; she addresses Walpole as if he were in the midst of writing his tale at that very moment and as if she could influence the outcome if she argues passionately enough. In all of these ways she is as susceptible a reader as Walpole fears.

Furthermore, Yearsley agreed with Walpole that his story was so terrifying that some readers should be protected from its effects—but the reader she in turn warned away was Walpole's fellow-member of the literary elite, Hannah More (referred to here as in other poems as Stella):

> Stella! if Walpole's spectres thus can scare,
> Then near that great Magician's walls ne'er
> tread,
> He'll surely conjure many a spirit there,
> Till, fear-struck, thou art number'd with the dead.
>
> Oh! with this noble Sorcerer ne'er converse,
> Fly, Stella, quickly from the magic storm;
>
> (ll. 81-86)

Clearly while she agrees that *Otranto* is not suitable for some readers, Yearsley does not share Walpole's belief that the better-educated and higher-class reader will prove less susceptible to the terrors of his story than she herself. Rather she assumes that she is hardy enough to converse "with this noble Sorcerer" Walpole, but that Stella, her superior in class, education, and literary background, is not. In fact, her entire poem stands on its head Walpole's assumption that those who are impressionable cannot also be sophisticated readers and critics. Her poem demonstrates that far from making her an unfit reader, being impressionable makes her instead the most passionately involved and generous reader of the *Castle of Otranto* that Walpole could have hoped for.

Yearsley is so willingly receptive to Walpole's text that she responds wholeheartedly even to those aspects of the story that he deemed inconsequential. She takes note of what goes on around the main action, in the lives of the women and the servants on the edges of the convoluted plot. For example, she uses Walpole's character Bianca, a servant in the castle, as the first-person speaker of her poem. As Bianca she addresses many of Walpole's other characters directly in her poem, identifying with them, and responding as if the tale depicted real people in intolerable situations. Her empathy for these characters prompts her to make their relationships and their internal struggles more important in her poem than the working out of the prophecy about who shall inherit the castle of Otranto. This shift in focus toward the characters and away from the plot leads her to criticize Walpole for the short shrift he gives those characters (especially the women) even as she praises him for his skill in creating the fictional world that has so captivated her. Speaking in the first person through Bianca, Yearsley addresses Walpole directly and, using both sticks and carrots, tries to cajole him into sharing her experience of the story he has written.

Yearsley's Bianca begins aggressively, venting her bitterness at the artificial limits Walpole has placed on her intelligence and her voice. In Walpole's tale Bianca seems to be merely a voluble and flighty servant in the castle, and Walpole is on record in his two prefaces as dismissing her as unimportant. In the first preface he offers this interpretation of the servants' roles in the story:

> Some persons may perhaps think the character of the domestics too little serious for the general cast of the story; but . . . [t]hey discover many passages essential to the story, which could not well be brought to light but by their *naivete* and simplicity; in particular, the womanish terror and foibles of Bianca, in the last chapter, conduce essentially towards advancing the catastrophe.[3]

According to Walpole the servants are not so much characters as they are devices to advance the plot. He goes further in his second preface to expand on this argument that the "domestics," as he calls them, function as a dramatic device (rather than as characters) to heighten the seriousness and the portentousness of the rest of the story. Here he appeals to both the "rule [of] nature" and to that "higher authority . . . [t]hat great master of nature, Shakespeare" for his assertion that:

> However grave, important, or even melancholy, the sensations of princes and heroes may be, they do not stamp the same affections on their domestics: at least the latter do not, or should not be made to express their passions in the same dignified tone. In my humble opinion, the contrast between the sublime of the one and the *naivete* of the other, sets the pathetic of the former in a stronger light.

> (*CO* [*The Castle of Otranto*], 8)

This argument continues for another four pages, with ample quotations from both Shakespeare and Voltaire, and I read it as Walpole's indirect acknowledgment that the servants end up occupying a large part of his tale and that he needs in some way to account for their prominence. His method is to say that although they take up space, they are not important in their own right.

Yearsley's Bianca takes offense at this characterization of her as a creature of "womanish terror and foibles" who is significant only for the ways in which she fur-

thers events or promotes the development of other characters. By choosing Bianca for her poetic persona Yearsley shows us that even in Walpole's version Bianca is the figure in the story who grasps the import of both the natural and the supernatural events and who sees the true nature of her fellow characters. In her poem Yearsley builds on Walpole's characterization to develop Bianca further into the figure who can address both praise and criticism to Walpole on behalf of his other characters. Bit by bit Yearsley's Bianca grows into a character who can assert that being a serving maid makes her a shrewd and necessary commentator on Walpole's story, not a flighty character whose "womanish foibles" obstruct the story's development. In Yearsley's poem Bianca achieves significance as an independent character because Yearsley makes hers the voice of the internal ideal reader of *The Castle of Otranto*. Thus Yearsley has Bianca demonstrate for the world within Walpole's fiction what her poem demonstrates for the world of the reader: just as Yearsley's passionate susceptibility to Walpole's authorial powers makes her an exceptional reader rather than an unfit one, so Bianca's supposed marginality as a servant turns out to be the asset that allows her a broader perspective on the work in which she appears.

As the poem opens, however, Yearsley's Bianca has not yet broken out of the role Walpole has given her. Instead she is chafing at that role from within its confines and bitterly decrying her inability to speak because of the limitations Walpole has placed on her:

> To praise thee, WALPOLE, asks a pen divine,
>   And common sense to me is hardly given,
> BIANCA's Pen now owns the daring line,
>   And who expects *her* muse should drop from
>   Heaven.

> (ll. 1-4)

At first Yearsley's Bianca can only repeat with bitter emphasis what Walpole would say of her:

> Supreme in prate shall woman ever sit,
>   While Wisdom smiles to hear the senseless squall;
> Nature, who gave me tongue, deny'd me wit,
>   Folly I worship, and she claims me all.

> (ll. 13-16)

And yet even in these opening lines we can see that although Yearsley has chosen one of Walpole's characters for her persona and so is speaking from inside the world of *Otranto*, she also uses Bianca to voice her own perspective so that Yearsley's Bianca is also the milkwoman poet addressing one of the most exalted aesthetes of the day. The poem is never a dramatic monologue; both the speaker and the implied audience shift back and forth from the world inside the poem to the world of the poet.

In these two stanzas Yearsley beats Walpole over the head with his portrait of Bianca. She has loosed his own character upon him, now giving Bianca's pen ownership of the "daring line" and forcing Walpole to attend to "The empty tattle, true to female rules, / In which thy happier talents ne'er appear" (ll. 9-10). And, she warns, there will be no praise of Walpole here, because that would take a "pen divine" and we all know Bianca's muse is not going to "drop from heaven." This aggressive beginning essentially dares Walpole to dismiss what Yearsley has to say because she has chosen to write in Bianca's voice.

Such a ferocious beginning would seem to promise a poem promoting literary anarchy, in which the fictional character chastises her creator and rewrites her story as she wants it to be told. But almost immediately Yearsley's poem turns away from such anarchy toward an awed, almost docile appreciation of Walpole's powers. The several stanzas which directly follow Bianca's opening outburst are more like the lines cited by W. S. Lewis; they narrate Bianca's empathetic involvement with the other characters and with the terrors they face.

This section begins with the lines, "The drowsy eye, half-closing to the lid, / Stares on OTRANTO's walls; grim terrors rise" (ll. 17-18). Here Yearsley's Bianca enters into a near dream state, in which she appears to be hypnotized by the specters and spectacles of Walpole's world of Otranto. "Funereal plumes now wave; ALPHONSO's ghost / Frowns o'er my shoulder;" (ll. 21-22). In this state she directly addresses her fellow characters and their mutual creator, Walpole. To Manfred she says, "I feel thy agonies in WALPOLE's line," (l. 30) and then she turns to Walpole himself, hailing his "magic pen" (l. 33) and then demanding, "Where's MANFRED's refuge? WALPOLE, tell me where?" (l. 37).

This challenge to the author marks another shift in the tone of Yearsley's poem from awe-struck admiration for Walpole to eager advocacy for his characters. After her address to Manfred, Yearsley's Bianca turns to the women: Matilda, Hippolita, and Isabella. As she addresses them, she becomes increasingly exercized at the positions in which Walpole and his character Manfred have the women confined. She moves from a more descriptive exclamation:

> MATILDA! ah, how soft thy yielding mind,
>   When hard obedience cleaves thy timid heart!
>
> (ll. 41-42)

to a more critical one:

> HYPOLITA! fond, passive to excess,
>   Her low submission suits not souls like mine;
> BIANCA might have lov'd her MANFRED less.[4]
>
> (ll. 49-51)

Over the course of these six stanzas which begin with her apostrophe to Matilda, Yearsley's Bianca moves from submissive awe at Walpole's powers to empathy with his downtrodden women characters, then to a declaration of her own "omnipotence," and finally to straightforward bargaining with the formerly awe-inspiring Walpole. This part of the poem is crucial to the development of Yearsley's Bianca and of her critique of Walpole's art.

Right after she asserts that she "might have lov'd her MANFRED less," Yearsley's Bianca emerges from the specifics of Walpole's story and characters to make a general pronouncement about the way women submit to men:

> Implicit Faith, all hail! Imperial man
>   Exacts submission; reason we resign;
> Against our senses we adopt the plan
>   Which Reverence, Fear, and Folly think divine.
>
> (ll. 53-56)

In these lines Yearsley's Bianca speaks from a perspective beyond the limits of what Walpole has allowed her. She has a greater scope than she does earlier in this same poem where she either chafes at her restrictions without being able to analyze them ("Supreme in prate shall woman ever sit," l. 13), or is wholly captivated by Walpole's spell ("grim terrors rise, / The horrid helmet strikes my soul unbid," ll. 18-19). As Bianca's voice develops we can also hear Ann Yearsley speaking from outside Walpole's story, expressing solidarity with the practically voiceless women in the text who must conceal what they know. Yearsley emerges even more directly in the next two stanzas in which she sets the terms for a deal with Walpole: Your character Bianca will keep silent about what she knows about "you MANFREDS," thereby leaving your tale intact, but in exchange you must "Ope the trap-door where all thy powers reside," and tell me your secrets, author to author:

> But be it so, BIANCA ne'er shall prate,
>   Nor ISABELLA's equal powers reveal;
> You MANFREDS boast your power, and prize your state;
>   We ladies our omnipotence conceal.
>
> But, Oh! then strange-inventing WALPOLE guide,
>   Ah! guide me thro' thy subterranean isles,
> Ope the trap-door where all thy powers reside,
>   And mimic Fancy real woe beguiles.
>
> (ll. 57-64)

In these stanzas Yearsley seems to abandon temporarily the persona of Bianca to speak to Walpole as a fellow author. For the plea to "ope the trap-door where all thy powers reside" is that of an author, not a character in *The Castle of Otranto*. It becomes clear that in the previous stanza it is Yearsley who will keep Bianca from "prating" and revealing "ISABELLA's equal powers," and who will her own "omnipotence conceal." In these stanzas Yearsley is making explicit the bargain she has fulfilled in this poem: I'll be an obedient and credulous participant in your fantasy (both the supernatural goings on at Otranto and the portraits of Manfred and others as "Imperial man") right down to giving up my voice for the voice of one of your own characters. But in exchange I want the secret of your literary power.

Certainly the poem's speaker is far more powerful and assertive in these lines than she was earlier in the poem when she was helpless before Walpole's literary power, either as his limited creation who can merely prattle, or as his spellbound reader who dies when his characters die (l. 20). However, Yearsley does not forfeit her susceptibility in order to claim this new forcefulness. For example, she wants access to Walpole's powers, but she has no desire to destroy or belittle them; she wants to be able to use them. For as Walpole saw, Yearsley's imagination was gloomy. And, as he does not mention, her life was hard.[5] She feels "real woe," and she is in need of "mimic Fancy" to beguile that woe away. Her poem returns to the power of that "mimic Fancy" right after this plea, narrating once again the susceptible reader's experience of *The Castle of Otranto*. Indeed, the awe-struck lines cited by Lewis appear just two stanzas after Yearsley/Bianca's attempt at blackmail. These heartfelt passages of pure readerly surrender further demonstrate that for all its aggression and criticism, Yearsley's poem is foremost an appreciation of Walpole's tale.

With this return to the effect *Otranto* has had on her, the poem's speaker also begins to consider other readers. She first turns to her primary interlocutor, the woman with whom she was engaged in an ongoing literary and personal conversation throughout the period in which she was writing the ***Poems on Several Occasions,*** Hannah More.[6] She warns "Stella" away from close conversation with Walpole's tale with the lines I've already quoted (ending with "Fly, STELLA, quickly from the magic storm" (l. 86). She then elaborates on the risks that reading Walpole entails:

> Trust not his art, for should he stop thy breath,
>   And good ALPHONSO's ghost unbidden rise;
> He'd vanish, leave thee in the jaws of death,
>   And quite forget to close thy aching eyes.

> (ll. 89-92)

Under the guise of warning Stella, Yearsley/Bianca here asserts that Walpole is raising specters he cannot control and creating images whose full effect on his readers he cannot possibly know. This suggestion is in keeping with the rest of Yearsley's reading of Walpole's tale: she asserts that in Bianca (and to some extent the other women) Walpole has created a character whose full powers and worth he ignores. She goes further to sug-

gest that in the tale as a whole, which he affected to dismiss as "a frantic thing," he has inserted challenges to the gender and class hierarchies that the world of *Otranto* seems so determinedly to support.

Like so much else in Yearsley's poem, these perceptions about the limits of Walpole's art and of his control over his characters contain a mixture of criticism and admiration. He has the power to "stop thy breath," the speaker says, but he'll "forget" to offer you comfort, "to close thy aching eyes." Similarly, he has the instinct to create the character of Bianca, but not the insight to use her fully in his tale.

Yearsley aims in her poem to add what she feels is missing from Walpole's tale. In this too she is following Walpole's lead, and even offering homage to him. For, although Yearsley broadens the scope of Walpole's Bianca as she enriches the character's voice in her poem, she is building on the character that Walpole created. Yearsley never strays too far from Walpole's Bianca. In fact, the argument that she makes for Bianca as well as for herself—that outsider status is a source of insight, not blindness—comes directly from something that Walpole's Bianca says in *The Castle of Otranto*: "A by-stander often sees more of the game than those that play" (*CO*, 43). When she says this, Walpole's Bianca is speculating to her mistress, Matilda, about an attachment between Matilda's friend, Isabella, and the mysteriously noble peasant, Theodore. Her assertion that "he tells you he is in love, or unhappy, it is the same thing" (43) is just one of the many instances in which Walpole's Bianca sees clearly what to other characters is shrouded in mist. At times her greater detachment even seems like a kind of readerly literary sophistication. In the matter of Theodore, for example, only Bianca seems to know the conventions of literary romance.

Walpole's own Bianca is clearly aware that her outsider status as a servant is anything but the handicap that it might seem to be. Instead it allows her greater mobility and more opportunity to speak than the other women characters. Especially in the last chapter, Bianca displays how she uses her "womanish terrors" to manipulate her master, Manfred, and her seemingly senseless prattle to speak the truth. In this chapter, she tortures Manfred with insinuations about Isabella's attachment to Theodore, and she thwarts his efforts to hide his stratagems from Isabella's father, Frederick. For example, when Manfred, plotting to marry Isabella himself, tries bribing Bianca to find out "how long . . . Isabella [has] been acquainted with Theodore," she effectively heightens his anxiety while telling him nothing:

> Nay, there is nothing can escape your highness . . .—
> not that I know anything of the matter. Theodore, to be
> sure, is a proper young man, and, as my lady Matilda

says, the very image of good Alfonso: Has not your highness remarked it? Yes, yes—No—thou torturest me, said Manfred: Where did they meet? when?—Who, my lady Matilda? said Bianca.

(CO, 97)

It is perhaps a mark of Walpole's backhanded acknowledgment of Bianca's power that he particularly cites this last chapter as evidence of Bianca's frivolity, and of her limited function as a device for advancing the plot, or as he put it, "the catastrophe" (*CO,* 4).

Walpole's instances of Bianca's foolishness paradoxically lead us—and presumably led Yearsley—to recognize how crucial she is to the story. The space he devotes in his prefaces to trying to confine Bianca to her role as a silly servant shows clearly that he knew that the character he had created didn't quite fit into the role he had assigned her. In her poem, Ann Yearsley pursues this belated insight of his and expands Bianca's role to fit the character Walpole had created. Instead of devaluing Bianca's insights by insisting that she is a mere prop to establish the greater nobility of the other characters as Walpole does in his prefaces, Yearsley lets her continue to speak as she does in Walpole's tale. As a result, Yearsley's poem, for all of its criticism of Walpole, offers us a generous reading of Bianca's character and of Walpole's novella as a whole. By setting up a dialogue between her poem and Walpole's novella, she gives more texture to the novella, which has been made richer by her attention to Bianca's character. In following his direction then, Yearsley continues to pay tribute to Walpole, even as she shows him how limiting his treatment of Bianca is.

Toward the end of the poem, when the speaker has clearly moved further outside the confines of Walpole's fictional world into the real world where Yearsley is both an admiring reader and an author in her own right, she professes to fear retaliation from Walpole and his dark art. Immediately after she warns Stella/More to "Trust not his art," Yearsley's Bianca asks:

> But is BIANCA safe in this slow vale?
>   For should his Goblins stretch their dusky wing,
> Would they not bruise me for the saucy tale,
>   Would they not pinch me for the truths I sing?
>
> Yet whisper not I've call'd him names, I fear
>   His ARIEL would my hapless sprite torment,
> He'd cramp my bones, and all my sinews tear,
>   Should STELLA blab the secret I'd prevent.

(ll. 93-100)

"Stella" might "blab the secret" to Walpole because he is a friend of hers. In fact, More had enlisted him in her campaign to publish Yearsley's poems and had sent him several of the early ones for his commentary.[7] And, of course, Yearsley is being coy here: she needs Stella to blab; she needs Walpole as a reader. Her poem is addressed to him, and he is the reader she most needs to convince of the validity of her version of Bianca's character and of the value of the laboring woman's perspective on events in *The Castle of Otranto.* Even her reference to Shakespeare's Ariel is an appeal to collaboration, echoing as it does Walpole's claim to be following Shakespeare in his comic treatment of the servants in his tale.

In these stanzas purporting to fear retribution, but more subtly enticing a reaction from Walpole, Yearsley is using the doubleness of her poetic persona to particular advantage. She plays on the contrast between her image as a lowly servant who has no protection against Walpole's Ariel who could "cramp my bones, and all my sinews tear," and her clear confidence in her voice as Walpole's fellow author. In these stanzas both the saucy yet powerless Bianca of the first part of the poem and the more aggressive Yearsley/Bianca of the quid pro quo offer in the middle of the poem appear again. Here Yearsley uses them together, carrot and stick, to flatter and correct Walpole into joining with her in a conversation about his work.

Building on Walpole's own Bianca, who uses her status as a mere by-stander to see the game more clearly than "those that play," Yearsley uses her awe-struck and impressionable reading to reveal to Walpole, as well as to us, the full richness of Bianca's power as a character. In her poem she suggests that Bianca—not coincidentally like Yearsley herself—is not entirely defined by her class status. Being a servant in the castle, then, does not make her a mere by-stander; it makes her a crucial by-stander—as important to the game as "those that play." Thus Bianca's presence in Walpole's story authorizes the reading Yearsley proposes in her poem. Using his own character, his own language, and his own observation about outsider status, Yearsley proposes to Walpole that there are hidden riches in his Gothic tale. That is, she proposes that it is also true of the relationship between reader and author that "a by-stander often sees more of the game than those that play."

Yearsley's attempt to claim Walpole as a kind of before-the-fact collaborator in her version of the tale of *The Castle of Otranto* is both "daring," as she first asserts when she gives "BIANCA's Pen" ownership of "the daring line," and hopeful—she's paying homage to his creation. By seizing the outsider's perspective that Walpole has given to Bianca and providing more scope for her insights (such as her criticism of "Imperial man" and of Walpole as an author), Yearsley rescues the class and gender dynamics of *The Castle of Otranto* from the subterranean passages where Walpole had buried them. In so doing, she lends the tale depth and rescues the women characters and their relationships from the burden of the plot which threatens to bury them. I use the word "subterranean" advisedly of course, for the subterranean is crucial to both the physical and metaphorical landscapes of the Gothic. Specifically, in *Otranto* a trap door and a subterranean passage provide the way out of the castle for the beautiful Isabella when Manfred threatens her with a quasi-incestuous marriage. Only her knowledge of that subterranean passage frees the young woman from Manfred's plots and gives her the chance to express her own perspectives and desires. Similarly, when Yearsley's Bianca explicitly situates Walpole's literary power in his "subterranean isles" (l. 62) and asks him to "ope the trap-door where all thy powers reside" (l. 63), she is pleading for a way out of the realm in which she can only sit "supreme in prate" (l. 13) toward one in which she can "sing . . . the truths" (l. 96) she sees.

The experience of rereading *The Castle of Otranto* after reading Yearsley's poem is one of noticing how central much of what Walpole has pushed to the margins turns out to be. Walpole's own description of the tale as a "frantic thing" is correct if you try to read for the plot, which is both confusing and oddly skeletal. It concerns a stolen kingdom, a prophecy, a search for a male heir, and giant body parts which appear abruptly to derail the plans of Manfred, the usurper. The narrative of this part of the tale is not coherent enough to keep our attention; instead we wander off into the tangle of protean relationships among family members in the castle. These relationships are what Yearsley's poem first prompts the rereader to notice. When we begin to take the characters seriously, as she does, we see that most of the story is concerned with the characters' unexpected links to each other and the passions the revelations about those links release. The second insight Yearsley's poem offers the reader is that the male princes and nobles make almost no sense as motivated characters: Conrad is a cipher; Manfred is an appalling tyrant about whom the narrator nevertheless says, "Manfred was not one of those savage tyrants who wanton in cruelty unprovoked" (*CO*, 30); and Frederick unreliably loses track of and then regains his desire to retrieve Isabella from Manfred's clutches. The third thing we notice is that the women and servants are far more richly drawn and are more consistent as characters than the men. Their motivations and actions make sense; they respond more credibly to events and to each other. These women and servants—and especially the women servants—precisely because they are less fantastic than the men—are the characters who give the reader a window into the tale. As we reread we see that the women emerge as the focal point of the tale. Even the plot finally works out to their advantage: Isabella marries Theodore; Hippolita retreats happily to a convent; even Matilda, who is sacrificed to her father's murderous rage is at least instrumental in his conversion (a fate which has been presaged by her otherworldliness). We are not told specifically what happens to Bianca, but we can bet that

she lands on her feet as the personal maid to the new queen. She keeps a careful eye on her own status from the beginning when she tries to persuade Matilda that marriage would not be so bad. "I would have you a great lady" (*CO*, 38) she says, knowing that she would then "have the honour of being your highness's maid of honour" (*CO*, 41).

By giving greater scope to Bianca's voice, then, Yearsley is making good on the hidden promises of Walpole's tale. By directing our attention away from the men contesting over the kingdom of Otranto, she restores coherence to our reading experience. Walpole had sacrificed this coherence by continually bringing the men and their plots back to the foreground of his story. While proposing that we (and Walpole) adopt her reading experience as her own, however, Yearsley is careful never to suggest that she wants to supplant Walpole as the author of *The Castle of Otranto*. On the contrary, she returns again and again to the source of her Bianca persona and her reading experience in Walpole's text. Reminding us how rooted her poem is in Walpole's creation is one of the purposes of the long passages of participatory reading, such as this stanza in which Yearsley's Bianca empathizes with Matilda, torn between duty and her love for Theodore:

> Ah, rigid duties, which two souls divide!
> Whose iron talons rend the panting breast!
> Pluck the dear image from the widow'd side,
> Where Love had lull'd its every care to rest.

> (ll. 45-48)

Even when she is most bitter, Yearsley's Bianca pays homage to Walpole's literary power. And even at the end of the poem, when Yearsley's Bianca has gained a more authoritative voice, she insists on Walpole's greater literary power. Each of her most daring moments, such as her offer of silence in exchange for guidance, and her daring Walpole to "bruise me for the saucy tale, / . . . pinch me for the truths I sing" (ll. 95-96) contains an acknowledgment of her susceptibility to Walpole's tale. She resists Walpole's either/or formulation: she is neither a susceptible nor a daring critic; she's both. The poem's ending acknowledges her susceptibility once more, and then goes a step further:

> But hush, ye winds, ye crickets chirp no more,
> I'll shrink to bed, nor these sad omens hear,
> An hideous rustling shakes the lattic'd door,
> His spirits hover in the sightless air.

> (ll. 101-04)

Just a few lines after she daringly and coyly warns Stella not to "blab the secret I'd prevent" (l. 100), Yearsley's Bianca succumbs once more to the terrifying images that Walpole has created. She "shrink[s] to bed" knowing that "his spirits" nevertheless "hover in the sightless air." The saucy and self-confident speaker who has earlier tried to cajole Walpole into seeing his own work through her eyes here longs to see nothing at all. She cannot free her mind of the spirits that Walpole has conjured there, so she pleads with a greater power, that of sleep, to "shut each entrance of my mind" and release her from Walpole's spell:

> Now, MORPHEUS, shut each entrance of my mind,
>   Sink, sink, OTRANTO, in this vacant hour;
> To thee, Oh, balmy GOD! I'm all resign'd,
>   To thee e'en WALPOLE's wand resigns its power.

(ll. 105-08)

It takes a god, not a mere milkmaid poet to make "WAL-POLE's wand resign its power." So Yearsley's poem concludes with great—if somewhat sad—admiration of Walpole. It also concludes with a retreat into silence, as if she is not quite sure she can sustain the voice she has created without Walpole's help.

Yearsley does not ask in this poem for Walpole to admire her as a fellow author. Rather she pleads for him to acknowledge her as a great reader of his work. She wants furthermore to show him that she is a great reader because of, rather than in spite of, the working-class and female perspective she brings to his work. These are some of her reasons for using Walpole's own character for the speaker of her poem; she wants to show him that her reading is as much a collaboration as a correction: she is following his lead.

In following that lead, and in expanding Bianca's character into what seems to be her more natural role, Yearsley is also participating in what was to become the great preoccupation of the Gothic novel in the eighteenth century: testing the limits of women's roles and exploring the indirect ways women might collaborate with—rather than simply be victimized by—the subterranean passions and powers beneath the roles that propriety allowed them. In the case of this milkmaid poet's daring to offer a corrective reading to Walpole's aesthetic experiment, this means most specifically suggesting that Walpole needs Yearsley as a sympathetic, collaborative reader to show him the riches in his own text. Still following his lead, Yearsley suggests to Walpole that this "bystander" has perhaps seen more in his novel than "those that play," that is, than he who first wrote it.

Notes

I presented a very early version of this paper at the conference "Rethinking Women's Poetry 1730-1930" in London, 21 July 1995. I am grateful for the feedback I got at that conference and for the travel grant from the American Council of Learned Societies, which enabled me to attend. I am also indebted to two of my best and most constant readers for their comments: Timothy Bishop and Cynthia Scheinberg. Thanks to Nancy Logan for the House of Work.

1. Horace Walpole to Hannah More, Saturday, 13 November 1784, in *Horace Walpole's Correspondence,* ed. W. S. Lewis, 48 vols. (New Haven: Yale University Press, 1938-83), 31 (1961): 221, n. 12.

2. Ann Yearsley, *Poems on Several Occasions* (London: Cadell, 1785), 87-96. Citations will be by line number in the text. In these quotations from Yearsley's poem I have modernized the eighteenth-century long "s" but have otherwise kept the spelling and punctuation intact. The full 1785 text of the poem is given in an appendix to this essay.

3. Horace Walpole, "Preface to the First Edition," *The Castle of Otranto,* ed. W. S. Lewis (New York: Oxford University Press, 1982), 4; hereafter *CO,* cited in the text.

4. Yearsley changes Walpole's spelling "Hippolita" to "Hypolita."

5. At one point Yearsley, her husband, her children, and her mother were homeless and starving. Her mother died from the prolonged period of starvation, shortly after they were rescued. For biographical information on Ann Yearsley, see Hannah More, "A Prefatory Letter to Mrs. Montagu. By a Friend," *Poems on Several Occasions*; J. M. S. Tompkins, *The Polite Marriage* (Cambridge: Cambridge University Press, 1938); Mary Waldron, "Ann Yearsley and the Clifton Records," *The Age of Johnson* 3 (1990): 301-29; and Linda Zionkowski, "Strategies of Containment: Stephen Duck, Ann Yearsley, and the Problem of Polite Culture," *Eighteenth-Century Life* 13, no. 3 (1989): 91-108.

6. For a detailed treatment of Yearsley's relationship to More as a collaborative one, see my article, "Hannah More and Ann Yearsley: A Collaboration across the Class Divide," *Studies in Eighteenth-Century Culture* 25 (1996): 203-23.

7. "I am surprised . . . at the dignity of her thoughts and the chastity of her style. Her ear, as you remark, is perfect . . . this good thing has real talents." Horace Walpole to Hannah More, 13 November 1784, *Correspondence,* 31: 219-20.

Mary Waldron (essay date 1999)

SOURCE: Waldron, Mary. "'This Muse-born Wonder': The Occluded Voice of Ann Yearsley, Milkwoman and Poet of Clifton." In *Women's Poetry in the Enlighten-*

ment: The Making of a Canon, 1730-1820, edited by Isobel Armstrong and Virginia Blain, pp. 113-26. Houndmills, England: Macmillan Press Ltd, 1999.

[*In the following essay, Waldron contends that Yearsley's poetic voice has been largely misunderstood by critics, claiming that rather than being an unlettered, simple, and rustic poet, Yearsley was self-educated, insightful, and sophisticated in her awareness of a broad range of literary and cultural issues.*]

The so-called primitive poets of the eighteenth century were seldom given a chance to define themselves and their aspirations; this privilege was claimed by those who considered themselves in charge, who believed themselves to be in an educational and social position which gave them the right to categorize these poets and require them to fulfil certain expectations.

The phrase 'muse-born wonder' was used of Yearsley in a letter written by Anna Seward in about 1787, and it gives expression to a persistent eighteenth-century illusion.[1] Seward was in general very supportive of Yearsley, especially in her quarrel with her patron, Hannah More, but, like many others, she wanted to believe that Yearsley's status and style of life gave her direct access to the 'muse'; she was a 'wonder', whose talents were supposed to have arisen directly from 'nature' without the necessity of much in the way of induction.

This belief in the existence of mysteriously endowed 'primitive' writers was related to the critical preoccupation with pastoral poetry which was a feature of much of the century. The mainstream debate was about Virgil and Theocritus and their later imitators, and about how much realism should be brought into the descriptions of the lives of shepherds and other rustic characters, but a minor tributary was concerned with the speculation that earlier poets such as Homer and Hesiod were themselves occupied in farming and other rural pursuits, were without education in the eighteenth-century sense, and were for this reason better poets than their modern descendants. Thomas Blackwell, writing about Homer and his times in 1735, says: 'The Talent of their poets was truly *natural,* and had a much better title to Inspiration than their learned Successors; I mean learned by Books . . .'.[2] In 1767 William Duff, in his *Essay on Original Genius,* is certain that poetry flourishes best in 'uncultivated' life: 'The efforts of Imagination, in Poetry at least, are impetuous, and attain their utmost perfection at once, even in the rudest form of social life'.[3] This quite widespread conviction also affected attitudes to Shakespeare—had indeed been around since Milton's 'l'Allegro': 'Then to the well-trod stage anon, / If Jonson's learned sock be on, / Or sweetest Shakespeare, Fancy's child, / Warble his native wood-notes wild'— but had become received opinion by mid-eighteenth century; Shakespeare was a difficulty which could only be got over by recourse to the supremacy of the 'wild and natural'; his work was supposed to be quite spontaneous and exceptional, and only likely to recur outside the restrictions of civilized urban life. Two further supposed advantages of the ancient poets—as well, presumably, of Shakespeare—in their rural Eden were tranquillity and innocence. Here is Duff once more:

> Genius naturally shoots forth in the simplicity and tranquility of uncultivated life. The undisturbed peace, and the innocent rural pleasures of this primeval state, are, if we may so express it, congenial to its nature. . . . Happily exempt from that tormenting ambition, and those vexatious desires, which trouble the current of modern life, he wanders with a serene, contented heart, through walks and groves consecrated to the Muses. . . .[4]

Duff's sentimental vision of the bucolic pleasures of ancient Greece translated itself perfectly naturally into a description of eighteenth-century 'uncultivated' life for those who insulated themselves from its hardships. But as time passed this notion of the origins of poetry underwent subtle changes.[5] Too much was known about the discomforts and incessant labour of those who actually worked the fields for the more honest and observant to give much credence to Duff's unrealistic constructions. Envy of their peaceful and uncluttered lives gave place to wonder that the muses ever got a look-in. Thus the idea of the 'natural poet' survived the transition to a more realistic view of the circumstances of those who toiled from morning to night and yet found time and energy to write. It seemed all the more certain that inspiration must be the source of their talent—a mysterious communion with an unseen power. These people had no access to teachers and very little to books—how could it be otherwise? The idea that such writers could have educated themselves did not enter into their calculations.

It is difficult, but interesting, to try to understand why the notion of the autodidact made so little headway against so much evidence at this time. Among men it is perhaps understandable, for the education of boys of the upper ranks, and increasingly of the 'middling sort' was stereotyped. It was entirely centred on classical literature and took place either in school or with a tutor; few saw any possibility of an alternative. But it is not so easy to explain why there was a similar resistance to the idea of self-education among women. Women's education in the same ranks of society was not stereotyped at all; it depended for its existence, its content, its extent and its duration on the vagaries of those who brought them up. Educated women could think themselves lucky for their opportunities and must have been aware of a certain amount of determination in themselves to sustain what was often circumscribed and curtailed by those who supported education for women in principle but believed that it should be restricted to matters not thought likely to tax the feeble female brain or—fearful prospect—turn them into unmarriageable pedants. Hannah More herself was thought by her father to be too precocious for her own good and, we are told by her nineteenth-century biographer, had to wring concessions from him when he wanted to limit her studies, especially in the classics, and in any case quietly went on with them in spite of him.[6] It is strange that women such as More failed to recognize the same phenomenon in writers who were financially less privileged than themselves—that having by good fortune made a start, they simply had to do the rest themselves. There seems to have been among those who regarded themselves as educated a need for an underclass incapable of helping themselves out of ignorance, an ineducable mass against which to rate their own prowess. The reality was that these writers were often better educated than many of their social superiors; there was probably an abundance of idle and dim-witted boys at the public schools for whom books had no charms; and most girls of the same rank received no effective education at all. So-called unlettered writers had, on the other hand, taken maximum advantage of their meagre opportunities. There was in fact no hard line between the educated and the 'unlettered'.

But the patrons of these writers, upon whom they were often totally dependent, preferred the more sensational 'muse-born wonder' to the patient and industrious self-taught student doing his or her best with the shreds and patches from the rich man's library which was ignored by the majority of people who had easy access to it. For one thing the marvel of nature was more saleable; writings were published by subscription, and the more apparently mysterious the protegé, the more people were likely to subscribe. But the result was that the actual writings were scarcely read—their content was virtually ignored and their real connection with or departure from mainstream writing of the time went unnoticed and uninvestigated.

Most of the poets from the lower ranks suffered in this way. Richard Greene and Betty Rizzo have observed in the work of Mary Leapor that such writers were often valued more for their status than for the content of their work.[7] Ann Yearsley had further problems: she was not only required to prove the truth of the origins of natural genius as laid down by William Duff, but also that its source lay in the exercise of the Christian religion. The last two decades of the century saw a marked change in attitudes to religion; it was increasingly a factor in social control: the exercise of religion was thought to ensure that the lower ranks remained content and functioning in the station to which they had been called. Hannah More, Yearsley's patron, though she certainly subscribed to this belief, did not at first perceive that it might not be wise to present this supposedly primitive poet as a devotee of the pagan classics. At this early,

harmonious stage of the patronage (it was very brief—no more than nine months) she was not averse to continuing the milkwoman's education, even with translations of Latin poetry (Yearsley had already told her that she had read Virgil's *Georgics*): 'I will get Ossian for her', she writes to Elizabeth Montagu, her fellow patron. 'As she has never read Dryden I have given her his Tales, and the most decent of the Metamorphoses.'[8] Montagu's reply is just as enthusiastic but sounds a subtle warning:

> Indeed she is one of nature's miracles. What force of imagination! What harmony of numbers! In Pagan times, one could have supposed Apollo had fallen in love with her rosy cheek, snatched her to the top of Mount Parnassus, given her a glass of his best helicon, and ordered the nine muses to attend her call: but, as this heathen fiction will not pass now, let us consider whether Christian faith may not serve better. . . . Her native fire has not been damped by a load of learning. . . . Avaunt! grammarians; stand away! logicians; far, far away all heathen ethics and mythology, geometry, and algebra, and make room for the Bible and Milton when a poet is to be made. The proud philosopher stands far short of what has been revealed to the simple in our religion. Wonder not, therefore, if our humble dame rises above Pindar, or steps beyond Aeschylus. I do not mean to affirm that such geniuses as do not want the help of art, instruction, and study, are not rare, but the temple of Jerusalem and the holy mount may form them, without the portico or the academic groves.[9]

There is a perceptible shift here—and it is noticeable that when Hannah More writes shortly to another friend on the subject of Yearsley, she refers to her as 'Heaven-taught'—the muses give place to the Christian God as the source of the primitive poet's inspiration.[10] For reasons which have more to do with the protection of social divisions than literature or religion, Yearsley is being deprived of her own voice. Expectation is gradually being built up—she must have read very few books; these books must be English rather than Latin or Greek, even in translation; and she must be presumed to be firmly Christian in her way of life. She must also be rural and simple. In another letter More refers to the 'wild Wood notes of the moaning Nightingale' and brushes aside the classics as useless:

> The *Night-Thoughts* and the *Paradise Lost* are the two poems she is best acquainted with, and on which she has formed her own style and the structure of her verse. But the Holy Scriptures, that rich and inexhaustible Treasury of divine Wisdom and Knowledge, have been the chief object of her Study, and the source of her Information. These have enriched her language and enlarged her Conceptions; and I am charmed to see how much our illiterate Christian rises superior to all Wit and learning, and Wisdom falsly so called of the Pagan World![11]

Very early in her career as an author, then, Yearsley is being forced into a mould which will satisfy the preconceptions—and the fears—of her patrons, and her actual experience and talent are being ignored. Hannah More, in her Prefatory Letter to *Poems on Several Occasions,* refers to 'the wild vigour of her rustic muse' and again asserts the sincerity of her simple Christian faith and ignorance of the classics.[12] All the time she and her friends were failing to notice that they were dealing with a living, breathing woman, who had read a great deal, within the limits of her opportunities, and was hardly about to unlearn it all in the interests of fulfilling the requirements of the establishment literati. Moreover, she had ideas of her own about religion.

Any subscriber who really examined the poems ought to have had inescapable doubts about More's assertions. The first poem invokes the muse of tragedy, Melpomene; the diction is that of an eighteenth-century cultured person; the versification only experimental within certain accepted parameters. Yearsley does not, like Burns, build on popular forms or local dialect, which she could easily have done; nor does she, like Blake, experiment with simple linguistic forms and eccentric collocations. The verse is not dull, but it lies within the range of eighteenth-century convention. It is the work of an educated person, an achievement which lay outside the reach of the overwhelming majority of those taught in contemporary schools and by private tutors at home. But it was consistently described as 'wild', 'simple', 'natural'.

The rustic simplicity of her Christian faith is also in doubt. Although in this she rather defies than follows convention, she still fails to fulfil the requirements of her patrons. There are clear signs in some of the poems that she has doubts about the religion in which she had been brought up, and that these doubts are of a highly sophisticated order. She is particularly concerned about the existence and nature of the afterlife:

> nature works
> Obedient and unseen forever: we
> May meet in spheres remote—If not, farewell!
> I feel and know, those wishes can arise
> But from affections growing with my life,
> Mingling with hope, oppress'd by fear. The change
> Fulfill'd in thee may chill me; ev'ry thought
> Oblit'rate; vision, fancy forms, be doom'd
> To sink, like beaming glory in the west;
> Whilst space contracts on my weak eye, and heav'ns
> By human artists coloured, fade away,
> As life goes gently from my beating heart.

> (From '**Soliloquy**', *The Rural Lyre,* 1796)

The proliferation of religious systems also gives her problems of acceptance, but it is the anthropomorphism in English Christianity—the making of a god in humanity's own image—which brings out her strongest expressions of rejection:

> . . . and say, what boasting fool,
> To great Omnipotence a debt can owe?

> Or owing, can repay it? Would'st thou dare
> Barter upon equality? Oh, man,
> Thy notion of a Deity is poor,
> Contracted, curb'ed, within a narrow space,
> Which must on finite rest.

> (From '**On Jephthah's Vow**', *Poems, on Various Subjects* 1787)

These ideas appear with increasing strength and clarity throughout the three volumes of poetry, and are noticeable too in her novel.[13] They are very much in line with contemporary discussions, which Yearsley had probably read, of what was called 'natural religion' or Deism. These ideas were disapproved of by the church, but no mention is made about this aspect of her work by anyone; it was simply overlooked, or not taken seriously. The import of what she had to say was of little interest—the surprise was that she had said anything at all.

Yearsley is no more satisfactory as a rural poet. She deals very little with rural occupations, and of rural persons of all ages she is often very critical:

> O! freeze, to hear the hoary-headed sinner,
> With ceaseless profanation, taint the air;
> Grown old in dark stupidity, he treads,
> Fearless tho' feeble; on the verge of fate
> Sin leaves him not; and innate flames of vice
> Still fiercely burn . . .

> The florid youth
> Robust, impetuous, ardent in his strength,
> Lively and bounding as the skipping roe,
> The blush of beauty glowing on his cheek;
> *Within,* a strong epitome of hell;
> *There* vices rage, and passions wildly roar;
> Strong appetites, which never knew restraint,
> Scream for indulgence . . .

> (From '**To Mr. R——, on His Benevolent Scheme for Rescuing Poor Children from Vice and Misery by Promoting Sunday Schools**', *Poems, on Several Occasions,* 1785)

She seems bent on destroying illusions about rural innocence. No contemporary comment seems to notice this. Time after time we find such phrases as 'favourite child of nature' used of her; her work is described 'as the wild and simple product of her genius'; and everywhere we find 'wild wood-notes', a ludicrous description of what she was actually producing.[14]

Most of this comment, however misguided and superficial, was positive—or at least indulgent; but some was the reverse. Mary Wollstonecraft noted the absence of rural simplicity and the attachment to the classics, and did not approve: Yearsley is not behaving as a rural, unlettered poet should. Wollstonecraft did not get an opportunity to say so publicly until 1790, when Yearsley published *Stanzas of Woe,* a piece of invective against a local enemy, Levi Eames, in the same pamphlet as a celebration of her eldest son's apprenticeship to an engraver, a poem called **'To William Cromartie Yearsley'**. Wollstonecraft says of *Stanzas* in the *Analytical Review*:

> The praise which she has received has been, in our opinion, much warmer than she ever merited. . . . Mrs. Y. certainly has abilities; but instead of 'native wood-notes wild', stale allusions obscure most of her poems, in which, however, we discover an independent mind and a feeling heart.

Those terrible wood-notes would continue to haunt Yearsley to the end. Of **'William Cromartie Yearsley'**:

> We now expected to have heard the simple effusions of maternal fondness; but trite illustrations from classical lore, which we have already noticed, met our view on every page; and the sense is rendered still more intricate by that confusion of thought, which shows struggling energy not sufficiently strong to cultivate itself, and give form to a chaotic mass.[15]

Wollstonecraft's attitude is difficult to analyse; her *Vindication* was to be directed at women of the middle and upper ranks forced by convention into idleness and langour; perhaps she thought women like Yearsley should be satisfied with independent and useful employment like milk-selling. It is clear that she sees little worth reading in her poems, and it is impossible to avoid the conclusion that she thought Yearsley was simply aping her betters by showing any sign of conventional education. Her criticism is unjust, too, on other grounds—Yearsley's poem to her son is a grave and thoughtful piece—anything but 'chaotic'.

In 1798, ironically, Yearsley is rapped over the knuckles by Richard Polewhele in *The Unsex'd Females* for her 'Gallic wanderings' in the wake of the 'Arch-priestess of female Libertinism', in other words, Mary Wollstonecraft, which illustrates the confusion created by the political situation at the time.[16] To Polewhele Yearsley was subversive by the very fact of writing. On the other hand, in comment on her third collection of poems in 1796, the *Critical Review* is dissatisfied with her reverence for her aristocratic patron, the Earl of Bristol,[17] clearly wanting her to be more democratic:

> The inequalities of nature . . . are good and useful; the inequalities of society are evil in themselves, and to be justified only as being necessary evils. . . . Mrs. Yearsley might have acknowledged, not without sighs, the necessity of such a state of society; but surely *she* should not have *exulted* in it. Dedications to great people are dangerous things. Woman, beloved by genius,

> 'Know thine own worth, and reverence the lyre!'[18]

It must have been galling to Yearsley to be both praised for her nonexistent rural charm and blamed for its absence, and into the bargain to receive brickbats from both the political left and right. Few seemed able to detach their comment on her work from her status. In fact, neither the approval nor the rebukes had very much to do with what she actually wrote. She herself clearly wanted to work in the mainstream of English poetry, but to use its forms for her own purposes. She used the materials at hand, but the energy which caused her to begin to write stayed with her and made something of her poetry that was different from what had gone before. Her anger is often transmuted into passionate invective which is energetic but controlled, and very effective. Here is an example of her use of the heroic couplet in denunciation of patronage as she had experienced it:

> The cooly-wise, with self-applauding glance,
> And taunting air, cries, 'Friendship's all romance:
> 'It ne'er existed but in pleasing sound;
> 'Nor has it been, or ever will be found.
> 'Have we not seen the World? Do we not know,
> 'How far its rapid streams *exactly* flow?
> ''Tis to relieve Distress—this is the sum,
> 'But let your Prudence point out what's to come.
> 'Keep wretches *humble,* for when once reliev'd,
> 'They oft-times prove our *Charity* deceiv'd:
> 'Therefore be *cautious,* nor their *merits* trust;
> 'They *may* have very few—if poor—they *must.*
> 'Think not a savage virtuous—but confine,
> 'His future acts by obligation's line:
> 'He surely *must* be humble, grateful, true,
> 'While *he's* dependent—the superior *you.*'

(From **'On Being Presented with a Silver Pen'**, *Poems, on Various Subjects,* 1787)

There is also present an element of self-analysis which does not even pay lip-service to the Johnsonian view that poetry should teach moral lessons. Her poetry often moves emphatically away from the general to the personal, and thus looks forward to what we recognize as 'romantic'. She writes of the death of her mother:

> How oft, with thee when life's keen tempest howl'd
> Around our heads, did I contented sit,
> Drinking the wiser accents of thy tongue,
> Listless of threat'ning ill! My tender eye
> Was fix'd on thine, inquisitively sad,
> Whilst thine was dim with sorrow; yet thy soul
> Betray'd no innate weakness, but resolv'd
> To tread thy sojourn calm and undismay'd:
> Thy fortitude threw on my weaker cheek
> Confusion's tinge; even now I faintly feel,
> Thus wanting thee, wrapt in whose fost'ring wing,
> I found a shelter from inclement skies.

(From **'On the Remembrance of a Mother'**, *Poems, on Various Subjects,* 1787)

Yearsley's feminism anticipates some aspects of Wollstonecraft's. In a poem called **'To Mira, on the Care of her Infant'** she stresses the importance of the mother's role in the physical care and education of children, and in another vindicates strong-mindedness and self-respect:

Why boast, O arrogant, imperious man,
Perfection so exclusive? are thy powers
Nearer approaching Deity? cans't thou solve
Questions which high Infinity propounds,
Soar nobler flights, or dare immortal deeds,
Unknown to woman, if she greatly dares
To use the powers assign'd her? Active strength,
The boast of animals, is clearly thine;
By this upheld, thou think'st the lesson rare
That female virtues teach; and poor the height
Which female wit obtains.

(From **'On Mrs Montagu'**, *Poems, on Several Occasions,*
1785)

Her attitudes to the political cross-currents of her time are usually centrist and conservative, though several of her poems inveigh against misused authority. Here she rebukes Levi Eames, a wealthy denizen of Clifton, for having two of her children beaten for trespassing:

What Daemon plac'd *Thee* in the council chair?
  Go back, thou novice to that glorious hour!
Where the bold Barons planted freedom here,
  And tore the vitals of tyrannic pow'r.

Hast thou read o'er the statutes of the land?
  In Magna-Charta hast thou ever found,
A *Mayor* trudging with his whip in hand,
  To give the schoolboy many a *lawful* wound?

(From *Stanzas of Woe,* 1790)

Particularly in her last book, **The Rural Lyre,** but also elsewhere, as in her poem **On the Inhumanity of the Slave Trade,** she shows a sophisticated awareness of the national and international problems of the time. She was both traditional and innovative. These extracts show that she was a poet worth listening to on her own terms, but she never got a hearing.

Misjudgement did not end after her death. Her quarrel with Hannah More and her great sin of ingratitude reverberated through the nineteenth century in reverent encomiums to More, to the exclusion of much comment on Yearsley's work. She has fared rather better in our own century, but still only as a representative of a distinct group of lower-status writers, never in the mainstream. J. M. S. Tompkins's otherwise sympathetic account in 1938 does not subject the poetry to genuine criticism, but describes it sweepingly as 'ungainly'.[19] The subtitle of Rayner Unwin's 1954 study refers to it as 'peasant poetry' and treats it rather as a minority-taste curiosity than as a serious literary endeavour.[20] Recently, interest in Yearsley has intensified, but the preoccupations of the present day are sometimes just as inimical to her poetic identity as were those of the past. Recovery of women writers has been mainly taken up by commentators who are interested in evidence for the exclusion of female and non-establishment writers by patriarchal and capitalist pressures. Such evidence can of course be found in abundance, but investigations

should not stop at this point. In many cases insufficient care has been taken to search out the details of the very varied situations within which so-called 'labouring' women writers produced their work, and important aspects of their writings have been ignored in the interests of proving a theory. Comment on Yearsley frequently still rests on unexamined eighteenth- and nineteenth-century statements of the kind discussed above. Especially in the work of commentators who want to see her as undeniably proletarian, there is a tendency to perpetuate such inaccuracies, in particular about her status and financial position, and to rely heavily on parts of the work which best support the overall theme of the study.[21] As more becomes known, comment is becoming less circumscribed, but some inaccuracies persist. For instance, she is often referred to as a 'milkmaid', although she was never any kind of servant, but a self-employed trader.[22]

While Yearsley's work is accessible only in the rare-books divisions of libraries, misrepresentations can attain the status of fact and omissions go undetected. What is obviously now needed, for Yearsley as for other recovered writers of the past, is a full and accurate republication of her œuvre in its entirety so that a well-based body of sensible criticism can emerge. Yearsley wished to be rated with other poets of her times, not imprisoned by ideological assumptions and seen only as a member of a subgroup. Our assessment of her writings continues to be influenced by our perception of her status, and so replicates the distortions of the past. It is time we ceased to deny her an independent and individual voice.

Notes

1. Anna Seward, *Letters: 1784-1807* (Edinburgh: George Ramsay, 1811), Letter 25. This letter, written to T. S. Whalley, is dated 1786, but its references to Yearsley's 'first publication' and to the poems of John Bryant, pipemaker poet of Bristol, suggest a date not earlier than 1787.

2. Thomas Blackwell, *An Enquiry into the Life and Writings of Homer* (London, 1735), p. 119.

3. William Duff, *Essay on Original Genius and its Various Modes of Exertion in Philosophy and the Fine Arts, Particularly in Poetry* (London: Dilly, 1767), p. 262.

4. Duff, ibid., pp. 271-2.

5. See John Barrell, *Literature in History, 1730-1780: An Equal, Wide Survey* (London: Hutchinson, 1983), p. 91.

6. William Roberts, *Memoirs of the Life and Correspondence of Mrs. Hannah More,* 4 vols (London: Seeley and Burnside, 1834), vol. 1, pp. 12-13.

7. See Richard Greene, *Mary Leapor: A Study in Eighteenth-Century Women's Poetry* (Oxford: Clarendon Press, 1993); and Betty Rizzo, 'The Patron as Poet-maker: the Politics of Benefaction', *Studies in Eighteenth-Century Culture*, 20 (1990), pp. 241-6.

8. This letter is held by the Huntington Library in the Montagu Collection (MO 3987). It is printed in Mary R. Mahl and Hélène Koon, *The Female Spectator: English Women Writers before 1800* (Bloomington and New York: Indiana Press and Feminist Press, 1977).

9. Roberts, op. cit., vol. 1, p. 362.

10. Letter to Mary Hamilton in the possession of Sir Peter Anson, Bart. Until 1782 she had been assistant sub-governess to the royal children. Printed in James Silvester, *Hannah More, Christian Philanthropist: A Centenary Biography* (London: Thynne, 1934), chapter 5.

11. Anson, unpublished letter to Mary Hamilton.

12. Prefatory Letter to the first edition of Yearsley's first collection of poems, *Poems, on Several Occasions* (London: Thomas Cadell, 1785).

13. *Poems, on Various Subjects* (1787); *The Rural Lyre* (1796); and *The Royal Captives* (1795). All were published by G. G. J. and J. Robinson, who took over Yearsley's work from Cadell after her quarrel with More.

14. William Matthews, *New History, Survey and Description of Bristol* (Bristol, 1793-4), p. 97; John Evans, *History of Bristol*, 2 vols (Bristol, 1816) vol. 2, p. 297.

15. *Analytical Review*, 9 (April 1791), pp. 447-8.

16. Richard Polewhele, *The Unsex'd Females* (London: Cadell, 1798), p. 20.

17. Frederick Hervey, Earl of Bristol and Bishop of Derry, whose patronage was more acceptable to Yearsley than that of Hannah More because he laid no heavy obligations of gratitude upon her.

18. *Critical Review*, 19 (April 1797), pp. 462-3.

19. J. M. S. Tompkins, *The Polite Marriage: Eighteenth-Century Essays* (Cambridge: Cambridge University Press, 1938), p. 58.

20. Rayner Unwin, *The Rural Muse: Studies in the Peasant Poetry of England* (London: Allen & Unwin, 1954), pp. 77-81.

21. A number of writers see Yearsley as a mouthpiece for emerging working-class politics, but have to be selective in the process of demonstrating this. See Donna Landry, *Muses of Resistance: Labouring-Class Women's Poetry in Britain, 1739-1796* (Cambridge: Cambridge University Press, 1990), pp. 11-16, 120-65, 260-7; Morag Shiach, *Discourse on Popular Culture* (Cambridge: Cambridge University Press[, 1989]), pp. 57-8; and Moira Ferguson, 'Resistance and Power in the Life and Writings of Ann Yearsley', *Eighteenth Century: Theory and Interpretation*, 27 (1986), pp. 247-68, and 'The Unpublished Poems of Ann Yearsley', *Tulsa Studies in Women's Literature* (Spring 1993), pp. 13-46.

22. Even Patricia Demers, in an otherwise excellently researched, informative and unbiased essay, uses this misleading description of Yearsley's occupation. See '"For mine's a stubborn and a savage will": Lactilla (Ann Yearsley) and "Stella" (Hannah More) Reconsidered', *Huntington Library Quarterly* (Spring, 1993), pp. 135-50. Yearsley's status, as well as the range and variety of her work, are discussed in my essay 'Ann Yearsley and the Clifton Records', *Age of Johnson*, 3 (1990), pp. 301-29 and forthcoming biography, *Lactilla: The Life and Writings of Ann Yearsley, 1753-1806* (Athens, GA: University of Georgia Press, in press).

Judith Dorn (essay date 2000)

SOURCE: Dorn, Judith. "*The Royal Captives, a Fragment of Secret History*: Ann Yearsley's 'Unnecessary Curiosity.'" In *1650-1850: Ideas, Aesthetics, and Inquiries in the Early Modern Era*. Vol. 5, edited by Kevin L. Cope, pp. 163-89. New York: AMS Press, 2000.

[*In the following essay, Dorn contends that with her Gothic romance* The Royal Captives, *Yearsley sought to exert her cultural significance as a socially suppressed writer.*]

Ann Yearsley was that sport of nature, a working-class woman who published poetry.[1] She produced four collections of poems (as well as works in other genres) during the '80s as the celebrated "Bristol Milk Woman and Poetess," a hybrid conferred on her by her patron Hannah More but whose class typing Yearsley herself found objectionable.[2] In 1795, however, she wrote a book that looks like an effort to diversify her portfolio to profit from the flourishing trade in long prose fictions: *The Royal Captives: A Fragment of Secret History*.[3] This work resembles Gothic romances by Ann Radcliffe whose success in the book trade Yearsley may have noticed while running her circulating library.[4] Where Yearsley's books of poetry had been printed by subscription, *The Royal Captives* was distributed by several booksellers at once in Ireland, England, and

America. In designing this prose commodity for a wider reading public, Yearsley offers insight into what publishing meant to her beyond sales and publicity. Her writing of the book contends with the institutions of public print culture that hold her "Truth" (Yearsley's own expression) in suspense.

The Royal Captives thematizes writing under duress, posing as a memoir handwritten in prison by one Henry Capet, son of Louis XIV's elder twin brother, also named Henry, a man who rightfully deserves the Sun King's place in the history of France. The usurping monarch's persecution of these two Henries and their extended family demonstrates that acts of domination by political power create public history at the expense of consigning the powerless to oblivion.

This story comes from gossip run rampant into myth after Voltaire hinted in *Siècle de Louis XIV* (1751) that a mysterious masked prisoner who figures in memoirs of Louis XIV's reign could be none other than the Sun King's own twin.[5] Yearsley's choice of this legend as material for a book written during the Terror implies a view of history that explains the present as the result of forces that had been set in motion during Louis XIV's time, forces unknown before their effects became public knowledge. Indeed, Yearsley does make such a theory of history explicit early in her narrative, projecting in turn the idea that unknown forces in motion during her own present will affect future events.

When Yearsley writes a Gothic romance that incorporates her poems and calls it "a fragment of secret history," she asserts her own agency in history by placing the public's national idea of history at stake. This motley text, whose form resembles Menippean satire, links her own survival in cultural memory to a collective vision of obscure ranks of people for whom public print culture's instituted protocols offer no place in historical narratives.[6]

Although Mary Waldron's biography of Yearsley can say, "This is not a novel that concerns itself very much with the lower ranks" (234), Yearsley's dislocation from her own rural origins haunts her Gothic romance as a mystery needing to be solved. This is not an interpretation that requires much allegorical depth of reading, since Yearsley's narrative represents characters in the act of reading poems written by herself that address this issue. These poems speak to politics and history rather than draw their readers' imaginations away to a domain of aesthetic and sentimental contemplation. Yearsley's narrative does lend itself to David Punter's theory that the Gothic responds transgressively to the pressure that social conditions place on bourgeois values.[7] By 1795, the French Revolution had shown to the world a case study of a nation calling a completely new understanding of itself into existence. Its aftermath, the Terror had

raised in England fears of the political and economic aspirations of Yearsley's own class.

If the Gothic romances studied by Kate Ellis delineate and subvert the domestic ideology that relegates men and women to the separate cultural spheres of public and private,[8] Yearsley's Gothic romance is remarkable for the directness with which it rewrites public knowledge of history. Her design does after all precede Alexandre Dumas's use of this legend to make readers of *The Man in the Iron Mask* imagine that France's most glorious reign had been a hoax contrived by a few friends working behind the scenes. Yearsley's version arrives at a ringing denunciation of "THE BRUTALITY OF A KING" by its last page.

Working on the edge of oblivion, Yearsley hedges her bets by manipulating the protocols of print genres to turn even her own obscurity into romance. She uses poems to link her own position in cultural memory to a larger argument in which she projects changes in readers' categories for evaluating historical significance. When she prints her name in block capitals at the end of her preface, she replaces her own voice with the narrator of the ensuing story. This narrative exposes the vulnerability of that signature to history, which Yearsley understands not only as material events but also as the re-narration of a cultural significance for reevaluation by readers over time. She has invested in a text that critiques her culture's inability to see her as significant, without knowing what the ultimate pay off will be.

1

Donna Landry honors Ann Cromartie Yearsley among "plebeian female poets" of the eighteenth century as the one who "most repays detailed historical study" (Landry, 120). Her metaphor of repayment exposes the economy by which literary criticism adds value to forgotten texts by recirculating them as the matter of history—as Landry is herself aware. *Muses of Resistance* uses Yearsley's revolt against the patronage of Hannah More as a parable warning critics that their own writing can continue the exploitation of working-class women into the present by turning them yet once more into commodities.[9]

Landry's implied analogy between historical representation and the process of negotiating the value of a commodity in a marketplace offers a model for understanding Yearsley as competing for the scarce resource of cultural significance. Scholars may increase *The Royal Captives'* value by representing it as a historical artifact now that the book has gained mystique from a two-hundred-year stint in special rare book collections, but the work's position in public recollection remains in doubt.[10]

Landry herself omits *The Royal Captives* from her account in *Muses of Resistance* of Ann Yearsley's contradictory, at once working-class and bourgeois identity

(124). Tellingly, Landry calls *The Royal Captives* a "novel," invoking a literary category that relieves her of responsibility for dealing not only with so lengthy a prose work, but even with the many poems included in it. Since the chapter on Yearsley is already the longest in *Muses of Resistance,* scarcity of time and space resources must have forced Landry to classify *The Royal Captives* out of her book's range.

It is precisely such material limitations on public knowledge that Yearsley addresses by critiquing print culture's literary and historical categories for measuring "significance." Indeed, it is the category of "critique" that can currently be used to give Yearsley value, as critics value in her their own critical agendas. Yearsley's critique works by exposing the relation between the genre of a text's construction and the power and authority it commands.

She announces in the preface to *The Royal Captives* that she has switched from poetry to prose in order to gain some influence over public knowledge of herself:

> I love Fame, though I have only heard her whispers; am sensible she incites towards the wonderful, the great and good; and that Authors, who affect to despise her, are cowards, insincere, and guilty of profanation; yet there is vast difference in being her lover and her slave. For me, I confess myself not deaf to, nor independent of the voice of the world, except in those enraptured moments when bewitching Fancy renders me insensible to the real dependencies of life. In poesy, I am her slave; in prose, I wish her to be mine.
>
> (i-ii)

It is a peculiar passage, in which Ann Yearsley imagines herself interchangeably loving or enslaved by the female personification Fame. Fancy, which gives poetry its power, would enslave Yearsley by numbing her awareness of "the real dependencies of life." The foremost of these "real dependencies" that Yearsley considers is "the voice of the world," on which Fame depends. This imagery suggests that the struggle that is real and material to her is that of a writer seeking a place in "the world." She turns to prose out of a desire (without clarifying how she distinguishes this "wishing" from the whims of poetic Fancy) to seize control of these real dependencies.

This preface demonstrates that Yearsley remains painfully conscious of her need to publish in defense of her reputation ten years after her breach with Hannah More. In his polemical poem *The Unsex'd Females* (1798), Richard Polwhele came to interpret *The Royal Captives*' preface as yet another offense against Hannah More (25), putting Yearsley on display as a public emblem of ingratitude fifteen years after the fact: "she spurned her benefactor from her door" (24). Yearsley's *Royal Captives* may consequently extend the strategy

that she resorted to in the defining moment of her break with More, when she justified her publication of *Poems, on Several Occasions* by attributing responsibility for the violation of her natural obscurity to More: "her arrows are of the most malignant kind—yet her endeavours to *crush* an insignificant wretch need not be so amazingly strenuous; for I should have sunk into obscurity again, had not my reputation been so cruelly wounded" (xxx).[11]

By writing to a "Public" she conceives of as setting the conditions for her fame, Yearsley demonstrates her sense of the conceptual boundaries marking the "bourgeois public sphere" of the late eighteenth century.[12] As reviewed by Oskar Negt and Alexander Kluge, the concept of the Public served bourgeois culture as a "horizon of experience," not a place but the embodiment in cultural practices of a set of conceptual boundaries. The "public sphere" consisted of a set of institutions—including especially the print media—through which the bourgeoisie gained a collective political agency apart from home, marketplace, or state.[13]

Since collective interpretation of representations of experience as "public" is what makes them so, not all of print culture counts as "public" (Landes, 11). Joan Landes has argued that women, who had found ways of exercising personal influence under the *ancien régime,* came to be marginalized in relation to the bourgeois public sphere forming in post-revolutionary France because of the public sphere's symbolic masculinity (Landes, 1-3). Negt and Kluge further observe that since bourgeois culture serves to measure which representations are of "public interest," working-class experience comes to be construed as "a gigantic, cumulative 'private interest'" and therefore as lacking in value or relevance to the collective "public" (Negt and Kluge, 7, 9, 13).

Yearsley's act of publishing *The Royal Captives* would have exposed the class and gender conditions of her writing, as well as its generic status, to literate culture's discriminating reading. At issue for her is whether readers will construe her text as a voice that has a place in the public sphere. Selling to readers isn't necessarily the same as going "public," although the literary marketplace features in her strategy for achieving that end.

2

Yearsley's understanding of publishing as material struggle appears from the dramatic way in which she ends her Preface. She first suggests that she is publishing in a fight to the death against the forces that interfere with the public's clear vision of her, and then asserts the ultimate truth of her own identity by coming to rest on her signature:

> The clouds that hang over my fortunes intervene between me and the Public. I incessantly struggle to dissipate them, feel those struggles vain, and shall drop in

the effort—This consolation I shall, however, bear with me to the verge of life, that to those who have guided me by the sacred and lambent flame of friendship, my memory will be dear, and that whilst Malice feebly breathes, Truth will boldly pronounce,

ANN YEARSLEY

Yearsley presents herself as a name spoken by truth personified, without reference to gender, class, or historical context. Of course her gender and her lack of title cannot be hidden unless she publishes anonymously. She may fix her signature materially in print in a multi-volume work for wide distribution, but that name remains subject to the constructions that the reading public makes of it.

My claims about the tendentiousness of Yearsley's views of history rest on the remarkable parallel between Yearsley's signature at the end of her Preface and her hero's act of signing off at the very end of the book. Young Henry, son of the legendary masked man whose existence proves Louis to be a usurper, has been driven with his family into exile in England by the king's unjust persecutions. When he signs his name, however, he accepts this fate and renounces his right to a royal place in history:

> Since our arrival [in England], two sons and a daughter have blessed the bosom of my Emily; from them we have concluded to keep the secret of their descent; and I hope, should those papers, hastily filled up, be ever found, my children will obey my command; which is, never to acknowledge themselves as the offspring of
>
> HENRY CAPET (IV:312)

The Royal Captives's last page appears to turn away from conflict with political power by coming to rest in the domain of private life and in the genre of domestic fiction apart from public history. But this narrative also ends with paradox. Young Henry signs his name in a self-contradictory act of renouncing his place in history by means of a document that itself serves as evidence of his existence. This gesture invokes the public authority of the law by binding Henry's children to erase his identity from memory. By the time any readers reach his command to abolish his name to oblivion, however, they will have read his whole story through and so given it at least an airing.

Yearsley's act of signing her name in *The Royal Captives* therefore invites comparison to the potentially revolutionary identity of her protagonist in the first-person narrative that follows. She presents *The Royal Captives* as "copied from an old manuscript," a document handwritten by a historical individual, Henry the nephew of Louis XIV. If read literally, his name could claim the greatest possible historical significance. The signature of Henry Capet invites literal reading as a sign of his substantial existence. His signature would then parallel Yearsley's own signature in the Preface, which stands in for her material presence as the author who produced this literary work—while provoking interest in whether she also means to sign off from further literary effort. Because signing off is an action that normally marks the signer as outside of the text, however, the parallel signatures become freighted with significant questions about this text's relation to "history," and consequently about the status of other printed texts that look like this one.

Support for this reading comes from the opening of the Preface, which challenges the literary authority of Shakespeare himself. Heading her text with nothing less than Hamlet's immortal line "To be, or not to be, that is the question" as an epigraph, Yearsley chides the Bard for failing to think through the line's philosophical implications: "When Shakespeare wrote this line, he had lost sight of congregated Nature; since, to exist, or not to exist, can never be a question from existing substance." Yearsley's diction suggests her self-conscious emulation of philosophical language. By subjecting even Hamlet's speech on suicide to critique, she assumes a posture of disinterested observation.

Her insistence that material existence cannot be questioned is the point crucial to the case she is making as she uses Hamlet's question to open the philosophical question of whether or not the hero of her own narrative exists: "Was Henry, or was not Henry, may be a question to which, if the following sheets find approbation, I may give, in future, the best answer I am capable of." Yearsley teasingly connects the question of her hero Henry's actual existence to her own survival as a publishing writer. That is, the public can never find out the truth unless they signify their approval of the first two volumes of *The Royal Captives,* presumably by buying them.[14] In comparison with Shakespeare, of course, the textual authority of her hero seems ephemeral indeed. She invites the public's skeptical curiosity about Henry's existence in order to maintain the place of her own name in public.

At issue, then, are the protocols by which the public makes historical knowledge into an institution and so constitutes an understanding of itself as a community. Yearsley engages and critiques these institutions by publishing her peculiar text. By placing her signature in tandem with Henry Capet's, Yearsley indicates that they depend on one another for their mutual survival. Yearsley insists on the ontological undeniability of "existing substance," but her own identity, like her hero's, becomes immaterial if the reading public fails to credit her text. Yearsley therefore takes issue with the most legitimate of historical figures, the Sun King, by showing that this king's established power succeeds in obscuring even subjects with a greater right than his own to a place in history. In the face of this power, she falls back on sheer "existing substance" as one truth that remains undeniable, but in doing so turns her own substantial existence into the object of a romance nostalgia by inviting the reading public to imagine her identity obscured.

Mary Waldron notes that Ann Yearsley overcame "health difficulties and lack of time and energy" (216) to compose and publish the first two volumes of *The Royal Captives* in early 1795. The work's preface appears unsure that it would be in her power to finish the project. Her own status as author of this novel is consequently linked with the tenuousness of Henry's fame in obvious ways. To see these parallel signatures as part of a larger historical argument requires reading the text for the protocols that Yearsley uses to signal its genre to readers.

While countless romances claim to be "copied from an old manuscript," Yearsley gives her book the physical resemblance of a documentary memoir bound in octavo. She writes in a first person narrative resembling Rousseau's *Confessions*, complete with effusions of feeling, accounts of the self as perceived by others, and the invention of proverbial formulations. Sophia Lee had called her historical novel *The Recess* (1789) "a tale," acknowledging the fictionality of its account of Mary Queen of Scots' hidden daughters, and noting only that the life of Queen Elizabeth proved that romances should not be blamed for improbability. Yearsley does not allow the terms romance or novel to be applied to her book.

Evidence that Yearsley strove to create a text different from its contemporaries comes from the contemporary reviewers who criticized her abrupt transitions between episodes, who found "the tale perplexed" and "too many inversions and uncouth metaphors," while praising it for provoking thought (Waldron, 220-21). Waldron notes that reviewers complimented Yearsley for taking on political themes in exchange for the sentimental world of "ordinary love-tales" (221).

Complex, experimental narratives were a frequent occurrence in the 1790s as novelists used their plots to reimagine society along lines which current political developments made to seem possible.[15] Reviewers apparently found the plot of *The Royal Captives* tortuous even among these extreme plots, however. Yearsley strives for the authentic look of private memoir by making little effort to accommodate a reader. She fragments the first volume to the point of incomprehensibility. The narrative makes abrupt shifts in time and place that deliberately lose the reader, and it takes the entire last volume to piece together all of the loose ends of this disconnected plot.

From the outset readers must work hard to orient themselves in the narrator's tormented point of view:

> Torn from the visions hope had been flattering me with, I was plunged into this dreary abode. In the fourth room on my left, I saw by the glimmering of a lamp the Marquis D****. He was reading; dejection had robbed his eyes of their brilliancy, his features were fixed by despair—I paused—one of the guards, I thought, looked sorrowfully at the Marquis, who raising his eyes towards Heaven, exclaimed, 'O merciful God! How long must I bear this thirst?'—A sigh broke from my bosom, but it availed not my friend, I was conducted to my cell, and left in awful silence to gloomy meditation.
>
> (I:1-2)

Like Helen Maria Williams's story of Monsieur du F—— in *Letters from France*,[16] *The Royal Captives* joins the struggle against the *ancien régime* by narrating the sufferings of an individual at the hands of tyrannical authority. These cumulative sentences not only grope moment by moment through the narrator's sensations but also omit contextual information that would explain the contexts that Henry alludes to here.

This narration raises a crucial issue for Yearsley as a writer with an interest in the public's understanding of history—the intensity with which readers scrutinized style in the eighteenth century for its viability in public. As Olivia Smith points out in *The Politics of Language*, strict class standards for judging discourse in the period made lower-class writers acutely conscious that their style discredited their arguments.[17] Yearsley had herself been warned not to write poetry that ventured beyond her limited personal experience as a laboring-class woman, and Hannah More had felt free to "correct" her poems (Landry, 163). Even to write this narrative consequently registers Yearsley's awareness, an awareness spreading among common folk in the age of Thomas Paine (Smith, 37), that to print her own unsophisticated prose was to assert the political viability of her own voice.

A prose narrative about lost French royalty takes Yearsley daringly far afield from her lived experiences and exposes her literacy skills for hundreds of pages at a stretch. Occasional breakdowns in grammar and coherence may indicate that the task taxes her ability to maintain narrative decorum, but more likely that she designs her prose to signal the authenticity of this first person memoir. She writes in a style easily distinguished from her own assertive voice in the Preface, for example in running sentences together to suggest the speed of young Henry's scribbling. Moreover, she is careful to explain away any lapses in the narrative's style from the decorum appropriate to the nephew of Louis XIV. In case young Henry's sufferings do not suffice to excuse his manner of writing, she goes out of her way to explain that he had been raised by peasants.

The resulting book may look of a kind with *Mysteries of Udolpho*, which was published in 1794 by Yearsley's own G. G. J. and J. Robinson, but Yearsley's text works to break the spell of aesthetic entertainment for the romance-reading public. *The Royal Captives* is not only "much more closely engaged with public affairs" (Waldron 219); the text also works to revise English readers' understanding of history by literalizing the materials of Gothic romance.

Yearsley takes her story from the legend of a masked prisoner in the Bastille that circulated in Revolutionary France as an illustration of the Old Regime's atrocities. Memoirs "documenting" the existence of this prisoner included Soulavie's sensational compilation of Richelieu's papers (1790) and Louis Pierre Anquetil's *Memoirs of the court of France, during the reign of Lewis XIV*, an English translation of the French original that had appeared as recently as 1791 (Edinburgh: Bell and Bradfute). Anquetil's memoir footnotes L'Abbe Lenglet du Fresnoy's account of a prisoner transferred to the Bastille from the island fortress of Sainte-Marguerite. The prisoner, whose bearing showed him to be lively and well-travelled, drew notice because his jailers kept him masked and treated him with unusual respect.[18]

Yearsley consequently makes her Gothic romance complement source materials that profess to supply evidence of the masked man's existence. Her text poses in public as primary, documentary evidence of the existence of a man whose historicity remains a question that makes the legitimacy of the Bourbon dynasty hinge on scanty traces in private memoirs. At the same time, Yearsley transforms this politically tendentious material into a bourgeois romance by surrounding the single masked prisoner with an extended family of "royal captives." This configuration allows Yearsley to show that bourgeois values have a stake in the events of international importance that she relates.

Because Yearsley tells the story from the point of view of the masked man's son, the plot absorbs itself in this son's search for his father and reconstitution of his family. The narrative begins as young Henry records his first impressions on being thrown into the dungeon of Sainte-Marguerite, where the concern that presides over his suffering is familial: his love for his guardian's daughter Emily and his will to reunite with his father and mother.

In this dungeon, young Henry must overcome the threat to domestic ideology represented by the fortress-prison's corrupt Governor, Dormoud, who views pleasure as the ultimate purpose of life and values even power only as a means of its pursuit, a principle whose contaminating influence Rousseau had feared.[19] The figure of Dormoud serves as an evil double for the father's authority and challenges Henry's faith in his own origins. Henry exclaims,

> 'I never saw a man so like my father—Your eyes, your hair, your voice; nay, your very shape is like his. He was very tall, so are you.'

> 'And how can you tell whether I am your father?' said the Governor. . . . Observing he had silenced me by putting a question which no man in the world is allowed to answer, he continued his merry jeer—'Can you be positive I am not your father?'

> (III:144-45)

Henry falls under Dormoud's spell because he has lost faith in the heroine Emily. Henry first mistakes Emily for his mother, then finds an affectionate letter she has written to the prison's monk, and sees Emily in his arms. When Henry confronts Emily, she gives an impassioned speech on Rousseau's principle that a union of natural virtue transcends human institutions such as marriage (II:225-26)[20] and scorns him for losing faith in her. In despair, Henry accepts the role of Dormoud's confidant in exchange for "freedom of the castle." Their reminiscences create flashbacks through which Yearsley recounts the events that lead to the imprisonment of Henry's whole family.

Young Henry roams the castle in search of his father. No sooner does a servant girl guide him into the presence of the masked man, however, than Dormoud attempts to execute both Henries by forcing them to drink poison, only to have them rescued by the Duke of B——, who is also Henry senior's brother-in-law. Leading a Protestant rebellion against Louis, the Duke has finally succeeded in breaking into the fortress of St. Marguerite. The narrative therefore presents a favorable image of revolutionary violence, but it is Young Henry who conceives of the ruse that ultimately liberates his family: he leaves Dormoud in his father's place under the mask, turning the false system against itself in order to deflect the king's power to persecute. Rejoined by his mother, who has been lodging safely with peasants, Henry must undergo one last trial. He learns that both "the Marquis" and the prison's monk are Emily's brothers—almost the entire extended family has been imprisoned in the castle—and must labor for much of volume four to regain Emily's trust. Then the family emigrates to England and takes up a life of peaceful obscurity.

3

Ian Duncan has called romance "modernity's vision of worlds it has superseded, charged with a magic of estrangement, peril and loss: a cultural uncanny."[21] The Gothic "names a broken historical descent, a cultural heritage grown balefully strange," thematizing "the structure of a dislocated origin: in the obsession with fragmented and contaminated genealogies, . . . usurped patrimony" (Duncan, 23). Yearsley associates her man in the mask with the class origins from which she has been dislocated, whose collective historical significance remains at issue together with her own. It is my argument that Gothic romance serves Yearsley as a strategy for turning her own problem of insignificance into a significant text. She places the figure of the masked man at the heart of her Gothic castle as a powerful symbol, turning historical obscurity into the sublime by gesturing toward his receding figure as the occluded, secret origin and aim of her work. Both father and True King, Henry senior embodies and romanticizes historical truths that have been masked and imprisoned by political forces that shape the nation's history and public knowledge.

The subtitle that Yearsley gives to **The Royal Captives, *A Fragment of Secret History,*** contributes to this argument. By calling her work a "secret history," Yearsley works to change the way in which readers read this text. That is, the term "secret history" breaches the habit of reading that would absorb **The Royal Captives** into the aesthetic appreciation encouraged by Gothic romances such as Radcliffe's. More to the point, the term "secret history" aligns Yearsley's work with a long legacy of politically engaged texts that claim to reveal information that defies the attempts of powerful persons and institutions to control public knowledge. A "secret history" contends for a more explicitly political voice in public than a novel or romance. "Secret histories" do claim to reveal historical truths, usually in opposition to dominant powers such as the French monarchy.

Genre reveals the conventions of the public sphere since to identify a genre requires the writer and reader's shared understanding of how a work is to be read and used. But the early so-called "secret histories" emerged during the forty years following 1688, when their chameleonic properties served writers who were renegotiating the reading public's relation to politics in the expanding market for printed texts. Yearsley's "Secret History" alludes to a genre with a century's worth of associations with political pamphleteering and scandal. For example, Louis XIV had long featured in anonymous secret histories that exposed his influence on international relations in Europe. These included John Oldmixon's Secret Histories of Europe and the anonymous *The Life, amours, and secret history of Francelia, late D——s of P———, favorite mistress to King Charles II* (1734), which sought to locate the dangers of absolutism in the power of seductive mistresses to influence the decisions of rulers.

Mary Delarivière Manley's *The Secret History of Queen Zarah and the Zarazians* and Eliza Haywood's *The Arragonian Queen: A Secret History* and *The Secret History of the Court of Caramania,* the first an attack on the Whig designs of the Duchess of Marlborough and the last a satire of George II's court, exemplify the cryptographic narratives used as weapons in the party conflicts of the early eighteenth century. None of these works calls itself a "novel," and all profess to represent the actual behind-the-scenes transactions of powerful figures whose identity would be transparent to any con-

temporary spectator of the news. Since these are texts representative of the scandal and sexual intrigue usually associated with the genre, it is evident that Yearsley has bourgeoisified the "secret history."

"Secret history" had been used to refer to an authentic memoir as recently as *The Secret History of the Court and Reign of Charles the Second* (1792), written by "A Member of His Privy Council." The term suggests the risky nature of these disclosures, usually published posthumously. Yearsley's "secret history" fills four volumes octavo, a plausible size for a memoir. Written in the voice of a man who professes to have been an actual individual living in Louis XIV's France and of the king's own blood, the work puts itself in a peculiar contiguity with historical texts and events. It also issues a challenge to the legitimacy of the French sovereign. Yearsley imagines the masked prisoner to be not only Louis XIV's twin but an elder brother at that, named Henry, whose right to the throne has been suppressed because he had been thought blind at birth. **The Royal Captives** represents the Sun King as a usurper who persecutes his own brother's family in order to maintain his hold on power. Yearsley consequently makes a common project out of both her attack on Louis XIV's legitimacy and her demand that the historical knowledge on public record be seen as a legacy of political coercion in need of drastic revision.

National historical narratives had become a genre carrying authority in the book trade by the late eighteenth century. The ideological warfare carried out via the printing presses of the early eighteenth century had produced limited runs of many versions of "the" history of England, which often asserted their high cultural value through their impressive dimensions and bindings.[22] Histories of the nation later came to circulate as commodities like other prose works, but served to establish print culture's understanding of which subjects count as "significant" and deserving of a place in the public record, conceived of as a coherent narrative of the nation's past. By mid-century, David Hume could remark that he had written *The History of England* (1752-61) in order to pursue a "literary fame" that his philosophical works had failed to achieve on account of their poor sales.[23]

Yearsley stakes her own fame on a narrative that exposes public history as an institution that embodies the State's coercive power. Her book points out that the national narrative of France celebrates Louis XIV's reign while excluding a family which by birthright deserves a prominent place in history; the public historical record has affirmed the raw power Louis wields in defense of his throne. By implication, Yearsley's own obscurity can be blamed on arbitrary operations of power that determine what knowledge becomes of public significance. If the public record can exclude the legendary true heir to the French throne, Yearsley's own obscurity can be critiqued as equally arbitrary.

The plausibility of this interpretation appears greater when we consider that Napoleon Bonaparte had himself encouraged circulation of a story that he descended from a marriage between the man in the iron mask and the daughter of the prison governor, "de Bonpart" (Noone, 11). The masked man remained a powerful symbol whose suggestive lineage evidently opened itself to identification.

The subtitle *A Fragment of Secret History* conveys Yearsley's understanding of history as an imaginable past expanding beyond the small part that is textually represented. If, moreover, her subtitle alludes to Desmoulins' *History of the Brissotins* (Girondins), published under the title *Fragment de l'histoire secrète de la Revolution* and translated into English in 1794, then **The Royal Captives** may be linked more directly with political commentary on the French Revolution. The term "fragment of secret history" implies that a large expanse of knowledge has been kept hidden from known history. Since this text reveals only a small part, the remainder must hint that greater revolutions in ideas must follow.

Yearsley articulates this vision of history more fully in a lecture that young Henry receives from his guardian:

> [L]ook behind you through the tracts of time, a vast desart of unnumbered ages lies open in the retrospect. Through this desart have your forefathers journeyed on, till wearied with years and sorrow they sank from the walk of man. You must leave them where they fell, and you are to go only a little further, where you will find eternal rest. Whatever you may encounter between the cradle and the grave be not dismayed. The universe is in endless motion, every moment big with innumerable events, which come not in slow succession, but bursting forcibly from a revolving and unknown cause, fly over this orb with diversified influence.
>
> (I:100-101)

The trudging anonymity of "the walk of man," an image that may derive from religious pilgrimage though with no heavenly goal in sight, offers a pessimistic view of Yearsley's chances of survival in cultural memory. But these generations subsiding successively into oblivion lead suggestively into a sublime vision of history as subject to unknowable, uncontainable forces that explosively create events on a cosmic scale instead of as causal sequence of events.[24] The passage opens the prospect of these trudging masses serving as the underlying force that transforms history through collective action, a revolutionary image that Henry's guardian presents as cause for hope.

Yearsley's principles show affinities with Helen Maria Williams's widely read *Letters from France*, which had rhapsodized over the founding of the new Republic be-

tween 1790 and 1792. The horror with which Williams describes the dungeons of the Bastille, which she accepts as a symbol of the justice of the revolutionary cause (Letter IV), make Yearsley's Gothic narrative sound less like psycho-sexual symbolism than like an imitation of eyewitness accounts of contemporary France.

Williams' account indicates that Yearsley's image of hidden, seemingly insignificant forces causing great events emerges out of contemporary discourse concerning the Revolution. Williams writes,

> The women have certainly had a considerable share in the French revolution: for, whatever the imperious lords of the creation may fancy, the most important events which take place in this world depend a little on our influence; and we often act in human affairs like those secret springs in mechanism, by which, though invisible, great movements are regulated.
>
> (Williams, I:37-38)

This version attributes motive force in history to the overlooked power of women, while Yearsley emphasizes an anonymous collective that shows bourgeois and laborer undifferentiated under tyranny.

Comparison to Williams's vision suggests that Yearsley avoids making an issue of women's position in history. She instead relies on a male protagonist to carry out her strategy of reconstituting the scope of political history. Yearsley does create in Emily a heroine whose strength of character far exceeds Henry's, and who delivers speeches on natural integrity and represents marriage as a chain used by fearful souls to bind themselves together (II:19-22; 225-33). But **The Royal Captives** may be more revealing of the political process forming historical narratives, and of Yearsley's own unconscious complicity in that process, than she is herself aware. Yearsley dates her narrative to 1685, the year when Louis heightened his persecution of Huguenots by revoking the Edict of Nantes, and shows Henry and his family supporting the Duke of B—— against Louis. While Yearsley uses this episode to let the Duke give a speech on how change in the political system will come about for "the strong, blind, obedient million" (IV:38) when *"the national soul has acquired new energy"* (IV:39), it is notable that Emily takes no part in the discussion of politics nor the military actions, a symptom of women writers' loss of continuity with early modern women's traditions by the late eighteenth century.

Joan DeJean has pointed out that French noblewomen of the seventeenth century had created a cult of female heroism which reflected the considerable political power women could wield while the nobility balanced the monarchy. The rebellion known as the Fronde against Louis XIV's regency in the 1650s was notable in particular for the number of aristocratic women who took leading parts in it, and for the erasure of these women from history by men of letters. Not only did the Duchesse de Longueville share leadership of the rebellion with her brother, but other noblewomen also contributed their political influence to the struggle and even took part in military actions. So dismayed were the literati by these "amazons" that after the rebellion failed, the women's militancy was first ridiculed, then left unmentioned by histories.[25] By the end of the eighteenth century, Yearsley's writing of *The Royal Captives* shows no trace of awareness that women could take active roles in warfare or in public historical events. Her "secret history" can call for inquiry into the knowledge suppressed by established histories, but remains limited by those histories.

4

The Royal Captives does give Yearsley the chance to compose a letter to Louis XIV himself in which she advises him to "Think little of your title" (IV:74). In the story, the letter is authored by the Duke of B—— and succeeds in stopping Louis from revoking the Edict of Nantes, a wishful rewriting of political history. Yearsley's activist and instrumental use of her mix of genres appears as well in the poems that she incorporates into the narrative. Where Ann Radcliffe strips quoted verses of their context in order to employ them as ornamental epigraphs to each chapter, or allows sentimental songs about insects, home, and landscape to heighten Emily St. Aubert's emotions during her sojourns in *Udolpho*, Yearsley's poems comment on the plot's action when they are read, often supplying politicized explanations of events.

The first poem young Henry reads exorcises his melancholy when he is reeling from the trauma of discovering the identity of his father and so of himself. This "Elegy of Laura" tells the story of a shepherd's daughter who "panted for Fame," possessing a spark of refinement "So deeply buried, none discern'd the flame; / Felt, though expressless, pow'rful though untaught!" This rural poet leaves home in search of a career and dies in the chilling sea. Swans rescue her poems (I:170). Whether or not Yearsley identified with Laura's yearnings, she repeats the pattern in the subplot of the peasant family that accompanies the Capet family through their ordeals. That is, Yearsley supplies an old peasant and his son Malnor to serve and rescue both Henries at regular intervals. Not that these peasants subsume their lives into serving the royals, as Radcliffe's do. They attend to their own business and are also preoccupied with the fate of Malnor's sister Anna who, like the shepherd poetess in "Elegy of Laura," has fled rural life. Literacy has led her away from home only to entangle her with an aristocratic betrayer. She dies in a dramatic episode in which young Henry, fighting off an ambush by Anna's false lover Antonio, accidentally

brings the dying villain to the cottage where Anna lies dying. Anna's servant promptly throws a book called *Resignation* onto the fire. While both Antonio and Anna breathe their last, Antonio reveals to Henry the secret of his father's birth as Louis XIV's elder twin. As we shall see, Henry always comes to knowledge of his father in the company of peasants.

In contrast to Radcliffe's use of poems in her romances, Yearsley's poems confront oppression directly. Young Henry finds one forceful poem written on the wall of Dormoud's execution chamber. He later learns that the poem's author was Maria, the working-class woman beloved by the Abbe of Dorovantes. Their love story closely parallels the account that Helen Maria Williams gives of Monsieur du F——, whose father imprisoned him because he wished to marry a woman of low birth. Harboring with Dorovantes after his escape from prison, Henry reads a pair of poems called "ANARCHY" and "PEACE," then Dorovantes gives Henry a lengthy poem "Dedicated to Louis XIV" that offers a "prophetic" vision of the revolution to ensue if the king disregards the balance his subjects' power and significance can give to his own:

> Know—tho' horrid gloom
> Wrap the lost captive from a social world;
> Not unobserving is that world: the bands
> Of Friendship bind the wretched link unseen;
> Millions of spirits, who to woe inur'd,
> Shall burst upon the light, when sanguine pow'r
> Shall sink abash'd, and see her fetters rust.
>
> (IV:112)

This passage overtly includes the humbler classes in the collective "world" whose watchfulness has the power to constitute order and whose united sense of injustice threatens to bring about the revolution that will "burst upon the light," an image of public knowledge. "Can such a mind as Dorovantes ever go extinct?" (IV:113), Henry asks himself. Since Yearsley saw herself primarily as a poet, it is telling that this narrative dramatizes poetry's agency in inspiring readers with visions of historical change in the midst of oppressive circumstances.

Unlike Horace Walpole, Clara Reeve, or Ann Radcliffe, Yearsley allows the Gothic usurper to retain his position of power and authority at story's end. The True King explains to his heir that a home with the woman he loves will give him more happiness than a kingdom. While Yearsley did not believe in the possibility of radical social and political change (Waldron, 206), however, her man of the mask represents unknown forces lying in wait for future transformations of history, not through bloodshed but perhaps through changes in the nation's soul, in public knowledge.

The masked man might be taken as symbolic of the usurped authority of Yearsley's own laboring-class origins. The True King himself dresses like a peasant (*sans culotte*?) and wishes nothing more than to be middle class. Young Henry perpetually encounters his father in association with working-class characters. At first glimpse, Henry senior easily passes for a common laborer and resides in an elaborately described Radcliffean landscape that renders his life of obscurity sublime. It is young Henry's fantasy that needy peasants live in the isolated cottage near his guardian's home that leads him to his father:[26]

> I again attempted to find an oblique passage—the effort was unavailing—my way was cut off by the horrid projections of the rock, and the smoke gradually dying away ceased to direct my curious eyes; I sat myself down, lamenting the calamities of innumerable beings . . . [who,] distant from the pale of society, pine unpitied and unseen in want even of frugal blessings.

> (I:118-19)

Of all the hardships of peasant life, Henry thinks of their obscurity with special melancholy. It is actually Henry's father who occupies the place of these imaginary peasants, however, having been excluded from the most renowned throne in history.

What distinguishes Yearsley's work from the Gothic of her predecessors is her treatment of laboring-class characters as subjects of her "history" in their own right. Where Walpole and Ann Radcliffe trivialize, even juvenilize servants and Clara Reeve ascribes them no independent plots of their own, Yearsley intertwines the story of Henry's family with the history of a family of peasants to which she devotes long tracts of narrative. Each member of this peasant family lives out a full biographical narrative, from the old man who assists Henry senior, to his daughter whose reading of books takes her away from her rustic home and to a tragic death, and to his son, Malnor, who pursues an independent heroic career that includes but is not subordinated to his job of rescuing the two Henries.

Yearsley's project of conveying the potential power of figures obscured from history appears most vividly in the threatening figure of Henry's prison guard. This soldier embodies the terrors of state power when he comes to poison the Marquis. In desperation, Henry beats on his prison door: "It was opened by a soldier, in whose countenance were discernible the tumultuous traits of unfinished murder. 'What would you have, Sir?—speak quickly—the Commandant would reprove me did he know I obey unnecessary curiosity—'" (I:2-3). Once we learn the guard's name, Malnor, however, this terrible guard turns out to be a peasant who is himself a prisoner of the system, since he must execute the Marquis or risk death himself. He even transforms into a romance hero who rescues the Marquis and other members of Henry's family. Despite his peasant origins, Malnor rises to the honor of killing the story's principal

villain, the aristocrat Roderique, in a duel. Indeed Yearsley elevates this peasant's story to the prestige of revenge tragedy because Roderique helped his brother Antonio destroy Malnor's sister Anna. Evil cannot be located even in Roderique, however. Breathing his last, Roderique admits the justice of his own death and bequeaths all of his estates to Malnor, whose class rise carries out the trajectory characteristic of bourgeois romance.

What takes the blame for everyone's sufferings in this account are the institutions through which the monarch maintains his state power, which make Malnor alien and force him to think of his humane interest in his fellow men as "unnecessary curiosity." This curiosity not only brings Malnor into Henry's company but also impels this wavering hero toward his father. Though not an ennobling, resistless, or even stable historical force, trivial curiosity has the potential to produce important consequences. Its revolutionary overtones appear in the anxiety characters express over this curiosity, calling it by turns "unnecessary," "impertinent," or even "dangerous."

Yearsley may not expect her text to provoke any passion in her readers stronger than "curiosity," but she invites inquiry into her Gothic architecture's monumentality, which is oddly complicated by the idea of an artistically crafted but ersatz antiquity:

> We stopped at the end of this long vault, and my conductor made me observe a small door so finely contrived, and so shadowed by the artist, that it wore the semblance of gothic stone, and appeared but as an entire part of this ancient structure. I should have passed it unperceived, had not the Governor slipped back a private spring, and opened it to awaken my curiosity.

> (I:48)

Even when young Henry penetrates this door to the corridors and chambers beyond, he can find only a cameo portrait of his mother as a token of his father's presence. His father has been removed to a chamber still deeper in the depths of this edifice and then masked. By stimulating young Henry's curiosity, the prison governor tempts him to investigate beyond the imprisoning cultural conditions these Gothic obstructions represent, but Dormoud only means to tease and frustrate Henry with this invitation. The two Henries do not escape until Yearsley's fourth volume, so that most of this narrative is contained by the fortress-prison.

Yearsley's Gothic challenges the authority of its own parents, Horace Walpole's *Castle of Otranto* and the romances of Ann Radcliffe. She adopts Walpole's pretense of transcribing an old manuscript, but uses this figure of the literal document against Walpole as well as, as we have seen, against history. Where Walpole relies on supernatural agents to overturn the usurper and restore the true heir, Yearsley refuses supernatural assistance and emphasizes that the usurping authority of Louis XIV remains on the throne.

Where Ann Radcliffe places her narratives at a feminized, "romance" remove from political history, Yearsley places the sufferings of a family of royal blood in textual contiguity with public history. The prisoners occupy the same castle on the "Isle of St. M*****" that is represented in the documents testifying to the material existence of Louis' masked prisoner. Her work's Gothic horrors represent the horrors of the castle dungeons where Louis XIV kept his prisoners, and the book's terrors are of a state whose representatives have material power over the narrator and his family. Yearsley challenges history in its institutional form as printed texts, and with it the assumption of the public sphere regarding the authority of historical knowledge. No longer a domain alien from domestic life, history becomes the ground her protagonists tread in the nation's vision of the past, knowing that but for the arbitrary workings of politics, the Sun King's historical position could have been theirs.

Ann Yearsley places herself by analogy with Louis XIV's legendary masked prisoner on the margins of history as a haunting presence. As she contemplates her own likely return to obscurity, Yearsley turns to prose in order to both assert her name as a literary author in the public sphere and critique the authority of the public record. She generates this narrative out of her perception that her voice lacks political viability in the public sphere in England. Knowing herself to be only an "unnecessary curiosity" from the perspective of public history, she uses the story of the masked man to suggest that historical significance is open to negotiation and subject to political changes in the public sphere.

The Royal Captives registers Yearsley's sense of loss at apprehending that the public's categorical reading of identity and genre forecasts doom for her own fame. Romance offers the consolation that in returning to obscurity she merges with a sublime vision of the unknown forces that shape historical events, and at the same time creates in readers a powerful nostalgia for individuals such as herself who have been lost to public knowledge. Yearsley consigns her textual identity to the process by which print culture reconceives and rewrites history over time, so that the changing status of her "Truth" reveals the transformations of interpretation that create history and implies that historical recollection can be critiqued as itself a romance projection.

Notes

1. Richard Polwhele refers to Yearsley satirically as "Nature's Child" in *The Unsex'd Females* (1798), which Donna Landry quotes in *The Muses of Resistance: Laboring-Class Women's Poetry in Britain, 1739-1796* (Cambridge, England: Cambridge University Press, 1990) in order to point out contemporary resistance to understanding working-class women as individual subjects, politically or culturally, 256. Linda Zionkowski studies the inequalities in print culture that ultimately disadvantaged Yearsley as well as Stephen Duck in her essay "Strategies of Containment," *Eighteenth-Century Life* 13 (1989): 91-108.

2. Landry, 153. Yearsley's books of poetry are: *Poems, on Several Occasions* (1785), *Poems, on Various Subjects* (1787), *Stanzas of Woe* (1789), and *The Rural Lyre* (1796), her last publication.

3. Page references in the present essay cite William W. Woodward's edition (Philadelphia, 1795). *The National Union Catalog* indicates that Yearsley published the book's first two volumes with a Dublin publisher (J. Stockdale) in 1795, marketing the work before completing the four-volume editions that appeared in London (G. G. J. and J. Robinson) and in Philadelphia (William W. Woodward and R. Campbell) in the same year. An additional edition appeared in Philadelphia (Thomas Bradford) in 1796.

4. 217 in Mary Waldron's biography, *Lactilla, Milkwoman of Clifton: The Life and Writings of Ann Yearsley 1753-1806* (Athens: University of Georgia Press, 1996), which establishes the context for the present essay. Yearsley's publishers, G. G. J. and J. Robinson, had produced *Mysteries of Udolpho* only the year before.

5. John Noone, *The Man Behind the Mask* (New York: St. Martin's Press, 1988) 2.

6. In "Resistance and Power in the Life and Writings of Ann Yearsley," *The Eighteenth Century: Theory and Interpretation* 27 (1986): 247, Moira Ferguson interprets Yearsley as taking unambiguous political positions in support of "artistic recognition and economic independence," the French Revolution, and the rights of British peasants. Ferguson emphasizes Yearsley's poetry in *Eighteenth-Century Women Poets: Nation, Class, and Gender* (Albany: State University of New York Press, 1995) chapter 4.

7. *The Literature of Terror* (London and New York: Longman, 1980) 402-27.

8. *The Contested Castle* (Urbana and Chicago: University of Illinois Press, 1989) x.

9. Landry, after Dominick LaCapra, 17.

10. Susan Stewart interprets "collections" as furthering "the process of commodification by which this

narrative of the personal operates within contemporary consumer society" in *On Longing* (Durham and London: Duke University Press, 1984, 1993) xii. I am grateful to the staff at the John Hay Library of rare books, Brown University, for assistance in researching the collection of Hammond Lamont.

11. *Poems, on Several Occasions,* 4th edition. (London: G. G. J. and J. Robinson, 1786) xviii.

12. For a recent review of the concept, see Margaret C. Jacobs, "The Mental Landscape of the Public Sphere: A European Perspective," *Eighteenth Century Studies* 28 (1994): 95-113.

13. Oskar Negt and Alexander Kluge, *Public Sphere and Experience,* trans. Peter Labanyi, Jamie Owen Daniel, and Assenka Oksiloff (Minneapolis and London: University of Minnesota Press, 1993) 9, a work that modifies Habermas by differentiating among diverse public spheres. It is Joan B. Landes, however, who points out the problematics of gender in the public sphere in *Women and the Public Sphere in the Age of the French Revolution* (Ithaca and London: Cornell University Press, 1988).

Yearsley's distance from even the alternative "sphere" of publishing radicals might be suggested by her absence from Eleanor Ty's account of the community ties among Mary Wollstonecraft, Mary Hays, Helen Maria Williams, Elizabeth Inchbald, and Charlotte Smith in *Unsex'd Revolutionaries* (Toronto: University of Toronto Press, 1993) 5.

14. Yearsley apparently published the first two volumes in a separate Dublin edition (not consulted) before completing work on all four volumes. The Preface alludes to the narrator breaking off his writing because of sickness. Since the second volume ends in precisely this fragmentary way, Yearsley evidently wrote the Preface to accompany this first, incomplete edition.

15. Patricia Meyer Spacks, "Energies of Mind: Novels of the 1790s," *Desire and Truth: Functions of Plot in Eighteenth-Century English Novels* (Chicago: University of Chicago Press, 1990) 178.

16. Helen Maria Williams, *Letters from France.* 2 vols. (New York: Delmar, rpt. 1975).

17. *The Politics of Language 1791-1819* (Oxford: Clarendon Press, 1984) 58. See also John Barrell, *English Literature in History 1730-80: An Equal, Wide Survey* (London: Hutchinson, 1983).

18. I:203 in the French version, *Louis XIV, sa cour, et le regent.*

19. Jean-Jacques Rousseau, *Emile or On Education,* ed. Allan Bloom (United States: Basic Books, 1979) 220-21.

20. Marilyn Butler traces the course of this radical, republican view of nature and marriage in Jacobin novels of the period and shows how dangerous it came to be seen, *Jane Austen and the War of Ideas* (Oxford: Clarendon Press, 1975) 28.

21. *Modern Romance and Transformations of the Novel: The Gothic, Scott, Dickens* (Cambridge, England: Cambridge University Press, 1992) 9.

22. See Joseph Levine's ninth chapter, "History and Theory," *The Battle of the Books: History and Literature in the Augustan Age* (Ithaca and London: Cornell University Press, 1991).

23. David Hume, *The History of England* (Indianapolis: Liberty Classics, 1983) I:xxx, xxxiii.

24. Yearsley's explosive imagery contrasts with Hume's more controlled view of history, in which "the connexion between all causes and effects is equally necessary, and that its seeming uncertainty in some instances proceeds from the secret opposition of contrary causes," *Enquiry Concerning Human Understanding,* ed. L. A. Selby-Bigge, 3rd edition (Oxford: Clarendon, 1975) 83, 87; ¶¶65, 67.

25. Joan De Jean, *Tender Geographies* (New York: Columbia University Press, 1991) 35ff.

26. Yearsley revises the traditions for depicting working-class figures surveyed by John Barrell in *The Dark Side of the Landscape* (Cambridge, England: Cambridge University Press, 1980) 16. Yearsley brings the figures out of the landscape to speak as subjects.

William J. Christmas (essay date 2001)

SOURCE: Christmas, William J. "Class Dialogue: Ann Yearsley, Hannah More, and the Power of Print." In *The Lab'ring Muses: Work, Writing, and the Social Order in English Plebeian Poetry, 1730-1830,* pp. 235-66. Newark: University of Delaware Press, 2001.

[*In the following essay, Christmas details the financial and literary quarrel between Yearsley and her patron Hannah More, suggesting that Yearsley's written commentary on the quarrel was a calculated and successful attempt to obtain support from her readers.*]

Slow rises worth, by poverty depress'd[1]

In the winter of 1784, Ann Yearsley and her family were most definitely suffering under the weight of poverty. Hannah More wrote to Elizabeth Montagu that

in the severity of last Winter, herself, husband, babes, and her aged Mother all got together into a Stable—to die of hunger!—the Mother actually perished; the rest were saved by a gentleman accidentally looking into the stable; they are now in a flourishing way, have nine Pigs and a Cow.[2]

Thanks to this gentleman, one Mr. Vaughan, and More herself, a desperate situation was transformed into a scene of rustic plenitude. More was spurred into action by her desire, as an evangelical Christian, to perform good works, and a genuine interest, as an author herself, in Yearsley's untutored poetical genius. More's letters over the next ten months show her tireless effort to ease Yearsley's pains and promote her poems among her wide circle of polite friends. In addition to rescuing the family from starvation, More hired a "*little* Maid" for Yearsley to "soften the rigours of the approaching Winter," and notes that she has "spent above eight months" and "written above a thousand pages" for the purpose of collecting a subscription toward publishing Yearsley's poems (*FS* [*The Female Spectator*], 280, 284). More's efforts did not escape the notice of Samuel Badcock, who reviewed Yearsley's **Poems, on Several Occasions** (1785) in *The Monthly Review*: "This rustic Poetess is under great obligations to Miss More, for bringing forward her productions to public notice, and for placing them and herself in the most advantageous light."[3] Perhaps no plebeian poet in the century owed a patron so much, only to rebel so forcefully.

And rebel Yearsley did, with a sense of moral authority and purpose we have hitherto seen only in the "unpublished" Woodhouse of *Crispinus Scriblerus*. In June 1785, More wrote to Montagu, with some pride, about the finished product and overall success of Yearsley's subscription:

> Were you not surprised, dear Madam, to see so magnificent a book? Really, the Crown subscribers have a bargain, to my great regret. We printed 1250 copies, and are obliged to sell the supernumerary copies at six to indemnify us a little; I paid near fourscore pounds *all* expenses, have lodged 350 in the Five per Cents which will produce about £18 a year, and shall take her down about £20 to cloathe her family and furnish her House. As I wished to have the honour of *your* name to sanction my own, I have laid out the money in your name, madam, and mine, having first had an instrument drawn up by the Lawyer signed by Yearsley and his wife, allowing us the controul of the money, and putting it out of the Husband's power to touch it.
>
> (*FS*, 282)

No previous record of the relationship between plebeian poet and patron provides so much detail about how the subscription money earned by the poet was disbursed or, in this case, controlled by the patron. The first edition garnered enough ready cash to pay off the publishing expenses and still realized a nice sum for investment in the "five per cent" stocks. But neither Yearsley nor her husband had access to this money, having signed over control to their benefactors, and Yearsley was thus

beholden to the handouts More deemed appropriate. It seems safe to assume that this elaborate plan was not common practice in late-century patron/poet relationships because More brings in a lawyer to draw up a special contract and wants Montagu's name to "sanction [her] own" in the business. More's best laid plans, however, would come back to haunt her within a month of the contract signing. On 21 July 1785, More wrote to Montagu complaining that Yearsley had treated her "with the blackest ingratitude" by accusing her "of a design to defraud her of the money" (*FS*, 283, 284). Over the next two years, Yearsley would successfully make her case against More in print through her controversial **"Narrative"** and the other prefatory material included in the fourth edition of **Poems, on Several Occasions** (1786), and reprinted in her second volume of poetry, **Poems, On Various Subjects** (1787).

Because the dispute between these two women is so well documented in contemporary historical records, there is a rich critical history on the subject. More's biographers, of course, sympathize with her in the affair, describing Yearsley's "bad conduct" and ascribing "the violent rupture" to Yearsley's unrefined nature.[4] Robert Southey affects an objective stance and terms the situation an "unfortunate difference" but he also notes that More's "benevolent intentions ought not to have been misunderstood."[5] J. M. S. Tompkins also sides with More in her account of "the Bristol Milkwoman," arguing that "prosperity had made [Yearsley] arrogant, and nature, it appeared, had made her malicious, since she was devising and spreading impossible slanders about Miss More."[6] Recent scholarship, however, has looked to justify Yearsley's claim to the subscription money and argues the strength of her commitment to resist the classist forces of polite culture.[7] In contrast to the tenor of this work, Mary Waldron, Yearsley's most recent (and most exhaustive) biographer, is more concerned with questioning received assumptions about Yearsley's status as a laboring-class woman than she is with taking sides in the dispute.[8] And Patricia Demers presents a balanced argument, noting that "it is as important to recognize Yearsley's expressions of gratitude as it is to note her corrosive anger; similarly, More's zeal and tirelessness in Yearsley's cause must be remembered as well as her miscalculations and intransigence."[9]

Whether or not More acted with prudence in the affair, and whether or not Yearsley was justified in her criticism, their dispute went far beyond the confines of any drawing room walls. In a letter to Weller Pepys, More writes, "There is hardly a species of slander the poor unhappy creature does not propagate against me, in the most public manner, because I have called her a *milkwoman*, and because I have placed the money in the funds, instead of letting her spend it."[10] It is Yearsley's "public manner" in this dispute, and More's apparent reluctance to respond in print, that interest me most.

When their normal dialogue ended, each woman in her own class-based way appears to have entered into a textual dialogue with a potentially supportive larger community: More with her polite friends and Yearsley with her reading public. Yearsley's intended audience was polite society, especially her subscribers (many of whom were friends of More), and so there was, no doubt, significant overlap between these two groups of readers. But Yearsley, the milkwoman-turned-poet, made her case in print while More, privileged and well-connected, confined herself to private letters. More's indefatigable work to promote Yearsley ironically provides the protégée with the means to combat her patron's contractual financial arrangement. Money, however, is not the only, or even the most important, issue at stake in their dispute; it also concerns issues of work, artistic autonomy, and control over public representation. For Yearsley, despite her plebeian social status, crossing the print line ultimately meant gaining control over her texts, her public image, and her "living." Yearsley effectively uses her access to commercial print culture to win the local battle with More between 1785 and 1787. But, in an ideological sense, she loses the war by the 1790s, when More begins her assault on the laboring classes, publishing imaginative texts intended to reform their increasingly incendiary politics. My purpose in this chapter is not to recap every aspect of the dispute that arose between Yearsley and More or to discuss all of their textual output. Rather, I will concentrate on the ways these two women manipulate dominant social values in their poetry and use the influential power late-eighteenth-century print culture offers to serve their respective agendas.

The correspondence between More and her set of polite friends shows that, from the beginning, Yearsley was subjected to the negative cultural attitudes about writing as work that were circulating in the late-century period. Yearsley's first benefactors genuinely wanted to relieve her penury, but were wary of indulging her poetical fancy, lest she should leave her appointed station and her God-given labors. Writing to More just after her discovery of Yearsley, Horace Walpole advises that Yearsley "must remember that she is a Lactilla, not a Pastora, and is to tend real cows, not Arcadian sheep."[11] Walpole's classical name for Yearsley—"Lactilla"—succinctly captures the view that one's social position is a fixed condition based on work; labor itself is both a defining feature of that condition as well as a restrictive boundary. Concerned about the potential for social climbing because Yearsley has published poetry, Walpole upholds this view throughout More's ordeal with her: "I am sick of these sweet singers, and advised that when poor Mrs Yearsley shall have been set at her ease by the subscription, she should drive her cows from the foot of Parnassus and hum no more ditties" (33:475). In his contempt for female poets in general, Walpole is even more specific on the subject of proper women's

work: "Am I in the wrong," he writes to Lady Ossory, "for thinking, that these Saphos had better be bound 'prentices to mantua-makers, than be appointed chambermaids to Mesdemoiselles the Muses!" (33:538). Although Walpole complimented Yearsley as a poet early on, pointing out "the dignity of her thoughts and the chastity of her style," and lauding her "real talents," he is set against "encouraging her propensity lest it should divert her from the care of her family" and her productive labor as a milkwoman (31:219, 220, 220). Walpole's operative assumptions about how social rank is defined indicate that he never considered his purchase of Yearsley's poems more than charity, and his view of her as a poet shifted remarkably when Yearsley's dispute with More deepened: Yearsley and other "harmonious virgins, have no imagination, no novelty," he wrote (33:533). Given the import of imagination, defined as originality, in late-century views of original genius, Walpole's criticism reads as a wholesale dismissal of Yearsley's status as one.

For her own part, More reproduces Walpole's class-based views in her letters and, more importantly, in the "Prefatory Letter to Mrs. Montagu" which appeared in print, prefixed to the first edition of Yearsley's poems. In an earlier letter to Montagu, written during the planning stages of their venture to support Yearsley, More states plainly: "I am *utterly* against taking her out of her station. *Stephen* was an excellent Bard as a *Thrasher,* but as a Court Poet, and rival of Pope, detestable" (*FS,* 279). More and Montagu concur that Yearsley "shou'd not be corrupted by being made *idle* or *useless*" by devoting herself to writing (*FS,* 280). It is clear that More's "Prefatory Letter" was written to be published in Yearsley's volume,[12] and so More uses the pretense of private correspondence to introduce Yearsley and her poetry to the subscribers. In the "Letter," More confidently assures Yearsley's polite readers that they are doing the right thing in supporting her:

> Pressing, as her distresses are, if I did not think her heart was rightly turned, I should be afraid of proposing such a measure, lest it should unsettle the sobriety of her mind, and, by exciting her vanity, indispose her for the laborious employments of her humble condition; but it would be cruel to imagine that we cannot mend her fortune without impairing her virtue.[13]

Thus More defines Yearsley's "virtue" in a class-specific way, in terms of her industry in performing her "laborious employments," and, given Yearsley's low social position, More's charity has its limits. The subscription, More continues, is "not intended to place [Yearsley] in such a state of independence as might seduce her to devote her time to the idleness of Poetry" (xi). Of course, writing poetry would interfere with Yearsley's proper work as a milkwoman and her responsibilities as wife and mother raising six young children. According to More, "it is not fame, but bread, which I am anxious to secure for her," yet the means for securing this "bread" is Yearsley's poetry (xii). That is, Yearsley worked for her bread by writing, a point she will use to her advantage in making her case for control of the money earned. More's text, then, reproduces a common paradox evident throughout the century regarding plebeian literary talent: Yearsley's laboring status makes her poetry a marketable commodity, but her success in print cannot raise her socially. A milkwoman, even one who is virtuous and exudes natural poetic talent, must remain a milkwoman.

Yearsley's early poems, however, show signs that she is not satisfied with the social limitations inherent in this view imposed upon her from above. As one would expect, the 1785 volume is rife with gratitude and high praise for her primary benefactors, More and Montagu. Yearsley acknowledges that "sunk in humble state, / With more than needful awe I view the great" (71). In the poem **"To Stella,"** Yearsley's classical pseudonym for More, she thanks both women openly:

> With deathless glories; every ardent prayer
> Which gratitude can waft from souls sincere,
> Each warm return to generous bounty due,
> Shall warm my heart for you and MONTAGU.
>
> (68)

But characteristic deference and gratitude aside, there are occasions when Yearsley voices her personal desires:

> Unequal, lost to the aspiring claim,
> I neither ask, nor own th' immortal name
> Of Friend; ah, no! its ardors are too great,
> My soul too narrow, and too low my state;
> STELLA! soar on, to nobler objects true,
> Pour out your soul with your lov'd MONTAGU;
> But, ah! shou'd either have a thought to spare,
> Slight, trivial, neither worth a smile or tear,
> Let it be mine; . . .
>
> (65-66)

Yearsley's plea for any Bluestocking intellectual table scraps seems heartfelt. Though she is careful to disown "the immortal name of Friend" because she is acutely aware of their differences in birth, she casts her desire (and claim) for her patrons' companionship in intellectual terms: "Quick let me from the hallow'd spot retire, / Where sacred Genius lights his awful fire" (66). In positioning herself, and not More or Montagu, on that "hallow'd spot" where "Genius" resides, Yearsley suggests she is at least worthy of their intellectual friendship.

Yearsley does have a mind of her own, despite her lack of formal education, evidenced by her answer to More about proper poetic compliments:

> For mine's a stubborn and a savage will;
> No customs, manners, or soft arts I boast,

> On my rough soul your nicest rules are lost;
> Yet shall unpolish'd gratitude be mine,
>
> (72)

The terms of Yearsley's self-description—"stubborn," "savage" and "rough soul[ed]"—serve, in one sense, an apparent accommodating function as Yearsley seems to acquiesce to the expected polite descriptions of a lower-class rustic poet. Yet, read with the benefit of hindsight in the context of the dispute with More that was about to erupt, this apparently self-deprecating image begins to look more socially disruptive. In other words, it is precisely Yearsley's "stubborn and savage will," her refusal to resign herself to polite patronly containment, that earns Yearsley her independence, and her "rough soul" will continue to sell poetry.

Despite Yearsley's private confrontation with More over control of the money, More continued with her investment plan and, as a testament to her love of good works, continued to promote Yearsley's interests by meeting the demand for a second edition. By September 1785, however, More notes that "they have put me in the Papers" and so the affair with Yearsley became a subject for gossip in Bristol (*FS*, 286). This prompted More's only public comment (as far as we know) on the dispute. It is merely a one-sentence, earnest statement of the facts appended to the "Advertisement" for the second edition of ***Poems, on Several Occasions***: "The Editor has raised a very handsome sum of money which is placed in the Public Funds, vested in Trustees hands for the benefit of the Author's Family" (*FS*, 286). Still, More chooses to hide behind the role-defining appellations of "editor" and "trustee," even though most readers would have known who was performing these duties. As she relates to Montagu, her confidante throughout the affair, More did her best to maintain a stiff upper lip through the public din: "I take not the least notice of any of *their* Scurrilities (for she has a low fellow, one Shiells, a Gardener in London, who assists her)" (*FS*, 286). That More did not defend herself explicitly against the "scurrilities" appearing in the press suggests that, for her, appealing to public opinion and defending herself in such a forum was itself scurrilous. Instead, she maintains her private correspondence throughout the affair with her polite friends—Montagu, Walpole, Pepys, and others—and refuses epistolary dialogue with either Yearsley or Shiells, her social inferiors. "Nor shall I answer any of their letters," More writes in a letter to Montagu (*FS*, 286).

While More closed her polite ranks privately and refused to respond to Yearsley either by letter or in the periodical press, for her part Yearsley seized the opportunity to reach the wider audience that print culture afforded. As Walpole succinctly observed: "Hannah will *not* write, and Lactilla *will*" (31:331). For Yearsley, publishing also provided the opportunity for upward mobility, and so it is not surprising that she produced the most significant public proclamation during the affair. Her **"Narrative,"** addressed "to the Noble and Generous Subscribers" of her first book of poems, is an effort to control her public image and to win supporters to her cause. And, as Linda Zionkowski has pointed out, the **"Narrative"** also shows Yearsley using "her access to print to further subvert More's authority."[14] Indeed, Yearsley's text was strategically placed after More's "Prefatory Letter" and before the poems in the fourth edition of *Poems, on Several Occasions* which Yearsley was responsible for bringing out in 1786. It also appeared, in exactly the same position, as part of the prefatory apparatus introducing Yearsley's second collection of poems, *Poems, on Various Subjects,* in 1787. The **"Narrative"** is often examined as a measure of Yearsley's individual mettle, but overlooked as the deft performance that it is in terms of her manipulation of class-based cultural values and her calculated appeal to garner the support of polite readers.

Yearsley's skill in constructing an image of herself that both caters to polite expectations and promotes her desire for independence serves her well in this text. For example, after the initial interview with More about the money, Yearsley describes her subsequent conduct in terms of labor, noting that she still "went daily to [More's] house for the dish-washings" in her effort to support her family.[15] On one level, the passage shows Yearsley to be submissive, not haughty. But in a footnote to this statement, she apologizes to her readers—"I am greatly hurt in obliging my readers to descend to this poor circumstance"—and intimates that More was irritated by the continued practice (xviii). Why does Yearsley go to the trouble of playing out this seemingly insignificant detail? The answer lies, I think, in the received cultural definitions of social rank that Yearsley both ventriloquized and tried to resist in her poetry. It is important that Yearsley collects More's hogwash because this is an aspect of her allotted vocation (More calls her "a milker of Cows and a feeder of Hogs"), the work she is supposed to do according to the classist biases we have seen expressed by More, Walpole, and many others throughout the century (*FS,* 281). But Yearsley's text also has the potential to make any polite reader uncomfortable with this occupation-based definition of social rank. The **"Narrative"** is Yearsley's first public performance free of More's editing and influence, and it showcases her rhetorical talents and her refined manners. This text, together with the new poems that follow, problematize typical polite views of Yearsley's proper vocation: should Yearsley, an established natural genius, be subjected to such low manual toils as collecting hogwash when her true vocation is writing verses?

Yearsley provides a good deal of evidence in her **"Narrative"** to promote the view that she is worthy of the title "poet." In one instance, she presents herself as an easy target for the well-connected More, but not without complicating the issue:

> Shielded by popular opinion, the ungenerous Stella aims at a defenceless breast—her arrows are of the most malignant kind—yet her endeavours to crush an insignificant wretch need not be so amazingly strenuous; for I should have sunk into obscurity again, had not my reputation been so cruelly wounded.
>
> (xxiv)

Yearsley's use of personal "reputation" here shows both her manipulation of mainstream constructions of lower-class "virtue" and her appropriation of upper-class "honor." As a milkwoman, to be deserving of patronage or even upper-class charity, Yearsley must exhibit good character. But in this passage, she is not simply trying to prove her virtue; rather, Yearsley is showing that in her own personal value system "character" is much like aristocratic "honor": "Character is more precious than life itself," she emphatically states (xxiv). Thus Yearsley appeals to her polite readers by suggesting that her values are like theirs; she also holds personal reputation in high regard. As always, even as she manipulates the cultural definitions of "reputation" to her advantage, Yearsley is careful to provide the basic road signs her polite readers would expect from a writer of her station. On the subject of her second volume of poems, for instance, Yearsley says she "will complete them with as much expedition as the more important duties of my family will permit" (xxiv).

This double-voiced movement of the **"Narrative"** is central to understanding how Yearsley uses the print medium to her advantage throughout her conflict with More. Yearsley, for instance, consistently seeks to combat the marginalizing social strictures placed upon her by More and late-eighteenth-century society in general, but she also continues to publish her laboring-class status. Early in the dispute, More wrote to Montagu that Yearsley complained openly "that it was the height of insult and barbarity to tell that she was poor and a Milkwoman" in the "Prefatory Letter" to her poems (*FS,* 284). In view of this statement, one might reasonably expect that Yearsley would discard these designations in the texts she published after gaining her autonomy. This was not the case, however. Yearsley herself controlled the production of *Poems, on Various Subjects* in 1787, and this volume maintains the bold reference to the author as "a Milkwoman of Clifton, near Bristol" on the title page. The opening address to Fredrick Augustus Hervey also reproduces the familiar tropes of "labor" and "disadvantage" she had criticized More for using: "On perusing them, you will remember, that they were written in the short intervals of a life of labour, and under every disadvantage which can possibly result from a confined education" (vi).

These conditions of her authorship advertised Yearsley as a poetic natural genius—a form of identification she well knew still helped sell books. Later, in a "Billet" addressed to Lord Courtdown, dated 24 July 1788, Yearsley refers to herself as "One who has had Nature only for her Tutor."[16] The title page to *Stanzas of Woe* shows that Yearsley was still using the "milk-woman of Clifton, near Bristol" advertisement as late as 1790.[17] She abandoned this practice in 1796 in her last volume of poems, *The Rural Lyre,* but Yearsley's statement in the "Dedication" to Hervey in this book reveals her understanding of the social limitations she was subjected to by More and her circle in the mid-1780s:

> Ten years are now elapsed, since in my cottage I was honoured by the presence of your Lordship. Through the cloud which then covered my confused spirit you had the goodness to discern an impatient desire for attainments so remote from my humble station, that by many they were deemed unnecessary, by most superfluous; and though by some a share of discrimination was allowed me, yet mental accomplishments were considered as incompatible with my laborious employment. This, my Lord, was not your opinion. You inspired me with hope, encouraged me to persevere, and enabled me to divide my domestic cares with the pleasures of meditation.[18]

This is a remarkable retrospective statement because it reveals Yearsley's sense of the protracted battle she fought against the restrictive, classist ideologies circulating in the late-century period. Yearsley purposefully distinguishes Hervey's view of her desire to indulge in "the pleasures of meditation" from the views of the "many"—including, we imagine, More's. In fact, Hervey was instrumental in assisting Yearsley after her break with More, providing the £50 she needed to bring out the controversial fourth edition of *Poems, on Several Occasions* (1786). If More was an enforcer of rigid social order, Hervey is presented here as an enabler of fluid social movement, at least in terms of labor. Unlike More, Hervey supports Yearsley's freedom to pursue Parnassian heights and, by extension, the life changes that might ensue.

Perhaps because Hervey was a wealthy, titled aristocrat whose high social position was less tenuous than More's, he harbors little anxiety over Yearsley's removing herself from her normal workaday labor in order to write and publish. Or, perhaps Hervey subscribed to more progressive ideas concerning political economy. It is instructive to view the differences in More's and Hervey's "patronage" of Yearsley through the lens of Adam Smith's influential *Wealth of Nations* (1776), specifically his notions regarding "the system of natural liberty." Gertrude Himmelfarb puts the case regarding the differences between "the old 'moral economy'" and Smith's political economy succinctly:

> The [old moral economy] depended, at least in principle, on a system of regulations derived from equity, tradition, and law, a system prescribing fair prices, just wages, customary rights, corporative rules, paternalistic obligations, hierarchical relationships—all of which were intended to produce a structured, harmonious, stable, secure, organic order. The 'system of natural liberty,' on the other hand, prided itself on being open, mobile, changeable, individualistic, with all the risks but also all the opportunities associated with freedom.[19]

Himmelfarb goes on to note that the contrast between the two systems is complicated in various ways; nevertheless, the terms of her description here resonate with Yearsley's very different experiences with patronage in the 1780s. As the representative of the old moral economy, More's benevolent paternalism certainly hindered Yearsley's freedom, especially her ability to earn her bread by her writing and so take advantage of the opportunities afforded by an expanding literary economy. Yearsley's construction of Hervey's patronage, quoted above, reads like a blueprint of Smith's ideas. Significantly, according to Yearsley, Hervey allows his charge her individualism; that is, the freedom to develop her talents and to take advantage of any and all opportunities available to her in a free society. While Hervey may well have seen his gift of £50 simply as an act of charity, it is Yearsley who represents the gesture in progressive political economical terms in print.

In addition to the **"Narrative,"** Yearsley includes "an exact copy" of the legal document in dispute, the "Deed of Trust," along with her counterproposal for "the consideration of the public" in her 1787 volume (xxv). Yearsley recounts in her **"Narrative"** the difficulty she had in obtaining a copy of this deed for herself, a detail which implicitly suggests the absolute power More wielded over her protégée. Providing this material to a waiting public produced the desired effect: both *The Monthly Review* and *The Critical Review* came down on Yearsley's side. Andrew Becket lauded Yearsley's rhetorical strategy throughout the prefatory material: "She defends herself with courage, but at the same time moderation; with a temper, in short, which would do honour to any cause. There is no retort, no recrimination whatever. It is simply a justification of, or apology for, her conduct."[20] *The Critical Review* reported that "the deed of trust" was "a very extraordinary one," in particular because it invested the trustees with "the power of disposing the principal and interest . . . in what manner they shall think proper."[21] "Miss More," the reviewer argues, "cannot escape the imputation of improper partiality, or unjust censure" and, after quoting Yearsley's counterproposal in full, observes that "surely a mother had reason to expect that some power would have been granted her in the disposal of that property her own abilities had acquired" (*CR* [*The Critical Review*], 64:435). It is interesting how quickly More's efforts in securing Yearsley a successful subscription are forgotten in favor of acknowledging Yearsley's own labors in composing poetry. In this reviewer's eyes, Yearsley is a legitimate working poet who, despite her lowly social position, has every right to the money earned by her published work. By late century, the commercial trade in literature allowed Yearsley (and others) to see the treatment by her patrons as repressive, especially in light of newly established laws governing literary property.[22]

Not content to rest on these laurels, Yearsley's counterproposal reveals her continued effort to exploit specific class-based social values to her advantage. More enacted her investment plan not only as a way of keeping Yearsley's husband away from the money, but also as a way to provide for Yearsley's children in the future. After the first confrontation with Yearsley, More asks Montagu, rhetorically, "Is such a Woman to be trusted with her poor Children's money?" (*FS*, 284). Later, when the trouble over the money reached a peak, More confided to Elizabeth Carter that "my conscience tells me I ought not to give up my trust for these poor children, on account of their mother's wickedness."[23] In the mid- to late-eighteenth century, there was an increasing concern among the upper and middling classes regarding motherhood and the proper methods for raising children.[24] Lawrence Stone observes that "there is no evidence" that this concern for children "penetrated much lower down the social scale" than the "high professional or bourgeois classes."[25] However, Yearsley writes in her **"Narrative"** that the deed More had her sign in fact makes no provision "whereby my children might have an undeniable claim in future" in the event of Yearsley's death (xvi). In effect, Yearsley argues that the deed usurps her "rights as a mother" (xvii). Her counterproposal, written pointedly "in Behalf of her Children," is an obvious attempt to rectify this problem while keeping within the boundaries of plebeian decorum:

> The money to continue in the future disposition of Mrs. Montague and Miss H. More, allowing Ann Yearsley to be admitted as a joint trustee, the money to be equally divided according to the number of her children, and subject to their demand on their arrival at the age of twenty-one years. Ann Yearsley, her present, or any future husband, *never* to have the least demand on the principal sum, but wishes to receive interest without controul.
>
> (xxx)

Significantly, Yearsley does not demand exclusive control over her invested earnings, but makes a judicious claim on the principal for her children in future, and seeks to use only the interest as she sees fit. In addition, the **"Narrative"** everywhere shows Yearsley to be a capable and caring mother. Yearsley, then, effectively neutralizes More's "family values" argument by using it against her, eventually securing control over her own earnings.

Yearsley's onslaught in print against More in particular[26] indeed brought her power over the funds in the trust by 1787, though it is difficult to ascertain exactly when Yearsley had the money at her disposal. More wrote to Montagu that she had "prevailed on a gentleman . . . to receive the trust" by October 1785, the handle already becoming too hot even before Yearsley's **"Narrative"** was in circulation.[27] But this capitulation to gendered authority did not mean that Yearsley controlled the funds—the situation was unchanged as far as she was concerned—and hence she went ahead with the publication of the **"Narrative"** and other prefatory material over the next eighteen months. This unnamed Bristol gentleman finally did make the money over to Yearsley, probably just prior to the publication of *Poems, on Various Subjects,* for More wrote to Walpole when that volume appeared to join her "in sincere compassion . . . for a human heart of such unaccountable depravity, as to harbour such deep malice for two years, though she has gained her point, and the money is settled to her wish."[28] Public support for Yearsley had been building for some time in the Bristol neighborhood. In a letter to Lady Ossory, dated the first of December, 1786, Walpole provides a glimpse of the support Yearsley had gained:

> I am not surprised that there should be a great party for the milkwoman. The wise people of Bristol have taken it into their heads that they have a manufacture of original genius *chez eux,* and the less foundation they have for their credulity, the stronger their faith is, as always is the case of fools.
>
> (33:550)

Walpole's contempt for the Bristol folk suggests that Yearsley had used the print medium to advantage and availed herself in the quarrel with More quite well.

Indeed, by 1787, Yearsley enjoyed a level of control over her writing and public image that few plebeian poets in the century ever attained. Her readers could now rest assured that her verses were the effusions of an untutored genius, now clearly uncorrupted because her work was uncorrected by More. We cannot recover the extent of More's editing of Yearsley's early poems because More had the manuscripts burned by her bookseller, a point which Yearsley also uses in her **"Narrative"** to illustrate the tyrannical power More held over her. Still, Yearsley used her wealth to remake herself in More's image, as evidenced by a portrait executed and published in 1787.[29] Wilson Lowry's engraving titled "The Bristol Milk Woman and Poetess" shows Yearsley dressed in the garb of a gentlewoman. This obvious change in Yearsley's dress is representative of those changes in material circumstance that More found socially disruptive in a patronized laboring-class poet: "I hear she wears very fine Gauze Bonnets, long lappets, gold Pins, etc.," More gossiped to Montagu (*FS,* 284). Similarly, Walpole noted that "[Yearsley] is grown extravagant and ostentatious" (33:538). The plate shows that, although the "gold Pins" might be absent, fine gauze is evident under Yearsley's hat, and "long lappets" are distinctly present. She appears dressed much as More is in a portrait of the same period,[30] and the whole is ornately framed, signifying the successful poet More no longer controls. The full caption continues Yearsley's practice of advertising her former workaday life in print, but the term "Poetess" best fits the image presented in the portrait.

I have been arguing that Yearsley achieved her independence as a poet by making a calculated appeal in print to her reading public. She successfully plays upon a series of dominant social values to show the public she is not, quoting More, the "'base,'" "'savage,'" "'bad woman'" that More and her circle say that she is (*POVS* [*Poems, on Various Subjects*], xix, xx). But there is another aspect to Yearsley's appeal to an anonymous reading public that remains largely unnoticed in discussions of her battle with More. After their break, Yearsley was taken on by the Robinsons, of Paternoster Row, when More's publisher, Thomas Cadell, would have nothing more to do with her. George Robinson, his son George, and his brother John were at the top of their profession in the mid-1780s; they had "the largest wholesale trade in London" and published many popular periodicals including *The Critical Review* and *The Town and Country Magazine*.[31] Robinson also "paid his authors well, believing that in this he was carrying out the true spirit of bookselling," and did not shy away from controversy.[32] The Robinsons published the controversial fourth edition of *Poems, on Several Occasions* and all of Yearsley's work until her death in 1806. Ferguson notes that they later advanced £200 to help Yearsley open a circulating library at Bristol Hotwells.[33] In this respect, aligning herself with such eminent and benevolent booksellers must have had a positive effect on both Yearsley's public image and her fortune. And the Robinsons knew a good business opportunity when they saw one, perhaps seeking to capitalize on Yearsley's notoriety at the time. They were no doubt rewarded for their risk because Yearsley's 1787 volume boasted another lengthy list of prepaid subscribers.

Yearsley's new poems, written during the height of her public quarrel with More, reflect an angry, less fettered critical voice. Although there are no overt references to "Stella" in this volume, More hovers everywhere over it.[34] For example, in **"To Those Who Accuse the Author of Ingratitude,"** Yearsley challenges the worldview of her polite detractors and implicates More in the process:

> You, who thro' optics dim, so falsely view
> This wond'rous maze of things, and rend a part
> From the well-order'd whole, to fit your sense
> Low, groveling, and confin'd; say from what source
> Spring your all-wise opinions?
> . . . .

> What are your boasts, ye incapacious souls,
> Who would confine, within your narrow orbs,
> Th' extensive All?
> . . . .
> A wish to share the false, tho' public din,
> In which the popular, not virtuous live;
> A fear of being singular, which claims
> A fortitude of mind you ne'er could boast;

(*POVS*, 57-59)

Beginning the poem with a generalized, second-person "You" suggests that Yearsley is addressing several "incapacious souls" who see the world through narrow lenses and "optics dim." As Landry has convincingly argued, Yearsley's use of "optics dim" and her focus on the "false" and "confin'd" worldviews of her polite critics suggests a class-specific sense of Yearsley's ideology critique.[35] Yet, as Yearsley continues to vent her spleen, her poem conjures up More as the primary addressee. This assertion is supported by the fact that **"To Those Who Accuse . . ."** represents a toned-down version of an unpublished poem titled **"To Stella"** penned by an angry Yearsley after her break with More, and before the publication of the 1787 volume of poems.[36] Yearsley's references to "narrow orbs" and the charges leveled in the last stanza above call attention to More's growing adherence to a dogmatic evangelical Christianity in the 1780s. Yearsley accuses More of finding comfort in numbers, amongst like-minded evangelical social and moral reformers "popular" in the period, and Yearsley claims a singularity and "fortitude of mind" for herself that her former patron lacks.

In another poem, **"Addressed to Ignorance, Occasioned by a Gentleman's desiring the Author never to assume Knowledge of the Ancients,"** Yearsley uses the verse epistle form to assert her right to ostensibly privileged categories of knowledge. The "gentleman" to whom Yearsley is responding in this piece apparently wanted Yearsley to discontinue her use of classical allusions, to which Yearsley responds by unleashing her "Fancy" in the face of forced "Ign'rance" (94). The final fifteen stanzas include no less than thirty-three references to ancient Greek figures and places, forming a wide survey of important warriors, writers, and philosophers from "Achilles" to "Zeno" (95, 96). At times, Yearsley seems content simply to show her reader that she possesses a surprising degree of classical learning for a milkwoman:

> Fond Paris, three changes with sighs has gone through,
>   First a Goat, then a Monkey compleat;
> Enrag'd, to the river Salmacis he flew,
>   Wash'd his face—and forgot his fair mate.

(95)

Yet this earnest display of classical knowledge more often ventures into ironic play:

> There's Virgil, the Courtier, with hose out at heel,
>   And Hesiod, quite shoeless his foot;

Poor Ovid walks shiv'ring, behind a cart-wheel,
  While Horace cries, "sweep for your soot."

(97)

One way to read Yearsley's zealousness with neoclassical imagery is to see her using the occasion of this gentleman's criticism to ironize a particular aesthetics of poetry which values finely turned classical allusions over anything else. In a moment of sharp defiance, Yearsley notes at poem's end: "this age I defy, / And the next cannot wound me, I know" (99). **"Addressed to Ignorance"** is both an angry response to literary criticism inspired by class difference, and also, in its very indulgence of classical references, an ironic dismissal of neoclassical poetics to make way for something different.

For Yearsley, this new poetics is deeply tied to what we now identify as the romantic—or more accurately preromantic[37]—ideal of personal self-expression in poetry. Samuel Badcock summed up his review of Yearsley's first volume of poems with the following statement: "On the whole, these Poems present us with a very striking picture of a vigorous and aspiring genius, struggling with its own feelings" (*MR* [*The Monthly Review*], 73:221). Badcock judges the strength of Yearsley's poetry by linking her "genius" to her ability to write about her internal struggles of feeling and emotion. Not only does Badcock's statement suggest a distinct shift from the 1730s in terms of the criteria for judging "good" poetry (plebeian or otherwise), but it also shows that Yearsley was writing the sort of poetry that appealed at least to contemporary critics, if not the reading public as well. Looking back to her poem answering the charge of ingratitude, Yearsley aptly exhorts her narrow-minded polite readers to "scan the feelings of Lactilla's soul" (*POVS*, 60). In another poem in the same volume, this one addressed **"To Mr. ****,"** a fellow "unletter'd poet," Yearsley links their shared natural genius to preromantic notions of self-expression in poetry: "Deep in the soul live ever tuneful springs, / Waiting the touch of Ecstasy, which strikes / Most pow'rful on defenceless, untaught Minds" (81). For Yearsley, the reasons for and the subjects of poetry lie within the individual "soul," and she turns the category of natural genius into an argument championing an unlettered poet's ability to produce this poetry of "artless Rapture":

I've patient trod the wild entangled path
Of unimprov'd Idea. Dauntless Thought
I eager seiz'd, no formal Rule e'er aw'd;
No Precedent controul'd; no Custom fix'd
My independent spirit: on the wing
She still shall guideless soar, nor shall the Fool,
Wounding her pow'rs, e'er bring her to the ground.

(80)

Again, More shows up in a negative light as the "Fool" steeped within the limitations of tradition and poetic

"precedent," but Yearsley defines herself and her work outside of those constrictions. It is not surprising, then, that those poems in which Yearsley enacts the poetic precepts she contends in **"To Mr. ****"** have been recently reprinted in anthologies which seek to widen the boundaries of English Romantic verse.[38]

"To Mr. **"** is significant also because it reveals Yearsley's superb self-management of her public image as a poet. Waldron notes that it is "a poem about poetry"[39]—which it is—but there is more going on within it that suggests what is at stake for Yearsley with the publication of *Poems, on Various Subjects*. While it may be true that Yearsley "sought success as a writer rather than a 'natural genius,'" she was not above using the period fascination with primitivism in poetry to her advantage.[40] "Mr. ****" has not been identified, and he could very well be an imaginary addressee, one that allows Yearsley to broach the subject of natural genius herself:

Ne'er hail the fabled Nine, or snatch rapt Thought
From the Castalian spring; 'tis not for *thee*,
From embers, where the Pagan's light expires,
To catch a flame divine. From one bright spark
Of never-erring Faith, more rapture beams
Than wild Mythology could ever boast.

(78-79)

We should remember that by 1787, after her break from More and Montagu, Yearsley no longer has patrons to trumpet her natural genius in print, so she seems to construct an opportunity for herself to do so in the course of her new volume. She makes it clear in this dogmatic passage that poetic genius emerges from within the poet; "one bright spark" of this is better than all that classical learning can provide: "the pen, / Tho' dipp'd in awful Wisdom's deepest tint, / Can *never* paint the wild extatic mood" (77-78). By placing untaught natural genius like hers at the top, Yearsley hierarchizes poetic genius in a way that Addison tried to avoid earlier in the century, as she also slyly reminds her readers of her status as one. As a verse epistle explicitly (if also ironically) addressed to someone else, the poem reveals more about Yearsley to her readers than it does about "Florus," the unknown addressee. It is not simply that Yearsley wants it both ways—to be recognized as a true, working poet and as a natural genius. The crucial point is she understands that defining the unique power of natural genius, and popularizing herself under its rubric, is the key to fashioning public success as a laboring-class poet. Yearsley thus embarks on her career as poet in her second volume without leaving the original signifiers of her popularity behind.

By 1787, Yearsley sees herself as a poet whose work is based on a conception of poetry which we understand as preromantic, and which Yearsley no doubt saw as contemporary and liberating: "What are the Muses, or Apollo's strains, / But harmony of soul?" (79). Like other late-century versifying plebeians, Yearsley does not make explicit use of a poetic discourse on work in her social criticisms. She never wrote a poem chronicling a milkwoman's labors, but she does maintain the designation "Lactilla" in her 1787 volume, perhaps as a critical gesture in the sense that she transforms the class-prejudice of her social betters into an ironic self-description by keeping it alive in her writing. When Yearsley does employ a poetic language of labor, she confines her use to the figures of metaphor and personification, as in the **"Ode, to Miss Shiells"**:

> Last, Industry, with features coarse and strong,
>   Rises behind, shaking his blister'd hand;
> The slow unwilling plough he drives along;
>   The dews of Labour on his forehead stand.
>
> (71)

And, "Winter" is an "unwelcome guest! / I hate his freezing toils," states Yearsley-the-poet, who nevertheless reminds her reader of her provincial roots: "But Rapture fills my rural breast" (75).

Yearsley, however, does not need a poetic discourse on work to communicate her social critique; hence her criticisms are aesthetically and qualitatively different from those articulated by the 1730s generation of plebeian poets. By 1787, Yearsley enjoyed a degree of independence as a publishing poet that neither Duck nor Collier ever achieved, and she is writing at a time when the expression of personal feeling in poetry was in vogue. Yearsley does not need to mask her thoughts as a plebeian woman struggling against the classist forces of her society the way that Collier did in the 1730s. For example, in **"On Being Presented with a Silver Pen,"** Yearsley uses a bold poetic strategy to criticize the class-specific ideology that seeks to limit her options in the world. The poem includes the following passage, one-half of a dialogue between imaginary polite society-types:

> "'Tis to relieve Distress—this is the sum,
> But let your Prudence point out what's to come.
> Keep wretches *humble*, for when once reliev'd,
> They oft-times prove our *Charity* deceiv'd:
> Therefore be *cautious*, not their *merits* trust;
> They *may* have very few—if poor—they *must*.
> Think not a savage virtuous—but confine,
> His future acts by obligation's line:
> He surely *must* be humble, grateful, true,
> While *he's* dependent—the superiour *you*."
>
> (88)

These are the sentiments of "the cooly wise" who speak condescendingly "with self-applauding glance, / And taunting air" (88). Yearsley intends to show that these are the words of a particular class of people, however indistinctly defined as those who patronize poor "wretches" (read poets), and not simply the words of More, though we know that More voiced similar ones to Yearsley. But here one member of "the cooly wise" is clearly addressing another, and Yearsley is imagining the tenor of their discussion (no doubt based on her own experience) when the subject is the patronage of poor "wretches." In her use of quotation marks and italics, Yearsley marks this speech as an intrusion into her own poetic discourse and distinguishes its ideological emphases: the goal in this passage is to "keep wretches humble" by controlling the potential long-term effects of patronage, that is, to raise the quality of life of the poor without raising them socially. The notion of confining "his future acts by obligation's line" reverberates with Yearsley's contractual arrangement with her patrons as well as the Montagus' plan to employ Woodhouse, who was just about to relieve himself of such "patronage" in 1787. Whereas Duck and Collier used a poetic discourse on work to describe the oppression enforced by their "Masters" and "Mistresses," Yearsley actually incorporates the polite dogma she wants to criticize into her verse, and will go so far as to respond with anger and purpose throughout this volume: "Independent, I smile at controul" (33).

Yearsley continues to air her independent voice in *A Poem on the Inhumanity of the Slave-Trade,* published by the Robinson brothers in 1788. The longest of her pamphlet-style occasional poems, this is an angry and graphic dramatic verse narrative that tells the story of Luco, an African slave torn from his "humble home," his "mourning father," and his beloved "Incilanda" by hypocritical Christian slave traders.[41] It is a powerful piece, full of Yearsley's characteristically exhortative and emotive blank verse. Andrew Becket judged the poem to be "a very affecting tale of a poor negroe, inhumanely butchered under the forms of law," though he goes on to laud Hannah More's poem on the same subject, *Slavery,* which also appeared in 1788, as "more philosophic" and "more elegant" than Yearsley's effort.[42] But, in calling attention to Yearsley's handling of "the forms of law" that sanction the exploitation of African slaves, Becket's language suggests that, though More's is the better poem, Yearsley's contains a stronger, more far-reaching political critique.

Indeed, *A Poem on the Inhumanity of the Slave-Trade* is the one poem in which Yearsley extends the concept of "Custom" in a critical poetic discourse aimed at exposing the hypocrisy of upper-class involvement in the slave trade and the unequal distribution of power within her society that enforces it. Early in the poem, Yearsley asks rhetorically, "Custom, Law / Ye blessings, and ye curses of mankind, / What evils do ye cause?," and follows with a grim reminder of Custom's sway: "We feel enslav'd, / Yet move in your direction" (2). For Yearsley, as for Jones before her, Custom is problematic because it represents a complex of contradictory social practices—in this case attending church and enslaving fellow human beings—as simply natural and socially acceptable. Yearsley's critique is explicit in this regard:

> Custom, thou
> Wilt preach filial piety; thy sons
> Will groan, and stare with impudence at Heav'n,
> As if they did abjure the act, where Sin
> Sits full on Inhumanity; the church
> They fill with mouthing, vap'rous sighs and tears,
> Which, like the guileful crocodile's, oft fall,
> Nor fall, but at the cost of human bliss.
> Custom, thou hast undone us! led us far
> From God-like probity, from truth, and heaven.
>
> (2-3)

Yearsley's imagery underscores the hypocrisy of Bristol merchants, those "grov'ling souls" who trade in human beings and attend church, seeking Christian salvation (1). And Custom in these passages is meant to represent what we might term the ideological apparatus behind the slave trade in the late eighteenth century. Yearsley thus exposes the process by which Custom, in this context, is internalized in the name of "Commerce" or, more precisely, economic prosperity and the maintenance of existing social relations (26). No doubt confident in her critique, at several points Yearsley baits her enemies to respond:

> Advance, ye Christians, and oppose my strain:
> Who dares condemn it? Prove from laws divine,
> From deep philosophy, or social love,
> That ye derive your privilege.
>
> (25-6)

The writer who advanced the most published work to counteract the radical potential of Yearsley's arguments was of course Hannah More. When More began writing again in earnest in the late 1780s, she saw a role for herself as a moral reformer, specifically in formulating and establishing the social codes for men, women, and children from all ranks of society. More's essays, poetry, and especially the Cheap Repository tracts—a collection of inexpensive ballads, broadsides, and chapbooks produced by More and her evangelical friends to combat the social unrest of the 1790s—show that she made "a vital contribution to the stabilizing of English society in the difficult years after the French Revolution."[43] More involved herself in the process of codifying domestic, religious, and social ideologies through her writing, she was a social ideologue extraordinaire, defining the proper place, the proper values, and the proper pursuits for working people in England in this contentious period. *Village Politics* (1793) and the Cheap Repository tracts (1795) were consciously written for a laboring-class audience, deploying mechanic caricatures and the simple language of the poor to appeal to the literate elements of this wide audience. In these texts, More commodifies the plebeian discourse on work to influence her intended audience. When More finally reenters print culture after the episode with Yearsley, she seeks to use the print medium—specifically lower forms such as the ballad and chapbook—to enter into dialogue with those potentially reformable readers of the laboring classes.

Because of her relatively high social position, public opinion of the sort that Yearsley had attained mattered very little to More. More still enjoyed the steadfast support of fashionable society. Her turn toward a conservative brand of evangelical Christianity and her correspondence during this period show that she met Yearsley's public onslaught with characteristic Christian stoicism: "I grieve most for poor fallen human nature; for, as to my own part, I am persuaded Providence intends me good by it. Had [Yearsley] turned out well I should have had my *reward*; as it is, I have my *trial*."[44] More emerged from her "trial" with Yearsley to embrace a higher calling to reform the lower classes. Although More never responded directly to Yearsley in print, her publications after 1787 at times seem directly informed by her experience with the upstart milkwoman. For instance, in *Thoughts on the Importance of the Manners of the Great to General Society,* published in 1788, More writes:

> The same principle in human nature by which the nabob, the contractor, and others, by a sudden influx of unaccustomed wealth, become voluptuous, extravagant, and insolent, seldom fails to produce the same effect on persons in [the] humbler stations, when raised from inferior places to the sudden affluence of these gainful ones. Increased profligacy on a sudden swell of fortune is commonly followed by desperate methods to improve the circumstances, when impaired by the improvidence attending unaccustomed prosperity.[45]

We can read More's experience with Yearsley in those "desperate methods" to which she alludes. More never gave up the ideal of securing upper-class charity for the needful members of the lower-classes, but hindsight dictated that the poor required moral reform to be worthy of, and to properly receive, such assistance.

In the aftermath of the Yearsley episode, Walpole pointed out that More "lov[ed] good works: a temper superior to revenge" (31:255), but, as Susan Pedersen has argued, More's post-Yearsley texts amount to "a deliberate assault on popular culture."[46] Pedersen is referring specifically to the Cheap Repository tracts, but *Village Politics,* published two years before the tracts began appearing, is also part of More's bombardment. *Village Politics* is explicitly addressed "to all the mechanics, journeymen, and day labourers, in Great Britain," and is written under More's pseudonymous plebeian persona, "Will Chip, a country carpenter."[47] One commentator has called this poem "Burke for beginners," a phrase which accurately sums up More's central purpose: to diffuse the critique against egalitarian ideas circulating in England amongst the lower social orders after the French Revolution.[48] The text takes the form of a political dialogue between two laboring men, "Jack Anvil" and "Tom Hod," one a blacksmith and the other a mason. Tom is a budding Painite republican who seeks "Liberty, Equality, and the Rights of Man," and so is in need of the moral and social enlightenment provided by Jack, a conservative ideologue who polemicizes against the reform movement in the interest of maintaining social harmony (3).

The subject of work is a primary feature of their dialogue, and thus is central to the didacticism of the poem as a whole. More has Tom admit early on that "work's plenty enough, if a man had but the heart to go to it," in effect positing the notion that real social problems are not plaguing the country, but instead radical social and political ideas are leading workers like Tom to stray from their proper labors (3). One of the points Tom raises in this discussion suggests that More understands work and leisure as specific class markers: "I don't see why we are to work like slaves, while others roll about in their coaches, feed on the fat of the land, and do nothing" (7). However, to illustrate More's appeal to a traditional social paradigm, Tom resigns himself to his fate of laboring for others in order to survive himself. When Tom asserts that "all men are equal," More, speaking through Jack, answers Tom's political query with a plea to religion: "If that's thy talk, Tom, thou dost quarrel with Providence and not with the government" (8). Jack chastises Tom further for not "go-[ing] oftner to church," and thus More effectively manipulates the contemporary discussion about social equality to serve her own ideological ends. That is, by shifting the issue of work and social equality from a political to a religious question precisely by appealing to larger theological imperatives, More defuses Tom's incendiary politics. Tom, of course, eventually capitulates to Jack's arguments. Yet, for many laboring-class people living in the last decade of the eighteenth century, the points and questions Tom raises in the poem were increasingly political, and only real political change would be entertained by the growing ranks of workers seeking better standards of living.

It is characteristic of More's politics that she looks back to an idealized past for the answers to present social ills. For example, through Jack, More paints an idyllic picture of rural laboring life and the earning power of a single family working on an aristocrat's estate. When "Sir John" and his Lady are down in summer, Jack notes that they

> [bring] such a deal of gentry that I have more horses than I can shoe, and my wife more linen than she can wash. Then all our grown children are servants in the

family, and rare wages they have got. Our little boys get something every day by weeding their gardens, and the girls learn how to sew and knit at Sir John's expence; who sends them all to school on a Sunday.

(11)

More's ideal case scenario describing a laboring family's earning power is strikingly similar to Arthur Young's, published in 1772. Young theoretically calculated that the average earnings of such a working family would have been close to £51 8s. per year, but Thorvald Rogers rightly notes that "it is plain that not one family in a thousand corresponded at that time to Young's hypothesis, and that, therefore, the calculations [with regard to] the remuneration of labour [are] entirely fictitious."[49] Tom complains that "there's not Sir John's in every village," to which Jack replies "the more's the pity" before pointing out the "other help" that is available in every parish (11). This assistance includes better management of parish poor rates and continued charity from benevolent aristocrats to raise the material conditions of the laboring poor—at least to basic subsistence levels. But the poor were required to be morally upright and productive: "no drinking, no riot, no bonfires," and they were to "'Study to be quiet, work with [their] own hands, and mind [their] own business'" in order to reap the benefits of what amounts to More's welfare package (16).

Clearly, More's ideas for social welfare were designed to maintain traditional hierarchical relations among the ranks of working people, the factory owners, and the landed gentry. The specter of riot haunted the Mores and Burkes of this period because it was only through insurrection that radical social change would be effected, as it was in France. More attacked this problem directly in one of her many contributions to the Cheap Repository tracts. "The Riot; or Half a Loaf is Better than No Bread" (1795) continues the dialogue between Jack Anvil and Tom Hod that was begun in *Village Politics*. The poem opens with Tom inciting a large group of workers to take to the streets:

> 'Come, neighbours, no longer be patient and quiet,
> Come let us kick up a bit of a riot;
> I am hungry, my lads, but I've little to eat,
> So we'll pull down the mills and seize all the meat:
> I'll give you good sport, boys, as ever you saw,
> So a fig for the justice, a fig for the law.'

> (*Works* [*The Works of Hannah More*], 6:62)

Again, More co-opts the language of the lower classes in order to speak as one of them and thus (potentially) influence their actions. "The Riot" was apparently successful in achieving this purpose; More wrote to Mrs. Boscawen that

> a very formidable riot among the colliers in the neighbourhood of Bath, was happily prevented by the ballad of "The Riot." The plan was thoroughly settled; they

were resolved to work no more, but to attack first the mills, and then the gentry. A gentleman of large fortune got into their confidence, and a few hundreds were distributed and sung with the effect, as they say, mentioned above. It is a fresh proof by what weak instruments evils are now and then prevented.[50]

More was becoming increasingly aware of the profound influence that such "weak instruments" as ballads and chapbooks could have as political and ideological tools.

Much of "The Riot," then, shows More presenting her own arguments, again through Jack, to counter Tom's incendiary rhetoric. Jack begins by pointing out the paradox inherent in the rioter's actions, noting the "whimsey" of destroying the infrastructure for producing food when food is in fact what they want (6:63). He then goes on to present a series of concisely argued points for Tom (and the reader) to consider. Jack appeals to national pride, observing that the Dutch and Spanish have it worse than the English; he exhorts Tom to cultivate patience because "prices will fall" (6:63), and to tighten his domestic economy in order to offset the current hardship—"The more ale we drink, boys, the less we shall eat" (6:63). Neither "Parliament" nor the King can control the weather, Jack argues, and so Nature, not government, is to blame for the bad harvests. This point eases into an insidious religious interpretation of the suffering experienced by the laboring poor:

> 'Besides, I must share in the wants of the times,
> Because I have had my full share in its crimes;
> And I'm apt to believe the distress which is sent
> Is to punish and cure us of all discontent.'
>
> (6:64)

Thus Jack argues that the poor are as culpable for the bad times—sent by Providence—as any other social group because they are equally morally corrupt. Finally, Jack glorifies manual labor, affirms his own piety, and places his faith in upper-class charity for his survival during hard times:

> 'And though I've no money, and though I've no lands,
> I've a head on my shoulders, and a pair of good hands;
> So I'll work the whole day, and on Sundays I'll seek
> At church how to bear all the wants of the week.
> The gentlefolks too will afford us supplies;
> They'll subscribe—and they'll give us their puddings
>   and pies.'
>
> (6:64)

"I'd rather be hungry than hanged," Jack exclaims, putting an end to the riotous rhetoric issued from Tom, who throws down his pitchfork "and went to his work" (6:65). Apparently the colliers in Bath did, too. More's success in "The Riot" can be attributed to her presentation of complex ideas in a language and form that working people could understand.

The overarching purpose of the Cheap Repository was very much defined by the evangelicals' desire to maintain traditional English values, and hence, the socioeconomic structure of traditional English society. The values that More proselytizes in the tracts—honesty, industry, domesticity, and piety—travel across class lines, though the lower-class people who cultivate these values do not. For instance, in "Patient Joe, the Newcastle Collier," the protagonist is held up as an example of laboring-class complacency and rightly-turned submission to both God and the class system:

> He prais'd his Creator whatever befell;
> How thankful was Joseph when matters went well!
> How sincere were his carols of praise for good health,
> And how grateful for any increase in his wealth!
> In trouble he bow'd him to God's holy will;
> How contented was Joseph when matters went ill!
> When rich and when poor he alike understood
> That all things together were working for good.
>
> (*Works*, 6:66)

Joe's Panglossian maxim that "all is for the best" includes an implicit justification for social difference. Although Joe is a collier, he represents one of the moral poor and so is counted as equal to any other Englishman before God in More's schema. In her effort to quell class antagonism, More uses Joe and other characters in her tracts to set out a program that simultaneously erases *and* upholds class difference: an ethereal equality before God is propagandized as reward for those who submit to God's will on earth, understood as their proper place within the social structure.

More thus employs the distinction between the moral and the material to manipulate class definitions in her work. Persons of all ranks can (and should) cultivate similar values and can thereby achieve equality in moral terms, according to More, but the Cheap Repositories as a whole never present material advancement of the sort that could blur social lines. The sheer number of tracts in circulation by March 1796—over two million—shows that More was successful in commodifying a fictional plebeian discourse on work and suggests a level of potential political and ideological influence that far surpasses the influence that Yearsley's public performances could have had.[51] Yearsley did publish consistently in the decade following her break with More, working in other genres with some critical acclaim.[52] More important, she succeeded in turning her writing into a career that would support her family, though her published pieces may not have had the same far-reaching political and ideological effects that More's did. Given their respective social positions, however, it is ironic that the print medium allowed Yearsley access to a potentially supportive community of polite readers, and More—in the case of the Cheap Repository—access to a potentially reformable community of low-order readers. Theirs was a textual dialogue fueled by the events of 1785, which led to a failed patron/poet relationship and an end to conventional lines of communication. One way to understand their texts published after this affair is to read Yearsley as using her knowledge of More and her polite social values to fashion herself as a successful plebeian author; and likewise, to read More as using her knowledge of Yearsley's values—the apparent source of her "ingratitude"—to formulate a poetic language to reform men and women like her.

While More may have won the larger, class-based ideological war with Yearsley with her Cheap Repository tracts, Yearsley's final volume of poems, *The Rural Lyre* (1796), is an important last retort in the dialogue between these two women writers. Given More's aggressive assault on popular culture in the Cheap Repository, we might have expected Yearsley to respond directly, with fire and purpose, continuing the angry poetics of class resistance begun in earnest in 1787 with *Poems, on Various Subjects.* However, Yearsley was never one to cede to expectations. At times, she echoes More in this volume on the subject of a poet's role in society, as in **"Remonstrance in the Platonic Shade,"** in which the poet tunes her "rural lay to universal love," in particular to her "social duties . . . / To Friendship, Virtue, Love, and Heav'n" (67, 73). Instead of pointedly engaging in the dialogue of social critique, Yearsley now pleads to Providence for assistance in finding social harmony: "O teach me Father! so to touch the lyre / That woe may smile, and social joy be near" (133).

But if Yearsley's new poems suggest a resignation on her part to the "social duties" defined by More and the dominant culture, they nevertheless point us toward recognizing her ultimate success: her achievement of personal "liberty," particularly from the economic constraints that plagued earlier plebeian poets. After Duck's elevation in Caroline's court, we have seen other plebeian poets throughout the century worry in print about worldly "cares" and attempt to use their writing to alleviate the penury they felt in varying degrees. Early in her career, Yearsley was no exception to this rule. But by the end of her career, she seeks to transcend the cash-nexus of poetry and print by means of a vision of pure poetry we have not yet witnessed from a plebeian pen. In the **"Familiar Poem to Milo, an Aged Friend, who Wished the Author Riches,"** Yearsley writes:

> You talk of wealth, dear Milo, as if I
> Could find no joy in Nature's purer gifts.
> . . . .
>   You are good and rich;
> I poor—a vot'ry of wild fancy. When
> You listen to my song, I am not poor;
> You have not wealth enough to buy my joys:—
>
>   (28, 34)

The notion of poetic "fancy" turns up in this poem and elsewhere in the volume to illustrate Yearsley's sense of herself as a true poet, as one who writes not for money, though her "purse is light," but because of a deep-seated passion to find and celebrate "Truth" (131). A decade after her experience with More, Yearsley distances herself from the worldly cares which defined her status as a plebeian poet:

> Fly me, Care! I will not be
> Through the world a slave to thee!
> Take thy fetters; know, my soul
> Laughs, old Friend, at thy controul
>
>   (82)

By 1796, perhaps Yearsley had earned enough money from her writing to feel free of worldly "care." But more important, this statement (and the many others like it that appear in this volume) presents an image of a poet now basking in her freedom as a writer.

In the last poem of the book, **"The Indifferent Shepherdess to Colin,"** Yearsley illustrates this "dominion bright and clear" over both gender and class oppression (139):

> For my eternal plan
>   Is to be calm and free.
> Estrang'd from tyrant man
>   I'll keep my liberty.
> . . . .
> I stray o'er rocks and fields
>   Where native beauties shine:
> All fetter'd fancy yields
>   Be, Colin, ever thine.
> Complain no more! but rove—
>   My cheek from crimson free,
> Within my native grove
>   I'll guard my liberty.
>
>   (141-42)

We might imagine Yearsley's speaking through the character of a lowly shepherdess in this poem in order to emphasize her own ideas, as a laboring-class woman, of maintaining personal "liberty" in the face of "tyrant man" and those forces originating from outside her "native grove." Thus, at the end of her career, Yearsley can imagine herself as having defeated such worldly cares and the oppression that stems from them. Her "liberty" of thought and expression is what marks her having achieved the status of poet. For Yearsley, the world always appeared "an empty bauble bound with chains," but she did much in her life and in her published poetry to resist the limiting effects of those chains—real and imaginary, material and ideological (86).

Notes

1. Samuel Johnson, "London," in *Works* [*The Yale Edition of the Works of Samuel Johnson,* 16 vols.

to date (New Haven and London: Yale University Press, 1958-)], 6:56.

2. More to Montagu, 27 August 1784, in Mahl, [Mary R., and Helen Koons, eds.], *The Female Spectator* [(Bloomington: Indiana University Press and The Feminist Press, 1977)], 277. Hereafter cited appropriately in the text.

3. *The Monthly Review* 73, part 2 (September 1785): 219.

4. William Roberts, *Memoirs of the Life and Correspondence of Mrs. Hannah More*, 2d ed. (London: R. B. Seeley and W. Burnside, 1834), 1:384 n. 1; and Mary Alden Hopkins, *Hannah More and Her Circle* (New York: Longmans, Green and Co., 1947), 124.

5. Southey, *Lives and Works of the Uneducated Poets*, [ed. J. S. Childers (London: Humphrey Milford, 1925),] 129, 130.

6. J. M. S. Tompkins, *The Polite Marriage: Eighteenth-Century Essays* (Cambridge: Cambridge University Press, 1938), 59.

7. See Moira Ferguson, "Resistance and Power in the Life and Writings of Ann Yearsley," [*The Eighteenth Century* 27 (1986): 247-68,] and her *Eighteenth-Century Women Poets* [(Albany: SUNY Press, 1995)], esp. 49-51; Donna Landry, *Muses* [*The Muses of Resistance* (Cambridge: Cambridge University Press, 1990)], esp. 120-85; Elizabeth Kowaleski-Wallace, *Their Fathers' Daughters: Hannah More, Maria Edgeworth, and Patriarchal Complicity* (New York: Oxford University Press, 1991), 3-5.

8. See Mary Waldron, "Ann Yearsley and the Clifton Records," *The Age of Johnson: A Scholarly Annual* 3, ed. Paul Korshin (New York: AMS Press, 1990), 310-18. For a judicious critique of Waldron's argument in this essay, see Landry, *Muses*, 303 n. 19. Waldron continues her argument in "'By no means milk and water matters': the contribution to English poetry of Ann Yearsley, milkwoman of Clifton, 1753-1806," *Studies on Voltaire and the Eighteenth Century* 304 (1992): 801-4); and *Lactilla, Milkwoman of Clifton: The Life and Writings of Ann Yearsley, 1753-1806* (Athens and London: University of Georgia Press, 1996), esp. 16-20. Waldron has continued to chastise critics who, she argues, see only what they want to see in Yearsley's life and poems: "In many cases insufficient care has been taken to search out the details of the very varied situations within which so-called 'labouring' women writers produced their work, and important aspects of their writings have been ignored in the interests of proving a theory" ("'This Muse-born Wonder': the Occluded

Voice of Ann Yearsley, Milkwoman and Poet of Clifton," in *Women's Poetry in the Enlightenment: The Making of a Canon, 1730-1820*, ed. Isobel Armstrong and Virginia Blain [London: Macmillan Press Ltd., 1999], 124). Waldron has in fact provided us with many significant details in Yearsley's case, and the question of Yearsley's plebeian status might be as dubious as, for example, that of John Bancks. But whether a "milkmaid" or a "self-employed trader" (as Waldron would have it), there can be little doubt that Yearsley was of the lower social strata in late-eighteenth-century English society, and that both she and her patrons constructed her public identity as a poet vis-à-vis the formulaic cultural tropes—poverty, hardship, natural genius, industriousness, Christian piety, and so on—of a plebeian poetic tradition (124).

9. Patricia Demers, "'For mine's a stubborn and a savage will': 'Lactilla' (Ann Yearsley) and 'Stella' (Hannah More) Reconsidered," *The Huntington Library Quarterly: Studies in English and American History and Literature* 56 (spring 1993): 135-50; quotation, 136.

10. Roberts, *Memoirs of Hannah More*, 1:387-88.

11. Walpole to More, 13 November 1784, in *Horace Walpole's Correspondence*, [ed. W. S. Lewis, et al., 48 vols. (New Haven: Yale University Press, 1961),] 31:221. Further references to Walpole's letters are from this edition and will appear appropriately in the text.

12. There is no extant manuscript of this "Letter" in the corpus of letters More sent to Montagu during this period. It also contains information that had been previously communicated to Montagu in earlier letters, and reveals a less personal voice than many of those same earlier epistles.

13. Hannah More, "A Prefatory Letter to Mrs. Montagu. By a Friend," in Yearsley's *Poems, on Several Occasions* (London, 1785), xi. Hereafter cited appropriately in the text.

14. Linda Zionkowski, "Strategies of Containment: Stephen Duck, Ann Yearsley, and the Problem of Polite Culture," *Eighteenth-Century Life* 13 (November 1989): 102.

15. Ann Yearsley, *Poems, on Various Subjects* (London, 1787), xviii. Hereafter cited appropriately in the text.

16. See Moira Ferguson, "The Unpublished Poems of Ann Yearsley," *Tulsa Studies in Women's Literature* 12 (spring 1993): 39. Yearsley provides a copy of the billet that was sent along with her unpublished poem addressed to George III, "To the King On His Majesty's arrival at Cheltenham

1788." Ferguson has discovered that Yearsley left behind several unpublished poems that were handwritten on the blank pages of what was probably Yearsley's own copy of *Poems, on Several Occasions* (1785). Ferguson generously appends the texts of these poems as well as the author's statements included in this volume, now housed in the Bristol Public Library, to her article for other scholars to use.

17. Ann Yearsley, *Stanzas of Woe, addressed from the Heart On A Bed Of Illness, to Levi Eames, Esq. Late Mayor Of the City Of Bristol* (London, 1790), title page.

18. Ann Yearsley, *The Rural Lyre* (London, 1796), vi. Hereafter cited appropriately in the text.

19. Himmelfarb, *The Idea of Poverty* [(New York: Alfred A. Knopf, 1984)], 63.

20. *The Monthly Review* 77, part 2 (December 1787): 485.

21. *The Critical Review* 64 (December 1787): 435-36.

22. See Zionkowski, who points out that "the increased commercial trade in literature strengthened [the] idea of authorial ownership, which the House of Lords in 1774 finally codified into law" ("Strategies of Containment," 102).

23. Roberts, *Memoirs of Hannah More,* 1:391.

24. See, for example, Leonore Davidoff and Catherine Hall, *Family Fortunes: Men and Women of the English Middle Class, 1780-1850* (Chicago: University of Chicago Press, 1987), esp. 321-56.

25. Lawrence Stone, *The Family, Sex and Marriage in England, 1500-1800,* abridged edition (New York: Harper & Row, 1979), 293. For the new emphasis on mothers in child-rearing practices in the eighteenth century, see 254-99.

26. Yearsley publicly vindicated Montagu because she felt Montagu was ignorant of the exact contents of More's "Deed of Trust": "Mrs. Montagu's name I think profaned in a proceeding of this nature; nor do I suppose that lady was ever made acquainted with the contents of the Deed before it was signed" (xxv). There is no evidence that Montagu was familiar with the document, but she did trust More implicitly and supported her decisions steadfastly.

27. More to Montagu, 20 October 1785, unpublished letter, Huntington Library manuscript MO 3993, quoted in Demers, "'Lactilla' and 'Stella' Reconsidered," 145.

28. Roberts, *Memoirs of Hannah More,* 2:81.

29. This engraving was cut by Wilson Lowry. See Freeman O'Donoghue, ed., *Catalogue of Engraved British Portraits* (London: Longmans and Co., 1914), 4:562.

30. This engraving was executed by James Heath from a portrait painted by John Opie in 1786. More is also wearing long lappets.

31. H. R. Plomer, ed., *A Dictionary of the Printers and Booksellers who were at work in England, Scotland and Ireland* (Oxford: Bibliographical Society at the Oxford University Press, 1932 [for 1930]), 215.

32. Ibid. Not only did the Robinsons take on Yearsley at the height of the controversy with More, but they were fined in 1793 for selling copies of Thomas Paine's *Rights of Man.* The Robinsons apparently had laboring-class sympathies.

33. Ferguson, "Resistance and Power," 253.

34. A point made by Landry, *Muses,* 157.

35. Ibid.

36. See Ferguson, *Eighteenth-Century Women Poets,* 76-77.

37. For the poetic movement toward meditation and self-expression in the late-century period, see Marshall Brown, *Preromanticism* (Stanford: Stanford University Press, 1991); and P. W. K. Stone, *The Art of Poetry, 1750-1820* (New York: Barnes & Noble, Inc., 1967), esp. 84-103.

38. See, for example, Jennifer Breen, ed., *Women Romantic Poets, 1785-1832: An Anthology* (London: J. M. Dent & Sons, Ltd., 1992), 96-103; and Jerome J. McGann, ed., *The New Oxford Book of Romantic Period Verse* (Oxford and New York: Oxford University Press, 1993), 7-8.

39. Waldron, *Lactilla, Milkwoman of Clifton,* 150.

40. Ibid., 46. I take issue with Waldron's overarching claim that Yearsley felt "misrepresented and miscategorized" by her patrons in print in 1785. Though plausible in the context of Yearsley's sense of class pride, there remains the issue of her natural genius, and the fact that Yearsley maintained specific features of her public representation left over from More's editorship. For a further discussion of Yearsley's relationship to contemporary theories of genius, see Tim Burke, "Ann Yearsley and the Distribution of Genius in Early Romantic Culture," in *Early Romantics: Perspectives in British Poetry from Pope to Wordsworth,* ed. Thomas Woodman (London and New York: Macmillan and St. Martin's, 1998), 215-30.

41. Ann Yearsley, *A Poem on the Inhumanity of the Slave-Trade* (London, 1788), 5.

42. *The Monthly Review* 78 (March 1788): 246. Perhaps for effect, the editors juxtaposed the reviews of each author's slavery poem.

43. Davidoff and Hall, *Family Fortunes,* 167.

44. Roberts, *Memoirs of Hannah More,* 1:390-91.

45. Hannah More, *Thoughts on the Importance of the Manners of the Great to General Society,* in *The Works of Hannah More* (London, 1834), 2:254-55. Hereafter cited appropriately in the text.

46. Susan Pedersen, "Hannah More Meets Simple Simon: Tracts, Chapbooks, and Popular Culture in Late Eighteenth-Century England," *Journal of British Studies* 25 (1986): 84-113; quotation, 106.

47. [Hannah More], *Village Politics* (Manchester, 1793), title page. Hereafter cited appropriately in the text.

48. M. G. Jones, *Hannah More* (Cambridge: Cambridge University Press, 1952), 134.

49. Rogers, *Work and Wages* [(London: Swan Sonnen Scein & Co., 1902)], 118.

50. Roberts, *Memoirs of Hannah More,* 2:386.

51. For information regarding publication and circulation figures of the Cheap Repository tracts, see Pedersen, "Hannah More Meets Simple Simon," 112.

52. For example, a reviewer of Yearsley's play *Earl Goodwin* (1790) wrote in the *GM* that: "In the evening was performed at the Theatre at Bath, a maiden tragedy of the celebrated Mrs. Yearsley, the Bristol milkwoman. It was called Goodwin, and was very much approved. And on Monday the 9th it was performed again at Bristol, to a very genteel and numerous audience.—The language is said to be highly poetical" (*GM* [*The Gentleman's Magazine*] 66, part 2 [November 1789]: 111).

FURTHER READING

Biography

Waldron, Mary. *Lactilla, Milkwoman of Clifton: The Life and Writings of Ann Yearsley, 1753-1806,* Athens: University of Georgia Press, 1996, 339 p.

Full-length bio-critical study of Yearsley.

Criticism

Cole, Lucinda, and Richard G. Swartz. "'Why Should I Wish for Words?': Literacy, Articulation, and the Borders of Literary Culture." In *At the Limits of Romanticism: Essays in Cultural, Feminist, and Materialist Criticism,* edited by Mary A. Favret and Nicola J. Watson, pp. 143-69. Bloomington: Indiana University Press, 1994.

Examines how Yearsley and Dorothy Wordsworth negotiated literary culture in their writings.

Kahn, Madeline. "The Milkmaid's Voice: Ann Yearsley and the Romantic Notion of the Poet." In *Approaches to Teaching British Women Poets of the Romantic Period,* edited by Stephen C. Behrendt and Harriet Kramer Linkin, pp. 141-47. New York: Modern Language Association of America, 1997.

Discusses Yearsley in the context of the canonical Romantic poets, especially William Wordsworth.

Kucich, Greg. "Women's Historiography and the (Dis)Embodiment of Law: Ann Yearsley, Mary Hays, Elizabeth Benger." *Wordsworth Circle* 33, no. 1 (winter 2002): 3-7.

Compares Yearsley's historical drama *Earl Goodwin* with histories written by Mary Hays and Elizabeth Benger, particularly studying their treatment of legal persecution of women.

Landry, Donna. "The Complex Contradictions of Ann Yearsley: Working-class Writer, Bourgeois Subject?" In *The Muses of Resistance: Laboring-class Women's Poetry in Britain, 1739-1796,* pp. 120-85. Cambridge: Cambridge University Press, 1990.

Examines Yearsley's writings in the historical and social context of late eighteenth-century England.

Mitchell, Robert Edward. "'The Soul That Dreams It Shares the Power It Feels So Well': The Politics of Sympathy in the Abolitionist Verse of Williams and Yearsley." *Romanticism on the Net,* nos. 29-30 (February-May 2003): <http://www.erudit.org/revue/ron/2003/v/n29/007719ar.html>.

Analyzes the sophisticated strategies that Yearsley and Helen Maria Williams employed for eliciting sympathetic identification with the enslaved in their respective long poems against the eighteenth-century slave trade.

Southey, Robert. "Ann Yearsley." In *Attempts in Verse, by John Jones, an Old Servant: With Some Account of the Writer, Written by Himself: And an Introductory Essay on the Lives and Works of Our Uneducated Poets, by Robert Southey, Esq., Poet Laureate,* pp. 125-34. London: John Murray, 1831.

Brief overview of Yearsley; admires her poetry for originality and depth of feeling.

Waldron, Mary. "'By No Means Milk and Water Matters': The Contribution to English Poetry of Ann Yearsley, Milkwoman of Clifton, 1753-1806." *Studies on Voltaire and the Eighteenth Century* 304 (1992): 801-04.

Sketch of Yearsley that briefly assesses her works, asserting that her poetry in particular is worthy of study.

Wordsworth, Jonathan. "Ann Yearsley to Caroline Norton: Women Poets of the Romantic Period." *Wordsworth Circle* 26, no. 3 (summer 1995): 114-24.

Overview of several women poets, giving particular attention to Yearsley and to Caroline Norton. Discusses the themes of their poetry, noting that the topic of injustice occurs frequently in Yearsley's writings.

Additional coverage of Yearsley's life and career is contained in the following sources published by Thomson Gale: *Dictionary of Literary Biography,* **Vol. 109; and** *Literature Resource Center.*

How to Use This Index

The main references

> **Calvino, Italo**
> 1923-1985 .... CLC 5, 8, 11, 22, 33, 39,
> 73; SSC 3, 48

list all author entries in the following Thomson Gale Literary Criticism series:

AAL = *Asian American Literature*
BG = *The Beat Generation: A Gale Critical Companion*
BLC = *Black Literature Criticism*
BLCS = *Black Literature Criticism Supplement*
CLC = *Contemporary Literary Criticism*
CLR = *Children's Literature Review*
CMLC = *Classical and Medieval Literature Criticism*
DC = *Drama Criticism*
FL = *Feminism in Literature: A Gale Critical Companion*
GL = *Gothic Literature: A Gale Critical Companion*
HLC = *Hispanic Literature Criticism*
HLCS = *Hispanic Literature Criticism Supplement*
HR = *Harlem Renaissance: A Gale Critical Companion*
LC = *Literature Criticism from 1400 to 1800*
NCLC = *Nineteenth-Century Literature Criticism*
NNAL = *Native North American Literature*
PC = *Poetry Criticism*
SSC = *Short Story Criticism*
TCLC = *Twentieth-Century Literary Criticism*
WLC = *World Literature Criticism, 1500 to the Present*
WLCS = *World Literature Criticism Supplement*

The cross-references

> See also CA 85-88, 116; CANR 23, 61;
> DAM NOV; DLB 196; EW 13; MTCW 1, 2;
> RGSF 2; RGWL 2; SFW 4; SSFS 12

list all author entries in the following Thomson Gale biographical and literary sources:

AAYA = *Authors & Artists for Young Adults*
AFAW = *African American Writers*
AFW = *African Writers*
AITN = *Authors in the News*
AMW = *American Writers*
AMWR = *American Writers Retrospective Supplement*
AMWS = *American Writers Supplement*
ANW = *American Nature Writers*
AW = *Ancient Writers*
BEST = *Bestsellers*
BPFB = *Beacham's Encyclopedia of Popular Fiction: Biography and Resources*
BRW = *British Writers*
BRWS = *British Writers Supplement*
BW = *Black Writers*
BYA = *Beacham's Guide to Literature for Young Adults*
CA = *Contemporary Authors*
CAAS = *Contemporary Authors Autobiography Series*
CABS = *Contemporary Authors Bibliographical Series*
CAD = *Contemporary American Dramatists*
CANR = *Contemporary Authors New Revision Series*
CAP = *Contemporary Authors Permanent Series*
CBD = *Contemporary British Dramatists*
CCA = *Contemporary Canadian Authors*
CD = *Contemporary Dramatists*
CDALB = *Concise Dictionary of American Literary Biography*

CDALBS = *Concise Dictionary of American Literary Biography Supplement*
CDBLB = *Concise Dictionary of British Literary Biography*
CMW = *St. James Guide to Crime & Mystery Writers*
CN = *Contemporary Novelists*
CP = *Contemporary Poets*
CPW = *Contemporary Popular Writers*
CSW = *Contemporary Southern Writers*
CWD = *Contemporary Women Dramatists*
CWP = *Contemporary Women Poets*
CWRI = *St. James Guide to Children's Writers*
CWW = *Contemporary World Writers*
DA = *DISCovering Authors*
DA3 = *DISCovering Authors 3.0*
DAB = *DISCovering Authors: British Edition*
DAC = *DISCovering Authors: Canadian Edition*
DAM = *DISCovering Authors: Modules*
   DRAM: *Dramatists Module;* **MST:** *Most-studied Authors Module;*
   MULT: *Multicultural Authors Module;* **NOV:** *Novelists Module;*
   POET: *Poets Module;* **POP:** *Popular Fiction and Genre Authors Module*
DFS = *Drama for Students*
DLB = *Dictionary of Literary Biography*
DLBD = *Dictionary of Literary Biography Documentary Series*
DLBY = *Dictionary of Literary Biography Yearbook*
DNFS = *Literature of Developing Nations for Students*
EFS = *Epics for Students*
EXPN = *Exploring Novels*
EXPP = *Exploring Poetry*
EXPS = *Exploring Short Stories*
EW = *European Writers*
FANT = *St. James Guide to Fantasy Writers*
FW = *Feminist Writers*
GFL = *Guide to French Literature,* Beginnings to 1789, 1798 to the Present
GLL = *Gay and Lesbian Literature*
HGG = *St. James Guide to Horror, Ghost & Gothic Writers*
HW = *Hispanic Writers*
IDFW = *International Dictionary of Films and Filmmakers: Writers and Production Artists*
IDTP = *International Dictionary of Theatre: Playwrights*
LAIT = *Literature and Its Times*
LAW = *Latin American Writers*
JRDA = *Junior DISCovering Authors*
MAICYA = *Major Authors and Illustrators for Children and Young Adults*
MAICYAS = *Major Authors and Illustrators for Children and Young Adults Supplement*
MAWW = *Modern American Women Writers*
MJW = *Modern Japanese Writers*
MTCW = *Major 20th-Century Writers*
NCFS = *Nonfiction Classics for Students*
NFS = *Novels for Students*
PAB = *Poets: American and British*
PFS = *Poetry for Students*
RGAL = *Reference Guide to American Literature*
RGEL = *Reference Guide to English Literature*
RGSF = *Reference Guide to Short Fiction*
RGWL = *Reference Guide to World Literature*
RHW = *Twentieth-Century Romance and Historical Writers*
SAAS = *Something about the Author Autobiography Series*
SATA = *Something about the Author*
SFW = *St. James Guide to Science Fiction Writers*
SSFS = *Short Stories for Students*
TCWW = *Twentieth-Century Western Writers*
WLIT = *World Literature and Its Times*
WP = *World Poets*
YABC = *Yesterday's Authors of Books for Children*
YAW = *St. James Guide to Young Adult Writers*

Literary Criticism Series
Cumulative Author Index

Archer, Lee
See Ellison, Harlan (Jay)

Archilochus c. 7th cent. B.C.- .... **CMLC 44**
See also DLB 176

Arden, John 1930- .... **CLC 6, 13, 15**
See also BRWS 2; CA 13-16R; CAAS 4;
CANR 31, 65, 67, 124; CBD; CD 5, 6;
DAM DRAM; DFS 9; DLB 13, 245;
EWL 3; MTCW 1

Arenas, Reinaldo 1943-1990 .. **CLC 41; HLC
1**
See also CA 124; 128; 133; CANR 73, 106;
DAM MULT; DLB 145; EWL 3; GLL 2;
HW 1; LAW; LAWS 1; MTCW 2; MTFW
2005; RGSF 2; RGWL 3; WLIT 1

Arendt, Hannah 1906-1975 .... **CLC 66, 98**
See also CA 17-20R; 61-64; CANR 26, 60;
DLB 242; MTCW 1, 2

Aretino, Pietro 1492-1556 .... **LC 12**
See also RGWL 2, 3

Arghezi, Tudor .... **CLC 80**
See Theodorescu, Ion N.
See also CA 167; CDWLB 4; DLB 220;
EWL 3

Arguedas, Jose Maria 1911-1969 .... **CLC 10,
18; HLCS 1; TCLC 147**
See also CA 89-92; CANR 73; DLB 113;
EWL 3; HW 1; LAW; RGWL 2, 3; WLIT
1

Argueta, Manlio 1936- .... **CLC 31**
See also CA 131; CANR 73; CWW 2; DLB
145; EWL 3; HW 1; RGWL 3

Arias, Ron(ald Francis) 1941- .... **HLC 1**
See also CA 131; CANR 81, 136; DAM
MULT; DLB 82; HW 1, 2; MTCW 2;
MTFW 2005

Ariosto, Lodovico
See Ariosto, Ludovico
See also WLIT 7

Ariosto, Ludovico 1474-1533 ... **LC 6, 87; PC
42**
See Ariosto, Lodovico
See also EW 2; RGWL 2, 3

Aristides
See Epstein, Joseph

Aristophanes 450B.C.-385B.C. .... **CMLC 4,
51; DC 2; WLCS**
See also AW 1; CDWLB 1; DA; DA3;
DAB; DAC; DAM DRAM, MST; DFS
10; DLB 176; LMFS 1; RGWL 2, 3;
TWA; WLIT 8

Aristotle 384B.C.-322B.C. .... **CMLC 31;
WLCS**
See also AW 1; CDWLB 1; DA; DA3;
DAB; DAC; DAM MST; DLB 176;
RGWL 2, 3; TWA; WLIT 8

Arlt, Roberto (Godofredo Christophersen)
1900-1942 .... **HLC 1; TCLC 29**
See also CA 123; 131; CANR 67; DAM
MULT; DLB 305; EWL 3; HW 1, 2;
IDTP; LAW

Armah, Ayi Kwei 1939- . **BLC 1; CLC 5, 33,
136**
See also AFW; BRWS 10; BW 1; CA 61-
64; CANR 21, 64; CDWLB 3; CN 1, 2,
3, 4, 5, 6, 7; DAM MULT, POET; DLB
117; EWL 3; MTCW 1; WLIT 2

Armatrading, Joan 1950- .... **CLC 17**
See also CA 114; 186

Armin, Robert 1568(?)-1615(?) .... **LC 120**

Armitage, Frank
See Carpenter, John (Howard)

Armstrong, Jeannette (C.) 1948- .... **NNAL**
See also CA 149; CCA 1; CN 6, 7; DAC;
SATA 102

Arnette, Robert
See Silverberg, Robert

**Arnim, Achim von (Ludwig Joachim von
Arnim)** 1781-1831 .. **NCLC 5, 159; SSC
29**
See also DLB 90

Arnim, Bettina von 1785-1859 ...... **NCLC 38,
123**
See also DLB 90; RGWL 2, 3

Arnold, Matthew 1822-1888 ..... **NCLC 6, 29,
89, 126; PC 5; WLC 1**
See also BRW 5; CDBLB 1832-1890; DA;
DAB; DAC; DAM MST, POET; DLB 32,
57; EXPP; PAB; PFS 2; TEA; WP

Arnold, Thomas 1795-1842 .... **NCLC 18**
See also DLB 55

Arnow, Harriette (Louisa) Simpson
1908-1986 .... **CLC 2, 7, 18**
See also BPFB 1; CA 9-12R; 118; CANR
14; CN 2, 3, 4; DLB 6; FW; MTCW 1, 2;
RHW; SATA 42; SATA-Obit 47

Arouet, Francois-Marie
See Voltaire

Arp, Hans
See Arp, Jean

Arp, Jean 1887-1966 .... **CLC 5; TCLC 115**
See also CA 81-84; 25-28R; CANR 42, 77;
EW 10

Arrabal
See Arrabal, Fernando

Arrabal (Teran), Fernando
See Arrabal, Fernando
See also CWW 2

Arrabal, Fernando 1932- ... **CLC 2, 9, 18, 58**
See Arrabal (Teran), Fernando
See also CA 9-12R; CANR 15; DLB 321;
EWL 3; LMFS 2

Arreola, Juan Jose 1918-2001 .... **CLC 147;
HLC 1; SSC 38**
See also CA 113; 131; 200; CANR 81;
CWW 2; DAM MULT; DLB 113; DNFS
2; EWL 3; HW 1, 2; LAW; RGSF 2

Arrian c. 89(?)-c. 155(?) .... **CMLC 43**
See also DLB 176

Arrick, Fran .... **CLC 30**
See Gaberman, Judie Angell
See also BYA 6

Arrley, Richmond
See Delany, Samuel R(ay), Jr.

Artaud, Antonin (Marie Joseph)
1896-1948 .... **DC 14; TCLC 3, 36**
See also CA 104; 149; DA3; DAM DRAM;
DFS 22; DLB 258, 321; EW 11; EWL 3;
GFL 1789 to the Present; MTCW 2;
MTFW 2005; RGWL 2, 3

Arthur, Ruth M(abel) 1905-1979 ..... **CLC 12**
See also CA 9-12R; 85-88; CANR 4; CWRI
5; SATA 7, 26

Artsybashev, Mikhail (Petrovich)
1878-1927 .... **TCLC 31**
See also CA 170; DLB 295

Arundel, Honor (Morfydd)
1919-1973 .... **CLC 17**
See also CA 21-22; 41-44R; CAP 2; CLR
35; CWRI 5; SATA 4; SATA-Obit 24

Arzner, Dorothy 1900-1979 .... **CLC 98**

Asch, Sholem 1880-1957 .... **TCLC 3**
See also CA 105; EWL 3; GLL 2; RGHL

Ascham, Roger 1516(?)-1568 .... **LC 101**
See also DLB 236

Ash, Shalom
See Asch, Sholem

Ashbery, John (Lawrence) 1927- .. **CLC 2, 3,
4, 6, 9, 13, 15, 25, 41, 77, 125, 221; PC
26**
See Berry, Jonas
See also AMWS 3; CA 5-8R; CANR 9, 37,
66, 102, 132; CP 1, 2, 3, 4, 5, 6, 7; DA3;
DAM POET; DLB 5, 165; DLBY 1981;
EWL 3; INT CANR-9; MAL 5; MTCW
1, 2; MTFW 2005; PAB; PFS 11; RGAL
4; TCLE 1:1; WP

Ashdown, Clifford
See Freeman, R(ichard) Austin

Ashe, Gordon
See Creasey, John

Ashton-Warner, Sylvia (Constance)
1908-1984 .... **CLC 19**
See also CA 69-72; 112; CANR 29; CN 1,
2, 3; MTCW 1, 2

Asimov, Isaac 1920-1992 ..... **CLC 1, 3, 9, 19,
26, 76, 92**
See also AAYA 13; BEST 90:2; BPFB 1;
BYA 4, 6, 7, 9; CA 1-4R; 137; CANR 2,
19, 36, 60, 125; CLR 12, 79; CMW 4;
CN 1, 2, 3, 4, 5; CPW; DA3; DAM POP;
DLB 8; DLBY 1992; INT CANR-19;
JRDA; LAIT 5; LMFS 2; MAICYA 1, 2;
MAL 5; MTCW 1, 2; MTFW 2005;
RGAL 4; SATA 1, 26, 74; SCFW 1, 2;
SFW 4; SSFS 17; TUS; YAW

Askew, Anne 1521(?)-1546 .... **LC 81**
See also DLB 136

Assis, Joaquim Maria Machado de
See Machado de Assis, Joaquim Maria

Astell, Mary 1666-1731 .... **LC 68**
See also DLB 252; FW

Astley, Thea (Beatrice May)
1925-2004 .... **CLC 41**
See also CA 65-68; 229; CANR 11, 43, 78;
CN 1, 2, 3, 4, 5, 6, 7; DLB 289; EWL 3

Astley, William 1855-1911
See Warung, Price

Aston, James
See White, T(erence) H(anbury)

Asturias, Miguel Angel 1899-1974 .... **CLC 3,
8, 13; HLC 1**
See also CA 25-28; 49-52; CANR 32; CAP
2; CDWLB 3; DA3; DAM MULT, NOV;
DLB 113, 290; EWL 3; HW 1; LAW;
LMFS 2; MTCW 1, 2; RGWL 2, 3; WLIT
1

Atares, Carlos Saura
See Saura (Atares), Carlos

Athanasius c. 295-c. 373 .... **CMLC 48**

Atheling, William
See Pound, Ezra (Weston Loomis)

Atheling, William, Jr.
See Blish, James (Benjamin)

Atherton, Gertrude (Franklin Horn)
1857-1948 .... **TCLC 2**
See also CA 104; 155; DLB 9, 78, 186;
HGG; RGAL 4; SUFW 1; TCWW 1, 2

Atherton, Lucius
See Masters, Edgar Lee

Atkins, Jack
See Harris, Mark

Atkinson, Kate 1951- .... **CLC 99**
See also CA 166; CANR 101, 153; DLB
267

Attaway, William (Alexander)
1911-1986 .... **BLC 1; CLC 92**
See also BW 2, 3; CA 143; CANR 82;
DAM MULT; DLB 76; MAL 5

Atticus
See Fleming, Ian (Lancaster); Wilson,
(Thomas) Woodrow

Atwood, Margaret 1939- . **CLC 2, 3, 4, 8, 13,
15, 25, 44, 84, 135; PC 8; SSC 2, 46;
WLC 1**
See also AAYA 12, 47; AMWS 13; BEST
89:2; BPFB 1; CA 49-52; CANR 3, 24,
33, 59, 95, 133; CN 2, 3, 4, 5, 6, 7; CP 1,
2, 3, 4, 5, 6, 7; CPW; CWP; DA; DA3;
DAB; DAC; DAM MST, NOV, POET;
DLB 53, 251, 326; EWL 3; EXPN; FL
1:5; FW; GL 2; INT CANR-24; LAIT 5;
MTCW 1, 2; MTFW 2005; NFS 4, 12,
13, 14, 19; PFS 7; RGSF 2; SATA 50,
170; SSFS 3, 13; TCLE 1:1; TWA; WWE
1; YAW

Bakunin, Mikhail (Alexandrovich)
1814-1876 .... **NCLC 25, 58**
See also DLB 277

Baldwin, James (Arthur) 1924-1987 . **BLC 1;**
CLC 1, 2, 3, 4, 5, 8, 13, 15, 17, 42, 50,
67, 90, 127; DC 1; SSC 10, 33; WLC 1
See also AAYA 4, 34; AFAW 1, 2; AMWR
2; AMWS 1; BPFB 1; BW 1; CA 1-4R;
124; CABS 1; CAD; CANR 3, 24;
CDALB 1941-1968; CN 1, 2, 3, 4; CPW;
DA; DA3; DAB; DAC; DAM MST,
MULT, NOV, POP; DFS 11, 15; DLB 2,
7, 33, 249, 278; DLBY 1987; EWL 3;
EXPS; LAIT 5; MAL 5; MTCW 1, 2;
MTFW 2005; NCFS 4; NFS 4; RGAL 4;
RGSF 2; SATA 9; SATA-Obit 54; SSFS
2, 18; TUS

Baldwin, William c. 1515-1563 .... **LC 113**
See also DLB 132

Bale, John 1495-1563 .... **LC 62**
See also DLB 132; RGEL 2; TEA

Ball, Hugo 1886-1927 .... **TCLC 104**

Ballard, J(ames) G(raham) 1930- . **CLC 3, 6,**
14, 36, 137; SSC 1, 53
See also AAYA 3, 52; BRWS 5; CA 5-8R;
CANR 15, 39, 65, 107, 133; CN 1, 2, 3,
4, 5, 6, 7; DA3; DAM NOV, POP; DLB
14, 207, 261, 319; EWL 3; HGG; MTCW
1, 2; MTFW 2005; NFS 8; RGEL 2;
RGSF 2; SATA 93; SCFW 1, 2; SFW 4

Balmont, Konstantin (Dmitriyevich)
1867-1943 .... **TCLC 11**
See also CA 109; 155; DLB 295; EWL 3

Baltausis, Vincas 1847-1910
See Mikszath, Kalman

Balzac, Honore de 1799-1850 ... **NCLC 5, 35,**
53, 153; SSC 5, 59; WLC 1
See also DA; DA3; DAB; DAC; DAM
MST, NOV; DLB 119; EW 5; GFL 1789
to the Present; LMFS 1; RGSF 2; RGWL
2, 3; SSFS 10; SUFW; TWA

Bambara, Toni Cade 1939-1995 .... **BLC 1;**
CLC 19, 88; SSC 35; TCLC 116;
WLCS
See also AAYA 5, 49; AFAW 2; AMWS 11;
BW 2, 3; BYA 12, 14; CA 29-32R; 150;
CANR 24, 49, 81; CDALBS; DA; DA3;
DAC; DAM MST, MULT; DLB 38, 218;
EXPS; MAL 5; MTCW 1, 2; MTFW
2005; RGAL 4; RGSF 2; SATA 112; SSFS
4, 7, 12, 21

Bamdad, A.
See Shamlu, Ahmad

Bamdad, Alef
See Shamlu, Ahmad

Banat, D. R.
See Bradbury, Ray (Douglas)

Bancroft, Laura
See Baum, L(yman) Frank

Banim, John 1798-1842 .... **NCLC 13**
See also DLB 116, 158, 159; RGEL 2

Banim, Michael 1796-1874 .... **NCLC 13**
See also DLB 158, 159

Banjo, The
See Paterson, A(ndrew) B(arton)

Banks, Iain
See Banks, Iain M(enzies)
See also BRWS 11

Banks, Iain M(enzies) 1954- .... **CLC 34**
See Banks, Iain
See also CA 123; 128; CANR 61, 106; DLB
194, 261; EWL 3; HGG; INT CA-128;
MTFW 2005; SFW 4

Banks, Lynne Reid .... **CLC 23**
See Reid Banks, Lynne
See also AAYA 6; BYA 7; CLR 86; CN 4,
5, 6

Banks, Russell (Earl) 1940- .... **CLC 37, 72,**
187; SSC 42
See also AAYA 45; AMWS 5; CA 65-68;
CAAS 15; CANR 19, 52, 73, 118; CN 4,
5, 6, 7; DLB 130, 278; EWL 3; MAL 5;
MTCW 2; MTFW 2005; NFS 13

Banville, John 1945- .... **CLC 46, 118, 224**
See also CA 117; 128; CANR 104, 150; CN
4, 5, 6, 7; DLB 14, 271, 326; INT CA-
128

Banville, Theodore (Faullain) de
1832-1891 .... **NCLC 9**
See also DLB 217; GFL 1789 to the Present

Baraka, Amiri 1934- .... **BLC 1; CLC 1, 2, 3,**
5, 10, 14, 33, 115, 213; DC 6; PC 4;
WLCS
See Jones, LeRoi
See also AAYA 63; AFAW 1, 2; AMWS 2;
BW 2, 3; CA 21-24R; CABS 3; CAD;
CANR 27, 38, 61, 133; CD 3, 5, 6;
CDALB 1941-1968; CP 4, 5, 6, 7; CPW;
DA; DA3; DAC; DAM MST, MULT,
POET, POP; DFS 3, 11, 16; DLB 5, 7,
16, 38; DLBD 8; EWL 3; MAL 5; MTCW
1, 2; MTFW 2005; PFS 9; RGAL 4;
TCLE 1:1; TUS; WP

Baratynsky, Evgenii Abramovich
1800-1844 .... **NCLC 103**
See also DLB 205

Barbauld, Anna Laetitia
1743-1825 .... **NCLC 50**
See also DLB 107, 109, 142, 158; RGEL 2

Barbellion, W. N. P. .... **TCLC 24**
See Cummings, Bruce F(rederick)

Barber, Benjamin R. 1939- .... **CLC 141**
See also CA 29-32R; CANR 12, 32, 64, 119

Barbera, Jack (Vincent) 1945- .... **CLC 44**
See also CA 110; CANR 45

Barbey d'Aurevilly, Jules-Amedee
1808-1889 .... **NCLC 1; SSC 17**
See also DLB 119; GFL 1789 to the Present

Barbour, John c. 1316-1395 .... **CMLC 33**
See also DLB 146

Barbusse, Henri 1873-1935 .... **TCLC 5**
See also CA 105; 154; DLB 65; EWL 3;
RGWL 2, 3

Barclay, Alexander c. 1475-1552 .... **LC 109**
See also DLB 132

Barclay, Bill
See Moorcock, Michael

Barclay, William Ewert
See Moorcock, Michael

Barea, Arturo 1897-1957 .... **TCLC 14**
See also CA 111; 201

Barfoot, Joan 1946- .... **CLC 18**
See also CA 105; CANR 141

Barham, Richard Harris
1788-1845 .... **NCLC 77**
See also DLB 159

Baring, Maurice 1874-1945 .... **TCLC 8**
See also CA 105; 168; DLB 34; HGG

Baring-Gould, Sabine 1834-1924 ... **TCLC 88**
See also DLB 156, 190

Barker, Clive 1952- .... **CLC 52, 205; SSC 53**
See also AAYA 10, 54; BEST 90:3; BPFB
1; CA 121; 129; CANR 71, 111, 133;
CPW; DA3; DAM POP; DLB 261; HGG;
INT CA-129; MTCW 1, 2; MTFW 2005;
SUFW 2

Barker, George Granville
1913-1991 .... **CLC 8, 48**
See also CA 9-12R; 135; CANR 7, 38; CP
1, 2, 3, 4, 5; DAM POET; DLB 20; EWL
3; MTCW 1

Barker, Harley Granville
See Granville-Barker, Harley
See also DLB 10

Barker, Howard 1946- .... **CLC 37**
See also CA 102; CBD; CD 5, 6; DLB 13,
233

Barker, Jane 1652-1732 .... **LC 42, 82**
See also DLB 39, 131

Barker, Pat 1943- .... **CLC 32, 94, 146**
See also BRWS 4; CA 117; 122; CANR 50,
101, 148; CN 6, 7; DLB 271, 326; INT
CA-122

Barker, Patricia
See Barker, Pat

Barlach, Ernst (Heinrich)
1870-1938 .... **TCLC 84**
See also CA 178; DLB 56, 118; EWL 3

Barlow, Joel 1754-1812 .... **NCLC 23**
See also AMWS 2; DLB 37; RGAL 4

Barnard, Mary (Ethel) 1909- .... **CLC 48**
See also CA 21-22; CAP 2; CP 1

Barnes, Djuna 1892-1982 .... **CLC 3, 4, 8, 11,**
29, 127; SSC 3
See Steptoe, Lydia
See also AMWS 3; CA 9-12R; 107; CAD;
CANR 16, 55; CN 1, 2, 3; CWD; DLB 4,
9, 45; EWL 3; GLL 1; MAL 5; MTCW 1,
2; MTFW 2005; RGAL 4; TCLE 1:1;
TUS

Barnes, Jim 1933- .... **NNAL**
See also CA 108; 175; CAAE 175; CAAS
28; DLB 175

Barnes, Julian 1946- .... **CLC 42, 141**
See also BRWS 4; CA 102; CANR 19, 54,
115, 137; CN 4, 5, 6, 7; DAB; DLB 194;
DLBY 1993; EWL 3; MTCW 2; MTFW
2005

Barnes, Julian Patrick
See Barnes, Julian

Barnes, Peter 1931-2004 .... **CLC 5, 56**
See also CA 65-68; 230; CAAS 12; CANR
33, 34, 64, 113; CBD; CD 5, 6; DFS 6;
DLB 13, 233; MTCW 1

Barnes, William 1801-1886 .... **NCLC 75**
See also DLB 32

Baroja, Pio 1872-1956 .... **HLC 1; TCLC 8**
See also CA 104; 247; EW 9

Baroja y Nessi, Pio
See Baroja, Pio

Baron, David
See Pinter, Harold

Baron Corvo
See Rolfe, Frederick (William Serafino Austin Lewis Mary)

Barondess, Sue K(aufman)
1926-1977 .... **CLC 8**
See Kaufman, Sue
See also CA 1-4R; 69-72; CANR 1

Baron de Teive
See Pessoa, Fernando (Antonio Nogueira)

Baroness Von S.
See Zangwill, Israel

Barres, (Auguste-)Maurice
1862-1923 .... **TCLC 47**
See also CA 164; DLB 123; GFL 1789 to
the Present

Barreto, Afonso Henrique de Lima
See Lima Barreto, Afonso Henrique de

Barrett, Andrea 1954- .... **CLC 150**
See also CA 156; CANR 92; CN 7

Barrett, Michele .... **CLC 65**

Barrett, (Roger) Syd 1946-2006 .... **CLC 35**

Barrett, William (Christopher)
1913-1992 .... **CLC 27**
See also CA 13-16R; 139; CANR 11, 67;
INT CANR-11

Barrett Browning, Elizabeth
1806-1861 ...... **NCLC 1, 16, 61, 66, 170;**
PC 6, 62; WLC 1
See also AAYA 63; BRW 4; CDBLB 1832-
1890; DA; DA3; DAB; DAC; DAM MST,
POET; DLB 32, 199; EXPP; FL 1:2; PAB;
PFS 2, 16, 23; TEA; WLIT 4; WP

Bird, Cordwainer
See Ellison, Harlan (Jay)
Bird, Robert Montgomery
1806-1854 .... **NCLC 1**
See also DLB 202; RGAL 4
Birkerts, Sven 1951- .... **CLC 116**
See also CA 128; 133, 176; CAAE 176;
CAAS 29; CANR 151; INT CA-133
Birney, (Alfred) Earle 1904-1995 .. **CLC 1, 4,**
6, 11; PC 52
See also CA 1-4R; CANR 5, 20; CN 1, 2,
3, 4; CP 1, 2, 3, 4, 5, 6; DAC; DAM MST,
POET; DLB 88; MTCW 1; PFS 8; RGEL
2
Biruni, al 973-1048(?) .... **CMLC 28**
Bishop, Elizabeth 1911-1979 ..... **CLC 1, 4, 9,**
13, 15, 32; PC 3, 34; TCLC 121
See also AMWR 2; AMWS 1; CA 5-8R;
89-92; CABS 2; CANR 26, 61, 108;
CDALB 1968-1988; CP 1, 2, 3; DA;
DA3; DAC; DAM MST, POET; DLB 5,
169; EWL 3; GLL 2; MAL 5; MBL;
MTCW 1, 2; PAB; PFS 6, 12; RGAL 4;
SATA-Obit 24; TUS; WP
Bishop, John 1935- .... **CLC 10**
See also CA 105
Bishop, John Peale 1892-1944 ..... **TCLC 103**
See also CA 107; 155; DLB 4, 9, 45; MAL
5; RGAL 4
Bissett, Bill 1939- .... **CLC 18; PC 14**
See also CA 69-72; CAAS 19; CANR 15;
CCA 1; CP 1, 2, 3, 4, 5, 6, 7; DLB 53;
MTCW 1
Bissoondath, Neil (Devindra)
1955- .... **CLC 120**
See also CA 136; CANR 123; CN 6, 7;
DAC
Bitov, Andrei (Georgievich) 1937- ... **CLC 57**
See also CA 142; DLB 302
Biyidi, Alexandre 1932-
See Beti, Mongo
See also BW 1, 3; CA 114; 124; CANR 81;
DA3; MTCW 1, 2
Bjarme, Brynjolf
See Ibsen, Henrik (Johan)
Bjoernson, Bjoernstjerne (Martinius)
1832-1910 .... **TCLC 7, 37**
See also CA 104
Black, Benjamin
See Banville, John
Black, Robert
See Holdstock, Robert P.
Blackburn, Paul 1926-1971 .... **CLC 9, 43**
See also BG 1:2; CA 81-84; 33-36R; CANR
34; CP 1; DLB 16; DLBY 1981
Black Elk 1863-1950 .... **NNAL; TCLC 33**
See also CA 144; DAM MULT; MTCW 2;
MTFW 2005; WP
Black Hawk 1767-1838 .... **NNAL**
Black Hobart
See Sanders, (James) Ed(ward)
Blacklin, Malcolm
See Chambers, Aidan
Blackmore, R(ichard) D(oddridge)
1825-1900 .... **TCLC 27**
See also CA 120; DLB 18; RGEL 2
Blackmur, R(ichard) P(almer)
1904-1965 .... **CLC 2, 24**
See also AMWS 2; CA 11-12; 25-28R;
CANR 71; CAP 1; DLB 63; EWL 3;
MAL 5
Black Tarantula
See Acker, Kathy
Blackwood, Algernon (Henry)
1869-1951 .... **TCLC 5**
See also CA 105; 150; DLB 153, 156, 178;
HGG; SUFW 1

Blackwood, Caroline (Maureen)
1931-1996 .... **CLC 6, 9, 100**
See also BRWS 9; CA 85-88; 151; CANR
32, 61, 65; CN 3, 4, 5, 6; DLB 14, 207;
HGG; MTCW 1
Blade, Alexander
See Hamilton, Edmond; Silverberg, Robert
Blaga, Lucian 1895-1961 .... **CLC 75**
See also CA 157; DLB 220; EWL 3
Blair, Eric (Arthur) 1903-1950 .... **TCLC 123**
See Orwell, George
See also CA 104; 132; DA; DA3; DAB;
DAC; DAM MST, NOV; MTCW 1, 2;
MTFW 2005; SATA 29
Blair, Hugh 1718-1800 .... **NCLC 75**
Blais, Marie-Claire 1939- .... **CLC 2, 4, 6, 13,**
22
See also CA 21-24R; CAAS 4; CANR 38,
75, 93; CWW 2; DAC; DAM MST; DLB
53; EWL 3; FW; MTCW 1, 2; MTFW
2005; TWA
Blaise, Clark 1940- .... **CLC 29**
See also AITN 2; CA 53-56, 231; CAAE
231; CAAS 3; CANR 5, 66, 106; CN 4,
5, 6, 7; DLB 53; RGSF 2
Blake, Fairley
See De Voto, Bernard (Augustine)
Blake, Nicholas
See Day Lewis, C(ecil)
See also DLB 77; MSW
Blake, Sterling
See Benford, Gregory (Albert)
Blake, William 1757-1827 . **NCLC 13, 37, 57,**
127, 173; PC 12, 63; WLC 1
See also AAYA 47; BRW 3; BRWR 1; CD-
BLB 1789-1832; CLR 52; DA; DA3;
DAB; DAC; DAM MST, POET; DLB 93,
163; EXPP; LATS 1:1; LMFS 1; MAI-
CYA 1, 2; PAB; PFS 2, 12, 24; SATA 30;
TEA; WCH; WLIT 3; WP
Blanchot, Maurice 1907-2003 .... **CLC 135**
See also CA 117; 144; 213; CANR 138;
DLB 72, 296; EWL 3
Blasco Ibanez, Vicente 1867-1928 . **TCLC 12**
See Ibanez, Vicente Blasco
See also BPFB 1; CA 110; 131; CANR 81;
DA3; DAM NOV; EW 8; EWL 3; HW 1,
2; MTCW 1
Blatty, William Peter 1928- .... **CLC 2**
See also CA 5-8R; CANR 9, 124; DAM
POP; HGG
Bleeck, Oliver
See Thomas, Ross (Elmore)
Blessing, Lee (Knowlton) 1949- .... **CLC 54**
See also CA 236; CAD; CD 5, 6; DFS 23
Blight, Rose
See Greer, Germaine
Blish, James (Benjamin) 1921-1975 . **CLC 14**
See also BPFB 1; CA 1-4R; 57-60; CANR
3; CN 2; DLB 8; MTCW 1; SATA 66;
SCFW 1, 2; SFW 4
Bliss, Frederick
See Card, Orson Scott
Bliss, Reginald
See Wells, H(erbert) G(eorge)
Blixen, Karen (Christentze Dinesen)
1885-1962
See Dinesen, Isak
See also CA 25-28; CANR 22, 50; CAP 2;
DA3; DLB 214; LMFS 1; MTCW 1, 2;
SATA 44; SSFS 20
Bloch, Robert (Albert) 1917-1994 .... **CLC 33**
See also AAYA 29; CA 5-8R, 179; 146;
CAAE 179; CAAS 20; CANR 5, 78;
DA3; DLB 44; HGG; INT CANR-5;
MTCW 2; SATA 12; SATA-Obit 82; SFW
4; SUFW 1, 2

Blok, Alexander (Alexandrovich)
1880-1921 .... **PC 21; TCLC 5**
See also CA 104; 183; DLB 295; EW 9;
EWL 3; LMFS 2; RGWL 2, 3
Blom, Jan
See Breytenbach, Breyten
Bloom, Harold 1930- .... **CLC 24, 103, 221**
See also CA 13-16R; CANR 39, 75, 92,
133; DLB 67; EWL 3; MTCW 2; MTFW
2005; RGAL 4
Bloomfield, Aurelius
See Bourne, Randolph S(illiman)
Bloomfield, Robert 1766-1823 ..... **NCLC 145**
See also DLB 93
Blount, Roy (Alton), Jr. 1941- .... **CLC 38**
See also CA 53-56; CANR 10, 28, 61, 125;
CSW; INT CANR-28; MTCW 1, 2;
MTFW 2005
Blowsnake, Sam 1875-(?) .... **NNAL**
Bloy, Leon 1846-1917 .... **TCLC 22**
See also CA 121; 183; DLB 123; GFL 1789
to the Present
Blue Cloud, Peter (Aroniawenrate)
1933- .... **NNAL**
See also CA 117; CANR 40; DAM MULT
Bluggage, Oranthy
See Alcott, Louisa May
Blume, Judy (Sussman) 1938- .... **CLC 12, 30**
See also AAYA 3, 26; BYA 1, 8, 12; CA 29-
32R; CANR 13, 37, 66; CLR 2, 15,
69; CPW; DA3; DAM NOV, POP; DLB
52; JRDA; MAICYA 1, 2; MAICYAS 1;
MTCW 1, 2; MTFW 2005; SATA 2, 31,
79, 142; WYA; YAW
Blunden, Edmund (Charles)
1896-1974 .... **CLC 2, 56; PC 66**
See also BRW 6; BRWS 11; CA 17-18; 45-
48; CANR 54; CAP 2; CP 1, 2; DLB 20,
100, 155; MTCW 1; PAB
Bly, Robert (Elwood) 1926- .... **CLC 1, 2, 5,**
10, 15, 38, 128; PC 39
See also AMWS 4; CA 5-8R; CANR 41,
73, 125; CP 1, 2, 3, 4, 5, 6, 7; DA3; DAM
POET; DLB 5; EWL 3; MAL 5; MTCW
1, 2; MTFW 2005; PFS 6, 17; RGAL 4
Boas, Franz 1858-1942 .... **TCLC 56**
See also CA 115; 181
Bobette
See Simenon, Georges (Jacques Christian)
Boccaccio, Giovanni 1313-1375 ... **CMLC 13,**
57; SSC 10, 87
See also EW 2; RGSF 2; RGWL 2, 3; TWA;
WLIT 7
Bochco, Steven 1943- .... **CLC 35**
See also AAYA 11, 71; CA 124; 138
Bode, Sigmund
See O'Doherty, Brian
Bodel, Jean 1167(?)-1210 .... **CMLC 28**
Bodenheim, Maxwell 1892-1954 .... **TCLC 44**
See also CA 110; 187; DLB 9, 45; MAL 5;
RGAL 4
Bodenheimer, Maxwell
See Bodenheim, Maxwell
Bodker, Cecil 1927-
See Bodker, Cecil
Bodker, Cecil 1927- .... **CLC 21**
See also CA 73-76; CANR 13, 44, 111;
CLR 23; MAICYA 1, 2; SATA 14, 133
Boell, Heinrich (Theodor)
1917-1985 ..... **CLC 2, 3, 6, 9, 11, 15, 27,**
32, 72; SSC 23; WLC 1
See Boll, Heinrich (Theodor)
See also CA 21-24R; 116; CANR 24; DA;
DA3; DAB; DAC; DAM MST, NOV;
DLB 69; DLBY 1985; MTCW 1, 2;
MTFW 2005; SSFS 20; TWA
Boerne, Alfred
See Doeblin, Alfred

Boyle, Mark
See Kienzle, William X(avier)
Boyle, Patrick 1905-1982 .... **CLC 19**
See also CA 127
Boyle, T. C.
See Boyle, T(homas) Coraghessan
See also AMWS 8
Boyle, T(homas) Coraghessan
1948- .... **CLC 36, 55, 90; SSC 16**
See Boyle, T. C.
See also AAYA 47; BEST 90:4; BPFB 1;
CA 120; CANR 44, 76, 89, 132; CN 6, 7;
CPW; DA3; DAM POP; DLB 218, 278;
DLBY 1986; EWL 3; MAL 5; MTCW 2;
MTFW 2005; SSFS 13, 19
Boz
See Dickens, Charles (John Huffam)
Brackenridge, Hugh Henry
1748-1816 .... **NCLC 7**
See also DLB 11, 37; RGAL 4
Bradbury, Edward P.
See Moorcock, Michael
See also MTCW 2
Bradbury, Malcolm (Stanley)
1932-2000 .... **CLC 32, 61**
See also CA 1-4R; CANR 1, 33, 91, 98,
137; CN 1, 2, 3, 4, 5, 6, 7; CP 1; DA3;
DAM NOV; DLB 14, 207; EWL 3;
MTCW 1, 2; MTFW 2005
Bradbury, Ray (Douglas) 1920- .... **CLC 1, 3,
10, 15, 42, 98; SSC 29, 53; WLC 1**
See also AAYA 15; AITN 1, 2; AMWS 4;
BPFB 1; BYA 4, 5, 11; CA 1-4R; CANR
2, 30, 75, 125; CDALB 1968-1988; CN
1, 2, 3, 4, 5, 6, 7; CPW; DA; DA3; DAB;
DAC; DAM MST, NOV, POP; DLB 2, 8;
EXPN; EXPS; HGG; LAIT 3, 5; LATS
1:2; LMFS 2; MAL 5; MTCW 1, 2;
MTFW 2005; NFS 1, 22; RGAL 4; RGSF
2; SATA 11, 64, 123; SCFW 1, 2; SFW 4;
SSFS 1, 20; SUFW 1, 2; TUS; YAW
Braddon, Mary Elizabeth
1837-1915 .... **TCLC 111**
See also BRWS 8; CA 108; 179; CMW 4;
DLB 18, 70, 156; HGG
Bradfield, Scott 1955- .... **SSC 65**
See also CA 147; CANR 90; HGG; SUFW
2
Bradfield, Scott Michael
See Bradfield, Scott
Bradford, Gamaliel 1863-1932 .... **TCLC 36**
See also CA 160; DLB 17
Bradford, William 1590-1657 .... **LC 64**
See also DLB 24, 30; RGAL 4
Bradley, David (Henry), Jr. 1950- .... **BLC 1;
CLC 23, 118**
See also BW 1, 3; CA 104; CANR 26, 81;
CN 4, 5, 6, 7; DAM MULT; DLB 33
Bradley, John Ed(mund, Jr.) 1958- . **CLC 55**
See also CA 139; CANR 99; CN 6, 7; CSW
Bradley, Marion Zimmer
1930-1999 .... **CLC 30**
See Chapman, Lee; Dexter, John; Gardner,
Miriam; Ives, Morgan; Rivers, Elfrida
See also AAYA 40; BPFB 1; CA 57-60; 185;
CAAS 10; CANR 7, 31, 51, 75, 107;
CPW; DA3; DAM POP; DLB 8; FANT;
FW; MTCW 1, 2; MTFW 2005; SATA 90,
139; SATA-Obit 116; SFW 4; SUFW 2;
YAW
Bradshaw, John 1933- .... **CLC 70**
See also CA 138; CANR 61
Bradstreet, Anne 1612(?)-1672 .... **LC 4, 30,
130; PC 10**
See also AMWS 1; CDALB 1640-1865;
DA; DA3; DAC; DAM MST, POET; DLB
24; EXPP; FW; PFS 6; RGAL 4; TUS;
WP
Brady, Joan 1939- .... **CLC 86**
See also CA 141

Bragg, Melvyn 1939- .... **CLC 10**
See also BEST 89:3; CA 57-60; CANR 10,
48, 89; CN 1, 2, 3, 4, 5, 6, 7; DLB 14,
271; RHW
Brahe, Tycho 1546-1601 .... **LC 45**
See also DLB 300
Braine, John (Gerard) 1922-1986 . **CLC 1, 3,
41**
See also CA 1-4R; 120; CANR 1, 33; CD-
BLB 1945-1960; CN 1, 2, 3, 4; DLB 15;
DLBY 1986; EWL 3; MTCW 1
Braithwaite, William Stanley (Beaumont)
1878-1962 .... **BLC 1; HR 1:2; PC 52**
See also BW 1; CA 125; DAM MULT; DLB
50, 54; MAL 5
Bramah, Ernest 1868-1942 .... **TCLC 72**
See also CA 156; CMW 4; DLB 70; FANT
Brammer, Billy Lee
See Brammer, William
Brammer, William 1929-1978 .... **CLC 31**
See also CA 235; 77-80
Brancati, Vitaliano 1907-1954 .... **TCLC 12**
See also CA 109; DLB 264; EWL 3
Brancato, Robin F(idler) 1936- .... **CLC 35**
See also AAYA 9, 68; BYA 6; CA 69-72;
CANR 11, 45; CLR 32; JRDA; MAICYA
2; MAICYAS 1; SAAS 9; SATA 97;
WYA; YAW
Brand, Dionne 1953- .... **CLC 192**
See also BW 2; CA 143; CANR 143; CWP
Brand, Max
See Faust, Frederick (Schiller)
See also BPFB 1; TCWW 1, 2
Brand, Millen 1906-1980 .... **CLC 7**
See also CA 21-24R; 97-100; CANR 72
Branden, Barbara .... **CLC 44**
See also CA 148
Brandes, Georg (Morris Cohen)
1842-1927 .... **TCLC 10**
See also CA 105; 189; DLB 300
Brandys, Kazimierz 1916-2000 .... **CLC 62**
See also CA 239; EWL 3
Branley, Franklyn M(ansfield)
1915-2002 .... **CLC 21**
See also CA 33-36R; 207; CANR 14, 39;
CLR 13; MAICYA 1, 2; SAAS 16; SATA
4, 68, 136
Brant, Beth (E.) 1941- .... **NNAL**
See also CA 144; FW
Brant, Sebastian 1457-1521 .... **LC 112**
See also DLB 179; RGWL 2, 3
Brathwaite, Edward Kamau
1930- .... **BLCS; CLC 11; PC 56**
See also BW 2, 3; CA 25-28R; CANR 11,
26, 47, 107; CDWLB 3; CP 1, 2, 3, 4, 5,
6, 7; DAM POET; DLB 125; EWL 3
Brathwaite, Kamau
See Brathwaite, Edward Kamau
Brautigan, Richard (Gary)
1935-1984 .... **CLC 1, 3, 5, 9, 12, 34, 42;
TCLC 133**
See also BPFB 1; CA 53-56; 113; CANR
34; CN 1, 2, 3; CP 1, 2, 3, 4; DA3; DAM
NOV; DLB 2, 5, 206; DLBY 1980, 1984;
FANT; MAL 5; MTCW 1; RGAL 4;
SATA 56
Brave Bird, Mary .... **NNAL**
See Crow Dog, Mary (Ellen)
Braverman, Kate 1950- .... **CLC 67**
See also CA 89-92; CANR 141
Brecht, (Eugen) Bertolt (Friedrich)
1898-1956 ..... **DC 3; TCLC 1, 6, 13, 35,
169; WLC 1**
See also CA 104; 133; CANR 62; CDWLB
2; DA; DA3; DAB; DAC; DAM DRAM,
MST; DFS 4, 5, 9; DLB 56, 124; EW 11;
EWL 3; IDTP; MTCW 1, 2; MTFW 2005;
RGHL; RGWL 2, 3; TWA

Brecht, Eugen Berthold Friedrich
See Brecht, (Eugen) Bertolt (Friedrich)
Bremer, Fredrika 1801-1865 .... **NCLC 11**
See also DLB 254
Brennan, Christopher John
1870-1932 .... **TCLC 17**
See also CA 117; 188; DLB 230; EWL 3
Brennan, Maeve 1917-1993 ... **CLC 5; TCLC
124**
See also CA 81-84; CANR 72, 100
Brenner, Jozef 1887-1919
See Csath, Geza
See also CA 240
Brent, Linda
See Jacobs, Harriet A(nn)
Brentano, Clemens (Maria)
1778-1842 .... **NCLC 1**
See also DLB 90; RGWL 2, 3
Brent of Bin Bin
See Franklin, (Stella Maria Sarah) Miles
(Lampe)
Brenton, Howard 1942- .... **CLC 31**
See also CA 69-72; CANR 33, 67; CBD;
CD 5, 6; DLB 13; MTCW 1
Breslin, James 1930-
See Breslin, Jimmy
See also CA 73-76; CANR 31, 75, 139;
DAM NOV; MTCW 1, 2; MTFW 2005
Breslin, Jimmy .... **CLC 4, 43**
See Breslin, James
See also AITN 1; DLB 185; MTCW 2
Bresson, Robert 1901(?)-1999 .... **CLC 16**
See also CA 110; 187; CANR 49
Breton, Andre 1896-1966 .. **CLC 2, 9, 15, 54;
PC 15**
See also CA 19-20; 25-28R; CANR 40, 60;
CAP 2; DLB 65, 258; EW 11; EWL 3;
GFL 1789 to the Present; LMFS 2;
MTCW 1, 2; MTFW 2005; RGWL 2, 3;
TWA; WP
Breytenbach, Breyten 1939(?)- .. **CLC 23, 37,
126**
See also CA 113; 129; CANR 61, 122;
CWW 2; DAM POET; DLB 225; EWL 3
Bridgers, Sue Ellen 1942- .... **CLC 26**
See also AAYA 8, 49; BYA 7, 8; CA 65-68;
CANR 11, 36; CLR 18; DLB 52; JRDA;
MAICYA 1, 2; SAAS 1; SATA 22, 90;
SATA-Essay 109; WYA; YAW
Bridges, Robert (Seymour)
1844-1930 .... **PC 28; TCLC 1**
See also BRW 6; CA 104; 152; CDBLB
1890-1914; DAM POET; DLB 19, 98
Bridie, James .... **TCLC 3**
See Mavor, Osborne Henry
See also DLB 10; EWL 3
Brin, David 1950- .... **CLC 34**
See also AAYA 21; CA 102; CANR 24, 70,
125, 127; INT CANR-24; SATA 65;
SCFW 2; SFW 4
Brink, Andre (Philippus) 1935- . **CLC 18, 36,
106**
See also AFW; BRWS 6; CA 104; CANR
39, 62, 109, 133; CN 4, 5, 6, 7; DLB 225;
EWL 3; INT CA-103; LATS 1:2; MTCW
1, 2; MTFW 2005; WLIT 2
Brinsmead, H. F.
See Brinsmead, H(esba) F(ay)
Brinsmead, H. F(ay)
See Brinsmead, H(esba) F(ay)
Brinsmead, H(esba) F(ay) 1922- ...... **CLC 21**
See also CA 21-24R; CANR 10; CLR 47;
CWRI 5; MAICYA 1, 2; SAAS 5; SATA
18, 78
Brittain, Vera (Mary) 1893(?)-1970 . **CLC 23**
See also BRWS 10; CA 13-16; 25-28R;
CANR 58; CAP 1; DLB 191; FW; MTCW
1, 2

Bruccoli, Matthew J(oseph) 1931- ... **CLC 34**
  See also CA 9-12R; CANR 7, 87; DLB 103
Bruce, Lenny .... **CLC 21**
  See Schneider, Leonard Alfred
Bruchac, Joseph 1942- .... **NNAL**
  See also AAYA 19; CA 33-36R; CANR 13, 47, 75, 94, 137; CLR 46; CWRI 5; DAM MULT; JRDA; MAICYA 2; MAICYAS 1; MTCW 2; MTFW 2005; SATA 42, 89, 131, 172
Bruin, John
  See Brutus, Dennis
Brulard, Henri
  See Stendhal
Brulls, Christian
  See Simenon, Georges (Jacques Christian)
Brunetto Latini c. 1220-1294 .... **CMLC 73**
Brunner, John (Kilian Houston)
  1934-1995 .... **CLC 8, 10**
  See also CA 1-4R; 149; CAAS 8; CANR 2, 37; CPW; DAM POP; DLB 261; MTCW 1, 2; SCFW 1, 2; SFW 4
Bruno, Giordano 1548-1600 .... **LC 27**
  See also RGWL 2, 3
Brutus, Dennis 1924- ... **BLC 1; CLC 43; PC 24**
  See also AFW; BW 2, 3; CA 49-52; CAAS 14; CANR 2, 27, 42, 81; CDWLB 3; CP 1, 2, 3, 4, 5, 6, 7; DAM MULT, POET; DLB 117, 225; EWL 3
Bryan, C(ourtlandt) D(ixon) B(arnes)
  1936- .... **CLC 29**
  See also CA 73-76; CANR 13, 68; DLB 185; INT CANR-13
Bryan, Michael
  See Moore, Brian
  See also CCA 1
Bryan, William Jennings
  1860-1925 .... **TCLC 99**
  See also DLB 303
Bryant, William Cullen 1794-1878 . **NCLC 6, 46; PC 20**
  See also AMWS 1; CDALB 1640-1865; DA; DAB; DAC; DAM MST, POET; DLB 3, 43, 59, 189, 250; EXPP; PAB; RGAL 4; TUS
Bryusov, Valery Yakovlevich
  1873-1924 .... **TCLC 10**
  See also CA 107; 155; EWL 3; SFW 4
Buchan, John 1875-1940 .... **TCLC 41**
  See also CA 108; 145; CMW 4; DAB; DAM POP; DLB 34, 70, 156; HGG; MSW; MTCW 2; RGEL 2; RHW; YABC 2
Buchanan, George 1506-1582 .... **LC 4**
  See also DLB 132
Buchanan, Robert 1841-1901 .... **TCLC 107**
  See also CA 179; DLB 18, 35
Buchheim, Lothar-Guenther 1918- .... **CLC 6**
  See also CA 85-88
Buchner, (Karl) Georg
  1813-1837 .... **NCLC 26, 146**
  See also CDWLB 2; DLB 133; EW 6; RGSF 2; RGWL 2, 3; TWA
Buchwald, Art(hur) 1925- .... **CLC 33**
  See also AITN 1; CA 5-8R; CANR 21, 67, 107; MTCW 1, 2; SATA 10
Buck, Pearl S(ydenstricker)
  1892-1973 .... **CLC 7, 11, 18, 127**
  See also AAYA 42; AITN 1; AMWS 2; BPFB 1; CA 1-4R; 41-44R; CANR 1, 34; CDALBS; CN 1; DA; DA3; DAB; DAC; DAM MST, NOV; DLB 9, 102; EWL 3; LAIT 3; MAL 5; MTCW 1, 2; MTFW 2005; RGAL 4; RHW; SATA 1, 25; TUS
Buckler, Ernest 1908-1984 .... **CLC 13**
  See also CA 11-12; 114; CAP 1; CCA 1; CN 1, 2, 3; DAC; DAM MST; DLB 68; SATA 47

Buckley, Christopher 1952- .... **CLC 165**
  See also CA 139; CANR 119
Buckley, Christopher Taylor
  See Buckley, Christopher
Buckley, Vincent (Thomas)
  1925-1988 .... **CLC 57**
  See also CA 101; CP 1, 2, 3, 4; DLB 289
Buckley, William F(rank), Jr. 1925- . **CLC 7, 18, 37**
  See also AITN 1; BPFB 1; CA 1-4R; CANR 1, 24, 53, 93, 133; CMW 4; CPW; DA3; DAM POP; DLB 137; DLBY 1980; INT CANR-24; MTCW 1, 2; MTFW 2005; TUS
Buechner, (Carl) Frederick 1926- . **CLC 2, 4, 6, 9**
  See also AMWS 12; BPFB 1; CA 13-16R; CANR 11, 39, 64, 114, 138; CN 1, 2, 3, 4, 5, 6, 7; DAM NOV; DLBY 1980; INT CANR-11; MAL 5; MTCW 1, 2; MTFW 2005; TCLE 1:1
Buell, John (Edward) 1927- .... **CLC 10**
  See also CA 1-4R; CANR 71; DLB 53
Buero Vallejo, Antonio 1916-2000 ... **CLC 15, 46, 139, 226; DC 18**
  See also CA 106; 189; CANR 24, 49, 75; CWW 2; DFS 11; EWL 3; HW 1; MTCW 1, 2
Bufalino, Gesualdo 1920-1996 .... **CLC 74**
  See also CA 209; CWW 2; DLB 196
Bugayev, Boris Nikolayevich
  1880-1934 .... **PC 11; TCLC 7**
  See Bely, Andrey; Belyi, Andrei
  See also CA 104; 165; MTCW 2; MTFW 2005
Bukowski, Charles 1920-1994 ... **CLC 2, 5, 9, 41, 82, 108; PC 18; SSC 45**
  See also CA 17-20R; 144; CANR 40, 62, 105; CN 4, 5; CP 1, 2, 3, 4, 5; CPW; DA3; DAM NOV, POET; DLB 5, 130, 169; EWL 3; MAL 5; MTCW 1, 2; MTFW 2005
Bulgakov, Mikhail 1891-1940 .... **SSC 18; TCLC 2, 16, 159**
  See also BPFB 1; CA 105; 152; DAM DRAM, NOV; DLB 272; EWL 3; MTCW 2; MTFW 2005; NFS 8; RGSF 2; RGWL 2, 3; SFW 4; TWA
Bulgakov, Mikhail Afanasevich
  See Bulgakov, Mikhail
Bulgya, Alexander Alexandrovich
  1901-1956 .... **TCLC 53**
  See Fadeev, Aleksandr Aleksandrovich; Fadeev, Alexandr Alexandrovich; Fadeyev, Alexander
  See also CA 117; 181
Bullins, Ed 1935- ... **BLC 1; CLC 1, 5, 7; DC 6**
  See also BW 2, 3; CA 49-52; CAAS 16; CAD; CANR 24, 46, 73, 134; CD 5, 6; DAM DRAM, MULT; DLB 7, 38, 249; EWL 3; MAL 5; MTCW 1, 2; MTFW 2005; RGAL 4
Bulosan, Carlos 1911-1956 .... **AAL**
  See also CA 216; DLB 312; RGAL 4
Bulwer-Lytton, Edward (George Earle Lytton) 1803-1873 .... **NCLC 1, 45**
  See also DLB 21; RGEL 2; SFW 4; SUFW 1; TEA
Bunin, Ivan Alexeyevich 1870-1953 ... **SSC 5; TCLC 6**
  See also CA 104; DLB 317; EWL 3; RGSF 2; RGWL 2, 3; TWA
Bunting, Basil 1900-1985 ...... **CLC 10, 39, 47**
  See also BRWS 7; CA 53-56; 115; CANR 7; CP 1, 2, 3, 4; DAM POET; DLB 20; EWL 3; RGEL 2

Bunuel, Luis 1900-1983 ... **CLC 16, 80; HLC 1**
  See also CA 101; 110; CANR 32, 77; DAM MULT; HW 1
Bunyan, John 1628-1688 .. **LC 4, 69; WLC 1**
  See also BRW 1; BYA 5; CDBLB 1660-1789; DA; DAB; DAC; DAM MST; DLB 39; RGEL 2; TEA; WCH; WLIT 3
Buravsky, Alexandr .... **CLC 59**
Burckhardt, Jacob (Christoph)
  1818-1897 .... **NCLC 49**
  See also EW 6
Burford, Eleanor
  See Hibbert, Eleanor Alice Burford
Burgess, Anthony . **CLC 1, 2, 4, 5, 8, 10, 13, 15, 22, 40, 62, 81, 94**
  See Wilson, John (Anthony) Burgess
  See also AAYA 25; AITN 1; BRWS 1; CD-BLB 1960 to Present; CN 1, 2, 3, 4, 5; DAB; DLB 14, 194, 261; DLBY 1998; EWL 3; RGEL 2; RHW; SFW 4; YAW
Burke, Edmund 1729(?)-1797 .... **LC 7, 36; WLC 1**
  See also BRW 3; DA; DA3; DAB; DAC; DAM MST; DLB 104, 252; RGEL 2; TEA
Burke, Kenneth (Duva) 1897-1993 ... **CLC 2, 24**
  See also AMW; CA 5-8R; 143; CANR 39, 74, 136; CN 1, 2; CP 1, 2, 3, 4, 5; DLB 45, 63; EWL 3; MAL 5; MTCW 1, 2; MTFW 2005; RGAL 4
Burke, Leda
  See Garnett, David
Burke, Ralph
  See Silverberg, Robert
Burke, Thomas 1886-1945 .... **TCLC 63**
  See also CA 113; 155; CMW 4; DLB 197
Burney, Fanny 1752-1840 .... **NCLC 12, 54, 107**
  See also BRWS 3; DLB 39; FL 1:2; NFS 16; RGEL 2; TEA
Burney, Frances
  See Burney, Fanny
Burns, Robert 1759-1796 ... **LC 3, 29, 40; PC 6; WLC 1**
  See also AAYA 51; BRW 3; CDBLB 1789-1832; DA; DA3; DAB; DAC; DAM MST, POET; DLB 109; EXPP; PAB; RGEL 2; TEA; WP
Burns, Tex
  See L'Amour, Louis (Dearborn)
Burnshaw, Stanley 1906-2005 ..... **CLC 3, 13, 44**
  See also CA 9-12R; 243; CP 1, 2, 3, 4, 5, 6, 7; DLB 48; DLBY 1997
Burr, Anne 1937- .... **CLC 6**
  See also CA 25-28R
Burroughs, Edgar Rice 1875-1950 . **TCLC 2, 32**
  See also AAYA 11; BPFB 1; BYA 4, 9; CA 104; 132; CANR 131; DA3; DAM NOV; DLB 8; FANT; MTCW 1, 2; MTFW 2005; RGAL 4; SATA 41; SCFW 1, 2; SFW 4; TCWW 1, 2; TUS; YAW
Burroughs, William S. 1914-1997 . **CLC 1, 2, 5, 15, 22, 42, 75, 109; TCLC 121; WLC 1**
  See Lee, William; Lee, Willy
  See also AAYA 60; AITN 2; AMWS 3; BG 1:2; BPFB 1; CA 9-12R; 160; CANR 20, 52, 104; CN 1, 2, 3, 4, 5, 6; CPW; DA; DA3; DAB; DAC; DAM MST, NOV, POP; DLB 2, 8, 16, 152, 237; DLBY 1981, 1997; EWL 3; HGG; LMFS 2; MAL 5; MTCW 1, 2; MTFW 2005; RGAL 4; SFW 4
Burroughs, William Seward
  See Burroughs, William S.

Challans, Mary 1905-1983
See Renault, Mary
See also CA 81-84; 111; CANR 74; DA3;
MTCW 2; MTFW 2005; SATA 23; SATA-
Obit 36; TEA

Challis, George
See Faust, Frederick (Schiller)

Chambers, Aidan 1934- .... **CLC 35**
See also AAYA 27; CA 25-28R; CANR 12,
31, 58, 116; JRDA; MAICYA 1, 2; SAAS
12; SATA 1, 69, 108, 171; WYA; YAW

Chambers, James 1948-
See Cliff, Jimmy
See also CA 124

Chambers, Jessie
See Lawrence, D(avid) H(erbert Richards)
See also GLL 1

Chambers, Robert W(illiam)
1865-1933 .... **SSC 92; TCLC 41**
See also CA 165; DLB 202; HGG; SATA
107; SUFW 1

Chambers, (David) Whittaker
1901-1961 .... **TCLC 129**
See also CA 89-92; DLB 303

Chamisso, Adelbert von
1781-1838 .... **NCLC 82**
See also DLB 90; RGWL 2, 3; SUFW 1

Chance, James T.
See Carpenter, John (Howard)

Chance, John T.
See Carpenter, John (Howard)

Chandler, Raymond (Thornton)
1888-1959 .... **SSC 23; TCLC 1, 7, 179**
See also AAYA 25; AMWC 2; AMWS 4;
BPFB 1; CA 104; 129; CDALB 1929-1941; CMW 4; DA3; DLB
226, 253; DLBD 6; EWL 3; MAL 5;
MSW; MTCW 1, 2; MTFW 2005; NFS
17; RGAL 4; TUS

Chang, Diana 1934- .... **AAL**
See also CA 228; CWP; DLB 312; EXPP

Chang, Eileen 1921-1995 .... **AAL; SSC 28**
See Chang Ai-Ling; Zhang Ailing
See also CA 166

Chang, Jung 1952- .... **CLC 71**
See also CA 142

Chang Ai-Ling
See Chang, Eileen
See also EWL 3

Channing, William Ellery
1780-1842 .... **NCLC 17**
See also DLB 1, 59, 235; RGAL 4

Chao, Patricia 1955- .... **CLC 119**
See also CA 163

Chaplin, Charles Spencer
1889-1977 .... **CLC 16**
See Chaplin, Charlie
See also CA 81-84; 73-76

Chaplin, Charlie
See Chaplin, Charles Spencer
See also AAYA 61; DLB 44

Chapman, George 1559(?)-1634 . **DC 19; LC
22, 116**
See also BRW 1; DAM DRAM; DLB 62,
121; LMFS 1; RGEL 2

Chapman, Graham 1941-1989 .... **CLC 21**
See Monty Python
See also CA 116; 129; CANR 35, 95

Chapman, John Jay 1862-1933 .... **TCLC 7**
See also AMWS 14; CA 104; 191

Chapman, Lee
See Bradley, Marion Zimmer
See also GLL 1

Chapman, Walker
See Silverberg, Robert

Chappell, Fred (Davis) 1936- .... **CLC 40, 78,
162**
See also CA 5-8R, 198; CAAE 198; CAAS
4; CANR 8, 33, 67, 110; CN 6; CP 6, 7;
CSW; DLB 6, 105; HGG

Char, Rene(-Emile) 1907-1988 .... **CLC 9, 11,
14, 55; PC 56**
See also CA 13-16R; 124; CANR 32; DAM
POET; DLB 258; EWL 3; GFL 1789 to
the Present; MTCW 1, 2; RGWL 2, 3

Charby, Jay
See Ellison, Harlan (Jay)

Chardin, Pierre Teilhard de
See Teilhard de Chardin, (Marie Joseph)
Pierre

Chariton fl. 1st cent. (?)- .... **CMLC 49**

Charlemagne 742-814 .... **CMLC 37**

Charles I 1600-1649 .... **LC 13**

Charriere, Isabelle de 1740-1805 .. **NCLC 66**
See also DLB 313

Chartier, Alain c. 1392-1430 .... **LC 94**
See also DLB 208

Chartier, Emile-Auguste
See Alain

Charyn, Jerome 1937- .... **CLC 5, 8, 18**
See also CA 5-8R; CAAS 1; CANR 7, 61,
101; CMW 4; CN 1, 2, 3, 4, 5, 6, 7;
DLBY 1983; MTCW 1

Chase, Adam
See Marlowe, Stephen

Chase, Mary (Coyle) 1907-1981 .... **DC 1**
See also CA 77-80; 105; CAD; CWD; DFS
11; DLB 228; SATA 17; SATA-Obit 29

Chase, Mary Ellen 1887-1973 .... **CLC 2;
TCLC 124**
See also CA 13-16; 41-44R; CAP 1; SATA
10

Chase, Nicholas
See Hyde, Anthony
See also CCA 1

Chateaubriand, Francois Rene de
1768-1848 .... **NCLC 3, 134**
See also DLB 119; EW 5; GFL 1789 to the
Present; RGWL 2, 3; TWA

Chatelet, Gabrielle-Emilie Du
See du Chatelet, Emilie
See also DLB 313

Chatterje, Sarat Chandra 1876-1936(?)
See Chatterji, Saratchandra
See also CA 109

Chatterji, Bankim Chandra
1838-1894 .... **NCLC 19**

Chatterji, Saratchandra .... **TCLC 13**
See Chatterje, Sarat Chandra
See also CA 186; EWL 3

Chatterton, Thomas 1752-1770 .... **LC 3, 54**
See also DAM POET; DLB 109; RGEL 2

Chatwin, (Charles) Bruce
1940-1989 .... **CLC 28, 57, 59**
See also AAYA 4; BEST 90:1; BRWS 4;
CA 85-88; 127; CPW; DAM POP; DLB
194, 204; EWL 3; MTFW 2005

Chaucer, Daniel
See Ford, Ford Madox
See also RHW

Chaucer, Geoffrey 1340(?)-1400 .. **LC 17, 56;
PC 19, 58; WLCS**
See also BRW 1; BRWC 1; BRWR 2; CD-
BLB Before 1660; DA; DA3; DAB;
DAC; DAM MST, POET; DLB 146;
LAIT 1; PAB; PFS 14; RGEL 2; TEA;
WLIT 3; WP

Chavez, Denise (Elia) 1948- .... **HLC 1**
See also CA 131; CANR 56, 81, 137; DAM
MULT; DLB 122; FW; HW 1, 2; LLW;
MAL 5; MTCW 2; MTFW 2005

Chaviaras, Strates 1935-
See Haviaras, Stratis
See also CA 105

Chayefsky, Paddy .... **CLC 23**
See Chayefsky, Sidney
See also CAD; DLB 7, 44; DLBY 1981;
RGAL 4

Chayefsky, Sidney 1923-1981
See Chayefsky, Paddy
See also CA 9-12R; 104; CANR 18; DAM
DRAM

Chedid, Andree 1920- .... **CLC 47**
See also CA 145; CANR 95; EWL 3

Cheever, John 1912-1982 ..... **CLC 3, 7, 8, 11,
15, 25, 64; SSC 1, 38, 57; WLC 2**
See also AAYA 65; AMWS 1; BPFB 1; CA
5-8R; 106; CABS 1; CANR 5, 27, 76;
CDALB 1941-1968; CN 1, 2, 3; CPW;
DA; DA3; DAB; DAC; DAM MST, NOV,
POP; DLB 2, 102, 227; DLBY 1980,
1982; EWL 3; EXPS; INT CANR-5;
MAL 5; MTCW 1, 2; MTFW 2005;
RGAL 4; RGSF 2; SSFS 2, 14; TUS

Cheever, Susan 1943- .... **CLC 18, 48**
See also CA 103; CANR 27, 51, 92; DLBY
1982; INT CANR-27

Chekhonte, Antosha
See Chekhov, Anton (Pavlovich)

Chekhov, Anton (Pavlovich)
1860-1904 .... **DC 9; SSC 2, 28, 41, 51,
85; TCLC 3, 10, 31, 55, 96, 163; WLC
2**
See also AAYA 68; BYA 14; CA 104; 124;
DA; DA3; DAB; DAC; DAM DRAM,
MST; DFS 1, 5, 10, 12; DLB 277; EW 7;
EWL 3; EXPS; LAIT 3; LATS 1:1; RGSF
2; RGWL 2, 3; SATA 90; SSFS 5, 13, 14;
TWA

Cheney, Lynne V. 1941- .... **CLC 70**
See also CA 89-92; CANR 58, 117; SATA
152

Chernyshevsky, Nikolai Gavrilovich
See Chernyshevsky, Nikolay Gavrilovich
See also DLB 238

Chernyshevsky, Nikolay Gavrilovich
1828-1889 .... **NCLC 1**
See Chernyshevsky, Nikolai Gavrilovich

Cherry, Carolyn Janice .... **CLC 35**
See Cherryh, C.J.
See also AAYA 24; BPFB 1; DLBY 1980;
FANT; SATA 93; SCFW 2; SFW 4; YAW

Cherryh, C.J. 1942-
See Cherry, Carolyn Janice
See also CA 65-68; CANR 10, 147; SATA
172

Chesnutt, Charles W(addell)
1858-1932 .... **BLC 1; SSC 7, 54; TCLC
5, 39**
See also AFAW 1, 2; AMWS 14; BW 1, 3;
CA 106; 125; CANR 76; DAM MULT;
DLB 12, 50, 78; EWL 3; MAL 5; MTCW
1, 2; MTFW 2005; RGAL 4; RGSF 2;
SSFS 11

Chester, Alfred 1929(?)-1971 .... **CLC 49**
See also CA 196; 33-36R; DLB 130; MAL
5

Chesterton, G(ilbert) K(eith)
1874-1936 . **PC 28; SSC 1, 46; TCLC 1,
6, 64**
See also AAYA 57; BRW 6; CA 104; 132;
CANR 73, 131; CDBLB 1914-1945;
CMW 4; DAM NOV, POET; DLB 10, 19,
34, 70, 98, 149, 178; EWL 3; FANT;
MSW; MTCW 1, 2; MTFW 2005; RGEL
2; RGSF 2; SATA 27; SUFW 1

Chettle, Henry 1560-1607(?) .... **LC 112**
See also DLB 136; RGEL 2

Chiang, Pin-chin 1904-1986
See Ding Ling
See also CA 118

Chief Joseph 1840-1904 .... **NNAL**
See also CA 152; DA3; DAM MULT

Clarke, Austin C(hesterfield) 1934- .. **BLC 1; CLC 8, 53; SSC 45**
See also BW 1; CA 25-28R; CAAS 16; CANR 14, 32, 68, 140; CN 1, 2, 3, 4, 5, 6, 7; DAC; DAM MULT; DLB 53, 125; DNFS 2; MTCW 2; MTFW 2005; RGSF 2

Clarke, Gillian 1937- .... **CLC 61**
See also CA 106; CP 3, 4, 5, 6, 7; CWP; DLB 40

Clarke, Marcus (Andrew Hislop)
1846-1881 .... **NCLC 19**
See also DLB 230; RGEL 2; RGSF 2

Clarke, Shirley 1925-1997 .... **CLC 16**
See also CA 189

Clash, The
See Headon, (Nicky) Topper; Jones, Mick; Simonon, Paul; Strummer, Joe

Claudel, Paul (Louis Charles Marie)
1868-1955 .... **TCLC 2, 10**
See also CA 104; 165; DLB 192, 258, 321; EW 8; EWL 3; GFL 1789 to the Present; RGWL 2, 3; TWA

Claudian 370(?)-404(?) .... **CMLC 46**
See also RGWL 2, 3

Claudius, Matthias 1740-1815 .... **NCLC 75**
See also DLB 97

Clavell, James (duMaresq)
1925-1994 .... **CLC 6, 25, 87**
See also BPFB 1; CA 25-28R; 146; CANR 26, 48; CN 5; CPW; DA3; DAM NOV, POP; MTCW 1, 2; MTFW 2005; NFS 10; RHW

Clayman, Gregory .... **CLC 65**

Cleaver, (Leroy) Eldridge
1935-1998 .... **BLC 1; CLC 30, 119**
See also BW 1, 3; CA 21-24R; 167; CANR 16, 75; DA3; DAM MULT; MTCW 2; YAW

Cleese, John (Marwood) 1939- .... **CLC 21**
See Monty Python
See also CA 112; 116; CANR 35; MTCW 1

Cleishbotham, Jebediah
See Scott, Sir Walter

Cleland, John 1710-1789 .... **LC 2, 48**
See also DLB 39; RGEL 2

Clemens, Samuel Langhorne 1835-1910
See Twain, Mark
See also CA 104; 135; CDALB 1865-1917; DA; DA3; DAB; DAC; DAM MST, NOV; DLB 12, 23, 64, 74, 186, 189; JRDA; LMFS 1; MAICYA 1, 2; NCFS 4; NFS 20; SATA 100; YABC 2

Clement of Alexandria
150(?)-215(?) .... **CMLC 41**

Cleophil
See Congreve, William

Clerihew, E.
See Bentley, E(dmund) C(lerihew)

Clerk, N. W.
See Lewis, C.S.

Cleveland, John 1613-1658 .... **LC 106**
See also DLB 126; RGEL 2

Cliff, Jimmy .... **CLC 21**
See Chambers, James
See also CA 193

Cliff, Michelle 1946- .... **BLCS; CLC 120**
See also BW 2; CA 116; CANR 39, 72; CD-WLB 3; DLB 157; FW; GLL 2

Clifford, Lady Anne 1590-1676 .... **LC 76**
See also DLB 151

Clifton, (Thelma) Lucille 1936- .... **BLC 1; CLC 19, 66, 162; PC 17**
See also AFAW 2; BW 2, 3; CA 49-52; CANR 2, 24, 42, 76, 97, 138; CLR 5; CP 2, 3, 4, 5, 6, 7; CSW; CWP; CWRI 5;

DA3; DAM MULT, POET; DLB 5, 41; EXPP; MAICYA 1, 2; MTCW 1, 2; MTFW 2005; PFS 1, 14; SATA 20, 69, 128; WP

Clinton, Dirk
See Silverberg, Robert

Clough, Arthur Hugh 1819-1861 .. **NCLC 27, 163**
See also BRW 5; DLB 32; RGEL 2

Clutha, Janet Paterson Frame 1924-2004
See Frame, Janet
See also CA 1-4R; 224; CANR 2, 36, 76, 135; MTCW 1, 2; SATA 119

Clyne, Terence
See Blatty, William Peter

Cobalt, Martin
See Mayne, William (James Carter)

Cobb, Irvin S(hrewsbury)
1876-1944 .... **TCLC 77**
See also CA 175; DLB 11, 25, 86

Cobbett, William 1763-1835 .... **NCLC 49**
See also DLB 43, 107, 158; RGEL 2

Coburn, D(onald) L(ee) 1938- .... **CLC 10**
See also CA 89-92; DFS 23

Cocteau, Jean (Maurice Eugene Clement)
1889-1963 ...... **CLC 1, 8, 15, 16, 43; DC 17; TCLC 119; WLC 2**
See also CA 25-28; CANR 40; CAP 2; DA; DA3; DAB; DAC; DAM DRAM, MST, NOV; DLB 65, 258, 321; EW 10; EWL 3; GFL 1789 to the Present; MTCW 1, 2; RGWL 2, 3; TWA

Codrescu, Andrei 1946- .... **CLC 46, 121**
See also CA 33-36R; CAAS 19; CANR 13, 34, 53, 76, 125; CN 7; DA3; DAM POET; MAL 5; MTCW 2; MTFW 2005

Coe, Max
See Bourne, Randolph S(illiman)

Coe, Tucker
See Westlake, Donald E(dwin)

Coen, Ethan 1958- .... **CLC 108**
See also AAYA 54; CA 126; CANR 85

Coen, Joel 1955- .... **CLC 108**
See also AAYA 54; CA 126; CANR 119

The Coen Brothers
See Coen, Ethan; Coen, Joel

Coetzee, J. M. 1940- ..... **CLC 23, 33, 66, 117, 161, 162**
See also AAYA 37; AFW; BRWS 6; CA 77-80; CANR 41, 54, 74, 114, 133; CN 4, 5, 6, 7; DA3; DAM NOV; DLB 225, 326; EWL 3; LMFS 2; MTCW 1, 2; MTFW 2005; NFS 21; WLIT 2; WWE 1

Coetzee, John Maxwell
See Coetzee, J. M.

Coffey, Brian
See Koontz, Dean R.

Coffin, Robert P(eter) Tristram
1892-1955 .... **TCLC 95**
See also CA 123; 169; DLB 45

Cohan, George M. 1878-1942 .... **TCLC 60**
See also CA 157; DLB 249; RGAL 4

Cohan, George Michael
See Cohan, George M.

Cohen, Arthur A(llen) 1928-1986 ...... **CLC 7, 31**
See also CA 1-4R; 120; CANR 1, 17, 42; DLB 28; RGHL

Cohen, Leonard 1934- .... **CLC 3, 38**
See also CA 21-24R; CANR 14, 69; CN 1, 2, 3, 4, 5, 6; CP 1, 2, 3, 4, 5, 6, 7; DAC; DAM MST; DLB 53; EWL 3; MTCW 1

Cohen, Leonard Norman
See Cohen, Leonard

Cohen, Matt(hew) 1942-1999 .... **CLC 19**
See also CA 61-64; 187; CAAS 18; CANR 40; CN 1, 2, 3, 4, 5, 6; DAC; DLB 53

Cohen-Solal, Annie 1948- .... **CLC 50**
See also CA 239

Colegate, Isabel 1931- .... **CLC 36**
See also CA 17-20R; CANR 8, 22, 74; CN 4, 5, 6, 7; DLB 14, 231; INT CANR-22; MTCW 1

Coleman, Emmett
See Reed, Ishmael (Scott)

Coleridge, Hartley 1796-1849 .... **NCLC 90**
See also DLB 96

Coleridge, M. E.
See Coleridge, Mary E(lizabeth)

Coleridge, Mary E(lizabeth)
1861-1907 .... **TCLC 73**
See also CA 116; 166; DLB 19, 98

Coleridge, Samuel Taylor
1772-1834 ...... **NCLC 9, 54, 99, 111; PC 11, 39, 67; WLC 2**
See also AAYA 66; BRW 4; BRWR 2; BYA 4; CDBLB 1789-1832; DA; DA3; DAB; DAC; DAM MST, POET; DLB 93, 107; EXPP; LATS 1:1; LMFS 1; PAB; PFS 4, 5; RGEL 2; TEA; WLIT 3; WP

Coleridge, Sara 1802-1852 .... **NCLC 31**
See also DLB 199

Coles, Don 1928- .... **CLC 46**
See also CA 115; CANR 38; CP 5, 6, 7

Coles, Robert (Martin) 1929- .... **CLC 108**
See also CA 45-48; CANR 3, 32, 66, 70, 135; INT CANR-32; SATA 23

Colette, (Sidonie-Gabrielle)
1873-1954 .. **SSC 10, 93; TCLC 1, 5, 16**
See Willy, Colette
See also CA 104; 131; DA3; DAM NOV; DLB 65; EW 9; EWL 3; GFL 1789 to the Present; MTCW 1, 2; MTFW 2005; RGWL 2, 3; TWA

Collett, (Jacobine) Camilla (Wergeland)
1813-1895 .... **NCLC 22**

Collier, Christopher 1930- .... **CLC 30**
See also AAYA 13; BYA 2; CA 33-36R; CANR 13, 33, 102; JRDA; MAICYA 1, 2; SATA 16, 70; WYA; YAW 1

Collier, James Lincoln 1928- .... **CLC 30**
See also AAYA 13; BYA 2; CA 9-12R; CANR 4, 33, 60, 102; CLR 3; DAM POP; JRDA; MAICYA 1, 2; SAAS 21; SATA 8, 70, 166; WYA; YAW 1

Collier, Jeremy 1650-1726 .... **LC 6**

Collier, John 1901-1980 . **SSC 19; TCLC 127**
See also CA 65-68; 97-100; CANR 10; CN 1, 2; DLB 77, 255; FANT; SUFW 1

Collier, Mary 1690-1762 .... **LC 86**
See also DLB 95

Collingwood, R(obin) G(eorge)
1889(?)-1943 .... **TCLC 67**
See also CA 117; 155; DLB 262

Collins, Billy 1941- .... **PC 68**
See also AAYA 64; CA 151; CANR 92; CP 7; MTFW 2005; PFS 18

Collins, Hunt
See Hunter, Evan

Collins, Linda 1931- .... **CLC 44**
See also CA 125

Collins, Tom
See Furphy, Joseph
See also RGEL 2

Collins, (William) Wilkie
1824-1889 .... **NCLC 1, 18, 93; SSC 93**
See also BRWS 6; CDBLB 1832-1890; CMW 4; DLB 18, 70, 159; GL 2; MSW; RGEL 2; RGSF 2; SUFW 1; WLIT 4

Collins, William 1721-1759 ...... **LC 4, 40; PC 72**
See also BRW 3; DAM POET; DLB 109; RGEL 2

Collodi, Carlo .... **NCLC 54**
See Lorenzini, Carlo
See also CLR 5; WCH; WLIT 7

Colman, George
See Glassco, John

Deschamps, Eustache 1340(?)-1404 .. **LC 103**
See also DLB 208

De Sica, Vittorio 1901(?)-1974 .... **CLC 20**
See also CA 117

Desnos, Robert 1900-1945 .... **TCLC 22**
See also CA 121; 151; CANR 107; DLB 258; EWL 3; LMFS 2

Destouches, Louis-Ferdinand
1894-1961 .... **CLC 9, 15**
See Celine, Louis-Ferdinand
See also CA 85-88; CANR 28; MTCW 1

de Tolignac, Gaston
See Griffith, D(avid Lewelyn) W(ark)

Deutsch, Babette 1895-1982 .... **CLC 18**
See also BYA 3; CA 1-4R; 108; CANR 4, 79; CP 1, 2, 3; DLB 45; SATA 1; SATA-Obit 33

Devenant, William 1606-1649 .... **LC 13**

Devkota, Laxmiprasad 1909-1959 . **TCLC 23**
See also CA 123

De Voto, Bernard (Augustine)
1897-1955 .... **TCLC 29**
See also CA 113; 160; DLB 9, 256; MAL 5; TCWW 1, 2

De Vries, Peter 1910-1993 ..... **CLC 1, 2, 3, 7, 10, 28, 46**
See also CA 17-20R; 142; CANR 41; CN 1, 2, 3, 4, 5; DAM NOV; DLB 6; DLBY 1982; MAL 5; MTCW 1, 2; MTFW 2005

Dewey, John 1859-1952 .... **TCLC 95**
See also CA 114; 170; CANR 144; DLB 246, 270; RGAL 4

Dexter, John
See Bradley, Marion Zimmer
See also GLL 1

Dexter, Martin
See Faust, Frederick (Schiller)

Dexter, Pete 1943- .... **CLC 34, 55**
See also BEST 89:2; CA 127; 131; CANR 129; CPW; DAM POP; INT CA-131; MAL 5; MTCW 1; MTFW 2005

Diamano, Silmang
See Senghor, Leopold Sedar

Diamond, Neil 1941- .... **CLC 30**
See also CA 108

Diaz del Castillo, Bernal c.
1496-1584 .... **HLCS 1; LC 31**
See also DLB 318; LAW

di Bassetto, Corno
See Shaw, George Bernard

Dick, Philip K. 1928-1982 ... **CLC 10, 30, 72; SSC 57**
See also AAYA 24; BPFB 1; BYA 11; CA 49-52; 106; CANR 2, 16, 132; CN 2, 3; CPW; DA3; DAM NOV, POP; DLB 8; MTCW 1, 2; MTFW 2005; NFS 5; SCFW 1, 2; SFW 4

Dick, Philip Kindred
See Dick, Philip K.

Dickens, Charles (John Huffam)
1812-1870 .... **NCLC 3, 8, 18, 26, 37, 50, 86, 105, 113, 161; SSC 17, 49, 88; WLC 2**
See also AAYA 23; BRW 5; BRWC 1, 2; BYA 1, 2, 3, 13, 14; CDBLB 1832-1890; CLR 95; CMW 4; DA; DA3; DAB; DAC; DAM MST, NOV; DLB 21, 55, 70, 159, 166; EXPN; GL 2; HGG; JRDA; LAIT 1, 2; LATS 1:1; LMFS 1; MAICYA 1, 2; NFS 4, 5, 10, 14, 20; RGEL 2; RGSF 2; SATA 15; SUFW 1; TEA; WCH; WLIT 4; WYA

Dickey, James (Lafayette)
1923-1997 .... **CLC 1, 2, 4, 7, 10, 15, 47, 109; PC 40; TCLC 151**
See also AAYA 50; AITN 1, 2; AMWS 4; BPFB 1; CA 9-12R; 156; CABS 2; CANR 10, 48, 61, 105; CDALB 1968-1988; CP 1, 2, 3, 4, 5, 6; CPW; CSW; DA3; DAM

NOV, POET, POP; DLB 5, 193; DLBD 7; DLBY 1982, 1993, 1996, 1997, 1998; EWL 3; INT CANR-10; MAL 5; MTCW 1, 2; NFS 9; PFS 6, 11; RGAL 4; TUS

Dickey, William 1928-1994 .... **CLC 3, 28**
See also CA 9-12R; 145; CANR 24, 79; CP 1, 2, 3, 4; DLB 5

Dickinson, Charles 1951- .... **CLC 49**
See also CA 128; CANR 141

Dickinson, Emily (Elizabeth)
1830-1886 ..... **NCLC 21, 77, 171; PC 1; WLC 2**
See also AAYA 22; AMW; AMWR 1; CDALB 1865-1917; DA; DA3; DAB; DAC; DAM MST, POET; DLB 1, 243; EXPP; FL 1:3; MBL; PAB; PFS 1, 2, 3, 4, 5, 6, 8, 10, 11, 13, 16; RGAL 4; SATA 29; TUS; WP; WYA

Dickinson, Mrs. Herbert Ward
See Phelps, Elizabeth Stuart

Dickinson, Peter (Malcolm de Brissac)
1927- .... **CLC 12, 35**
See also AAYA 9, 49; BYA 5; CA 41-44R; CANR 31, 58, 88, 134; CLR 29; CMW 4; DLB 87, 161, 276; JRDA; MAICYA 1, 2; SATA 5, 62, 95, 150; SFW 4; WYA; YAW

Dickson, Carr
See Carr, John Dickson

Dickson, Carter
See Carr, John Dickson

Diderot, Denis 1713-1784 .... **LC 26, 126**
See also DLB 313; EW 4; GFL Beginnings to 1789; LMFS 1; RGWL 2, 3

Didion, Joan 1934- . **CLC 1, 3, 8, 14, 32, 129**
See also AITN 1; AMWS 4; CA 5-8R; CANR 14, 52, 76, 125; CDALB 1968-1988; CN 2, 3, 4, 5, 6, 7; DA3; DAM NOV; DLB 2, 173, 185; DLBY 1981, 1986; EWL 3; MAL 5; MBL; MTCW 1, 2; MTFW 2005; NFS 3; RGAL 4; TCLE 1:1; TCWW 2; TUS

di Donato, Pietro 1911-1992 .... **TCLC 159**
See also CA 101; 136; DLB 9

Dietrich, Robert
See Hunt, E(verette) Howard, (Jr.)

Difusa, Pati
See Almodovar, Pedro

Dillard, Annie 1945- ...... **CLC 9, 60, 115, 216**
See also AAYA 6, 43; AMWS 6; ANW; CA 49-52; CANR 3, 43, 62, 90, 125; DA3; DAM NOV; DLB 275, 278; DLBY 1980; LAIT 4, 5; MAL 5; MTCW 1, 2; MTFW 2005; NCFS 1; RGAL 4; SATA 10, 140; TCLE 1:1; TUS

Dillard, R(ichard) H(enry) W(ilde)
1937- .... **CLC 5**
See also CA 21-24R; CANR 10; CP 2, 3, 4, 5, 6, 7; CSW; DLB 5, 244

Dillon, Eilis 1920-1994 .... **CLC 17**
See also CA 9-12R, 182; 147; CAAE 182; CAAS 3; CANR 4, 38, 78; CLR 26; MAICYA 1; SATA 2, 74; SATA-Essay 105; SATA-Obit 83; YAW

Dimont, Penelope
See Mortimer, Penelope (Ruth)

Dinesen, Isak ..... **CLC 10, 29, 95; SSC 7, 75**
See Blixen, Karen (Christentze Dinesen)
See also EW 10; EWL 3; EXPS; FW; GL 2; HGG; LAIT 3; MTCW 1; NCFS 2; NFS 9; RGSF 2; RGWL 2, 3; SSFS 3, 6, 13; WLIT 2

Ding Ling .... **CLC 68**
See Chiang, Pin-chin
See also RGWL 3

Diphusa, Patty
See Almodovar, Pedro

Disch, Thomas M(ichael) 1940- ... **CLC 7, 36**
See Disch, Tom
See also AAYA 17; BPFB 1; CA 21-24R; CAAS 4; CANR 17, 36, 54, 89; CLR 18; CP 5, 6, 7; DA3; DLB 8; HGG; MAICYA 1, 2; MTCW 1, 2; MTFW 2005; SAAS 15; SATA 92; SCFW 1, 2; SFW 4; SUFW 2

Disch, Tom
See Disch, Thomas M(ichael)
See also DLB 282

d'Isly, Georges
See Simenon, Georges (Jacques Christian)

Disraeli, Benjamin 1804-1881 ... **NCLC 2, 39, 79**
See also BRW 4; DLB 21, 55; RGEL 2

Ditcum, Steve
See Crumb, R.

Dixon, Paige
See Corcoran, Barbara (Asenath)

Dixon, Stephen 1936- .... **CLC 52; SSC 16**
See also AMWS 12; CA 89-92; CANR 17, 40, 54, 91; CN 4, 5, 6, 7; DLB 130; MAL 5

Dixon, Thomas, Jr. 1864-1946 ..... **TCLC 163**
See also RHW

Djebar, Assia 1936- .... **CLC 182**
See also CA 188; EWL 3; RGWL 3; WLIT 2

Doak, Annie
See Dillard, Annie

Dobell, Sydney Thompson
1824-1874 .... **NCLC 43**
See also DLB 32; RGEL 2

Doblin, Alfred .... **TCLC 13**
See Doeblin, Alfred
See also CDWLB 2; EWL 3; RGWL 2, 3

Dobroliubov, Nikolai Aleksandrovich
See Dobrolyubov, Nikolai Alexandrovich
See also DLB 277

Dobrolyubov, Nikolai Alexandrovich
1836-1861 .... **NCLC 5**
See Dobroliubov, Nikolai Aleksandrovich

Dobson, Austin 1840-1921 .... **TCLC 79**
See also DLB 35, 144

Dobyns, Stephen 1941- .... **CLC 37**
See also AMWS 13; CA 45-48; CANR 2, 18, 99; CMW 4; CP 4, 5, 6, 7; PFS 23

Doctorow, Edgar Laurence
See Doctorow, E.L.

Doctorow, E.L. 1931- . **CLC 6, 11, 15, 18, 37, 44, 65, 113, 214**
See also AAYA 22; AITN 2; AMWS 4; BEST 89:3; BPFB 1; CA 45-48; CANR 2, 33, 51, 76, 97, 133; CDALB 1968-1988; CN 3, 4, 5, 6, 7; CPW; DA3; DAM NOV, POP; DLB 2, 28, 173; DLBY 1980; EWL 3; LAIT 3; MAL 5; MTCW 1, 2; MTFW 2005; NFS 6; RGAL 4; RGHL; RHW; TCLE 1:1; TCWW 1, 2; TUS

Dodgson, Charles L(utwidge) 1832-1898
See Carroll, Lewis
See also CLR 2; DA; DA3; DAB; DAC; DAM MST, NOV, POET; MAICYA 1, 2; SATA 100; YABC 2

Dodsley, Robert 1703-1764 .... **LC 97**
See also DLB 95; RGEL 2

Dodson, Owen (Vincent) 1914-1983 .. **BLC 1; CLC 79**
See also BW 1; CA 65-68; 110; CANR 24; DAM MULT; DLB 76

Doeblin, Alfred 1878-1957 .... **TCLC 13**
See Doblin, Alfred
See also CA 110; 141; DLB 66

Doerr, Harriet 1910-2002 .... **CLC 34**
See also CA 117; 122; 213; CANR 47; INT CA-122; LATS 1:2

Domecq, H(onorio Bustos)
See Bioy Casares, Adolfo

Domecq, H(onorio) Bustos
See Bioy Casares, Adolfo; Borges, Jorge
Luis

Domini, Rey
See Lorde, Audre (Geraldine)
See also GLL 1

Dominique
See Proust, (Valentin-Louis-George-Eugene)
Marcel

Don, A
See Stephen, Sir Leslie

Donaldson, Stephen R(eeder)
1947- .... **CLC 46, 138**
See also AAYA 36; BPFB 1; CA 89-92;
CANR 13, 55, 99; CPW; DAM POP;
FANT; INT CANR-13; SATA 121; SFW
4; SUFW 1, 2

Donleavy, J(ames) P(atrick) 1926- .... **CLC 1,
4, 6, 10, 45**
See also AITN 2; BPFB 1; CA 9-12R;
CANR 24, 49, 62, 80, 124; CBD; CD 5,
6; CN 1, 2, 3, 4, 5, 6, 7; DLB 6, 173; INT
CANR-24; MAL 5; MTCW 1, 2; MTFW
2005; RGAL 4

Donnadieu, Marguerite
See Duras, Marguerite

Donne, John 1572-1631 ... **LC 10, 24, 91; PC
1, 43; WLC 2**
See also AAYA 67; BRW 1; BRWC 1;
BRWR 2; CDBLB Before 1660; DA;
DAB; DAC; DAM MST, POET; DLB
121, 151; EXPP; PAB; PFS 2, 11; RGEL
3; TEA; WLIT 3; WP

Donnell, David 1939(?)- .... **CLC 34**
See also CA 197

Donoghue, Denis 1928- .... **CLC 209**
See also CA 17-20R; CANR 16, 102

Donoghue, P. S.
See Hunt, E(verette) Howard, (Jr.)

Donoso (Yanez), Jose 1924-1996 ... **CLC 4, 8,
11, 32, 99; HLC 1; SSC 34; TCLC 133**
See also CA 81-84; 155; CANR 32, 73; CD-
WLB 3; CWW 2; DAM MULT; DLB 113;
EWL 3; HW 1, 2; LAW; LAWS 1; MTCW
1, 2; MTFW 2005; RGSF 2; WLIT 1

Donovan, John 1928-1992 .... **CLC 35**
See also AAYA 20; CA 97-100; 137; CLR
3; MAICYA 1, 2; SATA 72; SATA-Brief
29; YAW

Don Roberto
See Cunninghame Graham, Robert
(Gallnigad) Bontine

Doolittle, Hilda 1886-1961 . **CLC 3, 8, 14, 31,
34, 73; PC 5; WLC 3**
See H. D.
See also AAYA 66; AMWS 1; CA 97-100;
CANR 35, 131; DA; DAC; DAM MST,
POET; DLB 4, 45; EWL 3; FW; GLL 1;
LMFS 2; MAL 5; MBL; MTCW 1, 2;
MTFW 2005; PFS 6; RGAL 4

Doppo, Kunikida .... **TCLC 99**
See Kunikida Doppo

Dorfman, Ariel 1942- .... **CLC 48, 77, 189;
HLC 1**
See also CA 124; 130; CANR 67, 70, 135;
CWW 2; DAM MULT; DFS 4; EWL 3;
HW 1, 2; INT CA-130; WLIT 1

Dorn, Edward (Merton)
1929-1999 .... **CLC 10, 18**
See also CA 93-96; 187; CANR 42, 79; CP
1, 2, 3, 4, 5, 6, 7; DLB 5; INT CA-93-96;
WP

Dor-Ner, Zvi .... **CLC 70**

Dorris, Michael (Anthony)
1945-1997 .... **CLC 109; NNAL**
See also AAYA 20; BEST 90:1; BYA 12;
CA 102; 157; CANR 19, 46, 75; CLR 58;
DA3; DAM MULT, NOV; DLB 175;
LAIT 5; MTCW 2; MTFW 2005; NFS 3;
RGAL 4; SATA 75; SATA-Obit 94;
TCWW 2; YAW

Dorris, Michael A.
See Dorris, Michael (Anthony)

Dorsan, Luc
See Simenon, Georges (Jacques Christian)

Dorsange, Jean
See Simenon, Georges (Jacques Christian)

Dorset
See Sackville, Thomas

Dos Passos, John (Roderigo)
1896-1970 ... **CLC 1, 4, 8, 11, 15, 25, 34,
82; WLC 2**
See also AMW; BPFB 1; CA 1-4R; 29-32R;
CANR 3; CDALB 1929-1941; DA; DA3;
DAB; DAC; DAM MST, NOV; DLB 4,
9, 274, 316; DLBD 1, 15; DLBY 1996;
EWL 3; MAL 5; MTCW 1, 2; MTFW
2005; NFS 14; RGAL 4; TUS

Dossage, Jean
See Simenon, Georges (Jacques Christian)

Dostoevsky, Fedor Mikhailovich
1821-1881 .. **NCLC 2, 7, 21, 33, 43, 119,
167; SSC 2, 33, 44; WLC 2**
See Dostoevsky, Fyodor
See also AAYA 40; DA; DA3; DAB; DAC;
DAM MST, NOV; EW 7; EXPN; NFS 3,
8; RGSF 2; RGWL 2, 3; SSFS 8; TWA

Dostoevsky, Fyodor
See Dostoevsky, Fedor Mikhailovich
See also DLB 238; LATS 1:1; LMFS 1, 2

Doty, M. R.
See Doty, Mark (Alan)

Doty, Mark
See Doty, Mark (Alan)

Doty, Mark (Alan) 1953(?)- .... **CLC 176; PC
53**
See also AMWS 11; CA 161, 183; CAAE
183; CANR 110; CP 7

Doty, Mark A.
See Doty, Mark (Alan)

Doughty, Charles M(ontagu)
1843-1926 .... **TCLC 27**
See also CA 115; 178; DLB 19, 57, 174

Douglas, Ellen .... **CLC 73**
See Haxton, Josephine Ayres; Williamson,
Ellen Douglas
See also CN 5, 6, 7; CSW; DLB 292

Douglas, Gavin 1475(?)-1522 .... **LC 20**
See also DLB 132; RGEL 2

Douglas, George
See Brown, George Douglas
See also RGEL 2

Douglas, Keith (Castellain)
1920-1944 .... **TCLC 40**
See also BRW 7; CA 160; DLB 27; EWL
3; PAB; RGEL 2

Douglas, Leonard
See Bradbury, Ray (Douglas)

Douglas, Michael
See Crichton, (John) Michael

Douglas, (George) Norman
1868-1952 .... **TCLC 68**
See also BRW 6; CA 119; 157; DLB 34,
195; RGEL 2

Douglas, William
See Brown, George Douglas

Douglass, Frederick 1817(?)-1895 ..... **BLC 1;
NCLC 7, 55, 141; WLC 2**
See also AAYA 48; AFAW 1, 2; AMWC 1;
AMWS 3; CDALB 1640-1865; DA; DA3;
DAC; DAM MST, MULT; DLB 1, 43, 50,
79, 243; FW; LAIT 2; NCFS 2; RGAL 4;
SATA 29

Dourado, (Waldomiro Freitas) Autran
1926- .... **CLC 23, 60**
See also CA 25-28R; 179; CANR 34, 81;
DLB 145, 307; HW 2

Dourado, Waldomiro Freitas Autran
See Dourado, (Waldomiro Freitas) Autran

Dove, Rita (Frances) 1952- . **BLCS; CLC 50,
81; PC 6**
See also AAYA 46; AMWS 4; BW 2; CA
109; CAAS 19; CANR 27, 42, 68, 76, 97,
132; CDALBS; CP 5, 6, 7; CSW; CWP;
DA3; DAM MULT, POET; DLB 120;
EWL 3; EXPP; MAL 5; MTCW 2; MTFW
2005; PFS 1, 15; RGAL 4

Doveglion
See Villa, Jose Garcia

Dowell, Coleman 1925-1985 .... **CLC 60**
See also CA 25-28R; 117; CANR 10; DLB
130; GLL 2

Dowson, Ernest (Christopher)
1867-1900 .... **TCLC 4**
See also CA 105; 150; DLB 19, 135; RGEL
2

Doyle, A. Conan
See Doyle, Sir Arthur Conan

Doyle, Sir Arthur Conan
1859-1930 . **SSC 12, 83; TCLC 7; WLC
2**
See Conan Doyle, Arthur
See also AAYA 14; BRWS 2; CA 104; 122;
CANR 131; CDBLB 1890-1914; CLR
106; CMW 4; DA; DA3; DAB; DAC;
DAM MST, NOV; DLB 18, 70, 156, 178;
EXPS; HGG; LAIT 2; MSW; MTCW 1,
2; MTFW 2005; RGEL 2; RGSF 2; RHW;
SATA 24; SCFW 1, 2; SFW 4; SSFS 2;
TEA; WCH; WLIT 4; WYA; YAW

Doyle, Conan
See Doyle, Sir Arthur Conan

Doyle, John
See Graves, Robert (von Ranke)

Doyle, Roddy 1958- .... **CLC 81, 178**
See also AAYA 14; BRWS 5; CA 143;
CANR 73, 128; CN 6, 7; DA3; DLB 194,
326; MTCW 2; MTFW 2005

Doyle, Sir A. Conan
See Doyle, Sir Arthur Conan

Dr. A
See Asimov, Isaac; Silverstein, Alvin; Silverstein, Virginia B(arbara Opshelor)

Drabble, Margaret 1939- ...... **CLC 2, 3, 5, 8,
10, 22, 53, 129**
See also BRWS 4; CA 13-16R; CANR 18,
35, 63, 112, 131; CDBLB 1960 to Present;
CN 1, 2, 3, 4, 5, 6, 7; CPW; DA3; DAB;
DAC; DAM MST, NOV, POP; DLB 14,
155, 231; EWL 3; FW; MTCW 1, 2;
MTFW 2005; RGEL 2; SATA 48; TEA

Drakulic, Slavenka 1949- .... **CLC 173**
See also CA 144; CANR 92

Drakulic-Ilic, Slavenka
See Drakulic, Slavenka

Drapier, M. B.
See Swift, Jonathan

Drayham, James
See Mencken, H(enry) L(ouis)

Drayton, Michael 1563-1631 .... **LC 8**
See also DAM POET; DLB 121; RGEL 2

Dreadstone, Carl
See Campbell, (John) Ramsey

Dreiser, Theodore 1871-1945 .... **SSC 30;
TCLC 10, 18, 35, 83; WLC 2**
See also AMW; AMWC 2; AMWR 2; BYA
15, 16; CA 106; 132; CDALB 1865-1917;
DA; DA3; DAC; DAM MST, NOV; DLB
9, 12, 102, 137; DLBD 1; EWL 3; LAIT
2; LMFS 2; MAL 5; MTCW 1, 2; MTFW
2005; NFS 8, 17; RGAL 4; TUS

Dreiser, Theodore Herman Albert
See Dreiser, Theodore

Drexler, Rosalyn 1926- .... **CLC 2, 6**
See also CA 81-84; CAD; CANR 68, 124;
CD 5, 6; CWD; MAL 5

Dreyer, Carl Theodor 1889-1968 ...... **CLC 16**
See also CA 116

Drieu la Rochelle, Pierre(-Eugene)
1893-1945 .... **TCLC 21**
See also CA 117; DLB 72; EWL 3; GFL 1789 to the Present

Drinkwater, John 1882-1937 .... **TCLC 57**
See also CA 109; 149; DLB 10, 19, 149; RGEL 2

Drop Shot
See Cable, George Washington

Droste-Hulshoff, Annette Freiin von
1797-1848 .... **NCLC 3, 133**
See also CDWLB 2; DLB 133; RGSF 2; RGWL 2, 3

Drummond, Walter
See Silverberg, Robert

Drummond, William Henry
1854-1907 .... **TCLC 25**
See also CA 160; DLB 92

Drummond de Andrade, Carlos
1902-1987 .... **CLC 18; TCLC 139**
See Andrade, Carlos Drummond de
See also CA 132; 123; DLB 307; LAW

Drummond of Hawthornden, William
1585-1649 .... **LC 83**
See also DLB 121, 213; RGEL 2

Drury, Allen (Stuart) 1918-1998 .... **CLC 37**
See also CA 57-60; 170; CANR 18, 52; CN 1, 2, 3, 4, 5, 6; INT CANR-18

Druse, Eleanor
See King, Stephen

Dryden, John 1631-1700 ..... **DC 3; LC 3, 21, 115; PC 25; WLC 2**
See also BRW 2; CDBLB 1660-1789; DA; DAB; DAC; DAM DRAM, MST, POET; DLB 80, 101, 131; EXPP; IDTP; LMFS 1; RGEL 2; TEA; WLIT 3

du Bellay, Joachim 1524-1560 .... **LC 92**
See also DLB 327; GFL Beginnings to 1789; RGWL 2, 3

Duberman, Martin (Bauml) 1930- ..... **CLC 8**
See also CA 1-4R; CAD; CANR 2, 63, 137; CD 5, 6

Dubie, Norman (Evans) 1945- .... **CLC 36**
See also CA 69-72; CANR 12, 115; CP 3, 4, 5, 6, 7; DLB 120; PFS 12

Du Bois, W(illiam) E(dward) B(urghardt)
1868-1963 ..... **BLC 1; CLC 1, 2, 13, 64, 96; HR 1:2; TCLC 169; WLC 2**
See also AAYA 40; AFAW 1, 2; AMWC 1; AMWS 2; BW 1, 3; CA 85-88; CANR 34, 82, 132; CDALB 1865-1917; DA; DA3; DAC; DAM MST, MULT, NOV; DLB 47, 50, 91, 246, 284; EWL 3; EXPP; LAIT 2; LMFS 2; MAL 5; MTCW 1, 2; MTFW 2005; NCFS 1; PFS 13; RGAL 4; SATA 42

Dubus, Andre 1936-1999 ..... **CLC 13, 36, 97; SSC 15**
See also AMWS 7; CA 21-24R; 177; CANR 17; CN 5, 6; CSW; DLB 130; INT CANR-17; RGAL 4; SSFS 10; TCLE 1:1

Duca Minimo
See D'Annunzio, Gabriele

Ducharme, Rejean 1941- .... **CLC 74**
See also CA 165; DLB 60

du Chatelet, Emilie 1706-1749 .... **LC 96**
See Chatelet, Gabrielle-Emilie Du

Duchen, Claire .... **CLC 65**

Duclos, Charles Pinot- 1704-1772 .... **LC 1**
See also GFL Beginnings to 1789

Dudek, Louis 1918-2001 .... **CLC 11, 19**
See also CA 45-48; 215; CAAS 14; CANR 1; CP 1, 2, 3, 4, 5, 6, 7; DLB 88

Duerrenmatt, Friedrich 1921-1990 ... **CLC 1, 4, 8, 11, 15, 43, 102**
See Durrenmatt, Friedrich
See also CA 17-20R; CANR 33; CMW 4; DAM DRAM; DLB 69, 124; MTCW 1, 2

Duffy, Bruce 1953(?)- .... **CLC 50**
See also CA 172

Duffy, Maureen (Patricia) 1933- ...... **CLC 37**
See also CA 25-28R; CANR 33, 68; CBD; CN 1, 2, 3, 4, 5, 6, 7; CP 5, 6, 7; CWD; CWP; DFS 15; DLB 14, 310; FW; MTCW 1

Du Fu
See Tu Fu
See also RGWL 2, 3

Dugan, Alan 1923-2003 .... **CLC 2, 6**
See also CA 81-84; 220; CANR 119; CP 1, 2, 3, 4, 5, 6, 7; DLB 5; MAL 5; PFS 10

du Gard, Roger Martin
See Martin du Gard, Roger

Duhamel, Georges 1884-1966 .... **CLC 8**
See also CA 81-84; 25-28R; CANR 35; DLB 65; EWL 3; GFL 1789 to the Present; MTCW 1

Dujardin, Edouard (Emile Louis)
1861-1949 .... **TCLC 13**
See also CA 109; DLB 123

Duke, Raoul
See Thompson, Hunter S(tockton)

Dulles, John Foster 1888-1959 .... **TCLC 72**
See also CA 115; 149

Dumas, Alexandre (pere)
1802-1870 .... **NCLC 11, 71; WLC 2**
See also AAYA 22; BYA 3; DA; DA3; DAB; DAC; DAM MST, NOV; DLB 119, 192; EW 6; GFL 1789 to the Present; LAIT 1, 2; NFS 14, 19; RGWL 2, 3; SATA 18; TWA; WCH

Dumas, Alexandre (fils) 1824-1895 ...... **DC 1; NCLC 9**
See also DLB 192; GFL 1789 to the Present; RGWL 2, 3

Dumas, Claudine
See Malzberg, Barry N(athaniel)

Dumas, Henry L. 1934-1968 .... **CLC 6, 62**
See also BW 1; CA 85-88; DLB 41; RGAL 4

du Maurier, Daphne 1907-1989 .. **CLC 6, 11, 59; SSC 18**
See also AAYA 37; BPFB 1; BRWS 3; CA 5-8R; 128; CANR 6, 55; CMW 4; CN 1, 2, 3, 4; CPW; DA3; DAB; DAC; DAM MST, POP; DLB 191; GL 2; HGG; LAIT 3; MSW; MTCW 1, 2; NFS 12; RGEL 2; RGSF 2; RHW; SATA 27; SATA-Obit 60; SSFS 14, 16; TEA

Du Maurier, George 1834-1896 ..... **NCLC 86**
See also DLB 153, 178; RGEL 2

Dunbar, Paul Laurence 1872-1906 ... **BLC 1; PC 5; SSC 8; TCLC 2, 12; WLC 2**
See also AFAW 1, 2; AMWS 2; BW 1, 3; CA 104; 124; CANR 79; CDALB 1865-1917; DA; DA3; DAC; DAM MST, MULT, POET; DLB 50, 54, 78; EXPP; MAL 5; RGAL 4; SATA 34

Dunbar, William 1460(?)-1520(?) .... **LC 20; PC 67**
See also BRWS 8; DLB 132, 146; RGEL 2

Dunbar-Nelson, Alice .... **HR 1:2**
See Nelson, Alice Ruth Moore Dunbar

Duncan, Dora Angela
See Duncan, Isadora

Duncan, Isadora 1877(?)-1927 .... **TCLC 68**
See also CA 118; 149

Duncan, Lois 1934- .... **CLC 26**
See also AAYA 4, 34; BYA 6, 8; CA 1-4R; CANR 2, 23, 36, 111; CLR 29; JRDA; MAICYA 1, 2; MAICYAS 1; MTFW 2005; SAAS 2; SATA 1, 36, 75, 133, 141; SATA-Essay 141; WYA; YAW

Duncan, Robert (Edward)
1919-1988 .... **CLC 1, 2, 4, 7, 15, 41, 55; PC 2**
See also BG 1:2; CA 9-12R; 124; CANR 28, 62; CP 1, 2, 3, 4; DAM POET; DLB 5, 16, 193; EWL 3; MAL 5; MTCW 1, 2; MTFW 2005; PFS 13; RGAL 4; WP

Duncan, Sara Jeannette
1861-1922 .... **TCLC 60**
See also CA 157; DLB 92

Dunlap, William 1766-1839 .... **NCLC 2**
See also DLB 30, 37, 59; RGAL 4

Dunn, Douglas (Eaglesham) 1942- .... **CLC 6, 40**
See also BRWS 10; CA 45-48; CANR 2, 33, 126; CP 1, 2, 3, 4, 5, 6, 7; DLB 40; MTCW 1

Dunn, Katherine (Karen) 1945- .... **CLC 71**
See also CA 33-36R; CANR 72; HGG; MTCW 2; MTFW 2005

Dunn, Stephen (Elliott) 1939- .. **CLC 36, 206**
See also AMWS 11; CA 33-36R; CANR 12, 48, 53, 105; CP 3, 4, 5, 6, 7; DLB 105; PFS 21

Dunne, Finley Peter 1867-1936 ...... **TCLC 28**
See also CA 108; 178; DLB 11, 23; RGAL 4

Dunne, John Gregory 1932-2003 ..... **CLC 28**
See also CA 25-28R; 222; CANR 14, 50; CN 5, 6, 7; DLBY 1980

Dunsany, Lord .... **TCLC 2, 59**
See Dunsany, Edward John Moreton Drax Plunkett
See also DLB 77, 153, 156, 255; FANT; IDTP; RGEL 2; SFW 4; SUFW 1

Dunsany, Edward John Moreton Drax Plunkett 1878-1957
See Dunsany, Lord
See also CA 104; 148; DLB 10; MTCW 2

Duns Scotus, John 1266(?)-1308 ... **CMLC 59**
See also DLB 115

du Perry, Jean
See Simenon, Georges (Jacques Christian)

Durang, Christopher 1949- .... **CLC 27, 38**
See also CA 105; CAD; CANR 50, 76, 130; CD 5, 6; MTCW 2; MTFW 2005

Durang, Christopher Ferdinand
See Durang, Christopher

Duras, Claire de 1777-1832 .... **NCLC 154**

Duras, Marguerite 1914-1996 . **CLC 3, 6, 11, 20, 34, 40, 68, 100; SSC 40**
See also BPFB 1; CA 25-28R; 151; CANR 50; CWW 2; DFS 21; DLB 83, 321; EWL 3; FL 1:5; GFL 1789 to the Present; IDFW 4; MTCW 1, 2; RGWL 2, 3; TWA

Durban, (Rosa) Pam 1947- .... **CLC 39**
See also CA 123; CANR 98; CSW

Durcan, Paul 1944- .... **CLC 43, 70**
See also CA 134; CANR 123; CP 1, 5, 6, 7; DAM POET; EWL 3

Durfey, Thomas 1653-1723 .... **LC 94**
See also DLB 80; RGEL 2

Durkheim, Emile 1858-1917 .... **TCLC 55**
See also CA 249

Durrell, Lawrence (George)
1912-1990 ..... **CLC 1, 4, 6, 8, 13, 27, 41**
See also BPFB 1; BRWS 1; CA 9-12R; 132; CANR 40, 77; CDBLB 1945-1960; CN 1, 2, 3, 4; CP 1, 2, 3, 4, 5; DAM NOV; DLB 15, 27, 204; DLBY 1990; EWL 3; MTCW 1, 2; RGEL 2; SFW 4; TEA

Durrenmatt, Friedrich
See Duerrenmatt, Friedrich
See also CDWLB 2; EW 13; EWL 3; RGHL; RGWL 2, 3

Dutt, Michael Madhusudan
1824-1873 .... **NCLC 118**

Dutt, Toru 1856-1877 .... **NCLC 29**
See also DLB 240

Eliade, Mircea 1907-1986 .... **CLC 19**
See also CA 65-68; 119; CANR 30, 62; CD-
WLB 4; DLB 220; EWL 3; MTCW 1;
RGWL 3; SFW 4

Eliot, A. D.
See Jewett, (Theodora) Sarah Orne

Eliot, Alice
See Jewett, (Theodora) Sarah Orne

Eliot, Dan
See Silverberg, Robert

Eliot, George 1819-1880 ...... **NCLC 4, 13, 23, 41, 49, 89, 118; PC 20; SSC 72; WLC 2**
See Evans, Mary Ann
See also BRW 5; BRWC 1, 2; BRWR 2;
CDBLB 1832-1890; CN 7; CPW; DA;
DA3; DAB; DAC; DAM MST, NOV;
DLB 21, 35, 55; FL 1:3; LATS 1:1; LMFS
1; NFS 17, 20; RGEL 2; RGSF 2; SSFS
8; TEA; WLIT 3

Eliot, John 1604-1690 .... **LC 5**
See also DLB 24

Eliot, T(homas) S(tearns)
1888-1965 ...... **CLC 1, 2, 3, 6, 9, 10, 13, 15, 24, 34, 41, 55, 57, 113; PC 5, 31; WLC 2**
See also AAYA 28; AMW; AMWC 1;
AMWR 1; BRW 7; BRWR 2; CA 5-8R;
25-28R; CANR 41; CBD; CDALB 1929-
1941; DA; DA3; DAB; DAC; DAM
DRAM, MST, POET; DFS 4, 13; DLB 7,
10, 45, 63, 245; DLBY 1988; EWL 3;
EXPP; LAIT 3; LATS 1:1; LMFS 2; MAL
5; MTCW 1, 2; MTFW 2005; NCFS 5;
PAB; PFS 1, 7, 20; RGAL 4; RGEL 2;
TUS; WLIT 4; WP

Elisabeth of Schonau c.
1129-1165 .... **CMLC 82**

Elizabeth 1866-1941 .... **TCLC 41**

Elizabeth I 1533-1603 .... **LC 118**
See also DLB 136

Elkin, Stanley L(awrence)
1930-1995 .. **CLC 4, 6, 9, 14, 27, 51, 91; SSC 12**
See also AMWS 6; BPFB 1; CA 9-12R;
148; CANR 8, 46; CN 1, 2, 3, 4, 5, 6;
CPW; DAM NOV, POP; DLB 2, 28, 218,
278; DLBY 1980; EWL 3; INT CANR-8;
MAL 5; MTCW 1, 2; MTFW 2005;
RGAL 4; TCLE 1:1

Elledge, Scott .... **CLC 34**

Eller, Scott
See Shepard, James R.

Elliott, Don
See Silverberg, Robert

Elliott, George P(aul) 1918-1980 .... **CLC 2**
See also CA 1-4R; 97-100; CANR 2; CN 1,
2; CP 3; DLB 244; MAL 5

Elliott, Janice 1931-1995 .... **CLC 47**
See also CA 13-16R; CANR 8, 29, 84; CN
5, 6, 7; DLB 14; SATA 119

Elliott, Sumner Locke 1917-1991 ..... **CLC 38**
See also CA 5-8R; 134; CANR 2, 21; DLB
289

Elliott, William
See Bradbury, Ray (Douglas)

Ellis, A. E. .... **CLC 7**

Ellis, Alice Thomas .... **CLC 40**
See Haycraft, Anna
See also CN 4, 5, 6; DLB 194

Ellis, Bret Easton 1964- ...... **CLC 39, 71, 117**
See also AAYA 2, 43; CA 118; 123; CANR
51, 74, 126; CN 6, 7; CPW; DA3; DAM
POP; DLB 292; HGG; INT CA-123;
MTCW 2; MTFW 2005; NFS 11

Ellis, (Henry) Havelock
1859-1939 .... **TCLC 14**
See also CA 109; 169; DLB 190

Ellis, Landon
See Ellison, Harlan (Jay)

Ellis, Trey 1962- .... **CLC 55**
See also CA 146; CANR 92; CN 7

Ellison, Harlan (Jay) 1934- ... **CLC 1, 13, 42, 139; SSC 14**
See also AAYA 29; BPFB 1; BYA 14; CA
5-8R; CANR 5, 46, 115; CPW; DAM
POP; DLB 8; HGG; INT CANR-5;
MTCW 1, 2; MTFW 2005; SCFW 2;
SFW 4; SSFS 13, 14, 15, 21; SUFW 1, 2

Ellison, Ralph (Waldo) 1914-1994 .... **BLC 1; CLC 1, 3, 11, 54, 86, 114; SSC 26, 79; WLC 2**
See also AAYA 19; AFAW 1, 2; AMWC 2;
AMWR 2; AMWS 2; BPFB 1; BW 1, 3;
BYA 2; CA 9-12R; 145; CANR 24, 53;
CDALB 1941-1968; CN 1, 2, 3, 4, 5;
CSW; DA; DA3; DAB; DAC; DAM MST,
MULT, NOV; DLB 2, 76, 227; DLBY
1994; EWL 3; EXPN; EXPS; LAIT 4;
MAL 5; MTCW 1, 2; MTFW 2005; NCFS
3; NFS 2, 21; RGAL 4; RGSF 2; SSFS 1,
11; YAW

Ellmann, Lucy 1956- .... **CLC 61**
See also CA 128; CANR 154

Ellmann, Lucy Elizabeth
See Ellmann, Lucy

Ellmann, Richard (David)
1918-1987 .... **CLC 50**
See also BEST 89:2; CA 1-4R; 122; CANR
2, 28, 61; DLB 103; DLBY 1987; MTCW
1, 2; MTFW 2005

Elman, Richard (Martin)
1934-1997 .... **CLC 19**
See also CA 17-20R; 163; CAAS 3; CANR
47; TCLE 1:1

Elron
See Hubbard, L. Ron

El Saadawi, Nawal 1931- .... **CLC 196**
See al'Sadaawi, Nawal; Sa'adawi, al-
Nawal; Saadawi, Nawal El; Sa'dawi,
Nawal al-
See also CA 118; CAAS 11; CANR 44, 92

Eluard, Paul .... **PC 38; TCLC 7, 41**
See Grindel, Eugene
See also EWL 3; GFL 1789 to the Present;
RGWL 2, 3

Elyot, Thomas 1490(?)-1546 .... **LC 11**
See also DLB 136; RGEL 2

Elytis, Odysseus 1911-1996 .... **CLC 15, 49, 100; PC 21**
See Alepoudelis, Odysseus
See also CA 102; 151; CANR 94; CWW 2;
DAM POET; EW 13; EWL 3; MTCW 1,
2; RGWL 2, 3

Emecheta, (Florence Onye) Buchi
1944- ...... **BLC 2; CLC 14, 48, 128, 214**
See also AAYA 67; AFW; BW 2, 3; CA 81-
84; CANR 27, 81, 126; CDWLB 3; CN
4, 5, 6, 7; CWRI 5; DA3; DAM MULT;
DLB 117; EWL 3; FL 1:5; FW; MTCW
1, 2; MTFW 2005; NFS 12, 14; SATA 66;
WLIT 2

Emerson, Mary Moody
1774-1863 .... **NCLC 66**

Emerson, Ralph Waldo 1803-1882 . **NCLC 1, 38, 98; PC 18; WLC 2**
See also AAYA 60; AMW; ANW; CDALB
1640-1865; DA; DA3; DAB; DAC; DAM
MST, POET; DLB 1, 59, 73, 183, 223,
270; EXPP; LAIT 2; LMFS 1; NCFS 3;
PFS 4, 17; RGAL 4; TUS; WP

Eminem 1972- .... **CLC 226**
See also CA 245

Eminescu, Mihail 1850-1889 .. **NCLC 33, 131**

Empedocles 5th cent. B.C.- .... **CMLC 50**
See also DLB 176

Empson, William 1906-1984 ... **CLC 3, 8, 19, 33, 34**
See also BRWS 2; CA 17-20R; 112; CANR
31, 61; CP 1, 2, 3; DLB 20; EWL 3;
MTCW 1, 2; RGEL 2

Enchi, Fumiko (Ueda) 1905-1986 ..... **CLC 31**
See Enchi Fumiko
See also CA 129; 121; FW; MJW

Enchi Fumiko
See Enchi, Fumiko (Ueda)
See also DLB 182; EWL 3

Ende, Michael (Andreas Helmuth)
1929-1995 .... **CLC 31**
See also BYA 5; CA 118; 124; 149; CANR
36, 110; CLR 14; DLB 75; MAICYA 1,
2; MAICYAS 1; SATA 61, 130; SATA-
Brief 42; SATA-Obit 86

Endo, Shusaku 1923-1996 ..... **CLC 7, 14, 19, 54, 99; SSC 48; TCLC 152**
See Endo Shusaku
See also CA 29-32R; 153; CANR 21, 54,
131; DA3; DAM NOV; MTCW 1, 2;
MTFW 2005; RGSF 2; RGWL 2, 3

Endo Shusaku
See Endo, Shusaku
See also CWW 2; DLB 182; EWL 3

Engel, Marian 1933-1985 .... **CLC 36; TCLC 137**
See also CA 25-28R; CANR 12; CN 2, 3;
DLB 53; FW; INT CANR-12

Engelhardt, Frederick
See Hubbard, L. Ron

Engels, Friedrich 1820-1895 .. **NCLC 85, 114**
See also DLB 129; LATS 1:1

Enright, D(ennis) J(oseph)
1920-2002 .... **CLC 4, 8, 31**
See also CA 1-4R; 211; CANR 1, 42, 83;
CN 1, 2; CP 1, 2, 3, 4, 5, 6, 7; DLB 27;
EWL 3; SATA 25; SATA-Obit 140

Ensler, Eve 1953- .... **CLC 212**
See also CA 172; CANR 126; DFS 23

Enzensberger, Hans Magnus
1929- .... **CLC 43; PC 28**
See also CA 116; 119; CANR 103; CWW
2; EWL 3

Ephron, Nora 1941- .... **CLC 17, 31**
See also AAYA 35; AITN 2; CA 65-68;
CANR 12, 39, 83; DFS 22

Epicurus 341B.C.-270B.C. .... **CMLC 21**
See also DLB 176

Epsilon
See Betjeman, John

Epstein, Daniel Mark 1948- .... **CLC 7**
See also CA 49-52; CANR 2, 53, 90

Epstein, Jacob 1956- .... **CLC 19**
See also CA 114

Epstein, Jean 1897-1953 .... **TCLC 92**

Epstein, Joseph 1937- .... **CLC 39, 204**
See also AMWS 14; CA 112; 119; CANR
50, 65, 117

Epstein, Leslie 1938- .... **CLC 27**
See also AMWS 12; CA 73-76, 215; CAAE
215; CAAS 12; CANR 23, 69; DLB 299;
RGHL

Equiano, Olaudah 1745(?)-1797 . **BLC 2; LC 16**
See also AFAW 1, 2; CDWLB 3; DAM
MULT; DLB 37, 50; WLIT 2

Erasmus, Desiderius 1469(?)-1536 ..... **LC 16, 93**
See also DLB 136; EW 2; LMFS 1; RGWL
2, 3; TWA

Erdman, Paul E(mil) 1932- .... **CLC 25**
See also AITN 1; CA 61-64; CANR 13, 43,
84

Erdrich, Karen Louise
See Erdrich, Louise

Erdrich, Louise 1954- .... **CLC 39, 54, 120, 176; NNAL; PC 52**
See also AAYA 10, 47; AMWS 4; BEST 89:1; BPFB 1; CA 114; CANR 41, 62, 118, 138; CDALBS; CN 5, 6, 7; CP 6, 7; CPW; CWP; DA3; DAM MULT, NOV, POP; DLB 152, 175, 206; EWL 3; EXPP; FL 1:5; LAIT 5; LATS 1:2; MAL 5; MTCW 1, 2; MTFW 2005; NFS 5; PFS 14; RGAL 4; SATA 94, 141; SSFS 14, 22; TCWW 2

Erenburg, Ilya (Grigoryevich)
See Ehrenburg, Ilya (Grigoryevich)

Erickson, Stephen Michael 1950-
See Erickson, Steve
See also CA 129; SFW 4

Erickson, Steve .... **CLC 64**
See Erickson, Stephen Michael
See also CANR 60, 68, 136; MTFW 2005; SUFW 2

Erickson, Walter
See Fast, Howard (Melvin)

Ericson, Walter
See Fast, Howard (Melvin)

Eriksson, Buntel
See Bergman, (Ernst) Ingmar

Eriugena, John Scottus c. 810-877 .... **CMLC 65**
See also DLB 115

Ernaux, Annie 1940- .... **CLC 88, 184**
See also CA 147; CANR 93; MTFW 2005; NCFS 3, 5

Erskine, John 1879-1951 .... **TCLC 84**
See also CA 112; 159; DLB 9, 102; FANT

Eschenbach, Wolfram von
See Wolfram von Eschenbach
See also RGWL 3

Eseki, Bruno
See Mphahlele, Ezekiel

Esenin, Sergei (Alexandrovich) 1895-1925 .... **TCLC 4**
See Yesenin, Sergey
See also CA 104; RGWL 2, 3

Eshleman, Clayton 1935- .... **CLC 7**
See also CA 33-36R; 212; CAAE 212; CAAS 6; CANR 93; CP 1, 2, 3, 4, 5, 6, 7; DLB 5

Espriella, Don Manuel Alvarez
See Southey, Robert

Espriu, Salvador 1913-1985 .... **CLC 9**
See also CA 154; 115; DLB 134; EWL 3

Espronceda, Jose de 1808-1842 ..... **NCLC 39**

Esquivel, Laura 1951(?)- ... **CLC 141; HLCS 1**
See also AAYA 29; CA 143; CANR 68, 113; DA3; DNFS 2; LAIT 3; LMFS 2; MTCW 2; MTFW 2005; NFS 5; WLIT 1

Esse, James
See Stephens, James

Esterbrook, Tom
See Hubbard, L. Ron

Estleman, Loren D. 1952- .... **CLC 48**
See also AAYA 27; CA 85-88; CANR 27, 74, 139; CMW 4; CPW; DA3; DAM NOV, POP; DLB 226; INT CANR-27; MTCW 1, 2; MTFW 2005; TCWW 1, 2

Etherege, Sir George 1636-1692 . **DC 23; LC 78**
See also BRW 2; DAM DRAM; DLB 80; PAB; RGEL 2

Euclid 306B.C.-283B.C. .... **CMLC 25**

Eugenides, Jeffrey 1960(?)- .... **CLC 81, 212**
See also AAYA 51; CA 144; CANR 120; MTFW 2005

Euripides c. 484B.C.-406B.C. .... **CMLC 23, 51; DC 4; WLCS**
See also AW 1; CDWLB 1; DA; DA3; DAB; DAC; DAM DRAM, MST; DFS 1, 4, 6; DLB 176; LAIT 1; LMFS 1; RGWL 2, 3; WLIT 8

Evan, Evin
See Faust, Frederick (Schiller)

Evans, Caradoc 1878-1945 ... **SSC 43; TCLC 85**
See also DLB 162

Evans, Evan
See Faust, Frederick (Schiller)

Evans, Marian
See Eliot, George

Evans, Mary Ann
See Eliot, George
See also NFS 20

Evarts, Esther
See Benson, Sally

Everett, Percival
See Everett, Percival L.
See also CSW

Everett, Percival L. 1956- .... **CLC 57**
See Everett, Percival
See also BW 2; CA 129; CANR 94, 134; CN 7; MTFW 2005

Everson, R(onald) G(ilmour) 1903-1992 .... **CLC 27**
See also CA 17-20R; CP 1, 2, 3, 4; DLB 88

Everson, William (Oliver) 1912-1994 .... **CLC 1, 5, 14**
See Antoninus, Brother
See also BG 1:2; CA 9-12R; 145; CANR 20; CP 2, 3, 4, 5; DLB 5, 16, 212; MTCW 1

Evtushenko, Evgenii Aleksandrovich
See Yevtushenko, Yevgeny (Alexandrovich)
See also CWW 2; RGWL 2, 3

Ewart, Gavin (Buchanan) 1916-1995 .... **CLC 13, 46**
See also BRWS 7; CA 89-92; 150; CANR 17, 46; CP 1, 2, 3, 4, 5, 6; DLB 40; MTCW 1

Ewers, Hanns Heinz 1871-1943 ..... **TCLC 12**
See also CA 109; 149

Ewing, Frederick R.
See Sturgeon, Theodore (Hamilton)

Exley, Frederick (Earl) 1929-1992 .... **CLC 6, 11**
See also AITN 2; BPFB 1; CA 81-84; 138; CANR 117; DLB 143; DLBY 1981

Eynhardt, Guillermo
See Quiroga, Horacio (Sylvestre)

Ezekiel, Nissim (Moses) 1924-2004 .. **CLC 61**
See also CA 61-64; 223; CP 1, 2, 3, 4, 5, 6, 7; DLB 323; EWL 3

Ezekiel, Tish O'Dowd 1943- .... **CLC 34**
See also CA 129

Fadeev, Aleksandr Aleksandrovich
See Bulgya, Alexander Alexandrovich
See also DLB 272

Fadeev, Alexandr Alexandrovich
See Bulgya, Alexander Alexandrovich
See also EWL 3

Fadeyev, A.
See Bulgya, Alexander Alexandrovich

Fadeyev, Alexander .... **TCLC 53**
See Bulgya, Alexander Alexandrovich

Fagen, Donald 1948- .... **CLC 26**

Fainzilberg, Ilya Arnoldovich 1897-1937
See Ilf, Ilya
See also CA 120; 165

Fair, Ronald L. 1932- .... **CLC 18**
See also BW 1; CA 69-72; CANR 25; DLB 33

Fairbairn, Roger
See Carr, John Dickson

Fairbairns, Zoe (Ann) 1948- .... **CLC 32**
See also CA 103; CANR 21, 85; CN 4, 5, 6, 7

Fairfield, Flora
See Alcott, Louisa May

Fairman, Paul W. 1916-1977
See Queen, Ellery
See also CA 114; SFW 4

Falco, Gian
See Papini, Giovanni

Falconer, James
See Kirkup, James

Falconer, Kenneth
See Kornbluth, C(yril) M.

Falkland, Samuel
See Heijermans, Herman

Fallaci, Oriana 1930- .... **CLC 11, 110**
See also CA 77-80; CANR 15, 58, 134; FW; MTCW 1

Faludi, Susan 1959- .... **CLC 140**
See also CA 138; CANR 126; FW; MTFW 2; MTFW 2005; NCFS 3

Faludy, George 1913- .... **CLC 42**
See also CA 21-24R

Faludy, Gyoergy
See Faludy, George

Fanon, Frantz 1925-1961 .... **BLC 2; CLC 74**
See also BW 1; CA 116; 89-92; DAM MULT; DLB 296; LMFS 2; WLIT 2

Fanshawe, Ann 1625-1680 .... **LC 11**

Fante, John (Thomas) 1911-1983 .... **CLC 60; SSC 65**
See also AMWS 11; CA 69-72; 109; CANR 23, 104; DLB 130; DLBY 1983

Far, Sui Sin .... **SSC 62**
See Eaton, Edith Maude
See also SSFS 4

Farah, Nuruddin 1945- ...... **BLC 2; CLC 53, 137**
See also AFW; BW 2, 3; CA 106; CANR 81, 148; CDWLB 3; CN 4, 5, 6, 7; DAM MULT; DLB 125; EWL 3; WLIT 2

Fargue, Leon-Paul 1876(?)-1947 .... **TCLC 11**
See also CA 109; CANR 107; DLB 258; EWL 3

Farigoule, Louis
See Romains, Jules

Farina, Richard 1936(?)-1966 .... **CLC 9**
See also CA 81-84; 25-28R

Farley, Walter (Lorimer) 1915-1989 .... **CLC 17**
See also AAYA 58; BYA 14; CA 17-20R; CANR 8, 29, 84; DLB 22; JRDA; MAICYA 1, 2; SATA 2, 43, 132; YAW

Farmer, Philip Jose 1918- .... **CLC 1, 19**
See also AAYA 28; BPFB 1; CA 1-4R; CANR 4, 35, 111; DLB 8; MTCW 1; SATA 93; SCFW 1, 2; SFW 4

Farquhar, George 1677-1707 .... **LC 21**
See also BRW 2; DAM DRAM; DLB 84; RGEL 2

Farrell, J(ames) G(ordon) 1935-1979 .... **CLC 6**
See also CA 73-76; 89-92; CANR 36; CN 1, 2; DLB 14, 271, 326; MTCW 1; RGEL 2; RHW; WLIT 4

Farrell, James T(homas) 1904-1979 . **CLC 1, 4, 8, 11, 66; SSC 28**
See also AMW; BPFB 1; CA 5-8R; 89-92; CANR 9, 61; CN 1, 2; DLB 4, 9, 86; DLBD 2; EWL 3; MAL 5; MTCW 1, 2; MTFW 2005; RGAL 4

Farrell, Warren (Thomas) 1943- ...... **CLC 70**
See also CA 146; CANR 120

Farren, Richard J.
See Betjeman, John

Farren, Richard M.
See Betjeman, John

Fassbinder, Rainer Werner
1946-1982 .... **CLC 20**
See also CA 93-96; 106; CANR 31

Fast, Howard (Melvin) 1914-2003 .. **CLC 23, 131**
See also AAYA 16; BPFB 1; CA 1-4R, 181; 214; CAAE 181; CAAS 18; CANR 1, 33, 54, 75, 98, 140; CMW 4; CN 1, 2, 3, 4, 5, 6, 7; CPW; DAM NOV; DLB 9; INT CANR-33; LATS 1:1; MAL 5; MTCW 2; MTFW 2005; RHW; SATA 7; SATA-Essay 107; TCWW 1, 2; YAW

Faulcon, Robert
See Holdstock, Robert P.

Faulkner, William (Cuthbert)
1897-1962 .... **CLC 1, 3, 6, 8, 9, 11, 14, 18, 28, 52, 68; SSC 1, 35, 42, 92; TCLC 141; WLC 2**
See also AAYA 7; AMW; AMWR 1; BPFB 1; BYA 5, 15; CA 81-84; CANR 33; CDALB 1929-1941; DA; DA3; DAB; DAC; DAM MST, NOV; DLB 9, 11, 44, 102, 316; DLBD 2; DLBY 1986, 1997; EWL 3; EXPN; EXPS; GL 2; LAIT 2; LATS 1:1; LMFS 2; MAL 5; MTCW 1, 2; MTFW 2005; NFS 4, 8, 13; RGAL 4; RGSF 2; SSFS 2, 5, 6, 12; TUS

Fauset, Jessie Redmon
1882(?)-1961 .. **BLC 2; CLC 19, 54; HR 1:2**
See also AFAW 2; BW 1; CA 109; CANR 83; DAM MULT; DLB 51; FW; LMFS 2; MAL 5; MBL

Faust, Frederick (Schiller)
1892-1944 .... **TCLC 49**
See Brand, Max; Dawson, Peter; Frederick, John
See also CA 108; 152; CANR 143; DAM POP; DLB 256; TUS

Faust, Irvin 1924- .... **CLC 8**
See also CA 33-36R; CANR 28, 67; CN 1, 2, 3, 4, 5, 6, 7; DLB 2, 28, 218, 278; DLBY 1980

Fawkes, Guy
See Benchley, Robert (Charles)

Fearing, Kenneth (Flexner)
1902-1961 .... **CLC 51**
See also CA 93-96; CANR 59; CMW 4; DLB 9; MAL 5; RGAL 4

Fecamps, Elise
See Creasey, John

Federman, Raymond 1928- .... **CLC 6, 47**
See also CA 17-20R, 208; CAAE 208; CAAS 8; CANR 10, 43, 83, 108; CN 3, 4, 5, 6; DLBY 1980

Federspiel, J(uerg) F. 1931- .... **CLC 42**
See also CA 146

Feiffer, Jules (Ralph) 1929- ...... **CLC 2, 8, 64**
See also AAYA 3, 62; CA 17-20R; CAD; CANR 30, 59, 129; CD 5, 6; DAM DRAM; DLB 7, 44; INT CANR-30; MTCW 1; SATA 8, 61, 111, 157

Feige, Hermann Albert Otto Maximilian
See Traven, B.

Feinberg, David B. 1956-1994 .... **CLC 59**
See also CA 135; 147

Feinstein, Elaine 1930- .... **CLC 36**
See also CA 69-72; CAAS 1; CANR 31, 68, 121; CN 3, 4, 5, 6, 7; CP 2, 3, 4, 5, 6, 7; CWP; DLB 14, 40; MTCW 1

Feke, Gilbert David .... **CLC 65**

Feldman, Irving (Mordecai) 1928- ..... **CLC 7**
See also CA 1-4R; CANR 1; CP 1, 2, 3, 4, 5, 6, 7; DLB 169; TCLE 1:1

Felix-Tchicaya, Gerald
See Tchicaya, Gerald Felix

Fellini, Federico 1920-1993 .... **CLC 16, 85**
See also CA 65-68; 143; CANR 33

Felltham, Owen 1602(?)-1668 .... **LC 92**
See also DLB 126, 151

Felsen, Henry Gregor 1916-1995 ..... **CLC 17**
See also CA 1-4R; 180; CANR 1; SAAS 2; SATA 1

Felski, Rita .... **CLC 65**

Fenno, Jack
See Calisher, Hortense

Fenollosa, Ernest (Francisco)
1853-1908 .... **TCLC 91**

Fenton, James Martin 1949- .... **CLC 32, 209**
See also CA 102; CANR 108; CP 2, 3, 4, 5, 6, 7; DLB 40; PFS 11

Ferber, Edna 1887-1968 .... **CLC 18, 93**
See also AITN 1; CA 5-8R; 25-28R; CANR 68, 105; DLB 9, 28, 86, 266; MAL 5; MTCW 1, 2; MTFW 2005; RGAL 4; RHW; SATA 7; TCWW 1, 2

Ferdowsi, Abu'l Qasem
940-1020(?) .... **CMLC 43**
See Firdawsi, Abu al-Qasim
See also RGWL 2, 3

Ferguson, Helen
See Kavan, Anna

Ferguson, Niall 1964- .... **CLC 134**
See also CA 190; CANR 154

Ferguson, Samuel 1810-1886 .... **NCLC 33**
See also DLB 32; RGEL 2

Fergusson, Robert 1750-1774 .... **LC 29**
See also DLB 109; RGEL 2

Ferling, Lawrence
See Ferlinghetti, Lawrence

Ferlinghetti, Lawrence 1919(?)- .... **CLC 2, 6, 10, 27, 111; PC 1**
See also BG 1:2; CA 5-8R; CAD; CANR 3, 41, 73, 125; CDALB 1941-1968; CP 1, 2, 3, 4, 5, 6, 7; DA3; DAM POET; DLB 5, 16; MAL 5; MTCW 1, 2; MTFW 2005; RGAL 4; WP

Ferlinghetti, Lawrence Monsanto
See Ferlinghetti, Lawrence

Fern, Fanny
See Parton, Sara Payson Willis

Fernandez, Vicente Garcia Huidobro
See Huidobro Fernandez, Vicente Garcia

Fernandez-Armesto, Felipe .... **CLC 70**
See Fernandez-Armesto, Felipe Fermin Ricardo
See also CANR 153

Fernandez-Armesto, Felipe Fermin Ricardo
1950-
See Fernandez-Armesto, Felipe
See also CA 142; CANR 93

Fernandez de Lizardi, Jose Joaquin
See Lizardi, Jose Joaquin Fernandez de

Ferre, Rosario 1938- ...... **CLC 139; HLCS 1; SSC 36**
See also CA 131; CANR 55, 81, 134; CWW 2; DLB 145; EWL 3; HW 1, 2; LAWS 1; MTCW 2; MTFW 2005; WLIT 1

Ferrer, Gabriel (Francisco Victor) Miro
See Miro (Ferrer), Gabriel (Francisco Victor)

Ferrier, Susan (Edmonstone)
1782-1854 .... **NCLC 8**
See also DLB 116; RGEL 2

Ferrigno, Robert 1948(?)- .... **CLC 65**
See also CA 140; CANR 125

Ferron, Jacques 1921-1985 .... **CLC 94**
See also CA 117; 129; CCA 1; DAC; DLB 60; EWL 3

Feuchtwanger, Lion 1884-1958 .... **TCLC 3**
See also CA 104; 187; DLB 66; EWL 3; RGHL

Feuerbach, Ludwig 1804-1872 ..... **NCLC 139**
See also DLB 133

Feuillet, Octave 1821-1890 .... **NCLC 45**
See also DLB 192

Feydeau, Georges (Leon Jules Marie)
1862-1921 .... **TCLC 22**
See also CA 113; 152; CANR 84; DAM DRAM; DLB 192; EWL 3; GFL 1789 to the Present; RGWL 2, 3

Fichte, Johann Gottlieb
1762-1814 .... **NCLC 62**
See also DLB 90

Ficino, Marsilio 1433-1499 .... **LC 12**
See also LMFS 1

Fiedeler, Hans
See Doeblin, Alfred

Fiedler, Leslie A(aron) 1917-2003 ..... **CLC 4, 13, 24**
See also AMWS 13; CA 9-12R; 212; CANR 7, 63; CN 1, 2, 3, 4, 5, 6; DLB 28, 67; EWL 3; MAL 5; MTCW 1, 2; RGAL 4; TUS

Field, Andrew 1938- .... **CLC 44**
See also CA 97-100; CANR 25

Field, Eugene 1850-1895 .... **NCLC 3**
See also DLB 23, 42, 140; DLBD 13; MAICYA 1, 2; RGAL 4; SATA 16

Field, Gans T.
See Wellman, Manly Wade

Field, Michael 1915-1971 .... **TCLC 43**
See also CA 29-32R

Fielding, Helen 1958- .... **CLC 146, 217**
See also AAYA 65; CA 172; CANR 127; DLB 231; MTFW 2005

Fielding, Henry 1707-1754 .... **LC 1, 46, 85; WLC 2**
See also BRW 3; BRWR 1; CDBLB 1660-1789; DA; DA3; DAB; DAC; DAM DRAM, MST, NOV; DLB 39, 84, 101; NFS 18; RGEL 2; TEA; WLIT 3

Fielding, Sarah 1710-1768 .... **LC 1, 44**
See also DLB 39; RGEL 2; TEA

Fields, W. C. 1880-1946 .... **TCLC 80**
See also DLB 44

Fierstein, Harvey (Forbes) 1954- ..... **CLC 33**
See also CA 123; 129; CAD; CD 5, 6; CPW; DA3; DAM DRAM, POP; DFS 6; DLB 266; GLL; MAL 5

Figes, Eva 1932- .... **CLC 31**
See also CA 53-56; CANR 4, 44, 83; CN 2, 3, 4, 5, 6, 7; DLB 14, 271; FW; RGHL

Filippo, Eduardo de
See de Filippo, Eduardo

Finch, Anne 1661-1720 .... **LC 3; PC 21**
See also BRWS 9; DLB 95

Finch, Robert (Duer Claydon)
1900-1995 .... **CLC 18**
See also CA 57-60; CANR 9, 24, 49; CP 1, 2, 3, 4, 5, 6; DLB 88

Findley, Timothy (Irving Frederick)
1930-2002 .... **CLC 27, 102**
See also CA 25-28R; 206; CANR 12, 42, 69, 109; CCA 1; CN 4, 5, 6, 7; DAC; DAM MST; DLB 53; FANT; RHW

Fink, William
See Mencken, H(enry) L(ouis)

Firbank, Louis 1942-
See Reed, Lou
See also CA 117

Firbank, (Arthur Annesley) Ronald
1886-1926 .... **TCLC 1**
See also BRWS 2; CA 104; 177; DLB 36; EWL 3; RGEL 2

Firdawsi, Abu al-Qasim
See Ferdowsi, Abu'l Qasem
See also WLIT 6

Fish, Stanley
See Fish, Stanley Eugene

Fish, Stanley E.
See Fish, Stanley Eugene

Fish, Stanley Eugene 1938- .... **CLC 142**
See also CA 112; 132; CANR 90; DLB 67

Forsyth, Frederick 1938- .... **CLC 2, 5, 36**
See also BEST 89:4; CA 85-88; CANR 38, 62, 115, 137; CMW 4; CN 3, 4, 5, 6, 7; CPW; DAM NOV, POP; DLB 87; MTCW 1, 2; MTFW 2005

Forten, Charlotte L. 1837-1914 .... **BLC 2; TCLC 16**
See Grimke, Charlotte L(ottie) Forten
See also DLB 50, 239

Fortinbras
See Grieg, (Johan) Nordahl (Brun)

Foscolo, Ugo 1778-1827 .... **NCLC 8, 97**
See also EW 5; WLIT 7

Fosse, Bob .... **CLC 20**
See Fosse, Robert Louis

Fosse, Robert Louis 1927-1987
See Fosse, Bob
See also CA 110; 123

Foster, Hannah Webster
1758-1840 .... **NCLC 99**
See also DLB 37, 200; RGAL 4

Foster, Stephen Collins
1826-1864 .... **NCLC 26**
See also RGAL 4

Foucault, Michel 1926-1984 . **CLC 31, 34, 69**
See also CA 105; 113; CANR 34; DLB 242; EW 13; EWL 3; GFL 1789 to the Present; GLL 1; LMFS 2; MTCW 1, 2; TWA

Fouque, Friedrich (Heinrich Karl) de la Motte 1777-1843 .... **NCLC 2**
See also DLB 90; RGWL 2, 3; SUFW 1

Fourier, Charles 1772-1837 .... **NCLC 51**

Fournier, Henri-Alban 1886-1914
See Alain-Fournier
See also CA 104; 179

Fournier, Pierre 1916-1997 .... **CLC 11**
See Gascar, Pierre
See also CA 89-92; CANR 16, 40

Fowles, John 1926-2005 .... **CLC 1, 2, 3, 4, 6, 9, 10, 15, 33, 87; SSC 33**
See also BPFB 1; BRWS 1; CA 5-8R; 245; CANR 25, 71, 103; CDBLB 1960 to Present; CN 1, 2, 3, 4, 5, 6, 7; DA3; DAB; DAC; DAM MST; DLB 14, 139, 207; EWL 3; HGG; MTCW 1, 2; MTFW 2005; NFS 21; RGEL 2; RHW; SATA 22; SATA-Obit 171; TEA; WLIT 4

Fowles, John Robert
See Fowles, John

Fox, Paula 1923- .... **CLC 2, 8, 121**
See also AAYA 3, 37; BYA 3, 8; CA 73-76; CANR 20, 36, 62, 105; CLR 1, 44, 96; DLB 52; JRDA; MAICYA 1, 2; MTCW 1; NFS 12; SATA 17, 60, 120, 167; WYA; YAW

Fox, William Price (Jr.) 1926- .... **CLC 22**
See also CA 17-20R; CAAS 19; CANR 11, 142; CSW; DLB 2; DLBY 1981

Foxe, John 1517(?)-1587 .... **LC 14**
See also DLB 132

Frame, Janet .. **CLC 2, 3, 6, 22, 66, 96; SSC 29**
See Clutha, Janet Paterson Frame
See also CN 1, 2, 3, 4, 5, 6, 7; CP 2, 3, 4; CWP; EWL 3; RGEL 2; RGSF 2; TWA

France, Anatole .... **TCLC 9**
See Thibault, Jacques Anatole Francois
See also DLB 123; EWL 3; GFL 1789 to the Present; RGWL 2, 3; SUFW 1

Francis, Claude .... **CLC 50**
See also CA 192

Francis, Dick
See Francis, Richard Stanley
See also CN 2, 3, 4, 5, 6

Francis, Richard Stanley 1920- ... **CLC 2, 22, 42, 102**
See Francis, Dick
See also AAYA 5, 21; BEST 89:3; BPFB 1; CA 5-8R; CANR 9, 42, 68, 100, 141; CD-BLB 1960 to Present; CMW 4; CN 7; DA3; DAM POP; DLB 87; INT CANR-9; MSW; MTCW 1, 2; MTFW 2005

Francis, Robert (Churchill)
1901-1987 .... **CLC 15; PC 34**
See also AMWS 9; CA 1-4R; 123; CANR 1; CP 1, 2, 3, 4; EXPP; PFS 12; TCLE 1:1

Francis, Lord Jeffrey
See Jeffrey, Francis
See also DLB 107

Frank, Anne(lies Marie)
1929-1945 .... **TCLC 17; WLC 2**
See also AAYA 12; BYA 1; CA 113; 133; CANR 68; CLR 101; DA; DA3; DAB; DAC; DAM MST; LAIT 4; MAICYA 2; MAICYAS 1; MTCW 1, 2; MTFW 2005; NCFS 2; RGHL; SATA 87; SATA-Brief 42; WYA; YAW

Frank, Bruno 1887-1945 .... **TCLC 81**
See also CA 189; DLB 118; EWL 3

Frank, Elizabeth 1945- .... **CLC 39**
See also CA 121; 126; CANR 78, 150; INT CA-126

Frankl, Viktor E(mil) 1905-1997 ...... **CLC 93**
See also CA 65-68; 161; RGHL

Franklin, Benjamin
See Hasek, Jaroslav (Matej Frantisek)

Franklin, Benjamin 1706-1790 .... **LC 25; WLCS**
See also AMW; CDALB 1640-1865; DA; DA3; DAB; DAC; DAM MST; DLB 24, 43, 73, 183; LAIT 1; RGAL 4; TUS

Franklin, (Stella Maria Sarah) Miles (Lampe) 1879-1954 .... **TCLC 7**
See also CA 104; 164; DLB 230; FW; MTCW 2; RGEL 2; TWA

Franzen, Jonathan 1959- .... **CLC 202**
See also AAYA 65; CA 129; CANR 105

Fraser, Antonia (Pakenham) 1932- . **CLC 32, 107**
See also AAYA 57; CA 85-88; CANR 44, 65, 119; CMW; DLB 276; MTCW 1, 2; MTFW 2005; SATA-Brief 32

Fraser, George MacDonald 1925- ...... **CLC 7**
See also AAYA 48; CA 45-48; 180; CAAE 180; CANR 2, 48, 74; MTCW 2; RHW

Fraser, Sylvia 1935- .... **CLC 64**
See also CA 45-48; CANR 1, 16, 60; CCA 1

Frayn, Michael 1933- .... **CLC 3, 7, 31, 47, 176; DC 27**
See also AAYA 69; BRWC 2; BRWS 7; CA 5-8R; CANR 30, 69, 114, 133; CBD; CD 5, 6; CN 1, 2, 3, 4, 5, 6, 7; DAM DRAM, NOV; DFS 22; DLB 13, 14, 194, 245; FANT; MTCW 1, 2; MTFW 2005; SFW 4

Fraze, Candida (Merrill) 1945- .... **CLC 50**
See also CA 126

Frazer, Andrew
See Marlowe, Stephen

Frazer, J(ames) G(eorge)
1854-1941 .... **TCLC 32**
See also BRWS 3; CA 118; NCFS 5

Frazer, Robert Caine
See Creasey, John

Frazer, Sir James George
See Frazer, J(ames) G(eorge)

Frazier, Charles 1950- .... **CLC 109, 224**
See also AAYA 34; CA 161; CANR 126; CSW; DLB 292; MTFW 2005

Frazier, Ian 1951- .... **CLC 46**
See also CA 130; CANR 54, 93

Frederic, Harold 1856-1898 .... **NCLC 10**
See also AMW; DLB 12, 23; DLBD 13; MAL 5; NFS 22; RGAL 4

Frederick, John
See Faust, Frederick (Schiller)
See also TCWW 2

Frederick the Great 1712-1786 .... **LC 14**

Fredro, Aleksander 1793-1876 .... **NCLC 8**

Freeling, Nicolas 1927-2003 .... **CLC 38**
See also CA 49-52; 218; CAAS 12; CANR 1, 17, 50, 84; CMW 4; CN 1, 2, 3, 4, 5, 6; DLB 87

Freeman, Douglas Southall
1886-1953 .... **TCLC 11**
See also CA 109; 195; DLB 17; DLBD 17

Freeman, Judith 1946- .... **CLC 55**
See also CA 148; CANR 120; DLB 256

Freeman, Mary E(leanor) Wilkins
1852-1930 .... **SSC 1, 47; TCLC 9**
See also CA 106; 177; DLB 12, 78, 221; EXPS; FW; HGG; MBL; RGAL 4; RGSF 2; SSFS 4, 8; SUFW 1; TUS

Freeman, R(ichard) Austin
1862-1943 .... **TCLC 21**
See also CA 113; CANR 84; CMW 4; DLB 70

French, Albert 1943- .... **CLC 86**
See also BW 3; CA 167

French, Antonia
See Kureishi, Hanif

French, Marilyn 1929- .. **CLC 10, 18, 60, 177**
See also BPFB 1; CA 69-72; CANR 3, 31, 134; CN 5, 6, 7; CPW; DAM DRAM, NOV, POP; FL 1:5; FW; INT CANR-31; MTCW 1, 2; MTFW 2005

French, Paul
See Asimov, Isaac

Freneau, Philip Morin 1752-1832 .. **NCLC 1, 111**
See also AMWS 2; DLB 37, 43; RGAL 4

Freud, Sigmund 1856-1939 .... **TCLC 52**
See also CA 115; 133; CANR 69; DLB 296; EW 8; EWL 3; LATS 1:1; MTCW 1, 2; MTFW 2005; NCFS 3; TWA

Freytag, Gustav 1816-1895 .... **NCLC 109**
See also DLB 129

Friedan, Betty 1921-2006 .... **CLC 74**
See also CA 65-68; 248; CANR 18, 45, 74; DLB 246; FW; MTCW 1, 2; MTFW 2005; NCFS 5

Friedan, Betty Naomi
See Friedan, Betty

Friedlander, Saul 1932- .... **CLC 90**
See also CA 117; 130; CANR 72; RGHL

Friedman, B(ernard) H(arper)
1926- .... **CLC 7**
See also CA 1-4R; CANR 3, 48

Friedman, Bruce Jay 1930- ...... **CLC 3, 5, 56**
See also CA 9-12R; CAD; CANR 25, 52, 101; CD 5, 6; CN 1, 2, 3, 4, 5, 6, 7; DLB 2, 28, 244; INT CANR-25; MAL 5; SSFS 18

Friel, Brian 1929- .... **CLC 5, 42, 59, 115; DC 8; SSC 76**
See also BRWS 5; CA 21-24R; CANR 33, 69, 131; CBD; CD 5, 6; DFS 11; DLB 13, 319; EWL 3; MTCW 1; RGEL 2; TEA

Friis-Baastad, Babbis Ellinor
1921-1970 .... **CLC 12**
See also CA 17-20R; 134; SATA 7

Frisch, Max (Rudolf) 1911-1991 ... **CLC 3, 9, 14, 18, 32, 44; TCLC 121**
See also CA 85-88; 134; CANR 32, 74; CD-WLB 2; DAM DRAM, NOV; DLB 69, 124; EW 13; EWL 3; MTCW 1, 2; MTFW 2005; RGHL; RGWL 2, 3

Fromentin, Eugene (Samuel Auguste)
1820-1876 .... **NCLC 10, 125**
See also DLB 123; GFL 1789 to the Present

Frost, Frederick
See Faust, Frederick (Schiller)
Frost, Robert (Lee) 1874-1963 .. CLC 1, 3, 4, 9, 10, 13, 15, 26, 34, 44; PC 1, 39, 71; WLC 2
See also AAYA 21; AMW; AMWR 1; CA 89-92; CANR 33; CDALB 1917-1929; CLR 67; DA; DA3; DAB; DAC; DAM MST, POET; DLB 54, 284; DLBD 7; EWL 3; EXPP; MAL 5; MTCW 1, 2; MTFW 2005; PAB; PFS 1, 2, 3, 4, 5, 6, 7, 10, 13; RGAL 4; SATA 14; TUS; WP; WYA
Froude, James Anthony
1818-1894 .... NCLC 43
See also DLB 18, 57, 144
Froy, Herald
See Waterhouse, Keith (Spencer)
Fry, Christopher 1907-2005 ... CLC 2, 10, 14
See also BRWS 3; CA 17-20R; 240; CAAS 23; CANR 9, 30, 74, 132; CBD; CD 5, 6; CP 1, 2, 3, 4, 5, 6, 7; DAM DRAM; DLB 13; EWL 3; MTCW 1, 2; MTFW 2005; RGEL 2; SATA 66; TEA
Frye, (Herman) Northrop
1912-1991 .... CLC 24, 70; TCLC 165
See also CA 5-8R; 133; CANR 8, 37; DLB 67, 68, 246; EWL 3; MTCW 1, 2; MTFW 2005; RGAL 4; TWA
Fuchs, Daniel 1909-1993 .... CLC 8, 22
See also CA 81-84; 142; CAAS 5; CANR 40; CN 1, 2, 3, 4, 5; DLB 9, 26, 28; DLBY 1993; MAL 5
Fuchs, Daniel 1934- .... CLC 34
See also CA 37-40R; CANR 14, 48
Fuentes, Carlos 1928- .. CLC 3, 8, 10, 13, 22, 41, 60, 113; HLC 1; SSC 24; WLC 2
See also AAYA 4, 45; AITN 2; BPFB 1; CA 69-72; CANR 10, 32, 68, 104, 138; CDWLB 3; CWW 2; DA; DA3; DAB; DAC; DAM MST, MULT, NOV; DLB 113; DNFS 2; EWL 3; HW 1, 2; LAIT 3; LATS 1:2; LAW; LAWS 1; LMFS 2; MTCW 1, 2; MTFW 2005; NFS 8; RGSF 2; RGWL 2, 3; TWA; WLIT 1
Fuentes, Gregorio Lopez y
See Lopez y Fuentes, Gregorio
Fuertes, Gloria 1918-1998 .... PC 27
See also CA 178, 180; DLB 108; HW 2; SATA 115
Fugard, (Harold) Athol 1932- . CLC 5, 9, 14, 25, 40, 80, 211; DC 3
See also AAYA 17; AFW; CA 85-88; CANR 32, 54, 118; CD 5, 6; DAM DRAM; DFS 3, 6, 10; DLB 225; DNFS 1, 2; EWL 3; LATS 1:2; MTCW 1; MTFW 2005; RGEL 2; WLIT 2
Fugard, Sheila 1932- .... CLC 48
See also CA 125
Fujiwara no Teika 1162-1241 .... CMLC 73
See also DLB 203
Fukuyama, Francis 1952- .... CLC 131
See also CA 140; CANR 72, 125
Fuller, Charles (H.), (Jr.) 1939- .... BLC 2; CLC 25; DC 1
See also BW 2; CA 108; 112; CAD; CANR 87; CD 5, 6; DAM DRAM, MULT; DFS 8; DLB 38, 266; EWL 3; INT CA-112; MAL 5; MTCW 1
Fuller, Henry Blake 1857-1929 .... TCLC 103
See also CA 108; 177; DLB 12; RGAL 4
Fuller, John (Leopold) 1937- .... CLC 62
See also CA 21-24R; CANR 9, 44; CP 1, 2, 3, 4, 5, 6, 7; DLB 40
Fuller, Margaret
See Ossoli, Sarah Margaret (Fuller)
See also AMWS 2; DLB 183, 223, 239; FL 1:3

Fuller, Roy (Broadbent) 1912-1991 ... CLC 4, 28
See also BRWS 7; CA 5-8R; 135; CAAS 10; CANR 53, 83; CN 1, 2, 3, 4, 5; CP 1, 2, 3, 4, 5; CWRI 5; DLB 15, 20; EWL 3; RGEL 2; SATA 87
Fuller, Sarah Margaret
See Ossoli, Sarah Margaret (Fuller)
Fuller, Sarah Margaret
See Ossoli, Sarah Margaret (Fuller)
See also DLB 1, 59, 73
Fuller, Thomas 1608-1661 .... LC 111
See also DLB 151
Fulton, Alice 1952- .... CLC 52
See also CA 116; CANR 57, 88; CP 5, 6, 7; CWP; DLB 193
Furphy, Joseph 1843-1912 .... TCLC 25
See Collins, Tom
See also CA 163; DLB 230; EWL 3; RGEL 2
Fuson, Robert H(enderson) 1927- .... CLC 70
See also CA 89-92; CANR 103
Fussell, Paul 1924- .... CLC 74
See also BEST 90:1; CA 17-20R; CANR 8, 21, 35, 69, 135; INT CANR-21; MTCW 1, 2; MTFW 2005
Futabatei, Shimei 1864-1909 .... TCLC 44
See Futabatei Shimei
See also CA 162; MJW
Futabatei Shimei
See Futabatei, Shimei
See also DLB 180; EWL 3
Futrelle, Jacques 1875-1912 .... TCLC 19
See also CA 113; 155; CMW 4
Gaboriau, Emile 1835-1873 .... NCLC 14
See also CMW 4; MSW
Gadda, Carlo Emilio 1893-1973 ...... CLC 11; TCLC 144
See also CA 89-92; DLB 177; EWL 3; WLIT 7
Gaddis, William 1922-1998 ... CLC 1, 3, 6, 8, 10, 19, 43, 86
See also AMWS 4; BPFB 1; CA 17-20R; 172; CANR 21, 48, 148; CN 1, 2, 3, 4, 5, 6; DLB 2, 278; EWL 3; MAL 5; MTCW 1, 2; MTFW 2005; RGAL 4
Gaelique, Moruen le
See Jacob, (Cyprien-)Max
Gage, Walter
See Inge, William (Motter)
Gaiman, Neil 1960- .... CLC 195
See also AAYA 19, 42; CA 133; CANR 81, 129; CLR 109; DLB 261; HGG; MTFW 2005; SATA 85, 146; SFW 4; SUFW 2
Gaiman, Neil Richard
See Gaiman, Neil
Gaines, Ernest J(ames) 1933- .. BLC 2; CLC 3, 11, 18, 86, 181; SSC 68
See also AAYA 18; AFAW 1, 2; AITN 1; BPFB 2; BW 2, 3; BYA 6; CA 9-12R; CANR 6, 24, 42, 75, 126; CDALB 1968-1988; CLR 62; CN 1, 2, 3, 4, 5, 6, 7; CSW; DA3; DAM MULT; DLB 2, 33, 152; DLBY 1980; EWL 3; EXPN; LAIT 5; LATS 1:2; MAL 5; MTCW 1, 2; MTFW 2005; NFS 5, 7, 16; RGAL 4; RGSF 2; RHW; SATA 86; SSFS 5; YAW
Gaitskill, Mary 1954- .... CLC 69
See also CA 128; CANR 61, 152; DLB 244; TCLE 1:1
Gaitskill, Mary Lawrence
See Gaitskill, Mary
Gaius Suetonius Tranquillus
See Suetonius
Galdos, Benito Perez
See Perez Galdos, Benito
See also EW 7

Gale, Zona 1874-1938 .... TCLC 7
See also CA 105; 153; CANR 84; DAM DRAM; DFS 17; DLB 9, 78, 228; RGAL 4
Galeano, Eduardo (Hughes) 1940- . CLC 72; HLCS 1
See also CA 29-32R; CANR 13, 32, 100; HW 1
Galiano, Juan Valera y Alcala
See Valera y Alcala-Galiano, Juan
Galilei, Galileo 1564-1642 .... LC 45
Gallagher, Tess 1943- .... CLC 18, 63; PC 9
See also CA 106; CP 3, 4, 5, 6, 7; CWP; DAM POET; DLB 120, 212, 244; PFS 16
Gallant, Mavis 1922- ..... CLC 7, 18, 38, 172; SSC 5, 78
See also CA 69-72; CANR 29, 69, 117; CCA 1; CN 1, 2, 3, 4, 5, 6, 7; DAC; DAM MST; DLB 53; EWL 3; MTCW 1, 2; MTFW 2005; RGEL 2; RGSF 2
Gallant, Roy A(rthur) 1924- .... CLC 17
See also CA 5-8R; CANR 4, 29, 54, 117; CLR 30; MAICYA 1, 2; SATA 4, 68, 110
Gallico, Paul (William) 1897-1976 ..... CLC 2
See also AITN 1; CA 5-8R; 69-72; CANR 23; CN 1, 2; DLB 9, 171; FANT; MAICYA 1, 2; SATA 13
Gallo, Max Louis 1932- .... CLC 95
See also CA 85-88
Gallois, Lucien
See Desnos, Robert
Gallup, Ralph
See Whitemore, Hugh (John)
Galsworthy, John 1867-1933 .... SSC 22; TCLC 1, 45; WLC 2
See also BRW 6; CA 104; 141; CANR 75; CDBLB 1890-1914; DA; DA3; DAB; DAC; DAM DRAM, MST, NOV; DLB 10, 34, 98, 162; DLBD 16; EWL 3; MTCW 2; RGEL 2; SSFS 3; TEA
Galt, John 1779-1839 .... NCLC 1, 110
See also DLB 99, 116, 159; RGEL 2; RGSF 2
Galvin, James 1951- .... CLC 38
See also CA 108; CANR 26
Gamboa, Federico 1864-1939 .... TCLC 36
See also CA 167; HW 2; LAW
Gandhi, M. K.
See Gandhi, Mohandas Karamchand
Gandhi, Mahatma
See Gandhi, Mohandas Karamchand
Gandhi, Mohandas Karamchand
1869-1948 .... TCLC 59
See also CA 121; 132; DA3; DAM MULT; DLB 323; MTCW 1, 2
Gann, Ernest Kellogg 1910-1991 ..... CLC 23
See also AITN 1; BPFB 2; CA 1-4R; 136; CANR 1, 83; RHW
Gao Xingjian 1940- .... CLC 167
See Xingjian, Gao
See also MTFW 2005
Garber, Eric 1943(?)-
See Holleran, Andrew
See also CANR 89
Garcia, Cristina 1958- .... CLC 76
See also AMWS 11; CA 141; CANR 73, 130; CN 7; DLB 292; DNFS 1; EWL 3; HW 2; LLW; MTFW 2005
Garcia Lorca, Federico 1898-1936 ...... DC 2; HLC 2; PC 3; TCLC 1, 7, 49, 181; WLC 2
See Lorca, Federico Garcia
See also AAYA 46; CA 104; 131; CANR 81; DA; DA3; DAB; DAC; DAM DRAM, MST, MULT, POET; DFS 4, 10; DLB 108; EWL 3; HW 1, 2; LATS 1:2; MTCW 1, 2; MTFW 2005; TWA

Garcia Marquez, Gabriel 1928- .... **CLC 2, 3, 8, 10, 15, 27, 47, 55, 68, 170; HLC 1; SSC 8, 83; WLC 3**
See also AAYA 3, 33; BEST 89:1, 90:4; BPFB 2; BYA 12, 16; CA 33-36R; CANR 10, 28, 50, 75, 82, 128; CDWLB 3; CPW; CWW 2; DA; DA3; DAB; DAC; DAM MST, MULT, NOV, POP; DLB 113; DNFS 1, 2; EWL 3; EXPN; EXPS; HW 1, 2; LAIT 2; LATS 1:2; LAW; LAWS 1; LMFS 2; MTCW 1, 2; MTFW 2005; NCFS 3; NFS 1, 5, 10; RGSF 2; RGWL 2, 3; SSFS 1, 6, 16, 21; TWA; WLIT 1

Garcia Marquez, Gabriel Jose
See Garcia Marquez, Gabriel

Garcilaso de la Vega, El Inca
1539-1616 .... **HLCS 1; LC 127**
See also DLB 318; LAW

Gard, Janice
See Latham, Jean Lee

Gard, Roger Martin du
See Martin du Gard, Roger

Gardam, Jane (Mary) 1928- .... **CLC 43**
See also CA 49-52; CANR 2, 18, 33, 54, 106; CLR 12; DLB 14, 161, 231; MAICYA 1, 2; MTCW 1; SAAS 9; SATA 39, 76, 130; SATA-Brief 28; YAW

Gardner, Herb(ert George)
1934-2003 .... **CLC 44**
See also CA 149; 220; CAD; CANR 119; CD 5, 6; DFS 18, 20

Gardner, John (Champlin), Jr.
1933-1982 ...... **CLC 2, 3, 5, 7, 8, 10, 18, 28, 34; SSC 7**
See also AAYA 45; AITN 1; AMWS 6; BPFB 2; CA 65-68; 107; CANR 33, 73; CDALBS; CN 2, 3; CPW; DA3; DAM NOV, POP; DLB 2; DLBY 1982; EWL 3; FANT; LATS 1:2; MAL 5; MTCW 1, 2; MTFW 2005; NFS 3; RGAL 4; RGSF 2; SATA 40; SATA-Obit 31; SSFS 8

Gardner, John (Edmund) 1926- .... **CLC 30**
See also CA 103; CANR 15, 69, 127; CMW 4; CPW; DAM POP; MTCW 1

Gardner, Miriam
See Bradley, Marion Zimmer
See also GLL 1

Gardner, Noel
See Kuttner, Henry

Gardons, S. S.
See Snodgrass, W(illiam) D(e Witt)

Garfield, Leon 1921-1996 .... **CLC 12**
See also AAYA 8, 69; BYA 1, 3; CA 17-20R; 152; CANR 38, 41, 78; CLR 21; DLB 161; JRDA; MAICYA 1, 2; MAICYAS 1; SATA 1, 32, 76; SATA-Obit 90; TEA; WYA; YAW

Garland, (Hannibal) Hamlin
1860-1940 .... **SSC 18; TCLC 3**
See also CA 104; DLB 12, 71, 78, 186; MAL 5; RGAL 4; RGSF 2; TCWW 1, 2

Garneau, (Hector de) Saint-Denys
1912-1943 .... **TCLC 13**
See also CA 111; DLB 88

Garner, Alan 1934- .... **CLC 17**
See also AAYA 18; BYA 3, 5; CA 73-76; 178; CAAE 178; CANR 15, 64, 134; CLR 20; CPW; DAB; DAM POP; DLB 161, 261; FANT; MAICYA 1, 2; MTCW 1, 2; MTFW 2005; SATA 18, 69; SATA-Essay 108; SUFW 1, 2; YAW

Garner, Hugh 1913-1979 .... **CLC 13**
See Warwick, Jarvis
See also CA 69-72; CANR 31; CCA 1; CN 1, 2; DLB 68

Garnett, David 1892-1981 .... **CLC 3**
See also CA 5-8R; 103; CANR 17, 79; CN 1, 2; DLB 34; FANT; MTCW 2; RGEL 2; SFW 4; SUFW 1

Garnier, Robert c. 1545-1590 .... **LC 119**
See also DLB 327; GFL Beginnings to 1789

Garrett, George (Palmer, Jr.) 1929- . **CLC 3, 11, 51; SSC 30**
See also AMWS 7; BPFB 2; CA 1-4R, 202; CAAE 202; CAAS 5; CANR 1, 42, 67, 109; CN 1, 2, 3, 4, 5, 6, 7; CP 1, 2, 3, 4, 5, 6, 7; CSW; DLB 2, 5, 130, 152; DLBY 1983

Garrick, David 1717-1779 .... **LC 15**
See also DAM DRAM; DLB 84, 213; RGEL 2

Garrigue, Jean 1914-1972 .... **CLC 2, 8**
See also CA 5-8R; 37-40R; CANR 20; CP 1; MAL 5

Garrison, Frederick
See Sinclair, Upton

Garrison, William Lloyd
1805-1879 .... **NCLC 149**
See also CDALB 1640-1865; DLB 1, 43, 235

Garro, Elena 1920(?)-1998 .. **HLCS 1; TCLC 153**
See also CA 131; 169; CWW 2; DLB 145; EWL 3; HW 1; LAWS 1; WLIT 1

Garth, Will
See Hamilton, Edmond; Kuttner, Henry

Garvey, Marcus (Moziah, Jr.)
1887-1940 ... **BLC 2; HR 1:2; TCLC 41**
See also BW 1; CA 120; 124; CANR 79; DAM MULT

Gary, Romain .... **CLC 25**
See Kacew, Romain
See also DLB 83, 299; RGHL

Gascar, Pierre .... **CLC 11**
See Fournier, Pierre
See also EWL 3; RGHL

Gascoigne, George 1539-1577 .... **LC 108**
See also DLB 136; RGEL 2

Gascoyne, David (Emery)
1916-2001 .... **CLC 45**
See also CA 65-68; 200; CANR 10, 28, 54; CP 1, 2, 3, 4, 5, 6, 7; DLB 20; MTCW 1; RGEL 2

Gaskell, Elizabeth Cleghorn
1810-1865 .... **NCLC 5, 70, 97, 137; SSC 25**
See also BRW 5; CDBLB 1832-1890; DAB; DAM MST; DLB 21, 144, 159; RGEL 2; RGSF 2; TEA

Gass, William H(oward) 1924- . **CLC 1, 2, 8, 11, 15, 39, 132; SSC 12**
See also AMWS 6; CA 17-20R; CANR 30, 71, 100; CN 1, 2, 3, 4, 5, 6, 7; DLB 2, 227; EWL 3; MAL 5; MTCW 1, 2; MTFW 2005; RGAL 4

Gassendi, Pierre 1592-1655 .... **LC 54**
See also GFL Beginnings to 1789

Gasset, Jose Ortega y
See Ortega y Gasset, Jose

Gates, Henry Louis, Jr. 1950- ... **BLCS; CLC 65**
See also BW 2, 3; CA 109; CANR 25, 53, 75, 125; CSW; DA3; DAM MULT; DLB 67; EWL 3; MAL 5; MTCW 2; MTFW 2005; RGAL 4

Gatos, Stephanie
See Katz, Steve

Gautier, Theophile 1811-1872 .. **NCLC 1, 59; PC 18; SSC 20**
See also DAM POET; DLB 119; EW 6; GFL 1789 to the Present; RGWL 2, 3; SUFW; TWA

Gay, John 1685-1732 .... **LC 49**
See also BRW 3; DAM DRAM; DLB 84, 95; RGEL 2; WLIT 3

Gay, Oliver
See Gogarty, Oliver St. John

Gay, Peter 1923- .... **CLC 158**
See also CA 13-16R; CANR 18, 41, 77, 147; INT CANR-18; RGHL

Gay, Peter Jack
See Gay, Peter

Gaye, Marvin (Pentz, Jr.)
1939-1984 .... **CLC 26**
See also CA 195; 112

Gebler, Carlo 1954- .... **CLC 39**
See also CA 119; 133; CANR 96; DLB 271

Gee, Maggie (Mary) 1948- .... **CLC 57**
See also CA 130; CANR 125; CN 4, 5, 6, 7; DLB 207; MTFW 2005

Gee, Maurice 1931- .... **CLC 29**
See also AAYA 42; CA 97-100; CANR 67, 123; CLR 56; CN 2, 3, 4, 5, 6, 7; CWRI 5; EWL 3; MAICYA 2; RGSF 2; SATA 46, 101

Gee, Maurice Gough
See Gee, Maurice

Geiogamah, Hanay 1945- .... **NNAL**
See also CA 153; DAM MULT; DLB 175

Gelbart, Larry
See Gelbart, Larry (Simon)
See also CAD; CD 5, 6

Gelbart, Larry (Simon) 1928- .... **CLC 21, 61**
See Gelbart, Larry
See also CA 73-76; CANR 45, 94

Gelber, Jack 1932-2003 ...... **CLC 1, 6, 14, 79**
See also CA 1-4R; 216; CAD; CANR 2; DLB 7, 228; MAL 5

Gellhorn, Martha (Ellis)
1908-1998 .... **CLC 14, 60**
See also CA 77-80; 164; CANR 44; CN 1, 2, 3, 4, 5, 6 7; DLBY 1982, 1998

Genet, Jean 1910-1986 .. **CLC 1, 2, 5, 10, 14, 44, 46; DC 25; TCLC 128**
See also CA 13-16R; CANR 18; DA3; DAM DRAM; DFS 10; DLB 72, 321; DLBY 1986; EW 13; EWL 3; GFL 1789 to the Present; GLL 1; LMFS 2; MTCW 1, 2; MTFW 2005; RGWL 2, 3; TWA

Genlis, Stephanie-Felicite Ducrest
1746-1830 .... **NCLC 166**
See also DLB 313

Gent, Peter 1942- .... **CLC 29**
See also AITN 1; CA 89-92; DLBY 1982

Gentile, Giovanni 1875-1944 .... **TCLC 96**
See also CA 119

Gentlewoman in New England, A
See Bradstreet, Anne

Gentlewoman in Those Parts, A
See Bradstreet, Anne

Geoffrey of Monmouth c.
1100-1155 .... **CMLC 44**
See also DLB 146; TEA

George, Jean
See George, Jean Craighead

George, Jean Craighead 1919- .... **CLC 35**
See also AAYA 8, 69; BYA 2, 4; CA 5-8R; CANR 25; CLR 1; 80; DLB 52; JRDA; MAICYA 1, 2; SATA 2, 68, 124, 170; WYA; YAW

George, Stefan (Anton) 1868-1933 . **TCLC 2, 14**
See also CA 104; 193; EW 8; EWL 3

Georges, Georges Martin
See Simenon, Georges (Jacques Christian)

Gerald of Wales c. 1146-c. 1223 ... **CMLC 60**

Gerhardi, William Alexander
See Gerhardie, William Alexander

Gerhardie, William Alexander
1895-1977 .... **CLC 5**
See also CA 25-28R; 73-76; CANR 18; CN 1, 2; DLB 36; RGEL 2

Gerson, Jean 1363-1429 .... **LC 77**
See also DLB 208

Gersonides 1288-1344 .... **CMLC 49**
See also DLB 115

Gerstler, Amy 1956- .... **CLC 70**
  See also CA 146; CANR 99
Gertler, T. .... **CLC 34**
  See also CA 116; 121
Gertsen, Aleksandr Ivanovich
  See Herzen, Aleksandr Ivanovich
Ghalib .... **NCLC 39, 78**
  See Ghalib, Asadullah Khan
Ghalib, Asadullah Khan 1797-1869
  See Ghalib
  See also DAM POET; RGWL 2, 3
Ghelderode, Michel de 1898-1962 ..... **CLC 6,**
  11; DC 15
  See also CA 85-88; CANR 40, 77; DAM
  DRAM; DLB 321; EW 11; EWL 3; TWA
Ghiselin, Brewster 1903-2001 .... **CLC 23**
  See also CA 13-16R; CAAS 10; CANR 13;
  CP 1, 2, 3, 4, 5, 6, 7
Ghose, Aurabinda 1872-1950 .... **TCLC 63**
  See Ghose, Aurobindo
  See also CA 163
Ghose, Aurobindo
  See Ghose, Aurabinda
  See also EWL 3
Ghose, Zulfikar 1935- .... **CLC 42, 200**
  See also CA 65-68; CANR 67; CN 1, 2, 3,
  4, 5, 6, 7; CP 1, 2, 3, 4, 5, 6, 7; DLB 323;
  EWL 3
Ghosh, Amitav 1956- .... **CLC 44, 153**
  See also CA 147; CANR 80; CN 6, 7; DLB
  323; WWE 1
Giacosa, Giuseppe 1847-1906 .... **TCLC 7**
  See also CA 104
Gibb, Lee
  See Waterhouse, Keith (Spencer)
Gibbon, Edward 1737-1794 .... **LC 97**
  See also BRW 3; DLB 104; RGEL 2
Gibbon, Lewis Grassic .... **TCLC 4**
  See Mitchell, James Leslie
  See also RGEL 2
Gibbons, Kaye 1960- .... **CLC 50, 88, 145**
  See also AAYA 34; AMWS 10; CA 151;
  CANR 75, 127; CN 7; CSW; DA3; DAM
  POP; DLB 292; MTCW 2; MTFW 2005;
  NFS 3; RGAL 4; SATA 117
Gibran, Kahlil 1883-1931 . **PC 9; TCLC 1, 9**
  See also CA 104; 150; DA3; DAM POET,
  POP; EWL 3; MTCW 2; WLIT 6
Gibran, Khalil
  See Gibran, Kahlil
Gibson, Mel 1956- .... **CLC 215**
Gibson, William 1914- .... **CLC 23**
  See also CA 9-12R; CAD; CANR 9, 42, 75,
  125; CD 5, 6; DA; DAB; DAC; DAM
  DRAM, MST; DFS 2; DLB 7; LAIT 2;
  MAL 5; MTCW 2; MTFW 2005; SATA
  66; YAW
Gibson, William (Ford) 1948- ... **CLC 39, 63,**
  186, 192; SSC 52
  See also AAYA 12, 59; BPFB 2; CA 126;
  133; CANR 52, 90, 106; CN 6, 7; CPW;
  DA3; DAM POP; DLB 251; MTCW 2;
  MTFW 2005; SCFW 2; SFW 4
Gide, Andre (Paul Guillaume)
  1869-1951 ...... **SSC 13; TCLC 5, 12, 36,**
  177; WLC 3
  See also CA 104; 124; DA; DA3; DAB;
  DAC; DAM MST, NOV; DLB 65, 321;
  EW 8; EWL 3; GFL 1789 to the Present;
  MTCW 1, 2; MTFW 2005; NFS 21;
  RGSF 2; RGWL 2, 3; TWA
Gifford, Barry (Colby) 1946- .... **CLC 34**
  See also CA 65-68; CANR 9, 30, 40, 90
Gilbert, Frank
  See De Voto, Bernard (Augustine)
Gilbert, W(illiam) S(chwenck)
  1836-1911 .... **TCLC 3**
  See also CA 104; 173; DAM DRAM, POET;
  RGEL 2; SATA 36

Gilbert of Poitiers c. 1085-1154 .... **CMLC 85**
Gilbreth, Frank B(unker), Jr.
  1911-2001 .... **CLC 17**
  See also CA 9-12R; SATA 2
Gilchrist, Ellen (Louise) 1935- .. **CLC 34, 48,**
  143; SSC 14, 63
  See also BPFB 2; CA 113; 116; CANR 41,
  61, 104; CN 4, 5, 6, 7; CPW; CSW; DAM
  POP; DLB 130; EWL 3; EXPS; MTCW
  1, 2; MTFW 2005; RGAL 4; RGSF 2;
  SSFS 9
Giles, Molly 1942- .... **CLC 39**
  See also CA 126; CANR 98
Gill, Eric .... **TCLC 85**
  See Gill, (Arthur) Eric (Rowton Peter
  Joseph)
Gill, (Arthur) Eric (Rowton Peter Joseph)
  1882-1940
  See Gill, Eric
  See also CA 120; DLB 98
Gill, Patrick
  See Creasey, John
Gillette, Douglas .... **CLC 70**
Gilliam, Terry (Vance) 1940- .... **CLC 21, 141**
  See Monty Python
  See also AAYA 19, 59; CA 108; 113; CANR
  35; INT CA-113
Gillian, Jerry
  See Gilliam, Terry (Vance)
Gilliatt, Penelope (Ann Douglass)
  1932-1993 .... **CLC 2, 10, 13, 53**
  See also AITN 2; CA 13-16R; 141; CANR
  49; CN 1, 2, 3, 4, 5; DLB 14
Gilligan, Carol 1936- .... **CLC 208**
  See also CA 142; CANR 121; FW
Gilman, Charlotte (Anna) Perkins (Stetson)
  1860-1935 ...... **SSC 13, 62; TCLC 9, 37,**
  117
  See also AMWS 11; BYA 11; CA 106; 150;
  DLB 221; EXPS; FL 1:5; FW; HGG;
  LAIT 2; MBL; MTCW 2; MTFW 2005;
  RGAL 4; RGSF 2; SFW 4; SSFS 1, 18
Gilmour, David 1946- .... **CLC 35**
Gilpin, William 1724-1804 .... **NCLC 30**
Gilray, J. D.
  See Mencken, H(enry) L(ouis)
Gilroy, Frank D(aniel) 1925- .... **CLC 2**
  See also CA 81-84; CAD; CANR 32, 64,
  86; CD 5, 6; DFS 17; DLB 7
Gilstrap, John 1957(?)- .... **CLC 99**
  See also CA 160; CANR 101
Ginsberg, Allen 1926-1997 ... **CLC 1, 2, 3, 4,**
  6, 13, 36, 69, 109; PC 4, 47; TCLC
  120; WLC 3
  See also AAYA 33; AITN 1; AMWC 1;
  AMWS 2; BG 1:2; CA 1-4R; 157; CANR
  2, 41, 63, 95; CDALB 1941-1968; CP 1,
  2, 3, 4, 5, 6; DA; DA3; DAB; DAC; DAM
  MST, POET; DLB 5, 16, 169, 237; EWL
  3; GLL 1; LMFS 2; MAL 5; MTCW 1, 2;
  MTFW 2005; PAB; PFS 5; RGAL 4;
  TUS; WP
Ginzburg, Eugenia .... **CLC 59**
  See Ginzburg, Evgeniia
Ginzburg, Evgeniia 1904-1977
  See Ginzburg, Eugenia
  See also DLB 302
Ginzburg, Natalia 1916-1991 .... **CLC 5, 11,**
  54, 70; SSC 65; TCLC 156
  See also CA 85-88; 135; CANR 33; DFS
  14; DLB 177; EW 13; EWL 3; MTCW 1,
  2; MTFW 2005; RGHL; RGWL 2, 3
Giono, Jean 1895-1970 .... **CLC 4, 11; TCLC**
  124
  See also CA 45-48; 29-32R; CANR 2, 35;
  DLB 72, 321; EWL 3; GFL 1789 to the
  Present; MTCW 1; RGWL 2, 3

Giovanni, Nikki 1943- ..... **BLC 2; CLC 2, 4,**
  19, 64, 117; PC 19; WLCS
  See also AAYA 22; AITN 1; BW 2, 3; CA
  29-32R; CAAS 6; CANR 18, 41, 60, 91,
  130; CDALBS; CLR 6, 73; CP 2, 3, 4, 5,
  6, 7; CSW; CWP; CWRI 5; DA; DA3;
  DAB; DAC; DAM MST, MULT, POET;
  DLB 5, 41; EWL 3; EXPP; INT CANR-
  18; MAICYA 1, 2; MAL 5; MTCW 1, 2;
  MTFW 2005; PFS 17; RGAL 4; SATA
  24, 107; TUS; YAW
Giovene, Andrea 1904-1998 .... **CLC 7**
  See also CA 85-88
Gippius, Zinaida (Nikolaevna) 1869-1945
  See Hippius, Zinaida (Nikolaevna)
  See also CA 106; 212
Giraudoux, Jean(-Hippolyte)
  1882-1944 .... **TCLC 2, 7**
  See also CA 104; 196; DAM DRAM; DLB
  65, 321; EW 9; EWL 3; GFL 1789 to the
  Present; RGWL 2, 3; TWA
Gironella, Jose Maria (Pous)
  1917-2003 .... **CLC 11**
  See also CA 101; 212; EWL 3; RGWL 2, 3
Gissing, George (Robert)
  1857-1903 .... **SSC 37; TCLC 3, 24, 47**
  See also BRW 5; CA 105; 167; DLB 18,
  135, 184; RGEL 2; TEA
Gitlin, Todd 1943- .... **CLC 201**
  See also CA 29-32R; CANR 25, 50, 88
Giurlani, Aldo
  See Palazzeschi, Aldo
Gladkov, Fedor Vasil'evich
  See Gladkov, Fyodor (Vasilyevich)
  See also DLB 272
Gladkov, Fyodor (Vasilyevich)
  1883-1958 .... **TCLC 27**
  See Gladkov, Fedor Vasil'evich
  See also CA 170; EWL 3
Glancy, Diane 1941- .... **CLC 210; NNAL**
  See also CA 136; 225; CAAE 225; CAAS
  24; CANR 87; DLB 175
Glanville, Brian (Lester) 1931- .... **CLC 6**
  See also CA 5-8R; CAAS 9; CANR 3, 70;
  CN 1, 2, 3, 4, 5, 6, 7; DLB 15, 139; SATA
  42
Glasgow, Ellen (Anderson Gholson)
  1873-1945 .... **SSC 34; TCLC 2, 7**
  See also AMW; CA 104; 164; DLB 9, 12;
  MAL 5; MBL; MTCW 2; MTFW 2005;
  RGAL 4; RHW; SSFS 9; TUS
Glaspell, Susan 1882(?)-1948 ..... **DC 10; SSC**
  41; TCLC 55, 175
  See also AMWS 3; CA 110; 154; DFS 8,
  18; DLB 7, 9, 78, 228; MBL; RGAL 4;
  SSFS 3; TCWW 2; TUS; YABC 2
Glassco, John 1909-1981 .... **CLC 9**
  See also CA 13-16R; 102; CANR 15; CN
  1, 2; CP 1, 2, 3; DLB 68
Glasscock, Amnesia
  See Steinbeck, John (Ernst)
Glasser, Ronald J. 1940(?)- .... **CLC 37**
  See also CA 209
Glassman, Joyce
  See Johnson, Joyce
Gleick, James (W.) 1954- .... **CLC 147**
  See also CA 131; 137; CANR 97; INT CA-
  137
Glendinning, Victoria 1937- .... **CLC 50**
  See also CA 120; 127; CANR 59, 89; DLB
  155
Glissant, Edouard (Mathieu)
  1928- .... **CLC 10, 68**
  See also CA 153; CANR 111; CWW 2;
  DAM MULT; EWL 3; RGWL 3
Gloag, Julian 1930- .... **CLC 40**
  See also AITN 1; CA 65-68; CANR 10, 70;
  CN 1, 2, 3, 4, 5, 6

Glowacki, Aleksander
　　See Prus, Boleslaw
Gluck, Louise (Elisabeth) 1943- .. **CLC 7, 22, 44, 81, 160; PC 16**
　　See also AMWS 5; CA 33-36R; CANR 40, 69, 108, 133; CP 1, 2, 3, 4, 5, 6, 7; CWP; DA3; DAM POET; DLB 5; MAL 5; MTCW 2; MTFW 2005; PFS 5, 15; RGAL 4; TCLE 1:1
Glyn, Elinor 1864-1943 .... **TCLC 72**
　　See also DLB 153; RHW
Gobineau, Joseph-Arthur
　　1816-1882 .... **NCLC 17**
　　See also DLB 123; GFL 1789 to the Present
Godard, Jean-Luc 1930- .... **CLC 20**
　　See also CA 93-96
Godden, (Margaret) Rumer
　　1907-1998 .... **CLC 53**
　　See also AAYA 6; BPFB 2; BYA 2, 5; CA 5-8R; 172; CANR 4, 27, 36, 55, 80; CLR 20; CN 1, 2, 3, 4, 5, 6; CWRI 5; DLB 161; MAICYA 1, 2; RHW; SAAS 12; SATA 3, 36; SATA-Obit 109; TEA
Godoy Alcayaga, Lucila 1899-1957 .. **HLC 2; PC 32; TCLC 2**
　　See Mistral, Gabriela
　　See also BW 2; CA 104; 131; CANR 81; DAM MULT; DNFS; HW 1, 2; MTCW 1, 2; MTFW 2005
Godwin, Gail 1937- ...... **CLC 5, 8, 22, 31, 69, 125**
　　See also BPFB 2; CA 29-32R; CANR 15, 43, 69, 132; CN 3, 4, 5, 6, 7; CPW; CSW; DA3; DAM POP; DLB 6, 234; INT CANR-15; MAL 5; MTCW 1, 2; MTFW 2005
Godwin, Gail Kathleen
　　See Godwin, Gail
Godwin, William 1756-1836 .. **NCLC 14, 130**
　　See also CDBLB 1789-1832; CMW 4; DLB 39, 104, 142, 158, 163, 262; GL 2; HGG; RGEL 2
Goebbels, Josef
　　See Goebbels, (Paul) Joseph
Goebbels, (Paul) Joseph
　　1897-1945 .... **TCLC 68**
　　See also CA 115; 148
Goebbels, Joseph Paul
　　See Goebbels, (Paul) Joseph
Goethe, Johann Wolfgang von
　　1749-1832 . **DC 20; NCLC 4, 22, 34, 90, 154; PC 5; SSC 38; WLC 3**
　　See also CDWLB 2; DA; DA3; DAB; DAC; DAM DRAM, MST, POET; DLB 94; EW 5; GL 2; LATS 1; LMFS 1:1; RGWL 2, 3; TWA
Gogarty, Oliver St. John
　　1878-1957 .... **TCLC 15**
　　See also CA 109; 150; DLB 15, 19; RGEL 2
Gogol, Nikolai (Vasilyevich)
　　1809-1852 .... **DC 1; NCLC 5, 15, 31, 162; SSC 4, 29, 52; WLC 3**
　　See also DA; DAB; DAC; DAM DRAM, MST; DFS 12; DLB 198; EW 6; EXPS; RGSF 2; RGWL 2, 3; SSFS 7; TWA
Goines, Donald 1937(?)-1974 ... **BLC 2; CLC 80**
　　See also AITN 1; BW 1, 3; CA 124; 114; CANR 82; CMW 4; DA3; DAM MULT, POP; DLB 33
Gold, Herbert 1924- ... **CLC 4, 7, 14, 42, 152**
　　See also CA 9-12R; CANR 17, 45, 125; CN 1, 2, 3, 4, 5, 6, 7; DLB 2; DLBY 1981; MAL 5
Goldbarth, Albert 1948- .... **CLC 5, 38**
　　See also AMWS 12; CA 53-56; CANR 6, 40; CP 3, 4, 5, 6, 7; DLB 120
Goldberg, Anatol 1910-1982 .... **CLC 34**
　　See also CA 131; 117

Goldemberg, Isaac 1945- .... **CLC 52**
　　See also CA 69-72; CAAS 12; CANR 11, 32; EWL 3; HW 1; WLIT 1
Golding, Arthur 1536-1606 .... **LC 101**
　　See also DLB 136
Golding, William (Gerald)
　　1911-1993 ..... **CLC 1, 2, 3, 8, 10, 17, 27, 58, 81; WLC 3**
　　See also AAYA 5, 44; BPFB 2; BRWR 1; BRWS 1; BYA 2; CA 5-8R; 141; CANR 13, 33, 54; CD 5; CDBLB 1945-1960; CLR 94; CN 1, 2, 3, 4; DA; DA3; DAB; DAC; DAM MST, NOV; DLB 15, 100, 255, 326; EWL 3; EXPN; HGG; LAIT 4; MTCW 1, 2; MTFW 2005; NFS 2; RGEL 2; RHW; SFW 4; TEA; WLIT 4; YAW
Goldman, Emma 1869-1940 .... **TCLC 13**
　　See also CA 110; 150; DLB 221; FW; RGAL 4; TUS
Goldman, Francisco 1954- .... **CLC 76**
　　See also CA 162
Goldman, William 1931- .... **CLC 1, 48**
　　See also BPFB 2; CA 9-12R; CANR 29, 69, 106; CN 1, 2, 3, 4, 5, 6, 7; DLB 44; FANT; IDFW 3, 4
Goldman, William W.
　　See Goldman, William
Goldmann, Lucien 1913-1970 .... **CLC 24**
　　See also CA 25-28; CAP 2
Goldoni, Carlo 1707-1793 .... **LC 4**
　　See also DAM DRAM; EW 4; RGWL 2, 3; WLIT 7
Goldsberry, Steven 1949- .... **CLC 34**
　　See also CA 131
Goldsmith, Oliver 1730-1774 .... **DC 8; LC 2, 48, 122; WLC 3**
　　See also BRW 3; CDBLB 1660-1789; DA; DAB; DAC; DAM DRAM, MST, NOV, POET; DFS 1; DLB 39, 89, 104, 109, 142; IDTP; RGEL 2; SATA 26; TEA; WLIT 3
Goldsmith, Peter
　　See Priestley, J(ohn) B(oynton)
Gombrowicz, Witold 1904-1969 .... **CLC 4, 7, 11, 49**
　　See also CA 19-20; 25-28R; CANR 105; CAP 2; CDWLB 4; DAM DRAM; DLB 215; EW 12; EWL 3; RGWL 2, 3; TWA
Gomez de Avellaneda, Gertrudis
　　1814-1873 .... **NCLC 111**
　　See also LAW
Gomez de la Serna, Ramon
　　1888-1963 .... **CLC 9**
　　See also CA 153; 116; CANR 79; EWL 3; HW 1, 2
Goncharov, Ivan Alexandrovich
　　1812-1891 .... **NCLC 1, 63**
　　See also DLB 238; EW 6; RGWL 2, 3
Goncourt, Edmond (Louis Antoine Huot) de
　　1822-1896 .... **NCLC 7**
　　See also DLB 123; EW 7; GFL 1789 to the Present; RGWL 2, 3
Goncourt, Jules (Alfred Huot) de
　　1830-1870 .... **NCLC 7**
　　See also DLB 123; EW 7; GFL 1789 to the Present; RGWL 2, 3
Gongora (y Argote), Luis de
　　1561-1627 .... **LC 72**
　　See also RGWL 2, 3
Gontier, Fernande 19(?)- .... **CLC 50**
Gonzalez Martinez, Enrique
　　See Gonzalez Martinez, Enrique
　　See also DLB 290
Gonzalez Martinez, Enrique
　　1871-1952 .... **TCLC 72**
　　See Gonzalez Martinez, Enrique
　　See also CA 166; CANR 81; EWL 3; HW 1, 2

Goodison, Lorna 1947- .... **PC 36**
　　See also CA 142; CANR 88; CP 5, 6, 7; CWP; DLB 157; EWL 3
Goodman, Paul 1911-1972 ..... **CLC 1, 2, 4, 7**
　　See also CA 19-20; 37-40R; CAD; CANR 34; CAP 2; CN 1; DLB 130, 246; MAL 5; MTCW 1; RGAL 4
GoodWeather, Harley
　　See King, Thomas
Googe, Barnabe 1540-1594 .... **LC 94**
　　See also DLB 132; RGEL 2
Gordimer, Nadine 1923- ...... **CLC 3, 5, 7, 10, 18, 33, 51, 70, 123, 160, 161; SSC 17, 80; WLCS**
　　See also AAYA 39; AFW; BRWS 2; CA 5-8R; CANR 3, 28, 56, 88, 131; CN 1, 2, 3, 4, 5, 6, 7; DA; DA3; DAB; DAC; DAM MST, NOV; DLB 225, 326; EWL 3; EXPS; INT CANR-28; LATS 1:2; MTCW 1, 2; MTFW 2005; NFS 4; RGEL 2; RGSF 2; SSFS 2, 14, 19; TWA; WLIT 2; YAW
Gordon, Adam Lindsay
　　1833-1870 .... **NCLC 21**
　　See also DLB 230
Gordon, Caroline 1895-1981 . **CLC 6, 13, 29, 83; SSC 15**
　　See also AMW; CA 11-12; 103; CANR 36; CAP 1; CN 1, 2; DLB 4, 9, 102; DLBD 17; DLBY 1981; EWL 3; MAL 5; MTCW 1, 2; MTFW 2005; RGAL 4; RGSF 2
Gordon, Charles William 1860-1937
　　See Connor, Ralph
　　See also CA 109
Gordon, Mary 1949- .. **CLC 13, 22, 128, 216; SSC 59**
　　See also AMWS 4; BPFB 2; CA 102; CANR 44, 92, 154; CN 4, 5, 6, 7; DLB 6; DLBY 1981; FW; INT CA-102; MAL 5; MTCW 1
Gordon, Mary Catherine
　　See Gordon, Mary
Gordon, N. J.
　　See Bosman, Herman Charles
Gordon, Sol 1923- .... **CLC 26**
　　See also CA 53-56; CANR 4; SATA 11
Gordone, Charles 1925-1995 .. **CLC 1, 4; DC 8**
　　See also BW 1, 3; CA 93-96; 180; 150; CAAE 180; CAD; CANR 55; DAM DRAM; DLB 7; INT CA-93-96; MTCW 1
Gore, Catherine 1800-1861 .... **NCLC 65**
　　See also DLB 116; RGEL 2
Gorenko, Anna Andreevna
　　See Akhmatova, Anna
Gorky, Maxim .... **SSC 28; TCLC 8; WLC 3**
　　See Peshkov, Alexei Maximovich
　　See also DAB; DFS 9; DLB 295; EW 8; EWL 3; TWA
Goryan, Sirak
　　See Saroyan, William
Gosse, Edmund (William)
　　1849-1928 .... **TCLC 28**
　　See also CA 117; DLB 57, 144, 184; RGEL 2
Gotlieb, Phyllis (Fay Bloom) 1926- .. **CLC 18**
　　See also CA 13-16R; CANR 7, 135; CN 7; CP 1, 2, 3, 4; DLB 88, 251; SFW 4
Gottesman, S. D.
　　See Kornbluth, C(yril) M.; Pohl, Frederik
Gottfried von Strassburg fl. c.
　　1170-1215 .... **CMLC 10**
　　See also CDWLB 2; DLB 138; EW 1; RGWL 2, 3
Gotthelf, Jeremias 1797-1854 .... **NCLC 117**
　　See also DLB 133; RGWL 2, 3
Gottschalk, Laura Riding
　　See Jackson, Laura (Riding)

Gould, Lois 1932(?)-2002 .... **CLC 4, 10**
See also CA 77-80; 208; CANR 29; MTCW 1

Gould, Stephen Jay 1941-2002 .... **CLC 163**
See also AAYA 26; BEST 90:2; CA 77-80; 205; CANR 10, 27, 56, 75, 125; CPW; INT CANR-27; MTCW 1, 2; MTFW 2005

Gourmont, Remy(-Marie-Charles) de 1858-1915 .... **TCLC 17**
See also CA 109; 150; GFL 1789 to the Present; MTCW 2

Gournay, Marie le Jars de
See de Gournay, Marie le Jars

Govier, Katherine 1948- .... **CLC 51**
See also CA 101; CANR 18, 40, 128; CCA 1

Gower, John c. 1330-1408 .... **LC 76; PC 59**
See also BRW 1; DLB 146; RGEL 2

Goyen, (Charles) William 1915-1983 .... **CLC 5, 8, 14, 40**
See also AITN 2; CA 5-8R; 110; CANR 6, 71; CN 1, 2, 3; DLB 2, 218; DLBY 1983; EWL 3; INT CANR-6; MAL 5

Goytisolo, Juan 1931- .... **CLC 5, 10, 23, 133; HLC 1**
See also CA 85-88; CANR 32, 61, 131; CWW 2; DAM MULT; DLB 322; EWL 3; GLL 2; HW 1, 2; MTCW 1, 2; MTFW 2005

Gozzano, Guido 1883-1916 .... **PC 10**
See also CA 154; DLB 114; EWL 3

Gozzi, (Conte) Carlo 1720-1806 .... **NCLC 23**

Grabbe, Christian Dietrich 1801-1836 .... **NCLC 2**
See also DLB 133; RGWL 2, 3

Grace, Patricia Frances 1937- .... **CLC 56**
See also CA 176; CANR 118; CN 4, 5, 6, 7; EWL 3; RGSF 2

Gracian y Morales, Baltasar 1601-1658 .... **LC 15**

Gracq, Julien .... **CLC 11, 48**
See Poirier, Louis
See also CWW 2; DLB 83; GFL 1789 to the Present

Grade, Chaim 1910-1982 .... **CLC 10**
See also CA 93-96; 107; EWL 3; RGHL

Graduate of Oxford, A
See Ruskin, John

Grafton, Garth
See Duncan, Sara Jeannette

Grafton, Sue 1940- .... **CLC 163**
See also AAYA 11, 49; BEST 90:3; CA 108; CANR 31, 55, 111, 134; CMW 4; CPW; CSW; DA3; DAM POP; DLB 226; FW; MSW; MTFW 2005

Graham, John
See Phillips, David Graham

Graham, Jorie 1950- .... **CLC 48, 118; PC 59**
See also AAYA 67; CA 111; CANR 63, 118; CP 4, 5, 6, 7; CWP; DLB 120; EWL 3; MTFW 2005; PFS 10, 17; TCLE 1:1

Graham, R(obert) B(ontine) Cunninghame
See Cunninghame Graham, Robert (Gallnigad) Bontine
See also DLB 98, 135, 174; RGEL 2; RGSF 2

Graham, Robert
See Haldeman, Joe

Graham, Tom
See Lewis, (Harry) Sinclair

Graham, W(illiam) S(idney) 1918-1986 .... **CLC 29**
See also BRWS 7; CA 73-76; 118; CP 1, 2, 3, 4; DLB 20; RGEL 2

Graham, Winston (Mawdsley) 1910-2003 .... **CLC 23**
See also CA 49-52; 218; CANR 2, 22, 45, 66; CMW 4; CN 1, 2, 3, 4, 5, 6, 7; DLB 77; RHW

Grahame, Kenneth 1859-1932 ...... **TCLC 64, 136**
See also BYA 5; CA 108; 136; CANR 80; CLR 5; CWRI 5; DA3; DAB; DLB 34, 141, 178; FANT; MAICYA 1, 2; MTCW 2; NFS 20; RGEL 2; SATA 100; TEA; WCH; YABC 1

Granger, Darius John
See Marlowe, Stephen

Granin, Daniil 1918- .... **CLC 59**
See also DLB 302

Granovsky, Timofei Nikolaevich 1813-1855 .... **NCLC 75**
See also DLB 198

Grant, Skeeter
See Spiegelman, Art

Granville-Barker, Harley 1877-1946 .... **TCLC 2**
See Barker, Harley Granville
See also CA 104; 204; DAM DRAM; RGEL 2

Granzotto, Gianni
See Granzotto, Giovanni Battista

Granzotto, Giovanni Battista 1914-1985 .... **CLC 70**
See also CA 166

Grass, Guenter
See Grass, Gunter
See also CWW 2; RGHL

Grass, Gunter 1927- .. **CLC 1, 2, 4, 6, 11, 15, 22, 32, 49, 88, 207; WLC 3**
See Grass, Guenter
See also BPFB 2; CA 13-16R; CANR 20, 75, 93, 133; CDWLB 2; DA; DA3; DAB; DAC; DAM MST, NOV; DLB 75, 124; EW 13; EWL 3; MTCW 1, 2; MTFW 2005; RGWL 2, 3; TWA

Grass, Gunter Wilhelm
See Grass, Gunter

Gratton, Thomas
See Hulme, T(homas) E(rnest)

Grau, Shirley Ann 1929- .... **CLC 4, 9, 146; SSC 15**
See also CA 89-92; CANR 22, 69; CN 1, 2, 3, 4, 5, 6, 7; CSW; DLB 2, 218; INT CA-89-92; CANR-22; MTCW 1

Gravel, Fern
See Hall, James Norman

Graver, Elizabeth 1964- .... **CLC 70**
See also CA 135; CANR 71, 129

Graves, Richard Perceval 1895-1985 .... **CLC 44**
See also CA 65-68; CANR 9, 26, 51

Graves, Robert (von Ranke) 1895-1985 .. **CLC 1, 2, 6, 11, 39, 44, 45; PC 6**
See also BPFB 2; BRW 7; BYA 4; CA 5-8R; 117; CANR 5, 36; CDBLB 1914-1945; CN 1, 2, 3; CP 1, 2, 3, 4; DA3; DAB; DAC; DAM MST, POET; DLB 20, 100, 191; DLBD 18; DLBY 1985; EWL 3; LATS 1:1; MTCW 1, 2; MTFW 2005; NCFS 2; NFS 21; RGEL 2; RHW; SATA 45; TEA

Graves, Valerie
See Bradley, Marion Zimmer

Gray, Alasdair (James) 1934- .... **CLC 41**
See also BRWS 9; CA 126; CANR 47, 69, 106, 140; CN 4, 5, 6, 7; DLB 194, 261, 319; HGG; INT CA-126; MTCW 1, 2; MTFW 2005; RGSF 2; SUFW 2

Gray, Amlin 1946- .... **CLC 29**
See also CA 138

Gray, Francine du Plessix 1930- ..... **CLC 22, 153**
See also BEST 90:3; CA 61-64; CAAS 2; CANR 11, 33, 75, 81; DAM NOV; INT CANR-11; MTCW 1, 2; MTFW 2005

Gray, John (Henry) 1866-1934 ...... **TCLC 19**
See also CA 119; 162; RGEL 2

Gray, John Lee
See Jakes, John (William)

Gray, Simon (James Holliday) 1936- .... **CLC 9, 14, 36**
See also AITN 1; CA 21-24R; CAAS 3; CANR 32, 69; CBD; CD 5, 6; CN 1, 2, 3; DLB 13; EWL 3; MTCW 1; RGEL 2

Gray, Spalding 1941-2004 .... **CLC 49, 112; DC 7**
See also AAYA 62; CA 128; 225; CAD; CANR 74, 138; CD 5, 6; CPW; DAM POP; MTCW 2; MTFW 2005

Gray, Thomas 1716-1771 .... **LC 4, 40; PC 2; WLC 3**
See also BRW 3; CDBLB 1660-1789; DA; DA3; DAB; DAC; DAM MST; DLB 109; EXPP; PAB; PFS 9; RGEL 2; TEA; WP

Grayson, David
See Baker, Ray Stannard

Grayson, Richard (A.) 1951- .... **CLC 38**
See also CA 85-88; 210; CAAE 210; CANR 14, 31, 57; DLB 234

Greeley, Andrew M(oran) 1928- .... **CLC 28**
See also BPFB 2; CA 5-8R; CAAS 7; CANR 7, 43, 69, 104, 136; CMW 4; CPW; DA3; DAM POP; MTCW 1, 2; MTFW 2005

Green, Anna Katharine 1846-1935 .... **TCLC 63**
See also CA 112; 159; CMW 4; DLB 202, 221; MSW

Green, Brian
See Card, Orson Scott

Green, Hannah
See Greenberg, Joanne (Goldenberg)

Green, Hannah 1927(?)-1996 .... **CLC 3**
See also CA 73-76; CANR 59, 93; NFS 10

Green, Henry .... **CLC 2, 13, 97**
See Yorke, Henry Vincent
See also BRWS 2; CA 175; DLB 15; EWL 3; RGEL 2

Green, Julian .... **CLC 3, 11, 77**
See Green, Julien (Hartridge)
See also EWL 3; GFL 1789 to the Present; MTCW 2

Green, Julien (Hartridge) 1900-1998
See Green, Julian
See also CA 21-24R; 169; CANR 33, 87; CWW 2; DLB 4, 72; MTCW 1, 2; MTFW 2005

Green, Paul (Eliot) 1894-1981 .... **CLC 25**
See also AITN 1; CA 5-8R; 103; CAD; CANR 3; DAM DRAM; DLB 7, 9, 249; DLBY 1981; MAL 5; RGAL 4

Greenaway, Peter 1942- .... **CLC 159**
See also CA 127

Greenberg, Ivan 1908-1973
See Rahv, Philip
See also CA 85-88

Greenberg, Joanne (Goldenberg) 1932- .... **CLC 7, 30**
See also AAYA 12, 67; CA 5-8R; CANR 14, 32, 69; CN 6, 7; NFS 23; SATA 25; YAW

Greenberg, Richard 1959(?)- .... **CLC 57**
See also CA 138; CAD; CD 5, 6

Greenblatt, Stephen J(ay) 1943- ...... **CLC 70**
See also CA 49-52; CANR 115

Greene, Bette 1934- .... **CLC 30**
See also AAYA 7, 69; BYA 3; CA 53-56; CANR 4, 146; CLR 2; CWRI 5; JRDA; LAIT 4; MAICYA 1, 2; NFS 10; SAAS 16; SATA 8, 102, 161; WYA; YAW

Greene, Gael .... **CLC 8**
See also CA 13-16R; CANR 10

Author Index

Halldor Laxness .... **CLC 25**
See Gudjonsson, Halldor Kiljan
See also DLB 293; EW 12; EWL 3; RGWL
2, 3

Halleck, Fitz-Greene 1790-1867 .... **NCLC 47**
See also DLB 3, 250; RGAL 4

Halliday, Michael
See Creasey, John

Halpern, Daniel 1945- .... **CLC 14**
See also CA 33-36R; CANR 93; CP 3, 4, 5,
6, 7

Hamburger, Michael (Peter Leopold)
1924- .... **CLC 5, 14**
See also CA 5-8R, 196; CAAE 196; CAAS
4; CANR 2, 47; CP 1, 2, 3, 4, 5, 6, 7;
DLB 27

Hamill, Pete 1935- .... **CLC 10**
See also CA 25-28R; CANR 18, 71, 127

Hamilton, Alexander
1755(?)-1804 .... **NCLC 49**
See also DLB 37

Hamilton, Clive
See Lewis, C.S.

Hamilton, Edmond 1904-1977 .... **CLC 1**
See also CA 1-4R; CANR 3, 84; DLB 8;
SATA 118; SFW 4

Hamilton, Elizabeth 1758-1816 ... **NCLC 153**
See also DLB 116, 158

Hamilton, Eugene (Jacob) Lee
See Lee-Hamilton, Eugene (Jacob)

Hamilton, Franklin
See Silverberg, Robert

Hamilton, Gail
See Corcoran, Barbara (Asenath)

Hamilton, (Robert) Ian 1938-2001 . **CLC 191**
See also CA 106; 203; CANR 41, 67; CP 1,
2, 3, 4, 5, 6, 7; DLB 40, 155

Hamilton, Jane 1957- .... **CLC 179**
See also CA 147; CANR 85, 128; CN 7;
MTFW 2005

Hamilton, Mollie
See Kaye, M(ary) M(argaret)

Hamilton, (Anthony Walter) Patrick
1904-1962 .... **CLC 51**
See also CA 176; 113; DLB 10, 191

Hamilton, Virginia (Esther)
1936-2002 .... **CLC 26**
See also AAYA 2, 21; BW 2, 3; BYA 1, 2,
8; CA 25-28R; 206; CANR 20, 37, 73,
126; CLR 1, 11, 40; DAM MULT; DLB
33, 52; DLBY 2001; INT CANR-20;
JRDA; LAIT 5; MAICYA 1, 2; MAIC-
YAS 1; MTCW 1, 2; MTFW 2005; SATA
4, 56, 79, 123; SATA-Obit 132; WYA;
YAW

Hammett, (Samuel) Dashiell
1894-1961 .... **CLC 3, 5, 10, 19, 47; SSC
17**
See also AAYA 59; AITN 1; AMWS 4;
BPFB 2; CA 81-84; CANR 42; CDALB
1929-1941; CMW 4; DA3; DLB 226, 280;
DLBD 6; DLBY 1996; EWL 3; LAIT 3;
MAL 5; MSW; MTCW 1, 2; MTFW
2005; NFS 21; RGAL 4; RGSF 2; TUS

Hammon, Jupiter 1720(?)-1800(?) .... **BLC 2;
NCLC 5; PC 16**
See also DAM MULT, POET; DLB 31, 50

Hammond, Keith
See Kuttner, Henry

Hamner, Earl (Henry), Jr. 1923- ...... **CLC 12**
See also AITN 2; CA 73-76; DLB 6

Hampton, Christopher 1946- .... **CLC 4**
See also CA 25-28R; CD 5, 6; DLB 13;
MTCW 1

Hampton, Christopher James
See Hampton, Christopher

Hamsun, Knut .... **TCLC 2, 14, 49, 151**
See Pedersen, Knut
See also DLB 297; EW 8; EWL 3; RGWL
2, 3

Handke, Peter 1942- .... **CLC 5, 8, 10, 15, 38,
134; DC 17**
See also CA 77-80; CANR 33, 75, 104, 133;
CWW 2; DAM DRAM, NOV; DLB 85,
124; EWL 3; MTCW 1, 2; MTFW 2005;
TWA

Handy, W(illiam) C(hristopher)
1873-1958 .... **TCLC 97**
See also BW 3; CA 121; 167

Hanley, James 1901-1985 ..... **CLC 3, 5, 8, 13**
See also CA 73-76; 117; CANR 36; CBD;
CN 1, 2, 3; DLB 191; EWL 3; MTCW 1;
RGEL 2

Hannah, Barry 1942- .... **CLC 23, 38, 90**
See also BPFB 2; CA 108; 110; CANR 43,
68, 113; CN 4, 5, 6, 7; CSW; DLB 6, 234;
INT CA-110; MTCW 1; RGSF 2

Hannon, Ezra
See Hunter, Evan

Hansberry, Lorraine (Vivian)
1930-1965 ... **BLC 2; CLC 17, 62; DC 2**
See also AAYA 25; AFAW 1, 2; AMWS 4;
BW 1, 3; CA 109; 25-28R; CABS 3;
CAD; CANR 58; CDALB 1941-1968;
CWD; DA; DA3; DAB; DAC; DAM
DRAM, MST, MULT; DFS 2; DLB 7, 38;
EWL 3; FL 1:6; FW; LAIT 4; MAL 5;
MTCW 1, 2; MTFW 2005; RGAL 4; TUS

Hansen, Joseph 1923-2004 .... **CLC 38**
See Brock, Rose; Colton, James
See also BPFB 2; CA 29-32R; 233; CAAS
17; CANR 16, 44, 66, 125; CMW 4; DLB
226; GLL 1; INT CANR-16

Hansen, Martin A(lfred)
1909-1955 .... **TCLC 32**
See also CA 167; DLB 214; EWL 3

Hansen and Philipson eds. .... **CLC 65**

Hanson, Kenneth O(stlin) 1922- .... **CLC 13**
See also CA 53-56; CANR 7; CP 1, 2, 3, 4,
5

Hardwick, Elizabeth (Bruce) 1916- . **CLC 13**
See also AMWS 3; CA 5-8R; CANR 3, 32,
70, 100, 139; CN 4, 5, 6; CSW; DA3;
DAM NOV; DLB 6; MBL; MTCW 1, 2;
MTFW 2005; TCLE 1:1

Hardy, Thomas 1840-1928 .... **PC 8; SSC 2,
60; TCLC 4, 10, 18, 32, 48, 53, 72, 143,
153; WLC 3**
See also AAYA 69; BRW 6; BRWC 1, 2;
BRWR 1; CA 104; 123; CDBLB 1890-
1914; DA; DA3; DAB; DAC; DAM MST,
NOV, POET; DLB 18, 19, 135, 284; EWL
3; EXPN; EXPP; LAIT 2; MTCW 1, 2;
MTFW 2005; NFS 3, 11, 15, 19; PFS 3,
4, 18; RGEL 2; RGSF 2; TEA; WLIT 4

Hare, David 1947- . **CLC 29, 58, 136; DC 26**
See also BRWS 4; CA 97-100; CANR 39,
91; CBD; CD 5, 6; DFS 4, 7, 16; DLB
13, 310; MTCW 1; TEA

Harewood, John
See Van Druten, John (William)

Harford, Henry
See Hudson, W(illiam) H(enry)

Hargrave, Leonie
See Disch, Thomas M(ichael)

**Hariri, Al- al-Qasim ibn 'Ali Abu
Muhammad al-Basri**
See al-Hariri, al-Qasim ibn 'Ali Abu Mu-
hammad al-Basri

Harjo, Joy 1951- ..... **CLC 83; NNAL; PC 27**
See also AMWS 12; CA 114; CANR 35,
67, 91, 129; CP 6, 7; CWP; DAM MULT;
DLB 120, 175; EWL 3; MTCW 2; MTFW
2005; PFS 15; RGAL 4

Harlan, Louis R(udolph) 1922- .... **CLC 34**
See also CA 21-24R; CANR 25, 55, 80

Harling, Robert 1951(?)- .... **CLC 53**
See also CA 147

Harmon, William (Ruth) 1938- .... **CLC 38**
See also CA 33-36R; CANR 14, 32, 35;
SATA 65

Harper, F. E. W.
See Harper, Frances Ellen Watkins

Harper, Frances E. W.
See Harper, Frances Ellen Watkins

Harper, Frances E. Watkins
See Harper, Frances Ellen Watkins

Harper, Frances Ellen
See Harper, Frances Ellen Watkins

Harper, Frances Ellen Watkins
1825-1911 ..... **BLC 2; PC 21; TCLC 14**
See also AFAW 1, 2; BW 1, 3; CA 111; 125;
CANR 79; DAM MULT, POET; DLB 50,
221; MBL; RGAL 4

Harper, Michael S(teven) 1938- ... **CLC 7, 22**
See also AFAW 2; BW 1; CA 33-36R; 224;
CAAE 224; CANR 24, 108; CP 2, 3, 4, 5,
6, 7; DLB 41; RGAL 4; TCLE 1:1

Harper, Mrs. F. E. W.
See Harper, Frances Ellen Watkins

Harpur, Charles 1813-1868 .... **NCLC 114**
See also DLB 230; RGEL 2

Harris, Christie
See Harris, Christie (Lucy) Irwin

Harris, Christie (Lucy) Irwin
1907-2002 .... **CLC 12**
See also CA 5-8R; CANR 6, 83; CLR 47;
DLB 88; JRDA; MAICYA 1, 2; SAAS 10;
SATA 6, 74; SATA-Essay 116

Harris, Frank 1856-1931 .... **TCLC 24**
See also CA 109; 150; CANR 80; DLB 156,
197; RGEL 2

Harris, George Washington
1814-1869 .... **NCLC 23, 165**
See also DLB 3, 11, 248; RGAL 4

Harris, Joel Chandler 1848-1908 ..... **SSC 19;
TCLC 2**
See also CA 104; 137; CANR 80; CLR 49;
DLB 11, 23, 42, 78, 91; LAIT 2; MAI-
CYA 1, 2; RGSF 2; SATA 100; WCH;
YABC 1

**Harris, John (Wyndham Parkes Lucas)
Beynon** 1903-1969
See Wyndham, John
See also CA 102; 89-92; CANR 84; SATA
118; SFW 4

Harris, MacDonald .... **CLC 9**
See Heiney, Donald (William)

Harris, Mark 1922- .... **CLC 19**
See also CA 5-8R; CAAS 3; CANR 2, 55,
83; CN 1, 2, 3, 4, 5, 6, 7; DLB 2; DLBY
1980

Harris, Norman .... **CLC 65**

Harris, (Theodore) Wilson 1921- .... **CLC 25,
159**
See also BRWS 5; BW 2, 3; CA 65-68;
CAAS 16; CANR 11, 27, 69, 114; CD-
WLB 3; CN 1, 2, 3, 4, 5, 6, 7; CP 1, 2, 3,
4, 5, 6, 7; DLB 117; EWL 3; MTCW 1;
RGEL 2

Harrison, Barbara Grizzuti
1934-2002 .... **CLC 144**
See also CA 77-80; 205; CANR 15, 48; INT
CANR-15

Harrison, Elizabeth (Allen) Cavanna
1909-2001
See Cavanna, Betty
See also CA 9-12R; 200; CANR 6, 27, 85,
104, 121; MAICYA 2; SATA 142; YAW

Harrison, Harry (Max) 1925- .... **CLC 42**
See also CA 1-4R; CANR 5, 21, 84; DLB
8; SATA 4; SCFW 2; SFW 4

Houellebecq, Michel 1958- .... **CLC 179**
 See also CA 185; CANR 140; MTFW 2005
Hougan, Carolyn 1943- .... **CLC 34**
 See also CA 139
Household, Geoffrey (Edward West)
 1900-1988 .... **CLC 11**
 See also CA 77-80; 126; CANR 58; CMW
 4; CN 1, 2, 3, 4; DLB 87; SATA 14;
 SATA-Obit 59
Housman, A(lfred) E(dward)
 1859-1936 .... **PC 2, 43; TCLC 1, 10;**
 WLCS
 See also AAYA 66; BRW 6; CA 104; 125;
 DA; DA3; DAB; DAC; DAM MST,
 POET; DLB 19, 284; EWL 3; EXPP;
 MTCW 1, 2; MTFW 2005; PAB; PFS 4,
 7; RGEL 2; TEA; WP
Housman, Laurence 1865-1959 .... **TCLC 7**
 See also CA 106; 155; DLB 10; FANT;
 RGEL 2; SATA 25
Houston, Jeanne Wakatsuki 1934- .... **AAL**
 See also AAYA 49; CA 103, 232; CAAE
 232; CAAS 16; CANR 29, 123; LAIT 4;
 SATA 78, 168; SATA-Essay 168
Howard, Elizabeth Jane 1923- ..... **CLC 7, 29**
 See also BRWS 11; CA 5-8R; CANR 8, 62,
 146; CN 1, 2, 3, 4, 5, 6, 7
Howard, Maureen 1930- .... **CLC 5, 14, 46,**
 151
 See also CA 53-56; CANR 31, 75, 140; CN
 4, 5, 6, 7; DLBY 1983; INT CANR-31;
 MTCW 1, 2; MTFW 2005
Howard, Richard 1929- .... **CLC 7, 10, 47**
 See also AITN 1; CA 85-88; CANR 25, 80,
 154; CP 1, 2, 3, 4, 5, 6, 7; DLB 5; INT
 CANR-25; MAL 5
Howard, Robert E(rvin)
 1906-1936 .... **TCLC 8**
 See also BPFB 2; BYA 5; CA 105; 157;
 FANT; SUFW 1; TCWW 1, 2
Howard, Warren F.
 See Pohl, Frederik
Howe, Fanny (Quincy) 1940- .... **CLC 47**
 See also CA 117, 187; CAAE 187; CAAS
 27; CANR 70, 116; CP 6, 7; CWP; SATA-
 Brief 52
Howe, Irving 1920-1993 .... **CLC 85**
 See also AMWS 6; CA 9-12R; 141; CANR
 21, 50; DLB 67; EWL 3; MAL 5; MTCW
 1, 2; MTFW 2005
Howe, Julia Ward 1819-1910 .... **TCLC 21**
 See also CA 117; 191; DLB 1, 189, 235;
 FW
Howe, Susan 1937- .... **CLC 72, 152; PC 54**
 See also AMWS 4; CA 160; CP 5, 6, 7;
 CWP; DLB 120; FW; RGAL 4
Howe, Tina 1937- .... **CLC 48**
 See also CA 109; CAD; CANR 125; CD 5,
 6; CWD
Howell, James 1594(?)-1666 .... **LC 13**
 See also DLB 151
Howells, W. D.
 See Howells, William Dean
Howells, William D.
 See Howells, William Dean
Howells, William Dean 1837-1920 ... **SSC 36;**
 TCLC 7, 17, 41
 See also AMW; CA 104; 134; CDALB
 1865-1917; DLB 12, 64, 74, 79, 189;
 LMFS 1; MAL 5; MTCW 2; RGAL 4;
 TUS
Howes, Barbara 1914-1996 .... **CLC 15**
 See also CA 9-12R; 151; CAAS 3; CANR
 53; CP 1, 2, 3, 4, 5, 6; SATA 5; TCLE 1:1
Hrabal, Bohumil 1914-1997 ...... **CLC 13, 67;**
 TCLC 155
 See also CA 106; 156; CAAS 12; CANR
 57; CWW 2; DLB 232; EWL 3; RGSF 2

Hrabanus Maurus 776(?)-856 .... **CMLC 78**
 See also DLB 148
Hrotsvit of Gandersheim c. 935-c.
 1000 .... **CMLC 29**
 See also DLB 148
Hsi, Chu 1130-1200 .... **CMLC 42**
Hsun, Lu
 See Lu Hsun
Hubbard, L. Ron 1911-1986 .... **CLC 43**
 See also AAYA 64; CA 77-80; 118; CANR
 52; CPW; DA3; DAM POP; FANT;
 MTCW 2; MTFW 2005; SFW 4
Hubbard, Lafayette Ronald
 See Hubbard, L. Ron
Huch, Ricarda (Octavia)
 1864-1947 .... **TCLC 13**
 See also CA 111; 189; DLB 66; EWL 3
Huddle, David 1942- .... **CLC 49**
 See also CA 57-60; CAAS 20; CANR 89;
 DLB 130
Hudson, Jeffrey
 See Crichton, (John) Michael
Hudson, W(illiam) H(enry)
 1841-1922 .... **TCLC 29**
 See also CA 115; 190; DLB 98, 153, 174;
 RGEL 2; SATA 35
Hueffer, Ford Madox
 See Ford, Ford Madox
Hughart, Barry 1934- .... **CLC 39**
 See also CA 137; FANT; SFW 4; SUFW 2
Hughes, Colin
 See Creasey, John
Hughes, David (John) 1930-2005 ..... **CLC 48**
 See also CA 116; 129; 238; CN 4, 5, 6, 7;
 DLB 14
Hughes, Edward James
 See Hughes, Ted
 See also DA3; DAM MST, POET
Hughes, (James Mercer) Langston
 1902-1967 ..... **BLC 2; CLC 1, 5, 10, 15,**
 35, 44, 108; DC 3; HR 1:2; PC 1, 53;
 SSC 6, 90; WLC 3
 See also AAYA 12; AFAW 1, 2; AMWR 1;
 AMWS 1; BW 1, 3; CA 1-4R; 25-28R;
 CANR 1, 34, 82; CDALB 1929-1941;
 CLR 17; DA; DA3; DAB; DAC; DAM
 DRAM, MST, MULT, POET; DFS 6, 18;
 DLB 4, 7, 48, 51, 86, 228, 315; EWL 3;
 EXPP; EXPS; JRDA; LAIT 3; LMFS 2;
 MAICYA 1, 2; MAL 5; MTCW 1, 2;
 MTFW 2005; NFS 21; PAB; PFS 1, 3, 6,
 10, 15; RGAL 4; RGSF 2; SATA 4, 33;
 SSFS 4, 7; TUS; WCH; WP; YAW
Hughes, Richard (Arthur Warren)
 1900-1976 .... **CLC 1, 11**
 See also CA 5-8R; 65-68; CANR 4; CN 1,
 2; DAM NOV; DLB 15, 161; EWL 3;
 MTCW 1; RGEL 2; SATA 8; SATA-Obit
 25
Hughes, Ted 1930-1998 . **CLC 2, 4, 9, 14, 37,**
 119; PC 7
 See Hughes, Edward James
 See also BRWC 2; BRWR 2; BRWS 1; CA
 1-4R; 171; CANR 1, 33, 66, 108; CLR 3;
 CP 1, 2, 3, 4, 5, 6; DAB; DAC; DLB 40,
 161; EWL 3; EXPP; MAICYA 1, 2;
 MTCW 1, 2; MTFW 2005; PAB; PFS 4,
 19; RGEL 2; SATA 49; SATA-Brief 27;
 SATA-Obit 107; TEA; YAW
Hugo, Richard
 See Huch, Ricarda (Octavia)
Hugo, Richard F(ranklin)
 1923-1982 .... **CLC 6, 18, 32; PC 68**
 See also AMWS 6; CA 49-52; 108; CANR
 3; CP 1, 2, 3; DAM POET; DLB 5, 206;
 EWL 3; MAL 5; PFS 17; RGAL 4

Hugo, Victor (Marie) 1802-1885 .... **NCLC 3,**
 10, 21, 161; PC 17; WLC 3
 See also AAYA 28; DA; DA3; DAB; DAC;
 DAM DRAM, MST, NOV, POET; DLB
 119, 192, 217; EFS 2; EW 6; EXPN; GFL
 1789 to the Present; LAIT 1, 2; NFS 5,
 20; RGWL 2, 3; SATA 47; TWA
Huidobro, Vicente
 See Huidobro Fernandez, Vicente Garcia
 See also DLB 283; EWL 3; LAW
Huidobro Fernandez, Vicente Garcia
 1893-1948 .... **TCLC 31**
 See Huidobro, Vicente
 See also CA 131; HW 1
Hulme, Keri 1947- .... **CLC 39, 130**
 See also CA 125; CANR 69; CN 4, 5, 6, 7;
 CP 6, 7; CWP; DLB 326; EWL 3; FW;
 INT CA-125
Hulme, T(homas) E(rnest)
 1883-1917 .... **TCLC 21**
 See also BRWS 6; CA 117; 203; DLB 19
Humboldt, Alexander von
 1769-1859 .... **NCLC 170**
 See also DLB 90
Humboldt, Wilhelm von
 1767-1835 .... **NCLC 134**
 See also DLB 90
Hume, David 1711-1776 .... **LC 7, 56**
 See also BRWS 3; DLB 104, 252; LMFS 1;
 TEA
Humphrey, William 1924-1997 .... **CLC 45**
 See also AMWS 9; CA 77-80; 160; CANR
 68; CN 1, 2, 3, 4, 5, 6; CSW; DLB 6, 212,
 234, 278; TCWW 1, 2
Humphreys, Emyr Owen 1919- .... **CLC 47**
 See also CA 5-8R; CANR 3, 24; CN 1, 2,
 3, 4, 5, 6, 7; DLB 15
Humphreys, Josephine 1945- ..... **CLC 34, 57**
 See also CA 121; 127; CANR 97; CSW;
 DLB 292; INT CA-127
Huneker, James Gibbons
 1860-1921 .... **TCLC 65**
 See also CA 193; DLB 71; RGAL 4
Hungerford, Hesba Fay
 See Brinsmead, H(esba) F(ay)
Hungerford, Pixie
 See Brinsmead, H(esba) F(ay)
Hunt, E(verette) Howard, (Jr.)
 1918- .... **CLC 3**
 See also AITN 1; CA 45-48; CANR 2, 47,
 103; CMW 4
Hunt, Francesca
 See Holland, Isabelle (Christian)
Hunt, Howard
 See Hunt, E(verette) Howard, (Jr.)
Hunt, Kyle
 See Creasey, John
Hunt, (James Henry) Leigh
 1784-1859 .... **NCLC 1, 70; PC 73**
 See also DAM POET; DLB 96, 110, 144;
 RGEL 2; TEA
Hunt, Marsha 1946- .... **CLC 70**
 See also BW 2, 3; CA 143; CANR 79
Hunt, Violet 1866(?)-1942 .... **TCLC 53**
 See also CA 184; DLB 162, 197
Hunter, E. Waldo
 See Sturgeon, Theodore (Hamilton)
Hunter, Evan 1926-2005 .... **CLC 11, 31**
 See McBain, Ed
 See also AAYA 39; BPFB 2; CA 5-8R; 241;
 CANR 5, 38, 62, 97, 149; CMW 4; CN 1,
 2, 3, 4, 5, 6, 7; CPW; DAM POP; DLB
 306; DLBY 1982; INT CANR-5; MSW;
 MTCW 1; SATA 25; SATA-Obit 167;
 SFW 4
Hunter, Kristin
 See Lattany, Kristin (Elaine Eggleston)
 Hunter
 See also CN 1, 2, 3, 4, 5, 6

Hunter, Mary
See Austin, Mary (Hunter)
Hunter, Mollie 1922- .... **CLC 21**
See McIlwraith, Maureen Mollie Hunter
See also AAYA 13, 71; BYA 6; CANR 37, 78; CLR 25; DLB 161; JRDA; MAICYA 1, 2; SAAS 7; SATA 54, 106, 139; SATA-Essay 139; WYA; YAW
Hunter, Robert (?)-1734 .... **LC 7**
Hurston, Zora Neale 1891-1960 .... **BLC 2; CLC 7, 30, 61; DC 12; HR 1:2; SSC 4, 80; TCLC 121, 131; WLCS**
See also AAYA 15, 71; AFAW 1, 2; AMWS 6; BW 1, 3; BYA 12; CA 85-88; CANR 61; CDALBS; DA; DA3; DAC; DAM MST, MULT, NOV; DFS 6; DLB 51, 86; EWL 3; EXPN; EXPS; FL 1:6; FW; LAIT 3; LATS 1:1; LMFS 2; MAL 5; MBL; MTCW 1, 2; MTFW 2005; NFS 3; RGAL 4; RGSF 2; SSFS 1, 6, 11, 19, 21; TUS; YAW
Husserl, E. G.
See Husserl, Edmund (Gustav Albrecht)
Husserl, Edmund (Gustav Albrecht)
1859-1938 .... **TCLC 100**
See also CA 116; 133; DLB 296
Huston, John (Marcellus)
1906-1987 .... **CLC 20**
See also CA 73-76; 123; CANR 34; DLB 26
Hustvedt, Siri 1955- .... **CLC 76**
See also CA 137; CANR 149
Hutten, Ulrich von 1488-1523 .... **LC 16**
See also DLB 179
Huxley, Aldous (Leonard)
1894-1963 .... **CLC 1, 3, 4, 5, 8, 11, 18, 35, 79; SSC 39; WLC 3**
See also AAYA 11; BPFB 2; BRW 7; CA 85-88; CANR 44, 99; CDBLB 1914-1945; DA; DA3; DAB; DAC; DAM MST, NOV; DLB 36, 100, 162, 195, 255; EWL 3; EXPN; LAIT 5; LMFS 2; MTCW 1, 2; MTFW 2005; NFS 6; RGEL 2; SATA 63; SCFW 1, 2; SFW 4; TEA; YAW
Huxley, T(homas) H(enry)
1825-1895 .... **NCLC 67**
See also DLB 57; TEA
Huygens, Constantijn 1596-1687 .... **LC 114**
See also RGWL 2, 3
Huysmans, Joris-Karl 1848-1907 ... **TCLC 7, 69**
See also CA 104; 165; DLB 123; EW 7; GFL 1789 to the Present; LMFS 2; RGWL 2, 3
Hwang, David Henry 1957- .... **CLC 55, 196; DC 4, 23**
See also CA 127; 132; CAD; CANR 76, 124; CD 5, 6; DA3; DAM DRAM; DFS 11, 18; DLB 212, 228, 312; INT CA-132; MAL 5; MTCW 2; MTFW 2005; RGAL 4
Hyde, Anthony 1946- .... **CLC 42**
See Chase, Nicholas
See also CA 136; CCA 1
Hyde, Margaret O(ldroyd) 1917- ..... **CLC 21**
See also CA 1-4R; CANR 1, 36, 137; CLR 23; JRDA; MAICYA 1, 2; SAAS 8; SATA 1, 42, 76, 139
Hynes, James 1956(?)- .... **CLC 65**
See also CA 164; CANR 105
Hypatia c. 370-415 .... **CMLC 35**
Ian, Janis 1951- .... **CLC 21**
See also CA 105; 187
Ibanez, Vicente Blasco
See Blasco Ibanez, Vicente
See also DLB 322
Ibarbourou, Juana de
1895(?)-1979 .... **HLCS 2**
See also DLB 290; HW 1; LAW

Ibarguengoitia, Jorge 1928-1983 ..... **CLC 37; TCLC 148**
See also CA 124; 113; EWL 3; HW 1
Ibn Battuta, Abu Abdalla
1304-1368(?) .... **CMLC 57**
See also WLIT 2
Ibn Hazm 994-1064 .... **CMLC 64**
Ibsen, Henrik (Johan) 1828-1906 .... **DC 2; TCLC 2, 8, 16, 37, 52; WLC 3**
See also AAYA 46; CA 104; 141; DA; DA3; DAB; DAC; DAM DRAM, MST; DFS 1, 6, 8, 10, 11, 15, 16; EW 7; LAIT 2; LATS 1:1; MTFW 2005; RGWL 2, 3
Ibuse, Masuji 1898-1993 .... **CLC 22**
See Ibuse Masuji
See also CA 127; 141; MJW; RGWL 3
Ibuse Masuji
See Ibuse, Masuji
See also CWW 2; DLB 180; EWL 3
Ichikawa, Kon 1915- .... **CLC 20**
See also CA 121
Ichiyo, Higuchi 1872-1896 .... **NCLC 49**
See also MJW
Idle, Eric 1943- .... **CLC 21**
See Monty Python
See also CA 116; CANR 35, 91, 148
Idris, Yusuf 1927-1991 .... **SSC 74**
See also AFW; EWL 3; RGSF 2, 3; RGWL 3; WLIT 2
Ignatow, David 1914-1997 .... **CLC 4, 7, 14, 40; PC 34**
See also CA 9-12R; 162; CAAS 3; CANR 31, 57, 96; CP 1, 2, 3, 4, 5, 6; DLB 5; EWL 3; MAL 5
Ignotus
See Strachey, (Giles) Lytton
Ihimaera, Witi (Tame) 1944- .... **CLC 46**
See also CA 77-80; CANR 130; CN 2, 3, 4, 5, 6, 7; RGSF 2; SATA 148
Ilf, Ilya .... **TCLC 21**
See Fainzilberg, Ilya Arnoldovich
See also EWL 3
Illyes, Gyula 1902-1983 .... **PC 16**
See also CA 114; 109; CDWLB 4; DLB 215; EWL 3; RGWL 2, 3
Imalayen, Fatima-Zohra
See Djebar, Assia
Immermann, Karl (Lebrecht)
1796-1840 .... **NCLC 4, 49**
See also DLB 133
Ince, Thomas H. 1882-1924 .... **TCLC 89**
See also IDFW 3, 4
Inchbald, Elizabeth 1753-1821 ...... **NCLC 62**
See also DLB 39, 89; RGEL 2
Inclan, Ramon (Maria) del Valle
See Valle-Inclan, Ramon (Maria) del
Infante, G(uillermo) Cabrera
See Cabrera Infante, G(uillermo)
Ingalls, Rachel 1940- .... **CLC 42**
See also CA 123; 127; CANR 154
Ingalls, Rachel Holmes
See Ingalls, Rachel
Ingamells, Reginald Charles
See Ingamells, Rex
Ingamells, Rex 1913-1955 .... **TCLC 35**
See also CA 167; DLB 260
Inge, William (Motter) 1913-1973 ..... **CLC 1, 8, 19**
See also CA 9-12R; CAD; CDALB 1941-1968; DA3; DAM DRAM; DFS 1, 3, 5, 8; DLB 7, 249; EWL 3; MAL 5; MTCW 1, 2; MTFW 2005; RGAL 4; TUS
Ingelow, Jean 1820-1897 .... **NCLC 39, 107**
See also DLB 35, 163; FANT; SATA 33
Ingram, Willis J.
See Harris, Mark
Innaurato, Albert (F.) 1948(?)- ... **CLC 21, 60**
See also CA 115; 122; CAD; CANR 78; CD 5, 6; INT CA-122

Innes, Michael
See Stewart, J(ohn) I(nnes) M(ackintosh)
See also DLB 276; MSW
Innis, Harold Adams 1894-1952 .... **TCLC 77**
See also CA 181; DLB 88
Insluis, Alanus de
See Alain de Lille
Iola
See Wells-Barnett, Ida B(ell)
Ionesco, Eugene 1912-1994 ... **CLC 1, 4, 6, 9, 11, 15, 41, 86; DC 12; WLC 3**
See also CA 9-12R; 144; CANR 55, 132; CWW 2; DA; DA3; DAB; DAC; DAM DRAM, MST; DFS 4, 9; DLB 321; EW 13; EWL 3; GFL 1789 to the Present; LMFS 2; MTCW 1, 2; MTFW 2005; RGWL 2, 3; SATA 7; SATA-Obit 79; TWA
Iqbal, Muhammad 1877-1938 .... **TCLC 28**
See also CA 215; EWL 3
Ireland, Patrick
See O'Doherty, Brian
Irenaeus St. 130- .... **CMLC 42**
Irigaray, Luce 1930- .... **CLC 164**
See also CA 154; CANR 121; FW
Iron, Ralph
See Schreiner, Olive (Emilie Albertina)
Irving, John (Winslow) 1942- ... **CLC 13, 23, 38, 112, 175**
See also AAYA 8, 62; AMWS 6; BEST 89:3; BPFB 2; CA 25-28R; CANR 28, 73, 112, 133; CN 3, 4, 5, 6, 7; CPW; DA3; DAM NOV, POP; DLB 6, 278; DLBY 1982; EWL 3; MAL 5; MTCW 1, 2; MTFW 2005; NFS 12, 14; RGAL 4; TUS
Irving, Washington 1783-1859 . **NCLC 2, 19, 95; SSC 2, 37; WLC 3**
See also AAYA 56; AMW; CDALB 1640-1865; CLR 97; DA; DA3; DAB; DAC; DAM MST; DLB 3, 11, 30, 59, 73, 74, 183, 186, 250, 254; EXPS; GL 2; LAIT 1; RGAL 4; RGSF 2; SSFS 1, 8, 16; SUFW 1; TUS; WCH; YABC 2
Irwin, P. K.
See Page, P(atricia) K(athleen)
Isaacs, Jorge Ricardo 1837-1895 ... **NCLC 70**
See also LAW
Isaacs, Susan 1943- .... **CLC 32**
See also BEST 89:1; BPFB 2; CA 89-92; CANR 20, 41, 65, 112, 134; CPW; DA3; DAM POP; INT CANR-20; MTCW 1, 2; MTFW 2005
Isherwood, Christopher (William Bradshaw)
1904-1986 .... **CLC 1, 9, 11, 14, 44; SSC 56**
See also AMWS 14; BRW 7; CA 13-16R; 117; CANR 35, 97, 133; CN 1, 2, 3; DA3; DAM DRAM, NOV; DLB 15, 195; DLBY 1986; EWL 3; IDTP; MTCW 1, 2; MTFW 2005; RGAL 4; RGEL 2; TUS; WLIT 4
Ishiguro, Kazuo 1954- . **CLC 27, 56, 59, 110, 119**
See also AAYA 58; BEST 90:2; BPFB 2; BRWS 4; CA 120; CANR 49, 95, 133; CN 5, 6, 7; DA3; DAM NOV; DLB 194, 326; EWL 3; MTCW 1, 2; MTFW 2005; NFS 13; WLIT 4; WWE 1
Ishikawa, Hakuhin
See Ishikawa, Takuboku
Ishikawa, Takuboku 1886(?)-1912 ..... **PC 10; TCLC 15**
See Ishikawa Takuboku
See also CA 113; 153; DAM POET
Iskander, Fazil (Abdulovich) 1929- .. **CLC 47**
See Iskander, Fazil' Abdulevich
See also CA 102; EWL 3
Iskander, Fazil' Abdulevich
See Iskander, Fazil (Abdulovich)
See also DLB 302

Jerome, Jerome K(lapka)
1859-1927 .... **TCLC 23**
See also CA 119; 177; DLB 10, 34, 135;
RGEL 2

Jerrold, Douglas William
1803-1857 .... **NCLC 2**
See also DLB 158, 159; RGEL 2

Jewett, (Theodora) Sarah Orne
1849-1909 .... **SSC 6, 44; TCLC 1, 22**
See also AMW; AMWC 2; AMWR 2; CA
108; 127; CANR 71; DLB 12, 74, 221;
EXPS; FL 1:3; FW; MAL 5; MBL; NFS
15; RGAL 4; RGSF 2; SATA 15; SSFS 4

Jewsbury, Geraldine (Endsor)
1812-1880 .... **NCLC 22**
See also DLB 21

Jhabvala, Ruth Prawer 1927- . **CLC 4, 8, 29,
94, 138; SSC 91**
See also BRWS 5; CA 1-4R; CANR 2, 29,
51, 74, 91, 128; CN 1, 2, 3, 4, 5, 6, 7;
DAB; DAM NOV; DLB 139, 194, 323,
326; EWL 3; IDFW 3, 4; INT CANR-29;
MTCW 1, 2; MTFW 2005; RGSF 2;
RGWL 2; RHW; TEA

Jibran, Kahlil
See Gibran, Kahlil

Jibran, Khalil
See Gibran, Kahlil

Jiles, Paulette 1943- .... **CLC 13, 58**
See also CA 101; CANR 70, 124; CP 5;
CWP

Jimenez (Mantecon), Juan Ramon
1881-1958 .... **HLC 1; PC 7; TCLC 4**
See also CA 104; 131; CANR 74; DAM
MULT, POET; DLB 134; EW 9; EWL 3;
HW 1; MTCW 1, 2; MTFW 2005; RGWL
2, 3

Jimenez, Ramon
See Jimenez (Mantecon), Juan Ramon

Jimenez Mantecon, Juan
See Jimenez (Mantecon), Juan Ramon

Jin, Ba 1904-2005
See Pa Chin
See also CA 244; CWW 2

Jin, Xuefei
See Ha Jin

Jodelle, Etienne 1532-1573 .... **LC 119**
See also DLB 327; GFL Beginnings to 1789

Joel, Billy .... **CLC 26**
See Joel, William Martin

Joel, William Martin 1949-
See Joel, Billy
See also CA 108

John, Saint 10(?)-100 .... **CMLC 27, 63**

John of Salisbury c. 1115-1180 ..... **CMLC 63**

John of the Cross, St. 1542-1591 .... **LC 18**
See also RGWL 2, 3

John Paul II, Pope 1920-2005 .... **CLC 128**
See also CA 106; 133; 238

Johnson, B(ryan) S(tanley William)
1933-1973 .... **CLC 6, 9**
See also CA 9-12R; 53-56; CANR 9; CN 1;
CP 1, 2; DLB 14, 40; EWL 3; RGEL 2

Johnson, Benjamin F., of Boone
See Riley, James Whitcomb

Johnson, Charles (Richard) 1948- .... **BLC 2;
CLC 7, 51, 65, 163**
See also AFAW 2; AMWS 6; BW 2, 3; CA
116; CAAS 18; CANR 42, 66, 82, 129;
CN 5, 6, 7; DAM MULT; DLB 33, 278;
MAL 5; MTCW 2; MTFW 2005; RGAL
4; SSFS 16

Johnson, Charles S(purgeon)
1893-1956 .... **HR 1:3**
See also BW 1, 3; CA 125; CANR 82; DLB
51, 91

Johnson, Denis 1949- . **CLC 52, 160; SSC 56**
See also CA 117; 121; CANR 71, 99; CN
4, 5, 6, 7; DLB 120

Johnson, Diane 1934- .... **CLC 5, 13, 48**
See also BPFB 2; CA 41-44R; CANR 17,
40, 62, 95; CN 4, 5, 6, 7; DLBY 1980;
INT CANR-17; MTCW 1

Johnson, E(mily) Pauline 1861-1913 . **NNAL**
See also CA 150; CCA 1; DAC; DAM
MULT; DLB 92, 175; TCWW 2

Johnson, Eyvind (Olof Verner)
1900-1976 .... **CLC 14**
See also CA 73-76; 69-72; CANR 34, 101;
DLB 259; EW 12; EWL 3

Johnson, Fenton 1888-1958 .... **BLC 2**
See also BW 1; CA 118; 124; DAM MULT;
DLB 45, 50

Johnson, Georgia Douglas (Camp)
1880-1966 .... **HR 1:3**
See also BW 1; CA 125; DLB 51, 249; WP

Johnson, Helene 1907-1995 .... **HR 1:3**
See also CA 181; DLB 51; WP

Johnson, J. R.
See James, C(yril) L(ionel) R(obert)

Johnson, James Weldon 1871-1938 .. **BLC 2;
HR 1:3; PC 24; TCLC 3, 19, 175**
See also AFAW 1, 2; BW 1, 3; CA 104;
125; CANR 82; CDALB 1917-1929; CLR
32; DA3; DAM MULT, POET; DLB 51;
EWL 3; EXPP; LMFS 2; MAL 5; MTCW
1, 2; MTFW 2005; NFS 22; PFS 1; RGAL
4; SATA 31; TUS

Johnson, Joyce 1935- .... **CLC 58**
See also BG 1:3; CA 125; 129; CANR 102

Johnson, Judith (Emlyn) 1936- .... **CLC 7, 15**
See Sherwin, Judith Johnson
See also CA 25-28R; 153; CANR 34; CP 6,
7

Johnson, Lionel (Pigot)
1867-1902 .... **TCLC 19**
See also CA 117; 209; DLB 19; RGEL 2

Johnson, Marguerite Annie
See Angelou, Maya

Johnson, Mel
See Malzberg, Barry N(athaniel)

Johnson, Pamela Hansford
1912-1981 .... **CLC 1, 7, 27**
See also CA 1-4R; 104; CANR 2, 28; CN
1, 2, 3; DLB 15; MTCW 1, 2; MTFW
2005; RGEL 2

Johnson, Paul (Bede) 1928- .... **CLC 147**
See also BEST 89:4; CA 17-20R; CANR
34, 62, 100

Johnson, Robert .... **CLC 70**

Johnson, Robert 1911(?)-1938 .... **TCLC 69**
See also BW 3; CA 174

Johnson, Samuel 1709-1784 . **LC 15, 52, 128;
WLC 3**
See also BRW 3; BRWR 1; CDBLB 1660-
1789; DA; DAB; DAC; DAM MST; DLB
39, 95, 104, 142, 213; LMFS 1; RGEL 2;
TEA

Johnson, Uwe 1934-1984 .. **CLC 5, 10, 15, 40**
See also CA 1-4R; 112; CANR 1, 39; CD-
WLB 2; DLB 75; EWL 3; MTCW 1;
RGWL 2, 3

Johnston, Basil H. 1929- .... **NNAL**
See also CA 69-72; CANR 11, 28, 66;
DAC; DAM MULT; DLB 60

Johnston, George (Benson) 1913- .... **CLC 51**
See also CA 1-4R; CANR 5, 20; CP 1, 2, 3,
4, 5, 6, 7; DLB 88

Johnston, Jennifer (Prudence)
1930- .... **CLC 7, 150**
See also CA 85-88; CANR 92; CN 4, 5, 6,
7; DLB 14

Joinville, Jean de 1224(?)-1317 ..... **CMLC 38**

Jolley, (Monica) Elizabeth 1923- ..... **CLC 46;
SSC 19**
See also CA 127; CAAS 13; CANR 59; CN
4, 5, 6, 7; DLB 325; EWL 3; RGSF 2

Jones, Arthur Llewellyn 1863-1947
See Machen, Arthur
See also CA 104; 179; HGG

Jones, D(ouglas) G(ordon) 1929- ..... **CLC 10**
See also CA 29-32R; CANR 13, 90; CP 1,
2, 3, 4, 5, 6, 7; DLB 53

Jones, David (Michael) 1895-1974 .... **CLC 2,
4, 7, 13, 42**
See also BRW 6; BRWS 7; CA 9-12R; 53-
56; CANR 28; CDBLB 1945-1960; CP 1,
2; DLB 20, 100; EWL 3; MTCW 1; PAB;
RGEL 2

Jones, David Robert 1947-
See Bowie, David
See also CA 103; CANR 104

Jones, Diana Wynne 1934- .... **CLC 26**
See also AAYA 12; BYA 6, 7, 9, 11, 13, 16;
CA 49-52; CANR 4, 26, 56, 120; CLR
23; DLB 161; FANT; JRDA; MAICYA 1,
2; MTFW 2005; SAAS 7; SATA 9, 70,
108, 160; SFW 4; SUFW 2; YAW

Jones, Edward P. 1950- .... **CLC 76, 223**
See also AAYA 71; BW 2, 3; CA 142;
CANR 79, 134; CSW; MTFW 2005

Jones, Gayl 1949- ...... **BLC 2; CLC 6, 9, 131**
See also AFAW 1, 2; BW 2, 3; CA 77-80;
CANR 27, 66, 122; CN 4, 5, 6, 7; CSW;
DA3; DAM MULT; DLB 33, 278; MAL
5; MTCW 1, 2; MTFW 2005; RGAL 4

Jones, James 1921-1977 .... **CLC 1, 3, 10, 39**
See also AITN 1, 2; AMWS 11; BPFB 2;
CA 1-4R; 69-72; CANR 6; CN 1, 2; DLB
2, 143; DLBD 17; DLBY 1998; EWL 3;
MAL 5; MTCW 1; RGAL 4

Jones, John J.
See Lovecraft, H. P.

Jones, LeRoi .... **CLC 1, 2, 3, 5, 10, 14**
See Baraka, Amiri
See also CN 1, 2; CP 1, 2, 3; MTCW 2

Jones, Louis B. 1953- .... **CLC 65**
See also CA 141; CANR 73

Jones, Madison (Percy, Jr.) 1925- ...... **CLC 4**
See also CA 13-16R; CAAS 11; CANR 7,
54, 83; CN 1, 2, 3, 4, 5, 6, 7; CSW; DLB
152

Jones, Mervyn 1922- .... **CLC 10, 52**
See also CA 45-48; CAAS 5; CANR 1, 91;
CN 1, 2, 3, 4, 5, 6, 7; MTCW 1

Jones, Mick 1956(?)- .... **CLC 30**

Jones, Nettie (Pearl) 1941- .... **CLC 34**
See also BW 2; CA 137; CAAS 20; CANR
88

Jones, Peter 1802-1856 .... **NNAL**

Jones, Preston 1936-1979 .... **CLC 10**
See also CA 73-76; 89-92; DLB 7

Jones, Robert F(rancis) 1934-2003 .... **CLC 7**
See also CA 49-52; CANR 2, 61, 118

Jones, Rod 1953- .... **CLC 50**
See also CA 128

Jones, Terence Graham Parry
1942- .... **CLC 21**
See Jones, Terry; Monty Python
See also CA 112; 116; CANR 35, 93; INT
CA-116; SATA 127

Jones, Terry
See Jones, Terence Graham Parry
See also SATA 67; SATA-Brief 51

Jones, Thom (Douglas) 1945(?)- ..... **CLC 81;
SSC 56**
See also CA 157; CANR 88; DLB 244;
SSFS 23

Jong, Erica 1942- .... **CLC 4, 6, 8, 18, 83**
See also AITN 1; AMWS 5; BEST 90:2;
BPFB 2; CA 73-76; CANR 26, 52, 75,
132; CN 3, 4, 5, 6, 7; CP 2, 3, 4, 5, 6, 7;
CPW; DA3; DAM NOV, POP; DLB 2, 5,
28, 152; FW; INT CANR-26; MAL 5;
MTCW 1, 2; MTFW 2005

Kavan, Anna 1901-1968 .... **CLC 5, 13, 82**
See also BRWS 7; CA 5-8R; CANR 6, 57;
DLB 255; MTCW 1; RGEL 2; SFW 4

Kavanagh, Dan
See Barnes, Julian

Kavanagh, Julie 1952- .... **CLC 119**
See also CA 163

Kavanagh, Patrick (Joseph)
1904-1967 .... **CLC 22; PC 33**
See also BRWS 7; CA 123; 25-28R; DLB
15, 20; EWL 3; MTCW 1; RGEL 2

Kawabata, Yasunari 1899-1972 ..... **CLC 2, 5,
9, 18, 107; SSC 17**
See Kawabata Yasunari
See also CA 93-96; 33-36R; CANR 88;
DAM MULT; MJW; MTCW 2; MTFW
2005; RGSF 2; RGWL 2, 3

Kawabata Yasunari
See Kawabata, Yasunari
See also DLB 180; EWL 3

Kaye, M(ary) M(argaret)
1908-2004 .... **CLC 28**
See also CA 89-92; 223; CANR 24, 60, 102,
142; MTCW 1, 2; MTFW 2005; RHW;
SATA 62; SATA-Obit 152

Kaye, Mollie
See Kaye, M(ary) M(argaret)

Kaye-Smith, Sheila 1887-1956 .... **TCLC 20**
See also CA 118; 203; DLB 36

Kaymor, Patrice Maguilene
See Senghor, Leopold Sedar

Kazakov, Iurii Pavlovich
See Kazakov, Yuri Pavlovich
See also DLB 302

Kazakov, Yuri Pavlovich 1927-1982 . **SSC 43**
See Kazakov, Iurii Pavlovich; Kazakov,
Yury
See also CA 5-8R; CANR 36; MTCW 1;
RGSF 2

Kazakov, Yury
See Kazakov, Yuri Pavlovich
See also EWL 3

Kazan, Elia 1909-2003 .... **CLC 6, 16, 63**
See also CA 21-24R; 220; CANR 32, 78

Kazantzakis, Nikos 1883(?)-1957 .... **TCLC 2,
5, 33, 181**
See also BPFB 2; CA 105; 132; DA3; EW
9; EWL 3; MTCW 1, 2; MTFW 2005;
RGWL 2, 3

Kazin, Alfred 1915-1998 ..... **CLC 34, 38, 119**
See also AMWS 8; CA 1-4R; CAAS 7;
CANR 1, 45, 79; DLB 67; EWL 3

Keane, Mary Nesta (Skrine) 1904-1996
See Keane, Molly
See also CA 108; 114; 151; RHW

Keane, Molly .... **CLC 31**
See Keane, Mary Nesta (Skrine)
See also CN 5, 6; INT CA-114; TCLE 1:1

Keates, Jonathan 1946(?)- .... **CLC 34**
See also CA 163; CANR 126

Keaton, Buster 1895-1966 .... **CLC 20**
See also CA 194

Keats, John 1795-1821 ...... **NCLC 8, 73, 121;
PC 1; WLC 3**
See also AAYA 58; BRW 4; BRWR 1; CD-
BLB 1789-1832; DA; DA3; DAB; DAC;
DAM MST, POET; DLB 96, 110; EXPP;
LMFS 1; PAB; PFS 1, 2, 3, 9, 17; RGEL
2; TEA; WLIT 3; WP

Keble, John 1792-1866 .... **NCLC 87**
See also DLB 32, 55; RGEL 2

Keene, Donald 1922- .... **CLC 34**
See also CA 1-4R; CANR 5, 119

Keillor, Garrison 1942- ..... **CLC 40, 115, 222**
See also AAYA 2, 62; BEST 89:3; BPFB 2;
CA 111; 117; CANR 36, 59, 124; CPW;
DA3; DAM POP; DLBY 1987; EWL 3;
MTCW 1, 2; MTFW 2005; SATA 58;
TUS

Keith, Carlos
See Lewton, Val

Keith, Michael
See Hubbard, L. Ron

Keller, Gottfried 1819-1890 .... **NCLC 2; SSC
26**
See also CDWLB 2; DLB 129; EW; RGSF
2; RGWL 2, 3

Keller, Nora Okja 1965- .... **CLC 109**
See also CA 187

Kellerman, Jonathan 1949- .... **CLC 44**
See also AAYA 35; BEST 90:1; CA 106;
CANR 29, 51, 150; CMW 4; CPW; DA3;
DAM POP; INT CANR-29

Kelley, William Melvin 1937- .... **CLC 22**
See also BW 1; CA 77-80; CANR 27, 83;
CN 1, 2, 3, 4, 5, 6, 7; DLB 33; EWL 3

Kellogg, Marjorie 1922-2005 .... **CLC 2**
See also CA 81-84; 246

Kellow, Kathleen
See Hibbert, Eleanor Alice Burford

Kelly, Lauren
See Oates, Joyce Carol

Kelly, M(ilton) T(errence) 1947- ...... **CLC 55**
See also CA 97-100; CAAS 22; CANR 19,
43, 84; CN 6

Kelly, Robert 1935- .... **SSC 50**
See also CA 17-20R; CAAS 19; CANR 47;
CP 1, 2, 3, 4, 5, 6, 7; DLB 5, 130, 165

Kelman, James 1946- .... **CLC 58, 86**
See also BRWS 5; CA 148; CANR 85, 130;
CN 5, 6, 7; DLB 194, 319, 326; RGSF 2;
WLIT 4

Kemal, Yasar
See Kemal, Yashar
See also CWW 2; EWL 3; WLIT 6

Kemal, Yashar 1923(?)- .... **CLC 14, 29**
See also CA 89-92; CANR 44

Kemble, Fanny 1809-1893 .... **NCLC 18**
See also DLB 32

Kemelman, Harry 1908-1996 .... **CLC 2**
See also AITN 1; BPFB 2; CA 9-12R; 155;
CANR 6, 71; CMW 4; DLB 28

Kempe, Margery 1373(?)-1440(?) ... **LC 6, 56**
See also DLB 146; FL 1:1; RGEL 2

Kempis, Thomas a 1380-1471 .... **LC 11**

Kendall, Henry 1839-1882 .... **NCLC 12**
See also DLB 230

Keneally, Thomas (Michael) 1935- ... **CLC 5,
8, 10, 14, 19, 27, 43, 117**
See also BRWS 4; CA 85-88; CANR 10,
50, 74, 130; CN 1, 2, 3, 4, 5, 6, 7; CPW;
DA3; DAM NOV; DLB 289, 299, 326;
EWL 3; MTCW 1, 2; MTFW 2005; NFS
17; RGEL 2; RGHL; RHW

Kennedy, A(lison) L(ouise) 1965- ... **CLC 188**
See also CA 168; 213; CAAE 213; CANR
108; CD 5, 6; CN 6, 7; DLB 271; RGSF
2

Kennedy, Adrienne (Lita) 1931- .... **BLC 2;
CLC 66; DC 5**
See also AFAW 2; BW 2, 3; CA 103; CAAS
20; CABS 3; CAD; CANR 26, 53, 82;
CD 5, 6; DAM MULT; DFS 9; DLB 38;
FW; MAL 5

Kennedy, John Pendleton
1795-1870 .... **NCLC 2**
See also DLB 3, 248, 254; RGAL 4

Kennedy, Joseph Charles 1929-
See Kennedy, X. J.
See also CA 1-4R, 201; CAAE 201; CANR
4, 30, 40; CWRI 5; MAICYA 2; MAIC-
YAS 1; SATA 14, 86, 130; SATA-Essay
130

Kennedy, William (Joseph) 1928- ..... **CLC 6,
28, 34, 53**
See also AAYA 1; AMWS 7; BPFB 2; CA
85-88; CANR 14, 31, 76, 134; CN 4, 5, 6,
7; DA3; DAM NOV; DLB 143; DLBY
1985; EWL 3; INT CANR-31; MAL 5;
MTCW 1, 2; MTFW 2005; SATA 57

Kennedy, X. J. .... **CLC 8, 42**
See Kennedy, Joseph Charles
See also AMWS 15; CAAS 9; CLR 27; CP
1, 2, 3, 4, 5, 6, 7; DLB 5; SAAS 22

Kenny, Maurice (Francis) 1929- ..... **CLC 87;
NNAL**
See also CA 144; CAAS 22; CANR 143;
DAM MULT; DLB 175

Kent, Kelvin
See Kuttner, Henry

Kenton, Maxwell
See Southern, Terry

Kenyon, Jane 1947-1995 .... **PC 57**
See also AAYA 63; AMWS 7; CA 118; 148;
CANR 44, 69; CP 6, 7; CWP; DLB 120;
PFS 9, 17; RGAL 4

Kenyon, Robert O.
See Kuttner, Henry

Kepler, Johannes 1571-1630 .... **LC 45**

Ker, Jill
See Conway, Jill K(er)

Kerkow, H. C.
See Lewton, Val

Kerouac, Jack 1922-1969 ...... **CLC 1, 2, 3, 5,
14, 29, 61; TCLC 117; WLC**
See Kerouac, Jean-Louis Lebris de
See also AAYA 25; AMWC 1; AMWS 3;
BG 3; BPFB 2; CDALB 1941-1968; CP
1; CPW; DLB 2, 16, 237; DLBD 3;
DLBY 1995; EWL 3; GLL 1; LATS 1:2;
LMFS 2; MAL 5; NFS 8; RGAL 4; TUS;
WP

Kerouac, Jean-Louis Lebris de 1922-1969
See Kerouac, Jack
See also AITN 1; CA 5-8R; 25-28R; CANR
26, 54, 95; DA; DA3; DAB; DAC; DAM
MST, NOV, POET, POP; MTCW 1, 2;
MTFW 2005

Kerr, (Bridget) Jean (Collins)
1923(?)-2003 .... **CLC 22**
See also CA 5-8R; 212; CANR 7; INT
CANR-7

Kerr, M. E. .... **CLC 12, 35**
See Meaker, Marijane (Agnes)
See also AAYA 2, 23; BYA 1, 7, 8; CLR
29; SAAS 1; WYA

Kerr, Robert .... **CLC 55**

Kerrigan, (Thomas) Anthony 1918- .. **CLC 4,
6**
See also CA 49-52; CAAS 11; CANR 4

Kerry, Lois
See Duncan, Lois

Kesey, Ken (Elton) 1935-2001 ... **CLC 1, 3, 6,
11, 46, 64, 184; WLC 3**
See also AAYA 25; BG 1:3; BPFB 2; CA
1-4R; 204; CANR 22, 38, 66, 124;
CDALB 1968-1988; CN 1, 2, 3, 4, 5, 6,
7; CPW; DA; DA3; DAB; DAC; DAM
MST, NOV, POP; DLB 2, 16, 206; EWL
3; EXPN; LAIT 4; MAL 5; MTCW 1, 2;
MTFW 2005; NFS 2; RGAL 4; SATA 66;
SATA-Obit 131; TUS; YAW

Kesselring, Joseph (Otto)
1902-1967 .... **CLC 45**
See also CA 150; DAM DRAM, MST; DFS
20

Kessler, Jascha (Frederick) 1929- ...... **CLC 4**
See also CA 17-20R; CANR 8, 48, 111; CP
1

Kettelkamp, Larry (Dale) 1933- .... **CLC 12**
See also CA 29-32R; CANR 16; SAAS 3;
SATA 2

Key, Ellen (Karolina Sofia)
1849-1926 .... **TCLC 65**
See also DLB 259

Keyber, Conny
See Fielding, Henry

Keyes, Daniel 1927- .... **CLC 80**
See also AAYA 23; BYA 11; CA 17-20R,
181; CAAE 181; CANR 10, 26, 54, 74;
DA; DA3; DAC; DAM MST, NOV;
EXPN; LAIT 4; MTCW 2; MTFW 2005;
NFS 2; SATA 37; SFW 4

Keynes, John Maynard
1883-1946 .... **TCLC 64**
See also CA 114; 162, 163; DLBD 10;
MTCW 2; MTFW 2005

Khanshendel, Chiron
See Rose, Wendy

Khayyam, Omar 1048-1131 ... **CMLC 11; PC 8**
See Omar Khayyam
See also DA3; DAM POET; WLIT 6

Kherdian, David 1931- .... **CLC 6, 9**
See also AAYA 42; CA 21-24R, 192; CAAE
192; CAAS 2; CANR 39, 78; CLR 24;
JRDA; LAIT 3; MAICYA 1, 2; SATA 16,
74; SATA-Essay 125

Khlebnikov, Velimir .... **TCLC 20**
See Khlebnikov, Viktor Vladimirovich
See also DLB 295; EW 10; EWL 3; RGWL
2, 3

Khlebnikov, Viktor Vladimirovich 1885-1922
See Khlebnikov, Velimir
See also CA 117; 217

Khodasevich, Vladislav (Felitsianovich)
1886-1939 .... **TCLC 15**
See also CA 115; DLB 317; EWL 3

Kielland, Alexander Lange
1849-1906 .... **TCLC 5**
See also CA 104

Kiely, Benedict 1919- ... **CLC 23, 43; SSC 58**
See also CA 1-4R; CANR 2, 84; CN 1, 2,
3, 4, 5, 6, 7; DLB 15, 319; TCLE 1:1

Kienzle, William X(avier)
1928-2001 .... **CLC 25**
See also CA 93-96; 203; CAAS 1; CANR
9, 31, 59, 111; CMW 4; DA3; DAM POP;
INT CANR-31; MSW; MTCW 1, 2;
MTFW 2005

Kierkegaard, Soren 1813-1855 ..... **NCLC 34, 78, 125**
See also DLB 300; EW 6; LMFS 2; RGWL
3; TWA

Kieslowski, Krzysztof 1941-1996 .... **CLC 120**
See also CA 147; 151

Killens, John Oliver 1916-1987 .... **CLC 10**
See also BW 2; CA 77-80; 123; CAAS 2;
CANR 26; CN 1, 2, 3, 4; DLB 33; EWL
3

Killigrew, Anne 1660-1685 .... **LC 4, 73**
See also DLB 131

Killigrew, Thomas 1612-1683 .... **LC 57**
See also DLB 58; RGEL 2

Kim
See Simenon, Georges (Jacques Christian)

Kincaid, Jamaica 1949- ...... **BLC 2; CLC 43, 68, 137; SSC 72**
See also AAYA 13, 56; AFAW 2; AMWS 7;
BRWS 7; BW 2, 3; CA 125; CANR 47,
59, 95, 133; CDALBS; CDWLB 3; CLR
63; CN 4, 5, 6, 7; DA3; DAM MULT,
NOV; DLB 157, 227; DNFS 1; EWL 3;
EXPS; FW; LATS 1:2; LMFS 2; MAL 5;
MTCW 2; MTFW 2005; NCFS 1; NFS 3;
SSFS 5, 7; TUS; WWE 1; YAW

King, Francis (Henry) 1923- .... **CLC 8, 53, 145**
See also CA 1-4R; CANR 1, 33, 86; CN 1,
2, 3, 4, 5, 6, 7; DAM NOV; DLB 15, 139;
MTCW 1

King, Kennedy
See Brown, George Douglas

King, Martin Luther, Jr. 1929-1968 . **BLC 2; CLC 83; WLCS**
See also BW 2, 3; CA 25-28; CANR 27,
44; CAP 2; DA; DA3; DAB; DAC; DAM
MST, MULT; LAIT 5; LATS 1:2; MTCW
1, 2; MTFW 2005; SATA 14

King, Stephen 1947- .... **CLC 12, 26, 37, 61, 113; SSC 17, 55**
See also AAYA 1, 17; AMWS 5; BEST
90:1; BPFB 2; CA 61-64; CANR 1, 30,
52, 76, 119, 134; CN 7; CPW; DA3; DAM
NOV, POP; DLB 143; DLBY 1980; HGG;
JRDA; LAIT 5; MTCW 1, 2; MTFW
2005; RGAL 4; SATA 9, 55, 161; SUFW
1, 2; WYAS 1; YAW

King, Stephen Edwin
See King, Stephen

King, Steve
See King, Stephen

King, Thomas 1943- .... **CLC 89, 171; NNAL**
See also CA 144; CANR 95; CCA 1; CN 6,
7; DAC; DAM MULT; DLB 175; SATA
96

Kingman, Lee .... **CLC 17**
See Natti, (Mary) Lee
See also CWRI 5; SAAS 3; SATA 1, 67

Kingsley, Charles 1819-1875 .... **NCLC 35**
See also CLR 77; DLB 21, 32, 163, 178,
190; FANT; MAICYA 2; MAICYAS 1;
RGEL 2; WCH; YABC 2

Kingsley, Henry 1830-1876 .... **NCLC 107**
See also DLB 21, 230; RGEL 2

Kingsley, Sidney 1906-1995 .... **CLC 44**
See also CA 85-88; 147; CAD; DFS 14, 19;
DLB 7; MAL 5; RGAL 4

Kingsolver, Barbara 1955- .... **CLC 55, 81, 130, 216**
See also AAYA 15; AMWS 7; CA 129; 134;
CANR 60, 96, 133; CDALBS; CN 7;
CPW; CSW; DA3; DAM POP; DLB 206;
INT CA-134; LAIT 5; MTCW 2; MTFW
2005; NFS 5, 10, 12; RGAL 4; TCLE 1:1

Kingston, Maxine (Ting Ting) Hong
1940- .... **AAL; CLC 12, 19, 58, 121; WLCS**
See also AAYA 8, 55; AMWS 5; BPFB 2;
CA 69-72; CANR 13, 38, 74, 87, 128;
CDALBS; CN 6, 7; DA3; DAM MULT,
NOV; DLB 173, 212, 312; DLBY 1980;
EWL 3; FL 1:6; FW; INT CANR-13;
LAIT 5; MAL 5; MBL; MTCW 1, 2;
MTFW 2005; NFS 6; RGAL 4; SATA 53;
SSFS 3; TCWW 2

Kinnell, Galway 1927- ..... **CLC 1, 2, 3, 5, 13, 29, 129; PC 26**
See also AMWS 3; CA 9-12R; CANR 10,
34, 66, 116, 138; CP 1, 2, 3, 4, 5, 6, 7;
DLB 5; DLBY 1987; EWL 3; INT CANR-
34; MAL 5; MTCW 1, 2; MTFW 2005;
PAB; PFS 9; RGAL 4; TCLE 1:1; WP

Kinsella, Thomas 1928- .... **CLC 4, 19, 138; PC 69**
See also BRWS 5; CA 17-20R; CANR 15,
122; CP 1, 2, 3, 4, 5, 6, 7; DLB 27; EWL
3; MTCW 1, 2; MTFW 2005; RGEL 2;
TEA

Kinsella, W(illiam) P(atrick) 1935- . **CLC 27, 43, 166**
See also AAYA 7, 60; BPFB 2; CA 97-100,
222; CAAE 222; CAAS 7; CANR 21, 35,
66, 75, 129; CN 4, 5, 6, 7; CPW; DAC;
DAM NOV, POP; FANT; INT CANR-21;
LAIT 5; MTCW 1, 2; MTFW 2005; NFS
15; RGSF 2

Kinsey, Alfred C(harles)
1894-1956 .... **TCLC 91**
See also CA 115; 170; MTCW 2

Kipling, (Joseph) Rudyard 1865-1936 . **PC 3; SSC 5, 54; TCLC 8, 17, 167; WLC 3**
See also AAYA 32; BRW 6; BRWC 1, 2;
BYA 4; CA 105; 120; CANR 33; CDBLB
1890-1914; CLR 39, 65; CWRI 5; DA;
DA3; DAB; DAC; DAM MST, POET;
DLB 19, 34, 141, 156; EWL 3; EXPS;
FANT; LAIT 3; LMFS 1; MAICYA 1, 2;
MTCW 1, 2; MTFW 2005; NFS 21; PFS
22; RGEL 2; RGSF 2; SATA 100; SFW
4; SSFS 8, 21, 22; SUFW 1; TEA; WCH;
WLIT 4; YABC 2

Kircher, Athanasius 1602-1680 .... **LC 121**
See also DLB 164

Kirk, Russell (Amos) 1918-1994 .. **TCLC 119**
See also AITN 1; CA 1-4R; 145; CAAS 9;
CANR 1, 20, 60; HGG; INT CANR-20;
MTCW 1, 2

Kirkham, Dinah
See Card, Orson Scott

Kirkland, Caroline M. 1801-1864 . **NCLC 85**
See also DLB 3, 73, 74, 250, 254; DLBD
13

Kirkup, James 1918- .... **CLC 1**
See also CA 1-4R; CAAS 4; CANR 2; CP
1, 2, 3, 4, 5, 6, 7; DLB 27; SATA 12

Kirkwood, James 1930(?)-1989 .... **CLC 9**
See also AITN 2; CA 1-4R; 128; CANR 6,
40; GLL 2

Kirsch, Sarah 1935- .... **CLC 176**
See also CA 178; CWW 2; DLB 75; EWL
3

Kirshner, Sidney
See Kingsley, Sidney

Kis, Danilo 1935-1989 .... **CLC 57**
See also CA 109; 118; 129; CANR 61; CD-
WLB 4; DLB 181; EWL 3; MTCW 1;
RGSF 2; RGWL 2, 3

Kissinger, Henry A(lfred) 1923- ..... **CLC 137**
See also CA 1-4R; CANR 2, 33, 66, 109;
MTCW 1

Kittel, Frederick August
See Wilson, August

Kivi, Aleksis 1834-1872 .... **NCLC 30**

Kizer, Carolyn (Ashley) 1925- ... **CLC 15, 39, 80; PC 66**
See also CA 65-68; CAAS 5; CANR 24,
70, 134; CP 1, 2, 3, 4, 5, 6, 7; CWP; DAM
POET; DLB 5, 169; EWL 3; MAL 5;
MTCW 2; MTFW 2005; PFS 18; TCLE
1:1

Klabund 1890-1928 .... **TCLC 44**
See also CA 162; DLB 66

Klappert, Peter 1942- .... **CLC 57**
See also CA 33-36R; CSW; DLB 5

Klein, A(braham) M(oses)
1909-1972 .... **CLC 19**
See also CA 101; 37-40R; CP 1; DAB;
DAC; DAM MST; DLB 68; EWL 3;
RGEL 2; RGHL

Klein, Joe
See Klein, Joseph

Klein, Joseph 1946- .... **CLC 154**
See also CA 85-88; CANR 55

Klein, Norma 1938-1989 .... **CLC 30**
See also AAYA 2, 35; BPFB 2; BYA 6, 7,
8; CA 41-44R; 128; CANR 15, 37; CLR
2, 19; INT CANR-15; JRDA; MAICYA
1, 2; SAAS 1; SATA 7, 57; WYA; YAW

Klein, T(heodore) E(ibon) D(onald)
1947- .... **CLC 34**
See also CA 119; CANR 44, 75; HGG

Kleist, Heinrich von 1777-1811 ...... **NCLC 2, 37; SSC 22**
See also CDWLB 2; DAM DRAM; DLB
90; EW 5; RGSF 2; RGWL 2, 3

Klima, Ivan 1931- .... **CLC 56, 172**
See also CA 25-28R; CANR 17, 50, 91; CDWLB 4; CWW 2; DAM NOV; DLB 232; EWL 3; RGWL 3

Klimentev, Andrei Platonovich
See Klimentov, Andrei Platonovich

Klimentov, Andrei Platonovich
1899-1951 .... **SSC 42; TCLC 14**
See Platonov, Andrei Platonovich; Platonov, Andrey Platonovich
See also CA 108; 232

Klinger, Friedrich Maximilian von
1752-1831 .... **NCLC 1**
See also DLB 94

Klingsor the Magician
See Hartmann, Sadakichi

Klopstock, Friedrich Gottlieb
1724-1803 .... **NCLC 11**
See also DLB 97; EW 4; RGWL 2, 3

Kluge, Alexander 1932- .... **SSC 61**
See also CA 81-84; DLB 75

Knapp, Caroline 1959-2002 .... **CLC 99**
See also CA 154; 207

Knebel, Fletcher 1911-1993 .... **CLC 14**
See also AITN 1; CA 1-4R; 140; CAAS 3; CANR 1, 36; CN 1, 2, 3, 4, 5; SATA 36; SATA-Obit 75

Knickerbocker, Diedrich
See Irving, Washington

Knight, Etheridge 1931-1991 ... **BLC 2; CLC 40; PC 14**
See also BW 1, 3; CA 21-24R; 133; CANR 23, 82; CP 1, 2, 3, 4, 5; DAM POET; DLB 41; MTCW 2; MTFW 2005; RGAL 4; TCLE 1:1

Knight, Sarah Kemble 1666-1727 .... **LC 7**
See also DLB 24, 200

Knister, Raymond 1899-1932 .... **TCLC 56**
See also CA 186; DLB 68; RGEL 2

Knowles, John 1926-2001 ... **CLC 1, 4, 10, 26**
See also AAYA 10; AMWS 12; BPFB 2; BYA 3; CA 17-20R; 203; CANR 40, 74, 76, 132; CDALB 1968-1988; CLR 98; CN 1, 2, 3, 4, 5, 6, 7; DA; DAC; DAM MST, NOV; DLB 6; EXPN; MTCW 1, 2; MTFW 2005; NFS 2; RGAL 4; SATA 8, 89; SATA-Obit 134; YAW

Knox, Calvin M.
See Silverberg, Robert

Knox, John c. 1505-1572 .... **LC 37**
See also DLB 132

Knye, Cassandra
See Disch, Thomas M(ichael)

Koch, C(hristopher) J(ohn) 1932- .... **CLC 42**
See also CA 127; CANR 84; CN 3, 4, 5, 6, 7; DLB 289

Koch, Christopher
See Koch, C(hristopher) J(ohn)

Koch, Kenneth (Jay) 1925-2002 .... **CLC 5, 8, 44**
See also AMWS 15; CA 1-4R; 207; CAD; CANR 6, 36, 57, 97, 131; CD 5, 6; CP 1, 2, 3, 4, 5, 6, 7; DAM POET; DLB 5; INT CANR-36; MAL 5; MTCW 2; MTFW 2005; PFS 20; SATA 65; WP

Kochanowski, Jan 1530-1584 .... **LC 10**
See also RGWL 2, 3

Kock, Charles Paul de 1794-1871 . **NCLC 16**

Koda Rohan
See Koda Shigeyuki

Koda Rohan
See Koda Shigeyuki
See also DLB 180

Koda Shigeyuki 1867-1947 .... **TCLC 22**
See Koda Rohan
See also CA 121; 183

Koestler, Arthur 1905-1983 ... **CLC 1, 3, 6, 8, 15, 33**
See also BRWS 1; CA 1-4R; 109; CANR 1, 33; CDBLB 1945-1960; CN 1, 2, 3; DLBY 1983; EWL 3; MTCW 1, 2; MTFW 2005; NFS 19; RGEL 2

Kogawa, Joy Nozomi 1935- ...... **CLC 78, 129**
See also AAYA 47; CA 101; CANR 19, 62, 126; CN 6, 7; CP 1; CWP; DAC; DAM MST, MULT; FW; MTCW 2; MTFW 2005; NFS 3; SATA 99

Kohout, Pavel 1928- .... **CLC 13**
See also CA 45-48; CANR 3

Koizumi, Yakumo
See Hearn, (Patricio) Lafcadio (Tessima Carlos)

Kolmar, Gertrud 1894-1943 .... **TCLC 40**
See also CA 167; EWL 3; RGHL

Komunyakaa, Yusef 1947- .. **BLCS; CLC 86, 94, 207; PC 51**
See also AFAW 2; AMWS 13; CA 147; CANR 83; CP 6, 7; CSW; DLB 120; EWL 3; PFS 5, 20; RGAL 4

Konrad, George
See Konrad, Gyorgy

Konrad, Gyorgy 1933- .... **CLC 4, 10, 73**
See also CA 85-88; CANR 97; CDWLB 4; CWW 2; DLB 232; EWL 3

Konwicki, Tadeusz 1926- ...... **CLC 8, 28, 54, 117**
See also CA 101; CAAS 9; CANR 39, 59; CWW 2; DLB 232; EWL 3; IDFW 3; MTCW 1

Koontz, Dean R. 1945- .... **CLC 78, 206**
See also AAYA 9, 31; BEST 89:3, 90:2; CA 108; CANR 19, 36, 52, 95, 138; CMW 4; CPW; DA3; DAM NOV, POP; DLB 292; HGG; MTCW 1; MTFW 2005; SATA 92, 165; SFW 4; SUFW 2; YAW

Koontz, Dean Ray
See Koontz, Dean R.

Kopernik, Mikolaj
See Copernicus, Nicolaus

Kopit, Arthur (Lee) 1937- ...... **CLC 1, 18, 33**
See also AITN 1; CA 81-84; CABS 3; CAD; CD 5, 6; DAM DRAM; DFS 7, 14; DLB 7; MAL 5; MTCW 1; RGAL 4

Kopitar, Jernej (Bartholomaus)
1780-1844 .... **NCLC 117**

Kops, Bernard 1926- .... **CLC 4**
See also CA 5-8R; CANR 84; CBD; CN 1, 2, 3, 4, 5, 6, 7; CP 1, 2, 3, 4, 5, 6, 7; DLB 13; RGHL

Kornbluth, C(yril) M. 1923-1958 .... **TCLC 8**
See also CA 105; 160; DLB 8; SCFW 1, 2; SFW 4

Korolenko, V. G.
See Korolenko, Vladimir Galaktionovich

Korolenko, Vladimir
See Korolenko, Vladimir Galaktionovich

Korolenko, Vladimir G.
See Korolenko, Vladimir Galaktionovich

Korolenko, Vladimir Galaktionovich
1853-1921 .... **TCLC 22**
See also CA 121; DLB 277

Korzybski, Alfred (Habdank Skarbek)
1879-1950 .... **TCLC 61**
See also CA 123; 160

Kosinski, Jerzy (Nikodem)
1933-1991 .... **CLC 1, 2, 3, 6, 10, 15, 53, 70**
See also AMWS 7; BPFB 2; CA 17-20R; 134; CANR 9, 46; CN 1, 2, 3, 4; DA3; DAM NOV; DLB 2, 299; DLBY 1982; EWL 3; HGG; MAL 5; MTCW 1, 2; MTFW 2005; NFS 12; RGAL 4; RGHL; TUS

Kostelanetz, Richard (Cory) 1940- .. **CLC 28**
See also CA 13-16R; CAAS 8; CANR 38, 77; CN 4, 5, 6; CP 2, 3, 4, 5, 6, 7

Kostrowitzki, Wilhelm Apollinaris de
1880-1918
See Apollinaire, Guillaume
See also CA 104

Kotlowitz, Robert 1924- .... **CLC 4**
See also CA 33-36R; CANR 36

Kotzebue, August (Friedrich Ferdinand) von
1761-1819 .... **NCLC 25**
See also DLB 94

Kotzwinkle, William 1938- ..... **CLC 5, 14, 35**
See also BPFB 2; CA 45-48; CANR 3, 44, 84, 129; CLR 6; CN 7; DLB 173; FANT; MAICYA 1, 2; SATA 24, 70, 146; SFW 4; SUFW 2; YAW

Kowna, Stancy
See Szymborska, Wislawa

Kozol, Jonathan 1936- .... **CLC 17**
See also AAYA 46; CA 61-64; CANR 16, 45, 96; MTFW 2005

Kozoll, Michael 1940(?)- .... **CLC 35**

Kramer, Kathryn 19(?)- .... **CLC 34**

Kramer, Larry 1935- .... **CLC 42; DC 8**
See also CA 124; 126; CANR 60, 132; DAM POP; DLB 249; GLL 1

Krasicki, Ignacy 1735-1801 .... **NCLC 8**

Krasinski, Zygmunt 1812-1859 .... **NCLC 4**
See also RGWL 2, 3

Kraus, Karl 1874-1936 .... **TCLC 5**
See also CA 104; 216; DLB 118; EWL 3

Kreve (Mickevicius), Vincas
1882-1954 .... **TCLC 27**
See also CA 170; DLB 220; EWL 3

Kristeva, Julia 1941- .... **CLC 77, 140**
See also CA 154; CANR 99; DLB 242; EWL 3; FW; LMFS 2

Kristofferson, Kris 1936- .... **CLC 26**
See also CA 104

Krizanc, John 1956- .... **CLC 57**
See also CA 187

Krleza, Miroslav 1893-1981 .... **CLC 8, 114**
See also CA 97-100; 105; CANR 50; CDWLB 4; DLB 147; EW 11; RGWL 2, 3

Kroetsch, Robert (Paul) 1927- .... **CLC 5, 23, 57, 132**
See also CA 17-20R; CANR 8, 38; CCA 1; CN 2, 3, 4, 5, 6, 7; CP 6, 7; DAC; DAM POET; DLB 53; MTCW 1

Kroetz, Franz
See Kroetz, Franz Xaver

Kroetz, Franz Xaver 1946- .... **CLC 41**
See also CA 130; CANR 142; CWW 2; EWL 3

Kroker, Arthur (W.) 1945- .... **CLC 77**
See also CA 161

Kroniuk, Lisa
See Berton, Pierre (Francis de Marigny)

Kropotkin, Peter (Aleksieevich)
1842-1921 .... **TCLC 36**
See Kropotkin, Petr Alekseevich
See also CA 119; 219

Kropotkin, Petr Alekseevich
See Kropotkin, Peter (Aleksieevich)
See also DLB 277

Krotkov, Yuri 1917-1981 .... **CLC 19**
See also CA 102

Krumb
See Crumb, R.

Krumgold, Joseph (Quincy)
1908-1980 .... **CLC 12**
See also BYA 1, 2; CA 9-12R; 101; CANR 7; MAICYA 1, 2; SATA 1, 48; SATA-Obit 23; YAW

Krumwitz
See Crumb, R.

Landolfi, Tommaso 1908-1979 .... **CLC 11, 49**
See also CA 127; 117; DLB 177; EWL 3
Landon, Letitia Elizabeth
1802-1838 .... **NCLC 15**
See also DLB 96
Landor, Walter Savage
1775-1864 .... **NCLC 14**
See also BRW 4; DLB 93, 107; RGEL 2
Landwirth, Heinz 1927-
See Lind, Jakov
See also CA 9-12R; CANR 7
Lane, Patrick 1939- .... **CLC 25**
See also CA 97-100; CANR 54; CP 3, 4, 5,
6, 7; DAM POET; DLB 53; INT CA-97-
100
Lane, Rose Wilder 1887-1968 ...... **TCLC 177**
See also CA 102; CANR 63; SATA 29;
SATA-Brief 28; TCWW 2
Lang, Andrew 1844-1912 .... **TCLC 16**
See also CA 114; 137; CANR 85; CLR 101;
DLB 98, 141, 184; FANT; MAICYA 1, 2;
RGEL 2; SATA 16; WCH
Lang, Fritz 1890-1976 .... **CLC 20, 103**
See also AAYA 65; CA 77-80; 69-72;
CANR 30
Lange, John
See Crichton, (John) Michael
Langer, Elinor 1939- .... **CLC 34**
See also CA 121
Langland, William 1332(?)-1400(?) .... **LC 19,
120**
See also BRW 1; DA; DAB; DAC; DAM
MST, POET; DLB 146; RGEL 2; TEA;
WLIT 3
Langstaff, Launcelot
See Irving, Washington
Lanier, Sidney 1842-1881 . **NCLC 6, 118; PC
50**
See also AMWS 1; DAM POET; DLB 64;
DLBD 13; EXPP; MAICYA 1; PFS 14;
RGAL 4; SATA 18
Lanyer, Aemilia 1569-1645 .... **LC 10, 30, 83;
PC 60**
See also DLB 121
Lao Tzu c. 6th cent. B.C.-3rd cent.
B.C. .... **CMLC 7**
Lao-Tzu
See Lao Tzu
Lapine, James (Elliot) 1949- .... **CLC 39**
See also CA 123; 130; CANR 54, 128; INT
CA-130
Larbaud, Valery (Nicolas)
1881-1957 .... **TCLC 9**
See also CA 106; 152; EWL 3; GFL 1789
to the Present
Lardner, Ring
See Lardner, Ring(gold) W(ilmer)
See also BPFB 2; CDALB 1917-1929; DLB
11, 25, 86, 171; DLBD 16; MAL 5;
RGAL 4; RGSF 2
Lardner, Ring W., Jr.
See Lardner, Ring(gold) W(ilmer)
Lardner, Ring(gold) W(ilmer)
1885-1933 .... **SSC 32; TCLC 2, 14**
See Lardner, Ring
See also AMW; CA 104; 131; MTCW 1, 2;
MTFW 2005; TUS
Laredo, Betty
See Codrescu, Andrei
Larkin, Maia
See Wojciechowska, Maia (Teresa)
Larkin, Philip (Arthur) 1922-1985 ... **CLC 3,
5, 8, 9, 13, 18, 33, 39, 64; PC 21**
See also BRWS 1; CA 5-8R; 117; CANR
24, 62; CDBLB 1960 to Present; CP 1, 2,
3, 4; DA3; DAB; DAM MST, POET;
DLB 27; EWL 3; MTCW 1, 2; MTFW
2005; PFS 3, 4, 12; RGEL 2

La Roche, Sophie von
1730-1807 .... **NCLC 121**
See also DLB 94
La Rochefoucauld, Francois
1613-1680 .... **LC 108**
**Larra (y Sanchez de Castro), Mariano Jose
de** 1809-1837 .... **NCLC 17, 130**
Larsen, Eric 1941- .... **CLC 55**
See also CA 132
Larsen, Nella 1893(?)-1963 .... **BLC 2; CLC
37; HR 1:3**
See also AFAW 1, 2; BW 1; CA 125; CANR
83; DAM MULT; DLB 51; FW; LATS
1:1; LMFS 2
Larson, Charles R(aymond) 1938- ... **CLC 31**
See also CA 53-56; CANR 4, 121
Larson, Jonathan 1960-1996 .... **CLC 99**
See also AAYA 28; CA 156; DFS 23;
MTFW 2005
La Sale, Antoine de c. 1386-1460(?) . **LC 104**
See also DLB 208
Las Casas, Bartolome de
1474-1566 .... **HLCS; LC 31**
See Casas, Bartolome de las
See also DLB 318; LAW
Lasch, Christopher 1932-1994 .... **CLC 102**
See also CA 73-76; 144; CANR 25, 118;
DLB 246; MTCW 1, 2; MTFW 2005
Lasker-Schueler, Else 1869-1945 ... **TCLC 57**
See Lasker-Schuler, Else
See also CA 183; DLB 66, 124
Lasker-Schuler, Else
See Lasker-Schueler, Else
See also EWL 3
Laski, Harold J(oseph) 1893-1950 . **TCLC 79**
See also CA 188
Latham, Jean Lee 1902-1995 .... **CLC 12**
See also AITN 1; BYA 1; CA 5-8R; CANR
7, 84; CLR 50; MAICYA 1, 2; SATA 2,
68; YAW
Latham, Mavis
See Clark, Mavis Thorpe
Lathen, Emma .... **CLC 2**
See Hennissart, Martha; Latsis, Mary J(ane)
See also BPFB 2; CMW 4; DLB 306
Lathrop, Francis
See Leiber, Fritz (Reuter, Jr.)
Latsis, Mary J(ane) 1927-1997
See Lathen, Emma
See also CA 85-88; 162; CMW 4
Lattany, Kristin
See Lattany, Kristin (Elaine Eggleston)
Hunter
Lattany, Kristin (Elaine Eggleston) Hunter
1931- .... **CLC 35**
See Hunter, Kristin
See also AITN 1; BW 1; BYA 3; CA 13-
16R; CANR 13, 108; CLR 3; CN 7; DLB
33; INT CANR-13; MAICYA 1, 2; SAAS
10; SATA 12, 132; YAW
Lattimore, Richmond (Alexander)
1906-1984 .... **CLC 3**
See also CA 1-4R; 112; CANR 1; CP 1, 2,
3; MAL 5
Laughlin, James 1914-1997 .... **CLC 49**
See also CA 21-24R; 162; CAAS 22; CANR
9, 47; CP 1, 2, 3, 4, 5, 6; DLB 48; DLBY
1996, 1997
Laurence, (Jean) Margaret (Wemyss)
1926-1987 . **CLC 3, 6, 13, 50, 62; SSC 7**
See also BYA 13; CA 5-8R; 121; CANR
33; CN 1, 2, 3, 4; DAC; DAM MST; DLB
53; EWL 3; FW; MTCW 1, 2; MTFW
2005; NFS 11; RGEL 2; RGSF 2; SATA-
Obit 50; TCWW 2
Laurent, Antoine 1952- .... **CLC 50**
Lauscher, Hermann
See Hesse, Hermann

Lautreamont 1846-1870 .. **NCLC 12; SSC 14**
See Lautreamont, Isidore Lucien Ducasse
See also GFL 1789 to the Present; RGWL
2, 3
Lautreamont, Isidore Lucien Ducasse
See Lautreamont
See also DLB 217
Lavater, Johann Kaspar
1741-1801 .... **NCLC 142**
See also DLB 97
Laverty, Donald
See Blish, James (Benjamin)
Lavin, Mary 1912-1996 . **CLC 4, 18, 99; SSC
4, 67**
See also CA 9-12R; 151; CANR 33; CN 1,
2, 3, 4, 5, 6; DLB 15, 319; FW; MTCW
1; RGEL 2; RGSF 2; SSFS 23
Lavond, Paul Dennis
See Kornbluth, C(yril) M.; Pohl, Frederik
Lawes, Henry 1596-1662 .... **LC 113**
See also DLB 126
Lawler, Ray
See Lawler, Raymond Evenor
See also DLB 289
Lawler, Raymond Evenor 1922- .... **CLC 58**
See Lawler, Ray
See also CA 103; CD 5, 6; RGEL 2
Lawrence, D(avid) H(erbert Richards)
1885-1930 .... **PC 54; SSC 4, 19, 73;
TCLC 2, 9, 16, 33, 48, 61, 93; WLC 3**
See Chambers, Jessie
See also BPFB 2; BRW 7; BRWR 2; CA
104; 121; CANR 131; CDBLB 1914-
1945; DA; DA3; DAB; DAC; DAM MST,
NOV, POET; DLB 10, 19, 36, 98, 162,
195; EWL 3; EXPP; EXPS; LAIT 2, 3;
MTCW 1, 2; MTFW 2005; NFS 18; PFS
6; RGEL 2; RGSF 2; SSFS 2, 6; TEA;
WLIT 4; WP
Lawrence, T(homas) E(dward)
1888-1935 .... **TCLC 18**
See Dale, Colin
See also BRWS 2; CA 115; 167; DLB 195
Lawrence of Arabia
See Lawrence, T(homas) E(dward)
Lawson, Henry (Archibald Hertzberg)
1867-1922 .... **SSC 18; TCLC 27**
See also CA 120; 181; DLB 230; RGEL 2;
RGSF 2
Lawton, Dennis
See Faust, Frederick (Schiller)
Layamon fl. c. 1200- .... **CMLC 10**
See Laȝamon
See also DLB 146; RGEL 2
Laye, Camara 1928-1980 ..... **BLC 2; CLC 4,
38**
See Camara Laye
See also AFW; BW 1; CA 85-88; 97-100;
CANR 25; DAM MULT; MTCW 1, 2;
WLIT 2
Layton, Irving 1912-2006 ..... **CLC 2, 15, 164**
See also CA 1-4R; 247; CANR 2, 33, 43,
66, 129; CP 1, 2, 3, 4, 5, 6, 7; DAC; DAM
MST, POET; DLB 88; EWL 3; MTCW 1,
2; PFS 12; RGEL 2
Layton, Irving Peter
See Layton, Irving
Lazarus, Emma 1849-1887 ...... **NCLC 8, 109**
Lazarus, Felix
See Cable, George Washington
Lazarus, Henry
See Slavitt, David R(ytman)
Lea, Joan
See Neufeld, John (Arthur)
Leacock, Stephen (Butler)
1869-1944 .... **SSC 39; TCLC 2**
See also CA 104; 141; CANR 80; DAC;
DAM MST; DLB 92; EWL 3; MTCW 2;
MTFW 2005; RGEL 2; RGSF 2

Lonnbohm, Armas Eino Leopold 1878-1926
See Leino, Eino
See also CA 123
Lonnrot, Elias 1802-1884 .... **NCLC 53**
See also EFS 1
Lonsdale, Roger ed. .... **CLC 65**
Lopate, Phillip 1943- .... **CLC 29**
See also CA 97-100; CANR 88; DLBY
1980; INT CA-97-100
Lopez, Barry (Holstun) 1945- .... **CLC 70**
See also AAYA 9, 63; ANW; CA 65-68;
CANR 7, 23, 47, 68, 92; DLB 256, 275;
INT CANR-7, -23; MTCW 1; RGAL 4;
SATA 67
Lopez de Mendoza, Inigo
See Santillana, Inigo Lopez de Mendoza,
Marques de
Lopez Portillo (y Pacheco), Jose
1920-2004 .... **CLC 46**
See also CA 129; 224; HW 1
Lopez y Fuentes, Gregorio
1897(?)-1966 .... **CLC 32**
See also CA 131; EWL 3; HW 1
Lorca, Federico Garcia
See Garcia Lorca, Federico
See also DFS 4; EW 11; PFS 20; RGWL 2,
3; WP
Lord, Audre
See Lorde, Audre (Geraldine)
See also EWL 3
Lord, Bette Bao 1938- .... **AAL; CLC 23**
See also BEST 90:3; BPFB 2; CA 107;
CANR 41, 79; INT CA-107; SATA 58
Lord Auch
See Bataille, Georges
Lord Brooke
See Greville, Fulke
Lord Byron
See Byron, George Gordon (Noel)
Lorde, Audre (Geraldine)
1934-1992 .... **BLC 2; CLC 18, 71; PC
12; TCLC 173**
See Domini, Rey; Lord, Audre
See also AFAW 1, 2; BW 1, 3; CA 25-28R;
142; CANR 16, 26, 46, 82; CP 2, 3, 4, 5;
DA3; DAM MULT, POET; DLB 41; FW;
MAL 5; MTCW 1, 2; MTFW 2005; PFS
16; RGAL 4
Lord Houghton
See Milnes, Richard Monckton
Lord Jeffrey
See Jeffrey, Francis
Loreaux, Nichol .... **CLC 65**
Lorenzini, Carlo 1826-1890
See Collodi, Carlo
See also MAICYA 1, 2; SATA 29, 100
Lorenzo, Heberto Padilla
See Padilla (Lorenzo), Heberto
Loris
See Hofmannsthal, Hugo von
Loti, Pierre .... **TCLC 11**
See Viaud, (Louis Marie) Julien
See also DLB 123; GFL 1789 to the Present
Lou, Henri
See Andreas-Salome, Lou
Louie, David Wong 1954- .... **CLC 70**
See also CA 139; CANR 120
Louis, Adrian C. .... **NNAL**
See also CA 223
Louis, Father M.
See Merton, Thomas (James)
Louise, Heidi
See Erdrich, Louise
Lovecraft, H. P. 1890-1937 .... **SSC 3, 52;
TCLC 4, 22**
See also AAYA 14; BPFB 2; CA 104; 133;
CANR 106; DA3; DAM POP; HGG;
MTCW 1, 2; MTFW 2005; RGAL 4;
SCFW 1, 2; SFW 4; SUFW

Lovecraft, Howard Phillips
See Lovecraft, H. P.
Lovelace, Earl 1935- .... **CLC 51**
See also BW 2; CA 77-80; CANR 41, 72,
114; CD 5, 6; CDWLB 3; CN 1, 2, 3, 4,
5, 6, 7; DLB 125; EWL 3; MTCW 1
Lovelace, Richard 1618-1657 . **LC 24; PC 69**
See also BRW 2; DLB 131; EXPP; PAB;
RGEL 2
Lowe, Pardee 1904- .... **AAL**
Lowell, Amy 1874-1925 ... **PC 13; TCLC 1, 8**
See also AAYA 57; AMW; CA 104; 151;
DAM POET; DLB 54, 140; EWL 3;
EXPP; LMFS 2; MAL 5; MBL; MTCW
2; MTFW 2005; RGAL 4; TUS
Lowell, James Russell 1819-1891 ... **NCLC 2,
90**
See also AMWS 1; CDALB 1640-1865;
DLB 1, 11, 64, 79, 189, 235; RGAL 4
Lowell, Robert (Traill Spence, Jr.)
1917-1977 .... **CLC 1, 2, 3, 4, 5, 8, 9, 11,
15, 37, 124; PC 3; WLC 4**
See also AMW; AMWC 2; AMWR 2; CA
9-12R; 73-76; CABS 2; CAD; CANR 26,
60; CDALBS; CP 1, 2; DA; DA3; DAB;
DAC; DAM MST, NOV; DLB 5, 169;
EWL 3; MAL 5; MTCW 1, 2; MTFW
2005; PAB; PFS 6, 7; RGAL 4; WP
Lowenthal, Michael (Francis)
1969- .... **CLC 119**
See also CA 150; CANR 115
Lowndes, Marie Adelaide (Belloc)
1868-1947 .... **TCLC 12**
See also CA 107; CMW 4; DLB 70; RHW
Lowry, (Clarence) Malcolm
1909-1957 .... **SSC 31; TCLC 6, 40**
See also BPFB 2; BRWS 3; CA 105; 131;
CANR 62, 105; CDBLB 1945-1960; DLB
15; EWL 3; MTCW 1, 2; MTFW 2005;
RGEL 2
Lowry, Mina Gertrude 1882-1966
See Loy, Mina
See also CA 113
Lowry, Sam
See Soderbergh, Steven
Loxsmith, John
See Brunner, John (Kilian Houston)
Loy, Mina .... **CLC 28; PC 16**
See Lowry, Mina Gertrude
See also DAM POET; DLB 4, 54; PFS 20
Loyson-Bridet
See Schwob, Marcel (Mayer Andre)
Lucan 39-65 .... **CMLC 33**
See also AW 2; DLB 211; EFS 2; RGWL 2,
3
Lucas, Craig 1951- .... **CLC 64**
See also CA 137; CAD; CANR 71, 109,
142; CD 5, 6; GLL 2; MTFW 2005
Lucas, E(dward) V(errall)
1868-1938 .... **TCLC 73**
See also CA 176; DLB 98, 149, 153; SATA
20
Lucas, George 1944- .... **CLC 16**
See also AAYA 1, 23; CA 77-80; CANR
30; SATA 56
Lucas, Hans
See Godard, Jean-Luc
Lucas, Victoria
See Plath, Sylvia
Lucian c. 125-c. 180 .... **CMLC 32**
See also AW 2; DLB 176; RGWL 2, 3
Lucilius c. 180B.C.-102B.C. .... **CMLC 82**
See also DLB 211
Lucretius c. 94B.C.-c. 49B.C. .... **CMLC 48**
See also AW 2; CDWLB 1; DLB 211; EFS
2; RGWL 2, 3; WLIT 8
Ludlam, Charles 1943-1987 .... **CLC 46, 50**
See also CA 85-88; 122; CAD; CANR 72,
86; DLB 266

Ludlum, Robert 1927-2001 .... **CLC 22, 43**
See also AAYA 10, 59; BEST 89:1, 90:3;
BPFB 2; CA 33-36R; 195; CANR 25, 41,
68, 105, 131; CMW 4; CPW; DA3; DAM
NOV, POP; DLBY 1982; MSW; MTCW
1, 2; MTFW 2005
Ludwig, Ken 1950- .... **CLC 60**
See also CA 195; CAD; CD 6
Ludwig, Otto 1813-1865 .... **NCLC 4**
See also DLB 129
Lugones, Leopoldo 1874-1938 .... **HLCS 2;
TCLC 15**
See also CA 116; 131; CANR 104; DLB
283; EWL 3; HW 1; LAW
Lu Hsun .... **SSC 20; TCLC 3**
See Shu-Jen, Chou
See also EWL 3
Lukacs, George .... **CLC 24**
See Lukacs, Gyorgy (Szegeny von)
Lukacs, Gyorgy (Szegeny von) 1885-1971
See Lukacs, George
See also CA 101; 29-32R; CANR 62; CD-
WLB 4; DLB 215, 242; EW 10; EWL 3;
MTCW 1, 2
Luke, Peter (Ambrose Cyprian)
1919-1995 .... **CLC 38**
See also CA 81-84; 147; CANR 72; CBD;
CD 5, 6; DLB 13
Lunar, Dennis
See Mungo, Raymond
Lurie, Alison 1926- ..... **CLC 4, 5, 18, 39, 175**
See also BPFB 2; CA 1-4R; CANR 2, 17,
50, 88; CN 1, 2, 3, 4, 5, 6, 7; DLB 2;
MAL 5; MTCW 1; SATA 46, 112; TCLE
1:1
Lustig, Arnost 1926- .... **CLC 56**
See also AAYA 3; CA 69-72; CANR 47,
102; CWW 2; DLB 232, 299; EWL 3;
RGHL; SATA 56
Luther, Martin 1483-1546 .... **LC 9, 37**
See also CDWLB 2; DLB 179; EW 2;
RGWL 2, 3
Luxemburg, Rosa 1870(?)-1919 ..... **TCLC 63**
See also CA 118
Luzi, Mario (Egidio Vincenzo)
1914-2005 .... **CLC 13**
See also CA 61-64; 236; CANR 9, 70;
CWW 2; DLB 128; EWL 3
L'vov, Arkady .... **CLC 59**
Lydgate, John c. 1370-1450(?) .... **LC 81**
See also BRW 1; DLB 146; RGEL 2
Lyly, John 1554(?)-1606 .... **DC 7; LC 41**
See also BRW 1; DAM DRAM; DLB 62,
167; RGEL 2
L'Ymagier
See Gourmont, Remy(-Marie-Charles) de
Lynch, B. Suarez
See Borges, Jorge Luis
Lynch, David (Keith) 1946- ...... **CLC 66, 162**
See also AAYA 55; CA 124; 129; CANR
111
Lynch, James
See Andreyev, Leonid (Nikolaevich)
Lyndsay, Sir David 1485-1555 .... **LC 20**
See also RGEL 2
Lynn, Kenneth S(chuyler)
1923-2001 .... **CLC 50**
See also CA 1-4R; 196; CANR 3, 27, 65
Lynx
See West, Rebecca
Lyons, Marcus
See Blish, James (Benjamin)
Lyotard, Jean-Francois
1924-1998 .... **TCLC 103**
See also DLB 242; EWL 3
Lyre, Pinchbeck
See Sassoon, Siegfried (Lorraine)

Mason, Ernst
See Pohl, Frederik
Mason, Hunni B.
See Sternheim, (William Adolf) Carl
Mason, Lee W.
See Malzberg, Barry N(athaniel)
Mason, Nick 1945- .... **CLC 35**
Mason, Tally
See Derleth, August (William)
Mass, Anna .... **CLC 59**
Mass, William
See Gibson, William
Massinger, Philip 1583-1640 .... **LC 70**
See also BRWS 11; DLB 58; RGEL 2
Master Lao
See Lao Tzu
Masters, Edgar Lee 1868-1950 ...... **PC 1, 36;**
TCLC 2, 25; WLCS
See also AMWS 1; CA 104; 133; CDALB
1865-1917; DA; DAC; DAM MST,
POET; DLB 54; EWL 3; EXPP; MAL 5;
MTCW 1, 2; MTFW 2005; RGAL 4;
TUS; WP
Masters, Hilary 1928- .... **CLC 48**
See also CA 25-28R, 217; CAAE 217;
CANR 13, 47, 97; CN 6, 7; DLB 244
Mastrosimone, William 1947- .... **CLC 36**
See also CA 186; CAD; CD 5, 6
Mathe, Albert
See Camus, Albert
Mather, Cotton 1663-1728 .... **LC 38**
See also AMWS 2; CDALB 1640-1865;
DLB 24, 30, 140; RGAL 4; TUS
Mather, Increase 1639-1723 .... **LC 38**
See also DLB 24
Mathers, Marshall
See Eminem
Mathers, Marshall Bruce
See Eminem
Matheson, Richard (Burton) 1926- .. **CLC 37**
See also AAYA 31; CA 97-100; CANR 88,
99; DLB 8, 44; HGG; INT CA-97-100;
SCFW 1, 2; SFW 4; SUFW 2
Mathews, Harry (Burchell) 1930- ..... **CLC 6,**
52
See also CA 21-24R; CAAS 6; CANR 18,
40, 98; CN 5, 6, 7
Mathews, John Joseph 1894-1979 .. **CLC 84;**
NNAL
See also CA 19-20; 142; CANR 45; CAP 2;
DAM MULT; DLB 175; TCWW 1, 2
Mathias, Roland (Glyn) 1915- .... **CLC 45**
See also CA 97-100; CANR 19, 41; CP 1,
2, 3, 4, 5, 6, 7; DLB 27
Matsuo Basho 1644(?)-1694 ...... **LC 62; PC 3**
See Basho, Matsuo
See also DAM POET; PFS 2, 7, 18
Mattheson, Rodney
See Creasey, John
Matthews, (James) Brander
1852-1929 .... **TCLC 95**
See also CA 181; DLB 71, 78; DLBD 13
Matthews, Greg 1949- .... **CLC 45**
See also CA 135
Matthews, William (Procter III)
1942-1997 .... **CLC 40**
See also AMWS 9; CA 29-32R; 162; CAAS
18; CANR 12, 57; CP 2, 3, 4, 5, 6; DLB
5
Matthias, John (Edward) 1941- .... **CLC 9**
See also CA 33-36R; CANR 56; CP 4, 5, 6,
7
Matthiessen, F(rancis) O(tto)
1902-1950 .... **TCLC 100**
See also CA 185; DLB 63; MAL 5

Matthiessen, Peter 1927- ... **CLC 5, 7, 11, 32,**
64
See also AAYA 6, 40; AMWS 5; ANW;
BEST 90:4; BPFB 2; CA 9-12R; CANR
21, 50, 73, 100, 138; CN 1, 2, 3, 4, 5, 6,
7; DA3; DAM NOV; DLB 6, 173, 275;
MAL 5; MTCW 1, 2; MTFW 2005; SATA
27
Maturin, Charles Robert
1780(?)-1824 .... **NCLC 6, 169**
See also BRWS 8; DLB 178; GL 3; HGG;
LMFS 1; RGEL 2; SUFW
Matute (Ausejo), Ana Maria 1925- .. **CLC 11**
See also CA 89-92; CANR 129; CWW 2;
DLB 322; EWL 3; MTCW 1; RGSF 2
Maugham, W. S.
See Maugham, W(illiam) Somerset
Maugham, W(illiam) Somerset
1874-1965 .. **CLC 1, 11, 15, 67, 93; SSC**
8; WLC 4
See also AAYA 55; BPFB 2; BRW 6; CA
5-8R; 25-28R; CANR 40, 127; CDBLB
1914-1945; CMW 4; DA; DA3; DAB;
DAC; DAM DRAM, MST, NOV; DFS
22; DLB 10, 36, 77, 100, 162, 195; EWL
3; LAIT 3; MTCW 1, 2; MTFW 2005;
NFS 23; RGEL 2; RGSF 2; SATA 54;
SSFS 17
Maugham, William Somerset
See Maugham, W(illiam) Somerset
Maupassant, (Henri Rene Albert) Guy de
1850-1893 . **NCLC 1, 42, 83; SSC 1, 64;**
WLC 4
See also BYA 14; DA; DA3; DAB; DAC;
DAM MST; DLB 123; EW 7; EXPS; GFL
1789 to the Present; LAIT 2; LMFS 1;
RGSF 2; RGWL 2, 3; SSFS 4, 21; SUFW;
TWA
Maupin, Armistead 1944- .... **CLC 95**
See also CA 125; 130; CANR 58, 101;
CPW; DA3; DAM POP; DLB 278; GLL
1; INT CA-130; MTCW 2; MTFW 2005
Maupin, Armistead Jones, Jr.
See Maupin, Armistead
Maurhut, Richard
See Traven, B.
Mauriac, Claude 1914-1996 .... **CLC 9**
See also CA 89-92; 152; CWW 2; DLB 83;
EWL 3; GFL 1789 to the Present
Mauriac, Francois (Charles)
1885-1970 .... **CLC 4, 9, 56; SSC 24**
See also CA 25-28; CAP 2; DLB 65; EW
10; EWL 3; GFL 1789 to the Present;
MTCW 1, 2; MTFW 2005; RGWL 2, 3;
TWA
Mavor, Osborne Henry 1888-1951
See Bridie, James
See also CA 104
Maxwell, William (Keepers, Jr.)
1908-2000 .... **CLC 19**
See also AMWS 8; CA 93-96; 189; CANR
54, 95; CN 1, 2, 3, 4, 5, 6, 7; DLB 218,
278; DLBY 1980; INT CA-93-96; MAL
5; SATA-Obit 128
May, Elaine 1932- .... **CLC 16**
See also CA 124; 142; CAD; CWD; DLB
44
Mayakovski, Vladimir (Vladimirovich)
1893-1930 .... **TCLC 4, 18**
See Maiakovskii, Vladimir; Mayakovsky,
Vladimir
See also CA 104; 158; EWL 3; MTCW 2;
MTFW 2005; SFW 4; TWA
Mayakovsky, Vladimir
See Mayakovski, Vladimir (Vladimirovich)
See also EW 11; WP
Mayhew, Henry 1812-1887 .... **NCLC 31**
See also DLB 18, 55, 190
Mayle, Peter 1939(?)- .... **CLC 89**
See also CA 139; CANR 64, 109

Maynard, Joyce 1953- .... **CLC 23**
See also CA 111; 129; CANR 64
Mayne, William (James Carter)
1928- .... **CLC 12**
See also AAYA 20; CA 9-12R; CANR 37,
80, 100; CLR 25; FANT; JRDA; MAI-
CYA 1, 2; MAICYAS 1; SAAS 11; SATA
6, 68, 122; SUFW 2; YAW
Mayo, Jim
See L'Amour, Louis (Dearborn)
Maysles, Albert 1926- .... **CLC 16**
See also CA 29-32R
Maysles, David 1932-1987 .... **CLC 16**
See also CA 191
Mazer, Norma Fox 1931- .... **CLC 26**
See also AAYA 5, 36; BYA 1, 8; CA 69-72;
CANR 12, 32, 66, 129; CLR 23; JRDA;
MAICYA 1, 2; SAAS 1; SATA 24, 67,
105, 168; WYA; YAW
Mazzini, Guiseppe 1805-1872 .... **NCLC 34**
McAlmon, Robert (Menzies)
1895-1956 .... **TCLC 97**
See also CA 107; 168; DLB 4, 45; DLBD
15; GLL 1
McAuley, James Phillip 1917-1976 .. **CLC 45**
See also CA 97-100; CP 1, 2; DLB 260;
RGEL 2
McBain, Ed
See Hunter, Evan
See also MSW
McBrien, William (Augustine)
1930- .... **CLC 44**
See also CA 107; CANR 90
McCabe, Patrick 1955- .... **CLC 133**
See also BRWS 9; CA 130; CANR 50, 90;
CN 6, 7; DLB 194
McCaffrey, Anne 1926- .... **CLC 17**
See also AAYA 6, 34; AITN 2; BEST 89:2;
BPFB 2; BYA 5; CA 25-28R, 227; CAAE
227; CANR 15, 35, 55, 96; CLR 49;
CPW; DA3; DAM NOV, POP; DLB 8;
JRDA; MAICYA 1, 2; MTCW 1, 2;
MTFW 2005; SAAS 11; SATA 8, 70, 116,
152; SATA-Essay 152; SFW 4; SUFW 2;
WYA; YAW
McCaffrey, Anne Inez
See McCaffrey, Anne
McCall, Nathan 1955(?)- .... **CLC 86**
See also AAYA 59; BW 3; CA 146; CANR
88
McCann, Arthur
See Campbell, John W(ood, Jr.)
McCann, Edson
See Pohl, Frederik
McCarthy, Charles, Jr. 1933-
See McCarthy, Cormac
See also CANR 42, 69, 101; CPW; CSW;
DA3; DAM POP; MTCW 2; MTFW 2005
McCarthy, Cormac ...... **CLC 4, 57, 101, 204**
See McCarthy, Charles, Jr.
See also AAYA 41; AMWS 8; BPFB 2; CA
13-16R; CANR 10; CN 6, 7; DLB 6, 143,
256; EWL 3; LATS 1:2; MAL 5; TCLE
1:2; TCWW 2
McCarthy, Mary (Therese)
1912-1989 .. **CLC 1, 3, 5, 14, 24, 39, 59;**
SSC 24
See also AMW; BPFB 2; CA 5-8R; 129;
CANR 16, 50, 64; CN 1, 2, 3, 4; DA3;
DLB 2; DLBY 1981; EWL 3; FW; INT
CANR-16; MAL 5; MBL; MTCW 1, 2;
MTFW 2005; RGAL 4; TUS
McCartney, James Paul
See McCartney, Paul
McCartney, Paul 1942- .... **CLC 12, 35**
See also CA 146; CANR 111
McCauley, Stephen (D.) 1955- .... **CLC 50**
See also CA 141
McClaren, Peter .... **CLC 70**

Mehta, Ved (Parkash) 1934- .... **CLC 37**
See also CA 1-4R, 212; CAAE 212; CANR 2, 23, 69; DLB 323; MTCW 1; MTFW 2005

Melanchthon, Philipp 1497-1560 .... **LC 90**
See also DLB 179

Melanter
See Blackmore, R(ichard) D(oddridge)

Meleager c. 140B.C.-c. 70B.C. ...... **CMLC 53**

Melies, Georges 1861-1938 .... **TCLC 81**

Melikow, Loris
See Hofmannsthal, Hugo von

Melmoth, Sebastian
See Wilde, Oscar (Fingal O'Flahertie Wills)

Melo Neto, Joao Cabral de
See Cabral de Melo Neto, Joao
See also CWW 2; EWL 3

Meltzer, Milton 1915- .... **CLC 26**
See also AAYA 8, 45; BYA 2, 6; CA 13-16R; CANR 38, 92, 107; CLR 13; DLB 61; JRDA; MAICYA 1, 2; SAAS 1; SATA 1, 50, 80, 128; SATA-Essay 124; WYA; YAW

Melville, Herman 1819-1891 ..... **NCLC 3, 12, 29, 45, 49, 91, 93, 123, 157; SSC 1, 17, 46; WLC 4**
See also AAYA 25; AMW; AMWR 1; CDALB 1640-1865; DA; DA3; DAB; DAC; DAM MST, NOV; DLB 3, 74, 250, 254; EXPN; EXPS; GL 3; LAIT 1, 2; NFS 7, 9; RGAL 4; RGSF 2; SATA 59; SSFS 3; TUS

Members, Mark
See Powell, Anthony (Dymoke)

Membreno, Alejandro .... **CLC 59**

Menand, Louis 1952- .... **CLC 208**
See also CA 200

Menander c. 342B.C.-c. 293B.C. .... **CMLC 9, 51; DC 3**
See also AW 1; CDWLB 1; DAM DRAM; DLB 176; LMFS 1; RGWL 2, 3

Menchu, Rigoberta 1959- .. **CLC 160; HLCS 2**
See also CA 175; CANR 135; DNFS 1; WLIT 1

Mencken, H(enry) L(ouis)
1880-1956 .... **TCLC 13**
See also AMW; CA 105; 125; CDALB 1917-1929; DLB 11, 29, 63, 137, 222; EWL 3; MAL 5; MTCW 1, 2; MTFW 2005; NCFS 4; RGAL 4; TUS

Mendelsohn, Jane 1965- .... **CLC 99**
See also CA 154; CANR 94

Mendoza, Inigo Lopez de
See Santillana, Inigo Lopez de Mendoza, Marques de

Menton, Francisco de
See Chin, Frank (Chew, Jr.)

Mercer, David 1928-1980 .... **CLC 5**
See also CA 9-12R; 102; CANR 23; CBD; DAM DRAM; DLB 13, 310; MTCW 1; RGEL 2

Merchant, Paul
See Ellison, Harlan (Jay)

Meredith, George 1828-1909 .. **PC 60; TCLC 17, 43**
See also CA 117; 153; CANR 80; CDBLB 1832-1890; DAM POET; DLB 18, 35, 57, 159; RGEL 2; TEA

Meredith, William (Morris) 1919- .... **CLC 4, 13, 22, 55; PC 28**
See also CA 9-12R; CAAS 14; CANR 6, 40, 129; CP 1, 2, 3, 4, 5, 6, 7; DAM POET; DLB 5; MAL 5

Merezhkovsky, Dmitrii Sergeevich
See Merezhkovsky, Dmitry Sergeyevich
See also DLB 295

Merezhkovsky, Dmitry Sergeevich
See Merezhkovsky, Dmitry Sergeyevich
See also EWL 3

Merezhkovsky, Dmitry Sergeyevich
1865-1941 .... **TCLC 29**
See Merezhkovsky, Dmitrii Sergeevich; Merezhkovsky, Dmitry Sergeevich
See also CA 169

Merimee, Prosper 1803-1870 ... **NCLC 6, 65; SSC 7, 77**
See also DLB 119, 192; EW 6; EXPS; GFL 1789 to the Present; RGSF 2; RGWL 2, 3; SSFS 8; SUFW

Merkin, Daphne 1954- .... **CLC 44**
See also CA 123

Merleau-Ponty, Maurice
1908-1961 .... **TCLC 156**
See also CA 114; 89-92; DLB 296; GFL 1789 to the Present

Merlin, Arthur
See Blish, James (Benjamin)

Mernissi, Fatima 1940- .... **CLC 171**
See also CA 152; FW

Merrill, James (Ingram) 1926-1995 .. **CLC 2, 3, 6, 8, 13, 18, 34, 91; PC 28; TCLC 173**
See also AMWS 3; CA 13-16R; 147; CANR 10, 49, 63, 108; CP 1, 2, 3, 4; DA3; DAM POET; DLB 5, 165; DLBY 1985; EWL 3; INT CANR-10; MAL 5; MTCW 1, 2; MTFW 2005; PAB; PFS 23; RGAL 4

Merriman, Alex
See Silverberg, Robert

Merriman, Brian 1747-1805 .... **NCLC 70**

Merritt, E. B.
See Waddington, Miriam

Merton, Thomas (James)
1915-1968 . **CLC 1, 3, 11, 34, 83; PC 10**
See also AAYA 61; AMWS 8; CA 5-8R; 25-28R; CANR 22, 53, 111, 131; DA3; DLB 48; DLBY 1981; MAL 5; MTCW 1, 2; MTFW 2005

Merwin, W(illiam) S(tanley) 1927- ... **CLC 1, 2, 3, 5, 8, 13, 18, 45, 88; PC 45**
See also AMWS 3; CA 13-16R; CANR 15, 51, 112, 140; CP 1, 2, 3, 4, 5, 6, 7; DA3; DAM POET; DLB 5, 169; EWL 3; INT CANR-15; MAL 5; MTCW 1, 2; MTFW 2005; PAB; PFS 5, 15; RGAL 4

Metastasio, Pietro 1698-1782 .... **LC 115**
See also RGWL 2, 3

Metcalf, John 1938- .... **CLC 37; SSC 43**
See also CA 113; CN 4, 5, 6, 7; DLB 60; RGSF 2; TWA

Metcalf, Suzanne
See Baum, L(yman) Frank

Mew, Charlotte (Mary) 1870-1928 .. **TCLC 8**
See also CA 105; 189; DLB 19, 135; RGEL 2

Mewshaw, Michael 1943- .... **CLC 9**
See also CA 53-56; CANR 7, 47, 147; DLBY 1980

Meyer, Conrad Ferdinand
1825-1898 .... **NCLC 81; SSC 30**
See also DLB 129; EW; RGWL 2, 3

Meyer, Gustav 1868-1932
See Meyrink, Gustav
See also CA 117; 190

Meyer, June
See Jordan, June

Meyer, Lynn
See Slavitt, David R(ytman)

Meyers, Jeffrey 1939- .... **CLC 39**
See also CA 73-76, 186; CAAE 186; CANR 54, 102; DLB 111

Meynell, Alice (Christina Gertrude Thompson) 1847-1922 .... **TCLC 6**
See also CA 104; 177; DLB 19, 98; RGEL 2

Meyrink, Gustav .... **TCLC 21**
See Meyer, Gustav
See also DLB 81; EWL 3

Michaels, Leonard 1933-2003 ..... **CLC 6, 25; SSC 16**
See also CA 61-64; 216; CANR 21, 62, 119; CN 3, 45, 6, 7; DLB 130; MTCW 1; TCLE 1:2

Michaux, Henri 1899-1984 .... **CLC 8, 19**
See also CA 85-88; 114; DLB 258; EWL 3; GFL 1789 to the Present; RGWL 2, 3

Micheaux, Oscar (Devereaux)
1884-1951 .... **TCLC 76**
See also BW 3; CA 174; DLB 50; TCWW 2

Michelangelo 1475-1564 .... **LC 12**
See also AAYA 43

Michelet, Jules 1798-1874 .... **NCLC 31**
See also EW 5; GFL 1789 to the Present

Michels, Robert 1876-1936 .... **TCLC 88**
See also CA 212

Michener, James A(lbert)
1907(?)-1997 .. **CLC 1, 5, 11, 29, 60, 109**
See also AAYA 27; AITN 1; BEST 90:1; BPFB 2; CA 5-8R; 161; CANR 21, 45, 68; CN 1, 2, 3, 4, 5, 6; DAM NOV, POP; DLB 6; MAL 5; MTCW 1, 2; MTFW 2005; RHW; TCWW 1, 2

Mickiewicz, Adam 1798-1855 . **NCLC 3, 101; PC 38**
See also EW 5; RGWL 2, 3

Middleton, (John) Christopher
1926- .... **CLC 13**
See also CA 13-16R; CANR 29, 54, 117; CP 1, 2, 3, 4, 5, 6, 7; DLB 40

Middleton, Richard (Barham)
1882-1911 .... **TCLC 56**
See also CA 187; DLB 156; HGG

Middleton, Stanley 1919- .... **CLC 7, 38**
See also CA 25-28R; CAAS 23; CANR 21, 46, 81; CN 1, 2, 3, 4, 5, 6, 7; DLB 14, 326

Middleton, Thomas 1580-1627 ...... **DC 5; LC 33, 123**
See also BRW 2; DAM DRAM, MST; DFS 18, 22; DLB 58; RGEL 2

Migueis, Jose Rodrigues 1901-1980 . **CLC 10**
See also DLB 287

Mikszath, Kalman 1847-1910 .... **TCLC 31**
See also CA 170

Miles, Jack .... **CLC 100**
See also CA 200

Miles, John Russiano
See Miles, Jack

Miles, Josephine (Louise)
1911-1985 .... **CLC 1, 2, 14, 34, 39**
See also CA 1-4R; 116; CANR 2, 55; CP 1, 2, 3, 4; DAM POET; DLB 48; MAL 5; TCLE 1:2

Militant
See Sandburg, Carl (August)

Mill, Harriet (Hardy) Taylor
1807-1858 .... **NCLC 102**
See also FW

Mill, John Stuart 1806-1873 .... **NCLC 11, 58**
See also CDBLB 1832-1890; DLB 55, 190, 262; FW 1; RGEL 2; TEA

Millar, Kenneth 1915-1983 .... **CLC 14**
See Macdonald, Ross
See also CA 9-12R; 110; CANR 16, 63, 107; CMW 4; CPW; DA3; DAM POP; DLB 2, 226; DLBD 6; DLBY 1983; MTCW 1, 2; MTFW 2005

Millay, E. Vincent
See Millay, Edna St. Vincent

Monette, Paul 1945-1995 .... **CLC 82**
    See also AMWS 10; CA 139; 147; CN 6;
    GLL 1

Monroe, Harriet 1860-1936 .... **TCLC 12**
    See also CA 109; 204; DLB 54, 91

Monroe, Lyle
    See Heinlein, Robert A(nson)

Montagu, Elizabeth 1720-1800 .... **NCLC 7, 117**
    See also FW

Montagu, Mary (Pierrepont) Wortley
    1689-1762 .... **LC 9, 57; PC 16**
    See also DLB 95, 101; FL 1:1; RGEL 2

Montagu, W. H.
    See Coleridge, Samuel Taylor

Montague, John (Patrick) 1929- ..... **CLC 13, 46**
    See also CA 9-12R; CANR 9, 69, 121; CP
    1, 2, 3, 4, 5, 6, 7; DLB 40; EWL 3;
    MTCW 1; PFS 12; RGEL 2; TCLE 1:2

Montaigne, Michel (Eyquem) de
    1533-1592 .... **LC 8, 105; WLC 4**
    See also DA; DAB; DAC; DAM MST;
    DLB 327; EW 2; GFL Beginnings to
    1789; LMFS 1; RGWL 2, 3; TWA

Montale, Eugenio 1896-1981 ... **CLC 7, 9, 18; PC 13**
    See also CA 17-20R; 104; CANR 30; DLB
    114; EW 11; EWL 3; MTCW 1; PFS 22;
    RGWL 2, 3; TWA; WLIT 7

Montesquieu, Charles-Louis de Secondat
    1689-1755 .... **LC 7, 69**
    See also DLB 314; EW 3; GFL Beginnings
    to 1789; TWA

Montessori, Maria 1870-1952 ...... **TCLC 103**
    See also CA 115; 147

Montgomery, (Robert) Bruce 1921(?)-1978
    See Crispin, Edmund
    See also CA 179; 104; CMW 4

Montgomery, L(ucy) M(aud)
    1874-1942 .... **TCLC 51, 140**
    See also AAYA 12; BYA 1; CA 108; 137;
    CLR 8, 91; DA3; DAC; DAM MST; DLB
    92; DLBD 14; JRDA; MAICYA 1, 2;
    MTCW 2; MTFW 2005; RGEL 2; SATA
    100; TWA; WCH; WYA; YABC 1

Montgomery, Marion H., Jr. 1925- .... **CLC 7**
    See also AITN 1; CA 1-4R; CANR 3, 48;
    CSW; DLB 6

Montgomery, Max
    See Davenport, Guy (Mattison, Jr.)

Montherlant, Henry (Milon) de
    1896-1972 .... **CLC 8, 19**
    See also CA 85-88; 37-40R; DAM DRAM;
    DLB 72, 321; EW 11; EWL 3; GFL 1789
    to the Present; MTCW 1

Monty Python
    See Chapman, Graham; Cleese, John
    (Marwood); Gilliam, Terry (Vance); Idle,
    Eric; Jones, Terence Graham Parry; Palin,
    Michael (Edward)
    See also AAYA 7

Moodie, Susanna (Strickland)
    1803-1885 .... **NCLC 14, 113**
    See also DLB 99

Moody, Hiram (F. III) 1961-
    See Moody, Rick
    See also CA 138; CANR 64, 112; MTFW
    2005

Moody, Minerva
    See Alcott, Louisa May

Moody, Rick .... **CLC 147**
    See Moody, Hiram (F. III)

Moody, William Vaughan
    1869-1910 .... **TCLC 105**
    See also CA 110; 178; DLB 7, 54; MAL 5;
    RGAL 4

Mooney, Edward 1951-
    See Mooney, Ted
    See also CA 130

Mooney, Ted .... **CLC 25**
    See Mooney, Edward

Moorcock, Michael 1939- .... **CLC 5, 27, 58**
    See Bradbury, Edward P.
    See also AAYA 26; CA 45-48; CAAS 5;
    CANR 2, 17, 38, 64, 122; CN 5, 6, 7;
    DLB 14, 231, 261, 319; FANT; MTCW 1,
    2; MTFW 2005; SATA 93, 166; SCFW 1,
    2; SFW 4; SUFW 1, 2

Moorcock, Michael John
    See Moorcock, Michael

Moore, Brian 1921-1999 ... **CLC 1, 3, 5, 7, 8, 19, 32, 90**
    See Bryan, Michael
    See also BRWS 9; CA 1-4R; 174; CANR 1,
    25, 42, 63; CCA 1; CN 1, 2, 3, 4, 5, 6;
    DAB; DAC; DAM MST; DLB 251; EWL
    3; FANT; MTCW 1, 2; MTFW 2005;
    RGEL 2

Moore, Edward
    See Muir, Edwin
    See also RGEL 2

Moore, G. E. 1873-1958 .... **TCLC 89**
    See also DLB 262

Moore, George Augustus
    1852-1933 .... **SSC 19; TCLC 7**
    See also BRW 6; CA 104; 177; DLB 10,
    18, 57, 135; EWL 3; RGEL 2; RGSF 2

Moore, Lorrie .... **CLC 39, 45, 68**
    See Moore, Marie Lorena
    See also AMWS 10; CN 5, 6, 7; DLB 234;
    SSFS 19

Moore, Marianne (Craig)
    1887-1972 .... **CLC 1, 2, 4, 8, 10, 13, 19, 47; PC 4, 49; WLCS**
    See also AMW; CA 1-4R; 33-36R; CANR
    3, 61; CDALB 1929-1941; CP 1; DA;
    DA3; DAB; DAC; DAM MST, POET;
    DLB 45; DLBD 7; EWL 3; EXPP; FL 1:6;
    MAL 5; MBL; MTCW 1, 2; MTFW 2005;
    PAB; PFS 14, 17; RGAL 4; SATA 20;
    TUS; WP

Moore, Marie Lorena 1957- .... **CLC 165**
    See Moore, Lorrie
    See also CA 116; CANR 39, 83, 139; DLB
    234; MTFW 2005

Moore, Michael 1954- .... **CLC 218**
    See also AAYA 53; CA 166; CANR 150

Moore, Thomas 1779-1852 .... **NCLC 6, 110**
    See also DLB 96, 144; RGEL 2

Moorhouse, Frank 1938- .... **SSC 40**
    See also CA 118; CANR 92; CN 3, 4, 5, 6,
    7; DLB 289; RGSF 2

Mora, Pat(ricia) 1942- .... **HLC 2**
    See also AMWS 13; CA 129; CANR 57,
    81, 112; CLR 58; DAM MULT; DLB 209;
    HW 1, 2; LLW; MAICYA 2; MTFW
    2005; SATA 92, 134

Moraga, Cherríe 1952- ...... **CLC 126; DC 22**
    See also CA 131; CANR 66, 154; DAM
    MULT; DLB 82, 249; FW; GLL 1; HW 1,
    2; LLW

Morand, Paul 1888-1976 .... **CLC 41; SSC 22**
    See also CA 184; 69-72; DLB 65; EWL 3

Morante, Elsa 1918-1985 .... **CLC 8, 47**
    See also CA 85-88; 117; CANR 35; DLB
    177; EWL 3; MTCW 1, 2; MTFW 2005;
    RGHL; RGWL 2, 3; WLIT 7

Moravia, Alberto .... **CLC 2, 7, 11, 27, 46; SSC 26**
    See Pincherle, Alberto
    See also DLB 177; EW 12; EWL 3; MTCW
    2; RGSF 2; RGWL 2, 3; WLIT 7

More, Hannah 1745-1833 ...... **NCLC 27, 141**
    See also DLB 107, 109, 116, 158; RGEL 2

More, Henry 1614-1687 .... **LC 9**
    See also DLB 126, 252

More, Sir Thomas 1478(?)-1535 .... **LC 10, 32**
    See also BRWC 1; BRWS 7; DLB 136, 281;
    LMFS 1; RGEL 2; TEA

Moreas, Jean .... **TCLC 18**
    See Papadiamantopoulos, Johannes
    See also GFL 1789 to the Present

Moreton, Andrew Esq.
    See Defoe, Daniel

Morgan, Berry 1919-2002 .... **CLC 6**
    See also CA 49-52; 208; DLB 6

Morgan, Claire
    See Highsmith, (Mary) Patricia
    See also GLL 1

Morgan, Edwin (George) 1920- .... **CLC 31**
    See also BRWS 9; CA 5-8R; CANR 3, 43,
    90; CP 1, 2, 3, 4, 5, 6, 7; DLB 27

Morgan, (George) Frederick
    1922-2004 .... **CLC 23**
    See also CA 17-20R; 224; CANR 21, 144;
    CP 2, 3, 4, 5, 6, 7

Morgan, Harriet
    See Mencken, H(enry) L(ouis)

Morgan, Jane
    See Cooper, James Fenimore

Morgan, Janet 1945- .... **CLC 39**
    See also CA 65-68

Morgan, Lady 1776(?)-1859 .... **NCLC 29**
    See also DLB 116, 158; RGEL 2

Morgan, Robin (Evonne) 1941- .... **CLC 2**
    See also CA 69-72; CANR 29, 68; FW;
    GLL 2; MTCW 1; SATA 80

Morgan, Scott
    See Kuttner, Henry

Morgan, Seth 1949(?)-1990 .... **CLC 65**
    See also CA 185; 132

Morgenstern, Christian (Otto Josef
    Wolfgang) 1871-1914 .... **TCLC 8**
    See also CA 105; 191; EWL 3

Morgenstern, S.
    See Goldman, William

Mori, Rintaro
    See Mori Ogai
    See also CA 110

Mori, Toshio 1910-1980 .... **SSC 83**
    See also CA 116; 244; DLB 312; RGSF 2

Moricz, Zsigmond 1879-1942 .... **TCLC 33**
    See also CA 165; DLB 215; EWL 3

Morike, Eduard (Friedrich)
    1804-1875 .... **NCLC 10**
    See also DLB 133; RGWL 2, 3

Mori Ogai 1862-1922 .... **TCLC 14**
    See Ogai
    See also CA 164; DLB 180; EWL 3; RGWL
    3; TWA

Moritz, Karl Philipp 1756-1793 .... **LC 2**
    See also DLB 94

Morland, Peter Henry
    See Faust, Frederick (Schiller)

Morley, Christopher (Darlington)
    1890-1957 .... **TCLC 87**
    See also CA 112; 213; DLB 9; MAL 5;
    RGAL 4

Morren, Theophil
    See Hofmannsthal, Hugo von

Morris, Bill 1952- .... **CLC 76**
    See also CA 225

Morris, Julian
    See West, Morris L(anglo)

Morris, Steveland Judkins (?)-
    See Wonder, Stevie

Morris, William 1834-1896 . **NCLC 4; PC 55**
    See also BRW 5; CDBLB 1832-1890; DLB
    18, 35, 57, 156, 178, 184; FANT; RGEL
    2; SFW 4; SUFW

Morris, Wright (Marion) 1910-1998 . **CLC 1, 3, 7, 18, 37; TCLC 107**
See also AMW; CA 9-12R; 167; CANR 21, 81; CN 1, 2, 3, 4, 5, 6; DLB 2, 206, 218; DLBY 1981; EWL 3; MAL 5; MTCW 1, 2; MTFW 2005; RGAL 4; TCWW 1, 2

Morrison, Arthur 1863-1945 .... **SSC 40; TCLC 72**
See also CA 120; 157; CMW 4; DLB 70, 135, 197; RGEL 2

Morrison, Chloe Anthony Wofford
See Morrison, Toni

Morrison, James Douglas 1943-1971
See Morrison, Jim
See also CA 73-76; CANR 40

Morrison, Jim .... **CLC 17**
See Morrison, James Douglas

Morrison, John Gordon 1904-1998 ... **SSC 93**
See also CA 103; CANR 92; DLB 260

Morrison, Toni 1931- ..... **BLC 3; CLC 4, 10, 22, 55, 81, 87, 173, 194; WLC 4**
See also AAYA 1, 22, 61; AFAW 1, 2; AMWC 1; AMWS 3; BPFB 2; BW 2, 3; CA 29-32R; CANR 27, 42, 67, 113, 124; CDALB 1968-1988; CLR 99; CN 3, 4, 5, 6, 7; CPW; DA; DA3; DAB; DAC; DAM MST, MULT, NOV, POP; DLB 6, 33, 143; DLBY 1981; EWL 3; EXPN; FL 1:6; FW; GL 3; LAIT 2, 4; LATS 1:2; LMFS 2; MAL 5; MBL; MTCW 1, 2; MTFW 2005; NFS 1, 6, 8, 14; RGAL 4; RHW; SATA 57, 144; SSFS 5; TCLE 1:2; TUS; YAW

Morrison, Van 1945- .... **CLC 21**
See also CA 116; 168

Morrissy, Mary 1957- .... **CLC 99**
See also CA 205; DLB 267

Mortimer, John (Clifford) 1923- ..... **CLC 28, 43**
See also CA 13-16R; CANR 21, 69, 109; CBD; CD 5, 6; CDBLB 1960 to Present; CMW 4; CN 5, 6, 7; CPW; DA3; DAM DRAM, POP; DLB 13, 245, 271; INT CANR-21; MSW; MTCW 1, 2; MTFW 2005; RGEL 2

Mortimer, Penelope (Ruth)
1918-1999 .... **CLC 5**
See also CA 57-60; 187; CANR 45, 88; CN 1, 2, 3, 4, 5, 6

Mortimer, Sir John
See Mortimer, John (Clifford)

Morton, Anthony
See Creasey, John

Morton, Thomas 1579(?)-1647(?) .... **LC 72**
See also DLB 24; RGEL 2

Mosca, Gaetano 1858-1941 .... **TCLC 75**

Moses, Daniel David 1952- .... **NNAL**
See also CA 186

Mosher, Howard Frank 1943- .... **CLC 62**
See also CA 139; CANR 65, 115

Mosley, Nicholas 1923- .... **CLC 43, 70**
See also CA 69-72; CANR 41, 60, 108; CN 1, 2, 3, 4, 5, 6, 7; DLB 14, 207

Mosley, Walter 1952- .... **BLCS; CLC 97, 184**
See also AAYA 57; AMWS 13; BPFB 2; BW 2; CA 142; CANR 57, 92, 136; CMW 4; CN 7; CPW; DA3; DAM MULT, POP; DLB 306; MSW; MTCW 2; MTFW 2005

Moss, Howard 1922-1987 . **CLC 7, 14, 45, 50**
See also CA 1-4R; 123; CANR 1, 44; CP 1, 2, 3, 4; DAM POET; DLB 5

Mossgiel, Rab
See Burns, Robert

Motion, Andrew (Peter) 1952- .... **CLC 47**
See also BRWS 7; CA 146; CANR 90, 142; CP 4, 5, 6, 7; DLB 40; MTFW 2005

Motley, Willard (Francis)
1909-1965 .... **CLC 18**
See also BW 1; CA 117; 106; CANR 88; DLB 76, 143

Motoori, Norinaga 1730-1801 .... **NCLC 45**

Mott, Michael (Charles Alston)
1930- .... **CLC 15, 34**
See also CA 5-8R; CAAS 7; CANR 7, 29

Mountain Wolf Woman 1884-1960 . **CLC 92; NNAL**
See also CA 144; CANR 90

Moure, Erin 1955- .... **CLC 88**
See also CA 113; CP 5, 6, 7; CWP; DLB 60

Mourning Dove 1885(?)-1936 .... **NNAL**
See also CA 144; CANR 90; DAM MULT; DLB 175, 221

Mowat, Farley (McGill) 1921- .... **CLC 26**
See also AAYA 1, 50; BYA 2; CA 1-4R; CANR 4, 24, 42, 68, 108; CLR 20; CPW; DAC; DAM MST; DLB 68; INT CANR-24; JRDA; MAICYA 1, 2; MTCW 1, 2; MTFW 2005; SATA 3, 55; YAW

Mowatt, Anna Cora 1819-1870 ..... **NCLC 74**
See also RGAL 4

Moyers, Bill 1934- .... **CLC 74**
See also AITN 2; CA 61-64; CANR 31, 52, 148

Mphahlele, Es'kia
See Mphahlele, Ezekiel
See also AFW; CDWLB 3; CN 4, 5, 6; DLB 125, 225; RGSF 2; SSFS 11

Mphahlele, Ezekiel 1919- .. **BLC 3; CLC 25, 133**
See Mphahlele, Es'kia
See also BW 2, 3; CA 81-84; CANR 26, 76; CN 1, 2, 3; DA3; DAM MULT; EWL 3; MTCW 2; MTFW 2005; SATA 119

Mqhayi, S(amuel) E(dward) K(rune Loliwe)
1875-1945 .... **BLC 3; TCLC 25**
See also CA 153; CANR 87; DAM MULT

Mrozek, Slawomir 1930- .... **CLC 3, 13**
See also CA 13-16R; CAAS 10; CANR 29; CDWLB 4; CWW 2; DLB 232; EWL 3; MTCW 1

Mrs. Belloc-Lowndes
See Lowndes, Marie Adelaide (Belloc)

Mrs. Fairstar
See Horne, Richard Henry Hengist

M'Taggart, John M'Taggart Ellis
See McTaggart, John McTaggart Ellis

Mtwa, Percy (?)- .... **CLC 47**
See also CD 6

Mueller, Lisel 1924- .... **CLC 13, 51; PC 33**
See also CA 93-96; CP 6, 7; DLB 105; PFS 9, 13

Muggeridge, Malcolm (Thomas)
1903-1990 .... **TCLC 120**
See also AITN 1; CA 101; CANR 33, 63; MTCW 1, 2

Muhammad 570-632 .... **WLCS**
See also DA; DAB; DAC; DAM MST; DLB 311

Muir, Edwin 1887-1959 . **PC 49; TCLC 2, 87**
See Moore, Edward
See also BRWS 6; CA 104; 193; DLB 20, 100, 191; EWL 3; RGEL 2

Muir, John 1838-1914 .... **TCLC 28**
See also AMWS 9; ANW; CA 165; DLB 186, 275

Mujica Lainez, Manuel 1910-1984 ... **CLC 31**
See Lainez, Manuel Mujica
See also CA 81-84; 112; CANR 32; EWL 3; HW 1

Mukherjee, Bharati 1940- ..... **AAL; CLC 53, 115; SSC 38**
See also AAYA 46; BEST 89:2; CA 107, 232; CAAE 232; CANR 45, 72, 128; CN 5, 6, 7; DAM NOV; DLB 60, 218, 323; DNFS 1, 2; EWL 3; FW; MAL 5; MTCW 1, 2; MTFW 2005; RGAL 4; RGSF 2; SSFS 7; TUS; WWE 1

Muldoon, Paul 1951- .... **CLC 32, 72, 166**
See also BRWS 4; CA 113; 129; CANR 52, 91; CP 2, 3, 4, 5, 6, 7; DAM POET; DLB 40; INT CA-129; PFS 7, 22; TCLE 1:2

Mulisch, Harry (Kurt Victor)
1927- .... **CLC 42**
See also CA 9-12R; CANR 6, 26, 56, 110; CWW 2; DLB 299; EWL 3

Mull, Martin 1943- .... **CLC 17**
See also CA 105

Muller, Wilhelm .... **NCLC 73**

Mulock, Dinah Maria
See Craik, Dinah Maria (Mulock)
See also RGEL 2

Multatuli 1820-1881 .... **NCLC 165**
See also RGWL 2, 3

Munday, Anthony 1560-1633 .... **LC 87**
See also DLB 62, 172; RGEL 2

Munford, Robert 1737(?)-1783 .... **LC 5**
See also DLB 31

Mungo, Raymond 1946- .... **CLC 72**
See also CA 49-52; CANR 2

Munro, Alice (Anne) 1931- .... **CLC 6, 10, 19, 50, 95, 222; SSC 3; WLCS**
See also AITN 2; BPFB 2; CA 33-36R; CANR 33, 53, 75, 114; CCA 1; CN 1, 2, 3, 4, 5, 6, 7; DA3; DAC; DAM MST, NOV; DLB 53; EWL 3; MTCW 1, 2; MTFW 2005; RGEL 2; RGSF 2; SATA 29; SSFS 5, 13, 19; TCLE 1:2; WWE 1

Munro, H(ector) H(ugh) 1870-1916
See Saki
See also AAYA 56; CA 104; 130; CANR 104; CDBLB 1890-1914; DA; DA3; DAB; DAC; DAM MST, NOV; DLB 34, 162; EXPS; MTCW 1, 2; MTFW 2005; RGEL 2; SSFS 15

Murakami, Haruki 1949- .... **CLC 150**
See Murakami Haruki
See also CA 165; CANR 102, 146; MJW; RGWL 3; SFW 4; SSFS 23

Murakami Haruki
See Murakami, Haruki
See also CWW 2; DLB 182; EWL 3

Murasaki, Lady
See Murasaki Shikibu

Murasaki Shikibu 978(?)-1026(?) .. **CMLC 1, 79**
See also EFS 2; LATS 1:1; RGWL 2, 3

Murdoch, (Jean) Iris 1919-1999 .. **CLC 1, 2, 3, 4, 6, 8, 11, 15, 22, 31, 51; TCLC 171**
See also BRWS 1; CA 13-16R; 179; CANR 8, 43, 68, 103, 142; CBD; CDBLB 1960 to Present; CN 1, 2, 3, 4, 5, 6; CWD; DA3; DAB; DAC; DAM MST, NOV; DLB 14, 194, 233, 326; EWL 3; INT CANR-8; MTCW 1, 2; MTFW 2005; NFS 18; RGEL 2; TCLE 1:2; TEA; WLIT 4

Murfree, Mary Noailles 1850-1922 .. **SSC 22; TCLC 135**
See also CA 122; 176; DLB 12, 74; RGAL 4

Murnau, Friedrich Wilhelm
See Plumpe, Friedrich Wilhelm

Murphy, Richard 1927- .... **CLC 41**
See also BRWS 5; CA 29-32R; CP 1, 2, 3, 4, 5, 6, 7; DLB 40; EWL 3

Murphy, Sylvia 1937- .... **CLC 34**
See also CA 121

Murphy, Thomas (Bernard) 1935- ... **CLC 51**
See Murphy, Tom
See also CA 101

Murphy, Tom
See Murphy, Thomas (Bernard)
See also DLB 310

Murray, Albert L. 1916- .... **CLC 73**
See also BW 2; CA 49-52; CANR 26, 52, 78; CN 7; CSW; DLB 38; MTFW 2005

Murray, James Augustus Henry
1837-1915 .... **TCLC 117**

Murray, Judith Sargent
1751-1820 .... **NCLC 63**
See also DLB 37, 200

Murray, Les(lie Allan) 1938- .... **CLC 40**
See also BRWS 7; CA 21-24R; CANR 11,
27, 56, 103; CP 1, 2, 3, 4, 5, 6, 7; DAM
POET; DLB 289; DLBY 2001; EWL 3;
RGEL 2

Murry, J. Middleton
See Murry, John Middleton

Murry, John Middleton
1889-1957 .... **TCLC 16**
See also CA 118; 217; DLB 149

Musgrave, Susan 1951- .... **CLC 13, 54**
See also CA 69-72; CANR 45, 84; CCA 1;
CP 2, 3, 4, 5, 6, 7; CWP

Musil, Robert (Edler von)
1880-1942 .... **SSC 18; TCLC 12, 68**
See also CA 109; CANR 55, 84; CDWLB
2; DLB 81, 124; EW 9; EWL 3; MTCW
2; RGSF 2; RGWL 2, 3

Muske, Carol .... **CLC 90**
See Muske-Dukes, Carol (Anne)

Muske-Dukes, Carol (Anne) 1945-
See Muske, Carol
See also CA 65-68, 203; CAAE 203; CANR
32, 70; CWP; PFS 24

Musset, Alfred de 1810-1857 . **DC 27; NCLC
7, 150**
See also DLB 192, 217; EW 6; GFL 1789
to the Present; RGWL 2, 3; TWA

Musset, Louis Charles Alfred de
See Musset, Alfred de

Mussolini, Benito (Amilcare Andrea)
1883-1945 .... **TCLC 96**
See also CA 116

Mutanabbi, Al-
See al-Mutanabbi, Ahmad ibn al-Husayn
Abu al-Tayyib al-Jufi al-Kindi
See also WLIT 6

My Brother's Brother
See Chekhov, Anton (Pavlovich)

Myers, L(eopold) H(amilton)
1881-1944 .... **TCLC 59**
See also CA 157; DLB 15; EWL 3; RGEL
2

Myers, Walter Dean 1937- .. **BLC 3; CLC 35**
See also AAYA 4, 23; BW 2; BYA 6, 8, 11;
CA 33-36R; CANR 20, 42, 67, 108; CLR
4, 16, 35, 110; DAM MULT, NOV; DLB
33; INT CANR-20; JRDA; LAIT 5; MAI-
CYA 1, 2; MAICYAS 1; MTCW 2;
MTFW 2005; SAAS 2; SATA 41, 71, 109,
157; SATA-Brief 27; WYA; YAW

Myers, Walter M.
See Myers, Walter Dean

Myles, Symon
See Follett, Ken(neth Martin)

Nabokov, Vladimir (Vladimirovich)
1899-1977 .... **CLC 1, 2, 3, 6, 8, 11, 15,
23, 44, 46, 64; SSC 11, 86; TCLC 108;
WLC 4**
See also AAYA 45; AMW; AMWC 1;
AMWR 1; BPFB 2; CA 5-8R; 69-72;
CANR 20, 102; CDALB 1941-1968; CN
1, 2; CP 2; DA; DA3; DAB; DAC; DAM
MST, NOV; DLB 2, 244, 278, 317; DLBD
3; DLBY 1980, 1991; EWL 3; EXPS;
LATS 1:2; MAL 5; MTCW 1, 2; MTFW
2005; NCFS 4; NFS 9; RGAL 4; RGSF
2; SSFS 6, 15; TUS

Naevius c. 265B.C.-201B.C. .... **CMLC 37**
See also DLB 211

Nagai, Kafu .... **TCLC 51**
See Nagai, Sokichi
See also DLB 180

Nagai, Sokichi 1879-1959
See Nagai, Kafu
See also CA 117

Nagy, Laszlo 1925-1978 .... **CLC 7**
See also CA 129; 112

Naidu, Sarojini 1879-1949 .... **TCLC 80**
See also EWL 3; RGEL 2

Naipaul, Shiva(dhar Srinivasa)
1945-1985 .... **CLC 32, 39; TCLC 153**
See also CA 110; 112; 116; CANR 33; CN
2, 3; DA3; DAM NOV; DLB 157; DLBY
1985; EWL 3; MTCW 1, 2; MTFW 2005

Naipaul, V(idiadhar) S(urajprasad)
1932- .... **CLC 4, 7, 9, 13, 18, 37, 105,
199; SSC 38**
See also BPFB 2; BRWS 1; CA 1-4R;
CANR 1, 33, 51, 91, 126; CDBLB 1960
to Present; CDWLB 3; CN 1, 2, 3, 4, 5,
6, 7; DA3; DAB; DAC; DAM MST,
NOV; DLB 125, 204, 207, 326; DLBY
1985, 2001; EWL 3; LATS 1:2; MTCW
1, 2; MTFW 2005; RGEL 2; RGSF 2;
TWA; WLIT 4; WWE 1

Nakos, Lilika 1903(?)-1989 .... **CLC 29**

Napoleon
See Yamamoto, Hisaye

Narayan, R(asipuram) K(rishnaswami)
1906-2001 .... **CLC 7, 28, 47, 121, 211;
SSC 25**
See also BPFB 2; CA 81-84; 196; CANR
33, 61, 112; CN 1, 2, 3, 4, 5, 6, 7; DA3;
DAM NOV; DLB 323; EWL 3; MTCW
1, 2; MTFW 2005; RGEL 2;
RGSF 2; SATA 62; SSFS 5; WWE 1

Nash, (Frediric) Ogden 1902-1971 . **CLC 23;
PC 21; TCLC 109**
See also CA 13-14; 29-32R; CANR 34, 61;
CAP 1; CP 1; DAM POET; DLB 11;
MAICYA 1, 2; MAL 5; MTCW 1, 2;
RGAL 4; SATA 2, 46; WP

Nashe, Thomas 1567-1601(?) .... **LC 41, 89**
See also DLB 167; RGEL 2

Nathan, Daniel
See Dannay, Frederic

Nathan, George Jean 1882-1958 .... **TCLC 18**
See Hatteras, Owen
See also CA 114; 169; DLB 137; MAL 5

Natsume, Kinnosuke
See Natsume, Soseki

Natsume, Soseki 1867-1916 .... **TCLC 2, 10**
See Natsume Soseki; Soseki
See also CA 104; 195; RGWL 2, 3; TWA

Natsume Soseki
See Natsume, Soseki
See also DLB 180; EWL 3

Natti, (Mary) Lee 1919-
See Kingman, Lee
See also CA 5-8R; CANR 2

Navarre, Marguerite de
See de Navarre, Marguerite

Naylor, Gloria 1950- ..... **BLC 3; CLC 28, 52,
156; WLCS**
See also AAYA 6, 39; AFAW 1, 2; AMWS
8; BW 2, 3; CA 107; CANR 27, 51, 74,
130; CN 4, 5, 6, 7; CPW; DA; DA3;
DAC; DAM MST, MULT, NOV, POP;
DLB 173; EWL 3; FW; MAL 5; MTCW
1, 2; MTFW 2005; NFS 4, 7; RGAL 4;
TCLE 1:2; TUS

Neal, John 1793-1876 .... **NCLC 161**
See also DLB 1, 59, 243; FW; RGAL 4

Neff, Debra .... **CLC 59**

Neihardt, John Gneisenau
1881-1973 .... **CLC 32**
See also CA 13-14; CANR 65; CAP 1; DLB
9, 54, 256; LAIT 2; TCWW 1, 2

Nekrasov, Nikolai Alekseevich
1821-1878 .... **NCLC 11**
See also DLB 277

Nelligan, Emile 1879-1941 .... **TCLC 14**
See also CA 114; 204; DLB 92; EWL 3

Nelson, Willie 1933- .... **CLC 17**
See also CA 107; CANR 114

Nemerov, Howard (Stanley)
1920-1991 .... **CLC 2, 6, 9, 36; PC 24;
TCLC 124**
See also AMW; CA 1-4R; 134; CABS 2;
CANR 1, 27, 53; CN 1, 2, 3; CP 1, 2, 3,
4, 5; DAM POET; DLB 5, 6; DLBY 1983;
EWL 3; INT CANR-27; MAL 5; MTCW
1, 2; MTFW 2005; PFS 10, 14; RGAL 4

Neruda, Pablo 1904-1973 .. **CLC 1, 2, 5, 7, 9,
28, 62; HLC 2; PC 4, 64; WLC 4**
See also CA 19-20; 45-48; CANR 131; CAP
2; DA; DA3; DAB; DAC; DAM MST,
MULT, POET; DLB 283; DNFS 2; EWL
3; HW 1; LAW; MTCW 1, 2; MTFW
2005; PFS 11; RGWL 2, 3; TWA; WLIT
1; WP

Nerval, Gerard de 1808-1855 ... **NCLC 1, 67;
PC 13; SSC 18**
See also DLB 217; EW 6; GFL 1789 to the
Present; RGSF 2; RGWL 2, 3

Nervo, (Jose) Amado (Ruiz de)
1870-1919 .... **HLCS 2; TCLC 11**
See also CA 109; 131; DLB 290; EWL 3;
HW 1; LAW

Nesbit, Malcolm
See Chester, Alfred

Nessi, Pio Baroja y
See Baroja, Pio

Nestroy, Johann 1801-1862 .... **NCLC 42**
See also DLB 133; RGWL 2, 3

Netterville, Luke
See O'Grady, Standish (James)

Neufeld, John (Arthur) 1938- .... **CLC 17**
See also AAYA 11; CA 25-28R; CANR 11,
37, 56; CLR 52; MAICYA 1, 2; SAAS 3;
SATA 6, 81, 131; SATA-Essay 131; YAW

Neumann, Alfred 1895-1952 .... **TCLC 100**
See also CA 183; DLB 56

Neumann, Ferenc
See Molnar, Ferenc

Neville, Emily Cheney 1919- .... **CLC 12**
See also BYA 2; CA 5-8R; CANR 3, 37,
85; JRDA; MAICYA 1, 2; SAAS 2; SATA
1; YAW

Newbound, Bernard Slade 1930-
See Slade, Bernard
See also CA 81-84; CANR 49; CD 5; DAM
DRAM

Newby, P(ercy) H(oward)
1918-1997 .... **CLC 2, 13**
See also CA 5-8R; 161; CANR 32, 67; CN
1, 2, 3, 4, 5, 6; DAM NOV; DLB 15, 326;
MTCW 1; RGEL 2

Newcastle
See Cavendish, Margaret Lucas

Newlove, Donald 1928- .... **CLC 6**
See also CA 29-32R; CANR 25

Newlove, John (Herbert) 1938- .... **CLC 14**
See also CA 21-24R; CANR 9, 25; CP 1, 2,
3, 4, 5, 6, 7

Newman, Charles 1938-2006 .... **CLC 2, 8**
See also CA 21-24R; 249; CANR 84; CN
3, 4, 5, 6

Newman, Charles Hamilton
See Newman, Charles

Newman, Edwin (Harold) 1919- ...... **CLC 14**
See also AITN 1; CA 69-72; CANR 5

Newman, John Henry 1801-1890 . **NCLC 38,
99**
See also BRWS 7; DLB 18, 32, 55; RGEL
2

Newton, (Sir) Isaac 1642-1727 ...... **LC 35, 53**
See also DLB 252

Oneal, Elizabeth 1934-
  See Oneal, Zibby
  See also CA 106; CANR 28, 84; MAICYA 1, 2; SATA 30, 82; YAW

Oneal, Zibby .... **CLC 30**
  See Oneal, Elizabeth
  See also AAYA 5, 41; BYA 13; CLR 13; JRDA; WYA

O'Neill, Eugene (Gladstone)
  1888-1953 ... **DC 20; TCLC 1, 6, 27, 49; WLC 4**
  See also AAYA 54; AITN 1; AMW; AMWC 1; CA 110; 132; CAD; CANR 131; CDALB 1929-1941; DA; DA3; DAB; DAC; DAM DRAM, MST; DFS 2, 4, 5, 6, 9, 11, 12, 16, 20; DLB 7; EWL 3; LAIT 3; LMFS 2; MAL 5; MTCW 1, 2; MTFW 2005; RGAL 4; TUS

Onetti, Juan Carlos 1909-1994 ... **CLC 7, 10; HLCS 2; SSC 23; TCLC 131**
  See also CA 85-88; 145; CANR 32, 63; CDWLB 3; CWW 2; DAM MULT, NOV; DLB 113; EWL 3; HW 1, 2; LAW; MTCW 1, 2; MTFW 2005; RGSF 2

O Nuallain, Brian 1911-1966
  See O'Brien, Flann
  See also CA 21-22; 25-28R; CAP 2; DLB 231; FANT; TEA

Ophuls, Max 1902-1957 .... **TCLC 79**
  See also CA 113

Opie, Amelia 1769-1853 .... **NCLC 65**
  See also DLB 116, 159; RGEL 2

Oppen, George 1908-1984 ..... **CLC 7, 13, 34; PC 35; TCLC 107**
  See also CA 13-16R; 113; CANR 8, 82; CP 1, 2, 3; DLB 5, 165

Oppenheim, E(dward) Phillips
  1866-1946 .... **TCLC 45**
  See also CA 111; 202; CMW 4; DLB 70

Opuls, Max
  See Ophuls, Max

Orage, A(lfred) R(ichard)
  1873-1934 .... **TCLC 157**
  See also CA 122

Origen c. 185-c. 254 .... **CMLC 19**

Orlovitz, Gil 1918-1973 .... **CLC 22**
  See also CA 77-80; 45-48; CN 1; CP 1, 2; DLB 2, 5

O'Rourke, P(atrick) J(ake) 1947- .. **CLC 209**
  See also CA 77-80; CANR 13, 41, 67, 111; CPW; DAM POP; DLB 185

Orris
  See Ingelow, Jean

Ortega y Gasset, Jose 1883-1955 ...... **HLC 2; TCLC 9**
  See also CA 106; 130; DAM MULT; EW 9; EWL 3; HW 1, 2; MTCW 1, 2; MTFW 2005

Ortese, Anna Maria 1914-1998 .... **CLC 89**
  See also DLB 177; EWL 3

Ortiz, Simon J(oseph) 1941- ... **CLC 45, 208; NNAL; PC 17**
  See also AMWS 4; CA 134; CANR 69, 118; CP 3, 4, 5, 6, 7; DAM MULT, POET; DLB 120, 175, 256; EXPP; MAL 5; PFS 4, 16; RGAL 4; SSFS 22; TCWW 2

Orton, Joe ...... **CLC 4, 13, 43; DC 3; TCLC 157**
  See Orton, John Kingsley
  See also BRWS 5; CBD; CDBLB 1960 to Present; DFS 3, 6; DLB 13, 310; GLL 1; RGEL 2; TEA; WLIT 4

Orton, John Kingsley 1933-1967
  See Orton, Joe
  See also CA 85-88; CANR 35, 66; DAM DRAM; MTCW 1, 2; MTFW 2005

Orwell, George ...... **SSC 68; TCLC 2, 6, 15, 31, 51, 128, 129; WLC 4**
  See Blair, Eric (Arthur)
  See also BPFB 3; BRW 7; BYA 5; CDBLB 1945-1960; CLR 68; DAB; DLB 15, 98, 195, 255; EWL 3; EXPN; LAIT 4, 5; LATS 1:1; NFS 3, 7; RGEL 2; SCFW 1, 2; SFW 4; SSFS 4; TEA; WLIT 4; YAW

Osborne, David
  See Silverberg, Robert

Osborne, George
  See Silverberg, Robert

Osborne, John (James) 1929-1994 .... **CLC 1, 2, 5, 11, 45; TCLC 153; WLC 4**
  See also BRWS 1; CA 13-16R; 147; CANR 21, 56; CBD; CDBLB 1945-1960; DA; DAB; DAC; DAM DRAM, MST; DFS 4, 19; DLB 13; EWL 3; MTCW 1, 2; MTFW 2005; RGEL 2

Osborne, Lawrence 1958- .... **CLC 50**
  See also CA 189; CANR 152

Osbourne, Lloyd 1868-1947 .... **TCLC 93**

Osgood, Frances Sargent
  1811-1850 .... **NCLC 141**
  See also DLB 250

Oshima, Nagisa 1932- .... **CLC 20**
  See also CA 116; 121; CANR 78

Oskison, John Milton
  1874-1947 .... **NNAL; TCLC 35**
  See also CA 144; CANR 84; DAM MULT; DLB 175

Ossian c. 3rd cent. - .... **CMLC 28**
  See Macpherson, James

Ossoli, Sarah Margaret (Fuller)
  1810-1850 .... **NCLC 5, 50**
  See Fuller, Margaret; Fuller, Sarah Margaret
  See also CDALB 1640-1865; FW; LMFS 1; SATA 25

Ostriker, Alicia (Suskin) 1937- .... **CLC 132**
  See also CA 25-28R; CAAS 24; CANR 10, 30, 62, 99; CWP; DLB 120; EXPP; PFS 19

Ostrovsky, Aleksandr Nikolaevich
  See Ostrovsky, Alexander
  See also DLB 277

Ostrovsky, Alexander 1823-1886 .. **NCLC 30, 57**
  See Ostrovsky, Aleksandr Nikolaevich

Otero, Blas de 1916-1979 .... **CLC 11**
  See also CA 89-92; DLB 134; EWL 3

O'Trigger, Sir Lucius
  See Horne, Richard Henry Hengist

Otto, Rudolf 1869-1937 .... **TCLC 85**

Otto, Whitney 1955- .... **CLC 70**
  See also CA 140; CANR 120

Otway, Thomas 1652-1685 ... **DC 24; LC 106**
  See also DAM DRAM; DLB 80; RGEL 2

Ouida .... **TCLC 43**
  See De la Ramee, Marie Louise (Ouida)
  See also DLB 18, 156; RGEL 2

Ouologuem, Yambo 1940- .... **CLC 146**
  See also CA 111; 176

Ousmane, Sembene 1923- ... **BLC 3; CLC 66**
  See Sembene, Ousmane
  See also BW 1, 3; CA 117; 125; CANR 81; CWW 2; MTCW 1

Ovid 43B.C.-17 .... **CMLC 7; PC 2**
  See also AW 2; CDWLB 1; DA3; DAM POET; DLB 211; PFS 22; RGWL 2, 3; WLIT 8; WP

Owen, Hugh
  See Faust, Frederick (Schiller)

Owen, Wilfred (Edward Salter)
  1893-1918 ... **PC 19; TCLC 5, 27; WLC 4**
  See also BRW 6; CA 104; 141; CDBLB 1914-1945; DA; DAB; DAC; DAM MST, POET; DLB 20; EWL 3; EXPP; MTCW 2; MTFW 2005; PFS 10; RGEL 2; WLIT 4

Owens, Louis (Dean) 1948-2002 .... **NNAL**
  See also CA 137, 179; 207; CAAE 179; CAAS 24; CANR 71

Owens, Rochelle 1936- .... **CLC 8**
  See also CA 17-20R; CAAS 2; CAD; CANR 39; CD 5, 6; CP 1, 2, 3, 4, 5, 6, 7; CWD; CWP

Oz, Amos 1939- ...... **CLC 5, 8, 11, 27, 33, 54; SSC 66**
  See also CA 53-56; CANR 27, 47, 65, 113, 138; CWW 2; DAM NOV; EWL 3; MTCW 1, 2; MTFW 2005; RGHL; RGSF 2; RGWL 3; WLIT 6

Ozick, Cynthia 1928- .... **CLC 3, 7, 28, 62, 155; SSC 15, 60**
  See also AMWS 5; BEST 90:1; CA 17-20R; CANR 23, 58, 116; CN 3, 4, 5, 6, 7; CPW; DA3; DAM NOV, POP; DLB 28, 152, 299; DLBY 1982; EWL 3; EXPS; INT CANR-23; MAL 5; MTCW 1, 2; MTFW 2005; RGAL 4; RGHL; RGSF 2; SSFS 3, 12, 22

Ozu, Yasujiro 1903-1963 .... **CLC 16**
  See also CA 112

Pabst, G. W. 1885-1967 .... **TCLC 127**

Pacheco, C.
  See Pessoa, Fernando (Antonio Nogueira)

Pacheco, Jose Emilio 1939- .... **HLC 2**
  See also CA 111; 131; CANR 65; CWW 2; DAM MULT; DLB 290; EWL 3; HW 1, 2; RGSF 2

Pa Chin .... **CLC 18**
  See Jin, Ba
  See also EWL 3

Pack, Robert 1929- .... **CLC 13**
  See also CA 1-4R; CANR 3, 44, 82; CP 1, 2, 3, 4, 5, 6, 7; DLB 5; SATA 118

Padgett, Lewis
  See Kuttner, Henry

Padilla (Lorenzo), Heberto
  1932-2000 .... **CLC 38**
  See also AITN 1; CA 123; 131; 189; CWW 2; EWL 3; HW 1

Page, James Patrick 1944-
  See Page, Jimmy
  See also CA 204

Page, Jimmy 1944- .... **CLC 12**
  See Page, James Patrick

Page, Louise 1955- .... **CLC 40**
  See also CA 140; CANR 76; CBD; CD 5, 6; CWD; DLB 233

Page, P(atricia) K(athleen) 1916- ...... **CLC 7, 18; PC 12**
  See Cape, Judith
  See also CA 53-56; CANR 4, 22, 65; CP 1, 2, 3, 4, 5, 6, 7; DAC; DAM MST; DLB 68; MTCW 1; RGEL 2

Page, Stanton
  See Fuller, Henry Blake

Page, Stanton
  See Fuller, Henry Blake

Page, Thomas Nelson 1853-1922 .... **SSC 23**
  See also CA 118; 177; DLB 12, 78; DLBD 13; RGAL 4

Pagels, Elaine
  See Pagels, Elaine Hiesey

Pagels, Elaine Hiesey 1943- .... **CLC 104**
  See also CA 45-48; CANR 2, 24, 51, 151; FW; NCFS 4

Paget, Violet 1856-1935
  See Lee, Vernon
  See also CA 104; 166; GLL 1; HGG

Paget-Lowe, Henry
  See Lovecraft, H. P.

Paglia, Camille (Anna) 1947- .... **CLC 68**
  See also CA 140; CANR 72, 139; CPW; FW; GLL 2; MTCW 2; MTFW 2005

Paige, Richard
  See Koontz, Dean R.

Petry, Ann (Lane) 1908-1997 .. **CLC 1, 7, 18; TCLC 112**
See also AFAW 1, 2; BPFB 3; BW 1, 3; BYA 2; CA 5-8R; 157; CAAS 6; CANR 4, 46; CLR 12; CN 1, 2, 3, 4, 5, 6; DLB 76; EWL 3; JRDA; LAIT 1; MAICYA 1, 2; MAICYAS 1; MTCW 1; RGAL 4; SATA 5; SATA-Obit 94; TUS

Petursson, Halligrimur 1614-1674 .... **LC 8**

Peychinovich
See Vazov, Ivan (Minchov)

Phaedrus c. 15B.C.-c. 50 .... **CMLC 25**
See also DLB 211

Phelps (Ward), Elizabeth Stuart
See Phelps, Elizabeth Stuart
See also FW

Phelps, Elizabeth Stuart
1844-1911 .... **TCLC 113**
See Phelps (Ward), Elizabeth Stuart
See also CA 242; DLB 74

Philips, Katherine 1632-1664 . **LC 30; PC 40**
See also DLB 131; RGEL 2

Philipson, Morris H. 1926- .... **CLC 53**
See also CA 1-4R; CANR 4

Phillips, Caryl 1958- ..... **BLCS; CLC 96, 224**
See also BRWS 5; BW 2; CA 141; CANR 63, 104, 140; CBD; CD 5, 6; CN 5, 6, 7; DA3; DAM MULT; DLB 157; EWL 3; MTCW 2; MTFW 2005; WLIT 4; WWE 1

Phillips, David Graham
1867-1911 .... **TCLC 44**
See also CA 108; 176; DLB 9, 12, 303; RGAL 4

Phillips, Jack
See Sandburg, Carl (August)

Phillips, Jayne Anne 1952- .... **CLC 15, 33, 139; SSC 16**
See also AAYA 57; BPFB 3; CA 101; CANR 24, 50, 96; CN 4, 5, 6, 7; CSW; DLBY 1980; INT CANR-24; MTCW 1, 2; MTFW 2005; RGAL 4; RGSF 2; SSFS 4

Phillips, Richard
See Dick, Philip K.

Phillips, Robert (Schaeffer) 1938- .... **CLC 28**
See also CA 17-20R; CAAS 13; CANR 8; DLB 105

Phillips, Ward
See Lovecraft, H. P.

Philostratus, Flavius c. 179-c.
244 .... **CMLC 62**

Piccolo, Lucio 1901-1969 .... **CLC 13**
See also CA 97-100; DLB 114; EWL 3

Pickthall, Marjorie L(owry) C(hristie)
1883-1922 .... **TCLC 21**
See also CA 107; DLB 92

Pico della Mirandola, Giovanni
1463-1494 .... **LC 15**
See also LMFS 1

Piercy, Marge 1936- .... **CLC 3, 6, 14, 18, 27, 62, 128; PC 29**
See also BPFB 3; CA 21-24R, 187; CAAE 187; CAAS 1; CANR 13, 43, 66, 111; CN 3, 4, 5, 6, 7; CP 1, 2, 3, 4, 5, 6, 7; CWP; DLB 120, 227; EXPP; FW; MAL 5; MTCW 1, 2; MTFW 2005; PFS 9, 22; SFW 4

Piers, Robert
See Anthony, Piers

Pieyre de Mandiargues, Andre 1909-1991
See Mandiargues, Andre Pieyre de
See also CA 103; 136; CANR 22, 82; EWL 3; GFL 1789 to the Present

Pilnyak, Boris 1894-1938 . **SSC 48; TCLC 23**
See Vogau, Boris Andreyevich
See also EWL 3

Pinchback, Eugene
See Toomer, Jean

Pincherle, Alberto 1907-1990 ...... **CLC 11, 18**
See Moravia, Alberto
See also CA 25-28R; 132; CANR 33, 63, 142; DAM NOV; MTCW 1; MTFW 2005

Pinckney, Darryl 1953- .... **CLC 76**
See also BW 2, 3; CA 143; CANR 79

Pindar 518(?)B.C.-438(?)B.C. .... **CMLC 12; PC 19**
See also AW 1; CDWLB 1; DLB 176; RGWL 2

Pineda, Cecile 1942- .... **CLC 39**
See also CA 118; DLB 209

Pinero, Arthur Wing 1855-1934 .... **TCLC 32**
See also CA 110; 153; DAM DRAM; DLB 10; RGEL 2

Pinero, Miguel (Antonio Gomez)
1946-1988 .... **CLC 4, 55**
See also CA 61-64; 125; CAD; CANR 29, 90; DLB 266; HW 1; LLW

Pinget, Robert 1919-1997 .... **CLC 7, 13, 37**
See also CA 85-88; 160; CWW 2; DLB 83; EWL 3; GFL 1789 to the Present

Pink Floyd
See Barrett, (Roger) Syd; Gilmour, David; Mason, Nick; Waters, Roger; Wright, Rick

Pinkney, Edward 1802-1828 .... **NCLC 31**
See also DLB 248

Pinkwater, D. Manus
See Pinkwater, Daniel Manus

Pinkwater, Daniel
See Pinkwater, Daniel Manus

Pinkwater, Daniel M.
See Pinkwater, Daniel Manus

Pinkwater, Daniel Manus 1941- .... **CLC 35**
See also AAYA 1, 46; BYA 9; CA 29-32R; CANR 12, 38, 89, 143; CLR 4; CSW; FANT; JRDA; MAICYA 1, 2; SAAS 3; SATA 8, 46, 76, 114, 158; SFW 4; YAW

Pinkwater, Manus
See Pinkwater, Daniel Manus

Pinsky, Robert 1940- .... **CLC 9, 19, 38, 94, 121, 216; PC 27**
See also AMWS 6; CA 29-32R; CAAS 4; CANR 58, 97, 138; CP 3, 4, 5, 6, 7; DA3; DAM POET; DLBY 1982, 1998; MAL 5; MTCW 2; MTFW 2005; PFS 18; RGAL 4; TCLE 1:2

Pinta, Harold
See Pinter, Harold

Pinter, Harold 1930- .. **CLC 1, 3, 6, 9, 11, 15, 27, 58, 73, 199; DC 15; WLC 4**
See also BRWR 1; BRWS 1; CA 5-8R; CANR 33, 65, 112, 145; CBD; CD 5, 6; CDBLB 1960 to Present; CP 1; DA; DA3; DAB; DAC; DAM DRAM, MST; DFS 3, 5, 7, 14; DLB 13, 310; EWL 3; IDFW 3, 4; LMFS 2; MTCW 1, 2; MTFW 2005; RGEL 2; RGHL; TEA

Piozzi, Hester Lynch (Thrale)
1741-1821 .... **NCLC 57**
See also DLB 104, 142

Pirandello, Luigi 1867-1936 .. **DC 5; SSC 22; TCLC 4, 29, 172; WLC 4**
See also CA 104; 153; CANR 103; DA; DA3; DAB; DAC; DAM DRAM, MST; DFS 4, 9; DLB 264; EW 8; EWL 3; MTCW 2; MTFW 2005; RGSF 2; RGWL 2, 3; WLIT 7

Pirsig, Robert M(aynard) 1928- ... **CLC 4, 6, 73**
See also CA 53-56; CANR 42, 74; CPW 1; DA3; DAM POP; MTCW 1, 2; MTFW 2005; SATA 39

Pisan, Christine de
See Christine de Pizan

Pisarev, Dmitrii Ivanovich
See Pisarev, Dmitry Ivanovich
See also DLB 277

Pisarev, Dmitry Ivanovich
1840-1868 .... **NCLC 25**
See Pisarev, Dmitrii Ivanovich

Pix, Mary (Griffith) 1666-1709 .... **LC 8**
See also DLB 80

Pixerecourt, (Rene Charles) Guilbert de
1773-1844 .... **NCLC 39**
See also DLB 192; GFL 1789 to the Present

Plaatje, Sol(omon) T(shekisho)
1878-1932 .... **BLCS; TCLC 73**
See also BW 2, 3; CA 141; CANR 79; DLB 125, 225

Plaidy, Jean
See Hibbert, Eleanor Alice Burford

Planche, James Robinson
1796-1880 .... **NCLC 42**
See also RGEL 2

Plant, Robert 1948- .... **CLC 12**

Plante, David 1940- .... **CLC 7, 23, 38**
See also CA 37-40R; CANR 12, 36, 58, 82, 152; CN 2, 3, 4, 5, 6, 7; DAM NOV; DLBY 1983; INT CANR-12; MTCW 1

Plante, David Robert
See Plante, David

Plath, Sylvia 1932-1963 ..... **CLC 1, 2, 3, 5, 9, 11, 14, 17, 50, 51, 62, 111; PC 1, 37; WLC 4**
See also AAYA 13; AMWR 2; AMWS 1; BPFB 3; CA 19-20; CANR 34, 101; CAP 2; CDALB 1941-1968; DA; DA3; DAB; DAC; DAM MST, POET; DLB 5, 6, 152; EWL 3; EXPN; EXPP; FL 1:6; FW; LAIT 4; MAL 5; MBL; MTCW 1, 2; MTFW 2005; NFS 1; PAB; PFS 1, 15; RGAL 4; SATA 96; TUS; WP; YAW

Plato c. 428B.C.-347B.C. .... **CMLC 8, 75; WLCS**
See also AW 1; CDWLB 1; DA; DA3; DAB; DAC; DAM MST; DLB 176; LAIT 1; LATS 1:1; RGWL 2, 3; WLIT 8

Platonov, Andrei
See Klimentov, Andrei Platonovich

Platonov, Andrei Platonovich
See Klimentov, Andrei Platonovich
See also DLB 272

Platonov, Andrey Platonovich
See Klimentov, Andrei Platonovich
See also EWL 3

Platt, Kin 1911- .... **CLC 26**
See also AAYA 11; CA 17-20R; CANR 11; JRDA; SAAS 17; SATA 21, 86; WYA

Plautus c. 254B.C.-c. 184B.C. ...... **CMLC 24; DC 6**
See also AW 1; CDWLB 1; DLB 211; RGWL 2, 3; WLIT 8

Plick et Plock
See Simenon, Georges (Jacques Christian)

Plieksans, Janis
See Rainis, Janis

Plimpton, George (Ames)
1927-2003 .... **CLC 36**
See also AITN 1; CA 21-24R; 224; CANR 32, 70, 103, 133; DLB 185, 241; MTCW 1, 2; MTFW 2005; SATA 10; SATA-Obit 150

Pliny the Elder c. 23-79 .... **CMLC 23**
See also DLB 211

Pliny the Younger c. 61-c. 112 ...... **CMLC 62**
See also AW 2; DLB 211

Plomer, William Charles Franklin
1903-1973 .... **CLC 4, 8**
See also AFW; BRWS 11; CA 21-22; CANR 34; CAP 2; CN 1; CP 1, 2; DLB 20, 162, 191, 225; EWL 3; MTCW 1; RGEL 2; RGSF 2; SATA 24

Plotinus 204-270 .... **CMLC 46**
See also CDWLB 1; DLB 176

Plowman, Piers
See Kavanagh, Patrick (Joseph)

Rawlings, Marjorie Kinnan
1896-1953 .... **TCLC 4**
See also AAYA 20; AMWS 10; ANW;
BPFB 3; BYA 3; CA 104; 137; CANR 74;
CLR 63; DLB 9, 22, 102; DLBD 17;
JRDA; MAICYA 1, 2; MAL 5; MTCW 2;
MTFW 2005; RGAL 4; SATA 100; WCH;
YABC 1; YAW

Ray, Satyajit 1921-1992 .... **CLC 16, 76**
See also CA 114; 137; DAM MULT

Read, Herbert Edward 1893-1968 ..... **CLC 4**
See also BRW 6; CA 85-88; 25-28R; DLB
20, 149; EWL 3; PAB; RGEL 2

Read, Piers Paul 1941- .... **CLC 4, 10, 25**
See also CA 21-24R; CANR 38, 86, 150;
CN 2, 3, 4, 5, 6, 7; DLB 14; SATA 21

Reade, Charles 1814-1884 .... **NCLC 2, 74**
See also DLB 21; RGEL 2

Reade, Hamish
See Gray, Simon (James Holliday)

Reading, Peter 1946- .... **CLC 47**
See also BRWS 8; CA 103; CANR 46, 96;
CP 5, 6, 7; DLB 40

Reaney, James 1926- .... **CLC 13**
See also CA 41-44R; CAAS 15; CANR 42;
CD 5, 6; CP 1, 2, 3, 4, 5, 6, 7; DAC;
DAM MST; DLB 68; RGEL 2; SATA 43

Rebreanu, Liviu 1885-1944 .... **TCLC 28**
See also CA 165; DLB 220; EWL 3

Rechy, John 1934- ..... **CLC 1, 7, 14, 18, 107;
HLC 2**
See also CA 5-8R, 195; CAAE 195; CAAS
4; CANR 6, 32, 64, 152; CN 1, 2, 3, 4, 5,
6, 7; DAM MULT; DLB 122, 278; DLBY
1982; HW 1, 2; INT CANR-6; LLW;
MAL 5; RGAL 4

Rechy, John Francisco
See Rechy, John

Redcam, Tom 1870-1933 .... **TCLC 25**

Reddin, Keith 1956- .... **CLC 67**
See also CAD; CD 6

Redgrove, Peter (William)
1932-2003 .... **CLC 6, 41**
See also BRWS 6; CA 1-4R; 217; CANR 3,
39, 77; CP 1, 2, 3, 4, 5, 6, 7; DLB 40;
TCLE 1:2

Redmon, Anne .... **CLC 22**
See Nightingale, Anne Redmon
See also DLBY 1986

Reed, Eliot
See Ambler, Eric

Reed, Ishmael (Scott) 1938- . **BLC 3; CLC 2,
3, 5, 6, 13, 32, 60, 174; PC 68**
See also AFAW 1, 2; AMWS 10; BPFB 3;
BW 2, 3; CA 21-24R; CANR 25, 48, 74,
128; CN 1, 2, 3, 4, 5, 6, 7; CP 1, 2, 3, 4,
5, 6, 7; CSW; DA3; DAM MULT; DLB
2, 5, 33, 169, 227; DLBD 8; EWL 3;
LMFS 2; MAL 5; MSW; MTCW 1, 2;
MTFW 2005; PFS 6; RGAL 4; TCWW 2

Reed, John (Silas) 1887-1920 .... **TCLC 9**
See also CA 106; 195; MAL 5; TUS

Reed, Lou .... **CLC 21**
See Firbank, Louis

Reese, Lizette Woodworth
1856-1935 .... **PC 29; TCLC 181**
See also CA 180; DLB 54

Reeve, Clara 1729-1807 .... **NCLC 19**
See also DLB 39; RGEL 2

Reich, Wilhelm 1897-1957 .... **TCLC 57**
See also CA 199

Reid, Christopher (John) 1949- .... **CLC 33**
See also CA 140; CANR 89; CP 4, 5, 6, 7;
DLB 40; EWL 3

Reid, Desmond
See Moorcock, Michael

Reid Banks, Lynne 1929-
See Banks, Lynne Reid
See also AAYA 49; CA 1-4R; CANR 6, 22,
38, 87; CLR 24; CN 1, 2, 3, 7; JRDA;
MAICYA 1, 2; SATA 22, 75, 111, 165;
YAW

Reilly, William K.
See Creasey, John

Reiner, Max
See Caldwell, (Janet Miriam) Taylor
(Holland)

Reis, Ricardo
See Pessoa, Fernando (Antonio Nogueira)

Reizenstein, Elmer Leopold
See Rice, Elmer (Leopold)
See also EWL 3

Remarque, Erich Maria 1898-1970 . **CLC 21**
See also AAYA 27; BPFB 3; CA 77-80; 29-
32R; CDWLB 2; DA; DA3; DAB; DAC;
DAM MST, NOV; DLB 56; EWL 3;
EXPN; LAIT 3; MTCW 1, 2; MTFW
2005; NFS 4; RGHL; RGWL 2, 3

Remington, Frederic S(ackrider)
1861-1909 .... **TCLC 89**
See also CA 108; 169; DLB 12, 186, 188;
SATA 41; TCWW 2

Remizov, A.
See Remizov, Aleksei (Mikhailovich)

Remizov, A. M.
See Remizov, Aleksei (Mikhailovich)

Remizov, Aleksei (Mikhailovich)
1877-1957 .... **TCLC 27**
See Remizov, Alexey Mikhaylovich
See also CA 125; 133; DLB 295

Remizov, Alexey Mikhaylovich
See Remizov, Aleksei (Mikhailovich)
See also EWL 3

Renan, Joseph Ernest 1823-1892 . **NCLC 26,
145**
See also GFL 1789 to the Present

Renard, Jules(-Pierre) 1864-1910 .. **TCLC 17**
See also CA 117; 202; GFL 1789 to the
Present

Renart, Jean fl. 13th cent. - .... **CMLC 83**

Renault, Mary .... **CLC 3, 11, 17**
See Challans, Mary
See also BPFB 3; BYA 2; CN 1, 2, 3;
DLBY 1983; EWL 3; GLL 1; LAIT 1;
RGEL 2; RHW

Rendell, Ruth 1930- .... **CLC 28, 48**
See Vine, Barbara
See also BPFB 3; BRWS 9; CA 109; CANR
32, 52, 74, 127; CN 5, 6, 7; CPW; DAM
POP; DLB 87, 276; INT CANR-32;
MSW; MTCW 1, 2; MTFW 2005

Rendell, Ruth Barbara
See Rendell, Ruth

Renoir, Jean 1894-1979 .... **CLC 20**
See also CA 129; 85-88

Resnais, Alain 1922- .... **CLC 16**

Revard, Carter 1931- .... **NNAL**
See also CA 144; CANR 81, 153; PFS 5

Reverdy, Pierre 1889-1960 .... **CLC 53**
See also CA 97-100; 89-92; DLB 258; EWL
3; GFL 1789 to the Present

Rexroth, Kenneth 1905-1982 .... **CLC 1, 2, 6,
11, 22, 49, 112; PC 20**
See also BG 1:3; CA 5-8R; 107; CANR 14,
34, 63; CDALB 1941-1968; CP 1, 2, 3;
DAM POET; DLB 16, 48, 165, 212;
DLBY 1982; EWL 3; INT CANR-14;
MAL 5; MTCW 1, 2; MTFW 2005;
RGAL 4

Reyes, Alfonso 1889-1959 .... **HLCS 2; TCLC
33**
See also CA 131; EWL 3; HW 1; LAW

Reyes y Basoalto, Ricardo Eliecer Neftali
See Neruda, Pablo

Reymont, Wladyslaw (Stanislaw)
1868(?)-1925 .... **TCLC 5**
See also CA 104; EWL 3

Reynolds, John Hamilton
1794-1852 .... **NCLC 146**
See also DLB 96

Reynolds, Jonathan 1942- .... **CLC 6, 38**
See also CA 65-68; CANR 28

Reynolds, Joshua 1723-1792 .... **LC 15**
See also DLB 104

Reynolds, Michael S(hane)
1937-2000 .... **CLC 44**
See also CA 65-68; 189; CANR 9, 89, 97

Reznikoff, Charles 1894-1976 .... **CLC 9**
See also AMWS 14; CA 33-36; 61-64; CAP
2; CP 1, 2; DLB 28, 45; RGHL; WP

Rezzori, Gregor von
See Rezzori d'Arezzo, Gregor von

Rezzori d'Arezzo, Gregor von
1914-1998 .... **CLC 25**
See also CA 122; 136; 167

Rhine, Richard
See Silverstein, Alvin; Silverstein, Virginia
B(arbara Opshelor)

Rhodes, Eugene Manlove
1869-1934 .... **TCLC 53**
See also CA 198; DLB 256; TCWW 1, 2

R'hoone, Lord
See Balzac, Honore de

Rhys, Jean 1890-1979 .... **CLC 2, 4, 6, 14, 19,
51, 124; SSC 21, 76**
See also BRWS 2; CA 25-28R; 85-88;
CANR 35, 62; CDBLB 1945-1960; CD-
WLB 3; CN 1, 2; DA3; DAM NOV; DLB
36, 117, 162; DNFS 2; EWL 3; LATS 1:1;
MTCW 1, 2; MTFW 2005; NFS 19;
RGEL 2; RGSF 2; RHW; TEA; WWE 1

Ribeiro, Darcy 1922-1997 .... **CLC 34**
See also CA 33-36R; 156; EWL 3

Ribeiro, Joao Ubaldo (Osorio Pimentel)
1941- .... **CLC 10, 67**
See also CA 81-84; CWW 2; EWL 3

Ribman, Ronald (Burt) 1932- .... **CLC 7**
See also CA 21-24R; CAD; CANR 46, 80;
CD 5, 6

Ricci, Nino (Pio) 1959- .... **CLC 70**
See also CA 137; CANR 130; CCA 1

Rice, Anne 1941- .... **CLC 41, 128**
See Rampling, Anne
See also AAYA 9, 53; AMWS 7; BEST
89:2; BPFB 3; CA 65-68; CANR 12, 36,
53, 74, 100, 133; CN 6, 7; CPW; CSW;
DA3; DAM POP; DLB 292; GL 3; GLL
2; HGG; MTCW 2; MTFW 2005; SUFW
2; YAW

Rice, Elmer (Leopold) 1892-1967 ...... **CLC 7,
49**
See Reizenstein, Elmer Leopold
See also CA 21-22; 25-28R; CAP 2; DAM
DRAM; DFS 12; DLB 4, 7; IDTP; MAL
5; MTCW 1, 2; RGAL 4

Rice, Tim(othy Miles Bindon)
1944- .... **CLC 21**
See also CA 103; CANR 46; DFS 7

Rich, Adrienne (Cecile) 1929- ... **CLC 3, 6, 7,
11, 18, 36, 73, 76, 125; PC 5**
See also AAYA 69; AMWR 2; AMWS 1;
CA 9-12R; CANR 20, 53, 74, 128;
CDALBS; CP 1, 2, 3, 4, 5, 6, 7; CSW;
CWP; DA3; DAM POET; DLB 5, 67;
EWL 3; EXPP; FL 1:6; FW; MAL 5;
MBL; MTCW 1, 2; MTFW 2005; PAB;
PFS 15; RGAL 4; RGHL; WP

Rich, Barbara
See Graves, Robert (von Ranke)

Rich, Robert
See Trumbo, Dalton

Richard, Keith .... **CLC 17**
See Richards, Keith

Richards, David Adams 1950- .... **CLC 59**
See also CA 93-96; CANR 60, 110; CN 7;
DAC; DLB 53; TCLE 1:2

Richards, I(vor) A(rmstrong)
1893-1979 .... **CLC 14, 24**
See also BRWS 2; CA 41-44R; 89-92;
CANR 34, 74; CP 1, 2; DLB 27; EWL 3;
MTCW 2; RGEL 2

Richards, Keith 1943-
See Richard, Keith
See also CA 107; CANR 77

Richardson, Anne
See Roiphe, Anne

Richardson, Dorothy Miller
1873-1957 .... **TCLC 3**
See also CA 104; 192; DLB 36; EWL 3;
FW; RGEL 2

Richardson (Robertson), Ethel Florence
Lindesay 1870-1946
See Richardson, Henry Handel
See also CA 105; 190; DLB 230; RHW

Richardson, Henry Handel .... **TCLC 4**
See Richardson (Robertson), Ethel Florence
Lindesay
See also DLB 197; EWL 3; RGEL 2; RGSF
2

Richardson, John 1796-1852 .... **NCLC 55**
See also CCA 1; DAC; DLB 99

Richardson, Samuel 1689-1761 ...... **LC 1, 44;**
WLC 5
See also BRW 3; CDBLB 1660-1789; DA;
DAB; DAC; DAM MST, NOV; DLB 39;
RGEL 2; TEA; WLIT 3

Richardson, Willis 1889-1977 .... **HR 1:3**
See also BW 1; CA 124; DLB 51; SATA 60

Richler, Mordecai 1931-2001 .... **CLC 3, 5, 9,**
13, 18, 46, 70, 185
See also AITN 1; CA 65-68; 201; CANR
31, 62, 111; CCA 1; CLR 17; CN 1, 2, 3,
4, 5, 7; CWRI 5; DAC; DAM MST, NOV;
DLB 53; EWL 3; MAICYA 1, 2; MTCW
1, 2; MTFW 2005; RGEL 2; RGHL;
SATA 44, 98; SATA-Brief 27; TWA

Richter, Conrad (Michael)
1890-1968 .... **CLC 30**
See also AAYA 21; BYA 2; CA 5-8R; 25-
28R; CANR 23; DLB 9, 212; LAIT 1;
MAL 5; MTCW 1, 2; MTFW 2005;
RGAL 4; SATA 3; TCWW 1, 2; TUS;
YAW

Ricostranza, Tom
See Ellis, Trey

Riddell, Charlotte 1832-1906 .... **TCLC 40**
See Riddell, Mrs. J. H.
See also CA 165; DLB 156

Riddell, Mrs. J. H.
See Riddell, Charlotte
See also HGG; SUFW

Ridge, John Rollin 1827-1867 ...... **NCLC 82;**
NNAL
See also CA 144; DAM MULT; DLB 175

Ridgeway, Jason
See Marlowe, Stephen

Ridgway, Keith 1965- .... **CLC 119**
See also CA 172; CANR 144

Riding, Laura .... **CLC 3, 7**
See Jackson, Laura (Riding)
See also CP 1, 2, 3, 4, 5; RGAL 4

Riefenstahl, Berta Helene Amalia 1902-2003
See Riefenstahl, Leni
See also CA 108; 220

Riefenstahl, Leni .... **CLC 16, 190**
See Riefenstahl, Berta Helene Amalia

Riffe, Ernest
See Bergman, (Ernst) Ingmar

Riggs, (Rolla) Lynn
1899-1954 .... **NNAL; TCLC 56**
See also CA 144; DAM MULT; DLB 175

Riis, Jacob A(ugust) 1849-1914 ..... **TCLC 80**
See also CA 113; 168; DLB 23

Riley, James Whitcomb 1849-1916 .... **PC 48;**
TCLC 51
See also CA 118; 137; DAM POET; MAI-
CYA 1, 2; RGAL 4; SATA 17

Riley, Tex
See Creasey, John

Rilke, Rainer Maria 1875-1926 .... **PC 2;**
TCLC 1, 6, 19
See also CA 104; 132; CANR 62, 99; CD-
WLB 2; DA3; DAM POET; DLB 81; EW
9; EWL 3; MTCW 1, 2; MTFW 2005;
PFS 19; RGWL 2, 3; TWA; WP

Rimbaud, (Jean Nicolas) Arthur
1854-1891 ... **NCLC 4, 35, 82; PC 3, 57;**
WLC 5
See also DA; DA3; DAB; DAC; DAM
MST, POET; DLB 217; EW 7; GFL 1789
to the Present; LMFS 2; RGWL 2, 3;
TWA; WP

Rinehart, Mary Roberts
1876-1958 .... **TCLC 52**
See also BPFB 3; CA 108; 166; RGAL 4;
RHW

Ringmaster, The
See Mencken, H(enry) L(ouis)

Ringwood, Gwen(dolyn Margaret) Pharis
1910-1984 .... **CLC 48**
See also CA 148; 112; DLB 88

Rio, Michel 1945(?)- .... **CLC 43**
See also CA 201

Rios, Alberto (Alvaro) 1952- .... **PC 57**
See also AAYA 66; AMWS 4; CA 113;
CANR 34, 79, 137; CP 6, 7; DLB 122;
HW 2; MTFW 2005; PFS 11

Ritsos, Giannes
See Ritsos, Yannis

Ritsos, Yannis 1909-1990 .... **CLC 6, 13, 31**
See also CA 77-80; 133; CANR 39, 61; EW
12; EWL 3; MTCW 1; RGWL 2, 3

Ritter, Erika 1948(?)- .... **CLC 52**
See also CD 5, 6; CWD

Rivera, Jose Eustasio 1889-1928 ... **TCLC 35**
See also CA 162; EWL 3; HW 1, 2; LAW

Rivera, Tomas 1935-1984 .... **HLCS 2**
See also CA 49-52; CANR 32; DLB 82;
HW 1; LLW; RGAL 4; SSFS 15; TCWW
2; WLIT 1

Rivers, Conrad Kent 1933-1968 .... **CLC 1**
See also BW 1; CA 85-88; DLB 41

Rivers, Elfrida
See Bradley, Marion Zimmer
See also GLL 1

Riverside, John
See Heinlein, Robert A(nson)

Rizal, Jose 1861-1896 .... **NCLC 27**

Roa Bastos, Augusto 1917-2005 ...... **CLC 45;**
HLC 2
See also CA 131; 238; CWW 2; DAM
MULT; DLB 113; EWL 3; HW 1; LAW;
RGSF 2; WLIT 1

Roa Bastos, Augusto Jose Antonio
See Roa Bastos, Augusto

Robbe-Grillet, Alain 1922- .... **CLC 1, 2, 4, 6,**
8, 10, 14, 43, 128
See also BPFB 3; CA 9-12R; CANR 33,
65, 115; CWW 2; DLB 83; EW 13; EWL
3; GFL 1789 to the Present; IDFW 3, 4;
MTCW 1, 2; MTFW 2005; RGWL 2, 3;
SSFS 15

Robbins, Harold 1916-1997 .... **CLC 5**
See also BPFB 3; CA 73-76; 162; CANR
26, 54, 112; DA3; DAM NOV;
MTCW 1, 2

Robbins, Thomas Eugene 1936-
See Robbins, Tom
See also CA 81-84; CANR 29, 59, 95, 139;
CN 7; CPW; CSW; DA3; DAM NOV,
POP; MTCW 1, 2; MTFW 2005

Robbins, Tom .... **CLC 9, 32, 64**
See Robbins, Thomas Eugene
See also AAYA 32; AMWS 10; BEST 90:3;
BPFB 3; CN 3, 4, 5, 6, 7; DLBY 1980

Robbins, Trina 1938- .... **CLC 21**
See also AAYA 61; CA 128; CANR 152

Roberts, Charles G(eorge) D(ouglas)
1860-1943 .... **SSC 91; TCLC 8**
See also CA 105; 188; CLR 33; CWRI 5;
DLB 92; RGAL 2; RGSF 2; SATA 88;
SATA-Brief 29

Roberts, Elizabeth Madox
1886-1941 .... **TCLC 68**
See also CA 111; 166; CLR 100; CWRI 5;
DLB 9, 54, 102; RGAL 4; RHW; SATA
33; SATA-Brief 27; TCWW 2; WCH

Roberts, Kate 1891-1985 .... **CLC 15**
See also CA 107; 116; DLB 319

Roberts, Keith (John Kingston)
1935-2000 .... **CLC 14**
See also BRWS 10; CA 25-28R; CANR 46;
DLB 261; SFW 4

Roberts, Kenneth (Lewis)
1885-1957 .... **TCLC 23**
See also CA 109; 199; DLB 9; MAL 5;
RGAL 4; RHW

Roberts, Michele (Brigitte) 1949- .... **CLC 48,**
178
See also CA 115; CANR 58, 120; CN 6, 7;
DLB 231; FW

Robertson, Ellis
See Ellison, Harlan (Jay); Silverberg, Robert

Robertson, Thomas William
1829-1871 .... **NCLC 35**
See Robertson, Tom
See also DAM DRAM

Robertson, Tom
See Robertson, Thomas William
See also RGEL 2

Robeson, Kenneth
See Dent, Lester

Robinson, Edwin Arlington
1869-1935 .... **PC 1, 35; TCLC 5, 101**
See also AMW; CA 104; 133; CDALB
1865-1917; DA; DAC; DAM MST,
POET; DLB 54; EWL 3; EXPP; MAL 5;
MTCW 1, 2; MTFW 2005; PAB; PFS 4;
RGAL 4; WP

Robinson, Henry Crabb
1775-1867 .... **NCLC 15**
See also DLB 107

Robinson, Jill 1936- .... **CLC 10**
See also CA 102; CANR 120; INT CA-102

Robinson, Kim Stanley 1952- .... **CLC 34**
See also AAYA 26; CA 126; CANR 113,
139; CN 6, 7; MTFW 2005; SATA 109;
SCFW 2; SFW 4

Robinson, Lloyd
See Silverberg, Robert

Robinson, Marilynne 1944- ...... **CLC 25, 180**
See also AAYA 69; CA 116; CANR 80, 140;
CN 4, 5, 6, 7; DLB 206; MTFW 2005

Robinson, Mary 1758-1800 .... **NCLC 142**
See also DLB 158; FW

Robinson, Smokey .... **CLC 21**
See Robinson, William, Jr.

Robinson, William, Jr. 1940-
See Robinson, Smokey
See also CA 116

Robison, Mary 1949- .... **CLC 42, 98**
See also CA 113; 116; CANR 87; CN 4, 5,
6, 7; DLB 130; INT CA-116; RGSF 2

Roches, Catherine des 1542-1587 ...... **LC 117**
  See also DLB 327
Rochester
  See Wilmot, John
  See also RGEL 2
Rod, Edouard 1857-1910 .... **TCLC 52**
Roddenberry, Eugene Wesley 1921-1991
  See Roddenberry, Gene
  See also CA 110; 135; CANR 37; SATA 45;
    SATA-Obit 69
Roddenberry, Gene .... **CLC 17**
  See Roddenberry, Eugene Wesley
  See also AAYA 5; SATA-Obit 69
Rodgers, Mary 1931- .... **CLC 12**
  See also BYA 5; CA 49-52; CANR 8, 55,
    90; CLR 20; CWRI 5; INT CANR-8;
    JRDA; MAICYA 1, 2; SATA 8, 130
Rodgers, W(illiam) R(obert)
    1909-1969 .... **CLC 7**
  See also CA 85-88; DLB 20; RGEL 2
Rodman, Eric
  See Silverberg, Robert
Rodman, Howard 1920(?)-1985 .... **CLC 65**
  See also CA 118
Rodman, Maia
  See Wojciechowska, Maia (Teresa)
Rodo, Jose Enrique 1871(?)-1917 .... **HLCS 2**
  See also CA 178; EWL 3; HW 2; LAW
Rodolph, Utto
  See Ouologuem, Yambo
Rodriguez, Claudio 1934-1999 .... **CLC 10**
  See also CA 188; DLB 134
Rodriguez, Richard 1944- .... **CLC 155; HLC 2**
  See also AMWS 14; CA 110; CANR 66,
    116; DAM MULT; DLB 82, 256; HW 1,
    2; LAIT 5; LLW; MTFW 2005; NCFS 3;
    WLIT 1
Roelvaag, O(le) E(dvart) 1876-1931
  See Rolvaag, O(le) E(dvart)
  See also CA 117; 171
Roethke, Theodore (Huebner)
    1908-1963 .... **CLC 1, 3, 8, 11, 19, 46,
    101; PC 15**
  See also AMW; CA 81-84; CABS 2;
    CDALB 1941-1968; DA3; DAM POET;
    DLB 5, 206; EWL 3; EXPP; MAL 5;
    MTCW 1, 2; PAB; PFS 3; RGAL 4; WP
Rogers, Carl R(ansom)
    1902-1987 .... **TCLC 125**
  See also CA 1-4R; 121; CANR 1, 18;
    MTCW 1
Rogers, Samuel 1763-1855 .... **NCLC 69**
  See also DLB 93; RGEL 2
Rogers, Thomas Hunton 1927- .... **CLC 57**
  See also CA 89-92; INT CA-89-92
Rogers, Will(iam Penn Adair)
    1879-1935 .... **NNAL; TCLC 8, 71**
  See also CA 105; 144; DA3; DAM MULT;
    DLB 11; MTCW 2
Rogin, Gilbert 1929- .... **CLC 18**
  See also CA 65-68; CANR 15
Rohan, Koda
  See Koda Shigeyuki
Rohlfs, Anna Katharine Green
  See Green, Anna Katharine
Rohmer, Eric .... **CLC 16**
  See Scherer, Jean-Marie Maurice
Rohmer, Sax .... **TCLC 28**
  See Ward, Arthur Henry Sarsfield
  See also DLB 70; MSW; SUFW
Roiphe, Anne 1935- .... **CLC 3, 9**
  See also CA 89-92; CANR 45, 73, 138;
    DLBY 1980; INT CA-89-92
Roiphe, Anne Richardson
  See Roiphe, Anne
Rojas, Fernando de 1475-1541 ... **HLCS 1, 2;
    LC 23**
  See also DLB 286; RGWL 2, 3

Rojas, Gonzalo 1917- .... **HLCS 2**
  See also CA 178; HW 2; LAWS 1
Roland (de la Platiere), Marie-Jeanne
    1754-1793 .... **LC 98**
  See also DLB 314
**Rolfe, Frederick (William Serafino Austin
    Lewis Mary)** 1860-1913 .... **TCLC 12**
  See Al Siddik
  See also CA 107; 210; DLB 34, 156; RGEL
    2
Rolland, Romain 1866-1944 .... **TCLC 23**
  See also CA 118; 197; DLB 65, 284; EWL
    3; GFL 1789 to the Present; RGWL 2, 3
Rolle, Richard c. 1300-c. 1349 ...... **CMLC 21**
  See also DLB 146; LMFS 1; RGEL 2
Rolvaag, O(le) E(dvart) .... **TCLC 17**
  See Roelvaag, O(le) E(dvart)
  See also DLB 9, 212; MAL 5; NFS 5;
    RGAL 4
Romain Arnaud, Saint
  See Aragon, Louis
Romains, Jules 1885-1972 .... **CLC 7**
  See also CA 85-88; CANR 34; DLB 65,
    321; EWL 3; GFL 1789 to the Present;
    MTCW 1
Romero, Jose Ruben 1890-1952 .... **TCLC 14**
  See also CA 114; 131; EWL 3; HW 1; LAW
Ronsard, Pierre de 1524-1585 . **LC 6, 54; PC
    11**
  See also DLB 327; EW 2; GFL Beginnings
    to 1789; RGWL 2, 3; TWA
Rooke, Leon 1934- .... **CLC 25, 34**
  See also CA 25-28R; CANR 23, 53; CCA
    1; CPW; DAM POP
Roosevelt, Franklin Delano
    1882-1945 .... **TCLC 93**
  See also CA 116; 173; LAIT 3
Roosevelt, Theodore 1858-1919 ..... **TCLC 69**
  See also CA 115; 170; DLB 47, 186, 275
Roper, William 1498-1578 .... **LC 10**
Roquelaure, A. N.
  See Rice, Anne
Rosa, Joao Guimaraes 1908-1967 ... **CLC 23;
    HLCS 1**
  See Guimaraes Rosa, Joao
  See also CA 89-92; DLB 113, 307; EWL 3;
    WLIT 1
Rose, Wendy 1948- . **CLC 85; NNAL; PC 13**
  See also CA 53-56; CANR 5, 51; CWP;
    DAM MULT; DLB 175; PFS 13; RGAL
    4; SATA 12
Rosen, R. D.
  See Rosen, Richard (Dean)
Rosen, Richard (Dean) 1949- .... **CLC 39**
  See also CA 77-80; CANR 62, 120; CMW
    4; INT CANR-30
Rosenberg, Isaac 1890-1918 .... **TCLC 12**
  See also BRW 6; CA 107; 188; DLB 20,
    216; EWL 3; PAB; RGEL 2
Rosenblatt, Joe .... **CLC 15**
  See Rosenblatt, Joseph
  See also CP 3, 4, 5, 6, 7
Rosenblatt, Joseph 1933-
  See Rosenblatt, Joe
  See also CA 89-92; CP 1, 2; INT CA-89-92
Rosenfeld, Samuel
  See Tzara, Tristan
Rosenstock, Sami
  See Tzara, Tristan
Rosenstock, Samuel
  See Tzara, Tristan
Rosenthal, M(acha) L(ouis)
    1917-1996 .... **CLC 28**
  See also CA 1-4R; 152; CAAS 6; CANR 4,
    51; CP 1, 2, 3, 4, 5, 6; DLB 5; SATA 59
Ross, Barnaby
  See Dannay, Frederic; Lee, Manfred B.
Ross, Bernard L.
  See Follett, Ken(neth Martin)

Ross, J. H.
  See Lawrence, T(homas) E(dward)
Ross, John Hume
  See Lawrence, T(homas) E(dward)
Ross, Martin 1862-1915
  See Martin, Violet Florence
  See also DLB 135; GLL 2; RGEL 2; RGSF
    2
Ross, (James) Sinclair 1908-1996 ... **CLC 13;
    SSC 24**
  See also CA 73-76; CANR 81; CN 1, 2, 3,
    4, 5, 6; DAC; DAM MST; DLB 88;
    RGEL 2; RGSF 2; TCWW 1, 2
Rossetti, Christina 1830-1894 ... **NCLC 2, 50,
    66; PC 7; WLC 5**
  See also AAYA 51; BRW 5; BYA 4; DA;
    DA3; DAB; DAC; DAM MST, POET;
    DLB 35, 163, 240; EXPP; FL 1:3; LATS
    1:1; MAICYA 1, 2; PFS 10, 14; RGEL 2;
    SATA 20; TEA; WCH
Rossetti, Christina Georgina
  See Rossetti, Christina
Rossetti, Dante Gabriel 1828-1882 . **NCLC 4,
    77; PC 44; WLC 5**
  See also AAYA 51; BRW 5; CDBLB 1832-
    1890; DA; DAB; DAC; DAM MST,
    POET; DLB 35; EXPP; RGEL 2; TEA
Rossi, Cristina Peri
  See Peri Rossi, Cristina
Rossi, Jean-Baptiste 1931-2003
  See Japrisot, Sebastien
  See also CA 201; 215
Rossner, Judith 1935-2005 .... **CLC 6, 9, 29**
  See also AITN 2; BEST 90:3; BPFB 3; CA
    17-20R; 242; CANR 18, 51, 73; CN 4, 5,
    6, 7; DLB 6; INT CANR-18; MAL 5;
    MTCW 1, 2; MTFW 2005
Rossner, Judith Perelman
  See Rossner, Judith
Rostand, Edmond (Eugene Alexis)
    1868-1918 .... **DC 10; TCLC 6, 37**
  See also CA 104; 126; DA; DA3; DAB;
    DAC; DAM DRAM, MST; DFS 1; DLB
    192; LAIT 1; MTCW 1; RGWL 2, 3;
    TWA
Roth, Henry 1906-1995 ..... **CLC 2, 6, 11, 104**
  See also AMWS 9; CA 11-12; 149; CANR
    38, 63; CAP 1; CN 1, 2, 3, 4, 5, 6; DA3;
    DLB 28; EWL 3; MAL 5; MTCW 1, 2;
    MTFW 2005; RGAL 4
Roth, (Moses) Joseph 1894-1939 ... **TCLC 33**
  See also CA 160; DLB 85; EWL 3; RGWL
    2, 3
Roth, Philip 1933- ... **CLC 1, 2, 3, 4, 6, 9, 15,
    22, 31, 47, 66, 86, 119, 201; SSC 26;
    WLC 5**
  See also AAYA 67; AMWR 2; AMWS 3;
    BEST 90:3; BPFB 3; CA 1-4R; CANR 1,
    22, 36, 55, 89, 132; CDALB 1968-1988;
    CN 3, 4, 5, 6, 7; CPW 1; DA; DA3; DAB;
    DAC; DAM MST, NOV, POP; DLB 2,
    28, 173; DLBY 1982; EWL 3; MAL 5;
    MTCW 1, 2; MTFW 2005; RGAL 4;
    RGHL; RGSF 2; SSFS 12, 18; TUS
Roth, Philip Milton
  See Roth, Philip
Rothenberg, Jerome 1931- .... **CLC 6, 57**
  See also CA 45-48; CANR 1, 106; CP 1, 2,
    3, 4, 5, 6, 7; DLB 5, 193
Rotter, Pat ed. .... **CLC 65**
Roumain, Jacques (Jean Baptiste)
    1907-1944 .... **BLC 3; TCLC 19**
  See also BW 1; CA 117; 125; DAM MULT;
    EWL 3
Rourke, Constance Mayfield
    1885-1941 .... **TCLC 12**
  See also CA 107; 200; MAL 5; YABC 1
Rousseau, Jean-Baptiste 1671-1741 ...... **LC 9**

Rousseau, Jean-Jacques 1712-1778 .... **LC 14, 36, 122; WLC 5**
See also DA; DA3; DAB; DAC; DAM MST; DLB 314; EW 4; GFL Beginnings to 1789; LMFS 1; RGWL 2, 3; TWA

Roussel, Raymond 1877-1933 .... **TCLC 20**
See also CA 117; 201; EWL 3; GFL 1789 to the Present

Rovit, Earl (Herbert) 1927- .... **CLC 7**
See also CA 5-8R; CANR 12

Rowe, Elizabeth Singer 1674-1737 ..... **LC 44**
See also DLB 39, 95

Rowe, Nicholas 1674-1718 .... **LC 8**
See also DLB 84; RGEL 2

Rowlandson, Mary 1637(?)-1678 .... **LC 66**
See also DLB 24, 200; RGAL 4

Rowley, Ames Dorrance
See Lovecraft, H. P.

Rowley, William 1585(?)-1626 ... **LC 100, 123**
See also DFS 22; DLB 58; RGEL 2

Rowling, J. K. 1966- .... **CLC 137, 217**
See also AAYA 34; BYA 11, 13, 14; CA 173; CANR 128; CLR 66, 80, 112; MAICYA 2; MTFW 2005; SATA 109; SUFW 2

Rowling, Joanne Kathleen
See Rowling, J. K.

Rowson, Susanna Haswell
1762(?)-1824 .... **NCLC 5, 69**
See also AMWS 15; DLB 37, 200; RGAL 4

Roy, Arundhati 1960(?)- .... **CLC 109, 210**
See also CA 163; CANR 90, 126; CN 7; DLB 323, 326; DLBY 1997; EWL 3; LATS 1:2; MTFW 2005; NFS 22; WWE 1

Roy, Gabrielle 1909-1983 .... **CLC 10, 14**
See also CA 53-56; 110; CANR 5, 61; CCA 1; DAB; DAC; DAM MST; DLB 68; EWL 3; MTCW 1; RGWL 2, 3; SATA 104; TCLE 1:2

Royko, Mike 1932-1997 .... **CLC 109**
See also CA 89-92; 157; CANR 26, 111; CPW

Rozanov, Vasilii Vasil'evich
See Rozanov, Vassili
See also DLB 295

Rozanov, Vasily Vasilyevich
See Rozanov, Vassili
See also EWL 3

Rozanov, Vassili 1856-1919 .... **TCLC 104**
See Rozanov, Vasilii Vasil'evich; Rozanov, Vasily Vasilyevich

Rozewicz, Tadeusz 1921- ...... **CLC 9, 23, 139**
See also CA 108; CANR 36, 66; CWW 2; DA3; DAM POET; DLB 232; EWL 3; MTCW 1, 2; MTFW 2005; RGHL; RGWL 3

Ruark, Gibbons 1941- .... **CLC 3**
See also CA 33-36R; CAAS 23; CANR 14, 31, 57; DLB 120

Rubens, Bernice (Ruth) 1923-2004 . **CLC 19, 31**
See also CA 25-28R; 232; CANR 33, 65, 128; CN 1, 2, 3, 4, 5, 6, 7; DLB 14, 207, 326; MTCW 1

Rubin, Harold
See Robbins, Harold

Rudkin, (James) David 1936- .... **CLC 14**
See also CA 89-92; CBD; CD 5, 6; DLB 13

Rudnik, Raphael 1933- .... **CLC 7**
See also CA 29-32R

Ruffian, M.
See Hasek, Jaroslav (Matej Frantisek)

Ruiz, Jose Martinez .... **CLC 11**
See Martinez Ruiz, Jose

Ruiz, Juan c. 1283-c. 1350 .... **CMLC 66**

Rukeyser, Muriel 1913-1980 . **CLC 6, 10, 15, 27; PC 12**
See also AMWS 6; CA 5-8R; 93-96; CANR 26, 60; CP 1, 2, 3; DA3; DAM POET; DLB 48; EWL 3; FW; GLL 2; MAL 5; MTCW 1, 2; PFS 10; RGAL 4; SATA-Obit 22

Rule, Jane (Vance) 1931- .... **CLC 27**
See also CA 25-28R; CAAS 18; CANR 12, 87; CN 4, 5, 6, 7; DLB 60; FW

Rulfo, Juan 1918-1986 .. **CLC 8, 80; HLC 2; SSC 25**
See also CA 85-88; 118; CANR 26; CDWLB 3; DAM MULT; DLB 113; EWL 3; HW 1, 2; LAW; MTCW 1, 2; RGSF 2; RGWL 2, 3; WLIT 1

Rumi, Jalal al-Din 1207-1273 ...... **CMLC 20; PC 45**
See also AAYA 64; RGWL 2, 3; WLIT 6; WP

Runeberg, Johan 1804-1877 .... **NCLC 41**

Runyon, (Alfred) Damon
1884(?)-1946 .... **TCLC 10**
See also CA 107; 165; DLB 11, 86, 171; MAL 5; MTCW 2; RGAL 4

Rush, Norman 1933- .... **CLC 44**
See also CA 121; 126; CANR 130; INT CA-126

Rushdie, (Ahmed) Salman 1947- .... **CLC 23, 31, 55, 100, 191; SSC 83; WLCS**
See also AAYA 65; BEST 89:3; BPFB 3; BRWS 4; CA 108; 111; CANR 33, 56, 108, 133; CN 4, 5, 6, 7; DA3; DAB; DAC; DAM MST, NOV, POP; DLB 194, 323, 326; EWL 3; FANT; INT CA-111; LATS 1:2; LMFS 2; MTCW 1, 2; MTFW 2005; NFS 22, 23; RGEL 2; RGSF 2; TEA; WLIT 4

Rushforth, Peter 1945-2005 .... **CLC 19**
See also CA 101; 243

Rushforth, Peter Scott
See Rushforth, Peter

Ruskin, John 1819-1900 .... **TCLC 63**
See also BRW 5; BYA 5; CA 114; 129; CDBLB 1832-1890; DLB 55, 163, 190; RGEL 2; SATA 24; TEA; WCH

Russ, Joanna 1937- .... **CLC 15**
See also BPFB 3; CA 25-28; CANR 11, 31, 65; CN 4, 5, 6, 7; DLB 8; FW; GLL 1; MTCW 1; SCFW 1, 2; SFW 4

Russ, Richard Patrick
See O'Brian, Patrick

Russell, George William 1867-1935
See A.E.; Baker, Jean H.
See also BRWS 8; CA 104; 153; CDBLB 1890-1914; DAM POET; EWL 3; RGEL 2

Russell, Jeffrey Burton 1934- .... **CLC 70**
See also CA 25-28R; CANR 11, 28, 52

Russell, (Henry) Ken(neth Alfred)
1927- .... **CLC 16**
See also CA 105

Russell, William Martin 1947-
See Russell, Willy
See also CA 164; CANR 107

Russell, Willy .... **CLC 60**
See Russell, William Martin
See also CBD; CD 5, 6; DLB 233

Russo, Richard 1949- .... **CLC 181**
See also AMWS 12; CA 127; 133; CANR 87, 114

Rutherford, Mark .... **TCLC 25**
See White, William Hale
See also DLB 18; RGEL 2

Ruysbroeck, Jan van 1293-1381 ... **CMLC 85**

Ruyslinck, Ward .... **CLC 14**
See Belser, Reimond Karel Maria de

Ryan, Cornelius (John) 1920-1974 ..... **CLC 7**
See also CA 69-72; 53-56; CANR 38

Ryan, Michael 1946- .... **CLC 65**
See also CA 49-52; CANR 109; DLBY 1982

Ryan, Tim
See Dent, Lester

Rybakov, Anatoli (Naumovich)
1911-1998 .... **CLC 23, 53**
See Rybakov, Anatolii (Naumovich)
See also CA 126; 135; 172; SATA 79; SATA-Obit 108

Rybakov, Anatolii (Naumovich)
See Rybakov, Anatoli (Naumovich)
See also DLB 302; RGHL

Ryder, Jonathan
See Ludlum, Robert

Ryga, George 1932-1987 .... **CLC 14**
See also CA 101; 124; CANR 43, 90; CCA 1; DAC; DAM MST; DLB 60

S. H.
See Hartmann, Sadakichi

S. S.
See Sassoon, Siegfried (Lorraine)

Sa'adawi, al- Nawal
See El Saadawi, Nawal
See also AFW; EWL 3

Saadawi, Nawal El
See El Saadawi, Nawal
See also WLIT 2

Saba, Umberto 1883-1957 .... **TCLC 33**
See also CA 144; CANR 79; DLB 114; EWL 3; RGWL 2, 3

Sabatini, Rafael 1875-1950 .... **TCLC 47**
See also BPFB 3; CA 162; RHW

Sabato, Ernesto (R.) 1911- .... **CLC 10, 23; HLC 2**
See also CA 97-100; CANR 32, 65; CDWLB 3; CWW 2; DAM MULT; DLB 145; EWL 3; HW 1, 2; LAW; MTCW 1, 2; MTFW 2005

Sa-Carneiro, Mario de 1890-1916 . **TCLC 83**
See also DLB 287; EWL 3

Sacastru, Martin
See Bioy Casares, Adolfo
See also CWW 2

Sacher-Masoch, Leopold von
1836(?)-1895 .... **NCLC 31**

Sachs, Hans 1494-1576 .... **LC 95**
See also CDWLB 2; DLB 179; RGWL 2, 3

Sachs, Marilyn 1927- .... **CLC 35**
See also AAYA 2; BYA 6; CA 17-20R; CANR 13, 47, 150; CLR 2; JRDA; MAICYA 1, 2; SAAS 2; SATA 3, 68, 164; SATA-Essay 110; WYA; YAW

Sachs, Marilyn Stickle
See Sachs, Marilyn

Sachs, Nelly 1891-1970 .... **CLC 14, 98**
See also CA 17-18; 25-28R; CANR 87; CAP 2; EWL 3; MTCW 2; MTFW 2005; PFS 20; RGHL; RGWL 2, 3

Sackler, Howard (Oliver)
1929-1982 .... **CLC 14**
See also CA 61-64; 108; CAD; CANR 30; DFS 15; DLB 7

Sacks, Oliver 1933- .... **CLC 67, 202**
See also CA 53-56; CANR 28, 50, 76, 146; CPW; DA3; INT CANR-28; MTCW 1, 2; MTFW 2005

Sacks, Oliver Wolf
See Sacks, Oliver

Sackville, Thomas 1536-1608 .... **LC 98**
See also DAM DRAM; DLB 62, 132; RGEL 2

Sadakichi
See Hartmann, Sadakichi

Sa'dawi, Nawal al-
See El Saadawi, Nawal
See also CWW 2

Sade, Donatien Alphonse Francois
1740-1814 .... **NCLC 3, 47**
　　See also DLB 314; EW 4; GFL Beginnings
　　to 1789; RGWL 2, 3

Sade, Marquis de
　　See Sade, Donatien Alphonse Francois

Sadoff, Ira 1945- .... **CLC 9**
　　See also CA 53-56; CANR 5, 21, 109; DLB
　　120

Saetone
　　See Camus, Albert

Safire, William 1929- .... **CLC 10**
　　See also CA 17-20R; CANR 31, 54, 91, 148

Sagan, Carl (Edward) 1934-1996 .... **CLC 30, 112**
　　See also AAYA 2, 62; CA 25-28R; 155;
　　CANR 11, 36, 74; CPW; DA3; MTCW 1,
　　2; MTFW 2005; SATA 58; SATA-Obit 94

Sagan, Francoise .... **CLC 3, 6, 9, 17, 36**
　　See Quoirez, Francoise
　　See also CWW 2; DLB 83; EWL 3; GFL
　　1789 to the Present; MTCW 2

Sahgal, Nayantara (Pandit) 1927- .... **CLC 41**
　　See also CA 9-12R; CANR 11, 88; CN 1,
　　2, 3, 4, 5, 6, 7; DLB 323

Said, Edward W. 1935-2003 .... **CLC 123**
　　See also CA 21-24R; 220; CANR 45, 74,
　　107, 131; DLB 67; MTCW 2; MTFW
　　2005

Saint, H(arry) F. 1941- .... **CLC 50**
　　See also CA 127

St. Aubin de Teran, Lisa 1953-
　　See Teran, Lisa St. Aubin de
　　See also CA 118; 126; CN 6, 7; INT CA-
　　126

Saint Birgitta of Sweden c.
　　1303-1373 .... **CMLC 24**

Sainte-Beuve, Charles Augustin
1804-1869 .... **NCLC 5**
　　See also DLB 217; EW 6; GFL 1789 to the
　　Present

Saint-Exupery, Antoine de
1900-1944 .... **TCLC 2, 56, 169; WLC**
　　See also AAYA 63; BPFB 3; BYA 3; CA
　　108; 132; CLR 10; DA3; DAM NOV;
　　DLB 72; EW 12; EWL 3; GFL 1789 to
　　the Present; LAIT 3; MAICYA 1, 2;
　　MTCW 1, 2; MTFW 2005; RGWL 2, 3;
　　SATA 20; TWA

**Saint-Exupery, Antoine Jean Baptiste Marie
Roger de**
　　See Saint-Exupery, Antoine de

St. John, David
　　See Hunt, E(verette) Howard, (Jr.)

St. John, J. Hector
　　See Crevecoeur, Michel Guillaume Jean de

Saint-John Perse
　　See Leger, (Marie-Rene Auguste) Alexis
　　Saint-Leger
　　See also EW 10; EWL 3; GFL 1789 to the
　　Present; RGWL 2

Saintsbury, George (Edward Bateman)
1845-1933 .... **TCLC 31**
　　See also CA 160; DLB 57, 149

Sait Faik .... **TCLC 23**
　　See Abasiyanik, Sait Faik

Saki .... **SSC 12; TCLC 3; WLC 5**
　　See Munro, H(ector) H(ugh)
　　See also BRWS 6; BYA 11; LAIT 2; RGEL
　　2; SSFS 1; SUFW

Sala, George Augustus 1828-1895 . **NCLC 46**

Saladin 1138-1193 .... **CMLC 38**

Salama, Hannu 1936- .... **CLC 18**
　　See also CA 244; EWL 3

Salamanca, J(ack) R(ichard) 1922- .. **CLC 4, 15**
　　See also CA 25-28R; 193; CAAE 193

Salas, Floyd Francis 1931- .... **HLC 2**
　　See also CA 119; CAAS 27; CANR 44, 75,
　　93; DAM MULT; DLB 82; HW 1, 2;
　　MTCW 2; MTFW 2005

Sale, J. Kirkpatrick
　　See Sale, Kirkpatrick

Sale, John Kirkpatrick
　　See Sale, Kirkpatrick

Sale, Kirkpatrick 1937- .... **CLC 68**
　　See also CA 13-16R; CANR 10, 147

Salinas, Luis Omar 1937- ... **CLC 90; HLC 2**
　　See also AMWS 13; CA 131; CANR 81,
　　153; DAM MULT; DLB 82; HW 1, 2

Salinas (y Serrano), Pedro
1891(?)-1951 .... **TCLC 17**
　　See also CA 117; DLB 134; EWL 3

Salinger, J(erome) D(avid) 1919- .. **CLC 1, 3,
8, 12, 55, 56, 138; SSC 2, 28, 65; WLC
5**
　　See also AAYA 2, 36; AMW; AMWC 1;
　　BPFB 3; CA 5-8R; CANR 39, 129;
　　CDALB 1941-1968; CLR 18; CN 1, 2, 3,
　　4, 5, 6, 7; CPW 1; DA; DA3; DAB; DAC;
　　DAM MST, NOV, POP; DLB 2, 102, 173;
　　EWL 3; EXPN; LAIT 4; MAICYA 1, 2;
　　MAL 5; MTCW 1, 2; MTFW 2005; NFS
　　1; RGAL 4; RGSF 2; SATA 67; SSFS 17;
　　TUS; WYA; YAW

Salisbury, John
　　See Caute, (John) David

Sallust c. 86B.C.-35B.C. .... **CMLC 68**
　　See also AW 2; CDWLB 1; DLB 211;
　　RGWL 2, 3

Salter, James 1925- .. **CLC 7, 52, 59; SSC 58**
　　See also AMWS 9; CA 73-76; CANR 107;
　　DLB 130

Saltus, Edgar (Everton) 1855-1921 . **TCLC 8**
　　See also CA 105; DLB 202; RGAL 4

Saltykov, Mikhail Evgrafovich
1826-1889 .... **NCLC 16**
　　See also DLB 238:

Saltykov-Shchedrin, N.
　　See Saltykov, Mikhail Evgrafovich

Samarakis, Andonis
　　See Samarakis, Antonis
　　See also EWL 3

Samarakis, Antonis 1919-2003 .... **CLC 5**
　　See Samarakis, Andonis
　　See also CA 25-28R; 224; CAAS 16; CANR
　　36

Sanchez, Florencio 1875-1910 .... **TCLC 37**
　　See also CA 153; DLB 305; EWL 3; HW 1;
　　LAW

Sanchez, Luis Rafael 1936- .... **CLC 23**
　　See also CA 128; DLB 305; EWL 3; HW 1;
　　WLIT 1

Sanchez, Sonia 1934- .... **BLC 3; CLC 5, 116,
215; PC 9**
　　See also BW 2, 3; CA 33-36R; CANR 24,
　　49, 74, 115; CLR 18; CP 2, 3, 4, 5, 6, 7;
　　CSW; CWP; DA3; DAM MULT; DLB 41;
　　DLBD 8; EWL 3; MAICYA 1, 2; MAL 5;
　　MTCW 1, 2; MTFW 2005; SATA 22, 136;
　　WP

Sancho, Ignatius 1729-1780 .... **LC 84**

Sand, George 1804-1876 ..... **NCLC 2, 42, 57,
174; WLC 5**
　　See also DA; DA3; DAB; DAC; DAM
　　MST, NOV; DLB 119, 192; EW 6; FL 1:3;
　　FW; GFL 1789 to the Present; RGWL 2,
　　3; TWA

Sandburg, Carl (August) 1878-1967 . **CLC 1,
4, 10, 15, 35; PC 2, 41; WLC 5**
　　See also AAYA 24; AMW; BYA 1, 3; CA
　　5-8R; 25-28R; CANR 35; CDALB 1865-
　　1917; CLR 67; DA; DA3; DAB; DAC;
　　DAM MST, POET; DLB 17, 54, 284;
　　EWL 3; EXPP; LAIT 2; MAICYA 1, 2;
　　MAL 5; MTCW 1, 2; MTFW 2005; PAB;
　　PFS 3, 6, 12; RGAL 4; SATA 8; TUS;
　　WCH; WP; WYA

Sandburg, Charles
　　See Sandburg, Carl (August)

Sandburg, Charles A.
　　See Sandburg, Carl (August)

Sanders, (James) Ed(ward) 1939- .... **CLC 53**
　　See Sanders, Edward
　　See also BG 1:3; CA 13-16R; CAAS 21;
　　CANR 13, 44, 78; CP 1, 2, 3, 4, 5, 6, 7;
　　DAM POET; DLB 16, 244

Sanders, Edward
　　See Sanders, (James) Ed(ward)
　　See also DLB 244

Sanders, Lawrence 1920-1998 .... **CLC 41**
　　See also BEST 89:4; BPFB 3; CA 81-84;
　　165; CANR 33, 62; CMW 4; CPW; DA3;
　　DAM POP; MTCW 1

Sanders, Noah
　　See Blount, Roy (Alton), Jr.

Sanders, Winston P.
　　See Anderson, Poul (William)

Sandoz, Mari(e Susette) 1900-1966 .. **CLC 28**
　　See also CA 1-4R; 25-28R; CANR 17, 64;
　　DLB 9, 212; LAIT 2; MTCW 1, 2; SATA
　　5; TCWW 1, 2

Sandys, George 1578-1644 .... **LC 80**
　　See also DLB 24, 121

Saner, Reg(inald Anthony) 1931- .... **CLC 9**
　　See also CA 65-68; CP 3, 4, 5, 6, 7

Sankara 788-820 .... **CMLC 32**

Sannazaro, Jacopo 1456(?)-1530 .... **LC 8**
　　See also RGWL 2, 3; WLIT 7

Sansom, William 1912-1976 . **CLC 2, 6; SSC
21**
　　See also CA 5-8R; 65-68; CANR 42; CN 1,
　　2; DAM NOV; DLB 139; EWL 3; MTCW
　　1; RGEL 2; RGSF 2

Santayana, George 1863-1952 .... **TCLC 40**
　　See also AMW; CA 115; 194; DLB 54, 71,
　　246, 270; DLBD 13; EWL 3; MAL 5;
　　RGAL 4; TUS

Santiago, Danny .... **CLC 33**
　　See James, Daniel (Lewis)
　　See also DLB 122

**Santillana, Inigo Lopez de Mendoza,
Marques de** 1398-1458 .... **LC 111**
　　See also DLB 286

Santmyer, Helen Hooven
1895-1986 .... **CLC 33; TCLC 133**
　　See also CA 1-4R; 118; CANR 15, 33;
　　DLBY 1984; MTCW 1; RHW

Santoka, Taneda 1882-1940 .... **TCLC 72**

Santos, Bienvenido N(uqui)
1911-1996 ... **AAL; CLC 22; TCLC 156**
　　See also CA 101; 151; CANR 19, 46; CP 1;
　　DAM MULT; DLB 312; EWL; RGAL 4;
　　SSFS 19

Sapir, Edward 1884-1939 .... **TCLC 108**
　　See also CA 211; DLB 92

Sapper .... **TCLC 44**
　　See McNeile, Herman Cyril

Sapphire
　　See Sapphire, Brenda

Sapphire, Brenda 1950- .... **CLC 99**

Sappho fl. 6th cent. B.C.- ... **CMLC 3, 67; PC
5**
　　See also CDWLB 1; DA3; DAM POET;
　　DLB 176; FL 1:1; PFS 20; RGWL 2, 3;
　　WLIT 8; WP

Saramago, Jose 1922- .... **CLC 119; HLCS 1**
　　See also CA 153; CANR 96; CWW 2; DLB
　　287; EWL 3; LATS 1:2; SSFS 23

Sarduy, Severo 1937-1993 .... **CLC 6, 97; HLCS 2; TCLC 167**
See also CA 89-92; 142; CANR 58, 81; CWW 2; DLB 113; EWL 3; HW 1, 2; LAW

Sargeson, Frank 1903-1982 .... **CLC 31**
See also CA 25-28R; 106; CANR 38, 79; CN 1, 2, 3; EWL 3; GLL 2; RGEL 2; RGSF 2; SSFS 20

Sarmiento, Domingo Faustino
1811-1888 .... **HLCS 2; NCLC 123**
See also LAW; WLIT 1

Sarmiento, Felix Ruben Garcia
See Dario, Ruben

Saro-Wiwa, Ken(ule Beeson)
1941-1995 .... **CLC 114**
See also BW 2; CA 142; 150; CANR 60; DLB 157

Saroyan, William 1908-1981 ... **CLC 1, 8, 10, 29, 34, 56; SSC 21; TCLC 137; WLC 5**
See also AAYA 66; CA 5-8R; 103; CAD; CANR 30; CDALBS; CN 1, 2; DA; DA3; DAB; DAC; DAM DRAM, MST, NOV; DFS 17; DLB 7, 9, 86; DLBY 1981; EWL 3; LAIT 4; MAL 5; MTCW 1, 2; MTFW 2005; RGAL 4; RGSF 2; SATA 23; SATA-Obit 24; SSFS 14; TUS

Sarraute, Nathalie 1900-1999 .... **CLC 1, 2, 4, 8, 10, 31, 80; TCLC 145**
See also BPFB 3; CA 9-12R; 187; CANR 23, 66, 134; CWW 2; DLB 83, 321; EW 12; EWL 3; GFL 1789 to the Present; MTCW 1, 2; MTFW 2005; RGWL 2, 3

Sarton, (Eleanor) May 1912-1995 ..... **CLC 4, 14, 49, 91; PC 39; TCLC 120**
See also AMWS 8; CA 1-4R; 149; CANR 1, 34, 55, 116; CN 1, 2, 3, 4, 5, 6; CP 1, 2, 3, 4, 5, 6; DAM POET; DLB 48; DLBY 1981; EWL 3; FW; INT CANR-34; MAL 5; MTCW 1, 2; MTFW 2005; RGAL 4; SATA 36; SATA-Obit 86; TUS

Sartre, Jean-Paul 1905-1980 . **CLC 1, 4, 7, 9, 13, 18, 24, 44, 50, 52; DC 3; SSC 32; WLC 5**
See also AAYA 62; CA 9-12R; 97-100; CANR 21; DA; DA3; DAB; DAC; DAM DRAM, MST, NOV; DFS 5; DLB 72, 296, 321; EW 12; EWL 3; GFL 1789 to the Present; LMFS 2; MTCW 1, 2; MTFW 2005; NFS 21; RGHL; RGSF 2; RGWL 2, 3; SSFS 9; TWA

Sassoon, Siegfried (Lorraine)
1886-1967 .... **CLC 36, 130; PC 12**
See also BRW 6; CA 104; 25-28R; CANR 36; DAB; DAM MST, NOV, POET; DLB 20, 191; DLBD 18; EWL 3; MTCW 1, 2; MTFW 2005; PAB; RGEL 2; TEA

Satterfield, Charles
See Pohl, Frederik

Satyremont
See Peret, Benjamin

Saul, John (W. III) 1942- .... **CLC 46**
See also AAYA 10, 62; BEST 90:4; CA 81-84; CANR 16, 40, 81; CPW; DAM NOV, POP; HGG; SATA 98

Saunders, Caleb
See Heinlein, Robert A(nson)

Saura (Atares), Carlos 1932-1998 .... **CLC 20**
See also CA 114; 131; CANR 79; HW 1

Sauser, Frederic Louis
See Sauser-Hall, Frederic

Sauser-Hall, Frederic 1887-1961 ...... **CLC 18**
See Cendrars, Blaise
See also CA 102; 93-96; CANR 36, 62; MTCW 1

Saussure, Ferdinand de
1857-1913 .... **TCLC 49**
See also DLB 242

Savage, Catharine
See Brosman, Catharine Savage

Savage, Richard 1697(?)-1743 .... **LC 96**
See also DLB 95; RGEL 2

Savage, Thomas 1915-2003 .... **CLC 40**
See also CA 126; 132; 218; CAAS 15; CN 6, 7; INT CA-132; SATA-Obit 147; TCWW 2

Savan, Glenn 1953-2003 .... **CLC 50**
See also CA 225

Sax, Robert
See Johnson, Robert

Saxo Grammaticus c. 1150-c.
1222 .... **CMLC 58**

Saxton, Robert
See Johnson, Robert

Sayers, Dorothy L(eigh) 1893-1957 . **SSC 71; TCLC 2, 15**
See also BPFB 3; BRWS 3; CA 104; 119; CANR 60; CDBLB 1914-1945; CMW 4; DAM POP; DLB 10, 36, 77, 100; MSW; MTCW 1, 2; MTFW 2005; RGEL 2; SSFS 12; TEA

Sayers, Valerie 1952- .... **CLC 50, 122**
See also CA 134; CANR 61; CSW

Sayles, John (Thomas) 1950- .... **CLC 7, 10, 14, 198**
See also CA 57-60; CANR 41, 84; DLB 44

Scammell, Michael 1935- .... **CLC 34**
See also CA 156

Scannell, Vernon 1922- .... **CLC 49**
See also CA 5-8R; CANR 8, 24, 57, 143; CN 1, 2; CP 1, 2, 3, 4, 5, 6, 7; CWRI 5; DLB 27; SATA 59

Scarlett, Susan
See Streatfeild, (Mary) Noel

Scarron 1847-1910
See Mikszath, Kalman

Scarron, Paul 1610-1660 .... **LC 116**
See also GFL Beginnings to 1789; RGWL 2, 3

Schaeffer, Susan Fromberg 1941- ..... **CLC 6, 11, 22**
See also CA 49-52; CANR 18, 65; CN 4, 5, 6, 7; DLB 28, 299; MTCW 1, 2; MTFW 2005; SATA 22

Schama, Simon (Michael) 1945- ..... **CLC 150**
See also BEST 89:4; CA 105; CANR 39, 91

Schary, Jill
See Robinson, Jill

Schell, Jonathan 1943- .... **CLC 35**
See also CA 73-76; CANR 12, 117

Schelling, Friedrich Wilhelm Joseph von
1775-1854 .... **NCLC 30**
See also DLB 90

Scherer, Jean-Marie Maurice 1920-
See Rohmer, Eric
See also CA 110

Schevill, James (Erwin) 1920- .... **CLC 7**
See also CA 5-8R; CAAS 12; CAD; CD 5, 6; CP 1, 2, 3, 4, 5

Schiller, Friedrich von 1759-1805 ...... **DC 12; NCLC 39, 69, 166**
See also CDWLB 2; DAM DRAM; DLB 94; EW 5; RGWL 2, 3; TWA

Schisgal, Murray (Joseph) 1926- .... **CLC 6**
See also CA 21-24R; CAD; CANR 48, 86; CD 5, 6; MAL 5

Schlee, Ann 1934- .... **CLC 35**
See also CA 101; CANR 29, 88; SATA 44; SATA-Brief 36

Schlegel, August Wilhelm von
1767-1845 .... **NCLC 15, 142**
See also DLB 94; RGWL 2, 3

Schlegel, Friedrich 1772-1829 .... **NCLC 45**
See also DLB 90; EW 5; RGWL 2, 3; TWA

Schlegel, Johann Elias (von)
1719(?)-1749 .... **LC 5**

Schleiermacher, Friedrich
1768-1834 .... **NCLC 107**
See also DLB 90

Schlesinger, Arthur M(eier), Jr.
1917- .... **CLC 84**
See also AITN 1; CA 1-4R; CANR 1, 28, 58, 105; DLB 17; INT CANR-28; MTCW 1, 2; SATA 61

Schlink, Bernhard 1944- .... **CLC 174**
See also CA 163; CANR 116; RGHL

Schmidt, Arno (Otto) 1914-1979 .... **CLC 56**
See also CA 128; 109; DLB 69; EWL 3

Schmitz, Aron Hector 1861-1928
See Svevo, Italo
See also CA 104; 122; MTCW 1

Schnackenberg, Gjertrud (Cecelia)
1953- .... **CLC 40; PC 45**
See also AMWS 15; CA 116; CANR 100; CP 5, 6, 7; CWP; DLB 120, 282; PFS 13

Schneider, Leonard Alfred 1925-1966
See Bruce, Lenny
See also CA 89-92

Schnitzler, Arthur 1862-1931 ..... **DC 17; SSC 15, 61; TCLC 4**
See also CA 104; CDWLB 2; DLB 81, 118; EW 8; EWL 3; RGSF 2; RGWL 2, 3

Schoenberg, Arnold Franz Walter
1874-1951 .... **TCLC 75**
See also CA 109; 188

Schonberg, Arnold
See Schoenberg, Arnold Franz Walter

Schopenhauer, Arthur 1788-1860 . **NCLC 51, 157**
See also DLB 90; EW 5

Schor, Sandra (M.) 1932(?)-1990 ..... **CLC 65**
See also CA 132

Schorer, Mark 1908-1977 .... **CLC 9**
See also CA 5-8R; 73-76; CANR 7; CN 1, 2; DLB 103

Schrader, Paul (Joseph) 1946- . **CLC 26, 212**
See also CA 37-40R; CANR 41; DLB 44

Schreber, Daniel 1842-1911 .... **TCLC 123**

Schreiner, Olive (Emilie Albertina)
1855-1920 .... **TCLC 9**
See also AFW; BRWS 2; CA 105; 154; DLB 18, 156, 190, 225; EWL 3; FW; RGEL 2; TWA; WLIT 2; WWE 1

Schulberg, Budd (Wilson) 1914- .. **CLC 7, 48**
See also BPFB 3; CA 25-28R; CANR 19, 87; CN 1, 2, 3, 4, 5, 6, 7; DLB 6, 26, 28; DLBY 1981, 2001; MAL 5

Schulman, Arnold
See Trumbo, Dalton

Schulz, Bruno 1892-1942 .. **SSC 13; TCLC 5, 51**
See also CA 115; 123; CANR 86; CDWLB 4; DLB 215; EWL 3; MTCW 2; MTFW 2005; RGSF 2; RGWL 2, 3

Schulz, Charles M. 1922-2000 .... **CLC 12**
See also AAYA 39; CA 9-12R; 187; CANR 6, 132; INT CANR-6; MTFW 2005; SATA 10; SATA-Obit 118

Schulz, Charles Monroe
See Schulz, Charles M.

Schumacher, E(rnst) F(riedrich)
1911-1977 .... **CLC 80**
See also CA 81-84; 73-76; CANR 34, 85

Schumann, Robert 1810-1856 ...... **NCLC 143**

Schuyler, George Samuel 1895-1977 . **HR 1:3**
See also BW 2; CA 81-84; 73-76; CANR 42; DLB 29, 51

Schuyler, James Marcus 1923-1991 .. **CLC 5, 23**
See also CA 101; 134; CP 1, 2, 3, 4, 5; DAM POET; DLB 5, 169; EWL 3; INT CA-101; MAL 5; WP

Schwartz, Delmore (David)
1913-1966 ... **CLC 2, 4, 10, 45, 87; PC 8**
See also AMWS 2; CA 17-18; 25-28R;
CANR 35; CAP 2; DLB 28, 48; EWL 3;
MAL 5; MTCW 1, 2; MTFW 2005; PAB;
RGAL 4; TUS

Schwartz, Ernst
See Ozu, Yasujiro

Schwartz, John Burnham 1965- .... **CLC 59**
See also CA 132; CANR 116

Schwartz, Lynne Sharon 1939- .... **CLC 31**
See also CA 103; CANR 44, 89; DLB 218;
MTCW 2; MTFW 2005

Schwartz, Muriel A.
See Eliot, T(homas) S(tearns)

Schwarz-Bart, Andre 1928- .... **CLC 2, 4**
See also CA 89-92; CANR 109; DLB 299;
RGHL

Schwarz-Bart, Simone 1938- . **BLCS; CLC 7**
See also BW 2; CA 97-100; CANR 117;
EWL 3

Schwerner, Armand 1927-1999 .... **PC 42**
See also CA 9-12R; 179; CANR 50, 85; CP
2, 3, 4, 5, 6; DLB 165

**Schwitters, Kurt (Hermann Edward Karl
Julius)** 1887-1948 .... **TCLC 95**
See also CA 158

Schwob, Marcel (Mayer Andre)
1867-1905 .... **TCLC 20**
See also CA 117; 168; DLB 123; GFL 1789
to the Present

Sciascia, Leonardo 1921-1989 .. **CLC 8, 9, 41**
See also CA 85-88; 130; CANR 35; DLB
177; EWL 3; MTCW 1; RGWL 2, 3

Scoppettone, Sandra 1936- .... **CLC 26**
See Early, Jack
See also AAYA 11, 65; BYA 8; CA 5-8R;
CANR 41, 73; GLL 1; MAICYA 2; MAI-
CYAS 1; SATA 9, 92; WYA; YAW

Scorsese, Martin 1942- .... **CLC 20, 89, 207**
See also AAYA 38; CA 110; 114; CANR
46, 85

Scotland, Jay
See Jakes, John (William)

Scott, Duncan Campbell
1862-1947 .... **TCLC 6**
See also CA 104; 153; DAC; DLB 92;
RGEL 2

Scott, Evelyn 1893-1963 .... **CLC 43**
See also CA 104; 112; CANR 64; DLB 9,
48; RHW

Scott, F(rancis) R(eginald)
1899-1985 .... **CLC 22**
See also CA 101; 114; CANR 87; CP 1, 2,
3, 4; DLB 88; INT CA-101; RGEL 2

Scott, Frank
See Scott, F(rancis) R(eginald)

Scott, Joan .... **CLC 65**

Scott, Joanna 1960- .... **CLC 50**
See also CA 126; CANR 53, 92

Scott, Paul (Mark) 1920-1978 ...... **CLC 9, 60**
See also BRWS 1; CA 81-84; 77-80; CANR
33; CN 1, 2; DLB 14, 207, 326; EWL 3;
MTCW 1; RGEL 2; RHW; WWE 1

Scott, Ridley 1937- .... **CLC 183**
See also AAYA 13, 43

Scott, Sarah 1723-1795 .... **LC 44**
See also DLB 39

Scott, Sir Walter 1771-1832 .... **NCLC 15, 69,
110; PC 13; SSC 32; WLC 5**
See also AAYA 22; BRW 4; BYA 2; CD-
BLB 1789-1832; DA; DAB; DAC; DAM
MST, NOV, POET; DLB 93, 107, 116,
144, 159; GL 3; HGG; LAIT 1; RGEL 2;
RGSF 2; SSFS 10; SUFW 1; TEA; WLIT
3; YABC 2

Scribe, (Augustin) Eugene 1791-1861 . **DC 5;
NCLC 16**
See also DAM DRAM; DLB 192; GFL
1789 to the Present; RGWL 2, 3

Scrum, R.
See Crumb, R.

Scudery, Georges de 1601-1667 .... **LC 75**
See also GFL Beginnings to 1789

Scudery, Madeleine de 1607-1701 .. **LC 2, 58**
See also DLB 268; GFL Beginnings to 1789

Scum
See Crumb, R.

Scumbag, Little Bobby
See Crumb, R.

Seabrook, John
See Hubbard, L. Ron

Seacole, Mary Jane Grant
1805-1881 .... **NCLC 147**
See also DLB 166

Sealy, I(rwin) Allan 1951- .... **CLC 55**
See also CA 136; CN 6, 7

Search, Alexander
See Pessoa, Fernando (Antonio Nogueira)

Sebald, W(infried) G(eorg)
1944-2001 .... **CLC 194**
See also BRWS 8; CA 159; 202; CANR 98;
MTFW 2005; RGHL

Sebastian, Lee
See Silverberg, Robert

Sebastian Owl
See Thompson, Hunter S(tockton)

Sebestyen, Igen
See Sebestyen, Ouida

Sebestyen, Ouida 1924- .... **CLC 30**
See also AAYA 8; BYA 7; CA 107; CANR
40, 114; CLR 17; JRDA; MAICYA 1, 2;
SAAS 10; SATA 39, 140; WYA; YAW

Sebold, Alice 1963(?)- .... **CLC 193**
See also AAYA 56; CA 203; MTFW 2005

Second Duke of Buckingham
See Villiers, George

Secundus, H. Scriblerus
See Fielding, Henry

Sedges, John
See Buck, Pearl S(ydenstricker)

Sedgwick, Catharine Maria
1789-1867 .... **NCLC 19, 98**
See also DLB 1, 74, 183, 239, 243, 254; FL
1:3; RGAL 4

Sedulius Scottus 9th cent. -c. 874 .. **CMLC 86**

Seelye, John (Douglas) 1931- .... **CLC 7**
See also CA 97-100; CANR 70; INT CA-
97-100; TCWW 1, 2

Seferiades, Giorgos Stylianou 1900-1971
See Seferis, George
See also CA 5-8R; 33-36R; CANR 5, 36;
MTCW 1

Seferis, George .... **CLC 5, 11; PC 66**
See Seferiades, Giorgos Stylianou
See also EW 12; EWL 3; RGWL 2, 3

Segal, Erich (Wolf) 1937- .... **CLC 3, 10**
See also BEST 89:1; BPFB 3; CA 25-28R;
CANR 20, 36, 65, 113; CPW; DAM POP;
DLBY 1986; INT CANR-20; MTCW 1

Seger, Bob 1945- .... **CLC 35**

Seghers, Anna .... **CLC 7**
See Radvanyi, Netty
See also CDWLB 2; DLB 69; EWL 3

Seidel, Frederick (Lewis) 1936- .... **CLC 18**
See also CA 13-16R; CANR 8, 99; CP 1, 2,
3, 4, 5, 6, 7; DLBY 1984

Seifert, Jaroslav 1901-1986 . **CLC 34, 44, 93;
PC 47**
See also CA 127; CDWLB 4; DLB 215;
EWL 3; MTCW 1, 2

Sei Shonagon c. 966-1017(?) .... **CMLC 6**

Sejour, Victor 1817-1874 .... **DC 10**
See also DLB 50

Sejour Marcou et Ferrand, Juan Victor
See Sejour, Victor

Selby, Hubert, Jr. 1928-2004 ..... **CLC 1, 2, 4,
8; SSC 20**
See also CA 13-16R; 226; CANR 33, 85;
CN 1, 2, 3, 4, 5, 6, 7; DLB 2, 227; MAL
5

Selzer, Richard 1928- .... **CLC 74**
See also CA 65-68; CANR 14, 106

Sembene, Ousmane
See Ousmane, Sembene
See also AFW; EWL 3; WLIT 2

Senancour, Etienne Pivert de
1770-1846 .... **NCLC 16**
See also DLB 119; GFL 1789 to the Present

Sender, Ramon (Jose) 1902-1982 ...... **CLC 8;
HLC 2; TCLC 136**
See also CA 5-8R; 105; CANR 8; DAM
MULT; DLB 322; EWL 3; HW 1; MTCW
1; RGWL 2, 3

Seneca, Lucius Annaeus c. 4B.C.-c.
65 .... **CMLC 6; DC 5**
See also AW 2; CDWLB 1; DAM DRAM;
DLB 211; RGWL 2, 3; TWA; WLIT 8

Senghor, Leopold Sedar 1906-2001 ... **BLC 3;
CLC 54, 130; PC 25**
See also AFW; BW 2; CA 116; 125; 203;
CANR 47, 74, 134; CWW 2; DAM
MULT, POET; DNFS 2; EWL 3; GFL
1789 to the Present; MTCW 1, 2; MTFW
2005; TWA

Senior, Olive (Marjorie) 1941- .... **SSC 78**
See also BW 3; CA 154; CANR 86, 126;
CN 6; CP 6, 7; CWP; DLB 157; EWL 3;
RGSF 2

Senna, Danzy 1970- .... **CLC 119**
See also CA 169; CANR 130

Serling, (Edward) Rod(man)
1924-1975 .... **CLC 30**
See also AAYA 14; AITN 1; CA 162; 57-
60; DLB 26; SFW 4

Serna, Ramon Gomez de la
See Gomez de la Serna, Ramon

Serpieres
See Guillevic, (Eugene)

Service, Robert
See Service, Robert W(illiam)
See also BYA 4; DAB; DLB 92

Service, Robert W(illiam)
1874(?)-1958 ... **PC 70; TCLC 15; WLC
5**
See Service, Robert
See also CA 115; 140; CANR 84; DA;
DAC; DAM MST, POET; PFS 10; RGEL
2; SATA 20

Seth, Vikram 1952- .... **CLC 43, 90**
See also BRWS 10; CA 121; 127; CANR
50, 74, 131; CN 6, 7; CP 5, 6, 7; DA3;
DAM MULT; DLB 120, 271, 282, 323;
EWL 3; INT CA-127; MTCW 2; MTFW
2005; WWE 1

Seton, Cynthia Propper 1926-1982 .. **CLC 27**
See also CA 5-8R; 108; CANR 7

Seton, Ernest (Evan) Thompson
1860-1946 .... **TCLC 31**
See also ANW; BYA 3; CA 109; 204; CLR
59; DLB 92; DLBD 13; JRDA; SATA 18

Seton-Thompson, Ernest
See Seton, Ernest (Evan) Thompson

Settle, Mary Lee 1918-2005 .... **CLC 19, 61**
See also BPFB 3; CA 89-92; 243; CAAS 1;
CANR 44, 87, 126; CN 6, 7; CSW; DLB
6; INT CA-89-92

Seuphor, Michel
See Arp, Jean

Sevigne, Marie (de Rabutin-Chantal)
1626-1696 .... **LC 11**
See Sevigne, Marie de Rabutin Chantal
See also GFL Beginnings to 1789; TWA

Sevigne, Marie de Rabutin Chantal
See Sevigne, Marie (de Rabutin-Chantal)
See also DLB 268

Sewall, Samuel 1652-1730 .... **LC 38**
See also DLB 24; RGAL 4

Sexton, Anne (Harvey) 1928-1974 ..... **CLC 2, 4, 6, 8, 10, 15, 53, 123; PC 2; WLC 5**
See also AMWS 2; CA 1-4R; 53-56; CABS 2; CANR 3, 36; CDALB 1941-1968; CP 1, 2; DA; DA3; DAB; DAC; DAM MST, POET; DLB 5, 169; EWL 3; EXPP; FL 1:6; FW; MAL 5; MBL; MTCW 1, 2; MTFW 2005; PAB; PFS 4, 14; RGAL 4; RGHL; SATA 10; TUS

Shaara, Jeff 1952- .... **CLC 119**
See also AAYA 70; CA 163; CANR 109; CN 7; MTFW 2005

Shaara, Michael (Joseph, Jr.)
1929-1988 .... **CLC 15**
See also AAYA 71; AITN 1; BPFB 3; CA 102; 125; CANR 52, 85; DAM POP; DLBY 1983; MTFW 2005

Shackleton, C. C.
See Aldiss, Brian W(ilson)

Shacochis, Bob .... **CLC 39**
See Shacochis, Robert G.

Shacochis, Robert G. 1951-
See Shacochis, Bob
See also CA 119; 124; CANR 100; INT CA-124

Shadwell, Thomas 1641(?)-1692 .... **LC 114**
See also DLB 80; IDTP; RGEL 2

Shaffer, Anthony 1926-2001 .... **CLC 19**
See also CA 110; 116; 200; CBD; CD 5, 6; DAM DRAM; DFS 13; DLB 13

Shaffer, Anthony Joshua
See Shaffer, Anthony

Shaffer, Peter (Levin) 1926- .. **CLC 5, 14, 18, 37, 60; DC 7**
See also BRWS 1; CA 25-28R; CANR 25, 47, 74, 118; CBD; CD 5, 6; CDBLB 1960 to Present; DA3; DAB; DAM DRAM, MST; DFS 5, 13; DLB 13, 233; EWL 3; MTCW 1, 2; MTFW 2005; RGEL 2; TEA

Shakespeare, William 1564-1616 .... **WLC 5**
See also AAYA 35; BRW 1; CDBLB Before 1660; DA; DA3; DAB; DAC; DAM DRAM, MST, POET; DFS 20, 21; DLB 62, 172, 263; EXPP; LAIT 1; LATS 1:1; LMFS 1; PAB; PFS 1, 2, 3, 4, 5, 8, 9; RGEL 2; TEA; WLIT 3; WP; WS; WYA

Shakey, Bernard
See Young, Neil

Shalamov, Varlam (Tikhonovich)
1907-1982 .... **CLC 18**
See also CA 129; 105; DLB 302; RGSF 2

Shamloo, Ahmad
See Shamlu, Ahmad

Shamlou, Ahmad
See Shamlu, Ahmad

Shamlu, Ahmad 1925-2000 .... **CLC 10**
See also CA 216; CWW 2

Shammas, Anton 1951- .... **CLC 55**
See also CA 199

Shandling, Arline
See Berriault, Gina

Shange, Ntozake 1948- ... **BLC 3; CLC 8, 25, 38, 74, 126; DC 3**
See also AAYA 9, 66; AFAW 1, 2; BW 2; CA 85-88; CABS 3; CAD; CANR 27, 48, 74, 131; CD 5, 6; CP 5, 6, 7; CWD; CWP; DA3; DAM DRAM, MULT; DFS 2, 11; DLB 38, 249; FW; LAIT 4, 5; MAL 5; MTCW 1, 2; MTFW 2005; NFS 11; RGAL 4; SATA 157; YAW

Shanley, John Patrick 1950- .... **CLC 75**
See also AMWS 14; CA 128; 133; CAD; CANR 83, 154; CD 5, 6; DFS 23

Shapcott, Thomas W(illiam) 1935- .. **CLC 38**
See also CA 69-72; CANR 49, 83, 103; CP 1, 2, 3, 4, 5, 6, 7; DLB 289

Shapiro, Jane 1942- .... **CLC 76**
See also CA 196

Shapiro, Karl (Jay) 1913-2000 ...... **CLC 4, 8, 15, 53; PC 25**
See also AMWS 2; CA 1-4R; 188; CAAS 6; CANR 1, 36, 66; CP 1, 2, 3, 4, 5, 6; DLB 48; EWL 3; EXPP; MAL 5; MTCW 1, 2; MTFW 2005; PFS 3; RGAL 4

Sharp, William 1855-1905 .... **TCLC 39**
See Macleod, Fiona
See also CA 160; DLB 156; RGEL 2

Sharpe, Thomas Ridley 1928-
See Sharpe, Tom
See also CA 114; 122; CANR 85; INT CA-122

Sharpe, Tom .... **CLC 36**
See Sharpe, Thomas Ridley
See also CN 4, 5, 6, 7; DLB 14, 231

Shatrov, Mikhail .... **CLC 59**

Shaw, Bernard
See Shaw, George Bernard
See also DLB 10, 57, 190

Shaw, G. Bernard
See Shaw, George Bernard

Shaw, George Bernard 1856-1950 ..... **DC 23; TCLC 3, 9, 21, 45; WLC 5**
See Shaw, Bernard
See also AAYA 61; BRW 6; BRWC 1; BRWR 2; CA 104; 128; CDBLB 1914-1945; DA; DA3; DAB; DAC; DAM DRAM, MST; DFS 1, 3, 6, 11, 19, 22; EWL 3; LAIT 3; LATS 1:1; MTCW 1, 2; MTFW 2005; RGEL 2; TEA; WLIT 4

Shaw, Henry Wheeler 1818-1885 .. **NCLC 15**
See also DLB 11; RGAL 4

Shaw, Irwin 1913-1984 .... **CLC 7, 23, 34**
See also AITN 1; BPFB 3; CA 13-16R; 112; CANR 21; CDALB 1941-1968; CN 1, 2, 3; CPW; DAM DRAM, POP; DLB 6, 102; DLBY 1984; MAL 5; MTCW 1, 21; MTFW 2005

Shaw, Robert (Archibald)
1927-1978 .... **CLC 5**
See also AITN 1; CA 1-4R; 81-84; CANR 4; CN 1, 2; DLB 13, 14

Shaw, T. E.
See Lawrence, T(homas) E(dward)

Shawn, Wallace 1943- .... **CLC 41**
See also CA 112; CAD; CD 5, 6; DLB 266

Shaykh, al- Hanan
See al-Shaykh, Hanan
See also CWW 2; EWL 3

Shchedrin, N.
See Saltykov, Mikhail Evgrafovich

Shea, Lisa 1953- .... **CLC 86**
See also CA 147

Sheed, Wilfrid (John Joseph) 1930- . **CLC 2, 4, 10, 53**
See also CA 65-68; CANR 30, 66; CN 1, 2, 3, 4, 5, 6, 7; DLB 6; MAL 5; MTCW 1, 2; MTFW 2005

Sheehy, Gail 1937- .... **CLC 171**
See also CA 49-52; CANR 1, 33, 55, 92; CPW; MTCW 1

Sheldon, Alice Hastings Bradley
1915(?)-1987
See Tiptree, James, Jr.
See also CA 108; 122; CANR 34; INT CA-108; MTCW 1

Sheldon, John
See Bloch, Robert (Albert)

Sheldon, Walter J(ames) 1917-1996
See Queen, Ellery
See also AITN 1; CA 25-28R; CANR 10

Shelley, Mary Wollstonecraft (Godwin)
1797-1851 .... **NCLC 14, 59, 103, 170; SSC 92; WLC 5**
See also AAYA 20; BPFB 3; BRW 3; BRWC 2; BRWS 3; BYA 5; CDBLB 1789-1832; DA; DA3; DAB; DAC; DAM MST, NOV; DLB 110, 116, 159, 178; EXPN; FL 1:3; GL 3; HGG; LAIT 1; LMFS 1, 2; NFS 1; RGEL 2; SATA 29; SCFW 1, 2; SFW 4; TEA; WLIT 3

Shelley, Percy Bysshe 1792-1822 .. **NCLC 18, 93, 143; PC 14, 67; WLC 5**
See also AAYA 61; BRW 4; BRWR 1; CDBLB 1789-1832; DA; DA3; DAB; DAC; DAM MST, POET; DLB 96, 110, 158; EXPP; LMFS 1; PAB; PFS 2; RGEL 2; TEA; WLIT 3; WP

Shepard, James R. .... **CLC 36**
See also CA 137; CANR 59, 104; SATA 90, 164

Shepard, Jim
See Shepard, James R.

Shepard, Lucius 1947- .... **CLC 34**
See also CA 128; 141; CANR 81, 124; HGG; SCFW 2; SFW 4; SUFW 2

Shepard, Sam 1943- .... **CLC 4, 6, 17, 34, 41, 44, 169; DC 5**
See also AAYA 1, 58; AMWS 3; CA 69-72; CABS 3; CAD; CANR 22, 120, 140; CD 5, 6; DA3; DAM DRAM; DFS 3, 6, 7, 14; DLB 7, 212; EWL 3; IDFW 3, 4; MAL 5; MTCW 1, 2; MTFW 2005; RGAL 4

Shepherd, Jean (Parker)
1921-1999 .... **TCLC 177**
See also AAYA 69; AITN 2; CA 77-80; 187

Shepherd, Michael
See Ludlum, Robert

Sherburne, Zoa (Lillian Morin)
1912-1995 .... **CLC 30**
See also AAYA 13; CA 1-4R; 176; CANR 3, 37; MAICYA 1, 2; SAAS 18; SATA 3; YAW

Sheridan, Frances 1724-1766 .... **LC 7**
See also DLB 39, 84

Sheridan, Richard Brinsley
1751-1816 . **DC 1; NCLC 5, 91; WLC 5**
See also BRW 3; CDBLB 1660-1789; DA; DAB; DAC; DAM DRAM, MST; DFS 15; DLB 89; WLIT 3

Sherman, Jonathan Marc 1968- .... **CLC 55**
See also CA 230

Sherman, Martin 1941(?)- .... **CLC 19**
See also CA 116; 123; CAD; CANR 86; CD 5, 6; DFS 20; DLB 228; GLL 1; IDTP; RGHL

Sherwin, Judith Johnson
See Johnson, Judith (Emlyn)
See also CANR 85; CP 2, 3, 4, 5; CWP

Sherwood, Frances 1940- .... **CLC 81**
See also CA 146; 220; CAAE 220

Sherwood, Robert E(mmet)
1896-1955 .... **TCLC 3**
See also CA 104; 153; CANR 86; DAM DRAM; DFS 11, 15, 17; DLB 7, 26, 249; IDFW 3, 4; MAL 5; RGAL 4

Shestov, Lev 1866-1938 .... **TCLC 56**

Shevchenko, Taras 1814-1861 .... **NCLC 54**

Shiel, M(atthew) P(hipps)
1865-1947 .... **TCLC 8**
See Holmes, Gordon
See also CA 106; 160; DLB 153; HGG; MTCW 2; MTFW 2005; SCFW 1, 2; SFW 4; SUFW

Shields, Carol (Ann) 1935-2003 ...... **CLC 91, 113, 193**
See also AMWS 7; CA 81-84; 218; CANR 51, 74, 98, 133; CCA 1; CN 6, 7; CPW; DA3; DAC; MTCW 2; MTFW 2005; NFS 23

Shields, David (Jonathan) 1956- ...... **CLC 97**
See also CA 124; CANR 48, 99, 112

Shiga, Naoya 1883-1971 .... **CLC 33; SSC 23; TCLC 172**
See Shiga Naoya
See also CA 101; 33-36R; MJW; RGWL 3

Shiga Naoya
See Shiga, Naoya
See also DLB 180; EWL 3; RGWL 3

Shilts, Randy 1951-1994 .... **CLC 85**
See also AAYA 19; CA 115; 127; 144;
CANR 45; DA3; GLL 1; INT CA-127;
MTCW 2; MTFW 2005

Shimazaki, Haruki 1872-1943
See Shimazaki Toson
See also CA 105; 134; CANR 84; RGWL 3

Shimazaki Toson .... **TCLC 5**
See Shimazaki, Haruki
See also DLB 180; EWL 3

Shirley, James 1596-1666 .... **DC 25; LC 96**
See also DLB 58; RGEL 2

Sholokhov, Mikhail (Aleksandrovich)
1905-1984 .... **CLC 7, 15**
See also CA 101; 112; DLB 272; EWL 3;
MTCW 1, 2; MTFW 2005; RGWL 2, 3;
SATA-Obit 36

Shone, Patric
See Hanley, James

Showalter, Elaine 1941- .... **CLC 169**
See also CA 57-60; CANR 58, 106; DLB
67; FW; GLL 2

Shreve, Susan
See Shreve, Susan Richards

Shreve, Susan Richards 1939- .... **CLC 23**
See also CA 49-52; CAAS 5; CANR 5, 38,
69, 100; MAICYA 1, 2; SATA 46, 95, 152;
SATA-Brief 41

Shue, Larry 1946-1985 .... **CLC 52**
See also CA 145; 117; DAM DRAM; DFS
7

Shu-Jen, Chou 1881-1936
See Lu Hsun
See also CA 104

Shulman, Alix Kates 1932- .... **CLC 2, 10**
See also CA 29-32R; CANR 43; FW; SATA
7

Shuster, Joe 1914-1992 .... **CLC 21**
See also AAYA 50

Shute, Nevil .... **CLC 30**
See Norway, Nevil Shute
See also BPFB 3; DLB 255; NFS 9; RHW;
SFW 4

Shuttle, Penelope (Diane) 1947- .... **CLC 7**
See also CA 93-96; CANR 39, 84, 92, 108;
CP 3, 4, 5, 6, 7; CWP; DLB 14, 40

Shvarts, Elena 1948- .... **PC 50**
See also CA 147

Sidhwa, Bapsi 1939-
See Sidhwa, Bapsy (N.)
See also CN 6, 7; DLB 323

Sidhwa, Bapsy (N.) 1938- .... **CLC 168**
See Sidhwa, Bapsi
See also CA 108; CANR 25, 57; FW

Sidney, Mary 1561-1621 .... **LC 19, 39**
See Sidney Herbert, Mary

Sidney, Sir Philip 1554-1586 .... **LC 19, 39, 131; PC 32**
See also BRW 1; BRWR 2; CDBLB Before
1660; DA; DA3; DAB; DAC; DAM MST,
POET; DLB 167; EXPP; PAB; RGEL 2;
TEA; WP

Sidney Herbert, Mary
See Sidney, Mary
See also DLB 167

Siegel, Jerome 1914-1996 .... **CLC 21**
See Siegel, Jerry
See also CA 116; 169; 151

Siegel, Jerry
See Siegel, Jerome
See also AAYA 50

Sienkiewicz, Henryk (Adam Alexander Pius)
1846-1916 .... **TCLC 3**
See also CA 104; 134; CANR 84; EWL 3;
RGSF 2; RGWL 2, 3

Sierra, Gregorio Martinez
See Martinez Sierra, Gregorio

Sierra, Maria (de la O'LeJarraga) Martinez
See Martinez Sierra, Maria (de la
O'LeJarraga)

Sigal, Clancy 1926- .... **CLC 7**
See also CA 1-4R; CANR 85; CN 1, 2, 3,
4, 5, 6, 7

Siger of Brabant 1240(?)-1284(?) . **CMLC 69**
See also DLB 115

Sigourney, Lydia H.
See Sigourney, Lydia Howard (Huntley)
See also DLB 73, 183

Sigourney, Lydia Howard (Huntley)
1791-1865 .... **NCLC 21, 87**
See Sigourney, Lydia H.; Sigourney, Lydia
Huntley
See also DLB 1

Sigourney, Lydia Huntley
See Sigourney, Lydia Howard (Huntley)
See also DLB 42, 239, 243

Siguenza y Gongora, Carlos de
1645-1700 .... **HLCS 2; LC 8**
See also LAW

Sigurjonsson, Johann
See Sigurjonsson, Johann

Sigurjonsson, Johann 1880-1919 ... **TCLC 27**
See also CA 170; DLB 293; EWL 3

Sikelianos, Angelos 1884-1951 .... **PC 29; TCLC 39**
See also EWL 3; RGWL 2, 3

Silkin, Jon 1930-1997 .... **CLC 2, 6, 43**
See also CA 5-8R; CAAS 5; CANR 89; CP
1, 2, 3, 4, 5, 6; DLB 27

Silko, Leslie (Marmon) 1948- .... **CLC 23, 74, 114, 211; NNAL; SSC 37, 66; WLCS**
See also AAYA 14; AMWS 4; ANW; BYA
12; CA 115; 122; CANR 45, 65, 118; CN
4, 5, 6, 7; CP 4, 5, 6, 7; CPW 1; CWP;
DA; DA3; DAC; DAM MST, MULT,
POP; DLB 143, 175, 256, 275; EWL 3;
EXPP; EXPS; LAIT 4; MAL 5; MTCW
2; MTFW 2005; NFS 4; PFS 9, 16; RGAL
4; RGSF 2; SSFS 4, 8, 10, 11; TCWW 1,
2

Sillanpaa, Frans Eemil 1888-1964 ... **CLC 19**
See also CA 129; 93-96; EWL 3; MTCW 1

Sillitoe, Alan 1928- .. **CLC 1, 3, 6, 10, 19, 57, 148**
See also AITN 1; BRWS 5; CA 9-12R; 191;
CAAE 191; CAAS 2; CANR 8, 26, 55,
139; CDBLB 1960 to Present; CN 1, 2, 3,
4, 5, 6; CP 1, 2, 3, 4, 5; DLB 14, 139;
EWL 3; MTCW 1, 2; MTFW 2005; RGEL
2; RGSF 2; SATA 61

Silone, Ignazio 1900-1978 .... **CLC 4**
See also CA 25-28; 81-84; CANR 34; CAP
2; DLB 264; EW 12; EWL 3; MTCW 1;
RGSF 2; RGWL 2, 3

Silone, Ignazione
See Silone, Ignazio

Silver, Joan Micklin 1935- .... **CLC 20**
See also CA 114; 121; INT CA-121

Silver, Nicholas
See Faust, Frederick (Schiller)

Silverberg, Robert 1935- .... **CLC 7, 140**
See also AAYA 24; BPFB 3; BYA 7, 9; CA
1-4R; 186; CAAE 186; CAAS 3; CANR
1, 20, 36, 85, 140; CLR 59; CN 6, 7;
CPW; DAM POP; DLB 8; INT CANR-

20; MAICYA 1, 2; MTCW 1, 2; MTFW
2005; SATA 13, 91; SATA-Essay 104;
SCFW 1, 2; SFW 4; SUFW 2

Silverstein, Alvin 1933- .... **CLC 17**
See also CA 49-52; CANR 2; CLR 25;
JRDA; MAICYA 1, 2; SATA 8, 69, 124

Silverstein, Shel(don Allan)
1932-1999 .... **PC 49**
See also AAYA 40; BW 3; CA 107; 179;
CANR 47, 74, 81; CLR 5, 96; CWRI 5;
JRDA; MAICYA 1, 2; MTCW 2; MTFW
2005; SATA 33, 92; SATA-Brief 27;
SATA-Obit 116

Silverstein, Virginia B(arbara Opshelor)
1937- .... **CLC 17**
See also CA 49-52; CANR 2; CLR 25;
JRDA; MAICYA 1, 2; SATA 8, 69, 124

Sim, Georges
See Simenon, Georges (Jacques Christian)

Simak, Clifford D(onald) 1904-1988 . **CLC 1, 55**
See also CA 1-4R; 125; CANR 1, 35; DLB
8; MTCW 1; SATA-Obit 56; SCFW 1, 2;
SFW 4

Simenon, Georges (Jacques Christian)
1903-1989 .... **CLC 1, 2, 3, 8, 18, 47**
See also BPFB 3; CA 85-88; 129; CANR
35; CMW 4; DA3; DAM POP; DLB 72;
DLBY 1989; EW 12; EWL 3; GFL 1789
to the Present; MSW; MTCW 1, 2; MTFW
2005; RGWL 2, 3

Simic, Charles 1938- .... **CLC 6, 9, 22, 49, 68, 130; PC 69**
See also AMWS 8; CA 29-32R; CAAS 4;
CANR 12, 33, 52, 61, 96, 140; CP 2, 3, 4,
5, 6, 7; DA3; DAM POET; DLB 105;
MAL 5; MTCW 2; MTFW 2005; PFS 7;
RGAL 4; WP

Simmel, Georg 1858-1918 .... **TCLC 64**
See also CA 157; DLB 296

Simmons, Charles (Paul) 1924- .... **CLC 57**
See also CA 89-92; INT CA-89-92

Simmons, Dan 1948- .... **CLC 44**
See also AAYA 16, 54; CA 138; CANR 53,
81, 126; CPW; DAM POP; HGG; SUFW
2

Simmons, James (Stewart Alexander)
1933- .... **CLC 43**
See also CA 105; CAAS 21; CP 1, 2, 3, 4,
5, 6, 7; DLB 40

Simms, William Gilmore
1806-1870 .... **NCLC 3**
See also DLB 3, 30, 59, 73, 248, 254;
RGAL 4

Simon, Carly 1945- .... **CLC 26**
See also CA 105

Simon, Claude 1913-2005 ... **CLC 4, 9, 15, 39**
See also CA 89-92; 241; CANR 33, 117;
CWW 2; DAM NOV; DLB 83; EW 13;
EWL 3; GFL 1789 to the Present; MTCW
1

Simon, Claude Eugene Henri
See Simon, Claude

Simon, Claude Henri Eugene
See Simon, Claude

Simon, Marvin Neil
See Simon, Neil

Simon, Myles
See Follett, Ken(neth Martin)

Simon, Neil 1927- .... **CLC 6, 11, 31, 39, 70; DC 14**
See also AAYA 32; AITN 1; AMWS 4; CA
21-24R; CAD; CANR 26, 54, 87, 126;
CD 5, 6; DA3; DAM DRAM; DFS 2, 6,
12, 18; DLB 7, 266; LAIT 4; MAL 5;
MTCW 1, 2; MTFW 2005; RGAL 4; TUS

Simon, Paul 1941(?)- .... **CLC 17**
See also CA 116; 153; CANR 152

Smith, Stevie 1902-1971 .... **CLC 3, 8, 25, 44; PC 12**
See also BRWS 2; CA 17-18; 29-32R; CANR 35; CAP 2; CP 1; DAM POET; DLB 20; EWL 3; MTCW 1, 2; PAB; PFS 3; RGEL 2; TEA

Smith, Wilbur (Addison) 1933- .... **CLC 33**
See also CA 13-16R; CANR 7, 46, 66, 134; CPW; MTCW 1, 2; MTFW 2005

Smith, William Jay 1918- .... **CLC 6**
See also AMWS 13; CA 5-8R; CANR 44, 106; CP 1, 2, 3, 4, 5, 6, 7; CSW; CWRI 5; DLB 5; MAICYA 1, 2; SAAS 22; SATA 2, 68, 154; SATA-Essay 154; TCLE 1:2

Smith, Woodrow Wilson
See Kuttner, Henry

Smith, Zadie 1975- .... **CLC 158**
See also AAYA 50; CA 193; MTFW 2005

Smolenskin, Peretz 1842-1885 .... **NCLC 30**

Smollett, Tobias (George) 1721-1771 ... **LC 2, 46**
See also BRW 3; CDBLB 1660-1789; DLB 39, 104; RGEL 2; TEA

Snodgrass, W(illiam) D(e Witt) 1926- .... **CLC 2, 6, 10, 18, 68**
See also AMWS 6; CA 1-4R; CANR 6, 36, 65, 85; CP 1, 2, 3, 4, 5, 6, 7; DAM POET; DLB 5; MAL 5; MTCW 1, 2; MTFW 2005; RGAL 4; TCLE 1:2

Snorri Sturluson 1179-1241 .... **CMLC 56**
See also RGWL 2, 3

Snow, C(harles) P(ercy) 1905-1980 ... **CLC 1, 4, 6, 9, 13, 19**
See also BRW 7; CA 5-8R; 101; CANR 28; CDBLB 1945-1960; CN 1, 2; DAM NOV; DLB 15, 77; DLBD 17; EWL 3; MTCW 1, 2; MTFW 2005; RGEL 2; TEA

Snow, Frances Compton
See Adams, Henry (Brooks)

Snyder, Gary (Sherman) 1930- . **CLC 1, 2, 5, 9, 32, 120; PC 21**
See also AMWS 8; ANW; BG 1:3; CA 17-20R; CANR 30, 60, 125; CP 1, 2, 3, 4, 5, 6, 7; DA3; DAM POET; DLB 5, 16, 165, 212, 237, 275; EWL 3; MAL 5; MTCW 2; MTFW 2005; PFS 9, 19; RGAL 4; WP

Snyder, Zilpha Keatley 1927- .... **CLC 17**
See also AAYA 15; BYA 1; CA 9-12R; CANR 38; CLR 31; JRDA; MAICYA 1, 2; SAAS 2; SATA 1, 28, 75, 110, 163; SATA-Essay 112, 163; YAW

Soares, Bernardo
See Pessoa, Fernando (Antonio Nogueira)

Sobh, A.
See Shamlu, Ahmad

Sobh, Alef
See Shamlu, Ahmad

Sobol, Joshua 1939- .... **CLC 60**
See Sobol, Yehoshua
See also CA 200; RGHL

Sobol, Yehoshua 1939-
See Sobol, Joshua
See also CWW 2

Socrates 470B.C.-399B.C. .... **CMLC 27**

Soderberg, Hjalmar 1869-1941 ...... **TCLC 39**
See also DLB 259; EWL 3; RGSF 2

Soderbergh, Steven 1963- .... **CLC 154**
See also AAYA 43; CA 243

Soderbergh, Steven Andrew
See Soderbergh, Steven

Sodergran, Edith (Irene) 1892-1923
See Soedergran, Edith (Irene)
See also CA 202; DLB 259; EW 11; EWL 3; RGWL 2, 3

Soedergran, Edith (Irene) 1892-1923 .... **TCLC 31**
See Sodergran, Edith (Irene)

Softly, Edgar
See Lovecraft, H. P.

Softly, Edward
See Lovecraft, H. P.

Sokolov, Alexander V(sevolodovich) 1943-
See Sokolov, Sasha
See also CA 73-76

Sokolov, Raymond 1941- .... **CLC 7**
See also CA 85-88

Sokolov, Sasha .... **CLC 59**
See Sokolov, Alexander V(sevolodovich)
See also CWW 2; DLB 285; EWL 3; RGWL 2, 3

Solo, Jay
See Ellison, Harlan (Jay)

Sologub, Fyodor .... **TCLC 9**
See Teternikov, Fyodor Kuzmich
See also EWL 3

Solomons, Ikey Esquir
See Thackeray, William Makepeace

Solomos, Dionysios 1798-1857 .... **NCLC 15**

Solwoska, Mara
See French, Marilyn

Solzhenitsyn, Aleksandr I. 1918- .. **CLC 1, 2, 4, 7, 9, 10, 18, 26, 34, 78, 134; SSC 32; WLC 5**
See Solzhenitsyn, Aleksandr Isayevich
See also AAYA 49; AITN 1; BPFB 3; CA 69-72; CANR 40, 65, 116; DA; DA3; DAB; DAC; DAM MST, NOV; DLB 302; EW 13; EXPS; LAIT 4; MTCW 1, 2; MTFW 2005; NFS 6; RGSF 2; RGWL 2, 3; SSFS 9; TWA

Solzhenitsyn, Aleksandr Isayevich
See Solzhenitsyn, Aleksandr I.
See also CWW 2; EWL 3

Somers, Jane
See Lessing, Doris (May)

Somerville, Edith Oenone 1858-1949 .... **SSC 56; TCLC 51**
See also CA 196; DLB 135; RGEL 2; RGSF 2

Somerville & Ross
See Martin, Violet Florence; Somerville, Edith Oenone

Sommer, Scott 1951- .... **CLC 25**
See also CA 106

Sommers, Christina Hoff 1950- ...... **CLC 197**
See also CA 153; CANR 95

Sondheim, Stephen (Joshua) 1930- . **CLC 30, 39, 147; DC 22**
See also AAYA 11, 66; CA 103; CANR 47, 67, 125; DAM DRAM; LAIT 4

Sone, Monica 1919- .... **AAL**
See also DLB 312

Song, Cathy 1955- .... **AAL; PC 21**
See also CA 154; CANR 118; CWP; DLB 169, 312; EXPP; FW; PFS 5

Sontag, Susan 1933-2004 ... **CLC 1, 2, 10, 13, 31, 105, 195**
See also AMWS 3; CA 17-20R; 234; CANR 25, 51, 74, 97; CN 1, 2, 3, 4, 5, 6, 7; CPW; DA3; DAM POP; DLB 2, 67; EWL 3; MAL 5; MBL; MTCW 1, 2; MTFW 2005; RGAL 4; RHW; SSFS 10

Sophocles 496(?)B.C.-406(?)B.C. .... **CMLC 2, 47, 51, 86; DC 1; WLCS**
See also AW 1; CDWLB 1; DA; DA3; DAB; DAC; DAM DRAM, MST; DFS 1, 4, 8; DLB 176; LAIT 1; LATS 1:1; LMFS 1; RGWL 2, 3; TWA; WLIT 8

Sordello 1189-1269 .... **CMLC 15**

Sorel, Georges 1847-1922 .... **TCLC 91**
See also CA 118; 188

Sorel, Julia
See Drexler, Rosalyn

Sorokin, Vladimir .... **CLC 59**
See Sorokin, Vladimir Georgievich

Sorokin, Vladimir Georgievich
See Sorokin, Vladimir
See also DLB 285

Sorrentino, Gilbert 1929-2006 .... **CLC 3, 7, 14, 22, 40**
See also CA 77-80; CANR 14, 33, 115; CN 3, 4, 5, 6, 7; CP 1, 2, 3, 4, 5, 6, 7; DLB 5, 173; DLBY 1980; INT CANR-14

Soseki
See Natsume, Soseki
See also MJW

Soto, Gary 1952- ... **CLC 32, 80; HLC 2; PC 28**
See also AAYA 10, 37; BYA 11; CA 119; 125; CANR 50, 74, 107; CLR 38; CP 4, 5, 6, 7; DAM MULT; DLB 82; EWL 3; EXPP; HW 1, 2; INT CA-125; JRDA; LLW; MAICYA 2; MAICYAS 1; MAL 5; MTCW 2; MTFW 2005; PFS 7; RGAL 4; SATA 80, 120; WYA; YAW

Soupault, Philippe 1897-1990 .... **CLC 68**
See also CA 116; 147; 131; EWL 3; GFL 1789 to the Present; LMFS 2

Souster, (Holmes) Raymond 1921- .... **CLC 5, 14**
See also CA 13-16R; CAAS 14; CANR 13, 29, 53; CP 1, 2, 3, 4, 5, 6, 7; DA3; DAC; DAM POET; DLB 88; RGEL 2; SATA 63

Southern, Terry 1924(?)-1995 .... **CLC 7**
See also AMWS 11; BPFB 3; CA 1-4R; 150; CANR 1, 55, 107; CN 1, 2, 3, 4, 5, 6; DLB 2; IDFW 3, 4

Southerne, Thomas 1660-1746 .... **LC 99**
See also DLB 80; RGEL 2

Southey, Robert 1774-1843 .... **NCLC 8, 97**
See also BRW 4; DLB 93, 107, 142; RGEL 2; SATA 54

Southwell, Robert 1561(?)-1595 .... **LC 108**
See also DLB 167; RGEL 2; TEA

Southworth, Emma Dorothy Eliza Nevitte 1819-1899 .... **NCLC 26**
See also DLB 239

Souza, Ernest
See Scott, Evelyn

Soyinka, Wole 1934- .. **BLC 3; CLC 3, 5, 14, 36, 44, 179; DC 2; WLC 5**
See also AFW; BW 2, 3; CA 13-16R; CANR 27, 39, 82, 136; CD 5, 6; CDWLB 3; CN 6, 7; CP 1, 2, 3, 4, 5, 6 ,7; DA; DA3; DAB; DAC; DAM DRAM, MST, MULT; DFS 10; DLB 125; EWL 3; MTCW 1, 2; MTFW 2005; RGEL 2; TWA; WLIT 2; WWE 1

Spackman, W(illiam) M(ode) 1905-1990 .... **CLC 46**
See also CA 81-84; 132

Spacks, Barry (Bernard) 1931- .... **CLC 14**
See also CA 154; CANR 33, 109; CP 3, 4, 5, 6, 7; DLB 105

Spanidou, Irini 1946- .... **CLC 44**
See also CA 185

Spark, Muriel (Sarah) 1918-2006 . **CLC 2, 3, 5, 8, 13, 18, 40, 94; PC 72; SSC 10**
See also BRWS 1; CA 5-8R; CANR 12, 36, 76, 89, 131; CDBLB 1945-1960; CN 1, 2, 3, 4, 5, 6, 7; CP 1, 2, 3, 4, 5, 6, 7; DA3; DAB; DAC; DAM MST, NOV; DLB 15, 139; EWL 3; FW; INT CANR-12; LAIT 4; MTCW 1, 2; MTFW 2005; NFS 22; RGEL 2; TEA; WLIT 4; YAW

Spaulding, Douglas
See Bradbury, Ray (Douglas)

Spaulding, Leonard
See Bradbury, Ray (Douglas)

Speght, Rachel 1597-c. 1630 .... **LC 97**
See also DLB 126

Spence, J. A. D.
See Eliot, T(homas) S(tearns)

Stephens, James 1882(?)-1950 .... **SSC 50; TCLC 4**
    See also CA 104; 192; DLB 19, 153, 162; EWL 3; FANT; RGEL 2; SUFW

Stephens, Reed
    See Donaldson, Stephen R(eeder)

Steptoe, Lydia
    See Barnes, Djuna
    See also GLL 1

Sterchi, Beat 1949- .... **CLC 65**
    See also CA 203

Sterling, Brett
    See Bradbury, Ray (Douglas); Hamilton, Edmond

Sterling, Bruce 1954- .... **CLC 72**
    See also CA 119; CANR 44, 135; CN 7; MTFW 2005; SCFW 2; SFW 4

Sterling, George 1869-1926 .... **TCLC 20**
    See also CA 117; 165; DLB 54

Stern, Gerald 1925- .... **CLC 40, 100**
    See also AMWS 9; CA 81-84; CANR 28, 94; CP 3, 4, 5, 6, 7; DLB 105; RGAL 4

Stern, Richard (Gustave) 1928- .. **CLC 4, 39**
    See also CA 1-4R; CANR 1, 25, 52, 120; CN 1, 2, 3, 4, 5, 6, 7; DLB 218; DLBY 1987; INT CANR-25

Sternberg, Josef von 1894-1969 .... **CLC 20**
    See also CA 81-84

Sterne, Laurence 1713-1768 .... **LC 2, 48; WLC 5**
    See also BRW 3; BRWC 1; CDBLB 1660-1789; DA; DAB; DAC; DAM MST, NOV; DLB 39; RGEL 2; TEA

Sternheim, (William Adolf) Carl
    1878-1942 .... **TCLC 8**
    See also CA 105; 193; DLB 56, 118; EWL 3; IDTP; RGWL 2, 3

Stevens, Margaret Dean
    See Aldrich, Bess Streeter

Stevens, Mark 1951- .... **CLC 34**
    See also CA 122

Stevens, Wallace 1879-1955 . **PC 6; TCLC 3, 12, 45; WLC 5**
    See also AMW; AMWR 1; CA 104; 124; CDALB 1929-1941; DA; DA3; DAB; DAC; DAM MST, POET; DLB 54; EWL 3; EXPP; MAL 5; MTCW 1, 2; PAB; PFS 13, 16; RGAL 4; TUS; WP

Stevenson, Anne (Katharine) 1933- .. **CLC 7, 33**
    See also BRWS 6; CA 17-20R; CAAS 9; CANR 9, 33, 123; CP 3, 4, 5, 6, 7; CWP; DLB 40; MTCW 1; RHW

Stevenson, Robert Louis (Balfour)
    1850-1894 ...... **NCLC 5, 14, 63; SSC 11, 51; WLC 5**
    See also AAYA 24; BPFB 3; BRW 5; BRWC 1; BRWR 1; BYA 1, 2, 4, 13; CD-BLB 1890-1914; CLR 10, 11, 107; DA; DA3; DAB; DAC; DAM MST, NOV; DLB 18, 57, 141, 156, 174; DLBD 13; GL 3; HGG; JRDA; LAIT 1, 3; MAICYA 1, 2; NFS 11, 20; RGEL 2; RGSF 2; SATA 100; SUFW; TEA; WCH; WLIT 4; WYA; YABC 2; YAW

Stewart, J(ohn) I(nnes) M(ackintosh)
    1906-1994 .... **CLC 7, 14, 32**
    See Innes, Michael
    See also CA 85-88; 147; CAAS 3; CANR 47; CMW 4; CN 1, 2, 3, 4, 5; MTCW 1, 2

Stewart, Mary (Florence Elinor)
    1916- .... **CLC 7, 35, 117**
    See also AAYA 29; BPFB 3; CA 1-4R; CANR 1, 59, 130; CMW 4; CPW; DAB; FANT; RHW; SATA 12; YAW

Stewart, Mary Rainbow
    See Stewart, Mary (Florence Elinor)

Stifle, June
    See Campbell, Maria

Stifter, Adalbert 1805-1868 .. **NCLC 41; SSC 28**
    See also CDWLB 2; DLB 133; RGSF 2; RGWL 2, 3

Still, James 1906-2001 .... **CLC 49**
    See also CA 65-68; 195; CAAS 17; CANR 10, 26; CSW; DLB 9; DLBY 01; SATA 29; SATA-Obit 127

Sting 1951-
    See Sumner, Gordon Matthew
    See also CA 167

Stirling, Arthur
    See Sinclair, Upton

Stitt, Milan 1941- .... **CLC 29**
    See also CA 69-72

Stockton, Francis Richard 1834-1902
    See Stockton, Frank R.
    See also CA 108; 137; MAICYA 1, 2; SATA 44; SFW 4

Stockton, Frank R. .... **TCLC 47**
    See Stockton, Francis Richard
    See also BYA 4, 13; DLB 42, 74; DLBD 13; EXPS; SATA-Brief 32; SSFS 3; SUFW; WCH

Stoddard, Charles
    See Kuttner, Henry

Stoker, Abraham 1847-1912
    See Stoker, Bram
    See also CA 105; 150; DA; DA3; DAC; DAM MST, NOV; HGG; MTFW 2005; SATA 29

Stoker, Bram . **SSC 62; TCLC 8, 144; WLC 6**
    See Stoker, Abraham
    See also AAYA 23; BPFB 3; BRWS 3; BYA 5; CDBLB 1890-1914; DAB; DLB 304; GL 1; LATS 1:1; NFS 18; RGEL 2; SUFW; TEA; WLIT 4

Stolz, Mary (Slattery) 1920- .... **CLC 12**
    See also AAYA 8; AITN 1; CA 5-8R; CANR 13, 41, 112; JRDA; MAICYA 1, 2; SAAS 3; SATA 10, 71, 133; YAW

Stone, Irving 1903-1989 .... **CLC 7**
    See also AITN 1; BPFB 3; CA 1-4R; 129; CAAS 3; CANR 1, 23; CN 1, 2, 3, 4; CPW; DA3; DAM POP; INT CANR-23; MTCW 1, 2; MTFW 2005; RHW; SATA 3; SATA-Obit 64

Stone, Oliver 1946- .... **CLC 73**
    See also AAYA 15, 64; CA 110; CANR 55, 125

Stone, Oliver William
    See Stone, Oliver

Stone, Robert (Anthony) 1937- ... **CLC 5, 23, 42, 175**
    See also AMWS 5; BPFB 3; CA 85-88; CANR 23, 66, 95; CN 4, 5, 6, 7; DLB 152; EWL 3; INT CANR-23; MAL 5; MTCW 1; MTFW 2005

Stone, Ruth 1915- .... **PC 53**
    See also CA 45-48; CANR 2, 91; CP 5, 6, 7; CSW; DLB 105; PFS 19

Stone, Zachary
    See Follett, Ken(neth Martin)

Stoppard, Tom 1937- ... **CLC 1, 3, 4, 5, 8, 15, 29, 34, 63, 91; DC 6; WLC 6**
    See also AAYA 63; BRWC 1; BRWR 2; BRWS 1; CA 81-84; CANR 39, 67, 125; CBD; CD 5, 6; CDBLB 1960 to Present; DA; DA3; DAB; DAC; DAM DRAM, MST; DFS 2, 5, 8, 11, 13, 16; DLB 13, 233; DLBY 1985; EWL 3; LATS 1:2; MTCW 1, 2; MTFW 2005; RGEL 2; TEA; WLIT 4

Storey, David (Malcolm) 1933- . **CLC 2, 4, 5, 8**
    See also BRWS 1; CA 81-84; CANR 36; CBD; CD 5, 6; CN 1, 2, 3, 4, 5, 6; DAM DRAM; DLB 13, 14, 207, 245, 326; EWL 3; MTCW 1; RGEL 2

Storm, Hyemeyohsts 1935- ... **CLC 3; NNAL**
    See also CA 81-84; CANR 45; DAM MULT

Storm, (Hans) Theodor (Woldsen)
    1817-1888 .... **NCLC 1; SSC 27**
    See also CDWLB 2; DLB 129; EW; RGSF 2; RGWL 2, 3

Storni, Alfonsina 1892-1938 . **HLC 2; PC 33; TCLC 5**
    See also CA 104; 131; DAM MULT; DLB 283; HW 1; LAW

Stoughton, William 1631-1701 .... **LC 38**
    See also DLB 24

Stout, Rex (Todhunter) 1886-1975 ..... **CLC 3**
    See also AITN 2; BPFB 3; CA 61-64; CANR 71; CMW 4; CN 2; DLB 306; MSW; RGAL 4

Stow, (Julian) Randolph 1935- ... **CLC 23, 48**
    See also CA 13-16R; CANR 33; CN 1, 2, 3, 4, 5, 6, 7; CP 1, 2, 3, 4; DLB 260; MTCW 1; RGEL 2

Stowe, Harriet (Elizabeth) Beecher
    1811-1896 ... **NCLC 3, 50, 133; WLC 6**
    See also AAYA 53; AMWS 1; CDALB 1865-1917; DA; DA3; DAB; DAC; DAM MST, NOV; DLB 1, 12, 42, 74, 189, 239, 243; EXPN; FL 1:3; JRDA; LAIT 2; MAICYA 1, 2; NFS 6; RGAL 4; TUS; YABC 1

Strabo c. 64B.C.-c. 25 .... **CMLC 37**
    See also DLB 176

Strachey, (Giles) Lytton
    1880-1932 .... **TCLC 12**
    See also BRWS 2; CA 110; 178; DLB 149; DLBD 10; EWL 3; MTCW 2; NCFS 4

Stramm, August 1874-1915 .... **PC 50**
    See also CA 195; EWL 3

Strand, Mark 1934- .. **CLC 6, 18, 41, 71; PC 63**
    See also AMWS 4; CA 21-24R; CANR 40, 65, 100; CP 1, 2, 3, 4, 5, 6, 7; DAM POET; DLB 5; EWL 3; MAL 5; PAB; PFS 9, 18; RGAL 4; SATA 41; TCLE 1:2

Stratton-Porter, Gene(va Grace) 1863-1924
    See Porter, Gene(va Grace) Stratton
    See also ANW; CA 137; CLR 87; DLB 221; DLBD 14; MAICYA 1, 2; SATA 15

Straub, Peter 1943- .... **CLC 28, 107**
    See also BEST 89:1; BPFB 3; CA 85-88; CANR 28, 65, 109; CPW; DAM POP; DLBY 1984; HGG; MTCW 1, 2; MTFW 2005; SUFW 2

Straub, Peter Francis
    See Straub, Peter

Strauss, Botho 1944- .... **CLC 22**
    See also CA 157; CWW 2; DLB 124

Strauss, Leo 1899-1973 .... **TCLC 141**
    See also CA 101; 45-48; CANR 122

Streatfeild, (Mary) Noel
    1897(?)-1986 .... **CLC 21**
    See also CA 81-84; 120; CANR 31; CLR 17, 83; CWRI 5; DLB 160; MAICYA 1, 2; SATA 20; SATA-Obit 48

Stribling, T(homas) S(igismund)
    1881-1965 .... **CLC 23**
    See also CA 189; 107; CMW 4; DLB 9; RGAL 4

Strindberg, (Johan) August
    1849-1912 ... **DC 18; TCLC 1, 8, 21, 47; WLC 6**
    See also CA 104; 135; DA; DA3; DAB; DAC; DAM DRAM, MST; DFS 4, 9; DLB 259; EW 7; EWL 3; IDTP; LMFS 2; MTCW 2; MTFW 2005; RGWL 2, 3; TWA

Stringer, Arthur 1874-1950 .... **TCLC 37**
    See also CA 161; DLB 92

Stringer, David
    See Roberts, Keith (John Kingston)

Stroheim, Erich von 1885-1957 ..... **TCLC 71**

Tevis, Walter 1928-1984 .... **CLC 42**
See also CA 113; SFW 4

Tey, Josephine .... **TCLC 14**
See Mackintosh, Elizabeth
See also DLB 77; MSW

Thackeray, William Makepeace
1811-1863 ...... **NCLC 5, 14, 22, 43, 169;**
WLC 6
See also BRW 5; BRWC 2; CDBLB 1832-1890; DA; DA3; DAB; DAC; DAM MST, NOV; DLB 21, 55, 159, 163; NFS 13; RGEL 2; SATA 23; TEA; WLIT 3

Thakura, Ravindranatha
See Tagore, Rabindranath

Thames, C. H.
See Marlowe, Stephen

Tharoor, Shashi 1956- .... **CLC 70**
See also CA 141; CANR 91; CN 6, 7

Thelwall, John 1764-1834 .... **NCLC 162**
See also DLB 93, 158

Thelwell, Michael Miles 1939- .... **CLC 22**
See also BW 2; CA 101

Theobald, Lewis, Jr.
See Lovecraft, H. P.

Theocritus c. 310B.C.- .... **CMLC 45**
See also AW 1; DLB 176; RGWL 2, 3

Theodorescu, Ion N. 1880-1967
See Arghezi, Tudor
See also CA 116

Theriault, Yves 1915-1983 .... **CLC 79**
See also CA 102; CANR 150; CCA 1; DAC; DAM MST; DLB 88; EWL 3

Theroux, Alexander (Louis) 1939- .... **CLC 2, 25**
See also CA 85-88; CANR 20, 63; CN 4, 5, 6, 7

Theroux, Paul (Edward) 1941- ..... **CLC 5, 8, 11, 15, 28, 46, 159**
See also AAYA 28; AMWS 8; BEST 89:4; BPFB 3; CA 33-36R; CANR 20, 45, 74, 133; CDALBS; CN 1, 2, 3, 4, 5, 6, 7; CP 1; CPW 1; DA3; DAM POP; DLB 2, 218; EWL 3; HGG; MAL 5; MTCW 1, 2; MTFW 2005; RGAL 4; SATA 44, 109; TUS

Thesen, Sharon 1946- .... **CLC 56**
See also CA 163; CANR 125; CP 5, 6, 7; CWP

Thespis fl. 6th cent. B.C.- .... **CMLC 51**
See also LMFS 1

Thevenin, Denis
See Duhamel, Georges

Thibault, Jacques Anatole Francois
1844-1924
See France, Anatole
See also CA 106; 127; DA3; DAM NOV; MTCW 1, 2; TWA

Thiele, Colin (Milton) 1920- .... **CLC 17**
See also CA 29-32R; CANR 12, 28, 53, 105; CLR 27; CP 1, 2; DLB 289; MAICYA 1, 2; SAAS 2; SATA 14, 72, 125; YAW

Thistlethwaite, Bel
See Wetherald, Agnes Ethelwyn

Thomas, Audrey (Callahan) 1935- .... **CLC 7, 13, 37, 107; SSC 20**
See also AITN 2; CA 21-24R, 237; CAAE 237; CAAS 19; CANR 36, 58; CN 2, 3, 4, 5, 6, 7; DLB 60; MTCW 1; RGSF 2

Thomas, Augustus 1857-1934 .... **TCLC 97**
See also MAL 5

Thomas, D(onald) M(ichael) 1935- . **CLC 13, 22, 31, 132**
See also BPFB 3; BRWS 4; CA 61-64; CAAS 11; CANR 17, 45, 75; CDBLB 1960 to Present; CN 4, 5, 6, 7; CP 1, 2, 3, 4, 5, 6, 7; DA3; DLB 40, 207, 299; HGG; INT CANR-17; MTCW 1, 2; MTFW 2005; RGHL; SFW 4

Thomas, Dylan (Marlais) 1914-1953 .... **PC 2, 52; SSC 3, 44; TCLC 1, 8, 45, 105; WLC 6**
See also AAYA 45; BRWS 1; CA 104; 120; CANR 65; CDBLB 1945-1960; DA; DA3; DAB; DAC; DAM DRAM, MST, POET; DLB 13, 20, 139; EWL 3; EXPP; LAIT 3; MTCW 1, 2; MTFW 2005; PAB; PFS 1, 3, 8; RGEL 2; RGSF 2; SATA 60; TEA; WLIT 4; WP

Thomas, (Philip) Edward 1878-1917 . **PC 53; TCLC 10**
See also BRW 6; BRWS 3; CA 106; 153; DAM POET; DLB 19, 98, 156, 216; EWL 3; PAB; RGEL 2

Thomas, Joyce Carol 1938- .... **CLC 35**
See also AAYA 12, 54; BW 2, 3; CA 113; 116; CANR 48, 114, 135; CLR 19; DLB 33; INT CA-116; JRDA; MAICYA 1, 2; MTCW 1, 2; MTFW 2005; SAAS 7; SATA 40, 78, 123, 137; SATA-Essay 137; WYA; YAW

Thomas, Lewis 1913-1993 .... **CLC 35**
See also ANW; CA 85-88; 143; CANR 38, 60; DLB 275; MTCW 1, 2

Thomas, M. Carey 1857-1935 .... **TCLC 89**
See also FW

Thomas, Paul
See Mann, (Paul) Thomas

Thomas, Piri 1928- .... **CLC 17; HLCS 2**
See also CA 73-76; HW 1; LLW

Thomas, R(onald) S(tuart)
1913-2000 .... **CLC 6, 13, 48**
See also CA 89-92; 189; CAAS 4; CANR 30; CDBLB 1960 to Present; CP 1, 2, 3, 4, 5, 6, 7; DAB; DAM POET; DLB 27; EWL 3; MTCW 1; RGEL 2

Thomas, Ross (Elmore) 1926-1995 .. **CLC 39**
See also CA 33-36R; 150; CANR 22, 63; CMW 4

Thompson, Francis (Joseph)
1859-1907 .... **TCLC 4**
See also BRW 5; CA 104; 189; CDBLB 1890-1914; DLB 19; RGEL 2; TEA

Thompson, Francis Clegg
See Mencken, H(enry) L(ouis)

Thompson, Hunter S(tockton)
1937(?)-2005 .... **CLC 9, 17, 40, 104**
See also AAYA 45; BEST 89:1; BPFB 3; CA 17-20R; 236; CANR 23, 46, 74, 77, 111, 133; CPW; CSW; DA3; DAM POP; DLB 185; MTCW 1, 2; MTFW 2005; TUS

Thompson, James Myers
See Thompson, Jim (Myers)

Thompson, Jim (Myers)
1906-1977(?) .... **CLC 69**
See also BPFB 3; CA 140; CMW 4; CPW; DLB 226; MSW

Thompson, Judith (Clare Francesca)
1954- .... **CLC 39**
See also CA 143; CD 5, 6; CWD; DFS 22

Thomson, James 1700-1748 .... **LC 16, 29, 40**
See also BRWS 3; DAM POET; DLB 95; RGEL 2

Thomson, James 1834-1882 .... **NCLC 18**
See also DAM POET; DLB 35; RGEL 2

Thoreau, Henry David 1817-1862 .. **NCLC 7, 21, 61, 138; PC 30; WLC 6**
See also AAYA 42; AMW; ANW; BYA 3; CDALB 1640-1865; DA; DA3; DAB; DAC; DAM MST; DLB 1, 183, 223, 270, 298; LAIT 2; LMFS 1; NCFS 3; RGAL 4; TUS

Thorndike, E. L.
See Thorndike, Edward L(ee)

Thorndike, Edward L(ee)
1874-1949 .... **TCLC 107**
See also CA 121

Thornton, Hall
See Silverberg, Robert

Thorpe, Adam 1956- .... **CLC 176**
See also CA 129; CANR 92; DLB 231

Thubron, Colin (Gerald Dryden)
1939- .... **CLC 163**
See also CA 25-28R; CANR 12, 29, 59, 95; CN 5, 6, 7; DLB 204, 231

Thucydides c. 455B.C.-c. 395B.C. . **CMLC 17**
See also AW 1; DLB 176; RGWL 2, 3; WLIT 8

Thumboo, Edwin Nadason 1933- .... **PC 30**
See also CA 194; CP 1

Thurber, James (Grover)
1894-1961 .. **CLC 5, 11, 25, 125; SSC 1, 47**
See also AAYA 56; AMWS 1; BPFB 3; BYA 5; CA 73-76; CANR 17, 39; CDALB 1929-1941; CWRI 5; DA; DA3; DAB; DAC; DAM DRAM, MST, NOV; DLB 4, 11, 22, 102; EWL 3; EXPS; FANT; LAIT 3; MAICYA 1, 2; MAL 5; MTCW 1, 2; MTFW 2005; RGAL 4; RGSF 2; SATA 13; SSFS 1, 10, 19; SUFW; TUS

Thurman, Wallace (Henry)
1902-1934 ..... **BLC 3; HR 1:3; TCLC 6**
See also BW 1, 3; CA 104; 124; CANR 81; DAM MULT; DLB 51

Tibullus c. 54B.C.-c. 18B.C. .... **CMLC 36**
See also AW 2; DLB 211; RGWL 2, 3; WLIT 8

Ticheburn, Cheviot
See Ainsworth, William Harrison

Tieck, (Johann) Ludwig
1773-1853 .... **NCLC 5, 46; SSC 31**
See also CDWLB 2; DLB 90; EW 5; IDTP; RGSF 2; RGWL 2, 3; SUFW

Tiger, Derry
See Ellison, Harlan (Jay)

Tilghman, Christopher 1946- .... **CLC 65**
See also CA 159; CANR 135, 151; CSW; DLB 244

Tillich, Paul (Johannes)
1886-1965 .... **CLC 131**
See also CA 5-8R; 25-28R; CANR 33; MTCW 1, 2

Tillinghast, Richard (Williford)
1940- .... **CLC 29**
See also CA 29-32R; CAAS 23; CANR 26, 51, 96; CP 2, 3, 4, 5, 6, 7; CSW

Timrod, Henry 1828-1867 .... **NCLC 25**
See also DLB 3, 248; RGAL 4

Tindall, Gillian (Elizabeth) 1938- ...... **CLC 7**
See also CA 21-24R; CANR 11, 65, 107; CN 1, 2, 3, 4, 5, 6, 7

Tiptree, James, Jr. .... **CLC 48, 50**
See Sheldon, Alice Hastings Bradley
See also DLB 8; SCFW 1, 2; SFW 4

Tirone Smith, Mary-Ann 1944- .... **CLC 39**
See also CA 118; 136; CANR 113; SATA 143

Tirso de Molina 1580(?)-1648 .... **DC 13; HLCS 2; LC 73**
See also RGWL 2, 3

Titmarsh, Michael Angelo
See Thackeray, William Makepeace

Tocqueville, Alexis (Charles Henri Maurice Clerel Comte) de 1805-1859 .. **NCLC 7, 63**
See also EW 6; GFL 1789 to the Present; TWA

Toer, Pramoedya Ananta
1925-2006 .... **CLC 186**
See also CA 197; RGWL 3

Toffler, Alvin 1928- .... **CLC 168**
See also CA 13-16R; CANR 15, 46, 67; CPW; DAM POP; MTCW 1, 2

Toibin, Colm 1955- .... **CLC 162**
  See also CA 142; CANR 81, 149; CN 7;
  DLB 271

Tolkien, J(ohn) R(onald) R(euel)
  1892-1973 .... **CLC 1, 2, 3, 8, 12, 38;
  TCLC 137; WLC 6**
  See also AAYA 10; AITN 1; BPFB 3;
  BRWC 2; BRWS 2; CA 17-18; 45-48;
  CANR 36, 134; CAP 2; CDBLB 1914-
  1945; CLR 56; CN 1; CPW 1; CWRI 5;
  DA; DA3; DAB; DAC; DAM MST, NOV,
  POP; DLB 15, 160, 255; EFS 2; EWL 3;
  FANT; JRDA; LAIT 1; LATS 1:2; LMFS
  2; MAICYA 1, 2; MTCW 1, 2; MTFW
  2005; NFS 8; RGEL 2; SATA 2, 32, 100;
  SATA-Obit 24; SFW 4; SUFW; TEA;
  WCH; WYA; YAW

Toller, Ernst 1893-1939 .... **TCLC 10**
  See also CA 107; 186; DLB 124; EWL 3;
  RGWL 2, 3

Tolson, M. B.
  See Tolson, Melvin B(eaunorus)

Tolson, Melvin B(eaunorus)
  1898(?)-1966 .... **BLC 3; CLC 36, 105**
  See also AFAW 1, 2; BW 1, 3; CA 124; 89-
  92; CANR 80; DAM MULT, POET; DLB
  48, 76; MAL 5; RGAL 4

Tolstoi, Aleksei Nikolaevich
  See Tolstoy, Alexey Nikolaevich

Tolstoi, Lev
  See Tolstoy, Leo (Nikolaevich)
  See also RGSF 2; RGWL 2, 3

Tolstoy, Aleksei Nikolaevich
  See Tolstoy, Alexey Nikolaevich
  See also DLB 272

Tolstoy, Alexey Nikolaevich
  1882-1945 .... **TCLC 18**
  See Tolstoy, Aleksei Nikolaevich
  See also CA 107; 158; EWL 3; SFW 4

Tolstoy, Leo (Nikolaevich)
  1828-1910 . **SSC 9, 30, 45, 54; TCLC 4,
  11, 17, 28, 44, 79, 173; WLC 6**
  See Tolstoi, Lev
  See also AAYA 56; CA 104; 123; DA; DA3;
  DAB; DAC; DAM MST, NOV; DLB 238;
  EFS 2; EW 7; EXPS; IDTP; LAIT 2;
  LATS 1:1; LMFS 1; NFS 10; SATA 26;
  SSFS 5; TWA

Tolstoy, Count Leo
  See Tolstoy, Leo (Nikolaevich)

Tomalin, Claire 1933- .... **CLC 166**
  See also CA 89-92; CANR 52, 88; DLB
  155

Tomasi di Lampedusa, Giuseppe 1896-1957
  See Lampedusa, Giuseppe (Tomasi) di
  See also CA 111; DLB 177; EWL 3; WLIT
  7

Tomlin, Lily .... **CLC 17**
  See Tomlin, Mary Jean

Tomlin, Mary Jean 1939(?)-
  See Tomlin, Lily
  See also CA 117

Tomline, F. Latour
  See Gilbert, W(illiam) S(chwenck)

Tomlinson, (Alfred) Charles 1927- .... **CLC 2,
  4, 6, 13, 45; PC 17**
  See also CA 5-8R; CANR 33; CP 1, 2, 3, 4,
  5, 6, 7; DAM POET; DLB 40; TCLE 1:2

Tomlinson, H(enry) M(ajor)
  1873-1958 .... **TCLC 71**
  See also CA 118; 161; DLB 36, 100, 195

Tonna, Charlotte Elizabeth
  1790-1846 .... **NCLC 135**
  See also DLB 163

Tonson, Jacob fl. 1655(?)-1736 .... **LC 86**
  See also DLB 170

Toole, John Kennedy 1937-1969 ..... **CLC 19,
  64**
  See also BPFB 3; CA 104; DLBY 1981;
  MTCW 2; MTFW 2005

Toomer, Eugene
  See Toomer, Jean

Toomer, Eugene Pinchback
  See Toomer, Jean

Toomer, Jean 1894-1967 .. **BLC 3; CLC 1, 4,
  13, 22; HR 1:3; PC 7; SSC 1, 45;
  TCLC 172; WLCS**
  See also AFAW 1, 2; AMWS 3, 9; BW 1;
  CA 85-88; CDALB 1917-1929; DA3;
  DAM MULT; DLB 45, 51; EWL 3; EXPP;
  EXPS; LMFS 2; MAL 5; MTCW 1, 2;
  MTFW 2005; NFS 11; RGAL 4; RGSF 2;
  SSFS 5

Toomer, Nathan Jean
  See Toomer, Jean

Toomer, Nathan Pinchback
  See Toomer, Jean

Torley, Luke
  See Blish, James (Benjamin)

Tornimparte, Alessandra
  See Ginzburg, Natalia

Torre, Raoul della
  See Mencken, H(enry) L(ouis)

Torrence, Ridgely 1874-1950 .... **TCLC 97**
  See also DLB 54, 249; MAL 5

Torrey, E(dwin) Fuller 1937- .... **CLC 34**
  See also CA 119; CANR 71

Torsvan, Ben Traven
  See Traven, B.

Torsvan, Benno Traven
  See Traven, B.

Torsvan, Berick Traven
  See Traven, B.

Torsvan, Berwick Traven
  See Traven, B.

Torsvan, Bruno Traven
  See Traven, B.

Torsvan, Traven
  See Traven, B.

Tourneur, Cyril 1575(?)-1626 .... **LC 66**
  See also BRW 2; DAM DRAM; DLB 58;
  RGEL 2

Tournier, Michel 1924- .... **CLC 6, 23, 36, 95;
  SSC 88**
  See also CA 49-52; CANR 3, 36, 74, 149;
  CWW 2; DLB 83; EWL 3; GFL 1789 to
  the Present; MTCW 1, 2; SATA 23

Tournier, Michel Edouard
  See Tournier, Michel

Tournimparte, Alessandra
  See Ginzburg, Natalia

Towers, Ivar
  See Kornbluth, C(yril) M.

Towne, Robert (Burton) 1936(?)- ..... **CLC 87**
  See also CA 108; DLB 44; IDFW 3, 4

Townsend, Sue .... **CLC 61**
  See Townsend, Susan Lilian
  See also AAYA 28; CA 119; 127; CANR
  65, 107; CBD; CD 5, 6; CPW; CWD;
  DAB; DAC; DAM MST; DLB 271; INT
  CA-127; SATA 55, 93; SATA-Brief 48;
  YAW

Townsend, Susan Lilian 1946-
  See Townsend, Sue

Townshend, Pete
  See Townshend, Peter (Dennis Blandford)

Townshend, Peter (Dennis Blandford)
  1945- .... **CLC 17, 42**
  See also CA 107

Tozzi, Federigo 1883-1920 .... **TCLC 31**
  See also CA 160; CANR 110; DLB 264;
  EWL 3; WLIT 7

Tracy, Don(ald Fiske) 1905-1970(?)
  See Queen, Ellery
  See also CA 1-4R; 176; CANR 2

Trafford, F. G.
  See Riddell, Charlotte

Traherne, Thomas 1637(?)-1674 .. **LC 99; PC
  70**
  See also BRW 2; BRWS 11; DLB 131;
  PAB; RGEL 2

Traill, Catharine Parr 1802-1899 .. **NCLC 31**
  See also DLB 99

Trakl, Georg 1887-1914 .... **PC 20; TCLC 5**
  See also CA 104; 165; EW 10; EWL 3;
  LMFS 2; MTCW 2; RGWL 2, 3

Trambley, Estela Portillo .... **TCLC 163**
  See Portillo Trambley, Estela
  See also CA 77-80; RGAL 4

Tranquilli, Secondino
  See Silone, Ignazio

Transtroemer, Tomas Gosta
  See Transtromer, Tomas (Goesta)

Transtromer, Tomas (Gosta)
  See Transtromer, Tomas (Goesta)
  See also CWW 2

Transtromer, Tomas (Goesta)
  1931- .... **CLC 52, 65**
  See Transtromer, Tomas (Gosta)
  See also CA 117; 129; CAAS 17; CANR
  115; DAM POET; DLB 257; EWL 3; PFS
  21

Transtromer, Tomas Gosta
  See Transtromer, Tomas (Goesta)

Traven, B. 1882(?)-1969 .... **CLC 8, 11**
  See also CA 19-20; 25-28R; CAP 2; DLB
  9, 56; EWL 3; MTCW 1; RGAL 4

Trediakovsky, Vasilii Kirillovich
  1703-1769 .... **LC 68**
  See also DLB 150

Treitel, Jonathan 1959- .... **CLC 70**
  See also CA 210; DLB 267

Trelawny, Edward John
  1792-1881 .... **NCLC 85**
  See also DLB 110, 116, 144

Tremain, Rose 1943- .... **CLC 42**
  See also CA 97-100; CANR 44, 95; CN 4,
  5, 6, 7; DLB 14, 271; RGSF 2; RHW

Tremblay, Michel 1942- .... **CLC 29, 102, 225**
  See also CA 116; 128; CCA 1; CWW 2;
  DAC; DAM MST; DLB 60; EWL 3; GLL
  1; MTCW 1, 2; MTFW 2005

Trevanian .... **CLC 29**
  See Whitaker, Rod

Trevor, Glen
  See Hilton, James

Trevor, William .. **CLC 7, 9, 14, 25, 71, 116;
  SSC 21, 58**
  See Cox, William Trevor
  See also BRWS 4; CBD; CD 5, 6; CN 1, 2,
  3, 4, 5, 6, 7; DLB 14, 139; EWL 3; LATS
  1:2; RGEL 2; RGSF 2; SSFS 10; TCLE
  1:2

Trifonov, Iurii (Valentinovich)
  See Trifonov, Yuri (Valentinovich)
  See also DLB 302; RGWL 2, 3

Trifonov, Yuri (Valentinovich)
  1925-1981 .... **CLC 45**
  See Trifonov, Iurii (Valentinovich); Trifonov, Yury Valentinovich
  See also CA 126; 103; MTCW 1

Trifonov, Yury Valentinovich
  See Trifonov, Yuri (Valentinovich)
  See also EWL 3

Trilling, Diana (Rubin) 1905-1996 . **CLC 129**
  See also CA 5-8R; 154; CANR 10, 46; INT
  CANR-10; MTCW 1, 2

Trilling, Lionel 1905-1975 ..... **CLC 9, 11, 24;
  SSC 75**
  See also AMWS 3; CA 9-12R; 61-64;
  CANR 10, 105; CN 1, 2; DLB 28, 63;
  EWL 3; INT CANR-10; MAL 5; MTCW
  1, 2; RGAL 4; TUS

Trimball, W. H.
  See Mencken, H(enry) L(ouis)

Tristan
See Gomez de la Serna, Ramon

Tristram
See Housman, A(lfred) E(dward)

Trogdon, William (Lewis) 1939-
See Heat-Moon, William Least
See also AAYA 66; CA 115; 119; CANR 47, 89; CPW; INT CA-119

Trollope, Anthony 1815-1882 .... **NCLC 6, 33, 101; SSC 28; WLC 6**
See also BRW 5; CDBLB 1832-1890; DA; DA3; DAB; DAC; DAM MST, NOV; DLB 21, 57, 159; RGEL 2; RGSF 2; SATA 22

Trollope, Frances 1779-1863 .... **NCLC 30**
See also DLB 21, 166

Trollope, Joanna 1943- .... **CLC 186**
See also CA 101; CANR 58, 95, 149; CN 7; CPW; DLB 207; RHW

Trotsky, Leon 1879-1940 .... **TCLC 22**
See also CA 118; 167

Trotter (Cockburn), Catharine
1679-1749 .... **LC 8**
See also DLB 84, 252

Trotter, Wilfred 1872-1939 .... **TCLC 97**

Trout, Kilgore
See Farmer, Philip Jose

Trow, George W. S. 1943- .... **CLC 52**
See also CA 126; CANR 91

Troyat, Henri 1911- .... **CLC 23**
See also CA 45-48; CANR 2, 33, 67, 117; GFL 1789 to the Present; MTCW 1

Trudeau, Garry B. .... **CLC 12**
See Trudeau, G.B.
See also AAYA 10; AITN 2

Trudeau, G.B. 1948-
See Trudeau, Garry B.
See also AAYA 60; CA 81-84; CANR 31; SATA 35, 168

Truffaut, Francois 1932-1984 ... **CLC 20, 101**
See also CA 81-84; 113; CANR 34

Trumbo, Dalton 1905-1976 .... **CLC 19**
See also CA 21-24R; 69-72; CANR 10; CN 1, 2; DLB 26; IDFW 3, 4; YAW

Trumbull, John 1750-1831 .... **NCLC 30**
See also DLB 31; RGAL 4

Trundlett, Helen B.
See Eliot, T(homas) S(tearns)

Truth, Sojourner 1797(?)-1883 ...... **NCLC 94**
See also DLB 239; FW; LAIT 2

Tryon, Thomas 1926-1991 .... **CLC 3, 11**
See also AITN 1; BPFB 3; CA 29-32R; 135; CANR 32, 77; CPW; DA3; DAM POP; HGG; MTCW 1

Tryon, Tom
See Tryon, Thomas

Ts'ao Hsueh-ch'in 1715(?)-1763 .... **LC 1**

Tsushima, Shuji 1909-1948
See Dazai Osamu
See also CA 107

Tsvetaeva (Efron), Marina (Ivanovna)
1892-1941 .... **PC 14; TCLC 7, 35**
See also CA 104; 128; CANR 73; DLB 295; EW 11; MTCW 1, 2; RGWL 2, 3

Tuck, Lily 1938- .... **CLC 70**
See also CA 139; CANR 90

Tu Fu 712-770 .... **PC 9**
See Du Fu
See also DAM MULT; TWA; WP

Tunis, John R(oberts) 1889-1975 ..... **CLC 12**
See also BYA 1; CA 61-64; CANR 62; DLB 22, 171; JRDA; MAICYA 1, 2; SATA 37; SATA-Brief 30; YAW

Tuohy, Frank .... **CLC 37**
See Tuohy, John Francis
See also CN 1, 2, 3, 4, 5, 6, 7; DLB 14, 139

Tuohy, John Francis 1925-
See Tuohy, Frank
See also CA 5-8R; 178; CANR 3, 47

Turco, Lewis (Putnam) 1934- ..... **CLC 11, 63**
See also CA 13-16R; CAAS 22; CANR 24, 51; CP 1, 2, 3, 4, 5, 6, 7; DLBY 1984; TCLE 1:2

Turgenev, Ivan (Sergeevich)
1818-1883 ..... **DC 7; NCLC 21, 37, 122; SSC 7, 57; WLC 6**
See also AAYA 58; DA; DAB; DAC; DAM MST, NOV; DFS 6; DLB 238, 284; EW 6; LATS 1:1; NFS 16; RGSF 2; RGWL 2, 3; TWA

Turgot, Anne-Robert-Jacques
1727-1781 .... **LC 26**
See also DLB 314

Turner, Frederick 1943- .... **CLC 48**
See also CA 73-76, 227; CAAE 227; CAAS 10; CANR 12, 30, 56; DLB 40, 282

Turton, James
See Crace, Jim

Tutu, Desmond M(pilo) 1931- .. **BLC 3; CLC 80**
See also BW 1, 3; CA 125; CANR 67, 81; DAM MULT

Tutuola, Amos 1920-1997 ..... **BLC 3; CLC 5, 14, 29**
See also AFW; BW 2, 3; CA 9-12R; 159; CANR 27, 66; CDWLB 3; CN 1, 2, 3, 4, 5, 6; DA3; DAM MULT; DLB 125; DNFS 2; EWL 3; MTCW 1, 2; MTFW 2005; RGEL 2; WLIT 2

Twain, Mark .... **SSC 6, 26, 34, 87; TCLC 6, 12, 19, 36, 48, 59, 161; WLC 6**
See Clemens, Samuel Langhorne
See also AAYA 20; AMW; AMWC 1; BPFB 3; BYA 2, 3, 11, 14; CLR 58, 60, 66; DLB 11; EXPN; EXPS; FANT; LAIT 2; MAL 5; NCFS 4; NFS 1, 6; RGAL 4; RGSF 2; SFW 4; SSFS 1, 7, 16, 21; SUFW; TUS; WCH; WYA; YAW

Tyler, Anne 1941- . **CLC 7, 11, 18, 28, 44, 59, 103, 205**
See also AAYA 18, 60; AMWS 4; BEST 89:1; BPFB 3; BYA 12; CA 9-12R; CANR 11, 33, 53, 109, 132; CDALBS; CN 1, 2, 3, 4, 5, 6, 7; CPW; CSW; DAM NOV, POP; DLB 6, 143; DLBY 1982; EWL 3; EXPN; LATS 1:2; MAL 5; MBL; MTCW 1, 2; MTFW 2005; NFS 2, 7, 10; RGAL 4; SATA 7, 90; SSFS 17; TCLE 1:2; TUS; YAW

Tyler, Royall 1757-1826 .... **NCLC 3**
See also DLB 37; RGAL 4

Tynan, Katharine 1861-1931 .... **TCLC 3**
See also CA 104; 167; DLB 153, 240; FW

Tyndale, William c. 1484-1536 .... **LC 103**
See also DLB 132

Tyutchev, Fyodor 1803-1873 .... **NCLC 34**

Tzara, Tristan 1896-1963 .... **CLC 47; PC 27; TCLC 168**
See also CA 153; 89-92; DAM POET; EWL 3; MTCW 2

Uchida, Yoshiko 1921-1992 .... **AAL**
See also AAYA 16; BYA 2, 3; CA 13-16R; 139; CANR 6, 22, 47, 61; CDALBS; CLR 6, 56; CWRI 5; DLB 312; JRDA; MAI-CYA 1, 2; MTCW 1, 2; MTFW 2005; SAAS 1; SATA 1, 53; SATA-Obit 72

Udall, Nicholas 1504-1556 .... **LC 84**
See also DLB 62; RGEL 2

Ueda Akinari 1734-1809 .... **NCLC 131**

Uhry, Alfred 1936- .... **CLC 55**
See also CA 127; 133; CAD; CANR 112; CD 5, 6; CSW; DA3; DAM DRAM, POP; DFS 11, 15; INT CA-133; MTFW 2005

Ulf, Haerved
See Strindberg, (Johan) August

Ulf, Harved
See Strindberg, (Johan) August

Ulibarri, Sabine R(eyes)
1919-2003 .... **CLC 83; HLCS 2**
See also CA 131; 214; CANR 81; DAM MULT; DLB 82; HW 1, 2; RGSF 2

Unamuno (y Jugo), Miguel de
1864-1936 .. **HLC 2; SSC 11, 69; TCLC 2, 9, 148**
See also CA 104; 131; CANR 81; DAM MULT, NOV; DLB 108, 322; EW 8; EWL 3; HW 1, 2; MTCW 1, 2; MTFW 2005; RGSF 2; RGWL 2, 3; SSFS 20; TWA

Uncle Shelby
See Silverstein, Shel(don Allan)

Undercliffe, Errol
See Campbell, (John) Ramsey

Underwood, Miles
See Glassco, John

Undset, Sigrid 1882-1949 .. **TCLC 3; WLC 6**
See also CA 104; 129; DA; DA3; DAB; DAC; DAM MST, NOV; DLB 293; EW 9; EWL 3; FW; MTCW 1, 2; MTFW 2005; RGWL 2, 3

Ungaretti, Giuseppe 1888-1970 ... **CLC 7, 11, 15; PC 57**
See also CA 19-20; 25-28R; CAP 2; DLB 114; EW 10; EWL 3; PFS 20; RGWL 2, 3; WLIT 7

Unger, Douglas 1952- .... **CLC 34**
See also CA 130; CANR 94

Unsworth, Barry (Forster) 1930- .... **CLC 76, 127**
See also BRWS 7; CA 25-28R; CANR 30, 54, 125; CN 6, 7; DLB 194, 326

Updike, John 1932- . **CLC 1, 2, 3, 5, 7, 9, 13, 15, 23, 34, 43, 70, 139, 214; SSC 13, 27; WLC 6**
See also AAYA 36; AMW; AMWC 1; AMWR 1; BPFB 3; BYA 12; CA 1-4R; CABS 1; CANR 4, 33, 51, 94, 133; CDALB 1968-1988; CN 1, 2, 3, 4, 5, 6, 7; CP 1, 2, 3, 4, 5, 6, 7; CPW 1; DA; DA3; DAB; DAC; DAM MST, NOV, POET, POP; DLB 2, 5, 143, 218, 227; DLBD 3; DLBY 1980, 1982, 1997; EWL 3; EXPP; HGG; MAL 5; MTCW 1, 2; MTFW 2005; NFS 12; RGAL 4; RGSF 2; SSFS 3, 19; TUS

Updike, John Hoyer
See Updike, John

Upshaw, Margaret Mitchell
See Mitchell, Margaret (Munnerlyn)

Upton, Mark
See Sanders, Lawrence

Upward, Allen 1863-1926 .... **TCLC 85**
See also CA 117; 187; DLB 36

Urdang, Constance (Henriette)
1922-1996 .... **CLC 47**
See also CA 21-24R; CANR 9, 24; CP 1, 2, 3, 4, 5, 6; CWP

Uriel, Henry
See Faust, Frederick (Schiller)

Uris, Leon (Marcus) 1924-2003 ... **CLC 7, 32**
See also AITN 1, 2; BEST 89:2; BPFB 3; CA 1-4R; 217; CANR 1, 40, 65, 123; CN 1, 2, 3, 4, 5, 6; CPW 1; DA3; DAM NOV, POP; MTCW 1, 2; MTFW 2005; RGHL; SATA 49; SATA-Obit 146

Urista (Heredia), Alberto (Baltazar)
1947- .... **HLCS 1**
See Alurista
See also CA 182; CANR 2, 32; HW 1

Urmuz
See Codrescu, Andrei

Urquhart, Guy
See McAlmon, Robert (Menzies)

Verus, Marcus Annius
  See Aurelius, Marcus
Very, Jones 1813-1880 .... **NCLC 9**
  See also DLB 1, 243; RGAL 4
Vesaas, Tarjei 1897-1970 .... **CLC 48**
  See also CA 190; 29-32R; DLB 297; EW
  11; EWL 3; RGWL 3
Vialis, Gaston
  See Simenon, Georges (Jacques Christian)
Vian, Boris 1920-1959(?) .... **TCLC 9**
  See also CA 106; 164; CANR 111; DLB
  72, 321; EWL 3; GFL 1789 to the Present;
  MTCW 2; RGWL 2, 3
Viaud, (Louis Marie) Julien 1850-1923
  See Loti, Pierre
  See also CA 107
Vicar, Henry
  See Felsen, Henry Gregor
Vicente, Gil 1465-c. 1536 .... **LC 99**
  See also DLB 318; IDTP; RGWL 2, 3
Vicker, Angus
  See Felsen, Henry Gregor
Vidal, Eugene Luther Gore
  See Vidal, Gore
Vidal, Gore 1925- ...... **CLC 2, 4, 6, 8, 10, 22,**
  33, 72, 142
  See Box, Edgar
  See also AAYA 64; AITN 1; AMWS 4;
  BEST 90:2; BPFB 3; CA 5-8R; CAD;
  CANR 13, 45, 65, 100, 132; CD 5, 6;
  CDALBS; CN 1, 2, 3, 4, 5, 6, 7; CPW;
  DA3; DAM NOV, POP; DFS 2; DLB 6,
  152; EWL 3; INT CANR-13; MAL 5;
  MTCW 1, 2; MTFW 2005; RGAL 4;
  RHW; TUS
Viereck, Peter 1916-2006 .... **CLC 4; PC 27**
  See also CA 1-4R; CANR 1, 47; CP 1, 2,
  4, 5, 6, 7; DLB 5; MAL 5; PFS 9, 14
Viereck, Peter Robert Edwin
  See Viereck, Peter
Vigny, Alfred (Victor) de
  1797-1863 .... **NCLC 7, 102; PC 26**
  See also DAM POET; DLB 119, 192, 217;
  EW 5; GFL 1789 to the Present; RGWL
  2, 3
Vilakazi, Benedict Wallet
  1906-1947 .... **TCLC 37**
  See also CA 168
Villa, Jose Garcia 1914-1997 ... **AAL; PC 22;**
  TCLC 176
  See also CA 25-28R; CANR 12, 118; CP 1,
  2, 3, 4; DLB 312; EWL 3; EXPP
Villard, Oswald Garrison
  1872-1949 .... **TCLC 160**
  See also CA 113; 162; DLB 25, 91
Villarreal, Jose Antonio 1924- .... **HLC 2**
  See also CA 133; CANR 93; DAM MULT;
  DLB 82; HW 1; LAIT 4; RGAL 4
Villaurrutia, Xavier 1903-1950 ...... **TCLC 80**
  See also CA 192; EWL 3; HW 1; LAW
Villaverde, Cirilo 1812-1894 .... **NCLC 121**
  See also LAW
Villehardouin, Geoffroi de
  1150(?)-1218(?) .... **CMLC 38**
Villiers, George 1628-1687 .... **LC 107**
  See also DLB 80; RGEL 2
Villiers de l'Isle Adam, Jean Marie Mathias
  Philippe Auguste 1838-1889 ... **NCLC 3;**
  SSC 14
  See also DLB 123, 192; GFL 1789 to the
  Present; RGSF 2
Villon, Francois 1431-1463(?) . **LC 62; PC 13**
  See also DLB 208; EW 2; RGWL 2, 3;
  TWA
Vine, Barbara .... **CLC 50**
  See Rendell, Ruth
  See also BEST 90:4

Vinge, Joan (Carol) D(ennison)
  1948- .... **CLC 30; SSC 24**
  See also AAYA 32; BPFB 3; CA 93-96;
  CANR 72; SATA 36, 113; SFW 4; YAW
Viola, Herman J(oseph) 1938- .... **CLC 70**
  See also CA 61-64; CANR 8, 23, 48, 91;
  SATA 126
Violis, G.
  See Simenon, Georges (Jacques Christian)
Viramontes, Helena Maria 1954- .... **HLCS 2**
  See also CA 159; DLB 122; HW 2; LLW
Virgil
  See Vergil
  See also CDWLB 1; DLB 211; LAIT 1;
  RGWL 2, 3; WLIT 8; WP
Visconti, Luchino 1906-1976 .... **CLC 16**
  See also CA 81-84; 65-68; CANR 39
Vitry, Jacques de
  See Jacques de Vitry
Vittorini, Elio 1908-1966 .... **CLC 6, 9, 14**
  See also CA 133; 25-28R; DLB 264; EW
  12; EWL 3; RGWL 2, 3
Vivekananda, Swami 1863-1902 .... **TCLC 88**
Vizenor, Gerald Robert 1934- .... **CLC 103;**
  NNAL
  See also CA 13-16R, 205; CAAE 205;
  CAAS 22; CANR 5, 21, 44, 67; DAM
  MULT; DLB 175, 227; MTCW 2; MTFW
  2005; TCWW 2
Vizinczey, Stephen 1933- .... **CLC 40**
  See also CA 128; CCA 1; INT CA-128
Vliet, R(ussell) G(ordon)
  1929-1984 .... **CLC 22**
  See also CA 37-40R; 112; CANR 18; CP 2,
  3
Vogau, Boris Andreyevich 1894-1938
  See Pilnyak, Boris
  See also CA 123; 218
Vogel, Paula A(nne) 1951- ... **CLC 76; DC 19**
  See also CA 108; CAD; CANR 119, 140;
  CD 5, 6; CWD; DFS 14; MTFW 2005;
  RGAL 4
Voigt, Cynthia 1942- .... **CLC 30**
  See also AAYA 3, 30; BYA 1, 3, 6, 7, 8;
  CA 106; CANR 18, 37, 40, 94, 145; CLR
  13, 48; INT CANR-18; JRDA; LAIT 5;
  MAICYA 1, 2; MAICYAS 1; MTFW
  2005; SATA 48, 79, 116, 160; SATA-Brief
  33; WYA; YAW
Voigt, Ellen Bryant 1943- .... **CLC 54**
  See also CA 69-72; CANR 11, 29, 55, 115;
  CP 5, 6, 7; CSW; CWP; DLB 120; PFS
  23
Voinovich, Vladimir 1932- .. **CLC 10, 49, 147**
  See also CA 81-84; CAAS 12; CANR 33,
  67, 150; CWW 2; DLB 302; MTCW 1
Voinovich, Vladimir Nikolaevich
  See Voinovich, Vladimir
Vollmann, William T. 1959- ...... **CLC 89, 227**
  See also CA 134; CANR 67, 116; CN 7;
  CPW; DA3; DAM NOV, POP; MTCW 2;
  MTFW 2005
Voloshinov, V. N.
  See Bakhtin, Mikhail Mikhailovich
Voltaire 1694-1778 . **LC 14, 79, 110; SSC 12;**
  WLC 6
  See also BYA 13; DA; DA3; DAB; DAC;
  DAM DRAM, MST; DLB 314; EW 4;
  GFL Beginnings to 1789; LATS 1:1;
  LMFS 1; NFS 7; RGWL 2, 3; TWA
von Aschendrof, Baron Ignatz
  See Ford, Ford Madox
von Chamisso, Adelbert
  See Chamisso, Adelbert von
von Daeniken, Erich 1935- .... **CLC 30**
  See also AITN 1; CA 37-40R; CANR 17,
  44
von Daniken, Erich
  See von Daeniken, Erich

von Hartmann, Eduard
  1842-1906 .... **TCLC 96**
von Hayek, Friedrich August
  See Hayek, F(riedrich) A(ugust von)
von Heidenstam, (Carl Gustaf) Verner
  See Heidenstam, (Carl Gustaf) Verner von
von Heyse, Paul (Johann Ludwig)
  See Heyse, Paul (Johann Ludwig von)
von Hofmannsthal, Hugo
  See Hofmannsthal, Hugo von
von Horvath, Odon
  See von Horvath, Odon
von Horvath, Odon
  See von Horvath, Odon
von Horvath, Odon 1901-1938 .... **TCLC 45**
  See von Horvath, Oedoen
  See also CA 118; 194; DLB 85, 124; RGWL
  2, 3
von Horvath, Oedoen
  See von Horvath, Odon
  See also CA 184
von Kleist, Heinrich
  See Kleist, Heinrich von
von Liliencron, (Friedrich Adolf Axel)
  Detlev
  See Liliencron, (Friedrich Adolf Axel) De-
  tlev von
Vonnegut, Kurt, Jr.
  See Vonnegut, Kurt
Vonnegut, Kurt 1922- ... **CLC 1, 2, 3, 4, 5, 8,**
  12, 22, 40, 60, 111, 212; SSC 8; WLC 6
  See also AAYA 6, 44; AITN 1; AMWS 2;
  BEST 90:4; BPFB 3; BYA 3, 14; CA
  1-4R; CANR 1, 25, 49, 75, 92; CDALB
  1968-1988; CN 1, 2, 3, 4, 5, 6, 7; CPW 1;
  DA; DA3; DAB; DAC; DAM MST, NOV,
  POP; DLB 2, 8, 152; DLBD 3; DLBY
  1980; EWL 3; EXPN; EXPS; LAIT 4;
  LMFS 2; MAL 5; MTCW 1, 2; MTFW
  2005; NFS 3; RGAL 4; SCFW; SFW 4;
  SSFS 5; TUS; YAW
Von Rachen, Kurt
  See Hubbard, L. Ron
von Sternberg, Josef
  See Sternberg, Josef von
Vorster, Gordon 1924- .... **CLC 34**
  See also CA 133
Vosce, Trudie
  See Ozick, Cynthia
Voznesensky, Andrei (Andreievich)
  1933- .... **CLC 1, 15, 57**
  See Voznesensky, Andrey
  See also CA 89-92; CANR 37; CWW 2;
  DAM POET; MTCW 1
Voznesensky, Andrey
  See Voznesensky, Andrei (Andreievich)
  See also EWL 3
Wace, Robert c. 1100-c. 1175 .... **CMLC 55**
  See also DLB 146
Waddington, Miriam 1917-2004 .... **CLC 28**
  See also CA 21-24R; 225; CANR 12, 30;
  CCA 1; CP 1, 2, 3, 4, 5, 6, 7; DLB 68
Wagman, Fredrica 1937- .... **CLC 7**
  See also CA 97-100; INT CA-97-100
Wagner, Linda W.
  See Wagner-Martin, Linda (C.)
Wagner, Linda Welshimer
  See Wagner-Martin, Linda (C.)
Wagner, Richard 1813-1883 ..... **NCLC 9, 119**
  See also DLB 129; EW 6
Wagner-Martin, Linda (C.) 1936- .... **CLC 50**
  See also CA 159; CANR 135
Wagoner, David (Russell) 1926- .... **CLC 3, 5,**
  15; PC 33
  See also AMWS 9; CA 1-4R; CAAS 3;
  CANR 2, 71; CN 1, 2, 3, 4, 5, 6, 7; CP 1,
  2, 3, 4, 5, 6, 7; DLB 5, 256; SATA 14;
  TCWW 1, 2

Wah, Fred(erick James) 1939- .... **CLC 44**
See also CA 107; 141; CP 1, 6, 7; DLB 60
Wahloo, Per 1926-1975 .... **CLC 7**
See also BPFB 3; CA 61-64; CANR 73;
CMW 4; MSW
Wahloo, Peter
See Wahloo, Per
Wain, John (Barrington) 1925-1994 . **CLC 2,
11, 15, 46**
See also CA 5-8R; 145; CAAS 4; CANR
23, 54; CDBLB 1960 to Present; CN 1, 2,
3, 4, 5; CP 1, 2, 3, 4, 5; DLB 15, 27, 139,
155; EWL 3; MTCW 1, 2; MTFW 2005
Wajda, Andrzej 1926- .... **CLC 16, 219**
See also CA 102
Wakefield, Dan 1932- .... **CLC 7**
See also CA 21-24R, 211; CAAE 211;
CAAS 7; CN 4, 5, 6, 7
Wakefield, Herbert Russell
1888-1965 .... **TCLC 120**
See also CA 5-8R; CANR 77; HGG; SUFW
Wakoski, Diane 1937- ...... **CLC 2, 4, 7, 9, 11,
40; PC 15**
See also CA 13-16R, 216; CAAE 216;
CAAS 1; CANR 9, 60, 106; CP 1, 2, 3, 4,
5, 6, 7; CWP; DAM POET; DLB 5; INT
CANR-9; MAL 5; MTCW 2; MTFW
2005
Wakoski-Sherbell, Diane
See Wakoski, Diane
Walcott, Derek (Alton) 1930- ... **BLC 3; CLC
2, 4, 9, 14, 25, 42, 67, 76, 160; DC 7;
PC 46**
See also BW 2; CA 89-92; CANR 26, 47,
75, 80, 130; CBD; CD 5, 6; CDWLB 3;
CP 1, 2, 3, 4, 5, 6, 7; DA3; DAB; DAC;
DAM MST, MULT, POET; DLB 117;
DLBY 1981; DNFS 1; EFS 1; EWL 3;
LMFS 2; MTCW 1, 2; MTFW 2005; PFS
6; RGEL 2; TWA; WWE 1
Waldman, Anne (Lesley) 1945- .... **CLC 7**
See also BG 1:3; CA 37-40R; CAAS 17;
CANR 34, 69, 116; CP 1, 2, 3, 4, 5, 6, 7;
CWP; DLB 16
Waldo, E. Hunter
See Sturgeon, Theodore (Hamilton)
Waldo, Edward Hamilton
See Sturgeon, Theodore (Hamilton)
Walker, Alice 1944- ...... **BLC 3; CLC 5, 6, 9,
19, 27, 46, 58, 103, 167; PC 30; SSC 5;
WLCS**
See also AAYA 3, 33; AFAW 1, 2; AMWS
3; BEST 89:4; BPFB 3; BW 2, 3; CA 37-
40R; CANR 9, 27, 49, 66, 82, 131;
CDALB 1968-1988; CN 4, 5, 6, 7; CPW;
CSW; DA; DA3; DAB; DAC; DAM MST,
MULT, NOV, POET, POP; DLB 6, 33,
143; EWL 3; EXPN; EXPS; FL 1:6; FW;
INT CANR-27; LAIT 3; MAL 5; MBL;
MTCW 1, 2; MTFW 2005; NFS 5; RGAL
4; RGSF 2; SATA 31; SSFS 2, 11; TUS;
YAW
Walker, Alice Malsenior
See Walker, Alice
Walker, David Harry 1911-1992 ...... **CLC 14**
See also CA 1-4R; 137; CANR 1; CN 1, 2;
CWRI 5; SATA 8; SATA-Obit 71
Walker, Edward Joseph 1934-2004
See Walker, Ted
See also CA 21-24R; 226; CANR 12, 28,
53
Walker, George F(rederick) 1947- .. **CLC 44,
61**
See also CA 103; CANR 21, 43, 59; CD 5,
6; DAB; DAC; DAM MST; DLB 60
Walker, Joseph A. 1935-2003 .... **CLC 19**
See also BW 1, 3; CA 89-92; CAD; CANR
26, 143; CD 5, 6; DAM DRAM, MST;
DFS 12; DLB 38

Walker, Margaret (Abigail)
1915-1998 .... **BLC; CLC 1, 6; PC 20;
TCLC 129**
See also AFAW 1, 2; BW 2, 3; CA 73-76;
172; CANR 26, 54, 76, 136; CN 1, 2, 3,
4, 5, 6; CP 1, 2, 3, 4, 5, 6; CSW; DAM
MULT; DLB 76, 152; EXPP; FW; MAL
5; MTCW 1, 2; MTFW 2005; RGAL 4;
RHW
Walker, Ted .... **CLC 13**
See Walker, Edward Joseph
See also CP 1, 2, 3, 4, 5, 6, 7; DLB 40
Wallace, David Foster 1962- ... **CLC 50, 114;
SSC 68**
See also AAYA 50; AMWS 10; CA 132;
CANR 59, 133; CN 7; DA3; MTCW 2;
MTFW 2005
Wallace, Dexter
See Masters, Edgar Lee
Wallace, (Richard Horatio) Edgar
1875-1932 .... **TCLC 57**
See also CA 115; 218; CMW 4; DLB 70;
MSW; RGEL 2
Wallace, Irving 1916-1990 .... **CLC 7, 13**
See also AITN 1; BPFB 3; CA 1-4R; 132;
CAAS 1; CANR 1, 27; CPW; DAM NOV,
POP; INT CANR-27; MTCW 1, 2
Wallant, Edward Lewis 1926-1962 ... **CLC 5,
10**
See also CA 1-4R; CANR 22; DLB 2, 28,
143, 299; EWL 3; MAL 5; MTCW 1, 2;
RGAL 4; RGHL
Wallas, Graham 1858-1932 .... **TCLC 91**
Waller, Edmund 1606-1687 .... **LC 86; PC 72**
See also BRW 2; DAM POET; DLB 126;
PAB; RGEL 2
Walley, Byron
See Card, Orson Scott
Walpole, Horace 1717-1797 .... **LC 2, 49**
See also BRW 3; DLB 39, 104, 213; GL 3;
HGG; LMFS 1; RGEL 2; SUFW 1; TEA
Walpole, Hugh (Seymour)
1884-1941 .... **TCLC 5**
See also CA 104; 165; DLB 34; HGG;
MTCW 2; RGEL 2; RHW
Walrond, Eric (Derwent) 1898-1966 . **HR 1:3**
See also BW 1; CA 125; DLB 51
Walser, Martin 1927- .... **CLC 27, 183**
See also CA 57-60; CANR 8, 46, 145;
CWW 2; DLB 75, 124; EWL 3
Walser, Robert 1878-1956 ..... **SSC 20; TCLC
18**
See also CA 118; 165; CANR 100; DLB
66; EWL 3
Walsh, Gillian Paton
See Paton Walsh, Gillian
Walsh, Jill Paton .... **CLC 35**
See Paton Walsh, Gillian
See also CLR 2, 65; WYA
Walter, Villiam Christian
See Andersen, Hans Christian
Walters, Anna L(ee) 1946- .... **NNAL**
See also CA 73-76
Walther von der Vogelweide c.
1170-1228 .... **CMLC 56**
Walton, Izaak 1593-1683 .... **LC 72**
See also BRW 2; CDBLB Before 1660;
DLB 151, 213; RGEL 2
Wambaugh, Joseph (Aloysius), Jr.
1937- .... **CLC 3, 18**
See also AITN 1; BEST 89:3; BPFB 3; CA
33-36R; CANR 42, 65, 115; CMW 4;
CPW 1; DA3; DAM NOV, POP; DLB 6;
DLBY 1983; MSW; MTCW 1, 2
Wang Wei 699(?)-761(?) .... **PC 18**
See also TWA
Warburton, William 1698-1779 .... **LC 97**
See also DLB 104

Ward, Arthur Henry Sarsfield 1883-1959
See Rohmer, Sax
See also CA 108; 173; CMW 4; HGG
Ward, Douglas Turner 1930- .... **CLC 19**
See also BW 1; CA 81-84; CAD; CANR
27; CD 5, 6; DLB 7, 38
Ward, E. D.
See Lucas, E(dward) V(errall)
Ward, Mrs. Humphry 1851-1920
See Ward, Mary Augusta
See also RGEL 2
Ward, Mary Augusta 1851-1920 ... **TCLC 55**
See Ward, Mrs. Humphry
See also DLB 18
Ward, Nathaniel 1578(?)-1652 .... **LC 114**
See also DLB 24
Ward, Peter
See Faust, Frederick (Schiller)
Warhol, Andy 1928(?)-1987 .... **CLC 20**
See also AAYA 12; BEST 89:4; CA 89-92;
121; CANR 34
Warner, Francis (Robert le Plastrier)
1937- .... **CLC 14**
See also CA 53-56; CANR 11; CP 1, 2, 3, 4
Warner, Marina 1946- .... **CLC 59**
See also CA 65-68; CANR 21, 55, 118; CN
5, 6, 7; DLB 194; MTFW 2005
Warner, Rex (Ernest) 1905-1986 ...... **CLC 45**
See also CA 89-92; 119; CN 1, 2, 3, 4; CP
1, 2, 3, 4; DLB 15; RGEL 2; RHW
Warner, Susan (Bogert)
1819-1885 .... **NCLC 31, 146**
See also DLB 3, 42, 239, 250, 254
Warner, Sylvia (Constance) Ashton
See Ashton-Warner, Sylvia (Constance)
Warner, Sylvia Townsend
1893-1978 .. **CLC 7, 19; SSC 23; TCLC
131**
See also BRWS 7; CA 61-64; 77-80; CANR
16, 60, 104; CN 1, 2; DLB 34, 139; EWL
3; FANT; FW; MTCW 1, 2; RGEL 2;
RGSF 2; RHW
Warren, Mercy Otis 1728-1814 ..... **NCLC 13**
See also DLB 31, 200; RGAL 4; TUS
Warren, Robert Penn 1905-1989 .. **CLC 1, 4,
6, 8, 10, 13, 18, 39, 53, 59; PC 37; SSC
4, 58; WLC 6**
See also AITN 1; AMW; AMWC 2; BPFB
3; BYA 1; CA 13-16R; 129; CANR 10,
47; CDALB 1968-1988; CN 1, 2, 3, 4;
CP 1, 2, 3, 4; DA; DA3; DAB; DAC;
DAM MST, NOV, POET; DLB 2, 48, 152,
320; DLBY 1980, 1989; EWL 3; INT
CANR-10; MAL 5; MTCW 1, 2; MTFW
2005; NFS 13; RGAL 4; RGSF 2; RHW;
SATA 46; SATA-Obit 63; SSFS 8; TUS
Warrigal, Jack
See Furphy, Joseph
Warshofsky, Isaac
See Singer, Isaac Bashevis
Warton, Joseph 1722-1800 ... **LC 128; NCLC
118**
See also DLB 104, 109; RGEL 2
Warton, Thomas 1728-1790 .... **LC 15, 82**
See also DAM POET; DLB 104, 109;
RGEL 2
Waruk, Kona
See Harris, (Theodore) Wilson
Warung, Price .... **TCLC 45**
See Astley, William
See also DLB 230; RGEL 2
Warwick, Jarvis
See Garner, Hugh
See also CCA 1
Washington, Alex
See Harris, Mark

Wesker, Arnold 1932- .... **CLC 3, 5, 42**
See also CA 1-4R; CAAS 7; CANR 1, 33;
CBD; CD 5, 6; CDBLB 1960 to Present;
DAB; DAM DRAM; DLB 13, 310, 319;
EWL 3; MTCW 1; RGEL 2; TEA

Wesley, Charles 1707-1788 .... **LC 128**
See also DLB 95; RGEL 2

Wesley, John 1703-1791 .... **LC 88**
See also DLB 104

Wesley, Richard (Errol) 1945- .... **CLC 7**
See also BW 1; CA 57-60; CAD; CANR
27; CD 5, 6; DLB 38

Wessel, Johan Herman 1742-1785 .... **LC 7**
See also DLB 300

West, Anthony (Panther)
1914-1987 .... **CLC 50**
See also CA 45-48; 124; CANR 3, 19; CN
1, 2, 3, 4; DLB 15

West, C. P.
See Wodehouse, P(elham) G(renville)

West, Cornel (Ronald) 1953- .... **BLCS; CLC
134**
See also CA 144; CANR 91; DLB 246

West, Delno C(loyde), Jr. 1936- .... **CLC 70**
See also CA 57-60

West, Dorothy 1907-1998 ...... **HR 1:3; TCLC
108**
See also BW 2; CA 143; 169; DLB 76

West, (Mary) Jessamyn 1902-1984 ... **CLC 7,
17**
See also CA 9-12R; 112; CANR 27; CN 1,
2, 3; DLB 6; DLBY 1984; MTCW 1, 2;
RGAL 4; RHW; SATA-Obit 37; TCWW
2; TUS; YAW

West, Morris L(anglo) 1916-1999 ..... **CLC 6,
33**
See also BPFB 3; CA 5-8R; 187; CANR
24, 49, 64; CN 1, 2, 3, 4, 5, 6; CPW; DLB
289; MTCW 1, 2; MTFW 2005

West, Nathanael 1903-1940 .. **SSC 16; TCLC
1, 14, 44**
See also AMW; AMWR 2; BPFB 3; CA
104; 125; CDALB 1929-1941; DA3; DLB
4, 9, 28; EWL 3; MAL 5; MTCW 1, 2;
MTFW 2005; NFS 16; RGAL 4; TUS

West, Owen
See Koontz, Dean R.

West, Paul 1930- .... **CLC 7, 14, 96, 226**
See also CA 13-16R; CAAS 7; CANR 22,
53, 76, 89, 136; CN 1, 2, 3, 4, 5, 6, 7;
DLB 14; INT CANR-22; MTCW 2;
MTFW 2005

West, Rebecca 1892-1983 ... **CLC 7, 9, 31, 50**
See also BPFB 3; BRWS 3; CA 5-8R; 109;
CANR 19; CN 1, 2, 3; DLB 36; DLBY
1983; EWL 3; FW; MTCW 1, 2; MTFW
2005; NCFS 4; RGEL 2; TEA

Westall, Robert (Atkinson)
1929-1993 .... **CLC 17**
See also AAYA 12; BYA 2, 6, 7, 8, 9, 15;
CA 69-72; 141; CANR 18, 68; CLR 13;
FANT; JRDA; MAICYA 1, 2; MAICYAS
1; SAAS 2; SATA 23, 69; SATA-Obit 75;
WYA; YAW

Westermarck, Edward 1862-1939 . **TCLC 87**

Westlake, Donald E(dwin) 1933- . **CLC 7, 33**
See also BPFB 3; CA 17-20R; CAAS 13;
CANR 16, 44, 65, 94, 137; CMW 4;
CPW; DAM POP; INT CANR-16; MSW;
MTCW 2; MTFW 2005

Westmacott, Mary
See Christie, Agatha (Mary Clarissa)

Weston, Allen
See Norton, Andre

Wetcheek, J. L.
See Feuchtwanger, Lion

Wetering, Janwillem van de
See van de Wetering, Janwillem

Wetherald, Agnes Ethelwyn
1857-1940 .... **TCLC 81**
See also CA 202; DLB 99

Wetherell, Elizabeth
See Warner, Susan (Bogert)

Whale, James 1889-1957 .... **TCLC 63**

Whalen, Philip (Glenn) 1923-2002 .... **CLC 6,
29**
See also BG 1:3; CA 9-12R; 209; CANR 5,
39; CP 1, 2, 3, 4, 5, 6, 7; DLB 16; WP

Wharton, Edith (Newbold Jones)
1862-1937 ... **SSC 6, 84; TCLC 3, 9, 27,
53, 129, 149; WLC 6**
See also AAYA 25; AMW; AMWC 2;
AMWR 1; BPFB 3; CA 104; 132; CDALB
1865-1917; DA; DA3; DAB; DAC; DAM
MST, NOV; DLB 4, 9, 12, 78, 189; DLBD
13; EWL 3; EXPS; FL 1:6; GL 3; HGG;
LAIT 2, 3; LATS 1:1; MAL 5; MBL;
MTCW 1, 2; MTFW 2005; NFS 5, 11,
15, 20; RGAL 4; RGSF 2; RHW; SSFS 6,
7; SUFW; TUS

Wharton, James
See Mencken, H(enry) L(ouis)

Wharton, William (a pseudonym)
1925- .... **CLC 18, 37**
See also CA 93-96; CN 4, 5, 6, 7; DLBY
1980; INT CA-93-96

Wheatley (Peters), Phillis
1753(?)-1784 ... **BLC 3; LC 3, 50; PC 3;
WLC 6**
See also AFAW 1, 2; CDALB 1640-1865;
DA; DA3; DAC; DAM MST, MULT,
POET; DLB 31, 50; EXPP; FL 1:1; PFS
13; RGAL 4

Wheelock, John Hall 1886-1978 .... **CLC 14**
See also CA 13-16R; 77-80; CANR 14; CP
1, 2; DLB 45; MAL 5

Whim-Wham
See Curnow, (Thomas) Allen (Monro)

Whitaker, Rod 1931-2005
See Trevanian
See also CA 29-32R; 246; CANR 45, 153;
CMW 4

White, Babington
See Braddon, Mary Elizabeth

White, E. B. 1899-1985 .... **CLC 10, 34, 39**
See also AAYA 62; AITN 2; AMWS 1; CA
13-16R; 116; CANR 16, 37; CDALBS;
CLR 1, 21, 107; CPW; DA3; DAM POP;
DLB 11, 22; EWL 3; FANT; MAICYA 1,
2; MAL 5; MTCW 1, 2; MTFW 2005;
NCFS 5; RGAL 4; SATA 2, 29, 100;
SATA-Obit 44; TUS

White, Edmund (Valentine III)
1940- .... **CLC 27, 110**
See also AAYA 7; CA 45-48; CANR 3, 19,
36, 62, 107, 133; CN 5, 6, 7; DA3; DAM
POP; DLB 227; MTCW 1, 2; MTFW
2005

White, Elwyn Brooks
See White, E. B.

White, Hayden V. 1928- .... **CLC 148**
See also CA 128; CANR 135; DLB 246

White, Patrick (Victor Martindale)
1912-1990 ...... **CLC 3, 4, 5, 7, 9, 18, 65,
69; SSC 39; TCLC 176**
See also BRWS 1; CA 81-84; 132; CANR
43; CN 1, 2, 3, 4; DLB 260; EWL 3;
MTCW 1; RGEL 2; RGSF 2; RHW;
TWA; WWE 1

White, Phyllis Dorothy James 1920-
See James, P. D.
See also CA 21-24R; CANR 17, 43, 65,
112; CMW 4; CN 7; CPW; DA3; DAM
POP; MTCW 1, 2; MTFW 2005; TEA

White, T(erence) H(anbury)
1906-1964 .... **CLC 30**
See also AAYA 22; BPFB 3; BYA 4, 5; CA
73-76; CANR 37; DLB 160; FANT;
JRDA; LAIT 1; MAICYA 1, 2; RGEL 2;
SATA 12; SUFW 1; YAW

White, Terence de Vere 1912-1994 ... **CLC 49**
See also CA 49-52; 145; CANR 3

White, Walter
See White, Walter F(rancis)

White, Walter F(rancis) 1893-1955 ... **BLC 3;
HR 1:3; TCLC 15**
See also BW 1; CA 115; 124; DAM MULT;
DLB 51

White, William Hale 1831-1913
See Rutherford, Mark
See also CA 121; 189

Whitehead, Alfred North
1861-1947 .... **TCLC 97**
See also CA 117; 165; DLB 100, 262

Whitehead, E(dward) A(nthony)
1933- .... **CLC 5**
See Whitehead, Ted
See also CA 65-68; CANR 58, 118; CBD;
CD 5; DLB 310

Whitehead, Ted
See Whitehead, E(dward) A(nthony)
See also CD 6

Whiteman, Roberta J. Hill 1947- ...... **NNAL**
See also CA 146

Whitemore, Hugh (John) 1936- .... **CLC 37**
See also CA 132; CANR 77; CBD; CD 5,
6; INT CA-132

Whitman, Sarah Helen (Power)
1803-1878 .... **NCLC 19**
See also DLB 1, 243

Whitman, Walt(er) 1819-1892 .. **NCLC 4, 31,
81; PC 3; WLC 6**
See also AAYA 42; AMW; AMWR 1;
CDALB 1640-1865; DA; DA3; DAB;
DAC; DAM MST, POET; DLB 3, 64,
224, 250; EXPP; LAIT 2; LMFS 1; PAB;
PFS 2, 3, 13, 22; RGAL 4; SATA 20;
TUS; WP; WYAS 1

Whitney, Isabella fl. 1565-fl. 1575 ..... **LC 130**
See also DLB 136

Whitney, Phyllis A(yame) 1903- .... **CLC 42**
See also AAYA 36; AITN 2; BEST 90:3;
CA 1-4R; CANR 3, 25, 38, 60; CLR 59;
CMW 4; CPW; DA3; DAM POP; JRDA;
MAICYA 1, 2; MTCW 2; RHW; SATA 1,
30; YAW

Whittemore, (Edward) Reed, Jr.
1919- .... **CLC 4**
See also CA 9-12R; 219; CAAE 219; CAAS
8; CANR 4, 119; CP 1, 2, 3, 4, 5, 6, 7;
DLB 5; MAL 5

Whittier, John Greenleaf
1807-1892 .... **NCLC 8, 59**
See also AMWS 1; DLB 1, 243; RGAL 4

Whittlebot, Hernia
See Coward, Noel (Peirce)

Wicker, Thomas Grey 1926-
See Wicker, Tom
See also CA 65-68; CANR 21, 46, 141

Wicker, Tom .... **CLC 7**
See Wicker, Thomas Grey

Wideman, John Edgar 1941- ... **BLC 3; CLC
5, 34, 36, 67, 122; SSC 62**
See also AFAW 1, 2; AMWS 10; BPFB 4;
BW 2, 3; CA 85-88; CANR 14, 42, 67,
109, 140; CN 4, 5, 6, 7; DAM MULT;
DLB 33, 143; MAL 5; MTCW 2; MTFW
2005; RGAL 4; RGSF 2; SSFS 6, 12;
TCLE 1:2

Wiebe, Rudy (Henry) 1934- .. **CLC 6, 11, 14,
138**
See also CA 37-40R; CANR 42, 67, 123;
CN 1, 2, 3, 4, 5, 6, 7; DAC; DAM MST;
DLB 60; RHW; SATA 156

Wieland, Christoph Martin
    1733-1813 .... **NCLC 17**
    See also DLB 97; EW 4; LMFS 1; RGWL
    2, 3
Wiene, Robert 1881-1938 .... **TCLC 56**
Wieners, John 1934- .... **CLC 7**
    See also BG 1:3; CA 13-16R; CP 1, 2, 3, 4,
    5, 6, 7; DLB 16; WP
Wiesel, Elie 1928- ...... **CLC 3, 5, 11, 37, 165;**
    WLCS
    See also AAYA 7, 54; AITN 1; CA 5-8R;
    CAAS 4; CANR 8, 40, 65, 125; CDALBS;
    CWW 2; DA; DA3; DAB; DAC; DAM
    MST, NOV; DLB 83, 299; DLBY 1987;
    EWL 3; INT CANR-8; LAIT 4; MTCW
    1, 2; MTFW 2005; NCFS 4; NFS 4;
    RGHL; RGWL 3; SATA 56; YAW
Wiesel, Eliezer
    See Wiesel, Elie
Wiggins, Marianne 1947- .... **CLC 57**
    See also AAYA 70; BEST 89:3; CA 130;
    CANR 60, 139; CN 7
Wigglesworth, Michael 1631-1705 .... **LC 106**
    See also DLB 24; RGAL 4
Wiggs, Susan .... **CLC 70**
    See also CA 201
Wight, James Alfred 1916-1995
    See Herriot, James
    See also CA 77-80; SATA 55; SATA-Brief
    44
Wilbur, Richard (Purdy) 1921- ..... **CLC 3, 6,**
    9, 14, 53, 110; PC 51
    See also AMWS 3; CA 1-4R; CABS 2;
    CANR 2, 29, 76, 93, 139; CDALBS; CP
    1, 2, 3, 4, 5, 6, 7; DA; DAB; DAC; DAM
    MST, POET; DLB 5, 169; EWL 3; EXPP;
    INT CANR-29; MAL 5; MTCW 1, 2;
    MTFW 2005; PAB; PFS 11, 12, 16;
    RGAL 4; SATA 9, 108; WP
Wild, Peter 1940- .... **CLC 14**
    See also CA 37-40R; CP 1, 2, 3, 4, 5, 6, 7;
    DLB 5
Wilde, Oscar (Fingal O'Flahertie Wills)
    1854(?)-1900 .... **DC 17; SSC 11, 77;**
    TCLC 1, 8, 23, 41, 175; WLC 6
    See also AAYA 49; BRW 5; BRWC 1, 2;
    BRWR 2; BYA 15; CA 104; 119; CANR
    112; CDBLB 1890-1914; DA; DA3;
    DAB; DAC; DAM DRAM, MST, NOV;
    DFS 4, 8, 9, 21; DLB 10, 19, 34, 57, 141,
    156, 190; EXPS; FANT; GL 3; LATS 1:1;
    NFS 20; RGEL 2; RGSF 2; SATA 24;
    SSFS 7; SUFW; TEA; WCH; WLIT 4
Wilder, Billy .... **CLC 20**
    See Wilder, Samuel
    See also AAYA 66; DLB 26
Wilder, Samuel 1906-2002
    See Wilder, Billy
    See also CA 89-92; 205
Wilder, Stephen
    See Marlowe, Stephen
Wilder, Thornton (Niven)
    1897-1975 .. **CLC 1, 5, 6, 10, 15, 35, 82;**
    DC 1, 24; WLC 6
    See also AAYA 29; AITN 2; AMW; CA 13-
    16R; 61-64; CAD; CANR 40, 132;
    CDALBS; CN 1, 2; DA; DA3; DAB;
    DAC; DAM DRAM, MST, NOV; DFS 1,
    4, 16; DLB 4, 7, 9, 228; DLBY 1997;
    EWL 3; LAIT 3; MAL 5; MTCW 1, 2;
    MTFW 2005; RGAL 4; RHW; WYAS 1
Wilding, Michael 1942- ...... **CLC 73; SSC 50**
    See also CA 104; CANR 24, 49, 106; CN
    4, 5, 6, 7; DLB 325; RGSF 2
Wiley, Richard 1944- .... **CLC 44**
    See also CA 121; 129; CANR 71
Wilhelm, Kate .... **CLC 7**
    See Wilhelm, Katie
    See also AAYA 20; BYA 16; CAAS 5; DLB
    8; INT CANR-17; SCFW 2

Wilhelm, Katie 1928-
    See Wilhelm, Kate
    See also CA 37-40R; CANR 17, 36, 60, 94;
    MTCW 1; SFW 4
Wilkins, Mary
    See Freeman, Mary E(leanor) Wilkins
Willard, Nancy 1936- .... **CLC 7, 37**
    See also BYA 5; CA 89-92; CANR 10, 39,
    68, 107, 152; CLR 5; CP 2, 3, 4, 5; CWP;
    CWRI 5; DLB 5, 52; FANT; MAICYA 1,
    2; MTCW 1; SATA 37, 71, 127; SATA-
    Brief 30; SUFW 2; TCLE 1:2
William of Malmesbury c. 1090B.C.-c.
    1140B.C. .... **CMLC 57**
William of Ockham 1290-1349 ..... **CMLC 32**
Williams, Ben Ames 1889-1953 ..... **TCLC 89**
    See also CA 183; DLB 102
Williams, C(harles) K(enneth)
    1936- .... **CLC 33, 56, 148**
    See also CA 37-40R; CAAS 26; CANR 57,
    106; CP 1, 2, 3, 4, 5, 6, 7; DAM POET;
    DLB 5; MAL 5
Williams, Charles
    See Collier, James Lincoln
Williams, Charles (Walter Stansby)
    1886-1945 .... **TCLC 1, 11**
    See also BRWS 9; CA 104; 163; DLB 100,
    153, 255; FANT; RGEL 2; SUFW 1
Williams, Ella Gwendolen Rees
    See Rhys, Jean
Williams, (George) Emlyn
    1905-1987 .... **CLC 15**
    See also CA 104; 123; CANR 36; DAM
    DRAM; DLB 10, 77; IDTP; MTCW 1
Williams, Hank 1923-1953 .... **TCLC 81**
    See Williams, Hiram King
Williams, Helen Maria
    1761-1827 .... **NCLC 135**
    See also DLB 158
Williams, Hiram Hank
    See Williams, Hank
Williams, Hiram King
    See Williams, Hank
    See also CA 188
Williams, Hugo (Mordaunt) 1942- ... **CLC 42**
    See also CA 17-20R; CANR 45, 119; CP 1,
    2, 3, 4, 5, 6, 7; DLB 40
Williams, J. Walker
    See Wodehouse, P(elham) G(renville)
Williams, John A(lfred) 1925- . **BLC 3; CLC**
    5, 13
    See also AFAW 2; BW 2, 3; CA 53-56; 195;
    CAAE 195; CAAS 3; CANR 6, 26, 51,
    118; CN 1, 2, 3, 4, 5, 6, 7; CSW; DAM
    MULT; DLB 2, 33; EWL 3; INT CANR-6;
    MAL 5; RGAL 4; SFW 4
Williams, Jonathan (Chamberlain)
    1929- .... **CLC 13**
    See also CA 9-12R; CAAS 12; CANR 8,
    108; CP 1, 2, 3, 4, 5, 6, 7; DLB 5
Williams, Joy 1944- .... **CLC 31**
    See also CA 41-44R; CANR 22, 48, 97
Williams, Norman 1952- .... **CLC 39**
    See also CA 118
Williams, Roger 1603(?)-1683 .... **LC 129**
    See also DLB 24
Williams, Sherley Anne 1944-1999 ... **BLC 3;**
    CLC 89
    See also AFAW 2; BW 2, 3; CA 73-76; 185;
    CANR 25, 82; DAM MULT, POET; DLB
    41; INT CANR-25; SATA 78; SATA-Obit
    116
Williams, Shirley
    See Williams, Sherley Anne

Williams, Tennessee 1911-1983 . **CLC 1, 2, 5,**
    7, 8, 11, 15, 19, 30, 39, 45, 71, 111; DC
    4; SSC 81; WLC 6
    See also AAYA 31; AITN 1, 2; AMW;
    AMWC 1; CA 5-8R; 108; CABS 3; CAD;
    CANR 31, 132; CDALB 1941-1968; CN
    1, 2, 3; DA; DA3; DAB; DAC; DAM
    DRAM, MST; DFS 17; DLB 7; DLBD 4;
    DLBY 1983; EWL 3; GLL 1; LAIT 4;
    LATS 1:2; MAL 5; MTCW 1, 2; MTFW
    2005; RGAL 4; TUS
Williams, Thomas (Alonzo)
    1926-1990 .... **CLC 14**
    See also CA 1-4R; 132; CANR 2
Williams, William C.
    See Williams, William Carlos
Williams, William Carlos
    1883-1963 .... **CLC 1, 2, 5, 9, 13, 22, 42,**
    67; PC 7; SSC 31; WLC 6
    See also AAYA 46; AMW; AMWR 1; CA
    89-92; CANR 34; CDALB 1917-1929;
    DA; DA3; DAB; DAC; DAM MST,
    POET; DLB 4, 16, 54, 86; EWL 3; EXPP;
    MAL 5; MTCW 1, 2; MTFW 2005; NCFS
    4; PAB; PFS 1, 6, 11; RGAL 4; RGSF 2;
    TUS; WP
Williamson, David (Keith) 1942- ..... **CLC 56**
    See also CA 103; CANR 41; CD 5, 6; DLB
    289
Williamson, Ellen Douglas 1905-1984
    See Douglas, Ellen
    See also CA 17-20R; 114; CANR 39
Williamson, Jack .... **CLC 29**
    See Williamson, John Stewart
    See also CAAS 8; DLB 8; SCFW 1, 2
Williamson, John Stewart 1908-
    See Williamson, Jack
    See also CA 17-20R; CANR 23, 70, 153;
    SFW 4
Willie, Frederick
    See Lovecraft, H. P.
Willingham, Calder (Baynard, Jr.)
    1922-1995 .... **CLC 5, 51**
    See also CA 5-8R; 147; CANR 3; CN 1, 2,
    3, 4, 5; CSW; DLB 2, 44; IDFW 3, 4;
    MTCW 1
Willis, Charles
    See Clarke, Arthur C(harles)
Willy
    See Colette, (Sidonie-Gabrielle)
Willy, Colette
    See Colette, (Sidonie-Gabrielle)
    See also GLL 1
Wilmot, John 1647-1680 .... **LC 75; PC 66**
    See Rochester
    See also BRW 2; DLB 131; PAB
Wilson, A(ndrew) N(orman) 1950- .. **CLC 33**
    See also BRWS 6; CA 112; 122; CN 4, 5,
    6, 7; DLB 14, 155, 194; MTCW 2
Wilson, Angus (Frank Johnstone)
    1913-1991 . **CLC 2, 3, 5, 25, 34; SSC 21**
    See also BRWS 1; CA 5-8R; 134; CANR
    21; CN 1, 2, 3, 4; DLB 15, 139, 155;
    EWL 3; MTCW 1, 2; MTFW 2005; RGEL
    2; RGSF 2
Wilson, August 1945-2005 .. **BLC 3; CLC 39,**
    50, 63, 118, 222; DC 2; WLCS
    See also AAYA 16; AFAW 2; AMWS 8; BW
    2, 3; CA 115; 122; 244; CAD; CANR 42,
    54, 76, 128; CD 5, 6; DA; DA3; DAB;
    DAC; DAM DRAM, MST, MULT; DFS
    3, 7, 15, 17; DLB 228; EWL 3; LAIT 4;
    LATS 1:2; MAL 5; MTCW 1, 2; MTFW
    2005; RGAL 4
Wilson, Brian 1942- .... **CLC 12**
Wilson, Colin (Henry) 1931- .... **CLC 3, 14**
    See also CA 1-4R; CAAS 5; CANR 1, 22,
    33, 77; CMW 4; CN 1, 2, 3, 4, 5, 6; DLB
    14, 194; HGG; MTCW 1; SFW 4

Wilson, Dirk
See Pohl, Frederik
Wilson, Edmund 1895-1972 .. **CLC 1, 2, 3, 8, 24**
See also AMW; CA 1-4R; 37-40R; CANR 1, 46, 110; CN 1; DLB 63; EWL 3; MAL 5; MTCW 1, 2; MTFW 2005; RGAL 4; TUS
Wilson, Ethel Davis (Bryant)
1888(?)-1980 .... **CLC 13**
See also CA 102; CN 1, 2; DAC; DAM POET; DLB 68; MTCW 1; RGEL 2
Wilson, Harriet
See Wilson, Harriet E. Adams
See also DLB 239
Wilson, Harriet E.
See Wilson, Harriet E. Adams
See also DLB 243
Wilson, Harriet E. Adams
1827(?)-1863(?) .... **BLC 3; NCLC 78**
See also Wilson, Harriet; Wilson, Harriet E.
See also DAM MULT; DLB 50
Wilson, John 1785-1854 .... **NCLC 5**
Wilson, John (Anthony) Burgess 1917-1993
See Burgess, Anthony
See also CA 1-4R; 143; CANR 2, 46; DA3; DAC; DAM NOV; MTCW 1, 2; MTFW 2005; NFS 15; TEA
Wilson, Lanford 1937- .. **CLC 7, 14, 36, 197; DC 19**
See also CA 17-20R; CABS 3; CAD; CANR 45, 96; CD 5, 6; DAM DRAM; DFS 4, 9, 12, 16, 20; DLB 7; EWL 3; MAL 5; TUS
Wilson, Robert M. 1941- .... **CLC 7, 9**
See also CA 49-52; CAD; CANR 2, 41; CD 5, 6; MTCW 1
Wilson, Robert McLiam 1964- .... **CLC 59**
See also CA 132; DLB 267
Wilson, Sloan 1920-2003 .... **CLC 32**
See also CA 1-4R; 216; CANR 1, 44; CN 1, 2, 3, 4, 5, 6
Wilson, Snoo 1948- .... **CLC 33**
See also CA 69-72; CBD; CD 5, 6
Wilson, William S(mith) 1932- .... **CLC 49**
See also CA 81-84
Wilson, (Thomas) Woodrow
1856-1924 .... **TCLC 79**
See also CA 166; DLB 47
Wilson and Warnke eds. .... **CLC 65**
Winchilsea, Anne (Kingsmill) Finch
1661-1720
See Finch, Anne
See also RGEL 2
Winckelmann, Johann Joachim
1717-1768 .... **LC 129**
See also DLB 97
Windham, Basil
See Wodehouse, P(elham) G(renville)
Wingrove, David (John) 1954- .... **CLC 68**
See also CA 133; SFW 4
Winnemucca, Sarah 1844-1891 .... **NCLC 79; NNAL**
See also DAM MULT; DLB 175; RGAL 4
Winstanley, Gerrard 1609-1676 .... **LC 52**
Wintergreen, Jane
See Duncan, Sara Jeannette
Winters, Arthur Yvor
See Winters, Yvor
Winters, Janet Lewis .... **CLC 41**
See Lewis, Janet
See also DLBY 1987
Winters, Yvor 1900-1968 .... **CLC 4, 8, 32**
See also AMWS 2; CA 11-12; 25-28R; CAP 1; DLB 48; EWL 3; MAL 5; MTCW 1; RGAL 4

Winterson, Jeanette 1959- .... **CLC 64, 158**
See also BRWS 4; CA 136; CANR 58, 116; CN 5, 6, 7; CPW; DA3; DAM POP; DLB 207, 261; FANT; FW; GLL 1; MTCW 2; MTFW 2005; RHW
Winthrop, John 1588-1649 .... **LC 31, 107**
See also DLB 24, 30
Wirth, Louis 1897-1952 .... **TCLC 92**
See also CA 210
Wiseman, Frederick 1930- .... **CLC 20**
See also CA 159
Wister, Owen 1860-1938 .... **TCLC 21**
See also BPFB 3; CA 108; 162; DLB 9, 78, 186; RGAL 4; SATA 62; TCWW 1, 2
Wither, George 1588-1667 .... **LC 96**
See also DLB 121; RGEL 2
Witkacy
See Witkiewicz, Stanislaw Ignacy
Witkiewicz, Stanislaw Ignacy
1885-1939 .... **TCLC 8**
See also CA 105; 162; CDWLB 4; DLB 215; EW 10; EWL 3; RGWL 2, 3; SFW 4
Wittgenstein, Ludwig (Josef Johann)
1889-1951 .... **TCLC 59**
See also CA 113; 164; DLB 262; MTCW 2
Wittig, Monique 1935-2003 .... **CLC 22**
See also CA 116; 135; 212; CANR 143; CWW 2; DLB 83; EWL 3; FW; GLL 1
Wittlin, Jozef 1896-1976 .... **CLC 25**
See also CA 49-52; 65-68; CANR 3; EWL 3
Wodehouse, P(elham) G(renville)
1881-1975 . **CLC 1, 2, 5, 10, 22; SSC 2; TCLC 108**
See also AAYA 65; AITN 2; BRWS 3; CA 45-48; 57-60; CANR 3, 33; CDBLB 1914-1945; CN 1, 2; CPW 1; DA3; DAB; DAC; DAM NOV; DLB 34, 162; EWL 3; MTCW 1, 2; MTFW 2005; RGEL 2; RGSF 2; SATA 22; SSFS 10
Woiwode, L.
See Woiwode, Larry (Alfred)
Woiwode, Larry (Alfred) 1941- ... **CLC 6, 10**
See also CA 73-76; CANR 16, 94; CN 3, 4, 5, 6, 7; DLB 6; INT CANR-16
Wojciechowska, Maia (Teresa)
1927-2002 .... **CLC 26**
See also AAYA 8, 46; BYA 3; CA 9-12R; 183; 209; CAAE 183; CANR 4, 41; CLR 1; JRDA; MAICYA 1, 2; SAAS 1; SATA 1, 28, 83; SATA-Essay 104; SATA-Obit 134; YAW
Wojtyla, Karol (Jozef)
See John Paul II, Pope
Wojtyla, Karol (Josef)
See John Paul II, Pope
Wolf, Christa 1929- .... **CLC 14, 29, 58, 150**
See also CA 85-88; CANR 45, 123; CD-WLB 2; CWW 2; DLB 75; EWL 3; FW; MTCW 1; RGWL 2, 3; SSFS 14
Wolf, Naomi 1962- .... **CLC 157**
See also CA 141; CANR 110; FW; MTFW 2005
Wolfe, Gene 1931- .... **CLC 25**
See also AAYA 35; CA 57-60; CAAS 9; CANR 6, 32, 60, 152; CPW; DAM POP; DLB 8; FANT; MTCW 2; MTFW 2005; SATA 118, 165; SCFW 2; SFW 4; SUFW 2
Wolfe, Gene Rodman
See Wolfe, Gene
Wolfe, George C. 1954- .... **BLCS; CLC 49**
See also CA 149; CAD; CD 5, 6
Wolfe, Thomas (Clayton)
1900-1938 ...... **SSC 33; TCLC 4, 13, 29, 61; WLC 6**
See also AMW; BPFB 3; CA 104; 132; CANR 102; CDALB 1929-1941; DA; DA3; DAB; DAC; DAM MST, NOV;

DLB 9, 102, 229; DLBD 2, 16; DLBY 1985, 1997; EWL 3; MAL 5; MTCW 1, 2; NFS 18; RGAL 4; SSFS 18; TUS
Wolfe, Thomas Kennerly, Jr.
1931- .... **CLC 147**
See Wolfe, Tom
See also CA 13-16R; CANR 9, 33, 70, 104; DA3; DAM POP; DLB 185; EWL 3; INT CANR-9; MTCW 1, 2; MTFW 2005; TUS
Wolfe, Tom .... **CLC 1, 2, 9, 15, 35, 51**
See Wolfe, Thomas Kennerly, Jr.
See also AAYA 8, 67; AITN 2; AMWS 3; BEST 89:1; BPFB 3; CN 5, 6, 7; CPW; CSW; DLB 152; LAIT 5; RGAL 4
Wolff, Geoffrey 1937- .... **CLC 41**
See also CA 29-32R; CANR 29, 43, 78, 154
Wolff, Geoffrey Ansell
See Wolff, Geoffrey
Wolff, Sonia
See Levitin, Sonia (Wolff)
Wolff, Tobias (Jonathan Ansell)
1945- .... **CLC 39, 64, 172; SSC 63**
See also AAYA 16; AMWS 7; BEST 90:2; BYA 12; CA 114; 117; CAAS 22; CANR 54, 76, 96; CN 5, 6, 7; CSW; DA3; DLB 130; EWL 3; INT CA-117; MTCW 2; MTFW 2005; RGAL 4; RGSF 2; SSFS 4, 11
Wolfram von Eschenbach c. 1170-c. 1220 .... **CMLC 5**
See Eschenbach, Wolfram von
See also CDWLB 2; DLB 138; EW 1; RGWL 2
Wolitzer, Hilma 1930- .... **CLC 17**
See also CA 65-68; CANR 18, 40; INT CANR-18; SATA 31; YAW
Wollstonecraft, Mary 1759-1797 .... **LC 5, 50, 90**
See also BRWS 3; CDBLB 1789-1832; DLB 39, 104, 158, 252; FL 1:1; FW; LAIT 1; RGEL 2; TEA; WLIT 3
Wonder, Stevie 1950- .... **CLC 12**
See also CA 111
Wong, Jade Snow 1922-2006 .... **CLC 17**
See also CA 109; 249; CANR 91; SATA 112
Woodberry, George Edward
1855-1930 .... **TCLC 73**
See also CA 165; DLB 71, 103
Woodcott, Keith
See Brunner, John (Kilian Houston)
Woodruff, Robert W.
See Mencken, H(enry) L(ouis)
Woolf, (Adeline) Virginia 1882-1941 .. **SSC 7, 79; TCLC 1, 5, 20, 43, 56, 101, 123, 128; WLC 6**
See also AAYA 44; BPFB 3; BRW 7; BRWC 2; BRWR 1; CA 104; 130; CANR 64, 132; CDBLB 1914-1945; DA; DA3; DAB; DAC; DAM MST, NOV; DLB 36, 100, 162; DLBD 10; EWL 3; EXPS; FL 1:6; FW; LAIT 3; LATS 1:1; LMFS 2; MTCW 1, 2; MTFW 2005; NCFS 2; NFS 8, 12; RGEL 2; RGSF 2; SSFS 4, 12; TEA; WLIT 4
Woollcott, Alexander (Humphreys)
1887-1943 .... **TCLC 5**
See also CA 105; 161; DLB 29
Woolrich, Cornell .... **CLC 77**
See Hopley-Woolrich, Cornell George
See also MSW
Woolson, Constance Fenimore
1840-1894 .... **NCLC 82; SSC 90**
See also DLB 12, 74, 189, 221; RGAL 4
Wordsworth, Dorothy 1771-1855 . **NCLC 25, 138**
See also DLB 107

Literary Criticism Series
Cumulative Topic Index

This index lists all topic entries in Thompson Gale's *Children's Literature Review* (CLR), *Classical and Medieval Literature Criticism* (CMLC), *Contemporary Literary Criticism* (CLC), *Drama Criticism* (DC), *Literature Criticism from 1400 to 1800* (LC), *Nineteenth-Century Literature Criticism* (NCLC), *Short Story Criticism* (SSC), and *Twentieth-Century Literary Criticism* (TCLC). The index also lists topic entries in the Gale Critical Companion Collection, which includes the following publications: *The Beat Generation* (BG), *Feminism in Literature* (FL), *Gothic Literature* (GL), and *Harlem Renaissance* (HR).

Topic Index

Topic Index

Topic Index

NCLC Cumulative Nationality Index